102

D1093044

Marketing Leadership in Hospitality

Foundations and Practices

THIRD EDITION

Robert C. Lewis, Ph.D.

Professor Emeritus
Puslinch, Ontario

Richard E. Chambers, MBA

Vice President of Marketing
Leading Hotels of the World
New York, New York

JOHN WILEY & SONS, INC.

New York • Chichester • Weinheim • Brisbane • Singapore • Toronto

This publication is designed to provide accurate and authoritative information in regard to the subject matter covered. It is sold with the understanding that the publisher is not engaged in rendering professional services. If professional advice or other expert assistance is required, the services of a competent professional person should be sought.

Library of Congress Cataloging-in-Publication Data:

Lewis, Robert C., 1930–
    Marketing leadership in hospitality : foundations and practices /
Robert C. Lewis, Richard E. Chambers. — 3rd ed.
      p.   cm.
    ISBN 0-471-33270-4 (alk. paper)
    1. Hospitality industry—Marketing.   I. Chambers, Richard E.
(Richard Everett), 1956– .   II. Title.
TX911.3.M3L49 1999
674.94′068′8—dc21

                                                          99-19482

Printed in the United States of America.

10 9 8 7 6 5 4 3 2 1

To all those great students who worked so hard
and made teaching so rewarding
and to
Richard E. Chambers, Sr.

CONTENTS IN BRIEF

•◆•

CONTENTS

•◆•

PREFACE

•◆•

Since the second edition of this book came out five years ago, there have been many changes in the hospitality industry. On the hotel side we have witnessed a rapid consolidation phase with major companies integrating with others, through outright purchases or strategic alliances, on a worldwide basis. Hotel companies have entered the capital markets in a strong manner. Ten years ago there were less than 10 publicly traded hotel companies; now there are over 50. On the restaurant side we have seen many new concepts evolve and many fail. In both industries there has been great global expansion. Concurrently, there has been considerable change in the hospitality customer. The link between these two phenomena is marketing. This book is about that link.

Much of the hospitality industry today is made up of many sophisticated organizations. The Mom and Pop days are quickly receding into the sunset, especially for hotels. Branding has become the *modus operandi*. In both developed and less developed countries, like India and China, major hotel chains have opened properties or established franchises. So too have McDonald's, T.G.I. Friday's, KFC, Planet Hollywood, Hard Rock Cafe, Pizza Hut, Maxim's, and other restaurant companies. Independent operations have become increasingly fewer and will continue to be so. This is more true, of course, with hotels than with restaurants. But even the latter, with brand identity, are showing up in international hotels in joint ventures, as franchisor, or as leasers of space. The transition is not unlike that of the industrial revolution that began over two centuries ago. Cottage industries still exist and so does the individual entrepreneur in hospitality. It is these same entrepreneurs,

moreover, who have led the way in the growth explosion.

E. M. Statler, Conrad Hilton, Howard Johnson, Kemmons Wilson, J. Willard Marriott, and Ray Kroc were some of these early entrepreneurs whose legends and legacies survive today. All these people were marketers par excellence, albeit by a different standard than the one we apply to hospitality marketing today. No doubt terms like "segmentation," "positioning," "marketing mix," "consumer needs and wants," "product life cycle," "distribution channels," and many others you will find in this book, were not even part of their vocabulary. Nevertheless, they all had one thing in common: they solved consumers' problems. And that is what marketing is all about.

It was only natural that the legacies of these individuals, others like them, and today many unlike them who come from totally different backgrounds, would evolve in one form or another into large organizations. Growth comes from continued solving of consumers' problems. Growth, however, also brings with it growing pains. These are pains of organization, management, financing, distribution and, finally, competition.

The emphasis in the early growth years was on operations and costs. The people who could run a good operation and control their costs were likely to be successful. In hotels, many general managers rose through the ranks of food and beverage departments. In restaurants, the emphasis was primarily on food, beverage, and labor costs.

There were still (and always will be) the grand hotels and the grand restaurants, usually owned and run by entrepreneurs in the classic *mein host* style. By and large, however, customers took what they got for what they paid. There wasn't too much choice. Little attention was paid to selling and advertising, and marketing was a foreign word.

Marketing, in fact, did not truly begin to evolve to its present state of growth and recognition in any industry until the 1960s. It was a good 20 years later before it began to evolve in the hospitality industry. When this first happened, moreover, it was not in its present form. With the growth of chain operations and regional, if not nationwide, if not global, distribution, organizations began advertising more extensively. Hotels began to fill out their sales staffs. When marketing became an accepted word in the hospitality lexicon, selling and advertising were largely what marketing meant. Merchandising and promotion were added later.

Thus, until maybe 15 years ago, hospitality marketing consisted largely of what we know today as the communications mix, a subset of marketing. Today, personal selling is a major portion of the marketing mix for only some properties, both internally and externally. Extensive advertising is affordable by relatively few, although merchandising and promotion are quite common in all size operations.

Marketing has evolved similarly in restaurant and hospitality management academic progams. The early subjects were primarily merchandising and selling. Marketing was thought by many to be something intuitive that either you were good at, or you weren't, but there wasn't much point in spending an entire semester learning it. Hospitality marketing texts were largely nonexistent. What did exist concentrated primarily on merchandising, promotion, and selling.

A bare two decades ago, hospitality marketing began to acquire recognition. This came about primarily as a result of two forces. The first was the recognition of marketing in other industries and its increasingly frequent mention in the business press. Individuals who had degrees from business schools, and/or came from other industries, came into the hospitality industry and recognized the need for marketing. Former sales departments became marketing departments. By and large, however, much of the industry was unaware of the difference between sales and advertising, and marketing.

The second force occurred in the marketplace. As competition intensified, it was no longer a case of "build it and they will come." One had to begin to fight to obtain the business that the competiton was also seeking. The customer had also changed. Demographic lines began to blur. The customer became "educated" and more demanding. After all, he or she now had alternatives. Properties sought to differentiate from each other. Singular brands, such as Marriott, began to offer multiple levels of hotel offerings depending on the needs of the customer and location. The hospitality marketing trend that began in the United States is now in the heavy growth stage internationally. Businesses are now being challenged as never before to improve their marketing capabilites worldwide. Marketing has come of age in hospitality.

Coming of age, however, does not signify expertise. The transition has been slow, it seems, and there is still much to be learned. On the other hand, when one considers a 20 year span in the course of the long history of hospitality, the movement has been rapid, almost to the point of mindboggling. It is still the growth stage of hospitality marketing that exists today and that this book addresses.

Our Marketing Approach

This third edition of *Marketing Leadership in Hospitality* brings together what we, the industry, and academics, have learned in the past few years and a lot of what we are still learning. It is filled, as its subtitle indicates, with both *foundations* and *practices*. Our thesis is that the same situation rarely happens twice in the same way. Thus knowing a practice is of minimal help when faced with a situation that is not quite the same, and may be radically different. It is at these times that solid foundations lead the way to marketing leadership.

On the other hand, marketing decisions can be very elusive. Solutions to marketing problems are rarely simple. Two and two rarely add up to four; more likely they add up to three or five and sometimes 25. This is because they are based on human behavior; there is nothing we know that is more complex than the human being. Human behavior does not offer the concrete, factual, and ascertainable solutions that are presented by manufactured goods, financial equations, accounting manipulations, or even flights to the moon.

Five different marketers can arrive at five different solutions for the same problem. All may be right; all may be wrong. In marketing we really don't know the right decision from the wrong one until after it has been implemented. Further, all the marketing science in the world will never eliminate the gut instinct that seldom but sometimes works in spite of all the evidence to the contrary. Planet Hollywood is an example of where gut outruled evidence and success has turned into failure.

Nevertheless, there is a logic and a system to marketing. These can be learned. There are ways that we can understand, as best possible, the vagaries of customer behavior. There are ways to get at the issues and to reveal the substance of marketing problems. There are underlying principles that appear time and time again.

Although marketing's elusiveness is frustrating to many when first exposed to it, we have no choice in the hospitality industry today. Marketing is the umbilical cord that connects the business to the consumer. It is the means by which the organization adjusts to the ever changing needs of the marketplace. It is the force of change and growth and the exploration of new opportunities. It is the strongest weapon there is in fighting the competition. It is, in fact, the substance of survival in a dog-eat-dog business world.

Further, we do not believe that hospitality marketing is only for those titled "marketers." Rather, we believe that it is an essential and substantial portion of all hospitality management. This is because, unlike manufacturing, all management decisions in hospitality impact upon the customer—and the customer is the soul and substance of marketing.

This book takes a leadership approach to the study of marketing in hospitality organizations. Our target audience includes those in academic marketing courses. It also includes managers and marketers now operating in the real world of the hospitality industry, at any level, who feel a need for a more foundational view of marketing with applied examples.

We also focus on a long-range perspective, rather than an operational how-to approach, because marketing is long-range for any organization that seeks survival and growth. This also gives it an international perspective. Although many things may differ on the international scene, basic foundations of marketing do not change.

Our approach is a realistic one. We call it as we see it, but we don't do this lightly. Examples used come from many sources and have been checked and rechecked. Foundations presented are based on accepted principles and solid research. We editorialize and give opinions. These occasions should be clear to the reader, who should feel free to disagree. We will never claim that marketing is an exact science or that we have all the answers. No one does. That's why marketing is also fun—we can all disagree as long as we have the foundations on which to base our decisions.

A final note: Examples used, and the ads used to illustrate examples, are largely those of well-known and international companies. This should not be construed to imply that these companies do things any better or any worse than any other company. Rather, we have used them because they are readily available, and most of the companies are well-known and many readers, worldwide, will be familiar with the names and better able to identify with them. For students not that familiar with the industry, we have used these ads to create awareness as well as to demonstrate examples related to the text. Further, the use of ads does not contradict our thesis that advertising is but a small subset of marketing—as used here, these ads are simply the best source available to graphically demonstrate our points. They are carefully chosen for that reason.

This edition includes case studies at the back of the book. Although some of these have problem orientations, their main purpose here is to be descriptive of the book's context and to give life to it in a real world situation. All the cases are based on actual events, although in some instances names, places, and figures may be disguised.

Between us, we have 60 years of industry experience (not counting those summer jobs!). We started when the word marketing was Greek to most in the hospitality field, including us. We have seen marketing evolve in many different ways and, while we believe that today's operator needs the foundations and practices of this book, we also believe that there is no better way to learn to apply these concepts than with case studies.

The Third Edition

This edition maintains its tradition as the definitive text in hospitality marketing. To do that we have made a number of changes, not only to remain current but to stay ahead in the areas that have become front and center since the first and second editions.

Previous editions, as well as this one, have stressed customer, customer, customer. When we finished the first edition in 1988, it seemed that this emphasis was something little understood by much of the industry. By the time we finished the second edition in 1994, many in the industry had suddenly "discovered" the customer and the industry was changing. We'd like to think that we had some influence in this in our consulting and teaching, the feedback we get from former students, and the number of books the industry bought. Unfortunately, we still know too many situations where the customer is soon forgotten.

An excellent and very current example of this is Planet Hollywood, the *eatertainment* concept developed on "come see the movie stars, buy an $18.00 T-shirt, and don't worry about the food."

This company went public in 1996 and the stock reached $32.00 a share the first day of trading, a figure it never saw again. As we write this in early 1999, the stock is trading around $.75 a share with a 52 week high of $11.00. The company has reported a loss in the last quarter of $1.4 million versus a profit of $16.3 million a year earlier. Same store sales for Planet Hollywood are down over 30 percent from two years ago. There were 87 units opened, including Paris, Moscow, and Gurnee Mills, Illinois. But $250 million in junk bonds issued only six months ago to pay off debt and fund expansion are trading below 60 cents on the dollar. Even the celebrities, who got paid in stock and were supposed to be the main attraction, don't go there any more. And neither do the customers—once is enough for pallid, over priced food. They don't need any more T-shirts, the likes of which represented over 40 percent of sales. This is a company that developed a short-lived fad but never truly understood the customer.*

Along with the customers, we believe that there are three areas that will drive the industry leaders in the future. The first of these is technology. We mention it throughout and have added an appendix on the subject, which may be somewhat obsolete by the time you read this given the pace at which technology changes. Although technology is a critical marketing tool, and will be even more so in the future, we view it more as a cost of doing business today. This is because it is essential but also eminently copyable and offers no competitive advantage once everyone has it. Look at the computer and automobile industries for analogies. What has made Dell so successful, for example, is not its computers, which are like everyone else's, but the competitive advantage of its strong relationships with its customers.

And that brings us to two new chapters, the subjects of which we believe will make the leader-

---

*As we edit this in late 1999, Planet Hollywood has eliminated all stockholder's equity and sought protection under a Chapter 11 bankruptcy-law filing.

ship/follower difference tomorrow. The first is Chapter 3, Relationship Marketing. Marketing tomorrow, in any industry, will no longer be just giving the customer what he or she wants. There are too many competitors who can do that. Rather, it is about building relationships with customers so that they want to do business with you no matter what the competition offers. Competitive advantage is difficult in service industries because most innovations are soon copied. Relationship marketing, on the other hand, can be copied in effort (everyone says they're doing it!) but very few companies know how to do it well and do it right. In a financially driven, commodity product industry, many think the way to build loyalty is with frequent traveler points. This mindset will continue for some time to come. Future leaders, however, will use relationship marketing and true loyalty programs as a competitive advantage.

The second critical area is the need to thoroughly understand the competition. In our first two editions, competitive analysis was a small part of the marketing environment chapter. In this edition, it has become a chapter of its own, Chapter 6, and renamed "Understanding the Competition."

Technology is a necessity; understanding the competition and relationship marketing are the essential areas of competitive advantage. These new chapters, along with a number of other features such as 52 case studies, the book's easy reading, largely nonacademic style, and numerous actual examples, are what we think give this book a competitive advantage. Other chapters have been updated, rearranged, new material added, some old material deleted and, in general, freshened up but not radically changed, as the real world content has not radically changed. And a number of our users said, "Keep it like it is."

Some subjects are covered, albeit differently, in more than one chapter. The reasons for this redundancy are twofold: First, some topics are appropriate in more than one place and to put them in only one would be totally arbitrary. Second, few instructors use the entire text in one semester. Thus

subjects that might be left out because of an unassigned chapter are sometimes covered elsewhere.

We have listened to reviewers, both users and nonusers. As a result of their comments, we have added an "Overview" at the beginning of each chapter so that a reader can get a quick survey of what's in it. We have also added "Key Words and Concepts" at the end of each chapter for quick definition and review. At the same time, we have kept the glossary at the end of the book which includes more common words and a quick place to find them.

Another change, as a result of reviewers' comments, was to move the cases to the end of the book so that they can be used with different chapters. Thus, they are arranged randomly. In the Instructor's Manual, we have put a matrix of the cases and suggested how they would best fit. We have added some new cases and kept some timeless ones. The cases are intended to be explicative of the issues in the text, and not necessarily problem oriented, although many can be used for that purpose. Instructors, we find, use about 10 cases a semester. There are 52 cases so one can go at least four semesters without repeating.

Some instructors, we were surprised to learn, don't use the cases, something we don't really understand. We find them to be the best pedagogical tool for teaching marketing concepts. Our students love them and learn from them, and they help to make a class more interactive. Like the old Kellogg's commercial, we can only suggest: "Try it, you'll like it." For those who want to use more difficult and decision-oriented cases, we suggest, *Cases in Hospitality Marketing and Management,* second edition, and *Cases in Hospitality Strategy and Policy,* both by Robert Lewis and published by John Wiley.

Former Chapters 17 and 18, International Marketing and Tourism Marketing, have been removed. Users said they just never got to them. Many of their features, however, have been inserted throughout the text. Finally, the research section has become a stand-alone appendix. Several users wanted it separate and optional.

Usage of the Book

This book has been designed for different levels of expertise, background, and experience of the student, the instructor, and the practitioner. All chapters have been used, at one time or another, in the classroom at various different levels and/or in industry seminars at the line management, middle management, upper management, and executive levels.

We are acutely aware of the different class and instructor levels existing in academic institutions. For example, some programs require the intro marketing course in the business school followed by a second course in the hospitality program; some teach the intro course in the hospitality program. Some instructors have Ph.D.s in marketing; others, may be simply "assigned" the marketing course for a given semester. As much as possible, we have tried to accommodate all these needs. Suggestions for different uses are included in the *Instructor's Manual.*

One point of difference in this book is the terminology of the Marketing Mix. We do not feel that the "Four Ps" adequately serve the purpose in hospitality marketing. Some disagree with us. "They say the same thing," they argue. We agree. At the same time we have found, pedagogically, that the product/presentation/price/communications/distribution mix is a far more useful tool for understanding the hospitality marketing mix. We have used both this and the "Four Ps" in the classroom many times before coming to this conclusion. In the final analysis, either one is no more than a tool of understanding. When you have read Chapter 2 and the marketing mix chapters, and applied them to hospitality you may find, as we have, that the hospitality mix is a more useful tool. We have, however, made a concession to some who say it helps to have price as a separate part of the mix. We have done this but also kept it as small part of the presentation mix.

The book is intended to build one chapter upon the other. You will find common threads that run through the chapters to serve this purpose, as well as frequent referrals to previous chapters. You may, however, wish to change the chapter order. Many instructors do so to suit their own pedagogical method. This works just as well because of the numerous tie-ins. Some courses do not allow full usage of, or need, all the chapters, especially if you spend much time on cases. There is nothing wrong with skipping chapters. We do it all the time, depending on the class, and the book has been structured so you can do this without seriously disrupting the flow. We discuss this further in the Instructor's Manual which, incidentally, also includes test banks, overhead masters, and power point presentations.

Acknowledgments

Many people, friends, former students, colleagues, industry people, and customers, both advertently and inadvertently, have contributed to this book. Those who have directly contributed to a case are noted on the first page of that case. Most of these were graduate students at the University of Massachusetts/Amherst, the University of Guelph, Ontario, and Cornell/ESSEC Institut de Management Hôtelier International in France. Others were participants in executive seminars. Some will never realize how helpful they have been. We can only mention a few. We are grateful to these, and to many others unmentioned, especially some great graduate and undergraduate students, a few now teaching with this book.

We are especially thankful to Susan Morris and Ursula Geschke, our former master's students, who both contributed to Chapter 17 on personal selling. We are indebted to Stowe Shoemaker, Ph.D., University of Nevada/Las Vegas, who gave us a great deal of help with Chapter 3, Relationship Marketing, an area in which he has carved out a special niche. Peter Yesawich, CEO and President of Yesawich, Pepperdine & Brown, a specialist hospitality advertising agency based in Orlando, helped us locate many good ads to make our points, as well as provided information from his two annual National Travel Monitor studies, used in Chapters 5 and 8. Peter O'Connor at Cornell/ESSEC helped us with the technology section and contributed the last two cases which focus in that area. And, of course, our reviewers:

Dave Bojanic, University of Massachusetts/Amherst
Mark Bonn, Florida State University
Stanley Buchin, Boston University
Jeffrey Catrett, Ecole Hoteliere de Lausanne
Susan Gregory, Colorado State University
Plus many others who gave us helpful comments

We also thank Harsha Chacko, our third author on the second edition, who made many improvements, many of which we have kept.

Many companies, and individuals in those companies, who gave us permission to use their ads and/or material and/or provided information are especially thanked. These are the people who are true supporters of hospitality education, especially Mike Leven, CEO of US Franchise Systems® and Ingvald Fardal, senior vice president sales and marketing, of Radisson SAS Hotels.

In spite of all this help and support, we stand responsible for the entire contents.

Robert C. Lewis
Richard E. Chambers
Fall, 1999

ABOUT THE AUTHORS

Robert C. Lewis was professor of marketing and strategy in hospitality, and graduate coordinator at the University of Guelph, Ontario, Canada from which he is now retired. He previously served ten years in the same position at the University of Massachusetts/Amherst, where he is now Professor Emeritus. Dr. Lewis has also served as the Darden Eminent Scholar Chair in Hospitality Management at the University of Central Florida and is currently a visiting professor at Cornell/ESSEC *Institut de Management Hotelier International* in France. Prior to academe he spent 25 years in the hospitality industry in management and consulting before completing his Ph.D. in 1980. He continues to consult and teach in the industry.

Dr. Lewis is the author of *Cases in Hospitality Marketing Management,* second edition, and *Cases in Hospitality Strategy and Policy,* both published by John Wiley & Sons. He has published over 80 articles in hospitality and other journals, including 25 in the *Cornell Quarterly,* and has written or supervised over 100 case studies. He has taught, conducted executive seminars, and consulted on three continents.

Richard Chambers has worn many hats in the hospitality industry as an author, lecturer, consultant, and veteran hotelier. Richard earned his undergraduate degree from the University of Massachusetts and began his career in a variety of front office and sales positions at Sheraton franchises managed by Dunfey Hotels. After earning his M.B.A. from his alma mater, he joined the Berkshire Hilton in Pittsfield, Massachusetts as Director of Sales.

In 1983, after serving as Director of Marketing of a Cleveland-based Marriott hotel for Boykin Management, Mr. Chambers rejoined the new Omni/Dunfey organization for five years. With Omni, Mr. Chambers served as Director of Marketing for The Omni Berkshire Place, New York; Director of Sales for Omni Parker House, Boston; Director of Marketing and General Manager of the Omni Park Central, New York; Regional Director of Sales; and, ultimately, Corporate Director–Rooms Division.

After his departure from Omni in 1987, Mr. Chambers served as Vice President–Marketing for the regional New England chain, Sheraton Tara Hotels. It was after that that he struck out in an entrepreneurial direction, establishing his own consulting company, Directional Marketing, in New York and Boston. As its President, he built the company into a $5 million organization in seven years.

A challenge that The New York Palace presented to him, literally redesigning and repositioning the hotel over a period of four years, commencing in Fall of 1994, lured him away again as Director of Marketing. He is recently and currently Vice President of Marketing of HRI Companies, the parent company of Leading Hotels of the World and Prima Hotels, based in New York City.

Introduction to Hospitality Marketing

One

❖

THE CONCEPT
OF MARKETING

Overview

Chapter 1 reviews the fundamental marketing concept. It explains why everything that management does in a hospitality setting is an act of marketing. The definition of marketing is creating and keeping customers by communicating to and giving the target market customers what they want, when they want it, where they want it, at a price they are willing and able to pay. This concept is explained early in the chapter and developed to be the text's foundation. Most important, this book is about hospitality customers, because it is with the customer that marketing leadership begins and ends.

After reading this chapter you will understand why this is true. In short, you will understand the concept of marketing, the marketing philosophy, and the elements of marketing leadership. You will also understand why these factors are critical to future success in the hospitality industry. In the chapters that follow, you will learn how marketing leadership works.

FOUNDATIONS AND PRACTICES There are two purposes for being in business: creating customers and keeping customers. Marketing is the cornerstone in the process of achieving both these purposes. Marketing can bring the customer into the hotel or restaurant, and marketing can keep the customer as well.

THE CONCEPT OF MARKETING Creating and retaining customers can be accomplished by solving customers' problems. Customers want to solve their problems and they need to find solutions. Marketing communicates to the customers that their problems will be solved at a particular hotel, restaurant, destination area, or other hospitality enterprise. Marketing keeps these customers returning again and again by maintaining a trade-off balance among problems, solutions, and customer sacrifice.

MANAGEMENT ORIENTATIONS There are many types of hospitality management orientations. Operations-oriented organizations focus their managers' energies on making sure the operation runs smoothly. Product/service-oriented companies focus their energies on creating great products or services. A selling orientation emphasizes salespeople and promotions communicating the message to the customers. The most successful properties have a marketing orientation, as defined by the marketing concept.

THE MARKETING CONCEPT   Marketing-oriented companies employ the marketing concept. The marketing concept emphasizes the organization's ability to create products and services based on the problems (needs) of the customer with whom marketing activities begin and end. The marketing concept is a way of thinking to create customer value. Marketing-oriented companies communicate with customers. Marketing-oriented companies also utilize internal marketing to ensure their employees deliver good service, thereby ensuring return customers.

MARKETING LEADERSHIP   The organization that displays a vision for the future together with a systematic planning process will exhibit marketing leadership. Great marketing leaders in the hospitality industry recognized opportunities in the marketplace well before their competitors. Marketing leadership permeates every phase of the operation of the hospitality enterprise. The marketing system allows the marketing concept to work within the organization.

MARKETING IS EVERYTHING   Marketing is a way of doing business.

Everyone knows McDonald's. Even in Moscow, where 40,000 customers a day stood by the hundreds in long waiting lines, McDonald's is a household word. Why is this? Some will say it is the products, the Big Mac or the Chicken McNuggets or the french fries or milk shakes. Others might repeat the McDonald's slogan: QSC—quality, service, and cleanliness. All would be wrong. McDonald's had no monopoly on any of these features, yet its competition could not catch up with it. The reason McDonald's was a household word around the world was because its lifeblood was filled with the **concept of marketing** and it practiced it in nearly everything it did.

Practicing the concept of marketing means recognizing the relationship between marketing and management. Marketing and management in a service business, such as the hospitality industry, are one and the same. Practicing the concept of marketing means **marketing leadership,** which recognizes that it is marketing forces that shape the total organization.

Some fast-food chain manuals instruct management that the front windows must be washed every six hours, but the McDonald's manual states, "The front windows will never be dirty." In fact, some believe that the most innovative thing that Ray Kroc, founder of McDonald's, did was put large windows in front of every store. It was not enough that a McDonald's was clean inside; it was important that people could look in and see that it was clean. Before McDonald's you took your chances when you walked into a low-priced restaurant. Kroc went one step further. He also insisted that not only the outside of McDonald's be litter-free, but also the space next to them, even if McDonald's employees had to do the cleaning.

What do clean windows and clean sidewalks have to do with marketing? In hospitality, everything that management does affects the customer and everything that affects the customer is marketing, good or bad. We cannot repeat that often enough, because it may be the most important thing that you will ever learn about marketing. **Marketing** is:

Creating and keeping customers by communicating to and giving the target market customers what they want, when they want it, where they want it, at a price they are willing and able to pay.

This book is about marketing leadership in the hospitality industry. More specifically, it is about the causes and effects of marketing leadership. This book is about why people such as Ray Kroc and companies such as McDonald's succeeded, and why others don't succeed or succeed less well. It is about what it takes to succeed in the hospitality marketplace.

For 40 years McDonald's was a great success story, but this book is also about why the March 9, 1998 issue of *Business Week* carried an article entitled, "McDonald's: Can It Regain Its Golden Touch?" And readers responded with comments like,

> We don't like McDonald's food or its quality. . . . We drive past it for other fast food choices. We also don't think it is a place that is safe for us to be in or around. . . . We are not interested in free toys, playgrounds, or what the brand used to be.
>
> 13- AND 8-YEAR-OLD SISTERS

> I find McDonald's to serve tired food in remarkably dirty establishments, served by people with the uncanny propensity for messing up your order after they make you wait for no apparent reason. CEO Michael Quinlan obviously understands perfectly: McDonald's doesn't have to change [a quote by Quinlan in the article]; their customers are doing that for them.

> The reason my family and friends avoid the golden arches is because of lousy service. Sour employees in unkempt uniforms, dirty tables and counters, and sloppily slapped together Big Macs are the norm. . . . The pride and service is gone.[1]

This book is about why McDonald's, already one of the world's largest advertisers, increased its advertising outlays 27 percent from 1995 through 1997 and same store sales went down.[2] And why the American Customer Satisfaction Index in 1998 rated McDonald's number 189, second from the bottom, just above the Internal Revenue Service.[3]

And this book is about why McDonald's 53-year-old CEO Michael Quinlan, who started with the company in the mail room some 30 years before, lost his job of 12 years in 1998 to a 55-year-old accountant turned marketer, Jack M. Greenberg, who had been with the company only 16 years. Where did McDonald's go wrong after such a good start? Essentially, it forgot the customer.

FOUNDATIONS AND PRACTICES

Marketing-oriented companies and marketing-oriented people are the ones who are truly successful in the highly competitive hospitality market place. Does this mean that marketing has replaced operations and accounting? Of course not. The operations career individual will take fewer marketing courses, but must learn to apply marketing in his or her operations courses. When a menu is designed, the first question to be asked is, "How will the customer react to it?" When a hotel room is configured, the first question is, "How will the customer use it?" When prices are established, the first question is, "How will the consumer perceive the risk and the price/value relationship?" When engineering is taught and electric consumption is measured, the first question is, "Is the lighting appropriate for the customer?" When food, liquor, or labor cost controls are taught, we must ask how they impact upon the customer. The foundation is the concept of marketing; the application is its practice.

No company can continue to operate without a profit. But let's put first things first. No company can begin to operate without customers. Today we are in the "customer business." Without customers we are dead. And the way to have customers is to create them, and keep them, by satisfying their needs and wants and solving their problems.

This, then, is the foundation of marketing. Its practice starts at the highest level by deed and action, not just words, and it permeates down to the lowest level of the organization. Concern and responsibility for marketing are concerns and responsibilities of every person in a hospitality enterprise. At the highest level marketing shapes the corporate effort; at the lowest level it means the porter doesn't mop where the customer is walking.

THE CONCEPT OF MARKETING

For many, the term "marketing" conjures up images of selling and advertising. Because of this long-standing and common belief, we call selling and advertising **traditional marketing.** Restaurant management advertises, so they think they are marketing. Hotel management has four salespeople selling, so they think they are marketing. Actually, however, selling and advertising are only two subsets of the broad range of marketing. While they are important subsets, they are only subsets. Marketing is a philosophy or umbrella under which these communications are used to reach the customer.

All phases of marketing, both foundations and practices, derive from the customer. Sales- and advertising-oriented management may think in terms of the virtues of their product and how they can persuade the customer to buy. Consciously or unconsciously, they may be selling the operations or physical end of the business. They often think in terms of what they have to offer the customer. **Nontraditional marketing**–oriented management thinks in terms of customer needs at every step of the business: when designing the service or product before the sale or advertisement, when delivering the service after the sale, while the customer is consuming the service, and after the sale is over. They think in terms of what the customer wants.

The Twofold Purpose of Marketing

It is accepted without question that any business that fails to operate at a profit will eventually cease to exist. If goods and/or services cannot be offered at a price exceeding their total cost, then they should be removed from the market. Although essential to survival, however, profit is not the purpose of marketing but rather a way of measuring the success of management decisions made by a company. As well-known management guru, Peter Drucker, has stated:

> Profitability is not the purpose of but a limiting factor on business enterprise and business activity. Profit is not the explanation, cause, or rationale of business behavior and business decisions but the *test of their validity* [emphasis added].[4]

The only valid definition of business purpose, says Drucker, is to create a customer.

> It is the customer who determines what a business is. For it is the customer, and he alone, who through being willing to pay for a good or for a service, converts economic resources into wealth, things into goods. What the business thinks it produces is not of first importance—especially not to the future of the business and to its success. What the customer thinks he is buying, what he considers "value," is decisive—it determines what a business is, what it produces and whether it will prosper.[5]

Drucker wrote these words many years ago. No one since has said it better. Yet, amazingly, you can pick up a business publication or attend a conference to read or hear how someone has suddenly, in a stroke of genius, "discovered" the customer. Unfortunately there are businesses, including hospitality ones, that have still not discovered the customer. You will read many current examples of this throughout this book.

Creating a customer does not mean simply making a sale. It means creating a relationship wherein a buyer wants your product and/or service before that of the competition. In addition to creating a customer, the purpose of both marketing and business is also to keep a customer. A business's purpose and marketing's purpose, in fact, are really one and the same. Any definition of marketing must emphasize that creating and keeping customers is of primary importance.

Sometimes it is relatively easy to get a customer. Airlines, for example, do it with "seat sales." Restaurants do it with "**twofers.**" Hotels do it with off-season discounts. Tourist destinations do it with packages. Lest you be misled, let's make it clear that these are only small parts of marketing. They are promotions, enticements, inducements. They may get the customer in the door but they won't, by themselves, create and keep the customer. That will depend on how we handle the customer after he or she gets in the door. Thus creating and keeping are two inherent and inseparable words that define marketing. Compare, for example, the inducement versus marketing appeals of Figure 1-1 in light of this discussion.

The marketing challenge is a two-pronged approach: creating new customers while maintaining existing ones by establishing true relationships. Relationships can be as simple as a waitress smiling at a patron in a diner, or as extended as a vice president of marketing playing golf with a top travel manager. But they are a lot more than these examples, as we explain in Chapter 3.

Business revenues come from customers. The finest cost controls, the highest profit margins, the

SHERATON "9 TO 5" PLAN

YOU'VE ALWAYS WANTED TO COME AND GO AS YOU PLEASE.

NOW YOU CAN.

Sheraton
HOTELS & RESORTS
ITT

From now on, everything around here will run according to a very strict schedule.

Yours.

That's the whole idea behind the new Sheraton "9 to 5"℠ plan. The only plan that lets you check in as early as **9 a.m.** on arrival, and check out as late as 5 p.m. when you leave. It gives you more time to get things done. (And more time to fix things back at the office that have become undone.)

The Sheraton "9 to 5" plan is available to all guests paying corporate rates who are members of SCI, our frequent guest program. If you're not currently a member of SCI, simply inquire while making reservations or upon arrival.

And don't forget to use your Visa® card when calling your travel planner or **1-800-325-3535** to request the "9 to 5" plan. For reservations on-line, visit www.sheraton.com. Advance reservations required.

FIGURE 1-1 Sheraton confronts an age-old consumer problem.

most highly trained management, the most innovative products, and the most efficient production lines do not produce revenue and, ultimately, profit, if there are no customers.

There are only three ways to create customers: Get new ones, steal them from competitors, and build true loyalty in those you have and get. Creating new customers is difficult. Inducements may bring in customers who have had no need or desire to visit a particular restaurant or hotel; however, developing new products for nonusers is a limited activity and can be very expensive. In a stagnant or overbuilt market, stealing customers from competitors is the first marketing challenge. The second challenge is keeping them. Thus the first consideration of any management decision should be, "Will it create and/or keep customers?"

Often, decisions are made that are in the best interests of the customer. They may, in fact, create satisfaction, like cut-rate prices, but may not contribute to creating or keeping a customer. Although we certainly must satisfy customers to create and keep them, as we will shortly demonstrate, marketing means something more than simply "satisfying" them. It means understanding customers' needs and wants and solving their problems. It is not difficult to satisfy a customer if you want to give the store away. However, satisfaction alone will not necessarily ensure that customers will return if that satisfaction does not serve their needs and wants or solve their problems. As an actual case in point:

> Two focus groups—meetings customers and the executive committee of a hotel—were each given the assignment to design the "perfect" coffee break for a meeting setup. The executive committee diligently set out to design the "mother of all coffee breaks," including tri-level presentations, mirrors, ice carvings, lighting, flavored coffees, and so on. When costed out, the break had to be priced at $32 per person to make a profit. The meetings customers then turned in their "perfect" coffee break design: a simple coffee break with the table holding the break positioned about ten feet from the back wall. The purpose, they explained, was to alleviate the

congestion caused by a single line break. Their meetings could resume more quickly if the design of the table was simply moved a few feet!

This example shows how far management can be from understanding the real needs and problems of customers.

But, you might add, there are many ifs, ands, and buts to this scenario. True. For one, will the company achieve a sufficient profit in order to satisfy its owners and survive? That will be the test of the validity of its decisions and the extensions of marketing that we discuss in the remainder of this book. First, let's go back to the definition of marketing and look at what customers want and what they are willing to pay.

SOLVING CUSTOMERS' PROBLEMS

There is a basic premise of marketing that we must understand. Simply put, consumers do not buy something unless they have a problem to solve and believe that a purchase will provide the solution to the problem. An example, attributed to Charles Revson, founder of Revlon cosmetics, is: "In the factory we make cosmetics; in the store we sell hope." Another example is, "People don't buy quarter-inch drills; they buy quarter-inch holes."

In this sense, customers buy solutions, nothing else. If we can think of goods and services that we want to sell in this sense, we are a long way on the road to successful marketing. Thinking this way forces us to stand in the customer's shoes, to think like the customer thinks, and to understand what it is the customer wants, when, where, and at what price.

This point can be illustrated as follows. Perhaps you are driving down a highway and you become hungry, or you need a place to sleep. These are needs, and basic ones at that. Needs create problems—namely, how to satisfy them—so what you do next is seek a solution. You know that solution will have a cost. You have to give up something or make a sacrifice in order to get the solution. What

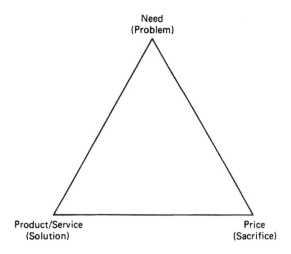

FIGURE 1-2 The trade-off of problem solutions.

emerges is a **trade-off** situation like that portrayed in Figure 1-2.

This is the trade-off thought process a consumer faces when contemplating a purchase. In general, the decision-making process becomes more complicated as the cost of the item to be purchased increases. A consumer may spend months selecting a honeymoon destination, and seconds selecting a can of soda. Nevertheless, the process takes place and the depth of deliberation depends on numerous factors, which are discussed in Chapter 6.

For the moment, let's continue the illustration and assume that a solution presents itself: a sign on the highway announces a motor inn ahead with rooms at $59.50. Rooms provide a solution for the need to sleep and $59.50 is a sacrifice you are willing to make. You decide to head for the motor inn rather than continue driving.

Now the situation becomes complicated. You *expect* that the solution is at hand, that is, you *expect* that you can get a good night's sleep at this motor inn. You *expect*, of course, that there will be a bed in the room, a bathroom, and other appointments. You also *expect* that the bed will be comfortable and that the room will be quiet so that you will sleep well. You may not verbalize these expectations, but subconsciously they exist. You also have, con-

sciously or unconsciously, made another decision: You have decided that spending $59.50 is worth the *risk* that your expectations will be met, that the solution will solve your problem, and that the value you will receive will be worth the sacrifice. The trade-off model now looks like that in Figure 1-3.

Obviously, consumers buy expectations at the same time that they buy solutions, both of which require a sacrifice. It then follows that the greater the sacrifice, the greater the risk, the greater the expectation, and the more demanding the customer is of the solution. To put it another way, if the solution meets the expectation and the value justifies the sacrifice, the risk becomes more justifiable, and a higher level of satisfaction becomes more likely. The result is a higher likelihood that we have created a customer. To put this in realistic terms, consider each element of Figure 1-3 in terms of going to eat at Pizza Hut versus Lutèce, a French restaurant in New York City where luncheon checks average over $150 per person.

Notice now what happens when the solution does not meet the expectation. This is the "potential gap" on the left-hand side of Figure 1-3, as indicated by the

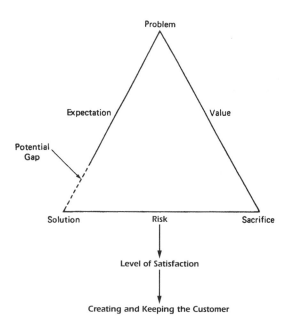

FIGURE 1-3 Expansion of the trade-off model.

dotted line. We have made the dotted line, let's say, "Pizza Hut length." We might make it a hair shorter for "McDonald's length," but for "Lutèce length" it might run almost to the peak of the triangle. The point is obvious: The greater the expectation, the greater the potential that it will not be fulfilled. We explore this point in more detail in later chapters. For now, you can see very clearly why marketing and management are one and the same. If management cannot fulfill customers' expectations, it won't create and keep customers; when it does, it is marketing.

Now notice in Figure 1-3 where satisfaction occurs—at the bottom of the triangle. This places satisfaction clearly as an end product of marketing, *not* as part of the process, in creating and keeping the customer. If the gap is too great between expectation and fulfillment, there will be a low level of satisfaction. Now you should understand why it is expectation that marketing must serve, not just satisfaction. While mints with the restaurant check and hotel bathroom amenities may create satisfaction in themselves, if they aren't expected and don't solve problems for the sacrifice made, the purchase may not be worth the risk or provide the overall level of satisfaction expected.

In essence, Figure 1-3 represents the concept and definition of marketing—creating and keeping customers by giving them what they want, when they want it, where they want it, at a price they are willing and able to pay (or a sacrifice they are willing to make). Each step in Figure 1-3 can also be shown to represent the process of marketing, as we now explain.

Marketing, of course, does not create the needs or problems associated with hunger or the need to sleep.* However, it does identify the needs associated with *what to eat* and *where to sleep*. Marketing differentiates among the available solutions through the creation of expectations. On the other side of the equation, having created expectation, marketing

needs to reduce perceived risk so that the prospective customer perceives the expectation as worth the risk.

This means not only that pricing is an important marketing tool, but also that marketing must persuade the customer that the solution is worth the price. The bottom line in the trade-off model is not profit. For the customer it is the level of satisfaction felt after making the sacrifice (Figure 1-3). For the business, if the satisfaction level is high enough, a customer has been created and kept. Table 1-1 explains this measurement in a little more detail. Keep in mind, of course, that the same tenets hold whether we apply them to a budget motel or a five-star luxury hotel.

Scores of 1 or 2 on such a scale are obviously a real problem—something needs to be done. A score of 5 looks like we've hit the mark. But how about scores of 3 and 4? Many organizations will be happy with 3s. Even more will be happy with 4s. But should they be? Should a level of satisfaction below Completely satisfied be acceptable? Can things ever be perfect?

Thomas Jones and W. Earl Sasser, among others, did some extensive research in this area. Table 1-2 shows some findings with some of our comments added.

Naturally, the solution to any problem rarely exists in a vacuum. That's why marketing becomes far more complex than the example presented. If a solution to the problem of needing a night's sleep was only a room and a bed at the right price in the right place, then there would be little need for marketing. Solutions aren't that simple and include

---

*This is not totally true. A billboard or television commercial depicting a steaming pizza, or a radio commercial describing an elegant dinner, can literally cause salivation. For our purposes of illustration, however, the assumption is normally true.

TABLE 1-1
Levels of Satisfaction

Hospitality customers, like many others, are often measured on the level of satisfaction with their experience(s). A typical scale looks like the following:

1	2	3	4	5
Very dissatisfied	Dissatisfied	Satisfied	Very satisfied	Completely satisfied

T A B L E   1 - 2
Research on Satisfied Customers[6]

1. Except in a few rare instances, complete customer satisfaction is the key to securing customer loyalty. *Note:* Research by Xerox has shown that completely satisfied customers were six times more likely to repurchase over the next 18 months than those who were simply satisfied. It has been found in services that only about 50 percent of those who rate their satisfaction a four plan to return, while this number jumps to 90 plus percent when they give a rating of five.[7]

2. Providing customers with outstanding value may be the only reliable way to achieve sustained customer satisfaction and loyalty. *Note:* Many factors can generate false loyalty, for example loyalty promotions such as frequent traveler programs. Conclusion: It is absolutely critical for a company to excel in both defining its target customers and delivering a product or service that completely meets their needs.

3. Very poor service or products are not the only cause—and may not even be the main cause—of high dissatisfaction. The company may have attracted the wrong customers or have an inadequate service recovery process for winning back the right customers when they have had a bad experience. *Note:* This can also work in reverse, for example, "perfect" service may not be desired or seen as value.

4. Different satisfaction levels reflect different issues and require different actions. *Note:* There are four elements that affect customer satisfaction:
   (a) Basic elements that customers expect to be delivered (e.g., comfortable bed, clean room);
   (b) Basic support services such as customer assistance that make the product more effective or easy to use (e.g., check-in, check-out services, no hassles);
   (c) A recovery process for counteracting bad experiences (e.g., removing a charge from the bill); and
   (d) Extraordinary services that excel in meeting customers' personal preferences, appealing to values, or solving particular problems (e.g., special feather pillows).
   Customers (target markets) determine which of these elements the company should especially focus on delivering.

5. Relying solely on results of customer satisfaction surveys can be fatal. *Note:* These surveys cannot supply the breadth and depth of information needed to guide strategy and product information. Companies must also utilize a variety of other methods to listen to existing, potential, and former customers.

many, many needs other than a simple bed in a simple room. The instant that one motor inn provides something different than another motor inn, competition is created and the mettle of marketing is tested. Instead of "here's a bed" (solution to problem), marketing creates "here's *this* bed," the *only* solution to *your* problem.

The goal for marketers is *to present the best solution to the problem as the lowest risk.* Marketing, however, does not stop there, especially in the hospitality industry. The creation of expectations might be classified as traditional marketing (selling and advertising). There are, however, those who believe that marketing does end there; that it is now operations management's job to assure that those expectations are fulfilled. Figure 1-4 depicts an advertising view of solutions to customers' problems that operations must fulfill.

While the fulfillment of expectations is surely operations management's responsibility, this means, further, that operations management is totally involved in the marketing effort: traditional marketing only brings the customer to the door; it is up to nontraditional marketing to *create* and *keep* the customer.

The trade-off model is critical to the understanding of marketing. The concept is developed further in the chapters to follow, but first we need to see how marketing influences the total picture.

MANAGEMENT ORIENTATIONS

All companies, firms, organizations, and other business entities operate under a basic philosophy or orientation. This philosophy may be spoken,

There's nothing a Regent concierge can't handle. *Even a lullaby or two.*

the Regent LONDON
A FOUR SEASONS · REGENT HOTEL

AUCKLAND. BANGKOK. BEVERLY HILLS. CHIANG MAI. FIJI. HONG KONG. JAKARTA. KUALA LUMPUR. LONDON. MELBOURNE. SINGAPORE. SYDNEY. TAIPEI. CONTACT YOUR TRAVEL COUNSELLOR OR CALL REGENT RESERVATIONS. TOLL FREE: (800) 545-4000.

FOUR SEASONS · REGENT. DEFINING THE ART OF SERVICE AT 40 HOTELS IN 19 COUNTRIES.

FIGURE 1-4   Regent's ad promises solutions to customers' problems.

written, or just simply implied. An organization's philosophy is part of its corporate culture—it emphasizes that "this is the way we do business around here." It is what drives the firm, what makes it work.

Orientations in the Hospitality Industry

The hospitality industry encompasses many philosophies and orientations at various times and places. These orientations may be based on opera-

tions, a product, a service, or selling, on some combination of these four, or, of course, on marketing.

Operations Orientation. An **operations orientation** is categorized by its emphasis on a "smooth operation," as symbolized by the anonymous wag who once stated, "This would be a great business to be in if only the customers didn't get in the way." Operations manuals provide prescriptions for direction and behavior for almost every conceivable occurrence—until the customer decides to do something differently.

Operations-oriented hotels and restaurants sometimes forget the customer in the interest of a smooth operation. Although these facilities run well, customers are fickle and procedures cannot be written for every kind of demand or problem. This does not mean that manuals are not desirable for operations purposes. In fact, in today's large chains it would be impossible to obtain consistency in service delivery without some of them.* Problems occur, however, when the manual becomes the "be-all and end-all" and there is no room for deviation on the customer's behalf. Or, what may be even worse, sometimes the manual is written only from an operations efficiency or cost perspective, without any consideration for the customer.

Operations philosophies, like all philosophies, come down from top management. When the company, or the company's executives, are very bottom line or profit driven, they tend to follow procedures based mainly on cost considerations, overlooking their impact on customers.

Consider, for example, the restaurant that has a slow night. Typically, management will send wait personnel home and close part of the dining room. The section that gets closed is often the exterior section, near the windows or with the view, because it is furthest away from the kitchen and takes more effort to serve. It is also the most desirable from the customer's perspective. The part that remains open, of course, is closest to the kitchen because it is most convenient to serve. Similarly, you may have had the experience of saying to a dining room hostess, "Can we have that table over there?" (instead of the one you were led to), and received the response, "I'm sorry, but it's not that waiter's turn." These practices, of course, can lead to even emptier dining rooms.

In another example, consider a large hotel of a major chain that claimed to be customer-oriented but rewarded all its people based on bottom-line results. This hotel was losing occupancy in the face of increasing competition, and was responding by cutting costs and raising prices. Management spent $17 million on a new entry way that had little if any effect on business. The problems were inside, where staff had been cut to save payroll. Normal check-in time took ten minutes, and that's when there wasn't a line. Check-out was about as bad. The widely advertised indoor pool didn't open until 9:00 A.M. (to save payroll), long after the business clientele had left for the day or was in meetings. The brightest light in the rooms was 67 watts (to save energy costs), difficult to use for paperwork or reading. The widest writing space in most rooms, including suites, was 16 inches.

These types of procedures are established in the name of operational or cost efficiency. Perhaps a better phrase might be, "customer blindness efficiency." Hotels and restaurants that operate by these kinds of procedures pride themselves on their operational efficiencies, rather than on their solutions to customers' problems. Obviously, such efficiencies may well cause problems instead of solving them for guests seeking a hassle-free experience.

Product/Service Orientation. Hospitality properties that operate under this orientation place their emphasis on the **product/service**. These properties market according to the concept of "build it and they will come." They trumpet that their property has the best food, the finest chefs, the ultimate in service, designer decorated lobbies, or even the best location. Consider, for instance, the previous example of the coffee break design, or the examples in Table 1-3.

Properties may have all the attributes they claim; sometimes they do not. Regardless, the claims, like the coffee break design, often fail to consider whether these factors are solutions to customers' problems. More than one group has been lost forever to a hotel because of inattentive personnel, inflexible policies, bad acoustics, or stale coffee, in spite of the beautiful and very expensive chandeliers and wallpaper. In the marketing sense, prod-

---

*Interestingly, when Bass PLC of England took over Holiday Inns in 1990, they reduced the stack of operations manuals from about three feet to about three inches.

T A B L E   1 - 3
Examples of Product/Service Orientations

A joint promotional brochure, directed at meeting planners, for some of Atlanta's hotels contained pictures of the hotels along with the following copy:

- At the Westin, after the hotel had spent $31 million, you could have a "more than successful" meeting because of "sumptuous new fabrics, elegant furnishings, Italian marble, and breath-taking views" and, for "meeting inspiration" there were "twinkling arches and hidden courtyards."
- At the Inter-Continental, you could have "a chauffeur-driven Rolls Royce meet your private airplane," and you could dine in "surroundings of hand-polished wood, antique crystal, and gleaming silver."
- At the Hyatt Regency, you would get to enjoy the hotel that, "20 years later continues to fulfill John Portman's vision."*a*
- At the Marriott Marquis, as a small group, you could "practically have the place to yourself . . . with its awesome atrium, ten restaurants and lounges."
- At the Ritz-Carlton, on the other hand, they "concentrate on the fine points of innkeeping like luxurious rooms, afternoon tea served in English bone china, and richly paneled walls graced by 18th and 19th century oils."

Then, in the same brochure, there was the Colony Square Hotel, a Preferred Hotel, which "assigns individuals who work behind the scenes to oversee every detail of your meeting—from planning to follow-up." Also in this ad was a picture and a quote of the manager of the Coca-Cola U.S.A. Training Center, who said, "The thing I appreciate most is the flexibility. They respond quickly to our last minute requests." Which of all these attributes do you suppose that meeting planners most prefer? That's a dumb question, isn't it? Yet tens of thousands of dollars were spent on these ads.

*a*In case you didn't know, and few today would, John Portman is the architect who created this hotel, with its first-of-a-kind atrium lobby, in the 1960s.

ucts and services should be defined only in terms of *what they do for the customer*. Whatever they do, they should not create even more problems.

Selling Orientation.

A **selling orientation** in hotel and restaurant companies is one where the effort to obtain customers emphasizes finding someone who will come through the doors, as opposed to marketing a solution to a designated market's needs. Hotel companies with this kind of orientation often have large sales forces and/or large advertising budgets. They are very conscious of their open periods and they push their salespeople to "go out and fill them" and to meet their sales quota. Or, in the case of restaurants, these properties may run frequent promotions and special offers. Whichever, everything is based on the sell, sell, sell edict rather than identifying customers' needs and wants.

There is obviously nothing wrong with running a good operation, having a good product/service, or employing an effective sales force. Well-run and successful companies accomplish all these and do them

well. A truly marketing-oriented company, however, views these achievements as subsets of marketing, that is, they are accomplished with the customer as the focal point. The operations manager says "I run a tight ship," but only after making sure that the customers' needs and wants have been considered. The service manager considers first what the service will do for the target market.[8] And the sales manager sells those benefits that will solve customers' problems and make their experiences hassle-free, as we discuss in Chapter 17. Last, however, there is an orientation that can be fatal. We'll discuss that next, and then go to the marketing-orientation philosophy.

Bottom-Line Orientation.

While the orientations mentioned above all have their place in different companies, the **bottom-line orientation** does not. This, in fact, is a dangerous orientation that has destroyed a number of companies in many industries. Twenty years ago this was very prevalent in hospitality companies, many of which did not survive. It is not as prevalent today. We'd like to think it is gone completely but unfortunately it still prevails in some places—from small owner-operated restaurants to some large companies.

The bottom line, of course, is profit. (See, however, Figure 1-5 for a different view.) A bottom-line orientation means that most, if not every thing, is done in the name of profit. In these cases, profit, or its reciprocal, cost, is the basis for decisions, not the test of their validity as we noted ear-

lier. This manifests itself most often in terms of cost—food cost, labor cost, beverage cost, marketing cost, refurbishment cost, and so forth. We discuss the fallacy of this more in the pricing chapter but suffice it to say for now that when the emphasis is on cost the customer is soon forgotten.

One of the authors confesses to being guilty at one time of this crime in running his own restaurant. After all he had gone to hotel school where he

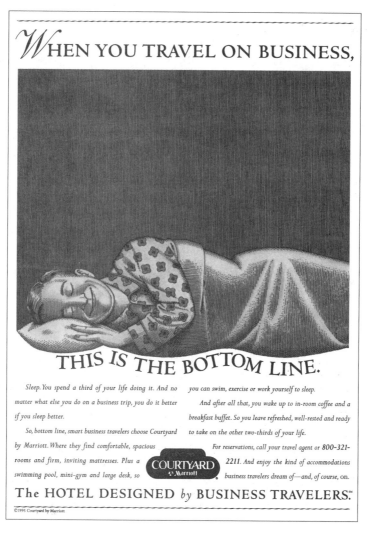

FIGURE 1-5 Marriott Courtyard offers a different view of the bottom line.

learned that the only thing that really mattered was 40 percent food cost, 30 percent labor cost, and 20 percent beverage cost. By this time, however, these standards had been dropped to 36, 26, and 18 percent. That's how he operated until he woke up one day and thought, "Boy, do I run a good operation—just look at those costs. Just one problem—there aren't too many customers."

Liquor bars in airports run a 14 percent liquor cost, but they have a captive audience. Some exclusive resorts get away with the same, but they have other attractions. For many businesses the mandate is cost-driven prices, not price-driven costs, which should be the case.

When we were writing the first and second editions of this book, we sometimes wondered how Sheraton Hotels, a well-known bottom-line organization noted for inconsistent service and poor maintenance, managed to survive. Well, guess what—it didn't. Starwood Hotels and Resorts completed its purchase of ITT Sheraton in 1998. That story is told in Table 1-4. Other examples of bottom-line losers who lost sight of the customer are the previously mentioned (old) Howard Johnson's

---

T A B L E   1 - 4
The Sheraton Story[9]

Sheraton was long noted for its bottom-line mentality. Staff was often short, service was poor, maintenance was deferred, and price/value was a stigma. Sheraton general managers and their staffs were rewarded for their low-cost efforts, largely based on percentages. Like all of us, they knew what influenced their paychecks. Sheraton was in trouble and top management knew it, but they weren't sure why. ITT bought the company in 1968 when Sheraton was as much a real estate company as a hotel company. The long-time CEO was soon "retired" in the 1970s. The successful manager of Sheraton's European operations became president and CEO, but operating Sheraton for ITT wasn't like managing hotels in Europe. In 1979, Rand Araskog became CEO of ITT and in 1980 he became CEO of the Sheraton division of ITT as well.

The New Sheraton

In the early 1980s Sheraton celebrated its 50th anniversary with an all-out bash in Hawaii that cost in the millions of dollars. All GMs, top staff, sales and marketing people, worldwide, were flown at company expense to Hawaii. Festive meals, cocktail hours, high-priced entertainment, all with plenty of ice carvings, decorations, music, and golf and other sports ensued for four days.

But there was a company message along with all this festivity, and it was pushed incessantly at many meetings throughout the conference. This message was called "The New Sheraton." Sheraton was going to change and you (the attendees) better get the message—better quality, better service, and better care for the customer. Costs were barely mentioned—this was the New Sheraton and we'd better get our act together if (implied) we are to survive.

On the last night, at a very gala banquet with all present, CEO Rand Araskog made a rousing closing speech, which ended with words to this effect: "Sheraton will never forgo quality or the customer, but let everyone in this room understand their responsibility, obligation, and contribution to the profits of this company."

What happened? Everyone went back to their jobs, some grousing about the money spent that might have given them raises instead. When back-home employees asked, "What's the New Sheraton?" the reply was, "Business as usual."

Sheraton Problems

Some five years later the newly appointed vice president–North America (a very successful previous Sheraton GM) invited one of the authors to the corporate office in Boston to discuss "strategy." His idea was to have strategy meetings with groups of GMs across the country. "What do you want to tell them?" the author asked. "Well, I just think we should get them to start thinking strategically," was the response.

(continued)

T A B L E   1 - 4   *(Continued)*

"What are your problems?" was the next question. "Oh, we don't have any problems," he replied. "I just think we should talk to them." The author had spent the previous night at the Sheraton Boston, the company's flagship hotel (in a large luxurious suite, in fact, due to a foul-up in room assignments). He related to the vice president a multitude of things that had "gone wrong" in that short 16-hour stay. The response was, "No, no, that's impossible. Those things don't happen at a Sheraton."

When we got down to the nitty-gritty, the VP admitted that Sheraton had a very bottom-line mentality and somehow this had to be changed. Stacked on the credenza behind his desk were maybe 50 to 100 copies of a book that had just been published. It was *Service America* by Karl Albrecht and Ron Zemke (Dow Jones-Irwin, 1985), probably the first, or at least the first best seller, of all the "service and customer" books that spewed out in the 1980s and 1990s. The VP was going to give a copy to each of his GMs. (He also gave one to the author.) That's as far as the meeting went. The strategy meetings were never held, and about five years later the VP left Sheraton to become VP of a Canadian hotel chain.

The Split-Up

Rand Araskog, once referred to by *The Wall Street Journal* as the "poster boy for overpaid executives," after he made $11.4 million in 1990 when ITT stock was grossly underperforming (when queried, his response was, "I feel I earned it.") marched forward. In 1995, he split ITT into three companies with himself as CEO of ITT Sheraton Hotels and Casinos company. He started the Sheraton Grand line of luxury hotels, putting millions into properties like the St. Regis in New York City, buying CIGA Hotels (a small luxury Italian chain), and other trophy hotels around the world. Mr. Araskog reportedly loved the grand life and was especially enthralled with the casino division. Knowing nothing about running casino hotels, however, he brought in at least two experienced casino operators, one after the other, to run that division. They soon left, in a matter of months. After all, Mr. Araskog knew how to squeeze profits out of these properties.

One good thing did happen along the way. Frank Camacho, head of research at Marriott, was hired as senior vice president–marketing and instituted a bonus system based one-third each on customer evaluations, employee evaluations, and return on investment. The old culture, however, by this time was too deeply imbedded, and this was not enough to save Sheraton.

The End

Fast forward to 1997. Steve Bollenbach, a financial wizard who had proven himself a highly capable turnaround artist with stints with Holiday Inn, Donald Trump, Marriott, and Disney, was named CEO of Hilton Hotels in 1996. Hilton had long been a stagnant company, like Sheraton never a leader, under Baron Hilton. Although Hilton owned a sizable portion of Hilton stock, he was usually preoccupied with his polo ponies and hot air balloon adventures, and the Hilton board finally made him hire a new CEO with full, 100 percent authority. Hilton's stock went up 16 percent in four days; within a year it was up 80 percent versus ITT Sheraton's 6 percent in the same period.

Within months, Bollenbach had bought Bally Casinos. On January 27, 1997 he led a $6.5 billion (later raised to $8.3 billion), plus assumption of $3 billion of debt, hostile takeover bid for ITT Sheraton. Among other things, he cited poor, weak, inefficient, self-serving top Sheraton management. Hilton would clean this up and turn Sheraton around. Well, you might as well have hit Mr. Araskog (now 65) over the head with a baseball bat. He spent $20 million to hire investment bankers Lazard Freres & Co. and Goldman, Sachs and Co., who had previously helped him fight off other predators like the Pritzker family (owners of Hyatt Hotels). Araskog also brought in the renowned New York City law firm of Cravath, Swaine & Moore (about $500 an hour), and planned his defense strategy.

Among other things, he sold off side businesses and some Sheraton hotels, postponed the annual shareholders' meeting (all directors were up for election at the same time—and Bollenbach was counting on replacing them with his own candidates), and took many other defensive actions including refusing to meet with or respond to Bollenbach. You might say that Mr. Araskog was slightly infuriated.

Finally, he found a "white knight," who came along in the form of 36-year-old Barry Sternlicht, CEO of Starwood Hotels and Resorts. Sternlicht had just completed the acquisition of Westin Hotels, the latest of many acquisitions, and

(continued)

was on the prowl for more with his tax-advantaged paired REIT.*a* Starwood won the bidding over Hilton, bought ITT Sheraton with a stock swap, and is now the largest hotel company in the world in market capitalization. Mr. Araskog "retired" with a $400,000 a year consulting contract through 2003, his car, driver, secretary, and use of the corporate jet. In case this wasn't enough; he received $15 million in severance pay and 162,500 new ITT stock options convertible into Starwood options. His existing stock options were valued at $64.4 million. Not exactly a "golden parachute"–*The Wall Street Journal* coined a new term calling it a "golden bungee."

Thus ends the saga of Sheraton Hotels, a company that survived for about 65 years but lost it all because of a bottom-line orientation. Thanks to Starwood, however, some latecomer shareholders doubled their investments.

---

*a*REIT stands for "real estate investment trust." These trusts get special tax treatment as they are required by law to pass 95 percent of their profits on to shareholders. They are not, however, allowed to operate the real estate. When this last ruling was made a special exemption was allowed for four existing publicly traded "paired share" trusts. These are REITs that own real estate and a management company that manages it, but trade as one stock. Starwood is one of the four. Steve Bollenbach, of course, cried foul, and he and others are trying to get Congress to revoke this special status. There is much speculation, however, that the consolidation of hotel brands by REITs may put the bottom line back before the needs of the customer. See, for example, Christina Binkley, "Young Mr. Sternlicht Built Hotel Empire; Now, He Must Run It," *Wall Street Journal,* March 5, 1998, pp. A1, A17.

and Victoria Station restaurants, many, many individual proprietor restaurants, and individual hotels, and more currently, Sizzler Restaurants.

THE MARKETING CONCEPT

If a firm adopts the marketing orientation as its philosophy, then the development and implementation of that philosophy is based on what has come to be known as the marketing concept. The marketing concept is based on the premise that the customer is king; the customer has a choice; the customer does not have to buy your product. Thus the best way to earn a profit is to serve the customer better.

> According to the marketing concept, an organization should try to provide products [and services] that satisfy customers' needs through a coordinated set of activities that also allows the organization to achieve its goals. . . . The organization must continue to alter, adapt and develop products to keep pace with customers' changing desires and preferences. . . . The marketing concept stresses the importance of customers and emphasizes that marketing activities begin and end with them.

> In attempting to satisfy customers, businesses must consider not only short-run, immediate needs but also broad, long-term desires. Trying to satisfy customers' current needs by sacrificing their long-term desires will only create future dissatisfaction. . . . To meet these short- and long-run needs and desires, a firm must coordinate all its activities. Production, finance, accounting, personnel and marketing departments must work together.

> . . . The marketing concept is not a second definition of marketing. It is a way of thinking—a management philosophy guiding an organization's overall activities. This philosophy affects all efforts of the organization, not just marketing activities. . . . The marketing concept stresses that an organization can best achieve its goals by [fulfilling customer expectations and solving customer problems].[10]

The marketing concept does not consist of advertising, selling, and promotion. It is a willingness to recognize and understand the consumer's needs and wants, *and* a willingness to adjust any of the marketing mix elements, including product, to satisfy those needs and wants.

Let us translate this definition into simpler language.

Having a marketing orientation is necessary, but not sufficient. We can believe that we are in the business of solving consumers' problems and serving their needs and wants, and we can have this philosophy permeate the entire firm, but until we do something about it—until we put it into practice—it will not suffice. Perhaps a better way of stating this is, "You have to put your money where your mouth is." Practicing the marketing concept does exactly that.

There is a fine but important distinction here: *a company can have a marketing orientation without practicing the marketing concept.* A company's having a marketing orientation without practicing the marketing concept is a good start, but it will not succeed in the long run. When the company dies, it will be said about it, "They were such nice people; I wonder why they didn't make it." On the other hand, practicing the marketing concept without a marketing orientation is like giving lip service to marketing; it constructs marketing as a company policy without permeating the firm as a shaper of the corporate effort. Both a marketing philosophy and the marketing concept must exist before we can define the firm as a true marketing company.

Practicing the marketing concept means putting yourself in the customer's shoes. It means selecting market segments that can be served profitably. This translates into profitable products and services that the company can produce. Practicing the marketing concept means making the business do what suits the customer's interests. For management, it has implications of integrating and coordinating the research, planning, and systems approaches of the firm. Practicing the marketing concept is a management approach to marketing that stresses problem-solving and decision-making responsibility to enhance the objectives of the entire firm. Marketing is not the clever selling of what you have to sell. It is, rather, the creation of genuine customer value. It is helping your customers to become better off.

Probably the most important management fundamental that is ignored is staying close to the customer to satisfy his needs and anticipate his wants. In too many companies, the customer has become a bloody nuisance whose unpredictable behavior damages carefully made strategic plans, whose activities mess up computer operations, and who stubbornly insists that purchased products should work.[11]

MARKETING LEADERSHIP

The guiding philosophy in any firm is established by the top management, which provides the leadership and direction for the organization. These leaders must believe in the marketing philosophy and the marketing concept and ensure that they pervade all levels of the organization. Marketing leadership accepts change as a constant. It not only recognizes needs and wants of the customer but it also recognizes that the customer changes; the customer is not in a static state and any successful company must change with, if not before, the customer. Business obituaries are replete with companies that failed to recognize changes in the marketplace.

An excellent example is that of the "old" Howard Johnson's. In 1965, Howard Johnson's annual sales were greater than the combined sales of McDonald's, Burger King, and KFC. By 1970, its sales were about the same as McDonald's. In 1984, when the company was broken up, its sales were less than three-fourths of a billion; McDonald's had grown to almost 3.5 billion.

When the customer changed, Howard Johnson's did not; slowly but surely its customer base eroded. As things got worse, Howard Johnson's concentrated on cutting costs rather than recognizing its customers' problems, and finding out what the customer wanted. Howard B. Johnson, son of the founder, said they ran a very tight operation. They were on top of the numbers daily. Others said, to the effect, if he'd eaten in his own restaurants more instead of lunching at 21 Club in New York City, he might have learned something.

On the other hand, take the example of Jan Carlzon. In 1981, he was picked by the Scandinavian Airways System (SAS) Board of Directors to be its president, with the challenge of turning around an ailing company. In what were tough times for the airlines, most other companies were cutting back. Carlzon went the other way; he poured it on. In a little over a year Carlzon took SAS from an $8 million loss to a gross profit of $71 million. He did it by going to the trenches, where the customer was. Carlzon initiated the marketing concept in SAS. He convinced employees that customer loyalty could be developed if employees fulfilled the needs and demands of travelers quickly and efficiently. SAS soon became one of the leading and most profitable international airlines. Carlzon understood the importance of the marketing concept, advocated it, and provided the leadership to permeate the marketing philosophy throughout the organization. In recent years we have seen companies as large as General Motors, IBM, Compaq, American Express, Sears Roebuck and Company, Holiday Inns, and Hilton Hotels turned around by new, customer-oriented leaders with new strategic plans, the type of plans we discuss in Chapter 3.

Opportunity

Great success stories in business almost always include tales of visionary leaders who saw and grasped opportunity, people like Howard Johnson (the founder), Kemmons Wilson, founder of Holiday Inns, and Ray Kroc, founder of McDonald's. These men were visionaries. They didn't create the needs, wants, or problems, but recognized them as opportunities.

Very few opportunities are as grand as these. To find the smaller ones, marketing concept managers don't look for opportunity first; they look for consumer problems because they are easier to identify. What is perceived as a consumer problem may well be the symptom of an operations problem. This, then, becomes an opportunity. For example, as previously mentioned, 67 watt light bulbs are real consumer problems to this day, caused by the management problem of wanting to cut costs.

Opportunity continues to be the lifeblood of successful marketing. It doesn't start with fancy drapery or upholstered walls; it starts with consumers' problems. Look for a problem, the real

problem, and you will find an opportunity. No industry, no business, and no product enjoys an automatically assured growth. It is only seeking, finding, and successfully exploiting opportunities that can assure growth.

Planning

Another element of practicing the marketing concept is planning. Planning is defining what has to be done and allocating the resources to do it. It means proacting rather than reacting. It means shaping your own destiny.

Although one would expect planning to be a given in most companies, it is not difficult to find companies that do not plan, plan haphazardly, or plan only as an exercise. Good planning follows from good leadership. Growth must be carefully planned. Opportunities must be sought and planned for in a systematic manner. This means planning with the customer in mind.

Many hotels develop annual marketing plans (restaurants rarely do), but they often have very little to do with planning. These marketing plans often turn into promotional objectives, advertising and sales allocations, budgets, and day by day occupancy forecasts. Rarely do they address the creation of customers or changes in current operating procedures to keep these customers coming back. While financial planning is often routine, true marketing planning has yet to achieve that status. Strange. Without customers there will be no finances to manage.

Control

Control is the third element of leadership, but it is also the glue that holds the others together and makes them work. When control is lacking, leadership and planning founder. Control in the marketing sense means control of your destiny through leadership, planning, and opportunity by control of the customer, the market, and the product.

Control is the feedback loop of the system that tells if the system is working and provides information to management on who the market is, and what the customer's problems, expectations, perceptions, and experiences are. Control is knowing whether perceptions equal reality, why the customers come or don't come, how they use the product, how their complaints are handled, and whether they return. In short, control is knowing and serving the customer. Control is also knowing your employees because, as we see later, every employee is an integral part of the marketing effort.

Control in marketing means a good management information system, which we discuss later in greater detail.

MARKETING IS EVERYTHING

Technology is transforming choice and choice is transforming the marketplace. Almost unlimited customer choice accompanied by new competitors is seen as a threat by many marketers. But the threat of new competitors is balanced by the opportunity of new customers.

> These new customers don't know about the old rules, the old understandings or the old way of doing business—and they don't care. What they do care about is a company that is willing to adapt its products or services to fit their strategies. This represents the evolution of marketing to the market-driven company.[12]

The alternatives to old traditional marketing approaches are what Regis McKenna calls **knowledge-based** and **experience-based** marketing. Knowledge-based marketing includes mastering the technology in which a company competes with knowledge of competitors and customers, the competitive environment, and the company's own organization, capabilities, and way of doing business. With this knowledge a company can integrate the customer into the process to guarantee a product or service that solves consumer problems, can identify segments of the market that the company can own, and can develop an infrastructure of suppliers, partners, and users to sustain a competitive edge.

Experience-based marketing means spending time with customers, constantly monitoring competitors, and developing a feedback system that turns this information into new product/service intelligence.

We have talked, and will talk more, about creating and keeping a customer and about customer loyalty. But today, with so much choice, customer loyalty may be short-lived. The only way to keep a customer may be to integrate him or her into the company and create and sustain a relationship between the customer and the company. This will be marketing's job. "Marketing will do more than sell. It will define the way a company does business."[13]

The old notion of marketing was based on certain assumptions and attitudes but:

> Marketing today is not a function. It is a way of doing business. . . . Marketing has to be all-pervasive, part of everyone's job description. . . . Its job . . . is to integrate the customer into the design of the product and to design a systematic process for interaction that will create substance in the relationship.[14]
>
> . . . Technology permits information to flow in both directions between the customer and the company. It creates the feedback loop that integrates the customer into the company, allows the company to own a market, permits customization, creates a dialogue, and turns a product into a service and a service into a product.[15]
>
> . . . The critical dimension of the company—including all the attributes that together define how the company does business—are ultimately the functions of marketing. That is why marketing is everyone's job, why marketing is everything and everything is marketing.[16]

Better yet, we might add, the customer is everything. The rest of this book is about customers.

SUMMARY

This chapter has introduced marketing as a philosophy and a way of life of the hospitality firm. We have defined marketing in terms of the customer and we have demonstrated how a marketing orientation, or the lack of it, impacts the entire organization. We have examined the concepts of internal and relationship marketing (although without using those terms), which are discussed in detail in Chapter 3.

We have shown that marketing is far more than selling and advertising, the traditional concepts of the field. In fact, it has been shown that advertising and selling, equated by some with the term marketing, are only subsets of marketing. The philosophy of marketing is needed before any communications vehicles are employed. In some cases, these activities may not even be necessary to marketing, as demonstrated by the many successful establishments that never advertise or practice direct selling.

The other side of this coin should also be apparent. You don't have to be a marketing professional to engage in marketing. Marketing is an integral part of management and the day-to-day business of running an operation.

Those readers for whom this chapter is their first real introduction to marketing may, in fact, be a little bewildered with this concept of marketing. Not to worry. In services industries, of which the hospitality industry is certainly a part, more than 80 percent of marketing may be nontraditional marketing. In Chapter 2 we explain why.

KEY WORDS AND CONCEPTS

Bottom-Line Orientation: A hospitality enterprise orientation that focuses on profit, the bottom line of an income statement.

Concept of Marketing: The art of creating customer value and helping the customer to be better off by fulfilling customers' expectations and solving customer problems.

Creating a Customer: Building a relationship that creates loyalty.

Experience-Based Marketing: Spending time with

customers, constantly monitoring competitors, and developing a feedback system that turns this information into new product/service intelligence.

Knowledge-Based Marketing: Mastering the technology in which a company competes, with knowledge of competitors and customers, the competitive environment, and its own organization, capabilities, and way of doing business.

Marketing Definition: Creating and keeping customers by communicating to and giving target market customers what they want, when they want it, where they want it, at a price they are willing and able to pay.

Marketing Leadership: A characteristic of hospitality enterprise that integrates marketing into every phase of its operation through opportunity, planning, and control. Marketing leadership combines a vision for the future with systematic planning for solving customers' problems.

Nontraditional Marketing: The concept of designing and delivering a product or service based on the needs of the customer.

Operations Orientation: A hospitality entity orientation that focuses on the execution of the operation to provide a smooth running organization.

Product/Service Orientation: A hospitality entity orientation that focuses on the product and service aspect of the organization to attract customers.

Selling Orientation: A hospitality entity orientation that focuses on utilizing salespeople and other communications to sell its product.

Trade-Off Model: The trade-off model is the concept of a customer's problems being satisfied by the solution provided by an organization for the sacrifice or risk the customer has to take, leading to customer loyalty

Traditional Marketing: The use of advertising and salespeople to communicate to customers what a company wants to sell.

Twofers: Two meals for the price of one.

Twofold Purpose of Marketing: The purpose of being in business is to create and to retain customers

DISCUSSION QUESTIONS

1. A very successful restaurateur says, "Who needs marketing? That's for big corporations and business students. I operate by hunch and common sense." Discuss this statement.
2. Give examples of hospitality operations with which you are familiar, or have read about, that seem to operate by the different philosophies discussed in the chapter. Relate their philosophy to their success or lack of it.
3. From some of your own experiences, apply the consumer trade-off model. How do you balance risk against problem solution? How does this affect your price/value perception and your expectations? Develop a scenario for how a hospitality customer might do the same thing.
4. The chapter states, "Having created expectation, marketing needs to reduce perceived risk." Discuss the ways in which marketing might do this in the hospitality industry.
5. Discuss the application of the marketing philosophy, and why it is needed before utilizing advertising and sales efforts.

GROUP PROJECTS

1. Design the "perfect" hotel room based on customer needs and wants. Be prepared to discuss in class.
2. Design the "perfect" restaurant experience based on customer needs and wants. Be prepared to discuss in class.

REFERENCES

1. Readers Report, *Business Week,* March 30, 1998, p. 16.
2. "McDonald's Sales Fail to Keep Pace with Ad Outlays," *The Wall Street Journal,* April 3, 1998, p. B2.
3. "Now Are You Satisfied?" *Fortune,* February 16, 1998, p. 164.
4. Peter F. Drucker, *Management: Tasks, Responsibilities, Practices.* New York: Harper & Row, 1974, p. 60.
5. Peter F. Drucker, *The Practice of Management.* New York: Harper & Row, 1954, p. 37.
6. Thomas O. Jones and W. Earl Sasser, Jr., "Why Satisfied Customers Defect," *Harvard Business Review,* November–December 1995, pp. 88–89. Copyright © 1995 by the President and Fellows of Harvard College; all rights reserved.
7. James L. Heskett, W. Earl Sasser, and Leonard A. Schlesinger, *The Service Profit Chain.* New York: Free Press, 1997, p. 22.
8. See, for example, Robert C. Lewis and Michael Nightingale, "Targeting Service to Your Customer," *Cornell Hotel and Restaurant Administration Quarterly,* August 1991, pp. 18–27.
9. Taken from trade publications, published news items, industry sources, and personal experiences and contacts.
10. William M. Pride, *Marketing: Concepts and Strategies.* Boston: Houghton Mifflin, 8th ed., 1997, pp. 13–14.
11. Thomas J. Peters and Robert H. Waterman, Jr., *In Search of Excellence.* New York: Harper & Row, 1982, p. 156.
12. Regis Mckenna, "Marketing Is Everything," *Harvard Business Review,* January–February 1991, p. 65.
13. *Ibid.,* p. 68.
14. *Ibid.,* p. 69.
15. *Ibid.,* p. 78.
16. *Ibid.,* p. 79.

Two

• ◆ •

MARKETING SERVICES AND THE HOSPITALITY EXPERIENCE

Overview

Chapter 2 focuses on services, the bedrock of hospitality in both marketing and operations. Hospitality is first and always a service industry. The differentiation between goods and services and the impact these differences have on customers and on marketers are fully covered and the characteristics of services that make them unique are explained. A model of service quality gaps is introduced. Finally, we discuss the specific elements of the hospitality product.

SERVICES VERSUS GOODS   Goods are tangible, meaning the consumer can take them home and use them. Services are different from goods because they are intangible and experienced, not tangible and possessed.

MARKETING OF SERVICES   This is different than marketing of goods for essentially four specific reasons:

Intangibility: Intangibility is a characteristic of services. The consumer of a service can only bring home an experience, very different than wearing a new sweater. The customer must be satisfied with the experience of the service itself.

Perishability: Services are perishable. They cannot be stored for later consumption and if unsold and unused at one particular time they cannot be redone or resold. This creates a greater need to manage demand and capacity.

Heterogenetity: The heterogeneity of service delivery is much different than that of goods delivery and creates special problems. Customers constantly interact with front desk, switchboard, sales, room service, and restaurant employees, among others, where there are constant vagaries in the service delivery. This poses special problems for both management and customers.

Simultaneity of Production and Consumption: Unlike its goods counterpart, whereby a car may be manufactured in Ohio and sold in Phoenix, services are consumed as they are produced in the same place and/or time. This means the customer is part of the production process, again leading to special problems.

SERVICE QUALITY AND SERVICE GAPS   A model know as SERVQUAL is used to demonstrate

where gaps occur in service delivery. The zone of customer tolerance is also explained.

COMPONENTS OF THE HOSPITALITY PRODUCT   These include goods and services as well as environment and experience. The marketing of the product is different because of these elements.

• ◆ •

Today, people doing knowledge work and service work account for three-fourths, if not four-fifths, of the work force in all developed countries—and their share is increasing. In 1955 these people formed less than one-third of the work force.[1] In the United States the service sector provides over three-fourths of the gross domestic product.

The hospitality industry is a service industry. This requires the need for special examination of the hospitality marketing activity as contrasted with the marketing of goods. The basic concept of marketing will not change, however, as it is concerned with the fulfilling of needs and wants, and solving consumer problems, in any industry.

It was argued in Chapter 1 that in the hospitality industry every act of management is also an act of marketing. When this notion is contrasted with the management of a manufacturing plant and the marketing of the goods produced by that plant, it can be seen that many differences exist between the two types of industry. These differences and the differences between services marketing and goods marketing are worth examining before we proceed to the special case of hospitality marketing.

SERVICES VERSUS GOODS

The major differentiation of **services** from **goods** is the notion of **intangibility.** Yet there is no such thing as a pure good without some elements of service attached to it. For example, an automobile is a manufactured good but few of us are strangers to

the service aspects of buying and owning a car. Thus even the purchase of a manufactured good will have some element of intangibility. Similarly, most services contain some element of **tangibility.** Airlines are considered part of the service sector but the seat you sit in is very tangible. What concerns us here is the marketing of the intangible aspects of the product, namely the service that accompanies it.

Essentially, the goods component of a product is different than the service component because you can see and feel goods, while services provide you with an intangible **experience.** A car is a good that can be driven and tested before being purchased. A hotel stay or a restaurant meal is a service, the room or food cannot be tried before purchase. A car buyer leaves with a car; a service buyer leaves with an experience. This explanation is somewhat simplistic. What we need to do is break the product down into its various components. Customers tend to view each component in terms of problems it solves.

As the state of the art of marketing services has developed over the past 20 years, it is clear that not only are services different from goods, but that services are different from services. The professional services of a doctor, lawyer, or accountant are not the same as those of a hospital, a dry cleaning service, a barber, or a hairdresser. Similarly, the hospitality product is different. Its components can be tangible and intangible and services and goods. It is all of these elements plus **environment** and experience that make the marketing of hospitality products a special case of nontraditional marketing. First, we need to understand the marketing of services, in general.

MARKETING OF SERVICES IS DIFFERENT

There are a number of important differences between services and manufactured goods. Four of these differences are those most frequently mentioned in discussions of services: **intangibility, perishability, heterogeneity,** and **simultaneous production and consumption.** It is important to understand these differences because they have major implications for marketing. For each difference, we discuss the implications from the perspective of both the consumer and the marketer.

Intangibility

In describing services, the term intangibility* has come to mean two things: one cannot grasp a service with any of the five senses, that is, one cannot taste, feel, see, smell, or hear a service, at least until one has consumed it, and one cannot easily grasp it conceptually. Although services will differ in some of these respects (and it is obvious that this description is not appropriate to the hospitality product in all cases), we continue to use the term in that common usage with license to violate it now and then.

Services are experienced rather than possessed, as shown in Figure 2-1. There is no passing of title when a service is purchased. Buyers have nothing to be displayed, to be shown to friends or family, to put on the shelf, or ever to use the same service again. In sum, buyers go away empty-handed. They

do not, however, go away empty-headed. They have an experience to remember and to talk about.

The Consumer. The intangibility of services has profound implications for consumers, and thus for marketers. In the extreme, buyers are not sure what they are buying, or what they will get. Even if they have bought it before, they cannot go back and say, "I want one of the same" and show the seller what it is that they want, or be sure they will get the same thing. Buyers cannot kick the tires, turn up the sound, smell the aroma, measure the size, or taste the flavor before buying. They are buying a "pig in a poke."*

The first service experience creates expectations for future experiences. This point demonstrates why each experience of a service rendered is a marketing effort. It is the only true way consumers have of valuing the purchase and determining if it is worth the sacrifice. Even then they are not sure if it will be repeated in an identical fashion. These factors increase the risk for customers. When buyers have not previously had the same experience, they may have to rely on similar experiences. If there have been none, then they may choose to rely on the experiences of others, either with the same experience or with similar experiences. Alternatively, they may rely on traditional marketing advertising. Any of these sources create perceptions and expectations.

For hospitality marketing, creating the right customer perception and expectation is critical. This is why traditional marketing may be counterproductive. A Howard Johnson hotel may advertise itself as a "Hotel and Conference Center." Similarly, a dedicated conference center, such as Arrowwood in Westchester County, New York, also advertises itself as such. Consumer perception and expectation may be the same but the service levels in these two "conference centers" will be vastly different.

---

*The word intangible is strictly defined as "being unable to be perceived by the sense of touch." The services marketing literature tends to use the term more loosely as being unable, or difficult, to be perceived by the five senses and by conceptualization. Thus the service of a waiter is intangible, while the steak served is tangible.

---

*This term is derived from the Scotch and, in turn, farmers of the American Midwest, where a poke is a bag or sack; it means that one cannot see what one is buying.

FIGURE 2-1   It's the experience that counts.

Further, a customer who has just held a meeting at the Arrowwood Conference Center would be very disappointed at the Howard Johnson version. Conversely, the Howard Johnson customer would be overwhelmed with the cost of holding a similar meeting at the Arrowwood Conference Center. Buyers who have only the advertising or the promise of the seller on which to rely may truly be buying a pig in a poke. In either case there will be different intangible experiences, as there will be in any hotel or restaurant experience. Thus hotels often advertise the intangible, as shown in Figure 2-2. Restaurants, however, rarely advertise the intangible, but probably should.

Business centers are another service that is offered to hotel customers with varying degrees of offerings. Hotel A may have a state-of-the-art business center with secretarial help, fax machines, computers, copiers, and so on, while Hotel B's business center may be the administrative assistant to the General Manager. Both market business centers, or tangible goods, as an amenity to their guests. Both offer very different levels of service and intangible experiences.

Words like "conference center," "fitness center," and "business center" create perceptions that may be far from the reality when encountered. Good marketing seeks to make perception and reality equal because, as we see later, **perception is reality** for the consumer. Thus, word of mouth, nontraditional marketing, may be the most potent force in creating a customer.

The Marketer. The intangibility of services creates several other challenges for marketers. It is not easy to display and communicate intangible services. Marketers must convince the prospective buyer that they offer the right solution to the buyer's problem. The first step is to develop the expectation. Traditional methods of doing this are through advertising, direct mail, personal selling, and public relations. Hospitality companies use these methods in many cases but there are inherent problems—it is not easy to advertise or sell an intangible service. You can use words, but often these

are as abstract as the service itself and may serve only to compound the intangibility (e.g., the finest, the ultimate). On the other hand, you can use tangible clues, sometimes called "tangibilizing the intangible." Refer again to Figures 2-1 and 2-2 for both these uses.

What we really do when we market a service is make promises; the greater the intangibility, the greater the promise, and the greater the risk for the buyer in terms of the sacrifice that has to be made. Customers have no choice but to believe us and take our word, or not believe us and go somewhere else where they will likely get the same promise and be faced with the same dilemma. It is because of this quandary that we say that traditional marketing is only a small part of hospitality marketing.

In fact, there are some who have raised serious questions about the value of advertising hospitality services except for purposes of creating awareness and as reminder, sometimes called maintenance, advertising. Research has shown that, barring first-hand experience, buyers of services rely on word of mouth more than any other source of information. We have now come full circle. If we want to create positive word of mouth, it is obvious that we must create positive experiences for customers. Thus it is clear that one of the most important elements of marketing a service lies in the handling of a customer's experience. The example is compounded even further. The typical customers who experience poor room service may not complain only about room service; they are as likely to complain about the total service in that hotel. The same analogy can be made for restaurants.

Intangibility also makes pricing decisions difficult. How much more will a customer pay for excellent service versus good service? In addition, buyers are more likely to equate higher prices with better quality. Consider this example. Prospective attenders of a large convention are sent a list of hotels and their rates for the city in which the convention is to be held. If one does not have any previous experience in that city, room rates may be the only indicator of quality. Buyers may speculate that

FIGURE 2-2 Radisson advertises the intangible.

lower room rates indicate a poor location, or poor upkeep or, very likely, poor quality and service, which is not necessarily the case. Branding, of course, attempts to assuage the fears of customers by giving them a sense of expectation at any price level. Nevertheless, the buyer cannot experience the service before making the choice.

Marketers are also affected by the fact that services, unlike tangible products, cannot be protected by patents. No one organization has the exclusive right to provide excellent service. In addition, most new services that a hotel may introduce can be easily copied by the competition, but the intangible customer satisfaction is not easily copied and is far more elusive.

Perishability

The second primary characteristic of services is their perishability. It has often been said, for example, that there is nothing as perishable as an airline seat or a hotel room. If not sold on a particular flight or for a particular night, that opportunity to sell it is gone forever. Initially, the impact of this characteristic appears to be a major problem for management rather than for the consumer. That is undoubtedly true, but the repercussions are felt by the consumer as well, as one cannot be told to "come back tomorrow." A hotel has a fixed number of rooms available for sale on any given day, and it is the task of management to create demand for these rooms. It is also management's task to have rooms available on consumer demand. There is probably no angrier a customer than one with a confirmed reservation who has been **walked.*** Some restaurants, however, do give out "rain checks" for another occasion (Figure 2-3).

The Consumer. Just as hotel room nights cannot be stored, other services provided also cannot be stored. A front desk clerk may be swamped during a busy check-in period and humanly incapable of providing good service to all customers. An hour later, however, he may be standing around with nothing to do. This fluctuating demand can cause service provided to customers to be uneven. The same is true, of course, in restaurants. The consumers don't care about perishability; what they care about is availability, and prompt and courteous service.

---

*To walk a customer is to deny a room that has been reserved but is not available. Many hotels today, to make up for this error, will provide taxi fare to another hotel and a free phone call home. Some will even pay for the first night at another hotel.

The Marketer. Just as inventory management and control are important to a goods manufacturing company, so management and control of inventory (i.e., a capacity to satisfy) are critical to a service company to supply the consumer upon demand. In essence, however, the service company—if it wants to be able to satisfy demand—must have the capacity and capability of producing satisfaction when demand occurs.

Hotels, airlines, and restaurants are unable to increase capacity in the short run. Not having enough rooms at certain times offers problems, as does having too many rooms available. The challenge, then, is to "manage" both demand and capacity. "Seat sales" for airlines, weekend packages and off-season rates for hotels are methods used to do this. So, too, are increased prices in times of heavy demand. In other words, the challenge for the marketer is to balance out the demand and the capacity as much as possible. This has led to a practice called yield management, or revenue management, which we discuss in detail in Chapter 14, on pricing. Many, many restaurants have excess demand on Saturday nights. So far, however, we have never seen an attempt to balance this out, for example by pricing, yet it seems a logical thing to do.[2]

One effect of low demand has been to push many hospitality managements into an operations mode and orientation to restrict costs in the event of unused supply. The emphasis on operations and cost control, while perhaps necessary in some cases for survival, may have an adverse effect on the customer relationship. Housekeeping staff, front desk staff, dining room staff, and other staff that serve the customer directly become the instruments of control. If overstaffing occurs, there is a high cost ratio and the labor cost percentage to sales is too high. Bottom-line management may resist this potential problem by understaffing. When unexpected demand occurs the service levels become too low.

One alternative has been to charge prices that are high enough so that overstaffing does not become too serious a problem. Four Seasons hotels followed this strategy and were known for their high level of service regardless of the level of de-

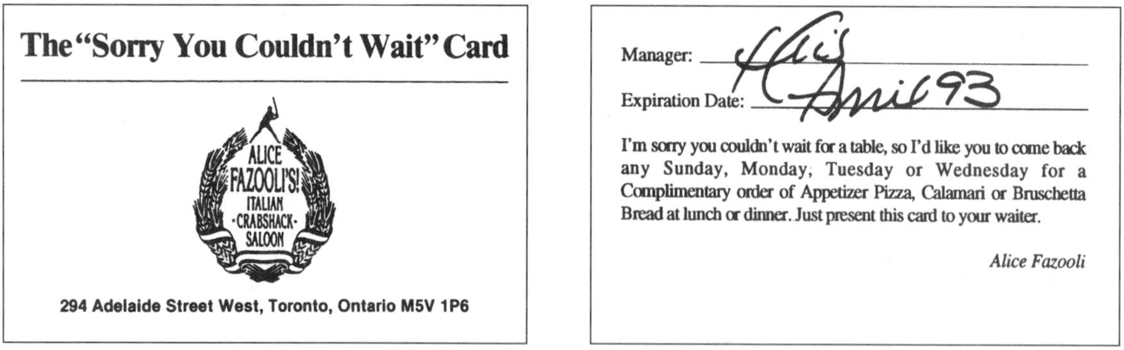

FIGURE 2-3   Alice Fazooli's offers a restaurant "rain check".

mand, but not without serious impact on the bottom line. In poor economic times, in which most hotels discounted severely, Four Seasons was unable to sustain their higher prices and had to accept the higher costs ratio. Many hotels and restaurants, however, cannot afford to discount and cut staff instead. The result is often irate customers.

While there is no easy solution to the problem, it is one in which, once again, marketing and management are inextricably intertwined. What this means is that reduction of staff is both a marketing decision and a management decision. The impact on the customer must be the first consideration. If service is an element that is being marketed, then service is an element of customer expectation that should be provided because service is being offered as a solution to the customer's problem. It is part of the value for which a sacrifice is made and the risk is taken.

Finally, while it is popular to talk about the perishability of the hospitality product, the oft-forgotten flip side of that characteristic is that the product can be sold over and over again. Doing this, of course, depends upon demand. There is nothing better than keeping customers for maintaining constant demand.

Heterogeneity

Heterogeneity of service is concerned with the variation and lack of uniformity in the service being performed. The service received by a guest at the front desk of a hotel may be much better (or much worse) than that received at the restaurant in the same hotel. Here we mean something different from lack of service caused by insufficient staff; instead we mean fluctuations in service caused by the human element, individual differences among employees and among customers themselves, as well as customers' perceptions of these differences.

On any given day, a hotel guest may come in contact with as many as a dozen or more different employees. The switchboard operator, front desk clerk, restaurant manager, and housekeeper may all have some contact with the guest. To have all these different contacts all go well for, perhaps, as many as 300 guests in one day, is a marketing task that is truly a special case. Jan Carlzon, formerly CEO of the Scandinavian airline, SAS, called each of these contacts a "moment of truth." Each of SAS' 10 million customers, he estimated, came in contact with approximately five SAS employees for an average of 15 seconds each trip, or a total of 50 million contacts a year. "These 50 million 'moments of truth' are the moments that ultimately determine whether SAS will succeed or fail as a company."[3]

Consistency of service may be very difficult if only because of the human-intensive nature of providing service. Manuals may well prescribe exactly what every employee in a large restaurant is supposed to do in any given situation, but they can never predict what various individuals with various backgrounds, various orientations, and various personalities will actually do in a given situation.

The Consumer. Understanding consumers' problems can mean a lot more than smiling at the customer and believing "the customer is always right." First of all, customers themselves are heterogeneous. Consider, for example, an elderly woman at the front desk of a hotel who needs considerable help in understanding where things are in the hotel, how to work the electronic key in her door, and how to get assistance when she needs it. The service-oriented desk clerk patiently and graciously explains these things to the woman, who will depart from the hotel to tell all her friends how nice the employees are. Unfortunately, the person waiting in line behind this woman may be a business person anxious to get to a meeting. As a frequent traveler, this individual knows the ropes and only wants to register, get the key, and be on the way. This person will depart from the hotel to tell friends about the wait in line and the poor service.

Another aspect of service heterogeneity is that the knowledge, experience, and proficiency of the customer affect the quality of consumption. One customer says, "Look at the full glass of wine they give you." Another says, "Don't they know that a glass of wine should never be more than half full?" One customer says, "That bellman was very helpful when he took me to my room and explained all the hotel's services." Another says, "The last thing I need is someone to carry my bag to my room the last 50 yards of my 2000 mile journey." Obviously, there is a wide variation in the consumers' measurement of quality, and what satisfies one may very well not satisfy another. Regardless, what consumers get they pay for; there is no opportunity to exchange their experience for another one.

The Marketer. Marketers of services who make promises to customers have two strikes against them. The first is the question of how the employee with whom customers come face to face will handle the situation. The second is the customers themselves; what is appropriate handling to

one is inappropriate to another; service to one customer may affect service to another. The consequence is that good service may equal bad service.

For the marketer, the heterogeneity of services constitutes a lack of assurance that the product you market or sell is actually the product the customer gets. For the consumer, it means risk and a lack of assurance that what you buy is what you get. In the hospitality industry, the consumer often perceives the personnel as the service, so that one unpleasant interaction with personnel can result in criticism of the entire experience. Customers' problems are infinite in number and diverse in scope but, petty or significant, they are real to the customer and a problem to the marketer.

Many companies have attempted to overcome the difficulties of heterogeneity through what Theodore Levitt has termed the industrialization of service.[4] Levitt sees these problems as special opportunities, and so they may well be, but it is folly to think that all services can be industrialized. (Certainly they should be analyzed closely with that possibility in mind, but the customer must be knowledgeable about service improvements—technological advances, such as utilizing electronic door locks and receiving your bill in your room on the television, fall into this category.) Some fast-food restaurants provide an excellent example of industrializing a service to near-uniform performance. Little room is left for human judgment or error. Salad bars in restaurants and budget motels are other examples.

Budget motels and salad bars are only two examples of a phenomenon to be pondered by the hospitality marketer: When is less service more service, and vice versa? Or, to put it another way, when should service be more personal and when should it be less personal? Numerous studies have shown that salad bars are very popular with a majority of the eating-out public because you can "do it yourself." Yet the salad bar is actually less service, since you have to get your own food. Whether in this case less service is more depends on the individual customer's own perception of salad bars, and clearly what satisfies one customer does not necessarily satisfy another.

Are budget motels offering service when they, sometimes, literally, just throw the key at you and make sure you pay first? For some, yes: you get what you pay for. For others, no. On the other hand, a friend told us how impressed he was when he came downstairs the first morning at a five-star hotel in New Delhi, India, and was greeted by name by all the staff. By the third day, however, he became irritated at having to go through this interchange of pleasantries every morning with at least a half dozen people.

It is not hard to see that the marketer faces many problems when trying to cope with the heterogeneity of services, or even when trying to provide solutions to consumers' problems. The answer, at least partially, lies in knowing your market and your customers and the custom-tailoring of services. This means the emphasis should be on the customer, not on the service.[5] We address this subject in more detail in later chapters.

Simultaneity of Production and Consumption

The service characteristic of simultaneous production and consumption is unique. It is also the strongest foundation for the premise that management *is* marketing in the hospitality industry. This is so because in the case of services the buyer must be present to experience (consume) the service provided (produced) by the seller. Thus, production and consumption occur simultaneously. These close interactions often result in interpersonal relationships between the buyer and seller that may supersede the service itself.

The Consumer. These types of personal interactions are not new, of course. We have them at the supermarket, the department store, the automobile dealership, and other places where intangible services sell very tangible goods. The difference, however, is critical. Unless the marketplace situation is totally unacceptable, people may still visit the same store to buy goods even if their relationship with one salesperson is not the best. This is because they are buying something other than the service. If the

goods customer responds to an advertisement for a brand of sneakers, she goes to purchase the sneakers. Let's say that her experience in the store is less than satisfactory—the clerk was not knowledgeable about the product and the checkout lines were too long. In any case, the customer purchased the sneakers, took them home and "consumed" them. If the sneakers fall apart the maker is far away, perhaps even in some foreign country, or the customer can go back and get another pair.

In hospitality, that is not the case. The entire product, service and goods, is consumed on premise with the seller (producer) on hand. The customer is buying the service. One individual can totally personify the service of a particular establishment and cause a customer not to return. A friendly, smiling, call-you-by-your-name clerk is not enough. Each employee is literally part of the product because each employee is producing while the customer consumes.

Another facet of the simultaneous production/consumption characteristic is that you don't know what you are buying until after you have consumed it. When you think about it that seems like a pretty stupid thing to do, but that's what we do when we buy a service, even if we have bought the same service before. The heterogeneity principle of services supports this premise.

Obviously, there are exceptions to this rule in services. If we have been to the same doctor 20 times, we pretty well know what to expect. In some cases this will also be true in hotels and restaurants, but to a lesser extent because of the heterogeneity principle, not to mention the personnel turnover. In most cases, however, it will be a new experience and every time we purchase we assume a new risk.

The Marketer. The interaction of marketing and simultaneous production and consumption is inescapable in the hospitality business, so let us go back to the friendly and smiling employee. The customer cannot consume what the employee cannot produce. Employees may be given "smile training," but still be restricted in their ability to solve consumers' problems. Smiles in these cases are of little avail.* Thus the marketer must be able to produce while the customer consumes and in a way that solves the customer's problem on the spot. To overcome this problem, some hotels **empower** their employees to take appropriate action on the spot and advertise this as an intangible, as shown in Figure 2-4.

To add insult to injury, another aspect of the simultaneous production and consumption of hospitality services is that the buyer is subject to the seller's rules for usage, and these rules become an element of the service. Some rules are necessary in hospitality premises, but many rules are operations-driven to prevent the customer from "getting in the way"; other rules may be totally frivolous or archaic but management doesn't stop to question why they exist or if they should. For example, "Sorry, that section is closed," or "It's not that waiter's turn," or "The pool doesn't open until 10:00," or, on a menu, "No substitutions allowed." Rules like these become part of the service because they restrict the consumer's consumption. It wouldn't hurt for every hospitality operation to periodically review rules that affect the customer and question why they exist (most likely to serve the operational efficiency or save costs).

Tying together the above four elements of service, we have come up with the following definition of the hospitality product:

> The hospitality product is something that prospective buyers, for the most part, cannot fully grasp with the senses before buying it. Buyers do not know if they will get what they think they are buying. After they buy it they must wait until the seller produces it before they can consume it, sometimes after having paid for it. It may be available today at $50.00 but not tomorrow at $150. The seller is not totally sure that he or she can produce it and the buyer must consume it at the same time according to the seller's rules. What's more, if buyers don't like what they get, they can't take it back, get an exchange, or, in most cases, get their money back.

Although this definition may appear to be a little extreme, perhaps we can better understand the problems of hospitality marketing if we consider the product in this light. After all, this does describe the position in which the buyer is placed.

Other Aspects of the Service Component

There are a number of other aspects of the service component of the hospitality product that impact on the marketing effort. One of these is that the needs of the buyers may be totally unrecognized by them; thus they do not notice something until it is missing. This factor places a burden on the marketer to anticipate buyers' needs. There is really only one way to do this and that is by putting yourself in the customer's shoes and thinking like a customer.* Mike Leven, CEO of United States Franchise Systems (Microtel, Hawthorne Suites, Best Inns) tells a story demonstrating this point by recounting an incident that took place when he was president of Americana Hotels.

> I was waiting in the lobby of our Jamaica property with some other of our executives about 6:00 A.M. one morning, waiting for the limo to take us to the airport. Also waiting for the same limo to catch the same flight were half a dozen guests who had just checked out. Suddenly, down the hallway came the F&B manager and a waiter wheeling a cart with fresh orange juice, coffee, and Danish. I thought to myself, "Now here's a management that knows how to take care of its customers," until I watched them wheel the cart right past the guests and in front of us. I immediately grabbed the cart, turned it around, and wheeled it back in front of the guests. I couldn't help but think, "If only we treated our customers as well as we treat ourselves."

---

*Consider an actual experience. A room service waiter in a top hotel arrived an hour and 15 minutes late with breakfast, after three follow-up phone calls by the guest who was about to miss an appointment, with a large smile and "How are you today?" but no explanation or regrets.

---

*And this in spite of the fact that all customers are different. We address that subject in Chapter 8.

FIGURE 2-4 Wyndham Hotels' employee empowerment in action.

The absence of the coffee cart might have had absolutely no effect on the guests' perception of the hotel's service quality. After all, that is not what they came to Jamaica to buy. On the other hand, the presence of the coffee cart could have considerable impact, because the customer leaves with a warm feeling about the concerns of this hotel for its customers. If they return to this hotel and the same situation, however, and there is no coffee cart, they will then question the service quality.

Another critical aspect of the hospitality product is that additional services affect the basic **core service** of rooms, meals, and so on. Although the customer reserves only a room or a table, an almost endless number of peripheral services are expected to accompany that room or table. In the extreme, such as at a resort hotel in Jamaica, this could even include whether the sun shines. Certainly it includes the beach, the pool, the entertainment, the sports facilities, and many other features that accompany the resort image. In a restaurant, it includes the lighting, the noise level, the print size on the menu, water glasses filled, and ash trays emptied and even, perhaps, where you have to park your car. The marketer and management cannot escape the responsibility for all of these surrounding attributes. The more obvious tangible components of the purchase bundle, however, may lead management to concentrate on those elements to the detriment of the peripheral elements, or the intangible elements. Thus the service delivery system must be designed with the presence of the consumer in mind (as, of course, must be the tangible aspects such as lighting, furnishings, and other accoutrements).

Table 2-1 summarizes what has been said about the differences between services and manufactured goods, and depicts some of the problems of the hospitality marketer.

COMPONENTS OF THE HOSPITALITY PRODUCT

There are four major elements that customers receive when purchasing and using the **hospitality product**—tangible goods, environment, intangible services, and experience.

Goods

Goods include the mostly physical factors over which management has direct, or almost direct, control. Management decisions or practices directly affect goods. In some cases management expertise determines the quality level of goods, as in the case of a chef. Alternatively, quality of goods may depend on management's willingness to spend or not spend money in pursuit of the target market it wishes to serve. In this category we place beds, food, room size, furnishings, location, bathroom amenities, elevator service, heating and air conditioning, TVs, things that don't work, and so forth. We also define price as tangible although it is a cost of services as well as goods, because it tangibilizes the intangible. To the consumer, price is very tangible in any purchase decision. In hospitality it is the goods components that, generally speaking, satisfy or don't satisfy the *basic* needs of customers, as we have illustrated in Chapter 1. The goods provide solutions to basic problems.

Environment

In the category of environment, we place those items over which management may also have some control, but not as directly and not as easily. While environmental items may or may not be tangible,

TABLE 2-1
Differences Between Services and Manufactured Goods

Functional Characteristics	Goods	Services
Unit definition	Precise	General
Ability to measure	Objective	Subjective
Creation	Manufactured	Delivered
Distribution	Separated from production	Same as production
Communications	Tangible	Intangible
Pricing	Cost basis	Limited cost basis
Flexibility of producer	Limited	Broad
Time interval	Months to years	Simultaneous or shortly after
Delivery	Consistent	Variable
Shelf life	Days to years	Zero
Customer perception	Standardized—what you see	Have to consume to evaluate
Marketing	Traditional, external	Nontraditional, largely internal

they are something the customer feels. And what we are marketing is that feeling. For example, putting electronic locks on bedrooms doors is something very physical and tangible, but we do not sell the electronic lock to the customer. What we sell, instead, is the benefit of the feature—a feeling of security, a very important but intangible attribute for many hotel customers (i.e., the customer needs a room with a lock, but wants a room with an electronic lock). Other attributes in this category are decor, atmosphere, comfort, ambience, architecture, and so forth. These attributes fall more in the "want," as opposed to the "need," category. They solve extended problems. A hotel room, for example, satisfies a basic need; a luxurious room satisfies a "want."*

Services

The third category, services, includes nonphysical, intangible attributes that management clearly does, or should, control. Items in this category depend heavily on the personal elements provided by employees, such as friendliness, speed, attitude, professionalism, responsiveness, and so on. But there are other factors as well: There are those that may depend on employee aptitude, but may also depend on the system, such as the handling of reservations. Then also there are those that may strictly depend on management decisions, such as whether to offer a service. Room service is an example of this. In fact, we can use room service to demonstrate the complexity of the interrelationships among the four components of the hospitality product.

Management must first decide to offer room service. Obviously, this decision is relevant to many things including the particular property and the target market. The first question to be answered, of course, is whether offering room service will solve a problem for customers at this property. If an alert management decides that the answer is

yes, it will then analyze demand, cost, resources, and facilities. If customers expect room service and it is not offered, there will be dissatisfaction.

Deciding to offer room service is not the end. There are still many opportunities to fulfill or not fulfill expectations. First, there is the service element. How many times does the phone ring before the room service department answers it? What is the attitude of the person who does answer? Is the order delivered when promised?* What is the attitude of the room service waiter? Did he remember the rolls, the sugar, and enough cream for the coffee? When the meal is finished and the tray is put out in the hallway, how long does it stay there before someone takes it away?

Now let's look at the goods element. Is the orange juice fresh, the coffee hot? Is the silverware clean? Is the bacon crisp or the toast soggy? Is the price fair?

What about the environment? Is there a table to put the food on without rearranging the bedroom, perhaps even a balcony where one can enjoy the view? Are there chairs to sit on that enable one to reach the table? Is the tray well presented?

If all these things are done well, consistent with the target market that determines what "well" is, does the customer say, "Boy, this is a well-managed hotel?" Probably not. But if one thing is not done well, the customer may well say the opposite. Why should this be? Because it is *expected* to be done well. That is the solution to the customer's problem. That is how the customer measures the price/value relationship. This is why the "risk" was taken. *All* these lead to the ultimate level of satisfaction. There is no opportunity to return room service for another room service in the same way a good can be exchanged. You can see now that room service, like all parts of hospitality operations, is *marketing*—it solves or causes problems, it can

---

*The same argument can be made, of course, for a car—we need a car but we want a Mercedes. The difference lies in the intangibility and nonpossessiveness of the hospitality environment.

*Failure to deliver room service when promised, which is a nonsolution to a customer's problem, is such a frequent complaint that some companies put all their emphasis on delivery. See Marriott's ad in Figure 2-5. The promise was based, however, on service having been ordered the night before.

You can't be late for
your business appointments,
and neither can we.

At Marriott, if your breakfast doesn't show up on time, it won't show up on your bill.
That's because we take our business just as seriously as you take yours. And our business
is service. This commitment is what makes Marriott the business traveler's first choice.
See for yourself. Call **1-800-228-9290** or your Travel Professional.

SERVICE. THE ULTIMATE LUXURY.℠

F I G U R E 2 - 5 Marriott emphasizes timeliness of room service delivery.

keep or lose a customer. Look now at Marriott's later ad in Figure 2-6. Comparing it to Figure 2-5 you can see that Marriott went from a stance of timely delivery to one of having your breakfast "perfect in every way."

Experience

There is a fourth component of the hospitality product that may, in fact, be the most important. This is *experience*, which is most likely an outcome of the other three components. While buyers of the

"I'M A REAL STICKLER ABOUT BREAKFAST. SO IF YOURS ISN'T JUST RIGHT, I'LL PAY FOR IT MYSELF."

Bill Marriott

We want your breakfast to be perfect in every way –
preparation, presentation, service and timing. If everything isn't
just so, it's on us. Call your travel agent or 1-800-228-9290.

Marriott.
HOTELS · RESORTS · SUITES

WE MAKE IT HAPPEN FOR YOU.

Not available at Courtyard by Marriott, Residence Inn by Marriott or Fairfield Inn. ©1993 Marriott Corp.

FIGURE   2-6   Marriott emphasizes all elements of room service breakfast.

hospitality product may not always seek an experience, *per se*, that is inevitably what they come away with and what they most remember.

Consider the value of experience from the viewpoint of the humble coffee bean. It begins life as a *commodity*. At about three dollars a pound, its cost translates to three or four cents a cup. Someone roasts, grinds, and packages it, turning it into a

good, costing 5 to 25 cents a cup. Brewed and served in a diner, it becomes a *service* at perhaps $1 per cup. Then we add the *environment* of, say, an upscale restaurant or an espresso bar, and consumers gladly pay $2 to $5 a cup. At a place like Fouquet's on the Champs-Elysées in Paris, a single cup of coffee may run $15 to $20 a cup.

So coffee is a commodity and a good. It is purchased as a service in an environment. But how can one place charge more than another, up to $15 to $20? Because each one adds a distinctive *experience.* Experiences are a distinct economic offering, as different from services as services are from goods.[6]

How are experiences different from goods and services? Experiences are *memorable,* experiences *unfold over a period of time,* and experiences are *inherently personal.* Thus experiences can create new and greater economic value. They are not merely entertainment, such as at theme restaurants like Planet Hollywood, where food is just a prop for what has become known as an "eatertainment" experience. Rather they *engage* the customer, connecting with him or her in a personal, memorable way.

Effective service providers use experiences to increase the attractiveness of their offering—to bring customers back to the same hotel or restaurant. As services increasingly become copied and commoditized, successful hospitality operators will create memorable experiences to create and keep customers.

Now you can see why marketing the hospitality product is not exactly like marketing tires, stereo sets, a doctor's services, a hospital room, or a haircut. In the room service case, the person who answered the phone, the person who took the order, the person who fixed the breakfast, the person who delivered the meal, the person who designed the room, the person who retrieved the tray, the china, the silver, and the room itself are all part of the experience. More important, they are all part of the marketing effort.

In this chapter our concern is with the special case of nontraditional marketing of hospitality products, with special attention to the services element. We should bear in mind, however, that whether we call the hospitality product a good (steak), environment (decor), or service (service), in essence the entire hospitality product can be classified as an intangible experience or, even better, a total experience.

This is true for two reasons. First, the hospitality product is personal. The customer interacts with all phases of the product at a very personal level and judges them on the basis of personal experiences. Judgment is usually based not so much on the quality that the manufacturer puts into the product, as on the personal relationship of the customer to the product. For example, a Rolls Royce is a luxury car no matter how you look at it. Four Seasons, considered one of the top luxury hotel chains in the world, may not be experienced as luxurious by some guests if the light bulbs are only 60 watts or if there is only one comfortable chair in the room. Those situations would create a different experience than if the bulbs were 100 watts and there were two chairs.

In fact, Isadore Sharp, CEO of Four Seasons, once gave a speech on services to a large conference at which one of the authors was present. He went on at some length on the virtues of Four Seasons hotels and how they took such good care of their customers. As an example, Sharp said, "We insist that room service be delivered within 20 minutes [plus or minus] of the time it is requested." The entire audience spontaneously booed Sharp, apparently to his consternation. Given the expectation gap of a Four Seasons (as explained in Chapter 1) even a five-minute leeway would barely be tolerable to "stand around" wondering what to do next, not knowing when your breakfast is coming. That's a negative experience.

The second reason for classifying the hospitality product as an intangible experience is that it is always "left behind," that is, customers do not take it with them and it can never be redone. The moment has passed forever. Customers go away empty-handed, with nothing to show for their money. Even the services of a doctor or a barber, which are considered by many to qualify more purely as services than hospitality, have some elements that you can take with you. You can show your friends the scar left by the surgeon's knife, and, generally, your hair will grow in again. The hospitality product is unique in that there is no cure and no second chance. All you take away with you is an experience. This has incredible implications for hospitality marketing and operations.

SERVICE GAPS

We now come back to expectations, because it is the fulfillment of expectations, or lack of it, that creates experiences. Perception, once again, is reality. The differences between what was expected and what was perceived (the customer's), if any, constitute service gaps, and we now discuss these gaps in some detail.

Expectation Gaps

In Chapter 1, we considered the potential gaps that may occur in expectation between the problem and the solution. Figure 2-7 is a model that illustrates potential "gaps" in service delivery and where they may occur. Gaps arise because of differences between expectations and perceptions, but they occur for different reasons. In Table 2-2 we apply this model to the hospitality industry to show the challenges that hospitality marketers face in eliminating gaps.

It is clear that all of these gaps may overlap and affect each other. Yet each is critical to creating experiences and keeping customers and can have serious consequences. Any gap may cause a difference between expectation and reality because perception is reality. Again, all management is marketing.

The gap in Figure 2-7 that we are most concerned with is Gap 4, because this gap is really the

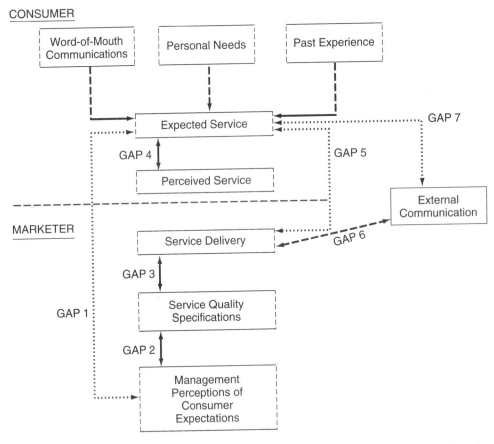

F I G U R E   2 - 7   The SERVQUAL Model: Potential gaps that can occur in delivering expected services.[7]

T A B L E   2-2
Potential Gaps in Hospitality Service[7]

Gap 1—Gap between services expected by the consumer and management perceptions of consumers' expectations: Management has to decide the range of services to offer. Two comfortable chairs, 100 watt light bulbs, coffeemaker, room service, computer hookups, free local phone calls, and an airport shuttle are just a few of the services that may be offered, plus all the service intangibles. A well-traveled international tourist may find it unbelievable that most hotels in the United States have no currency exchange facility. This is a service that most American hotels consider to be unnecessary, even though they consider themselves full-service hotels, but this same service is almost always offered in foreign hotels, and for numerous different currencies. The gap will result if management doesn't fully understand and thus offer the services that fulfill the expectations of the market segments that the property is trying to attract. This type of gap is a common one in hospitality when sometimes customer expectations are not really understood.

Gap 2—Gap between management perceptions of consumer expectations and service quality specifications: Specifications dictate how the service will be implemented by the company. Let's say a hotel realizes that a free airport shuttle is a service that customers expect. They offer the service but vans are scheduled to leave the hotel only once every hour, causing long, inconvenient waits for customers. The gap arises from the difference between what management thinks the customer wants (free airport shuttle) and how management decides to implement the service (only once an hour).

Gap 3—Gap between service quality specifications and service delivery: This is a common gap in almost any business and is caused by the failure of employees to provide services in accordance with the procedures established by the company. An example of this would be when room service with a specified delivery time shows up half an hour late.

Gap 4—Gap between service expected by the consumer and perceived service: Figure 2-7 shows that expected service is affected by consumers' past experience, personal needs, and exposure to communications such as word-of-mouth recommendations. Again, perception is reality. This gap can be as simple as a desk clerk who is helpful by property standards but not helpful enough by consumer expectations. Thus consumers have a certain level of expectations even before they arrive at a hotel or restaurant. A gap here could be caused by the heterogenity principle or, worse, a failure in any of the other gaps. This gap can be especially difficult for marketers to avoid, even with the best of intentions.

Gap 5—Gap between service expected by the customer and the service delivered when the customer really wanted something different: Even when management has been able to monitor customer expectations, it may be difficult to provide services to meet those expectations. Heterogeneity, again, may often be the cause. Even though the specifications are accurate, mistakes happen. Forgetting the cream on a room service tray would fall into this category. After all, when services are performed by humans there are bound to be fluctuations in service delivery.

Gap 6—Gap between service delivery and external communication: Firms often make promises in their advertisements that are difficult to live up to or that imply something that is not fulfilled (e.g., the moon). Holiday Inn's "No Surprises" campaign of a few years ago is an example. The implication was that everything would be "right." It soon became apparent that this promise could not be delivered and the advertising campaign was dropped after angering a lot of customers.

Gap 7—Gap between expected service and external communication: This is one of the most serious gaps caused by advertising claims and puffery. Gap 7 is more blatant   advertising intentionally builds expectations that are knowingly not realistic, or that are unlikely to be fulfilled. This gap could also arise because of any or all of the other gaps. Figure 2-8, for example, shows an ad with great potential to create Gap 6 and Gap 7.

outcome of all the others. In other words, any gaps in the other six measures will likely cause a Gap 4. The developers of the SERVQUAL model have also, through their research, identified the nature and determinants of customer expectations of service and linked it to what they call the "**zone of tolerance,**" as shown in Figure 2-9.

The zone of tolerance in Figure 2-9 fills the gap between expected and the perceived service. The smaller the gap, the closer the expected is to the

FIGURE 2-8 New York Hemsley's ad displays great Gap 6 and Gap 7 potential.

perceived. Note, however, that there is a "desired" service that may be less than the expected service, and an "adequate" service that may just be acceptable. In between is the area where customers may tolerate the level of service but not be particularly thrilled by it. This goes back to our discussion in Chapter 1 on levels of satisfaction. The service can-

not be returned so, while the customer may be somewhat satisfied, he or she will not be totally satisfied. Thus the customer may not complain but also may never return.

Figure 2-9 also shows the determinants of customer expectations, which are discussed in various sections of this text, especially in Chapter 8 on con-

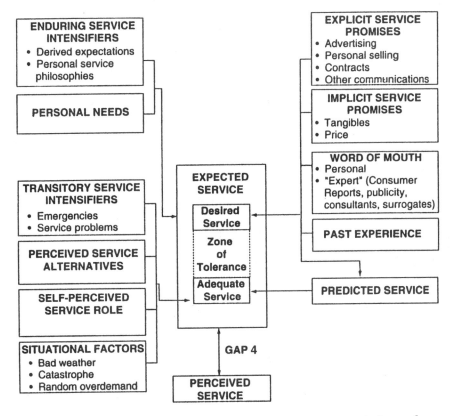

F I G U R E   2 - 9   Nature and determinants of gaps, and the zone of tolerance.[8]

sumer behavior. Overall, these gap models are valuable tools in tracing customer satisfaction and dissatisfaction.

The researchers who developed the SERVQUAL model also identified five service quality dimensions that customers use to assess a service multidimensionally.[9] These dimensions are:

- *Reliability:* Ability to perform the promised service dependably and accurately
- *Responsiveness:* Willingness to help customers and provide prompt service
- *Assurance:* Employees' knowledge and courtesy and their ability to inspire trust and confidence
- *Empathy:* Caring, individualized attention given to customers

- *Tangibles:* Appearance of physical facilities, equipment, personnel, and written materials

Of these five dimensions, none of which stands alone, reliability has been consistently shown to be the most important determinant of perceptions of service quality. What reliability means is, "What you promise me is what I get." Note, again, that promises may be implicit or explicit. The other dimensions are self-explanatory and, of course, will vary in importance from person to person. All dimensions together result in the total experience that the customer takes away. Clearly, a hospitality mission statement that contained these elements, and had them fulfilled by all employees, would be a long way on the road to keeping customers. In Chapter 3 we discuss this in more depth under the term "relationship marketing," a concept for gaining competitive advantage.

International Gaps

It should be noted that the previous discussion on gaps, and the research done to identify them, is all based on the U.S. consumer. Thus, these concepts may or may not apply in other countries or with customers who come from other countries. The culture of service varies widely around the world. It is one thing to identify the need for quality service, but entirely another matter to determine how such a service might be supplied to customers of a different nationality.

Each actor in the service encounter brings to the interaction his or her own ethnic/national identity. Ideas about personal space, for example, vary from culture to culture. In some cultures, making eye contact during verbal communication is unacceptable; in other cultures eye contact is an important sign of openness. In some cultures, friendliness is the ultimate service; in others it is disdained as "getting too close." While reliability may be the most important service dimension in the United States, it is not difficult to think of countries where responsiveness would be more highly valued by most, at least in a hospitality setting. Thus we caution about overgeneralizations of these concepts although basic gaps, such as Gap 4, the expectations/perception gap, would probably apply anywhere. The trick is to know what the expectations really are. The hospitality worker, at any level, is likely to work in a multicultural environment. There must be a genuine appreciation of the values underlying the culture of service and an understanding of what constitutes a positive total experience for guests.

SUMMARY

The world's economy can be broadly divided into manufacturing and service sectors. The hospitality industry is part of the service sector, which has grown to become three times larger than its manufacturing counterpart in many countries. In this chapter it was argued that the differences between the nature of services and manufactured goods require different approaches to their marketing. Services are essentially intangible, heterogeneous, and perishable. In addition, services are produced and consumed at the same time. Of course, hospitality services are also different from other services such as health care, education, banking, and insurance, and require different marketing strategies. Most important, the hospitality product, all things combined, is a total experience, the only thing the customer takes away.

The elements of services and the fact that management and marketing are inseparable in hospitality creates unique problems for the keeping of customers. This is because most of what hospitality products **do** for the customer takes place at the property. The solutions to those problems require a further extension of nontraditional marketing, which is often referred to as relationship marketing, the subject of Chapter 3.

KEY WORDS AND CONCEPTS

Core Services: Services that are based on central rather than peripheral market needs, such as checking into a hotel or being seated in a restaurant.

Employee Empowerment: Allowing the employee to make decisions that will solve customers' needs. Employee empowerment is part of internal marketing in that it brings the decision-making process to the closest point of contact with the customer.

Environment: The items that create the atmosphere experienced by the customer. The environment includes both tangible and intangible items.

Experience: The total outcome to the customer from the combination of environment, goods, and services purchased.

Goods: The physical factors over which management has direct, or almost direct, control.

Heterogeneity of Service: The inconsistent delivery of service levels provided by many different employees, affected by many different customers.

Hospitality Product: The combination of goods, services, environment, and experience that the customer buys.

Intangibility: The attribute of services that the customer cannot grasp with any of the five senses. That is, customers cannot taste, feel, see, smell, or hear a service, until they've consumed it, and one cannot easily grasp it, conceptually.

Perception Is Reality: If the customer doesn't perceive it, it doesn't exist for that customer.

Perishability: The life cycle of the hospitality service. A room is only available for a 24 hour period, making it very perishable.

Services: The nonphysical and intangible items that management does, or should, control.

Simultaneous Production and Consumption: Consumption of the purchase while it is being produced.

Tangibility: The attribute of products or components that the customer can grasp with any of the five senses.

Walked: The industry term for denying a room to a person with confirmed reservation.

Zone of Tolerance: That area between desired service and adequate service that the customer will tolerate, even if not totally satisfied.

DISCUSSION QUESTIONS

1. Discuss the argument that the marketing of services is different from the marketing of goods. Give examples, both pro and con, from your experiences.
2. Discuss and explain the goods/environment/services trichotomy of the hospitality product. When is one more/less important than the others?

4. How can you tangibilize the intangible in hospitality marketing?
5. Why is the total experience so important in hospitality?
6. Keep a service journal for a week or two and document your use of services in any hospitality establishment. Before each service encounter, indicate your predicted service. Afterward, note whether your expectations were met or exceeded. How does your encounter affect your desire to return to that establishment again?
7. Interview someone with a non-U.S. cultural background. Ask that person about the five dimensions of service quality in a hospitality experience, how relevant they are, and which are most important.

GROUP PROJECTS

1. Take some actual situations that people in your group have experienced in a hospitality service operation and write a short composite case like those in Cases 10, 12, 24, 42, or 50 at the end of the book. Make it come "alive," like that case. Then write an analysis of what should be done by the hypothetical operation. Be prepared to present and discuss in class.
2. Consider all the service elements (intangible, etc.) of a hospitality experience. Make a list of these. Now write different ways that these impact the consumer and the marketer in a restaurant, as we did at the beginning of the chapter. Analyze these and develop marketing strategies or tactics that could be used to deal with them.

REFERENCES

1. Peter Drucker, *Post-Capitalist Society*. New York: Harper Business, 1993.
2. For an interesting and extended discussion on this subject, see Sheryl E. Kimes, Richard B. Chase, Sunmee Choi, Philip Y. Lee, and Elizabeth N. Ngonzi, "Restaurant

Revenue Management: Applying Yield Management to the Restaurant Industry," *Cornell Hotel and Restaurant Administration Quarterly*, June 1992, pp. 32–39.

3. Jan Carlzon, *Moments of Truth.* Cambridge, MA: Ballinger Publishing Company, 1987.

4. Theodore Levitt, "The Industrialization of Service," in Theodore Levitt (Ed.), *The Marketing Imagination.* New York: Free Press, 1986, pp. 50–71.

5. See, for example, Robert C. Lewis and Michael Nightingale, "Targeting Service to Your Customer," *Cornell Hotel and Restaurant Administration Quarterly*, August 1991, pp. 12–27.

6. B. Joseph Pine, II, and James H. Gilmore, "How to Profit from Experience," *The Wall Street Journal*, August 4, 1997, p. A24.

7. Based on A. Parasuraman, V. A. Zeithaml, and L. L. Berry, "A Conceptual Model of Service Quality and Its Implications for Future Research," *Journal of Marketing*, Fall 1985, pp 41–50, published by the American Marketing Association.

8. Valerie A. Zeithaml, Leonard L. Berry, and A. Parasuraman, "The Nature and Determinants of Customer Expectations of Service," *Journal of the Academy of Marketing Science*, 21, 1 (1993), pp. 1–12.

9. Valerie A. Zeithaml, A. Parasuraman, and Leonard L. Berry, "Strategic Positioning on the Dimensions of Service Quality," in *Advances in Services Marketing and Management*, Vol. 2, Teresa A. Swartz, David E. Bowen, and Stephen W. Brown (Eds.). Greenwich, CT: JAI Press, 1993.

Three

◆•◆

RELATIONSHIP MARKETING

Overview

The concept of relationship marketing is introduced in this chapter. In this concept, customers are valuable assets to be retained and with whom to build ongoing relationships in order to develop loyalty. Relationship marketing is also applied to employees for the same reason. The chapter deals with the "whys" and "hows" of relationship marketing.

WHAT RELATIONSHIP MARKETING IS AND WHAT IT IS NOT Relationship marketing is about creating customer value and long-term relationships. It is not about databases or travel frequency programs, which may enhance it but do not create value.

NEED FOR RELATIONSHIP MARKETING This section demonstrates the role of relationship marketing in a hospitality firm and why it is so important.

LIFETIME VALUE OF A CUSTOMER Here we discuss how to go about converting the subjective concept to concrete results.

CUSTOMER ANALYSIS Different customers need different types of care and recognition.

SERVICE RELATIONSHIPS These are based on trust and commitment, or lack of them. Each and together, they have antecedents and consequences that can build or destroy them. Service relationships are built on core, customized, and augmented products and services.

BUILDING LOYALTY True loyalty is not based on behaviors but vice versa—behavior is based on loyalty, which is emotional and psychological. Thus, frequent guest programs are unlikely to build true loyalty. We also discuss what loyalty programs don't do and what makes them work.

WHY RELATIONSHIP MARKETING DOESN'T WORK In spite of all that's been said about it, and all good intentions by many, there are still too many flaws in relationship marketing.

CUSTOMER COMPLAINTS This section deals with "service recovery"—the impact of resolving/not resolving complaints, and how to benefit from them in maintaining relationships. It also discusses how to handle complaints.

EMPLOYEE RELATIONSHIP MARKETING

We develop relationships with customers largely through our employees. Thus it is essential that we develop similar relationships with employees.

THE PAST, AND THE FUTURE OF RELATIONSHIP MARKETING

Past practices are not going to work in the future. The companies that shun them forever and take a new perspective on relationships are going to have the competitive advantage in the years ahead.

Customers are assets. They are the most important assets a company can have. It is good management in business to protect your assets, but assets like buildings, or a warehouse of goods, do not produce profits; the customer that buys the goods does. One way to define **relationship marketing** is as marketing to protect the customer base. (We define it in other ways later on.) Relationship marketing sees the customer as an asset. Its function is to attract, maintain, and enhance customer relationships. To put this in perspective, consider the hypothetical abbreviated balance sheets in Table 3-1.

You don't have to have had a finance course to know that total assets always equal total liabilities plus shareholders' equity, or to know that to improve equity you must either increase assets, decrease liabilities, or both. If you succeed in doing this in the second balance sheet (**B**), it is not hard to see the effect it will have on the first balance sheet (**A**). This is what relationship marketing is all about: get more customers, keep more customers, and lose fewer customers. Well, come to think of it, that's what marketing is all about, isn't it? But relationship marketing adds an element—this is not just giving the target market what they want, when they want it, where they want it, at a price they are willing and able to pay. Rather, this is about building a relationship with them so that they come back for more, and more, and tell many others. Relationship marketing is a competitive advantage.

There is, however, a tendency to concentrate efforts on obtaining new customers while doing a poor job of handling the present customer rela-

tionship. Yet, the cost of the former is considerably greater than the cost of the latter. Sometimes, in fact, it would seem that customers are perceived as liabilities to be disposed of as soon as possible. Consider the situation in Table 3-2.

WHAT RELATIONSHIP MARKETING IS AND WHAT IT IS NOT

Relationship marketing is nontraditional marketing and is different than traditional marketing as we mentioned in Chapter 1. Some of these differences are delineated in Table 3-3.

On the other hand, relationship marketing is not, contrary to some beliefs, database marketing, frequent traveler programs, partnerships, or relationship selling. While some of these may be used to enhance relationships they are not, in themselves, the bases of relationships.

Relationship marketing, then, is an ongoing process of identifying and creating new value with individual customers for mutual value benefits and then sharing the benefits from this over a lifetime of association. In this sense it differs from our usual definition of marketing, although it is certainly part of it, in the following ways.

- It seeks to create *new* value for customers and *share* the value so created.
- It recognizes the key role of *individual* customers in defining the value they want, that is,

T A B L E   3-1
Customers as Assets on the Balance Sheet

A. Hypothetical Standard Balance Sheet for a Hotel

Current assets:

Cash and investments	$120,000
Receivables	30,000
Inventory	50,000
Total current assets	200,000

Fixed assets:

Properties and land	25,000,000
Investments	2,500,000
Total assets	27,700,000

Liabilities:

Current debt	100,000
Accounts payable	50,000
Long-term debt	20,000,000
Shareholders' equity: Capital stock	7,550,000
Total liabilities and equity	27,700,000

B. Hypothetical Customer Balance Sheet for the Same Hotel

Current assets:

Probable customers: 2000 @$2000 a year	$4,000,000
Receivables: 1000 customer prospects @ $2000 a year	2,000,000
Inventory: guaranteed customer deposits for future year 1400 @$500	700,000
Total current assets	6,700,000

Fixed assets:

Investments: 10,500 loyal customers@$2000	21,000,000
Total assets	27,700,000

Liabilities:

Current debt: loss of upset customers 500 @ $2000	1,000,000
Accounts payable: pay back irate customers	100,000
Long-term debt: loss of customers by word of mouth	19,050,000
Shareholders' equity: Capital stock	7,550,000
Total liabilities and equity	27,700,000

value is created *with* customers, not *for* customers.

- It requires that a company define its organization to support the value that individual customers want.
- It is a continuously cooperative effort between buyer and seller.
- It recognizes the value of customers over their purchasing *lifetimes*.
- It seeks to build a chain of relationships between the organization and its main stakeholders to create the value that customers want.
- It focuses on the processes and whatever else is needed to advance the customer relationship.[1]

Later in this book we talk about segmentation and target marketing and we have defined marketing as "giving the target market. . . ." With relationship marketing we take this one step further to develop customer-specific objectives and strategies that are unique to each customer or to each group of similar customers, that are part of a larger target market.

THE NEED FOR RELATIONSHIP MARKETING

Nowhere is relationship marketing more applicable than in service industries in general and the hospitality industry in particular. Relationship marketing is most applicable when:

1. There is an ongoing and periodic desire for service by the customer,
2. The service customer controls the selection of the service supplier,
3. There are alternative supplier choices,
4. Customer loyalty is weak and switching is common and easy, and
5. Word of mouth is an especially potent form of communication about a product.

These conditions are obviously quite prevalent in the hospitality industry. We don't sell one-time

T A B L E   3-2
Undoing a Relationship

A couple had gone to a certain hotel within 25 miles of their home following their marriage. The time was early December, when the hotel traditionally ran 20 percent occupancy. They continued going there weekends on their anniversary for five years, each time spending about $600. They also went there other times, or ate there, during the year, sometimes with friends.

On the fifth year, they arrived about 7:00 P.M. and were welcomed by the desk clerk, whom they had come to know. They went to their room and ordered champagne and dinner. They also had their remaining meals in the hotel and spent time in the hotel lounge. When they checked out three days later, they asked for the 10 percent room discount they were entitled to as members of an organization with which the well-known hotel chain had an agreement. The same clerk's response was that he could not grant the discount as they had not asked for it when they checked in, according to the standard operating procedure. When they got home they wrote to the general manager, asking for the discount. In a two-page letter the discount was refused in no uncertain terms. They then wrote to the vice president–marketing of the company, enclosing a copy of the manager's letter.

Shortly afterward, they received a polite letter from the general manager starting, "We are always glad to know of our customers' complaints because it helps us to improve our operations," and an invitation to spend a weekend at the hotel as his guests. They never went back and never will, nor will many of their friends.

Consider the cost of granting the discount, about $25.00, against the business lost. Customers are assets—too many managers still don't get it!

services, and the consumer has many choices. In an era of heavy hotel building and restaurant openings, or excess capacity, any hotel or restaurant is especially vulnerable to competition. Most everyone likes to try a new place. The question, when they've tried your place, is will they come back? Do we offer a competitive product on dimensions that are meaningful to customers, solve customer problems, and are difficult for competitors to duplicate? Do we have a meaningful relationship? This is what relationship marketing is all about, and when the above conditions pertain the opportunities to practice it are abundant.

In relationship marketing, moreover, the process doesn't stop there. The relationship marketer works to maintain the relationship long after the formal production/consumption process has ended, seeking not only to keep customers but to bring them back as well. Theodore Levitt compares the relationship to something like a marriage.

T A B L E   3-3
Traditional Marketing versus Relationship Marketing[2]

Traditional Focus	*Relationship Focus*
Orientation to single sales	Orientation to customer retention
Discontinuous customer contact	Continuous customer contact
Focus on product features	Focus on customer value
Short time scale	Long time scale
Token emphasis on customer services	High emphasis on customer services
Token commitment to customer expectations	High commitment to customer expectations
Quality is the concern of production staff	Quality is concern of all staff

The sale merely consummates the courtship. Then the marriage begins. How good the marriage is depends on how well the relationship is managed by the seller. That determines whether there will be continued or expanded business or troubles and divorce, and whether costs or profits increase.

. . . It is not just that once you get a customer you want to keep him. It is more a matter of what the buyer wants. He wants a vendor who will keep his promises, who'll keep supplying and stand behind what he promised. The age of the blind date or the one-night stand is gone. Marriage is both more convenient and more necessary. . . . In these conditions success in marketing, like success in marriage, is transformed into the inescapability of a relationship.[3]

Service is not an event any more than a marriage is. It is a process, creating for the customer an environment of information, assurance, empathy, and reliability. It has its focus on building loyal customer relationships.

The Lifetime Value of a Customer

The **lifetime value of a customer,** in short, is the net profit received from doing business with a given customer during the time that the customer continues to buy from you. In fact, according to some Harvard business faculty, "[T]he life time value of a loyal customer can be astronomical, especially when referrals are added to the economics of customer retention." These researchers calculate that the lifetime revenue from a loyal pizza customer can be greater than $8000.[4]

Others estimate that a 5 percent increase in customer loyalty can produce *profit* increases from 25 to 85 percent. These authors conclude that *quality* of market share, measured in terms of customer loyalty, deserves as much attention as *quantity* of market share. Taco Bell, in fact, measures "share of stomach" to compare the company's sales against all other food purchases a customer can potentially make. As a result, Taco Bell tries to reach customers through kiosks, carts, trucks, and the shelves of supermarkets.[5]

Worksheets can be developed for calculating the lifetime value of customers.[6] What one needs to know is the retention rate, the spending rate, the variable costs, and the discount rate to compute net present value (i.e., the value today of the customer over a period of time). While few properties or companies in hospitality will do this, there is no question but that loyal customers can add greatly to profits. Figure 3-1 gives one view on profits from loyal customers.

With relationship marketing, the emphasis is on which customers are to be served, as well as on understanding their expectations and delivering to those expectations, not to mention figuring out how more similar customers can be created and kept. Thus we have switched from product and service profitability to customer profitability. This is a radical move in the hospitality industry but an especially necessary one in an industry with high fixed costs and capital investment. We discuss it more in later chapters, including the marketing mix chapters. For the moment, however, look at the list of questions in Table 3-4. The answers to these questions form the bases of relationship marketing, yet there are few hospitality companies that can accurately answer them.

When you think about it, there is nothing very new in what we have just discussed, and also nothing that should be very difficult for management to

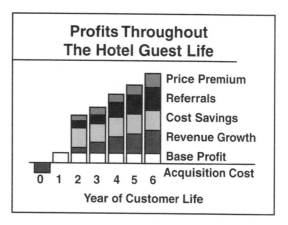

FIGURE 3-1 Profits throughout the hotel guest life.[7]

TABLE 3-4
Information Needed for Relationship Marketing

- How much does it cost to get a new customer?
- How much does it cost to keep that customer?
- What is the revenue from that customer—each visit, annually, lifetime?
- What is the cost of serving that customer—each visit, annually, lifetime?
- What are the retention rates of customers?
- If we are losing loyal customers for reasons beyond our control, for example, death, moving away, are we replacing them and with whom? (We address this later, but keep in mind that grandiose statements like, "We have 80 percent repeat customers" can be dangerous if you are not also acquiring new ones. See next question.)
- What is a repeat customer? For example, is it someone who comes only on Saturday night when the restaurant is always full? Someone who stays every time he is in town but who's in town only once a year? Someone who wants us to stay as we are when we know we have to change? Someone who stays in this hotel but who, when she's in other cities, goes to a different chain? Someone who's loyal as long as we give him an upgrade? As you can imagine, this list could go on and on. The questions can, however, be turned around to make them positive examples.
- What is the revenue and profitability from repeat customers versus those we might replace them with? (For example, in hotels, do our repeat customers buy the cheapest rooms and always eat out? In other words, what is the total revenue and profitability they provide?)
- What other opportunities are there for revenue from our customers for things that we don't now provide?
- Do our customers really want all the things in our package bundles?
- If our customers weren't here, where would they be or where might they go?
- What value do our customers get from us?
- Do we have a "relationship" with our customers or are they just customers?
- How frequently do we communicate (Internet, telephone, mail, mass media) with our customers? Is this favorable to them and to us?

acquire. Any actions that a property can take to increase customer trust will lead toward commitment. Yet we know that, overall, hotel loyalty, at least, is not very strong. Why can't this information be acquired at all hotels? Clearly, relationship marketing is more noticeable for its absence, which is why it can be a competitive advantage for those who adopt it.

CUSTOMER ANALYSIS

Going back to our customer balance sheet at the beginning of the chapter, we can now begin to develop a **customer analysis,** in a sense, for each customer. Which customers are profitable, now and in

the future? Some customers add value, while others may have negative value, that is, they require too much time and effort to ever make them profitable. The customer matrix shown in Figure 3-2 helps to make the point.

What Figure 3-2 means is that different customers have different priorities on the part of management, depending on their "income statement." Perhaps the best example, albeit ironic, of this matrix being put into practice in the hospitality industry is in the casino business, where the individual income statement is based on how much the customer wagers, or puts at risk. The high roller gets free rooms (possibly suites), free liquor, maybe even free airfare, and lots of management attention, and many other perks ("reward and invest").

		UNPROFITABLE	PROFITABLE
C U R R E N T **C U S T O M E R S**	**P R O F I T A B L E**	**MANAGE** Issues need to be addressed. Create mutual value that will enhance business prospects.	**REWARD AND INVEST** Ideal customers. Assign priorities. Invest time. Reward with special benefits.
	U N P R O F I T A B L E	**FIRE** Analyze and assess. If no benefits, now or future, have friendly parting of ways.	**DISCIPLINE** Make profitable. May be able to reduce costs or to charge more while maintaining the relationship.
		UNPROFITABLE	**PROFITABLE**
		CUSTOMERS — FUTURE	

FIGURE 3-2 Customer Analysis[8]

Under "manage" is the customer who may become unprofitable in the future because he requires too much attention, tends to go from casino to casino, and thus prospects don't look good down the road. He can be managed with more attention, getting him to stay at our casino or to play other games where he wagers more. In other words, mutual value needs to be created.

Under "discipline" we have an unprofitable customer who may not wager enough, stays and eats at another hotel, requires a lot of attention, and so forth. If she looks profitable in the future we may need to cultivate her into a bigger wagerer or, contrarily, take away the free drinks.

Not all customers are worth having. Some may be too costly to serve and sell. They may buy only on specials and low margin items. They may not be personally desirable due to dress or manner. They may be constant complainers who require undue atten-

tion. The customer we "fire" is a low wagerer and is just not profitable and never will be. He takes a place at the crap table but only bets now and then. He just likes the atmosphere and watching others. Maybe he can't even really afford to be in a casino. We don't want to alienate him so we have to be careful. Perhaps if he doesn't get enough attention he'll go elsewhere.

What the matrix shows is that different kinds of customers require different types of relationships. In a way we seem to be contradicting our definition of marketing. But not really. It is the *target market* that we need to determine and then apply the marketing concept. Remember, too, from Chapter 1 that it is the resulting profits that are the *test of the validity* of our decisions. If we cultivate too many of the customers in the "fire" category, we may have many completely satisfied customers that we've created and can keep but we will not have a profitable business that will survive.

Types of Customers

There is another way to categorize a portfolio of customers. Table 3-5 shows these types as well as ways to deal with them.

SERVICE RELATIONSHIPS

It is good at this point to understand service relationships and just what they are. A good relationship involves **commitment** and **trust** and, as in our personal lives, there are numerous antecedents that bring this about. There are also numerous consequences when they don't exist. Figure 3-3 shows a model of service relationships developed by Bowen and Shoemaker based on their research. This model illustrates the antecedents and consequences of commitment and trust in service relationships, as indicated by the plus and minus signs. We explain the model as follows. [10]

Antecedents that affect trust and commitment are:

- Fair costs, that is, perceived value of prices and their fairness (+)

T A B L E   3-5
Classifying and Dealing with Customers[9]

Suspects: Anyone who might buy our product or service. Called suspects because we suspect they might buy our service, but don't know enough to be sure.

Focus: Learn more about them.

Prospects: Someone who has a need for our product or service, the ability to buy, has heard of us, but has not yet purchased.

  Focus: Overcome apprehension with empathy/encouragement, client "success stories," site visits, product/service guarantees. (Hampton Inns gave an unconditional guarantee starting in 1990. In the first year they sold about 157,000 rooms to first-time users because of the guarantee. This grossed an additional $7 million. Of those who invoked the guarantee, 3300 returned the same year and 61 percent of these said the reason was the guarantee. The payout on the guarantee was $350,000. The total additional revenue was $8 million.)

Disqualified Prospects: Those about whom we have learned enough to know that they do not need or do not have the ability to buy our product. Present customers who are unprofitable and likely to remain so also fall into this group.

  Focus: Fire them.

First-Time Customer: May have come from the competition.

  Focus: Meet or exceed expectations. Build a promise for return visits. Thank for business, invite to return.

Repeat customer: Those who have purchased two or more times.

  Focus: Provide value-added benefits with each repeat purchase. Uncover needs. Seek regular feedback.

Client: Customer who buys regularly all or most of our products/services. Strong ongoing relationship that makes him or her immune to the competition.

  Focus: Tailor service to this customer's needs. Customize care. Don't take business for granted. Let this customer know it's smart to do business with us. Continually seek input and feedback.

Advocate: Like a client but also encourages others to buy from us. Does our marketing for us and brings additional customers.

  Focus: Get these customers to sell for us. Encourage advocacy through letters of endorsement and referral acknowledgments. Communicate with regularly.

Inactive Customer or Client: Has not bought from us in a period longer than the normal purchase cycle.

  Focus: Develop "win back" plan based on inactivity diagnosis. Detect as soon as possible. Let the customer know he or she's been missed. Activate special communication/purchase offers to win back. If defection is certain, ask "What can we do to win you back?" and listen closely. Meet requirements, communicate changes, and ask for the business. Be patient. Stay in touch.

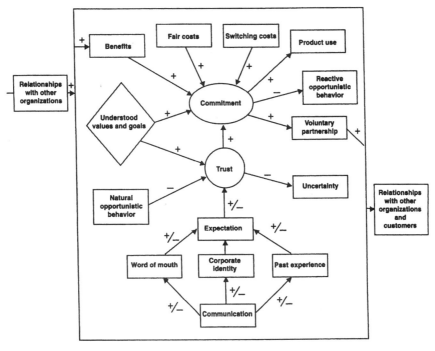

FIGURE 3-3 Model of service relationships.[11]

- Switching costs, that is the costs and troubles of going somewhere else (+)
- Benefits, that is all the things that the customer will receive that provide value and trust, for example, the extent to which the provider's word can be relied upon (+)
- Understood values and goals, that is, the extent to which two parties have beliefs in common that speak to the actions that they should identify and perform to be appropriate or inappropriate (+)

Consequences that result from trust and commitment, or lack of it, are:

- Increased product usage, for example, using the hotel's restaurant versus going elsewhere (+)
- Voluntary activities that one partner is likely to undertake on behalf of the other, such as strong word of mouth and business referrals (+)

Note that the above are all positive outcomes. Negative outcomes result from lack of trust and commitment. These are:

- Uncertainty, that is, feeling a lack of trust in the service delivery (−)
- Natural and reactive opportunistic behavior, where one party takes advantage of the other, for example, a hotel changing rates according to demand (natural) or a reaction to a particular action of one party, for example a customer getting irate when the room desired is not available (−)

Trust is the belief that an individual or exchange partner can be relied on to keep his or her word and promise. Trust is an antecedent of loyalty because the customer trusts the organization to do the things that it is supposed to do, implicitly or explicitly. Any actions taken to increase feelings of trust will lead to commitment.

Commitment is the belief that an ongoing relationship is so important that the partners are willing to work at maintaining it and are willing to make short-term sacrifices to realize long-term benefits.

Building the Service Relationship

So far, we have largely discussed understanding the customer relationship, classifying the customer, and what relationship marketing is all about. The relationships that customers have directly with the service is, as we have mentioned, a personal one in hospitality. Thus another facet of relationship marketing is to enhance the service according to customer needs and wants. Following are some strategies for doing this.

Core Services. **Core services** are based on central rather than peripheral market needs. It is the service around which the customer relationship is built because it attracts new customers by meeting their needs, cements the business through its quality and enduring nature, and provides the means for offering additional services over time. An example of offering a new core service is the suite hotel concept—a suite, including breakfast and drinks, for the price of a regular room. There are more simple examples that we've mentioned before: a large working desk, sufficient and appropriate lighting, comfortable chairs, a television that can be seen from different angles, large soap bars, security peepholes, and so forth. Examples for restaurants would include large enough tables, appropriate lighting for the atmosphere, clean, easy-to-read menus, service people who know the menu and can explain it, bringing the check at the appropriate time, and so forth.

Customizing Services. Because hospitality services are flexible to a large degree, they can often be **customized.** Here, hospitality businesses have a considerable advantage over goods manufacturers because they have the customer in-house, on premises. There is tremendous opportunity to

learn about particular customers and their specific problems and to tailor the service to solve those problems. At Caneel Bay Resort on St. John in the Caribbean, for example, guests are allowed to store anything that they do not want to carry back home, including such items as suntan lotion, swimsuits, and snorkel gear. For their next visit, these belongings are placed in their rooms before arrival. Another example is asking hotel guests if they want help to get to their room or are happy to find their own way and carry their own bags. Video checkout and bed turndown on *request* are still other possible customizations. Figure 3-4 shows some methods of delivering amenities that build relationships but cost little, plus a rate integrity guarantee, something that Bowen and Shoemaker found very important in developing guest loyalty.

Service Augmentation. **Service augmentation** means building extras into the service, especially those that it is difficult for the competition to copy. The extras must be genuine extras that have meaning and value for the customer. Bathroom amenities and mints on pillows, although introduced in this sense, do not fill the criteria unless they are something the customer genuinely values. When the customer simply packs them to take home, they add only cost. It is augmented services, particularly, that can be used to build lasting relationships, but only after the more basic services have been correctly provided first.

Consider Little Dix Bay Resort on Virgin Gorda in the Caribbean. Accessibility to this island requires several changes in flights on small commuter airlines. Guests often arrive at the resort before their baggage. The hotel assigns one person the responsibility of tracing and retrieving lost baggage. In addition, these guests are given a free "survival" kit of essential toiletries in a bag with the hotel's logo on it.

In a hotel or restaurant, it is not easy to add amenities or augmented services that the competition cannot duplicate. This should not deter the effort when it serves a need. Recall the previous comment that one problem with services is that they are not noticed until they are missing; in these

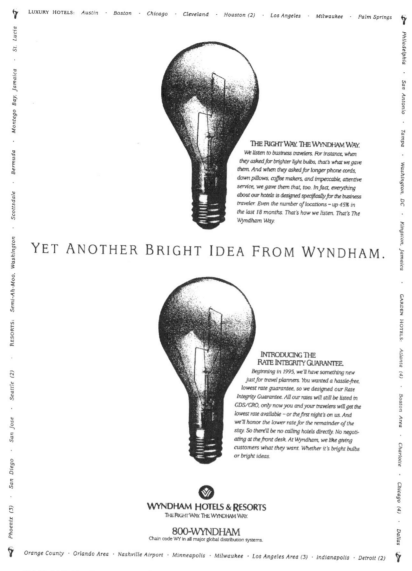

THE RIGHT WAY. THE WYNDHAM WAY.
We listen to business travelers. For instance, when they asked for brighter light bulbs, that's what we gave them. And when they asked for longer phone cords, down pillows, coffee makers, and impeccable, attentive service, we gave them that, too. In fact, everything about our hotels is designed specifically for the business traveler. Even the number of locations – up 45% in the last 18 months. That's how we listen. That's The Wyndham Way.

YET ANOTHER BRIGHT IDEA FROM WYNDHAM.

INTRODUCING THE
RATE INTEGRITY GUARANTEE.
Beginning in 1995, we'll have something new just for travel planners. You wanted a hassle-free, lowest rate guarantee, so we designed our Rate Integrity Guarantee. All our rates will still be listed in GDS/CRO, only now you and your travelers will get the lowest rate available – or the first night's on us. And we'll honor the lower rate for the remainder of the stay. So there'll be no calling hotels directly. No negotiating at the front desk. At Wyndham, we like giving customers what they want. Whether it's bright bulbs or bright ideas.

WYNDHAM HOTELS & RESORTS
THE RIGHT WAY. THE WYNDHAM WAY.

800-WYNDHAM
Chain code WY in all major global distribution systems.

FIGURE 3-4 Wyndham advertises amenities that build relationships.

cases just the presence of a service becomes a service augmentation.

An example that demonstrates this point is the pull-out clothesline that many hotels, even older ones, have installed in bathrooms to solve a problem of women travelers. When a new 1200-room hotel of a national chain opened recently, the director of housekeeping was asked why these clotheslines had not been installed. The response was, "They're too much trouble." This management didn't understand service augmentation.

There are many ways that today's hotels and restaurants can augment, or personalize, service. One way to find out what they are is to talk to customers, something the relationship marketer will do on a regular basis. Customers will always have problems that need solving. Later, we show what features Bowen and Shoemaker found to contribute most to creating loyalty; most of these features are solutions to problems.

Pricing. Hotels commonly give "quantity discounts" to companies that agree to book so many room-nights a year. They also discount rooms for large groups. Relationship pricing can go far beyond these practices, which ignore a large part of the market. Relationship pricing should deal with rewarding loyalty, rather than charging whatever the market will bear at different points of time, and depending on where/how the reservation is made.

Suppose, for example, that regular hotel customers were allowed to order wine or liquor room service, by the bottle, without paying the 300 to 500 percent markups that appear on most room service lists. Not only would customers feel privileged, they wouldn't feel taken advantage of. The hotel would also benefit, not just from the customers' loyalty but also from the service being purchased in the hotel instead of at the package store across the street, where many hotel guests now go. All customers have pet peeves about "extras" they have to pay for, plus they like to feel they are getting something "free." Figure 3-5 shows some of both. We discuss rate integrity in more detail in Chapter 14 on pricing.

BUILDING LOYALTY

The true sense and purpose of relationship marketing is to maintain the customer relationship and build loyalty with the expectation of mutual benefit. As we have shown, satisfaction does not necessarily build loyalty. To offer special attractions and rewards to obtain customers, and to continue to give those rewards to keep customers, are in the vein of traditional marketing, not loyalty marketing.

Frequent Guest Programs

Frequent guest programs do not constitute relationship marketing in the true sense. The reason is

that these programs are really "buying" customers and "buying" their repeated patronage; they are not creating or keeping customers in the marketing sense of creating loyalty. Most frequent guest beneficiaries are unfaithful: They will go where the grass looks the greenest, without remorse. The reason for this is readily apparent; frequent guest programs do not solve consumers' problems. In addition, these plans are very expensive to operate. In effect, they have, for many, become no more than a "cost of doing business."*

The measurable impact of these programs, as they all became essentially the same, has been questionable, in spite of industry claims. When markets are down, as in the early 1990s, cost pressures caused these programs to reduce both awards and frequency of communications. Even in times of greater demand potentially valuable customer databases languish. Frequency Marketing, Inc., a firm that studies and consults on these programs, found that

> [Hotel programs offer] little differentiation, and little competitive advantage. [Calls] to customer service . . . voice response units [eliminate] direct interaction with customers. . . . Hotel databases [are] an unexplored opportunity. . . . Hotel marketers are absurdly neglectful of the customer information they collect. Program mailings are [often] generic and irrelevant to [customers]. [In most cases] database information [is kept secured] at headquarters [so that property marketing directors cannot decide for themselves how to] market directly to program members.[13]

Repeated research has shown that only a minority of business travelers say that these programs influence their hotel decision. For these reasons both the Inter-Continental and Radisson chains ended their plans some time ago with no apparent ill ef-

---

*Research has shown, however, that until the industry as a whole drops these programs most airlines and hotel companies will be forced to maintain them so as not to be at a competitive disadvantage.[12]

FIGURE 3-5 Clubhouse's relationship pricing.

fects.* So-called affinity programs are even less likely to build loyalty. For example, American Express Membership Miles allows application of mileage points on a choice of airlines, forcing the loyalty to American Express rather than to the airlines.

Restaurant Programs

So-called "twofer" programs (two for the price of one) and other types of restaurant promotions, such as couponing, have also been found lacking. Those who take advantage of these promotions often would

---

*Radisson subsequently developed its "Look to Book" program, which rewards travel agents with points. Inter-Continental developed its Six Continents Club, which provides benefits at the hotel such as upgrades every stay and priority reservations, but no points.

not come to the restaurant otherwise, and won't come back. Thus some restaurant chains established frequent dining programs, including Chart House, Chili's (ended July 31, 1997), Charlie Brown's, and T.G.I. Friday's, with limited success. All of these programs give points for dollars spent and various other benefits *at the restaurant,* but mostly not with airlines or others. Some use the programs to collect data on how often these members visit, and how much they spend and, to a limited degree, on what their customers eat. Frequency Marketing, Inc. says:

> All-in-all, these programs have not proved their worth and, in fact, are struggling to survive. The programs are costly, communications with members end at point of sale, there is no real dialogue, there is no special recognition or treatment of any kind, and there is a blatant lack of true relationship content. Essentially, all these programs assume that offering points for free food is all it takes to constitute a viable marketing relationship with a customer. Wrong![14]

True Loyalty

Relationship marketing means getting and keeping the customer because of his or her relationship with you. It should not be necessary to give away something that you would not give away otherwise. In fact, if the relationship is strong the customer may even be willing to pay more because of it. The traditional view of marketing as only an external activity is both short-sighted and self-defeating.

Figure 3-6 shows what can be called "the customer loyalty ladder." The obvious effort is to move the customer from the state of awareness (suspect/prospect) to a brand advocate.

Steps 2 through 5 in Figure 3-6 provide opportunities to build or maintain loyalty through a loyalty program. The potential trap is to confuse purchase frequency with customer loyalty, that is, to confuse the ends with the means. As we have shown, it is not frequency that builds loyalty but loyalty that builds frequency. The focus on frequency behavior ignores the emotional and psychological factors that build real commitment. Without that commitment, customers focus on the "deal," not the brand or product

relevance. Sales may increase, as they would with price discounts. Repeat purchase may increase, but the focus is on the rewards, not on product superiority or brand relevance. Thus awards programs are tactical solutions to a strategic problem—an awards program for unprofitable customers, parity instead of differentiation. This behavior focus makes bribing the customer the line of reasoning. Over time, the economics of bribery begin to collapse with greater and greater bribes, eventually eroding the brand image and diminishing product/service differentiation. The differences are shown in Table 3-6 and illustrated in Figure 3-7.

So, what, really is loyalty? When the customer feels strongly that you can best meet his or her relevant needs, your competition is virtually excluded from the considered set, and the customer buys almost exclusively from you—referring to you as "her restaurant" or "his hotel." The customer focuses on your brand, offers, and messages to the exclusion of others. Price is not a dominant consideration, but only one component in the larger value proposition.

Loyalty provides critical inoculation. Loyal customers are less likely to ask about price. Competitive offers face a higher hurdle. The customer becomes more forgiving when you make a mistake because there is good will equity. In fact, loyal customers are more likely to report service failures. *Loyalty begets loyalty.* Further, marketing and sales costs are lower, as are transactions costs. Research has shown that if companies increase their customer retention by 2 percent, it is the equivalent of cutting their operating costs by 10 percent.[15]

What Loyalty Programs Don't Do

Sometimes the wrong things are expected from loyalty programs. These programs are not "quick fixes." They will not fix an essential problem in the operation that may be costing customers. They won't show a profit in the short run—these are dedicated long-term efforts. They are not a temporary promotion, or, worse, a promotion that becomes part of the product, raising costs without raising profits. And loyalty programs won't bring in new customers—as was shown in Figure 3-6 the

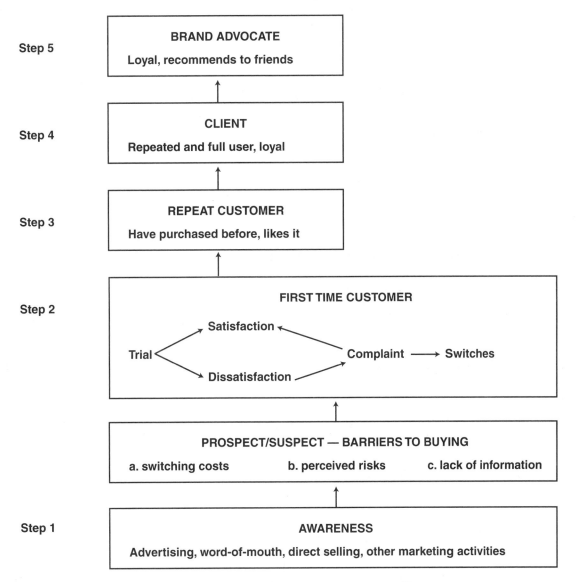

FIGURE 3-6 The customer loyalty ladder.[16]

brand has to overcome the barriers to first trial before the loyalty program can kick in.

What Makes Loyalty Programs Work

According to Richard Dunn at Carlson Group Marketing, the following elements are essential to a successful relationship program:[17]

- A vital database—the relationship foundation
- Targeted communications—the relationship dialogue
- Meaningful rewards—relationship recognition
- Simplicity—easy to participate and understand
- Attainability—motivational rewards must be attainable (e.g., upgrades)
- Sustainability—don't let it lapse, keep it active

TABLE 3-6
Frequency versus Loyalty

Frequency		*Loyalty*
Objectives	Build traffic, sales, profit	Build sales, profits, brand desirability
Strategy	Incentivize repeat transactions	Build personal brand relationship
Focus	Segment behavior and profitability	An individual's emotional and rational needs and their value
Tactics	Free/discounts/rewards, profitability	Individual value, tenure, preferred status, "insider," value-added upgrades, add-ons, tailored offers/messages, emotional rewards
Measurement	Transactions, sales growth	Individual lifetime value, attitudinal change, emotional response

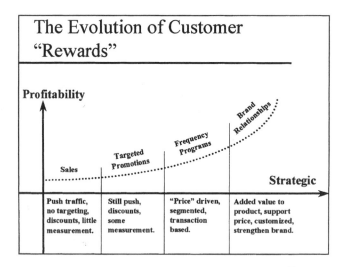

FIGURE 3-7 The evolution of customer awards.[18]

- Measurability—make sure it is working in the right ways
- Management—full commitment and behind it all the way
- Manageability—don't let it get out of hand
- Profitability—is it really working in the long term?

Further caveats from Dunn are these:

- Don't treat the program like a promotion.
- Don't focus excessively on rewards, but on the relationship.
- Don't shortchange the communications component.

- Don't underestimate the importance of internal support.
- Don't pretend to care more than you really do.
- Tailor the value of benefits to specific customers based on their achieved or expected value.

Table 3-7 provides an outline for establishing a loyalty program.

Relationship marketing means thinking in terms of the customers we have, rather than just in terms of the ones we hope to acquire. This is crucial in the hospitality industry. Competition is standing by, all too ready and willing to take the customers you can't

T A B L E   3 - 7
Setting Up a Loyalty Program[19]

Management Commitment
- Long-term business growth vs. short-term costs
- Reallocation of resources
- Need a champion
- Need to get all areas of the company sold on the idea

Set Objectives
- Are objectives to solve a problem? Capitalize on an opportunity? Try to avoid being left behind?
- Program objectives must support strategic objectives
- Objectives must be measurable

Design Program
- Need to focus on the customer
  - What's your vision for your relationship with the customer?
  - What do your customers want (does it add value)?
  - Do your customers want a relationship with you?
  - What can you give the customer to make it worthwhile for them?
  - Is it simple and understandable?
- Need to consider the competition
  - Develop a sustainable point of difference
  - Make it difficult to copy
  - Create a reluctance to defect
- Need to consider program structure
  - Promotional currency? (rewards or recognition)
  - Plateau
  - Qualification to play
  - Lifetime of rewards (i.e., are there expiration dates?)
  - What are overall costs (costs to be addressed shortly)?
  - Free or fee?
  - Voluntary enrollment or automatic?
- Need an exit strategy

Logistics and Accounting
- Enrollment
- How to handle rewards given out

- How to handle customers' questions
- Start and end dates
- Tracking program performance
- Reporting
- Liability reporting
- Partnering billing
- Renewals
- Measurement

Examine Issues of Partnerships
- With whom?
- How long?
- Arrangements

Make Budget Calculations
- Cost of communication
  - acknowledgment (welcome to new members: includes individual letter, membership card, program guide, initial benefits credentials)
  - ongoing communications (program mailings, statement mailings)
  - must include materials, printing, postage, assembly, storage, translation
- Cost of Administrative
  - operations + database (equipment, data entry, printing, MIS people, etc.)
  - accounting department
  - reward fulfillment
  - management of the program

Decision to Test Program
- Pros: an opportunity to refine before rollout; can avoid mistakes
- Cons: gives competition an early look at your program; high cost per customer; delays impact of rollout

Finalize Program

Train Employees
- Get employees involved in the development and maintenance of the program (e.g., set up teams to perform "loyalty duties" such as retention evaluation, etc . . .)

TABLE 3-8
Features of a Hotel That Create Trust
and Loyalty[20]

Trust

- I always feel safe at this hotel.
- The management of this hotel knows the luxury hotel business.
- When an employee at this hotel says he or she will do something, I am sure it will get done.
- If I ask management or an employee a question, I feel I will get a truthful answer.
- If I make a request, no matter how trivial, it gets taken care of.
- Any communication, including reservations, will always be accurately received and recorded or filed.

Loyalty

- The hotel provides upgrades.
- You can check in and check out at a time that suits you.
- The hotel uses information from previous stays to customize service for you.
- You can request a specific room.
- Employees communicate the attitude that your problems are important to them.
- When you return to a hotel, your registration process is expedited.

keep. What specific things create trust and loyalty? Many things to be sure, and not always the same things at different properties. Bowen and Shoemaker found, for example, that the features in Table 3-8 have the greatest impact on the creation of trust and loyalty for business travelers in luxury hotels.

WHY RELATIONSHIP MARKETING DOESN'T ALWAYS WORK

Everyone, it seems, extols the virtues of relationship marketing. Entire courses are taught on the subject, entire books have been written about it,

and there is probably at least part of a chapter on it in any recent marketing text. Yet it does not seem to be working in many instances in many businesses where, instead, customers feel harried, confused, manipulated, trapped, and victimized. Companies may, in fact, be wasting money on misdirected relationship programs or providing customer benefits that bring little return.[21]

Presumably, companies know more about us than ever before. Huge databases tell them when we shop, what we buy, how much, why, and numerous other factors, not to mention all the demographics they have on us. Try to get on some Web sites without giving your life away! Frequent flyer and frequent guest programs have us all in their databases. What do we, as individuals, get for all this?

In most cases, barring perhaps the 5 percent of the population who travel often and/or stay in luxury hotels and are readily recognized, the answer seems to be "not much." We get bombarded with promotions in which we have little interest, we get special "price breaks" that can be beat by calling an 800 number, we get phone calls in the evening when we're eating dinner that inevitably start with, "How are you today?" (as if it's any of their business!), we get no better seats on airplanes (unless of course we use our points to upgrade), and we seldom get better rooms in hotels unless we demand them. In fact, although your hotel member card probably says "free upgrade if available" it is often not available unless you ask for it and not often then. And we fill out questionnaire after questionnaire. Not to mention all that stuff that comes in the mail. In fact,

> Customer satisfaction rates in the United States are at an all-time low, while complaints, boycotts, and other expressions of consumer discontent rise.... Ironically, the very things that marketers are doing to build relationships with customers are often the things that are destroying those relationships.... Relationship marketing is powerful in theory but troubled in practice.[22]

Fournier et al. make the points in Table 3-9; our comments are added. Some examples of these problems are given in Table 3-10.

T A B L E   3-9
Problems with Relationships[23]

- The number of one-on-one relationships that consumers are asked to maintain are untenable. Thus many marketing initiatives seem trivial and useless instead of unique and valuable.
  Note: With so many similar offers to choose from, what does it matter which company you do business with?
- When companies ask their customers for friendship, loyalty, and respect, too often they don't give it in return.
  Note: For all the information we are asked for and give, what do we get back? Is what we ask for one time necessarily what we want the next time? They can call you at home but how do you get in touch with them without going through a recorded "press key" runaround?
- Do they really "value" our relationship as they say? How do they show it? "Best" customer treatment may leave other revenue-generating customers feeling left out.
  Note: As we previously pointed out in this chapter (Figure 3-2), some customers should be "fired," but others need to be managed and disciplined. Companies cannot survive on only their "reward and invest" customers.
- Companies need people to think of them as allies and friends, but more often than not they come across as enemies. They claim to offer solutions but too often create more problems than they solve.
  Note: Hotels, in particular, often advise you to, say, call housekeeping if you need something (that should have been there in the first place). It can take 10 minutes on the phone until you get the right person, and 30 minutes later someone delivers the wrong thing. Or, when you call for a reservation, the person on the other end of the call starts by offering you a $300 room until, ten minutes later, she suddenly "discovers" a room for $129. Customers, in fact, develop coping strategies to deal with many of these situations.

T A B L E   3-10
Troubled Relationships

- "[Senator Pat Carney is upset over] a decision by the Citadel [Hotel in Ottawa, a popular residence for MPs and senators] to stop serving cereal and bagels as part of its complimentary breakfast. When Ms. Carney complained, [the manager indicated the hotel was reassessing aspects of its food service and had also upgraded amenities in all rooms with, especially, a hair dryer.]
  "The senator [trying to shed 18 kilograms] responded that her heart was more important than her hair. [She sent a letter about the Citadel to all MPs and senators including a rhyme]: 'They don't care if we live or die/They just care if our hair is dry.'
  "[The manager, is contemplating the complaint]and says, 'We take our clients' comments very seriously.'"[24]
- "Hotels call them 'loyal guest programs.' [At one Chicago hotel members have their bags rushed] to their rooms ahead of other guests' [while others wait]. [To get this preferential treatment, guests had to have stayed with the hotel at least 35 times."][25]
- "Some hotels have introduced 'intelligent' systems. [These tell] when guests are in their rooms and raise or lower temperatures accordingly. Previous systems that [do the same thing have caused some guests] to jam any card into the key-card slots so the temperature stays where they want it.
  "To save even more [money] hotels can set the temperature. [higher or lower when the guest is not in the room]. [The more money a hotel wants to save] the less comfort they're providing the guest.'"[26]

Thus the real effort in relationship marketing is to understand that it is a two-way street. We need to convince customers, not just ourselves, that the relationship is worthwhile. Somehow, at least in the hotel business, we need to learn not only that a guest wants a feather pillow but also what he or she doesn't want, the things that frustrate customers. When hotels started charging guests for local phone calls there was a burst of anger. Some listened; many did not and still don't. (Interestingly, you are more likely to pay for these calls in a $300 a night room than in a $69 budget property!) A Holiday Inn recently charged us $32.00 for a 12-page incoming fax. But we got points!(We won't go back there!) For all the evidence that frequent travelers carry light bulbs in their briefcases to replace the hotel's low wattage bulbs, some hotels still don't get it. And far too many hotels still offer weekend packages to couples with rooms clearly furnished for the single traveler.

A true customer relationship requires an understanding of how our products and services are used, a singular view of consumer behavior. Marriott, which advertises its Courtyard brand as the "hotel designed by business travelers" is right on. It actually did that—asked a multitude of business travelers how they use a hotel room. This led to long phone cords, a large desk for work, a bright lamp over the desk rather than on it, and numerous other conveniences. Courtyard has been copied, but most imitations don't work as well as the original. Many companies do not have a realistic grasp of what their customers *and* employees actually think and do.

The usual customer satisfaction surveys don't do the trick, as we explained in Chapter 1. Too often, in fact, they simply measure how well a customer's expectations were met. They don't really tell us how to make our service better. Customer satisfaction is a requisite for loyalty. However, customer satisfaction does not always build loyalty. It must be met or exceeded in order to build loyalty, yet it may not necessarily do that. A satisfied customer who does not return and does not spread positive word of mouth does not contribute additional value to the company.[27] Relationship marketing means we have to get inside the head of customers and understand their

experiences, and what truly builds loyalty. Fournier et al. sum it up this way: "Relationship marketing can work if it can deliver on the principles on which it was founded. . . .[I]t is alarming how quickly and thoughtlessly relationships can be destroyed through the muddled actions we often engage in. . . . It's time to think about—and act on—what being a partner in a relationship really means."[28]

All of this is not to say that many companies don't "talk the talk." Management speaks with great conviction about empowerment and customer focus, and puts a great deal of attention on employee training. Unfortunately, too many employees really don't understand the point of it all or grasp their own role in it. Once the energy and excitement have peaked, too many fall back in relief and reassume bad habits. They don't really understand what they are supposed to be doing differently. Sometimes it is the frontline employees who seem to be the only people in the company who understand why the company is in trouble with its customers, but somehow they can't get that message through to management.

Canadian Pacific Hotels (CP) of Canada is one company that has tried to put its brand on every aspect of its customer relationships. Its survey of individual business travelers found that what they wanted most was recognition of their individual quirks and preferences. CP started mapping every bit of the guest's experience (sometimes called "service blueprinting") from the first approach to a hotel to the last thing before leaving. It then analyzed how it could make good on the highest level of service: What products or services could be offered? What processes needed to be put in place to offer them? What did employees have to do or learn to deliver them? Management structures had to change: At each hotel a champion was appointed and given broad, cross-functional authority to see that the staff understood and lived up to the expanded promise the company had made to its most valuable customers. Within slightly more than a year CP's share of Canadian business travel increased 16 percent while the market as a whole increased only 3 percent. Further, a quarter of CP "club members" stopped spreading their business around and are sticking with CP.

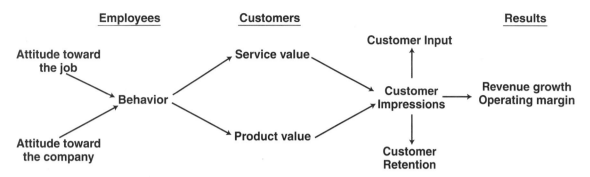

F I G U R E 3 - 8 A model of relationship management.

Figure 3-8 presents a model that ties all this together.

CUSTOMER COMPLAINTS

If there is one place where internal marketing and relationship marketing come together, it is in the handling of customer complaints, sometimes called **service recovery.** Customer complaints deserve special treatment in this chapter because they are one of the most misunderstood and mishandled areas of customer relations in the hospitality industry. Let us look first at what customer complaints are:

- *Inevitable:* Nothing is perfect. The diversity of the hospitality customer and the heterogeneity of the hospitality product absolutely ensure that there will be complaints. This will be true even when everything goes according to plan. Of course, when everything doesn't go according to plan, and it almost never does, there will be additional problems and there will be more complaints.
- *Healthy:* The old army expression is, "If the troops aren't griping look out for trouble." An absence of complaints may be the best indication management has (along with declining occupancies or covers) that something is wrong. Hospitality customers are never totally satisfied, especially over a period of time. Probably, instead, they are simply not talking to you or you are not

talking to them. The communication process is not working; the relationship is deteriorating. By the time it explodes, it will be too late. Some say, "If it isn't broken, don't fix it." First, you have to know if it's broken; the ones who know first are your customers. And, incidentally, the ones they tell first are your employees, which means that you had better listen to your employees as well.
- *Opportunities:* Customer complaints are opportunities to learn of customers' problems, whether they are idiosyncratic or caused by the operation itself. If it's broken, you have an opportunity to fix it. We call this "service recovery." If it's not broken, you have an opportunity to make it better, to be creative, to develop new product, to learn new needs, and to keep old customers.
- *Marketing Tools:* If marketing is to give customers what they want, then marketing must know what they want. All the customer surveys in the world won't tell you as much as customer complaints will tell you.*
- *Advertising:* Yes, advertising. The advertising is negative if you don't resolve the problems, and there is nothing more devastating in the hospitality business than negative word of mouth. It is positive if you fix the problem. Research has shown that one of the best and most loyal customers is the one who had a complaint that was

*Year after year we see research on what customers want. The top of the list is most often "clean rooms." Great. We know that limited response surveys tell us the same thing over and over. Complaints tell us about the multitude of things that are not on the survey.

satisfactorily resolved. And this customer loves to tell others about it. The research reported in Table 3-11[29] demonstrates this.

The research detailed in Table 3-11 shows that once the cause of the complaint has occurred, the level of stress becomes a function of the handling of the situation. The disturbance level can be reduced if the complainant actively believes in management. This means it is important for management to direct its efforts toward creating an attitude that will minimize the negative effect of the complaint.

Complainants want to feel that management is sincere and will make a sincere effort to correct the situation. If this belief is supported, they will probably choose the same hotel again. The tendency of complainants, however, is not to believe. Interestingly enough, 29 percent of the still unsatisfied complainants indicated they would have ben satisfied simply with a proper response from management rather than what they felt were token gestures.

More recent research has similar findings. These are depicted in Figure 3-9.[30] Additionally, Bowen and Shoemaker found that a guest who feels loyalty toward a specific hotel will tell an average of 12 people positive things about the hotel.

These studies demonstrate the opportunities inherent in the proper handling of consumer complaints. Appropriate complaint handling just may be relationship marketing at its finest; certainly it is a tremendous marketing opportunity, which is why a marketing-oriented management should actually seek out complaints.

What to Do About It

Practicing relationship marketing through consumer complaint handling is not the easiest task in the world. Many discontented customers will not take the trouble to complain. Actually encouraging complaints becomes the necessary objective.

Research has shown that people do not complain for three primary reasons:

It is not worth the time and effort.

They don't know where or how to complain.

They believe that nothing will be done even if they do complain.

Marketing's task is to overcome these obstacles by making it easy to complain, making it known where and how to complain (see Figure 3-10), and truly doing something about the complaint if it is reasonable, and over three-fourths of all complaints appear to fall into that category. This means setting up specific procedures.[31] Such an action will also constitute internal marketing; when employees see management taking complaints seriously they will feel more inclined to do likewise.

Categorically, there are four ways complaints are usually handled as shown in Table 3-12[32] along with strategies for complaint handling.

The benefits are clear: long-term profit from loyal customers, and more positive, and less negative, word-of-mouth advertising. There are other ancillary benefits, such as new product ideas, new product information, improved image, better-educated customers, and higher productivity and service. For line employees there are also the benefits of less customer conflict, better image and word of mouth about the company, and better respect for the company and the product.

Each company must devise its own system for soliciting and handling complaints. Handling satisfied customers is easy; handling dissatisfied customers is the acid test of marketing and management.

EMPLOYEE RELATIONSHIP MARKETING

Employee relationship marketing, often referred to as **internal marketing,** means applying marketing principles to the people who serve the customers. The emphasis of internal marketing is on the employee as the internal customer who also has needs, wants, and problems. What this customer is buying is his or her job. Thus the job is the product that satisfies the needs and wants of these internal customers so that they, in turn, will better satisfy the needs and wants of the external customer. In fact, Taco Bell, by examining employee turnover records for individual stores, found that the 20 percent of the stores with the lowest turnover rates have double the sales and

T A B L E   3-11
Customer Complaint Research[29]

- One hundred twenty previous guests of a specific hotel who had communicated with the hotel were surveyed by mail as to their feelings, actions, and behaviors. About 50 percent of those surveyed had written only complaints, 20 percent had written only compliments, and 30 percent had written both to complain and to compliment. Of the complainers, 60 percent had complained to management in person before leaving the hotel.

- Of the guests who had complained, 71 percent said they never used guest comment cards to register their complaints. Thirty-eight percent of those who complained said they would never return, while 25 percent were unsure. For those who would choose to return, the major factor in their decision was the way the complaint was handled. Of those who complained, 63 percent were highly likely to make a point of telling others about their complaint, and 21 percent were unsure if they would; 47 percent were highly likely to tell others not to use the hotel, and 12 percent were unsure if they would.

- These percentages were even higher when the complaint was not handled satisfactorily. On the other hand, the percentages decrease substantially when the complaint was handled satisfactorily; as few as 14 percent would tell others not to use the hotel under this condition. From these findings it could also be inferred that for every 10 complaints received there were 25 that were not expressed.

- In another study, 479 of those people who had written complaints to managements of 9 hotels in a 21-hotel chain over a 2-month period were surveyed by written questionnaire. Sixty-four percent had made their complaint in person at the time of the incident; 66 percent said they were extremely disturbed at the time.

- Of the respondents, 50 percent said it was highly unlikely that they would ever stay at the same hotel again. Of those who had been in the area of the hotel since their complaint, 75 percent had purposely not returned to the hotel; 32 percent had purposely not returned to other hotels in the chain. An analysis of their word-of-mouth behavior is shown below.

  Likely to tell others outside family about the complaint?

Highly likely	62%
Undecided	18%

  Number of people actually told (average)   12

  If the complaint was not resolved?

Highly likely	75%
Not sure	15%

  Likely to tell others not to use the hotel?

Highly likely	43%
Not sure	13%

  Number of people actually told (average)   8

  If complaint was not resolved?

Highly likely	71%
Not sure	11%

- Fifty-eight percent of the respondents in this study reported that they were led to complain by a series of problems or incidents. This indicates that the hotel managements involved had a number of opportunities, if they had known of them, to resolve difficulties for the same customer. After the complaints were received, management had additional opportunities, which it failed to take advantage of in 61 percent of the cases.

- This 61 percent indicated that they believed their complaint could have been better handled. How? Only 19 percent felt that they should have received a rebate or complimentary rooms or meals. Thirty-four percent thought the situation could have been better handled at the time the incident occurred. A whopping 47 percent stated they would have been satisfied with a better response from management in terms of more detailed and speedier communication or a more pleasant tone.

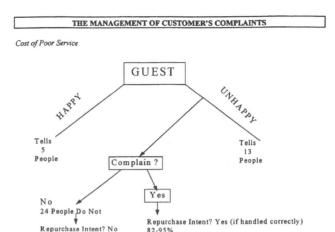

FIGURE 3-9   The effect of complaint behavior.

55 percent higher profits than the 20 percent of the stores with the highest turnover rates.[33]

Sheraton found likewise. It determined that its employee satisfaction index accounted for 50 percent of the variance in its customer satisfaction index, which in turn, accounted for 50 percent of the variance in its revenue per available room (REVPAR).

To create customer value, the company must create employee value. Employees, after all, manage the process, provide the imagination, implement the policies, and derive the insight to help deepen customer bonding. This is especially true when we are dealing with so many intangibles that make for customer value and can never be explicit in the policies ordained. Without the commitment of employees, relationship marketing is doomed to fail. This may mean looking at employees in a new light, like customers. To do this, it is useful to apply the matrix in Figure 3-2 to employees with some minor adaptations. Instead of using the words "profitable"/ "unprofitable," we can replace them with "creates customer value"/"doesn't create customer value." This, of course, is the view of the employer, who must also create value for the employee.

At first glance, this may appear to be a strange way to look at marketing; it is certainly not the way that we look at the marketing of goods. However, a closer look makes the case obvious: One of the first tasks of marketing and management is to have the employees believe in their job, which is the product that they represent to the customer. To wit, the successful hospitality firm must first sell its jobs to employees before it can sell its services to its customers. If this is not done, we end up with dissatisfied customers (employees) who will, one way or another, express their dissatisfaction to the paying customers. Paying customers, in turn, find that their problems are not adequately solved, so they go elsewhere. Clearly, this is not the way to keep customers. Thus what is practiced in the creation and keeping of customers needs to also be practiced in the creation and keeping of employees. Relationships with customers often depend on employees' going beyond standard policies and procedures to make a big difference in problem resolution and the feeling a customer has for the company.

Again, Bowen and Shoemaker shed some light on what this means. When asked, what does it mean to have trust in a luxury hotel, these were the leading responses:

- "The hotel does things as promised."
- "The feeling that my personal property is safe in my room."
- "If I receive a fax, I know it will be delivered to my room."

Dear Guest:

At Doubletree Hotels and Doubletree Guest Suites, our employees are dedicated to one objective – the highest standards of hospitality, to ensure that your stay is enhanced by sweet dreams.

Each hotel has its own CARE Committee where employees work together to improve Guest services in every department, from the front desk to housekeeping to restaurants. And management at each hotel are full partners in the philosophy of CARE...putting the emphasis on Guest Satisfaction.

Your evaluation of our performance is our most valuable source of information. Please take a moment to complete this form and let us know of anything that did not measure up to your expectations. We'd also like to hear what pleased you as well.

For an immediate response to any concerns, this form is addressed to the General Manager of the hotel and may be dropped in the CARE Box at the front desk. However, please feel free to write me directly at Doubletree Hotels Corporation, 410 N. 44th Street, Suite 700-1A, Phoenix, AZ 85008.

On behalf of all of us at Doubletree Hotels and Doubletree Guest Suites, thank you for your loyal and continued patronage.

Richard M. Kelleher
President & CEO

BECAUSE WE CARE

	Yes	No
1. Did we recognize you by name?	☐	☐
2. Was our staff friendly?	☐	☐
3. Did we provide professional service?	☐	☐
4. Did we respond to your needs?	☐	☐
5. Will you return?	☐	☐
6. Have you been to this hotel before?	☐	☐

7. What was the purpose of your stay?
   ☐ Business ☐ Meeting ☐ Leisure

8. We sincerely appreciate any written comments you have about our performance, including the names of staff members who were particularly helpful or friendly to you during your stay.

_____

_____

_____

Hotel Location _____ *Room Number*

Name _____

Address _____ *Telephone*

City, State, Zip _____

FIGURE 3-10 Doubletree encourages customer input.

- "Employees provide quick and correct answers."
- "*I trust a hotel that trusts its employees*" (emphasis added).[34] One respondent commented that if management could not trust an employee with a $30 decision (of another guest), he could not feel comfortable leaving a $4000 computer and other valuables in his room.[35]

Management Practices

Keeping good employees leads to keeping good customers (Figure 3-11). The quality of services depends in large measure on the skills and attitudes of the people producing the services. An acceptable product is necessary to appeal to the external market. The same is true of the internal market.

TABLE 3-12
Postures of Complaint Handling[32]

Company's Reception	Company's Response	
	Defensive	*Corrective*
Passive	Deflects complaints	Reacts to needs
Active	Lip service, illusionary	Relationship management

Reactions

Defensive/Passive Deflection Reaction: "I'm sorry you're not happy. Here is your bill."

Defensive/Active Lip Service Reaction: Management solicits complaints but does nothing about them.

Corrective/Passive Reaction: Management resolves complaint but does nothing to prevent it from happening again.

Corrective/Active Reaction (Relationship Management): Management resolves complaint. Finds out why it happened. Fixes cause. Follows up to make sure customer is fully satisfied. Encourages customer to return.

Strategies for Relationship Management Complaint Handling

- Make it easy for customers to give feedback. Show willingness to hear complaint. Get employees in the habit of asking about complaints and writing them down on a standard form.
- Provide help to customers quickly. People who have to ask more than once for a resolution are less satisfied. Inform them of approximate length of time to fix problem.
- Give authority to line staff to settle complaints. Having to get permission only delays the resolution and creates further dissatisfaction. Also gives a feeling of trust.
- Learn how to comfort an angry customer:
  - (a) Let them blow off steam. Ask open-ended questions. Listen attentively. Do not interrupt. Do not be defensive. Keep the customer talking until you get all the facts.
  - (b) Let the customer know you understand the problem. Repeat it back. Write it down.
  - (c) Find out what the customer wants and how they would like it resolved. Ask what is fair. If he or she offers a solution, take it.
  - (d) Suggest a solution if the customer doesn't. Make sure it will satisfy the customer.
  - (e) For any significant complaint, make a follow-up satisfaction call.
- Make sure to not further inconvenience the customer. Doing so will only make him or her angrier.
- Provide an alternative if an immediate solution can not be found.
- Tell the guest what will be done so it doesn't happen again.

Employees, an integral part of the product in hospitality, must also be marketing oriented. Unless a firm has something to offer to its employees, it should not expect marketing-oriented behavior. Just as we select customers whose needs we can best meet, we must select employees whose needs can be met through a job in our organization.

Understanding the simultaneous production and consumption nature of services is helpful in understanding what has just been stated. Many companies conduct employee courses in customer handling, including what trainees have dubbed "smile training." Smile training, as we have previously said, is not enough. Consider the previous example of a room service waiter who arrived an hour late with breakfast, a big smile and a "How are you folks today?" instead of a somber, "I'm sorry." Or, the following anecdote, told to one of the authors by a front desk clerk of a large convention hotel:

FIGURE 3-11 Oriental finds that keeping employees means keeping customers.

A large convention was checking into the hotel all day and we never had a chance to get away from the desk and take a break for coffee, or even for lunch. We were smiling our damnedest, dealing with all the problems, and things were going fairly smoothly considering the circumstances. After a while, however, it begins to get to you so we devised a little sing-song communication and banter among us which helped to keep our sense of

humor and keep us going. While all this was going on, our supervisors were sitting in a room behind the front desk, talking and drinking coffee. Occasionally, one would step out and, seeing that all was going well, would go back to the room leaving us to carry on. When they heard our banter, however, things changed. One of us was called into the backroom and told to tell the others to cut it out. Our attitudes changed immediately. We kept on working but we couldn't have cared less about the customers and it showed.

The impact of this anecdote is that marketing principles have not been applied to these employees' jobs. Customer satisfaction has been given token attention rather than being treated as a philosophy. Employees will not "buy" the product, customer service, when it appears that management is not willing to deliver on its promise of what it is "selling." The old expression "practice what you preach" is also the essence of internal marketing. There is a natural conflict between company policies and the ability of the employee to satisfy customers. The very nature of the service business implies that it is impossible to anticipate all the needs and wants of customers. Obviously, there must be policies to guide employee actions, and no one is suggesting that there are easy solutions to these conflicts. But it is just as obvious that there must be flexibility. Progressive companies, like Marriott, are embracing the concept of **employee empowerment** (Figure 3-12). Line employees are allowed to make decisions that will solve guests' immediate problems without seeking prior approval from their supervisors.

The Peabody Hotel in Orlando, FL, and the Opryland Hotel in Nashville, TN, are two properties that have managed to "break the mold" for customer service. Visiting these hotels, both over 1000 rooms, one is completely impressed with the level of service offered by *everyone*. These hotels each have 800 plus employees continuously interacting with the guests. Every employee verbally and visually engages the customer and is empowered to satisfy that customer's needs and ask questions later. Ritz-Carlton employees are empowered to spend up to $2000 to satisfy a customer. According to Patrick Mene, head of quality control at Ritz-Carlton, "To us, empowerment means giving the employees responsibility for solving guests' problems."[36]

Consider the following anecdote from Eddystone C. Nebel, who followed and observed ten hotel general managers as part of a qualitative research study:

This general manager . . . tries very hard to communicate what is important to his employees. He's developed a series of sayings to help guide the thinking and actions of the entire hotel staff. His first saying which he preaches with missionary zeal to his staff of 850 employees and executives is, "Talk to the guests." Talking to the guest is meant to convey a number of things. It means that a pleasant hello from all the staff is a sign of hospitality, even in a 1000 room hotel. But talking to the guests means much more; it means finding out from the guests if things are going well or if they need anything. In short, "talk to the guests" means constant and total communication, one-on-one, between as many employees and as many guests as possible. How is your stay? What do you need? Are there any problems? How can I help? These are the kinds of questions his staff is continuously asking the guests. . . . [His] goal is to not only talk to the guest but also to get the *guest talking* [emphasis added].[37]

Customers have a wide variety of expectations. Although the customer is not always right, there is not much to be gained in proving the customer wrong. Employees, instead, must be empowered to make the customer "feel right." This constitutes marketing to both the customer and the employee—what influences customers must be marketed to all employees.

Noncontact Employees

We have discussed internal marketing from the point of view of the customer-contact employee. This is certainly the most obvious way to look at it, but it doesn't stop there. The engineers, the housekeepers, the night porters, the cooks, the dishwashers, the storeroom people, and even the accountants are part of the internal marketing effort in hospitality. Management's task is to get employees to realize and feel that they are part of the effort.

It is a dishwasher, for example, who can stop a chipped glass or stained plate from going back into the dining room. It is the storeroom person who can make certain that the right degree of freshness is received. It is the housekeeper who can make sure that all the light bulbs in a room are working. It is the engineer—well, you get the point. **All** employ-

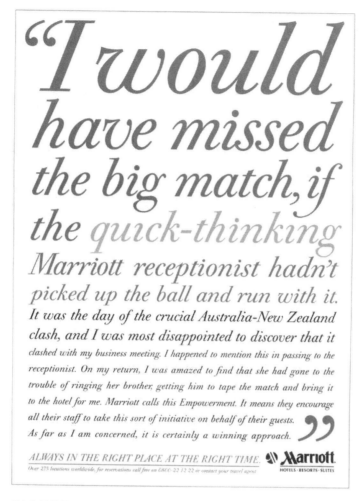

"I would have missed the big match, if the quick-thinking Marriott receptionist hadn't picked up the ball and run with it.

It was the day of the crucial Australia-New Zealand clash, and I was most disappointed to discover that it clashed with my business meeting. I happened to mention this in passing to the receptionist. On my return, I was amazed to find that she had gone to the trouble of ringing her brother, getting him to tape the match and bring it to the hotel for me. Marriott calls this Empowerment. It means they encourage all their staff to take this sort of initiative on behalf of their guests. As far as I am concerned, it is certainly a winning approach. "

ALWAYS IN THE RIGHT PLACE AT THE RIGHT TIME. **Marriott** HOTELS · RESORTS · SUITES

Over 275 locations worldwide, for reservations call free on 0800-22 12 22 or contact your travel agent

FIGURE 3-12 Marriott uses employee empowerment to benefit the customer.

ees in hospitality are part of the marketing effort. If you said this to back-of-the house employees, most of them would probably say, "Hunh?" What influences customers must be *marketed* to all employees. Consider, for example, housekeepers talking (or even shouting) in a hallway at 8:00 A.M. One could tell them not to do this; better, one could tell them the effect it has on customers in their rooms.

Employees will not only need to understand how what they do impacts the customer but they will need also to broaden their scope of knowledge of more processes, technologies, and people with whom they must interact. They need to understand how everything the company does comes together for the customer as each customer expects. Ian Gordon suggests the following:

1. Identify the relationship marketing skills required from employees who are to participate in all the processes that impact customer value.

2. Assess the performance of employees in respect of these skills and determine any knowledge gaps, by working this through with employees and communicating effectively in real time, not just in an impersonal manner.

3. Develop training programs and technology support to re-skill and/or de-skill processes where employees require additional knowledge or context.[38]

As Gordon points out, "Many companies establish major training initiatives, putting vast amounts of information into three-ring binders and then attempting to drill this into the skulls of their staff."[39] This approach is likely to fail more often than not.

The Internal Marketing Concept

Motivating employees is not a new management task but neither is it only a function of the organization's personnel department. The effort that supports the concept of internal marketing starts with top management and involves management at every level of the organization. Lower-level employees, whether they are customer contact or not, cannot be expected to be customer conscious if management above them is not similarly involved. Management style and decisions must support this orientation, not counteract it. Personnel policies, likewise, must reflect this orientation and practice it in the form of job-filling, recruiting, and promotion. We can take this one step further: If internal marketing is not incorporated into the management culture, the direction of the firm may make implementation of internal marketing difficult or even impossible at lower levels. Successful internal marketing considerably eases the task of implementing relationship marketing, or the primary task of keeping customers.

In fact, Bowen and Shoemaker discovered that a final barrier to loyalty can be employees. Their findings indicate that if employees do not communicate the attitude that a guest's problems are important to them, guests will not become loyal to a hotel.[40]

Traditional marketing activities can also play a role in influencing personnel as much as they are designed to influence customers. Employees should be kept abreast of new products, new developments, and new consumer promises even before the consumer. If a consumer wishes to claim an advertised benefit, it is self-evident that the employee to whom the claim is made should know exactly what the customer is talking about, and be enthused about promoting it. Too many times have we called the 800 reservation number of a national chain to request a rate advertised in a full page newspaper ad only to find that the reservation agent knows nothing about it. "It's not on my screen," is a frequent response.

Here's a great story that makes the point.

Mike Leven, now CEO of U.S. Franchise Systems, was once honored by Washington State University as "Hotel Marketer of the Year." Two students from the hotel school picked him up at the Seattle airport. "Tell us about marketing," they said. "Just watch," said Mike. When they got to the Holiday Inn in Pullman (the other end of the state) there on the hotel sign in large neon lights were the words, "Welcome Mike Leven, Hotel Marketer of the Year." "Neat," thought Mike. When he went to check in, however, the clerk proclaimed that he had no reservation. More than a little tired, and now a little irate, Mike asked how that could be when his name was in neon lights at the front of the hotel. "How would I know that?" responded the clerk, "I came in the back door."

Clearly, figuratively speaking, employees need to come in the front door to understand the customer. Okay, but was this the clerk's fault or management's?

Employees need to be aware of what is going on, and not only so that they can respond to customers. Unawareness leads to embarrassment, disappointment, reduced motivation, and lack of support for marketing efforts. Employees are, in fact, as much vital recipients of marketing campaigns as are consumers. Robert Kelley put this all together quite well in a "Manager's Journal" column in the *Wall Street Journal:*

Service providers treat customers similar to the way they, as employees, are treated by management. . . . If management treats employees' concerns with indifference, then employees will not care about the customers' complaints.

. . . If managers want to improve service quality they must treat employees the same way they want employees to treat customers.[41]

Kathy Ray was the new GM of the Sheraton Grand in Washington D.C. when it was in bad shape—occupancy was down, employee morale was low, and, it was said, "It was beyond hope," and this was the Sheraton flagship hotel in the city. Ray gathered all employees together for a meeting. She put an organizational chart of the hotel on the wall. At the top were the employees. She ate in the employees' dining room. Former GMs had never done that. She went into the kitchen to talk to the employees, not to have coffee with the chef or to have a special omelette prepared. She made her employees "believe," the customers noticed, and she turned the hotel around.

The success of the internal marketing concept ultimately lies with management. Lower-level employees cannot be expected to be customer-conscious if the management above them does not display the same focus. Operations-oriented managers who concern themselves primarily with policies and procedures, often instituted without regard to the customer, undermine the firm's internal marketing effort, reducing employees' jobs to mechanical functions that offer little in the way of challenge, self-esteem, or personal gratification. Moreover, by requiring employees to adhere rigidly to specific procedures, the operations-oriented manager ties their hands and restricts their ability to satisfy the customer. All this means that the organization that practices relationship marketing has to change from the old traditional style. Table 3-13 delineates these differences.

THE PAST, AND THE FUTURE OF RELATIONSHIP MARKETING

Although, as we have said, everyone talks about the customer and relationship marketing, that isn't the way it necessarily works in the organization. In fact, the way that too many organizations work is as follows:

TABLE 3-13
Traditional versus the Relationship Marketing Organization[42]

Traditional	Relationship
Functional departments	Process teams with customer focus
Simple tasks, checking, monitoring	Little checking on, trust
Lots of controls	Empowerment
Hire for skills	Hire for team spirit, broad education, self-discipline
Teaching *how* of job	Teaching *why* of job
Boss appraisal	Customer appraisal, impact on satisfaction
Small merit increases	Bonuses
Advancement based on performance	Advancement based on ability and leadership potential, customer handling
"Boss pays my salary"	"Customer pays my salary"
"I'm just a cog in the wheel"	"Every job is important; I make a difference"
"The higher my title, the more important I am"	"My importance is based on my contribution to customer loyalty"
"Tomorrow will be just like today"	"We live with constant change—I must constantly learn"

- Some organizations only talk about treating customers better. Management doesn't always understand what outstanding service looks like and aren't ready to turn their organization upside down to provide it. They paint happy faces on frontline people. Or they conduct a service program for employees, but don't make it a part of their core strategy. Rhetoric does not become reality.

- The organization tries to be everything to everybody. Customers are lumped together as one big mass. Their separate expectations are not known, or aren't weighted and prioritized.

- Customer surveys are acknowledged when they are positive, but negative data is often denied. Budget priorities are set and resources allocated with little, if any, connection to customer expectations. Priority is on what management or the company thinks is important.

- Customers are not part of research and development of new services and products.

- Employees are seen as the cause of service breakdowns when research shows that a large majority of service breakdowns are caused by the system, the process, or the structure, and only a few by the people in the trenches.

- Focus is on customer acquisition rather than customer retention. Sales and marketing efforts are aimed more at bringing in new customers than at keeping or expanding the business of old customers.

The future promises something different for those companies that deal with these negatives and focus on the positives. In today's technological world there is little reason for failing to understand the customer and what he or she expects, and thus generating more profitably for the company. Technology, however, only provides the means; it doesn't by itself change attitudes or behavior, and if attention is not paid to these changes, the technology becomes no more than a costly, fruitless expense.

Innovative leaders in the hospitality marketplace are not only translating guest experience and expectation data into operational changes, they are forging links between data acquisition, analysis, and delivery. They are rethinking customer and service strategy, and improving customer services and value by providing frontline employees with the information they need to provide higher quality customer service and retention. These will be the companies with the sustainable competitive advantage of the future.

KPMG Peat Marwick LLP, a leading consultant to the hospitality industry, has developed an integrated management approach to improve interaction with the customer, in order to maximize profitability from each individual guest, an approach they refer to as "Customer Concentric Management (CCM)." This system focuses on managing guest behavior and guest requirements to differentiate services and gain a competitive edge. Call it CCM, call it micro-marketing, loyalty marketing, one-to-one marketing, wrap-around marketing, customer partnering, symbiotic marketing, interactive marketing, mass customization (all terms being used), or call it relationship marketing, or call it something else, this is what will matter in the future and will, if soundly based on the customer, separate the leaders from the followers.

SUMMARY

A technique of nontraditional marketing is relationship marketing. Relationship marketing creates customer bonding and understanding, which is an integral part of any company's sustenance and growth. Relationships must be developed and sustained so they build loyalty and increase the lifetime value of a customer. In a services business, this is hardly possible without similar employee relations. The principle of internal marketing is to market hospitality jobs to employees just as we market hotels or restaurants to customers.

Relationship marketing, however, has not been the great success that it is touted to be. Companies need to rethink this entire process and how the three-way relationship—management, employees, and customers—really works.

Establishing good customer relations also involves creating an atmosphere where customers complaints are sincerely addressed. We call this service recovery. One way to do this is to talk to the customer and to make it easy for the customer to talk back. Complaints are healthy, customer problems are opportunities, and marketers must be opportunists. Innovative relationship marketing will make tomorrow's leaders' and their companies' sustainable competitive advantage.

KEY WORDS AND CONCEPTS

Advocate: A customer who encourages others to buy from us.

Client: A client who regularly buys our services.

Commitment: A willingness to work at maintaining a relationship.

Core Services: The central or major component of the service that the customer buys.

Customer Analysis: Analyzing customers in terms of how to focus on them.

Customized Service: Customization to specific needs and wants.

Employee Empowerment: Empowering employees to settle service discrepancies with customers.

Employee Relationship Marketing: Applying marketing principles to those who serve the customers, and building a bond and trust with them that is shared.

Internal Marketing: See Employee Relationship Marketing.

Lifetime Value of a Customer: The total value of a customer based on repeat purchase and word of mouth to others, less costs.

Relationship Marketing: Marketing to protect an existing customer base through an ongoing process by creating new value for customers and sharing this over a lifetime association. Relationship marketing ensures a loyal base of customers.

Service Augmentation: Building extras into a service, especially those that it is difficult for the competition to copy.

Service Recovery: Correcting a failure in service delivery to a customer's satisfaction.

Trust: The belief that an individual or entity can be relied on to keep their word and promise, explicit or implicit.

DISCUSSION QUESTIONS

1. Which is the end and which is the means—frequent patronage or loyal patronage? Why? Discuss.
2. Discuss what relationship marketing is not. Why is this so?
3. What are the important elements in computing the lifetime value of a customer? How can you establish the value?
4. What is the importance of doing a customer analysis when establishing a relationship marketing program?
5. What is the difference between a customized service and service augmentation?
6. What are the problems with frequent guest/dining programs? What are the virtues?
7. What are some reasons that relationship marketing doesn't work?
8. Consider a complaint you have made in a hotel or restaurant. How was it handled? How would you have handled it?
9. In the hospitality industry, we have many uneducated and/or foreign speaking employees. Can these employees be taught relationship marketing? How?

GROUP PROJECTS

1. Develop a model for determining the lifetime value of a hotel or restaurant customer. Put some numbers to it.
2. Develop a loyalty program for a specific hotel or restaurant with which you are familiar.

REFERENCES

1. Adapted from Ian Gordon, *Relationship Marketing,* Toronto: Wiley Canada, 1998, p. 9. Readers interested in learning more on this subject than we can cover in one chapter are urged to read this book.

2. Adapted from notes of Stowe Shoemaker, Ph.D., Harrah College of Hotel Administration, University of Nevada, Las Vegas, 1998. We are indebted to Dr. Shoemaker for much input into the discussion on loyalty as well as other parts of this chapter.

3. Theodore Levitt, "Marketing Intangible Products and Product Intangibles," *Harvard Business Review,* May–June 1981, pp. 94–102. Copyright 1981 by the President and Fellows of Harvard College; all rights reserved.

4. James L. Heskett, Thomas O. Jones, Gary W. Loveman, W. Earl Sasser, Jr., and Leonard A. Schlesinger, "Putting the Service-Profit Chain to Work," *Harvard Business Review,* March–April 1994, p. 164. Copyright 1981 by the President and Fellows of Harvard College; all rights reserved.

5. Frederick F. Reiccheld and W. Earl Sasser, Jr., "Zero Defections: Quality Comes to Services," *Harvard Business Review,* September–October 1990. Copyright 1981 by the President and Fellows of Harvard College; all rights reserved.

6. The objective is to get as close as possible to an evaluation of the net present value of all future profits from a particular customer. The profit from a customer is the profit margin on sales to that customer, less the cost of maintaining the relationship, plus any incremental benefits the customer brings, such as recommendations to other customers. For formulas see, for example, Joan Koob Cannie, *Turning Lost Customers into Gold,* New York: American Management Association, 1994.

7. Adapted from Shoemaker, *op. cit.*

8. The idea for this matrix was suggested by Gordon, *op. cit.*

9. Shoemaker, *op. cit.*

10. Adapted from John T. Bowen and Stowe Shoemaker, "Loyalty: A Strategic Commitment," *Cornell Hotel and Restaurant Administration Quarterly,* February 1998, pp. 14–17.

11. Bowen and Shoemaker, *op. cit.,* p. 15.

12. Ken W. McCleary and Pamela A. Weaver, "Are Frequent-Guest Programs Effective?" *Cornell Hotel and Restaurant Administration Quarterly,* August 1991, p. 45.

13. Anonymous, "Hotel Frequent-Guest Programs ... A Slumbering Opportunity." *Colloquy,* Vol. 5, Issue 3, 1996, pp. 14–16.

14. Anonymous, "Frequent-Dining Programs—Missing Some Key Ingredients," *Colloquy,* Vol. 5, Issue 4, 1997, p. 49.

15. Shoemaker, *op. cit.*

16. Adapted from Shoemaker, *op. cit.*

17. Richard Dunn, Carlson Marketing Group, Minneapolis.

18. Shoemaker, *op. cit.*

19. Thomas Campbell, Frequency Marketing Inc., in a presentation for the Strategic Research Institute, December 9–10, 1996, Chicago.

20. Bowen and Shoemaker, *op. cit.,* p. 19.

21. Bowen and Shoemaker, *op. cit.,* p. 13.

22. Susan Fournier, Susan Dobscha, and David Glen Mick, "Preventing the Premature Death of Relationship Marketing," *Harvard Business Review,* January– February 1998, pp. 43–51. Copyright © 1998 by the President and Fellows of Harvard College; all rights reserved.

23. Based in part on findings of Fournier et al., *op. cit.*

24. *The Toronto Globe and Mail,* March 7, 1998, p. A4.

25. *The Wall Street Journal,* March 13, 1998, p. B11.

26. *Ibid.*

27. While we don't have space to go into all the details here, an excellent and succinct explanation and analysis of what we have been saying is contained in J. L. Heskett, T. O. Jones, G. W. Loveman, W. E. Sasser, Jr., and L. Schlesinger, "Putting the Service-Profit Chain to Work," *Harvard Business Review,* March–April 1994, pp. 164–174.

28. Fournier et al., *op. cit.,* p. 51.

29. Robert C. Lewis, "When Guests Complain," *Cornell Hotel and Restaurant Administration Quarterly,* August 1983, pp. 23–32. Susan Morris, "The Relationship Between Company Complaint Handling and Consumer Behavior," Master's Thesis, University of Massachusetts, 1985.

30. Bowen and Shoemaker, *op. cit.*

31. For more discussion of this subject, see Robert C. Lewis and Susan V. Morris, "The Positive Side of Guest Complaints," *Cornell Hotel & Restaurant Administration Quarterly,* February 1987, pp. 13–15.

32. Shoemaker, *op. cit.*

33. Heskett et al., *op. cit.,* pp. 169–170.

34. Bowen and Shoemaker, *op. cit.,* p. 24.

35. Bowen and Shoemaker, *op. cit.,* p. 24.

36. Quoted in Charles G. Partlow, "How Ritz-Carlton applies TQM," *Cornell Hotel & Restaurant Administration Quarterly,* August 1993, p. 20.

37. Eddystone C. Nebel, *Managing Hotels Effectively: Lessons from Outstanding General Managers.* New York: Van Nostrand Reinhold, 1991, p. 37.

38. Gordon, *op. cit.,* p. 275.

39. Gordon, *op. cit.,* p. 275.

40. Bowen and Shoemaker, op. cit., p. 25.

41. Robert E. Kelley, "Poorly Served Employees Serve Customers Just as Poorly," *The Wall Street Journal,* October 12, 1987, p. 20.

42. Shoemaker, *op. cit.*

The Marketing System

Four

STRATEGIC MARKETING

Overview

As Chapter 4 is quite long and does not easily split into two chapters, it has been divided into two parts, A and B. Part A, The Concept of Strategy, discusses strategic planning and how it should impact and guide whatever a firm does. We differentiate between strategy, operational effectiveness, and marketing management. The importance of strategic leadership and strategic vision are emphasized. Discussion of various levels and types of strategy, including the value chain and generic strategies, are discussed.

Part B, The Strategic Marketing System, starts by discussing the mission statement and leads into a full discourse of the strategic marketing system, including SWOT analysis—analysis of strengths, weaknesses, opportunities, and threats—and development of a strategic marketing plan.

For upper level classes, we suggest the entire chapter be assigned, especially in a case study course. A good grasp of strategy and its importance, and developing a strategic plan before developing a marketing plan, can be obtained by using only Part B.

PART A
• ◆ •
THE CONCEPT OF STRATEGY

──────────── *Overview* ────────────

STRATEGIC MARKETING VERSUS MARKETING MANAGEMENT

Strategy   Strategy takes a long-range view. It is about creating "fit" to develop competitive advantage. Once objectives have been established, the strategies for obtaining those objectives must be developed to fit the rest of the organization's activities. Strategy must not be confused with tactics, which are the specific steps necessary to execute the strategy.

Strategic Leadership   Many strategies fail for lack of strategic leadership. This section tells why and provides examples.

Strategic Marketing   The overall view of marketing, which allocates the resources and sets the objectives after defining the market, as opposed to the day-to-day management of marketing. This section delineates the difference between strategic marketing and marketing management.

Marketing Management   The day-to-day handling of the marketing process, which we discuss in more detail in Chapter 7.

THE CONCEPT OF STRATEGY   A view of the big picture and the end result that guides the day-to-day tactical decisions.

STRATEGIC PLANNING   Considers all elements of what business we are in and what takes place at various levels of an organization. A systematic approach that reviews business objectives, matching services with customers, identifying competition, allocating resources, and implementing measurement tools to judge success.

THE LEVELS OF STRATEGIC PLANNING

Corporate, Business, and Functional Level Strategies   The strategies implemented at different levels of the organization are delineated. We discuss, as part of these, the way companies grow, generic competitive strategies, and the value chain.

EMERGENT STRATEGIES   In spite of all the planning efforts, sometimes strategies simply emerge, often as a result of changes in the environment that create new opportunities or threats.

• ◆ •

Today's complex hospitality industry environment requires organizations to be better prepared to anticipate and proact to internal and external changes. Successful achievement of a firm's objectives depends on the ability of management to respond to opportunities in an ever-changing environment. Strategic marketing includes all the decisions and

actions used to formulate and implement strategies designed to achieve those objectives.

First, we clarify the use of the word "strategy" in the marketing or management context. We then enlarge upon the process of strategic marketing planning and demonstrate its importance in any marketing context. We introduce several topics that are discussed only briefly in this chapter: in Chapter 5 we discuss broad environmental influences, in Chapter 6 we explain the competitive environment, and in Chapter 7 we deal with how a marketing plan that includes these strategies and influences is developed.

STRATEGIC MARKETING VERSUS MARKETING MANAGEMENT

First, we need to differentiate between marketing management and strategic marketing. Some people place strategy largely at the corporate or strategic business unit (SBU) level and management at the local level; we believe that both belong at both levels when good marketing leadership is practiced.

It is essential, then, that we distinguish between **management effectiveness** and strategy, as too often management tools have replaced strategy. Management effectiveness refers to activities that allow a company to operate more smoothly, produce better. They are necessary but not sufficient. **Strategic effectiveness** means performing activities that differ from those of competitors' or performing similar activities in different ways. A company can outperform others only if it can preserve an established difference.

We do not discuss here, in detail, management effectiveness, which includes such things as employee motivation, technological advances, total quality management (TQM), better salesmanship, yield management, global distribution, and employee empowerment, among others. All of these create important differences in profitability among competitors, but competitors can imitate these and the advantages are soon lost. Too often, management effectiveness is emphasized in lieu of **strategic thinking**, a long-range view, which must precede it in order for management effectiveness to work.

Strategy

Competitive strategy is about being different. A classic case is Southwest Airlines, which offers short-haul, low-cost, quick plane turnaround, frequent departures, no meals, no assigned seating, and flights between only secondary airports. Southwest's strategy is to perform things differently and to perform different things. Southwest does what it does well because it sticks to what it does best, and it keeps its promises to customers.

Strategic competition is the process of perceiving new positions that bring new customers from competitors, or bring new customers into the market, as Southwest has done and does. Often these positions open up, or close, because of environmental change or because they have been ceded by competitors. Strategy is a function of differences on the supply side, differences in activities that do not rely on customer differences, although strategic positionings often accompany customer needs differences.

What, then, is strategy?[1]

1. Strategy is the creation of a unique and valuable position. If there were only one ideal position, there would be no need for strategy. The idea is to choose activities that are different from competitors.
2. Strategy is making trade-offs in competing, for the strategy to be sustainable. Companies cannot be all things to all customers. Trade-offs purposefully limit what a company offers. An essential part of strategy is also choosing what not to do.
3. Strategy is creating **"fit,"** combining activities, as in the case of Southwest Airlines, whose competitive advantage comes from the way its activities fit and complement one another. Fit locks out competitors by creating a chain that is as strong as its *strongest* link. The best fits are strategy-specific because they enhance the company's uniqueness. The whole matters more than any individual part, and sustainable competitive advantage grows out of the entire system of activities.

Many companies lack marketing strategies, or fail to make strategic choices, or let their strategies disintegrate and disappear. Although this may be due partially to external causes (e.g., changes in technology or competition), more often it comes from within—a misguided view of competition, organizational failure, or an undisciplined desire to grow "bigger and better."

Managers are under increasing pressure to deliver measurable performance growth. Managerial effectiveness becomes the goal and strategic thinking gets bypassed. Companies imitate one another in a kind of follow the leader behavior. This has been especially true in the hotel industry. Recall the case of Sheraton in Chapter 1.

Then there is the desire to grow with steps that blur a company's strategic position. Attempts to compete on many fronts can create confusion and cause organizational chaos. The goal is for more revenue even if profits fall. Meanwhile, uniqueness is fuzzy, compromises are made, fit is reduced, and competitive advantage is lost. Rather than deepen a strategic position, it is broadened and compromised. Again, Sheraton. Consider, as well, Darden Restaurants, operators of Red Lobster and Olive Garden, which tried to grow through a Chinese food concept called China Coast—after opening 55 units across the United States they were all shuttered and the concept abandoned. China Coast lacked strategic fit and competitive advantage.

On the positive side, consider the successful growth strategies of Marriott International, which has acquired Residence Inn, Renaissance, Ritz-Carlton, and developed a number of successful new product lines. How does Marriott do it? According to Arne Sorenson, Executive Vice President of Strategy Development, who is the key player for Marriott in acquisitions, there are four major criteria: (1) *the strategic fit,* (2) the net present value of ten years out, (3) earnings per share, and (4) the reputability of the company.

Success, ironically, can be one of the greatest threats to survival and future success because it may invoke the attitude, "We can do no wrong." Examples of the past include IBM, General Motors, Apple, Michelin, Philips, Digital Equipment, Sears Roebuck, International Harvester, Western Union, Japanese bankers, Korean investors, Holiday Inn,

Sheraton, Howard Johnson's, Planet Hollywood and, perhaps, McDonald's (see Table 4-3 below). Bill Gates of Microsoft, an astute observer, has vowed never to be afflicted by the same mentality.

Strategic Leadership

Strategic leadership is the fundamental element necessary to establish or reestablish a clear strategy. This requires strong leaders willing to make choices. Leadership in many companies, however, satisfies itself with making operational improvements and making "deals." (Again, Sheraton example.) Michael Porter describes his view of strategic leadership in Table 4-1.

The views laid out in Table 4-1 make more sense and are easier to grasp when applied to a real situation. As it is important to grasp the overall concepts before we move on to more detailed explanations and applications of strategic thinking and planning and of strategic choice, we provide real situations in Tables 4-2, Hyatt Hotels, and 4-3, McDonald's. You will recall that we began Chapter 1 with the example of McDonald's—because McDonald's is a marketing concept company that demonstrates all the principles of marketing. Later in that chapter we took a different and more current view of McDonald's and some of its problems. In 2005, will McDonald's still "Do it all for you?" Let us say now that the answer to that question may well depend on what we have just written about, strategic leadership. Table 4-3 takes this view. Analyze this and the Hyatt example in Table 4-2 in terms of strategic leadership.

Hyatt, after the travails outlined in Table 4-2, is now developing new strategies. It has begun franchising, and operating time-share resorts. It is looking for more acquisitions. But the competition is fierce as Hyatt, no longer trying to be an elitist chain, is competing with Marriott, Radisson, Hilton, Sheraton, and others in unfamiliar territory with well-entrenched foes in an industry where brand loyalty is fading. Hyatt needed a new strategic position, strategic trade-offs, and better strategic fits.

T A B L E   4-1
Michael Porter's View of Strategic Leadership[2]

General management is more than the stewardship of individual functions. Its core is strategy: defining and communicating the company's unique position, making tradeoffs and forging fit among activities. The leader must provide the discipline to decide which industry changes and customer needs the company will respond to, while avoiding organizational distractions and maintaining the company's distinctiveness. . . .One of the leader's jobs is to teach others in the organization about strategy—and to say no.

Strategy renders choices about what not to do as important as choices about what to do. . . . Deciding which target group of customers, varieties, and needs the company should serve is fundamental to developing a strategy. But so is deciding not to serve other customers or needs and not to offer certain features or services. Thus strategy requires constant discipline and clear communication. Indeed, one of the most important functions of an explicit, communicated strategy is to guide employees in making choices that arise because of tradeoffs in their individual activities and day-to-day decisions.

. . . A company may have to change its strategy if there are major structural changes in its industry. In fact, new strategic positions often arise because of industry changes, and new entrants unencumbered by history often can exploit them more easily. However, a company's choice of a new position must be driven by the ability to find new tradeoffs and leverage a new system of complementary activities into a sustainable advantage.

McDonald's was built on the concept of "quality, service, cleanliness." But customers today seem to want better food and more variety. Recent surveys have shown that Wendy's and Burger King offer better-tasting fare. In one survey in which 2800 consumers graded chains on the taste of their food, McDonald's ranked 87th out of 91—just behind Hooters. McDonald's is counting on its new cooking system to change this.

With many choices today, consumers no longer choose McDonald's just because there's one around the corner. Fast-food no longer means fried food. McDonald's has stuck to hamburgers but not for lack of trying. One claim they make is that new items don't fit peoples' expectations of McDonald's. Others, however, say that too often the new products just don't taste good. A survey of McDonald's franchisees indicated that only 28 percent thought McDonald's was on the right track. McDonald's says the biggest problem with the brand is the media's view of it.

In short, McDonald's management lost the strategic leadership of its founder, Ray Kroc.

Strategic leadership is the ability of the leader to articulate a strategic vision for the company, or division of the company (e.g., one hotel in a chain) and to motivate others to buy into that vision. Characteristics of this type of leadership also include commitment, being well informed, willingness to delegate and empower, and astute use of power.

Strategic Marketing

We return now to the differences between marketing management and strategic marketing. Strategic marketing takes an overall view, allocating resources and setting objectives after defining the market; *marketing management* develops the product/service, prices it, tells the customer about it, and gets it to the customer. Thus strategy must precede management. A hotel's restaurant, for example, cannot be appropriately designed without first correctly designating the market it is to serve. Table 4-4 delineates the differences between strategic marketing and marketing management.

Strategic marketing deals with the long-term view of the market and the business to be in; marketing management stresses running that business and the implementation of the strategies on a daily basis. We emphasize this distinction for a specific reason. Far too many annual marketing plans fail because they are based on the wrong strategy, or fail to flow from the right strategy. An excellent example of this is the strategy of a hotel to target an upscale market when that market does not exist, is already overcrowded, or the product is not ade-

TABLE 4-2
Hyatt Hotels—A Strategic Transition[3]

In the 1980s, Hyatt Hotels was the epitome of grandeur. Soaring atrium lobbies, huge multihundred million dollar mega resorts with $700 gourmet picnics atop a waterfall, $1000 a night rooms, and grandiose buffets with multiple ice carvings were some of the symbols of a Hyatt experience. Costs didn't bother management: they just charged for it and if you had to ask the price you shouldn't be there. The hotels' owners, not Hyatt, in most cases bore the financial losses from this management philosophy.

But the industry structure changed starting in 1990—the market for luxury hotels crashed. Many of these hotels were saddled with empty rooms, huge debts, and unserviceable mortgages. The Hyatt chain is controlled by Chicago's Pritzker family (worth an estimated $4 billion) and runs over 100 hotels in North America, Hawaii, and the Caribbean, not to mention Hyatt International, a separate worldwide division. The Pritzkers own some of the hotels, the land under some others, and manage the remainder. In the early 1990s they had to help restructure some that they managed, one of which was a $360 million resort in Waikoloa, which was sold to Hilton Hotels for $60 million in 1993, besides the ones they owned.

Hyatt became a much chastened and far more cost-conscious company in order to banish the image of an all-frills hotelier. CEO Darryl Hartley-Leonard, who concentrated on burnishing Hyatt's image but lacked strategic vision, was replaced with Douglas Geoga, a lawyer credited for his understanding of changed industry economics.

The transition wasn't easy. After years of adding services and amenities regardless of cost, Hyatt was in danger of losing many of its management contracts, or of not getting many more. Hyatt studied what services guests *really* wanted. Wine lists were pared down as much as 90 percent. Turndown service came only on request, and mints on the pillow were eliminated.

Many mid-level jobs were eliminated. The corporate management staff was reduced severely. Central purchasing was instituted and the number of providers drastically reduced. When it was discovered that delivering room service coffee was losing money, coffeemakers were put in every room. All in all, $100 million annually was cut from operating costs. Hyatt claimed that it was cutting where it didn't hurt the guest. In five years, revenues were up 13 percent while gross operating profit was up 45 percent. Owners stopped complaining.

quate to serve it. A marketing plan is then developed to implement the strategy, and fails.

If the strategy cannot be implemented, it may be the wrong strategy. Too often a marketing plan is developed with the final conclusion drawn before the work begins, and the data collected are summarily "fitted" to the conclusion. The result is a marketing plan that is both unrealistic and unworkable.

THE CONCEPT OF STRATEGY

We begin with the standard textbook definition of strategy versus **tactics,** which is directly derived from the military: Tactics are the way to win the battle; strategy is the way to win the war. In a simplistic example, we could demonstrate this as follows:

Objective: Surround the enemy.
Strategy: Take one area at a time.
Tactic: Use armored tank divisions.

Actually, marketing is not much different. The objective is to increase revenues. Strategy is the way to gain and keep customers; tactics are the step-by-step procedure of how to do it. For example:

Objective: Increase revenues by being perceived as the hotel of choice.
Strategy: Always give customers better value.
Tactics: Always have their reservation and room (tables) ready; call them by name; make sure they receive their wake-up call; have full-length mirrors and good bathroom lighting in their rooms; offer fresh-brewed coffee as soon as they sit down for breakfast; have

McDonald's—A Loss of Strategic Leadership[4]

Ray Kroc is reported to have said something like, "I don't know what we'll be serving in the year 2000, but we'll be serving more of it than anybody." As America's tastes changed, McDonald's changed with them. The changes were vital, but never radical. The Golden Arches became one of the world's most recognized symbols. For 40 years, the future of McDonald's seemed assured, but today that is not so true. In fact, McDonald's may have lost some of its relevance to American culture—a culture that it helped to shape. And overseas the same thing is happening. Some facts:

- The last new successful product was Chicken McNugget in 1983.
- Tests with pizza, veggie burgers, fajitas, pasta, McLean Deluxe, Arch Deluxe, and discount promotions have confused the public, and most were discontinued shortly after they were initiated.
- Since 1987, McDonald's share of fast-food sales in the United States has declined two percentage points to 16.2 percent even as it has increased its number of restaurants by 50 percent.
- Operating profits haven't kept up with inflation—they've risen just 2 percent in 10 years. Per store profits have declined over 20 percent in the same period, from $125,000 to $97,000.
- In two years, McDonald's stock price increased just 3 percent, compared to Coca-Cola's 71 percent and Walt Disney's 78 percent, companies that changed their position, made trade-offs, and created better fits, and the S&P 500's 63 percent increase.
- A price promotion in 1997 offering 99 cent Big Macs caused a furor among franchisees and was quickly and embarrassingly abandoned.

In short, McDonald's has been unable to use its brand strength to grow beyond its basic formula of hamburgers and french fries.

In 1997, CEO Michael Quinlan reorganized and decentralized the management team in an attempt to recreate some entrepreneurial spirit. Fundamentally, however, McDonald's didn't change. "Do we have to change?" asked Quinlan. "No, we don't have to change. We have the most successful brand in the world. We will extend our line, rather than go in more radical, different directions."[5]

One industry observer put it this way. "McDonald's seems to have fallen into the hell that traps many of the best companies at some point in their lives. Having established a dominant position under a previous generation, it is bedeviled by a reverence for the old formulas, while its leadership takes weak steps and then denies all problems."[6]

In 1997 top management outlined plans to improve its domestic business, calling for "value" pricing and improvements to the current menu, but no new products. They said they would restore momentum by concentrating on improving the taste of current products and re-emphasizing clean restaurants and fast, accurate service.

In 1998 McDonald's announced that it would kill the year-old Arch Deluxe sandwich (designed to attract adults), which Quinlan said had exceeded all expectations when everyone knew it hadn't, and push franchisees to upgrade their kitchens. Made-to-order sandwiches would be the new feature, based on a new computerized production system called "Made for You." This system would send orders directly from the cash register to the griller or sandwich maker even before the customer had finished ordering. Heat lamps would be phased out.

In essence, McDonald's asked, "How can we sell more hamburgers?" rather than "What does our brand allow us to consider selling to our customers?" McDonald's tried to make the same formula appeal to everyone. It could have used its credibility to develop new approaches, but it was stuck in a 50-year-old rut lacking innovativeness.

McDonald's is an insular company. The Board of Directors is filled with current and former executives, vendors, and service providers. Top executives blame others, for example dissident franchisees, once their most notable source of new ideas. Management does not communicate with the investment community. McDonald's clings to the McFamily philosophy it started with, rewarding long-term managers who stay for life.

McDonald's international business earnings have doubled in the past five years, but as it expands out of the big city markets, its margins are dropping. Objectives of 18–20 percent growth have been missed by at least half. One consultant reported, "If the same set of conditions duplicate themselves abroad, than you have a dead end waiting to happen."[7] Imagine, he notes, if McDonald's used low-margin burgers to sell a line of high-margin toys, instead of low-margin toys to sell low-margin burgers. McDonald's says that is not its core business.

TABLE 4-4
Major Differences Between Strategic Marketing and Marketing Management*,[8]

Point of Difference	Strategic Marketing	Marketing Management
Timeframe	Long-range; i.e., decisions have long-term implications	Day-to-day; i.e., decisions have relevance in a given financial year
Orientation	Inductive and intuitive	Deductive and analytical
Decision process	Primarily bottom-up	Mainly top-down
Relationship with environment	Environment considered everchanging and dynamic	Environment considered constant with occasional disturbances
Opportunity sensitivity	Ongoing to seek new opportunities	Ad hoc search for a new opportunity
Organizational behavior	Achieve synergy between different components of the organization, both horizontally and vertically	Pursue interests of the decentralized unit
Nature of job	Requires high degree of creativity and originality	Requires maturity, experience, and control orientation
Leadership style	Requires proactive perspective	Requires reactive perspective
Mission	Deals with what business to emphasize	Deals with running a delineated business

*Their differences are relevant, not opposite ends of a continuum.

room service delivered on time; have the print on the menu large enough to read; offer a selection for those who are light eaters; and so forth.

From this example it can be seen that tactics flow from strategy. That means that the first thing we have to do is develop the appropriate strategy. It is the strategy that drives the firm and specifies the direction in which it is going?

If that is the case, you might ask, if no strategy has been developed then what drives the firm? The answer is that there is always a strategy, in one way or another. If there is no explicit strategy, then there is an implicit one. In fact, too often strategies exist by default. Here's a simple example.

One of the basic tenets of marketing strategy is market segmentation, which involves dividing the total market into smaller groups of customers who have similar needs. We then select those markets that we can serve best. Suppose no one has even given this a thought, much less developed a strategy. The result is that "we'll take any customers we can get." The strategy, by default, is to take anyone as customers. Along comes a bus tour group; we take it and it fills the lobby. The result may be our corporate customers saying, "What's going on here? We thought this was a businessperson's hotel. Let's go somewhere else next time."

The default strategy in this case is counterproductive. That is why strategy should never be left to chance. It should be both planned and executed very carefully, although it may also emerge, as we discuss later.

Strategic Planning

The essence of **strategic planning** is "how to get from here to there." This process follows, in short,

Visioning Process

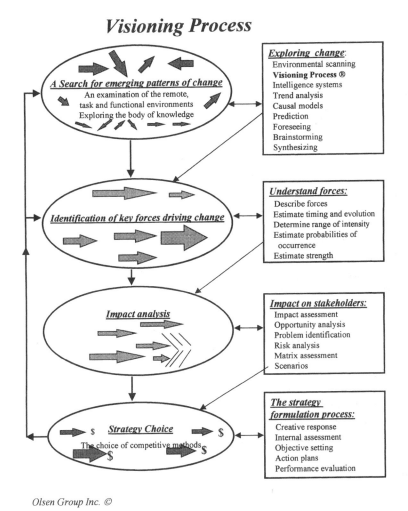

Olsen Group Inc. ©

FIGURE 4-1 Strategic visioning model.[9]

strategic visioning and is demonstrated by the model in Figure 4-1. (We explain this model more thoroughly in the rest of this chapter and the next.) It naturally follows that there are two things inherent in such a statement: If you want to get from "here" you have to know where "here" is; if you want to get to "there" you have to know where "there" is. In strategic planning, the first is called a situation analysis, or "where we are now"; the second is called objectives, or "where we want to go." Strategic planning fills the gap: How do we get from where we are now to where we want to go?

In a more formal sense, strategic planning is concerned with **environmental scanning,** estimating the impact of the environment, the setting of business objectives, the match between products and markets, the choice of competition, the allocation of resources, and the proactive planning and **competitive advantages** needed to reach the objectives. Although some people believe that strategic planning is complicated and difficult to understand, it is really an everyday, basic concept. We'll explain this with another simple example.

Consider a high school graduate. Where is he now? Seventeen years old, no real skills, no profession, and certainly little chance for professional growth in a solid career path. Where does he want to be? A solid candidate for a good job in a firm that will offer opportunities for growth and advancement. Strategy? Get a good education and enhance his capabilities and potential in the business world. Tactic? Go to college.

Although most strategic planning is done at the higher levels of a business organization, this should not necessarily be the case. *Strategic marketing planning is appropriate at any level.* We repeat this because of the common perception to the contrary. In fact, this has been one of the major failings of strategic planning: it often takes place only at higher levels and doesn't filter down to strategic management that focuses on implementation of the strategic plan.

To use the same example as above, giving the customer better value can be a strategy at any level. If this is the actual corporate strategy of a 300-property hotel chain, let's see how it translates down to the strategic management of a coffee shop in only one of those 300 units.

The manager, a recent college graduate, thinks, "If that's the corporate strategy, then how does it affect me—how do I give better value?" She looks around and says, "Right now [situation analysis] we're just another coffee shop. What we'd like to be [objective] is the best coffee shop in town." The answer is [strategy] giving the customer better value [competitive advantage]. How that is done [tactics] is always to have fresh orange juice and fresh-brewed coffee, offer coffee as soon as a customer is seated for breakfast, never close off the most desirable part of the dining room no matter how slow it is, don't "push" customers so we can turn the tables over, don't put singles next to the kitchen door, and be sure that prices are competitive.

In contrast, a fast-food operation works on volume. The objective is to maximize patronage and turnover. The strategy is to give the customer every reason to move on quickly. The tactics are to have food all ready, accept payment for food when it is

picked up, and minimize table setting so the table can be ready for another party almost immediately.

This, then, is the concept of strategic planning: decide where you are now, decide where you want to go, and develop and manage the strategy that will get you there. From that strategy, let flow everything else that you do, including all tactics.

The strategic marketing planning and management process has many interrelationships between the various elements and requires a systems perspective. The strategic framework model for this perspective is illustrated later; we first discuss the levels of strategic planning and then discuss the systems model step by step and cover each step in more detail in later chapters.

THE LEVELS OF STRATEGIC PLANNING

Although we have clearly stated that strategic thinking and planning is necessary at any level of management, there are usually certain strategic functions at certain levels, commonly called corporate, business, and functional. This is not to say that, depending on the business, they may not all come togther in the same place. For example, if you are Joe, the owner and operator of Joe's Hot Dog Stand, all these strategies fall on your shoulders. Keep this in mind as you read the following.

Corporate-Level Strategy

Strategy at this level must address the issue of what business should we be in to maximize the long run viability of the firm. This involves not only issues of position, trade-offs, and fit, but also how to maximize these capabilities through the following types of strategies, among others.

Vertical Integration. This means moving backward into the production process (upstream) or forward into the distribution process (downstream). Suppose Joe decides he should make his own hot dog rolls because he can make them better and/or cheaper (upstream). Or maybe, instead of waiting for students to come and buy his hot dogs, he can hire students to deliver them to dorm rooms (downstream). Nouvelles Frontières, a French travel agency, bought an airline and hotels (upstream) for its customers, and had exclusive arrangements with tour operators and agencies (downstream) to sell its packages.

Diversification. Diversification means entering into a new business activity that complements (is related to) the present business, or using extra resources to enter into a different business (unrelated). Joe decides to set up a hamburger stand next to his hot dog stand (related), or decides to set up a souvenir stand (unrelated). Sheraton diversified into luxury hotels and casinos (related) as well as publication houses and Madison Square Garden (unrelated).

Acquisitions, New Ventures, and Restructuring. All companies, especially publicly traded ones, have a mandate to grow to increase shareholder value. McDonald's has done this internally by international expansion and franchising more and more units, without acquisitions or new ventures.

Marriott developed a limited service internal new venture called Courtyard and, eventually, franchised it for faster growth. In the luxury category, the J. W. Marriott brand was growing too slowly, so Marriott acquired Ritz-Carlton Hotels to take a strong position in the luxury market. In 1998, Marriott wanted to grow faster internationally (having already acquired Renaissance Hotels, based in Hong Kong, for the same reason) and made a bid for Inter-Continental Hotels. Bass Breweries of England, however, which had already acquired Holiday Inns (later Holiday Hospitality, now Bass Hotels and Resorts), overcoming entry barriers into the international hotel market, had the same strategy and outbid Marriott. Four Seasons acquired Regent Hotels to get quick Pacific Rim exposure.

Marriott also started a new restaurant venture called Allie's, which failed, and eventually sold off its entire restaurant division in a restructuring that eventually split the company in two parts—Marriott International, the hotel management company, and Host Marriott, the real estate company that owns hotel properties and manages airport and turnpike food concessions.

General Mills restructured by divesting (spinning off) its restaurant unit, which became Darden Restaurants. PepsiCo did the same with Pizza Hut, Taco Bell, and KFC, now all part of a company called Tricon Global with the stock symbol YUM. Both Darden and Tricon kept their management. Thus these are also referred to as management buyouts or spinoffs.

Strategic Alliances and Joint Ventures. These are situations where two or more parties get together to enhance the overall value of each. SAS International Hotels (SIH) of Brussels wanted exposure outside of Europe and formed a strategic alliance with Radisson Hotels (Figure 4-2), which wanted exposure in Europe. Radisson SAS now has rights to the brand in Europe, the Middle East, and North Africa. Radisson has the rest of the world. Both share the same worldwide reservation system (Pierre), and togther they have tripled their marketing clout through economies of scope.

Four Seasons found it couldn't handle growth of the Regent brand after buying it and formed a strategic alliance with Carlson Hospitality (owners of Radisson), which now has all rights to the expansion and growth of Regent.

United States Franchise Systems (USFS) was started in 1995 by acquiring Microtel. In 1996 it formed a joint venture with Hawthorne Suites (then controlled by the Pritzker family) to expand that brand and, in 1998, acquired all the rights to the brand. It later did the same thing with Best Inns.

These kinds of corporate level strategies, while heavily financially oriented, are definitely corporate marketing strategies. While they may reduce costs, provide better management, and have other benefits, their primary objective is to reach different markets, or the same markets differently, and gain competitive advantage. This is strategic visioning and leadership. These companies saw their industries consolidating, understood the forces of branding, analyzed the opportunities and risks,

FIGURE 4-2 SAS strategic alliance with Radisson.

and chose expanded branding and international growth as prime competitive methods.

Business-Level Strategy

Business-level strategy is the overall competitive theme of a company and the way it positions itself in the marketplace.* We cover this in more detail in a moment in connection with the strategic market-

---

*This also applies to **strategic business units (SBUs)** of a company. In a sense an SBU is a company by itself, but it is subject to corporate level strategies above.

ing systems model. For now, we take a broader view based on Porter's three generic competitive strategies at the business level.[10] These three approaches are cost leadership, differentiation, and focus.

Cost Leadership Strategy.

This strategy aims to outperform competitors by producing goods and services at a lower cost. This enables a business to charge a lower price but realize the same profits, or charge a similar price but make higher profits.

The low cost leader chooses a low level of product differentiation or uniqueness. It usually targets a mass market, and its distinctive competency is the management of the materials and production process. McDonald's and Burger King immediately come to mind. So do Microtel of the United States (Figure 4-3) and Formule1 of France (an Accor brand), both low budget properties with tremendous cost savings built into their design as well as their operation. Southwest Airlines is another example. Customers may not be totally happy with these products, but are attracted by the lower prices. Any customer loyalty is likely based on that factor.

Differentiation Strategy.

This approach is designed to achieve a competitive advantage by creating

No Other Hotel Chain Offers Its Franchisees So Much For So Little

Microtel Inn franchise fees are highly competitive with other national hotel chains. The combined marketing and reservations fee is 3 percent for the first year of a Microtel Inn franchise. This drops to 2.5 percent in the second year, and 2 percent in the third year. Royalties are 4 percent during the first year, 5 percent in the second year and 6 percent in the third year. The initial fee is $350.00 per room with a minimum of $35,000.

That's it! Nothing hidden. No "per room" charges. No "per reservation" charges. NO OTHER CHARGES!

And what does the Microtel Inn franchisee get for those fees?

SUPERIOR CURB APPEAL

The exterior of a Microtel Inn has a residential look in the style of a low-rise, suburban apartment complex with appealing landscaping. The interior corridor design is contemporary, clean and inviting. Microtel Inn properties really stand out from the tired, older properties that currently line the highways.

DESIGN AND CONSTRUCTION ASSISTANCE

Microtel Inn properties are 100 percent new construction, ensuring that guests will experience clean, fresh, comfortable rooms with every stay. Knowing what to expect at every location builds brand loyalty. To that end, US Franchise Systems will provide Microtel Inn franchisees with a full set of working plans for building a variety of Microtel prototypes. These plans need only to be site adapted and approved by a local architect before construction begins.

NATIONAL PURCHASING DISCOUNTS

US Franchise Systems has established national vendor accounts to help shave the costs off of building, furnishing and decorating Microtel properties.

LOW COST/HIGH YIELD RESERVATIONS

The unique reservations system employed by Microtel Inns allows all guests to have total last-room availability. Guests call the toll-free reservations system, and are connected directly to the property of their choice. Every hotel has its own toll-free number.

For the owner, the cost of reservations training and equipment is greatly reduced, and on-site personnel "sell" the hotel. US Franchise Systems charges no "per reservation" fee, driving down the cost of reservation delivery.

MARKETING TO BUILD BRAND AWARENESS

Microtel Inns is investing in a brand awareness campaign that will grow as the system grows. This strong marketing and advertising support includes print advertising in appropriate business and leisure travel locations, combined with extensive billboard advertising to enhance each individual location, and listings in the Automobile Association of America (AAA) directory.

A Microtel Inns directory will be published twice each year for distribution through direct mail and at existing properties.

SUPERIOR TRAINING FOR MANAGEMENT AND STAFF

Experienced hotel operations professionals have designed full training programs for all levels of hotel employees. Emphasis is placed on getting a hotel up and running quickly.

LOW OVERHEAD/LOW OPERATING COST

Compact guest rooms, and built-in furniture make cleaning the guest rooms faster and easier for the housekeeping staff. Smaller total size, limited use of public space and elimination of food and beverage outlets result in lower operating costs (labor, maintenance and utilities) and less overhead.

GUARANTEED SYSTEMWIDE QUALITY ASSURANCE

Because meeting guest expectations is vital to building and maintaining brand loyalty, Quality Assurance is strictly maintained. Two unannounced inspections are conducted every year with an emphasis on teaching employees what they need to know to achieve the highest possible scores. A minimum of 450 out of a possible 500 points must be achieved prior to opening.

SAFETY AND SECURITY FOR GUESTS AND STAFF

Each hotel is interior corridor. This provides a greater sense of safety and security for guests, a special concern for the growing segment of female business travelers. As an added unique safety and security measure, these hotels have only one after-hours entrance for non-registered guests — through the lobby — and guests must use a room key or summon the front desk for entry. Recently constructed properties and all Microtel Inn construction going forward will feature electronic locks on guest room doors and hotel entry doors. Lobbies, corridors and parking areas are well-lighted.

APPEALING ROOM RATES THAT THE GUEST AND THE OWNER CAN AFFORD

Microtel is a true budget brand. In its rate category, Microtel Inn properties have significant advantages over their older, exterior corridor competition.

FIGURE 4-3   Microtel is a low-cost leader.

a product or service that is perceived to be unique in some meaningful way. This strategy may target a number of different market segments, often charge a premium price, and its distinctive competency is in research and development, sales, and marketing.

Planet Hollywood and its ilk fall into this category. So, too, do all-suite hotels and all-inclusive resorts. Regent Hotels (Figure 4-4) and Ritz-Carlton differentiate on their level of service. Ruth's Chris Steak House (Figure 4-5) differentiates on the quality of its steaks. Singapore Airlines (Figure 4-6) differentiates on the graciousness of its service. Customer loyalty in these cases is based on unique characteristics. The difficulty with this strategy is the company's long-term ability to maintain the perceived uniqueness of the product/service.

It is one thing to say "differentiate"; it is another thing to do it. There are many who say that hotel

FIGURE 4-4 Regent Hotels differentiate on level of service at any hour.

FIGURE 4-5 Ruth's Chris differentiates on the quality of its steaks.

rooms and airline seats have become commodities, like a pound of salt, in that there is very little left to differentiate among them within the same product class. It is at this point, however, that marketing imagination comes to the forefront. Sometimes the way a company manages its marketing may be the most powerful form of differentiation.

Focus Strategy. This is aimed at serving the needs of a limited customer group or segment, one or a few, based on any kind of distinctive competency. Using a focus strategy a company specializes in some way. This may be by differentiation or as a cost leader, but in a more specialized sense than

those two as a core generic strategy. The New York Palace Hotel Towers, with 173 rooms out of 900 in the entire hotel, would fit this category because, although it competes with the 360 room Four Seasons in New York, it targets a smaller and more select market of individuals. Other unique hotels fit this category of a focus strategy, such as the Pierre in New York, the Ritz or Bristol in Paris, the Claridge, Savoy, and Connaught (Figure 4-7) in London, and so forth. Lutèce Restaurant in New York, Taillevant in Paris, certain ethnic restaurants, and the Concorde of British Airways/Air France are other examples, as are top drawer casinos in Las Vegas that focus on "high-rollers." These companies' **distinctive competence** is their competitive advantage.

Some companies use both cost leadership and differentiation strategies, and focus strategists may use either, so there is a lack of clear cut distinction in many cases. This does not, however, void the need to determine the strategy to use. Without doing so, a company may easily be "caught in the middle" to its detriment.

This happened to Holiday Inns. A low cost producer, Holiday Inns tried to respond to a growing upscale differentiated market at the same time. Crowne Plazas, the upscale line, were no more than overpriced Holiday Inns and headed for disaster. Holiday Inns was subsequently bailed out by Bass Breweries, which also took a long time to recognize the problem. Today, Crowne Plaza is its own brand, still owned by Bass but with no Holiday Inn identification.

The same thing occurred in reverse at Continental Airlines, which initiated "Continental Lite" service to compete with Southwest Airlines. This so confused Continental's customers that it turned into a marketing disaster, put the company back in bankruptcy, and cost the CEO his job. It has since been abandoned as Continental has reemerged as a strong carrier and struck a strategic alliance with Northwest Airlines.

Functional-Level Strategy

Functional level strategies are aimed at improving the effectiveness of functional operations, which

FIGURE 4-6 Singapore Airlines differentiates on graciousness of service and amenities.

we detail later in this chapter. Here we discuss, again in a generic sense, what is commonly referred to as the **value chain,** or the generic building blocks of competitive advantage. Each activity in the value chain adds value to the final offering of the product/service, presentation, communication, and distribution. The cross-functional goals that do this are efficiency, quality, innovation, and customer responsiveness.[11]

Efficiency refers to economies of scale (the more

we do it, the lower the costs), learning effects (the more we do it, the better we do it), experience effects (the more we do it, the more we learn better ways to do it), and economies of scope (the sharing of resources such as distribution channels so that each business unit has to invest less). In other words, efficiency means increasing employee productivity, which lowers costs of production.

Quality enhances a company's reputation so it can charge higher prices and/or create customer

FIGURE 4-7 The Connaught Hotel uses a focus strategy.

loyalty. It also decreases defects in the service process, thus increasing efficiency and lowering costs. Quality is especially market-driven, as it means that goods and services do what they were designed to do and do it well.

Innovation is more than developing new products and services. It is doing things in better ways that better satisfy the customer, and give the company a competitive edge. Innovation in the five functional areas, although it may eventually be copied, is what drives a firm to a superior position. As noted earlier, innovation may lie in strategic thinking itself.

Customer responsiveness means giving customers what they want when they want it to build brand loyalty and create competitive advantage. This includes, as previously discussed, customer focus leadership at the top, employee attitudes,

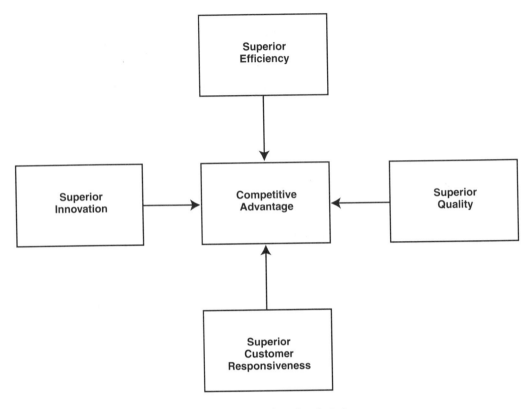

FIGURE 4-8   The value chain impact.

complaint handling, and a system that serves the customer rather than getting in the customer's way, as so many "house rules" seem to do. Customer response time—the time it takes for a service to be performed—is an important part of this phase of the value chain. Figure 4-8 shows how the value chain impacts on competitive advantage.

EMERGENT STRATEGIES

All strategies are not carefully and rationally planned and followed. In fact, many seem to emerge in response to unforeseen circumstances. Henry Mintzberg, a strategy guru at McGill University, says that strategy is more than what a company intends or plans to do; it is also what it actually does, which may be more appropriate than that intended.

Mintzberg also talks about **crafting strategy** and likens this to working at a potter's wheel. As the wheel turns, the potter crafts the vase with his hands, slowly developing the final product in a form that he likes.[12] In the final analysis, strategies are probably a combination of planned, crafted, and emergent. Either one, at any stage, requires strategic thinking, but the formulation of intended strategies is essentially a top-down process, crafted strategies are ongoing adjustments to strategies, and emergent strategies come from a bottom-up process. Figure 4-9 shows the two types of formulation, while crafting strategies would apply to either.

Intended Strategy

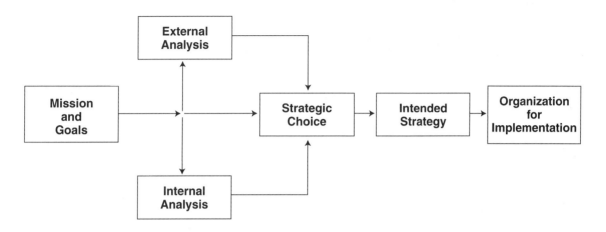

Emergent Strategy

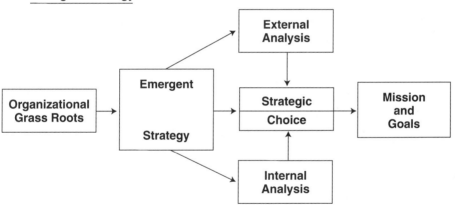

F I G U R E   4 - 9   Intended and emergent strategies.

PART B

•◆•

THE STRATEGIC MARKETING SYSTEM

──────────── *Overview* ────────────

STRATEGIC MARKETING SYSTEM   The open system of strategies, impacted by the environment, that flow from the corporate mission or vision through each strategic level with two feedback control loops.

MISSION STATEMENT   The strategic system begins with a mission statement. The mission statement identifies what the hospitality entity wants to be, and where it wants to go, in terms of owners, customers, and employees.

MASTER MARKETING STRATEGY   The master marketing strategy reviews the situation analysis and shapes the firm's long-range marketing objectives through its distinctive competence.

SITUATION ANALYSIS   A first step in developing strategies: finding out where we are now. This includes external factors, called opportunities and threats, and internal factors, called strengths and weaknesses.

OBJECTIVES AND MASTER STRATEGIES   The strategies that flow from the corporate mission at the highest level and determine what business the firm is in and "where" it wants to go. These strategies guide all the substrategies to get the firm

where it's going, after performing a thorough situation analysis.

BUSINESS STRATEGIES   The business strategies are the "how" that follow the master marketing strategies. These strategies take form in target market strategy, product strategy, competitive strategy, market strategy, and positioning strategy.

FUNCTIONAL STRATEGIES   The functional strategies are the "what" that follow the business marketing strategies. Functional strategies lead to the marketing mix, five forms of substrategy: product/service, presentation, price, communication, and distribution.

FEEDBACK LOOPS   The feedback loops question the risk and fit involved with the master strategy as well as providing feedback on the success of the strategy once it is in place.

STRATEGY SELECTION   Choosing the right strategy and evaluating it in terms of measurable criteria.

STRATEGIC PLANS   These plans often fail. This final section provides some reasons why.

•◆•

Figure 4-10 shows the strategic marketing system model, which starts with the firm's mission statement. This beginning with the mission is true whether you are Hilton Hotels or Joe's Hot Dog Stand. Both Hilton and Joe have specific objectives

and missions. Hilton's may be put together by an executive committee of senior vice presidents. Joe may carry his around in his head and, if you asked him, might be unable to articulate them. It doesn't matter; they are still there and they will drive the

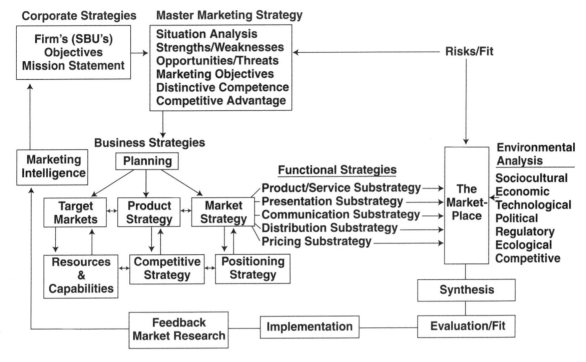

FIGURE 4-10 The strategic marketing system model.

operation of the Hot Dog Stand, for better or for worse, every bit as much as Hilton's will guide the operations of that large corporation. The mission statement usually includes the broad long-term goals of an organization.

THE MISSION STATEMENT

Any firm has certain financial objectives and we do not dwell on those here, keeping in mind that profit is the test of the validity of decisions. In addition, the firm has competitive objectives, consumer objectives, and company objectives, all of which are related. These objectives are brought together in what constitutes the **mission statement.**

The mission statement defines the purpose of a business. It states why we exist, who we compete against, who our market is, and how we serve our constituents—those who have an interest in what we do. These include customers, employees, owners, financial backers, and the local community, all of whom are commonly called stakeholders.

Mission statements exist not only at the corporate level, but also at the level of every **strategic business unit (SBU)** within the firm. An SBU is a unit of a business that serves a clearly defined product-market segment with its own strategy, but in a manner consistent with the overall corporate strategy, its own mission, and its own identifiable competitors.

As Marriott Hotels and Resorts has a mission, so too does the Courtyard by Marriott division, the Fairfield Inns division, and the Residence Inn division. The same is true of the Marriott Long Wharf and the Marriott Copley Place, both in Boston. These hotels not only have their individual competitors but also compete against each other, not to mention against three other Marriotts in the

Boston area. By the same token, the restaurants and lounges at the Marriott Copley Place should each have their own objectives and mission, and their own identifiable competitors.

It is the corporate mission statement, however, from which all other mission statements in the organization flow, as shown in Figure 4-10. Figure 4-10, on the other hand, can be applied just as well to any strategic business unit. Thus in the case of Marriott Copley Place, we could replace "Firm's" objectives with "Hotel's" objectives. By the same token, we could replace "Hotel's" objectives with "Restaurant's" objectives. Strategic planning occurs at every level where an SBU exists. We should bear that in mind as we discuss the remainder of the strategic marketing systems model.

A firm's (or SBU's) objectives may include growth, return on investment, profit, leadership, industry position, or other factors. These are included in the mission statement. Thus, developing the mission statement is a crucial assignment. Since the mission statement indicates the purpose of the business, and is a statement of why the business exists, it drives all subsets of the business. Most importantly, mission statements must be realistic. For a mission statement to say, as some do, "we will be known as the leader in the hotel industry," when such a possibility is not realistic or meaningful, only leads to confusion at lower levels of the organization.

The mission statement should be something in which all employees can believe. It sets goals and it urges everyone in the organization to meet those goals. Properly, it is communicated throughout the organization for all to follow. That, in fact, is one of its purposes—to unify the organization. When the response at lower levels is "Who are they kidding?" (as we saw in the Sheraton case in Chapter 1), the entire effort becomes a meaningless and self-defeating endeavor. Although some mission statements are quite brief, an effective mission statement, which is nothing less than an overall strategy statement, should fulfill the criteria shown in Table 4-5, either implicitly or explicitly.

Consider the mission statement of Ritz-Carlton, probably one of the more complete ones in hospitality, in Figure 4-11. Evaluate this mission statement in light of the criteria in Table 4-5.

MASTER MARKETING STRATEGY

Developing the **master marketing strategy** is the next stage in the strategic marketing system, as shown in Figure 4-10. The master strategy is designed to be long term, not short. This does not mean it will never change; if conditions change, then so too should the master strategy.

We saw earlier how Hyatt changed its strategy and McDonald's hadn't. Consider, again, Marriott, which was initially founded as a foodservice organization. In the 1980s, Marriott's Restaurant Division pursued a master strategy of growth and acquisition. To implement this, one substrategy aimed at creating a mid-priced restaurant chain (named Allie's) to complement Marriott's fast-food branch (Roy Rogers). The long-term objective of the division was to have 3000 Allie's units after ten years; 600 of these were to be completed in three years at a budgeted cost of $250 million.[13] By the end of 1989, however, and after completing another situation analysis, Marriott decided to divest its entire restaurant division. A company that was founded on foodservice had to face the realities of the environment. It changed its corporate master strategy and placed its emphasis where its strengths and opportunities lay—in hotels and institutional feeding.

The original intention, however, of master strategies is that they will endure for some time. This means that they take a long-range perspective of the environment, as opposed to the short-range perspective of the marketing plan (discussed in Chapter 7), even though many of the issues are the same.

The master strategy shapes objectives after developing and weighing alternatives. It specifies where the firm is going and thus is the framework of the entire marketing effort. Derived from the mission statement and objectives, the master mar-

T A B L E   4-5
Criteria of an Effective Mission Statement

1. It states what business the company (or SBU) is in, or will be in. This goes considerably beyond being in the hotel, restaurant, or food business. Instead, it is more specific and states how we serve our customers and specifies who they are. For example:

    Hotel XYZ is in the business of providing the traveling and price-sensitive public with modern, comfortable, and clean accommodations at a very reasonable price.

    Accordingly, it recognizes the basic needs of travelers as well as the need for a pleasant and hassle-free experience, but without the amenities for which this market is unwilling to pay. Hotel XYZ wants to be known as the best buy at the moderate price level, satisfying all essential needs for the motoring public.

    You can see that this statement has numerous ramifications such as how, what, when, and where. These are enumerated later in the strategic plan, but the answers will be driven by the mission statement.

2. It identifies the special competency of the firm and how it will be unique in the marketplace.

    XYZ hotel company is and will continue to be a leader in its field because of its special identification with the budget-minded traveling public and its needs. By continuous communication with its market and regular adaptation to the changing needs of that market, Hotel XYZ will maintain its position as the hotel of choice of its customers.

    Again, it can be seen that the mission statement has committed the firm to a definite course of action. Its competency and uniqueness is special knowledge of the target market and a commitment to maintain and implement that knowledge.

3. In a market position statement it defines who the competition will be—that is, it actually chooses against whom it will compete and does not leave this to chance.

    Hotel XYZ's niche in the market will be between the full economy, highly price-sensitive market that chooses accommodations almost solely by price, and the middle-tier market that will pay $20 more for additional amenities and services. Accordingly, XYZ competes only tangentially against ABC and DEF, on the one hand, and GHI and JKL on the other hand. XYZ competes directly for the same market against MNO and PQR, as well as other companies that choose to enter this market.

    As Burger King knows it has to beat McDonald's and Pepsi Cola knows it has to beat Coca-Cola, XYZ knows it has to beat MNO and PQR and will watch these competitors very closely.

4. It identifies the needs of its constituents.

    Customers: XYZ will conduct ongoing research of its customers' needs, both at the corporate and unit levels. It will continuously seek to satisfy those needs within the constraints of its mission.

    Employees: XYZ recognizes all employees as internal customers with their own varying needs and wants. Accordingly, it will attend to those needs and wants with the same attitude it holds toward its paying customers and will maintain an open line of communication for that purpose.

    Community: XYZ recognizes its position in the economic, political, and social communities. Thus it will maintain a role of good citizenship in all endeavors and efforts.

    Owners: XYZ has committed itself to a 15 percent ROI for its investors as well as a positive image of which they can be proud. XYZ will function both in the marketplace and in its operations to maintain these commitments.

5. It identifies the future.

    Hotel XYZ will develop and expand through controlled growth in suitable locations. Its strategy will be to develop regional strength as a gradual development toward national strength, with the objective of reaching that goal by the year 2005.

MISSION STATEMENT

The Ritz-Carlton Hotel Company will be regarded as the quality and market leader of the hotel industry worldwide.

We are responsible for creating exceptional, profitable results with the investments entrusted to us by efficiently satisfying customers.

The Ritz-Carlton Hotels will be the clear choice of discriminating business and leisure travelers, meeting planners, travel industry partners, owners, partners and the travel agent community.

Founded on the principles of providing a high level of genuine, caring, personal service; cleanliness; beauty; and comfort, we will consistently provide all customers with their ultimate expectation, a memorable experience and exceptional value. Every employee will be empowered to provide immediate corrective action should customer problems occur.

Meeting planners will favor The Ritz-Carlton Hotels. Empowered sales staff will know their own product and will always be familiar with each customer's business. The transition of customer requirements from Sales to Conference Services will be seamless. Conference Services will be a partner to the meeting planner, with General Managers showing interest through their presence and participation. Any potential problem will be solved instantly and with ease for the planner. All billing will be clear, accurate and timely. All of this will create a memorable, positive experience for the meeting planner and the meeting participants.

Key account customers will receive individualized attention, products and services in support of their organization's objectives.

All guests and customers will know we fully appreciate their loyalty.

The Ritz-Carlton Hotels will be the first choice for important and social business events and will be the social centers in each community. Through creativity, detailed planning, and communication, banquets and conferences will be memorable.

Our restaurants and lounges will be the first choice of the local community and will be patronized on a regular basis.

The Ritz-Carlton Hotels will be known as positive, supportive members of their community and will be sensitive to the environment.

The relationships we have with our suppliers will be one of mutual confidence and teamwork.

We will always select employees who share our values. We will strive to meet individual needs because our success depends on the satisfaction, effort and commitment of each employee. Our leaders will constantly support and energize all employees to continuously improve productivity and customer satisfaction. This will be accomplished by creating an environment of genuine care, trust, respect, fairness and teamwork through training, education, empowerment, participation, recognition, rewards and career opportunities.

Source: Reprinted with permission of the Ritz-Carlton Hotel Company

F I G U R E   4 - 1 1   The Ritz-Carlton mission statement.

keting strategy turns to the marketing emphasis to fulfill those missions.

The mission statement of the hypothetical hotel company XYZ in Table 4-5 noted that it wanted to be perceived as the best buy at the moderate price level. The master marketing strategy, then, should deal with the accomplishment needed to make it happen.

SITUATION ANALYSIS

The master strategy begins with a situation analysis of *strengths* and *weaknesses,* again asking the questions, "Where are we now?" and "Where do we want to go?" It is the "where" of the strategic marketing system that shapes objectives and sets the

stage for all decision aspects. A master strategy deals with the generic stages we have just discussed such as positions, trade-offs, and fit. It also deals with such issues as new markets, growth sectors, customer loyalty, repeat business, quantity versus quality, cheap versus expensive, best versus biggest, high or low markups, quick turnover, product/service range, building brand name, consumer awareness and perception, and a host of other things that will guide the business strategies. Marketing objectives are identified in the master strategy in these contexts.

To address these issues it is clear that one must first know their current state. We continue with an environmental analysis (see Figure 4-10), looking especially at the long-range trends and effects. These trends could be economic (the state of the international, national, or local economy); sociocultural (the graying of America, Generation X); lifestyle (interest in fitness and health); legal (laws pertaining to employees such as minimum wage requirements); ecological (a greater awareness of environmental concerns); political (room taxes), technological (Internet reservations), and competitive (industry consolidation). The major purpose of environmental analysis is to identify external *opportunities* and *threats* to the organization.

An opportunity is a favorable trend in the environment such as an emerging market segment, or a need or demand for certain specialized services. On the other hand, a threat is an unfavorable trend such as reduced demand or new competition. External opportunities and threats will evolve when various questions are asked about the organization, along with its internal strengths and weaknesses, in a situation analysis. This is discussed further in Chapters 5 and 6. Analysis of strengths, weaknesses, opportunities, and threats is often called SWOT analysis. Examples are shown in Table 4-6.

The main objective of a SWOT analysis is to identify strategies that fit a company's resources and capabilities to the demands of the environment in which the company operates. The purpose of the strategic alternatives developed by a SWOT analysis

TABLE 4-6
Some Elements of a Situation Analysis

Internal—Strengths and Weaknesses

Brand Demand: Who is our customer? Why? What is our position? Who are our market segments and target markets? To which do we appeal the most? What use do they make of our product/service? What benefits do we offer? What problems do we solve or not solve? What are the levels of awareness, preference?

Customer Profile: What do they look like—demographically, psychographically, socially? Are they heavy users or light users? How do they make the decision? What influences them? How do they perceive us? What do they use us for? Where else do they go? What needs and wants do we fulfill? What are their expectations?

Organizational Values: What are the values that guide us? What is the corporate culture? What drives us in a real sense? Do these limit alternatives?

Resources: What are our distinctive capabilities and strengths? What do we do particularly well? How do these strengths compare to the competition? What are our physical resources? Are there any conflicts among our resources, our values, and our objectives? Do we have a good fit?

Product/Service: What is it? What benefits does it offer or problems does it solve? How is it perceived, positioned? What are the tangibles/intangibles? What are our complementary lines? What are our strengths and weaknesses?

Objectives: Where do we want to go? What do we want to accomplish? How do we want to be perceived? What are the long-/short-range considerations? What trade-offs do we need to make?

Policies: What rules do we have now? How do we operate? What guides us? Are any rules conflicting?

Organization: How are resources, authority, and responsibility organized and implemented? Do we proact rather than react? Does the organization enhance the strategy or does the organization need to be changed?

External—Opportunities and Threats

Generic Demand: How are we positioned? Why do people come here and why do they use this product? Where else do they go? What do they need, want, demand? Are there unmet needs? What do users/nonusers look like? What are the segments for this product category? What are the alternatives? What are the trend patterns—cyclical, seasonal, fashionable?

Competition: Who are they? Where are they? What do they look like? How are they positioned against us? In what market segments are they stronger/weaker? Why do people go there? What do they do better/poorer than us? What is their market share? What are their strengths and weaknesses? What are their expectations? What are their strategies? What are they doing and where are they going? Are there new ones coming?

Environment: What are the impacts of technology and sociocultural changes, economic, political and regulatory trends?

---

is to build on a company's strength by exploiting the opportunities, countering the threats, and overcoming the weaknesses, thus developing distinctive competencies and competitive advantage.

The distinctive competency of an organization is more than what it can do; it is what it can do particularly well. It often takes a great deal of self-analysis to understand this and to abide by it. Objective situation analysis is the tool to lay bare the facts. Abiding by it is sometimes more difficult.

Holiday Inns learned this when they diversified into over 30 different businesses in which they lacked strength or distinctive competency. In many cases, failure to recognize strengths and weaknesses results in targeting the wrong markets. Strategically speaking, a firm should do only what it has the competency and resources to do well. Ignoring this fact may result in a colossal strategic error.

Too often SWOT analysis is primarily indications of past performance that are unlikely to produce assessments of future opportunities. Some methods to avoid this are:

- Involve the managers who will make the final strategic choices.
- Test alternative strategies against strengths and weaknesses.
- Evaluate strengths and weaknesses in terms of the future and their strategic significance, and relative to the competition.
- Separate weaknesses from simple problems "to be overcome."

The final output should be a list of the most significant strengths, on which the future should be planned, and the most important weaknesses, which should be targeted for solution and avoided as underpinnings of strategy.

Solid strength and weakness analysis may be the most neglected phase of strategic planning in the hospitality industry. Without a doubt, this lack was a major contribution to the failure of Howard Johnson's, the stages of which are shown in Table 4-7. In less than ten years Howard Johnson went from boom to bust. Eventually, it was broken up and sold off in pieces, all because management failed to understand its strengths and weaknesses or to see its opportunities and threats. Many opportunities and threats spring from the changing environment, as seen in this case, as well as from consumers' problems, which you can conjecture from Table 4-7.

USING THE STRATEGIC MARKETING SYSTEM MODEL

Rather than discourse further on the model in Figure 4-10 we will make it come alive by illustrating the stages with excerpts from the actual strategic marketing plan of an international hotel that we will call the International. The mission of this hotel was to be the top upscale hotel of choice in its city for the international traveler. Without going

into the full situation analysis, covered above, that forms the basis of the strategy, we have placed some key questions in brackets. Three years after this strategic plan was drawn, this hotel was devastated by new competition. Examine its analysis and plan and see if you can understand why.

Objectives and Master Strategy

Marketing Objective. To be perceived as a premier super deluxe hotel marketed to the connoisseur consumer.

Master Marketing Strategy. To create an image of exclusivity and uniqueness with premium quality facilities and services.

Strengths

Personalized and professional service
Prime strategic location
Part of chain that has already made its mark
High standards of food and service
Newly refurnished outlets
Renowned shopping arcade on premise
Wide variety of excellently appointed suites

[Do these strengths represent unique competitive differences perceived by the customer that build defenses against competitive forces or find niche positions in the market? What is the hotel's distinctive competency?]

Weaknesses

Higher room and F&B rates make it difficult to secure international conference business
Market sensitivity that we are more pro-foreigner and have less identification with local community
Lower percentage of national clientele
Marketing is more product-oriented than customer-oriented
Lack of exclusive executive club

T A B L E   4-7
Chronology of Howard Johnson's Failure Due to Lack of Diligent SWOT Analysis and Strategic Planning

[1979:] Daiquiris, discos and candlelight dinners: that's what Howard Johnson's is serving up these days. . . . The bastion of the highway travel market is out to change its image. . . . Says Johnson, "We know where our operations will be in the 1980s, but the question is will we be in the right spot?'" . . . "I still don't think the food business is a marketing business." . . . "I'm sure that we're making the right long-term moves."[14]

[1983:] The wraps are slowly coming off a new strategic business plan at the Howard Johnson Co. Key to the sluggish giant's assault on its problems is a carefully planned, major reorganization of the way the company manages and markets its restaurants and lodges. . . . "It's just a case of reorienting the thinking under new leadership."[15]

[1983:] "Everybody has a theme restaurant, but I think Ground Round [a restaurant concept division of Howard Johnson's] has a unique niche among them. Both families and singles are comfortable with us. We have done the one thing older chains have failed to do: marry the family trade with strong liquor sales."[16]

[1984:] Bettering the chain's infamously undependable service has suddenly become a priority.[17]

[1985—after the fall:] Howard Johnson's restaurants had become overpriced and understaffed purveyors of pallid food, hamstrung by outdated ideas. . . . Howard Johnson's troubles [were blamed] on everything but incompetent management. . . . Howard Johnson's stood fast with a diversified menu while it was being "segmented" to death. . . . for two decades, what an opportunity was blown![18]

Absence of well-located properties in chain, which reduces chain utilization

[Are these weaknesses, or problems that need to be solved?]

Opportunities

The commercial market in the city is very active and our location is strategic.
Development in this area is strong and has strong affiliation with our hotel.
Entrepreneurial market is growing and most are locating in this area.

[Is this a matching of strengths and competencies to opportunity?]

Threats

Foreign traffic will be dependent on political stability of the country.
Corporations are developing own facilities to encourage privacy and reduce expenditures.
Renovated rooms at biggest competitor.
Some corporations are moving to suburbs.

[Are these threats caused by weaknesses? Can they be avoided? Can resources be better deployed?]

Business Strategies

Referring back to Figure 4-10 it can be seen that the next stage in strategic marketing, and one flowing from the master strategy, is the planning stage, or what are called the operational or **business level strategies.** These strategies are the "how" of strategic marketing—that is, "how" we're going to get from "here" to "where" we want to go. Strategies at this point are more easily measurable and may have time and performance requirements.

This is the stage at which the organization acts in advance, rather than reacts, by planning for change. It is here that the organization shapes its own destiny. It is at this stage that the company attempts to minimize risk, maintain control, and allocate resources to keep in focus and reach its objectives.

The planning stage is also the stage of specific matching of the product to the market, of understanding where the business is going to come from, of developing new products and services, and of influencing demand. You should take special note of the interrelationship among the various elements of the business strategies.

Target Market Strategy.

Target market strategy clearly depends on, among other things, resources and capabilities. To target a market with similar needs and wants is grossly insufficient, if not fatal, when the resources and competencies are not there to serve that market. The appropriate strategy is to target not just markets that appear to have the most opportunity, but also those that the firm can best serve and, one hopes, serve better than the competition.

A common failing in this respect are hotels that target the upscale market and price accordingly. If the firm does not have the resources and capabilities to sustain an advantage in that market, such strategies often fail. The hotel then has to accept lower-rated business while management continues to vehemently maintain that it is in the upscale market. The result is a confused image and failure to fulfill potential. Such strategies are often built on egos and wishful thinking rather than on unbiased analysis.

Another area of weakness in target market strategy is targeting too many different markets—a strategy of providing something for everyone, which lacks focus and results in confusion for anyone.

Target market strategy means defining the right target market within the broader market segment. The strategy of the International Hotel we have been discussing is to target the following market.

Age: 35 plus

Income: High

Lifestyle: Result-oriented, professional businessperson, aristocratic with a modern outlook on life, respected in the community, voices an opinion, a leader, an active socializer

Desired consumer response:

Rational: I like staying here because the rooms are spacious and beautiful. I like the computerized telephone exchange with its automatic wake-up call and direct international dialing. The executive club with computers and fax machines is time-saving, smooth, and trouble-free. Check-in/checkout is fast and efficient. Because the hotel is so exclusive I don't encounter undesirable people. Service is smooth, courteous, and efficient.

Emotional: I like staying here because everyone knows me and takes care of me. I feel very much at home with the room service and restaurants. They know my likes and dislikes and make it a point to remember. It is so exclusive, I like to be seen here.

Target marketing is discussed further in Chapter 8.

Product Strategy.

Product strategy is concerned with the offering of different products and services to satisfy market needs. It deals with the benefits the product provides, the problems it solves, and how it differentiates from the competition. Product strategies should be based on opportunities in the environment and customer needs rather than be based on owners' or managements' concept of what the product should be. For example, it is quite common in popular Asian cities for upscale hotels to have as many as five formal dining rooms. These will inevitably be Chinese, Japanese, and French, plus one native to the country. The other is likely to be Italian or American. The reasoning, of course, is that all these geographic markets are served by the hotel. Each room usually seats 100 or more and in most cases is fortunate if it is 50 percent occupied.

The low patronage does not occur because there is no market need. Demand exists for all these ethnic foods, but at varying levels. Further, there are numerous freestanding restaurants in the city also filling these needs—at least the Chinese, Japanese, and native. Regardless, the product strategy is to have something for everyone instead of defining the specific needs of the target market.

The essence of marketing is to design the product to fit the market. Sometimes, however, the product, like a hotel, already exists and the situation is reversed: the market must be found that fits the product. Such a case might exist when the market changes or new competition takes it away. Product strategy is discussed further in Chapter 12.

Competitive Strategy. In developing **competitive strategy,** the firm actually chooses its competition and when and where it will compete, as well as if it will be a low cost producer, a differentiator, a focuser, or some combination of these. This is realistic provided the choice is realistic, and if it is based on an objective situation analysis. Take the case of Wendy's Restaurants, which used a focus strategy.

In the early 1970s, when McDonald's and Burger King were already well established, industry experts did not think that there was room for another hamburger chain to enter the market and grow to any substantial size. However, in less than ten years after opening their first restaurant in 1969, Wendy's had grown to a chain of 1000 units. Wendy's did not compete head to head with McDonald's or Burger King, but rather it focused on a special niche in the crowded hamburger market. It went after the baby-boomers who were young adults in their 20s and 30s. Surveys showed that over 80 percent of Wendy's business came from those over 25 years old. Compare this with McDonald's, which derived 35 percent of its business from those under 19 years.

The secret to a successful competitive marketing strategy is to find a market where there is a clear advantage or a niche in the market that can be defended. The trick, then, is to match the firm's product strengths with the market or niche. It does not matter whether this niche occurs in the high or low end of the market. Consider examples on both ends of the spectrum.

Ritz-Carlton Hotels uses a differentiation strategy and is positioned at the top of the market. Their product is "top drawer" and it is almost never compromised. Even after being bought by Marriott, Marriott has clearly indicated they will never put the Marriott name on the brand. On the other hand, Microtel has maintained its position in the budget segment as a low cost leader. Both these companies chose their competition, stuck to it in the marketplace, and were realistic about the choice. This is the essence of formidable competitive strategy. These are single product companies that compete in a single niche.

Other companies, like Choice International, choose their competition in different niches with different brand lines—Clarion, Quality, Comfort, and Sleep Inns—and market them together, giving the customer a choice. Taj Hotels, in India, uses one brand name on six different product lines (Figure 4-12), while Groupe Accor of France has six brand lines—Sofitel, Novotel, Mercure, Ibis, Etap, and Formule1, plus Motel 6 and Red Roof in the United States—but markets them separately.

On the other hand, poor strategic planning leads to choosing the wrong competitors to compete against with the wrong product. When Omni Hotels took over the New York Sheraton and refurbished it, management chose as its competition upscale hotels such as the Essex House and the Parker Meridien, but failed to come even close to offering a comparable product; hence they damaged the Sheraton's identity. Gross operating profit doubled when new management chose instead to compete against the lower scale hotels in the marketplace.

In some companies with widely varied product carrying the same name, each property has to choose its own competition. This is sometimes difficult when the brand name is carried on all products. For example, Sheraton operated the deluxe Sheraton St. Regis in New York City, the convention hotel Sheraton New York a few blocks away, a mid-scale Sheraton Inn in Bordentown, New Jersey (50 miles away), and a franchised basic low-tier Sheraton Inn in Westchester County, a half an hour from New York City. Each of these Sheratons had markedly different competition and customers, but all were marketed together under the Sheraton flag. More recently, hoping to correct this situation, Sheraton has established the Four Points (*by*

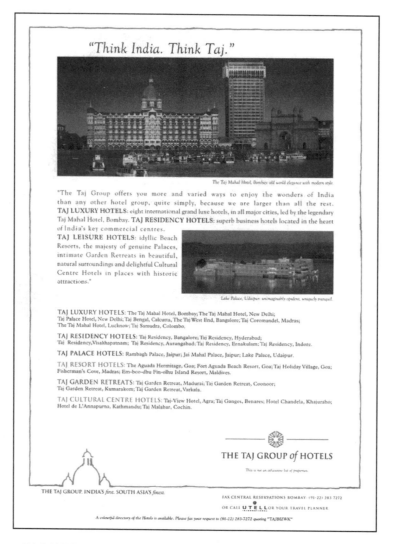

FIGURE 4-12   Taj Group offers one brand with six product lines.

Sheraton) hotel brand. These are new properties or former Sheraton Inns that have been required to improve their standards or lose their franchise.

Conversely, Marriott, Westin, Canadian Pacific, and Hyatt have all maintained similar competitors in all markets. When Marriott decided to go "down market" it followed the Choice and Groupe Accor lead with new products, Courtyard and Fairfield Inn (*by Marriott*), aimed at different markets and with very different competition.

Market Strategy. **Market strategy** is concerned with reaching the market with the product. In the final analysis, if you can't reach the market, the best product and the most well-defined strategy will fail. For the hospitality industry, reaching the market can be looked at in two ways. The first is taking the product to the market; the second is bringing the market to the product. By contrast with manufactured goods, taking the product to the market is a major commitment and, in some cases, a major capital investment. For multiunit hotel and restaurant companies, taking the product to the market is part of the distribution system. This is the area where location becomes a major factor. The strategy involved concerns the appropriate markets to enter.

For multiunit companies that seek growth, the case is multiplied many times. When McDonald's saw its growth limited in freestanding, drive-up stores, it changed its market strategy. Soon McDonald's appeared in inner-city locations, office buildings, universities, and almost anywhere else one looked. It then headed overseas to both the European and Asian markets. In Singapore, on the main road of the city and right next to the Hilton International, sits what became the highest-grossing McDonald's in the world, later supplanted by the one in Red Square, Moscow. Market strategy has been a major factor in McDonald's success.

Hilton International's market strategy was to be in major capital cities throughout the world. Inter-Continental aimed for cities where Pan American Airlines, its former owner, flew. Le Meridien Hotels chose to enter primary cities like Boston, New York, and San Francisco when it expanded into the United States. Marriott likes to saturate an area with multiple units, as it has done in Boston, Washington, DC, Atlanta, Dallas, and other cities.

Getting the market to the product involves a new set of strategies. When resources are scarce, as they usually are, the market strategy must designate where to use those resources. A restaurant may choose the surrounding neighborhood and concentrate on word of mouth. McDonald's, on the other hand, uses national television to cover the entire United States, as well as other countries. The Stanhope Hotel in New York City uses the International Herald Tribune in Europe to attract the European market, a focus strategy. Hyatt concentrates heavily on airline magazines, meeting planner journals, and travel agent indexes. Marriott concentrates on its frequent traveler program and business publications. Many hotels, especially in Asia and southern Europe, rely heavily on tour operators to get their customers to them.

Positioning Strategy. The last, but by no means least, of the business strategies is the **positioning strategy.** Market positioning means to create an image in the consumer's mind. Positioning strategy is no less than the presentation of the product strategy directed at the target markets, consistent with the resources and capabilities of the firm, aimed at specific markets, vis-à-vis the competition. It is important to note the relationship between positioning and the other business strategies, as shown in Figure 4-10. Positioning is discussed in greater detail in Chapter 11.

The strategic plan for positioning the International Hotel to its market is specified as follows.

> The hotel will be positioned as a super-deluxe property for the "up" market. It will be positioned to image-conscious elitists and high-flying business executives. All marketing will be geared to the top-brass higher-echelon bracket of both the social and business circles, for whom facilities, specialties and personalized attention are the main criteria for selection. The exclusive executive club, the businessman's club with business equipment, and the rooms with antiques, objets d'art, and special butler service, will symbolize luxury plus.

Functional Strategies

Functional strategies (refer again to Figure 4-10) are the "what" of the strategic system—that is, the "what" we are going to do to get "where" we want to go. The important thing to remember is that these are still strategies, not tactics, which come immediately afterward. It is this set of strategies that flows directly to the consumer in the form of the value chain. For example, in the International Hotel situation the communication strategy might be to portray luxury, the presentation strategy to price exclusively, with luxurious rooms, the product/service strategy to render personal attention (e.g., butler service), and the distribution strategy to use exclusive referral systems and select travel agents. The functional strategies are the substrategy implementation of the business strategies. They are commonly referred to as the marketing mix, which is discussed in detail in Chapters 12 to 18. Strategies at this level of the hierarchy represent shorter-term and more flexible strategies. All include value chain elements.

Product/Service Substrategy. The **product/service** mix is:

The combination of products and services, whether free or for sale, aimed at satisfying the needs of the target market.[19]

In the better known "Four Ps" (product, price, place, promotion) developed for goods marketing this is the product. Ritz-Carlton Hotels has a top-of-the-line product/service strategy at the master and business strategy levels. At the functional strategy level, strategic decisions must be made on the level of service to offer, and when and how to offer it. The same criteria, of course, apply: What is important to the target market? What does the target market expect? What problems does the target market have?

Let's say the product/service substrategy is to provide luxury. This would be a natural derivation from the master strategy and the business strategies. The question is how to put it into practice. These are the tactics. Consider terry cloth bathrobes in each room—is this important to the market? Does the market expect it? Does it solve a problem for the customer? For Ritz-Carlton the answer may be yes, and the customer is willing to pay the additional cost. For most other hotels the answer is probably no. We carry this discussion further in Chapter 12.

The Oberoi Hotel chain in India once changed its master strategy and decided to aim at the super luxury market. Into the rooms went antique desks, personalized stationery, beautiful brass ashtrays, and terry cloth bathrobes, among other things. The rooms themselves weren't much different; it was the symbols of luxury that made the difference and

the product/service strategy had to change. Many other changes were also made in the hotel's marketing mix to carry out this strategy. Table 4-8 gives some examples of tactics that belied the strategies of other companies and properties.

These examples demonstrate that product/service functional strategies concern the level of product and service offered consistent with higher-level strategies. Because higher-level strategies must be built around the target markets and the product, so too should the functional strategies that flow from them and the tactics that are implemented. As shown in Table 4-8, this is sometimes not the case in practice.

Presentation Substrategy. The **presentation** mix is defined as:

All elements used by the firm to increase the tangibility of the product/service mix in the perception of the target market at the right time and place.[20]

These include the physical plant, atmospherics, employees, customers, location, and price and are further elaborated on in Chapter 11. The same rules apply to this strategy as to the product/service strategy. Much of what we have said above could also be applied here—that is, this strategy is no less than a carryover of the product/service strategy. This mix has no true counterpart in the Four Ps but includes price.

Physical plant and *atmosphere* must be consistent with the product/service strategy. This means they shouldn't be overdone or underdone.

Employees must be hired and trained accordingly. Certainly we expect a bigger smile and quieter maids at a four-star than at a two-star hotel, and better service at a three-star than at a one-star restaurant. In either case, we expect an emphasis on the customer rather than on the service. This difference, in fact, is why Ritz-Carlton does so well at what it does. The reverse is also true, at McDonald's we expect service to be consistent with

TABLE 4-8
Tactics That Fail to Support Strategies

Hyatt Hotels once had a policy that every dish that went out of its restaurants must have fresh fruit on it; strawberries showed up in the strangest places but the tactic, at least, was consistent with the strategy of fresh quality. This was also the communications strategy at that time and ads portrayed fresh fruit (tactic). In other situations this was not the case. The Sheraton Towers in Boston had a product/service strategy of exclusiveness and provided bathrobes, but didn't open the pool until 9:00 A.M., and all the light bulbs in the rooms were only 67 watts. Marriott's Courtyards didn't open the pool until 10:00 A.M., in spite of the people trying to get in at 8:00 A.M. The Southampton Princess Hotel in Bermuda emphasized service, convenience, and told you that its coffee shop was open until 1:00 A.M., but closed it if no one happened to be there at 10:00 P.M. It also closed its lobby restrooms and waterfront pool and bar in the slow season to keep down costs, but maintained expensive bathroom amenities and high room rates in the largely empty rooms.

The Americana Dutch in Orlando offered nightly dancing but only disco, and only "locals" went. The hotel was full of families, its target market. The Holiday Inn in Kuala Lumpur offered fresh orange juice but not before 10:00 A.M. (because "the juicer is in the bar") and targeted Americans. The Asia hotel in Bangkok, catering to an American and European market, had minibars in the rooms but no wine in them. The Harbour Castle Westin in Toronto had "Do Not Disturb" signs to hang on your door knob. The maid knocked at 8:00 A.M. anyway.

The Marriott Copley Place in Boston had drapes that didn't close all the way to shut out the morning light, no pull-out clotheslines in the bathroom because they're "too much trouble," and a restaurant with coffee shop decor, appointments, and service, but fine dining room prices. The Park Hotel in Sognefjord, Norway, billed itself as the finest hotel in Norway, charged $200 for a double room, had tiny soap bars (albeit in a fancy box) reminiscent of the early American motels.

the product strategy; for example, McDonald's expects you to clear your own tray when finished!

The *customer* mix strategy is very important. In some four-star deluxe hotels in Paris and London men don't get in the door without a coat and tie. At other places you may be an "oddball" if you have them on. There is a basic strategy here that really applies in almost all cases: don't mix incompatible markets if you can possibly help it; if you have to deal with incompatible markets, keep them separated in both time (e.g., seasonally) and space (e.g., separate dining rooms).

Location strategy means being where the customer can get to you or you can get to the customer. Again, McDonald's, in its infinite ubiquitousness, is a prime example of this element, being located in just about every conceivable type of facility or location that one can imagine.

Pricing strategy, again, should be consistent with the other functional strategies. In too many cases, in fact, there seems to be no strategy at all.

Prices sometimes seem to be set totally independently of all other strategies and without regard to their interrelationship. Price creates many expectations, which is why we consider it part of the presentation mix, as well as a separate part of the marketing mix.

Consider the airline passenger who pays $2000 to fly first class versus the one who pays $600 in economy. They leave and arrive at the same time and travel at the same speed. What does $1400 tell you? That's an easy one. What does $200 in a hotel room tell you? Or $100, or $75, or $35? In Toronto we found a hotel that charged $150 for a room service imperial quart bottle (40 ounces) of liquor, plus tax and tip, that sold in the liquor store for under $30.00. The room cost $119.00. Although the customer is the same for both, there is clearly no relationship between the pricing strategies.

Pricing Substrategy. The **pricing** mix is the combination of prices used by the firm to represent the value of the offering. The pricing mix is how the customer values what is being offered and what is received.

The following points have been considered by the International Hotel in developing the pricing strategy (note the last line):

- The special features of the product.
- The spending power of the market.
- The traffic movement of the market.
- The possibility of losing regular users of high-rate rooms to lower-rate rooms.
- Pricing of the competition.
- Management policy to avoid discounted business, group business, and any upgrading to the new rooms.
- The rates will be raised in three months.

As Jain states,

Increase [in price] should be considered for its effect on long-term profitability, demand elasticity, and competitive moves. Although a higher price may mean higher profits in the short run, the long-run effect of a price increase may be disastrous. The increase may encourage new entrants to flock to the industry and competition from substitutes. . . . Further, an increase in price may lead to shifts in demand that could be detrimental.[21]

All of the possibilities mentioned by Jain have happened in the hotel and restaurant industries in recent years, because of overpricing in the short run. We spend all of Chapter 14 on pricing, as a separate part of the marketing mix, so it is not belabored further here. Suffice it to say that pricing is both a powerful and a dangerous strategic tool.

Communication Substrategy. The **communications** mix is:

All communications between the firm and the target market that increase the tangibility of the product/service mix, that establish or monitor consumer expectations, or that persuade customers to purchase.[22]

The communication mix replaces promotion in the 4 Ps.

The issue here is obviously the strategy to be used to communicate all of the above to the marketplace. The strategic issue is what to say, not how to say it. The "how to say it" requires exceptional creativity in many cases and is often best left to those with that kind of expertise. The "what to say," however, is a strategic management decision and should not be left for advertising agencies to decide without extensive consultation.

Management's failure to clarify its strategy will not stop the agency from being creative. But it could, and too often does, result in advertising that does not clearly communicate the desired or appropriate message. The finished ads, the "how to say it," should always be checked back against the strategy to be certain that the two are consistent with each other.

A common example is advertising copy that places a hotel or restaurant at a higher level than its positioning strategy calls for. The property may be at three-star level and aimed at the corresponding target market. The "creative" agency, however, gets carried away with terms like "luxurious," "elegant," and so on. The appropriate target market feels it cannot afford the facility, and the upscale market, which is attracted, is disappointed. The result is a net loss for everyone.

Advertising, of course, is not the only part of the communications mix strategy. The strategy will also dictate the methods of communication. Under the umbrella of the overall communications strategy and what to say is the mix of personal selling, public relations, promotion (including frequent traveler programs), merchandising, direct mail, and today the World Wide Web. The strategy will indicate where the emphasis and what proportion of the budget will be placed on each. All these are discussed further in Chapters 15 to 17.

An excerpt from the strategic plan of the International Hotel follows.

Objective: To creatively highlight the uniqueness of the product.

Strategy: To convince customers, especially the FIT (Foreign Independent Traveler) and corporate segments, that we have a unique hotel in terms of its being traditional in decor, being equipped with the most modern business aids, and having a greater accent on personalized service. To create awareness of the new F&B outlets.

Mix: [This is followed by an extensive list including advertising media, in-house materials, sales materials, direct mail, publicity materials, brochures, sales trips and blitzes, research, personal invitations, travel agencies, and other strategic and tactical plans.]

Distribution Strategy. The **distribution** mix is made up of all channels available between the firm and the target market that increase the probability of getting the customer to the product.

Strategies for distribution deal with channels and, in the case of most hospitality services, how to move the customer physically to the product. These include travel agents, tour brokers, wholesalers, referral services, reservations systems, Web sites, airlines, travel clubs, and so forth. Strategies involve the emphasis placed on each (or none) as well as the channels used. Distribution replaces "place" in the Four Ps.

Destination hotels and resorts will place special emphasis on utilizing these channels. Distribution systems have become increasingly complex in the hotel industry and for many companies require far more attention today than they did ten years ago. New technologies are discussed in Chapter 16.

Club Med presents a somewhat unusual example. The Club Med vacation is generally all-inclusive (meals, transfers, hotel room, and sometimes airfare are packaged on a per person pricing). Accordingly, Club Med at one time tended to act largely as its own travel agent. This strategy was less than optimally effective in penetrating the American market, however, so a revised strategy was implemented, cultivating specific markets and select travel agencies. Club Med personally trained these agencies in the "Club Med concept" and made them "Club Med specialists." This strategy established a special distribution channel that turned out to be very effective.

The International Hotel in our example belongs to a consortium that advertises as a group but represents many hotels and hotel chains in the world in a similar product class. This enables it to benefit from international advertising that it otherwise could not afford.

Restaurants are also involved in distribution channels. Restaurants in New Orleans, where there is heavy convention and tourist traffic, work closely with tour operators and incentive travel planners to bring in customers. There are other special cases, too. Many restaurants utilize the services of concierges at hotels to make recommendations to out-of-town guests. This distribution channel in many cases is worked every day, with financial rewards to the concierges that send the most business to certain restaurants.

In fact, destination management companies (DMCs) are increasingly becoming strong channels of distribution. Originally designed to handle the land transportation need of groups, the DMCs quickly recognized the ability to steer potential customers to restaurants, catering facilities, attractions, and other related hospitality providers. Chapter 18 elaborates more on distribution strategies.

Feedback Loops

There are two **feedback loops** in the strategic marketing systems model in Figure 4-10. One is the *risk/fit* loop. Feeding back to the master strategy, this loop questions the risks if the strategy is pursued and the strategic fit. Some of the risk questions to be asked are "What can happen? Will it work? What if it doesn't? How will competitors react? What are the economics? Does it meet objectives? Is there a fit between the marketplace and the master strategy?" These are critical questions that must be asked. If answers are negative, reevaluation must take place. This is far better than following hunches that often end in failure.

The second loop starts with **synthesis** of all the

analysis that has been done. In analysis we learn to break a problem into its many parts such as the marketing, financial, organizational, and environmental components. Many students and managers are good at this, but what they often do not do is put the pieces back together again. Too often the ability to analyze is valued over the ability to synthesize. Danny Miller states it this way:

> Analytical skills are fine for delving into problems, but they are inadequate for generating the insight needed for a workable solution. Analysis requires systematic probing, thoroughness, and logic. Synthesis, on the other hand, calls for artful pattern recognition, receptiveness, and magical insight—traits much neglected in the western world.[23]

In other words, synthesis means putting the pieces back together in a meaningful way that separates the wheat from the chaff. This means restating the pertinent elements in a concise, clear summation in a reconfiguration that considers the needs of the firm, the needs of its customers, and the challenges of its competitors. It means identifying a theme or a vision for a configuration that is durable, defensible, and feasible.

Synthesis is followed by *evaluation/fit*. Here we ask some of the same questions that we asked in the risk loop. We also make value judgments about whether the strategy matches capabilities and if the organization can support it, that is, can it be successfully implemented and, if so, what will it take? Evaluation is the summation of the upside and the downside.

Once the strategy is planned and approved, of course it has to be *implemented*. Unfortunately, this is sometimes where it all falls apart, especially if the previous planning stages haven't been analyzed thoroughly. Implementation may require a number of events.

First, there is the organization. Strategy is implemented through organizational design. This means creating an organizational structure that will spot its own weaknesses and make the strategy work. Too often, strategies are put in place with an existing organizational structure that doesn't allow them to

work or, worse, the strategy is designed around the existing structure. *Structure follows strategy.* This is critical. Employees activities must be coordinated and employees must be motivated to make the strategy work—to create value and obtain competitive advantage. The organization must also be designed to have an effective control system that compares actual performance against established targets, evaluates the results, and takes action if necessary.

As this is a marketing text, we won't elaborate further on organizational structure and implementing change. These issues, however, are not to be taken lightly and should be considered in any strategic plan.

The second feedback loop continues with the feedback on whether the strategy is working once it is in place. *Marketing research* is fed into the *marketing intelligence system*. This is the control that warns management to act before the possibility arises of the system's being out of control.

STRATEGY SELECTION

As we have progressed through the strategic marketing systems model illustrated in Figure 4-10, we have provided a framework on which we can later expand. We have probably raised more questions than we have provided answers. That is because there is no single right marketing strategy for any situation; there are simply right alternatives. The situation analysis, if done objectively, should lay bare the facts. The environmental analysis provides the bases for assumptions. From these sources, the strategic planner develops alternative courses of action.

Which one should be chosen? That is a simple question that has no simple answer. When you consider that there are also alternatives at every step of the strategic planning process, you find that you have dozens, perhaps hundreds, of choices to make. That seems like a formidable task and it may well be. Some are better at it than others. Good common sense, wisdom, judgment, and intuition still have their place. Interpreting information, while objective, is not mechanical. The functions of strategic planning are to define objectives in terms other than profit, to plan ahead, to influence and not just react to change, and to inspire organizational commitment. Once your strategy has been formulated, it should also be evaluated for content. Table 4-9 is a checklist for that purpose. Strategy selection should also include understanding the customer's role in the process, to wit:

> A business . . . is defined by the want the customer satisfies when he buys a product or service. . . . To the customer, no product or service, and certainly no company, is of much importance. . . . The customer only wants to know what the product or service will do for him tomorrow. All he is interested in are his own values, his own wants, his own reality. For this reason alone, any serious attempt to state "what our business is" must start with the customer, his realities, his situation, his behavior, his expectations, and his values.[24]

WHY STRATEGIC PLANS SOMETIMES FAIL

The best formulated strategy in the world can fail if it is badly implemented. In some quarters, strategic planning has acquired a bad name because of these failures. It is better to understand the reasons for

TABLE 4-9
Strategy Checklist

Is it identifiable and clear in words and practice?

Does it fully exploit opportunity?

Is it consistent with competence and resources?

Is it internally consistent, synergistic?

Is it a feasible risk in economic and personal terms?

Is it appropriate to personal values and aspirations?

Does it provide stimulus to organizational effort and commitment?

Are there indications of responsiveness of the market?

Is it based on reality to the consumer?

Is it workable?

failure than to blame the process. Research has shown that many of the reasons for failure are those below. We have added some comments to each.

- *Poor Preparation of Line Managers:* Too often managers are rewarded solely or largely on the bottom line. The emphasis remains on short-term objectives. Owners demands become the compelling decision process.
- *Faulty Definition of Business Units:* Too often structure comes before strategy and the organization does not support the development and execution of strategy. The role of top management is not to spot and solve problems as much as to create an organization that can spot and solve its own problems. Organizations need to determine whether they have the right structure to implement the preferred strategy.
- *Vaguely Formulated Goals:* Too often goals are largely financially oriented or based too much on average rate, occupancy, and/or market share rather than on share of customer, customer loyalty, or long-range strategic advantage.
- *Inadequate Information Bases for Action Planning:* Planning in detail should be used as a further test of a strategy's feasibility, requiring the participation of middle and lower management and the workforce. Lower level participation is essential to working out practical steps. Pushing strategic planning out into the organization by exhortation or one-way communication is not effective.
- *Inadequate Linkage of Strategic Planning with Other Control Systems:* These would include budgets, information systems, and reward systems. Strategic planning is a way of thinking about a business and how to run it.

SUMMARY

Strategic planning is a difficult but essential process. At the highest level of the firm, it drives the firm. At the lowest management level, it drives day-to-day activities. It is an essential phase of marketing and management leadership. In the short term, however, it is the annual marketing plan, to which we turn in Chapter 7, that makes the strategic plan work.

Good strategic planning rests on knowing where you are now and where you want to go, and finding the best way to get there. Its success rests on objective analysis, knowing what business you are in, understanding markets, integrating within the firm, and creating an organizational structure that will provide the implementation. In essence, there is no substitute for strategic planning and execution in today's competitive environment.

At the same time, all strategic thinking and planning need not take place only at the corporate or higher levels of management. Unit managers have to be involved in strategic planning. We have given numerous examples of what happens when strategic planning is not done, or is done poorly, or is poorly executed. At the least, every manager should be thinking strategically at every level.

Strategic planning occurs at the functional level, following the strategies set forth at the higher levels. It may occur for a 60-seat coffee shop or a 20-unit motel. Regardless, it is strategy that drives tactics and that, when done and executed properly, will optimize marketing performance. Even Joe at Joe's Hot Dog Stand will sell more hot dogs when he plans strategically. The functions of strategic planning are to define objectives in terms other than profit, to plan ahead, to influence and not just react to change, and to inspire organizational commitment.

KEY WORDS AND CONCEPTS

Business Strategies: The "how" of the strategic marketing system:

> **Competitive Strategy:** Defining the competition for products and services; also defining when, where, and against whom the hospitality entity will compete.
>
> **Market Strategy:** Strategy for reaching the market with the product.

> **Positioning Strategy:** Creating the image of the product or service in the mind of the customer.
>
> **Product Strategy:** Focusing on the offering of different products and services to satisfy the needs of the customer.
>
> **Target Market Strategy:** Defining the right target market within a broader market segment.

Competitive Advantage: The edge by which an organization hopes to beat the competition.

Competitive Strategy: About being different in a way that gains competitive advantage.

Cost Leadership Strategy: Outperforming competitors by producing at a lower cost.

Crafted Strategy: A strategy that evolves, as time passes, from either a planned or and emergent strategy.

Differentiation Strategy: Achieving competitive advantage by producing in a manner that is perceived to be unique.

Distinctive Competence: That which a firm does particularly well, giving it a competitive advantage.

Diversification: Entering into a new business activity that is related or unrelated to the current business.

Emergent Strategy: Strategy that is developed and shaped by the business, rather than planned.

Environmental Scanning: Analyzing the forces that cause change.

Feedback Loops: Mechanisms to measure the success of the strategic marketing process. Loops question the risk if the master strategy is pursued and provide feedback on whether the strategy is working once it is in place.

Fit: How activities match and complement each other to gain the strongest possible force.

Focus Strategy: Serving the needs of a limited customer group based on a distinctive competency.

Functional Strategies: These substrategies are the "what" of the strategic marketing strategy:

> **Communications:** This strategy outlines the use of the communications mix: advertising, promotion, merchandising, public relations, direct sales, and Web sites.

Distribution: This strategy outlines how a hospitality entity brings the customer to the product/service.

Presentation: This strategy employs elements of the presentation mix: physical plant and atmosphere, employees, customers, location, and pricing.

Pricing: One of the first visible signs to the market, this strategy must be consistent with the other four functional strategies.

Product/Service: This strategy focuses on what level of product/service to offer and how.

Management Effectiveness: Activities that enable a company to operate more smoothly and produce better.

Master Marketing Strategy: This strategy reviews the strengths, weaknesses, opportunities, and threats of the hospitality entity and shapes its long-range marketing objectives.

Mission Statement: Defines the purpose of a business and may include many ways to achieve that in terms of all stakeholders. It should drive all subsets of the business.

Strategic Business Unit (SBU): A unit of a business that serves a clearly defined product-market segment with its own strategy.

Strategic Effectiveness: Performing different activities from competitors or performing similar activities in different ways.

Strategic Leadership: Leadership that thinks strategically, rather than tactically, by viewing the big picture beyond the everyday management aspects.

Strategic Planning: A systematic planning process that reviews business objectives, matches service with customers, identifies competition, allocates resources, and implements measurement tools.

Strategic Thinking: Thinking long range of the big picture and the impact of environmental forces.

Strategic Visioning: Visioning the future by exploring potential change, understanding the forces driving change, analyzing the impacts, and formulating strategic competitive methods.

Synthesis: The process of putting back together the parts from an analysis to form a new and succinct whole.

Tactics: The specific action steps employed to execute the strategy.

Value Chain: The four major components or generic building blocks that add value to a company's offering: efficiency, quality, innovation, and customer responsiveness.

Vertical Integration: Expanding backward (upstream) into the production process or forward (downstream) into the distribution process.

DISCUSSION QUESTIONS

1. Discuss the key differences between strategies and tactics. List three examples of each as they apply to the hospitality industry. Do the tactics flow from the strategies?
2. Discuss why a mission statement and objectives are needed at the highest and lowest levels of management.
3. How is product/service strategy different from target market strategy in strategic planning?
4. What are the most critical factors in strategy selection? Discuss why.
5. Why does marketing strategy have to come before the marketing plan?
6. Explain the differences and similarities among corporate, business, and functional level strategies.
7. What is meant by "strategy is making trade-offs" and "strategy is creating fits"?

GROUP PROJECTS

1. Use the strategic marketing systems model in Figure 4-10 to analyze a local operation with which you are all familiar such as a bar, restaurant, or even campus food service. Pinpoint each stage of the model.

2. From a recent publication such as *The Wall Street Journal, Business Week, Fortune, Forbes,* and so on, clip a critical article on the problems of a hospitality enterprise. Analyze the organization in terms of the model in Figure 4-10. Where did the company go wrong? Where could it, should it have corrected the situation? How?

REFERENCES

1. We have borrowed some ideas here and in other parts of this section from Michael Porter's writings. See Michael Porter, *Competitive Advantage:* Creating and Sustaining Superior Performance. New York: The Free Press, 1985; and Michael Porter, "What Is Strategy?," *Harvard Business Review,* November–December 1996, pp. 61–78.

2. Source: Porter, "What Is Strategy?" *op. cit.* pp. 77, 78.

3. This section is taken from various trade publications, published news items, industry sources, and personal contacts.

4. This section is taken from various industry sources, trade and business publications. Direct quotes, however, are credited separately.

5. David Leonhardt, "McDonald's. Can It Regain Its Golden Touch?" *Business Week,* March 9, 1998, pp. 70–77.

6. *Ibid.*

7. Holman W. Jenkins, Jr., "How to Save McDonald's," *The Wall Street Journal,* March 18, 1998, p. A23.

8. Subash C. Jain, *Marketing Planning and Strategy,* 5th ed. Cincinnati: South-Western Publishing, 1997, p. 32.

9. Source: Michael D. Olsen, Michael D. Olsen Associates, Blacksburg, VA.

10. Michael E. Porter, *Competitive Strategy: Techniques for Analyzing Industries and Competitors.* New York: The Free Press, 1980.

11. For more detailed discussion on the value chain, see Porter, *Competitive Advantage, op. cit.* Chapters 2 and 3.

12. Henry Mintzberg, "Crafting Strategy," *Harvard Business Review,* July–August 1987, pp. 66–75. It is worth noting here, as this is a marketing not a strategy book, that our discussion on strategies is limited to the most generally accepted and used versions. Other versions exist and are rising. Mintzberg, in fact, proposes 10 different schools of thought on strategy formation. See Henry Mintzberg, Bruce Ahlstrand, and Joseph Lampel, *Strategy Safari: A Guided Tour Through the Wilds of Strategic Management.* New York: The Free Press, 1998.

13. Christopher Muller, "The Marriott Divestment: Leaving the Past Behind," *The Cornell Hotel and Restaurant Administration Quarterly,* February 1990, pp. 7–13.

14. "The Howard Johnson Team: Razing the Orange Roof," *Restaurant Business,* February 1, 1979, pp. 123–134

15. "Hojo Unveils New Strategy to Overcome Sluggish Sales," *Nation's Restaurant News,* January 17, 1983, p. 1.

16. "Welcome Back, Howard Johnson's," *Restaurants and Institutions,* December 28, 1983, p. 88.

17. "Howard Johnson: Is It Too Late To Fix Up Its Faded 1950s Image?" *Business Week,* October 22, 1984, p. 90.

18. "The Sad Case of the Dwindling Orange Roofs," *Forbes,* December 30, 1985, pp. 75–79.

19. Leo M. Renaghan, "A New Marketing Mix for the Hospitality Industry," *Cornell Hotel and Restaurant Administration Quarterly,* April 1981, p. 32.

20. *Ibid.*

21. Jain, *op. cit.,* p. 410.

22. Renaghan, *op. cit.* p. 32.

23. Danny Miller, *The Icarus Paradox: How Exceptional Companies Bring About Their Own Downfall.* New York: Harper Business, 1990, p. 208.

24. Peter F. Drucker, *Management: Tasks, Responsibilities, Practices.* New York: Harper & Row, 1974, pp. 79–80.

Five

THE MARKETING ENVIRONMENT

Overview

Environmental impacts on hospitality enterprises are accelerating at a fast pace and changing the competitive scene. This chapter reviews the different types of marketing environments and analyzes opportunities and threats.

ENVIRONMENTAL SCANNING This is the process of observing uncontrollable forces that will affect the business environment in the near- and far-term future and looking for ways to benefit or guard the business from them.

TYPES OF ENVIRONMENTS These are the many uncontrollable forces that affect the business and competitive environments. These types of environment include technological, political, eco-

nomic, sociocultural, regulatory, and ecological impacts.

OPPORTUNITIES AND THREATS Marketing opportunities begin with identifying unmet customer needs in a changing environment. Threats to these opportunities include the flip side of not seizing opportunity, as well as threats from other environmental forces.

PORTER'S FIVE FORCES MODEL This is a way of looking at the complete environment, both macro and micro, and depicts opportunities, threats, and competitive forces from an industry perspective.

Every organization is part of a larger environment that includes many forces beyond the control of any one firm. As discussed in the previous chapter, a careful assessment of these environmental forces is necessary before any strategic plans can be implemented. As the world's economies become more intertwined, the environment of a company becomes larger and more complex than ever before. Events in faraway places have an impact close to home. Customer needs and wants are also ever-changing, creating an environment that is dynamic and demanding.

Environmental impacts such as the North American recession of the early 1990s changed the buying habits of consumers, just as the strong economy days of the late 1990s did. The customer today is looking for "value-added" in every purchase, from cars to homes to hotel rooms to fast food. As one hotel executive stated, off the record, "During the 80s, we just provided the product. The 90s is a service decade. Unless we are able to provide the service, we cannot compete."

These demands create **opportunities** to serve customers in new and better ways. There is no other choice. The right choice means reading the environment, understanding that change is constant, and developing the products and services that anticipate customers' problems. Yesterday's success is tomorrow's failure if there is no constant adaptation to the environment. Opportunities lie in the environment and in the future, and so do **threats.** It is being alert to that environment and those opportunities and threats, while understanding the competition, that brings success in the future. This calls for constant and careful **environmental scanning** and analysis.

ENVIRONMENTAL SCANNING

Marketing leadership means planning for the future. Trying to determine what the future holds in store has come to be known as environmental scanning. This simply means, "What is going on out there in the environment that is going to impact on our busi-

ness?" What this also means is having an awareness of the need to proact, rather than react, and the need to constantly perceive what is happening and to anticipate what will occur. Environmental scanning as a systematic approach is an essential leadership tool. All of this, of course, is relative to the competition, which is also an environmental force. We discuss competitive analysis in the next chapter.

TYPES OF ENVIRONMENTS

Macroenvironmental forces, other than competitive, can be broadly classified into **technological, political, economic, sociocultural, regulatory,** and **ecological** environments. We discuss some of the impacts of these changing **environments** upon the hospitality industry.

Technological Impacts

When we think about scanning in the technological environment from a marketing viewpoint, we need to think about the impact of technology upon the customer. In the restaurant business, the improvement in credit card processing technology has prompted even quick service chains such as Burger King and Pizza Hut to provide that convenience to their customers. In addition, a number of U.S. table service restaurants provide customers with a fax number for placing orders and, of course, airline, car rental, and hotel reservations can be made online all over the world. Further technological advances have brought us things like better and faster elevators, in-room movies, immediate credit card approval, electronic door locks, and many other amenities. In 1998, in fact, the 2041-room Hilton New York was the first hotel to install in all its guest rooms a "SmartLock" system. This system recognizes information stored on a microchip imbedded in the hotel's "SmartKeys" or the guest's multifunction "Smartcard," providing the ultimate in room security and a competitive advantage for the hotel.

Computerization has certainly been one of the greatest technological advances. Awareness of this fact in environmental scanning leads to analysis of its uses—that is, leads to asking how this advance can be used to customer and competitive advantage. For a long time, most hospitality firms viewed computerization only from the perspective of how it could be used to improve operations.

There is nothing wrong with improving operations. In fact, computerization soon became a necessity to many aspects of running a hospitality firm, but from a marketing perspective it did not always deal with the needs of the consumer. At the front desk of a hotel, for example, computers improved operational control immensely, but left the customer standing in line just as long, if not longer, to check in. To make matters worse, employees had their eyes glued to the computer screen instead of looking at the customer, creating a more sterile environment for the traveler. Things are better today, especially in the check-out area where it is possible to do this from the TV screen in your room (Figure 5-1). The situation is getting better in the check-in area too (Figure 5-2), perhaps even with customers checking themselves in.

Welcome to our Hotel. Our Associates have been looking forward to providing you with exceptional service in a World Class Facility.

We want to exceed your expectations inclusive of your departure. When checking out, there is a potential for line ups and some delays at the Guest Service Desk.

We have a solution! If you are paying your account by credit card this will allow you to use the following service and avoid any delay in your departure.

> o   *On the morning of your departure a copy of your charges and credit card voucher will be placed under your door for you to review. Simply tell Guest Services when you have checked out of your room.*

> *or*

> o   *Use our Video Check Out Services. Touch Channel "88" on the free TV Keys; follow the simple instructions and you will have checked yourself out without having to say anything or stop off anywhere! (You will already have a copy of your account from under your door).*

Our check out time is 1pm. Taking advantage of Sunday Shopping and wish to check out later than 1pm? Just call the Guest Service Desk (Dial 3) and let us know.

Thank you for staying at the Toronto Marriott Eaton Centre Hotel. It has been a pleasure to serve you; and have a safe trip home.

Sincerely,

TORONTO MARRIOTT EATON CENTRE

William J. Saitta
Front Office Manager

WJS/gv

FIGURE 5-1 Marriott Toronto—Technology makes check-out easier.

FIGURE 5-2 Hyatt—Technology makes check-in easier.

Another trend in TV technology is to use it as a high-tech concierge. Guests at a number of hotels can watch video channels describing local attractions, shops, and restaurants and see what, for example, the restaurant looks like and hear about its specialties. Upon pressing another button guests learn not only the address but also what the cab fare should be for the ride over. Another channel provides information on special exhibits at museums and whether tickets are hard to get. Guests can also order breakfast in advance in six different languages. Some hotels have a system through which guests can buy theater tickets and shop at local merchants directly through their in-room television.

For the business traveler, computer technology has produced the portable laptop. Now many of these customers expect a second phone line in their rooms for their computer modem or fax machine. Figure 5-3 shows how Canadian Pacific Hotels offers both high-tech and low-tech amenities.

Guest **databases** have been a major benefit of computer technology. Newer integrated guest history databases connect the central reservations office to the front office **property management system (PMS)**. Some advantages of database systems are shown in Table 5-1.

Database marketing and other uses of today's advanced technology in hospitality have become so pervasive that we devote an entire appendix to it in this edition.

Technology and travel are natural partners. The rapid growth of travel and tourism in the last 20 years has been fostered by technological developments, such as in air transport through the development and refinement of the jet engine, more sophisticated aircraft design, and improved systems management. The original Boeing 747 had to make a refueling stop at an intermediary location in making a flight from Los Angeles to Tokyo. Newer Boeings makes the same flight nonstop. This capability affected many destination points, both pro and con, with flights that no longer made intermediary stops.

Wide use of technology has brought another leap of advance to the travel industry. Software has been designed to facilitate a wide range of activities undertaken by the travel trade (e.g., information retrieval, reservations, ticketing, and invoicing), not to mention the impact of the Internet and World Wide Web, as we discuss further in Appendix B. Future technological developments will result in more revolutions in the distribution and marketing of the various travel and tourism services throughout all segments of the industry and the world. We must never forget, however, that in hospitality there are always customers who want the "human touch."

According to recent research, technology is shaping up to be one of the most significant competitive advantages a hospitality firm can have. Technology will permeate customer service, information management, and hotel design and create

FIGURE 5-3 Canadian Pacific Hotels offer both high-tech and low-tech amenities.

alternatives to existing products and services. The advent of technology-based management information and decision support systems, property management, yield management, and database marketing has improved management control and, in turn, its efficiency and effectiveness. Given the speed of change, firms cannot wait. They must invest today, not only in the opportunities presented, but also in systems that help them monitor changes and their impact on the evolution of customer expectations.[1] Unfortunately, this will not provide *sustainable* competitive advantage, as technology can be copied by all.

Political Impacts

Political impacts upon the hospitality industry vary both with the stability of government and with the interest of government in developing tourism. In the United States there has been rela-

tively little interest at the federal level in developing tourism. The U.S. federal government typically ranks about twentieth in the world, behind such countries as Korea, Malaysia, and Greece, in the amount of money allocated to market to international visitors. This has placed a far greater burden on the states and industry to develop international trade. In other stable governments, such as Singapore and Bermuda, the governmental interest and investment in developing tourism has been a tremendous asset to the industry. Even some unstable governments, such as the Philippines, make strong political efforts to boost tourism.

Political uprisings, of course, can kill tourism in destination areas. Contrarily, political calming, such as in the former Soviet Union, can greatly boost tourism. Political differences between countries, such as the airline route squabble between the United States and Canada, can also impede tourism. Positive agreements, on the other hand, can enhance

TABLE 5-1
Advantages of Database Systems

- Databases speed the taking of reservations.
- A guest's record can be located quickly.
- Guest history reports can be reviewed and rooms prepared accordingly. A guestroom can be stocked with a guest's preferences.
- Guest preferences in the aggregate can be reviewed to see if guests have a common need for which the hotel is not providing.
- Profiles of frequent guests can be established. Guests' demographics and spending patterns can be used to "fingerprint" trends of current customers. This fingerprint is then used to obtain lists of customers with similar demographics and spending patterns to be used to prospect for new customers.
- Sales and marketing can track the effectiveness of advertising campaigns and promotional rates.
- Hotels in a chain can fulfill guests' needs on the first visit when that guest has stayed at other hotels in the chain.

it, such as the agreements between the United States and China, and between Canada and Cuba.

The political environment is particularly critical for large and multinational companies in many areas of the world. The opening of the People's Republic of China to trade led to many opportunities for both hotel and fast-food companies, as did the opening of the former Soviet Union. One of the most successful KFC restaurants is now in Tiananmen Square, Beijing (scene of a disastrous student political uprising in 1989 that shook the world), and one of the largest McDonald's is in Red Square, Moscow. On the other hand, the American owner of the Radisson Kanapolsky was gunned down in front of his hotel in Moscow by political dissidents in 1996.

Globalization has become so predominant in the hospitality industry, in fact, that no company so involved can remain aloof from international politics. Formerly American companies like Holiday Inns, Omni, Westin, and Motel 6 were bought by British, Hong Kong, Japanese (then

Mexican, then American again), and French companies. Sydney-based Southern Pacific Hotels, owned by the Pritzker family of Chicago (Hyatt Hotels), operates a floating hotel in Calcutta, India, and is opening Travelodge properties (an American brand once owned by Forte Hotels of England) in India in agreement with Shri Tribura Sundari Hotels of that country. Queens Moat Houses of England owns HI Management, a French hotel management company. Reso of Sweden manages the Royal Classic Hotels of Denmark. Thousands of other hotels are operated in countries other than those of their owners like Sol Hotels (Spain), which operates in Australia, Indonesia, Malaysia, Thailand, Singapore, Andorra, Venezuela, Colombia, Cuba, Mexico, Moscow, Brazil, and the Dominican Republic. Sheraton has properties in 65 countries and Radisson (Minneapolis) in about 40 countries.* All of these companies must understand and deal with political conditions in all of these countries.

India now allows foreign corporations to hold more than 50 percent ownership in a firm, but only after driving out Coca-Cola and keeping out McDonald's, Holiday Inns, and others, with charges that they were imperialists. A new political government now seeks foreign investment but, still, three KFC units were shut down in 1997 by political movements claiming unsanitary conditions but actually trying to stave off competition. Disneyland of Paris has faced all sorts of political confrontations from those French who don't like the "Americanization" of their country.

Other political impacts occur within a nation's borders and are either to be taken advantage of or counteracted. Within the United States, both the National Restaurant Association and the American Hotel & Motel Association maintain lobbyists in Washington, D.C., to fight taxes and minimum wage laws and lobby for a greater emphasis on

---

*World maps are provided in an appendix to this book so you can become familiar with the location of these countries where you may be working some day!

tourism. State and provincial politics can be equally important. Florida (United States), Ontario (Canada), Loire Valley (France), Algarve (Portugal), Costa del Sol (Spain), and the Bosporus (Turkey) are examples of locations where state and provincial politics have had major impacts in helping tourism.

Local politics can be equally important, and often critical. No operator can afford to ignore them. When the state of Louisiana licensed a casino in New Orleans, the local restaurant association lobbied to prevent the casino from having any substantial food and beverage services that would compete with existing local restaurants. At the even more local level, politics—town, village, or city—control such things as liquor licenses, zoning variances, building permits, and hours of operation.

Government interest in tourism has stemmed primarily from its economic significance, particularly tax earning and employment potentials. Tourism demand, however, is also largely influenced by legislative actions at various levels of government and intergovernmental agencies (e.g., World Tourism Organization (WTO) and International Air Transport Association (IATA)). As well, international politics play a significant role in the volume of travel and tourism business, especially when there are warring factions and terrorist activity.

The air transport industry was liberalized in most tourist generating countries in the 1980s, although the European Union (EU) did not give full freedom to intracountry flights of foreign national airlines (called cabotage) until 1997, which increased competition and reduced fares. The deregulation of the airline industry in North America further generated a significant increase in intercontinental flights, which in turn positively contributed to the growth of world tourism. The adoption of an open sky policy in Asian countries resulted in a substantial increase of air traffic within Asia and fostered the introduction of new carriers like Eva Airways (Taiwan) and Asian Airlines (South Korea).

Relaxed travel restrictions and increased leisure time and income of residents in newly industrial-ized countries contribute significantly to a growth of tourism within, to, and from Asia. In the past, both the Taiwanese and South Korean governments restricted or limited overseas travel by their citizens. With rapid economic growth and an increase in consumer disposable income, the concept of leisure travel became widespread in these countries, and their governments gradually lifted overseas travel bans. Once, for example, the Korean government prevented its citizens from obtaining a passport for "sightseeing" purposes or pleasure travel; at one time an applicant had to be at least 50 years old. Eventually, the government eliminated all age restrictions on the issuance of passports to its citizens. The Taiwanese government followed the same course. The number of outbound tourists from Taiwan increased more than threefold in four years. The number of South Korean outbound travelers increased fivefold during the same period.

Economic Impacts

There are many obvious economic factors affecting any business—recessions, inflation, employment levels, interest rates, personal discretionary income, and so forth. Currency fluctuations affect international travel. If the U.S. dollar is strong relative to other international currencies, it allows Japanese tourists, for example, to purchase fewer dollars with their yen, thus making the United States a less attractive place to visit. In the late 1990s, with the Canadian dollar at $1.50 to the U.S. dollar, Americans flocked to Canada for the bargains of their lives, while many Canadians decided to "visit" their own country. The so-called "Asian contagion" of the late 1990s, when many southeast Asian economies and currencies essentially collapsed, caused that area also to become a bargain for travelers from other parts of the world, but virtually stopped many Asians from traveling. British Columbia, Canada, heavily dependent on this market, went into official recession while eastern Canada was thriving.

All the above factors and many more must be analyzed and considered in environmental scanning, even at the local level. In Seattle the economy rises and falls based on the fortunes of Boeing Aircraft. In depressed Toronto, Ontario, in the early 1990s, with at least five major hotels in receivership, Delta Chelsea management successfully practiced "marketing in a down market" to maintain market share. Some other hotel managements simply complained about the economy—which didn't help much when lenders wanted their money; there were numerous ownership and management changes. But by 1998, Ontario was selling out versus British Columbia's empty rooms.

Among other economic factors affecting the hospitality industry is price resistance, strong in many world areas. The expense account customer, whom many hoteliers had classified as "nonprice-sensitive," is resisting higher prices. Corporate controllers have forced cutbacks in expense accounts, and organizational travel planner buyers are seeking reduced price contracts with both airlines and hotel companies. Corporate travel planners reduce airline costs by negotiating a flat per mile charge per ticket used. Tickets cost the company the same per mile from New York to Paris as from New York to Boston. Hotel costs are reduced by the same travel managers, who choose two or three hotels in a given travel destination. Once rates are negotiated with these select properties, they are placed in a directory for use by company travelers, who can use only the selected properties or their hotel expenses will not be reimbursed. Tax laws have further decreased the deductibility of meals from corporate expense accounts and room tax increases have deterred travel.

Tiering. As some companies choose to ignore these trends, others choose to capitalize on them; this is the best use of environmental scanning. The economic impacts of the environment are, of course, the main reason behind the tier structure of the hotel industry today, started by Quality Inns, now Choice International. This "reading" of the environment by Robert Hazard of Choice, and others who soon followed, gave these companies a large head start and competitive advantage. They grouped hotels into different categories based on the price levels that customers would be willing to pay. Choice developed Comfort Inns for the budget traveler, Quality Inns for the middle tier, and Clarion Hotels for those customers willing to pay a higher price, added Sleep Inns for the low budget, and then bought Econo Lodge, Friendship, and Rodeway to fill out the budget categories (see Figure 5-4). Other hotel companies have followed suit.

As the economies of many countries have grown stronger, particularly those of developing nations that had not previously introduced their own upscale hotel chains, two things happened. The first was that foreign developers began to invest. Many at first brought in North American companies to manage their properties. Eventually, they developed their own chains, also initially in the upscale market.

The second thing that happened was that the traveler changed. Persons of lower income or not on expense accounts began to travel, both abroad and in their own countries. These people resisted the high prices of the upscale hotels and searched for alternatives. The result was that many hotel companies had to learn to adjust to the local economy.

Hotel companies of countries other than the United States also tended to enter foreign markets at the upper end of the scale. An exception was Accor of France. This company took its two- and three-star concepts into neighboring European countries and Asia, as well as the United States, under the names of Ibis and Novotel, and bought Motel 6, a U.S. budget chain. Accor's strategy, as it turned out, was a forerunner of the future as economic conditions continued to change. Days Inn and Choice International budget properties are now worldwide, Holiday Inn has Garden Courts in Europe (Figure 5-5) and Africa and Holiday Express in India, and Country Lodging by Carlson has expanded globally.

There are still many countries without sufficient satisfactory middle-tier hotel accommodations to serve the market, countries as diverse as Finland and India, which has a middle class of 200 million people. Residents of these countries, as well as in-

1. In the beginning, there was Quality. But we've changed with the times. Since 1981, more than half of the original Quality Inns have been eliminated for failure to meet our new, stricter standards. Yet today there are nearly three times as many properties as there were in 1981, including our beautiful all-suites hotels. And nearly 60% of the chain has achieved a three-diamond or better rating.

2. In 1981, we entered the luxury-budget hotel market with Comfort Inns. Since then, Comfort has grown to over 850 properties, becoming the fifth largest lodging chain in the U.S. in its own right. But we didn't stop there. Comfort is still one of the fastest-growing chains in the country. And with good reason. We've earned three times as many three-diamond or better ratings than our nearest economy competitor.

3. In 1981, we introduced our first luxury hotel chain. Since then, Clarion has grown into a worldwide network of distinctive upscale hotels. Today, there are over 80 Clarion hotels open or under development around the world, from our convention hotels to our quaint Clarion Carriage House Inns, all meeting the highest standards in the industry.

4. Sleep Inns are Choice's newest lodging concept. The all new construction, limited-service hotels offer travelers amenities such as oversized showers, large desks, and color televisions with VCRs at a budget rate. At the same time, they offer hotel owners the opportunity to build an attractive property for an affordable price. In just two years, 50 Sleep Inns are open or under development, and there's no end in sight.

5. The Friendship Inns chain includes over 100 budget hotels nationwide. Friendship strengthens our presence in the super-economy segment, making us the number one choice for the price-conscious traveler.

6. **Econo Lodge** With about 800 hotels open or under development in the U.S. and Canada, Econo Lodge gives Choice the strongest presence in the economy segment. Econo Lodge has a national average room rate of about $35 a night, and continues to grow very quickly as the most recognized name in the economy segment.

7. **RODEWAY** Rodeway is an economy chain with 160 hotels in the U.S. and Canada. For years it has courted a loyal following of economy travelers. Its affiliation with Choice brings it the marketing muscle and services necessary to compete on a national scale.

FIGURE 5-4 Choice International's segmented brand line.

ternational travelers who visit them in increasing numbers, must often choose between top-rate hotels or less-than-desirable facilities. Many companies are moving to take advantage of these opportunities. Microtel, for example, a U.S. budget chain, is franchising in South America.

Asia is a special case because it was economically less developed for so long. Strong economic growth, coupled with greater political stability in many Asian countries, were the major reasons for the strong growth surge. Higher disposable incomes of the Asian population, increased leisure time, and relaxation of travel restrictions added to these promising trends until the 1998 economic collapse. Now, of course, the Asian economies are reviving and the cycle will begin all over again.

Of all environmental concerns, the economic environment may be the most universally critical to the company doing business in foreign lands. It is the economic environment that opens doors to

opportunities, and also closes them. This is because countries differ greatly in areas of growth rate, consumer consumption, level of economic development, and discretionary income.

The Macroeconomy. Every nation's economy is at a certain stage of economic development or collapse at any given time. Western Europe, Japan, and the United States are fully industrialized, while Indonesia, Malaysia, Brazil, and Argentina are developing. In 1998, however, Japan, Indonesia, and Malaysia were all in economic crisis stages. On the other hand, the economies of India (where the average annual wage is under U.S. $500 but the "middle class" population is more than half as large as that of the entire United States) and China are less developed but on the verge of taking off. These different stages of economic development often determine the kinds of opportunities available for hospitality firms.

LE BON STYLE • LE BON PRIX • LE BON CHOIX
RIGHT STYLE • RIGHT PRICE • BRIGHT CHOICE

FIGURE 5-5 Holiday Inns goes downscale in Europe.

In the meanwhile, the macroeconomic environment changes continually, sometimes slowly if not drastically. If the economy declines, the market picture changes as well, and the marketing plan has to be altered accordingly. High-priced goods and services tend to suffer more in a declining economy. Conversely, McDonald's and Burger King have done well in international markets in spite of weak economies.

We've talked mostly about economic impacts of the past. Now consider the advent of the euro, the currency introduced in most of Europe in 1999, before this book was published, and the only currency in those countries in 2002, after this book was published. Table 5-2 provides the scenario and the threats and opportunities. Figure 5-6 shows the countries involved.

The Microeconomy. On the other side of the coin exists the microeconomic environment. This environment is concerned with use of the product, awareness levels, and the competitive situation. A good example is Singapore. Once upon a time the Singapore economy was booming. Both tourism and international business travel were on the increase. Inter-Continental, another Sheraton, and Westin entered the market with over 2000 rooms. Mandarin, New Otani from Japan, Peninsula from Hong Kong, and others also opened new hotels. By the time most of these hotels were built (and others were still building or had construction halted), the macroeconomy had softened.

The microeconomy now presented a totally different picture. Rate-cutting practices became intense, and consumers could almost name their own price for hotel rooms. Eventually, occupancy caught up, and a new hotel building binge began. In Hong Kong, this binge has been almost continuous, in spite of hotel closings, due to the ability of their owners to get higher, more profitable rents by converting their hotels into office buildings.

In the final analysis, any company seeking to do business in an international market must carefully weigh all the economic considerations. Each country requires specific strategic approaches and marketing plans that must fit the company's resources, culture, and capabilities. The long-term economic environment is the primary consideration. Although many developing countries offer inducements such as tax incentives and low-cost employment, they may still be very unstable for market entry.

Foodservice companies entering international markets almost totally deal with the local consumer and the microeconomy. Although there are obvious exceptions—for example, there are restaurants in Paris and other cities geared to Americans or Britons—these generally are not the purpose of entry for a foreign firm. This means that understanding population size, wage levels, disposable income, standards of living, and other economic factors is important. Conventional wisdom of the home base country often does not apply. In Australia, for example, KFC chicken is considered to be expensive.

For hotel companies seeking to expand interna-

TABLE 5-2
Advent of the Euro in Europe

The European Monetary Union's (EMU's) "euro" became a currency in its own right on January 1, 1999. On that date the currency exchange rates of participating nations was irrevocably converted to the euro, although national currencies still exist. The conversion process will be completed by January 1, 2002. Six months later, national currencies will be withdrawn from circulation.

The first wave of countries includes Germany, France, Belgium, The Netherlands, Luxembourg, Austria, Ireland, Finland, Italy, Spain, and Portugal. The United Kingdom is not scheduled to participate; however, UK companies will be significantly affected. The same holds true for other nonparticipating nations—Denmark, Sweden, Greece, Norway, and Switzerland, as well as international hotel chains based elsewhere in the world. Conversion potentially sets the stage for new strategic opportunities and improved competitive positions for many companies in the global hospitality industry.

The implications are significant. Conversion will affect virtually every aspect of hotel operations. Immediate savings from eliminating foreign exchange risk will be realized by hotels no longer needing to include a margin in their price to hedge against adverse movements in exchange rates. Strategic opportunities need to be identified.

For multinationals operating in euro countries, the single currency provides the opportunity to budget, forecast, report, and account in the same unit, settle all intercompany transactions in euros, and instantly compare the performance of business units across national boundaries. A major challenge will be converting financial systems. For example, yield management systems, which rely on historical rate and occupancy data, will have to be translated to the new currency.

The euro also has significant strategic implications and benefits in sales and marketing. A customer booking a conference a year in advance, for example, will not have to deal with potential changes in the exchange rate between the booking and conference dates. Thus, properties in euro companies will have a competitive advantage in attracting these customers.

Conversion to the euro will also have a broad impact on customer relations. Business and leisure travelers, as well as conference planners, will be able to compare prices with much greater ease. Customers can be expected to shop for the best deal and to become more knowledgeable than under the system of multiple national currencies. Thus various opportunities will present themselves:

- The conference market will be stimulated because the exchange rate risk is eliminated.
- Package tours and holidays will become more affordable, due to the elimination of hedging. Demand will increase and potentially reduce prices even more.
- Investment in vacation ownership (time-sharing) will be stimulated since euro investors will not be exposed to exchange loss on capital.
- Lower travel costs, due to airline fuel (now fixed in U.S. dollars) not being hedged because of the reduced volatility of the euro, are likely to increase demand.
- Transparent and consistent pricing can strengthen brands. International hotel chains can gain advantage through consistent euro pricing in different tiers. This could be particularly advantageous in the budget sector and as a means of attracting business off peak in companies with very similar products.

Hotel companies may have to restructure sales and marketing as relationships with key customers will need to be established on a pan-European basis rather than at the national or even local property level, as is commonly the case today. Companies will need to consider ways of redefining their products to take advantage of new marketing opportunities, increase differentiation to offset price comparability, and consider revision and maintenance of psychological price points in euro currency. For example, in Italy millions of lira will become hundreds of euro.

The significance in the change to euro is largely in strategic opportunities and threats for hospitality organizations and their impact on a global industry. The single euro currency will be a driver of change, creating opportunities for many and threats for others.

FIGURE 5-6 Eleven countries adopting the euro first (*The Wall Street Journal*).

tionally, there are two considerations. One concerns the local economic climate. The geographic and demographic customer mix and that portion of room nights sought from the domestic market are very important.

The other consideration is the international travel market: will it be sought, where will it come from, and what economic factors will affect it? Regardless of its decision, the international hotel company will still have to confront the local market for its food and beverage outlets as well as for a portion of its meetings business. Although hotel dining and drinking is not necessarily fashionable in the United States or countries like France and England, in some countries, such as India, hotels are where almost all "better" dining takes place.

Consumption patterns in international tourism are largely dependent upon the economic conditions in the market. These conditions in the countries or regions in which prospective visitors live strongly influence total visitor volume. Developed and growing economies sustain large numbers of trips away from home for business purposes of all kinds. Business meetings, attendance at conferences and trade shows, and travel on government business are all important parts of the travel and tourism industry. The influence of economic conditions is even more obvious in leisure travel where, in many countries with advanced and developed economies, average disposable income per capita has grown to a size large enough to enable a majority of the population to take vacation trips in foreign lands. A strategist today, for example, must look to the future to decide the risks to be taken in Asia before its economies rebound.

Sociocultural Impacts

Although the economic environment will probably have the greatest impact upon major international marketing decisions, it is certainly the cultural environment that will most deeply affect marketing behavior. Culture is the common set of values shared by most citizens in any country. This includes personal beliefs and aspirations, values and attitudes, opinions and lifestyles, interpersonal relationships, religion, and social structure.

Because hospitality is a personal business and of a personal nature to everyone who buys its product, it is extremely vulnerable to social and cultural change. Subhash C. Jain states, "The ultimate test of a business is its social relevance. It therefore behooves the strategic planner to be familiar with emerging social trends and concerns."[2] A summary of the social climate in the United States in 1997 is given in Table 5-3. This is a clear departure from the negativity of the late 1980s and early 1990s.

T A B L E 5-3
Summary of the United States Current Social Climate[3]

Today's customer is in an essentially positive state of mind—forward looking and forward thinking. Some consumers are living Possibility (an emerging upbeat consumer perspective), while others are only aspiring to it. More than eight in ten Americans say it is important to feel in charge. Nonetheless, trust has bottomed out at stable, yet low, levels. Nevertheless consumers are more likely to say brands are a strong influence on purchase decisions. Particularly significant to travel marketers is the notion that "fun is the number one thing that consumers are looking for" for the third year in a row (see Figure 5-7). Thus it is a challenge to understand the consumer mind-set as they seek to fulfill Possibility.

The bottom line is that Americans are realistic in an imperfect world. They have a "grip." It is this paradox that presents travel marketers with new opportunities to empower consumers to maintain their grip. This is the next big move about to happen in the marketplace. A focal point in assisting consumers is to recognize that stress and confusion continue to plague the vast majority of Americans.

In the past, the key for consumers dealing with the tough times of the 1980s and 1990s was balance. The thinking was, "If I simultaneously embrace a little of everything, I will make it." All too frequently this led to trade-offs. Today, balance is seen as an undesirable compromise, a paradox in itself as it leaves them betwixt and between true satisfaction. They live neither here nor there. As a result their lives become more unbalanced.

So, today's customers are leaving behind compromise characterized by seeking balance, ambiguity, confusion, mediocrity, giving up idealism, and trading off. Instead, they are adopting clarity where little compromise is required and they can take a stand and establish higher expectations. Taking a stand means doing what makes sense to you personally. Taking a stand is increasingly looking to what a brand can do. Brands must give up image-making for tool-making [tools that make self-reliance work and empower them to move forward] in order to be a viable presence in tomorrow's marketplace. Travel marketers who stand in the middle by attempting to be all things to all people are unlikely to enjoy support. Ambiguous offerings where it is hard to figure out the value and nature of the experience is not the direction consumers want to go. Currently, the desire to buy brands is at odds with the inability of Americans to believe marketers' claims. A known and *trusted* brand as an influence on purchase decisions is now as important as low price.

Things that are extremely important in taking a vacation have changed considerably in the past 10 years. Today they are: Top Five—spend time with family, experience new/different things, relax and do nothing, spend time with friends, and catch up with things at home; Bottom Five—have time away from kids, play golf/tennis/ski/sports, be pampered, fulfill sense of adventure, and celebrate holidays.

Source: Courtesy of Yesawich, Pepperdine & Brown, Orlando.

FIGURE 5-7   Customers are looking for fun.[4]

Two-income families, later marriages, higher divorce rates, AIDS, fewer children, female careerism, physical fitness and well-being, escape from monotony and boredom, return to nature, greater sophistication, and many other social changes worldwide have affected the hospitality industry in recent years, and many hotels and restaurants have reflected these changes—some sooner, some later.

The sociocultural environment also includes demographics (e.g., aging of the population), socioeconomics (e.g., increasing dual-income households), cultural values (e.g., the changing role of women), and consumerism (e.g., certain "rights" like full information, safety, and ecology). Contained in the sociocultural environment is the marketplace itself and the characteristics of society. Many of these trends started in the United States and have moved, or are moving, abroad. Others came from the opposite direction. While the hospitality industry has not been

oblivious to these trends, it is sometimes slow in catching up with them. This is hardly surprising, since so many have come so quickly, but the organization that is constantly alert and adapts to cultural change will have a lead on the others.

Let's consider an example. The single woman traveler, now almost 50 percent of the U.S. business travel market, initially said, "I just want to be treated the same way as men." But her wants also included special hangers, full-length mirrors, better lighting around mirrors (never fluorescent!), irons, softer colors, and a myriad of other things that never occurred to men. Electronic door lock security has become critical, as have lobby lounges that are out in the open, and room service to avoid going to restaurants. Today, however, this woman says, "I just want to be treated like a person, like myself (i.e., I don't care how men are treated)." The woman traveler has established her own identity (Figure 5-8).

F I G U R E 5 - 8   Westin—The woman traveler has her own identity.

In restaurants, sociocultural changes are affecting menus and concepts. Trends toward healthier foods have increased the consumption of salads, fish, pasta, and chicken at the expense of red meat. Interesting food and presentation is replacing quantity. Decaffeinated coffee, tea, substitutes for sugar and salt, truth-in-menu, and nonsmoking sections are "in." In restaurants in Los Angeles, New York City, and Toronto, as well as on airplanes, in fact, *all* smoking is "out." Consider Dunkin' Donuts doughnuts without egg yolks to make them cholesterol free, and dealcoholized wines and beers. Moderately priced, casual restaurants are succeeding at the expense of both high-priced gourmet and fast-food restaurants. Table 5-4 provides a commentary on change in the U.S. restaurant market.

Generation Gaps. Consider the **baby boomers** (those born from 1946 through 1964), a term applied to the outcome of the high birth rate in the 20-year period following World War II, some of whom are now in their fifties. They won't tolerate old product or poor service. They are taking many short vacations, they are eating out frequently, they are more sophisticated than their parents, they have more choices, and they are more demanding.

TABLE 5-4
Overview of the U.S. Restaurant Industry by the Way Customers Use Restaurants[5]

The modern foodservice industry began in the 1950s by offering one primary service: home meal replacement. In other words, the average 1950s family typically visited a restaurant so that Mom didn't have to cook. As times have changed, we now believe that customers use restaurants in four primary ways—corresponding to either eating a daytime or evening meal, and either sitting down and enjoying themselves or eating on the go. We classify the four primary foodservice businesses as follows: 1) Eat-ertainment (dine-in dinner), 2) home meal replacement (take-home dinner), 3) sandwich (sit-down breakfast/lunch, and 4) fast-fuel (fast-food breakfast/lunch).

The underlying premise of our long-term investment thesis about the restaurant industry is based on our belief that social, demographic and lifestyle trends (longer work weeks, rising birth rates, more dual-income households, and the aging of baby boomers) are forging a divergence in what customers are demanding from these four core dining occasions—and, as a result, these four businesses are growing more distinct. Therefore, we believe that the best-positioned players are those that cater to only one business. In essence, this trend will help to accelerate the inevitable transformation of the foodservice industry—which the "generalist" restaurants still dominate—into a much more specialized industry.

[Authors' note: The word "eatertainment" is not used in this book as defined by Salomon Brothers. We find the more common usage to be eating where there is a surrounding entertainment atmosphere, such as Planet Hollywood, Hard Rock, or Rain Forest.]

They want five-star standards in four-star hotels at three-star prices. They want personal service and they don't want excuses for inferior performance. They want added value—a superior product and better service at a reasonable price.

Many of the baby boomers were categorized as **"yuppies,"** young, urban, professionals with high incomes on the fast track, who never worried about tomorrow but spent for today. Now we have the "DINKS," Double Income, No Kids, with high discretionary dollars, and the "DEWKS," Dual Earnings With Kids. Dewks, who don't get to see much of their children, now take them with them but still want escape. **"Generation Xers"** (adults born since 1964), now in their twenties and thirties, want "answers" and high tech. In the year 2000 there will be 62 million of them in the United States. Tables 5-5[6] and 5-6[7] show some recent research on pleasure travel differences among boomers, Xers, and **"matures"** (those born before 1946). Other acronyms and names will arise to categorize particular population segments as they develop, all important to hospitality marketers.

The sociocultural environment facing the hospitality industry continues to change. The "can you top this" policies of coupons, twofers, concierge floors, frequent traveler give-aways, pillow mints, and extended bathroom amenities are not going to satiate these social changes or take the place of better price/value relationships. The hospitality industry works hard at increasing customer expectations; but it has to deliver. Michael Diamond, when senior vice-president of marketing at the Boca Raton Hotel and Club in Florida, a five-star resort hotel, stated it this way:

> [W]hatever their needs, travelers want those needs met. You can have all the amenities you want, but unless there's a friendly, knowledgeable, caring person to make those amenities work, you have nothing. . . . It's knowing what travelers need and want in a hotel and then providing it that keeps us in the travel business. If we lose sight of that, then we might as well forget the concierge floors, special menus and technologies. We're here to serve our customers' needs.[8]

Contrast this with the case of Holiday Inns, which in 1987 faced a system occupancy below 60 percent for the first time in its history:

> The tale shows a company can fall victim to its own success, how a business that rode up on the demographics and developments of one time [the '50s] can be laid low by those of another. . . . By the

T A B L E 5-5
Differences Among Three Generations of Pleasure Travelers[6]

	Xers %	Boomers %	Matures %
Weekenders	28	43[a]	29
Extended (5+ nights)	22[a]	36	42[a]
Weekday	26[a]	42	32
Likes to stay at lodging that makes me feel like I've "made it"	69[c,d]	51	56
Usually stay in same brand friends use	5[c]	38	44
Well-known brand is important in choosing	65	60	64
Usually stay at same brand as last time	41[c,d]	54	60
Difficult to get me to change	48	55	60
Risky to stay at brand not familiar with	53	43	48
Try to negotiate the best rates	77	83	86
Some preferred brands			
Holiday Inn	62[c,d]	50[d]	36
Marriott	23	25[d]	15
Best Western	15	16	21
Ramada	21	13	14
Hilton	29[c,d]	12	9
Comfort Inn	26[d]	17	14
Hyatt	5	13[b]	7
Take one or more trips a year:			
With another adult without children	71	57[b]	79[b,c]
With children	27	47[b]	15[b,c]
Alone	26	26	27

[a]Significantly different from the general population profile; percentages expressed as percentage of all respondents in the trip type.
[b]Significantly different from Xers.
[c]Significantly different from boomers.
[d]Significantly different from matures.
Source: Courtesy of Yesawich, Pepperdine & Brown, Orlando.

mid-1960s, Holiday was vulnerable because it hadn't much changed and consumers had. They demanded more—and instead of getting better, many Holiday Inns had gone downhill.[9]

Holiday Inns is now part of Bass Hotels & Resorts and owned by Bass Plc of England where marketing-oriented leadership (from Procter & Gamble in the goods industry) is taking it on a different track.

International Impacts. The sociocultural environment is also changing, of course, in different parts of the world. International cable television and World Wide Web sites provide viewers direct access to latest trends and have a great influence on people all over the world. Social changes occurring in foreign countries often mirror the changes in the United States and are expected to lead to a greater demand for meals away from home, and global interest

TABLE 5-6
What Different Generations Are Looking for in a Pleasure Travel Experience[7]

	1996			1997		
	Xers %*	*Boomers* %*	*Matures* %*	*Xers* %*	*Boomers* %*	*Matures* %*
Attributes Considered Extremely/ Very Desirable:						
Familiarity/Control:						
Safety of destination	81	86	84	77bc	86	86
Safety of hotel or motel	85	85	87	82	86	85
Visiting friends and family	70	69	74	72	67	75b
A place I have visited before	47	45	55	44	40	54ab
Having separate children's and teen programs	30	30	24	31	28	21ab
Pricing:						
An all-inclusive vacation price that includes air transportation, accommodations, food, transfer to the hotel or resort, and some recreation	61	54	61	61b	54	56
An all-inclusive resort price (one price that includes accommodations, food, and recreation)	53	54	54	59bc	51	50
The lowest-priced vacation	48	44	36	47	46	41
Staying at the best hotels or resorts	38	38	47†	44b	35	39
Convenience/Accessibility:						
A destination that I can drive to within 3 hours	37†	49	46	50	46	51
A destination that I can fly to within 6 hours	N/A	N/A	N/A	45	40	45
A destination that I can fly to within 3 hours	31†	39	44	45	40	42
Having a cellular phone available to stay in touch with home or office	N/A	N/A	N/A	40bc	28	31
Having access to the Internet or an online service to stay in touch with home or office	N/A	N/A	N/A	19	19	16
Experimentation/Fantasy:						
A place I have never visited before	72	72†	70	75b	65	69
An opportunity to eat different and unusual cuisines	46	50	49	49	50	51
A vacation at sea on a cruise ship	51	40	43	45bc	38	37
Learning a new skill or activity	41	34	33	46bc	31	34
A destination that is remote and untouched	48	43†	31	44bc	36	31
Going to theme parks	43	44	34	49bc	41c	30
Being able to gamble	30	20	29	33bc	20	24
Going to a spa	31	21	20	30bc	24	21

(continued)

TABLE 5-6   *(Continued)*

	1996			1997		
	Xers %*	*Boomers* %*	*Matures* %*	*Xers* %*	*Boomers* %*	*Matures* %*
Physical Activities:						
Getting exercise	51	50	51	50	50	50
Hiking and outdoor adventure	44	48†	29	45	39	25ab
Playing golf	21	16	16	17	12ac	17
Participation in water sports	43	36	17	40bc	33c	15
Snorkeling or scuba diving	34†	26	12	27	25	10ab
Snow skiing	33†	18	12	25bc	16c	8
Playing tennis	13	10	8	13c	10	7
Other Activities:						
Visiting arts/architectural/historical sites	46	54	59	49	49	54
Shopping	46	39	42	44	39	44

a = statistically significant difference from Xers, b = significant difference from boomers, c = significant difference from matures.

*Does not equal 100% due to multiple responses.

†Denotes statistically significant difference from 1997.

Courtesy of Yesawich, Pepperdine & Brown, Orlando.

in American popular culture continues to create a demand for American foodservice establishments.

The major difference, in fact, other than more discretionary income, at least as regards the more developed countries, is in the education of the consumer. **Consumerism** has had no small part in the movement of social change affecting business in many countries. The same is true of marketing itself. Marketing, particularly as evidenced by advertising as you can see from the ads in this book, has conditioned consumers to greater and greater expectation. When consumers don't get what they expect, or have been promised, they are not hesitant to make an issue of it.

In other countries of the world, including those of a less-developed nature, the hospitality industry has long catered to the foreign traveler. In these countries, there is a new awareness of their own domestic traveler. There is also a need by the industry to find other markets, and it is looking inward. In these countries, too, the environment continuously changes.

Hospitality marketers need to be keenly aware of cultural norms of both the countries in which they operate and the countries or nationalities from which their customers come. Establishing a hotel in a foreign land requires giving up some preconceived notions. The astute company will first go into the marketplace and determine the cultures, social customs, dining-out habits, and other environmental elements of the populace, and do a competitive analysis. Of course, all this is no different from knowing your market, wherever you are—it just takes a little more effort.

If you want to learn from guest complaints, for example, it will be difficult in Asia. Asian cultures emphasize always smiling and being pleasant, and never disagreeing.

In Moslem countries such as Kuwait, alcoholic beverages are totally banned. This is no idle gesture. Imagine developing weekend packages for a hotel in Kuwait, when Cairo with all its nightclubs is just a short flight away. In India, four out of five people are

Hindu and eat no beef. McDonald's uses a nonbeef (lamb) substitute and spikes it for Indian tastes.

Values that are important to one culture may mean little to another. These conflicts become more intense in an industry that sells very personal services to a very diversified clientele. Preconceived notions of what the hotel guest wants may conflict with the guest's own notions in any country; these can result in disaster when marketing to other cultures. Cultural differences have a tremendous impact upon marketing mix decisions in international operations.

In Thailand, for example, most business dealings are transacted among friends. So a new element of the marketing mix is relying on your friends, clients, and guests to increase your business. In most of the western world kickbacks are illegal. In some parts of Asia, people may think you're strange if you refuse to accept them. Attracting and retaining skilled labor is a huge challenge in Asia and Africa. Hotel GMs are constantly looked to for guidance by the rank and file as "providers for their families." Training, motivating, and compensating staff is much different than in the United States and Europe.

Many Americans are familiar with demographic shifts taking place in the United States, like Generation X, the aging of the baby boomers, and increasing purchasing power of the mature market. There are similar demographic trends shaping the population in every nation. In addition to the size of the population, the per capita income or purchasing power of citizens must be evaluated. Even though China and India are the world's most populous countries, only about 10 percent of the population can actually afford to purchase services offered by the hospitality industry. Still, these markets have a huge potential. Mathematically, 10 percent of India's population represents a market of almost 100 million people.

What this means is that no longer does an international company like Sheraton, Hyatt, Days Inn, Holiday Inn, or Accor simply assume a management contract in, say, Taipei, bring in a European management staff, and set up business for the international traveler. To be successful today, these companies must understand the local populace and the local trends, as well as the other environmental factors.

Regulatory Impacts

Regulations tell restaurateurs to whom they can sell liquor and when. They tell hoteliers what information they must obtain from a guest; in many countries, this includes a passport number, where you came from, where you are going, how and when, and a multitude of other details. Regulations tell us how much tax to add to a bill, what we can say on the menu, how much we have to pay employees, what to do with our waste, where to smoke, and whom we must accept as a customer. This is not to mention the mass of paperwork required just to comply with city, state, and national government information requirements, or the taxes we have to pay.

In fact, costs and profits can sometimes be affected almost as much by regulations as by management decisions or customers' preferences. This, of course, is why hospitality professional associations have lobbyists in Washington, as well as in state capitals. In many countries there is no such luxury—if the government decides it wants to do something, it simply does that thing. Wherever regulations come from, including the smallest town's local ordinance, opposing, supporting, or dealing with regulations is a science of its own. We are more concerned here with the marketing implications.

Aside from fighting proposed regulations that will affect a business, scanning the environment means preparing for the event if and when it materializes. A good example is the somewhat recent and continuing banning of "Happy Hours" with reduced drink prices in various American states and municipalities. While there has been no definitive evidence, before or after, that this would decrease drunk driving, the climate (or social environment) was ripe for such action. There was, and is, actually no concrete evidence that banning happy hours would hurt business either. They also were not the reason that people drank at that time of the day. Astute operators read the writing on the wall and, before the laws were passed, turned to other promotions, such as free snacks, that have been just as successful. If people drink less now it is because of society and driving laws, not the banning of happy hours.

On a national scale, a similar event occurred with the passage of the U.S. 1986 tax law allowing only 80 percent of meal expenses as a business deduction, reduced to 50 percent in 1993. Many restaurant operators, especially those that counted heavily on the expense account customer, seemed to go into panic. After all, who else could afford to pay the exorbitant prices they were charging?

More astute operators quietly went about their business, adjusted their menus, and provided other inducements. Most realized that few good business people would jeopardize a business relationship by not taking a customer to lunch to save a few dollars in tax benefits. Some, wisely, began to target other market segments that they had previously ignored.

Regulatory impacts are bound to be with us for a long time to come. There is no way that they can be successfully ignored. The marketer's task is to be aware of them, prepare for them, and develop a contingency plan before they occur.

It is clear that regulatory and legal environments of countries other than one's own will differ from each other, and often radically. These elements are intertwined with economic and cultural differences. Many times it is largely who you know and who you pay "extra to" that will determine when, or if, it will be done. It may take economic influence to get the political influence to get around the regulatory barriers. Sometimes, competitors know someone higher than you do. That's the culture! Problems of political and regulatory environments are not limited only to developing countries; they occur in almost all countries. All of these problems impact marketing strategies and tactics.

Despite perceived difficulties, companies from all countries with expanding economies will increasingly go abroad. Domestic markets get overbuilt and the need to continually expand the customer base and revenues leads in one direction—international.

Ecological Impacts

As consumers become more aware of the fragility of our natural environment, issues relating to ecol-ogy have risen to the forefront. In fact, one of the buzzwords of the travel industry is ecotourism. Belize, a small country nestled in between Mexico and Guatemala, is trying to create an image of an ecotourist paradise. With many unspoiled natural resources, ranging from tropical mountains to the second largest barrier reef in the world, Belize is approaching tourism with caution and has positioned itself to attract the growing number of environmentally conscious travelers.

Among environmental concerns, waste disposal, recycling, and pollution are all attracting attention not only from customers but from regulators as well. Cruise ships are no longer allowed to dump their wastes into the sea, and some even have biodegradable golf balls so that their customers can practice from an on-board driving range without polluting the sea! McDonald's Corporation, which was committed to the use of Styrofoam containers, realized that customers' attitudes had changed and switched to paper wrappers. Golf courses are looking for new strains of grass to minimize the use of pesticides, and hotels are slowly moving toward recycling of solid wastes, not to mention asking you to reuse your towel. In Germany, ecological concerns of citizens are so strong that McDonald's totally revised its waste handling. This was as much a marketing move as anything else. Increasingly, the hospitality industry is expected by the public to incorporate ecological concerns into their decision making. Some have already started and even found it profitable.

It is interesting that so much of the progress in ecological management in hotels and restaurants has been made outside the United States. Steigenberger Hotels of Germany now places unwrapped soap in guest rooms and saves 50 percent. When it changed from portion packs for butter and jams it estimated the saving at 40 percent. The Crowne Plaza in Wiesbaden uses low energy light bulbs and a central switch to make it easy to turn them all off. The Thai Wah Group of Thailand won the International Hotel Association Environmental Award for converting an abandoned denuded former tin mining area into the luxurious Laguna Beach resort on Phukat Island with a total commitment to the physical, cultural, and social environment. Wood was not used as a structural material in the hotel. All organic waste is composted. Treated sewage is cycled into a chemically treated system and recycled into the gardens. Figure 5-9 shows how Canadian Pacific Hotels is dealing with ecological concerns.

So far, we have discussed the different components of the environment and how they affect the hospitality industry. However, it must be noted that these components are dynamic and often tied to each other. Table 5-7 shows the *major* events driving change over a recent ten-year period as determined by Olsen and his colleagues in their study for the International Hotel Association.[10] One can see how these events interact with each other. The major task of environmental scanning is not only to

identify those elements that will affect the firm but also to assess the nature of the effect. A favorable effect is an opportunity, while an unfavorable effect is often a threat. Figure 5-10[11] is a model demonstrating the flow of environmental scanning information to the development of strategy and marketing planning. The steps are explained in Table 5-8.

OPPORTUNITIES AND THREATS

Opportunities occur when environmental trends create the potential of achieving competitive advantage. But let us begin with a basic premise that never hurts repeating: Finding marketing opportunities means finding customers, creating customers, and

Our program ...

In 1990, Canadian Pacific Hotels & Resorts undertook the development of a green program for our hotels in Canada. Our aim was to institute the highest possible standards of environmental responsibility throughout the chain.

Environmental Committees were formed at every one of our properties to lead the green program in-house. An Environmental audit was conducted in all our hotels in Canada, looking for areas where we could introduce more nature-friendly products and practices.

We asked professional environmental consultants for ideas on "going green." And most importantly, we asked our 10,000 employees in Canada how they felt about introducing a green program. Our employees gave us an overwelming vote of support as well as lots of great ideas on where to start greening our hotels....

Exciting results...

- Each year the Royal York collects over 496,000 bottles.
- We also collected and recycled over 24,000 aluminum cans!
- Last year, over 224,000 pounds of paper were recycled - a savings of 2,128 trees!
- ✓ Organic waste from the kitchen has been cut by approximately 2,000 pounds per day through the use of a Hobart Press waste disposal system!
- ✓ A $25,000 program of replacing leaky steam traps and fixing leaks brought stream consumption levels down from 160 million to 130 million pounds per year, with corresponding energy production savings.

Other achievements...

- Extensive recycling program for aluminum, metal, glass, cardboard, newsprint, paper and plastic have resulted in the reduction of over 1 million pounds of waste annually.

- Our discard bedding, linens, hand soap and unused portions of hotel amenities are distributed to a variety of local relief agencies and Third World Countries.
- Guest laundry bags on Business Class floors are made from discarded bedding, thereby eliminating quanties of plastic bags.
- Unused portions of facial and toiletry tissue are placed in staff locker rooms.
- Blue boxes are in all guest rooms to encourage hotel guests to participate in the hotel's recycling program.
- ✓ Conversion to more energy effecient light bulbs throughout the hotel is in progress.
- Installation of a freon management system recaptures old freon gas when chillers are being repaired.
- Our kitchens supply local organizations such as Second harvest with leftover baked goods and hot food.
- Our food and beverage outlets are phasing in recycled paper with environmentally friendly coatings on all menus.
- All office stationery and paper suppies are being converted to products that are made from 100% recycled paper with a high post-consumer content.
- ✓ Elimination of all aerosols within the hotel.

The Royal York is "Toronto's most advanced hotel" on the environmental front.
- Meeting & Incentive Magazine, Spring 92

Toronto Region of Canadian Pacific Hotels and Resorts are winners of the 1992 Lieutenant Governor's Conservation Award.

What some of our sister hotels have been doing....

CHATEAU WHISTLER
Commercial pesticides on its rose bushes have been replaced by lady bugs, which are equally effective in controlling aphids and similar pests. They also have a reforestation program whereby Christmas trees used in the hotel over the holiday season are kept in pots, and are replanted locally in the summer.

LE CHATEAU MONTEBELLO
Two particularly interesting projects undertaken at this hotel are the construction of a compost site to fertilize the hotel's own herb garden and natural fish fertilizer being used on the golf course!

LE CHATEAU FRONTENAC
Every month, two metric tons of cardboard are sold to a local recycler for $60 per ton. Proceeds from this sale help a local charity, Reves d'enfants (Children's Wish) which raises money for terminally ill children.

HOTEL NEWFOUNDLAND
Without the support of recycling programs which exist in other areas of Canada, ingenuity was the key here. They now work with a local wine supply store. The hotel sends its glass and plastic bottles (over 70 cases per month) to the store, which in turn recycles them to their customers who make home-made wine!

HOTEL VANCOUVER
One of the hotel's most successful environmental moves took place in the hotel laundry. The engineering department installed 82 steam guards in the laundry, and in just 3 weeks, saved 1.25 million pounds of steam.

SKYDOME HOTEL
The hotel was the first hotel in the chain to start a blue box program, a program which helped inspire Canadian Pacific Hotels & Resorts to make this a chain-wide project.

BANFF SPRINGS HOTEL
All non-refundable cans are being collected both within the hotel and in staff accommodations, and shredded in the hotel's new Rabco recycling machine. Every month over 1,000 pounds of cans are recovered in this way, and sent to a recycling plant in Calgary.

L'HÔTEL
The most striking example of L'Hôtel's environmental program success is in the area of energy conservation. With the involvement of Ontario Hydro, L'Hôtel switched its 40-W fluorescent tubes to 34-W tubes, an investment of $10,000 which paid off swiftly: the first energy year saving was over $25,000, and to top it off, L'Hôtel qualified for an Ontario Hydro conservation rebate of $1,900!

F I G U R E 5 - 9   CP Hotels deal with guests' ecological concerns.

TABLE 5-7

Major Events That Drove Recent Change in the International Hotel Industry[12]

- The ideological shift to free market economies
- The drop of the U.S. dollar from historic highs (note the reverse situation in 1998)
- A global recession
- The Gulf war
- Corporate downsizing and cost containment
- Increase in buying power by consumer and corporate groups
- Increased interest by the capital market community in hotels
- An increasingly price/value–oriented consumer
- Lifestyle changes, two-income households, and short break vacations
- Growing disposable income in parts of the developing world
- The information age and technology advancement
- Tax reform in the United States
- Crash in the global real estate market
- Lower valuation of hotel assets

keeping customers. By contrast, many financial opportunities begin with the "chance to make a lot of money." Many defunct multimillion dollar projects (such as mega resorts in Hawaii) have been based on that premise, and many supposedly great ideas have failed for lack of customers. Here we are concerned with customer opportunities.

Ray Kroc's original concept remains a classic case of seized market opportunity, as we saw in Chapter 1. Kroc saw sociocultural changes of families who moved to the suburbs, with discretionary income and children, having a real hassle in finding a place to eat that was quick, clean, and dependable. Howard Johnson (the founder) saw an opportunity in nationwide consistent restaurants; Kemmons Wilson saw the same thing with motels for Holiday Inns. More currently, developers of suite hotel and budget motel chains saw opportunities in changing needs in the lodging market. Total conference center hotels were an opportunity

that grew out of companies' dissatisfaction with what they were being offered at standard hotels. Domino's saw an opportunity in home-delivered pizza, McDonald's in their product on airlines and in volume discount stores, Whattaburger in gourmet hamburgers, PepsiCo in Mexican food (Taco Bell), Boston Market in upscale takeout, and hotels in fitness and business centers. All of these opportunities occurred because of environmental changes and where there was a consumer problem.

New markets come from only three places: They are *stolen* from the competition, they are *created*, or they are ***cannibalized***, that is, we take them from ourselves. If they are to come from the competition, we have to do something better than the competition, or we have to do something the competition isn't doing at all. If new markets are to be created, we have to find a undeveloped need that either isn't recognized or isn't being fulfilled. An example of creating a new market is McDonald's introduction of breakfast, which turned out to fill a real need that no one was really sure was there. In most of these cases, however, of the stolen customer or the created customer, the window of opportunity closes very quickly.

Stolen customers must be convinced to make the change—that is, they must get everything they were promised, or they will not stay stolen. This makes the task of stealing customers all the more difficult. Furthermore, competition will act quickly to get them back. Created customers, on the other hand, will soon be offered an abundance of similar products and/or services, sometimes at lower prices, by others. The answer to this problem is to be continuously seeking new opportunities, since successes can often be short term.

In cannibalizing we steal from ourselves. We get customers to buy something instead of what they were previously buying. When Marriott developed its Courtyard by Marriott concept (an opportunity well filled), a major concern was that these hotels might draw away too many regular Marriott customers from higher-priced properties. Today, Marriott Hotels and Courtyards, Quality Inns and Comfort Inns, Sofitels and Novotels, and other segmented brands of the same company, sit side by side

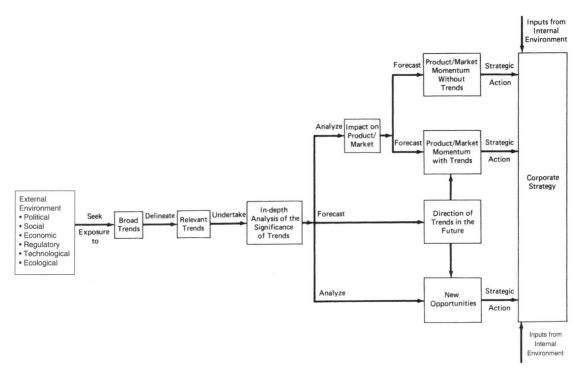

FIGURE 5 - 1 0   Linking environmental scanning to marketing.[13]

in many locations. The answer here, usually, is that it is better to steal from yourself than to let someone else steal from you, but don't rob Peter to pay Paul. New dining concepts in a hotel, for example, sometimes decimate the old ones with no net gain or loss, except for the expense of opening the new space.

Another way to look at opportunity is through consumer demand. **Existing demand** is demand for a good or service that is available from one or more sources. **Latent demand** is demand where there is a need but no suitable product available to satisfy it. **Incipient demand** is demand for which even the customer may not yet recognize the need as it is just beginning to exist or appear. There are opportunities at all three levels of demand but especially the latter two.

Trends indicate that there will be opportunities for international hospitality marketers but that these opportunities will not come without risks and challenges. Nevertheless, most marketing decisions

relevant to marketing principles remain the same in whatever country one does business. It is the environment in which these decisions are made that remains unique, determines the outcome, and makes international marketing different from marketing in one's home country. In short, scanning the environment means looking for new opportunities.

Marketing Threats

Scanning the environment also means looking for new threats. Threats are the other side of opportunities. They occur when environmental trends endanger the competitive advantage of a firm. Often one needs only to look at the other side of the coin. For example, computers are an opportunity. If not seized, they become a threat when a competitor adopts the new technology. Competition is only one threat in the environment, but a powerful one. Competitive threats mean that the enemy did, or

T A B L E 5-8
The Steps of Environmental Scanning

Figure 5-9 demonstrates the flow of environmental scanning information to the development of strategy and marketing planning. The steps are discussed below.

Watch for Broad Trends   Examples of this are the American change in social mores regarding drinking, smoking, later marriages, two-income families, increased travel, diet consciousness, "grazing" eating habits and those items shown in Table 5-6. Even locally, there may be broad trends occurring. For example, as more and more New Yorkers bought second homes in Vermont, the demand for better restaurants there increased dramatically. In Europe and Asia more vacation time and discretionary income are examples.

Determine Relevant Trends   Not everything that happens in the environment is relevant, nor can an organization adapt to everything that is relevant. The problem is determining what is relevant and what is irrelevant. Certainly, there are no hard and fast rules. Creativity, imagination, and farsightedness play an important role in this process. Some people are better at this than others and these people should be singled out. Another method is to circulate a short memo to key people (these could very well include line employees who are close to the action) and ask for reactions.

Analyze the Impact   Assuming relevance, what is the possible impact of the change, both sooner and later? Analyze it in terms of product, price, target market, competition, cost, employee attitude, and other variables that could be affected. Does it present a threat or an opportunity? If it is a threat, can it be turned into an opportunity? Again, get reactions from key people and from line employees where appropriate. At the same time, beware of those who automatically resist change and will try to minimize any impact. Two examples of very noticeable trends that were virtually ignored for years by many hoteliers were the increase of single women travelers, and the price sensitivity to increasing rack rates. Substantial competitive advantage was gained by those who acted early on these trends; such as those who moved into the middle tier market.

Forecast Direction   This is a difficult stage. One method is to use people to develop scenarios. For example, when the forthcoming increase in women travelers became apparent companies might have brought together groups of its women employees to do this. While that does not constitute scientific research, it is a start. The general manager or marketing director of an individual hotel could do the same, and so too could the manager of a restaurant. Another method is to use an outside consultant unconstrained by past experiences and personal biases.

Intuitive reasoning by one person alone should not be used. That person's view may be too narrow—for example, one might see the marketing impact but not the financial implications, or vice versa. Alternatively, one's impact may be clouded by one's own set of values, beliefs, experiences, likes, and dislikes. Playing off opposites may not lead to consensus, but it can certainly help in getting all viewpoints. This helps particularly when management may perceive a trend but can't conceive of its relationship or impact. Serious research is another way to develop forecasting accuracy.

Assess Opportunity   As with the 1986 tax act, the banning of happy hours, the raising of drinking ages, and the banning of smoking, it is too easy to look at the bad side of things. Look too for the opportunities. Remember that "necessity is the mother of invention."

Relate the Outcome   Relate the outcome of the above five steps to the marketing strategy or marketing plan, now, next year, and five years from now. Are changes needed? If so, what are the full implications?

Environmental scanning is too important to any organization to be approached haphazardly. A systematic method is needed to fully utilize this critical marketing tool.

---

will, get there first or will soon follow. We hope to be able to react quickly enough to turn a threat into an opportunity, but this may not be possible; we may just be too late.

Michael Porter has delineated the competitive threats in the environment into a framework of five forces that shape competition within an industry.[14] Porter argues that a company's ability to raise prices and achieve greater profits is limited by the strength of these forces; a strong force is a threat, a weak force is an opportunity. Thus a strategy should recognize each when they occur or change, and formulate appropriate responses to the company's advantage. Porter's five forces are diagramed in Figure 5-11 and explained in Table 5-9.

The macroenvironment, as we have previously discussed, impacts of course on all five of these forces in many ways, as Figure 5-11 shows. As well, there are many forms of threats and opportunities in each force beyond those we have discussed in this short space. From a strategic marketing perspective, what we must do is constantly analyze each force in view of the changing environment. Failing to do so can leave a company "caught with its pants down,"

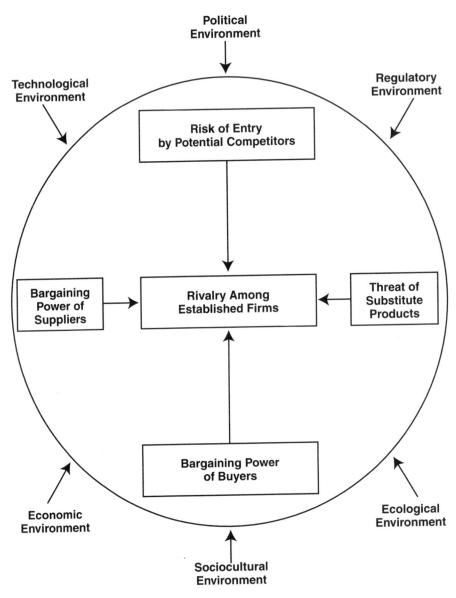

FIGURE 5-11 Porter's five forces model.

TABLE 5-9
Porter's Five Forces

---

1. *Rivalry among established firms* is the central and first force, and is largely a function of three factors—*industry competitive structure* (fragmented vs. consolidated), *demand conditions* (declining vs. increasing), and *exit barriers* (how easy is it to get out). A fragmented industry is a threat, because others can more easily enter. A consolidated one may be an opportunity for those already in the industry, such as Marriott, but may also be a threat because the action of one company threatens the market share of its rivals. This can lead to price wars; thus a company must compete on other features. Declining demand is a threat, increasing demand an opportunity—growing demand gives a company an opportunity to expand; declining demand increases rivalry intensity for market share. Exit barriers are a threat when there is no other use for the facilities. In hospitality, however, it seems that there is always another use, be it as condominiums or a new restaurant brand or, in Hong Kong, a new office building.

     Rivalry among established firms is impinged on every side by four other forces.

2. *Risk of entry by potential competitors* who are not already in the industry. There are three main barriers to entry—*brand loyalty, absolute cost advantages,* and *economies of scale.* Thus entering the fast-food industry on a national or international scale against McDonald's and Burger King would have serious barriers to entry in the United States, but perhaps not in some other countries such as Australia. In the hotel industry, the situation might seem the same but we have seen various new entries in recent years, particularly in the budget area by companies like Microtel. Microtel, in one short year, 1997–1998, was able to establish a strong foothold because of lack of loyalty to budget brands and new cost advantages, and is a real threat to its competition. In the late 1990s we also saw REIT companies like Starwood and Patriot American find strong opportunities in the middle and upscale hotel categories by acquiring brand names and having a distinctive cost advantage because of their tax status.

3. *The bargaining power of buyers* is a threat when buyers can force prices down, demand higher quality or better service, or when there are numerous other choices or substitute products and switching costs are low, which is generally the case with hotels and restaurants. This often happens in a weak economy such as the early 1990s when fliers forced airlines to make concessions just to fill their planes. In the late 1990s, however, a strong economy was seen as an opportunity by the airlines, even when oil prices fell, as they delivered poorer service and charged more and more, probably for most fliers destroying any true loyalty left among their customers. Thus the real opportunity in this time might have been to treat their customers better and *develop* loyalty. The only airline that seemed to realize that was Southwest.

4. *The bargaining power of suppliers* is a threat when they are able to force up the prices a company must pay for its supplies, or reduce the quality. Weak suppliers, such as the oil companies experiencing a glut in world oil supplies, provide the airlines an opportunity to force down prices.

5. *The threat of substitute products* is the fifth force that can threaten an industry. Grocery stores take-out meals, both fresh and frozen, and convenience stores with ready-to-go meal products are threats to the restaurant industry. Recreation vehicles (RVs), camping, time-share condominiums, and staying with friends are threats to the hotel industry. Buses, trains, and cars are threats to the airline industry on short distances. Herb Kelleher, who founded Southwest Airlines, however, saw this as an opportunity. By departing from city center airports and charging low no-frills fares, Southwest actively competes for both time and money against alternative means of transportation.

---

something that happened to many companies we have already mentioned in previous chapters.

Globalization

Today, we must be aware of the globalization of markets, in which we are moving away from the notion of national markets isolated from other national markets. This is probably more true in the hospitality industry than in most others. Simply put, people worldwide eat, sleep, and fly on airplanes. Cultural differences in these basic needs are not all that different, at least as far as the basic products are concerned. At the same time, global communications and technology are helping to create a worldwide culture. Thus hospitality industry boundaries do not stop at national borders. Foreign competitors, as we have already shown a number of times, have increased the impact of the macroenvironment and Porter's five forces in every respect, opening up both threats and opportunities of a new kind. Thus our strategic choices today must be international in scope and to ignore this is to do so at one's peril.

Whistler, British Columbia, for example, is probably one of the greatest ski and golf course areas in North America. It can compete against Vail, CO, or Mount Snow, VT, and thus, for example, worry about discretionary income in the United States and Canada. A major part of its market, however, comes from Japan, an economy which in the late 1990s was down, while the North American one is up. Can Whistler, thus, concentrate its marketing strategies on the North American market? If it does, what will happen when the Japanese market is booming again in 2002? Similar scenarios can be found worldwide in the entire hospitality business. When conference rates are too high in Paris, more conferences will go to Frankfurt, or Bangkok, or Buenos Aires. Almost no hospitality enterprise today, with the possible exception of Joe's Hot Dog Stand, can afford not to think globally—if your business isn't located there, there's a good chance that many of your customers are! (That is why there are world maps in the back of this book—know your world!)

THE FUTURE

Michael D. Olsen and Ewout Cassee conducted exhaustive research and held worldwide "think tanks" with hospitality industry people on "visioning the future" (another phrase for environmental scanning), for the International Hotel Association. As a conclusion of that work, they identified a number of future perspectives, at least for the start of the next millennium. As these should be of great interest to future hoteliers, these findings are presented here in Tables 5-10 through 5-13.

Now that we understand what environmental opportunities and threats are, in the next chapter we can go about understanding competition in order to find opportunities and diminish threats.

SUMMARY

Today's complex and dynamic marketing environment requires hospitality firms to constantly look out for new and evolving opportunities and threats. Environmental scanning has become increasingly relevant for all businesses in this fast-moving and fast-changing world. Without it, a company is relegated to being able only to react to what happens in the environment. The basis of hospitality marketing, which was presented in the first part of this book, and the application of hospitality marketing, which will be presented in the remainder of the book, lie in what is happening in the environment.

Environmental scanning looks at the big picture, the broad view, and the long range. Marketing

---

T A B L E 5-10
The Five Events Shaping the Future of the Lodging Industry[15]

- Capacity control (control is falling into the hands of those who own and manage global reservations systems and/or negotiate for large buying groups)
- Safety and security (increasing confrontation with potential risks to personal safety and health from both a macro- and microperspective)
- Assets and capital (hyper-competition for whatever capital is available)
- Technology (navigating this emerging medium in order to successfully market and manage products and services)
- New management (a new definition of what it takes to succeed in the increasingly complex and volatile world of the hospitality professional—see Table 5-11)

TABLE 5-11
New Management and Major Competencies[16]

- Handling the speed of change (ability to adapt)
- Boundary spanner (capable of balancing time between internal operations and the scanning of the external environment in order to incorporate important trends into daily operating decisions)
- Behaviorally driven (learning how to obtain, motivate, and develop human resources that are becoming increasingly scarce, diverse, and expensive)
- Blending functional skills (greater knowledge of each functional area and more diligence in monitoring changes)
- Thinking skills (enhance thinking skills to synthesize large amounts of information from diverse sources)
- Respect for cultural tradition (both employees and customers will require better understanding of diversity)
- Technology astute (see Appendix B)
- Managing by competitive methods (see Chapter 6)
- A strategist (see Chapter 4)
- Service mentality (see Chapters 2 and 3)
- Communication skills in a new era (that acknowledge cultural diversity)
- Craft versus business manager (combining these to create effective competitive methods for survival in an environment where both customer and competitor are demanding more—balancing craft skills necessary to deliver outstanding service with the conceptual skills that assure a strong strategic position in the competitive marketplace)

TABLE 5-12
The Hotel of the Future[17]

- Communication center
- Employee/management relationships will demand a respect for differences
- Rational user of scarce resources
- Compete primarily using the "purpose of visit" formula
- An extremely secure and healthful haven
- Pricing activities will be driven less by inflation and more by broad-based demand/supply conditions reflecting the capacity control environment
- Technology dependent, focusing upon the time, information and convenience needs of the traveler
- Personal encounters with the guest will be highly customized with high performance expectations
- Less human resource dependent with higher skill level expectations per employee
- The hotel cost structure will be less labor intensive but with a higher cost per unit of input

TABLE 5-13
Tomorrow's Hotel Manager[18]

- Direct to consumer marketing
- Discriminate and filter information inflow
- How to buy and sell your way into the information highway
- Evaluating and maintaining the best strategic alliances
- Recognize, interact with, and utilize the resources of those who will own the information systems of the information highway
- Capable of receiving, analyzing, and synthesizing incredible amounts of information regarding the guest, internal operations, and external data from capacity controllers
- Utilize information to adjust to the speed of change
- Monitor changes in an increasingly diverse/complex demand curve
- Provide information to guests to satisfy their needs for safety and security

builds on this by approaching it in an increasingly narrower perspective, resting ultimately on the individual consumer.

Environmental scanning, both in textbooks and the real world, has been largely constrained to the corporate level and to strategic planning. By definition, environmental scanning presents a macroview. We believe, however, that this macroview can be given a microperspective. In other words, we believe that every individual or unit operator, as well as corporate and higher-level management, must be conscious of and continuously analyzing the environment, and forecasting its impact upon each unit operation. The hospitality industry today is too broad-based, too diversified, and too much operated in multiple microenvironments to ignore this technique at any level.

Opportunities are the bedrock of marketing, the chink in the competitor's armor. They are the unsolved consumer problem or the unfulfilled consumer need and want. They come from the changing environment and changing customers. Marketing threats come from all sides and directions in the same changing environment. The obvious goal is to seize opportunity and overcome threats, some of which can be turned into opportunities.

This chapter has examined the changing environment and explored the opportunities available to alert marketers. Understanding these things, and the actors that make them work, requires constant analysis. Without this, and often good research to explain it, marketing is doomed to ignore opportunity and the property is doomed to the status of "also ran" when the final count is in.

KEY WORDS AND CONCEPTS

Baby Boomers: Those born from 1946 through 1964.

Cannabilizing: Stealing business from your own product line rather than the competitor's.

Consumerism: Efforts by consumers to establish their rights as buyers to obtain certain features from sellers.

Databases: Computerized information on customers that contain personal information so that they can be reached and served better.

DEWKS: Families with dual earnings with kids.

DINKS: Families with double income, no kids.

Environmental Scanning: Literally scanning the environment in search of future impacts. The "OT" part of SWOT analysis (opportunities and threats) that are created because of environmental change.

Environments: Forces that impact the hospitality industry:

Ecological: Natural environmental concerns such as product usage and waste disposal that concern customers and governments.

Economic: Recession, inflation, discretionary income, and currency exchange rates are just some of the more visible economic impacts that affect the hospitality industry.

Political: Government and anti-government movements and positions that affect consumers and businesses such as feminism, discrimination, funding, tourism support, uprisings, border crossings, truth in menu regulations, monetary policy, freedom of choice, and so on.

Regulatory: Government rulings at any level such as taxes and work practices that affect both a business' operations and/or consumers' behavior.

Sociocultural: Cultural values, customs, habits, trends, taste, demographic changes, and so on that affect consumer behavior.

Technological: Advances in technology from electronic door locks to computerization to informations systems that drive change and create marketing opportunities.

Existing Demand: Demand for a good or service that is already available.

Generation Xers: adults born since 1964.

Incipient Demand: Demand for which even the customer may not yet recognize the need.

Latent Demand: Demand where there is need but no suitable product to fill it.

Matures: Those born before 1946.

Opportunities: Marketing opportunities begin with finding unmet customer needs and serving customers in new and better ways in a changing environment.

Property Management Systems (PMS): Computerized systems in a property that make it more efficient to handle operations, reservations, and customer needs.

Threats: Threats include competition and environmental situations that can affect businesses negatively.

Yuppies: Young, urban professionals on the fast track—a class of the baby boomers.

DISCUSSION QUESTIONS

1. Consider a local restaurant or hotel. What environmental factors are impacting it in a macro sense? In a micro sense? Explain. How is it affected by the three types of consumer demand?
2. Consider some current fads in eating such as Planet Hollywood. How long will they last? Will they turn into trends? Why/why not? If you were a restaurateur, how would you capitalize on them? What environmental changes may impact them?
3. Political impacts on the hospitality business environment can be enormous. Discuss some present potential impacts in your country or area.
4. Discuss some of the actions taken by hotels and restaurants to keep up with the growing ecological movement.
5. Evaluate the arrival of the euro in Europe. Other than what is stated in the chapter discuss further ramifications, opportunities, and threats.
6. Analyze the use of modern and future technological advances. What is needed? How could it be used to benefit the customer?
7. Under what environmental conditions are price wars likely to occur in the hospitality industry? What are the implications of price wars for a company in the industry? How should a company try to deal with the threat of a price war?
8. Discuss Porter's five forces model with reference to what you know about the hotel industry. What does the model tell you about the level of competition in the industry?
9. How do you think the trend toward greater globalization is likely to be impacted by the five forces model?

GROUP PROJECTS

1. Using the model in Figure 5-10, develop a scenario for opening a new hotel or restaurant.
2. Consider a hotel or restaurant chain with which you are familiar, for example, Sheraton.

Delineate how it should develop marketing strategy for the next ten years to take advantage of the environment.

3. Assume your group is one of experienced hoteliers who have been made redundant by a major hotel chain that is undergoing financial restructuring. You are considering establishing a regional moderate-price hotel chain. You are due to make a presentation to a group of investors who have expressed an interest in funding the first four properties. Before they commit funds, the investors want you to undertake a thorough analysis of the nature of environmental forces in the market.
   a. Use Porter's five forces model to carry out this analysis.
   b. Perform a scan and analysis of the environmental forces.
   c. On the basis of these analyses, try to predict the opportunities and threats that you might encounter.
   d. Sketch out the basic strategy that you would pursue in order to compete in the market.
   e. On the basis of the above, if you were one of the investors would you fund this venture?

REFERENCES

1. Michael D. Olsen and Ewout Cassee, "The International Hotel Industry in the New Millennium: Visioning the Future," In *Into the New Millennium, A White Paper on the Global Hospitality Industry.* Paris: International Hotel Association, 1997, pp. 58–60.
2. Subhash C. Jain, *Marketing Planning and Strategy,* 5th ed. Cincinnati: South-Western Publishing Co., 1997, p. 134.
3. Abstracted from *The YP&B Yankelovich Partners 1998 National Travel Leisure Monitor*[SM], pp. 3–12. Copyright Yesawich, Pepperdine & Brown and Yankelovich Partners Inc., 1998. All rights reserved. Used by permission.
4. Courtesy of Yesawich, Pepperdine & Brown, Orlando.
5. Paul L. Westra and L. Kepler Sweeney, *The Right Moves in the Wrong Environment,* New York: Salomon Brothers, November 20, 1996, p. 5.
6. YP&B Yankelovich Partners, *op. cit.,* pp. 19–21, 30, 33.

7. *Ibid.*, p. 62.

8. Presentation at World Hospitality Congress III, March 9, 1987, Boston.

9. John Helyar, "The Holiday Inns Trip: A Breeze for Decades, Bumpy Ride in the '80s," *The Wall Street Journal,* February 19, 1987, pp. 1, 23.

10. Michael D. Olsen, Jin Lin Zhao, Wanae Cho, Eliza Tse, "Hotel Industry Performance and Competitive Methods: A Decade in Review: 1985–1994." In *Into the New Millennium, A White Paper on the Global Hospitality Industry.* Paris: International Hotel Association, 1997, p. 30.

11. Jain, *op. cit.*, p. 141

12. Olsen et al., *op. cit.*

13. Jain, *op. cit.*

14. Michael E. Porter, "How Competitive Forces Shape Strategy," *Harvard Business Review,* March–April 1979. Copyrighted 1979 by the President and Fellows of Harvard College; all rights reserved.

15. Olsen and Cassee, *op. cit.*, pp. 53–60.

16. *Ibid.*, pp. 60–61.

17. *Ibid.*, p. 63.

18. *Ibid.*, p. 67.

Six

◆

UNDERSTANDING COMPETITION

Overview

This chapter takes a closer look at the competition, the different types, how to defend against it, how to determine it, compare it, and measure it.

MACROCOMPETITION This is the broad-based industry competition or, in fact, any one competing for the same consumer's dollar.

MICROCOMPETITION We use this term to describe any business competing for the same customer in the same product class at the same point in time.

CHOOSING THE RIGHT COMPETITION Businesses need to know and choose whom they compete against, not leave it to chance or pick the wrong competition.

COMPETITIVE INTENSITY This is the intensity with which competing companies do battle with each other.

COMPETITIVE INTELLIGENCE Management should know everything possible about competi-

tors in their attempt to help their firm gain sustainable competitive advantage.

COMPETITIVE ANALYSIS Competitive intelligence needs to be carefully analyzed to determine its impact on the firm as well as how the firm can use it to advantage.

COMPETITIVE MARKETING Porter's three generic strategies for beating the competition are strategic starting points for developing competitive weapons.

FINDING MARKETING OPPORTUNITIES The search for unfilled or unsatisfied consumer problems is the search for marketing opportunity.

COMPETITIVE ADVANTAGE A firm gains a competitive advantage when it can beat something better than the competition can do.

MARKET FEASIBILITY STUDIES These involve analyzing projects to see if they are feasible in customer and financial terms.

◆◆

In marketing, opportunity and understanding competition go hand in hand. This is so because opportunity means being where the competition isn't, or being where the competition is weak, or being there first. Someone once said that marketing opportunity is "the niche that cries out to be filled." That statement may be a little melodramatic but it does make the point. The only problem is that most opportunities don't cry out; in fact, they can be very well hidden. Perhaps it would be better to say "the niche that cries out to be found."

In marketing, competition is the enemy. To outmaneuver the enemy we have to know its strengths and weaknesses, what it does and doesn't do well, who its customers are, why they go there, and what they do when they get there. We would also like to know something about customer loyalty, dissatisfaction, what needs and wants are not being fulfilled, and what problems customers are having. This calls for a great deal of marketing intelligence.

Competitive analysis is not limited to investigating bricks and mortar, number and size of meeting rooms, decor, what grade beef is bought, what size drink is poured, or what prices are charged. That would amount to a product orientation, and we don't want to be any more product-oriented in analyzing the competition than we do in analyzing ourselves. Of course, if the competition itself is product-oriented, we should know that as well. It may be our marketing opportunity.

If, on the other hand, the competition is marketing-oriented, how marketing-oriented are they? Are they creative, do they adapt quickly, will they accept short-term losses for long-term gains, do they worry about the customer, and how soon will they copy or react to what we do (or, how short-lived will any advantage we gain be)? In other words, we have to get to know the competition. Of course, we have to know something about their facilities, product, services, and resources, but here's a basic truism that is often ignored: The competition is not simply other hotels and restaurants; it is the people who manage and operate those hotels and restaurants, the strategies they employ, and the tactics with which they carry them out. Understanding the competition means understanding these people. As Subhash C. Jain states:

> Some firms fail to identify the true sources of competition; others underestimate the capabilities and reactions of their competitors. In the current [business] environment, business strategies must be competitively oriented.[1]

Consider, for example, the Japanese auto industry. When Toyota wanted to learn what Americans preferred in a small, imported car, it didn't ask the people who owned Chevrolets and Pontiacs as General Motors did; it asked the owners of Volkswagens what they liked or disliked about the Beetle. They looked for the "niche crying out to be found!" They identified the true competition and then addressed consumers' problems.

Any organization is a creature of its environment. Scanning the environment is an organization's method of improving its ability to deal with a rapidly changing world. Understanding competition is a vital part of that analysis. First, however, we have to know who the competition is. It is too easy to identify the wrong competition or to fail to identify the right competition. Because it is so easy, misidentity often occurs. Second, we have to decide what information is important, and we have to obtain it. Third, we have to understand competitors' future moves and reactions. Finally, we need to determine what we can do to gain competitive advantage, now and in the future.

MACROCOMPETITION

How do we define competition? There are actually two broad forms of competition, macro, or industry competition, and micro, or product class competition. We discuss the macro here and the micro later.

In a macro sense, competition is anyone competing for the same consumer's dollar. This means that any restaurant represents competition to any other restaurant, at least in the same area, and any hotel is competition with any other hotel. We can carry it even further: We can say that any supermarket is competition to any restaurant, or that a new car is competition to a two-week cruise, even though it is satisfying a different need and solving different problems.

Several changes take place in the competitive environment as an industry reaches the maturity stage of its life cycle. Some that have particularly impacted the hospitality industry are the following:

- Competition for **market share** has become more intense as firms are forced to achieve sales growth at one another's expense.
- Firms are selling increasingly to experienced, repeat buyers who are making choices from known alternatives.
- Competition has become more oriented to cost and service as knowledgeable buyers expect similar price and product and service features.
- New products and services and new applications are harder to come by.
- Branding has become a more powerful force in consumer selection.
- Fragmented industries start to consolidate, creating bigger and more powerful competition.
- Substitute products become more prevalent.

Tablecloth restaurant operators are threatened by the competition they are getting from supermarkets (especially prepared dinners), take-out services, catering services, and casual dining. Hotel and motel operators are threatened by the competition they are getting from campers, recreational vehicles, and the hospitality of friends and relatives. Condominiums that couldn't be sold have been marshaled to accommodate transient guests at resorts, leaving some hotel rooms empty. One thing about services is that one can often readily substitute for another, maybe even at a much lower price. The above examples are environmental changes that are taking place, in which the macro competition is moving in to fulfill a need.

Why are these other businesses competition? Because they are satisfying the same needs and solving the same problems, albeit in a different way. The customer wants it more cheaply, quickly, easily, or conveniently, with less hassle. The hospitality industry is not, of course, totally oblivious to this. McDonald's, Burger King, Wendy's, Boston Market, and others have gone back to drive-up windows. Many tablecloth restaurants, especially in hotels, have gone into catering and/or casual dining. Marriott, Choice International, and Groupe Accor of France have bought or built in every tier of the hotel industry. All-suite and luxury budget hotels have become commonplace. All these started out as opportunities in a changing environment. Someone saw an opportunity—a niche, if you will—in the marketplace left void by the competition as the environment changed.

Environmental changes should not be confused with fads, although there is no reason not to make an opportunity out of a fad. Fads tend to be short lived, whereas environmental changes are major shifts in the environment and society. The point at which a fad ends and a shift or trend begins can be problematic; marketing can take advantage of either. The risk lies in making substantial investment in what turns out to be a fad. A food item may be a fad, but this should not inhibit the opportunity to make a few menu changes that can easily be reversed. On the other hand, fantasy mega-resorts in Hawaii, with multimillion dollar investments, turned out to have been fads and many have been sold for less than half the cost of building them. Planet Hollywood and its ilk, **eatertainment** restaurants with poor food, may turn out to be the next fad that didn't survive.

MICROCOMPETITION

At the microcompetition level, we define competition as any business that is competing for the same customers in the same product class at the same point in time—in other words, a business that is a direct competitor with a similar product in a similar context. By this definition, the gourmet restaurant does not compete with fast-food restaurants, and upscale hotels do not compete with budget motels.

Caution is necessary to avoid overgeneralizing these contrasts. As mentioned above, an alternative in a different product class can become a competitor if the one product class is not fulfilling the customer's need. In other words, we would not normally think that a three-star hotel would be a direct competitor of a four-star hotel. The situation changes, however, if the four-star hotel prices itself too high and consumers turn to lower-priced alternatives. The situation is reversed in markets where upscale hotels with full services offer rates almost as low as limited service properties. Perhaps the toughest part of competitive analysis is recognizing the realities of it.

Conversely, for marketing planning at a given time, a greater failing may be to consider as competition properties that are actually in different product classes. This failing can lead to major strategic errors. If the operator of a French restaurant says his competition is the Red Lobster across the street, he is probably basing his statement on geographic proximity rather than product class or customer needs, wants, and demand. Let us analyze this point in some detail to be certain that it is clear.

The people who eat at the French restaurant may also eat at the Red Lobster—they may even eat there more often—but this does not make the two restaurants direct competitors. The reason is that customers are fulfilling different needs and wants at the two restaurants. Except in rare cases, one of these restaurants would not be an alternative to the other.

Suppose these are the only two restaurants within 100 miles. Does the situation change? If the Red Lobster disappeared, would patronage increase at the French restaurant? Probably very little. Those times that people would have gone to the Red Lobster, they may now be likely to stay home.

Suppose, however, that the Red Lobster is doing volume business and the French restaurant is doing zilch. Now does the situation change? Yes, but. . . . The but is not that the Red Lobster is the competition; it is that the French restaurant, assuming it is a good operation, has misjudged the market and is not catering to the needs and wants of the marketplace. These examples assume prices consistent with the product, but even at the same price level there would be some noncompetitive separation of needs and wants.

CHOOSING THE RIGHT COMPETITION

Choosing the right competition is very critical in competitive analysis because it has tremendous bearing on the marketing strategy and tactics of any hospitality operation. Choosing the "wrong" competition is an error that can be illustrated with a restaurant and two hotel examples.

In the first example, management of the only French restaurant in a small city was unhappy with the volume they were doing. They were at a loss to explain this, since they received very favorable customer comments. In fact, cursory research showed that they were overwhelmingly rated the best restaurant in the city in terms of food, service, and atmosphere. In final desperation, after scouting all the "competition," management decided to "do as the Romans do." They put in a prime rib buffet, added steaks and chops to the menu, and did various other things that other restaurants were doing. A little less than a year later business had fallen to the point where ownership sold out.

Two things contributed to this failure. First, the new menu had alienated the old clientele. Second, the restaurant had failed to attract a new clientele, as potential diners still perceived it as an expensive French restaurant. The failing was management's failure to recognize that their major competition was not in the same city; the competition was in adjoining cities where this restaurant lacked awareness. The appropriate strategy would have been to develop the strong niche they had and pull in customers from out of town who would have been willing to go a distance for that kind of food and service.

The second case is one of a 300-room resort hotel on Cape Cod, MA, in a remote seasonal, ocean-side location. In an attempt to build the off-season business, management did extensive refurbishing and remodeling so as to have expansive conference facilities. It was the only hotel in the area with the capacity and the facilities to draw groups of substantial size. In a market analysis two large cities 75 and 175 miles away, Boston and New York, were designated as the markets. The only lodging properties within 25 miles, a Holiday Inn, a Sheraton franchise, and three or four individual properties, were designated as the competition. Marketing efforts were aimed at competing with these properties. However, the effort to build off-season business failed, as did the hotel.

Once again, management failed to recognize that the customers who went to the "competition" were not the same ones or in the same market segment as the ones the property was trying to attract. The competition in this case was hundreds of miles away in similar properties that drew from diverse markets for conference and meetings business which, in the winter, largely went south or to nearby conference centers.

A third example occurred in a hotel in Bangkok. This hotel was located near the airport, by itself but off a very busy highway with limited exits and divided lanes going in each direction—in other words it was a considerable nuisance for hotel guests to go elsewhere to eat. Many of the guests, in fact, had no cars because they were airline crews or Asian people in transit to and from the airport. These guests were construed as a captive market. The hotel had a fine dining room with elegant service and an American-Continental menu featuring steak, lobster, shrimp, and so forth. Prime rib was rolled out

on a silver gueridon. The restaurant didn't open until 8:00 P.M. because that is the time that fashionable dining starts in Bangkok. On a good night, this restaurant did about a dozen covers. Meanwhile, the coffee shop was packed from 5:00 to 9:00 P.M. Management decided to cut the high prices and run special promotions in the main dining room to increase business. The effort failed. Why?

In the first place, airline crews are on a per diem food allowance (fixed amount per day) and rarely eat in restaurants of this kind. In the second place, guests at the hotel were largely Thai or at least Asian. These people rarely include these types of menu items in their eating-out choices, especially when in transit. Thus guests either ate in the coffee shop, in this case the competition, or "found" the real competition.

Managements that, in designing their property, concentrate on the concept rather than the customer and the competition have what we call **"conceptitis."** One former food and beverage vice-president of a hotel chain suffered greatly from conceptitis. He was noted for his public statements that he developed great hotel restaurants not just for hotel guests but for a clientele outside the hotel. This is a fine idea, provided the market is there, provided you are not at the same time losing all your hotel customers, and provided the concept fits the needs of the designated market that the competition is not filling. More than one "great" concept designed by this vice-president did poorly because these rules were violated. (After being fired he became a consultant!) The basis of this violation was twofold: conceptitis emphasizes the concept as opposed to either the customer or the competition.

With all the possible alternatives, then, how do we compete? Unfortunately, there is no simple answer to that question. The answer requires thorough analysis of any given situation. We can suggest, however, two launching points, after determining who is after the same customers in the same product class, at the same point in time.

First, deliberately choose whom you want to,

FIGURE 6-1 Stealing customers from the competition.

and can, compete against. Rarely do markets simply appear out of nowhere; most of the time you have to steal them, like Crowne Plaza tries to do in Figure 6-1. As Michael Porter has pointed out in his extensive writings on competition, choosing whom you want to compete against is one of the first decisions that has to be made in developing a product or business.[2]

Second, ask your customers where they would

be if they weren't at your property. Why? Or, if you're developing a new product, research the market. Where does your target market go now? Why? The answers to these questions will tell you, at least, who the market perceives as your competition. The answers will also tell you what you have to compete against in terms of attributes and services. If the answers from the market are different from the properties you have chosen to compete against, it is clear that your perception differs from the market's.* It may be necessary to rethink your competitive strategy.

We can illustrate these two points with further reference to hotel F&B outlets. Astute marketers will first determine who they want as customers and what their needs and wants are. (This includes in-house customers and the local market.) Then they will ask where these customers go now, or will go. Next, they will do a thorough analysis of this competition. Then they will go to the architect, the F&B director, and other involved parties and say, "This is what we need to do to keep/steal these customers." Then, and only then, should concept development begin because you have now chosen whom you will compete against. You have also determined the weapons you need to compete.

COMPETITIVE INTENSITY

The **competitive intensity** in a marketplace is the fierceness with which competing companies do battle with each other. It is an important measurement in competitive analysis because the level of intensity will often dictate the way a firm does business. In general, competitive intensity is very high in the hospitality industry. This can lead to less-than-wise decisions to gain competitive advantage. Jain puts it as follows:

The degree of competition in a market depends upon the moves and countermoves of the various firms active in the market. It usually starts with one firm trying to achieve a favorable position by pursuing appropriate strategies [or tactics]. Because what is good for one firm may be harmful to rival firms, however, rival firms respond with counter strategies [or tactics] to protect their own

interests. Intense competitive activity may or may not be injurious to the industry as a whole.[3]

Table 6-1 shows some factors contributing to competitive intensity in the hospitality industry.

Competitive intensity can be illustrated with what took place in the so-called hotel amenities wars, because it is a marketing truism that all opportunities are not necessarily competitive advantages.

The amenities wars started in the United States in the early 1980s with one hotel chain adopting the European custom of putting a mint on the pillow and turning the bed down. Other hotel chains followed suit, and the mints got better and more expensive. Then someone started with special soaps, soon followed by shampoos, body lotions, shoe horns, and so on, and then a choice of soaps, body lotions, shampoos, bubble baths, and so on. In some cases all this added well over $5.00 per occupied night to the cost of the room for the hotel.

No hotel company bothered to do research to determine what effect all these amenities really did have on the customer, or read the research others were doing.[4] At the same time, hotel guests were filling their suitcases with the amenities and stocking their home medicine cabinets. Finally, Michael Leven, then president of Holiday Inn, Americas Division, called a halt, "Bubble bath is not [in]. We are off Vidal Sassoon and into reality."[5] Today, the amenities wars are over with no winners except the manufacturers who made them.

The amenities wars story demonstrates some important things about competitive intensity. First, services that can be easily duplicated offer only short-term advantage, if that, when you have aggressive competitors. When those services are not perceived as a determinative advantage by consumers and instead end up costing them more for the core product, such services may in fact become a negative factor for the entire product class. At one point, Marriott quietly cut down their bathroom amenities package from a cost of five dollars to

---

*In a study we did in Boston, the Parker House management viewed its major competitor as the Ritz-Carlton. Very few of its customers, however, gave the Ritz-Carlton as an alternative; no Ritz-Carlton guests gave the Parker House as an alternative.

T A B L E   6-1
Factors Contributing to Competitive Intensity

Opportunity Potential: A promising market increases the number of firms interested in sharing the pie, thus increasing the rivalry.

Ease of Entry: When entry into an industry is relatively easy, the existing firms try to discourage potential entrants by adopting strategies that increase competition.

Nature of Product: When the products offered are perceived by the market as more or less similar, properties are forced into price and service competition, which can be quite severe in some locations.

Exit Barriers: High investments in assets for which there may not be a readily alternative use and top management's emotional attachment force companies into competitive methods in order to improve, or even survive.

Homogeneity of the Market: When segments of the market are more or less homogeneous, the competitive intensity is increased to gain market share.

Industry Structure: When the number of firms active in the market is large, one or more may aggressively seek an advantageous position, leading to intense competitive activity as other firms retaliate.

Commitment to the Industry: When a company has committed itself, it will do most anything to hang on without worrying about the impact on either the industry or its own resources.

Technological Innovations: In industries where these are frequent, each firm tries to cash in on the latest technology by quickly copying what other firms do, creating competitive activity.

Scale Economies: Attempts to gain scale economies may lead a firm to aggressively compete for market share, escalating pressure on other firms. Alternatively, when fixed costs are high, a firm tries to spread them over larger volume.

Economic Climate: When the economy is down and growth is slow, competition is much more volatile as each firm tries to make the best of a bad situation.

Diversity of Firms: New entries into an industry do not necessarily play by the rules of a kind of industry standard of behavior. Instead, they may have different strategic perspectives and be willing to go to any lengths to achieve their goals.

under one dollar, and suffered no ill effects. Figure 6-2 shows how another hotel company loudly countered the amenities war for its own competitive advantage.

Second, when introducing an additional service, you need to have an idea of how your competitors will react.

Third, competitive tactics should, as much as possible, be based on the needs of the customer, not on the competition's tactics, unless matching the competition is necessary for the firm's self-protection. This is essentially what happened in the amenities war, which was brought on by competitive intensity and ended up being overdone.

Does this mean that a hotel or restaurant should not try to gain competitive advantage by introducing services that are easily duplicated? No, it does not, or else there would never be growth or improvement. There is also something to be said for being there first. It does mean, however, that the intensity of the competition is a critical factor and should be carefully weighed before making the decision.

It also means going back to the customer first. Does a new service create or keep customers? If yes, at what cost to them and at what cost to the property? Does it increase the price/value relationship, or just price? If it is to be done, in what meaningful way can it be done—that is, do we know what the customer really wants? If the competition follows suit, do we retain an advantage or just an additional cost? The best competitive advantages are those that are **sustainable,** but these are few and far between in hospitality.

When the needs of the market are similar, the intensity of competition is much greater as many

Welcome basket filled with things you won't eat.

Free local calls.

What's really important to you is all that's important to us. That's how to run a hotel. For reservations at Quality Inn or Quality Suites, visit www.qualityinn.com or call 1-800-228-5151 or your travel agent.

Quality
Inns · Hotels · Suites

HOW TO RUN A HOTEL.™

A chocolate covered mint and a form letter from the manager.

A big desk and a place to plug in your computer.

What's really important to you is all that's important to us. That's how to run a hotel. For reservations at Quality Inn or Quality Suites, visit www.qualityinn.com or call 1-800-228-5151 or your travel agent.

Quality
Inns · Hotels · Suites

HOW TO RUN A HOTEL.™

A shoe horn and a polishing cloth in your room.

A coffee maker and coffee in your room.

Multi-cup coffee-maker, Maxwell House coffee. Sorry, nothing for your feet. What's really important to you is all that's important to us. That's how to run a hotel. For reservations at Quality Inn or Quality Suites, visit www.qualityinn.com or call 1-800-228-5151 or your travel agent.

Quality
Inns · Hotels · Suites

HOW TO RUN A HOTEL.™

The radio tuned to a station that will put you to sleep.

A Serta Sleeper mattress.

What's really important to you is all that's important to us. Like getting a great night's sleep on the Quality Sleeper by Serta. That's how to run a hotel. For reservations at Quality Inn or Quality Suites, visit www.qualityinn.com or call 1-800-228-5151 or your travel agent.

Quality
Inns · Hotels · Suites

HOW TO RUN A HOTEL.™

FIGURE 6-2 Quality counters the amenities wars.

entries in the market are competing for the same customer. See the example in Figure 6-3 (Hilton cried foul!). Some companies, in fact, may resort to misleading information (Figure 6-4) or even lawsuits (Figure 6-5). Small competitive advantages can become large ones if they can be sustained. On the other hand, it may be mandatory for one firm to copy another that is aggressively seeking an advantageous position, if it can do so, in order to eliminate the advantage. The hotel "business

FIGURE 6-3 Renaissance makes a play for Hilton customers.

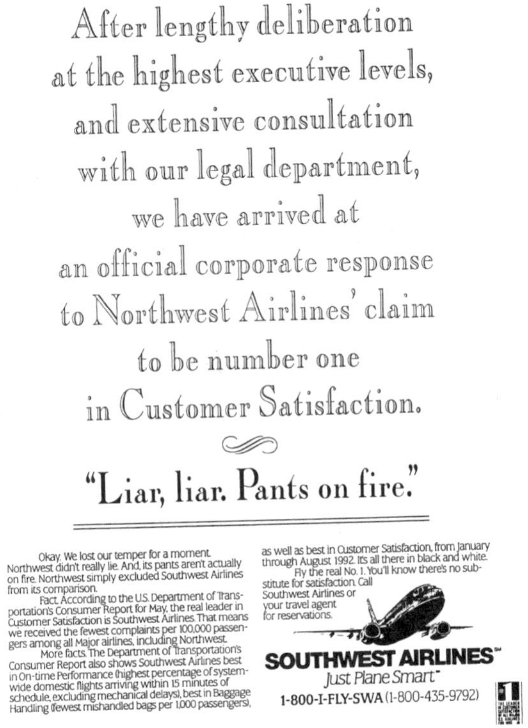

FIGURE 6-4 Northwest Airlines calculates to its own advantage, and Southwest responds.

room" (Figure 6-6), for example, has been copied by many so the advantage has not been sustainable by whoever did it first. It has, however, filled a need, solved problems, added value for the customer, and today is an essential part of the product offering for many hotels.

Michael Olsen and his colleagues' extensive international research uncovered major hotel industry competitive innovations over the past few years. Their findings are shown in Table 6-2. All were quickly copied by competitors. Some have added value, some have not. In other words, some were successful and some were not in gaining and keeping customers.

COMPETITIVE INTELLIGENCE

In business, as in war, one always wants to know what the enemy is doing, their position and inten-

tions, strengths and weaknesses, where they are most vulnerable and least vulnerable, and where the best place is to attack. There are a number of ways to get this information, and it is well worth getting. It goes beyond physical property descriptions. The movie **Godfather II** taught us one thing about this: Be close to your friends, but closer to your enemies.

First, there is public information. The media (especially the World Wide Web today), annual reports if a publicly held company, company brochures, flyers and ads, publicity releases, and so forth are some sources. Then there is trade gossip—information from vendors and others who deal with the competition, for example, consulting and accounting firms, universities, local convention and visitors' bureaus, and local hotel and restaurant associations.

Another technique for getting information is

What's The World Coming To?
Now Goliath Is Suing David
For Pain and Suffering.

We guess Pizza Hut subscribes to that old adage: when all else fails, sue. Armed with a slew of lawyers, the pizza giant is trying to do in court what they can't do in the marketplace: stop Papa John's increasing market share. They filed a lawsuit charging our advertising and "Better Ingredients. Better Pizza." slogan is misleading. We think it's an act of desperation.

OUR ADVERTISING IS TRUTHFUL AND ACCURATE.
Pizza Hut has challenged Papa John's advertising a number of times in a variety of forums. And we've always met their challenge. In fact, we have worked with the most respected self-regulatory advertising body in the country (on two separate occasions) to ensure that Papa John's advertising is truthful and accurate.

CONSUMERS SAY WE'RE BETTER.
Papa John's pizzas are preferred over comparable Pizza Hut pizzas in independent taste tests.* Maybe that's because our sauce is made from fresh tomatoes canned the day they're picked. Pizza Hut uses remanufactured paste to make its sauce.

BEST PIZZA CHAIN IN AMERICA.
For two consecutive years, Papa John's has been named Best Pizza Chain in America by *Restaurants & Institutions* (1997-1998). An honor previously reserved for the pizza giant.

YOU BE THE JUDGE.
The pizza wars won't be won or lost in the courtroom. You, the consumer, have the final verdict. Which makes us wonder: instead of wasting all this time with frivolous lawsuits, why doesn't Pizza Hut put all that energy into making a better pizza?

*Based on regional taste tests of Papa John's Works™ and Pizza Hut's Supreme™ traditional and thin crust pizzas, among those with a preference.

©1998 PJI, Inc.

FIGURE 6-5 Fast-food chains fight competition hard.

FIGURE 6-6   Delta Hotels Delta Hotels "BusinessZone^{SM}" room adds value for the customer.

simply to talk to your competitors. You might do this one on one, or at industry meetings. You can also talk to your customers, who might have been their customers. You can talk to your employees, who might have been their employees, or at least might know some of their employees. Finally, physical evidence can be obtained by visiting or using the competitor's product. Don't forget, of course, that while you are doing this, so is the competition! Finally, there are measurable differences that can be determined.

Measurable Differences

Market Share. In some areas, hotels exchange room occupancy percentages and average rate figures nightly by mutual arrangement. Many restaurant operators do likewise. (An old restaurant trick is to drive around and count cars in parking lots, but beware of employee cars!) Actually such arrangements are mutually beneficial because all they tell you is how you are doing relative to the others. The refusal of some managements to share this information, or their attempts to lie to each other, are generally self-defeating. It still remains to be discovered why you are doing better or worse.

Comparison figures of occupancy and covers are called market share figures and are used to compare actual market share with fair market share. In computing **fair market share** it is important to be certain that you are comparing apples with apples—in other words, with other properties in the same product class competing for the same customer. To do this you divide your capacity by total capacity in the product class. The resulting figure is your percentage of fair market share. To

T A B L E   6-2
Competitive Innovations in Hotels over the Past Few Years[6]

Frequent Guest Programmes: Programmes designed to build customer loyalty by providing special privileges and free travel opportunities to frequent guests.

Strategic Alliances: Efforts made by firms to formally cooperate in such programmes as advertising and marketing, sharing products and customers, and financing activities designed to maximize hotel occupancy.

Computer Reservation Systems: First pioneered by Holiday Inn, these programmes work similarly to airline reservation systems. Designed to fill rooms at rates that maximize the revenue yield per room, these programmes also make it easier for the customer and travel agent to secure desired accommodations at appropriate prices.

Amenities: Added products and services available to the guest once they have registered. Often include toiletries and in-room services.

Branding: Attempts by hotel companies to create and deliver new products to the customer. Often thought of as levels of service such as budget, economy, luxury and business class hotels. Each product is associated with specific products and services to differentiate it from the competition. Brands are available in several of these segments as well.

Technological Innovation: This method includes a wide array of advancements designed to improve the products and services offered by hotels. They include all elements of communication systems, decision support systems for management, accounting services, safety and security programmes, energy and conservation programmes, automated check-in and check-out services etc.

Niche Marketing and Advertising: These programmes were designed to zero in on specific target markets emphasizing special products and services to those markets.

Pricing Tactics: This method is generally viewed as discounting and yield management (maximising the revenue per room based upon demand projections).

Cost Containment: The attempt to operate as efficiently as possible by reducing all costs associated with running a hotel.

Service Quality Management: The attempt by hotels to improve service quality by such techniques as Total Quality Management, continuous process improvement etc.

International Expansion: As current markets become saturated, hotel firms seek expansion into new overseas markets.

Travel Agent Valuation: This method seeks to improve relations with the travel agent industry in order to secure greater volumes of business. This includes agent reward and incentive schemes.

Franchising and the Management Fee: This method of growth is viewed as a competitive method for those firms that possess unique capacity to deliver the necessary capabilities in each case.

Employees as Important Assets: This method places new value on the role of the employee in delivering and executing high quality products and services.

In-Room Sales and Entertainment: This method offers an array of possibilities to improve the revenue yield of each rented room by providing such items as pay-per-view on-demand movies, beverages, snacks and concierge services.

Special Services for Frequent Guests: This programme goes beyond the early frequent guest programmes and offers such attributes as automated check-in and out, special seating, lounges, merchandise discounts in the hotel and overall improved choices and upgrades for all products and services.

Conservation/Ecology Programmes: Methods in this category are designed to address the guest's growing awareness for conservation and desire for clean air in the hotel and its rooms. It is seen as a way of attracting guests who value these efforts.

Business Services: Designed to meet the needs of the increasingly pressured business traveller, these methods include a full range of business services in the hotel and/or room as well as a full range of communication services.

Database Management: This method takes advantage of growing technological capabilities to fully track the guest and his/her habits. This information is now being fully integrated into all other information systems utilized by the hotel.

Core Business Management: The recognition of doing one or few things well underpins this method. Firms have divested themselves of peripheral business units in order to concentrate on the core business of hotel management.

Direct to Consumer Marketing: The information highway and advancing technology now make it possible for firms to sell directly to the consumer using information provided by database marketing programmes. This method will grow in popularity as more travellers seek to make their own travel plans through such channels as the Internet.

T A B L E 6-3
Hypothetical Example of Market Share

Hotel	Actual Rooms	Rooms Sold	Occupancy %	Fair Share %	Actual Share %
Upper-Tier Hotels					
A	300	220	73.3	11.5	15.5
B	500	350	70.0	19.2	24.7
C	1200	500	41.7	46.2	35.2
Yours	600	350	58.3	23.1	24.7
Total	2600	1420	54.6	100.0	100.0
Middle-Tier Hotels					
E	275	220	80.0	31.3	30.6
F	425	360	84.7	48.3	50.0
G	180	140	77.8	20.4	19.4
Total	880	720	81.8	100.0	100.0

compute **actual market share** you divide your actual occupancy (or covers) by total product class occupancy. You then compare actual to fair market share as a measure of how well you are doing relative to the competition.

Consider the hypothetical example shown in Table 6-3 for one city area for one night. All the participants in the arrangement are not in the same product class. This does not mean that you are not interested in their occupancy—for instance, it would be worthwhile to know why middle-tier properties are running at higher occupancy than upper-tier properties. It might indicate that the upper-tier properties are pricing themselves out of the market, or it could mean something entirely different, for instance, concerning the type of business that was in town last night.

Now consider the market shares of the properties in your product class, as shown in the table. Hotel C's actual share is considerably lower than its fair share. But look at the size of this hotel; it is still filling more rooms than any of the others in the product class. Perhaps this is primarily a convention hotel with widely fluctuating occupancies; perhaps it should not be included in the same

product class. What this means is that one has to interpret these figures with discretion before making judgments.

As you can see, your hotel is barely getting its fair market share and would not be doing even that if Hotel C's occupancy was up. Hotels A and B, however, are substantially exceeding their fair share. What, you might ask, are they doing right? Or what are you doing wrong? This calls for an examination of their segments and marketing strategies.

REVPAR. While market share is one method of measuring position in the marketplace, the calculation of Revenue Per Available Room (REVPAR) is another method being employed in the hotel industry (REVPAR = room revenue/number of rooms available for sale or Average Daily Rate (ADR) × occupancy percentage). The fallacy of market share is that a competitor can gain actual share in the market at the expense of room rates. If a hotel drops its rates $10, more people may book at that hotel. REVPAR measures the revenue generated per available room and, in fact, is the method most widely used in the industry today.

T A B L E 6 - 4
Hypothetical Example of REVPAR

Hotel	Actual Rooms	Rooms Sold	Occupancy %	Average Daily Rate (ADR)	Revenue	REVPAR
Upper-Tier Hotels						
A	300	220	73.3	$120	$ 26,400	$88.00
B	500	350	70.0	130	45,500	91.00
C	1200	500	41.7	150	75,000	62.50
Yours	600	350	58.3	140	49,000	81.67
Total	2600	1420	54.6	137.96	195,900	75.35
Middle-Tier Hotels						
E	275	220	80.0	$110	$ 24,200	$88.00
F	425	360	84.7	100	36,000	84.70
G	180	140	77.8	90	12,600	70.00
Total	880	720	81.8	101.11	72,800	82.70

This calculation more accurately measures the balance of marketing efforts, as shown in Table 6-4, using the same hotels as in Table 6-3. The middle-tier hotels indicate better asset management. Their REVPARS are comparable to the upper-tier hotels, or better, and they undoubtedly are lower cost producers. One possible conclusion is that they are stealing business from the upper-tier hotels with lower rates. Another is that, on this particular day, the upper-tier hotels had booked lower rate conference groups. In any case, the reason needs to be examined on a regular basis. Trends are more enlightening than single days, and other conclusions might be drawn.

REVPOR. Another, less widely used, measurement tool is Revenue Per Occupied Room (REVPOR). This method includes all revenue attributed to each room such as food and beverage expenses, telephone and minibar charges, room service, and so forth. Assume, in the example in Table 6-4 above, that in "Yours" hotel you had additional room charges that night of $10,000. Your REVPOR would be $10,000 plus $49,000 divided by 350 rooms, or $168.57. This tool can also be used per individual room to indicate who your most valuable customers are in terms of how much they spend in total. In the example above, your average is $168.57. Any customer exceeding this amount would be more valuable in total expenditure than any customer spending less than this amount.

Of course, you could apply the same logic to REVPAR, but we would have to find a new acronym. (Maybe TOTREVPAR, Total Revenue Per Available Room?) We have not seen this done yet but it may still come and has merit. The difficulty in either case, however, arises when guests don't charge their other expenses to the rooms. For example, someone might use a credit card or pay cash in the restaurant. To confuse matters more, how do you handle the restaurant room charge when someone takes others to dinner and charges it all to his or her room? How do you handle a conference food bill? All this would have to be sorted out in order to develop a protocol, but for some hotels it would be revealing information.

REVPAC. What some consider a major measurement tool of the future is Revenue Per Available Customer (REVPAC). This acronym was suggested by Roger Cline, worldwide director of hospitality consulting for Arthur Andersen Worldwide. The method requires advanced technology in a fully integrated system tying reservations to the Property Management System (PMS) across all units of the company including all Strategic Business Units (SBUs). What is being measured is total yield per available customer.* From a marketing point of view this makes a great deal of sense.

Marriott, for one, has appointed a committee to try and work this out so it can be implemented. Consider this: Marriott has a business customer who stays regularly at their hotels and charges everything in the hotel to his room. At conferences, he often stays at a Marriott Marquis. For getaway weekends, he stays at a Marriott Courtyard, except when he goes on a golfing vacation when he plays on a Marriott golf course. When he goes to see his grandchildren, he likes a Marriott Fairfield Inn nearby. For vacations he buys a Marriott timeshare. When his company relocates him he stays at a Marriott all-suite Residence Inn until he finds a place to live. When he travels to the Far East, he prefers a Marriott Renaissance Hotel. For his 25th wedding anniversary he stays at a Marriott Ritz-Carlton. And, when he finally gives it all up, he lives in a Marriott retirement community. Developing an integrated system to keep track of all this is daunting, but the marketing information derived could be a very powerful tool for use in developing profiles for others.

In a lesser form, REVPAC is used today primarily by resorts to measure total spending of the customer including golf, skiing, spa, tennis, and so forth.

Purchased Data. More sophisticated operators use third party services to gain market share data (and avoid possible antitrust violations). Smith Travel Research (STR) of Hendersonville, Tennessee is a primary provider of this information to the hotel industry in the United States. Each month, STR generates STAR reports for more than 15,000 lodging establishments in the United States. Table 6-5 is an example of this information.

Table 6-5 is for a fictitious property located near the Nashville airport for the month of November. The data for ABC Inn is real (derived by adding the performance of several properties in the area and dividing through by a constant), and the results shown on the report are valid. A brief review indicates a property with below average performance. We explain this in Table 6-6.

Restaurant Comparisons. Restaurant Market Share Revenue per square Foot (RsqFt) and Revenue Per Available Seat (REVPAS) are two very new methods developed for restaurants. Both calculate competitive restaurant share by measuring one's own position against that of the competition. Table 6-7 shows how this is done.

Perceptual Mapping. Another form of competitive intelligence is with the use of mapping your own and your competitors' positions in the marketplace based on research of consumers' perceptions. This technique may involve simple plotting on an arbitrary scale, or sophisticated statistical methods known as multidimensional scaling or discriminant analysis. In Figure 6-7 mapping is used to place various competitive positions on a two-dimensional scale, along with an "ideal" position, in order to locate the gaps and niches or, conversely, the crowded areas. This shows the results of customer research and how customers position, in their own minds, various restaurants on the two dimensions of service quality and price. It also shows how they would position an "ideal" restaurant.

The "ideal" restaurant in this case has fairly high service quality and fairly high prices. There is no one restaurant that actually fits this ideal in the customers' minds. Restaurant A is perceived as having even better service but also higher prices. The customers' ideal would be to have less service that cost less. Restaurant E is at the other extreme, with low service and low price. This target market wants lower prices than A, but it wants more service than E has to offer at that price. You can com-

---

*REVPAC is somewhat akin to, but still different from, lifetime value of a customer, as discussed in Chapter 3.

TABLE 6-5
Example of a STAR Report from Smith Travel Research[7]

Performance Report	Occupancy Percent	Average Room Rate	Room Sales Per Available Room	Room Sales	Market Share Report Room Supply	Room Demand
Market Segment						
ABC Inn	56.8	$41.93	$23.81			
Market						
Nashville, Tenn.	66.1	$58.07	$38.38	100.0	100.0	100.0
ABC Inn				.4	.6	.5
Price Level						
Mid-Price	62.5	$42.90	$26.81	21.4	30.7	29.0
ABC Inn				1.7	2.0	1.8
Selected Competitors						
Competitors	75.0	$46.74	$35.06	4.4	4.8	5.5
ABC Inn				8.5	12.5	9.5
Market Tract						
Nashville E. Airport	68.1	$68.44	$46.61	51.8	42.6	43.9
ABC Inn				.7	1.4	1.2
Tract by Price Tier						
Middle Tier	57.1	$41.87	$23.91	9.5	18.6	15.5
ABC Inn				7.6	7.6	7.6
Tract by Chain Segment						
Small Chains/Ind.	62.6	$41.60	$26.04	16.0	28.7	26.4
ABC Inn				4.5	4.9	4.5

Source: Smith Travel Research.

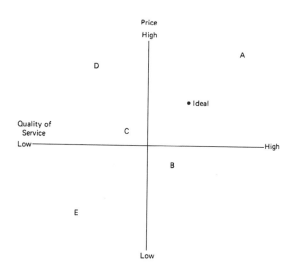

FIGURE 6-7 A positioning map for competitive analysis.

pare these two, in the same manner, against restaurants B, C, and D.

Which restaurant has the best opportunity in this hypothetical situation? Probably B. If B can raise its service level, or the perception of its service level, just a little, it can raise its prices quite a bit (assuming, of course, that all other things are equal). On the other hand, to get closer to the ideal, A would have to lower its perceived prices, but could also give up some service refinements.

In analyzing the position of the competition, marketers also want to be able to protect the position they hope to establish. This means anticipating possible competitive reactions and taking measures to reduce their impact. In Figure 6-7, restaurant B could raise its prices "very cautiously" so that A would have to come down substantially to match them. If B knew its competitors, it might

---

T A B L E   6 - 6
Explanation of the STAR Report in Table 6-5[8]

With an occupancy of 56.8 percent, the ABC occupancy is nearly 10 percentage points below the Nashville market and 12 points less than the Nashville East airport tract. The difference narrows somewhat when you compare the ABC Inn's occupancy performance with its specific price tier and chain segment. Relative to other properties in the middle-price tier in this tract, the ABC Inn is comparable in terms of both occupancy and room rates.

The most important comparison is with its selected competitors. These properties have a substantial occupancy premium and nearly a $5 rate premium above the ABC Inn. As a result, REVPAR for the competitive set is nearly $12 or 50 percent more than the ABC Inn. This difference is highlighted in the market share section of the report, where ABC Inn has 12.5 percent of the supply, but only 9.5 percent of the demand and 8.5 percent of the room sales.

Based on this data, ABC Inn has a penetration index of 76.0 (computed by dividing 56.8 percent property occupancy by 75 percent competitive set occupancy, or by dividing 9.5 percent demand share by 12.5 percent supply share) and a yield index of 68 percent (computed by dividing $23.81 property room rate by $35.06 competitive set room rate, or by dividing 8.5 percent revenue share by 12.5 percent supply share). Since both indices are less than 100, the property is not obtaining its fair market share of rooms sold or rooms revenue. Further, REVPAR has declined by 1.6 percent for ABC, but rose 4.9 percent for the competitive set.

All this does not bode well for ABC. One next step might be to review the competitors' facilities. This might indicate a need for renovation to restore ABC's competitive position. Another review might be that of the marketing program and sales effort. In any case, a competitive analysis is called for. A competitive market analysis is an essential first step in evaluating whether a problem is property specific or a function of the competitive market.

"know" that this is something A would be reluctant to do.

In Figure 6-8, we show a more sophisticated mapping, based on multidimensional scaling and discriminant analysis, of the perception of casinos in Las Vegas. The discriminant analysis enables the researcher to categorize the different perceptions of the casinos. The net effect of this is the ability of the casino that commissioned the research to see not only how it is perceived, but also who its competition is in that category.

Types and Objectives of Competitive Intelligence

Competitive intelligence involves close observation of competitors to learn what they do best and why, and where they are weak and why. There are three major types and objectives of this information:

Defensive Intelligence: This involves keeping track of competitors' moves to avoid being caught off guard. For example, you need to know if the restaurant across the street is planning to feature early bird specials.

Passive Intelligence: This is obtained in order to make specific decisions. For example, what markets do a competing hotel's sales force cover? What discounts do they offer to groups?

Offensive Intelligence: This is for the purpose of identifying new opportunities. For example, some hotels have their salespeople spend a night in competitor hotels to learn where there may be opportunities to do something better.

Any kind of competitive intelligence has three major objectives:

1. To understand your position of comparative advantage and disadvantage,
2. To understand competitors' strategies and tactics, and
3. To help you develop your own strategies and tactics that may create competitive advantage.

Table 6-8 pulls all this together in a step-by-step procedure for gathering and using competitive intelligence.

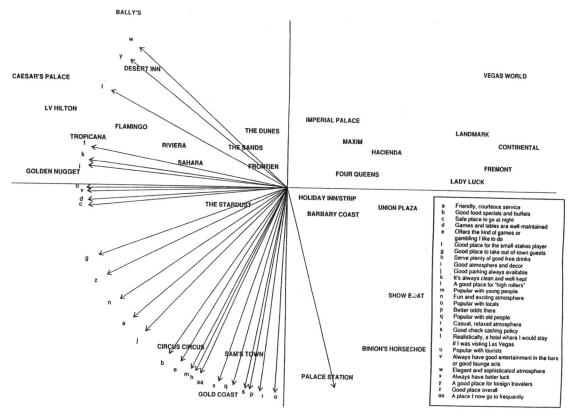

FIGURE 6-8 A positioning map for classifying competitors.[9]

In the final analysis, the management that obtains the most information will be the one that moves around, keeps its eyes and ears open, and uses good intuitive judgment. Close observation can tell you a lot about what the competition does best and why, where they are off the mark and why, what their strengths are and their weaknesses, and what they plan next. All this is good marketing intelligence, and it can go a long way in helping you to develop your own marketing strategy.

COMPETITIVE ANALYSIS

The purpose of competitive intelligence, of course, is to use it to your best advantage. Figure 6-9 provides a model of broad dimensions for competitor analysis. If you are behind, you need to seek and increase competitive advantage. If you are ahead, you need to sustain and increase competitive advantage. In the first case, you need to overcome barriers to move ahead. In the second case you need to erect barriers to stay ahead.

A barrier may be raised based on size in the targeted market, better access to resources or customers, and limitations on what competitors can do. Scale economies, for example, may be an unbeatable cost advantage. In the hotel industry, this is especially true today in the use and cost of the latest technology. This technology also gives a firm preferred access to customers. This helps to explain at least one reason that the industry has been in such a consolidation stage.

Barriers are also raised based on cost differentials or on price and service differentials. A suc-

TABLE 6-7
Calculating Competitive Restaurant Share for One Month

1	2	3	4	5	Revenue Per Square Foot (RsqFT)				Revenue Per Available Seat (REVPAS)				
					6	7	8	9	10	11	12	13	14
Comp Set	Avg Check	Covers	Revenue	AMS % of Total Revenue	Avail Sq.Ft	Revenue per Sq. Foot	FMS % of Available Sq. Feet	Penetration Index on Square Footage	Available Seats	FMS %	Revenue Per Available Seat	AMS %	Penetration Index on Available Seats
Istana	$ 45	7,500	$ 337,500	10.0%	60,000	$ 5.63	11.8%	−1.8%	3,300	12.2%	$ 102.27	9.7%	−2.5
Tokyo Rose	$ 70	5,250	$ 367,500	10.9%	60,000	$ 6.13	11.8%	−.9%	2,800	10.4%	$ 131.25	12.5%	2.1
Marty's	$ 63	9,000	$ 567,000	16.9%	80,000	$ 7.09	15.7%	1.2%	2,100	7.8%	$ 270.00	25.7%	17.9
Dice	$ 73	6,000	$ 438,000	13.0%	75,000	$ 5.84	14.7%	−1.7%	4,000	14.8%	$ 109.50	10.4%	−4.4
Balche	$ 77	6,300	$ 485,100	14.4%	70,000	$ 6.93	13.7%	.7%	3,600	13.3%	$ 134.75	12.8%	−.5
Fellini	$ 78	5,700	$ 444,600	13.2%	70,000	$ 6.35	13.7%	−.5%	3,800	14.1%	$ 117.00	11.1%	−3.0
Sushi House	$ 76	7,000	$ 532,000	15.8%	60,000	$ 8.87	11.8%	4.0%	4,100	15.2%	$ 129.75	12.3%	−2.9
Cellantro	$ 48	4,000	$ 192,000	5.7%	35,000	$ 5.49	6.9%	−1.2%	3,315	12.3%	$ 57.92	5.5%	−6.8
Average	66.25	6,344	$ 420,462		63,750	$ 6.54			3,377		$ 131.56		
Totals		50,750	$3,363,700	100%	510,000		100%		27,015	100%	$1,052.44	100%	

Column:

1 is the competitive set of restaurants

4 is average check × covers = revenue

5 AMS = % of total revenue is a restaurant's revenue / total revenue

7 revenue per square foot is revenue / square footage

8 FMS is square footage / total square footage

9 penetration index (PI) on square footage is FMS subtracted from AMS

Cellantro's PI is a negative 1.2 so it is not getting its FMS; Sushi House is getting the largest market share with a penetration index of 4.0

10 available seats = number of seats × days in the month

11 is FMS percentage of all available seats

12 is revenue / available seats

13 is AMS percentage of revenue per available seat

14 penetration index on available seats is FMS subtracted from AMS

Cellantro's PI is a negative 6.8 so it is not getting its FMS but, in this case, based on available seats, Marty's is doing the best with a 17.9 PI

Average checks, number of covers, or some combination can be reviewed to ascertain where the differences lie.

176

TABLE 6-8
Obtaining and Using Competitive Intelligence

---

1. Setting up the process:
   - Identify competitors in all relevant market segments.
   - Identify your target, that is, define your competition.
   - Identify the unique characteristics of the customers in each market segment.
   - Determine what specific information you need. The most commonly sought data are on pricing, sales statistics, strategic plans, market share changes, key customers, new product developments, and growth plans, but there are obviously many others, as shown below.
   - Decide who will get and use the intelligence and what will be done with it.
   - Identify the most likely sources of the data.
   - Develop research strategies and techniques, not hit-or-miss methods.
2. Collecting the raw data:
   - Determine the performance record of each competitor. This includes such things as market share, REVPAR, pricing, sales growth, and profitability.
   - Determine the offerings of each competitor such as discounts, packages, guest amenities, loyalty programs, room sizes, physical condition, F&B outlets, and so forth.
   - Construct a profile of each competitor's marketing strategy. This includes goals and objectives, strengths and weaknesses, distinctive competence, target markets, resources, positioning, sales efforts, and the full marketing mix.
3. Evaluate and analyze the data:
   - Ask, where are they most vulnerable?
   - Predict any future strategies and tactics. This is a qualitative exercise shared among managers. It is based on the information gathered in the previous stages and managers' own experience in the industry.
   - Evaluate the impact of competitors' strategies and tactics upon the property or firm.
4. Draw conclusions and use the data:
   - Is the data reliable? Do we have all we need?
   - Develop, on an ongoing basis, defensive, passive, or offensive strategies and tactics that will counter or lead to competitive advantage.

---

cessful barrier returns higher margins if it is sustainable and unbreachable by the competition; that is it must cost the competition more to overcome it than it costs the firm to defend it. Figure 6-10 shows a Ritz-Carlton approach to this. To continue to perform the promise in the ad can be an expensive proposition that many firms cannot yet sustain. As technology becomes cheaper, however, this service may well expand to all levels of the industry. Doubletree, on the other hand, has found a very simple approach to competitive advantage (Figure 6-11), one so simple, in fact, that no one *dares* to copy it.

Another example of a cost barrier is in advertising. Marriott, for example, can get twice the impact from national advertising as that of a firm with half the market share. In other words, the same advertising spreads over a much larger customer base and quantity of hotel rooms. A wide product line, large sales and service forces, and systems capabilities (again Marriott) are other examples of major barriers. Each is effective against smaller competitors who are attempting to overcome the leader but have less volume over which to spread the costs.

These, and many more, are all reasons why hotel and restaurant companies grow larger and develop

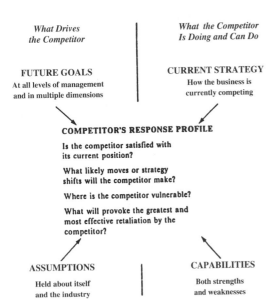

FIGURE 6-9 The components of a competitor analysis.[10]

some sustainable advantages as they do so. On the other hand, there is an anomaly in this situation that is peculiar to the industry: in many cases, each unit (hotel or restaurant) stands largely on its own. Although all chains have loyal customers, many hospitality customers make their choices based on individual properties. Thus The Mansion on Turtle Creek in Dallas, for example, can and does compete against the Four Seasons with some premium service advantages that are unique and sustainable in spite of being one of a kind and not having economies of scale or scope.

A sustainable competitive advantage in marketing strategy happens only when (1) customers perceive a consistent difference in important attributes between a firm or property and its competition; (2) the difference is the result of a capability gap between the firm and its competitors, and (3) both the difference in important attributes and the capability gap can endure over time.[11]

The essence of opportunity is beating the competition. Intense competition in an industry is neither coincidence nor bad luck. It is a fact of business life. The competitive objective is to find the

position where you can break down or influence the barriers, or where you can erect the best defense barriers. This means finding what makes the competition vulnerable. Attacking vulnerability, as in the military sense, means attacking the weaknesses and avoiding the strengths in the line. The latter is as important as the former.

Wendy's is one fast-food operator that has proven the above point. Wendy's attacked where McDonald's was weak in two areas. One was the area of "adult" hamburgers. Wendy's saw that McDonald's was not really serving this market, so they set out to carve their own niche. The second area was in the product. Wendy's saw a dislike in the market for the frozen, pre-cooked hamburger, especially among a portion of the adult market, and offered fresh hamburgers. Wendy's has survived where many others that copied McDonald's failed. The budget portion of the hotel industry has done likewise.

Avoid the competition's strength, at least until you are strong enough and have the resources to challenge them with a meaningful differentiation. Look for the weaknesses. These may be in the product line, in positioning, in segmentation and target markets, in capacity, in resources, in cost disadvantages, in product differentiation, in customer loyalty, or in distribution channels.

COMPETITIVE MARKETING

Michael E. Porter suggests three strategies for beating the competition: positioning to provide the best defense, influencing the balance by taking the offense, and exploiting industry change.[12]

Defensive positioning means matching strengths and weaknesses against the competition by finding positions where it is the weakest (as Wendy's above), and developing strengths where the company is least vulnerable. Ritz-Carlton Hotels have accomplished this by maintaining their level of service at all costs.

Influencing the balance by taking the offensive,

FIGURE 6-10 Ritz-Carlton attempts to erect intangible barriers for competitive advantage.

or proacting, means attempting to alter the industry structure and its causes. It calls for marketing innovation, establishing brand identity, or otherwise differentiating the product. Darden is a restaurant example with Olive Garden, Red Lobster, and Bahama Breeze. This has also happened with suite hotels, conference center hotels and, especially, luxury budget hotels; also with Marriott entering every product class and buying Ritz-Carlton and Renaissance.

Exploiting industry change means anticipating

shifts in the environment, forecasting the effect, constructing a composite of the future, and positioning accordingly. Taco Bell and Domino's pizza delivery are two examples. Robert Hazard accomplished this in his successful metamorphosis of Quality Inns (now Choice International) in the early 1980s, when he offered three different product levels to the marketplace. All-suites have done the same thing, as has SAS Hotels in its strategic alliance with Radisson.

A successful company must look beyond today's competitors to those that may become competitors

FIGURE 6-11 Doubletree features a sustainable competitive advantage with simplificity.

tomorrow (à la convenience stores and take-out versus the fast-food industry). It must also watch out for new entries in the race (e.g., conference center hotels), and the threat of substitute products (e.g., supermarket "make your own meal" bars).

The key to growth, even survival, is to obtain a position that is less vulnerable to direct attack, old or new, and less vulnerable to consumer manipulation and substitute products. This can be done by relationship marketing, actual or psychological product differentiation, and constant and foresighted competitive awareness and analysis.

FINDING MARKETING OPPORTUNITIES

To be sure, all marketing opportunities begin with consumers' problems. Well-known management author Peter Drucker calls these opportunities "incongruities."[13] Incongruities here are discrepancies between what is and what ought to be. As far as the customer is concerned, this may be the difference between expectation and reality; it also may be the difference between what the customer would like it to be and what is available. These are both true opportunities. Drucker states,

> Of all incongruities, that between perceived and actual reality may be the most common. Producers and suppliers almost always misconceive what it is that the customer actually buys. They assume that what represents "value" to the producer and supplier is equally "value" to the customer. . . . And yet, no customer ever perceives himself as buying what the producer or supplier delivers. Their expectations and values are always different.[14]

Even if Drucker is only half right, it is clear that within consumer incongruities there are tremendous opportunities. Every one is familiar with the expression "there ought to be a better way." It is in that better way that opportunities lie. Consider the case of the atrium hotel lobby, now common all over the world.

John Portman was an architect who decided there ought to be a better way to design a hotel. At the time, hotel architecture had reached a degree of sameness that was so "commodity-laden" that no one thought hotels could ever be other than what they were, architecturally speaking. The first Portman-designed atrium hotel was opened by Hyatt in Atlanta in 1967 and the industry was shocked, primarily because of the perceived energy costs. Everyone criticized, but the customers kept coming, and Hyatt became a major chain as a result.

Was this a consumer problem solved? Was this a case of consumer expectations being unfulfilled? Of course it was. Hotels were dull, dreary places with long, dark corridors and dull lobbies with couches built around the antiquated concept of "a home away from home." Customers didn't want a

home away from home; they wanted a new and exciting experience. They wanted something different, and Hyatt gave it to them. The decision by Hyatt to build an atrium lobby hotel did more than start Hyatt on its way; it started hotel architecture on its way, and today's many examples are a result of that initial Portman design and Hyatt decision.

Consider the now popular restaurant salad bar. Who knows where or when it started? Someone saw an opportunity arising from a consumer problem. Fine wine by the glass, thanks to nitrogen-filled, partially empty wine bottles, and coffee, juice, and roll carts on hotel elevators solved other consumer problems. Environmental changes present other, more macro problems and opportunities. If you want to find an opportunity, look for a consumer problem.

Opportunity solutions, to be effective, have to be simple. They have to be easily understandable by the consumer. They have to avoid increased customer risk. Opportunities call for innovation, leadership, and a constant awareness that there ought to be a better way. Opportunities are out there, crying for solutions, but innovation to fulfill them doesn't fall in your lap. Sometimes it takes hard work, sometimes just a little common sense.

The search for opportunity begins with knowing your market, knowing your customers, and understanding your customer's problems. But never forget the first rule of marketing when you get a great opportunity idea: Will it create and/or keep a customer? When you can answer yes, then and only then ask what will it cost to do it and if you can afford it.

All opportunities to create and keep a customer are not "great" ideas. Some are just common sense. For example, consider the American chain hotel in Kuala Lumpur, Malaysia, that offered freshly squeezed orange juice, but you couldn't get it until after 10:00 A.M. Why not? "The juicer is in the bar and the bar doesn't open until 10:00 o'clock." The service personnel don't tell you this; they simply serve canned orange juice until 10:00 o'clock! Opportunity lost, along with common sense.

Marketing intelligence and marketing research are critical activities in marketing and getting to know the customer. They are particularly vital parts of environmental scanning and opportunity and competitive analysis. They also constitute of course, a subject of their own. We introduce readers to a once-over-lightly but more detailed treatment of both subjects in Appendix A of this edition. We urge you to read this (even if it is not assigned), and then go take a marketing research course.

FEASIBILITY STUDIES

Another form of marketing opportunity differs somewhat from that in the previous discussion. Instead of looking for opportunities, market **feasibility studies** are conducted to verify whether an opportunity exists. When feasibility studies are conducted, someone already believes that there is an opportunity, such as to build a hotel or open a restaurant in a certain location. The purpose of the feasibility study is to verify that belief (and prove to the lender that it is a viable one). Measurement of market potential, or feasibility, aims to gain knowledge of market size, market growth, market segments, profitability, demand and type of buying decision, and competition. In essence, the feasibility study should ask these questions:

Is there a market for this property (business, concept, operation) in this location? If so, where is it, how large is it, or will it be, what are its needs, and how is it currently served by the competition? What market share can be captured? Will they use our property? Who are its members? Other related questions will follow naturally.

How does the answer to the first question project into financial realities—for example, room rates or check averages, revenue, profit, return on investment, and other quantitative financial considerations?

The answers to the second question obviously depend upon the answers to the first question. Our interest here is only in the first question.

Market feasibility studies are concerned with both marketing opportunities and competitive analysis. Feasibility studies deserve an entire chap-

ter to themselves, but that is not within the scope of this text. Instead, we place the emphasis on the analysis of the marketing opportunity. Studying markets, as we know by now, involves studying consumers or consumer groups and how they will respond (in this case) to a given offering. In other words, having decided that we would like to do something (e.g., build a new hotel or restaurant), we seek to determine whether the opportunity is there. The opportunity, of course, lies in consumers who are ready, willing, and able to buy.

The marketing opportunity depends on the consumer. If the consumer is not willing, there is no marketing opportunity. By the same token, the competitive analysis of this marketing opportunity must be restricted to focus on those who are competing for the same customer under the same conditions. The six motels within a five-mile area have little to do with the competition for a proposed 300-room conference center.

A market feasibility study should have only one purpose: to show the opportunity to attract that many customers, to pay that price, to come to that property, over a period of time. That's the hard part. Once done, the easier part is to estimate revenue, subtract cost, predict net and cash flow, and determine whether the project is "feasible"—that is, a financial opportunity.

A true market feasibility study depends, totally, on customers—whether they will come and what they will pay. This is the competitive opportunity, or lack of it. Unfortunately, most feasibility studies crunch numbers with only a remote idea of where the customers are, whether they will come, or who the real competition is. In marketing, opportunities depend on creating paying customers—nothing else.

SUMMARY

Although we tend to think of marketing as a managerial activity in reaching the customer, we have shown in this chapter that there are other elements involved. Marketing, in fact, is enemy warfare and includes outwitting, outflanking, and outdoing the competition in the battle for consumer loyalty. Marketing does not live in a vacuum in solving consumers' problems and satisfying their needs and wants. A firm's marketing must perform these tasks better than the competitors do. This is the only answer to sustained advantage and growth in the hospitality industry.

There are, without doubt, many firms in the hospitality industry that maintain the status quo and still survive, but maintenance and survival are not the true sense of marketing. Neither objective will fulfill the potential of the firm.

This chapter has shown that identifying and understanding the competition does not mean just understanding bricks and mortar. Rather, understanding all facets, and the actors that make them work, requires constant analysis. Without this understanding, and often good research to explain it, marketing is doomed to ignore opportunity and the property is doomed to the status of "also ran" when the final count is in.

Sustainable competitive advantage is hard to come by in the hospitality industry. Regardless, it is an essential competitive element. As we said in Chapter 3, we think, at least in the immediate future and some time to come, it will lie in understanding the competition and relationship marketing.

KEY WORDS AND CONCEPTS

Actual Market Share (AMS): The share of business generated in a competitive area that a property actually obtains, relative to other properties in the same product class.

Competitive Intelligence: Information obtained on the competition that can be used to understand what it is doing and, perhaps, can be used to develop better strategies and tactics to obtain competitive advantage.

    Defensive: Keeping track of competitors' moves to avoid being caught off-guard.

    Passive: Obtaining information in order to make a specific decision.

    Offensive: Identifying new opportunities.

Competitive Intensity: The fierceness in the marketplace with which competitors compete, for example matching prices and offerings, or even skullduggery.

Conceptitis: A term we have coined for when the emphasis is on the concept, rather than on the market.

Eatertainment: An industry term for restaurants whose primary emphasis is on the entertainment part, such as Planet Hollywood.

Fair Market Share (FMS): A property's "fair" share of business based on its capacity relative to the competition in the same product class.

Feasibility Study: A business study that is based on present and future competitive data and consumer demand to determine if a project is feasible, followed by financial analysis.

Market Share: A property's or company's share of the business, regardless of whether it is "fair" or not. For example, Marriott might have *X* percent share of all lodging business in the United States.

Perceptual Mapping: A method of visually comparing competitors' products against one's own, based on consumer perception.

REVPAC (Revenue Per Available Customer): The lifetime, or lifetime span, revenue generated from a single person or company.

REVPAR (Revenue Per Available Room): Average revenue obtained per room on a given night or period of time. Total room revenue divided by the number of available rooms.

REVPAS (Revenue Per Available Seat in a restaurant): Total revenue divided by the number of seats available per month.

REVPOR (Revenue Per Occupied Room): Average or specific revenue derived from room night including all hotel expenditures by the occupant.

RsqFt (Revenue per square Foot in a restaurant): Total revenue divided by number of square feet available.

Sustainable Competitive Advantage: Advantages

over the competition that can be sustained for at least some period of time, that is, advantages that are not quickly copyable.

DISCUSSION QUESTIONS

1. What are the basic elements of strategic competition? Discuss.
2. Identify, with examples, different sources of competition.
3. How does industry structure affect intensity of competition?
4. What are the major sources of competitive intelligence?
5. How can a company or property maintain sustainable competitive advantage?
6. Consider a local restaurant or hotel. What is its competition in a macro sense? In a micro sense? Explain.
7. Explain competitive intensity. How does it impact upon marketing? Give examples and discuss.
8. Make a list of new competitive advantages that a hotel or restaurant might achieve. Could they be sustainable?

GROUP PROJECTS

1. Consider a hotel or restaurant chain with which you are familiar. Delineate how it should develop marketing strategy in order to build and sustain competitive advantage for the next ten years.
2. Marriott needs a hand in establishing protocol to measure REVPAC. Develop a model that would provide a framework to address this.
3. Blindly, have each member of your group categorize along specified dimensions a restaurant or hotel with which you are all familiar, considering

any thing that might be a competitive advantage. Draw a positioning map for this property.

REFERENCES

1. Subhash C. Jain, *Marketing Planning and Strategy*, 5th ed. Cincinnati:South-Western Publishing, 1997, p. 70.
2. Michael E. Porter, *Competitive Strategy: Techniques for Analyzing Industries and Competitors*, New York: Free Press, 1980.
3. Jain, *op. cit.*, pp. 76–77.
4. In one study, for example, of 1314 hotel guests of six hotels, amenities were found to be nonsignificant in determining the choice of hotel and nonsignificant in importance when staying at a hotel, for both business and pleasure travelers. See Robert C. Lewis, "Predicting Hotel Choice: The Factors Underlying Perception," *Cornell Hotel and Restaurant Administration Quarterly*, February 1985, pp. 82–96.
5. Quoted in "Industry Rethinks Amenities and Value," *Business Travel News*, September 27, 1993, p. 20.
6. Michael D. Olsen, Jin Lin Zhao, Wanae Cho, and Eliza Tse, "Hotel Industry Performance and Competitive Methods: A Decade in Review: 1985–1994." In *Into the New Millennium, A White Paper on the Global Hospitality Industry*. Paris: International Hotel Association, 1997, p. 33.
7. Randell A. Smith, Smith Travel Research, "How to Succeed by the Numbers," *Lodging*, February 1994, p. 19. Used by permission.
8. *Ibid.*, pp. 19–21.
9. We thank Professor Stowe Shoemaker of the Harrah College of Hotel Administration, University of Nevada/Las Vegas for this example, which is derived from research he conducted.
10. Porter, *op. cit.*, p. 49.
11. Jain, *op. cit.*, pp. 96–98.
12. Michael E. Porter, "Note on the Structural Analysis of Industries," *Harvard Business School Case Services*, 1975, p. 22.
13. Peter F. Drucker, *Innovation and Entrepreneurship*. New York: Harper & Row, 1985, p. 57.
14. *Ibid.*, p. 66.

Seven

THE MARKETING PLAN

The marketing plan is the management tool that steps down the strategic planning process to the action stage for the forthcoming year. It provides the road map to operate by during the year. The marketing plan is a working document, used throughout the year, to guide the organization in its strategic direction toward goals and objectives.

REQUIREMENTS OF A MARKETING PLAN
These are the essential elements that make the plan work—it must be doable, realistic, and measurable.

DEVELOPMENT OF A MARKETING PLAN
The discussion goes through the various stages of putting a plan together.

DATA COLLECTION This is the first stage. Workable, effective, and realistic marketing plans can be developed only through the gathering of complete and adequate information and its thorough and objective analysis.

External environment data includes international and domestic trends, both in the environment and in the marketplace.

Competitive environment data collection reviews the status of direct competitors, including their physical condition, market segments, their behavior, and other pertinent matters.

Internal environment data collection includes bringing together all the information about the property and its customers, information that will reveal its strengths and weaknesses.

DATA ANALYSIS Once the data has been collected, it has to be analyzed.

Environmental analysis dissects the trends and forces of the business environment and their potential impact.

Competitive analysis reveals the trends of the competition, strengths and weaknesses, successes and failures, looking for opportunities for competitive advantage.

Demand analysis shows the overall customer needs in the marketplace and how they are being fulfilled.

Property needs analysis covers the internal opportunities to improve the customer base where business is now weak.

Internal analysis dissects the current business and customer base and the overall present property situation.

Market analysis brings all other phases of the data analysis together to focus on the customer in the search for opportunities.

MISSION AND MARKETING POSITION STATEMENT   After all of the data collection and analysis are completed, the mission statement, broad objectives, and positioning for the next year are created for the business unit. This mission statement follows the conclusions of the research, not the other way around. Customer opportunities and objectives follow from the marketing plan.

OPPORTUNITY ANALYSIS   This is the analysis of the opportunities in the marketplace.

OBJECTIVES AND METHODS   The objectives and methods for fulfilling the mission are established.

ACTION PLANS   The action plans are devised, based on the mission statement and overall marketing plan, and detail who will do what and when.

MARKETING FORECAST   This is the projection of objectives and action plans into results.

MARKETING BUDGETS   These budgets are created to fund the overall marketing plan.

MARKETING CONTROLS   These are the monitoring of the marketing plan throughout the year.

• ◆ •

The **marketing plan** is the working document that the hospitality enterprise develops for action during the forthcoming year. Although sometimes marketing plans are written for future years, and in fact often give at least some brief mention to the next two to five years, for the sake of consistency, they are usually written for just one year at a time. Shorter plans to capture, for example, group bookings two to five years down the road may also be utilized.

The marketing plan of a business unit flows from its own strategy and mission statement, which, of course, derive from the corporate strategy and corporate mission statement.* In many hospitality firms the corporate level and the business unit level are one and the same, so the strategic plan and the marketing plan will be at one level only. On the other hand, many hospitality firms do not do strategic planning, develop annual marketing plans, or even have mission statements. This can be a mistake. Marketing plans are quite common in hotel

chains and large restaurant companies, but not so common in smaller companies, especially restaurants. Our focus here is on the individual property, the most common usage in hospitality.

REQUIREMENTS FOR A MARKETING PLAN

There are three key elements to a successful marketing plan: (1) that it is workable, (2) that it is realistic and flexible, and (3) that it has measurable, achievable goals. Too many plans fail in one or all of these respects, which by their nature overlap each other.

The marketing plan has to remain simple and easy to execute. Two hundred page marketing plans with a list of 100 action steps may be impressive, but they are unproductive. Too many businesses confuse activity with productivity. The result is poorer performance and frustration. The marketing plan that is the simplest, with a few key items to be completed, will be the most focused and successful.

---

*It may be helpful to refer back to Table 4-4 to review the differences between strategic marketing and marketing management.

The marketing plan must also be realistic and flexible.

A road map is useful if one is lost in a highway system, but not in a swamp whose topography is constantly changing. A simple compass that indicates the general direction and allows you to use your own ingenuity in overcoming difficulties is far more valuable.[1]

The topography of the hospitality industry changes rapidly these days. Marketing plans, even more than strategic plans, should always be adaptable to changes in the business topography. Thus marketing plans must constantly be reviewed and reevaluated. This is not to say that they should be changed at the sign of the slightest aberration; a good marketing plan has a certain stability to it. It simply means you mustn't be locked into a position when the situation changes and there is evidence that this position no longer is the most effective one in which to be.

The marketing plan must be appropriate for the business in terms of capacity, image, scope, and risk, as well as being feasible in terms of time and resources. This would seem to be a fairly obvious statement, but it is often violated. Owners' demands, corporate's demands, management's demands, and others lead to many marketing plans that simply have little or no chance of success. Although a marketing plan will have objectives, they should be based solely and entirely on the characteristics of the market and the resources to implement the plan. Wild-eyed dreams and wishful thinking will not overcome these realities just because someone higher up says, "**Raise the numbers**" (a hotel industry expression meaning increase occupancy and average rate).

The marketing plan should assign specific responsibility, with times and dates for accomplishment of measurable and achievable goals, both individually and as a total effort, for example, "raise occupancy four percentage points," or "raise REVPAR four dollars." Continuous follow-up assures that these responsibilities will be met, or changed, as need be. This provision requires that the plan be thoroughly understood by everyone in the organization. A good plan indicates how marketing activities are integrated with all other activities of the operation. What this means is that the marketing plan doesn't stop at the door of the marketing office. Although the details of the entire plan will not go to every person in the workforce, the essence of the plan should do exactly that.

A Bangkok hotel, for example, planned to attract a market segment of German families with children on vacation at a package rate. The promotion was a success and the families came, but no one had made adequate plans, as promised in the promotion, for children's activities, babysitters, or even extra beds to be placed in the rooms.

A Valentine's Day promotion at a large New York City hotel was part of a well-written marketing plan. The hotel "sold out" on the promotion, making it a financial success. Unfortu-nately, the front office manager forgot to tell the garage that the promotion that included free parking was such a success. The result was a one and a half hour wait to park, and another hour to retrieve a car the next day. A full hotel with angry customers is not an example of a well-executed marketing plan.

Any plan that succeeds in attracting the market but fails to fulfill its promises, explicit or implicit, to that market will in the long term be self-defeating. Personnel cannot deliver what marketing promises if they don't know what those promises are or don't have the tools to deliver on them.

A good marketing plan provides direction for an operation. It states where you are going and what you are going to have to do to get there. It builds employee and management confidence through shared effort and teamwork toward common goals. It recognizes weaknesses, emphasizes strengths, and deals with reality. It seeks and exploits opportunities. And last but certainly not least, a good marketing plan gets everyone into the act.

Some marketing plans are no more than a description of the facility, a list of possible competitors and their facilities, an advertising and sales plan, and a forecast and budget. These are necessary but not sufficient elements of a marketing plan that succeeds. Like everything else we have said in this book, the test of the marketing plan is embodied in the question "How will the customer be served?"

DEVELOPMENT OF THE MARKETING PLAN

As in strategic planning, the marketing plan begins with a situation analysis. Here, however, we are dealing with greater specifics. Our goal is to decide how our marketing resources will be used to best attract and serve designated markets.

It is well to begin, then, with a short, simple version of the mission statement of the individual property, the strategic statement that sets out the property's broad mission, keeping in mind the corporate philosophy and the master strategy. For example, The Doubletree Guest Suites on Times Square in New York City picks up on the corporate mission and adds a short mission for each of its functional departments, as shown in Table 7-1.

Following is the property mission statement from a five-star (four-star deluxe by French nomenclature) hotel in Paris, part of a small luxury chain, that we will be using as an example throughout this chapter.

Grand expectations. . .
Pleasant surprises. . .
We will consistently serve our guests, employees, and owners by exceeding expectations and continually enhancing our standards of service excellence.
Listening, not hearing. . .
Doing, not just acting. . .
Anticipating, not just serving. . .
Caring, genuinely.

This will establish the context within which the marketing plan will be developed, which will be restated later as mission objectives.

A further statement at this point should include what has worked well in the past and broad objectives for the coming year, such as to increase actual market share from 8 to 10 percent,* or, qualitatively, to reach new markets or to expand old ones, or to project a better image.

The next step is to complete the first major portion of the plan, **data collection.**

Data Collection

External Environment. Data collection can be divided into two parts: external and internal. **External data** deals with the environment, including international and domestic trends as mentioned in Chapter 4 and further explained in Chapters 5 and 6. There are also numerous industry trends to be considered, such as growth or decline of various market segments, building trends affecting future supply, room occupancy and eating-out trends, and new concept trends.

Then there are external impacts such as state, regional, or national tourism promotions, major new tourist attractions, new industries in the area, new office buildings being built, airline routes added or removed, plant closings, companies merged and moved, new sources of visitor origin, and new convention centers being built. Every factor does not affect every operation; the key is to recognize those that may affect yours. The marketing plan has to deal with these factors, prepare for them, and, whenever possible, capitalize on them or counteract them.

For example, we know of one restaurateur who had operated a very successful restaurant for a number of years until business began declining quite drastically. Because this operation was in the country and some distance off a main highway, the operator concluded that people were simply not traveling as often or as far, because of the cost of gasoline. Closer analysis, however, revealed that his

---

*An interesting side note: Jack Welch, CEO of General Electric for many years, and considered by many to be one of the top CEOs in industry, is noted for saying, "I don't want my fair share; I want my UNfair share."

TABLE 7-1
Doubletree Guest Suites New York City Mission Statement

Corporate: Doubletree Hotels Corporation is a socially sensitive organization committed to its team members, customers, and to the communities in which we do business.

Doubletree Hotels Corporation is committed to the recognition and satisfaction of human needs through integrity, quality, and communications.

Doubletree Hotels Corporation is an industry leader, creating a quality product and work environment, which will result in superior financial performance and long-term asset appreciation.

Functional Areas:

Human Resources: We are the human tools that ensure the success of our team members by providing a healthy environment through competitive recruitment, development recognition, and compensation.

Housekeeping: We will do our best to provide you with clean and comfortable accommodations each and every day.

Engineering: We are committed to doing it right the first time.

Food and Beverage: We provide each and every guest with an exceptional dining experience, utilizing the freshest ingredients available, and present our products in an interesting, efficient, friendly, and professional manner.

Front Office: We are empowered and committed to providing quality service and a friendly atmosphere—at your home away from home.

Reservations: There are no hesitations when you call for reservations.

Sales: We will demonstrate and encourage a level of service that inspires our fellow team members. We will respect each team member as we work together to achieve excellence and have fun in the process.

competition was doing better than ever. In fact, the tastes of the market had changed and new markets had emerged. Instead of adapting to the market (e.g., he refused to change his menu, which had remained pretty much the same for 30 years, because his remaining old long-time customers "loved it as it is"), he watched his business gradually disappear.

Competitive Environment. The second area of external data collection is concerned with **competitive data.** It is important that the local marketing team collect data on all feasible competitors within logical boundaries. Understand that "logical boundaries" may mean the hotel or restaurant across the street or it may mean the one 3000 miles away. The competition for the convention market for the Hotel del Coronado off the coast of southern California includes the Homestead Hotel in Virginia, the Greenbriar Hotel in West Virginia, the Cloisters Hotel in Georgia, the Breakers Hotel in Florida, and the Hyatt Regency in Maui, not to mention many others.

The motel in North Overshoe, Maine, competes with the motel in South Skislope, Maine, even though they are 30 miles apart. The Club Med in Eleuthera in the Bahamas competes with the all-inclusive Couples in Jamaica.* The restaurant in the city competes with the one in the suburbs. And McDonald's competes with the convenience store but, by the same token, neither one competes with the French restaurant located between them. **Competition,** as defined by the marketing plan, is anyone competing for the same customer with the same or a similar product, or a reasonable alternative, that the customer has a reasonable opportunity to purchase at the same time and in the same context. Sometimes you can learn who your competition is from their advertising, as indicated in Figure 7-1.

---

*An "all-inclusive" resort contains all product/services, for example, food, drink, lodging, sports activities, in one all-inclusive price.

FIGURE 7-1   Four Points Hotels—Learning from advertising who your competition is

As in everything, of course, there may be exceptions. We may want to expand even from this perspective of competition in a highly competitive environment or from the perspective of a period of slow economic growth. At these times it may be necessary to reach down-market from the current level of product in order to maintain acceptable profit margins.

These different views of who the competition is have been discussed in the previous chapter on competitive analysis. Let it suffice here to say that the marketing plan should include data on any competitor from which, in the forthcoming year, we can reasonably expect to take customers, or to which we could conceivably lose customers.

The marketing team must take an objective stance when it comes to evaluating the competition. While we all like to believe we have the best product to sell in our product class, this may lull us into a false sense of security, and the competition can move by us very quickly. The marketing plan must be truly objective and realistic about the products evaluated for the best results. After making a list of all competitors for your product, the minimum information shown in Table 7-2 will be needed.

TABLE 7-2
Competitive Information Needed in the Marketing Plan

Description: A brief description of the physical attributes of the competing hotel or restaurant or lounge (or, for tourism, countries, states, or cities, etc.). Emphasize strengths as well as weaknesses. Determine such things as when the product was last renovated, plans for upgrading in the near future, physical facilities, and all features that compete with yours—that is, the product/service mix. The description includes quality and level of both tangible and intangible features, personnel, procedures, management, reservations systems, distribution networks, marketing efforts and successes and failures, promotions, market share, image, positioning, chain advantages/disadvantages, and so forth. All of these items will be important in the final analysis. A physical description—number of rooms, meeting space, F&B outlets, and so on—is simply not enough. All strengths and weaknesses need to be defined.

Customer Base: Who are their customers? Why do these customers go there? Are they potentially your customers? Part of the marketing plan will focus on creating demand for your product. Much of the plan will focus on taking customers directly from your competitors. It will be difficult to take customers from your competition if you do not know who those customers are. In a restaurant situation, for example, do your competitors have a high volume of senior citizens eating at traditionally quiet times, a group that you desire? Does their lounge have a successful happy hour that you could improve on for your lounge and, if so, what type of people go there? Does a competitive hotel have a higher percentage of transient guests than your own? What particular market segments does the competition attract?

Price Structure: Where is your competition in relation to price? While food and beverage prices are relatively easy to obtain, the product delivered for the price is also important. Is their $6.95 chef's salad as good as yours for $8.95? When analyzing prices it is important to compare "apples with apples." Published guest room prices are relatively easy to discover. Prices negotiated with volume producers take a little more effort but can usually be obtained from purchasers, or from directories made available to the public.

Future Supply: It is important to determine if there are any new projects that will affect your competitive environment in the future. This information can normally be obtained from the Chamber of Commerce or other local sources. The fact that a new 300-room hotel is scheduled to break ground soon is very important in the development of the marketing plan. Likewise, if the building that houses a major food and beverage competitor is scheduled for demolition to make way for a new office park, this could also influence your decision-making process for the following year.

Once again, keep in mind that competition is all relative. Traditional boundaries of location may no longer apply. For a restaurant in New York City the competition may encompass a three-block radius that is less than one-quarter square mile. For a five-star resort hotel the competition might be located thousands of miles away. When determining who your competition is, the question must be asked; "Where else do/might my customers/potential customers go?" Other competitive information that might be needed has been detailed in Chapter 6.

In the development of the marketing plan, it is also critical to keep in mind the fact that you want new customers and that you are looking for opportunities to get them. This means that sometimes you have to break the "rules" of competition. For example, a Hilton property might normally be positioned against Sheraton, Hyatt, and Westin as competition. In good times this might be correct. However, when occupancies are low the Hilton hotel might consider customers that it could capture at a profit from other competition. If rooms are going vacant, a "normal" Holiday Inn customer might be a target of the marketing plan of the hypothetical Hilton. A Holiday Inn customer might only be williling to pay $95 for a room that usually goes for $125. If the room costs $25 to prepare, however, that $95 customer may be a good customer to have when the room might otherwise be vacant. In addition, there might be a synergistic effect in being able to retain this person as a regular customer. On the other hand, the Red Roof Inn customer, who only wants a room at $59, would not be considered as an alternative target.

Internal Environment. The third area of collection is that of **internal data.** One hopes that accurate and adequate records have been kept; if so much of this information will be readily at hand. Once you have prepared your first marketing plan you will have said, at least a dozen times, "I wish I knew that." Thus you will have set up procedures so that next year you will know "that."

Hotels and/or restaurants should have current data at all times on occupied rooms, occupancy ratio, fair market share (FMS), actual market share (AMS), revenues, average rate (totally and by market segment), REVPAR, market segments served, restaurant covers, seat turnovers, menu abstracts, average check, food to beverage check ratios (totally and for each outlet), and ratios as a percentage of gross revenue. These figures should be broken down by month, seasonally, and by days of the week. This is also the place to identify market segments and target markets—past, present, and future.

These are the "hard" data and the easiest to obtain, but not the place to stop. List now what you know about the markets. Who are they, what do they like, what are their needs and wants? Why do they come here? Where would they go if they didn't come here? What are their complaints? Describe their characteristics, attitudes, opinions, and preferences. What is the market's perception and awareness? If you don't know the answers to these questions, it is time to start doing some research. At the minimum, start talking to your customers. Have personnel in every single department keep logs on all customer comments—good, bad, and otherwise.

Formal research is even better. The basic tenet of all marketing is to know your market. It is surprising how few hospitality establishments do. This is why so many marketing plans, rather than discuss what they will do for the customer, deal with bricks and mortar, physical facilities, inaccurate definition of competition, too broad market segments (e.g., the business traveler), vague budgets and forecasts, and undirected advertising.

The second category of internal data collection is the objective listing of resource strengths and weaknesses, including the bricks and mortar. What is the condition of the property? Where is it weak and where is it strong? How can/should it be improved? What does it offer in terms of facilities? How effective is the location?

Then, the hardest part—how strong is management? The marketing staff? Personnel training, experience, and attitude? How are guests being treated? What do complaints look like? How successful have marketing efforts been in the past? What is the consumer image of the property? What is the position in the marketplace? This is the time for realistic objectivity, not glossing over or wishful thinking. Finally, make a list of what you do not know, that is, what research is needed.

To give an idea of how all this comes together, some abstractions from the data collection portion of the actual marketing plan of a five-star hotel in Paris are shown in Table 7-3.*

Data Analysis

Thus far we have been engaged only in the collection of data. It is wise to complete this stage first without attempting any **data analysis,** because you want to obtain the complete picture. Analyzing different factors in isolation can be misleading.

Analysis follows the same flow as the data collection process. Essentially, we want to draw some conclusions about market position, market segments, customer behavior, environmental impacts, growth potential, strengths and weaknesses, threats and opportunities, performance trends, customer satisfaction, resource needs and limitations, and other factors that will be pertinent to the marketing plan.

Environmental and Market Trend Analysis. Look first at environmental and market trends. Are they positive or negative? How will/can they affect us? How can we take advantage of, or compensate,

---

*Note that the entire marketing plan is 78 pages long, so we can only show excerpts.

T A B L E   7-3
Data Collection Abstracts from a Paris Hotel Marketing Plan

Economy: The economy in France is wrestling with the creation of the postwar socialist state, the European Union (EU), and the forthcoming EU currency, the euro. The latter, especially, will have multiple effects on pricing and operating costs. High unemployment (12%) has put pressure on the government to reduce benefits to workers to increase jobs. Neighboring European states are producing quality goods with one-third of the fixed labor costs.

External Impacts: While Paris remains a strong destination in the worldwide marketplace, pricing has become an issue. Five-star hotel rooms in Los Angeles go for $450 a night, New York $500, London $600, and Paris $700. The results are occupancies in the mid-fifty percent range, making most hotels unprofitable. Customers are coming to Paris from other European destinations for only one- and two-day trips, leaving rooms empty almost one-half of the time. The results of low occupancies have been delayed renovations. This year the Crillon, Bristol, Plaza Athenee, and the Meurice will all complete total renovations. The Ritz finished its two years ago.

Internal Impacts: While service levels remain high, workers share the growing anxiety of the French economy. Will jobs be combined or eliminated to meet owners' needs? Will the customers return after the renovations, or be absorbed by another hotel in the area? Will the new hotel opening on the Champs Elysée be accepted by the local French, or will they like other competitors better?

Future of Our Markets: The European Union makes travel among members much easier, as will a single currency. Overall, the economy of Europe itself is growing, led by the United Kingdom, Paris' largest feeder market. Tourists, however, are more prone to short holidays, and weekends, and packages, especially in summer, our busiest season. Company individual bookings have also declined.

for them? What are our alternatives? How long will they last? What courses of action are possible and feasible? How do these fit together?

Competitive and Demand Analysis. What are the potentials and opportunities in the marketplace? Determining this requires a close analysis of all the demand factors, various market segments, and target markets—for instance, what are the strongest market segments; what is their potential for further growth; are they steady, growing, or in decline; what is their contribution in room nights, covers, revenue; what can be done to accelerate a growing trend, begin growth in a steady trend, or reverse the direction of a declining trend? What other segments are there, perhaps untouched, that could be developed?

How do these segments affect our market mix? Are they compatible? Can they be expanded to fill gaps such as seasonal or day-of-the-week fluctuations? What types of business would complement these segments? What types of action could be taken to attract more business during low-occupancy periods? How does the competitive situation affect all these factors?

Property Needs Analysis. Here we have added a new category. A **property needs analysis** means analyzing major profit areas to see what gaps have to be filled. These gaps could be in occupancy, market share, average room rates, market segments, food sales, beverage sales, seasonal needs, and many other areas. In other words, instead of looking at where we can cut costs, we want to look at where we can obtain business. When we have done that we can match property needs with market needs to determine target markets and how to reach and serve them.

Needs analysis also means identifying other marketing problems. For example, this might be marketing strategies that aren't working, image changes that are needed, ineffective advertising or promotion, pricing problems, losing business to a particular competitor (perhaps because of a new facility, new product or service, or even just better marketing), or changing needs of a market segment that we can't meet.

In short, property needs analysis is an identification of problems to be overcome. It makes the case clearer if we can apply some quantitative measurements to our analysis, which is no more than a best estimate based upon all of the data assembled. To demonstrate this we will use a simplified case to determine what the overall increase or decrease for the product will be for the forthcoming year. Ideally, this would be done by market segment.

In this example, we will say that we are anticipating an increase of 2 percent in demand for both group and transient hotel rooms in the product class category. From the data collected, a competitive universe can be compiled, as shown in Table 7-4. Assume, for the purpose of discussion, that a Holiday Inn Crowne Plaza of 200 rooms is opening next year with a projected occupancy of 55 percent. Its forecasted market mix is 50 percent group and 50 percent transient.

Now, for the purpose of developing the marketing plan, we have some quantitative data with which to work. One thing is immediately obvious: ABC Hotel has a relatively low occupancy and is barely getting fair market share. After all the data collected in the situation analysis have been analyzed, two main areas of concentration are ready to be addressed: creating new business and capturing competitors' business.

Creation of New Business. Given the current situation, what plans can be developed to create a new demand for the product? McDonald's created a new demand for its product by opening for breakfast. Package weekends have created new demands for hotel products in the past. Creating a new demand in the hospitality industry, however, may be the toughest part of marketing. The important point to remember is that we are creating demand that until now did not exist for a product. This usually means creating a new use.

Leading Hotels "Manhattan Summer Sale" is an example of a promotion to create new business (Figure 7-2). In this case, the target market is couples who enjoy luxury but normally can't afford it, including luxury shopping. They might stay home except for this exciting opportunity, or perhaps they have been enticed away from a competitor offering only a standard package. The objective of the hotel, of course, is to build new business. This is different from, for example, selling a corporate meeting package where meeting planners have already decided what they want to do, the only question being "where." That constitutes direct marketing against the competition, rather than creating a new use for the product. Other parts of the marketing plan will carry out and specify the implementation of the Summer Sale concept in terms of the specific target market.

Capturing Competitors' Business. Most efforts of the marketing plan will concentrate in this area. Specifically, let's return to the competitive universe depicted in Table 7-4. ABC Hotel's main competitors are Westin, Hyatt, and Hilton, plus the new

TABLE 7-4
Hypothetical Competitive Universe of ABC Hotel

Hotel	Number of Rooms	Rooms Available/Year	FMS[a]	% Rooms Occupied	Rooms Sold	AMS[b] Variance		Rank
ABC Hotel	200	73,000	20%	67	48,910	20%	0	3
Westin	350	127,750	35%	73	93,258	38.2%	3.2	1
Hyatt	250	91,250	25%	72	65,700	26.9%	1.9	2
Hilton	200	73,000	20%	50	36,500	14.9%	(5.1)	4
Total	1000	365,000	100%	67	244,368	100%		

[a]FMS (Fair Market Share) is the number of available rooms per hotel divided by total available rooms.
[b]AMS (Actual Market Share) is the number of rooms sold per hotel divided by the total number of rooms sold.

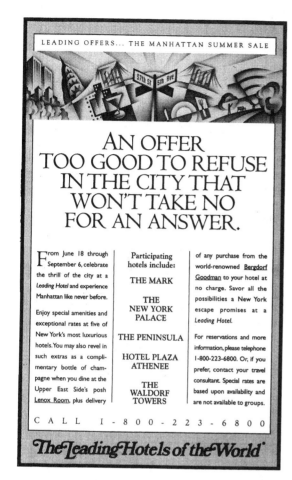

FIGURE 7-2 Leading Hotels advertise a special summer package intended to create new business.

Crowne Plaza being built. A demand analysis for these five hotels, two of which are capturing more than their fair market share, while ABC and Hilton are not, might appear as shown in Table 7-5.

A red flag should be raised with this scenario. Although the forecast is an increase in demand for the hotel product, the increase in supply will be greater than the increase in demand. Each hotel will now be fighting for a smaller piece of the pie. If ABC Hotel does everything the same as the year before, they will be drawing on a smaller pool of rooms and occupancy will drop lower. In fact, ABC and its four competitors are now competing for

209,105 rooms versus 244,368 of the previous year, after the new Crowne Plaza takes its share.

ABC's marketing team can now see the task that lies before it. In order just to maintain the occupancies of the year before, it will have to create new demand for the product, aggressively attack competitors for new business, and maintain its own customer base, which the competition will be trying to lure away with their own marketing plans. It will also have to exceed its new FMS by 2.95 percentage points, something it hasn't been able to do in the past. ABC's strength may be as a transient hotel while this may be a weakness of the other properties. In this case, ABC might choose to direct its major marketing effort at that market.

Another possibility is that ABC has neglected the group market and needs to direct greater effort in that direction. Then, of course, it may have to make major efforts in both directions. Let us assume, for the sake of argument and because it is easier to demonstrate, that there is high price sensitivity in the market in either one or both of these segments. In either case, specific marketing plans must be made to attack the competitive hotels in order to capture rooms from them. The plans might, perhaps, be directed at lowering prices specific days of the week or times of the year when ABC's occupancy suffers the most.

The ABC example is clearly an oversimplified one. There are innumerable other factors affecting any similar situation, and numerous alternative approaches. In fact, we haven't even mentioned the consumer in this discussion, and that database would be the first one to consider! The point we want to make is that there is an absolute need for complete and adequate data and information followed by thorough analysis of all possible considerations. It is only through such methods that workable, realistic, and effective marketing plans can be developed.

Internal Analysis. We now turn to the **internal analysis.** Using the realistic and objective data we have gathered, we start by asking questions such as those shown in Table 7-6. We would do this by segment and target market. Strategies by segment for a

T A B L E   7-5
Hypothetical Demand Analysis

	Total	Group Segment	Transient Segment	New ABC FMS	@20%AMS
Rooms sold previous year	244,368	146,231	98,137		
Next year projection with 2% increase in demand	249,255	149,156	100,099		
New supply—Crowne Plaza	40,150	20,075	20,075	16.7%	49,851

hotel might include group sales, consortia, national sales, local corporate, weekends, or international markets. Catering might include segments like free-standing, local corporate, evenings, and social markets. Descriptions on how each market should be addressed would be outlined in this section.

Once again, a list like the one in Table 7-6 could go on indefinitely. Once again, we have to state that workable, effective, and realistic marketing plans can be developed only through the gathering of complete and adequate information and its thorough and objective analysis.

Market Analysis.   Our final step in analysis is the market itself, the customer. Because this entire book is about the hospitality customer, it would be redundant to repeat here all that we will say about this strange individual who is the reason for the existence of any hospitality enterprise. For purposes of devel-oping the marketing plan, this step means determining where the gaps are, where needs are unfulfilled, where problems are not being solved, and where the niches are that the competition is not filling.

This analysis must be matched with the environmental trends, the competitive and demand analysis, the property needs analysis, and the internal analysis. We would, of course, combine all these analyses by segment and target market. We are then ready to develop a mission statement for the property, determine opportunities, establish objectives, and begin the actual marketing plan, which will include a plan and course of action for each segment or target market.

The Mission and Marketing Position Statement

The mission statement at the beginning of the marketing plan flows from the strategic mission state-

T A B L E   7-6
Internal Analysis Questions

What is the gap between what your customers want and need, what you promise them, and the product/service that is provided? How well do you meet or exceed customer expectations?

How does the market's estimation of your product/service agree with yours? What makes you think so?

What items, product improvements, or services are needed to improve customer satisfaction?

Are you actually delivering what you think you are?

What patterns are appearing in guest comments? What types of problems seem to recur? What areas seem to need improvement?

Do you have the proper organization to accomplish what you are trying to? For instance, although the manager is a strong operations person does he or someone else understand the customer?

Do you reward your staff strictly on bottom-line results? If so, does it show up in matters affecting the customers?

Do you know, identify, and deal with your real strengths and weaknesses?

ment and from the corporate mission statement and differs in that it is a broad statement of objectives at the unit level. The general guideline of the corporate mission statement is a good starting point. In multi-unit organizations, however, there can be great variety. Many chains have diversified products selling in diversified markets for diversified uses. Corporate strategies established in corporate headquarters in Atlanta, Chicago, New York, London, Paris, or Tokyo do not necessarily fit the situation in India, Germany, Kuwait, New York City, Minneapolis, or Los Angeles.

It is the situation analysis of the marketing plan that provides the test of the strategy and necessitates rewriting the local mission statement. Thus only after the situation analysis has been completed do we recommend writing the marketing plan mission statement and, if necessary, adjusting the strategic mission statement. Recall, moreover, that the latter is the long-term mission; the marketing plan mission is designed for one year at a time. This mission statement will have specific objectives such as "to be the business traveler's hotel of choice in the city." More specific objectives will be contained in the statement of objectives, such as ". . . by increasing our ratio of business customers to pleasure travelers from 55 to 65 percent."

Further, the marketing position will be identified. This statement flows from the strengths and weaknesses of the competition as well as the property for which the plan is written. For example, our Paris hotel example would be positioned, at minimum, as one of the top five luxury hotels in Paris. Other attributes, such as a "corporate luxury hotel," might also be part of the positioning to that market segment. Market positioning is discussed in detail in Chapter 11.

Opportunity Analysis

If a thorough job of data collection and analysis has been done, we should now be able to determine the opportunities available. The section heading is self-explanatory and can best be discussed by example. Therefore, we abstract again from the marketing plan of the Paris hotel previously mentioned, as shown in Table 7-7.

T A B L E 7-7
Marketing Plan Opportunity Analysis of Paris Hotel

---

1. Market segments relating to existing customer mix:
   - Corporate groups
   - Corporate individual bookings
   - Leisure travelers from abroad
   - Weekend packages with special features
   - Special off-season incentives
2. New markets:
   - Packages for individual travelers
   - U.S. upscale travel agencies
   - Incentive market—London, New York
   - High ranking government officials
3. Image
   - More professional and colorful F&B promotions
   - Improved reputation for service and cuisine
   - Provide better background information about city, emphasize price/value
   - Professional advertising to improve hotel image

The opportunities in Table 7-7, although perhaps too general, have been derived after analysis of the market, market segments, the competition, trends, the needs of the property, and so forth. Its brief form belies the groundwork that goes into identifying opportunities. Sometimes this groundwork is not done—that is, someone says something like, "How about the incentive market? We don't have any of that business. That's an opportunity! Let's put it down." Of course, a thorough study of the incentive market, its needs and wants, and the organization's ability to serve them is necessary first. Opportunities, in the true sense, are not just something that's "out there"; they are, instead, a match between consumer needs and an organization's competencies and, one hopes, a lapse in the competition.

Objectives and Methods

The next step in the marketing plan is to establish the objectives and how they are to be accomplished. Again, this is better explained by doing, so we continue to abstract from the marketing plan of the French five-star hotel, as shown in Table 7-8.

The objectives listed in Table 7-8 are specific and fairly typical of hotel marketing plans. Many are directly measurable. Action plans are designed to carry out each one. There could be many other kinds of objectives, including strategic ones, particularly those that derive from the identification of market needs, such as those in Table 7-9.

We caution again not to try to do too many things at once. Make objectives reasonable, so they can be accomplished and can be done well.

A marketing plan needs to be employed for existing customers as well. Relationship marketing can always be improved. These customers may, in fact, be the best opportunity and the target of the most important objectives. This part of the plan addresses current patrons, and should be designed to make them "competition proof." Because the main emphasis of the marketing plan will be on capturing competitors' business, so too will be the emphasis of competitors' marketing plans. If the

focus is entirely on bringing in new customers and the present customers are forgotten, then the marketing plan is simply going to be one of robbing Peter to pay Paul. Replacing current customers with new customers is never cost-efficient.

A documented plan to keep guests coming back and to reduce exposure to competitors' attempts to steal customers should be an integral part of any marketing plan. Once again, however, this does not necessarily mean giveaway programs. The basic task of marketing is to fulfill its promises, not give away the product.

Action Plans

Action plans dictate how the marketing plan will be carried out. They assign specific responsibility to individuals and dates for accomplishment. An action plan is a detailed list of the action steps necessary for carrying out the strategies and tactics for reaching each objective. One format for an action plan is shown in Table 7-10, but there are numerous variations on the theme.

Action plans deal with the various parts of the marketing mix, which of course is the implementation of the marketing plan. For example, the action plan for the communications mix would incorporate advertising, direct mail, personal sales efforts, promotions, merchandising, and public relations campaigns. Each of these is coordinated for maximum impact of the strategies that are derived from the conclusions drawn from the creation of business and competitive strategies section of the plan.

The action plan should be developed for a full year, updated quarterly with all products and actions for new business, keeping current business, and strategies for taking business from competitors outlined in time frames that reflect achievable goals.

In the previous example of the Summer Sale, advertising support may be necessary in designated months to create awareness and accommodate requests for more information. An ad in a sophisticated magazine would be in support of the

---

T A B L E 7-8
Objectives and Methods from Paris Hotel Marketing Plan

A. To increase yearly occupancy from 58 to 64 percent:
1. Review annual forecast on a monthly and weekly basis to ensure an overall and continuous view of occupancies and early actions where problem periods or days exist.
2. Develop and advertise more attractive, unique weekend packages to increase weekend occupancy by 15 percentage points.
3. Orient the room rate structure to the market and similar destinations worldwide.
4. Conduct permanent hard and aggressive sales actions to increase:
   - Corporate rate business—increase 10 percent from present 38 percent of occupancy.
   - Seminars and small conferences, especially in winter.
   - Winter weekend business with high end travelers.
   - Incentive travel year-round—now 1 percent of occupancy, increase to 5 percent.
B. To keep up with the competition and increase our actual market share among direct competitors in Paris from 14.7 to 16.5 percent (FMS is 15.2 percent):
1. Provide better technological amenities for business travelers.
2. Make better use of database on regular customers and their needs.
3. Spruce up hospitality service and well-trained staff.
4. Continuous sales follow-up on existing corporate clients.
5. Continuous sales calls to potential new customers.
6. Offer clients "just a little more" in rooms and restaurant, which will make their stay with us different from the others.
7. Develop more creativity in sales and F&B.
C. To level out occupancy throughout the year:
1. Develop attractive (but not bargain) offers during weak periods for seminars and conferences, emphasize price/value.
2. Develop winter all-inclusive packages for individuals.
3. Develop new initiatives, such as room here and lunch on Champs Elysee.
4. Develop incentive tie-ins with exclusive Parisian boutiques.
D. To level out occupancy over the week:
1. Lower rates for winter seminars during the week.
2. Develop packages for individuals to be distributed to London travel agents with special commission rates.
3. Create special activities for upscale consortia to sell in United Kingdom, Japan, and the United States.
E. To increase average rate from 3400 FF to 3800 FF:
1. Increase corporate rates and add value with business amenities.
2. Increase rates in the commercial business market by 10 percent.
3. Build higher rate in suites through luxury room amenities, upgrades, and services.
4. Try to reduce low-rate contracts during high season.
5. Develop exclusive weekend packages at higher prices where the market is not price sensitive.

(continued)

TABLE 7-8 *(Continued)*

F. To increase F&B sales by 10 percent overall and average check in signature dining room from 1400 FF to 1600 FF:

1. Improve signature restaurant image with better selling of individual items (versus degustation menu) and wines.

2. Appeal more to in-house guests through:
   - Tasteful promotional material in rooms, lobby, reception, and other guest service areas.
   - Food promotion frames inside and in front of elevators.
   - Sales-trained people in bar, restaurant.
   - Training guest service agents to ask at check-in if guests want to reserve table in restaurant.

3. Develop the local market through promotions:
   - Special chef presentation dinner promotions.
   - Wedding promotions for exclusivity and security.
   - Charity dinners at the high end.
   - Attract traders in the financial sector with an after-work promotion.

package, designed to counter a competitor's offering during the traditionally slower months in the summer. An advertisement in a travel agency index might be intended to offer an alternative to competition presently more frequently utilized by travel agencies.

Yearly schedules for other support mechanisms of the communications mix are needed to coordinate the entire plan. A direct mail campaign might be used in conjunction with the advertising for the Summer Sale to generate the highest volume. Without action plans, too many things are forgotten too often, or are done too late to be effective.

There are other concerns as well. The communications mix is expensive to execute. The aggressive marketing executive will constantly be looking for ways to maximize communications mix dollars. Co-advertising is possible with related travel

TABLE 7-9
Some Possible Marketing Plan Objectives

Changes in marketing direction

Defensive or offensive marketing moves

New opportunities

Other specific product line objectives

Market share objectives—overall and by market segment, such as geographic, demographic, psychographic, group, FIT (free independent traveler), package, and so on

Pricing objectives

Sales and promotion objectives

Advertising objectives

Channel, distribution, and intermediary objectives, such as travel agents

Research objectives

Awareness, perception, image, and positioning objectives

Double occupancy objectives

Customer loyalty and repeat business objectives

Customer satisfaction objectives

T A B L E   7 - 1 0
Marketing Plan Action Plan

XYZ Hotel Marketing Action Plan

Name: Quarter:

Booking Goals

__1000__ Month   __250__ Week   __50__ Day

New Accounts Opened

__20__ Month   __5__ Week   __1__ Day

Action Plan By Week: Person Responsible:

Week 1   _____ Begin advertising campaign, corp group _____
Week 2   _____ Trade show schedule, third quarter _____
Week 3   _____ Direct mail, corporate transient _____
Week 4   _____ Good accounts function, associations _____
Week 5   _____ Public relations for catering _____
Week 6   _____ Public relations for catering _____
Week 7   _____ Focus groups, meeting planners _____
Week 8   _____ Focus groups, travel agents _____
Week 9   _____ Image advertising campaign begins _____
Week 10   _____ Strategy session, tour and travel _____
Week 11   _____ Direct mail, past users _____
Week 12   _____ Develop co-marketing partners _____

---

industries, such as American Express (Figure 7-3). Airlines are increasingly willing to work with hotels to generate business through collective advertising and direct mail. Credit card companies are doing dual promotions with restaurants and lounges on a consistent basis to differentiate their products and combine resources. Telephone companies are now aggressively marketing together with hotels (see Figure 7-1 again). All these efforts require considerable advance planning and specific actions being done on time.

Except for forecasts and budgeting, the marketing plan is now complete. Remember, this should be a "fluid" document, ready to be changed with shifts of the marketplace. This is not to suggest that the entire marketing plan be rewritten every time there is a shift in the market; if the situation analysis was done properly, the conclusions drawn should not change readily or dramatically.

Some opportunities, however, that present themselves during the year should be incorporated into an effective marketing plan. If an opportunity arose to do a combined direct mail piece to selected guests of a reputable credit card company, for example, it should not be passed up just because it's not in the marketing plan. The plan should be analyzed and resources reallocated if necessary.

The Marketing Forecast

Making accurate **marketing forecasts** is one of the most difficult stages of the marketing plan. Regardless, the best attempt possible is essential. Forecasts are a venture into the unknown that are subject to any number of alterations in the marketplace. The answer to accuracy lies in the best information available, thorough analysis, and the best judgment of the forecaster.

F I G U R E   7 - 3   Renaissance co-advertises with American Express.

Many hotel marketing plan formats require the projection of room nights for every day of the forthcoming year to forecast, by segment and day of the week, the upcoming year's business. It is not uncommon for forecasters to use some figure, say 5 percent, as the projected increase in sales over the previous year. Such a method is purely arbitrary and of little advantage. It is better to start with a zero base each year and build according to the marketing plan. In this way, room nights, covers, and other sources of revenue are based on the marketing objectives that have been realistically established. Monetary amounts such as average room

rate per segment, average breakfast, lunch, and dinner check, and so on are used as the multipliers to forecast revenue.

Table 7-11 illustrates a forecast form used by one hotel company. Again, there are many variations on the theme according to the particular situation or needs of the operation.

The Marketing Budget

Industry-wide averages for **marketing budgets** of U.S. hotels are between 5 and 7 percent of total sales. (There are no reported averages for restaurants ex-

TABLE 7-11
Hotel Occupancy Forecasting Form, by Month

	LAST YEAR ACTUAL Rooms Occupied	LAST YEAR ACTUAL Average Rate	LAST YEAR ACTUAL Revenues	BUDGET Revenues	BUDGET Average Rate	BUDGET Rooms Rented	J	F	M
Pure/Transient									
Meeting Conv.									
Tour & Travel									
Individual									
Wholesaler									
Group									
Total Tour & Travel									
Contract									
Charter									
Other									
Total Contract									
Commercial									
Preferred Co.									
Pref. Guest									
Other									
Total Commercial									
Special Programs									
W/E Package									
Other									
Other									
Other									
Other									
TOTALS									
Rooms Avail.									
% of Occ.									

cept a general figure of 2 to 3 percent of sales spent on advertising for an individual sit-down, mid-to-upper scale operation.) As a rule of thumb, the marketing payroll expenses are normally about one half of the marketing budget. Traditionally, resorts have slightly higher marketing expenses, as do new properties with high opening costs. The overall trend in the industry has been toward increasing the marketing budget as a total percentage of sales. Hotel advertising today, for example, has proliferated considerably over ten years ago.

An actual brief description of a marketing budget for a convention chain hotel in a major U.S. city is as follows:

Sales revenues	$50 million
Marketing budget:	2.5 million
Includes wages, supplies, local and corporate advertising, direct mail, public relations, entertainment, national sales office support, travel	
Does not include chain reservation system fees or travel agency fees	
Sales staff: One director of marketing	
Two directors of sales	
Eight sales managers	
Support of chain's frequent traveler program	$400,000

Internationally, the expenses for marketing average slightly lower, in Asia between 5 and 6 percent of total sales. Latin America and Caribbean hotels spend over 6 percent of sales for their marketing budget, while hotels in Europe and Africa spend under 4 percent of their total sales.[2]

Unfortunately, these industry averages mean very little in the increasingly competitive environment that has been created in the hospitality industry. The traditional 5 percent of hotel sales allocated to marketing was sufficient for a property to maintain its market share and occupancies consistently in the days when the increase in demand for hotel rooms was exceeding the number of rooms being built.

While demand continues to be strong for the lodging product, supply of the product in many markets will eventually eclipse the growth curve, once again. Some markets have seen a 20-plus percent increase in supply of hotel rooms, with a 5 percent increase in demand. To attack a problem of this kind with a traditional marketing budget of 5 percent of total sales would be like David fighting Goliath. (Recall, however, that David won, because he had a better strategy.) More important, for marketing planning, what is taking place is a shift in the market into different product classes.

The marketing budget should be a natural extension of the marketing plan—no more and no less. Once a strategy has been developed to create, steal, or keep customers, the funds need to be allocated to ensure success.

The budget will normally include the following categories in some degree, regardless of the size or type of the operation. This even includes a case in which, for example, the manager of a restaurant (chain, individual, or within a hotel) performs all the marketing and sales duties. Parts of that person's salary and expenses should be allocated to the marketing budget.

Payroll will include all marketing and sales time plus any secretarial or related work.
Communication includes all advertising, promotion, direct mail, public relations, collateral, and related items.
Travel includes all related travel.
Office expenses include telephone and related office supplies.
Research includes all research expenses.
Entertainment includes entertainment of clients or prospective clients, both in-house and out.

The above are broad and fairly obvious categories. Further breakdown depends on the needs of the operation. What is important is that marketing expenses be clearly and appropriately assigned. As with any other budget items, they are a cost of operating a particular department. Table 7-12 shows one hotel's monthly spreadsheet for allocating particular expenses to a given time period.

The budget should be carefully prepared, not done haphazardly or by guesswork. If you are not your own boss, you will probably have to have it approved by someone. In that case, you may have to justify each cost item as one that will produce tangible results.

The marketing budget should also be a fluid tool, reacting to the changes in the marketing plan. It is critical to protect the integrity of the budget and plan throughout the planning year. The plan and budget should be changed if results are falling

T A B L E   7-12
Monthly Spreadsheet for Allocating Expenses to a Given Month

	Dates	Market Segment
Sales Trips/Trade Shows		
Washington (WSAE)	5/00	Group
Atlanta/Delta & Agents	5/00	T&T/Whlslrs
Incentive House Trip	5/00	T&T
Advertising		
Hotel Trvl Index 1 pg 4 c	Quarterly	T&T
Fla Resident Ad 2 col 5″	1 week	Special
Southern Living 4″ ad	Monthly	Trans.
Airport Display	Monthly	Trans.
Travel Agent Mktplc	Bi-monthly	T&T
Trvl Weekly 20″ 4c	6×	T&T
F&B Advertising		
Fla. Tour. News	6×	F&B
Orlando Mag ½ pg BW	Monthly	F&B
Dining Out 1 pg BW	Monthly	F&B
Orlando Sentinel	5×	F&B
Local News	1×	F&B
Special Promotions		
Mother's Day Coll. & Menu	Annual	F&B
Samantha's Calendar	Monthly	F&B
Direct Mail		
Bus. Reply	Ongoing	Group
Samantha's Mailing	Monthly	F&B
Mother's Day Mailing	Annual	F&B
Collateral Proration		
5000 Rack Brochures	Ongoing	Group
5000 IT Brochures	Ongoing	T&T
7000 F&B Brochures	Ongoing	F&B

short of forecasts. For instance, the Summer Sale might be considered cost-effective if it produced 50 rooms for a given week. If after three or four attempts, the demand never exceeds 35 rooms nights, the responsive marketing team will reevaluate the feasibility of the project.

The decision might be to try the promotion again at a later date, or to scrap it altogether and al-locate the funds elsewhere. The difficult decisions when cutting the marketing budget occur when managers think only in terms of short-range objectives (i.e., improving short-term financial performance by cutting costs) rather than executing longer-range strategies to increase and retain customers.

This type of situation occurs frequently in the

careers of sales and marketing professionals. Although there is no clear-cut answer to the dilemma, the need to create and keep customers should be the paramount consideration for any successful organization. Short-term rewards are gained too many times at the expense of future business.

MARKETING CONTROLS

There is a final step, and it's an important one—monitoring the marketing plan throughout the year and evaluating it periodically and at the end of the year.

The first step, of course, is to continuously match performance against the desired results and to detect when and where deviations occur. The extent of each deviation should be measured and the worst ones addressed. The cause of the deviation should be determined and dealt with, either by bringing it into line or by adjusting the plan.

Yardsticks are set up in advance. These could include any of the following as well as others: market share, occupancy figures, covers served, seat turnovers, check averages, F&B ratios, revenue per available guest room, average room rate by segment, product mix, business mix by segments, advance bookings, advertising results, return per marketing dollar, customer satisfaction, complaints/compliments, repeat business, revenue, and profit.

A feedback system should be established to synchronize with the yardsticks. You should be able to answer questions such as the following: Is the product meeting needs of the segment(s)?

Is the segment growing, static, or declining?
Is the segment profitable?
Is customer perception as intended?
Is your positioning correct?
How are you doing vis-à-vis the competition?
Are you solving consumers' problems?
Are weaknesses showing?

Are strengths being exploited?
Is there price resistance?
Are you having selling problems?
What are the reasons for the variances?

You may have to make changes where necessary and/or move in contingency plans. You may have to reanalyze your strategy or your plan, or perform a new situation analysis. Marketing plans are not static, but dynamic; they operate under dynamic conditions and must be monitored in the same way.

A final word: The marketing-driven organization must not be susceptible to a short-term mentality that will eventually lose customers. The marketing budget and plan should be adjusted according to the customers, not the accountants. To do otherwise is not unlike deferring maintenance to improve short-term bottom-line figures, and then having to buy new equipment at some time in the future. Even so, accountants must have their say. Thus plans and budgets must ultimately stand the test of concrete cost-effective results and proven revenues.

SUMMARY

The marketing plan and the marketing budget are fluid tools designed to create, capture, and retain customers. The process begins early in the year and continues until fall. It is based on a sound and realistic situation analysis, which requires good data collection, research where necessary, and acute analysis. Instead of relying on traditional methods to deal with unique situations, the marketing team needs to develop innovative strategies based on solid information. The funding of these strategies must then be realistic, to get the job done.

Table 7-13 has been designed as a template that can be used to develop a marketing plan. The chapter fills in many of the empty spaces with explanations, but the actual data must come from those who work the plan.

TABLE 7-13
Marketing Plan Template

1. *Overall Mission Statement:* This statement is broad-based, to serve as a guideline, and subject to revision later.

2. *Situation Analysis:* The situation analysis describes the business climate of the hospitality entity. This portion of the plan gives an overview of the business, recapping what worked well in the current year, and what needs to be accomplished for the upcoming year. It also indicates environmental and industry trends.

   - Recap of Past Year: What works well, what doesn't, and broad needs for next year.
   - Environmental Trends: Possible major shifts that affect customers or operations: political, economic, social, technological, ecological, regulatory.
   - Market Trends: Provide the foundation for the marketing plan: possible major or minor shifts that affect customers: international, national, regional, local. Statistics are gathered for analysis. Market potential is an important part of this. Macro statistics can be obtained from sources such as a Visitors and Convention Bureau or the National Restaurant Association. Micro statistics, such as local trends, can be obtained from Smith Travel Research for rooms, or Fasttrack for food and beverage.
   - Competitive Trends and Forces: Both current and forecasted are needed to anticipate competitive moves, strengths and weaknesses. A competitive review needs to be completed at least yearly. Current supply of hotel rooms or restaurants should be documented with not only the obvious statistics, such as number of guest rooms, seats, or square footage of function space, but also a determination of the direction of each competitor in terms of the overall market place. Strengths and weaknesses of each should be documented. Any new or lost supply of rooms or restaurants should be identified.

3. *Internal Data:* This includes all pertinent data and statistics on the operation, including both financial and customer data, including segments and target markets.

4. *Data Analysis:* This involves analyzing the data collected in steps 2 and 3. We add, however, one new category called "property needs analysis." In this category we analyze the internal gaps to be filled so that we can match them with the opportunities revealed by analysis of the other stages.

5. *Mission and Market Position Statement:* The mission and objectives for the forthcoming year are detailed. Although this is not done until all the previous above work is done, it will be inserted at the beginning of the marketing plan right after the broad mission statement. The market positioning follows. With the statistics gathered and the competitors reviewed, the hospitality entity has to state clearly where it belongs in the marketplace. For example, Mary's Restaurant will be positioned just below Cathy's Restaurant, directly in competition with Jenny's Restaurant, and above Meagan's Restaurant. The market position statement gives direction for the marketer as well as the employees as to what the hospitality entity expects of itself.

6. *Opportunity Analysis:* This analysis involves identifying all the opportunities in the marketplace, revealed by all the previous analyses, that are consistent with the mission and market position adopted. Once the positioning has been established, a strategy for each market segment needs to be developed. This can be as simple as break fast and lunch segments for Mary's Restaurant or as complex as identifying 22 segments of customers at The Grand Hyatt in New York City. Each segment has to be defined and planned for in the marketing program.

7. *Objectives and Methods:* Objectives must be measurable where appropriate. Together the objectives and methods lay out where we want to go and how we plan to get there.

8. *Action Plans:* This step sets specific responsibility for every member of the team, and even for some who are not direct members, such as a chef, who will be become involved here, if not before, in laying out the action necessary by him.

(continued)

TABLE 7-13   *(Continued)*

9. *Marketing Communications:* Each segment responds to different communication vehicles. The corporate market for rooms has to be called upon by salespeople, while customers for a restaurant "two-fers" offer read newspaper ads or listen to the radio. The marketing communications portion of the marketing plan establishes how we are going to tell our customers what we have to offer. Clearly there are multiple communication vehicles available for singular market segments. The corporate customer, for example, not only responds to a salesperson, he or she also reads corporate directories and advertisements.

10. *Market Forecast and Revenue Projections:* The revenue forecast takes all of the assumptions of the marketing program and establishes a financial goal for the upcoming year. In many cases revenue goals by market segment are determined to track the progress of the marketing programs.

11. *Marketing Budget:* With the data collection in place and strategies by segment outlined, the allocation of marketing resources such as advertising, public relations, direct sales, and database marketing are dedicated to support the strategies.

12. *Marketing Controls:* The old expression, "What gets measured gets done," applies here. Controls are the follow-up that will let you stay on track, see what is working and what isn't, and determine if any changes or new directions are needed.

KEY WORDS AND CONCEPTS

Action Plans: The action plans detail putting the marketing plan into action by specific assignment. While the marketing plan and mission statement are both written yearly, the action plans are updated at least quarterly to keep the planning process current.

Competition: Anyone competing for the same customer with the same or similar product, or reasonable alternative, that the customer has a reasonable opportunity to purchase at the same time and in the same context.

Data Analysis: This is the tearing apart of all the information collected so it can be analyzed and later synthesized to provide the course and structure of the marketing plan.

    Competitive analysis: This is a dissection of the competition and everything it does or doesn't do in the search for competitive advanatage.

    Demand Analysis: This searches the overall customer needs and demand factors for rooms or restaurant or other services.

    Environmental and Market Trend Analysis: This reveals the trends in the business environment and looks at their potential impact for opportunities and threats.

    Internal Analysis: This reflects the trends of the current customer base and the successes and failures of the property, and looks for strengths and weaknesses.

    Market Analysis: This is the consideration of all other phases of the data analysis together to focus on the customer, in the search for opportunities.

    Property Needs Analysis: This identifies the areas where the property needs improvement in developing the market.

Data Collection: The gathering of complete and adequate information for the marketing plan.

    Competitive Environment Data Collection: This includes the status of direct competitors and any information that can be obtained about them, including things like their renovation status, their markets, and their plans.

    External Environment Data (technological, economic, social, regulatory, political, ecological): This includes international and domestic trends. Industry trends such as the increase or decrease in certain market segments, new room or restaurant supply, and new concept trends are also included.

Internal Environment Data: This encompasses how well the property is operating, the current customer base, and the strengths and weaknesses.

Marketing Budgets: The financial planning to fund the overall marketing plan.

Marketing Forecast: This portion of the marketing plan requires forecasting the statistics for the forthcoming year of rooms sold, covers sold, financial results, and so on, to accurately forecast future results.

Marketing Plan: The marketing plan is the management tool that steps down the strategic planning process to the unit managers. The marketing plan provides the road map to operate during the year. The marketing plan needs to be a working document, used throughout the year to guide the organization toward its strategic direction.

Raise the Numbers: A hotel industry expression meaning increase the average rate and occupancy.

DISCUSSION QUESTIONS

1. Discuss the key differences between strategic marketing and marketing management in the development of the marketing plan.
2. Formulate a situation analysis for a restaurant or hotel where you have worked or with which you are familiar. Analyze the internal and external factors.
3. Construct a detailed property needs analysis for the same restaurant or hotel that will form the basis of a marketing plan.

4. Develop an internal marketing plan for a real or hypothetical hotel or restaurant.
5. Why is the realistic and objective analysis of the data collection critical to a successful marketing plan? Discuss. What happens when this is lacking?
6. Write a mission statement for the restaurant or hotel analyzed in question 2.

GROUP PROJECTS

1. Develop a marketing plan for a hotel or restaurant with which you are all familiar. If that is not possible, develop a plan for one of the cases at the end of the book, for example, Cases 2, 9, 17.
2. If you can, obtain an actual hotel marketing plan. One of you may be able to obtain one where you work, or your instructor may have some copies. Do a thorough analysis of this plan, good and bad, as outlined in this chapter.

REFERENCES

1. Robert H. Hayes, "Why Strategic Planning Goes Awry," *New York Times,* April 20, 1986.
2. Percentages are from *Trends in the Hotel Industry, USA Edition* and *Trends in the Hotel Industry, International Edition,* published annually by Pannell Kerr Forster, Houston, TX.

Three

The Hospitality Customer

C H A P T E R

Eight

UNDERSTANDING INDIVIDUAL CUSTOMERS

Overview

This chapter reviews the consumer behavior process in meeting needs and wants, solving problems, making decisions, and making choices, with special emphasis on hospitality purchases. The second part of the chapter deals with the behaviors of two broad-based segments—business travelers and pleasure travelers.

BASIC TENETS   There are five basic tenets of consumer behavior: (1) consumer behavior is purposeful and goal-oriented; (2) consumers have free choice; (3) consumer behavior is a process; (4) consumer behavior can be influenced; and (5) there is a need for consumer education.

CHARACTERISTICS OF CUSTOMERS   Abraham Maslow developed a hierarchy of needs, showing needs such as thirst and hunger as base needs, moving up to safety needs, social needs, esteem needs, and then graduating to the need of self-actualization. Once basic needs are satisfied, the

consumer gradually becomes more sophisticated in the needs process. Needs drive purchase decisions.

THE BUYING DECISION PROCESS   The consumer begins by having a problem (need) that can be solved or satisfied by the hospitality offering. Initially the consumer searches past experiences for a solution, but may graduate to searching outside information. Customers selectively choose stimuli for the decision-making process, which can be made with high involvement (an important decision for the consumer) to low involvement (a relatively unimportant decision). Customer perceptions of the product or service are critical in the buying decision process. Beliefs are derived from perceptions, and in the consumer's mind reflect the position of the hospitality offering.

ALTERNATIVE EVALUATION   Consumers have many choices in most cases. These choices allow the customer to employ a variety of thought processes to make the final buying selection. Attitudes are the emotional tendencies to respond to beliefs. Alternative comparisons allow the consumer to evaluate similar offerings, by measuring expectations that lead to the buying choice. Perception by the consumer of the hospitality offering may or may not become reality, which results in satisfaction or dissatisfaction.

TYPES OF HOSPITALITY CUSTOMER Hospitality consumers display different buying behaviors.

Business travelers are the largest segment for the hospitality industry. They tend to be short-term stays in hotels or one-hour lunch users in restaurants, although there are many exceptions. Business travelers have needs such as convenience, location, business services, and, at some point, price.

Pleasure travelers tend to be more price sensitive and are big weekend users, although they may be the same persons who are the business travelers on Friday and Monday. This group also includes many resort users.

Package customers buy a hotel room wrapped with added-value items such as continental breakfast, free drinks, or parking.

Mature travelers are a growing segment of the hospitality industry.

International customers are a growing market everywhere, due to lower airfares and increasingly easier access to most countries.

Individual resort goers are there for pleasure and activity.

If the first step in marketing is to recognize customers' needs, wants, and problems, then it is obvious that we must understand how and why customers behave the way they do, as well as what leads them to behave in that manner. This is no small task.

There are no easy and definite answers to these questions. Instead, there are many theories, concepts, and models that have been developed to explain this complex being, the customer. These have been derived from many disciplines, such as sociology, psychology, social psychology, anthropology, philosophy, and economics, and these approaches must be integrated before we can approach even a limited understanding. Our ultimate goal, of course, is to be able to influence buyer behavior. We may fall far short of that goal in its full sense but we will learn, at least, to understand some hows and whys and their causes.

It is important to begin with some basic and generally agreed upon **tenets of consumer behavior,** because effective marketing must be based on these premises. Managerial decisions that ignore these premises will tend to lead to marketing failures.

Premise 1: Consumer behavior is purposeful and goal-oriented. What may appear to be completely irrational to the outside observer is, nevertheless, the action that an individual views as the most appropriate at the time. To assume otherwise is to underestimate the consumer.

Premise 2: The consumer has free choice. Messages and choices are processed selectively. The frequency of these messages is increasing daily. Those that are not felt to be pertinent are either ignored, disregarded, or forgotten.

Premise 3: Consumer behavior is a process. The specific act of buying is only an intermediate stage in that process. There are many influences on consumer behavior both before and after purchase. The purchase may be a culmination of the marketing effort and its influence on the process.

Premise 4: Consumer behavior can be influenced, but only if we address perceived problems and potential needs and wants, a task of marketing.

Premise 5: There is a need for consumer education. In all their wisdom and purposeful behavior, consumers may still behave unwisely, against their own interest. Marketers have a responsibility in this effort.

Are hospitality customers any different from customers of other goods and services? Probably not. After all, they are the same people regardless of the type of purchase they are contemplating or making at any given time. It would seem, then, that basic buyer behavior theories would apply and we could confine ourselves to that domain. There is a difference, however, and it lies in the context of the purchase.

Buying a stereo is certainly not in the same context as buying a hotel room or a restaurant meal. The characteristics that distinguish services from products, such as intangibility, perishability, heterogeneity, and simultaneous production and consumption, create different contexts in which hospitality purchases take place. In the first part of this chapter we look at a few theories of consumer behavior that have been developed in other contexts and then apply them to the hospitality context. In the second part we look at specific types of hospitality customers.

level needs have to be met before the higher level needs become important. Thus until physiological needs of hunger and thirst are satisfied, they remain primary in human motivation. Once these are satisfied, our safety needs of security and protection become primary, and so forth on up the pyramid. Of course, all of us will not act in exactly the same manner, but it has been shown, in a general sense, that the order prevails. (Recall from Chapter 1 that in marketing jargon we translate these into problems to be solved.)

Maslow *did not claim that the hierarchy was completely rigid or necessarily exclusive.* In fact, it should be noted that we may seek to satisfy two or more diverse needs at the same time; for instance, reserving a hotel suite instead of just a room might be an attempt to satisfy needs at opposite ends of the hierarchy. Or, in another marketing sense, we might *need* a room but *want* a suite.

Maslow also identified two categories of cognitive needs that he did not specifically place on the hierarchy, but that he felt belonged fairly high on the scale. These additional needs are the need to know and understand, and aesthetic needs, which are designated as needs for things that are pleasing to the eye. These needs, of course, certainly apply to hospitality.

It should also be noted that we may satisfy the same need in different ways, depending on the occasion, the availability, and the appropriateness at

CHARACTERISTICS OF CUSTOMERS

Needs and Wants

Abraham Maslow was a psychologist who wanted to explain how people are motivated. What he learned was that motivations are based on different needs in different contexts. Maslow labeled his theory of motivation the "hierarchy of needs."[1] This hierarchy model has stood the test of time and is the basis of much of what we know about human behavior. The model is shown in Figure 8-1.

The thrust of **Maslow's hierarchy** is that lower-

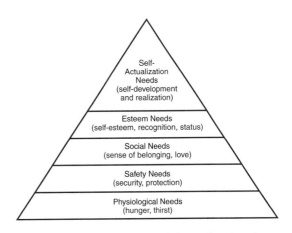

F I G U R E   8 - 1   Maslow's hierarchy of needs.

the time. This leads us into a useful second-level theory called **behavior primacy theory.** This theory holds that behavior is a reaction to the environment—that is, behavior changes as the environment changes or, to use the same term used previously, as the context changes.

Application of the Theories

Do we have to know a psychological theory to know that when we say we are "starving," the first thing we want to do is eat, or to know that we have higher-level needs of belonging, esteem, and self-actualization? The reason the answer is yes will become clearer when we get to Chapter 10 on segmentation and target marketing, both of which mean pinpointing particular customers. In the meantime, let us consider the need/context relationship.

Businesspeople who travel have the need to sleep, shower, change their clothes, and perhaps watch a little TV. These are basic needs, so almost any hotel will satisfy them. But they also may have the need for esteem and will select a hotel to fulfill that need.

At the same time, they will have other needs, such as a desk to write at, good lighting to read by, good telephone service, a wake-up call on time, and perhaps a modem for their laptop. These are not needs in the sense of Maslow's hierarchy; they are needs, or more likely wants, in the sense of what we mean when we say "the consumer has a problem." They seek solutions to those problems and are willing to pay for them (or have their companies pay).

Beside these, they have other wants. They want the bed to be comfortable, the room to be large, the chair to comfortable to sit in; they want to be able to see the TV while lying in bed, to be able to have breakfast in the room. Furthermore, they want the front desk to have their reservation so they can check in without any hassle.*

---

*Marriott research found that the five "key drivers" of guest satisfaction are the qualities of check-in speed, friendliness, cleanliness, value, and breakfast. *Trends in the Hotel Industry,* PKF Consulting, Houston, August 1993.

They definitely do not want to stand in line, to wait an hour for breakfast to be delivered, to have the telephone ring 15 times before the operator answers, and to hear the housekeepers yelling at each other in the hallway. In this sense, customers have **contrary needs** or "do not wants," which really means that needs are not being satisfied.

For the sake of example, the same people go home on Friday, after a very hectic week. They say to their families, "Let's get out of here. I just need to relax." Let's say they go back to the same hotel. Their basic needs haven't changed; they still need to sleep, shower, and change clothes, but the environment or context has changed. Now price is a factor; the cost comes out of their own pocket. The phone is unnecessary and there is no need for a desk. They want the TV away in the corner so they won't be disturbed when the children are watching it. They still don't want housekeepers yelling in the hall, but they aren't too disturbed when their kids run up and down the hallway screaming at each other. The hotel restaurant that was perfect for entertaining their clients is now too expensive; besides the kids won't eat that "stuff!" and the service is too slow for them. Where's the nearest McDonald's? In short, the needs are the same whether for business or pleasure: What has changed is the wants and problems.

The upshot of all this is that we have to understand the needs hierarchy, the wants that go with each level of the hierarchy, the "problems" of given individuals, and we have to understand the context or environment in which they will consume the hospitality product. Still, needs and wants cannot be generalized across the entire population and, especially, the international market. Consider, then, what hoteliers and restaurateurs might like to know of the needs and wants of women versus men, meeting planners versus corporate planners, incentive planners, tour planners, and self-employed business travelers, just to mention a few of the broader possibilities.

Maslow's hierarchy of needs is a critical foundation of human behavior. At the same time it is only a foundation upon which we must build. Motives activate people's behavior but perceptions determine the course of that behavior.

THE BUYING DECISION PROCESS

It was stated at the beginning of this chapter that consumer behavior is a process and many influences affect this process both before and after the act of purchase. We now examine the **buying decision** process as shown in Figure 8-2 in some detail. Only by understanding the process can the marketer hope to influence it.

Needs, Wants, and Problems

The process normally begins with needs, wants, and problem recognition or identification. Sometimes the need, want, or problem recognition will come as a response to stimuli, for example, a TV commercial, an ad, or a billboard.

In the case of problem recognition coming first, consumers know, or think, they have a problem and begin a search for a solution. We should understand that this may be a very subtle stage. Consumers do not suddenly jump up and shout, "I have a problem." In fact, consumers may not even think of it as a problem; they might simply say:

> "I'm hungry [problem].
> Let's eat [solution]."

On the other hand, they might think:

> "I'd really like to go to a quiet [want]
> place for a good [want]
> dinner [need] tonight.
> Where should we go [problem]?"

Search Process

Consumers then begin the **search process** for a solution. They may simply search their memories, they may ask others, they may look to the newspa-

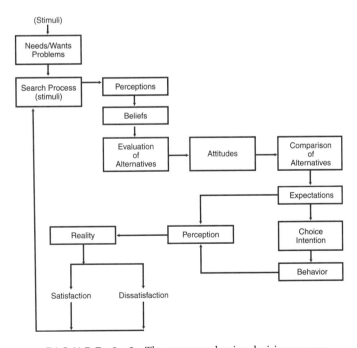

F I G U R E 8 - 2   The consumer buying decision process.

per or the telephone directory, they may search the Web, or they may do any number of other things to obtain either new information or additional information. They may do this in split seconds if there is a suitable restaurant right around the corner, or they may take a year to do it, as in planning an annual vacation. They may give the task to someone else, such as a subordinate, a secretary, a spouse, an airline, or a travel agency.

In the example given above the consumer has recognized the problem unaided. Marketing has had little, if any, impact upon that recognition. Once the problem has been recognized, however, marketing can begin to take an active role. Where consumers go for information, what they read or hear there, whether the information was already in their memory, for whatever reason—marketing can have an influence on this part of the process.

At other times the problem may arise not through recognition, but through identification. In this case, consumers are unaware that they have a problem until it is presented to them and identified for them. Now marketing has a role right from the beginning. Let us say that these same consumers plan, as usual, to eat at home tonight. They are reading the newspaper or watching television when suddenly they see an ad for what appears to be a nice quiet restaurant. They think, "Boy, wouldn't that be nice for a change?" Their wants and problem have been identified for them. Marketing has not created a need—that was already there. Marketing has created a want and caused a problem that needs a solution.

These simplistic examples can be applied to the beginning of any purchase decision process, whether it be for an ice cream cone or a year-long trip around the world. For simple purchases the process may be totally subconscious and/or parts of it may be skipped. For similar decisions that have been made many times before, the process may be instantaneous because of what has become a learned reaction. Of course, the process could also end in a decision not to purchase. This might be the case when marketing has not done its job adequately. Regardless, the role of marketing is ap-

parent even at this early stage. It is also apparent that if marketers want to affect the process at this stage, they must be aware of the complexities of the decision and the influences that will modify it.

Stimuli Selection

In the first case above, consumers determined their own problem; in the second case it was caused by a stimulus. In either case, **stimuli** may affect the process at some stage. The degree of impact, as well as the intensity of the entire search process, is determined by the level of involvement the consumer has with the purchase decision.

The impact and intensity is greater in cases of **high involvement.** These are cases when the decision has high personal importance or relevance to the consumer, such as high cost, high risk, or high effect on self-image. For example, selecting the place where customers are going on their honeymoon is usually a high involvement decision. When **low involvement** exists (selecting a fast-food restaurant) the process is similar except that it proceeds far more quickly and some stages may be skipped, especially when information is readily at hand. Regardless, consumers are affected only by stimuli that they **selectively** choose.

The process of selective choice represents a hierarchy, that is, the steps are taken in sequence, or dropped at any point, as follows:

Selective Attention: We attend only to that which is of interest to us. Advertisers may use graphics or headlines to get this attention.
Selective Comprehension: We try to comprehend that which is still of interest.
Selective Acceptance: We accept or reject what we comprehend.
Selective Retention: We retain in memory what we want to remember.

Because consumers selectively attend, comprehend, accept, and retain messages, we should be aware that much of what we direct at them does not sink in. Unless we can bombard them, à la

McDonald's, we need to be certain that what we want them to select is directed in a manner that appeals to their needs, wants, and problems. This truism applies not only in advertising but also in personal selling, in-house merchandising, public relations, and any other way in which consumers gather information or consumers communicate it. A good test of this concept is to skim through the ads in this book, then close the book and apply the four stages of selectivity.

Perceptions

For the consumer, *perception is reality,* as we have previously noted. Perhaps one of the greatest mistakes we can make as marketers is thinking that what we perceive is also what the customer perceives. If the customer doesn't perceive it, it doesn't exist. If the customer does perceive it, it does exist. You cannot make something what it is not by simply saying so; you have to change perception.

Perceptions are meanings we assign to what we see, hear, and sense around us. Our perceptions are heavily influenced by sociocultural and psychological forces. Sociocultural forces include the culture of society, social class, and small reference groups among others. A **reference group** may be defined as people who influence a person's attitudes, opinions, and values such as family, friends, or business associates. Reference groups are especially important in the purchase of hospitality services where word-of-mouth recommendations play a major role in the buying decision. Psychological forces that influence consumer behavior generally come from within a person and include learning experiences, personality, and self-image.

Hotels and restaurants that brag about how great they are must be able to live up to their boasts. Figure 8-3 is an example. When a hospitality firm promises the moon and then fails to deliver the moon (in fact, is bewildered when the customer asks for the moon), that firm has defeated its own purpose: it has alienated a customer. Expectations arise from initial perceptions and may be disconfirmed by subsequent perceptions.

FIGURE 8-3 The Grand Bay Hotel sets itself a high standard to live up to. Courtesy of Yesawich, Pepperdine & Brown, Orlando.

Initial perceptions depend on stimulus factors. This is the area of traditional marketing.

A resort hotel brochure illustrates an indefinitely long (as far as the eye can see) stretch of white sandy beach, a quiet remote setting, elegant dining on your own private patio overlooking the ocean, and a romantic full moon.

These are stimulus factors and your perception is, "What a perfect place for a honeymoon!" You book your honeymoon with great expectations.

Actual perception depends on personal factors: needs, moods, experiences, values, and, most of all, expectations, as we showed in Chapter 2.

> You find the beach all right. It's on the other side of the island; the one at the hotel is the size of a postage stamp. When you check in, you find that a 300-room convention is checking in ahead of you. The remote setting is in the flight path of the airport. The private patio overlooking the ocean is in the $800 suite, which you didn't reserve. You can eat in your room or in the enclosed dining room without view, or even windows. It rains the entire week.

Now, reality is perception: expectations were not fulfilled and your perceptions are negative. You go back home and say, "What a bummer!"

> Then you meet a couple who stayed in the suite the following week, when the convention was gone and the moon shone. They couldn't have cared less about the beach; they spent all their time in their suite, and had room service for every meal. They tell you what a fantastic place it is.

Reality is perception. These differences in perceptions create many problems for service marketers.

Perception is selective. We cannot possibly perceive all the stimulus objects that are presented to us, so we select what we want to perceive. If you are looking for a honeymoon spot, you select to perceive the beach, the patio, the quiet, and the moon from the brochures, ads, or materials presented you. If you are looking for a spot for your company's next sales meeting, you select to perceive the meeting rooms, the banquet facilities, and the sports facilities from the very same brochures, ads, and materials. When you are at a hotel you may select to perceive the decor, elevator service, the bar,

the golf course, or anything that you felt was promised you. Perceptions are images, and images influence purchase behavior.

Marketers must deal very acutely with perceptions. Marketers must create images with the stimuli pertinent to the specific target market they are trying to attract. They must use stimuli that are relevant to that market, and they must be certain that reality equals, or almost equals, expectation, so that reality doesn't negatively influence perception. Failure to do this will create a dissatisfied customer and negative word-of-mouth. Recall, that it is not enough just to create a customer; it is necessary, as well, to keep the customer.

Beliefs

Beliefs can be defined as something we actually think is fact; they derive from perceptions. We attach a belief to an object. An object could be a restaurant, and a belief could be that it is expensive. Whether or not the restaurant is expensive is incidental to the belief. Beliefs are *cognitive;* they exist in the mind regardless of where or whom they come from. If beliefs are accurate—if the restaurant is expensive—and we want consumers to have that belief, then we can be satisfied with the status quo in that respect.

Sometimes, however, marketers want to change or create beliefs. The restaurant is really not expensive, we say. But how can we say that? For some people it may be very expensive, and for others it may be quite inexpensive. The solution lies in the definition of the target market. These are the people we want as customers; what are their beliefs? We have to learn this before we decide whether we want to change them.

The same is true if we want to create beliefs, as for a new restaurant. Creating beliefs, however, is much easier than changing them, because essentially what exists already is a vacuum and all we have to do is fill it. When we want to change a belief we have to both get rid of the old one and replace it with a new one. This is why it is important that we try to "do things right" in the first place.

People change beliefs frequently without any effort on the part of marketers, or maybe because of lack of effort. Consider the case of Howard Johnson's restaurants. Customers changed their beliefs over time to include unclean facilities, poor service, and mediocre food. This belief became so ingrained that a massive effort was necessary to change it. Howard Johnson's tried to clean up their act and then tried to persuade the public that it had done so. The persuasion effort failed, and not only because they failed to clean up their act sufficiently. They also failed to understand that their orange roofs epitomized negative beliefs. People were not going to be persuaded simply because they were told that things were different.

Research by Howard Johnson's failed to uncover this problem. Howard Johnson's research analyzed attitude. They responded to this analysis with the notion that if they could change attitude they would change behavior. But the problem wasn't attitudes. People's attitudes were and continued to be negative toward unclean restaurants with poor service. The problem was the belief that these elements were inherent in Howard Johnson's. Howard Johnson's then committed a major blunder.

Their research showed that people's attitude toward family restaurants was that they liked them to be "homelike." Based on this revelation, Howard Johnson's commenced an advertising campaign to convince the public that its restaurants were homelike. The headline of the campaign was, "If it's not your mother, it must be Howard Johnson's." Consider the subliminal impact: First, I still believe that Howard Johnson's is unclean and has poor service; and second, I'm insulted by your telling me that my mother has an unclean house and poor service. Of course, beliefs did not change, they only became more negative. With a better understanding of consumer behavior, the story might have had a different ending.

Alternative Evaluation

Rarely is there only one possible solution, and the consumer now has to process **alternative evaluations.** Reference groups and other evaluative criteria have strong impact at this stage. More important, how well have the marketers done their job? Has the case been well presented? Does the solution look viable? Is the risk worth it? Is the price/value relationship appropriate? Does it cover the necessary needs and wants? What is the word-of-mouth reputation? Is it different or better than the other alternatives, and if so, why? These are the thoughts that are going through the mind of the consumer. Again, the higher the involvement, the lengthier and more deliberate the process, and the greater the search for more information.

The marketer's most critical impact is probably at this stage, at least for medium- to high-involvement purchases. The level of involvement will vary with the individual. Eating at McDonald's is low involvement but that does not stop McDonald's from having one of the largest advertising budgets in the country. McDonald's truly wants you to have high involvement with them.

As the price gets higher and, in the hospitality industry, as the service element becomes more important, the level of involvement increases. But the involvement level in choosing a hotel or upscale restaurant is always relatively high, because the product is consumed as purchased, unlike a good, which can be returned if it doesn't work. It is also because the entire hotel experience is personal; if it's a bad experience, it affects the user personally. Alternative evaluation is the point at which the total marketing effort, including especially internal and relationships marketing, will pay off.

Attitudes

Attitudes are the *affective* component of the belief, attitude, intention trilogy that consumers often follow. Affective means the subjective and emotional feelings toward the belief. Attitudes are tendencies to respond toward beliefs, as in the Howard Johnson's case above. If you believe that a restaurant is expensive, how do you actually feel about going there? In a sense, this is the application of our beliefs; this is how we judge our beliefs and how we react to them.

Let's assume that our restaurant is expensive and our target market believes this. There is no point here in trying to change belief, because it is true. Yet people are not coming to the restaurant because of their response to their belief that it's too expensive. Unless, of course, we want to change the restaurant to lower prices (and research may show that to be the only viable course of action, given this market), what we have to change is attitude and affect. One way to do this might be to try and persuade people that the restaurant is expensive but worth the price. If we succeed in this effort, we will have changed attitude toward the restaurant while maintaining the same belief.

Research contrary to that of Howard Johnson's makes this point. Coca-Cola found that a significant majority of 40,000 people who taste-tested "new" Coke against "old" Coke preferred the new variety. When they switched their formula to the new Coke, however, the market revolted. What Coca-Cola's research did was to measure beliefs and ignore attitudes. People believed that new Coke was better, but not better enough to make the change because their attitude toward changing was negative.

Alternative Comparison

Hospitality purchase choices often include many elements. There are the obvious elements such as price, location, accessibility, reputation, and quality. There are also the less obvious or anticipated elements such as service, ambience, attitude, newness, and other clientele. Researchers have developed different models to explain how consumers compare alternative choices. One assumption is that consumers will make trade-offs of one attribute for another, that is, a weakness in one attribute can be made up by a strength in another. For example, we might select a hotel, on the outskirts of town (weak in location) because the price is very reasonable (strong in price). Another model would have the consumer establish a minimum level on only one or a few attributes—for example, price. These choice models and others require consumer research to determine the target market's choice process.

Expectations

All the steps of the process in Figure 8-2 through which the consumer has now proceeded lead to expectations (we might even say "great expectations"), as we explained in Chapters 1 and 2.

Choice Intentions

The final stage of the belief, attitude, intention trilogy* is called the *conative* stage, covering what people *intend* to do. This is not behavior, but it may be as close to behavior as we can get, as we discuss shortly. There is no way we can positively be assured of behavior until after it happens. Failing this, we want to know what people intend to do.

Let us assume that there is a restaurant that you believe to be expensive but worth it. You have a positive disposition to this restaurant. Do you intend to go there? No! You can't afford it. Your positive attitude thus turns out to mean nothing for the marketer who wants your patronage. Of course, the specific context may change: Would you intend to go there on your tenth wedding anniversary next week? Perhaps now the answer will be yes. It can be seen now how context can change behavior, or at least intended behavior. It can also be seen that simply asking people what they intend to do can be very misleading without also measuring belief, attitude, time, and context.

Behavior

Intention is followed by actual behavior. This may mean doing nothing; that is still behavior. But assume that the consumer does "behave," that is, make a choice and act upon it. Now we have a new stage

---

*Note that this trilogy is often stated "belief → attitude → intention," but in many cases this is not so. For example, we may intend to do something and then develop beliefs and attitudes toward doing it.

of perception—the one that comes *after* the fact—face-to-face with reality,[2] as shown in Figure 8-2.

Perception Versus Reality

We now come back to perception: Were expectations met or not? Perception now, once again, is reality. The differences between what was expected and what is perception/reality, if any, are the gaps that can occur, which we have discussed in Chapter 2.

Outcomes—Satisfaction or Dissatisfaction

The choice is made and the performance takes place. What is the outcome? Does performance match expectation? Is perception changed? We have managed to create a customer, but have we managed to keep one? Will he or she come back? Tell others? Is the new customer satisfied, dissatisfied, or just so-so?

We could never hope to know if every customer left satisfied or dissatisfied but we certainly should have a good idea of many of them. With individuals, we will have to randomly sample to find this out; with groups and large parties, we should have some contact with some members of each.

Marketing hasn't stopped yet. Remember, we want to keep these new customers. As much as we can, let's follow up with them. If they are satisfied, let's find out why. Maybe it will teach us something.

If they are not satisfied, why not ? What can we do about it ? Can we still get them to come back ? Can we correct the problem ? Perhaps they are suffering from a reality called **cognitive dissonance,** a state of mind in which attitudes and behaviors don't mesh—in other words, when what we did is not the same as our present attitude toward it. This state causes us to have second thoughts or doubts about the choice that we made. This is especially true when the choice was an important one pschologically and/or financially and when there were alternative choices with a number of favorable features.

Most people try to reduce their own cognitive dissonance. We can't change the behavior, so we try to change our attitude to feel better about having done it. Marketers can help customers reduce cognitive dissonance by convincing them that they did, in fact, make the right choice.

Research has shown that people try to reduce dissonance by seeking or choosing to perceive information that supports the wiseness of the decision, by finding fault with the alternatives so that they look less favorable, and by downplaying the negative aspects of the choice and enhancing the positive elements. Advertising that supports the choice or personal communication that commends the wisdom of the choice have been found to be helpful in reducing dissonance and increasing loyalty.

Now let us apply the consumer behavior process to the hotel industry. The process shown in Figure 8-4 is one of choosing a vacation destination but it is easily adaptable to other choices such as for a restaurant. It is self-explanatory so further discussion here is unnecessary, but the reader should trace through the steps to see how they fit the elements of consumer behavior we have discussed thus far. This analysis will make the theory more practical. You might even attempt fitting the model to your own particular mental process on a recent or proposed purchase to see how it fits. Better yet, think of how marketing could impact upon each stage of the process. You will find ads (only one phase of marketing) in this book that address each step.

Figure 8-4 is an oversimplification of a very complex process. In fact, this process is so complex that only one's own mind can process it for oneself, as it is full of many different variables. The process in an overall consumer behavior sense, however, is important, and marketers should understand it. Here, we tie the thought processes together in a hypothetical sequential order so as to understand how they are interrelated.

So far we have discussed hospitality customers and their purchase behavior in a general sense. Now we look at some specific types of customers, as commonly defined in the industry.

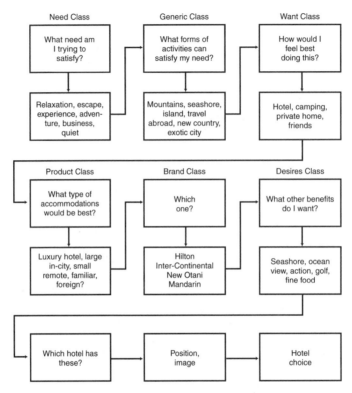

F I G U R E 8 - 4   Consumer mental evaluation process (conscious and/or unconscious).

TYPES OF HOSPITALITY CUSTOMERS

There are various ways of grouping different types of hospitality customers based on common needs and wants, and this is discussed in greater detail in Chapter 10, Market Segmentation. Here we try to understand these customers in broad category types so that we can make an effort to influence their purchase behavior.

The Business Traveler

The business traveler market segment is one of the most desirable for the hospitality marketer. This market consists of over 50 million travelers a year in the United States alone. It is not only the largest major segment, but it is also considered the least price-sensitive market available. The business traveler is defined as a customer who is utilizing the product because of a need to conduct business in a particular destination area. While the hotel facility or restaurant may be used during business, the facility is not the sole reason for the buy. Purposes of the business trip include company-related business, consulting, sales trips, personal business, and trips required to fulfill managerial functions. Most of these travelers spend between two and three nights away from home on each trip.

On the surface, the needs of this market are simple; in practice, they are far more complex and not so simple to deliver. One thing is certain: The business traveler group contains the greatest "demanders"—best explained by considering the nature or purpose of their travels. They would rather be home, they may have had a bad flight or business dealing, they are quickly in and out, and they want everything to go like clockwork.

Business Traveler Needs

Whereas business travelers (like others) once complained loudly about the small towels and the soap bar, they now have other things to complain about. The industry has changed radically and so has the customer. In the past, a hotel served the purpose of providing a place to sleep while a customer was on a business trip. Today, a hotel has to provide the services for a successful business trip, and may just happen to be a place to sleep as well. Research has shown that when business travelers are asked open-ended questions on their first consideration when selecting a hotel, convenience of location receives the highest response. This is followed by reputation and price. It is useful to go through the actual decision process.[3]

First, business travelers consider location, and many hotels emphasize it in their ads. If the location is inappropriate, the hotel is out of the running. This rarely happens because business travelers look at location first, and then only at the hotels that are situated within that location. Many hotel companies try to circumvent the location issue by offering strong "bonus awards" to their customers. Giving the customer frequent stay points for staying at their hotel, versus staying with a competitor in a better location, companies attempt to influence the location choice of the business traveler.

Second, business travelers look at rate ranges impacted by any company mandates or personal limitations. This is a determination by product class—that is, all hotels within the product class are assumed to be in the appropriate rate range, be it upscale, middle-tier, or budget. This is why descriptive research with close-ended questions often does not indicate price as an important factor—that decision has already been made and is no longer a factor. Furthermore, price is a factor only relative to what is available. If the product class desired is middle-tier (Ramada), and the only other available choice is upscale (Four Seasons), then price may be the single most important factor in the decision, including location.

Most hotels have what are called corporate rates. To get them all you have to do is ask. These are not necessarily the lowest rates but often are better rooms, better furnished for the business traveler at a discount from the rack rate. Some are on concierge floors where, for a higher price, special services, a lounge, and complimentary continental breakfast are available. The concept is that the business traveler will pay more for less hassle. In other cases, corporate rates apply to specific corporations that book so many room nights a year, either at a particular hotel or at any hotel of a chain.

Today, in many locations all over the world, there is an alternative to high prices that includes clean, comfortable rooms and good locations as well as security, prompt/courteous service, friendliness, and other factors. In understanding the business traveler, one has to understand the *role* of price—its role lies in designating a price range. Once that price range is determined, price is a minor factor unless, of course, the same or better value can be found at a lower price.

Business travelers do not really think much about cleanliness when making an initial choice; they assume it exists unless they have had a previous bad experience. Cleanliness is almost never given as a reason for choosing a particular hotel at a particular time, but it is always an important consideration when travelers get there. What they want to know next is the reputation of the hotel or, barring that, the chain. This will come from their own personal experiences or from conversations with others. (They have little, if any, faith in "highfalutin" hotel ad claims unless there is a promise behind it that can be backed up.)

We are now past the "threshold" items and a level where the issues become myriad and idiosyncratic depending on the individual, but can be lumped together by target market. These are the service aspects. Each hotel should do its own research on these aspects as these will often be the determining factors in choosing among competitors in similar locations at similar rates. Again, most of these will be based on reputation and previous experience. If these are unknown the first two items, general location and price, will prevail.

One most important aspect, according to one hotel company's research, is covered by the question "Will they have what I ordered and have it on time?" This may include things like floor level, exposure, bedroom configuration, type of bed, working space, telephone location, lighting, and so on. This is consistent with the notion that hotels today have a greater role to play in the success of a business trip. This was echoed by Nan K. Moss, Assistant Vice President of Hyatt Hotels:

> Customers tell us that they basically want what they need when they need it. They need a hotel to be flexible in meeting their needs because what they are looking for is enhanced productivity.[4]

Other concerns are check-in lines, employee attitudes, deferential treatment, lighting, skirt hangers, mirrors, security, type of clientele, coffeemakers, business services, noise (some business travelers avoid convention, atrium-lobby hotels and prefer more boutique, smaller properties), operational efficiency, hotel "rules," limousine service to the airport, and a host of other things.

On the whole, business travelers who are choosing a hotel do not consider bathroom amenities, shoe polishers, bathrobes, turndown service, chocolates on the pillow, and other such factors, except, perhaps, in luxury hotels where they are expected. These may be nice "extras" but are not critical, and customers have come to expect certain amenities, such as a decent size bar of soap. Goat's milk shampoo, herbal soap, and bubble bath are mostly "take home" items. Even when some are used, their absence wouldn't be considered serious. These travelers are more concerned with how the shower works.

An even better example is that of a new president of a major hotel company in India. Seeing competition increasing, he decreed that business travelers would get a box of chocolates, a bathrobe, a copy of *Time* magazine (expensive in India), and other amenities, adding about $10.00 to the variable room cost. "Whoa!" said the director of marketing in the London office that booked many of these guests. "What our customers want is to get through the airport hassle-free," a real hassle in India but easily relieved by a little know-how. The president prevailed, but added only costs not revenue—he left the company soon afterward.

For many hotels superfluous amenities have become a cost they can no longer afford at the prices travelers are willing to pay. A better way, perhaps, is the approach now taken by some hotels to provide amenities only when really needed, as shown in Figure 8-5. " 'Amenity creep'. . . is coming to a halt. It appears the clear winners in the future will be hotel management which is truly committed to customer satisfaction, value, and consistent provision of the basic lodging fundamentals," plus the availability of things that certain business travelers want.[5] Many hotels, for example, now offer special "business plan" rooms as shown in Figure 8-6.

FIGURE 8-5 Holiday Inn provides amenities on demand when needed.

FIGURE 8-6 Business plan rooms at Westin hotels.

Further, simply having a swift, friendly check-in, with all of the information being correct the first time, solves many problems and greatly improves customer satisfaction.

Most business travelers visiting cities do not consider hotels' restaurants as a determining factor, simply because there are usually numerous alternatives available. A good breakfast room is as-

sumed and a quick and easy "grazing" restaurant open all hours is desired; having other restaurants in a hotel is considered convenient, sometimes, but not totally necessary. A majority of city hotel customers, in most developed countries, eat out for lunch and dinner. This somewhat contradicts the notion of convenient location, which tends to reappear when staying at a roadside hotel. (This does not mean that an upscale hotel should not have good restaurants, but that they are seldom determinant in the choice of hotel.) These are generalizations. As we have said, each hospitality establishment has to know its own target market.

The Yesawich, Pepperdine & Brown and Yankelovich *National Business Travel Monitor* for 1997 provides some interesting statistics, which are shown in Table 8-1. Table 8-2 shows what business travelers are looking for in a hotel/motel experience and some differences between men and women.

Dealing with the Business Segment

While the corporate office is saying, "Raise the rates," the local marketing team will frequently feel that lower pricing is the means necessary for capturing new customers, or for keeping existing customers. Naturally, if a hotel is significantly higher or lower in price than its competition, a choice may be made on price, but this alone is not the answer—and there is no one answer. What it is necessary to know is the appropriate price range for existing market conditions. This is not an arbitrary decision, as is sometimes assumed. An inherent conflict often exists, in this regard, between the local sales department and the corporate office of hotel chains. For example:

A 1400-room hotel was undergoing a three-year, $100 million renovation program. This had caused considerable customer discontent and some serious loss of business at the same time that the economy had turned down. Although hotel management felt that there was no problem in selling the 600 renovated rooms at a higher rate, there was a problem with the rest of the hotel and the disrupting construction. The corporate rate for this hotel was $144. The corporate rate of the major competitor was $135. The corporate office of the hotel under renovation, in the midst of this situation, mandated that the property increase its corporate transient room nights sold from 60 to 65 thousand. At the same time, it mandated a corporate rate increase to $158, *while* the disrupting renovations continued. This mandate left the property sales staff in an impossible and noncompetitive situation and caused the eventual loss of a considerable amount of business, much of which was never regained.

Most business travel is affected by prevailing economic conditions. The early 1990s were difficult times for many corporations worldwide, and this resulted in declines in business travel. The late 1990s saw very heavy hotel demand in many parts of the world (except Asia) and the luxury hotel market, especially, saw some of its best days ever. It is true, of course, that the business traveler who always stays at a Four Seasons or a comparable hotel is probably less price-sensitive. In fact, all upscale hotels have some of these customers. The question is: Are there enough of them? For most hotels, the basic premise is simple: If a hotel is providing what the customers want at a reasonable price, then market share will be obtained.

For the restaurant industry, business travelers mean expense account travelers. Like hotels, a sizable number of restaurants would not be in business today were it not for these customers. Although, restaurant meals became only 50 percent tax-deductible in 1993, this issue is not the primary factor in the eating out decision, and restaurants that serve the needs of this market well will prosper even if the tax laws are changed. No logical businessperson would decide not to take a good customer to lunch for lack of a $25 tax deduction. On the other hand, restaurants have needed to adjust menus and prices with more creativity to charge lower prices and/or create greater value perception.

The hospitality industry, worldwide, cherishes the business travel segment—which, sometimes or in some cities, is simply not large enough to go around. The property that gets its fair market share, and more, will be the one that truly understands the needs, wants, and problems of this market. It will not be the one that tries to win it by giveaways and gimmicks. The business traveler segment is not homogeneous. All of its members want convenience of location and cleanliness. The irony is that some want price, some want service, some want room appointments (like a large desk with good lighting), and some want a number of other things. Separating the "somes" is the essence of target marketing. Figure 8-7 shows some other different views of the business traveler—what they like, what they don't like, and what they do.

The Pleasure Traveler

The leisure market is comprised of travelers that individually, in couples, in families, or in small groups visit a hotel or restaurant for nonbusiness purposes. They may be traveling on vacation but often are not. Many, of course, are weekend, or other package users. Others travel to cities for shopping, visiting friends, going to the theater, "just for a change," personal business, and various other purposes.

Increasingly, many pleasure travelers and business travelers are becoming the same person, as

TABLE 8-1
U.S. Business Travel Behavior[6]

Behavior	%
Extend business trip for pleasure purposes whenever possible	69
(Of those who do) With spouse	56
With children	24
With grandchildren	5
Think technology will reduce business travel in future	70
Find business travel a hassle	36
When traveling, prefer: Hotel/motel chains	87
Independents	13
Economy	9
Moderate	72
Luxury	19
Traditional hotel room	72
All-suite	28
Full service	80
Limited service	20
Like to stay at hotels/motels:	
That make me feel like I've made it	50
That have a well-known brand name	76
Usually at the same brand I did last time	71
Try to negotiate the best rates when making a reservation	79
Things that influence hotel choice decision:	
Previous experience with hotel	90
Location	84
Reputation of hotel/chain	77
Recommendation of friend/associate	76
Price	74
Things read/seen	44
Frequent guest program	40
Travel agent recommendation	39

continued

TABLE 8-1 *(Continued)*

When considering a hotel, have a confidence in:

	Some Confidence	Great Confidence
Recommendation of a friend/associate	78	43
Recommendation of a travel agent	47	15
Articles in publications or programs on TV/radio	24	4
Information in travel brochures	28	6
Traditional advertising	21	4
Web site or on-line service	25	9

Hotel service issues:

	Agree
Quality is improving	77
Service is generally excellent	73
Prefer to dine in restaurant outside hotel	64
Service is generally poor	11

Primary decision maker:

Self	59
Travel manager/company travel office	18
A business associate	10
Secretary	5
Travel agent	5
Other	3

Some conclusions from this research:

- The extended-stay market (five nights or more in the same location) is quite high with four in ten taking one or more of these trips.
- The probability of combining leisure with business is quite high; seven out of ten say they do.
- Business travelers tend to be more responsive to brand image than to brand loyalty and brand loyalty may be declining.
- While business travelers value brands, a substantial proportion are not loyal to any one. Changes in ownership and management, franchising, product disparities, and inconsistent operations among locations have a net effect of watering down any particular brand significance.
- The most influential criterion in the selection of a hotel/motel is prior experience with the particular property. Properties need to be truly differentiated and consistently stand for something relevant.
- Past guests are the most powerful promotional force when it comes to credibility. Traditional advertising methods are suspect.
- Preference for eating outside the hotel is a shortcoming of hotels and a substantial revenue loss.

Source: Courtesy of Yesavich, Pepperdine & Brown, Orlando.

T A B L E   8 - 2
What Business Travelers Are Looking for in a Hotel/Motel Experience and Gender Differences[7]

	Business MONITOR			
	1996		1997	
	Men %	*Women* %	*Men* %	*Women* %
Attributes Considered Extremely/Very Desirable:				
Mastery of Basics:				
Clean/well-maintained rooms	95	99†	94	92
Friendly, efficient service	91	95	91	90
Safe place to stay	91	96†	92	88
Electronic door locks on guest rooms	56	79	55	73a
Pricing/Value:				
No phone access charges	72	81	78	85
Discounts for advance reservations	63	76	68	73
Complimentary shuttle service to and from the airport	71	76	66	71
Breakfast with the room rate	58†	72	66	71
Free coffee service in room	53	64	49	68a
Promotional pricing	59	64	57	64
Free in-room movies	45	46	46	45
Streamlining/Simplification:				
Complimentary shuttle service to and from the airport	71	76	66	71
Free coffee service in room	53	64	49	68a
Self check-in and checkout	58	62	59	64
Bathroom amenities (e.g., shampoo, conditioner, sewing kit)	55	62	58	62
Baggage check-in and ticketing for the airline you are flying	54	64	47	58a
Check-in for your flight at hotel	52†	59	44	54a
24-hour room service	51	50	47	49
Automated airline arrival and departure information system in lobby	42	50	41	48
Microwave in room	28	36†	30	48a
Minibar or snack bar in room	34†	31	25	29
Cordless telephone in room	24	27	22	24
Business Services/Command Center Concept:				
Business services (e.g., copying, faxing, etc.)	60	62	60	53
Free newspaper delivered to the guest room	N/A	N/A	47	50
Automated airline arrival and departure information system in lobby	42	50	41	48
Voice mail	33	32†	38	45

continued

TABLE 8-2   *(Continued)*

	Business MONITOR			
	1996		1997	
	Men %	Women %	Men %	Women %
Computer dataports in room	36	33	36	40
Computer in room	35	28†	31	40a
Access to the Internet or online service	N/A	N/A	39	37
VCR in room	31	36	30	35
Multiline telephone in room	36†	30	28	31
Fax in room	31	23	27	30
Telephone in bathroom	18	23	20	26
Cordless telephone in room	24	27	22	24
Creature Comforts:				
Nonsmoking rooms	65	74	70	73
Free coffee service in room	53	64	49	68a
Specially equipped rooms for female travelers (e.g., separate vanities, makeup mirrors, hair dryers, increased security)	29	71	30	66a
Iron and ironing board in room	31	57	38	65a
Diversity of restaurants on premises	64†	65	49	63a
Bathroom amenities (e.g., shampoo, conditioner, sewing kit)	55	62	58	62
King-size bedding	67	54	69	59a
Fine dining restaurant	58	54	53	57
Hair dryer in room	18	55	20	54a
Free newspaper delivered to the guest room	N/A	N/A	47	50
24-hour room service	51	50	47	49
Delicatessen on premises	38†	38†	30	48a
Microwave in room	28	36†	30	48a
Exercise facilities	36†	50†	47	37a
VCR in room	31	36	30	35
Stereo system in room	29	25	24	32
Concierge or executive floor	31	34	25	29
Minibar or snack bar in room	34†	31	25	29
Pay-per-view movies	26	32	29	28
Bar or lounge	35	28	33	27
Spa services	N/A	N/A	34	26
Interior decor specially designed for women	12	33	13	24a
A sports bar	29	16	24	21
Programs that encourage socializing with other guests	18	23	19	20

continued

TABLE 8-2   *(Continued)*

	Business MONITOR			
	1996		1997	
	Men %	*Women* %	*Men* %	*Women* %
Live entertainment	21	19	18	16
In-room video games	13†	11	6	9
Perks:				
Hotel frequent guest points	38	52	39	45
Airline frequent flyer points	41	52†	38	43

One Conclusion: Women are predisposed to different desires than men, particularly in creature comfort attribute preferences. Other research supports this finding.[8] Women travelers should be targeted with more relevant marketing programs.

a = statistically significant difference from men.

†Denotes statistically significant difference from 1997.

Source: Courtesy of Yesawich, Pepperdine & Brown, Orlando.

Table 8-1 shows. With significant airfare reductions being offered for Saturday night stay overs, many business people do just that to see the sights of a destination, or just plain relax as the ad in Figure 8-8 entices. One survey of a Wall Street (New York City's financial district) hotel's weekend guests found that 95% were originally there because of business. We described some of the idiosyncracies of this market at the beginning of this chapter. As we showed, the same individual has different needs at different times.

In the restaurant business, the leisure segment includes a very large market of those who eat out just for pleasure. In many cities, both large and small, this is a powerful segment with many diverse needs and wants. Not as constrained as the business customer by having to "get back to the office," the pleasure diner tends to be more relaxed and casual. At the same time, since the primary purpose of being there is to eat and socialize, these diners have more time to be critically conscious of the product/service delivery.

Some pleasure travelers use the best hotels and visit the best restaurants. In recent years, however, there has been a growing trend toward short pleasure trips and frequent dining out at less expensive

properties by those with limited budgets. This has considerable impact on the hospitality industry both in expanding the industry and in the need to better serve this market.

Many destinations have recognized the value and significance of tourism, and there is intense competition among countries and states to attract the pleasure traveler. For example, residents of New Orleans are exposed to advertising campaigns from the states of Texas, Arkansas, Mississippi, and Tennessee, all of which compete heavily for visitors from that area. Malaysia seeks Singaporeans and vice versa. Advertising campaigns have raised the awareness of customers as to their many vacation choices, such as the ad shown in Figure 8-9. Thus demand for hospitality services is being created and spurred on by foreign, state, and local governments, which reap their share from taxes levied on visitors. The international tourism market has grown huge and is still growing with many different needs and wants.

The pleasure market is a high growth potential market. While the business market remains relatively stable, and travels and eats out when it has to, a large portion of the pleasure market stays home and has yet to be developed. This is even more true in countries other than the United States. Many

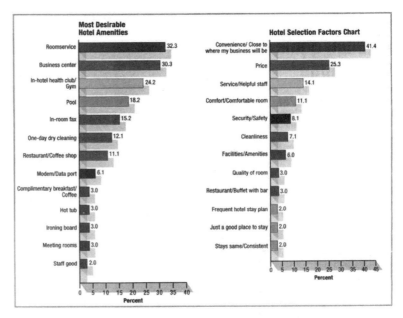

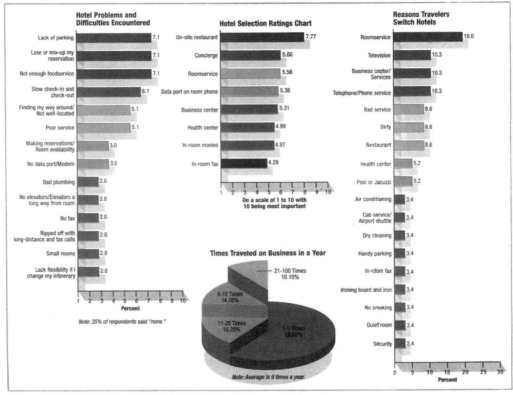

FIGURE 8-7 Views on business travelers, likes, dislikes, and behaviors.[9]

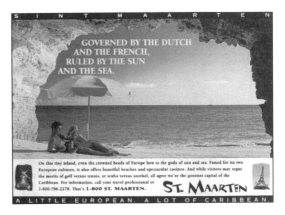

FIGURE 8-9 Advertising to the vacationer by St. Maarten, an international destination area. Courtesy of Yesawich, Pepperdine & Brown, Orlando.

countries have only recently seen a large growth in the so-called middle class with more discretionary income. As they are not "big spenders," however, they are often closed out of a market that caters and prices to the expense account customer. Lower cost options of hotels and restaurants in some countries have expanded this market.

A major part of the pleasure market is made up of family travelers. Even in tough economic times a family vacation has become an essential part of many lifestyles. This market is more price-sensitive than the business segment and is more fickle about choices of destinations and hotels. Just as hotels must learn the needs of business travelers, however, they must also determine the underlying rea-

sons and needs of pleasure travel. Peter Mason, Travel Marketing Director for *Better Homes and Gardens* magazine, revealed the results of research on the family vacation market:

> The number one reason is *To Be Together as a Family.* . . . The next most important reason was *The Need to Get Away from the Stress of Balancing a Home and a Career.* . . . *Rest and Relaxation* is number three. This all boils down to the fact that the Boomer Generation, the two income households, who are so important to the travel industry, are stressed out. They feel that they have got to get away.[10]

Table 8-3 shows some research results on what people are looking for in a pleasure travel hotel experience. You can contrast this with Table 8-2 to see some of the differences between business and pleasure travel needs for both men and women.

Another important pleasure market is made up of people traveling to visit friends and relatives. Although many of these travelers stay with friends and relatives at their final destination, they often seek out lodging accommodations along the way. This is generally a value-conscious market that is attracted to budget hotels and eating places like McDonald's and family restaurants. In these lower-tier markets, pleasure travelers are actually less demanding than

T A B L E 8-3
What Men and Women Are Looking for in Pleasure Experience[11]

	Leisure MONITOR			
	1996		1997	
	Men %*	Women %*	Men %*	Women %*
Attributes Considered Extremely/Very Desirable:				
Familiarity/Control:				
Safety of hotel or motel	83	88	81	88a
Safety of destination	79	88	80	87a
Visiting friends and family	66	76	65	77a
A place I have visited before	47	51	42	48a
Having separate children's and teen programs	27†	28	20	32a
Pricing:				
An all-inclusive vacation price that includes air transportation, accommodations, food, transfer to the hotel or resort, and some recreation	55	61	51	61a
An all-inclusive resort price (one price that includes accommodations, food, and recreation)	51	56	49	56a
The lowest-priced vacation	40	44	41	48a
Staying at the best hotels or resorts	42†	40	35	41a
Convenience/Accessibility:				
A destination that I can drive to within 3 hours	40	50	43	53a
A destination that I can fly to within 3 hours	35	42	37	46a
A destination that I can fly to within 6 hours	N/A	N/A	39	46a
Having a cellular phone available to stay in touch with home or office	N/A	N/A	28	35a
Having access to the Internet or an online service to stay in touch with home or office	N/A	N/A	18	18
Experimentation/Fantasy:				
A place I have never visited before	71	72	66	72a
An opportunity to eat different and unusual cuisines	51	47†	47	53a
A vacation at sea on a cruise ship	43†	44	37	42
Going to theme parks	39	41	36	42a
Learning a new skill or activity	36	36	34	37
A destination that is remote and untouched	46†	34	39	34
Going to a spa	20	27	17	31a
Being able to gamble	26	25	25	25

continued

TABLE 8-3 *(Continued)*

| | Leisure MONITOR | | | |
| | 1996 | | 1997 | |
	Men %*	Women %*	Men %*	Women %*
Physical Activities:				
Getting exercise	51	49	49	51
Hiking and outdoor adventure	43	37	39	34
Participation in water sports	34	28	30	27
Snorkeling or scuba diving	30†	17	23	18a
Snow skiing	22	18†	18	14a
Playing golf	24†	11	19	12a
Playing tennis	10	11	10	10
Other Activities:				
Visiting arts/architectural/historical sites	52	55	47	54a
Shopping	31	51	31	52a

Some Conclusions: Women are more predisposed than men to familiarity and control aspects of safety, all-inclusive pricing, the lowest-priced vacations, and staying at the best resorts. They are also more convenience oriented, and more responsive to select experimentation and fantasy attributes, but less predisposed to selected physical attributes. In contrast, they have more interest in historical sites and shopping.a = statistically significant difference from men.

a = statistically significant difference from men.

*Does not equal 100% due to multiple responses.

†Denotes statistically significant difference from 1997.

Source: Courtesy of Yesawich, Pepperdine & Brown, Orlando.

customers in almost any other market. One reason for this is the lack of experience. Travelers may not realize just what is available and/or they may simply not know how to demand. (The exceptions, of course, are the business travelers now turned pleasure travelers.) They do, however, have long memories. These customers are prone to simply walk out of a bad experience without complaining, never to return. They also are very prone to spread negative word-of-mouth. They are and will become, however, more demanding as their travel experience increases.

Resorts. The resort leisure market is also unique from the consumer viewpoint. Business travelers stay at a hotel or resort because they have business to do or a conference to attend. The resort leisure market, however, travels to resorts because it wants to be there, and to get away from it all. This has led to a proliferation of both upscale and downscale resorts, and quiet country inns where you can spend a week in a rocking chair on the front porch. Again, the wants and needs of these customers are different from those of the nonresort traveler. We showed the decision process of these customers in Figure 8-4, but the possibilities are almost endless.

Resort leisure guests need to fulfill their idea of a vacation. Whether it be total, quiet relaxation or a sports/recreation schedule busier than their job back home, they must feel satisfied that their idea of relaxation was met.

The complexion of resort guests is different from that of guests at commercial hotels. Almost two-thirds may be pleasure travelers while the rest are attending a conference, or vice versa, participating in an incentive junket or on business, depending of course on the hotel and the location. This varied market poses inherent problems, especially when it comes together at the same time, which should be avoided whenever possible. The hotel staff must be trained to deal with the diverse needs of the leisure traveler on vacation, at the same time that it executes complicated conferences with infinite details. The needs of the meeting planner and the leisure resort market come into conflict. A hotel has to be prepared to serve them both.

For example, a major conference at a hotel may want to use the pool area for a cocktail reception, worth $20,000 to the resort. Should the manager shut down the pool area to leisure guests to accommodate the needs of the conference? (It too often does!) This integration of diverse customers is more amplified in the resort setting. Many times—in fact, too often—the exclusive nature of the facility lends itself to these conflicts, as, for example, when there are so many conferees on the golf course that it is impossible for an individual to get a tee time. The marketing-driven manager will understand the needs of both customers, develop operating standards for both, and sell the facility so that revenues will be maximized without losing guests.

Weekend escape travel is another part of the pleasure market. Dual income households provide better incomes for people, but make the scheduling of vacations much harder. There is a trend toward shorter, more frequent vacations taken by travelers who will be more demanding during the use of their precious vacation time. Much of this is part of the package market.

The Package Market

This increasingly popular method of attracting customers during low-demand periods is becoming more crowded with offerings every day. In the *New York Times* Sunday Travel Section, hotels from the upscale Ritz Carlton on Central Park and the Carlyle on the upper east side, to the Waldorf-Astoria on Park Avenue, to the convention-type Hotel Pennsylvania in the garment district, and the downscale Milford Plaza on Broadway, are all offering weekend packages. The same is true in major cities throughout the United States, at resorts, and in London, Paris, Rome, Athens, Singapore, Bangkok, and just about any other place you look. Some include air fare. Another popular version of packages is the "escape" or "getaway theme," as shown in Figure 8-10.

The hotel package market is defined as the offering of a combination of room and amenities to consumers for an inclusive price. While normally these packages are designed to boost occupancy during low-demand time periods, such as weekends and off-seasons, cases exist where packages are used to maximize revenues at all times.

An example of this might be a resort, where a package includes three nights' accommodations and breakfast and dinner daily. The purpose of this combined package is to ensure that while the hotel is full, the guests are required to make use of the food and beverage facilities. Also, the three nights are sold at once, ensuring their occupancy over the period. If sold individually, one night might sell out before the others, eliminating longer, more desirable bookings. Naturally, the hotel would have to forecast some significant demand to be able to force the customer to purchase that type of package.

We define a package as bundling of goods and services, be it food and beverage, coupons to a nearby retailer, or a welcome gift upon arrival. Often the term is misused to describe blatant discounting. Offering a guest room at a significant discount is nothing more than that; it certainly does not package anything for the consumer.

An example of this "bundling" of services is Le Meridien in Boston. This hotel worked closely with a famous retailer, Saks Fifth Avenue, on joint marketing promotions as shown in Figure 8-11. The

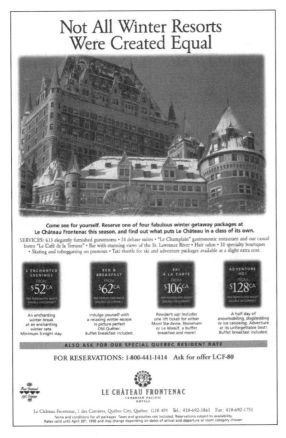

FIGURE 8-10 Chateau Frontenac's winter "Getaway" packages.

FIGURE 8-11 The New York Meridien Hotel Bundles a package with a retailer.

result was satisfied customers and significant business increases for both parties.

Developing Packages.

In developing packages, the needs and problems of the customer must be first understood in order to succeed in developing the target package market. What works in one section of the country, or the world, may be completely foreign in another market.

Once the needs of the target package consumer have been identified, the competition needs to be analyzed. As mentioned earlier, there are very few places left that do not have a myriad of packages for the consumer to buy. Again, the key is the differentiation of the product to the target market. With so many different packages available, and plenty of availability on weekends, or in off-season or, for some resorts, midweek, the creation must, to capture the market, clearly be better from an offering or price advantage.

From the customer's point of view there are four different advantages to packages, assuming the initial motivation is there from the needs and wants perspective. In other words, why buy a package when you can do the same thing on your own?

The first advantage is price. The implication with package prices is that the sum is cheaper than the individual parts. This is usually but not always true, and depends heavily on the quality of the parts. A low-rated, obscure room and an inexpensive split of champagne might have been bought cheaper on your own, but many people don't know this and either don't want or don't know how to take the trouble to find out, so they buy on price. Even when the price is not less, there is a *perception* of value in packages.

The second reason is that packages offer something that people want but probably would not request by itself—for example, breakfast in bed. "It's too expensive, but look, it's included." Or perhaps it's something like horseback riding: "I always wanted to do that but never would have thought of it." Packages remove the worry of "how to," and make it easier for the customer to do whatever it is.

The third reason, and sometimes the greatest, is that packages should be hassle-free. The customer doesn't have to make decisions about where to eat, where to dance, where to go to the theater, how to get there, and so on. This is particularly true for the inexperienced traveler. It is also why carefully thought-out packages can sometimes be priced at more than the sum of their parts. The package removes much of the hassle for customers, and they will pay for that, even though they probably think they are getting it cheaper. Packages make the multiple-purchase decision much simpler.

Club Med has become a master at this art by offering a total week's experience at their resorts, including airfare, ground transportation, all food, wine, and sports activities. All you pay for is drinks and you do that with beads, for which you are charged on departure. In fact, Club Med is an excellent example of a marketing-oriented packaging company (Figure 8-12).

When Club Med was first conceived, its packages appealed to the younger single set that wanted to get away and meet members of the opposite sex. There was a definite hedonistic overtone to the advertising messages. The market has since changed. Consumers are more conservative, and many of today's Club Med customers are older and married with children. Club Med's product has changed with them, offering a much more wholesome package, including a staff pediatrician in some locations.

Other companies have taken this one step further to what is called the all-inclusive resort—for instance, Sandals in Jamaica. These packages don't include airfare but they include everything else—all you can drink, for instance, and cigarettes. The price is high but is paid only once. The customer feels that a problem is solved: "I can do whatever I want and don't have to worry about what it costs." Figure 8-13 is an example of such an offering.

The fourth appeal of some packages is that buyers get something they would not get without the package. That something appeals to a particular interest.

FIGURE 8-12 A Club Med package offering.

One example is the "murder weekend" packages that started in England and have had mixed success in the United States. With these packages, a couple goes to a hotel for the weekend and spends the weekend, with other couples, trying to solve a murder that is literally enacted before their eyes, with all the appropriate clues. With the package, of course, comes room, food, and beverages. Murder mystery nights are now sometimes available at restaurants. Other packages of this type are designed for "buffs." For example, there are rock buffs, sea shell buffs, birdwatcher buffs, and others. Special activities are planned for these buffs, who know they will be sharing the experience with others of like interest.

"Hey sleepyhead, wake up…"

there's a big, beautiful beach waiting right outside the door.

Mmmm. It'll be there later, trust me.

We're booked for later. We're going to snorkel or windsurf or maybe play volleyball.

Wait a minute. I came down here with my husband Jerry the accountant and I wake up with Superjock?

OK, after breakfast we'll just lounge around in the swim-up pool bar and then we'll devour…

Don't tell me. Lunch.

Hey, at least I worked it off yesterday in the fitness center. All you did was veg out in the whirlpool, putting away those endless cocktails.

I was saving my energy for later.

Now that was a workout.

Get used to it. I meant the romantic candlelight dinner, the wine, the dancing.

Yeah…

And that's why I'm staying right here in this big beautiful bed.

Move over…

Sandals

Exclusive features found only at Sandals Resorts.
Rooms and suites right on the beach. King-size beds, hair dryers, clock/radios in every air-conditioned room • Elegant full-service evening dining • Specialty dining by reservation • Snacks anytime • At least 2 freshwater pools and whirlpools
At least four bars including swim-up pool bars serving unlimited name brand liquors.

Jamaica's #1 All-Inclusive Resorts for Couples Only
Stay at one, play at all four resorts. Sandals Royal Caribbean • Sandals Montego Bay • Sandals Ocho Rios • Sandals Negril
Contact your travel agent or call toll-free in North America **1-800-SANDALS**

FIGURE 8-13 Sandals all-inclusive resort package for couples. (Carlson wagonlit)

There is an important warning about packages that too often is violated: Provide what you promise in the package! This advice is obvious, but is not always followed, resulting in very negative feedback for the property. For example, we know one small city hotel that offered the usual weekend package. The main appeal of this package in the winter in New England was the indoor pool and lounge area. People from only a few miles away bought the package for that reason. More often than not, however, the hotel had a wedding party on Saturday afternoon that was held by the pool. Because of the weddings, including set-up and break-down time, package customers could not use the pool for much of their stay.

Too often hotels do not deliver on the promises made with their packages. The main reasons for this seem to be that they do not plan for packages and consider them secondary, low-rated business. This is self-defeating and results in extremely negative word-of-mouth. Research on customer complaints has revealed a disproportionate number of complaints about package "promises."

There is another kind of package—the tour group package that includes air and accommodations. This will be described in the chapter on distribution.

The Mature Traveler

The mature traveler market, actually a subsegment of the pleasure market, is another important growth segment for both the hotel and restaurant marketer. Usually defined as aged 55 and over, this market's size is on the increase as people tend to live longer and better. This segment is important to the hospitality industry not just for its size but for other reasons. These consumers travel extensively, spending over 50 percent more of their time away from home than the younger pleasure segments. Members of this market today live longer, healthier, and more vigorous lives, are better educated, and have wider interests and activities. Their children are grown, their mortgages are paid, and they have the time, energy, and inclination to travel.

The needs and wants of the mature market are different from those of other segments discussed in this chapter. Studies have reported that "to visit new places" was the number one reason for trips taken by mature travelers, followed by "to visit friends and family." Many mature travelers are price-sensitive and getting a discount is an important attraction. Because they have the flexibility to plan trips any time, they can take advantage of the lowest prices. These travelers use hotels of all price ranges, from luxury to budget, but hotels must be able to provide those attributes that are important to this segment. Some of these attributes include increased security, well-lit public areas, legible signage, no-smoking rooms, easily maneuverable door handles, grab-bars and supports in bathrooms, and wide doorways to accommodate wheelchairs and walkers.

The senior citizen market is not homogeneous. This market can be segmented in a variety of ways: travel habits of mature travelers differ depending on retirement status; travel habits are likely to be affected by travelers' life stage as they grow older and encounter physical restrictions; and some mature travelers may prefer to travel as part of a group while others travel in pairs.

Many hotel chains are aggressively pursuing this market. Choice Hotels has long featured famous but active seniors in its television advertising. Hilton has a Seniors HHonors program where members can receive up to a 50 percent discount on room rates. Radisson SAS once gave discounts by age starting at age 65. Best Western provides the following advertising guidelines to hotel members who want to target this market:

Keep ads and collateral pieces upbeat and positive.

Always depict older customers as active, healthy, and involved.

Use language that is sensitive to mature audiences.

Emphasize convenience.

Show price/value relationship.

Stress service, reliability, and savings.

Restaurants also tap into this market. Active senior citizens spend a large proportion of their food budgets on food away from home, and most prefer mid-scale restaurants. Many are bargain hunters who are conservative in their eating habits.

Restaurants should have good lighting to avoid safety hazards and menus should be easily readable with enough variety to satisfy senior citizens' nutritional needs. Service staffs should be trained to recognize changes in vision and hearing so that people with special needs can be provided better service without calling attention to their impairments.

The restaurateur can fill some seats early in the evening, since seniors tend to eat dinner earlier. In fact, "sunset dinners" or "early-bird specials" have become quite popular in attracting diners from 5:30 to 6:30 P.M., before regular patrons arrive. These menu offerings normally include beverage and dessert at an attractive price.

The needs of the senior citizen are basically simple. They are not, as a group, a demanding one. They want rooms close to the lobby, they want help with luggage, and they want information. Like most customers they want clean rooms, convenient location, and value. They do not want to be publicly singled out for service, but at the same time hospitality employees must recognize their special needs and provide them in a subtle way. This market tends not to be rushed through their stay like conferees or businesspeople.

Senior citizens tend to travel outside traditional patterns, such as the businessperson's Monday through Thursday, the weekend package guest's Friday and Saturday, or the busier times of the year. They are also more flexible in rearranging their schedules. Senior travelers can often check in on a Thursday and stay through Monday, making their stay attractive to the hotelier.

As the baby-boom generation matures, it is possible that the needs of this market will further evolve and change, as it has in only the past ten years. It is up to hospitality corporations to research these needs as they evolve so that this market can be better served.

International Travelers

Tourism is already the world's largest retail industry, and travel between nations is expected to continue to grow. International visitor spending in the United States is growing each year and may now account for over 25 percent of total tourist spending in the United States.

Canada and Mexico provide the most tourists to the United States, and vice versa, because of their contiguous borders. Overseas visitors are led by the Japanese, followed by Europeans from the United Kingdom, Germany, France, and Italy. Growth markets in the future are visitors from Argentina and South Korea, which have shown huge increases. In Singapore they target Australians and Japanese. In Thailand they target Germans. In Portugal, Spain, and Turkey they target the British. And so it goes.

The international market is staggering in its size and complexities. Over 400 million people travel outside their own countries every year. This market is obviously not homogeneous, and hospitality marketers must be sensitive to the cultural differences of visitors from different nations. Since it is expensive and risky to try to directly market to individual international visitors, hospitality operators often seek out an intermediary, such as a consortium, reservation system, referral network, or tour operator with which to establish marketing relationships. We discuss these in Chapter 18.

International trade shows, like the Travel Industry Association's Annual POWWOW, are also essential for reaching this market. This show brings together tour operators from all over the world who meet with hospitality industry representatives to conduct business. The tour operators account for over 70 percent of all international tourist arrivals to the United States and as much as 90 percent at some international destinations. As the number of international travelers has increased, hospitality corporations and tourist destinations have become more user-friendly. However, there is much that can be done.

Not long ago, most U.S. hospitality companies, both small and large, could disregard the international market unless they deliberately chose to enter it. This situation is changing quickly. To this day, foreign visitors to the United States can go to only a very few select hotels in major cities like New York and expect to find someone who speaks their language and exchanges their money, not to mention understanding their needs. The situation is even worse in restaurants; the singular hope for a foreign speaker in this case is to go to a purely ethnic restaurant or hope to have an immigrant waiter or waitress who speaks the same language.

On the other hand, an American can travel almost anywhere overseas and find hotels and restaurants in which at least someone will speak English, or make an honest attempt at it. The overseas hospitality enterprise has long recognized the value of the American market. Even in some remote European or Asian villages it is possible for Americans to communicate basic needs and wants. Contrarily, foreign visitors to the United States are too often greeted with a "Huh?" when trying to communicate in an American hospitality enterprise. This problem goes far beyond the problem of language difficulties; it extends into the area of basic consumer needs and wants. Because many foreign visitors to the United States are able to speak some English, Americans are relieved of the burden of understanding another language, but this does not relieve them of the burden of understanding the customer.

The basic principles of marketing to the international traveler are no different wherever you go—they always involve the needs and wants and solutions of problems of customers. Likewise, the concepts of positioning, segmentation, and marketing planning or strategy are no different. What changes, of course, are the consumers. International marketing does not involve changes in marketing concepts; instead, it involves understanding the changes in consumers.

Worldwide the customer is looking for the same thing, to establish a relationship, to be sure that they will "be taken care of" on arrival. Communicating the message that a property will do this may vary by country of origin but the meaning will be the same. Vagaries such as a Japanese breakfast or directional arrows to Mecca for Arabs are like mints on the pillow—nice to have but without trust and relationship, a nonissue.

When McDonald's first opened in Moscow, they served 35,000 customers a day. Russians, however, ate with utensils and were not accustomed to picking up food with their hands. So McDonald's created brochures and tray liners explaining *how* to eat a hamburger, not *why* to buy one. Burger King had similar experiences in Venezuela—hamburger buns there no longer have sesame seeds (the Venezuelans kept brushing them off), the catsup is sweeter as are milkshakes, the menu includes ice cream (everyone's favorite dessert there), and the outlets stay open as late as 1:30 A.M., as Venezuelans eat late.

Burger King also realized that mere adaptation to cultural differences does not mean that one gets to know the market. Burger King originally served wine in its restaurants in France, but customers tended to linger longer over glasses of wine. This slowed table turnover, so wine was removed from the menu. Conversely, Disney did not allow alcoholic beverages to be served at Euro Disney. The French were outraged and Disney now sells wine.

But what do you do when your customer mix originates in 10, 20, or more countries, as is the case for many hotels worldwide in major destination areas, and some not so major? This is the challenge that faces hospitality firms that have an international focus.

Free Independent Travelers (FIT)

There is a final category of individual travelers that is somewhat of a catch-all for everyone that is left over. In fact, in many hotels' segment breakdowns of their customer base, this may be quite a substantial proportion. That is because everyone that is not known to fit into some other category will fall into this one.

The FIT traveler is a "nonorganized" visitor who does not belong to a group. While these travelers may well participate in tours during their visit, they essentially come on their own and do as they please. Unidentified business travelers will also be lumped into this category. Hotels catering to the FIT market will usually set aside a block of rooms a year in advance, and fill them in as reservations are made. The lead time may be three to six months in advance. The hotel releases the unused blocked space according to its buy-time schedule.

Both wholesalers and retail agents (who are discussed in Chapter 18 on distribution) handle the FIT. This segment is normally willing to pay higher rates than group customers. However, a conflict arises with this situation. While the FIT is willing to pay a higher rate because of a lack of volume, the wholesaler and retailer are able to negotiate large discounts due to aggregate FIT bookings.

The resulting savings are not always passed on to the traveler. Therefore, the guest may pay a high price while the hotel receives a relatively low room rate. Often the FIT booked by an intermediary may get the poorest room in the house based on the rate being paid to the hotel. The traveler is at a disadvantage in these situations, and is surprised at the accommodations. This can hurt the hotel that is caught in the middle.

Incidentally, the term FIT is also used by some to designate "free individual traveler," or "free international traveler."

SUMMARY

There is a tremendous amount of research on the topic of consumer behavior, and it is impossible to review all of it in any one chapter. However, we have tried to show how some of these theories can be applied to understand the behavior of hospitality customers. This chapter has also shown that this can be very difficult, because we cannot be sure what goes on in a person's mind. Maslow's hierarchy of needs forms a foundation but perceptions and expectations play an important role. Differences between perceptions and expectations creates many challenges for hospitality marketers, as seen in the gap model.

Perceptions lead to beliefs, which in turn affect attitudes, and much of marketing deals with attitudes and the changing of attitudes. Positive attitudes toward a product or service are required before customers will include it among their choices. Consumer behavior is a complex process, and the different stages are need or problem recognition, search, stimuli selection, alternative evaluation, alternative comparison, and choice.

The key to marketing today is to understand the customer. Good theory provides the basis for that understanding. Applying it will put you light years ahead of those who are still selling when they should be marketing.

In the latter part of this chapter we reviewed the most common broad individual market segments, business and pleasure, that are encountered in the marketing of hospitality. There are numerous other segments, as well as more specifically defined target markets. The most important point to remember is that market segments represent groupings of customers with similar needs and problems. Ideally, the scenario would be to operate a hotel or restaurant that catered to one market segment year-round. Unfortunately, this is seldom realistically possible. In fact, different segments will often be on premise at the same time, making service and execution of the product difficult. The marketing-oriented team responds to this challenge by truly understanding the needs of the customer, and communicating these needs to the staff that will deliver the product promised. When all is said and done it will be relationship marketing that provides the tie that binds.

KEY WORDS AND CONCEPTS

Alternative Evaluation: Alternative comparisons allow the consumer to evaluate similar offerings, by measuring expectations and leading to choice intentions.

Attitudes: The affective component of the belief, attitude, intention trilogy of the buying process.

Behavior Primacy Theory: The theory that behavior is not always based on needs but may, in fact, be a reaction to the environment.

Buying Decisions: The consumer has a problem (need/want) that can be solved or satisfied by the hospitality offering. To resolve this, a decision process is followed.

> **Beliefs:** Derived from perceptions, and in the consumer's mind reflecting the position of the hospitality offering.
>
> **High Involvement:** When a purchase has high relevance, for example, a customer actively researching a honeymoon destination.
>
> **Low Involvement:** When a purchase has low relevance, for example, a customer chooses one fast-food restaurant over seven others.
>
> **Perceptions:** Perceptions of the product or service are critical in the buying decision process.
>
> **Search Process:** Initially the consumer searches past experiences to solve the problem, but may graduate to seeking outside information.
>
> **Stimuli:** These provide an impetus for the buy/not buy decision.

Choice Intentions: Customers choose what they intend to do. Whether the customer actually does what he or she intends to do cannot be determined until after the fact.

Cognitive Dissonance: A state of mind after behavior is performed that is not consistent with a new attitude, like, "Why did I buy that? I could have found one cheaper."

Contrary Needs: "Do not wants" or things like a missed wake-up call that lead to need dissatisfaction.

FIT (Free Independent Traveler): Defined as a nonorganized visitor who does not belong to a group.

Hospitality Customers: There are a variety of customer types that display different buying behaviors:

> **Business Customers:** The largest segment for

the hospitality industry, these customers have needs such as convenience, location, business services, and, at some point, price.

International Customers: A growing segment due to lower airfares and increasingly easier access to most countries.

Mature Travelers: A strong segment of the hospitality industry. Seniors are traveling to hotels and eating in restaurants at an ever-increasing rate.

Package Customers: Travelers that are buying a hotel room wrapped with added-value items such as continental breakfast, free drinks, or parking.

Pleasure Travelers: These travelers tend to be more price sensitive, stay over in hotels or eat in restaurants over the weekends, and visit relatives and attractions during their stays. Resorts represent the upper end of the pleasure travel segment.

Maslow's Hierarchy: A hierarchy of needs that begins with physiological needs, such as thirst and hunger, moves to safety needs, up to social needs, onto esteem needs, and finally graduates to the need of self-actualization, but not always necessarily followed in that order.

Reference Group: People who influence a person's attitudes, opinions, and values.

Selectivity: Customers selectively choose what they pay attention to, perceive, comprehend, accept, and retain.

Tenets of Consumer Behavior: Consumer behavior is purposeful and goal-oriented; consumers have free choice; consumer behavior is a process; consumer behavior can be influenced; and there is a need for consumer education.

DISCUSSION QUESTIONS

1. Consider Maslow's hierarchy in terms of a hotel and of a restaurant. In each case, name as many attributes as you can that fit each level of the hierarchy. Be prepared to discuss.

2. From a recent paper or magazine, collect a half-dozen hotel or restaurant ads. Discuss them in terms of perception, expectation, beliefs, attitudes, and intentions.

3. List the reference groups that you belong to and how they can shape your choices of hospitality facilities.

4. Explain the relationship among beliefs, attitudes, and intentions. Discuss how all these interrelate in hospitality consumer behavior.

5. Consider Figure 8-2. Take an example of something you have done or might want to do in terms of a hospitality purchase. Apply the model.

6. What are the major factors that business travelers consider when selecting a hotel or restaurant? Pleasure travelers?

7. "We do not sell hotel rooms to business travelers; we improve their productivity." Discuss.

8. Mature travelers' needs will change as the baby-boom generation ages into this market. Discuss.

GROUP PROJECTS

1. Consider a particular market segment, such as students on a spring break. Develop and price realistically the "perfect" package for this segment.

2. Do the same as Project 1 for mature travelers. This will be a lot harder because you are not one of them, so you may have to do some research. This is more realistic than Project 1 because hotel marketers usually do not belong to the groups for whom they design packages.

3. Consider either the business or pleasure market. Develop a mini-marketing plan that considers the needs and wants of both men and women.

REFERENCES

1. Abraham H. Maslow, *Motivation and Personality.* New York: Harper & Row, 1954.

2. This discussion of consumer information processing is quite limited. Those who would like to take it a step further are referred to Icek Ajzen and Martin Fishbein, *Understanding Attitudes and Predicting Social Behavior.* Englewood Cliffs, NJ: Prentice-Hall, 1980.

3. This discussion is based on extensive research by the authors and others.

4. Reported in "1993 Outlook for Travel and Tourism," *Proceedings of the U.S. Travel Data Center's 18th Annual Travel Outlook Forum,* p. 94.

5. PKF Consulting, "Trends in the Hotel Industry," August 1993.

6. Yesawich, Pepperdine & Brown and Yankelovich Partners, Inc., *National Business Monitor*[SM], 1998, pp. 18, 20, 21, 27, 40–42, 75–79.

7. Yesawich, Pepperdine & Brown and Yankelovich Partners, *op. cit.,* pp. 59–60, 79.

8. See, for example, Ken W. McCleary, Pamela A. Weaver, and Li Lan, "Gender-Based Differences in Business Travelers' Lodging Preferences," *Cornell Hotel and Restaurant Administration Quarterly,* April 1994, pp. 51–58.

9. Courtesy of On Target Research.

10. Reported in "1993 Outlook for Travel and Tourism," *op. cit.,* pp. 107–108.

11. Yesawich, Pepperdine & Brown and Yankelovich Partners, Inc., *National Leisure Travel Monitor*[SM], 1998, p. 60.

Nine

•❖•

UNDERSTANDING THE ORGANIZATIONAL CUSTOMER

Overview

The organizational customer is described as the purchaser of hospitality products for a group or an organization that has a common purpose. There are several subsegments of the organizational customer market, described in detail in this chapter.

GENERIC ORGANIZATIONAL MARKET The customer in this market is the meeting planner or travel manager, buying hospitality services for the end user. The needs of the planner/manager and the needs of the end user are not necessarily the same, although the former's job is to serve the latter.

MEETING PLANNERS These are the people who plan meetings for different organizations. These customers have different buying cycles. Each of them and their end users have different needs. Corporate customers need business centers, for example, while association planners need off-site functions. These customers need to set measurable goals, develop a plan, and be prepared to work in

tandem with the hospitality enterprise to make everything go well and to resolve any conflicts. Finally, these customers must be prepared to evaluate the results and relay them to both the hospitality enterprise and the end user.

CORPORATE TRAVEL MARKET This market includes the individual corporate travel segment with arrangements made by a travel manager. These mangers have specific requirements, and the need to manage costs. They tend to negotiate on volume.

CORPORATE MEETINGS MARKET Most corporate meetings in an off-premise facility are handled by a corporate or professional meeting planner. This very sizable market requires considerable special attention from a property that caters to it. After booking one of these meetings, on-site conference coordinators handle the details.

CONFERENCE CENTERS These are facilities built specifically to address the needs of the meetings customer. They are usually connected to, or part of, a hotel or resort that also takes nonconference guests. A "dedicated" conference center serves, almost solely, the meetings market.

INCENTIVE MARKET   This is a subsegment of the corporate market where incentive planners organize trips as rewards for top performers within the end user organization. The needs of the incentive market, while still having corporate end users, are considerably different than those of the corporate meetings market. The incentive market needs less meeting space and more recreational activities.

ASSOCIATION, CONVENTION, AND TRADE SHOW MARKETS   These customers normally have a long buy-time, need a significant amount of meeting space, may block rooms in multiple hotels for the same meeting, and have several off-site programs.

CONVENTION CENTERS AND CONVENTION AND VISITORS BUREAUS (CVB)   Most convention centers have large capacity and, while separated from hotels, need the hotels to room their attendees. CVBs facilitate the selling of a city or destination to large groups and help them make arrangements.

AIRLINE MARKET   The airline market is either courted or ignored, depending on the hotel demand at a destination. In soft market times, the personnel of the airlines may be sought to ensure a base of business. In better market climates these lower rated customers are not solicited by upscale hotels, except outside North America. These customers purchase blocks of rooms for a continuous period of time, making them a unique organizational entity.

SMERF AND GOVERNMENT MARKETS   Like the airline crews, these organizational customers are price sensitive and are viewed as base business for soft occupancy periods. In some cases the SMERF customer can fill in weekend time periods, adding value to the hotel's booking pattern.

GROUP TOUR AND TRAVEL   This organizational customer in the United States primarily represents the mature market, seniors traveling by bus to various attractions and destinations. This market is also price sensitive. Worldwide, however, it may represent all levels of the market as a group traveling together with a common interest, such as seeing historical sites.

•◆•

The **organizational customer** is defined as the purchaser of hospitality products for a group or organization that has a common purpose. This customer's needs are somewhat different from those of the individual customers described in Chapter 8. Although all of the basic principles are the same as described in Chapter 8—stimuli, search, perceptions, beliefs, attitudes, and so on—organizational customers are essentially buying for someone else who is the actual user. Although both the **meeting planner** (or **travel manager**) and the actual user are organizational customers, we use the term "user" (or "end user") for the actual user who is not the buyer. We use the term "planner" (or "manager") for the buyer who is not the end user.

Planners and managers act as intermediaries to satisfy the needs and wants of the users, as a group, which is why this is often called the group market. They may "sell" to the organizational customer, just as travel agents, tour operators, and incentive travel planners do. On the other hand, as is the case with meetings and convention planners, they may organize and plan meetings on demand of the organizational customer. Another possibility, as in the case with travel managers, is that they will "manage" the travel arrangements for organizational customers.

Although there are a number of target market categories in the organizational market, we can define them in seven major segments: the corporate travel market; the corporate meetings market; the incentive market; the association, convention, and trade show market; the airline crew market; the social, military, education, religious, and fraternal (SMERF) and government markets; and the group tour and travel market.

THE GENERIC ORGANIZATIONAL MARKET

When a couple books a hotel room on a weekend package, it knows what its expectations will be: The expectations are their own. Similarly, business travelers may choose to be close to their business location for the next day, sometimes at the expense of comfort. The needs and purpose of these customers are individualized. The planner or manager, however, intends to satisfy, perhaps, 25 to 5000 individual needs. Although the group may have a common purpose—such as a business meeting of a corporation, a computer industry convention, or an incentive trip for insurance salespeople—each member of the group may have somewhat different individual needs. This makes the overall task somewhat more formidable for the planner or manager. The similarity, of course, is that in either case if expectations are not met, the customer may go somewhere else the next time.

The problem has grown greater in recent years due to the corporate trend toward "downsizing." Large corporations have trimmed their work forces by tens of thousands of employees. Many meeting planners and travel managers have been included in the downsizing, leaving these tasks to administrative assistants who lack experience in this field, or to travel agents or travel planners, who don't know the organization as intimately. This gives the hotel marketer an even more critical task and need to understand the buyer. This has also led to more independent professional meeting planners, who do not work for just one company but plan meetings for any number of company clients.[1]

Specifically, the planner or manager must try to anticipate the needs of the group, as well as to select the proper facilities to accomplish the common purpose. For example, the meeting planner of a corporation may be given the task of planning a sales conference for the international division. The planner must understand the needs of that particular department within the company, with which he or she normally has very little contact, as well as the needs of the individual members.

At times, planners or managers may not even visit the hotels or restaurants to which they send their organizational group. Thus to make the right decision, they need to rely on a different set of stimuli from those used by other customers. Word-of-mouth from fellow planners or managers ranks first as probably the predominant factor in choosing facilities. Recommendations from others within the organizational group rank second in the decision-making process, with direct sales efforts by suppliers ranking third. Advertising ranks far down the list of possible influences. Regardless, hotels are heavy advertisers in publications such as *Meetings & Conventions, Successful Meetings,* and *Corporate Meetings and Incentives,* such as shown in Figure 9-1.

MEETING PLANNERS

Planners rely on hotel salespeople, unlike individual customers. Also, *conference coordinators* of the hotel, who handle the details during an event, become extremely important in the decision to book, and to rebook after the event is over. Even the chef, who is going to be serving perhaps 300 attendees three meals a day, becomes critical. The organizational planner is at far more risk from a bad meal than the weekend package customer who is not pleased with an individual meal.

As planners gain more experience on the job, however, they are less influenced by salespeople. In the case of the incentive buyer, it has been found that only about 25 percent of those planners with

WE CAN ONLY OFFER YOU
ONE KIND OF MEETING.

FLAWLESS.

• 29 PRESTIGIOUS CONFERENCE ROOMS
• 32,000 SQUARE FEET OF FLEXIBLE MEETING SPACE
• AN IMPRESSIVE HEALTH AND RACQUET CLUB
• ALL AMID 18 ACRES OF LUSH, GRACEFUL FOREST

THE HOUSTONIAN
HOTEL, CLUB & SPA

AS UNIQUE AS THE PEOPLE WHO COME HERE.™

111 NORTH POST OAK LANE (BETWEEN WOODWAY & MEMORIAL) HOUSTON, TEXAS 77024
713/680-2626 FAX 713/688-6305 FOR TOLL-FREE RESERVATIONS, CALL 1-800-231-2759
PLEASE VISIT OUR WEBSITE AT WWW.HOUSTONIAN.COM

FIGURE 9-1   A *meetings* publication ad directed to planners.

more than five years' experience are greatly influenced by salespeople. These people and many other planners want to see for themselves, and will often visit the property before booking it. There is an increased professionalism among experienced planners, evident in the way they go about inspecting properties and setting up meetings. All planners, no matter what their depth of competence, are most concerned that the hotel and its staff perform so that their meetings are successful. Quite often a planner's promotion—or even his or her job—is on the line, and hotels often target this in their advertising (Figure 9-2). Even if the hotel was entirely at fault for a mishap, it is ultimately

the responsibility of the planner who chose the wrong site for the meeting. At least one planner has said:

> You can have the most gorgeous facility in the world. . . . I still need professional staff to augment what I do. . . . I often follow the same people as they move from hotel to hotel. The people I do meetings for like to be pampered a little bit. A property may be less than desirable, but if they can provide service and if the food is good we can overlook the other things. What's important to me is . . . that everything I've ordered is there. Problems occur when hotels don't deliver what they say they can deliver.[2]

Table 9-1 shows the highest 16 site selection criteria generally agreed on by association and corporate meeting planners.[3]

Planning the Event

To begin to understand the needs of the **organizational planner,** it is important to see how the planning process should go for a meeting or function. Understanding this, the sales and operations departments of a hotel can anticipate problems before they happen, perhaps preserving the success of an entire meeting.

Buy Time. Each segment of customers has different **buy times** (also called **lead time**) for purchasing the hotel product. A corporate traveler may make reservations one week in advance of an upcoming trip. The convention planner is booking business as far as five years in advance. Over 80 percent of corporate meetings are booked for a date less than four months in advance, with close to 40 percent done within a 60-day window.[4] The tour operator will have routes calculated a year or more in advance.

Knowing the timing of the purchase is important in selecting potential market segments. In order to maximize revenues, the ideal business mix of segments may include a variety of customers. With the different room rate potential of each cus-

FIGURE 9-2 Westin targets the meeting planner's need for success.

tomer grouping, managing the inventory becomes critical.

For example, a 400-room hotel may have an opportunity to sell out to a midweek convention three years in advance at a rate of $100. At first glance, this might appear to be a good sale; the sales department can spend its time trying to fill other, less busy time periods. More careful analysis, however, might show that this hotel has an average of 300 rooms per night occupied by business travelers during the week. The rate this year is $125, and in three years is expected to be at $150.

Few, if any, business travelers plan business trips three years in advance. These travelers will be calling the hotel a few days in advance for their room reservations, unaware of the convention that is being held there at that time. If all patterns hold, the hotel will lose $50 per room on the 300 rooms that it could have held for the segment that pays a higher rate, but books the shortest lead time. Mistakes like this are very subtle, because the hotel is sold out, yet the room revenues are decreased by $5000 a night. The hotel may also alienate some regular customers who cannot get rooms. It does

T A B L E   9-1
Site Selection Criteria of Association and Corporate Meeting Planners[3]

Corporate Planners	*Association Planners*
1. Service at hotel	Availability of hotel rooms
2. Availability of hotel rooms	Service at hotel
3. Overall service at destination	Overall service at destination
4. Security at hotel	Hotel room rates
5. Security at destination	Square footage available for meetings
6. Hotel room rates	Security at hotel
7. Availability of air service	Security at destination
8. Cost of air transportation	Cost of food and beverage
9. Distance of hotels from meeting site	Availability of air service
10. Cost of food and beverage	Cost of meeting space
11. Cost of meeting space	Time of year available
12. Type of hotel chains available	Distance of hotels from meeting site
13. Distance of airport from meeting site/hotel	Service at convention center
14. Square footage available for meetings	Type of hotel chains available
15. Time of year available	Service by convention and visitors bureau
16. Service at convention center	Square footage available for exhibits

not take many miscalculations like this to bring home the importance of the lead time of market segments.* Dealing with this has led to a practice called yield management, which is discussed in detail in an appendix to Chapter 14, on pricing.

On the other hand, another buy time variable is the use of a property at different periods of time. City hotels generally target business travelers and conventions during the week and pleasure travelers on weekends. The same variation occurs between summer and winter. Thus many hotels offer "package" meetings at special rates during slow periods, just as they offer packages for individual travelers. Resort hotels have similar situations depending on the season of the year. At one time, many of these hotels simply closed during the "off-season." Now

most stay open year-round but seek different markets such as meetings and conventions.

Assess the Needs. Each body of people with a common purpose has different needs as an organization. The Elks Club, a fraternal organization, certainly has different reasons for a meeting at a convention than does the new product development team for Eastman Kodak Co., yet both of these organizations may meet in the same meeting room, in the same hotel, at the same time of the year. Both the planner and the hotel employees must understand the purpose of the meeting. If, in fact, the meeting is purely a social one, theme parties, golf outings, fashion shows, and so on are expected and welcomed. If, in fact, the purpose of the meeting is to devise strategies that will bring a corporation out of bankruptcy, the entire agenda will be altered accordingly. These are obvious differences; there are many far more subtle ones.

The most common complaint planners have

---

*With convention: 400 rooms @ $100 = $40,000. Without convention: 300 rooms @ $150 = $45,000. This calculation, of course, ignores F&B revenues from the convention, which could change the picture. Still, the question of alienation remains.

about hotel salespeople does not relate either to high-pressure selling or to cold calls—though they don't particularly like either one. It is that the salesperson has not taken enough time to find out about their business. They may be pitched by a property unsuited to their needs and resent the fact that their time is being wasted by someone who didn't make enough effort to find out what they were like.

Set Measurable Goals. For the planner, it is critical that the needs of the meeting be translated into measurable results. Corporate planners can measure results from their agenda. If the meeting purpose is to brainstorm for a new product, the success of the meeting may be partially judged on how the hotel helped to facilitate the process. For the incentive planner, posttrip evaluations are helpful. The goal may be that 90 percent of the winners of the incentive would return next year if given the opportunity. From the hotel side, if the planner does not have measurable goals set, success for the meeting becomes subjective rather than objective, and minor discrepancies are subject to magnified scrutiny.

Develop a Plan. The plan needs to be concise and to lead directly from the goals and needs of the organization. The planner should include hotel and nonhotel related activities. Airline tickets, ground transportation to and from the airport, excursions, and transportation of materials are all items that must be incorporated into the plan. An organizational planner without a plan is one who must be helped through the process by the hotel staff.

It is the responsibility of the hotel that wants satisfied customers to assist inexperienced planners with all phases of the meeting. Many hotels have been accustomed to working with meeting professionals. Now, these duties in some cases have been assigned to staff with little experience in this area. For example, the bylaws of the organization may stipulate that the secretary of the group is responsible for the annual convention. If the newly elected secretary has no prior planning experience, the hotel staff needs to give assurance that all phases of the meeting will be accommodated. It will do the hotel no good to have a disorganized function come to fruition, no matter whose fault. Once the salesperson senses an absence of knowledge, a different selling scenario should be employed.

During the planning process, for example, it may be found that the planner did not allow the proper timing between sessions for the group to move from the meeting rooms to the ballroom for lunch. The conference coordinator must be knowledgeable enough to steer the planner toward the correct time frame. An example occurred in the city of Boston, where two hotels formed a strategic alliance to market themselves. The "Copley Connection" combined the guest rooms of the Marriott Copley Place and Westin Hotel (Figure 9-3). Together their facilities offered the planner 1500 guest rooms with 100,000 plus square feet of function space. The hotels were marketed together, as one big place to have a meeting. Although the hotels were connected by a skywalk, planners soon found out it took 30 minutes to move a group from the ballroom of the Marriott to a function room at the Westin. Experienced planners adjusted their agendas accordingly; others found the spaces and distances to be problematic.

On the other hand, professional planners are also becoming more educated as to what is best for their meetings. For example, a hotel salesperson might book another group into the meeting room next to the general session of the conference. The planner might, in this instance, insist that the space be utilized for his or her luncheon, thereby preventing any unanticipated interruptions from the group next door.

Resolve Conflicts. Planners have to work in tandem with both the hotel and their own organizations to anticipate and resolve potential problems. While planning may alleviate possible conflicts, the hotel may be only half of the problem. The organization itself presents problems that

FIGURE 9-3 Westin and Marriott formed a strategic alliance to attract large groups.

must be addressed before the function occurs. There may be a hierarchy within the organization that needs suites, first-class travel, and seats at the head table. Failing to accommodate these needs can cause conflicts that ruin the meeting through no fault of the hotel. A hotel staff can anticipate these needs by asking to review the VIP list and discussing its needs.

There are numerous other potential issues. Nonsmoking guestrooms and meeting rooms are entering into the spectrum of worries. Individual special meals during a banquet are no longer limited to just kosher meals. Many banquet meals now require low salt or vegetarian plates to satisfy the needs of attenders.

The best way to resolve possible conflicts for both sides is to have a **preconference meeting.** The term preconference is generic, and can be applied to incentive trips as well as to corporate meetings. At this meeting, the planner reviews the details of

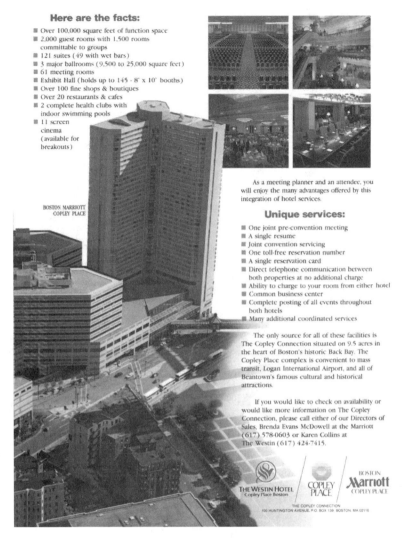

Here are the facts:

- Over 100,000 square feet of function space
- 2,000 guest rooms with 1,500 rooms committable to groups
- 121 suites (49 with wet bars)
- 3 major ballrooms (9,500 to 25,000 square feet)
- 61 meeting rooms
- Exhibit Hall (holds up to 145 - 8' x 10' booths)
- Over 100 fine shops & boutiques
- Over 20 restaurants & cafes
- 2 complete health clubs with indoor swimming pools
- 11 screen cinema (available for breakouts)

BOSTON MARRIOTT
COPLEY PLACE

As a meeting planner and an attendee, you will enjoy the many advantages offered by this integration of hotel services.

Unique services:

- One joint pre-convention meeting
- A single resume
- Joint convention servicing
- One toll-free reservation number
- A single reservation card
- Direct telephone communication between both properties at no additional charge
- Ability to charge to your room from either hotel
- Common business center
- Complete posting of all events throughout both hotels
- Many additional coordinated services

The only source for all of these facilities is The Copley Connection situated on 9.5 acres in the heart of Boston's historic Back Bay. The Copley Place complex is convenient to mass transit, Logan International Airport, and all of Beantown's famous cultural and historical attractions.

If you would like to check on availability or would like more information on The Copley Connection, please call either of our Directors of Sales, Brenda Evans McDowell at the Marriott (617) 578-0603 or Karen Collins at The Westin (617) 424-7415.

THE WESTIN HOTEL
Copley Place Boston

COPLEY PLACE

BOSTON
Marriott
COPLEY PLACE

THE COPLEY CONNECTION
100 HUNTINGTON AVENUE, P.O. BOX 139, BOSTON, MA 02116

FIGURE 9-3 *(Continued)*

the meeting with each department to ensure that communications have not been distorted through the conference coordinator. The front office, housekeeping, and banquet managers, and general manager if the situation warrants, should be in attendance with the salesperson and conference coordinator to ensure that all potential conflicts are discussed and remedied before the function occurs.

Execute the Meeting. This may be the simplest phase of the planner's job, if all the previous steps were followed and done well. If they were not, this is certainly the hardest portion of the process. The execution of the meeting could occur without the planner being in attendance. The needs of the planner are now being transposed onto the group.

Sometimes, even if the organizational planner is on the site, the end users' needs are not met. For example, the association planner may want the general session set up theater-style, with the room having chairs that face the podium for a guest speaker. The guest speaker might demand that the room be set up classroom-style, with each chair having a desk in front of it so that participants can write in conjunction with the presentation. One of the authors attended a function in Chicago where the meeting specifications called for a podium on the platform. At the last minute it was decided that a sit-down panel format would be more appropriate. The flustered setup man clearly was annoyed at the last minute change.

These are classic examples of how the planner is not the end user, and the needs of the group change right up to the last minute. The hotel that adjusts accordingly will be the one that receives the future business. There are no right and wrong sides to this scenario. The task must be completed to satisfy the needs of both the end user and the organizational planner. It really does not matter how many times a group changes their minds about the setup of a room. The hotel is responsible for making the changes.

Evaluate the Results. Based upon the goals of the organization, was the meeting a success? The hotel should be interested in the results as much as is the planner. The evaluation process can take place in a **postconference meeting** held shortly after the conclusion of the function. Department heads and the planner can review face-to-face all the things that went right, as well as those that went wrong. The marketing-oriented organization will take immediate steps to correct the malfunctions and to reinforce the positive aspects.[5]

The evaluation process is also critical for the planner. When these customers are the buyers, but may not be present at the actual event, it may be difficult for them to understand exactly what took place. Even when the hotel delivered as promised, the organization may not have accomplished its goals. The planner will need to assess the results before starting to plan the next similar function, and should be made aware of the problem areas by the hotel that wants to recapture the business.

THE CORPORATE TRAVEL MARKET

The corporate travel manager or coordinator plans the travel and entertainment for a company's employees. Corporate travel managers are different from corporate meeting planners in that they plan for a group of people with individual travel schedules. A common purpose still may exist, since the corporate entity is relatively homogeneous, but people at different levels of the organization will be traveling on different missions. In some organizations, the travel manager and the meeting planner are the same person. Corporate meeting planning is discussed in the next section.

The size of the corporate travel market is very large, running into tens of millions of business travelers, worldwide. Behind salaries and technology, travel and entertainment costs are the third largest controllable expense of United States private sector companies.[6] About half of these end users are directed or influenced by the corporate travel manager who plans, controls, mediates, negotiates, evaluates and/or approves over 40 percent of U.S. travel expenditures of those companies having corporate travel managers.[7] This market is very desirable for hotels because it tends to pay good rates, is large in size, and travels consistently throughout most of the year. Hotel executive clubs are popular with this market.

The corporate travel manager needs to find the correct products for the entire group of corporate travelers. Once the product is identified, the best rates are negotiated. The supplier needs to understand the culture of the organization to fulfill its needs. For example, some companies go to the top of the line for their hospitality and service needs. From first-class airplane seats, to limousines for ground transport, to the best hotel in the area, some companies spare no expense when entertaining themselves or their customers.

Some corporate cultures are just the opposite. They use hotel rooms sparingly, have meetings in their own offices, and use cabs or airport shuttles to reach hotels. The sales staff of the Embassy

Suites Hotel in Boca Raton ran into this culture during negotiations with the travel planner for a large corporation. After renovation, the hotel approached this major customer for a rate increase. During the sales call, the customer did not disagree that the hotel was new, and worth more money. The customer simply said that the company at this time would not pay more than $125 for a hotel room, even if it was the Ritz-Carlton. The Embassy Suites lost the business. Most companies, however, fall somewhere in between these two extremes.

Typically, corporate executives get the best treatment and company trainees the least. It mostly comes down to examining the purpose of travel, who is traveling, and what is their position.

Many companies have come to realize the extent of their travel and entertainment budgets. In some cases, this can be as much as 25 percent of an organization's costs. Thus many corporations are tightening the screws on travel costs. As one corporate travel manager told us, "You can't believe what $5 a night means over a year's time." Figure 9-4 shows a hotel company advertising to this need.

The way corporations spend their travel and entertainment dollars significantly affects the revenues of the hospitality industry. The emergence of corporate travel buyers is a result of this cost control effort. Essentially, such people's task is to control the cost without losing the quality of the product. Corporate travel buyers first ascertain the level and service of product that the organization is willing to accept; they then negotiate the prices and proceed more or less as follows.

Dealing with the Corporate Travel Market

Know the Volume. It is difficult to negotiate anything without knowing the parameters with which both parties are dealing. A hotel might give a discount based upon expected volume, only to find that the volume never materializes. A corporation, on the other hand, might be unaware of its true rooms volume at a destination and be paying more than it could negotiate at that volume. The same is true with airline travel, where companies can often negotiate volume discounts.

With hotel rack rates at their present heights, the travel manager has come to expect a discount no matter what the volume. One of the authors once received a call from a corporate travel department asking for a discounted rate. The company, which happened to make shoes, claimed its volume

FIGURE 9-4 Ala Moana Hotel addresses the budget needs of the corporate travel manager.

would be about 100 room nights annually. The hotel happened to enjoy high occupancies and rarely discounted rooms, even for 1500 room nights a year. The shoe company planner was not convinced that his perception of volume did not apply in this case. Finally, the author asked if he could get a discount on shoes if he bought three pairs a year. The response was, "Of course not! You have to be a big retailer to command a discount!" The point was finally made.

Hotel room rates are negotiated initially from the published or rack rates. Rarely, today, do customers pay the rack rate unless they are uneducated enough not to ask for the myriad array of other rates available, or are traveling during peak demand periods. Corporate or commercial rates are usually at least 10 to 15 percent lower than the rack rate, if not more.

Hotels now negotiate individual corporate rates with individual corporate customers. Volume corporate customers recognize the widescale availability of corporate rates for anyone, and demand their own corporate rate relative to their volume. These rates can run 15 to 35 percent below the rack rate. This, of course, makes the rack rate a ridiculous pretension, so hotels regularly raise the rack rate, say 10 percent, in order to raise the corporate and volume rates.

Large travel agencies, or consortia, provide mega-purchasing power for their customers. Woodside Travel in Boston, American Express in New Jersey, or Rosenbluth Travel in Philadelphia all are considered consortia, or a large umbrella under which smaller agencies can access the technology and buying power of larger entities by combining the volume of a number of corporations to get the best rate for all. These specific corporate rates are called "volume negotiated rates," which are framed in **"rate buckets,"** based on volume. An example is shown in Table 9-2.

Corporate travel managers also like hotel chain representatives to negotiate rates that will apply chain-wide. A chain that provides the convenience of "one-stop shopping," or one place where corporate travel managers can negotiate room rate

TABLE 9-2
Volume Negotiated Corporate Rate Buckets

Hotel Rate Structure

Rack[a]	$200
Corporate[b]	$180
Consortia[c]	$170

Rate Buckets

Volume Promised per Year	Negotiated Rate
250 plus rooms	$165
400 plus rooms	$160
500 plus rooms	$155
1000 plus rooms	$145

[a]Rack rate is the published room rate.

[b]Corporate rate is the rate quoted to anyone asking for a corporate rate.

[c]Consortia rates are given to large groupings of travel agencies that pool their buying power for the purpose of getting lower rates. To be accepted into their distribution channel, consortia demand rates at least 15 percent below rack and below the available corporate rates. Salespeople use these rates to negotiate with large rooms producers in a destination.

agreements for all hotels in the chain, would have a competitive advantage in this market.[8]

Understanding Travel Patterns. The corporate travel manager uses knowledge of corporate travel patterns to negotiate with hotel suppliers; the supplier responds in kind. For example, if the corporation has people traveling to a given city mainly when occupancy is already high, the manager will have far greater difficulty in negotiating preferred rates. On the other hand, if travel can be planned during low-occupancy periods, the manager may obtain not only high discount rates but also preferred availability during periods of high occupancy. The corporate customer tries to anticipate travel patterns, reserve in advance, and not just react to travel trends.

Controlling the Costs. When low room rates are negotiated, the corporate customer tries to ensure that they are used. If rates were negotiated on the basis of volume, then lack of volume may forfeit the rate. This stipulation is often inserted in the contract by the hotel. Of course, if lower rates are negotiated and company personnel don't utilize them, the cost savings are not realized.

Some companies develop policies to enforce their negotiated rates. The corporate travel manager might go into a marketplace and negotiate (or ask for bids) with hotels at various levels of product class and cost. For example, in Denver a company might have three preferred hotels: Holiday Inn, Sheraton, and Hyatt. Who stays at which depends upon the management level of the employee. To enforce compliance, the company may not reimburse hotel bills at alternative hotels unless the others are sold out.

There is a trend by companies to hire outside professionals to handle this phase of the business, such as Thomas Cook, American Express, and IVI Business Travel International. As rates for hotels and airlines become more complicated, as do the benefits of frequent traveler programs, the task of managing individual travel for corporations has become increasingly complex.

Another solution has been the hiring of "**in-plants**" by companies with large travel budgets. An "in-plant" is a division of a travel agency that is located within the corporate offices of the organizational customer. The equipment and employees belong to the travel agency, but their utilization is dedicated to the one company's needs. These employees become the travel manager, although they technically work for the travel agency. The in-plant receives either straight fees, commissions on bookings, or a combination of both for services rendered.

The in-plants offer unique resources to the corporation that might not be otherwise accessible. Specifically, the in-plant can leverage its business with the one company plus other companies also served by the agency, to negotiate even lower rates. For example, XYZ Company may have 500 rooms being used annually in Denver. This volume might justify a 10 percent discount off rack rates. The in-plant agency, however, might also represent four other companies with equal room usage in Denver. Thus the in-plant can negotiate on the basis of 2500 room nights to receive a 25 percent discount for all, the same as the travel agent consortia mentioned above.

Of course, costs are not the only consideration of travel managers. Research has shown the most important factors and the priority given them by travel managers in negotiating contracts; these are shown in Table 9-3.[9]

THE CORPORATE MEETINGS MARKET

The corporate meetings market covers a wide range of organizational customers. This market represents some 800,000 off-site meetings annually with 50 million attendees in the United States alone.[10] Although a part of a large market, individual corporate meetings are relatively small, requiring an average of only 60 hotel rooms.[11] Some hotel companies aim to specifically attract this business (Figure 9-5). The most common type of corporate meeting is a management meeting, where executives meet to discuss company business. These tend to be smaller in size with largely only senior mangers attending. Another kind of meeting is the sales meeting, which is usually organized once or more a year to discuss and review company sales goals and strategies and "pump up" the sales team. A third major type is training meetings and seminars, which provide corporations avenues to exchange information and improve their personnel's performance. These are often for new recruits, to ensure their indoctrination into the corporate culture. The corporate planner is responsible for all three types of meetings, and any others. Some incentive type meetings are also in this bailiwick but this unique type of meeting is usually handled by incentive houses.

To understand the needs of the corporate meeting planner, one must review all the components of the organizational customer. In a nutshell, meeting

TABLE 9-3
Major Considerations of Corporate Travel Managers in Negotiating Hotel Contracts[9]

Attribute	Utility Score[a]
1. Rating of hotel brand by the company's travelers	143
2. Guaranteed availability of negotiated rate	142
3. Convenience of location	140
4. Hotel brand reputation	134
5. Amount of the negotiated rate—on target or better	134
6. Willingness to negotiate policy on late cancellation of room reservation	105
7. Business services available and where	91
8. "Quality" of national sales manager	91
9. Provision of complimentary breakfast	91
10. Room upgrade policy	88
11. Complimentary airport shuttle	88
12. Free local telephone and waived access charges	87
13. Prior experience with the property or chain	85
14. Fitness facilities	78
15. Fax charges	76
16. Room configurations	72

[a]The research was done using conjoint analysis, which is a method of selecting the best combination of attributes. In this type of analysis, the higher the utility score the more important the attribute.

planners need to "look good." They need to look good to their boss, to the person whose meeting they organize, and also to the hotel, if they want to continue to look good to the first two people. At least one hotel company was advertising to appeal to this need of meeting planners, as shown in Figure 9-6.

What meeting planners do not need is for hotels to mislead them in regard to the capabilities of the physical plant and the personnel. The sometimes short-term thinking of the hotel business may lend itself to this undeliberate type of misrepresentation, and eventual loss of the customer. With as much as a 70 percent annual turnover in many hotel sales offices, and bonuses based on room nights sold, the reward system essentially mandates that you make your quota quickly to increase your income or get promoted. Sales offices are told to "book it, not cook it," meaning get the signed contract and go find more business. Many experienced planners, however, have little need for the salesper-

son, requiring instead the attention of a professional **conference coordinator,** who works for the hotel, to service the meeting. Conference coordinators are the on-site need fulfillers (see Figure 9-7). All the detail work will be done with this person who, like salespeople, may also be on a similar "fast track," often leaving the meeting planner in the hands of inexperienced new people.

Meeting planners need meeting rooms that will suit the purpose of the event. They also want a quiet room. Often, hotel ballrooms are divided by thin, movable walls that allow noise from the meeting next door to filter through. One of the authors recently gave an all-day seminar on research methods directly across a narrow hallway from a national convention of gospel singers. Guess what?

Hotel employees may also be a source of disruptive noise. While it is operationally convenient to have the kitchen right next to the ballroom, meeting attendees are disconcerted when the

FIGURE 9-5 Embassy Suites ad pursuing the small meetings market.

kitchen crew bangs pots and pans throughout a meeting. Doors that bang when people go in and out of meeting rooms are another source of high irritation.

The meeting planner needs an efficient front desk that will assign rooms to the right people: the VIPs in the suites and the attenders in the regular rooms. The billing needs to be right: Some rooms may be billed to the organization, some attendees may have to pay for their own. The meeting planner needs meeting rooms to be set up on time, and coffee breaks to arrive when ordered. The audiovisuals need to be in the meeting room at the right time, and in working order. The spare bulb for the projector should be on the cart, not locked in a closet at the other end of the building.

Meeting planners, like all customers, do not need excuses. It is not their problem that the banquet manager did not show up for work, or that the linen was supposed to be delivered at 10:00 A.M., or that they should not have scheduled the break so close to lunch time. The hotel staff assumes all responsibility for the "well-being" of the meeting.

In short, meeting planners expect all of the de-

tails to be handled absolutely professionally. If a hotel is able to provide planners not only with what they think they need, but also with what they don't realize they need, the planners will return. The above concerns, and much else, fall on the shoulders of the conference coordinator assigned to service a group.

From the hotel's side, there are problems with the corporate meetings market. While attendance at these meetings is usually compulsory, thus assuring the planned rooms and meal counts, cancellation of the entire meeting is often a threat. At the last minute, a corporation can cancel a meeting for hundreds of people that has been in the planning stage for months. Economic conditions, failure to develop a new product on schedule, or simply whim may provoke such a decision. This has led to more large up-front nonrefundable deposits. Corporate meetings also have shorter lead times but often demand what they want when they decide that they want it.

Corporate meeting planners need as much help as they can get and may require a great deal of guidance in accomplishing their company's objec-

At The Ritz-Carlton, we want to help you project a winning image. Whether you're holding a board meeting or a sales meeting, a conference or a seminar, our goal is to help you achieve yours. To make every meeting run like clockwork. And it all starts with a Conference Services Manager who's reliable as well

as available, 24 hours a day. A seasoned professional whose primary purpose is to coordinate every phase of your event, from the gearing up to the winding down. So you can relax. Everything will be taken care of. Please call your travel professional or 800-241-3333. If you'd like your company to look good, take a good look at us.

OUR OBJECTIVE AT THE RITZ-CARLTON IS MORE THAN MAKING YOUR MEETING LOOK GOOD. IT'S MAKING YOUR BUSINESS LOOK GOOD.

THE RITZ-CARLTON
HOTELS

Atlanta • Barcelona • Boston • Buckhead • Cleveland • Dearborn • Double Bay • Hong Kong • Houston • Huntington Hotel • Kansas City • Marina del Rey
New York • Pentagon City • Philadelphia • Phoenix • San Francisco • Seoul • St. Louis • Sydney • Tysons Corner • Washington, D.C. • 1995 Singapore

FIGURE 9-6 Ritz-Carlton makes meeting planners look good.

tives. On average, corporate planners plan 5 management meetings, 14 training meetings, 7 sales meetings, 1 incentive program, and 6 conferences in a year.[12] The hotel staff that provides the right guidance will often secure the business. Figure 9-8 shows an ad addressing this issue.

CONFERENCE CENTERS

Today there is a multitude of hotels from which meeting planners can choose. With this additional supply in most marketplaces, the need to attract meeting planners' business has grown. Some hotels claim to be **conference centers** by adding the words to their name, believing they can establish a new identity (i.e., XYZ Motor Inn becomes XYZ Motor Inn and Conference Center). Howard Johnson properties have, for example, in many areas, adopted the practice of adding the term "conference center" on their signs. These properties are not, however, conference centers in the true sense. In fact, many are far from it and may, in the long run, be hurting themselves with this pretension. On the other hand there are many large hotels that

FIGURE 9-7 A conference coordinator (Radisson's Meeting Solutions Manager) can guide meetings' progress.

have excellent conference centers connected to them or on the same grounds as shown in Figure 9-9, in this case called a convention center.

One way the industry has responded to the unique needs of the meeting planner is by developing "dedicated" conference centers, reserved mainly for meetings, and doing an excellent job specializing in this market. Pure conference centers are interested entirely in meetings. Scanticon Conference Center in New Jersey or Arrowwood Conference Center in Westchester, NY, are pure conference centers. IACC (International Associa-

tion of Conference Centers) sets a criterion of at least 60 percent of business coming from meetings or conferences to qualify as a "legitimate" conference center, as described in Figure 9-10. Even this may be suspect, however, unless the appropriate facilities exist and transient business is not allowed to interfere with conference participation. The needs of the meeting attendee are very different from those of leisure guests or business travelers. Figure 9-11 shows an example of a dedicated resort conference center.

According to the IACC the big difference be-

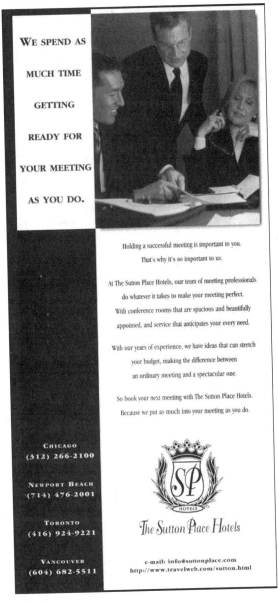

FIGURE 9-8 Sutton Place addresses the concerns of corporate meeting planners.

tween a combined hotel-and-conference center and a legitimate conference center is not just technical services but human services. The IACC claims that the business of the typical hotel is transient, limiting the attention and service it can give to every meeting, and that conference centers have a stronger commitment to conferences as essentially the only market they have.

In some cases, the combination of hotel and conference center works well when the markets are separated by time of the week or season. In other cases conflicts are created that can be detrimental. The ballroom that is ideal for weddings, or for trade shows, may be entirely inappropriate for meetings. For example, in the first case, wedding guests would probably not hear noise from the kitchen. During a meeting sales presentation, however, those noises can break the concentration of the speaker and ruin the meeting. The dividing walls of the same ballroom may be ideal for the separation of a cocktail reception and a dinner, while too porous for the holding of two meetings simultaneously. There are very few facilities that are ideal for all markets.

True conference centers attempt to serve one market only, the meetings market. They offer strictly meetings in controlled environments. With soundproof meeting rooms, dedicated audiovisual rooms with state-of-the-art equipment, and conference coordinators whose sole job is to facilitate the needs of the meetings, these properties offer a serious environment for conducting meetings. Most are located outside and away from major cities so that distractions are held to a minimum.

Many conference centers offer a full package rate that includes all the necessary services for one per-person price. These centers are dedicated to the needs of the meeting planners and serve them well. At the same time, some are having a difficult time making ends meet. High occupancy occurs during selected time periods and the shoulder and low periods incur very high costs without compensating revenues. For this reason most dedicated conference centers do attempt to fill in open dates with the social transient market.

THE INCENTIVE MARKET

The **incentive planner** has a unique problem (need) when compared with other customers of the hospitality product. The incentive planner has to provide not only for the accommodation of a group, but also for the group's idea of "fun," such as entertainment, golf, sightseeing, and a multitude of other activities. This is a difficult task. When you think of your own idea of a good time, it is probably quite different from that of some people you know. This problem of disparity is one with which the incentive planner is challenged.

The incentive planner organizes travel as a reward for superior performance within a group. For example, the sales team of a computer manufacturer may have exceeded its sales quota by 30 percent. The reward is a trip to the Caribbean for a week, with spouses. Managers of a retail store chain may be eligible for travel incentives if their profit margins are above a certain quota.

The Society of Incentive Travel Executives (SITE), defines incentive travel as follows: "Incentive travel is a modern management tool that motivates salespeople, dealers, distributors, customers, and internal employees by offering rewards in the form of travel for participation in the achievement of goals and objectives."[13]

The United States incentive travel market generates over $10 billion a year, including airfare and ground service. Over 50 percent is hotel related. Trip sizes range from 2 to 2000 people, with an average of over 100 people per trip. Most trips include spouses. About 50 percent of locations are resorts.[14]

Travel certainly is not the only method of incentive reward, but it is one that projects an image of excitement and relaxation away from the job. When this is done in the group format, teamwork and morale increase with the sense of accomplishment. Merchandise rewards, such as television, stereos, and cash bonuses, are the competition to travel rewards. Travel rewards are preferred by many companies, and managing that travel becomes an important task.

This has led to the growth of **"incentive houses,"** companies that provide professional incentive planning and hope to assure no-hassle, successful, and satisfying trips. As the value of the incentive travel market has become recognized by the hotel industry, companies are trying to better meet this market's needs. According to J. J. Gubbins, former vice-president of Sheraton:

> Incentives really taught the hotel industry to be creative. It got us to focus on the idea of travel as entertainment. Through servicing incentives we learned how to develop the creative aspects of our own industry, which has affected nearly every aspect of our operation—even in the way hotels and resorts are designed.[15]

Incentive Travel

The incentive planner often becomes involved in the development of criteria for incentive success. In order to have winners to send on trips, the framework of the incentive must be established. In order to have a successful incentive, the reward must be different and worth wanting.

Once the framework of the incentive has been developed, the incentive planner must formulate the appropriate travel prizes. Even if incentive planners do not specifically design the promotion, it is critical for them to have a full understanding of the composition of the group and its achievements. Incentive planners need to establish the perceived level of incentive, and plan accordingly.

The Incentive Trip. The actual incentive trip can take three forms: pure incentive, incentive plus, and incentive weekends. The pure incentive trip is dedicated to having a good time without any business-related activities. The incentive plus is a more popular form of incentive trip and is used in over 70 percent of the cases. Incentive plus trips combine pleasure with some form of meetings or new product introductions. In this way, companies maximize use of their incentive travel dollars. The company can disseminate valuable information without having another meeting elsewhere. Incentive weekends are increasingly being used as rewards for good, but less than superior, performance. Companies recognize that while incentive trips are productive, they also take time away from the workplace. Three-day weekend incentives are more cost effective from a time management viewpoint.

FIGURE 9-9 Brochure pages for Rodos Palace, a hotel/convention (conference) center.

The incentive planner has a multifaceted job when planning the actual trip. Specifically, all phases of the excursion must be minutely planned to enhance the end user experience. This is different from planning corporate or association meetings, or conventions. In those cases, the planner plans the functions but leaves it to the individuals to get there and participate. The incentive planner, on the other hand, arranges for literally everything: air and land travel, hotel, food, excursions, sightseeing, entertainment, sports, and anything else

that might take place during the trip. Each and every one of these categories can be critical to the success of the trip.

This is why incentive planners have almost always visited the site, and the hotels, restaurants, and ground operators at the site, before developing the package. They want to make sure not only that everything is up to par, but that every detail will be taken care of; they or their representatives go on the trip as a final security. This means that a hotel has a special challenge in booking and handling in-

FIGURE 9-9 *(Continued)*

centive travel. We know of one case, for example, when the planner ruled out an upscale hotel on an inspection trip because the sand urns had cigarette butts in them and facial tissue was missing in some of the rooms. "If they can't take care of the little things, they'll never take care of the big ones," was this planner's comment.

Incentive trip planning also differs from that of other organizational customers in that the destination is of primary importance. (See, for example, Figure 9-12.) The corporate customer or meeting planner may choose a facility because of the hotel itself or because of its proximity to business-related activities; for the incentive planner, the choice of hotel comes after the choice of destination.

Many companies are not large enough or skilled enough to develop incentive trips through their internal organization. A company may have a full-time corporate travel manager and a meeting planner, but the complexities of the incentive purchase are entirely different. For example, staying familiar with different destination areas and necessary ground arrangements is incredibly time-consuming.

BURT CABAÑAS TALKS ABOUT EFFECTIVE MEETINGS.

A CANDID CONVERSATION WITH AN INDUSTRY LEADER

BURT CABAÑAS
PRESIDENT AND CEO
BENCHMARK HOSPITALITY, INC.

■ **IN A NUTSHELL, WHAT DIFFERENTIATES A CONFERENCE CENTER FROM A TRADITIONAL HOTEL?**

"To begin with, conference centers are designed, built and managed with one primary purpose in mind . . . maintaining the balanced environment of "Living, Learning and Leisure"™ in order to ensure productive meetings. Unlike hotels, this means that everything from the physical facilities to the operating policies to conference services maintains

the meeting planners' needs as the number one priority."

■ **ARE THERE GUIDELINES THAT A PROPERTY MUST FOLLOW TO BE CONSIDERED A "CONFERENCE CENTER"?**

"While the term 'conference center' is not protected, IACC (International Association of Conference Centers) has worked hard to identify the criteria for inclusion. Membership in IACC–of which we are one of the founders–is usually a good

indicator that the property is getting at least 60% or more of its business from meetings and conferences and its facilities and operating focus are geared toward the service of conferences."

■ **WHAT KIND OF MEETINGS ARE BEST SUITED TO A CONFERENCE CENTER?**

"Any time the ultimate goal of a meeting is information retention and learning, a conference center–with its more focused environment–is an ideal setting. Management training meetings

to teach managers about new products or management methods . . . or meetings focusing on marketing and financial strategies . . . are well suited to conference centers where the average group size is less than 50 people."

■ **DO CONFERENCE CENTERS PROVIDE RECREATION?**

"Conference centers are not designed for all work and no play. Benchmark understands how critically important the "leisure" aspect of a meeting is–not just for relaxation but as an important way to foster interaction among the conference attendees. As a pioneer of the "conference resort" concept, Benchmark offers worldclass recreation that ranks with the nation's best. Championship golf, Olympic-calibre skiing, tennis, swimming, hike and bike trails, and extensive executive fitness centers featuring state-of-the-art exercise equipment and spa facilities all help attendees unwind."

■ **IS THE CONFERENCE CENTER DINING EXPERIENCE FLEXIBLE?**

"The conference center dining concept–three meals per day served 'kiosk' style–provides the quality of first-class dining. Our "America's Harvest" approach to menu planning offers guests tremendous variety at each meal as opposed to pre-set banquet menus and allows meetings to break at a time that's convenient for the planner. It also includes flexible continuous coffee breaks with an abundance of choices."

■ **THERE'S A MYTH THAT CONFERENCE CENTERS ARE NOT AESTHETICALLY APPEALING. IS IT TRUE?**

"In generations past, conference centers were more utilitarian than luxurious, but that's not the case today. Baby Boomers expect a higher level of comfort. At a Benchmark property, you will find recreational facilities, guest room amenities and customer service delivered at a four-star level."

■ **WHAT ABOUT PRICE? IS IT COMPETITIVE?**

"Myth versus reality . . . the conference center's value to a meeting goes beyond dollars and cents. The fact of the matter is that conference centers are not only competitive, but when you take advantage of the Complete Meeting Package (CMP), which generally covers in excess of 90% of the total meeting costs, there are no surprises at check out."

■ **WHAT IS CMP AND IS THERE ANY ROOM FOR NEGOTIATION?**

"The Complete Meeting Package (CMP) includes the meeting space, refreshment breaks, all meals, guest room, most audio-visual equipment, conference services and concierge and some recreational activities. Negotiations are based on supply and demand coupled with our strong desire to meet the meeting planner's objective and to establish a long-term working relationship. In general, our pricing varies as much as 30%."

FIGURE 9-10   Dedicated conference center criteria.

FIGURE 9-11 The Woodlands, a dedicated conference center and resort.

Incentive houses are a popular intermediary for the companies that need the dedicated attention of a professional. The incentive house is more than a travel agent; professional incentive planners help in all phases of incentive management. Broad experience with specialized organizational needs supplements seasoned knowledge in even first-time attempts.

Overall, the incentive organizational customer has a unique job among hotel customers. The "fun" aspect of the planning can be anything but that. Hotels that want a greater share of the incentive market must be extremely flexible in their approach to this marketplace. Standardized approaches to capturing this market are likely not to be fruitful.

The world's most rewarding incentive destination.
Combine the myriad sights of an ancient culture with a rich variety of beach and city hotels; add sunshine, theme parties, shopping and nightlife; and you have the perfect incentive: Thailand

FIGURE 9-12 An ad aimed by Thailand at the incentive market.

ASSOCIATION, CONVENTION, AND TRADE SHOW MARKETS

These three markets overlap. Association and convention customers have similar needs, although they are somewhat different types of groups. Both tend to have large guestroom and function space requirements. An **association meeting** can comprise a group of people convening on a social basis to elect officers, have social functions, and organize activities on a regional and/or a national basis. This category of organizational customer also tends to meet throughout the year in smaller groups, and social contacts are a major reason for attendance. There are, of course, innumerable professional

(e.g., American Medical Association) and business associations (e.g., National Association of Manufacturers) that meet both regionally and nationally to present papers, have board meetings, and set policy.

Convention planners are more focused on annual activities, such as annual meetings of delegates for a political caucus. Other examples are union gatherings to decide policies for the coming year, or a fishermen's convention to plan lobbying efforts. The participants may or may not meet throughout the year, and dissemination of information, more than social contacts, is the primary objective.

Finally, the main purpose of **trade shows** is to sell products. This takes wide open space, as advertised in Figure 9-13. The hotel's task in booking trade shows is not only to provide the space, but also to provide ease of access for products to be brought in and the facilities, such as electric power and lighting, to display the products. This requires a great deal of work, which can be disruptive to other guests. In addition, the hotel sells rooms and meals to exhibitors and those who attend. Exhibitors also make wide use of "hospitality suites" where they can entertain customers. This puts heavy pressure on the hotel's room service division, although at high cost to the exhibitors.

While each of these three planners (association, convention, and trade show) has a different reason for purchasing the hospitality product, the needs are similar and sometimes interchangeable. For example, an association may meet as a convention in connection with a trade show. At times, an entire facility will be purchased for a two- or three-day period. Usually, the planner arranges for guestrooms to be held, but reservations are made individually by the participants. The organizer will have a list of VIPs, but the majority of guestrooms are booked by direct calls or through the use of reservation cards.

Reservations cards are essentially order forms that are provided by the hotel and are designed specifically for the use of attendees. Attendees, of course, are always free to stay somewhere else if

We've got 299,999 more of these.

So if you need a lot of square feet to make your trade show work, call the Opryland Hotel.

Whatever your trade, the Opryland Hotel has the spaces to show it off–including 145,000 square feet of dedicated exhibit space on one level. The Opryland Hotel has the square footage and more...superior service, outstanding facilities, state-of-the-art technology and spaces that work hard to make your trade show work:

☐ 145,000 square feet of exhibit space, all on one level
☐ 300,000 total square feet of magnificently designed public space
☐ 1,900 deluxe guest rooms, including 120 suites
☐ three expansive ballrooms, totalling 68,000 square feet–each divisible into smaller areas
☐ the new Cascades–a 2½-acre indoor water garden with dancing waters, brooks, waterfalls and fountains
☐ the Conservatory–a two- acre, year-round tropical garden under glass

☐ 29 front desk stations–more per room than any other hotel our size in the nation
☐ conveniently adjacent to the 4,400-seat Grand Ole Opry House
☐ part of Opryland USA, including Opryland, America's Musical Showplace, the *General Jackson* showboat and The Nashville Network.

We invite you to discover the superb spaces and facilities of the Opryland Hotel. Please call George Aguel, Vice President/Marketing, or Jerry Wayne, Director of Sales, at (615) 889-1000. Or write Opryland Hotel, 2800 Opryland Drive, Nashville, TN 37214.

OPRYLAND HOTEL

FIGURE 9-13 Opryland ad soliciting trade show business.

they prefer. Thus, the hotel sales department tries to make it conducive for them to stay there. Handling reservations in this manner can make coordination difficult. The hotel must be flexible to the needs of the attendees, many of whom are buying the hotel sight unseen. Strict inventory control is necessary. If, for example, the hotel accepts more king-size bedroom requests than it can accommodate, it may have many unhappy customers.

Food and beverage is also a unique proposition for hotels in these markets. The organizational buyer tries to be as precise as possible in the num-

ber of people who will attend meal functions, but the actual attendance can vary widely. If there are alternatives, as in a large city, many attendees will go out for meals. Attendance at different meal functions can vary widely even within the same meeting. The first night's award banquet might have close to 100 percent attendance. The following night might have a boring speaker, and half the attendees will go elsewhere.

Association, convention, and trade show planners need extremely good coordinators within the hotel to execute all phases of the event. These coordinators are far more important than the sales-people in delivery of the final product. Rutherford and Umbreit found that convention-services managers of hotels had the greatest number of encounters with meeting planners during the process of planning and executing an event of any hotel personnel.[16] This may be true for any meeting of size, but it is especially true for these large complex ones. Technical details such as the voltage in the main ballroom, the delivery space for exhibits, and the audiovisuals for the speakers are all critical to the success of the function.

The hotel staff also needs to have good relations with the unions that are involved in handling large affairs. Not only are union members within the hotel utilized, but often there are members of other unions who set up booths, deliver products to the display area, and so forth. A convention planner working at too much of a distance will be unaware of the vagaries of local unions. A mistake in procedures can ruin the setup or breakdown of a function very easily.

Delegates to these kinds of functions often will not stay for the duration of the meeting. They may book for three nights and stay two, and not give any notice of doing it (although hotels are beginning to penalize for this behavior). Many are small business people who cannot make definite plans for the future; others will simply feel they've had all they want and decide to leave.

Delegates to these functions also tend to be quite price-sensitive. The organizer, who wants to keep the delegates happy, looks for low rates and for low-cost or free meeting space. All three of these markets are tough to sell and tough to service, but they can represent lucrative business, especially if booked during slow business periods.

CONVENTION CENTERS AND CONVENTION AND VISITORS BUREAUS

There are two external bodies often closely involved in the handling of association, convention, and trade show marketing that need brief mention.

The first is the freestanding **convention center,** sometimes called a conference center, but generally meaning a freestanding, independent property such as that shown in Figure 9-14. Most major cities in the world, small countries, and many secondary and tertiary cities, especially in the United States, have such convention centers. In these cases, the "main event" takes place in the convention center, which is usually publicly owned but privately operated. The trade show or convention itself, on the other hand, may be handled by a private organizing firm.

The National Restaurant Association (NRA) trade show in Chicago or the annual technology show in Las Vegas are examples of trade shows held in convention centers. Either booths or space are sold to purveyors, and attendees peruse the offerings under one roof. Although informational seminars may be given during the show, the main purpose of the event is to display products and take orders. The trade show organizer makes money from the booth or space sales. In turn, the purveyors hope to write enough business to make their expenses worthwhile.

The convention center works closely with the city's hotels and restaurants for lodging and feeding. In New York City, for example, the annual American Hotel & Motel Association (AH&MA) trade show is held in Jacob Javits Convention Center. The collateral sent out by the show operator includes hotels' locations and rates, free bus schedules, and restaurant and theater ads, all intended to make it easier for attenders to plan their stay. Hotels may get individual groups and functions from this event, but they are not the main center of focus.

Many such events are arranged, at least initially, with **convention and visitors bureaus (CVBs),** such as that shown in Figure 9-15. These organizations are publicly and privately supported by those they serve—convention centers, hotels, restaurants, merchants, theaters, airlines, and so forth. A tradi tional distribution channel, the CVB is becoming less of a factor in the booking process. Often a planner contacts the local CVB for housing, transportation, and entertainment coordina-

We Hosted The Globe

Sherb🌀urne
CONFERENCE CENTRE

Prestige in Paradise
A modern state-of-the-art meeting facility with extraordinary experience. In 1994 the Sherbourne Conference Centre was the venue for the United Nations Global Conference on Sustainable Development for Small Island Developing States. That's a world class endorsement. And your assurance that the Sherbourne Conference Centre offers the facilities, the technology, the know-how and the service excellence you wish for your conference.

- Just 2 miles from the capital, Bridgetown
  15 minutes from the international airport;
  close to commercial centres, luxury hotels, etc.
- Main hall seats up to 1000 theatre style, other meeting rooms accommodate 250 to 859 persons.
- Simultaneous translation in 6 languages.
- Media Centre with microwave link video conference facilities.
- Over 25,000sq. ft. of exhibition space.

Sherbourne Conference Centre,
Two Mile Hill, St, Michael,
Barbados, West Indies.
Tel: (246) 434-3000 or 428-5980/1
Fax: (246) 431-9795
TOLL FREE: 888-851-9400

CONFERENCING IN BARBADOS...

...THE BEST UNDER THE SUN

*B*ARBADOS

JUST BEYOND YOUR IMAGINATION

FIGURE 9-14 Sherbourne/Barbados, a freestanding convention/conference center.

tion. Planners in the association and convention markets relied on local CVBs for 41 percent of their bookings in 1995. This number shrank to 35 percent in 1997, and is expected to slide further to 22 percent in 2000. Third party meeting planners, primarily independents, are replacing the traditional CVBs for planning large group meetings. They are able to provide the personal service that CVBs have yet to master for the customer.[17]

CVB organizations are nonprofit, serving their constituents, who pay annual fees. They exist in both large and small cities. Their main mission is to promote the city as a destination area. Hotels and restaurants still need to work very closely with CVBs. If the CVB can sell the city to a group, it then provides information on hotel accommodations, restaurants, and other attractions that are part and parcel of the overall enticement.

THE AIRLINE MARKET

The **airline market** is defined as the housing of airline employees and crew members on a contract

FIGURE 9-15 A solicitation from convention and visitors bureau (CVB) of Baton Rouge.

basis. When an airline's employees fly a designated number of hours, as established by government aviation bodies, the airline has to provide a place for the crew to rest for a designated number of hours. In the past, hotels chosen for this purpose have been low-priced and located near the airport for reasons of reduced transportation costs. Two factors have changed the traditional scenario, however; one is the supply/demand ratio in the hotel marketplace, and the other is the unions that participate in the bargaining process on behalf of their members.

In the first case, as more hotels have been built in relatively stable demand centers, the competition for customers has increased. This has put pressure on hotels to find new customers to fill their hotel rooms, especially in soft economic periods. In the second case, although airline unions may not get the wage increases they would like, they have been successful in keeping and improving other benefits for their members, such as housing. Crew unions have hotel committees, members of which go on hotel inspection trips with theirs airlines' hotel buyers. They keep databases of crew complaints and a list of the hotels they dislike.

The net result has been that the airline buyer, who negotiates for crew accommodations, finds a number of better products to choose from, with pressure from the unions to make the best possible facilities available to their members. On the hotel's part, however, facilities alone will not hold the contract. Unless the hotel understands these customers and their unique needs, it will not be able to deliver the product and will eventually lose the business to the hotel that does understand airline and crew members' problems. Some airlines have a "chief of flight crew accommodations" who regularly evaluates contracted rooms and facilities for their suitability.

Airline crew members have many needs and problems different from those of other travelers. Due to tight flight schedules, there are relatively few hours available to rest between flights. Airline crews must have all of their rooms available and assigned before they arrive, which may be at odd hours, for instantaneous check-in. The aircraft captain is always in charge of the crew, even off the plane. All unusual situations need to be discussed with him or her before any decisions can be made.

Once in their rooms, airline crews do not necessarily like street views with street noises! Here is a market segment that would gladly take the rooms facing an inner courtyard or another building. Some airline crews have very unusual hours of sleep—for instance, some international flight crews check in at 8:00 A.M. and need to sleep immediately. Therefore heavy blackout drapes are also necessary to enable crew members to sleep during the day, a feature that would not affect most other customers of the hotel. Flight crews abhor any kind of noise, and want 24-hour room service, cheap meals, and free coffee.

Coordination is needed in all phases of the operation. For the corporate client who is at a meeting, 11:00 A.M. may be the best time to have a houseman vacuum the hallways, but this is not true for the crew that checked in at 8:00 A.M. Wake-up calls are critical. Delayed flights can cost an airline thousands of dollars if an operator making $8.50 per hour forgot to make wake-up calls at 3 P.M. There are numerous other seemingly small details that are critical for crew members, such as locating them away from elevators and ice machines, and putting female crew members into adjacent rooms that have only other crew members next door.

Finally, integration of the food and beverage offerings needs to occur. Recognizing that crews are not on expense accounts (like many government employees, they are on **per diem**—a fixed daily allowance) the lunch menu with an $18.00 average check will probably not be utilized by them. However, there is potential in these extra customers and special menu discounts can provide additional revenues and profits.

How much is too much? Airline crews were once largely contracted on a yearly basis for a set number of rooms, but this has changed as the airlines insist on short-term contracts to give them more flexibility. Rates can sometimes be very low (as low as 40 percent of rack rate) in comparison to the printed rack rates, or even the corporate rates. At one time many hotels displaced their crew rooms because demand was so strong from more lucrative market segments. The pendulum always swings back, however, and now many hotels are seeking the airline market.

Airline contracts are obtained by a low-rated bid practice. Some managers shy away from airline business because of the low rates and/or because they think it gives a negative image to a hotel and/or because of the hassle they cause. Airline crews may not be considered "appropriate" in the lobby of a luxury hotel in the United States; overseas, however, in many countries they are accepted as adding prestige to the hotel.

In fact, many hoteliers admit that the clients who annoy them most are flight crews, with whom they have a love-hate relationship. Hotels cater to crews because their business is sizable and steady, providing a comfortable cushion when the economy is soft. American Airlines alone buys 1.8 million room nights a year for its crews. Some hotels derive 30 percent or more of their revenue from airline contract business.[18] Besides the image/trouble factor, the real test of accepting airline business depends on the net revenue generated by the business and the compatibility with the segment mix. To determine the profit margins of an airline contract, a displacement study needs to be done. First, management must estimate how many nights during the contract period the hotel will run a high enough occupancy that it could not accommodate under the crew contract. For example, if an airline wants 100 rooms in a 500-room hotel, how many nights would the hotel likely have between 80 and 100 percent occupancy? The number of possible lost nights becomes the basis for revenue displacement. In other words, how many nights could the guestrooms be sold to a guest at a higher rate, and what would be the net gain or loss?

Revenue can be calculated for both scenarios—with and without the crew contract. From this should be deducted variable cost. For example, if the variable cost to service a room is $20.00 and the airline contract is for $60.00 a room, and the otherwise obtainable rate is $120.00, the hotel has to sell two and one-half airline rooms to make the same gross margin as one regular room. It may also be wise to calculate additional margins such as from food and beverages where crews tend to spend very little. If the gross margin earned from an airline crew contract is greater than the gross margin from the displaced rooms, then the airline business should be considered.

THE SMERF AND THE GOVERNMENT MARKETS

The **SMERF** market is not solicited by many major hotels. Their inventory is being used by more upscale corporate customers and associations. Other hotels, however, those in poor supply/demand positions, are looking for SMERF customers. The SMERF market is now considered a "segment" by Professional Conference Managers Association (PCMA). SMERF customers are comprised of all organizational customers who do not fit into the other categories, a "catchall" market. Major submarkets of SMERF—social, military, education, religious, and fraternal—cover most of the complexion of this market.

So what is a SMERF market? It is a price sensitive, nonprofit organization market. All social related group business is considered SMERF. Wedding parties needing overnight accommodations, rehearsal dinner parties, society events, fund raisers, and so on, all these are considered within this market. So are gospel singers on tour; military customers using hotel rooms for reunions or for travel on business; the education subsegment, consisting of groups such as faculty and school sports teams; religious groups, from large Baptist conventions that can fill a city to the Order of the Rising Star meeting in a hotel. Finally, fraternal orders, such as the Elks Clubs or the Benevolent Order of Moose, all fall into the SMERF segment.

Although the SMERF segment has the reputation of being low rated, the customers nevertheless fill guestrooms, ballrooms, and local restaurants, especially during slow periods. The "Head Buffalo" of an Elks group can be no less important a customer to some hotels than a corporate meeting planner.

The **government market** is also low rated but in the United States it is a $12 billion market, and it is large in other countries as well. Again, economic slumps in bookings lead hoteliers to see government as an attractive market. This market is a reliable source of incremental revenue for many budget and mid-level properties. Upscale properties also cannot ignore the upper end of this business.*

Government at all levels is engaged in many activities that tend to be travel-intensive: research, regulation, investigation, enforcement, oversight, litigation, education, and coordination. Government employees travel anywhere and everywhere people are to be found.

Although government employees may be end users, they may not be the customers to whom to make the sale. Government travel planning is a bureaucratized affair. A program manager or travel coordinator is probably responsible for employees' reservations, and per diem rates are set by state or national capitals. As with airline crews, hotels can target this market for rooms that might otherwise be left empty. Careful planning and marketing is needed and, again, segment mix must be considered.

THE GROUP TOUR AND TRAVEL MARKET

This market is defined as leisure travelers who travel in groups, with or without an escort. This is a wide-ranging market that has changed dramatically in recent times, and is no longer characterized by hordes of ignorant travelers visiting five countries in four days. Tours may range from trekking in the Himalayas to whale-watching in the Pacific; from a ladies' garden club tour of Japan to a high school senior trip to Spain; other tour groups may be simply individual parties on the same plane going to the same destination. Group tour travelers have different motivations for selecting this form of travel, most important being the convenience of

---

*It should be noted that in some countries outside the United States (for example Saudi Arabia), much government business is akin to royalty and is *top-rated*.

having all arrangements made for them. Other motivations include companionship (especially among mature travelers), lower travel costs, and planned itineraries that will ensure that travelers will not miss the "must-see" places. Regardless of motivation or type of tour, hotel accommodations may be the most important part of a group tour package. As Stanley C. Plog states:

> An adequate hotel room is important in travelers' itineraries because it becomes a stable base for almost everything that vacationers want to do, whether they are the venturesome types or the more timid souls. They do not want to worry about making wrong choices, in terms of quality or price, because so much of an always short vacation can be ruined by the discomforts and indignities that accompany the wrong choice of hotel. The assumption exists that the travel organizer, whether an airline or a tour wholesaler, can obviate the need for the vacationer to go through the learning curve on how to select hotels of adequate quality and that they will do this for a relatively reasonable price because of the buying power of large organizations.[19]

There are over 2000 tour operators in the United States, and many more around the world. Tour operators usually belong to trade associations such as the National Tour Association, American Bus Association, or the United Bus Owners of America. Member directories provide useful information and are a good starting point for hospitality marketers interested in pursuing this type of business. Although there are many kinds of tours, a common type is the escorted motorcoach tour or the Group Inclusive Tour (GIT), arranged by wholesale tour brokers, which is discussed further in Chapter 18.

Hotels and restaurants will have to deal with the travel organizers for these groups, who may be tour operators, travel agents, or both.

Motorcoach Tour Travelers

In the United States, this market segment has traditionally been made up mostly of older travelers.

In other parts of the world, however, where owning cars is not as prevalent, **motorcoach tours** have long been a popular mode of sightseeing and vacationing. Things are changing in the United States, as well. Many younger travelers are utilizing motorcoach tours to see domestic sights inexpensively.

The motorcoach tour market for hotels and restaurants can be defined as five or more travelers arriving at a hospitality establishment by motorcoach, as part of a total tour package. This market really has to be separated from other travelers arriving at the hotel by bus, simply because of their original reason for the purchase. A group of corporate business people could arrive at a hotel by bus, yet their sole purpose for the visit would be a corporate meeting, making them a corporate group. A convention could have an entire delegation from a single geographic area arrive by bus, but again, the reason would be to attend the convention, not to visit local attractions. The size of the motorcoach tour market is ever expanding. Although the majority of these trips are within one day, almost 40 percent stay overnight in a lodging establishment. Motorcoach tours from the United States to Canada generate over $1 billion a year in Canada, according to the National Tour Association. Every "bus night" (average of 40 passengers) generates many thousands of dollars. More than one-third of this goes to hotels.

Motorcoach tours are arranged in two formats, series and ad hoc groups. A tour series is a prearranged link of stopovers, usually carrying a theme. An example is a motorcoach tour to see the New England autumn foliage. Stopovers include country inns and landmark restaurants, with occasional visits to local museums.

An ad hoc group has a specific destination in mind, for example, Disneyworld in Orlando, FL, or Disneyland of Paris. A group arranges to travel there by motorcoach and stay several nights to take advantage of the attraction. While ad hoc groups might also have another stopover, this is normally just a stopover, not the initial reason for the trip.

When soliciting the motorcoach market, responding to its specific needs makes the marketing more successful. Tours employ tour leaders responsible for the well-being of the group as well as the satisfaction of its individual members. Tour leaders are also, in essence, sales representatives for the tour company. The hotel salesperson sells the hotel to the tour company, but the tour leader is the one who has to travel with the group and ensure their satisfaction. As with most other products, there are many similar tours available to the consumer, and often the tour leader develops a following of repeat customers.

The group requires special room key assignment, all being preassigned before the bus arrives. The keys are distributed by the tour leader, and the baggage is unloaded and tagged. The luggage is a critical need for this customer. It is unacceptable to have to wait over half an hour for luggage to arrive in the rooms, after a long day on the road and before an inflexible dinner time. Whether luggage is carried to the rooms by bellmen, or by the customer directly, this relatively simple yet unusual situation can, if not handled correctly, cause many dissatisfied customers.

Although the median age of motorcoach tour travelers is dropping into the 50s, generally older travelers prefer rooms that do not require the use of stairs. They prefer rooms with views, they like being close to each other, and they want the correct bedding configuration—areas in which misunderstanding this market may arise. A weekend package user might ask for a double room, and be completely satisfied with a queen bed assignment. The same double room for the motorcoach guest may indicate a need for two beds in the same room—and a roll-away is not an acceptable substitute.

Motorcoach tour groups are a viable market for many hotels; in fact, some hotels survive on them. The warning here is the one we have mentioned before: Tour groups do not mix well with some other market segments, and special care is needed to see that this mix is not a problem. Motorcoach tour operators traditionally seek out medium-priced hotels but one study showed that tour operators used four-star hotels for over 30 percent of their business.[20]

Regardless of their budget, these travellers' needs come all at once. An average busload of 40 means 40 bags all at once (maybe 80), 40 luncheons all at once, and 40 breakfasts all at once. Staffing to handle this is critical, especially when these customers don't tip well and employees are not especially eager to serve them. Disgruntled tour groups make a great deal of noise!

SUMMARY

Organizational meeting planners and travel managers are unique to the hospitality industry in that they plan travel for others in groups, or individually, but they themselves are not the end users. These planners/managers are responsible to the organizations they represent. They have to anticipate the wide variety of needs that members of these organizations represent.

Overall, organizational planners and travel managers are better educated about, and have more experience in, the hospitality industry than the individual purchaser of the hotel and restaurant product. The single most important factor in their decision-making process remains the word of mouth of their fellow professionals. Second, references from someone within their organization help steer this customer toward a hotel choice. The conference coordinator at the hotel is probably more significant than the salesperson, in most cases, in creating and keeping customers. Advertising ranks low on the scale of influence for the organizational customer.

KEY WORDS AND CONCEPTS

Airline Market: This organizational customer purchases rooms for airline personnel in an extended time frame up to one year, subject to renewal.

Association Meetings: Organizational customers

that use hospitality services for organizations like the Elks Club and Alzheimer's Association, which may also be conventions.

Buy Time: The time span before an actual event that the product is bought. Also, the calendar time that a group books.

Conference Centers: Facilities specifically built and designed to accommodate corporate and other meetings and within or connected to a hotel.

Conference Coordinator: A hotel employee who handles the details of a meeting before and when it happens.

Convention and Visitors Bureau (CVB): A local, business-supported, nonprofit organization that facilitates the selling of a city or destination to groups.

Convention Centers: Freestanding, usually independent facilities specifically built and designed to accommodate large conventions and trade shows; provide catering service but not lodging.

Convention Planners: Organizational customers who arrange conventions and may purchase or organize hospitality services for large organizations or associations.

Government Market: Organizational customers who purchase hospitality services for government employees, or, government employees on per diem.

Incentive Houses: Companies that provide high quality incentive planning for organizations.

Incentive Planners: Incentive planners are a sub-segment of the corporate market, who provide trips as rewards for top performers within the end user organization.

In-Plant: A division of a travel agency located on corporate premises to handle travel management.

Lead Time: See Buy Time.

Meeting Planner: Person who plans the group travel and meeting arrangements of the end user. In some cases they also plan incentive travel.

Motorcoach Tour: This organizational customer represents the market of people traveling by bus to various attractions and destinations.

Organizational Customer: This customer is both the meeting planner or travel manager, buying hospitality services for the end user, an organization, and the people in the organization who will actually use the product. For ease of presentation, we use the term end user to apply to the actual user.

Organizational Planner: A generic term, regardless of title, for the purchaser of hospitality services for a group or an organization that has a common purpose.

Per Diem: A fixed daily allowance for employees to spend on travel and be reimbursed.

Postconference Meeting: A meeting to recap the event to determine if there were shortfalls in expectations.

Rate Buckets: Rate brackets for customers gaining discounts based on volume.

Preconference Meeting: A method to arrange details and resolve conflicts during the meeting planning/execution process. The planner and the hospitality enterprise meet prior to the event to ensure there are no misunderstandings as to the expectations of either party.

SMERF Market: Organizational customers who purchase hospitality services in the Social, Military, Education, Religious, or Fraternal categories.

Trade Shows: Organizational customers that purchase hospitality services for industry groups displaying products, like the Toy Fair and Printing/Stationery Show.

Travel Manager: Person who oversees, negotiates arrangements, and sometimes plans the individual travel and entertainment of the end users. In some cases they also plan meetings.

DISCUSSION QUESTIONS

1. What is the essential difference between the organizational customer and other customers discussed earlier in this book?
2. Why do hotel convention and conference coor-

dinators play a more important role in the decision-making process of the organizational customer?

3. How do the corporate travel manager customers and the corporate meeting planner customers differ?

4. Describe the three types of different incentive trips. How would each of these affect the choice of destination and hotel?

5. Why is the preconference meeting and the postconference evaluation process critical for organizational customers?

6. Describe the similarities and differences among the association, the convention, and the trade show segments in terms of the end users.

GROUP PROJECTS

1. Act as a meeting planner for a designated group and develop a list of their needs and a list of their requirements that you would expect a hotel to deliver.

2. Act as a corporate travel manager for a designated well-known corporation where employees at all levels travel frequently. Develop a Request for Proposal (RFP) that you would send to hotel chains to get them to bid on your business.

REFERENCES

1. In 1994, *Successful Meetings Magazine* conducted a survey of corporations on the use of independent planners. At that time, 15 percent of the respondents used independent planners. The most recent study, in 1997, showed 20 percent of the corporation planners to be independent. In a survey of planners, corporate planners were 63 percent of the total, independent planners 20 percent, and association planners 7 percent. Julie Barker, "State of the Industry," *Successful Meetings Magazine,* January 1997, p. 44.

2. Quoted in Kathy Seal, "Staff, Service, Top Priorities Planners," *Hotel & Motel Management,* July 20, 1987, pp. 40, 42, 43.

3. Abbreviated and abstracted from *Successful Meetings Magazine,* July 1993, pp. 60–61.

4. *Ibid.*

5. Some details of meeting rights and wrongs are revealed in a critical incident study, which is recommended for additional insight into this critical process. See Denny G. Rutherford and W. Terry Umbreit, "Improving Interactions Between Meeting Planners and Hotel Employees," *Cornell Hotel and Restaurant Administration Quarterly,* February 1993, pp. 68–80.

6. *American Express 1994 Survey of Business Travel Management.* New York: American Express Travel Related Services Company, Inc.

7. *Ibid.*

8. Russell A. Bell, "Corporate Travel-Management Trends and Hotel-Marketing Strategies," *Cornell Hotel and Restaurant Administration Quarterly,* April 1993, pp. 31–39.

9. Ursula B. Geschke, "Relative Importance of Attributes Entering into the Corporate Travel Manager's Selection of Preferred Hotel Properties." Unpublished Master's Thesis, University of Guelph, 1996.

10. State of the Industry, *Meetings and Conventions Magazine,* July 1995.

11. *Ibid.*

12. Barker, *op. cit.,* p. 52.

13. Quoted in Margaret Shaw, *The Group Market: What It Is and How to Sell It,* Washington D.C.: The Hotel Sales and Marketing Association International Foundation, 1985, p. 45.

14. "State of the Industry," *Successful Meetings Magazine,* July 1993, pp. 7, 30.

15. Quoted in Vincent Alonzo, "A Wider World for Winners," *Meetings and Conventions,* August 1991, p. 101.

16. Rutherford and Umbreit, *op. cit.*

17. Caren Meyers, "The Great Bed Race," *Successful Meetings Magazine,* February 1998, p. 97.

18. Susan Carey, "Harried Hoteliers Say Flight Crews Demand Perfect Landing Pads," *The Wall Street Journal,* January 3, 1995, p. A1.

19. Stanley C. Plog. *Leisure Travel—Making it a Growth Market Again.* New York: Wiley, 1991, p. 98.

20. Harsha E. Chacko and Eddystone C. Nebel, "The Group Tour Industry: An Analysis of Motorcoach Tour Operators," *Journal of Travel & Tourism Marketing,* August 1993, pp. 69–83.

Defining the Market

DIFFERENTIATION, SEGMENTATION, AND TARGET MARKETING

Overview

The concepts of differentiation, segmentation, and target marketing are discussed in this chapter. These concepts, while related, are separate tools used in the marketing of the same product.

DIFFERENTIATION Differentiation means making your product or service different, or appear different, from the competition. The customer has to perceive the difference as adding value, making them want to buy your product over another. In goods marketing, differentiation can occur in the size of the package, or the components used in the making of the product. While the restaurant or hotel may also be physically different, the intangibility of the service aspect of hospitality is more difficult to differentiate in the same product class. There are both tangible and intangible

ways to differentiate, as well as many subtle ones, as we discuss.

MARKET SEGMENTATION Market segmentation is a complementary strategy to differentiation, but instead of differentiating the product it differentiates the customers. Product segmentation differentiates the offering and then finds the appropriate customer segment to purchase it. True market segmentation addresses the needs and wants of differentiated customers and then creates the product to fulfill them.

SEGMENTATION VARIABLES Potential customers can be segmented by several variables. The most basic segmentation is geographic, addressing the business or residence location of the customers. Customers may be identified by demographics, which creates customer sets by income, race, age, nationality, religion, culture, gender, education, and so forth. Customers can also be grouped by psychographic segmentation, based on personality traits, self-concepts, and lifestyle behaviors. Usage segmentation covers a wide range of categories such as purpose, frequency of purchase, size of purchase, or time of purchase. Usage can also segment on nature of the purchase, where customers go, on what occasions they purchase, and whether these customers are heavy, medium, or light users. Benefit segmentation clusters customers by the needs and wants that they seek when buying a product or service. Price segmentation separates product classes and, sometimes, offerings within a product class. This section also discusses segmentation variables in international settings.

SEGMENTATION STRATEGIES   This section deals with segmentation criteria and application of the variables.

TARGET MARKETING   Target markets are subsegments. Many of the same principles of segmentation apply, but are refined. Undifferentiated target marketing assumes that all customers within a segment have similar needs and wants, so only one type of product/service is offered. Concentrated target marketing has a firm identify one target market, among a number, and allocate all of its resources to attracting those customers. Differentiated multitarget marketing chooses a limited number of target markets and develops a product/ service mix for each one. Mass customization is targeting one customer at a time, the ultimate in target marketing.

In previous chapters we have talked about **differentiation, market segmentation,** and **target marketing** without really explaining those concepts in detail. It is time that we did so, since each is a vital and integral part of marketing. Differentiation, segmentation, and target marketing are tools that help us to understand and analyze the market. They are tools by which the marketer hopes to outflank the competition, seize marketing opportunity, maximize marketing efforts, and satisfy customer needs and wants. They are separate concepts and tools but, at the same time, they are highly interrelated—that is, all three are almost always involved in the marketing of the same product. We will define how they are different and how they work together.

DIFFERENTIATION

Differentiation in its simplest form means distinguishing your product/service from that of the competition, so that customers will come your way, instead of someone else's. The assumption is that the customer will *perceive* greater utility, better price value, and/or better problem solution in your product/service. Notice the use of the word perceive, a word that we expanded on at some length in Chapter 8; it is not necessary that there be an actual difference, only that the market perceives there to be one. It is just as important to note the converse situation: If the market does not perceive a difference, then for all intents and purposes it doesn't exist. It is the role of the marketer to convince the customer that a difference exists. It is the role of operations to deliver the difference.

There are numerous examples of this strategy in the hospitality industry. One is that of Peabody Hotels, which differentiate in a unique way. A family of ducks is housed in each hotel and they are brought down in an elevator each morning to spend the day at a fountain in the hotel lobby. In the evening the ducks troop back into the elevator to return to their quarters. This ritual attracts many spectators to the Peabody lobbies. The lobby bar does a roaring business every evening as people wait to see the ducks march into the elevator. In fact, the logo of the Peabody Hotels is a duck (Figure 10-1). Does this make the Peabody a better hotel? Probably not, but it certainly differentiates it.

Bases of Differentiation

The **bases for differentiation** can be minor product features. In themselves, they may be unimportant, but they can be very effective when (1) they cannot be easily duplicated, (2) they appeal to a particular need and/or want, and (3) they create an image or impression that goes beyond the specific difference itself. (Like ducks?)

Consider the Fairmont Plaza Hotel or the Waldorf-Astoria, both in New York City. Both are eminent hotels with a great deal of history behind them, which have been frequented in the past by people of international fame. These hotels' histories cannot be duplicated by other hotels in New York. This differentiation has considerable appeal for consumers who like the old world and the feeling of blending with the past. Further, there is an

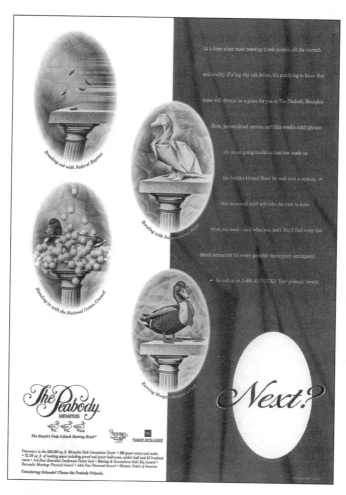

F I G U R E   1 0 - 1   Peabody Hotels differentiate on ducks.

image or impression that these hotels, because of their past, will have great service and unmatched elegance. In sum, companies that differentiate products must also instill an image in the minds of customers that distinguishes their products from others, and causes the customer to react more favorably toward them.

Differentiation of Intangibles

Because much of the hospitality product is largely intangible, differentiation in traditional marketing often centers largely on "tangibilizing the intangible." Making a tangible representation out of something abstract, such as using an atrium lobby (tangible) to represent an "exciting" (intangible) hotel, was an example of this in the first atrium hotels. Today, atriums are so common that few differentiate any more. Many hotels try to differentiate on the basis of better service quality. However, this is somewhat suspect until customers experience the service first and then decide if it was indeed better. If tangible proof is offered, then differentiating on this basis can be successful. For example, the Windsor Court Hotel in New Orleans is perceived to have the best service in town. Proof—The Windsor Court is the only Five-Diamond hotel in New Orleans. Renaissance Hotels, as a chain, has done likewise with the J. D. Power award (Figure 10-2).* Similarly, restaurants sometimes differentiate by their "famous" chef.

The Roger Smith Hotel has differentiated itself in the New York City marketplace by creating an artistic guest experience. The exterior, lobby, and restaurant all feature original art designed by the owner and others. This "thinking man's" boutique hotel is unique in a city full of medium to large commercial hotels. Starwood Lodging's 1998 "W" concept, also in New York City in a refurbished property, promises to uniquely differentiate by of-fering "business chic" to attract the Generation X business people who are upwardly mobile and "bored" with their parents' choice of lodging.

Differentiation as a Marketing Tool

Differentiation is an important marketing tool, whether the differences are real or only perceived. For one thing differentiation helps to create awareness and trial by the consumer. Atrium lobbies once did that, famous person artifacts did it for Planet Hollywood, "infinite attention to detail" service does it for Mandarin Oriental hotels, ducks do it for Peabody Hotels, superior steaks do it for Ruth's Chris Steak House, chocolate chip cookies do it for Doubletree, and consistency of service does it for Marriott. Note that these differentiating factors are both tangible and intangible and all, more or less, fit our three criteria above. Yes, some can be duplicated but not really that easily.

As we see later in this chapter, sometimes the only thing we can do when we compete with others in the *same* market segment or **product class** is attempt to differentiate the product. It is a world of limited opportunities, in this respect, when the product approaches commodity status and differentiation may occur only, as pointed out in Chapter 3, in the marketing. When these attempts violate our three rules above, however, such as extensive bathroom amenities and mints on the pillow, the differential advantage is soon lost, and the cost of the differential becomes a cost burden without producing additional revenue.

There is a way out of this, however, and it lies in marketing in its true sense, rather than in essentially giving things away. This means, of course, going back to the customer. Days Inn research in 1985 revealed that guests prefer in-room coffee service over such basic amenities as shampoo, lotions, and shower caps: 87 percent indicated they would even pay an increased room rate if rooms were supplied with such a service; 78 percent indicated an in-room coffee system would influence their selection of a hotel the next time they traveled. In-room coffee, of course, can be duplicated and has been

---

*Five diamonds is the highest and most exclusive rating given by the American Automobile Association (AAA), a respected authority that personally inspects all rated properties. J. D. Power awards have similar credibility.

F I G U R E   1 0 - 2   Renaissance Hotels tangibilize the intangible with a highly respected award.

many times over. Days, however, set itself apart by inaugurating this service in budget hotels. They appealed to a particular need and created an impression that went beyond the service itself.

Foodservice establishments actually have greater opportunity to differentiate than do hotels. Although some foodservice product classes may be somewhat close to commodity status, there is a wide variety of ways that restaurants can differentiate their product; in other words, it is much easier to be creative, economically, with a menu and decor in a restaurant than with a hotel room. Lettuce Entertain You Enterprises has been very successful with its creativity in Chicago, as shown in Figure 10-3. In spite of this potential, however, restaurant advertising tends to be blandly and boringly the same (Figure 10-4). Figure 10-5 shows an exception to this; this ad clearly creates a perceived differentiation, as opposed to those in Figure 10-4.

Hotel managements have also begun to realize

FIGURE 10-3 Lettuce Entertain You, one organization that differentiates its restaurants.

the need to differentiate restaurants and have developed more creative concepts. The traditional hotel had a coffee shop, a fine dining room, and a lounge, often with little imagination or creativity and often not fulfilling customers' needs. Rather than be creative and seek new opportunities, it was simply accepted that food and beverage departments would hopefully operate at a small profit and there wasn't much that could be done about it. The frequent customer reaction was, "That's hotel food; let's go out to eat."

The situation is quite different outside the United States. Both in Europe and in Asia it is not uncommon for hotel dining rooms to be among the best restaurants in the city. Both hotel guests and the local populace patronize them heavily. In France, for example, one can find a two-star hotel with minimal rooms that includes a dining room superior to most in New York City. In Japan, where eating out is such a common practice, F&B can contribute as much as 70 percent of a hotel's revenue.

FIGURE 10-4   The sameness of restaurant advertising.

If a hotel restaurant is going to compete with a freestanding restaurant, management has to think, look, and act like its freestanding competition. Jim Nassikas did this when he opened the Stanford Court Hotel in San Francisco. Nassikas opened Fournou's Ovens, an upscale restaurant, within the hotel, but didn't tell the hotel guests. There was no mention of the restaurant in the guest rooms or within the hotel. To get there, guests were instructed to go out the front door and around the corner. In fact, one of Nassikas' favorite stories is of the hotel guests who hailed a cab in order to get to the restaurant. Nassikas' strategy not only added a mystique to the restaurant, it also differentiated it

in the perception of nonguests who fastidiously avoided "hotel food." The result was a very successful, differentiated hotel gourmet restaurant. In a similar manner, after noted failures, the St. Regis Hotel built one of the most famous restaurants in New York City, Lespinasse; the Nikko Essex House developed Les Célébrités; and the New York Palace leased its restaurant space to Le Cirque; all creating tremendous differentiated in-house dining experiences for guests, as well as outside customers.

Today there are hotels with "fast-break" bars for juice, coffee, and rolls; lounges with deli bars as well as liquor bars, lobby lounges with entertainment, grazing restaurants, and so forth. When the

Filet of Sole   *11 Duncan Street*   *Toronto 598-3256*

F I G U R E   1 0 - 5   Filet of Sole uses creative restaurant advertising.

basic hotel room doesn't change much, these are excellent opportunities to differentiate in areas that are not as susceptible to copying and can offer unique and distinct advantages. Some hoteliers, however, don't seem to have a lot of marketing imagination when it comes to F&B facilities, especially if they came up through the F&B ranks. We gave an example of this in Chapter 5 with an F&B vice president. As a result, there is an increasing frequency of leased restaurants in hotels by established operators such as Champions, TGI Friday, Henry Bean, Grill Concepts, and others.

Differentiation—Of Anything

Goods manufacturers seek competitive difference through features that may be seen and measured or sometimes just implied. This is also true, says Theodore Levitt in a classic article, with services:

> Commodity exchange dealers trade in totally undifferentiated generic goods such as pork bellies and metals; what they sell is the claimed distinction of their execution, their efficiency, their responsiveness to customers' buy and sell orders . . . In short, the "offered" product is differentiated, although the "generic" product is identical. When the generic product is undifferentiated, the offered product makes the difference in getting customers, and the delivered product in keeping them.[1]

Product differentiation, then, is any perceived difference in a product when compared with others. It is what makes Smirnoff a premium vodka when it is fairly well established that all American vodkas are, by legal specification, very much the same. It is what makes Stolichnaya or Absolut vodka even more premium than Smirnoff even when used in a mixed drink where the subtle difference is indistinguishable to most. It is what makes waiting in a single line at a Burger King different than multiple lines at a McDonald's. It is what makes a person respond, "I just like it there," when asked why he or she goes to a particular restaurant. It is what makes one hotel appear more friendly, another more efficient.

In short, the marketer seeks differentiation whether perceived or real. The differentiation may be product-specific or it may be brand-specific. The latter is more difficult to achieve in the hospitality industry because of the heterogeneity of services but, because of that, even more desirable for chain operations.

Levitt states the case for differentiation as follows:

> To attract a customer, you are asking him to do something different from what he would have done in the absence of the programs you direct at him. He has to change his mind and his actions. The customer must shift his behavior in the direction advocated by the seller. . . . If marketing is seminally about anything, it is about achieving customer-getting distinction by differentiating what you do and how you operate. All else is derivative of that and only that. . . . To differentiate an offering effectively requires knowing what drives and attracts customers. It requires knowing how customers differ from one another and how those differences can be clustered into commercially meaningful segments. If you're not thinking segments, you're not thinking.[2]

Differentiation also separates product classes. The luxury hotel is different from the budget hotel. Choice International tries to differentiate Sleep from Comfort from Quality from Clarion. Within the same product class differentiation separates the competition. Days Inn strives to be different from La Quinta and Wendy's differentiates from McDonald's and Burger King. In traditional marketing, differentiation is essentially a promotional or advertising strategy that attempts to control demand. In nontraditional marketing, it is an internal strategy that attempts to create demand. For this reason, the best differentiation may be in the marketing itself, such as relationship marketing. Differentiation provides an opportunity in competitive strategy, as discussed in Chapter 6, and it forms the basis of positioning strategy, as will be discussed in Chapter 11.

MARKET SEGMENTATION

Differentiation and market segmentation are not competing but complementary strategies. While the first is what is done with a product or service to differentiate it, the second is what is done with the marketplace to differentiate the customers. It is useful to clarify this point.

Product differentiation is based on an assumption that customers' needs and wants are quite alike but that some aspect of the product offered separates it from other product offerings. Coca-Cola and Pepsi-Cola, for example, both market to a number of segments and the segments are the same for both. Each, of course, tries to create a perceived, if not real, difference between its products and the other's. They try to get each of the segments to perceive this difference, which is not just based on taste.

Segmentation, on the other hand, starts with the customer. It assumes that the market is made up of customers whose needs and wants are different. The product is defined for specific market segments based upon these differences. This calls for a more precise adjustment of the product to requirements of specific market segments. Market segments are no more than groups of people who are in some way alike—that is, who have the same needs or

wants on one or more dimensions. We discuss these groups specifically later in the chapter.

Which Comes First?

Differentiation can lead to market segmentation, and market segmentation can lead to product differentiation. In the first case, the product differentiates for essentially the same market—that is, the product does the segmenting (called **product segmentation**). Of course, as Levitt says, this requires knowing what drives and attracts customers. In the second case, the market is segmented first and then this segmentation is followed by differentiation of the product among competitors in the same segment, based on needs and wants (called **market segmentation**). This requires, first, knowing how people differ, segmenting them accordingly, and then developing the product to meet their needs and wants.

An excellent example of this process is the "product segmentation" practice in the hotel industry. This practice has hotel companies featuring a number of product lines such as budget, economy, suite, middle-tier, and upscale properties. As an analogy, this is similar to General Motors' offering five different product lines of automobiles, a practice which started out as successful market segmentation in the 1920s, but that now has become primarily product segmentation.

Product segmentation within the same company in the hotel industry had its inception in the 1980s, when Robert Hazard became CEO of Quality Inns (now Choice International), a hotel franchisor. Hazard inherited a wide variety of franchisees with diverse properties, ranging from the barely adequate to the middle tier of quality, all called Quality Inn. The result had been a very confused consumer image with mixed expectations and a high risk factor. To counteract this, Hazard differentiated the product into three categories: Comfort Inns, Quality Inns, and Quality Royale (now called Clarion), and advertised to create different perceptions of each category. What resulted was a market segmented by the product. Hazard's concept was highly successful and other operators soon jumped on the bandwagon. Eventually, true market segmentation evolved in some, but not all, cases.*

True market segmentation practices the marketing concept. In fact, a major reason for studying consumer behavior is to aid in the development of segmentation strategies. Segmentation distinguishes groups of customers, their needs and wants, and develops the product specifically for them. The essence of this development is Marriott's "Courtyard by Marriott" product line. What Hazard had started as product differentiation became product segmentation; Marriott developed the concept as market segmentation. Marriott went to self-employed, independent, restricted, or non-expense-account customers, a subset of the business traveler market, and asked what they wanted in a relatively low-cost hotel room, what trade-offs they would make, and what they would give up in order to pay less. The product was then designed to fit the demand. This is true market segmentation.†

The result, of course, was much copying by oth-

ers. In fact, some hotel chains blatantly stated that their new products would be copies of Marriott's Courtyards. Hilton, for example, followed years later with Garden Inns. Today, there are many hotel companies competing in the same market segment as Courtyard. The astute marketer now must turn back to differentiation within the product class.

Another example is the all-suite hotel concept pioneered by Granada Royale Hometels. The all-suite hotel was designed for the extended-stay business traveler who wanted a little more room to spread out. At the time the all-suite was a differentiated product; today it is a full-blown market segment with a number of individual target markets, with upscale and downmarket offerings.

Segmentation Comes First

At first glance, it may appear that we have really been saying the same thing in different ways. Who cares if we first segment, then differentiate, or vice versa? The difference, of course, is in customers' needs and wants. Numerous cases exist where attempts to differentiate have been less than fulfilling and failure to recognize market segments has resulted in loss of market share. In some cases this has been carried to the extreme, when a company tries to be "all things to all people," the antithesis of market segmentation. Strategies of segmentation and differentiation may be employed simultaneously,‡ but more commonly they are applied in sequence in response to changing market conditions.

The Process of Market Segmentation

With all of the above in mind, let us proceed through the market segmentation process. The basic assump-

---

*Eventually, more confusion evolved as product lines began to overlap each other. Studies have shown that consumers see broad price ranges greatly overlapping so-called segments. One of the authors, in fact, was "socked" $100 for a turnpike Comfort Inn (luxury budget) room, after leaving the Chicago Hyatt Regency Chicago at $105 (group rate), when down the highway Holiday Inn was selling a better room for $63.00. A year later he paid $63 for an "upscale" Quality Inn Suites room with all-suite amenities in Burlington, Vermont; $60 for a noisy "budget" Friendship Inn room in Hadley, Massachusetts; $42 for an Econo Lodge "economy" room in Plattsburgh, New York, which was the best room of the bunch (except for the Quality Suites) and had the best-service of them all. For examples of many overlaps in hotel brands, see Robert C. Lewis, "Positioning Holiday Inn Worldwide" in *Cases in Hospitality Marketing and Management*, 2nd ed. New York: John Wiley & Sons, 1997, pp. 181–215.

†The industry's common use of the term segmentation is that if a company has different levels of product class they are segmenting. This may or may not be true (i.e., it could be simple differentiation, product line extension, or product segmentation). However, contrary to trade press usage, segmentation most definitely occurs with one product line (e.g. Four Seasons and Microtel). Such companies have segmented on one end of the market and designed the product to fit it. These so-called "nonsegmenters" are, in truth, the strongest segmenters of all. This is exactly what Levitt means when he says (above), "If you're not thinking segments, you're not thinking."

‡One example of this is in Vancouver, British Columbia where there are two Starbucks coffee houses kitty-corner from each other. One is an arc of funky glass and steel. Young people wearing trendy black, lots of tattoos, and facial hair extend out to the sidewalk patio. These are the Generation Xers. Across the street, the other is in a brick heritage building, more modest, no patio, and a cozy, wood interior. The patrons are older, wealthier, and more subdued. These are the Yuppies. According to Starbucks, the twain never meets and both are quite successful.

tion, once again, is that the marketplace is heterogeneous; customers have different needs and wants. If we are to establish a more precise definition of the needs and wants of the marketplace, it is clear that we will need to locate those segments of the market with similar needs and wants—in other words, we need to break the market down into smaller homogeneous segments. Our need is better served if we take this in stages, since there are a number of elements that we will need to consider along the way.

Needs and Wants of the Marketplace. In an oversimplification of the problem, we could conduct a giant research survey in which we asked consumers what it was they wanted in a hotel or restaurant. The complexity of this question is immediately apparent: Where? When? With whom? For what purpose? At what price? It is clear that we will not get very far with this approach, so the first thing we will have to do is to set some parameters. Let us proceed with a hypothetical example.

We are considering opening a restaurant in a city whose population is a million people, including the environs. We have decided that this will not be a fast-food restaurant but could be anything from an inexpensive family restaurant to a very expensive gourmet restaurant. We analyze what already exists and find that there is no high-quality French restaurant in the area. With this existing void, we could go this route and, without too much difficulty, clearly differentiate our restaurant from the competition, on French cuisine.

But what if no one wants French cuisine? We would be in serious trouble. Already we see the hazards of differentiating before segmenting. Instead, at this stage, let's ignore the competition and what already exists because, even if it exists, we really don't know if it is satisfying the needs and wants of the marketplace. Maybe it is not as successful as it looks; maybe it is successful only because there is no alternative.

So, let us reset the parameters. To simplify the example, let's say we have found a location and we have decided to open for lunch and dinner. Otherwise, there are no restrictions. Now we can conduct our survey.

Assume that we take a random sample of those with household incomes of $40,000 or more per year (10 percent of the population). The questions we could ask are almost unlimited but we will have to narrow them down: How often do you go out for lunch/dinner? Where do you go? What do you order? Are you satisfied with the offering? What would you like to have instead? How much do you spend? How far do you travel? Do you like the atmosphere? Would you like a different atmosphere? What? Where would you like to go? How often? How much would you be willing to spend? What would you order? and so forth.

Our survey shows that 20,000, or 20 percent of the population with incomes greater than $40,000 (i.e., 20 percent of 100,000), would go to a gourmet restaurant with some frequency. They will go there an average of twice a month for lunch with an average of three other persons, and once a month for dinner with an average of two other persons. They would spend $18 per person for lunch and $45 per person for dinner.

Of course, the other 80 percent of the same population is saying something else that, having open minds, we could not ignore. For purposes of illustration, however, let us concentrate on this 20 percent. This is a market segment: a relatively homogeneous segment of the market that likes, and will patronize, a gourmet restaurant. Armed with this information we can proceed to the second stage.

Projecting Wants and Needs into Potential Markets. This stage is called demand analysis. Demand analysis includes needs and wants plus willingness and ability to pay. Willingness and ability to pay are critical, and we cannot afford to overlook them. For example, we may truly need a car to get to work every day, and we may truly want a Mercedes, but if we are unwilling to pay the price of a Mercedes, we are clearly not in the demand segment for that car. On the other hand, if we are willing but unable to pay, we are also not in the appropriate demand segment. Demand analysis means projecting needs, wants, and willingness and ability to pay into a potential market.

Our survey has shown that we have needs, wants, and willingness and ability to pay. What does this mean in terms of potential market? If we can believe the figures (again, this is an oversimplification to make the point), we have calculated that 20,000 people in the market segment (20 percent of 100,000) would be interested in the restaurant. If we accept the frequency figures and assume that those who would accompany them are also in the population surveyed, we calculate 10,000 [(20,000/4) × 2] lunches a month for a gross of $180,000 (10,000 @ $18). For dinner we calculate 6,667 covers [(20,000/3) × 1] a month for a gross of $300,000 (6,667 @ $45). The total potential of this market is perceived to be approximately $480,000 gross per month or $5,760,000 a year. This appears to be sufficient, so we proceed to step 3.

Matching the Market and Capabilities. Recall that when we surveyed the market, we had open minds about the type of restaurant we would open. Now that we have found an effective demand, the question is, do we have the capabilities to meet that demand? In this case, because we are starting from scratch, we have to consider dollar resources and all the financial implications of a major undertaking; designing and equipping a gourmet restaurant is not the same as designing and equipping a family restaurant. But we also have to consider the expertise in the firm: Who will manage it? What is their experience? Is this our mentality or philosophy? Does it fit with other things we are doing? Do we need outside help? and so forth. It is important, but often overlooked, that a firm's capabilities be matched to the market it is trying to serve.

If we have successfully passed the first three steps, we can proceed to step 4.

Segmenting the Market. We have determined the needs and wants of the marketplace, projected them into potential markets, and matched them with our capabilities. But gourmet is a very broad category; in fact it is quite heterogeneous in composition. Not only does gourmet mean different things to different people, there are also many forms of gourmet. So we turn to further segmentation. To simplify the case, let's assume that we found a strong preference for French food in our survey; we decide to segment the market on those who have a high preference for French food. Now we have to go back through steps 2 and 3, and reevaluate the situation once more.

Selecting Target Markets from Identified Segments. Just as gourmet food is not all the same, neither is all French food. To take an example, this fact was learned the hard way by a restaurateur in a mid-sized New England city:

> This operator opened a French restaurant because "there weren't any around." He managed to build a small, loyal, steady clientele as well as an infrequent special-occasion following. When he closed, unsuccessful, two and a half years later his comment was, "The people in this city think French cuisine is quiche Lorraine."

So we have to select specific target markets from the broader market segment. This is discussed in more detail later, but we might target on occasion, on nouvelle French, on income bracket, on age, on business entertaining, or any number of other things.

Tailoring the Product to the Wants and Needs of the Target Market. Now we see the advantages of segmenting and target marketing in terms of the marketing concept. Let's look at these advantages more specifically.

- *We are better able to identify and evaluate opportunities in the marketplace.* By knowing our target market, we can track it, identify what is missing, find niches, and discover consumers' problems.
- *We can better mesh our product with the needs of the market.* Consider the survey we did of the entire population, an expensive and time-consuming chore. Now we can be more specific as to who the market is. We can ask more spe-

cific questions and get higher response rates because we now have people interested in the subject. We can identify better who those people are. We can have a much better idea of the acceptance of any innovation.

- *We can optimally allocate and direct our resources.* As in the case described above, we wouldn't build a fancy French restaurant for a market that wanted quiche, nor would we need the same level of manpower and expertise. Perhaps we could determine that there is a take-out market for quiche and develop that end of the business. In short, the potential for wasting resources is greatly decreased.

- *We can use relevant market intelligence to sense change and to change strategies.* Because we now have a smaller market and are closer to it, we can keep in touch with it better. We have more opportunity to "talk" to the customer. We are better able to determine cultural and reference group influences, to understand beliefs and attitudes, to recognize and influence perceptions, to use tangible evidence of intangible constructs, to understand the information processing of the consumer, and to give more "control" to both consumers and employees.

- *We have greater ability to tailor our behavior, promotion, logistics, distribution channels, and marketing mix to the market.* Essentially, this means we are better able to reach customers both by knowing where they are and by knowing what appeals to them, what they pay attention to, what they react to, and what media they use.

- *We are better able to be unique and to differentiate from the competition.* We can determine more readily what the competition is doing for this segment or target market. We know better what to copy, what not to copy, and what we do that will be copied. We have more opportunity to find competitive advantage and to exploit the weaknesses of the competition.

- *We are better able to determine strategies to develop and enlarge the core market.* Take again the example of take-out quiche. Initially we might not think this was a viable opportunity at all; by knowing our market we might learn that it was and start offering take-home quiche to our customers. Eventually we could expand this market by selling it to noncustomers—those who would not come to eat but would come to take it home.

SEGMENTATION VARIABLES

There is no one best way to segment the market but there is no shortage of different ways to do it. What's more, they are certainly not mutually exclusive. First, we discuss some of the more commonly used **segmentation variables** and then we take a look at how they overlap.

Geographic Segmentation

Geographic location is probably the original segmentation variable and one of the most widely used. It has its strengths and its weaknesses.

Geographically speaking, we can segment by country, city, town, part of city, or even neighborhood. The essence and the substance of geographic segmentation is that certain geographic locations are the major sources of our business. A hotel in San Francisco might draw most of its business from Los Angeles and New York. A hotel in Singapore might draw most of its business from Australia and Japan. A restaurant in New York City might draw most of its business from a five-block radius. A restaurant in Hartford, Connecticut, might draw most of its business from suburban towns.

If geographic segments can be pinpointed, then the problem of reaching those segments is greatly facilitated, especially if they are in concentrated areas. Both direct mail and media forms of communication are more easily specified. It is also possible to utilize available resources to learn more about the denizens of these areas.

The U.S. federal government defines large metropolitan areas in terms of supposed economic boundaries called **standard metropolitan statisti-**

cal areas (SMSA), for example, the New York City SMSA. The government produces reams of data on these areas—population, ethnic mix, growth, income, discretionary spending, household size, occupations, and so forth. The use of SMSAs in hospitality marketing is probably greatest when the market is being segmented on certain demographic variables. SMSAs can be analyzed for the existence of these variables.

Another geographic division is the **designated market area (DMA),** developed by the A. C. Nielsen research company. These designations are based on geographic areas served by television stations. Their data also include demographic characteristics that can be used for reaching specific audiences by television. Fast-food chains such as McDonald's and Burger King use these designations.

A final, widely used geographic designation is the **area of dominant influence (ADI).** These designations are also based on television coverage but are used as well by newspaper and magazine media for distribution of their regional editions. Thus one could use ADIs for print communication as well as television.

Geographic segmentation is the easiest segmentation to define but it is also the most fallible for the hospitality industry. The local neighborhood eatery doesn't have to employ SMSAs, DMAs, or ADIs (more widely used in goods industries) to know where its business comes from. Broader-based operations draw from a wide variety of geographic locations and need to use more specific and economical means to reach their markets. In fact, one of the problems of individual restaurants is that they cater to numerous small segments that are difficult and prohibitively expensive to reach through traditional advertising media.

The other problem with geographic segments is that such definitions tend to arise largely after the fact. Once we have determined where our customers will or do come from, we then establish that area as the target of our marketing efforts. This may help in developing the area but may ignore other areas and does not necessarily influence buyers—that is, just because they are from that area does not mean they will come to our property, and does not tell us what their needs and wants are.

On the other hand, geographic segmentation can be very useful in concentrating resources. The tourism board of Bermuda knows that most of Bermuda's tourism comes from the northeastern United States, eastern Canada, and the United Kingdom, and their advertising dollar is concentrated in those three areas. The New York City restaurant that knows most of its business comes from within a five-block radius can use direct mail and flyers to reach that market. Singapore can spend a major share of its marketing resources in Australia and Japan.

While all this is both true and helpful, it helps us only to reach the market; it is not of much assistance in determining the needs and wants of the market, because geographic segments, unless they are very small ones, are still very heterogeneous in terms of consumer profiles, needs, and wants.

Demographic Segmentation

Demographic segmentation is widely used in almost all industries. One reason for this is that, like geographic segments, demographics are easily measured and classified. Demographic segments are segments based on income, race, age, nationality, religion, gender, education, cultural, and so forth. For some goods, demographic segments are clearly product specific—for instance, children's clothes, lipstick, Rolls Royces, and denture cleaners.

For the hospitality industry, however, these segments may be somewhat moot. Knowing that someone is 30 years old, earns $40,000 a year, is married, and has a child may not be too helpful in separating a truck driver, a college professor, and an accountant. Each of these people will have different needs and seek different benefits, but for a large majority of hotels and restaurants the demographics will not distinguish among them.

Demographic lines have, in many cases, become very blurred and fuzzy. Plumbers may have higher incomes than accountants with MBAs. Everyone wears jeans, regardless of social standing. Executives check into hotels on weekends looking as if they had just finished mowing the lawn. Some of the wealthy get wealthier by eating cheap, staying at budget motels, and fighting over the last nickel on their check. In fact, demographic lines have become so blurred that it is hard to tell what they mean anymore unless, of course, you operate something like a specific neighborhood ethnic restaurant.

For the hospitality industry today, one of the most useful demographic parameters may be age—age in the sense of attracting children who bring with them parents à la McDonald's, or age in the sense of senior citizens, a vast and rapidly growing market with distinctive needs and wants, not to mention discretionary income. We defined these groups somewhat in Chapter 8.

Another demographic variable that may be useful in some operations, particularly restaurants and resorts, is the **family life-cycle** stage. The cycle runs, of course, from the single young person, to the married couple, the married couple with children, the married couple with grown children, the matures, to the widow or widower. In between there are, increasingly today, couples who don't have children and both have incomes, single parents and nonparents, and second and third marriages. Each of these stages contains, for most people, its own level of discretionary income, personal time freedom, specific buying needs, and patterns of behavior. Marketers can tap into this information, as has been demonstrated by singles resorts, early-bird dinners, special tours, and packages. Econo Lodge claimed generation of over one million dollars of additional revenue in the first four months of offering designated "senior rooms."

Demographic market segments, like geographic ones, are also largely nonpredictive because they too are post hoc. We may know that older people with high incomes come to our property, but we still need to find out why; what needs and wants of these people are being satisfied or not? Age, income, education, nationality, and other demographic or sociodemographic characteristics are limited in informing us of the needs and wants of these segments.*

Does this mean that demographics are an unimportant segmentation variable? No, it does not. It means that we have to understand the meaning of those demographics and how they relate to other segmentation variables. Demographics serve as gross parameters within which are found more specific subsegments, as shown in Figure 10-6.

 ## Psychographic Segmentation

Psychographic segments are segments based on **attitudes, interests, and opinions (AIO)**, self-concepts, and lifestyle behaviors. AIOs are personality traits and the word psychographic actually means the measurement of personality traits. First, we need to understand what psychographics are.

According to Joseph Plummer, a former advertising executive and one of the leading proponents of lifestyle segmentation, the concept is defined as follows:

> Life style as used in life style segmentation research measures people's activities in terms of (1) how they spend their time; (2) their interests, what they place importance on in their immediate surroundings; (3) their opinions in terms of their view of themselves and the world around them; and (4) some basic characteristics such as their stage in life cycle, income, education, and where they live [i.e., demographics and geographics].[3]

Those who are strong advocates of psychographic segmentation argue that lifestyle patterns

---

*One exception, however, as we showed to some extent in Chapter 8 is, at least in some instances, that between men and women. Some complaints of women, according to Total Research, are lack of feeling secure, being treated as second-class customers, lack of pleasantness, preferential treatment, and respect (as opposed to men) by employees, treated as poor drivers by car rental staff, and being treated rudely, among others. According to David Dower, Total Research marketing director, "Our survey suggests the travel trade still doesn't really understand the female business traveler. A change in attitude which wouldn't cost anything, could have a major impact on the bottom line."[4]

FIGURE 10-6 Westin segments on demographics.

combine the virtues of demographics with the way people live, think, and behave in their everyday lives. Psychographers attempt to correlate these factors into relatively homogeneous categories using classification terms such as homebodies, traditionalists, swingers, loners, jet-setters, conservatives, socialites, baby boomers, yuppies, DINKS, DEWKS, Generation X and, most recently, Generation Y (born since about 1985). The classifications are then correlated with product usage,

desired product attributes, and media readership and viewing. This has led to the VALS™ approach.

The VALS™ Approach. SRI International, a major research firm, is responsible for introducing the **Values And Lifestyles (VALS™)** approach, a consumer psychographic segmentation tool. It has proven an effective tool for categorizing Americans into various lifestyle groups, using values, beliefs, and lifestyles to do this. For example, Merrill Lynch replaced its "Bullish on America" herd of bulls with one bull after analysis revealed that the target market that Merrill Lynch wanted to attract saw themselves as self-made visionaries rather than as part of a herd.

VALS™ 2, introduced in 1989, presented eight segments of adult consumers and three major categories or "orientations" (as shown in Table 10-1): principle-oriented, status-oriented, and action-oriented. Within each segment, people's resources were arranged, from abundant to minimal.

Orientations classify three different ways of buying: (1) principles or beliefs rather than feelings, events, or desire for approval; (2) status or other people's actions, approval, or opinions; and (3) action prompted by a desire for social or physical activity, variety and risk taking. Resources include education, income, self-confidence, health, eagerness to buy, intelligence, and energy level (ranging from minimum to abundant, increasing through middle age and decreasing with extreme age), de-

---

T A B L E   1 0 - 1
VALS™ 2 Psychographic Segments

---

1. *Actualizers*—successful, sophisticated, active, "take-charge" people with high self-esteem and abundant resources. They are interested in growth and seek to develop, explore, and express themselves in a variety of ways. Their possessions and recreation reflect a cultivated taste for the finer things in life.

- -

Principle-oriented:

2. *The Fulfilled*—mature, satisfied, comfortable, reflective people who value order, knowledge, and responsibility. Most are well-educated, well-informed about world events, and professionally employed. Fulfillers are conservative, practical consumers; they are concerned about value and durability in the products they buy.

3. *Believers*—conservative, conventional people with concrete beliefs and strong attachments to traditional institutions—family, church, community, and nation. As consumers they are conservative and predictable, favoring American products and established brands.

Status-oriented:

4. *Achievers*—successful career- and work-oriented people who like to, and generally do, feel in control of their lives. Achievers live conventional lives, are politically conservative, and respect authority and the status quo. As consumers they favor established products and services that demonstrate success to their peers.

5. *Strivers*—people who seek motivation, self-definition, and approval from the world around them. They are easily bored and impulsive. Money defines success for strivers, who lack enough of it. They emulate those who own more impressive possessons, but what they wish to obtain is generally beyond their reach.

Action-oriented:

6. *Experiencers*—young, vital, enthusiastic, and impulsive. They seek variety and excitement and combine an abstract disdain for conformity and authority with an outsider's awe of others' wealth, prestige, and power. Experiencers are avid consumers and spend much of their income on clothing, fast food, music, movies, and video.

7. *Makers*—practical people who value self-sufficiency. They live within a traditional context of family, practical work, and physical recreation and have little interest in what lies outside that context. They are unimpressed by material possessions other than those with a practical or functional purpose (for example, tools, pickup trucks, or fishing equipment).

- -

8. *Strugglers*—people whose lives are constricted—chronically poor, ill-educated, and low-skilled. They lack strong social bonds; aging strugglers are concerned about their health; they are focused on meeting the urgent needs of the present moment. Strugglers are cautious consumers who represent a very modest market for most products and services but are loyal to favorite brands.

Source: Adapted from *Values and Lifestyles*™: *The VALS*™ *2 Typology.* Menlo Park, Cal.: SRI International, © 1994.

pression, financial reverses, and physical or psychological impairment. VALS™ defines these segments with different attitudes and distinctive behavior and decision-making patterns.

The assumption is that product attributes can be tailored to psychographic segments and that the product will thus have special appeal to those segments. The greatest proponents and users of psychographics are advertising agencies, which use the classification elements to reach the segments via specific media, and to communicate the product attributes via the lifestyle factors. Lifestyle research provides advertisers with insight into the setting, the type and appearance of the characters, the music, the tone, self-perceived roles, and the rewards people seek. Thus in the past, we saw on television the "typical" housewife, whose main concern was taking care of her family, standing by the washing machine extolling the virtues of a laundry detergent. Today, there is a different kind of woman, as well as man, washing clothes.

Psychographics may be used in developing hospitality advertising messages such as that of McDonald's and Burger King. Another user has been Club Med resorts, which for years promoted a hedonistic and singles lifestyle for the swinger segment. More recently, Club Med has been trying to reposition for both family groups and conferences and has incorporated some lifestyles of these segments into their advertising. In some cases, however, it has been found that lifestyle variables themselves are more important than media exposure in planning vacations, and that media exposure alone may be an inadequate influence.

Critics of psychographics express concern whether these variables can be defined, are valid, and are stable. Lifestyle variables not only are difficult to define but also overlap greatly. Because of this there is considerable room for error variance in establishing the classifications. Furthermore, people change, and do so rapidly, in today's society: Today's lifestyle may not be tomorrow's.

Regardless of the criticisms and failings of psychographic segmentation, it remains a rich area for marketing effectiveness in the hospitality industry.

New hotels and restaurants are sometimes designed and built, and old ones refurbished, by architects, designers, and developers with little attention to consumers and how they "use" a property. Architects and designers want their creations to be artistic, developers want them to be built at minimum cost, operators wants them to be functional, and marketers want them to be marketable. It is possible that psychographic research can tell us a great deal about what the customer wants and how to build and market to those wants. Figure 10-7 shows an lifestyle example ad in hospitality.

Usage Segmentation

Usage segmentation is a broad umbrella that covers a wide range of categories that probably apply more specifically to hospitality businesses than any other type of segmentation. Although we often accept these categories as givens, some are not always well utilized in market segmentation strategies. The basic question of all is, "How do customers use the product/service?" We discuss them one at a time.

Purpose. **Purpose** is a common segment category. Often market breakdowns of occupancy are kept on a daily basis categorized by purpose. Approximately 80 percent of urban hotel occupancy in the United States, on average, derives from business travelers. The business expense account customer is also a source of sizable patronage in many restaurants. Business purpose can be broken down into submarkets such as conventions, associations, corporate, expense account, nonexpense account, and so forth. These subcategories are important because each one will have somewhat different needs and wants and should be marketed to accordingly. These categories were discussed in Chapters 8 and 9.

The other major purpose category is called social or pleasure or leisure. This market actually has a number of specific purposes, and a better term would probably be, simply, nonbusiness or personal. For restaurants this segment will represent a larger proportion of business than for hotels.

FIGURE 10-7 Morton's Restaurant ad aimed at modern lifestyle.

Frequency. Frequency segments have to do with regularity of usage. Repeat business is well recognized as highly desirable, and programs like frequent traveler plans are geared to this element. Again, however, there are subsegments that should not be ignored. High frequency might mean once a week to a restaurant, once a month to a commercial hotel, and once a year to a resort hotel. Low frequency can also be an important segment, especially if it occurs with regularity. A restaurant might have certain customers who come only once a year on an anniversary date. A few hundred of these, however, constitute an important segment that needs special attention.

Purchase Size. We might call the important members of this segment "big spenders." **Purchase size** is the high check average in a restaurant, the

expensive wines, even the big tippers can be a vital segment. In hotels this segment might use the better rooms or suites, eat in the hotel's restaurants, or order expensive room service. Obviously, this type of behavior should be encouraged by marketing. Purchase size is also the low spenders; we may have to consider whether they are desirable customers.

Timing. Timing deals with days, months, or seasonal periods of the calendar. The Monday night customer can be icing on the cake for a restaurant, the weekend customer for a hotel, and the off-season customer for a resort. These segments may include people who don't like crowds, or simply those on different schedules. Of course, those who come at busy times also represent a timing subsegment.

Timing segments also can be based on when the

customer buys as explained in Chapter 9. For a wedding anniversary dinner, it might be two weeks ahead; but for a wedding, six months; for a simple dinner out, two hours. A meeting planner may buy one or more years in advance; the business traveler, two days in advance.

Nature of Purchase. Consumer behaviorists often categorize buyers by the **nature of purchase:** convenience—buy a particular product because it's convenient to do so; impulse—buy products on impulse without much forethought; and rational—buy only after careful consideration. Each of these subsegments is susceptible to a different approach.

Convenience buyers, for example, are probably more apt to utilize in-room refrigerator bars, or room service if it is convenient to get it. Impulse buyers are highly subject to suggestions such as menu clip-ons, wine carts, the server's dessert suggestions, and a higher-priced room with a view. Rational buyers need more information; they are more apt to be influenced by descriptions on wine lists, in-room descriptive materials, and ads or brochures with more detailed information.

Where They Go. Some segments can be identified by **where they go.** Many might go to certain destinations on a regular basis. For vacation, they might always go to the Caribbean; for a hotel, they might always go near the theater district; for a restaurant they might always go to the suburbs. Some, in fact, might always go some place different. They can be marketed to according to these inclinations.

Purchase Occasion. **Purchase occasion** represents special-occasion segments. They go to restaurants for birthdays and anniversaries, or use hotels for the same occasions. Some may use hotels only for visiting relatives or when on vacation, or when going to the theater in a large city.

Heavy, Medium, and Light Users. **Heavy, medium, and light users** often get special attention from marketers. An old marketing shibboleth states that 80 percent of purchases are made by 20 percent of the people (often referred to as the 80/20 rule). Any marketing research needs to pay special attention to separating these categories. As a total group, customers might have a mean of 2.5 on a scale of five when evaluating an attribute. Broken down, it might be that light users have a 1.7, medium users a 3.2, and heavy users a 4.4. Changes made to please heavy users might alienate light users, a consideration that management must evaluate before making changes. Degree of usage is similar to, but something more than, frequency. For example, a restaurant customer, frequent or not, who always orders expensive wine would be a heavy user of that product.

There tends to be a heavy concentration in marketing circles on the so-called heavy user. This is probably advisable but at the same time it should not distract from the light user or, to coin a new phrase perhaps, the "other-user." Hypothetically, let's suppose the heavy user represents 80 percent of an establishment's patronage while the other 20 percent represents a mix of various segments. That 20 percent may well also represent five more percentage points of occupancy or, in a volume sensitive business, its spending may come 90 percent down to the bottom line. Frequent traveler programs tend to be biased against these customers.

It would not be too difficult to suggest even more user segments than those mentioned above. The point that has to be made is that each of these segments has some different needs and wants. They may also have many needs and wants in common, but it is catering to the different, special needs and wants that creates and keeps customers.

A given restaurant or hotel may well have every segment mentioned above as customers or potential customers. This is not as impossible a situation as it may at first seem; it is simply the nature of the hospitality business and demonstrates why paying attention to only broad segments, such as business/pleasure, may constitute falling into a trap. With few exceptions, a hotel or restaurant that wants to maximize its potential simply cannot afford to treat all people the same.

The Saturday night hotel guest is simply not the same as the Wednesday night one—even when it is the same person. Likewise, the Monday night restaurant customer is not the same as the Saturday night one. The anniversary dinner is not the same as the business dinner. One restaurant of one of the authors' acquaintance had a heavy weekday lunch patronage of businessmen but wondered why they never appeared for dinner or on weekends. Subsequent research revealed that these men found the restaurant convenient for lunch but did not find it satisfactory as a place to bring their wives for dinner.

User segments have an advantage over geographic, demographic, and psychographic segments. By their nature and narrowness they are more predictable. In other words, if we know what influences them (i.e., why they constitute a segment), the chances are good that they can be influenced. This is not necessarily the case simply because we know someone's age, income, sex, or geographic origin. In fact, Holiday Inn claims that, "Today, 'purpose of trip' and 'experiences desired' are the prime reasons for choosing a hotel. Though a mid-market consumer always retains the same mid-market values and demographics, her or his 'ideal hotel' concept changes depending on the occasion of travel. . . .The future lies with innovative customer-focused lodging concepts that serve the needs of specifically defined segments of traveling customers."[4] Figure 10-8 illustrates segmenting customers on usage categories.

Benefit Segmentation

Benefit segments are based on the benefits that people seek when buying a product. Benefits are very akin to need satisfaction: comfort, prestige, low price, recognition, attention, romance, quiet, and safety are just a few of the possible benefits sought in a hospitality purchase. Like psychographic segments, benefits have the disadvantage of being more difficult to measure. Similarly, they are subject to whimsy and change. On the other hand, when measurement is reliable, benefit segments may be the most basic reasons for true market segments and the most predictable of all segments. Knowing what benefits people seek provides a basis for predicting what people will do. Benefit segmentation is a market-oriented approach consistent with the marketing concept.

From these segments can be derived other characteristics such as demographics, psychographics, usage patterns, and so forth; in other words, benefit segments can be used to identify relevant descriptive variables and consumer behavior. Benefit segmentation is also concerned with total satisfaction from a service rather than simply individual benefits. This phenomenon has been termed the **benefit bundle** and is a significant factor in segmenting markets by benefits. An example is shown in Figure 10-9.

A group of Finnish researchers studied the benefit segments of Scandinavian hotel business customers. They found that business customers do not evaluate hotels homogeneously. Six distinct segments emerged, plus a seventh one that the authors called the "idiosyncratics." Benefits sought by the six different segments varied primarily on the use of business services, efficiency, friendliness, quiet, restaurants, image, clientele, interior decor, and location. These benefit segments were related to background data for each segment: travel-related attributes, company-related attributes, demographics, geographics, hotel-related attitudes, and behavior. This study demonstrated both the power of benefit segmentation and the error of treating business travelers as one homogeneous segment.[5]

There are two important distinctions between benefit and other forms of segmentation. Benefits are the needs and wants of the consumer. More than that, benefits are what the product/service does for the customer. Other segmentation strategies only assume a relationship between the segment variables and consumer needs and wants. We all know that McDonald's makes a special effort to appeal to children, a strong demographic segment. The next time you go to a McDonald's look around at the people and see if you can place them into a segment category. Chances are it will be a benefit segment; quick and cheap.

FIGURE 10-8   American Express segments hotel customers on various usage categories.

Second, understanding benefits enables marketers to influence behaviors. (Consider the discussion of selective perception in Chapter 8 to see how it pertains to benefit segments.) Other segmentation variables are often merely descriptive. The marketer can only try to appeal to what exists and its assumed relationship. Consider the singles or mature category, fairly large market segments: Is each group relatively homogeneous, so it can be treated as one major seg-

ment? Not at all, but break them down by benefits sought and you will find high degrees of similarity.

In summary, benefit analysis can be a powerful segmentation tool. Its best utilization lies in good research—research that can pay off in terms of understanding customers and what motivates them. Taco Bell research found wide variation in U.S. geographic areas. For instance, "customers in Minneapolis don't care how long it takes as long as employees are cour-

FIGURE 10-9 Regal Hotels use benefit bundle advertising.

teous. In New York City, they don't care how courteous you are, they want it fast."[6]

Price Segmentation

Price segmentation is actually a form of benefit segmentation, only more visible and more tangible. There are two ways to look at price segments: One is between product classes; the other is within the product class. Price segments within the product class, at least in hospitality, are limited. A lower price may increase the value of the benefit bundle, other things being equal, but customers will generally not make major trade-offs for a small gain in price; that is, they won't accept a poor location or poor service just to save a few dollars within the same product class. Price segmentation is nearly nonexistent in these cases in hospitality.

Price segmentation between product classes is a different matter. Five-star hotels and budget motels both provide lodging but they are each a different product class. Gourmet restaurants and fast-food restaurants are also separate product classes. The inference is that one product class does not truly compete with another on the same occasion, given the same circumstances. If we go to New York City we do not choose between the Waldorf-Astoria and Days Inn. In these cases, price is clearly a segmenting factor. While the initial determination by the customer may be based on price range, it is the other elements of the bundle that will influence the final choice. No one rationally pays more for something without expecting to get more. In cases like these, markets are segmented within broad price ranges.

In the U.S. hotel industry today, we have low budget, middle budget, upper budget, and luxury budget, and the same four classifications apply to the middle- and upper-tier categories. Amazingly, with today's modern construction, the physical product is not all that different, within ranges, and in some cases neither is the price. In many cases lower prices have been obtained by lower construction and operating costs and through elimination of public space and food and beverage facilities. Surely as one moves up the ladder, the furniture gets better, the walls and the carpet get thicker, the atrium gets higher, and the bathroom (sometimes) gets larger and has more amenities. No longer, necessarily, does the bed sag in a budget motel, or is the furniture scratched, broken, and torn, or the soap in the bathroom by definition minuscule. In other words, the basic needs are still fulfilled.

Why, then, are customers willing to pay more for relatively little more? And is this really price segmentation? Well, in many cases they are not, and in many cases it really isn't. Those cases when customers are willing to pay more are largely because of the intangibles and tangibles that they receive in return: service, prestige, professionalism, larger, higher quality, and others. These are benefits and the net result is actually benefit, not price, segmentation.

The other answer is somewhat ambiguous because, for most, price is a major consideration in any purchase, and varying price sensitivities will stratify any market. In the final analysis, however, within the same product class, it is rarely price alone that determines the segment. Price is only the risk that the willing and able buyer will take based on the intensity of the problem and the perceived value and expectation of the solution. This analysis applies to both the hotel and restaurant industries.

Now that you know all the segmentation variables, look at the drawing in Figure 10-10 and see if you can specify the different segments and their variables. Also, in Table 10-2 you can see how Marriott has touched on just about all the segmentation variables we have discussed.

International Segmentation

Segmentation takes on a different perspective for hospitality companies in the international arena.

Movable Feasts: More People Dine and Drive

FIGURE 10-10 A variety of different segments.

TABLE 10-2
Marriott Segmented Hotel Brands

Brand Name	Double Occupancy Price Range	Market Segment
Fairfield Inn	$45–65	Upper economy business and leisure travelers
TownePlace Suites	$55–70	Moderate level travelers with weekly or multi-weekly stays
SpringHill Suites	$75–95	Business and leisure travelers seeking more space and amenities
Courtyard	$75–100	"Designed for the road warrior," quality and affordable accommodations
Residence Inn	$85–110	Travelers looking for a "residential-style" hotel
Marriott Hotels & Resorts	$90–250	"Achievers" who seek consistent quality—business and leisure
Renaissance Hotels & Resorts	$90–250	More discriminating travelers who want attention to detail—business and leisure
Ritz-Carlton	$175–300	Luxury, unique, personalized stay for senior executives

The potential market is so diverse that special care must be taken in regard to customer mix. For the individual restaurant, segmentation strategies are developed based on whether the intended market is native, or international, or both. The hotel restaurant will likewise segment both by its in-house market and by the local market it wishes to attract.

Hotel companies in countries other than the United States, at least those in major cities, have long had to deal with wide geographic and cultural segmentation. Groupe Accor's Formule1, Etap, Ibis, Mercure, Novotel, and Sofitel divisions all segment both on the native and various international markets. In some small countries, such as Singapore, the upscale hotels are almost totally dependent on the international market. Even in large countries like India and China this is also largely true in major cities. In the United States relatively few hotels segment on the international market at all. However, as international tourism and business travel into the U.S. continues to grow rapidly, many hotels in gateway cities such as New York, Los Angeles, and Miami actively seek out foreign visitors.

When a hotel company strays to foreign lands, the picture changes. The company must first seek geographic and cultural definition of its markets. The Nikko hotel in New York City and the New Otani in Los Angeles initially (both Japanese owned hotels) sought to capture the Japanese market. More specifically, they segmented on both the Japanese business and pleasure travel markets. Other companies like those from France, such as Meridien and Sofitel, do not necessarily seek the same nationality as their origin. Instead, this segment will be just one of a number of segments they hope to attract. When either these companies or American companies locate in other parts of the world, they seek a diverse international clientele.

International hotel marketers must first make conscious decisions about the geographic segments they wish to attract. The Japanese market, the Taiwanese market, the Australian market, the ASEAN (Association of South East Asia Nations) market, the German market, the European market, and the North American market, all have special significance for hotels in ASEAN countries (Philippines, Singapore, Malaysia, Thailand, Indonesia, and Brunei). This is true whether the hotels are operated by companies of the native country, United States, Hong Kong, Japan, or any other country. This situation is even more apparent in Hong Kong where, like Singapore, very few guests will be national residents.

It is also possible, of course, for some of these hotels to have guests from over 20 different countries at one time or another, as we have previously shown. Resources would be spread too thin, however, if a hotel made concentrated efforts to appeal to all of them. Many hotels try to avoid the stigma of being a one-origin hotel—a Japanese hotel, an Arab hotel, an American hotel.

A case in point is the Oberoi hotel in Bombay, which tried to shed the image of catering primarily to the international traveler while its rival, the Taj Hotel, skimmed off the cream of the Indian market. Another case is a former Holiday Inn in Antwerp, Belgium, that wanted to dispel the image of being an "American" hotel, especially when the American market weakened. Focusing too narrowly on a major share of just one market can be misleading and counterproductive when you consider that no one geographic market is large enough to maintain necessary occupancy in spite of the potential of obtaining a major share of that market.

Fine-Tuning Segments. It can be a mistake to segment on very broad geographical or cultural areas. All Europeans are clearly not the same, nor are all Moslems, all French, nor all Americans. Thus some international hotel companies are beginning to fine-tune their segmentation strategies with a global perspective. This could mean, for example, a certain level of business executive regardless of geographic origin. This segment, composed of diverse cultures, is more difficult and expensive to reach, but increasingly global communication media and distribution channels are easing the task. A good example of this is the Century Park Sheraton in Singapore, an All Nippon Airways (ANA) managed hotel. The prime market for this hotel is the business traveler. Main sources of this market are Japan, the United States, the United

Kingdom, and Europe. All this hotel's business travelers have essentially the same needs—to wit, a business center, a location near the business area, dining and entertainment facilities, and a good communication infrastructure. Each ethnic group may have different priorities but the needs remain the same. The Century Park segments as follows:

Sheraton: Business generated by the Sheraton reservation system
Corporate: Business generated from companies located in Singapore
Diplomatic: Business generated by local diplomatic missions
Crew: Airline crew rooms booked by contract, travel agency, and airline personnel, and business generated by airline reservations systems

By carefully targeting these markets, the hotel has been able to maintain its image even in bad times by refusing tour groups. This hotel is a good example of avoiding the trap that some other Singapore hotels fell into of not utilizing careful segmentation strategies.

Fine-tuning follows the pattern of good segmentation strategy—that is, complementary target markets. The Meridien at Porte Maillot in the heart of Paris, a 1000-room hotel, had considerable segmentation difficulties with the mixture of executives and tour groups. The company took over another hotel in Montparnasse, a commercially less desirable (for the businessperson) location in Paris, where it booked most of its tour groups. This move considerably enhanced the position of the Porte Maillot property.

One way to fine-tune is to look at the business market as something other than one vast market and segment on benefits and usage. Moller and colleagues found that business segments included a larger share of top and middle management personnel, who travel more than the average business customers, and do more work during their stay at the hotel. Another segment had additional, fairly unique, features. Its members were keen on hotel advice, using the "right" hotels, and included a high share of U.S. and UK visitors. This segment also had more loyal patronizing behavior than other segments, were more favorable toward international "luxury" chains, and exhibited a more active recreation pattern.[7]

Radisson/SAS Hotels of Brussels was particularly successful in using psychographic segmentation, concentrating on the "efficiency-minded" segment. In Stavanger, Norway, Radisson/SAS operates an "efficient" businesspersons' hotel without the usual flourish of varied restaurants and lounges usually associated with upscale hotels.

The pitfalls of concentrated segmentation are more acute with international markets. Some geographical markets collapse overnight, as occurred with the fall of the North American market in Europe due to terrorism activities and the Gulf War. The same thing happened in Florida in the 1990s with the German market, as foreign tourists were the victims of violent crimes that received tremendous publicity. Of course, there is no way to foresee these types of events but being forewarned means not depending on one segment too heavily.

Globalization of Markets

Theodore Levitt considered that the era of multinational marketing must move to one of "globalization of markets." Levitt argued, in another classic article:

. . . Though companies always customize for specific segments, success in a world whose wants become more homogenized requires of such companies strategic and operating modes that search for opportunities to sell to similar segments throughout the globe to achieve the scale economies that keep their costs competitive.

Seldom these days is a segment in one country unique to that country alone. It is found everywhere, [and is] thus available to sellers from everywhere. Small local segments in this fashion become globally standardized, large, and therefore subject to global competition, especially price competition. . . . [T]he successful global corporation does not abjure customization or differentia-

tion for the requirements of markets that differ in product preferences, spending patterns, shopping preferences. . . . But the global corporation accepts and adjusts to these differences only reluctantly, only after relentlessly testing their immutability—after trying in various ways to circumvent and reshape them.[8]

Does Levitt argue against segmentation? If a country or even a segment within that country is not homogeneous, can the world be one homogeneous marketplace? Does this apply to the hospitality industry? Is a hotel room, or a restaurant meal, basically the same worldwide with minor modifications? Should the marketer adjust only after testing the waters? In the final analysis, other than catering to cultures and differences, if you agree with Levitt (and many don't) it is probably benefit segmentation that are the "similar segments throughout the globe," and whose "immutability" can be relied upon. Inter-Continental has long capitalized on Levitt's thesis, as shown in Figure 10-11.

SEGMENTATION STRATEGIES

No segments exist in isolation and there is considerable overlap and sharing of the variables. Also, few hotels or restaurants today can survive on only one market segment. It is likely that there will be numerous segments and numerous segmentation strategies. The foundation of any segmentation strategy is behavioral differences. No segment is meaningful if it does not behave differently from another segment—the same factor that leads to conflict between segments. Whether you use geographics, demographics, psychographics, benefits, or usage, the test of the segment is the differentiation of behavior. Thus, in the final analysis, it is the behavior of segments that is the true test of their validity. Consider the following example.

A suburban hotel suffering from slow weekend occupancy surveyed the market for new sources

One World. One Hotel.
Uniquely Inter-Continental.

FIGURE 10-11   Inter-Continental's advertising strategy to fit a global environment.

of business. Two distinct segments were discovered, but neither one was large enough to create the desired weekend occupancy. It was decided to market to both and separate strategies based on the needs and wants of each segment were developed and implemented. The segments were romantic couples who wanted to get away for a peaceful and quiet weekend, and families who wanted to take their children for a mini-vacation with lots of activities. It wasn't long before the two segments collided head-on. The potential damage is obvious.

These two segments behave differently, so they are both valid segments. The problem arose only when the two came together. Knowing how consumer behaviors change, it is readily apparent that segments also change over time. We have argued already that one of the advantages of segmentation is the ability to stay closer to the customers and understand them better. This advantage should never be neglected and a constant alert must always be maintained for changing, merging, or dividing segments. Too much segmentation can lead to too many markets and an inability to serve anyone well, or profitably.

In the final analysis, market segmentation is a scientific procedure requiring scientific analysis. It cannot be a casual or haphazard exercise. What strategic thinking management does is seek the "ideal business mix." Table 10-3 shows the tests to which each market segment should be subjected. Figure 10-12 shows the relationship between analysis and segmentation and marketing strategies to help to do this.

The necessity of market segmentation in the hospitality industry has become increasingly critical due to the intense competition that has become even more so over the last ten years. In many cases, market segmentation may be a prerequisite to growth. In some cases, large or major segments may have reached their level of fulfillment. Smaller segments, unimportant individually but critical in the aggregate, may be the next wave.

Product differentiation, as a *singular* market strategy, may have seen its day in the hospitality industry. As product classes become more crowded, however, it will remain as a key competitive strategy within the same product class segments.

TABLE 10-3
Tests for Segmentation

---

1. Is it homogeneous? Homogeneity on every aspect is not necessary, or even possible, but certain key aspects should be identified in this respect. These aspects form the basis of the segment.

2. Can it be identified? Certainly we can identify segments based on gender or geographic origin, but other measures are not so easy. For example, suppose we wanted to segment on psychographic dimensions of conservative, moderate, and liberal. The segment would be of little value if we could not identify those who fit those dimensions.

3. Can it be measured? Suppose we could identify a conservative segment. We would then need to be able to measure the level of conservatism and the accompanying needs and wants.

4. Can it be reached economically? The segment will not be much use to us, beyond present customers, if we cannot build upon it. Through media, direct mail, or even internal marketing we need to be able to get to the segment.

5. Can a differential in competitive advantage be maximized and preserved? In the hospitality industry this is one of the toughest tests of segmentation, but one that should be constantly sought if not always reached.

6. Is the segment large enough and/or profitable enough? There is a large bus tour segment for hotels that many would find unprofitable. There is a very small segment of visiting royalty that a few hotels may find very profitable. The cost and effort of serving each segment must be weighed against the return.

7. Is it compatible with others segments we may have at the same time?

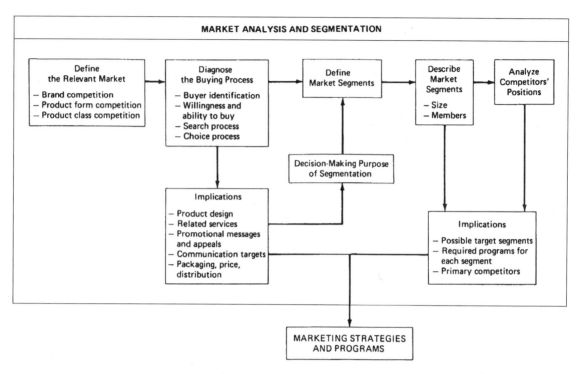

FIGURE 10-12   Relationship between market and segmentation strategies.[9]

TARGET MARKETING

Target markets are drawn from segments. They might be called subsegments, but the word target has a more active connotation that is important. Once we have segmented the market and examined the market potential, we must select those specific markets that we can best serve by designing our products and services directly to them. Many of the same segmentation rules apply; we just refine them further. For example, earlier in the chapter we segmented the restaurant market on gourmet and then targeted a smaller portion of that segment.

There are three strategies for selecting target markets. *An undifferentiated* targeting strategy assumes that customers within a segment have similar needs so only one type of product or service is offered to that segment. This is common practice in the hospitality industry, for example the business traveler.

A *concentrated* targeting strategy results when a firm selects a target group within one market segment and pursues it aggressively. For example, Ritz-Carlton targets executives who demand a top hotel experiences, while Microtel goes after business travelers who merely need a place to sleep.

The third strategy is *differentiated multi-target* marketing. Marriott International, as previously shown in Table 10-2, is the perfect example, targeting specific business needs with Marriott Hotels, Courtyard by Marriott, Fairfield Inn, and Residence Inn, all serving distinct target markets within the business segment and doing it without the confusion that Choice International has created with its overlapping of products. Within any one hotel, multi-target strategy is also in effect. Numerous hotels have "towers"— "a hotel within a hotel" or concierge floors, or "business plan" rooms with special services that target differentiated business travelers with specific business needs.

Concentrated or differential target marketing

means aiming specifically at one or more portions of a market. One travel researcher found, for example, that the vacation market segment could be broken down into ten target markets. Each one represents an isolation of interests and behavior based on benefits, usage, demographics, and psychographics. Each one has different needs and wants, and requires a different package, a different positioning, and different communication. These target markets and some of their specific characteristics are shown in Table 10-4.

As with segmentation criteria, there are criteria for choosing target markets. They overlap the segmentation criteria but are a little more precise. These are shown in Table 10-5.

Target marketing is practiced at the unit level also. A property may use concentrated targeting and select one market and serve it well. The Delta Queen Steamboat Company, which operates three-day to one-week cruises on the Mississippi River, effectively targets the mature traveler market that likes to gamble. The risk of concentrated targeting is that of putting all our eggs into one basket. If environmental or other changes negatively affect the demand, we may not have any market left to serve.

On the other hand, a hotel may select several markets to serve but there are risks to this strategy too, as we noted above. These markets must be compatible and seek similar benefits from our establishment.

Take the case of one very successful resort in the Virgin Islands. One target market was honeymoon couples and the other was high-income senior executives and their spouses, usually over 55 years old (employees referred to these markets, tongue-in-cheek, as newlyweds and nearly-deads, respectively). At first glance, these segments do not appear to have much in common but in reality they complemented each other. Both segments wanted isolation, peace, and quiet. The resort was on a small remote island and rooms did not have air conditioning, radios, television, or telephones. The resort pursued these two markets aggressively and ran an annual occupancy rate of over 85 percent. In order to increase low-season occupancy rates, the resort decided to book group leisure travelers from Italy. These guests were on holiday and rightfully sang and danced until the wee hours

---

TABLE 10-4
Vacation Target Markets

- The Carriage Trade: Desire a change of scene but not of style, secure in wealth and position, play golf and tennis year round and when traveling, tend to vacation as a family.
- The Comfortables: The largest group, insecure, seek social and psychological comfort, like recommended restaurants, guided tours, and organized activities.
- The Venturers: Want to see new things, have a thirst for fresh ideas, information, and education, seek the new and the different, don't travel in groups, collect experiences.
- The Adventurers: The venturer advanced one step—seeks risk, danger, and the unknown.
- The Inners: Jet-setters, go somewhere because of who is there rather than what is there, they "make" destinations like Acapulco, Majorca, Costa del Sol.
- The Buffs: Strongly subject oriented, travel because of particular interest or hobby.
- The Activists: Not content to sit by the pool and bask in the sun, want constant activities.
- The Outdoorsers: Want camping, hiking, birdwatching, bicycling, and other outdoor recreations.
- The Restless: Travel for something to do, tend to be senior citizens, retired, widowed, collect travel experiences, travel all the time including off-seasons.
- The Bargain Hunters: Can afford to travel but compulsively seek the best deal.

TABLE 10-5
Target Market Criteria

1. What is the potential revenue and market share?
2. What are the demand characteristics? Are the target customers able and willing to buy?
3. How are they currently being served by the competition?
4. Are they compatible with the objectives of the firm?
5. Are they compatible with each other?
6. Do they fit the resources of the firm?
7. Do they fit the tastes and values of the firm?
8. What is the feasibility of exploiting them?

of the morning, alienating the resort's traditional target markets. Needless to say, this experiment was quickly ended. Consider, however, the unique target markets in Table 10-6. These are obviously quite small but may also be high-rated.

MASS CUSTOMIZATION

While we have talked about criteria for market segments and target markets, such as homogeneity, size, and so forth, modern technology is bringing us closer to target markets of one, sometimes called by the oxymoron, **mass customization.** This possibility arises largely because of the computer databases that contain vast amounts of guest information. According to Terry Ortt, president of Journey's End Hotels, "You take your orientation to the customer from a very broad brush down to the individual."[10]

Often considered the domain of upscale hotels with their frequent traveler plans and finicky customers (feather pillows, special amenities, etc.), this computer power is now coming down to the budget level properties such as Journey's End. When Ortt took over as president in 1992, he ordered a search of 10 million guest registration cards kept, but never read, in an old warehouse. Instead of the presumed 72 percent of guests who were supposed to be city-based, they found that 45

TABLE 10-6
Unique Target Markets

Equinox Hotel, Manchester, VT: Mastering falconry—handling birds of prey; Land Rover—handling four-wheel drive vehicles on ice-slicked roads or steep terrain; fly fishing.

Disney Institute hotels, Buena Vista, FL: Inner workings of show business; self-defense; TV production; outdoor photography; culinary training.

Hyatt, Scottsdale, AZ: Hopi Indian learning center; "hop on a Harley"—motorcycle riding.

Forte Hotel, Guyana: Timberland, a rainforest retreat.

Accor Lake Manyana Hotel, Tanzania: Safari jungle romp.

Mauna Lani Bay Hotel, HI: Explore hidden pools, ravines, and guava forest.

Praia do Forte, Brazil: Turtle mating and procreation.

Four Seasons, Chicago; Sofitel, Miami; Vista, Pittsburgh: Cigar smoking salons and dinners.

percent came from rural areas or small towns. This brought a change in marketing efforts.*

This led to more surveys to find out how customers at the 120 properties really think and act. These, in turn, led to changes from how employees are paid to what guests are offered for breakfast. The next step was to the chain's check-in counters, compiling a database to track every guest, every stay, every wake-up call. "Eventually, Journey's End will be able to pitch its specials to guests by name, reward them for stays at other properties in the chain, and perhaps remember to turn up the thermostat to just the temperature they requested last time."[11]

Marketers are taking the database far beyond a simple electronic Rolodex of names and addresses. It is possible to talk to customers as individuals, then reconstruct the product/service to aim at target groups and to reward loyal customers. Databases can measure what the customer does, not just what they say they do. This information can drive the entire marketing strategy. Much of this, of course, is based on the heavy user segment that accounts for a large proportion of sales.

Hotel databases have not yet reached their potential. Data are often collected *en masse* without first knowing what will be done with them. Customer loyalty is the ultimate goal. Knowing why you want to know the customer better, you know what questions to ask. Databases are rich sources when they combine demographics with buying habits. These will become even more potent marketing tools in the future. All this, of course, is relationship marketing on which we spent all of Chapter 3, but the flip side of that is mass customization.

The economic logic behind mass customization is, today, as inevitable and irresistible as the logic of the assembly line 100 years ago. It will happen and marketers will have to think in terms of share of cus-

tomer, rather than market share. Mass customization, if done right, represents keeping a satisfied, loyal, long-term customer. It is the ultimate form of customer differentiation to capture the greatest possible share of every single individual's business. It is the key to success in tomorrow's hospitality business.

Once target markets have been determined, the next step is to tailor the marketing effort to the needs and wants of each market. In Chapter 11, we discuss this under the term "positioning." In subsequent chapters, we discuss it in terms of the product/service, the presentation, and the communication effort.

SUMMARY

Differentiation, market segmentation, and target marketing are alternate and complementary marketing strategies. In a highly competitive marketplace, each one alone and all together are critical to the marketing effort.

Differentiation is used to create real or perceived differences between products and services offered by hospitality organizations. The objective is for the customer to perceive a positive difference between our hotel or restaurant and the competition and thus react more favorably toward us.

The differences among customers form the basis for using segmentation. Segmentation is the way in which the firm attempts to match its marketing effort to the unique behavior of specified customer groups in the marketplace, through the use of segmentation variables.

Several criteria guide the process of segmentation and differentiation. It is necessary first to identify the bases for segmenting the market. Profiles of the resulting segments are then determined and matched with the firm's capabilities, followed by the projection of potential markets and segment attractiveness. The market is then segmented and target markets are selected from the identified segments. Positioning is developed for each target market as well as the tailoring of the marketing mix.

---

*Similar market research was done in an upscale hotel in Philadelphia. The executive committee was asked, "Where do your weekend customers come from?" The answer was Boston, New York, and Washington, DC. A review of 1000 registration cards of weekend guests indicated that 945 came from the greater Philadelphia area.

Each segment or target market must be examined competitively. Where others are targeting the same market, as will usually be the case, a final differentiation strategy is needed. Increasingly, it is customer differentiation that is the goal and the application of mass customization to build loyalty.

KEY WORDS AND CONCEPTS

Area of Dominant Influence (ADI): A geographic division of customers that is determined by both television viewers and print media readership.

Attitudes, Interests, and Opinions (AIO): A segmentation of customers based on concepts and lifestyle behaviors.

Bases for Differentiation: The features of the product/service that cannot be easily duplicated, that appeal to a particular need or want, and that create an image or impression that goes beyond the difference itself.

Benefit Bundle: The group of benefits that consumers get from a purchase.

Designated Market Areas (DMA): A geographic division of customers as developed by A.C. Neilsen Research Company. This geographic division is determined by television viewers.

Differentiation: The concept of making the product or service distinctively different, or appear so, than those of other firms.

Family Life Cycle: The age cycle that runs from young single to widow/widower.

Market Segmentation: A process of separating and selecting customers that have similar needs and wants on one or more dimensions. The customer comes first, before the product.

Mass Customization: Target markets of one, or the ultimate form of customer differentiation.

Product Class: A product class is a group of similar products basically serving the same needs, for example fast-food versus gourmet, upscale versus budget.

Product Segmentation: Cases in which a differentiated product segments the market by its differ-

ences, rather than developing the product based on the segment.

Segmentation Variables: There are a variety of methods to segment a given market. These are:

Benefit Segmentation: Customer segments that are based on the benefits that people seek when buying a product.

Demographic Segmentation: Groupings of customers based on income, race, age, culture, nationality, religion, gender, education, and other similar categories.

Geographic Segmentation: Grouping customers by where they come from, either residence or place of business.

Price Segmentation: A process of selecting customers that choose products in a similar price range.

Psychographic Segmentation: Grouping customers by personality traits, self-concepts, and lifestyle behaviors.

Usage Segmentation: See below

Standard Metropolitan Statistical Areas (SMSA): Federally defined large metropolitan areas in terms of supposed economic boundaries.

Target Marketing: The process of choosing subsegments of customers and allocating marketing resources toward developing an individual product/service for each target market.

Usage Segmentation: A umbrella concept of segmenting a market. These are:

Frequency Segmentation: The customer is segmented by the frequency of which they visit an establishment.

Heavy, Medium, and Light Users: Customers segmented by their degree of usage of a product.

Nature of Purchase Segmentation: The customer is segmented by how the decision was made to purchase the product/service.

Purchase Occasion Segmentation: The customer is segmented by special purchase occasions such as anniversaries or birthdays.

Purchase Size Segmentation: The customer is segmented by how much they spend.

Purpose Segmentation: The customer is segmented by the reason for the purchase, such as business or pleasure.

Timing Segmentation: The customer is segmented by the time of day or time of year that they purchase, also by how far in advance.

Where They Go Segmentation: The customer is segmented by any routine of where they purchase.

Values and Lifestyles (VALS™): This is a consumer psychographic segmentation tool for categorizing the way people think, live, and act.

DISCUSSION QUESTIONS

1. Distinguish between product differentiation and product segmentation. Discuss how they relate. Which would you use, and how, if your product was a pure commodity? Why?
2. Consider a restaurant with which you are familiar. Apply strategies for differentiation and segmentation. Discuss.
3. Using the same restaurant, discuss the various segmentation variables. How do they fit? How can they be better targeted.
4. The text argues that price segmentation is really benefit segmentation. Explain and discuss.
5. What is the difference between a target market and a market segment? Give some examples and explain them.
6. Considering your answers to questions 2 and 3, how would you develop these or a marketing program for the restaurant?
7. Develop a list of unique target markets, for a specific hotel or restaurant, that would meet the target market criteria in Table 10-5.
8. Using yourself as the guinea pig, develop a mass customization program for you as a customer.

GROUP PROJECTS

1. Try segmenting your group on the different segmentation criteria discussed in the chapter. Then, given a specific time, place, and purpose, try to pick a hotel or restaurant product for each segment.
2. Develop a mass customization program for each member of your group. Are they feasible? How would you set up the program?

REFERENCES

1. Theodore Levitt, "Marketing Success Through Differentiation—Of Anything." *Harvard Business Review,* January-February 1980, p. 73. Copyright 1980 by the President and Fellows of Harvard College; all rights reserved.
2. Theodore Levitt, *The Marketing Imagination.* New York: Free Press, 1986, p. 128.
3. Joseph T. Plummer, "The Concept and Application of Life Style Segmentation," Reprinted from the *Journal of Marketing,* January, 1974, pp. 33–37, published by the American Marketing Association.
4. Standards Manual: Holiday Inn Sunspree Resort.
5. K. E. K. Moller, J. R. Lehtinen, G. Rosenqvist, and K. Storbacka, "Segmenting Hotel Business Customers: A Benefit Clustering Approach." In T. Bloch et al. (Eds.), *Services Marketing in a Changing Environment.* Chicago: American Marketing Association, 1985, pp. 74–75. Published by the American Marketing Association.
6. From a speech by Blaise Mercadente, Taco Bell Research Director, at the American Marketing Association Conference on Customer Satisfaction, Sheraton Palace Hotel, San Francisco, May 1993.
7. K. E. K. Moller et al., *op. cit.,* pp. 72–77.
8. Theodore A. Levitt, "The Globalization of Markets," *Harvard Business Review,* May/June 1983, pp. 92–102.
9. Joseph P. Guiltinan and Gordon W. Paul, *Marketing Management: Strategies and Programs,* 5th ed. New York: Mcgraw-Hill, 1993, Chapter 3.
10. John Southerst, "Customer Crunching," *Canadian Business,* September 1993, p. 28.
11. *Ibid.*

Eleven

❖

MARKET POSITIONING
AND BRANDING

Overview

Market positioning means creating an image in the mind of the consumer as to what the product/service is, what it does, and what it stands for. As we have learned, many purchases are made, or not made, based on perception. Without effective positioning a property can get lost in the marketplace. Branding, among other things, is a way to position a property, or group of properties, in a product line to create recognition and perception.

SALIENCE, DETERMINANCE, AND IMPORTANCE In order to develop positioning strategies, it is important to be able to determine why the customer is buying a product or service. Once this reasoning has been determined, the positioning of the product or service becomes more natural.

Salience determines the "top of the mind" attributes that consumers use in selection of a product or service. Determinance attributes are those that actually determine the choice. Importance attributes are those that are important to the consumer in making, or after making, a hospitality choice. These attributes are complementary concepts and are important to the positioning effort.

OBJECTIVE POSITIONING This positioning creates an image about a product based on the objective attributes of the physical product. Hyatt Hotels, for example, has positioned itself objectively by offering towering atrium lobbies. Objective positioning is based on features that we would all more or less agree upon.

SUBJECTIVE POSITIONING This positioning is more difficult to convey than objective positioning because it presents an image, not a physical product, to the consumer. Attributes such as service and prestige are less tangible than the physical characteristics of the product. Positioning tangible features requires developing intangible mental perceptions. Intangible positioning requires tangible evidence to create the image.

EFFECTIVE POSITIONING In order for the product or service to be effectively positioned, it has to create an image and be differentiated from the competition. The customer needs to be able to perceive the difference between this property and hundreds of others. Effective positioning must also promise and deliver the benefit that the customer will receive while creating expectations and offering solutions to the customer's problem.

REPOSITIONING Repositioning requires a change of image about a product or service. There are a number of reasons for repositioning. They arise from lack of performance or market recognition, new target markets, or rebranding.

DEVELOPING POSITIONING STRATEGIES All positioning strategies need to be based on a thorough situation analysis.

COMPETITIVE POSITIONING This allows the marketer to position the hospitality offering vis-à-vis the competition. This positioning can be done by any number, or combination of, attributes.

BRANDING AND POSITIONING Brands also have their own positioning image. Individual properties of the brand need to be consistent in meeting that image, differentiation, and promise.

MULTIPLE BRAND AND PRODUCT POSITIONING Multiple brand positioning gives major hospitality companies the ability to service many markets from budget to deluxe, under similar brand offerings.

INTERNATIONAL BRANDING Multiple brands face even greater challenges in the global environment.

INTERNAL POSITIONING ANALYSIS Positioning maps can also be used to measure expectations against performance to determine how well a property is meeting its positioning.

—————————————— •◆• ——————————————

Market positioning is the natural follow-through of market segmentation and target marketing. In fact, it is upon those strategies that positioning is built because they define the market to which the positioning is directed. Therefore, it is necessary to select and understand our target markets before effective and efficient positioning strategies can be developed. The objective of positioning is to create a distinctive place in the minds of potential customers, a place where customers know who we are, how we are different from our competition, and how we can satisfy their needs and wants. It is about *creating* the perception that we have talked about so much in this book.

There are several pitfalls if we do not create this distinctive place for ourselves.

1. The firm is forced into a position of competing directly with stronger competition. For example, an independent midscale hotel may be pushed into a losing competition with a clearly positioned Courtyard by Marriott.
2. The firm's position is unclear so that it lacks true identity and customers do not know what it offers and what needs can be fulfilled. In other words, there is no clear perception. This often happens when a property or chain tries to be all things to all people.
3. The firm has no position in customers' minds so that it lacks top-of-the-mind awareness and is not part of the customer's **evoked set.** The name Joe's Restaurant, for example, provides no perception or image by itself.

There are actually two kinds of positioning in marketing: objective positioning and subjective positioning. Each has its appropriate place and usage. Each is concerned with its position vis-à-vis the competition. Before we explain these, however, we need to deal with three consumer attributes that are important when positioning to them.

SALIENCE, DETERMINANCE, AND IMPORTANCE

In evaluating and developing effective positioning strategies, we need to understand how consumers perceive and differentiate among salient, determinant, and important product attributes or benefits. One might, for example, position on a salient benefit with poor results because those benefits are not necessarily determinant or important in the consumer choice process.

Salience

Salient attributes are those that are "top of the mind." They are the ones that readily come to mind when you think of an object. Because of this, a list of strictly salient attributes obtained from customers may be totally misleading in describing how they make choices. If you were asked, "Why did you buy that shirt?" you might say because it was on sale. If we then assumed that the next shirt you buy will also be one on sale, we could be making a completely erroneous assumption. What really determines your choice could be the style of the shirt: the sale price was just an inducement.

Salient factors might also be determinant factors, but they are not determinant when they are not the true differentiating factor the consumer is looking for, or when they are common throughout the product class. In the first case, let's go back to the chocolates on the pillow. This could be very salient and be remembered by customers, but it is doubtful that they would base their choice of hotel on chocolates.

In the second case, an excellent example is location. Take a survey of almost any set of hotel customers and ask what is important to them in choosing a hotel. At the top of the list will almost always be location, as we have previously discussed

and as descriptive, multiple-answer questionnaires will always reveal. Location is a very salient attribute, but if six restaurants are within four blocks of each other in Chicago, or right next to each other as in "fast-food rows" everywhere, or if eight resort hotels are withing five miles of each other in Palm Springs, as is the case in so many areas today, location is not likely to be a determinant factor. In marketing, we most often use salient factors to get attention and create awareness.

Determinance

In one study, 81 percent of respondents said location was salient in choosing a hotel, 82 percent said it was determinant, but only 18 percent said location was the reason they chose the hotel at which they were staying.[1] The frequency of consumers' naming an attribute does not necessarily indicate its relative determinance as the true differentiating factor in the choice process.

Determinant attributes are those that actually determine choice such as reputation, price/value, or level of service. These are the attributes most closely related to consumer preferences or to actual purchase decisions—in other words, these features predispose consumers to action. These attributes are critical to the consumer choice process. The research problem, as indicated above, is that consumers do not always know exactly what it is that forms the basis of their choice.

An example here is the same one we have used before, bathroom amenities. Bathroom amenities may not be very salient, but they could be quite important after we have become used to having them. If every hotel in the product class has them, however, they are hardly determinant any more, if they ever were. There is a caveat here, however: If we were now to remove the extended line of bathroom amenities, they might become negatively determinant—people might say, "I won't go there because they don't have good bathroom amenities." The implication is that perhaps hotels in this product class should now have the amenities, but promoting them or positioning on them would be to little avail.

This is also true of location and cleanliness, supposedly the main reasons that people choose hotels. People don't choose hotels simply because of location and cleanliness; they do choose against specific hotels because of their lack of location and cleanliness. In marketing we most often use determinant factors to persuade customers to make a choice.

Importance

Importance attributes are those that are important to the consumer in making a choice, or after having made a choice. The example above of bathroom amenities demonstrated this. It is important that they be there, once the customer is accustomed to their being there, but they are still not determinant. Once the choice has been made, what was salient or determinant fades into the background unless, of course, they are found not to exist. Now it is important that the room be clean and the bed comfortable. In marketing, we most often use importance factors to arouse interest and create a benefit bundle that will lead to determinance.

Salience, determinance, and importance are complementary concepts and they are all significant in the positioning effort. It is critical to understand the place of each. Recall the discussion in Chapter 8 of selective perception, selective acceptance, and selective retention. Salient factors may cause all three to operate. Determinant and important factors are more likely to cause selective retention, but determinant factors are most vital in the actual choice process. Much positioning that is done only on salient factors—for instance, location or an atrium lobby—is less than successful when these factors are not determinant. In sum, good positioning rests on three criteria—creating an image, differentiating the product/service, and making a promise, all based on salient and/or determinant and/or importance factors. The uses and interpretations of each concept depend highly on the nature of the target market.

OBJECTIVE POSITIONING

Objective positioning is concerned almost entirely with the objective attributes of the physical product. It means creating an image about the product that reflects its physical characteristics and functional features. It is usually concerned with what actually is, what exists. For example, take the statement "The car is red." We can all see that it is red. If the company that makes this car makes only red cars, we might call it "the red car company." We would carry an image of these cars as opposed to those made by "the green car company." Or, we could say, "That building is tall." Again, we would all likely agree.

That's a little simplistic so let's apply it to the hospitality industry. Econo Lodge is a low-cost motel; the Cerromar Beach Hotel is on the beach; Ponderosa Steak House sells steaks; Marriott Marquis are convention hotels. All of these businesses conjure up specific images based on their product. In three of the cases the image comes from the name itself; it derives from an objective, concrete, specific attribute. If we know anything about the product, we know at least that much.

Objective positioning need not always be concrete, however. It may be more abstract than these examples. Mazeratis are not only red; they also go fast. A Ritz-Carlton is a luxury hotel; McDonald's offers quick service; Le Cirque offers gourmet meals and fine wines. Again, these images derive from the product itself.

Objective product positioning can be very important and is often used in the hospitality industry. Hyatt Regencys have atrium lobbies, Red Lobster positions on seafood and Olive Garden on Italian food. The Fairmont Plaza Hotel in New York City positions on its proximity to Central Park. If a product has some unique characteristic or unique functional feature, that feature may be used to objectively position the product, to create an image, and to differentiate it from the competition, such as the ad in Figure 11-1. Again, we would all pretty much agree.

FIGURE 11-1 This Rainforest Cafe ad creates an objective unique position that differentiates the facility.

Less successful objective positioning occurs when the feature is not unique, for example when an ad simply shows a picture of a hotel building. In other words, this ad would create no real position in our mind about the property, although it may create awareness, which is probably its intent. Totally unsuccessful, typical approaches include a picture of two people in a hotel room or, worse, a picture of an empty restaurant with waiters standing at attention.

SUBJECTIVE POSITIONING

Subjective positioning is a lot more difficult in practice than objective positioning. It is concerned with *subjective* attributes of the product or brand. Subjective positioning is the image, not the physical aspects of the product, but of other attributes as perceived by the customer—they belong not necessarily to the product but to the customer's mental perception. These perceptions and the resulting image may or may not reflect the true state of the product's characteristics. They may simply exist in the customer's mind, and it is possible that we could find many who would disagree with particular perceptions and images. What the marketer hopes is that the people in the target market will agree on a favorable image or characteristic, whether or not it is factual. This is the test of effective subjective positioning.

Hilton Hotels' former ad campaign, "When American business hits the road, American business stops at Hilton," and its slogan "America's Business Address" are examples of attempts at subjective positioning. The desired image, obviously, is that businesspeople prefer Hilton Hotels. One reason that people might not accept this positioning is because it lacks uniqueness and does not differentiate from the competition. For example, one Hilton advertisement showed an empty conference room with a conference table surrounded by chairs. These are objective product characteristics that clearly are no different from characteristics at thousands of other hotels.

Another, more intangible, example is a Hyatt ad campaign, which used the slogan, "Feel the Hyatt Touch" and showed a picture of an atrium lobby. This replaced a former slogan, "Capture the Spirit," which featured a smiling employee. These campaigns failed to differentiate because many companies could say the same thing.

Tangible Positioning

There are two very important differences in the types of positioning when they are used in the hospitality industry. The first occurs in **tangible positioning** because the industry's product has almost reached **commodity status.** In other words, many of the rooms in hotels of the same product class are almost exactly alike. The same is true, to a lesser degree, in restaurants. Consider, for example, McDonald's versus Burger King or Le Cirque versus Le Célébrités. We need to understand what this means for positioning.

Consider the ultimate commodity, salt. How would you use positioning to create a unique image and differentiate your salt from someone else's salt? Morton tries it with the positioning statement "When it rains, it pours." This is intended to imply that Morton salt is free-flowing even when the weather is damp, whereas other salts are not. It is not necessarily true that others are not, but if you buy into it you do so because you differentiate Morton's salt from other salts based on the physical characteristic of being free-flowing. Salt is a very tangible good; it would be difficult to argue that salt is exotic, tantalizing, or romantic.

Those arguments, however, could be made for cosmetics, and they certainly are, as we all know. Cosmetics are mostly tangible. However, their successful marketing is based on mental perceptions of intangible results. As Charles Revson, founder of Revlon, said, "In the factory we make cosmetics; in the drugstore we sell hope." If we are selling a near-commodity product like a hotel room that is mostly tangible, then we need to develop intangible mental perceptions that may or may not actually belong to the product. Thus arose the expression: "Sell the sizzle, not the steak."

Consider again a hotel ad showing a picture of a couple in a hotel room. A hotel room is very tangible. It looks like thousands of other hotel rooms. As with salt, it is very hard to develop a mental perception of a hotel room that creates an image and differentiates from other hotel rooms. Two people in the room are also tangible. What's more, they are no different from two people in any other hotel room. Now you see the problem that advertisers have been struggling with for years: How to position a tangible product that has very little means of differentiation?

It's difficult but not impossible. One common practice is shown in Figure 11-2. But does the view of a city from one room really create a position in your mind? On the other hand, what is more dull, plain, ordinary, and undifferentiated than a pre-frozen, overcooked hamburger? But notice the next McDonald's commercial that you see. Notice the emphasis on people, fun, good times, convenience, or whatever. Figure 11-3 shows an attempt to create a subjective position from the tangibleness of a hotel room. Subjective positioning of tangible features requires developing intangible images.

Intangible Positioning

The second important difference in the positioning of hospitality products resides in the converse situation, **intangible positioning.** What we are largely marketing is not tangible, it is intangible. Some would say that is nonsense, because what's

FIGURE 11-2 Mandarin Oriental attempts to create a subjective position with a view.

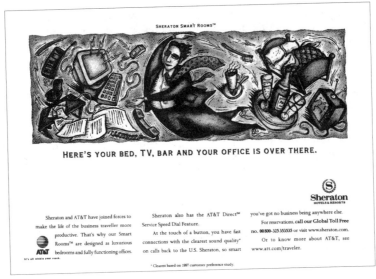

FIGURE 11-3   Sheraton attempts to create a subjective position for a tangible product.

more important than the room or the meal? They would be right, but that's what we're selling, and not what we're marketing. If we were selling only rooms and beds, or steaks and sushi bars, what difference would it make to the customer where he or she went, assuming a comparable level of quality? And comparable quality is an assumption we have to make within the same product class, so it doesn't get us very far.

So, again, what we are largely marketing are intangibles. The tangibles are essential and necessary but as soon as they reach a certain level of acceptance, they become secondary. Because they are so difficult to differentiate, to be competitive we have to market the intangibles. Even when tangible (e.g., a steak) they have a measure of intangibility because they are consumed rather than taken home to be possessed. We have referred to this as *tangibilizing the intangible*. The intangible elements are abstract. To emphasize the tangible elements is to fail to differentiate from the competition. To emphasize the abstract (e.g., with words like "escape to the ultimate") is to compound the intangibility. Thus hospitality positioning needs to focus on enhancing and differentiating the intangible realities through the manipulation of tangible cues.

Some hotels do this with atrium lobbies. People don't buy atrium lobbies; they buy what the lobbies tangibilize. We might not all agree, but some would say atrium lobbies are exotic, full of grandeur, majestic, or exciting. These are intangible images and nothing more than mental perceptions. Of course, check-in may be just as slow, and the rooms may be no different from those in other hotels, but the image is there, not just the physical characteristics.

What we want to do is create a subjective "position" in the consumer's mind. You can see now why positioning follows so closely on target marketing—we need to know what mental constructs are held by the consumer in the target market, and what tangible evidence sustains them.

Return for a moment to the steak-and-sizzle argument. If we want to sell the steak, this argument goes, we need to market the sizzle. But our steak is just like all the others, so what we have to do is sell the sizzle, the intangible. How do we tangibilize the sizzle?

There is probably no better example, even 30 years

later, than what Jim Nassikas did at the Stanford Court Hotel in the 1970s. In fact, he was so successful in positioning the Stanford Court that Nassikas virtually stopped advertising and still ran one of the highest occupancies and ADRs in San Francisco, until he sold the hotel to Stouffers in 1988. Examples of the ads Nassikas ran are shown in Figure 11-4.

Note the **positioning statement** in the Stanford Court ads, "For people who understand the subtle differences." Note the tangible evidence in the pictures. Finally, note the caption, "You're as finicky about choosing a fine hotel as you are about. . . . We designed the Stanford Court for you."

Positioning, then, is a relative term. It is not just how the brand is perceived alone but how the perceived image stands in relation to competing im-

F I G U R E   1 1 - 4   Tangibilizing the intangible for the Stanford Court.

ages. It is the consumer's mental perception, which may or may not differ from the actual physical characteristics. It is most important when the product is intangible and there is little difference from the competition on physical characteristics. For two examples of this kind of restaurant positioning, see the ads in Figure 11-5.

Effective Positioning

Our discussion so far has dwelled largely on image, the mental picture the consumer has of the product or service. We have also discussed the need for the image to *differentiate* the brand from the product class. These are two essential criteria for effective positioning, but there is one more.

This will take us back to the basic marketing concept, the notion of needs and wants and problem solutions—the promise we make to the customer. It also takes us back to Chapter 8, on consumer behavior in terms of customer attitudes. Images and differentiation mean creating beliefs. Next we have to develop the affective reaction, the attitude toward the belief, and the action that will create the intention to buy.

Thus effective positioning also must *promise the benefit* the customer will receive, it must create the expectation, and it must offer a solution to the customer's problem. Furthermore that solution, if at all possible, should appear to be different from and better than the competition's, especially if five of one's competitors are already offering the same solution.

David Ogilvy, a long time advertising guru and former head of the international firm, Ogilvy and Mather, states in his classic book:

> Advertising which promises no benefit to the consumer does not sell, yet the majority of campaigns contain no promise whatever. (That is the most important sentence in this book. Read it again.)[2] [His parentheses]

Notice how the Stanford Court ads in Figure 11-5 fill all three of good positioning requirements—create an image, differentiate, and promise a benefit. If we're lucky we can capture all this in a single positioing statement as Nassikas did.

FIGURE 11-5 Tangibilizing the intangible for restaurants.

Here are some better-known positioning statements of the past with which many of us are familiar. As you read each one consider the image, the differentiation, and the promised benefit, as well as the tangible and intangible aspects.

U.S. Army—Be all that you can be.
Toyota—I love what you do for me.
IBM—Solutions for a small planet.
McDonald's—We do it all for you.
Burger King—Have it your way.
Harvey's—We make you spoiled for char-broiled.
General Electric—We bring good things to life.
Microsoft—Where do you want to go today?
Holiday Inn—Stay with someone you know.
Marriott—Service. The ultimate luxury.
Embassy Suites—Twice the hotel
Nike—Just do it.

Not all positioning statements are as short and simple as these. Examine the ad in Figure 11-6. The ad differentiates La Quinta from similar properties: it gives you what others give you but at a lower price. Also, it promises a benefit—quality at a low price. This ad clearly positions to the target market: the self-employed or nonexpense account business traveler who wants a reasonable level of amenities without paying an arm and a leg for them.

How do we determine the desired position for our product/service? Table 11-1 provides a brief checklist for this purpose. This tells us that one may position in a number of different ways, all related to segmentation strategies. As discussed, positioning may be achieved on specific product features, product benefits, or a specific usage or user category. In sum, an effective position is one that clearly distinguishes from the competition on factors important to the relevant target market in everything an operation does. Table 11-2 is a checklist of positioning approaches.

Positioning's Vital Role

We have dealt with positioning so far in the context of advertising, only because it is easier to illustrate that way. This is by no means, however, the only context in which positioning should be used. Positioning should be a single-minded concept, an umbrella from which everything else in the organi-

How Does La Quinta® Deal With Hungry, Talkative, Claustrophobic Business Travelers On A Budget?

Simple. We give them a free continental breakfast, free local calls, big comfortable rooms and great low rates.

And since ninety-nine percent of our inns are company owned, when you book with us you can expect consistency from every La Quinta, coast-to-coast, no matter which of our over 200 locations you choose.

Your travelers work hard out on the road. That's why we offer them so much more.

You're Not Staying At A Hotel.
You're Staying With Us.

FIGURE 11-6 La Quinta's positioning statement for business travelers.

TABLE 11-1
Checklist for Determining a Desired Position[3]

- Analyze product attributes that are salient and/or determinant and/or important to customers.
- Examine the distribution of these attributes among different market segments.
- Determine the optimal position for the product/service in regard to each attribute, taking into consideration the positions occupied by existing brands.
- Choose an overall position for the product, based on the overall match between product attributes and their distribution in the population and the positions of existing brands.

zation flows. Bill Dowling, a noted hotel marketing consultant, states, "Properly targeted, single-minded positioning affects everything a hotel [or restaurant] does or stands for—not only advertising but also all of its promotions, brochures, facilities—even its decor."[4]

Dowling stops short, however. Positioning also affects policies and procedures, employee attitudes, customer relations, complaint handling, and the myriad other details that combine to make a hospitality experience. Positioning plays a vital role in the development of the entire marketing mix, which we discuss in the next few chapters. Hospitality services compete on more than just image, differentiation, and benefits offered. There must be a consistency among the various offerings, and it is the positioning statement that guides this consistency. Likewise, although positioning can be applied for a given unit, or a specific service, chain operations should develop a consistency if the company desires to use one unit to generate business for another.

Kyle Craig, former president and CEO of S&A Restaurant Corp., operators of the Steak & Ale, Bennigan's, JJ Muggs, and Bay Street chains, says:

> When we talk about a marketing niche we are really talking about positioning. You must position your concept as offering a unique product or service. The key is to understand the consumer decision and then use it to your advantage to successfully stimulate sales. Once you understand what the customer wants and match that against what your chain has to offer, you have a better chance of success.

> . . . Finding a niche is tough but delivering the restaurant experience the niche demands is tougher. . . .Once the concept matches consumer needs there are two litmus tests. First, your position must be believable in the consumer's mind. Second, you must deliver on the promise on a consistent basis. [Craig also warns us to] watch out for a niche that is restaurant-driven rather than consumer-driven.[5]

Subjective positioning is a strategy for creating a unique product image with the objective of creating and keeping customers. It exists solely in the mind of the customer. It can occur automatically, without any effort on the part of the marketer, and any kind of positioning may result. Two very dissimilar products may be perceived as the same; two similar products may be perceived as different. What the marketer hopes to do is to control the positioning, not just let it happen. Failure to select a position in the marketplace and to achieve and hold that position by delivering it, moreover, may lead to various consequences, all undesirable, as pointed out earlier.

REPOSITIONING

Repositioning, as the name implies, constitutes changing a position or image in the marketplace. The process is the same as initial positioning with the addition of one other element—removing the old positioning image.

There may be a number of reasons for wanting

TABLE 11-2
Checklist for Positioning Approaches

1. *Positioning by Attribute, Feature, or Customer Benefit:* This approach emphasizes the benefits of particular features or attributes of the service or product: "What you do with the extra room you get at Guest Quarters is your business." "Where else can you promise a party for 4,000 without bursting anyone's balloom." (Loew's Anatole, Dallas, referring to their banquet space). Swissotels offers to come to the rescue of the customer, using a St. Bernard dog with a safety kit around its neck to prove the point.

2. *Positioning by Price/Quality:* Price is a powerful positioning tool because it is perceived to say a great deal about the product. It also supports a level of quality. This is one reason that upscale hotel chains maintain high rack rates and then discount them severely. To lower the published price is perceived as lowering the image and positioning downscale. More commonly, price is used to position the lower end of the marketplace for both hotels and restaurants.

3. *Positioning with Respect to Use or Application:* Here a service is positioned on the reasons for using it. Often hotels will direct this positioning toward specific markets that have been segmented by purpose of use. Wingate Inns says, "We are built for business, every amenity, absolutely free, everywhere you are." Harrah's in Lake Tahoe goes after incentive travel business with "Tell your best people to go jump in the lake." The Ventana Canyon Golf & Racquet Club in California sets itself apart as a place for meetings that require golf as an essential amenity. McDonald's used "You deserve a break," as a contrast to cooking at home.

4. *Positioning According to the Users or Class of Users:* This positioning features the people who use the product. Choice Hotels' uses advertising showing famous, but active, senior citizens as users of their hotels. Fisher Island, a luxury residential development in Florida, positions itself as the place "Where people who run things can stop running." Westin once used the line, "If *The Wall Street Journal* were a hotel, it would be a Westin."

5. *Positioning with Respect to a Product Class:* This technique is often used to position a product in a certain product class. Preferred Hotels, a referral group of independent hotels, shows their exclusivity with the statement, "We made it impossible to join. That's why every hotel wants to get in." The Beverly Wilshire Hotel says, "If Hollywood is indeed ruled by czars, The Regent Beverly Wilshire is their palace." La Quinta, as shown in Figure 11-6, positions to the budget market.

6. *Positioning vis-à-vis the Competition:* This approach is sometimes called "head-on" positioning to bring out differences among services. Visa credit cards competes with American Express by showing examples of places all over the world where they do not accept American Express, and only Visa cards are accepted. As we saw in Chapter 6, Southwest Air and Burger King have used this approach. Ritz-Carlton is a little more subtle when they say, "After a day of competition, you deserve a hotel that has none." Avis' now famous campaign was against Hertz, "We're #2 so we try harder."

---

to reposition. One reason may be that you are occupying an unsuccessful position in the first place. Another is that you may have tried and failed to fully achieve a desired position. Also, you might find that competitors, too many and/or too powerful, have moved into the same position, making it overcrowded. Another reason could be in perceiving a new niche opportunity of which you wish to take advantage.

All of these situations are relatively common in the hospitality industry. Hamburger chains have tried repositioning as "gourmet" hamburger restaurants. Friendly's, originally an ice cream and sandwich chain, repositioned as a family restaurant. Howard Johnson's, among other things, tried repositioning from being only a family restaurant to being that plus a young adult restaurant with bar and live music. This served only to confuse an already tarnished image. McDonald's is promising to reposition with "Made for You" fresher and hotter food, but may have trouble getting rid of its old image. Many restaurants, which change hands

T A B L E   1 1 - 3
The Repositioning of Dunkin' Donuts[6]

By 1994, Dunkin' Donuts' growth, after 30 years with virtually the same menu and the same positioning statement ("America's Number One Donut Chain"), had slowed to a crawl. William A. Kussell was brought in from Reebok to spice up the menu and reputation. He dumped the old slogan and replaced it with "Dunkin' Donuts: Something fresh is always brewing here," and began a play to become the breakfast king. Dunkin' adopted the latest in fast-food cool, from specialty coffees to oven-baked bagels and fat-free muffins. The tacky old pink decor was replaced with a more upscale "ripe raisin" hue.

Dunkin' introduced four or more blends of fresh-brewed coffee and hot and cold specialty drinks, all at a fraction of the Starbucks price. Value and no-nonsense service has positioned Dunkin' against Starbucks and McDonald's in a serious battle for the breakfast buck. Same store sales are up over 20 percent compared to the fast-food industry's average of 2 percent. For 1998, Dunkin' predicts $200 million in bagel sales, six times the year before, gaining on the industry leader Einstein/Noah, which had total sales of $303 million. Overall coffee sales have jumped 40 percent. In a further repositioning, Dunkin' has now set its sights on the noontime crowd and wants to "eat the competitors' lunch."

often, are constantly repositioning with new names. A more complete example of restaurant repositioning is given in Table 11-3.

Repositioning might also be used to appeal to a new segment, to add a new segment while trying to hold on to an old one, or to increase the size of a segment. Club Med, as we have noted, repositioned to the family market but still keeps its old market (and some of its old image) at some well-defined properties. Another reason could be that new ownership desires a new position or wishes to merge the position of a newly acquired property into that of other properties already owned. Finally, repositioning would be called for in developing a partially or totally new concept, or downgrading a property that has become distressed, or upgrading one that has been refurbished.

Examples of the above are Holiday Inns separating its upscale Crowne Plaza line by removing the Holiday name and marketing it separately. In New York City, Shrager Hotels renovated a run-down hotel, Morgans, and repositioned it as a chic, trendy hotel. It did similarly with the Paramount, Barbizon, and St. Moritz. Manhattan East hotels repositioned the old two-star Beverly Hotel into a four-star product called the Benjamin. Starwood Hotels bought the Doral Hotels, also in New York, and is repositioning them as its new luxurious brand, "W."

The former Stouffer Hotels is a good example of a successful repositioning of an entire chain. Stouffer hotels had been little more than a sideline for the Stouffer restaurant company. New owners, the Nestle Company of Switzerland, wanted to change that. They established what the identity should be and defined the company's niche in the upscale market. Refurbishing followed, some properties were eliminated, including franchises, and a one-segment successful market repositioning was instituted.

In another case, Ramada tried to go upscale with hotels called Ramada Renaissance Hotels. The Ramada name, however, had a downscale stigma, which stuck and was eventually dropped, to better position Renaissance Hotels as upscale. Renaissance is now owned by Marriott but keeps only the Renaissance name. An example of a single property repositioning is given in Table 11-4.

Renovating and repositioning old hotels has become a common practice today. Stephen Taylor describes the problem:

The art of repositioning is coming into its own. Repositioning, the economic [marketing] revival of troubled properties and the renovation and revitalization of old/outdated ones, can provide an alternative to the more traditional routes taken when hotels stop making good economic sense.

TABLE 11-4
Repositioning the Nikko/Atlanta[7]

When the Nikko Atlanta Hotel opened in the exclusive Buckhead area of the city, there were four other major hotels close by: Ritz-Carlton, Westin, Embassy Suites, and Holiday Inn. The city and the area were suffering low occupancy rates that affected all. In fact, the Westin was in foreclosure by its owners and later became a Marriott. Ritz was the occupancy leader with 75 percent and an ADR of $120 from a single rack rate of $140–$185. Westin was running 55 percent and an ADR of $100 from single rack rate of $130–$170. The others were further below. Nikko set its rack rates at $135–$185 and positioned directly against the Ritz, whom it saw as its only real competition. A year later, Nikko was running 35 percent occupancy and drastically discounting to pick up market share. The situation did not improve even when the market picked up. A year later new management was brought in.

According to the new GM, "The hotel wasn't marketed right, it was more concerned with competing with the Ritz. Nikko management looked at what was good for operations. We were providing customers what we wanted, not what the customers wanted. While the customer experience at the Nikko could be just as good as one at the Ritz, that wasn't the way the customer perceived the hotel."

The Nikko had to first reconceive, then reposition itself. The goal became to be the area's value leader among luxury hotels. Nikko's rack rate was dropped $15 below that of the Ritz while also adding room upgrades. That positioned the hotel lower than the Ritz but slightly higher than the J. W. Marriott (former Westin) and a new Swissotel. "The intent was to encourage more trial visits and create more awareness. Although we lowered the rates, average rates actually went up." Weekend packages were instituted for $125 on an executive floor and $139 in an executive suite, including valet parking and a $20 credit in the signature restaurant. In the first month, Nikko sold 1000 packages generating more than $100,000 in revenue. "By finding the right market niche and positioning ourselves appropriately, we became the growth leader among our primary competitors. We've grown 18 percent in occupancy and 24 percent in revenue this year over last. Our closest competitor grew 10 percent and 16 percent, respectively," said the GM.

The task of repositioning is not as simple as creating a market slot for a brand-new hotel. A repositioner has to deal with two consumer images—the existing one and a new one that must be projected.

Repositioning is a two-pronged effort. In most cases, a negative image and consumer ill-will must be overcome before a new impression can be created. To achieve the goals which define the success of a repositioning effort . . . it needs to be finely tuned to fit the specific situation, and it takes thought, perceptiveness, and careful planning. . . . The successful repositioning of any hotel property begins with an intensive examination of the market the repositioner intends to enter.[8]

The Art of Repositioning

Repositioning rests on a change of image. The appropriate procedure for doing this is shown in Table 11-5.

The application of the first four criteria in Table 11-5 is evident in the effort of the Waldorf-Astoria Hotel to reposition. The Waldorf was perceived as the hotel of royalty, and top business executives, and as being very expensive, even though it was actually in the same price range as its competition. Management wanted to position to customers at the middle-management level. Research revealed lifestyles of this level of the Waldorf's customers. The repositioning campaign emphasized these lifestyles as well as the attributes and the affordability of the Waldorf.

Hilton, which owns the Waldorf, had a different repositioning problem for the elite Towers section at the hotel. Billed as an upscale "hotel within a hotel," this product did not match the affordability positioning of the Waldorf. The Towers successfully aligned itself with a different reservations system, Leading Hotels of the World, and marketed itself separately from the main hotel, as shown in Figure 11-7.

T A B L E   11-5
Procedures for Repositioning

1. Determine the present position. It is essential to know where you are now, before you determine how you are going to get to where you want to go. In repositioning, this is absolutely critical because the consumer's image may not be at all what you think it is. Before trying to change a perception, you have to know what that perception is.

2. Determine what position you wish to occupy. This calls for thorough and objective research of both the market and the competition, as well as the resources and ability to occupy that position. One has to be very realistic at this stage and not simply engage in wishful thinking.

3. Make sure the product is truly different for the repositioning. Telling a customer that the product has changed, and is therefore now attractive, had better be followed through operationally.

4. Initiate the repositioning campaign based on the three criteria of effective positioning formulated from the research of the target market: image, differentiation, and promised benefits.

5. Remeasure to see if the position has significantly changed in the desired direction. This too is critical. It is naive to assume that perceptions have changed simply because they are expected to. Do not simply measure this in terms of sales or profits; changes there may be due to other causes. What you want to know is whether perceptions have truly changed.

There are pitfalls of which to be wary. The short-run effect may be a loss of sales while the repositioning is being accomplished. A gain in sales, on the other hand, may occur only because people are "giving it another chance." There may be a sales drop because the new position was a poor choice and the market is too limited or already dominated by a competitor. It is important to find out why something has happened; it is never good business sense to assume that you know why.

DEVELOPING POSITIONING STRATEGIES

Strategies are necessary whether initially positioning or repositioning. This means doing a thorough situation analysis. Christopher Lovelock suggests the model shown in Figure 11-8 as appropriate for developing market positioning strategies. This model is no different than one might use for selecting target markets. A major distinction, however, would occur in the thrust of the research. In this case we would need to know a great deal more about perceptions, what they mean and what they reflect. A benefit is not a benefit unless it is perceived to be one.

Once again, positioning is not in the product, in the brand, or even in the advertising; it is in the consumer's mind. It is definitely and positively not in management's mind. This is why it is so important for management to understand true positioning. It can be a perilous trap to assume that customers position in the same way as management.

A checklist for developing positioning strategies is presented in Table 11-6. All this, of course, has to be based on the target markets.

COMPETITIVE POSITIONING

One way to visualize some of the elements in Table 11-6 is through the use of positioning maps. We introduced this idea in Chapter 6 with positioning maps based on competitive restaurants and Las Vegas hotels. Here we carry the idea further.

In developing positioning strategies, a critical element is the positioning vis-à-vis the competition. It is necessary first to examine images and po-

NINETY-SIX PERCENT OF ALL BUSINESS PEOPLE
ARE UNCOMFORTABLE DOING BUSINESS IN NEW YORK.
(THE REST STAY AT THE WALDORF TOWERS.)

It has often been noted many successful business trips begin at The Waldorf Towers. And it is really no wonder. From our private entrance and lobby to our beautifully appointed executive guest rooms, individually decorated suites, and legendary impeccable service, you will feel very much at home and yet, curiously far from it. For reservations, call your professional travel agent, or call us at 1-888-WATOWER.

The Waldorf Towers

100 East 50th Street, New York, NY 10022
A member of
The Leading Hotels of the World

The Waldorf Towers is a registered trademark of Hilton Hotels Corp. ©1998 Hilton Hotels

FIGURE 11-7 Positioning the Towers aways from the main Hotel Waldorf-Astoria..

sitions of all entities that may compete. One should then try to anticipate the effects of the proposed positioning and the reactions of competitors. Examining strengths and weaknesses of **competitive positioning** can identify positions to adopt, to stay away from, and areas of dissatisfaction where a new positioning could generate new customers or lure others from the competition. If the segment is

expanding, this process could also identify a growth opportunity.

Many hospitality entities today focus too closely on their immediate adjacent competition. As the economy becomes more global, newer markets and competitors must be understood to effectively market a hotel. There is a temptation to judge success by looking at the competition down the street.

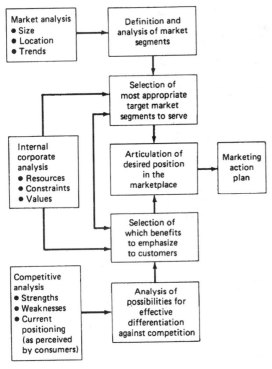

The flowchart contains these boxes:
- Market analysis: Size, Location, Trends
- Definition and analysis of market segments
- Selection of most appropriate target market segments to serve
- Internal corporate analysis: Resources, Constraints, Values
- Articulation of desired position in the marketplace
- Marketing action plan
- Selection of which benefits to emphasize to customers
- Competitive analysis: Strengths, Weaknesses, Current positioning (as perceived by consumers)
- Analysis of possibilities for effective differentiation against competition

F I G U R E   1 1 - 8   Developing a market position strategy.[9]

For example:

A Marriott-franchised hotel in east Cleveland, Ohio, was concerned about its rate structure for the upcoming year. After doing a quick review of the destination it was found that the hotel was competitive with the local hotel offerings. The determination of the pricing should have come not from the local competition, but from the target markets. Research indicated that a majority of customers, business travelers, at this hotel could be segmented on similar characteristics and came from certain east coast cities. Travel agencies from these "feeder cities" were booking thousands of room nights per quarter. These customers were used to paying $300 plus per night in New York, $250 in Boston and Chicago. Why, then, $159 in Cleveland? By positioning the hotel vis-à-vis its local competitors, money was being lost. When the hotel positioned itself against other destinations, the results improved dramatically.

The risks involved in positioning or repositioning are high. Thus it is important to position on customer perception, not management's, vis-à-vis the competition. The technique of **perceptual mapping** can be used to substantially reduce the risks. It helps the marketer to:

- Understand how competing product/services are perceived by the target markets in terms of strengths and weaknesses.
- Understand the similarities and dissimilarities between competing product/services.
- Position or reposition a product/service in the marketplace.
- Track the progress of a marketing campaign on the perceptions of the target markets.

Focus groups (small groups of consumers gathered together for the express purpose of analyzing a product's image and gaps), or other forms of research, can be very useful at this point of exploration. Mapping is used to place various competitive positions on a two-dimensional scale, sometimes with an "ideal" position, in order to locate the gaps and niches or, conversely, the crowded areas. This technique may involve simple plotting on an arbitrary scale, or sophisticated statistical methods known as multidimensional scaling or discriminant analysis, of which we showed an example in Figure 6-8.

The perceptual map in Figure 11-9, on the other hand, shows how customers positioned an actual restaurant. Respondents were asked to rate the importance of certain attributes in choosing an upscale restaurant at which to have dinner. Respondents were also asked to rate this particular restaurant on a scale ranging from poor to excellent. No one rated it poor, but Figure 11-9 shows the quadrants in which are located those who rated

TABLE 11-6
Checklist for Developing Positioning Strategies

1. *Company:* What are our strengths and weaknesses, resources, management capabilities, present market position, values, objectives, and policies? Where are we now? Where do we want to go?

2. *Product/Service:* What are facilities, location, attributes (salient, determinant, important), physical condition, level of service? What is it? What does it do, in functional terms? Why do/should people come?

3. *Brand Position:* What are the levels of awareness and loyalty? What is our image? How do these compare to the competition's? What are the market segments? What are the perceived attributes and how are they distributed among the segments? Where are we positioned?

4. *Customers:* What are their segments and needs and wants? What benefits do they seek? What is the optimal position of attributes for each segment?

5. *Competition:* Who is their customer and why does he or she go there? What do they do or not do better? How are we differentiated? What positions do they occupy?

6. *The Marketplace:* Where is it? What are the segments? What is the generic demand? What is our market share? How are the segments reached?

7. *Opportunities:* What needs are unmet? Can we meet them? Can we improve on them? What innovations are needed? Are they worth going after? Are there new uses, new users, or greater usage?

8. *Decision:* What is the best overall position?

TABLE 11-7
Examples of Poor Positioning that Positioning Maps Would Uncover

- We once had cocktails with the controller of a large, major hotel in New York City in a beautiful new lounge that seated over 100 people, off the main lobby of the hotel. The hotel was full, but the lounge was empty and it was cocktail time. We discussed the problem as well as a similar problem with one of the hotel's dining rooms. "What are your liquor and food cost percentages?" we asked. "Fourteen percent and 24 percent," he proudly answered. The emphasis was on cost and the lounge and dining room were positioned as far too expensive.

  This same hotel had a coffee shop in which one could obtain juice, coffee, and a roll for $15.95 plus tax and tip. Across the street, one could obtain juice, coffee, roll, two eggs, bacon, and hash browns for $7.95, plus tax and tip. Obviously, there was a big difference between the two operations, but the waitresses were as surly in one as in the other, and both operations paid the same union wages. The $7.95 restaurant also had to pay its own rent, heat, light, and power. One was definitely cleaner and you had to wait for a hostess to take you to your table. But the food, for breakfast, was comparable.

  People who stayed in the hotel, mostly on expense account, surely could afford to have breakfast there, and many did. A great many also went across the street. This was not price segmentation, but benefit segmentation. Some liked the "benefit" of staying in the hotel in cleaner and more prestigious surroundings; others liked the "benefit" of feeling they got their money's worth. The two restaurants were subjectively positioned on benefits, and value was the positioning tool. As the GM of a Boston hotel said, "Then there's the guest who takes a suite, has rack of lamb and fine wine for dinner, and goes across the street to Dunkin' Donuts for breakfast."

- In another hotel in New York City, a new restaurant concept was designed to appeal to the local neighborhood. Seating 125, it averaged 40 to 50 covers a night and most house guests ate elsewhere. A quick look at the menu made one imagine a check average of around $55.00, although there were a few lower-priced items available, such as salads. The actual check average was about $24.00, which should tell somebody something. To counter this, menu prices were raised! This is a case, as mentioned above by Kyle Craig of S&A Restaurant Corporation, where the positioning was restaurant driven rather than customer driven.

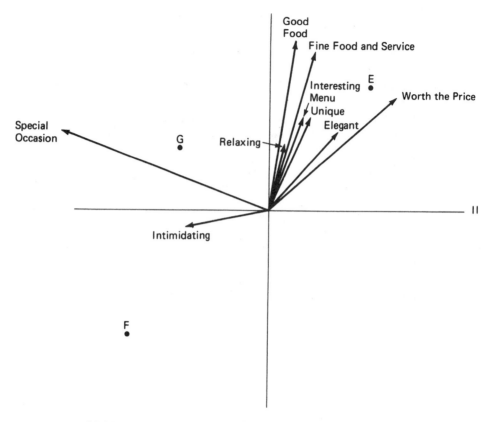

FIGURE 11-9   Perceptual mapping of restaurant attributes.

it Fair (F), Good (G), and Excellent (E). Similar mapping of another restaurant would reveal the competitive differences.

Positioning Hotel Restaurants. A case in point, in a general sense, is that of U.S. hotel restaurants, which for years have been perceived as overpriced. At the same time, they have been perceived as offering "hotel food." The current trend is to reposition hotel dining rooms by offering different food types. Although the change in hotel restaurant concepts is apparent everywhere, the change in the prices, in many cases, is not. In fact, it appears that customers are against paying almost the same prices for trendy food with less service that they used to pay for a "fine dining" experience.

While some hotel restaurants concentrate on the neighborhood customer, their own house guests continue to go out. In this sense, hotel restaurants, generically speaking, are positioned against non-hotel restaurants, as we discussed earlier. Two examples that perceptual maps could have easily uncovered are given in Table 11-7.

Some hotel restaurants have a major repositioning to undertake and many are doing it. They not only need to be more realistic about current eating trends, but they have a major job in changing consumers' perceptions. Products must be matched with their market segments. Positioning makes a statement of what the product is and how it should be evaluated. True positioning is accomplished by using all the marketing mix variables. This includes the products and services offered, how they are presented to the customer, the price, and all the methods used to communicate to the customer. Not a single one can be ignored, because it is there whether or not a conscious effort is made to use it.

Once the positioning goal has been established, every effort must be made to be certain that the product or brand actually achieves the position. Even with all the necessary ingredients of good positioning, there is no assurance of success until "share of mind" is achieved. This is where promotional strategy comes into play. Whether this level of awareness results from advertising or in-house promotions, desired positions do not wait to be discovered. Success here means the realization of all positioning efforts. Table 11-8 provides a checklist for your positioning or desired positioning.

BRANDING AND POSITIONING

Branding in the hospitality industry is a major factor in positioning because brand names carry their own positioning status. Because of this, or maybe in spite of it, hotel and motel properties are continuously going through a process called **brand switching** or, vernacularly, "switching flags."* This is an interesting phenomenon because so many travelers tend to be, if anything, hotel loyal rather than brand loyal. In fact, all this flag switching (averaging about 1500 a year in the United States) has tended to erode brand loyalty—to which every company in the industry is aspiring.

But it is not really because of loyalty that hotels switch brands. Rather it is more because of reservation systems, new owners, failed operators, investment status, and repositioning. Another cause lies in positioning in a certain product class or to a certain market segment in a continuing search for

greater market share. Nevertheless, the result is often a confused customer who gets mixed brand signals. In the United States, approximately 70 percent of hotel properties are branded, but in Canada it is closer to 30 percent. In other parts of the world it can drop to 10 to 15 percent. Regardless, it is definitely on the increase for the reasons given above, plus "instant recognition." Some new brands, however, are barely surviving and many have been taken over by "bigger brands."

Branded properties are becoming ever more important in the marketing realm. Companies that control well-recognized and highly regarded brands will be the winners, depending on how they handle their brand identity. To be effective, brands must take advantage of the mass media, which has become increasingly expensive as the channels of distribution expand along with the communications revolution. The result will be more direct and highly focused marketing driven by sophisticated, identified customer tracking, putting even more emphasis on the relationship marketing that we discussed in Chapter 3.

Another impact, however, will be on frequent traveler programs. These programs have become an expensive luxury that many companies cannot afford (but also cannot afford to give up). As brands expand, however, these programs are perceived by management as providing a form of "loyalty" that can be "bought." In a positioning sense, these programs thus become a positioning statement, and a very poor one at that. They attempt to create an image that a particular brand has the best plan; they seek to differentiate themselves on numbers of "points" given, and they make a promise of the best rewards. A vicious competitive circle of "can you top this?" results.

Technology has had a significant impact on brand marketing. Reservation systems have shifted from voice to global to internet distribution. This has considerable implications for the benefits associated with branding. For one, it brings branded properties wider recognition. On the other hand, when properties can be accessed visually and di-

---

*Restaurants also close and reopen with new names but not usually for the same reasons of brand identity.

T A B L E   1 1 - 8
Checklist for Evaluating Positioning Strategy

1. Does it say who you are and what you stand for? Does it create a mental picture?
2. Does it set you apart and show how you are different?
3. Does it preempt a benefit niche and capitalize on an advantage?
4. Does it turn any liability into an asset?
5. Does it have benefits for the target market you are trying to reach?
6. Does it provide tangible evidence or clues?
7. Does it feature the one or two things that your target market wants most?
8. Is it consistent with strategy—for instance, does it expand or exchange usage patterns? Create new awareness? Project the right image?
9. Does it have credibility?
10. Does it make a promise you can keep?

rectly by worldwide customers, the positioning of brand identities will be more closely scrutinized, putting more pressure on properties to deliver what they profess (i.e., stand for).

The industry, in general, does a poor job of monitoring consumer awareness and marketing effectiveness, including advertising effectiveness. Few companies can tell themselves what works and what doesn't, or what the behavioral responses are to the product/service being delivered. True understanding of who the customers are, what they think

and do, when they do it and why are needed. Brand managers need to learn these things and adjust their positioning accordingly. Technology is providing that possibility. In the franchise world, whether the brand's positioning matches the properties' optimal segment mix and image, and whether the brand delivers on its promise of customer development and loyalty are vital concerns in consumers selecting the brand. Product consistency and integrity of branded properties affect the positioning of the entire brand. Inconsistent brand

T A B L E   1 1 - 9
Value of a Brand Positioning Strategy[10]

Brand Equity: The net result of all the positives and negatives linked to the brand and that add value to, or subtract value from, the brand. These include brand loyalty, name awareness, perceived quality, and associations.

Brand Loyalty: The loyalty of the customer base—the degree to which customers are satisfied, have switching costs, like the brand, and are committed to it.

Brand Awareness: The strength of recognition and top-of-mind recall.

Perceived Quality: Improves prices and market share. Provides a reason to buy and a point of differentiation.

Brand Associations: Anything mentally linked to the brand. These include a point of differentiation, a reason to buy, positive attitudes and feelings, customer benefits.

Brand Position: How the brand is perceived—the image, the dfferentiation, and the promise it makes.

Brand Name and Symbols: Serve as indicators of the brand and are central to brand recognition and brand associations. Suggest the positioning.

portfolios that cannot meet this challenge will soon become the wayward cousins and will lose out in the competitive marketplace. Table 11-9 provides some details of the value of a brand positioning strategy. Under-standing these components is essential to positioning a property to the market sector it serves and the clientele it will attract.

Hotel Restaurant Branding

An interesting part of the branding phenomenon has been the outsourcing of F&B outlets to recognized brand names. U.S. hotel F&B outlets have been notoriously unprofitable. For some, this is changing with new brand identities.

The UK-based Regal Hotel group in 1998 bought a $600,000 equity position in The Restaurant Partnership, a company that provides F&B solutions to the hotel industry through expertise and the installation of branded outlets. Hotel guests have notoriously "eaten out" on a majority of occasions going, instead, to a recognized brand restaurant. The new trend is to put those brand names in-house to keep customers and as a point of differentiation among hotels.

The F&B branding trend works, generally speaking, in one of three ways. The first is for the hotel to lease the space for a flat fee and/or a percentage of sales. In this case, the hotel loses control to another operator. The second method is for the hotel to acquire a franchise and become a franchisee, paying fees and royalties to the franchisor. Marriott was one of the first to do this, with Pizza Hut in 1989. The third method is to undertake a joint venture where both the hotel and the restaurant operator share the costs and the profits. Radisson SAS Hotels has used both the first and third methods. It has also developed a strategy of having a range of branded F&B outlets. For example, in Hamburg, Germany, their hotel has a Trader Vic's (U.S. brand), in Berlin it has a T.G.I. Friday's (U.S. brand), while in Copenhagen, there's a Blue Elephant (Thai brand), and in Brussels, a Henry J. Bean's (UK brand).

MULTIPLE BRAND AND PRODUCT POSITIONING*

Hospitality companies develop multiple brands for growth purposes and for market niches. Sometimes this is through development of a new concept, sometimes through acquisition, and sometimes through both. Marriott, for example, developed the Courtyard (midprice) and Fairfield Inn (budget) lodging concepts to develop new segments, purchased Residence Inns for quick entry into extended stay properties, developed Marriott Marquis as convention hotels and Marriott Suites as luxury all-suites, and initiated J. W. Marriotts as upscale luxury hotels. Between 1995 and 1998, at least 34 new hotel brands were introduced in the United States alone. All of these are extensions of existing hotel companies.[11]

While development of multiple brands provides growth, it also provides protection from the competition against a single brand. Marriott saw other chains moving into lower-tier markets and threatening the middle-to-upper tier in which Marriott hotels were positioned. Marriott felt it might as well steal its own customers (also called **cannibalization**), as let someone else steal them. It also realized that there were markets that the existing concept was neglecting.

Multiple brands, of course, are common practice in other industries, for instance, Procter & Gamble and General Motors. The restaurant industry has long had multiple brands, as in the case of Darden Restaurants, which owns Red Lobster, Olive Garden, and a new Carribean restaurant concept, Bahama Breeze. Tricon Global owns Pizza

---

*The usage of the terms brand, product, and product line can be confusing. As commonly used and used here, a brand is a brand name that identifies a set of products called the product line. Thus Chrysler Corporation has four car brands—Chrysler, Dodge, Plymouth, and Eagle. The brand Chrysler has a product line with different products such as Concorde, Neon, Intrepid, Cirrus, Sebring, LHS (and maybe something else by the time you read this).

Hut, Taco Bell, and KFC. Brinker International has 11 different restaurant brand concepts.

The issue here is one of **multiple brand positioning** for each brand. In the case of Tricon Global, positioning Pizza Hut, Taco Bell, and KFC is not much different from positioning against an outside competitor in terms of positioning strategy, with one exception: It could be self-defeating for the parent company if these three chains cannibalized each other, which to some extent they now do by offering similar products such as chicken. What they want to do, instead, is to position to different market segments, as Darden's three brands do.

The different market segments may include many of the same people. They belong, however, to a different segment when they use restaurants for different purposes, in different contexts, or at different times. Thus the positioning of each chain should be managed so that they do not steal from each other, and then the standard positioning rules can be applied.

This is easier to do when your chains are named Pizza Hut and Taco Bell and many people don't even know they belong to the same company, than when they are named Ramada Inn, Ramada Hotel, Ramada Plaza, Ramada Suites, and Ramada Resorts, often leading to multiple confusion. This is actually one brand (Ramada) with five products in its product line.

Ever since Quality Inns was successfully broken into Comfort Inns, Quality Inns, and Quality Royale (now Clarion), there have been a number of hotel chains with properties under the same or similar name, each trying to position to a different market segment. This is commonly referred to as brand proliferation.

Quality Inns subsequently created Sleep Inns and renamed itself Choice International Hotels with four brands. Management claims that there is no question about the difference between the four brand names. This may not be the case when a Comfort Inn (so-called luxury budget segment) charges $100, as we previously noted, denying the positioning of that brand name. Further, the purchase addition of Rodeway, Friendship and Econo

Lodge to the Choice fold may have created some very confused customers, particularly as all brands answer to the same 800 number. Choice now has seven brands with 13 different products, some being different versions of the same product, (e.g., Clarion hotels, suites, resorts, and inns). The overlap is obvious as shown in their own (understated) brand positioning (Figure 11-10).

A *Cornell Quarterly* article contained some comments on this situation:

> Yesawich [president of the hospitality advertising firm Yesawich , Pepperdine & Brown] said that the success of brands depends on creating a clear differentiation in the minds of customers. With only few exceptions, the advertising and promotion that has been initiated on behalf of new product concepts has failed to communicate clearly or convincingly the basis of the differentiation. Consumers are quick to discern the availability of free drinks or free breakfasts, but it takes much more to constitute a new product in consumers' minds. . . . If advertising doesn't communicate the perception of a new product, then maybe the product isn't really new at all.
>
> Some observers are concerned that consumers may be confused by a chain that has one name on a variety of hotels. Yesawich noted that chains pursuing diversification by introducing new products under different names have so far met with greater success.
>
> "In general terms, a brand name is an asset, as long as it stands single mindedly for a specific package of value and benefits. Call it a personality," said Robert Bloch [then senior vice-president for marketing at Four Seasons]. "Leaving a midprice brand name on an upscale property, as some operators are doing, may confuse some customers."[12]

Ramada had this very problem with Renaissance, and Holiday Inns with Crowne Plaza, as we have already noted. But notice in Figure 11-11 how a franchisee tries to position the basic Holiday Inn product. Holiday (Bass Hotels & Resorts) still has problems with a confused product line of Holiday Inn, Holiday Express, and Holiday Inn Select.

Even worse, and totally confusing to the market,

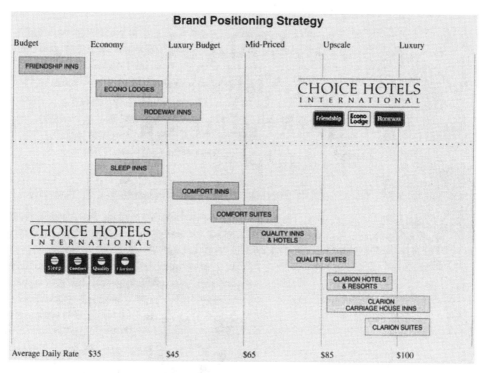

FIGURE 11-10   Choice International's self-positioning of brands and product line.

was what Howard Johnson did when it instituted five products—Lodge, Plaza-Hotel, Hotel, Park Square Inn, Suites—all with the exact same signage, a large Howard Johnson on top and the product line names in small letters at the bottom. After this, and following its sale to HFS when its parent Prime Motor Inns went into bankruptcy, Howard Johnson developed still another brand and opened 165 HoJo Inns, limited service properties. Eventually, expansion of HoJo Inns was aborted. Eric Pfeffer, former Howard Johnson president, reported:

> [R]esearch shows that 80 percent of American travelers believe the name HoJo is synonymous with Howard Johnson, so when they show up at a HoJo Inn "their expectations are fried clams, 28 flavors of ice cream and a full-service lodging facility, complete with meeting rooms and swimming pool," not a budget motel.[13]

Sheraton and Hilton have wrestled with a similar image problem. The vast difference between the Sheraton Wayfarer Motor Inn in Bedford, NH, and the Sheraton St. Regis (now a luxury brand name that the new owners, Starwood, plan to take worldwide) in Manhattan was about the same difference as the Berkshire Hilton Inn and the Waldorf-Astoria, two hotels sporting the Hilton name brand. Customers can be very confused with what position the brand name actually conveys. Hilton has recently developed Hilton Garden Inns; Sheraton has created a new brand called Four Points, and required all the former "inns" to come up to standard to use this name or otherwise be disenfranchised, to deal with this problem, which has existed for many years.

Marriott debated long and hard, when developing the Courtyard concept, as to whether to call it a Marriott. The final decision was to call it Courtyard by Marriott with the Marriott in smaller letters. Today, the "by" has been dropped. Thus Courtyard can trade on its famous brand

GO FROM PLANE TO LUXURIOUS AT THE HOLIDAY INN– JFK AIRPORT.

In a matter of minutes. The Holiday Inn - JFK Airport offers luxurious rooms, exquisite dining, spectacular meeting rooms and state-of-the-art health facilities, without Manhattan prices or hassles. Shouldn't luxury be a convenience?

1-800-692-5358

Holiday Inn

JFK AIRPORT
114-02 135th Ave., Jamaica, NY 11436
718-659-0200

Stay With Someone You Know.

FIGURE 11-11   Positioning a Holiday Inn above its product class.

name without creating expectations of the same product/service. The same was done with the Fairfield Inn brand line. Marriott, in fact, has probably been the hotel company in the United States that has most successfully differentiated its brands and kept them clearly in their product class. The problem for others is not necessarily in the name (only a possible compounding of the problem), but in the positioning.

Can hotel concepts under the same or similar names make the same claim? In other words, is each brand or product positioned to a different specific target market, each with specific needs that relate to the positioning? Furthermore, if the company succeeds with this positioning, can the customers who make up these markets differentiate the positioning of each brand or product name so that they know which one "belongs" to them? This is the crucial question and is the concern of positioning any multiple brands, more so when the problem is compounded by similar names. If the answers to the above questions are no, then there will be a clear case of cannibalization and customer confusion.

Multiple brand positioning can be done successfully as Marriott has shown. Groupe Accor, a French firm, has developed lodging concepts called Formule1, Ibis, Mercure, Novotel, and Sofitel, and now owns Motel 6 in the United States. By French government rating these are one-, one-, two-, three-, and four-star properties, respectively. Each is based on the needs of a specific target market.

Each is clearly differentiated from the other three; in fact, you might say that no customer would ever choose one when he or she wanted the other. In fact, in at least one site in Paris, a Novotel and a Sofitel sit side by side; only a common wall divides them, but they have separate entrances, a practice not uncommon among multibrand hotel companies in the United States. The traveler has a choice in the exact same location. Each hotel was clearly positioned to its own market segment, but eventually the Novotel started to cannibalize the Sofitel.

INTERNATIONAL BRANDING

Brand names also need to be considered for positioning in international markets. There are essentially three different common practices: single name, multinames, and individual names.

Perhaps the most common practice is to use a single name, as do Sheraton and Meridien. The purpose in this case is to create immediate identity. As Sheraton proclaimed in one ad:

Knowing where you're going is knowing where to stay. In Sana'a [the capital of Yemen, in the Middle East], and around the world, that can only mean Sheraton Hotels. Where the art of hospitality finds new expressions of excellence. And sensitivity to the needs of the business and leisure traveler results in a superior guest experience. So when you come to Sana'a come to Sheraton to stay.

One of the more perplexing brand name situations occurrs with Hilton. In the United States, the name Hilton is used by the original company. Overseas, however, the same company is not allowed to use the Hilton name, because of the terms of the original Hilton split-up. Therefore, it uses the name Conrad to represent Hilton-managed hotels overseas. To confuse issues further, a now totally different company, based in England, uses the brand name Hilton International overseas, at the same time using the name Vista in the United States. Hilton International hotels are generally more upscale than U.S. Hilton hotels. Thus, it is not unusual for a European or Asian to reserve at a Hilton hotel when coming to the United States, unaware of the separate companies, and to be quite shocked by the property.

The multiname practice is followed by Groupe Accor to differentiate its product line. The corporate name is never used, other than a very small symbol. To many people in the 60-plus foreign countries in which Accor operates, perhaps even in France, Sofitel, Novotel, Mercure, Ibis, Etap, and Formule1 may be perceived as six separate and distinct chains, as its acquisition in the United States, Motel 6, surely is. In mid-1999, however, Accor, thinking it might be losing a great deal of crossover business, was considering a full branding with the Accor name.

A company that maintained individual names, and still largely does although under new ownership, throughout the world was Trusthouse Forte of England. This company operates over 200 hotels in the United Kingdom and over 600 outside of it. Customers can stay at the Compleat Angler (Marlow, England) for a country inn; the Wynnstay (Machynlleth, Wales) for a small-town hotel; the Old England (Bowness-on-Windermere, England) for a lakeside resort; the Post House (Edinburgh, Scotland) for an outside-the-city hotel; the Strand Palace (London) for a touristy group hotel; or the George V (Paris), the Dom (Cologne), the Plaza Athenee (New York), the Ritz (Madrid), or the Sandy Lane (Barbados) for top-of-the-line luxury hotels—all without knowing they are in a Trusthouse Forte property, unless they recognized the small but ubiquitous "thf" initials.

Somewhat similarly, Movenpick, a Swiss company, uses its name alone, and in combination, to position its four-star, three-star, and two-star properties (Figure 11-12), in this case to an Italian market.

In short, when going international, some companies have attempted to market all their brands in an integrated message, whereas others have focused on each brand separately. There are clearly advantages to both strategies—the halo effect of a strong brand supporting weaker properties in the case of the former, and the focused segmentation approach, allowing brands of differing quality to be positioned separately, in the latter case.

FIGURE 11-12 Movenpick positions its product line with different names.

348

The first approach has had its difficulties in many cases, especially in the lower tiers. A $70 Best Western in the United States can be $180 a night in Paris, in New Delhi $140, and all of different quality. In fact, many of the "budget" hotels are hardly cheap outside North America. Quality Inn, which may charge $70 in the United States, gets $170 in Rome. In Beijing, a Holiday Inn is $180. Some of this, of course, is caused by the exchange rate but that doesn't alleviate the shock when the hotel room is about as large as a closet, is well-worn, and doesn't have many of the basic services.

Many local companies are moving in on this situation, especially in countries where the choice is largely between five-star properties and others that are little more than a hostel. Out of Hong Kong, Shangri-La, a very upscale chain, has introduced a consistent midmarket model called Traders, which offers genuine value for the money. Southern Pacific Hotels of Sydney is expanding its midmarket brand franchise, Travelodge, throughout Asia with midprice standards. Upscale Indian operators, such as Oberoi, are diversifying downmarket with branded products to compete against Days Inn and Quality Inn, which are already there, but as franchises without the home control over quality.

In Europe, there are many unbranded properties, both upscale and downscale, of varying distinction. Upscale ones, often chateaus or old mansions, often have very clear positions in the marketplace and may belong to a consortium like Relais & Chateaux as a means of branding and obtaining reservations. In the lower end of the market, the properties, by and large, lack positioning identity. Some of these, of course, are quite small but many are joining affiliations or taking on brand identities such as Best Western, more for their reservation systems and international travelers than for their positioning quality, which seems to be sporadic.

A survey by Business Development Research Consultants of London, England, found that 70 percent of international travelers and 64 percent of domestic travelers felt that branding was important in choosing a hotel. However, this varied by market: 41 percent at luxury hotels were influenced a "great deal" by branding, 27 percent in the middle market, and 19 percent in the lower market. Much of this may be due, of course, to lack of brands in the lower end of the market. Overall, the total brand line of Accor is the most powerful one, with clear positioning at all its brand levels.

INTERNAL POSITIONING ANALYSIS

Positioning maps, mentioned above, help to determine positioning strategies vis-à-vis the competition. They are also very useful methods for analyzing one's own position on a number of different attributes or benefits (as was done in Figure 11-9). In these cases, a different procedure is to use expectations, salient, determinant, or important factors as one scale and performance perception as the other. Customers then are asked their rating on each scale. For example, we might find, on a one to five scale, that cleanliness was a 5 in expectation and a 4 in perception, thus showing that the property is not living up to expectations. All attributes so measured can be shown on one two-dimensional plot, such as the hypothetical example in Figure 11-13.

Internal analysis indicates where the operation may be failing both internally and relative to the competition. Further, it aids in the best use of resources by indicating where they will count the most for the customer.

The hard questions that have to be asked are these: What is the expectation of the target market and how does it perceive our performance on these attributes? Similar maps can be drawn for the competition to learn where they stand.

The reality is that if the target market doesn't perceive the image, it doesn't exist; if the target market doesn't believe that what you have to offer is a benefit, it isn't a benefit; if customers do not believe that you can deliver the benefit, your promises are meaningless; if the benefit isn't important to the target market, it isn't important; if

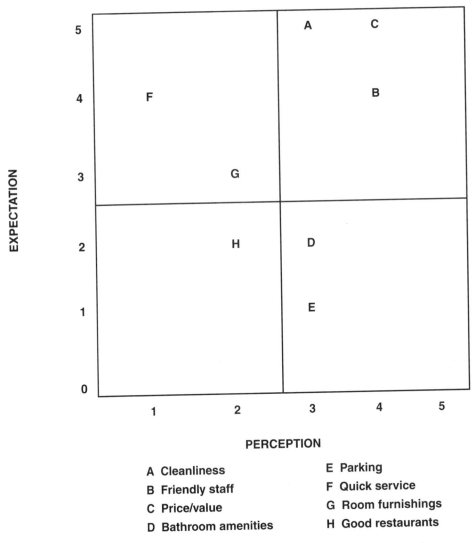

FIGURE 11-13 A perceptual map of consumer expectations and perceptions.

A Cleanliness   E Parking
B Friendly staff   F Quick service
C Price/value   G Room furnishings
D Bathroom amenities   H Good restaurants

your benefit is not perceived as different from that of the competition, you haven't differentiated. In short, images, benefits, and differentiation are solely the perception of the consumer, not management. We keep repeating these statements intentionally—they are the most often forgotten or neglected truths of marketing. Let us also repeat, as a reminder, that these statements are especially pertinent to hospitality marketing because of the intangibility of the services offered and the simul-

taneous production and consumption of the offering, which permits evaluation only after the purchase, but also leaves plenty of room for wrong images before the purchase.

Hospitality research too often fails to identify the vital elements of benefits. Comment cards, for example, ask customers whether they liked certain features of the property or operation. What those features do for the customer or how important they are even when satisfactorily rated is not revealed.

The architecture of a property, the decor, and the furnishings are examples of attributes that may produce a benefit, or may be tangible representation of an intangible benefit, but are not themselves the benefit. The benefit itself is what the attributes do for the customer—for instance, give a sense of security, a sensation of grandeur, an aura of prestige, or a feeling of comfort. The credibility of these benefits may diminish rapidly if an expectation is not fulfilled. Decor is soon forgotten if the service takes an hour. The impression of security loses credibility if the guest encounters slovenly characters in the lobby. It is this fulfillment of expectations or lack of it that creates the perception of deliverability for the consumer.

Finally, as previously mentioned, competing properties may be seen to offer the same senses of security, grandeur, prestige, and comfort. The tangible attributes have lost their ability to differentiate and, at the same time, are no longer determinant in the consumer choice process.

Benefits, then, like positioning, exist in the mind of the consumer and are determinable only by asking the consumer. This information is essential to proper positioning analysis.

In sum, positioning is the ultimate weapon in niche marketing. Stripped of all its trappings, positioning analysis answers the following questions:

1. What position do you own now ? (In the mind of the target market.)
2. What position do you want to own ? (Look for positions or holes in the marketplace.)
3. Whom must you out position ? (Manipulate what's already in the mind.)
4. How can you do it ? (The attributes or benefits that are salient, determinant, and important to the target market and which the firm can deliver.)

SUMMARY

Market positioning is a valuable weapon for hospitality marketers. To position successfully requires recognizing the marketplace, the competition, and consumers' perceptions. Positioning analysis on a target market basis provides the tools to identify opportunities for creating the desired image that differentiates from the competition, and for serving the target market better than anyone else.

Positioning may be objective, where images of the physical characteristics of the product are used, or subjective, where customer's mental perceptions play a greater role. Positioning of a tangible good is often accomplished through association with intangible notions; alternatively, it is better to position intangible services with tangible clues.

Repositioning may be necessary when a hospitality firm is in an unacceptable position or when trying to appeal to a new market segment. Old hotels with poor images are often renovated and repositioning them is crucial to their success. Six approaches to positioning were discussed and marketers may select the ones that will be most effective after selecting the desired position.

The differences between salient, important and determinant attributes must be considered, especially if the firm is being positioned by benefit or attribute. All three are complementary and it is crucial to understand their place.

As many hotel and restaurant chains grow by adding new brands and concepts, multiple brand positioning becomes important. The chains must prevent one brand from cannibalizing the other and also be able to create separate images and benefits for each one. Finally, internal positioning analysis can be used to examine one's own position to see how it is perceived by its customers.

KEY WORDS AND CONCEPTS

Brand Switching: When properties change brands for supposed better marketing pull.

Cannibalization: Taking customers away from one of your own products.

Commodity Status: When there is little or no differentiation in the product among producers.

Competitive Positioning: Creating an image of a product or service vis-à-vis the competition.

Determinance: Attributes of a product or service that actually determine the purchase choice.

Evoked Set: A customer's evoked set is the group of products in a category that quickly come to mind when considering a purchase.

Importance: Attributes of a product or service that are important to a consumer in making a choice, or after making a choice.

Intangible Positioning: Creating a tangible, objective image based on intangible attributes such as service and guest experience.

Multiple Brand Positioning: Hospitality companies that offer different levels of product and service for different target markets.

Objective Positioning: Creating an image about a product based on the objective attributes of the physical product.

Perceptual Mapping: A method of plotting a property's attributes against those of the competition to determine strengths and weaknesses, or of plotting one's own strengths and weaknesses based on customer perception.

Positioning Statement: This is a singular expression by a property or brand that captures its intended position in the marketplace.

Repositioning: Creating a change of position or image about a product or service in the marketplace.

Salience: Attributes of a product or service that are "top of mind" reasons for considering a product.

Subjective Positioning: Creating a position in the consumer's mind that belongs to the consumer's mental perception.

Tangible Positioning: Creating an intangible, subjective image based on a tangible attribute.

DISCUSSION QUESTIONS

1. What are the different kinds of hospitality positioning? Give examples of when you would use each one and why.
2. Discuss the problems a product can incur with a weak or undefined position.

3. Identify a hotel or restaurant you know that is in need of repositioning, and outline the steps needed to achieve the repositioning.
4. Take two competing hotels you are familiar with and position them using the six approaches (Table 11-2) to positioning.
5. Discuss the salient, determinant, and important attributes of the same hotel or restaurant.
6. Develop a list of questions that you would pose to a focus group of customers of a cocktail lounge that seeks to establish a position in the marketplace.
7. How does competition affect the positioning of a product? Discuss.
8. Draw a positioning map like that in Figure 11-9 for a group of restaurants or hotels with which you are familiar, based on your own perceptions.
9. Draw another positioning map like that in Figure 11-13 on your own expectations and perceptions of a particular property.
10. Discuss how a company may avoid problems of cannibalization among competing brands.
11. Conceptualize how a lagging brand may be repositioned for new uses.
12. What criteria may be employed to determine the viable position for a brand in the market?

GROUP PROJECTS

1. Consider a hotel, restaurant, or chain not mentioned in the chapter and consider how it is positioned, both objectively and subjectively, and why. Does this positioning reflect reality?
2. Take a different hotel, restaurant, or chain that is poorly positioned and outline how you would reposition it.
3. Do a Web search for a branded franchise, for example, Holiday Inn. Compare a dozen or so different properties on attributes, price, and so on. Are they consistent? Can you explain the differences as a consumer?

REFERENCES

1. Robert C. Lewis, "The Basis of Hotel Selection," *Cornell Hotel and Restaurant Administration Quarterly,* May 1984, pp. 54–69.

2. David Ogilvy, *Ogilvy on Advertising.* New York: Vintage Books, 1985, p. 160.

3. Adapted from Subhash C. Jain, *Marketing Planning & Strategy,* 5th ed. Cincinnati: South-Western College Publishing, 1997, p. 345.

4. William Q. Dowling, "Creating the Right Identity for Your Hotel," *Lodging,* September 1980, p. 58.

5. Quoted in Denise M. Brennan, "Niche Marketing," *Restaurant Business,* May 1, 1986, pp. 186, 189.

6. Abstracted from William C. Symonds, "Dunkin' Donuts is on a Coffee Rush," *Business Week,* March 16, 1998, pp. 107–108.

7. Abstracted from Carlo Wolff, "When Reconception Means Repositioning," *Lodging Hospitality,* November 1994, pp. 28, 30.

8. Stephen P. Taylor, "Repositioning: Recovery for Vintage and Distressed Hotels," *HSMAI Marketing Review,* Fall 1986, pp. 12–15.

9. Christopher Lovelock, *Services Marketing,* 2nd ed. Englewood Cliffs, NJ: Prentice-Hall, 1991, p. 112. Reprinted by permission of Prentice-Hall Inc.

10. Abstracted in part from Ronald A. Nykiel, "Brand marketing paramount to success," *Hotel & Motel Management,* October 6, 1997, pp. 22, 51.

11. Marty Whitford, "New Brands Sprint for Survival," Hotel & Motel Management, May 4, 1998, p. 48.

12. Glenn Withiam, "Hotel Companies Aim at Multiple Markets," *Cornell Hotel and Restaurant Administration Quarterly,* November 1985, pp. 39–51.

13. Ed Watkins, "The Forum," *Lodging Hospitality,* September 1993, p. 2.

The Marketing Mix

C H A P T E R

Twelve

❖

THE HOSPITALITY MIX AND THE PRODUCT/SERVICE MIX

Overview

The marketing mix involves developing and implementing an appropriate mix of marketing activities directed toward both market segments and target markets. In this chapter we explain the marketing mix and one of its elements, the product/service mix, by which the hospitality firm decides what products and services to offer.

HOSPITALITY MARKETING MIX The hospitality marketing mix is comprised of five sub mixes:

Product/service mix is the combination of products and services, whether free or for sale, that are aimed at satisfying the needs of the target market. Presentation mix is all of the elements used by the hospitality firm to increase the tangibility of the product/service mix in the perception of the target market at the right place and time.

Pricing mix is the combination of prices that customers pay for products/services.

Communications mix is all communications between the firm and the target market that increase the tangibility of the product/service mix, that establish or monitor consumer expectations, or that persuade customers to purchase.

Distribution mix is all channels available between the hospitality firms and its target market that increase the probability of getting the customer to the product.

HOSPITALITY PRODUCT/SERVICE MIX This mix is the integration of the product, which is an offering by a hospitality firm as it is perceived by present and future customers, into a benefit bundle that will solve a customer's problem. The hospitality firm offers a formal product, which is what customers think they are buying, together with the core product, which is what the customer is really buying. The augmented product is the totality of all benefits received or experienced by the customer.

COMPLEXITY OF THE PRODUCT/SERVICE MIX Standard products have the advantage of providing a cost benefit derived from standardization. The customer knows just what he or she is getting. Standard products with modifications are those designed to differentiate and meet particular segment needs. Customized products are designed to fit the specific needs of a particular target market. Internationally, there are even more reasons to modify the product. The product decision, in the final analysis, should be based on the target market.

PRODUCT LIFE CYCLE (PLC) Every product has a "life cycle" through which it passes. The timing of the PLC varies. The stages of the PLC include the introduction, when customers are just

learning about the offering(s). Growth follows as more customers buy and refer the product to others. Maturity settles in as new customers dwindle and competition begins to enter the marketplace. Finally, the decline stage shows business falling off, employees disgruntled, and unhappy customers. Some properties then go into a death spiral.

LOCATING PRODUCTS IN THEIR LIFE CYCLES There are many telltale signs that must be evaluated for this purpose.

DEVELOPING NEW PRODUCTS AND SERVICES New products start with consumer problems. There are means to evaluate the probability of success.

The marketing mix involves the developing and implementing of an appropriate mix of marketing activities directed toward market segments and target markets. These activities include the creation and presentation of products and services; the methods used to get the customer to these products and services (or vice versa) for an appropriate price; and the various techniques employed to communicate with customers. We have mentioned these activities briefly in Chapter 4, and we now elaborate further. In this chapter we define the marketing mix, especially as it relates to the hospitality industry, and then discuss in detail its first element, namely the product/service mix. The other elements are discussed in future chapters.

The marketing mix is the stage of marketing management and strategy that directly affects the customer, but it is also a stage where the company has the most control. We can decide what kind of products and services to offer, or the kinds of hotels and restaurants we want to build. We can also select the magazines or radio stations to carry our message and, of course, we determine the price. Finally, we select the distribution channels. Naturally, all these activities will take place only

after we have studied the external environment and learned the needs and wants of our target markets and determined our positioning. The marketing mix is the ultimate outcome of the company's philosophy and mission statement, and the final delivery of the company's offering to the marketplace. It is the culmination of everything we have discussed so far, including both traditional and nontraditional marketing.

The marketing mix was originally developed by Professor Neil Borden of Harvard in what have come to be known, through subsequent alteration, as the "**Four Ps.**"[1] Borden's six original elements—product planning, pricing, distribution, promotion, servicing, and marketing research—were later reduced to four elements by E. Jerome McCarthy—product, price, place (distribution), and promotion.[2] Although we change the names of these elements to better fit the hospitality industry, it is necessary to understand the concept.

The problem that we have with the four Ps in hospitality marketing is not their concept, but the elements of the mix that are essentially based on the marketing of goods. Consistent with our previous arguments in Chapter 2, we believe that the marketing of hospitality services is different from the marketing of goods and thus requires a different approach to the marketing mix. The point in redefining the mix elements for this purpose is not to change their meanings—essentially, they remain the same—but to make the concept of the marketing mix more useful and applicable for hospitality marketing decisions.

THE HOSPITALITY MARKETING MIX

The first attempt at developing a new marketing mix for the hospitality industry was undertaken by Leo M. Renaghan.[3] The hospitality marketing mix, according to Renaghan, contains three major sub-mixes: the product/service mix, the presentation mix, and the communications mix. To this trio we add back two of the original elements defined by Borden—price and distribution.

The Product/Service Mix

The **product/service mix** is the combination of products and services, whether free or for sale, that are factually offered to satisfy the needs of the target market. The product/service mix is what customers see, get, and perceive when they go to a hotel, restaurant, or other hospitality entity.

This definition is consistent with our discussion of the hospitality product in Chapter 2. An important addition here, however, is the word free. This, again, is an important distinction between the marketing of manufactured goods and the marketing of hospitality services. We can infer "free" as including those supporting goods that the customer does pay for, but indirectly. In this category would be placed swimming pools, exercise facilities, free airport transportation, linen tablecloths, china and silverware, fresh flowers on the table, and so forth. These are items over which manage-

ment has control, that thus become part of the offering decision process.

There are other "free" features over which management may have little or no control but that are part of the consumer's expectation. These items include such things as the sun, the moon, the stars, the ocean, the beach, and the weather. We include these because they can have considerable bearing on customers' expectations and resulting satisfaction. The product/service mix is discussed in detail later in this chapter.

The Presentation Mix

The **presentation mix** is all of the elements used by the firm to increase the tangibility of the product/service mix in the perception of the target market at the right place and time. The presentation mix is how the product/service is presented for the customer to sense; it is what the customer perceives.

There are six elements of the presentation mix that can be utilized to make tangible the product/service mix and to differentiate it from the competition's offerings. These elements are: the physical plant, the location, atmospherics, price, employees, and customers. The presentation mix is discussed in detail in Chapter 13.

Although price stands alone as part of the marketing mix, we also include it here because price is a highly tangible element that increases the tangibility of the product/service mix in the perception of the target market. For example, if you believe that the check average at a certain restaurant is $50, or that the price of a hotel room is $45, you immediately sense how the product/service should be presented.

The Pricing Mix

The **pricing mix** is the combination of prices used by the firm to represent the value of the offering. The pricing mix is how the customer values what is being offered and what is received. We discuss it at length in Chapter 14.

The Communications Mix

The **communications mix** is all communications between the firm and the target market that increase the tangibility of the product/service mix or the presentation mix, that establish or monitor consumer expectations, build relationships, or that persuade consumers to purchase.

This area is similar to that of traditional marketing, although with some new twists due to the intangibility of the product. Except for these new twists, this part of the marketing mix is no different from the promotion element of the Four Ps. The word communication, however, covers a far broader expanse than the word promotion. In fact, we will show that promotion is but one subset of communications. The communications mix is discussed in detail in Chapters 15, 16, and 17.

The Distribution Mix

The **distribution mix** is all channels available between the firm and the target market that increase the probability of getting the customer to the product. This is how the customer can buy and use the services offered.

The general concept of services, as opposed to goods, is that rather than the good being taken to the customer (e.g., through retail outlets), the customer must come to the service. Thus a hotel or restaurant chain that has 500 locations nationwide is "distributing" the product so that the customer can come to it.

The Four Ps approach typically assumes that decisions relative to product design and product distribution are largely independent of one another. In hospitality, however, a customer must come to the place where a service is produced in order to experience it, making production and distribution largely inseparable. The complexities of selling the hospitality product, however—especially in the case of hotel rooms sold through 800 telephone reservation numbers, wholesalers, tour brokers, travel agents, and others—have become so confounded that location itself is no longer adequate to describe this phenomenon. We treat distribution and its supporting technology as a separate element of the marketing mix and discuss it in detail in Chapter 18.

THE HOSPITALITY PRODUCT/SERVICE MIX

We have defined the product/service mix in general terms as the combination of products and services, whether free or for sale, that are factually offered to satisfy the needs of the target market. We need now to be more specific. From here on we may use the word "product" as a generic term to describe product/service or the offering of a hospitality entity.

A product is an offering or a bundle of benefits designed to satisfy the needs and wants, and solve the problems of specified target markets. A product is composed of both tangible and intangible elements; it may be as concrete as a chair or a dinner plate, or as abstract as a "feeling." The value of a product derives from what it does for the customer. What it does for the customer depends also on customer perception.

What it does for the customer is critical. We have covered this ground before but it bears repeating. "People don't buy quarter-inch drills, they buy quarter-inch holes." It is what the drills do, not what they are. Recall that we are in the business of solving consumers' problems, as abstract as they may be. Solving problems, then, is what the product does for the customer.

Designing the Hospitality Product

If a product is defined in terms of what it does for the customer, then it becomes immediately obvious that the design of a product begins with what the customer wants done. In the case of goods, that is often easier to determine. People who buy tires want safety and endurance. People who buy music want good sound reproduction. People who buy a Mercedes want prestige. But what do people want when they buy hotel rooms and restaurant meals? A comfortable bed and a good meal? Of course this is what they want, but we know that their desires go far beyond those basic minimums.

An important feature of the product/service mix is the bundle purchase concept. Consumers do not purchase individual elements of the offering; rather, they purchase a bundle or unified whole. When buying a hotel room, the customer is also buying the bed, bathroom, restaurant, wake-up call, and many more bundled items. The restaurant customer is buying food, as well as the service and atmosphere of the restaurant. It is clear that a delicate balance exists in the mix and that management must be aware of how the various elements of the bundle interact. Every element of this bundle is an integral part of the product, and a change in one element can affect the perception of the entire product. Thus it is useful to break the bundle down into its component parts: the formal product, the core product, and the augmented product.

The Formal Product

The **formal product** can be defined as what customers think they are buying. This may be as simple as a bed or a meal, or it may be as elusive as quality or elegance; it may be as intangible as environment or class, or as specific as location. The formal product, in fact, might be defined as what the customer can easily articulate. Because of this, it is easy to be misled by what the customer does articulate.

It has been noted that hotel and restaurant customers frequently name location and good food as their primary reasons for choosing a particular hotel or restaurant. In many cases, however, this is only because location and good food are elements that can be easily articulated. In fact, if these were really major reasons for determinance we could dispense with the bundle concept and concentrate on these elements alone. Such, of course, is not the

case, and it would be a serious mistake to believe that it is.

The Core Product

The **core product** is what the customer is really buying. This often consists of abstract and intangible attributes. Some examples of core products are experience, atmosphere, relaxation, celebration, and convenience. These are actually core benefits rather than product attributes. By now, of course, we know that what the customer is really buying is, in fact, benefits rather than product attributes. Understanding the core product—what the customer is really buying—means understanding the customer's problems. This has two very important implications. First, understanding customers' problems is where product design should begin. Too often it begins, instead, with management's problems.

Consider, for example, the case of large banquet rooms that can be divided into smaller meeting rooms through the use of folding accordion doors. The innovation of doors of this kind came about some years ago because of a critical management problem: how to accommodate both large and small groups in the same space. The solution solved the problem for management, but caused one for the customer. In many hotels, even today, one can sit in a small meeting room and listen not only to what is occurring in that room, but also to what is occurring in the rooms on either side, not to mention the banquet kitchen. This is an aggravating and ongoing problem for meeting groups. Today, better folding or collapsing doors are built that almost eliminate this problem, but they can be found largely only in the newer or more recently renovated hotels.

The formal product, what customers think they are buying, is the meeting room and the seating capacity, and that's what the hotel is selling. The core product, what they are really buying, is a quiet, controlled, hassle-free, successful meeting. That's what the hotel should be marketing, and many do, as we saw in Chapter 9.

The formal product, of course, is the meeting space and unless it meets a minimum standard, it will be unacceptable. This is also the salient product. The core product, that which is also determinant and important, is how the entire facility deals with the meeting planner's problems.

The Augmented Product

The **augmented product** is the totality of all benefits received or experienced by the customer. It is the entire system with all accompanying services. It is the way the customer uses the product. The augmented product may include both tangible and intangible attributes. These attributes range from the manner in which things are done, the assurance that they will be done, the timeliness, the personal treatment, and the no-hassle experience, to the size of the bath towels, the cleanliness of the restrooms, the decor, and the honored reservation.

The augmented product even includes the sun and the moon. As any resort manager can testify, there is nothing worse than three or four rainy days with all your guests locked inside on their vacation, or a ski area with unskiable conditions. The frequent effect is that customers go away angry over something management can do nothing about. Or can it? For a marketing-oriented management the answer is yes. This is a customer problem that management anticipates and for which it prepares by developing alternative activities.

The augmented product is the total product bundle that should solve all the customers' problems, and even some they haven't thought of yet. In designing the product, it is critical to understand the augmented concept and its basis in consumer problems. This is different from simply augmenting for the sake of augmenting. Mints on pillows don't make up for poor lighting. Elaborate bathroom amenities don't make up for a businessperson's having no place to write, or for a couple not having two chairs to sit in.

The success of the all-suite hotel concept is based on the augmented product. This concept provides guests with a total living experience rather than simply meeting their basic needs. The success of McDonald's was based on the augmented product, which included, among other things, cleanliness and fast service. In fact, the success of any hospitality enterprise begins with an understanding of the core product and its augmentation to solve consumers' problems.

Examine the ad in Figure 12-1. What do you consider to be the formal, the core, and the augmented products?

THE COMPLEXITY OF THE PRODUCT/SERVICE MIX

Now that we understand what a product is and what it does, it should be easy enough to go out and design a hotel or restaurant that will solve consumers' problems. Ah, if only life were that simple. Obviously, we have a multitude of consumers with a multitude of problems, and we can never hope to satisfy all the consumers or solve all the problems. We narrow the problem down, of course, by segmentation and target marketing, which is why these strategies are so critical to effective marketing. Even within these submarkets, however, we can never hope to be all things to all people.

It is clear, however, that we need to go beyond the basic and formal product when designing the hospitality product/service. Certain characteristics of products and services come to be taken for granted by consumers, especially those concerned with basic functional performance. If these are missing in a product, the user may well be upset. But if they are present, the seller gets no special credit, because quite logically every other seller is assumed to be offering the equivalent. In other words, the values that are salient in decision-making are the values that are problematic—that are important, to be sure, but also those which differentiate one offering from another. One thing is for sure—the product/service shouldn't cause problems.

Consider, for example, the experiences of Stanley Turkel, a hotel consultant, described in

IN THE AGE OF THE
VIRTUAL OFFICE

WE'RE PROUD TO INTRODUCE
THE ACTUAL PERSON.

DISCOVER   THE   PEOPLE   WITH   THE   HYATT   TOUCH™

FIGURE 12-1 Hyatt ad showing the formal, core, and augmented product.

Table 12-1. Too often, designers, architects, or whomever, don't understand how people use a hotel room.

Today's hospitality customers are much more well-traveled and sophisticated than previous generations. Thus the basic functions served by a hotel are taken for granted. Customers expect a good location, clean room and bath, comfortable beds, and pleasant service from all hotels. However, customers look for other benefits, which may be unique to a particular hotel, benefits which differentiate one hotel from others. For example, business travelers will look for a hotel that offers services that will increase their productivity. A family on vacation will look for services that allow them to be together as a family but, perhaps, also separate to enjoy their own activities, as advertised in

Figure 12-2. Another way to look at a product offering is as a standard product, a standard product with modifications, or a customized product.

Standard Products

Standard products have the advantage of providing a cost benefit derived from standardization. They are also more amenable to efficient national marketing. Holiday Inns' original motels are an example of a successful standardized product. No matter where in the country customers stayed at a Holiday Inn, they could just about find their way blindfolded to the front desk, their room, the lounge, or the dining room, Today, Microtel, Formule1, and Etap would be prime examples, as well as fast-food chains. In hospitality, this kind of

TABLE 12-1
User-Friendly Guest Rooms[4]

Staying recently in a five-star, five-diamond hotel, the guest rooms were oversized and expensively decorated by a well-known hotel designer who, apparently, never stayed in a hotel room:

- The blackout draperies did not protect against the morning sunrise and allowed a "halo of light" to penetrate around the periphery of the draperies.
- The lamp on the light table did not encourage reading in bed. Its 65-watt bulb was inadequate even when the lamp shade was tilted.
- The guest room doors had no electronic door locks, but the old fashioned metal key and lock cylinder.
- A low-quality clock radio–alarm perched on the night table but the variety and quality of music was nil.
- The television did not provide recent release movies.
- The desk chair and upholstered chair were too low to allow comfortable dining from the room service table.
- There was no telephone on the desk. One had to sit, unsupported, on the edge of the bed to make calls.

standardization exists, justifiably, almost entirely at the lower end of the price scale. Upscale properties, however, are sometimes guilty of standardization as well, as documented in Table 12-1.

A problem with standardized products, however, and one that befell Holiday Inns for awhile, is the emphasis placed on cost-savings so that needed, and sometimes more expensive, variations in the product in certain markets are ignored. Eventually this results in a loss of customers who either want something different or want a more modified or customized product. Even McDonald's, which has been successful with a highly standardized product, allows its franchisees to make variations on the theme. The effect has been a major contribution to their success. In Canada, for example, McDonald's allows franchisees to incorporate a maple leaf (the national symbol) into the traditional golden arches. Canadian consumers feel that the restaurant has addressed their nationalist needs, while serving the same fare as the outlet in the next town over the U.S. border.

Standard Products with Modifications

The **standard product with modifications** is a compromise between the standard product and the customized product. An example is the concierge floor of a hotel. In such cases, the scale economies of building and furnishing a standard room remain unchanged; the modifications are easily added to only those rooms requiring them, and an additional charge is often extracted for them.

This strategy has one considerable advantage: The modifications, or added amenities, are sometimes easily added, removed, or changed as the market changes. Thus the property maintains a flexibility that in itself may be perceived as a desirable attribute because the property can more easily meet customer requirements and encourage new uses of the product. Another advantage that accrues is differentiation within the product class, while maintaining the same strategic position. In restaurants, one example of a standard product with modifications is to offer different-size portions of menu items. Such a policy has a high level of flexibility as well as the ability to cater directly to changing market needs. (The popularity of doggie bags indicate that many people don't eat all they order.) Burger King's "We do it your way" campaign had considerable impact on McDonald's method of doing it only their way. Starbucks coffee shops are a very successful standard product with modifications.

HOW DOES IT FEEL TO SQUISH

FINGERPAINTS IN CIRCLES

WITH A DOZEN NEW FRIENDS.

OR LEARN ABOUT COMPUTERS ONE DAY

AND HULA DANCING THE NEXT.

IT FEELS LIKE HYATT.®

CAMP HYATT® AT THE HYATT RESORTS

THESE HYATT RESORTS OFFER CAMP HYATT WITH SUPERVISED ACTIVITIES FOR THE KIDS
AND PEACE OF MIND FOR THE PARENTS.

HYATT REGENCY ARUBA • HYATT REGENCY BEAVER CREEK® • HYATT REGENCY CERROMAR BEACH
HYATT DORADO BEACH • HYATT REGENCY GRAND CAYMAN • HYATT GRAND CHAMPIONS
HYATT REGENCY GRAND CYPRESS® • HYATT REGENCY HILTON HEAD • HYATT REGENCY KAUAI
HYATT REGENCY LAKE TAHOE • HYATT REGENCY MAUI • HYATT REGENCY SCOTTSDALE
HYATT REGENCY ST. JOHN • HYATT REGENCY WAIKIKI • HYATT REGENCY WAIKOLOA • GRAND HYATT WAILEA

FEEL THE HYATT TOUCH®

For more information about Camp Hyatt, the supervised vacation world
for children ages 3-12 at participating Hyatt Resorts, call 1-800-233-1234.

Hyatt Hotels and Resorts encompasses hotels managed or operated by two separate groups of companies—
companies associated with Hyatt Corp. and companies associated with Hyatt International Corp.

HYATT
R E S O R T S

FIGURE 12-2 As Hyatt shows, some families want to have it both ways.

Customized Products

Customized products are based on the premise of designing the product to fit specific needs of a particular target market, or even one individual's needs, as we discussed in Chapter 10 as "mass customization." Price may not be a large consideration for the buyer of customized products, because he or she expects to pay a premium to have it exactly the way it is wanted. On the other hand, Marriott has demonstrated with Courtyard a customized product for the price-conscious business traveler. Business traveler rooms with all the business amenities are examples of customized products that are now branded with names like "Smart Room" (Sheraton), "The Room that Works" (Marriott), "The Guest Office" (Westin), "The Wyndham Way" (Hyatt), "Business Plan," and "The Business Class Room" (Loews).

The growth of all-suite hotel concepts has led to both modifications in the standard product and some degree of customization. Free breakfasts and free cocktail hours have been two of the modifications, while the perceived price/value of the suite is still maintained. One all-suite in San Francisco, however, charges over $250 a night. This property stocks the suite with cooking and eating equipment, foods and snacks, liquors and wines, stereo, cassette recorders, and a VCR with a choice of movies and free exchange for other ones. The concept is customized to a very specific target market. In 1998, Chicago's Ritz-Carlton introduced "allergy sensitive" rooms with hypoallergenic mattress guards, feather-free bedding, and super powered vacuums to do the clean up.

Hotel bathrooms may be the latest version of customized products in the hotel industry. In the world's deluxe hotels, the bathroom frills once considered lavish (telephones, TV, marble) have now become commonplace. Designers are looking for new attractions. The Takeshiba Hotel in Tokyo has bathroom scales built directly into the tile, ballet bars to be used for exercise, and a soft light with dimmers above the toilet. The Beverly Hills Hotel has antifog mirrors. Three rotating shower heads, heated towel racks, dual-line telephones, remote controls for the television, and other deluxe amenities are appearing in mainstream hotel chain bathrooms, as well.

THE INTERNATIONAL PRODUCT/SERVICE

The question of standardization versus customization is an even more complex one when dealing with international markets. "Think global, act local," say some. "Think local, act global," say others. And Theodore Levitt, as we previously pointed out, says that high-touch products are as globalized as high-tech ones and the global organization should seek global standardization.[5] As with all product decisions, however, the answer should lie in the needs and wants of the marketplace and the degree of difference among the markets being served.

There are pitfalls in either case. Hilton International's standardization of product helped it to establish a common image worldwide so that first Americans, and then other international travelers, became accustomed to it and bought Hilton when available. This standardized product, however, did not match the conditions in every market. Holiday Inn, by contrast, has been more successful in foreign markets where it has adapted the product than in those where it has not. Fast-food firms have been quick to adapt internationally. In Australia, KFC has delivery service and a "smorgasbar" deli case, Pizza Hut has spicy sauces, barbecue, and all-you-can-eat dessert bars, and Sizzler includes pumpkin soup on its menu. In India McDonald's has mutton burgers. All of these are adaptations to popular items in the countries.

Jollibee, a burger chain in the Phillipines, however, has taken advantage of McDonald's pattern of standardization. First, it borrowed every trick in McDonald's Book—from child-friendly spokescharacters to prime locations. Instead of selling a generic burger, however, it caters to a local penchant for sweet and spicy flavors, which it also puts in its fried chicken and spaghetti. It is the dominant chain in the Phillipines with over 200 outlets and 46 percent market share versus McDonald's 100 outlets and 16 percent market share, even though McDonald's has now introduced its own Filipino-style menu items.

Each international expansion requires designing the product line for the location and the markets to be served. Products such as hotels and restaurants may need to be adapted to different countries and cultures. The product objectives for each country and market must be clearly delineated and related to the local situation as well as to the overall corporate objectives. On the other hand, TGI Friday's adapted to French customs when it opened in Paris with a dismal performance. Research finally revealed, "If we're going to go to an American concept, we want it to be American." Subhash C. Jain states the case this way:

[The international] product decision must be made on the basis of careful analysis and review. The nature, depth, and breadth of the product line; the possibilities of new product development and product innovation; . . . the adaptation and customization of products to suit local conditions vis-a-vis standardization, . . . and a planned screening and elimination of unsuccessful products bear heavily on success in foreign markets.[6]

MAKING THE PRODUCT DECISION

Standardizing, modifying, and customizing are important marketing decisions in designing the hospitality product/service. Although the examples used here have been on a fairly large scale, these decisions also apply to all facets of the product. To illustrate this point, let's examine a relatively minor product decision in the light of the criteria that have been proposed.

If a restaurant has rack of lamb on its menu, or Dover sole, or Caesar salad, does it carve, filet, or mix these in the kitchen or at tableside? To do it in the kitchen is to standardize it. This provides cost efficiencies, and presumably the finished product offered to the customer is identical to the one offered when the work is done at tableside.

The decision, however, is a marketing one, not a cost one. To perform the work at tableside has elements of both the core and augmented product in it. First, we would have to identify the target market. Does this market expect, want, and appreciate the additional effort and cost to customize the product at tableside? Is it willing to pay an additional price for it?

What does the modified or customized product do for customers? Does tableside service make customers feel better and more prestigious? Does it impress their guests, add perceived quality, or add romance or mysticism to the product? Or, does it simply delay the service delivery?

What business are we in? Are we in the business of serving quality food at a fair price, or providing a dining experience? Are we providing elegance, flair, or entertainment?

Finally, do we have the capabilities? Is the staff properly trained, or can they be trained? If trained to do the carving, fileting, or mixing properly, can they do it with flair and finesse? If not, we may defeat the entire purpose.

The hospitality product/service includes everything we have to offer the guest, whether "free" or for sale. It contains the basic elements of what guests think they are buying, what they really hope to get, and the total augmentation of the product that constitutes the entire experience in purchasing it. From the budget motel in North Overshoe to the Bristol Hotel in Paris, from the hot dog vendor at Fenway Park to Paul Bocuse's widely acclaimed restaurant in Burgundy, the hospitality product/service determination is a marketing decision based on the target market. The problem for the marketer is to determine the effective demand for the various product features and the total benefit bundle.

Table 12-2 provides a checklist for analyzing the hospitality product. This is a marketer's checklist for an existing product, because the answers will give the marketer the necessary tools to market the product. When applying the list, keep in mind the two critical definitions of a product: How is it perceived, and what does it do for the customer? See if you can apply these criteria to the ad in Figure 12-1, or to other ads in this book. Is the product standardized, modified, or customized?

There is one more thing to be said about designing the hospitality product, which has been said before but bears repeating: No matter how successful your product is now, never forget that the customer changes. The hospitality product re-

T A B L E   12-2
Analyzing the Hospitality Product/Service

As Seen by the Target Market:

What is it in terms of what it does for the customer?

How does it solve problems?

What benefits does it offer?

How does it satisfy demand?

Who uses it? Why? How?

How does it compete?

What are the occasions for its use?

What are its attributes?

What is the perception of it?

How is it positioned?

Which attributes are salient? Determinant? Important?

quires constant evaluation and reevaluation. We discuss this in more detail in the next section on the product life cycle.

THE PRODUCT LIFE CYCLE

The concept of the **product life cycle (PLC)** is basic to the marketing literature. It rests on the premise that a product goes through various stages during its lifetime, much as individuals do. There is the introduction, or embryonic, stage followed by the growth stage, the mature stage, and the stage of decline. Each stage calls for different strategies and tactics.

The product life cycle concept may be applied in four ways. It may refer to all products within a product class, such as all fast-food restaurants or all-suite hotels, sometimes called an industry life cycle. On the other hand, the product life cycle may be used in reference to one particular brand, such as McDonald's or Burger King; it may be used in terms of one particular property such as the Waldorf-Astoria. Finally, it may apply to one specific product line such as Burger King's "Whopper,"

or McDonald's "Arch Deluxe," which died in about a year. The traditional and widely used perspective of the product life cycle is shown in Figure 12-3.

The Nature of Product Life Cycles

Life cycles of products can vary widely in time span. Researchers have identified some as long as 100 years (Ivory Soap) and some as short as six months (pet rocks). The life cycle of the fast-food industry, which is now considered to be in the mature stage in the United States, had its major introduction in the 1950s. In retrospect, products with very short life cycles are usually referred to as fads.

Product life cycles do not always follow the familiar S-shaped curve shown in Figure 12-3. An example of a variation of the curve is the growth of the highway motel. This product had a fast growth period following World War II and the end of gas rationing. It never really matured. It fell into disrepute (as well as disrepair), went into decline and became moribund, to finally emerge on a new growth curve as the motor inn with full hotel facilities. Today, there is another new growth curve in what was the motel life cycle fueled by the boom in budget properties without full facilities.

Product life cycles may be in different stages in different parts of the world. The hotel industry is considered mature in the United States but is still in its introductory stage in China. Upscale hotels are in the mature stage in India while middle-tier properties (budget in the U.S., e.g., Microtel, Holiday Express) are in the growth stage. Similarly, the fast-food industry is in an introductory phase in Russia and in a growth phase in parts of Asia.

Regarding brands, Rodeway Hotels had been in the decline stage for some time, which took it through six owners. Now franchised by Choice Hotels International, it is being revitalized as senior citizen hotels with special senior citizen pretested amenities. Planet Hollywood has reached decline. Rainforest Cafe is in the growth approaching maturity stage, and Boston Market (formerly Boston Chicken) is in sharp decline. All of this occurred in about four to five years each. Time will

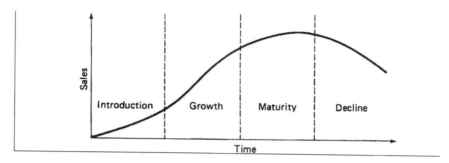

F I G U R E   1 2 - 3   Classic stages of the product life cycle.

tell if there is a demand for theme restaurants outside a few select destinations. In New York City there is a Hard Rock Cafe, Fashion Cafe, Harley Davidson Cafe, and a Planet Hollywood, all within a couple of blocks of each other. With the exception of New York City, it is unlikely that there are many other markets that can absorb this level of theme restaurants, yet each of these restaurants needs to be in every major city to develop brand awareness.

With regard to product modifications in the hospitality field, mints and fancy bathroom amenities are largely dead while business rooms and large working desks are in the growth stage. In restaurants similar examples apply. Nouvelle cuisine came and grew fast and is now all but dead. Hard liquor is in decline and bottled water is in sustained growth. Good wine has been in the growth stage for about 40 years. All these examples should make clear how products, brands, and product lines go through life cycle stages. How this relates to marketing is the issue that now needs to be addressed.

It is well to keep in mind that the introductory, growth, and decline stages of the product life cycle must, at some point in time, come to an end. The mature stage, at least theoretically, could go on forever. Our argument, then, is that the mature stage is the most critical to the marketer. This is not to say that introduction and growth are not marketing challenges as well. It is at the mature stage, or that of early decline, that the introductory and/or growth stage must be reincarnated if the product is to survive in some form.

The growth of a product is to some extent a function of the strategy being pursued. Thus a product is not necessarily predestined to decline as propounded by the traditional concept of the product life cycle, but can be kept profitable and mature by proper adaptation to the evolving market environment. As an analogy, Crest toothpaste has been reintroduced several times with special plaque fighters, new flavors, baking soda, a new dispensing cap, and other alterations. Fast-food hamburgers, introduced by White Castle in 1921, have had numerous incarnations. On the other hand, there are many products that just decline and die, such as motels, and are replaced with something else.

Perhaps what is most important, then, is to recognize the stage in which the product presently resides—for instance, to see that one's product is in the mature stage. Too often, management may be unaware of the product's stage, believing that growth will go on forever.

STAGES OF THE PRODUCT LIFE CYCLE

The Introductory Stage

The introductory stage of a product is its entry into the marketplace; the new restaurant that opened down the street, or the new hotel that was just built in Las Vegas are entering the introductory phase of their product life cycles.

As well, some products in the later years of their product life cycles begin anew with new names. The Park Suites Hotel in Boca Raton, Florida entered the decline stage with declining occupancies and revenues. By reflagging the hotel with the Embassy Suites name, and investing capital for refurbishment, the existing real estate structure entered a new introductory stage of its life cycle. Often, as we discussed in Chapter 11, a repositioning of a refurbished individual property does exactly that.

The very nature of the hospitality product often may make test-marketing prohibitive before introduction, although not for a new brand or new restaurant item. Ideally, the product should be developed on the basis of as much consumer research as possible. Frequently, however, this is not done and a new hotel or restaurant is opened on the opinions of the owner, developer, and/or management. An exception was the Marriott Courtyard concept. Extensive consumer research was conducted before three Courtyards were built in the Atlanta area to test the concept before further expansion ensued. Darden Restaurants tested two Bahama Breeze units in Orlando before deciding whether to take the concept elsewhere. If the property is truly innovative, the marketer holds a two-edged sword: The product will be easier to differentiate, but may create more resistance to achieving trial and acceptance.

The introductory stage may also be one of high costs. Before McDonald's could open its first restaurant in Moscow, the company had to build a 100,000 square-foot distribution center that included a meat plant, a bakery, a potato plant, and a dairy. McDonald's even had to work with Russian farmers to raise the appropriate breed of cattle, from which the meat would be obtained, and the appropriate potato for its french fries.

Whereas goods manufacturers often shroud their new products in secrecy as long as possible before introduction (Gillete's new razor, introduced in 1998, was a closely guarded secret in development for five years), hotels and restaurants do not have the same luxury. Construction time may

be as long as three to four years and is often preceded by publicity due to zoning changes, financial arrangements, and other events that must occur long before the actual opening. This is considered an advantage to the property because it is all free publicity.

Whereas goods manufacturers may work with only two or three months lead time to promote the introduction of their product, hotels seek two to three years of lead time and restaurants may use up to a year. For hotels this is because groups, conventions, corporate accounts, and others must be solicited well in advance of actual purchase and usage. Thus the property's marketing team arrives well in advance of the opening.

Introduction begins with a "soft" opening that may be a few days to a few weeks before the official opening. Word-of-mouth brings some customers, small groups (sometimes large ones) are booked, and various people, such as dignitaries, are invited to "test" the facility. This is the shakedown period, when management hopes to get a smooth operation going before the expected deluge.

Marketing's concern is very different with hospitality than with a manufactured good. The good has been built to specification and tested, so many units have been produced and distributed, and one hopes they will be sold. Hospitality marketers have a different problem. Instead of producing just so many units to be sold, they must produce on demand. They hope they can "handle the crowds," that the staff is trained and ready, that everything has been thought of, and that there are no major snafus. Chances are that the product is not even totally complete since construction never seems to finish quite on time, and not quite all the furniture and equipment ever arrives on time. Hospitality products depend on repeat purchases. Business may boom initially; the question is "Will they come back?"

In the marketing sense, initial hospitality customers are less innovators in the marketing sense than are new goods buyers, although initial hospitality customers may be more innovative with restaurants. More likely, people who try new hotels or restaurants are variety seekers who want to try something different and who may not be too willing to forgive when everything doesn't go right the first night. Also, competitors may be many and customers can always go back to where they came from. Switching costs are low.

The same factors apply, only to a lesser degree, to the introductory stage of a new cocktail lounge or restaurant concept. The lead times will be shorter, more publicity and advertising will be needed to create awareness, but the same concerns pertain. This is also true for a new service, menu item, or other smaller part of the product mix. Obviously, advance time is less, if it exists at all, and the risk is far lower, but the elements are the same.

The marketing objectives at this stage include creating product awareness, inducing trial, and establishing a position in the marketplace. When the property is part of a known chain this is easier to do than if it is an independent entity. However, brand name alone is insufficient to establish a firm position because of the often wide variations between properties, especially in the case of hotels. Research has shown that businesspeople, at least, judge far more by the individual property than by the chain name.

There is still a far more important marketing objective in the case of introducing the hospitality product; it points out the use of recognizing the stages of the product life cycle concept. It is critical and essential that, for a product to enter the growth stage, the customer must be persuaded in the introductory stage. Awareness and trial will come, relatively easily, through advance publicity, advertising, and word of mouth if the demand forecast is accurate. It is what happens to the customer during trial that determines the slope of the growth curve. Although selling and advertising to get new customers is important, it is secondary to the critical need for relationship marketing.

Consider a case in point. A new large hotel opened in Atlanta with existing ample competition and wholesale rate-cutting being practiced. The corporate office of the hotel company was so con-

vinced that they had a winner and that there would be a deluge to stay at the new hotel, that it issued orders not to offer discounts to get business. The sales staff was literally laughed at, and advance bookings remained minimal. After six months, corporate rescinded the order. The sales staff was laughed at again; they had alienated a major part of the market. The hotel survived because it was one of a large national chain with an excellent reputation, but millions of dollars in revenue had been lost in the process.

New product introductions rarely go perfectly, especially when they are major products such as a hotel or restaurant. This is the high-cost, low-profit stage of the life cycle. It is the stage when the customer has to be wooed and won at any cost. Failure to recognize this can be suicidal. Most of all, the emphasis must be on internal and relationship marketing.

The Growth Stage

Many newly developed manufactured goods, in fact most, fail in the introductory stage and never reach the growth stage. This is not as true in the hospitality world, where there is large investment capital. If a new menu item does not sell, of course, it can be discontinued with minimal loss. McDonald's twice pretested pizza in selected restaurants and withdrew it from the market when it did not receive a favorable reception. If the new product is a $50 million hotel or a $5 million restaurant, however, it is more difficult simply to "discontinue" it. Generally, the property will find a new owner who buys it at the right price and has pockets deep enough to ride out the slow growth period. It may also emerge in a new form such as condominiums. This has happened to numerous hotels such as the Mayfair Hotel in New York City. There is an old saying in the restaurant industry that it is the third owner who succeeds, having bought it at the right price after two failures. But even the high rate of restaurant failures occurs mostly in the growth stage.

The growth stage of a hospitality entity is one of

excitement and pitfalls. Sales may be growing monthly, there may not be enough seats in the restaurant, or the hotel may be filled on many nights. Customers who tried the facility in the introductory stage have told others who are now trying it. Business is booming, but there are many marketing issues at hand.

Survivors of the introductory stage will proceed into a period of growth—slow, rapid, or somewhere in between. It is during the growth stage that the previous relationship marketing pays off. Customers come back and they tell others. This is what the growth stage of a hospitality product is all about. Although, like goods, new customers are needed for rapid growth, the hospitality product depends far more on repeat customers. Good relationship marketing must, of course, continue. The hospitality customer is very fickle and management must be ever alert, unlike the management, in the following example, of the trendy new Aurora restaurant in New York City, which treated its customers haughtily, ignored complaints, and closed a few months after opening:

> "The trendy places take success for granted, and that hurts many of them eventually," says Paul Emmett, who manages Jake's Restaurant in New York. "You see places that were hot a year ago become lackadaisical, then sales drop precipitously and they fold."[7]

The growth stage is also the time of product refinement. Continuous customer research and feedback should result in both elimination of flaws and fine-tuning of the product to the target market. This is by no means a time to rest on one's laurels over the introductory stage having been a booming success. Products must be improved and ways must be found to serve the target markets better than ever before. A frequent mistake made with hospitality products is for management to assume that initial fast growth gives them automatic license to raise prices. In the short term, this means higher profits; in the long term, it can mean disaster; this is the time for building loyalty, not for gouging the customer.

Here are some of the tactical things that managements do to alienate the market after a successful introduction:

- Charge for coffee formerly included with the meal
- Raise prices of alcoholic beverages
- Raise prices of menu entrees that are selling well
- Create artificial price levels of guest room product, and restrict access to affordable accomodations during busy periods
- Stop taking reservations or fail to honor them on time
- Move tables closer together to get more people in
- Refuse to serve arrivals who come at closing time
- Not provide rooms requested
- Raise room rates
- Overbook and have to "walk" too many customers
- Dismiss complainants as a nuisance
- Overcharge for small extras or room service items
- Fail to honor special requests like bedboards

Consider the above list. It is operations that makes these decisions 99 times out of 100, but you can see that they are really marketing decisions. Every one affects the customer. It is poor management that would make such decisions without a marketing perspective. Once again, we repeat, hospitality management is inseparable from hospitality marketing. Typically, instead, while these decisions are being made, management is exhorting its salespeople to "get out there and get more customers." And, believe it or not, when decline comes the only question management can ask is, "What happened?" Many will answer, "Overbuilding," "Too much competition," "Everyone's going to Europe these days," or "They rerouted the highway."

The growth stage of a product is the time for fortification and consolidation. It is the time to plow back both money and good will, not take away; it is the time to sow not reap. It is the time to reward your good staff and to keep them enthusiastic and motivated. It is the time to listen to your customers and your employees for constant improvement of the product. It is the time to steal customers from the competition.

The marketing objectives at this stage are to solidify, to price for penetrating the market, and to keep customers. Every customer you keep at this stage will create other customers. This is the stage when you not only have to do things right; you also have to do the right things. This is the stage that will make or break the product. Finally, it is the time to start planning, if you haven't already, for extension of the mature stage.

The Mature Stage

The mature stage of the product life cycle, as we have already said, can continue for a long period of time. It can also end very abruptly. Once more, complacency is a bitter foe. If the product has successfully and correctly traversed the introductory and growth stages, the market should now be pretty well in place. The product's positioning should be established, its niche carved out, and its target market steady and loyal. There is a temptation at this stage to say, "We've got it made!" Nothing could be further from the truth. Never forget that fickle customer out there, the one who says, "What have you done for me lately?"

The characteristics of the mature stage are usually easy to diagnose—leveling off of sales levels, good repeat business, and general settling down of the operation. Things finally seem to be getting easier, but now is the time for marketing management to be at its best.

At the mature stage, the product sometimes begins to get a little frayed around the edges—not just the furniture, carpet, and drapes, but also the concept and the execution. All elements need refurbishing. Too frequently, management thinks that a face-lift is all that is needed, and then wonders why business continues to slip. Table 12-3 gives an example.

The example in Table 12-3 is a classic case of a management not understanding the ramifications of having reached the mature stage of its life cycle, of not having prepared for that stage, and of not taking the appropriate actions when it reached that stage. Even a customer research study showing that this hotel was perceived as the poorest in the city in its product class failed to daunt management. The hotel survived because of its size, location, and membership in a large chain, but it took years and new management to recover its former position.

In the mature stage of the product life cycle the product has to run harder just to stand still. Competition abounds, market segments have been tapped, and the product and product concept are old hat. The best defense at this stage is to have built the loyalty and fortification in the growth stage, but this alone will not be enough to contend with the newcomers on the block. One must also go on the offensive.

The best offenses are innovativeness, staying close to the customer, finding new markets, seeking and solving consumers' problems, and doing this better than the competition. McDonald's, for example, reached this stage around the mid-1970s. It developed the breakfast concept and Egg McMuffin. It researched its market to see what it could do better. It went overseas, into malls, office buildings, museums, and other unexpected places to find new markets. It developed new products, such as styrofoam take-out containers, to solve consumers' problems—and it did this all better than the competition.

You don't have to be a McDonald's to survive in the mature stage. You can be Joe's Bar and Grill down on the corner. The concepts, principles, and practices are the same; the difference is only a matter of scale. Sales growth slows down in this stage; that is to be expected. This is a maintenance stage, not a period of creating interest, but of maintaining it. This is a stage of developing new users and new uses, and new variations on the theme. It is a stage when product quality is paramount, and to slip now is to court disaster. This is a stage when customers have gotten to know us well and will not

T A B L E   12-3
The Mature Life Cycle Stage for a Hotel

Consider a 1400-room hotel in a large city, for years the largest hotel and the major convention property in town. Other chains started to move into the city with brand new state-of-the-art properties. Occupancy in this hotel began slipping. The corporate office's decision was to put $27 million into refurbishing the property. Instead of putting the money into meaningful renovations, two-thirds of the monies went into building a new exterior carriageway.

This hotel essentially had had the market to itself for a number of years with relatively little effort. It had stayed in the mature stage largely because there was no serious competition to stop it. It did need refurbishing, but probably could have done what was necessary for less than half the amount spent—but the condition of the property wasn't the real problem.

The real problem was that management didn't communicate with the customer. It virtually ignored complaints or dismissed them with trite responses. It was notorious for snafus at the front desk—lost reservations, overbooking and walking, putting people in rooms not made up, making people wait until 5:00 P.M. to get into a room, long lines and waiting, incredibly slow room service, lost telephone messages, overpricing, and other related problems.

The hotel also had waited too long for refurbishment because management thought it had a captive market. Instead of building customer loyalty at the right time, according to many who stayed there, the hotel seemed to delight in alienating customers even to the point of refusing such simple requests as to split a bill on two credit cards. One large group that occupied a very sizable block of rooms four times a year had been complaining for years, to no avail, about both the services and the prices. This group, for one, moved en masse as soon as another hotel opened that could handle it.

tolerate our blunders. This is the time to augment the product. This is the stage when Total Quality Management (TQM) proves itself. TQM is a classic example of the principle that, in services, management and marketing are the same.

If the product is not maintained during the mature stage, it will enter into the decline stage. In some cases, this is a natural and appropriate thing to happen when the product was a short-lived fad that has run its course. Menu items lose their freshness, tastes change, the customer changes, and it is time to go on to bigger and better things. When the product is something like a hard piece of real estate, however, the situation is somewhat different. To avoid decline, sooner or later the product must be reanalyzed, refurbished, renovated, reformatted, redesigned, repositioned, and/or remarketed. This is the time to reverse the curve before it heads south with abandon.

McDonald's did it with innovativeness and new markets. Burger King did it with head-on competitive advertising. Days Inn did it with new leadership. The Greenbriar and Homestead Resorts in West Virginia and Virginia did it by targeting con-

vention business instead of primarily the leisure market. Pinehurst Resort, in the golf capital of North Carolina, did it by repositioning from a golf resort to a family sport resort. Club Med is trying to do it by targeting families instead of singles and yuppies, as in the past.

Although all this may sound fairly easy, it is not. It takes real marketing leadership to know which way to go, to understand the market, and to take the risk involved. Often it demands a change in attitude, as with the case of the hotel discussed in Table 12-3. The main point is that the mature stage is the critical stage: Sooner or later it will end in decline if something isn't done, and done right.

The Decline Stage

Decline has a tendency to accelerate even faster than growth. Actually, some of the above examples of reversing the life cycle curve have occurred in, or very close to, the decline stage. Alert leadership does not wait that long; it knows when it is in the mature stage and that something has to be done. Even more alert leadership starts planning before it reaches the mature stage. We use the term decline stage here, then, to mean that the end is near. Although there may be a rebirth in some other form, for all intents and purposes the product, as we know it, is finished.

Howard Johnson's failed because it waited too long, couldn't change its attitude, was too solidified in a negative position, and didn't understand the customer. Its third owner has revitalized it. Victoria Station and Valle's Steak House failed because they waited too long, didn't understand what was happening, and didn't know what to do. Sambo's Restaurants failed because it took away management's incentive and didn't understand its employees. The company has now disappeared. Many restaurants fail simply because they allow product quality to slip. Some hotels fail because management thinks the way to survive, when the product slips and business declines, is to raise prices and cut costs. These responses only serve to grease the skids. Figure 12-4 shows a simple schematic of what can happen in the decline stage of the product life cycle, called the product **death spiral.**

Management, faced with declining revenues, takes the easiest course of action, reducing expenses. This is done by reducing the number of desk clerks, housekeepers, servers in the restaurant, telephone operators and others. Other reductions follow such as no new carpet for the ballroom, cheaper soap in the bathroom, and smaller shrimp on the menu. Customers begin to notice the decline in service and product. With so many options in the marketplace, they begin to go to competitors. The results are more revenue decline, resulting in more dissatisfied customers, resulting in further revenue declines. The product death spiral continues until someone finally wakes up and says, "Hey, let's do some marketing to bring in customers instead of cutting costs." Of course, by that time it may be too late.

Some products, of course, should die. They have lived their time and served their purpose. We may even push them into oblivion to make room for new products. Others, like many fast-food franchises of the 1960s and 1970s, simply become extinct. When demise is not natural, not anticipated, and not desired, however, marketing probably has not done its job.

LOCATING PRODUCTS IN THEIR LIFE CYCLES

How do you know what stage the product is in at any given point in time? Such an evaluation is highly subjective, prone to error due to irregularities in the S curve, and inconclusive. There are guidelines that, along with good management acumen, marketing leadership, and willingness to objectively accept reality, make determining the life cycle stage for hospitality products not as difficult as it might seem.

The first step in locating a product in its life cycle is to study its performance, competitive history, and current position and match this information with the characteristics of a particular stage of the life cycle. Past performance can be analyzed as follows:

- Sales growth and market share progression in comparison with the best fitting curve that one would expect for the particular product
- Alterations and enhancements that have to be made to the product
- Sales and profit history of similar, related, complementary, or comparable products
- Casualty history of similar products in the past

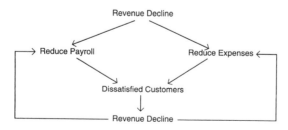

FIGURE 12-4 The product death spiral in the decline stage.

- Customer feedback
- Repeat and new business ratios (heavy repeat business with declining overall business is a sign of maturity or decline)
- Competitive growth and decline
- New competition and new concept introduction
- Number of competitors and their strengths/weaknesses
- Industry life cycle progressions
- Critical factors for success of the product

Current situations should be reviewed to gauge whether sales are on the upswing, have leveled out, or are heading down; whether any competitive products are moving up to replace the product under consideration; whether customers are becoming more demanding vis-à-vis price, service, or special features; whether additional sales efforts are necessary to keep the sales going up; and whether it is becoming harder to work through the distribution network.

Such an analysis is not a task for amateurs; managerial intuition and judgment are critical. As our thinking tends to be strongly tainted or biased after the fact, a wise move could be to develop a model, based on the above, prior to introduction of the product. The model will then serve as a yardstick for future measurement.

DEVELOPING NEW PRODUCT/SERVICES

It is clear by now that the development of a new product or service should start with customers' needs and wants and problems. This does not prohibit someone with a stroke of genius shouting, "Eureka, I've got it!" and coming up with just the right new idea that customers will love. It also does not necessarily mean that finding new ideas comes from asking customers what they want. In fact, research has long shown that customers are really not very good sources for new product ideas if we ask them directly. Customers have difficulty articulating just what it is they would like to have in a new product that they haven't seen. Nevertheless, it is around the customer that most new products should be developed.

Having said that, we hasten to add that this is often not the case in the hospitality industry. It is doubtful that anyone has ever asked customers whether they wanted a mint on their pillow or their bed turned down. If they had, of course, the reply would no doubt be a unanimous "Yes." Why not? It doesn't hurt, and it's "free."

When the bathroom amenities "war" started, no one asked customers what amenities they wanted; management made that decision. Since then, it is true, customers have been surveyed as to which ones they use. One company found, to no one's surprise, that soap is the most frequently used bathroom amenity. No one has yet scientifically determined, to our knowledge, which of the amenities people take and use at home.

When frequent traveler plans were developed, how often were customers asked what should be included? When a hotel is built how many ask customers how they "use" it? (Actually, today, some chains do ask.) How often is the market asked what items it would like to see on a menu? (Some restaurant chains do ask.) Or how it would prefer the seating and lighting in a restaurant? Or whether it really likes that loud music or blaring TV in the lounge (often the preference of the employees who work there), especially when the lounge is empty most of the time?[8]

The point of all these questions is to emphasize that too many new hospitality products originate from the mind of someone other than the customer—yet their purpose is usually to enhance the product, increase satisfaction, create and keep a customer, and generally to fulfill the customer's needs and wants. With these objectives, the customer should be consulted more often. There is, however, a definite emerging trend with more and more companies conducting consumer research.

Those operators who do, in fact, introduce successful new products are usually those who have based the product on solving consumers' problems. Adding a sports bar to some hotels was a

FIGURE 12-5   Ibis demonstrates the relationship between product and need.

trend of the early 1990s; it separated those who wanted to watch sports on TV from those who didn't and were annoyed by it. Champions was introduced at the Marriot Copley Place in Boston, and was copied by other Marriots and convention hotels throughout the United States. No-smoking sections came from an obvious consumer problem even though, in most cases, it had to be mandated by law before restaurants would offer a solution. All-suite hotels came from consumers' problems of where to stay on extended stays. Directories in hotel rooms came from problems of wanting information, and keyless door locks came from consumers' problems with security.

But mints on pillows, turndown service, the extravagance of bathroom amenities, and TVs in bathrooms (but not telephones) were ideas that originated from management. As we have noted, the worst part of this kind of product development

is that once the competition does the same thing, the differential advantage is lost, and what remains is a higher cost structure.

What we are saying is not that a new or improved product should not be developed to try and gain a marketing edge and differentiate from the competition. What we are saying is that products and services should be developed for the purpose of creating and keeping a customer and that, if you are in the new product development game, the best place to start is with customer needs. Figure 12-5 demonstrates this point. Table 12-4 provides a question checklist for evaluating new products.

What Succeeds?

Many new products fail, as we have previously said. What about those that succeed? Researchers have

TABLE 12-4
Checklist for New Product Appraisal

Question	Best Response	Worst Response
Is it compatible with current product line?	Complements and reinforces	No fit, will hurt present line
Do we have know-how and appropriate skills?	Can handle with minimal training	Will need new staff and training
Will it be stable?	Will always have high use	Fad—short-lived
Will target market grow?	Increasing demand	Declining
Size of target market?	Large, only need small share	Not large enough to support
Can we reach target market?	Easily	Difficult, expensive
Communication efforts?	Easy, present channels	Difficult
Price/value?	Excellent	Difficult to sell
Versus competition?	Clear advantage	No advantage
Loyalty impact?	High	One shot, no repeat
Differentiation	Original, fills need	No distinctive advantage
Copy possibilities?	Unique to us, difficult to copy	Would be copied immediately
Market life?	Long	Quick obsolescence
Customer acceptance?	Eager	Nil
Marketing ease?	Easily advertised, sold, promoted	No promotable advantages
Measure of success	Dollar and customer increases	Hard to tell
Capital available?	No problem	Will be costly
Continuing costs?	Minimal	High
ROI?	High	Minimal
Profit margin?	High	Minimal
Contribution margin?	High	Minimal

found the following factors most likely to be associated with successful new products:

- The ability to identify customer needs
- Use of existing company know-how and resources
- Development of new products in the company's core markets
- Measurement of performance during the development stage
- Screening and testing of ideas before money is spent on development
- Coordination between research and development and marketing
- An organizational environment that encourages entrepreneurship and risk-taking
- Linking new product development to corporate goals

New product development is a total company effort. Successful new products very often come from the bottom up rather than the top down. This is especially true in the hospitality business, because it is the bottom line of employees that is closest to the customer. It is often these people who can best tell you what the customer's problems are. Of course, you can always ask customers as well; do not ask what they would like to see, but what their problems are. Marriott Suites Hotel in Downers Grove, IL, has a General Manager's breakfast twice a week. Ten guests are treated to a complimentary buffet. Each is asked to bring questions and concerns of the hotel operation to discuss.

SUMMARY

The marketing mix consists of various activities directed toward the customer. Most day-to-day marketing efforts take place in the implementation of this stage of the marketing effort. The importance of the marketing mix is evident in the marketing of any good or service. Because of this, Borden's original marketing mix and McCarthy's popularization of it have made the Four Ps common terms in the language of marketers. The Four Ps have survived for many years and it has been difficult for marketers to break away from this constraint in terms of marketing services. Renaghan, however, has shown that traditional marketing-mix concepts have limited utility for hospitality marketers because they reflect strategies for marketing goods and ignore the unique complexities of marketing hospitality services.

The product/service mix represents what the hospitality firm has to offer to the consumer, both tangible and intangible, both "free" and for sale. The product/service mix drives the other elements of the marketing mix; in some cases it may even drive the strategy of the firm. Accordingly, it is not just the marketer's job to "sell" the product/service. More important, it is the marketer's job to design in accordance with the needs and wants of the target markets.

A product/service has three elements: the formal element, the core element, and the augmented element. These elements are closely related to the concepts of salience, determinance, and importance discussed in Chapter 11. The astute marketer will develop products/services with these relationships in mind.

The product life cycle is concerned with the various stages of a product's growth in the marketplace. The best use of the product life cycle is not so much to predict the future, but to recognize its existence and preplan for it, and to recognize the product's present stage and the appropriate actions necessary.

Product innovation is a characteristic of marketing leadership. The place to look for new product ideas is in consumers' problems. Too many new products are designed without considering the customer's real needs.

KEY WORDS AND CONCEPTS

Augmented Product: The totality of all benefits received or experienced by the customer.

Communications Mix: All communications between the firm and the target market that increase the tangibility of the product/service mix, that establish or monitor consumer expectations, or that persuade consumers to purchase.

Core Product: What the customer is really buying (see Formal Product).

Customized Products: Customized products are designed to fit the specific needs of a particular target market.

Death Spiral: The spiral of cutting back on costs, leading to less business, leading to more cost cutting.

Distribution Mix: All channels available between the firm and the target market that increase the probability of getting the customer to the product.

Formal Product: What the customers think they are buying (see Core Product).

Four Ps: A term applied to a common marketing mix for goods: product, price, place, and promotion.

Presentation Mix: All of the elements used by the firm to increase the tangibility of the product/service mix in the perception of the target market at the right place and time.

Pricing Mix: The combination of prices that consumers pay for a product/service.

Product Life Cycle (PLC): A product goes through several stages during its lifetime. These stages are introduction, growth, maturity, and decline.

Product/Service Mix: The combination of products and services, whether free or for sale, that are aimed at satisfying the needs of the target market.

Standard Product: Products that appear similar and standard to the customer, albeit in different locations.

Standard Product with Modifications: A product that has been embellished with new elements but the basic product remains essentially the same.

What It Does for the Customer: The absolute critical test of a product fulfilling customer needs and wants and solving problems.

DISCUSSION QUESTIONS

1. Discuss the virtues of the hospitality marketing mix against those of the Four Ps. Do you think, as some do, that the Four Ps are adequate for the hospitality market? Argue why they are or are not.
2. List the formal, core, and augmented products of an all-inclusive resort hotel in the Caribbean.
3. Give examples of various hospitality products that are in various stages of the product life cycle. How do you define which stage they are in? What specific implications does this have for marketing them?
4. Discuss the following: Hospitality customers really have no choice in product determination. They can't articulate what they want until they have it. Therefore, there really is no alternative but to determine the product for them.
5. Consider a common customer complaint—for instance, waiting for the elevator, waiting at the front desk, hearing the telephone ring 15 times before the operator answers. Develop a new

"product/service" that is economically feasible to solve these customers' problems.
6. Which part of the hospitality product is most important to the customer—the tangible or the intangible? Discuss.

GROUP PROJECTS

1. Analyze the product/service mix at a local establishment. Does it fulfill the criteria outlined in the chapter? How? How not?
2. Develop a new product/service for a hotel or restaurant and match it against the criteria in Table 12-4.

REFERENCES

1. Neil Borden, "The Concept of the Marketing Mix," *Journal of Advertising Research,* June 1964, pp. 2–7.
2. E. Jerome McCarthy, *Basic Marketing: A Managerial Approach.* Homewood, IL: Richard D. Irwin, 1975, pp. 75–80.
3. Leo M. Renaghan, "A New Marketing Mix for the Hospitality Industry," *Cornell Hotel and Restaurant Administration Quarterly,* April 1981, pp. 31–35. The definitions that follow are adapted from Renaghan.
4. Stanley Turkel, Hotel Consultant, 10 Rockefeller Plaza, Twelfth Floor, New York, NY 10020.
5. Theodore A. Levitt, "The Globalization of Markets," *Harvard Business Review,* May/June 1983, pp. 92–102.
6. Subhash C. Jain, *International Marketing Management.* Boston: Kent Publishing, 1984, p. 345.
7. Kathleen A. Hughes and Laura Landro, "A Lot of Restaurants Now Serve Rudeness with the Rigatoni," *The Wall Street Journal,* November 12, 1986, p. 22.
8. An insight into new product development in restaurants, as well as an excerpt on the development of Courtyard by Marriott, can be found in Tom Feltenstein, "New-Product Development in Food Service: A Structured Approach," *Cornell Hotel and Restaurant Administration Quarterly,* November 1986, pp. 63–71.

Thirteen

◆

THE HOSPITALITY PRESENTATION MIX

Overview

The hospitality presentation mix is what the customer perceives, as opposed to what he or she gets. It includes the headings listed below. This chapter discusses each one in turn.

PHYSICAL PLANT   The physical plant is a tangible package that makes a statement to the market.

LOCATION   A salient attribute but not necessarily a determinant one.

ATMOSPHERICS   A critical force in how customers feel about a property.

EMPLOYEES   In hospitality, employees are both part of the product and part of the presentation.

CUSTOMERS   Who they are and what they do is part of the presentation mix.

PRICES   The most visible and flexible part of the presentation mix.

◆

The second part of the hospitality marketing mix is the presentation mix. It is helpful to repeat the definition given in Chapter 12: *All elements used by the firm to increase the tangibility of the product/service mix in the perception of the target market at the right place and time.* There are some places, of course, where the presentation mix will overlap with the product/service mix as the two are very complementary. Once we understand the mind and the decision-making process of the hospitality customer, we can see why the presentation mix is such an important tool in marketing. This chapter proceeds with that understanding and considers the six elements of the presentation mix: physical plant, location, atmospherics, employees, customers, and price.

PHYSICAL PLANT

The term **physical plant** represents everything physical and quickly perceptible to the senses in the hospitality property. It is bricks and mortar, marble columns, potted plants, wallpaper and paint, flowers, gardens, sand urns, and a vast multitude of other things. It is also how it "works," that is, how it makes life easier for the customer. That should make life easy for us; all we have to do is hire a good architect and a good interior designer, and the problem takes care of itself.

What is so easy to forget is that all of this must begin with the customer. Did you ever inspect a factory before you bought the stereo produced there? Did you care what the factory looked like after you bought the stereo? Do you suppose the marketing department of the stereo company was consulted before building the plant? Why not? Because, of course, it has nothing to do with the customer.

Does this mean stereos are built without regard to the customer? Again, no; knowledge of what the target market wants in a stereo is taken back to the design team and the engineers. The stereo is built. If the research was well done, the marketing team can now take over. The job is relatively easy because the product has been built to the desired specifications. All that is needed now is basic traditional marketing and assurance to customers that this stereo does what they want better than the competition's. But because sound also cannot be seen, even the stereo company has to do some tangibilizing to create expectation and reduce risk. This is done with packaging. In the final analysis, however, the customer listens to the stereo, and

judges by the sound before buying. In hospitality things are different.

Developing the Physical Plant Package

The physical plant element of the hospitality presentation mix is nothing more than packaging, only in this case the customer has to largely consume and judge after buying. Packaging helps in attracting and creating the customer, and good packaging will help to bring the customer back; this is nontraditional marketing.

There are numerous examples of what we are saying. Atrium lobbies, elegant chandeliers, luxurious bathrooms are all statements about a property and are tangible entities in the presentation mix. (So, too, are dingy lobbies, burned out light bulbs, chipped columns, and stained sinks.) Rarely are these decisions based directly on consumer needs and wants, nor would it be too feasible if they were. For example, we would never be able, even if consumers had the knowledge, to get a consumer consensus on the appropriate chandelier, or wallpaper. We have little choice but to rely on the expertise of architects and designers for these decisions. Their judgments, in turn, are often strongly influenced by the owner's or executive officers' "gut feeling" and personal likes and dislikes.

When this happens, the consumer sometimes gets left out. Marketing plays little if any direct part in the physical plant decisions but is left with the job of selling the property in order to pay for the cost of those decisions. Sometimes management gets an **edifice complex.** It is little wonder that a product orientation often develops.

Although it is not feasible to ask customers to make all these decisions, it is feasible to ask, "What will this do for the customer? How will the customer use this property? What kind of tangible presentation does this make of what our product really is?" The principles are the same for a luxury hotel, a budget property, a pizza parlor, or a McDonald's. Some examples of failures to ask these questions are given in Table 13-1.

There are, of course, thousands of examples of

TABLE 13-1
Examples of Poor Physical Plant Presentation

- A relatively new hotel in a major U.S. city has a beautiful lobby and two-story waterfall. So as not to impose on the aesthetic sense, the front desk was tucked into a corner on the second floor. What did the lobby and waterfall tangibilize for the new customer who spent five to ten minutes wandering around trying to find the front desk?
- Another new hotel in the same city has rooms with wall-to-wall windows covered by expensive drapes about two inches too narrow. If the drapes are closed in the middle, they leave a narrow slit on the ends, and vice versa. If you had a room on the east side on a sunny morning you never had to leave a wake-up call.
- There are still any number of hotels targeting the business market that have desks in the rooms hardly large enough for two pads of paper, never mind the telephone, a lamp (often with a low-watt bulb), and other paraphernalia.
- Targeting the weekend market, a new upscale hotel in Toronto had only one comfortable chair in each room. When queried, the general manager said, "That was a big mistake. Now we're trying to find the money to buy the chairs."
- A real-estate developer decided to get into the hotel business. He bought a 300-room resort that was in the decline stage of its product life cycle, with plans to refurbish it. As sometimes happens, his wife became the interior designer and set up three beautifully refurbished rooms as prototypes. No one stopped to think how the guest would use the room. Here were some of the problems:
  - The television was hidden in the bottom level of a console across from the end of the bed. It was impossible to lie in bed and see the television.
  - The exquisite bedside lamps were about a foot tall. It was impossible to read in bed without leaning over the side to get enough light.
  - The bed headboards were covered with a fine satin that absorbed hair stains, giving the appearance of uncleanliness.

the physical plant elements making a positive presentation: lobbies, dining rooms, spacious seating, room arrangements, grounds, decor, space, lobby cocktail lounges, and so forth. What we have cited in Table 13-1 are design failures that created customer problems rather than solve them, the kinds of things we want to avoid.

The physical plant is an integral part of nontraditional marketing. When it "works," it makes a strong and positive statement about the property and the product it has to offer. When it doesn't work, it makes the opposite statement—in fact, it becomes a major source of customer complaints. Marketing should be involved in initial management decisions; management should be practicing marketing in subsequent operational decisions. There are always two lines of inquiry to be considered:

1. What statement does the physical plant make to the target market—that is, how does it tangibi-

lize the core product? Will it help to create customers?
2. How does/will the customer use it—in other words, does it solve problems? Will it keep customers?

Pursuing these two lines of inquiry, we should make note that physical plants do not necessarily always have to be top drawer facilities. A physical plant can also say to the right target market, "Relax, don't worry; throw your peanut shells and your cigarette butts on the floor."

Consider the example of Caneel Bay, a very successful resort in the Virgin Islands, where room rates are over $500 per night. The resort sits on land that is now part of a national park and its core product is peace, quiet, prestige, and total relaxation. The physical plant consists of mostly one or two storied units that blend in with the environment, with the 168 units spread out over 170 acres. The rooms are very simply, but elegantly, decorated and, surprisingly, do not have any air-conditioning, radios, television, or telephones. Peace, quiet and relaxation is effectively tangibilized. The resort solves the problems of the mostly urban, highly successful professionals who lead hectic lives and need a place to get away from it all.

LOCATION

Location is a limited but useful element of the presentation mix. Its limitation lies in three factors.

First, location is inflexible once the property has been erected. A hotel is on the beach or it isn't.

Second, location is a minimum threshold attribute. By this we mean that location is in a somewhat black-or-white category with little gray in between. If the location is desirable, it then becomes secondary as a determinant or important factor, and other factors take over in the decision process. If the location is not desirable, other attributes may have little meaning.

The third limitation of location is that it tangibilizes only one attribute of the product—namely, convenience. There is no other reason for location to be a determinant factor in choosing a hotel or restaurant.* In spite of these limitations, location plays a major role in the minds of many hospitality marketers as well as hospitality customers. Exploring why this is so will provide some insight into the use of location in the presentation mix.

Location's Role

The major role of **location** for hospitality customers derives from its salient nature. As we have previously noted, almost any survey will show location as one of the most frequently mentioned attributes in choosing a hotel or restaurant. This response is strongly related to the tangible nature of location as well as its salience. When we think of choosing a restaurant or of staying in a city away from home, we immediately think of what is most convenient. (If we do not, such as wanting to go to a particular restaurant wherever it is, then location is a nonfactor.) Location tends, in many cases, to become the first consideration. Whether it is the final consideration depends on two factors. First, customers look at what else is available in relatively the same location. Second, the customers examine any other criteria that are important to them. Research has shown that when a number of different variables are considered at the same time in relation to each other, location is a less important variable.

The most important use of location in marketing is obviously in its initial selection relevant to target markets and competition. To build a hotel or restaurant where no one ever goes would not be too wise unless, of course, one could then get people to go there. Some years ago no one went to Cancún, Mexico, because there was nothing there but a large sandbar. Today, after a massive concentrated effort, there are thousands of hotel rooms and accompanying facilities, and Cancún is a major destination area for those who like to frolic in the sun and sand. Cancún, however, does have a location advantage. It is attractive to Americans because it is not too far or "too" foreign.

On the other hand, very few would ever go to Hot Springs, Virginia, or White Sulphur Springs, West Virginia, except for the hotels that are there, The Homestead and The Greenbriar, respectively. It is true that both hotels are in beautiful country settings, but it is also true that there are many other beautiful country settings in that part of the country. People go there specifically because of The Homestead and The Greenbriar; in other words, location is not a strong tangible presentation of convenience for these hotels.

A similar but converse situation is the Banff Springs Hotel in the Rocky Mountains in Alberta,

---

*There are, of course, exceptions to this rule. A location may be quite inconvenient but still be desirable as regards privacy, seclusion, vista, prestige, or other intangible elements. (An example is Caneel Bay, cited above.) This, however, falls outside the comon usage of the word location. We use the word here in its more common usage.

Canada. This hotel is also in beautiful countryside and people go to Banff because of that feature. While there, they stay at the Banff Springs Hotel because it is there. For the Banff Springs Hotel, location is a strong tangible presentation of convenience.

These examples are given to demonstrate the increasing or diminishing importance of location. Location today has been strongly affected by modern methods of transportation. Because of major expansion of air travel, for example, very few destination locations at this time can be considered "bad," as far as reaching them is concerned. While some are clearly more desirable, modern transportation has diminished location's importance.

The same thing applies within a city. Few go to the Millennium Hilton Hotel in New York City for reasons other than its being the only deluxe hotel in the Wall Street area. Those who go to the Waldorf-Astoria on Park Avenue, however, have many other choices and choose the Waldorf for reasons other than location. In fact, some of them endure the long taxi ride to Wall Street by choice.*

We have a similar situation with restaurants. Like car dealerships, fast-food restaurants tend to cluster on so-called fast-food rows. These rows are where the heavy traffic is and where the target markets for these restaurants prevail. Location is critical for fast-food restaurants because of the need for population density, which is why so many of them group together, giving the fast-food customer a choice in the same area. Many contend that all the good fast-food locations in the United States are now gone. Paradoxically, once established, location has little marketing value for a fast-food restaurant, and one rarely sees it emphasized in their advertising. Starbucks Coffee, on the other hand, in

its fast expansion surge, went into a new location, identified the thriving properties, and rented prime space just down the street.

Upscale restaurants face a different situation. To locate on fast-food row would probably be the kiss of death. Remoteness can well be an asset for these restaurants. In fact, there are many successful ones in the world in small towns that make this their claim to fame. Many upscale restaurants strive to be a destination in themselves. Durgin Park Restaurant in Boston was famous as a restaurant long before the development of the Faneuil Hall area as a major tourist attraction near it. One of the authors remembers vividly being brought there by his grandfather in the 1960s, when the area was run down and unsafe. The restaurant was always full, despite its poor location. Now the restaurant is still full and has a superior location.

One of the most successful restaurants in the United States is Anthony's Pier 4 in Boston ("You haven't been to Boston if you haven't been to Anthony's"). Although it is on the waterfront, that factor has little appeal once you are inside. When you finally get to your table, after enduring the long wait, you find yourself elbow to elbow with hundreds of others. Anthony's is also not that easy to get to from downtown Boston, with constant construction on the major throughway in the center of the city. Once there, the customer finds the restaurant is situated among several abandoned warehouses. There are better restaurants in Boston with lower prices, better atmosphere, easier to find locations, and shorter taxi rides. Is location an important attribute for Anthony's? Not at all. Its target market doesn't much care where the restaurant is.

Location as a Marketing Tool

Let us go back now to the three limitations of location in the presentation mix to see when and how location can be an important attribute.

We said, first, that location is inflexible. This means that marketing must enter into the decision process at the first step, which, once decided, is unchangeable. The importance of the decision at this

---

*At the same time, there is another location aspect that may be important only because it exists in the consumer's mind. For example, hotels in New York City may sell a location advantage as little as two blocks apart. A hotel on the east side of town traditionally commands higher room rates than those of comparable quality on the west side. It is unimportant that the east and west sides are separated by a street only 150 feet wide.

FIGURE 13-1   Manapany and Little Dix Bay position their remoteness as a location advantage.

stage is directly related to the target market. The presentation element comes in "being there." As we have said in the case of fast-food operators, it would be of little use for them to promote location, but being in the right location itself makes the tangible presentation of convenience.

For the Banff Springs Hotel the situation is reversed. Its major attraction is its location. Thus the location becomes the tangible presentation of the product/service, is a very important factor in its promotion, and should be used as a marketing tool. This is also true of remote island resort hotels that are located in areas of great natural beauty, as seen in Figure 13-1.

The second limitation is that of minimum threshold. This limitation is more relevant to immediate competition. If you have a motel in North Overshoe, Maine, and the next nearest motel is 25 miles away, and your market wants to do business in North Overshoe, it may not matter too much what else you do. Location is your major asset and possibly the sole criterion in the choice of your motel—that is, it is a determinant attribute.

On the other hand, a hotel in Boston faces a dif-

ferent situation. Like business travelers in North Overshoe, people who go to Boston to do business in the downtown area also don't want to stay at a hotel 25 miles away. Given, however, that there are 20 plus hotels within a 20-block radius, any hotel in that area has passed the minimum threshold; for most it is "close enough." Location is salient but not determinant. This does not mean that if, for example, you intended to do business in the Prudential Center, it wouldn't be most convenient for you to stay at the Sheraton next door, or that you wouldn't prefer to do that. It means that you would introduce other, more determinant, criteria in making your choice. In such cases, where competition possesses relatively the same location, location goes from being salient to being minimally determinant in the choice process.

The third limitation of location is its singular tangible presentation of the attribute of convenience. To turn this to advantage, we again must examine the target market. If convenience is a determinant attribute for the target market, location should be stressed; otherwise, it has little appeal. But, if numerous other properties are similarly convenient, other determinant factors must also be stressed.

Location is a significant but sometimes overrated variable in hospitality marketing. While salient, it has limited use. Hospitality customers today have both many other choices and many other reasons for choosing a property. The strength of location in the presentation mix—the tangibilization of the product—lies in knowing when and how to use it in marketing.

ATMOSPHERICS

The third element of the presentation mix is a powerful one. Most of us are fully aware of this element—we often say that we like or don't like the **atmosphere** somewhere. Atmosphere is a quality of the immediate environment that is recognized by all the senses except taste, although taste can be influenced by the other senses. Thus wine or food may seem to taste better when other atmospheric dimensions are positive.

Atmosphere constitutes a sensory experience. This is done in a number of ways. Visual sense is influenced by color, light, size, and shape. Hearing sense is influenced by volume and pitch, smelling sense by scent, and feeling sense by texture and temperature. Atmospherics is often one element of the bundle that customers buy. It is often the atmospherics that tangibilize all those intangible benefits that are sought—comfort, good feeling, excitement, serenity, contentment, romance, or any number of others. If atmosphere is not part of the core product that consumers buy, it can at least greatly influence the purchase decision. Marketers can use atmospherics as consciously and skillfully as they use other tools of marketing.

Atmospherics as a Marketing Tool

Atmospherics should have an emotional effect on buyers that will increase the likelihood of purchase. The hospitality customer learns to expect certain atmospheric conditions and often makes a purchase decision based on those expectations. A convention hotel is crowded, noisy, and boisterous; avoid it for a quiet weekend. A certain restaurant is dark and quiet, another is bright and happy. The task for the marketer is to create the atmosphere that it is hoped will be perceived.

This is not as easy as it may sound, if only because of the individuality of customers. Many people will not equate the intended atmosphere with the perceived atmosphere simply because we all react differently to lighting, colors, sounds, and temperatures. The dimly lit restaurant is romantic for a young couple; for an older couple it makes reading the menu difficult. The finely decorated restaurant is elegant for some; for others, it looks too expensive. The large hotel is "where things happen" for some; for others it is noisy and intimidating. The more heterogeneous the customers, the more varied their perceptions will be. Selecting and knowing target markets that are compatible become critical in this situation.

There are a number of situations where atmospherics can be particularly important as a marketing tool. The following pertain especially to hospitality establishments.

1. In situations where the product is purchased and consumed on premise
2. In situations where the seller has numerous design options
3. In situations where atmospherics help to create or increase the buyer's rate of consumption
4. In situations where there are a number of competitors, and atmospherics can be used to differentiate the product
5. In situations where the objective is to attract and hold a particular target market segment
6. In situations where product and price differences are small for products that are very similar
7. In situations where one wants to create a price difference for products that are very similar

Probably nowhere else in the presentation mix

does a hospitality marketer have as much ability to manipulate tangible clues. The decor in a hotel creates perceptions as to the kind of the hotel. The Mirage Hotel in Las Vegas uses atmospherics as a major differentiating feature in the following message in its ads geared toward meeting planners:

> Undoubtedly, people are influenced by the location of your meeting. What you call distractions, they call attractions. And the Mirage has plenty of them. Here, they can wander through our tropical rainforest to the most elegant casino on the strip. Visit our white tigers, sharks or dolphins. . . . Or just relax near waterfall, poolside. All between your meetings, of course.

Thus atmospherics can be used to get attention, create retention, and manipulate perception. Accordingly, atmospherics are a message creating medium by which marketers say certain things about the establishment. By this means they can communicate to the target market what they intend to offer. They can differentiate from other establishments. Affective states are enhanced by arousing sensations that create a desire for goods, services, and experiences. In this role, atmospherics help to convert behavioral intentions into actual buying behavior.

Over approximately the last 25 years there has been a greater emphasis on atmospherics in restaurants. Before that, restaurants tended to be quite plain and basic in their decor. Emphasis was on prices and the quality of food. It still is in many countries. There is no doubt that today, given a moderate level of food quality and the right price range, that atmosphere can often make or break a restaurant in many locations. Even institutional dining rooms have been caught up in the trend and few now look like the army dining halls they used to resemble.

There is a very important warning here, however. Restaurants' atmospheres are likely to have a very fast growth period, early maturity, and quick decline. "Fern bars" (loaded with ferns just as the name implies), for example, which were extremely popular in the 1980s, are largely moribund in their life cycle. The public is extremely fickle in this respect and today's "in" decor is tomorrow's "out" decor. Most vulnerable seem to be those restaurants that are also called theme, or even atmosphere, restaurants in which the decor follows a particular theme such as Nautical, Western, or early American. Similarly, the latest big trend, now in decline, are what are called "eatertainment" restaurants like Rainforest Cafe, Harley Davidson Cafe, and Planet Hollywood.

Atmospheres must be continually reevaluated in relation to the changing market, new possibilities, and competitive developments. Effectiveness also declines because of imitation or changing styles. Management must be constantly alert to the need for refreshing or revising atmospheres. Using atmosphere as a marketing tool for restaurants thus becomes a tricky proposition.

Atmosphere Planning

There are numerous other facets of atmospherics that the reader should have no problem identifying, including music, color, lighting, and design. We need, however, to take a more general approach to discussing the marketing elements of atmosphere planning.

If atmospherics play an important role in the buying process, then we need to apply the same regimen to their planning that we would to any other consumer behavior process. What atmospherics do, of course, is create a feeling; that is, the best atmosphere is one that makes the customer "feel good" in a particular environment. Feeling good can take on many dimensions depending on the purpose and the use—for instance, it can mean exciting, romantic, or relaxed. Our first criterion, then, as usual, is to recognize who the target market is, for example:

> What is the target market seeking from the buying experience?
> What atmospheric variables can fortify the beliefs and emotional reactions the buyers are seeking?

Will the resulting atmosphere compete effectively with competitors' atmospheres?

These are necessary questions but not easy ones to answer. It is often for lack of answers to these questions that some "great" atmospheres fail—that is, atmospheres considered "great" by the owner or management, the architect, the designer, and often their spouses and friends. But somehow they don't capture the right feeling, create the right emotional reactions, or compete effectively with the competition. Also, a "failed" atmosphere just may not suit the target market—not an excusable mistake given today's marketing consciousness. Probably the most frequent reason for this occurring is that marketers had minimum input into the decision and/or no one took time to fully analyze the target market. As in any type of marketing planning, the more homogeneous the target market, the easier it will be to design the appropriate atmosphere.

Restaurants can be very different in their food and finesse, but design problems "are overwhelmingly similar," say Susan Davidson and David Schultz, owners of DAS Architects Inc., Philadelphia. They identify ten common pitfalls: inconsistent ambience, too many designers, a poorly defined target market, improper spacing of tables, greedy use of space, inefficient traffic patterns, poor lighting, unrealistic budgets, offensive colors, and a lack of provision for growth. As for color, orange enhances appetites; red, brown, pink, and other warm colors make diners look their best. The biggest flaw they see when dining out? "Bad lighting."[1]

Pretesting and Research. It would be nice if one could construct an "atmosphere" and pretest it on the target market. Although scale models are recommended, they are not overly effective for pretests simply because one has to live with an atmosphere in order to experience it realistically. Hospitality customers are not just buying, they are also consuming on-premises. "Living" with an atmosphere for two or more hours can provoke very different reactions than those from simply walking in and out. After a period of time, noise can seem louder, colors can be annoying, and decor can be distracting. Thus one must recognize what experience the customer is seeking not only immediately, but over a period of time. It must also be recognized that emotional reactions can change over the same period of time.

Homestead Villages, a limited-service extended-stay hotel company, has a full design shop at their headquarters in Altanta, Georgia. Customers are researched, then model rooms are constructed for the customers to use and critique the layout of the rooms and amenities. Presenting a new atmosphere should be followed by immediate research on customer reaction, rather than waiting until the concept has failed. Small changes, such as lighting or sound, can often turn a disaster into a triumph.

In one example, a restaurant chain hired a research firm to survey its customers before and after a major change in decor. The research firm planned to conduct the "after" survey in the first two months after the work was completed. The chain's management, however, disagreed and said, "Let's wait six months and let them get used to it." Of course, by that time the people who liked the change would still be there, those who didn't like it would be long gone, and the research would have lesser value.

Atmospherics, needless to say, are greatly, but not always, influenced by local mores and traditions in international locations. Amazingly enough, there are still properties like a Holiday Inn in Kuala Lumpur, Malaysia, where one could easily believe he was in a Holiday Inn in Des Moines, Iowa. Consider, instead, the case of Forte's Grand Hotel in Abu Dhabi, opened in the 1990s: This hotel entered a well-established market of international hotel chains and independents. It used the presentation mix to get an edge in the market. The Forte Grand is the tallest building in the city and easily spotted on the road from the airport. Its design is unmistakable—a lean ellipse of sheer blue glass. The local market in Abu Dhabi is important because government laws allow alcoholic licenses only in hotel outlets. Consequently, hotels compete to attract local residents as well as international travelers.

The designer arrived at a feel that is understated European with the opulence of Arabian motifs and furnishings. The lobby reflects the local tradition of *majlis*—an open meeting place—with Arabic seating areas on a sweep of marble. The overall effect is one of clear coolness, [important in a climate that can reach daytime temperatures of 110 F (43 C) and 100% humidity]. All bedrooms have natural lighting, a sea view, and a comfortable window seat spanning an arc of glass.[2]

Atmosphere is always a factor in a hospitality purchase situation, whether it be at the local pub, a ski lodge, or a resort in the Caribbean. It is not only a presentation of the offering but also a powerful competitive tool. More research is needed to understand just how different atmospheric elements work and what messages they communicate. Atmospherics call for conscious, not casual, planning because they represent tremendous potential for differential advantage when there are few other ways to achieve it. Figure 13-2 shows one of many companies that specializes in creating atmospheric settings for hotels.

EMPLOYEES

It is more than obvious that **employees** are an important part of the presentation mix. In some cases they may be the most important part. The hospitality industry is one in which management, the entire property, the service, and the quality of the product can be judged in the consumer's mind by employee contact, sometimes even by a single incident.

The initial tangibilization is in the presentation itself—the appearance of employees. This is usually paramount. Customers arriving at the front door of an establishment are no longer looking at the architectural design. What they see is the employees who greet them: the doorman, parking valet, bellhop, desk clerk, host or hostess, waiter or waitress.

On the other hand, as with the physical plant and atmospherics, there are many times when the staff's being well groomed not only is unnecessary but also is not expected. A guest at a budget property doesn't really expect to see a uniformed person behind the desk who might, in fact, be the franchisee. A family-run neighborhood restaurant gains much of its charm from family members working in various forms of dress. Today, in fact, casualness seems to be "in" in many places. Tangibilization sets no standards; it simply implies the presentation, in whatever form, of the desired product to the target market.

What this means is that employees should "fit" the presentation mix. For example, a French brasserie, in a New York City hotel, formerly a coffee shop, was staffed with 15-year veteran union coffee shop employees. The result: surly waiters posing in the "brasserie" model of service. The staff didn't fit the concept or the intended market.

These people immediately became, if only temporarily, the product itself. They are the physical manifestation of what the establishment has to offer. Most people accept this premise. What many don't realize is that it is not just that employees should "look good," it is also that they are part of the marketing team, and this means they should also "look right." Looked at this way, employee appearance takes on a slightly different perspective and should receive more attention than it does in some cases.

What about casual or noncontact employees such as maids, engineers, servicepeople, maintenance workers, chefs and cooks, and so forth? How does their presentation affect the tangibilization of the product? Consider the following analogy.

Few airline passengers see the cockpit crew except for a goodbye when deplaning or when walking through the terminal. The crews almost always look neat and well groomed and have all the other desired qualities. So far, so good.

Now, suppose you stopped for dinner at a restaurant on the way home. While waiting in the cocktail lounge you see an airline captain—neat, well groomed, and all the rest—sitting at

FIGURE 13-2 TreeScapes International is one company that specializes in creating hotel atmospheres.

the bar having what looks like a double martini on the rocks. How would you feel? Chances are you might never fly that airline again. Perhaps he is only on his way home as well; perhaps he is only drinking mineral water while waiting for someone. It wouldn't matter, would it? The tangibilization of airline safety just became something else. This, of course, is why airline crews are forbidden to frequent such places when in uniform.

The point made by this analogy is the one we have made numerous times before. It is the perception that counts, not the reality. Think back to a hotel or restaurant situation. It is with perception that we are concerned. Every single employee is part of the marketing team. Some managers allow employee appearance to slip when business gets bad. They want to save on the cost of uniforms as well as laundry and cleaning. The man who comes to fix the TV is in jeans and a torn shirt, and the maids slouch around in old slippers: These are signs of the beginning of a product death spiral, described in Chapter 12.

"Smile training" plays a role in the presentation mix as well. Greeting guests, calling them by name, offering to help, and all the rest that goes with generally accepted public contact behavior is important. It is not always easy to extend this practice to noncontact employees. Frequently these people are of strong ethnic backgrounds and may speak no or limited English. Also, they are not always happy with their jobs (internal marketing). But people smile in every language in the world, and often that is all it takes. Although it may seem like a worn-out cliché, it is still nothing short of amazing what a smile can do for a tired, irritable, unhappy, or discontented customer. While not sufficient, smiling is a necessary requisite in employee presentation.

Employees as a Marketing Tool

The importance of the role of all employees in marketing is being recognized. Employee empowerment requires a change in the culture of an organization and includes total employee involvement, a customer focus, continuous improvement of operations, and a spirit of teamwork. One company that does this well is described in Table 13-2.

Employees are one of the most powerful parts of the presentation mix and can be used to tangi-

---

T A B L E   1 3 - 2
Peabody Hotels Gets Employee Involvement

A two-hotel chain in the United States has taken a dramatic lead in the level of service offered by its employees. Peabody Hotels, with locations in Memphis and Orlando, has taken the term "service" to a new level. Faced with increased supply in both markets, and limited name brand recognition (as opposed to Hyatt, Marriott, etc.), Peabody Hotels made a strategic decision to invest in its employees. Instead of cutting costs (product death spiral), or spending money on advertising and promotions, Peabody Hotels gave the customers what they wanted: good service.

Peabody Hotels faced the same labor problems that every one else does—turnover, multiethnic staff, limited educations, and so on. But, across the board, all Peabody employees go out of their way to satisfy the needs of customers. Repeated stays in these hotels have yielded similar results, impeccable service.

One common theme comes from repeated employee interviews: the company cares. Many companies have "smile" programs, where everyone wears a button for two weeks and management feels they are addressing customers' needs. Peabody Hotels have gone further. Its management trained employees to not only be nice to customers, *but to be nice to the other employees!* The good will naturally flows to the customers.

Simple gestures are also part of the training. The hotels are vast structures, with multiple levels of restaurants and meeting space. Every employee, when asked for directions within the hotel, personally escorts a guest to the area he or she is seeking. Compare this service standard to a typical "it's over there" with a wave of the hand, and you can begin to see the real difference of employee marketing.

There are thousands of first class hotel rooms in the Orlando area. The transient and group customer has hundreds of options of similar products from which to choose. Peabody Hotels has differentiated from the competition by offering superior service and, incidentally, runs some of the best occupancy and average rates in the area, without a national brand affiliation.

3:13 p.m.
San Francisco
Concierge
Addis Rezene

*Conversant
in Japanese
and French.
Fluent in
English and
2-year-old.*

Radisson
HOTELS WORLDWIDE
The difference is genuine."

The difference. You notice it the minute you arrive. In people like Addis Rezene. And the rest of our staff. People who are helpful and courteous not because it's their job. But because it's their nature. We invite you to experience the difference at any Radisson.

For reservations call 1-800-333-3333, visit us at www.radisson.com or contact your travel professional.

FIGURE 13-3 Radisson's employees tangibilize the product.

bilize the product, as shown in Figure 13-3. This is commonly accepted wisdom in the hospitality business. The only problem seems to come in its execution. Management needs to be constantly aware of this critical aspect of the marketing concept and to understand the motivations of employees.

In one case, a waiter received the "employee of the month reward" because he came in during a heavy snowstorm, slept in the hotel, and worked long hours to compensate for the shortage of other employees. When asked privately why he did this, he said, "I knew there would be a shortage of help and I could make lots of money. I made $600 in two days."

In another case, an uneducated maid, a single mother with three children who had trouble paying the rent, also won the employee of the month award. Her reward? An IBM desktop computer!

Understanding employees' needs is every bit as important as understanding customers' needs!

CUSTOMERS

How can **customers** constitute a marketing tool? Think about it—when you go into a restaurant or bar, do you look to see who else is there? Of course you do, and not just to see whether there is someone you know. You look at the type of people, how they are dressed, how they behave, and how they look.

This is an area where hospitality truly departs from manufactured goods. We buy goods without too much concern for who else is buying them, unless we want an opinion on a major item like a computer. When we buy a hospitality product we are concerned because we share space, noise, atmosphere, and other elements with people who are there to consume the same product or service.

Consider two extreme cases to make the point:

The Ritz-Carlton hotel in Boston once did not allow in its dining rooms or lounges men without coats and ties, or women in slacks. In fact, it was about all you could do to walk through the lobby without the designated dress without feeling out of place. The Ritz-Carlton wanted only a certain class of people in its hotel. One of their means of discriminating was through clothing requirements. They have since relaxed these stringent rules but still expect conservative dress. The presentation of the customers is clear.

The other extreme is at the opposite end of the scale, a blue-collar bar. If a man goes there in a three-piece suit he will surely feel out of place. Those who are regular patrons will look at him in a way that will make him feel out of place, if he doesn't already.

In between there are many variations on the theme. No longer, in the vast majority of places, do hospitality establishments discriminate by dress. People who wear jeans drive Mercedes, and people who wear three-piece suits may not be able to afford them. So we use other means to judge the patronage and to see if we "belong." In effect, the *customers become part of the product*. They are a tangible manifestation of the product/service being offered. We can tell a great deal about that product/service by looking at the people who use it. In effect, we are asking, "Are we in this target market?"

Positioning the Customer Mix

Does this mean we "kick out" those who don't fit the right image? Not necessarily. What it means is that by our positioning, the level of the product/service, or the target markets we designate, we establish the types of customers we expect to come to our establishment. Would you expect to see a bus tour unloading at a Ritz-Carlton hotel as you were checking in yourself? Consider the following incident.

A couple went to a resort in the Bahamas for their honeymoon. They chose this destination because the brochures had pictured it as a quiet, remote place on the ocean, with individual bungalows and a romantic setting. When they arrived they found 85 percent of the rooms occupied by a tour group that was drinking heavily, carousing most of the day and night, and making an incredible amount of noise. When they went to the dining room for dinner they found that it looked like a university dining hall. They had to wait an hour before reaching the front of the line. They were then told they would have to share a table with a couple from the tour group. It is not surprising that they and many others checked out the next morning and found another resort (or that the hotel went into receivership six months later!).

Today, except at the highest and lowest ends of the scale, we are accustomed to seeing people of all kinds in hotels and restaurants. Yet it is a task of marketing to attempt to sort out these groups so as to establish specific target markets and cater to their needs and wants. It does this, in fact, by catering to the needs and wants of the specific target markets and not to those of the other customers.

A business traveler's hotel doesn't feature cribs, baby-sitters, or entertainment for children, although it may have them available for select instances. A family hotel doesn't feature conference rooms. A gourmet restaurant doesn't offer children's portions. McDonald's, at least in the United States, doesn't serve alcoholic beverages.

At the root of market segmentation is the question of what sorts of customers should be served. Although many hotels and restaurants would like to cater to one customer segment, economics dictate other action. If the property is unable to obtain enough of the most desired target customers, a decision must be made: either accept other customers or don't pay the mortgage.

Once a decision is made to accept alternative market segments, marketing needs to be involved. For example:

A mid-sized hotel decided to accept an airline crew contract, to provide a base of business for the next few years. The introduction of the crew business could have been traumatic for both employees and costumers. The hotel was insightful, however, from a marketing perspective. A separate airline check-in desk was created to alleviate congestion at the front desk during busy periods. Airline floors were established, separating the crew from other customers. An airline crew lounge was carved out of an existing suite, creating a separate area for crews to wait for their airport transportation. A full time housekeeping staff was assigned to the airline floors, with housemen scheduled to vacuum at 4 P.M. instead of 11 A.M., recognizing the unusual sleep patterns of the crews. The result: two segments of customers using the same hotel with no negative interaction.

The customer mix is an issue that must be ad-

dressed if an establishment hopes to avoid conflict between market segments, as in the honeymoon example above. The hospitality industry is a high public contact business, where even the customers interact and share services. These customers contribute to the atmosphere of the establishment. As such, they should be aware of some of the rules—regarding dress, decorum, behavior, and courtesies. Management cannot mandate these rules, but it can create awareness by careful selection of the target markets.

Refusal to admit people is today both unethical and illegal in many countries. That is the way it was done in the old days. Today it is done by good marketing that identifies to the marketplace the positioning of the property and the kinds of people who go there (Figure 13-4). This takes careful planning.

Market segments that are fully compatible are not easy to find. This is a greater problem for hotels and restaurants that are large in size. With many rooms to fill and a perishable product, many properties have to respond to two or more different segments, which may or may not mix well. When they do not mix, it is wise to keep them separated. For example, a hotel might have primarily business customers during the week and families on the weekend, with children who love to run around the hotel.

Sometimes it is possible to separate by different sections of a restaurant. Some hotels try to separate by using different floors, as in the airline case above. This doesn't always work because sooner or later the two groups are likely to come together in the public spaces. Pricing is another, and simpler, method to separate groups, as long as it doesn't lead to the alienation of a desired segment.

The best customer mix, sometimes called the ideal business mix, varies from one establishment to another. The important point is that it shouldn't be allowed to just happen.

Hospitality marketers need to be concerned about who their customers are because customers help to define the character of the organization. Selective targeting is mandatory for the most po-

FIGURE 13-4   Morton's Steak House's presentation of the customer mix.

tentially successful operation. The customer is a tangible presentation of the product/service.

PRICE

Prices are the most visible and the most flexible part of the presentation mix. This is of critical importance. Flexibility means, at least in the United States, where prices are not regulated, that prices can be changed at any time—on a whim, in response to competition, to make a deal, or just to fill more rooms or sell more steaks. Visibility means that the use of price to influence the consumer is rapid—in some cases, instant. This flexibility and visibility provides management with a very versatile and useful sales tool.

The flip side is that price flexibility can lead to

misuse. Using price flexibility strictly as a revenue generator or a financial tool ignores the fact that pricing is best used as a marketing tool. The visibility of prices makes them the most tangible aspect of the presentation mix. Prices undeniably say something about the product. Prices are a critical factor in the risk/return trade-off and the value/expectation relationship discussed in Chapter 1. This means that prices should invariably be consumer-based according to the target markets.

The development of pricing strategies is discussed in Chapter 14 as a separate part of the marketing mix. Here we extract only minimally from that discussion to place pricing in its appropriate place in the presentation mix. What we need to keep in mind is that the ultimate objective of pricing strategy from a marketing viewpoint is to present the desired tangible surrogate of the product/service. Chapter 14 deals with how we go about doing that, along with the financial ramifications of pricing. The discussion here deals only with the end result.

One of the objectives of pricing concerns how we want to influence the customer—that is, what tangible presentation we wish to achieve. Because customers use price to make judgments too readily when other information is unavailable, price is a potent force in creating perception. That perception represents reality to consumers until they learn otherwise. Because price is so visible it may be the only variable on which a judgment is made. If that judgment is negative, there is a good chance that consumers will go no further and will not buy, and that their negative judgment will be a lasting one. Our first decision, then, is what it is that we want price actually to say to the marketplace.

In the above sense, price is a potent force in positioning either a product or a brand in the marketplace. Because of this, much of the hotel industry has segmented the market by price. What this strategy says is that there are segments of the market that buy hotel rooms based on price. This is a product-oriented strategy seeking a market. Thus if price says something about product, the effect may be to position a low-priced property as an inferior product.

No one, admittedly or intentionally, buys an inferior product. On the other hand, we can utilize price as the tangible symbol of the "bargain" or "good value" that our product represents. This is the appropriate use of price in the presentation mix. Instead of segmenting by price, we segment by benefit bundle and use price to represent that bundle. This is a fine but important distinction: It is the difference between being product-oriented and marketing-oriented.

Another customer objective of pricing is to use it to differentiate the product from that of the competition. This is something more than price segments because it assumes that the competition is competing for the same market segment. Customers use price to make a judgment about value; they use price to develop expectations; they use price to assess risk. All these uses are part of the trade-off decision process of the consumer. Realizing this, marketers or price-setters have a complex situation on their hands. The tools for dealing with this situation are discussed in Chapter 14.

We have mentioned before the new W Hotel that Starwood Hotels and Resorts is developing. The first opened in New York City at the end of 1998. Its preopening promotion piece contained the wording in Table 13-3 and the pictures in Figure 13-5. Consider how this does/does not capture the total presentation mix.

SUMMARY

The presentation mix of the hospitality product makes a statement to the marketplace. It consists of the physical plant, location, atmospherics, employees, customers, and price. Especially where the product is abstract and intangible, as it is with services and as it is with customer experiences, the presentation mix may be all the customer has to "hang on to."

As with products, the presentation mix is a hospitality marketer's major tool for communicating with the customer in the sense of nontraditional marketing. Using tangible aspects to communicate with the customer in the sense of traditional marketing is part of the communication mix, which is discussed in Chapters 15 through 17.

This promotion piece came in a $5\frac{1}{2}$ inch by $5\frac{1}{2}$ inch spiral-bound little "booklet" with eight pages plus the covers, in two shades of beige and and one of blue gray. We will go through the contents in order.

Front cover:	A leaf and the words "What is the sound of W New York?"
Inside front cover:	it is whimsical,
	In the heart of the city stands a sanctuary. Conceived by Barry Sternlicht, one of the world's leading hoteliers, it is inspired by nature and dedicated to service.
	By gathering three masters of their trades who embraced his vision, Sternlicht has created a new era in hotels—a place where every whim is within arm's reach.
First page:	Surrender your cares to our meticulously trained staff. At W New York, service is a priority. Our staff is considerate, discreet and attentive. And we specialize in wish fulfillment.
	a wish come true.
Second page:	the sound of water,
	From a wall of running water to free-flowing fabric dancing in the breeze, award winning architect David Rockwell has created a lobby spacious enough to lose yourself—and intimate enough to meet your friends.
Third page:	Inspired by the feeling of a forest, the windows of the lobby are detailed with jewel-colored glass—
	the leaves in the woods.
	casting a brilliant illumination inside, as well as a magical glow onto the street.
Fourth page:	it is the silence of a wanderer. . .
	When you're ready to retreat from everything, we've created rooms that are sanctuaries to solace and sleep. From feather beds and down comforters to CD players, cable television, voicemail and computer data ports—you'll have all the comfort of W New York and all the convenience of home.
Fifth page:	it's warm
	Fueling the energy of W New York is Heartbeat—the newest restaurant from New York's own Dave Nieporent. Keeping with the hotel's philosophy of balance and well-being, Heartbeat offers a menu of whole, healthful cuisine that entices the taste buds through flavor, not fat.
Sixth page:	From entrepreneur Rande Gerber comes Whiskey Blue, the perfect place to end your day or begin your night. You can fall into a couch and hide away, or if you're feeling more adventurous, an inviting aura makes it easy to jump right in.
	it's whiskey
Seventh page:	it is wisdom being revered.
	Take on the world from the comfortable furnishings in our 4,000 square foot ballroom, 2,000 square foot meeting space or technologically advanced boardroom. From high-tech conference equipment to restaurant style catering facilities—everything here has been orchestrated to insure that wisdom takes center stage.
Eighth page:	a want being fulfilled.
	Our thoughtfully designed spa offers anything you could want. From on-site trainers, weight machines and state-of-the-art cardiovascular equipment to facials, massages, and hydrotherapy sessions—this is a place where you worship you.
Inside back cover:	This is the sound of New York. CD disc in slot with following: Rawhide (Link Wray & The Wraymen), Black Coffee (Sarah Vaughn), I & I (Taja Seyvelle), Inhaler (Hooverphonic), Are You Lonely for Me Baby (Freddie Scott), Drive (Bic Runga), Solitude (Billie Holiday), Are You Hep to the Jive? (Cab Calloway).
Back cover:	W NEW YORK opening November 1998
	541 lexington avenue new york, new york 10022
	phone: 212 755-1200 fax: 212 319-8344
	Starwood Hotels & Resorts Worldwide, Inc.

(a)

(b)

(c)

FIGURE 13-5 Photos in W Hotel promotion piece (*a*) A place of magic, mystery and meetings. (*b*) The new definition of nightlife—Whiskey blue. (*c*) Come to a place where sleep itself is inspired.

KEY WORDS AND CONCEPTS

Atmosphere: The overall sensual environment of a property and its parts.

Customers as part of the presentation mix: People who represent the product and its usage and the kind of place it is.

Edifice Complex: A play on words from an Oedipus complex (see below) where management/owners are so proud of the physical property that they forget how it affects the customer.

Employees: Manner, appearance, and attitude tangibilize the service delivery.

Location: The primary use of location is convenience, although there are extenuating circumstances that change this.

Oedipus Complex: From Greek mythology, Oedipus was sent away as a baby and later returned to, unknowingly, kill his father and marry his mother. In psychoanalysis, the strong desire of a son for his mother to the exclusion of his father.

Physical Plant: The tangible "bricks and mortar" of a property and how it "works."

Prices: A very tangible presentation of the property.

DISCUSSION QUESTIONS

1. How is the physical plant different for hospitality presentations than for consumer goods? Give some examples from personal experience.

2. Discuss the limitations and roles of location in the presentation mix.

3. Define and discuss how atmospherics would influence your choice of a restaurant.

4. Describe how the customer integrates with the product/service mix. Give positive and negative examples.

5. What is the role of pricing in the presentation mix?

6. Establish the advantage of recognizing the customer in the design of the physical plant of a hospitality product.

GROUP PROJECTS

1. Visit a major hotel and analyze its total presentation mix and how it is utilized. Write and/or make a report to the class. Are there any flaws?

2. As a group, "design" a hotel or restaurant's presentation mix that would suit you as the target market whether your group is homogeneous or heterogeneous.

REFERENCES

1. Business Bulletin column, *The Wall Street Journal,* September 10, 1998, p. A1.

2. Abstracted from "Hotel Design—Forte Means Business in Abu Dhabi," *Hotels,* April 1994, pp. 62–65.

Fourteen

❖

THE HOSPITALITY PRICING MIX

Overview

Prices are the only part of the marketing mix that directly create revenue. On the other hand, prices are how customers value what is being offered and what they receive. Setting prices requires a thorough decision-making process. This chapter discusses all the nuances of arriving at the appropriate pricing mix.

PRICING PRACTICES This section reviews past pricing practices in the hospitality industry. We do this to create reader awareness because we believe that the industry history is likely to repeat itself.

BASIS OF PRICING These include five major categories, which are discussed in order in the text: pricing objectives, cost-based pricing, competitive pricing, market demand pricing, and consumer pricing.

PRICING OBJECTIVES These include:

Financial objectives such as profit maximization, return on investment, price stabilization, and cash flow pricing.

Volume objectives such as increasing market share and/or the customer base, occupancy or seat turnover, and contribution to fixed costs.

Customer objectives including price stability, inducement to try, enhancing the image, desensitizing the customer, price/value relationship, differentiation, and added value services.

COST BASED PRICING This section considers prices set on a cost basis such as cost plus, cost percentage, mark-up, break-even, and one dollar per thousand.

COMPETITIVE PRICING Pricing against the competition can be handled in various ways but should be based on good information.

MARKET DEMAND PRICING Pricing based on market demand must carefully measure that demand and its purposes.

CUSTOMER PRICING Pricing based on the customer more than other factors, includes price/value, value pricing, expectation pricing, psychological pricing, and Veblen effects. Value-added services pricing is also discussed in this section.

INTERNATIONAL PRICING Currency exchange rates add to the complexity of pricing for international companies and international travelers.

THE LAST WORD ON PRICING This system sums up information needs and pitfalls in hospitality pricing, and some effects on customers.

YIELD MANAGEMENT This subject and how it works is covered in an appendix to the chapter.

The pricing mix is the combination of prices used by the firm to represent the value of the offering and the value of what is received. Price is of unique importance to marketers for a number of reasons. It is the only directly revenue-producing part of the marketing mix. It is the matching of supply to demand so that financial objectives can be achieved. It is also a powerful force in attracting attention and increasing sales. It establishes the market positioning of the product, and it is part of relationship marketing, a part that can help build loyalty. For all these reasons, price should be based on a thorough decision-making process by the seller that will communicate the worth of the total offering; a worth that is consistent with the market's perception of the offering's value. The importance of price in the marketing mix is explained by Martin L. Bell as follows:

> Price is a dangerous and explosive marketing force. It must be used with caution. The damage done by improper pricing may completely destroy the effectiveness of the rest of a well-conceived marketing strategy. . . . As a marketing weapon, pricing is the "big gun." It should be triggered exclusively by those thoroughly familiar with its possibilities and dangers. But unlike most big weapons, pricing cannot be used only when the danger of its misuse is at a minimum. Every marketing plan involves a pricing decision. Therefore, all marketing planners should be equipped to make correct pricing decisions.[1]

Product and price decisions are inseparable because of the importance that buyers place on price in relation to value. The buyer uses price to esti-

mate value received even when competitive prices are the same. This means that there is a real opportunity to enhance the product's acceptance with the proper pricing decision. If the customer won't pay the price, it makes little matter how high or low your costs are or what your profit goals are. Price, like product, flows from the consumer; the integration of product and price is critical. Notice how this is done in Figure 14-1.

Setting prices is a complex exercise, with any number of strategic and tactical implications. The hospitality industry has fixed physical plant products and locations. Sometimes we have to work with the product we have and set prices accordingly. In other words, rather than set the price to the target market, we may have to find the target market that will accept a given product at a given price. This is called **product-driven pricing,** but it is still the customer who will determine the acceptable price. Given all this, it is worth noting Subhash C. Jain's comments:

> [W]hile everybody thinks businesses go about setting prices scientifically, very often the process is incredibly arbitrary. Although businesses of all types devote a great deal of time and study to determine the prices they put on their products, pricing is often more art than science. . . . In many cases, the equation includes psychological and other such subtle factors that the pricing decision may essentially rest on gut feeling.[2]

In the final analysis, pricing, like product, is consumer-driven. Utilizing all of the models of pricing only gets the end price closer to what the consumer will pay. If the price is too high, cus-

FIGURE 14-1   The integration of price and product as established by Cambridge Suites.

tomers will not pay for the service. If the price is too low, many customers will pay for the service. Ultimately, the customer determines the price at which a product/service will be successfully offered. It is this thesis that we pursue in this chapter. First, we set the stage by discussing pricing history in the restaurant and hotel industries.

PRICING PRACTICES

Restaurant Pricing

The concept of consumer-based pricing has sometimes been ignored in the hospitality industry. The restaurant industry, which traditionally has used cost-based pricing, was seriously affected when inflation became rampant in the 1970s. The industry responded by continuously increasing prices. Whenever the cost of staples of the industry (e.g., butter, beef, sugar, coffee) went up, restaurant prices quickly followed suit. The result was that the consumer eventually said, "Whoa!" and turned to other alternatives, including staying home.

Eventually, the industry caught on. It found new ways to do things, new items to put on menus, new ways to prepare menu items, and new ways to serve them (e.g., the salad bar) to cut labor costs. In the restaurant industry consumer reaction to price can be very swift, if only because it is relatively simple for someone else to enter the market with a new idea and/or a better price.

Hotel Room Pricing

The hotel industry fell into the same trap. Throughout the 1970s and early 1980s, average hotel rates increased at a pace considerably exceeding the increase in the inflation rate. Rack rates increased even faster, average rates being held down only by heavy discounting. A major factor was the demand by owners, who were rarely hoteliers, for greater profits through higher prices. Due to highly favorable tax laws before the U.S. 1986 tax act, many hotels were built with little regard to customer demand or customer needs. Many hotel owners were financially oriented, which had considerable impact on hotel pricing and severely strained its relationship to marketing. By 1989, the slide in national occupancy rates was accelerated and the early 1990s saw some of the worst years the hotel industry had ever experienced. Cumulatively, U.S. hotels lost $14 billion between 1986 and 1992. For the first time in many years, U.S. hotel room rates grew at a slower rate than that of inflation. Customers became more aware that they were in a buyer's market and bargaining for discounted hotel rooms became rampant.

By 1999, many of the least successful owners were gone, having been bought out at bargain prices; there was also a swarm of takeovers by chains. Demand caught up with supply, and hotels once again went on a rate-raising binge even though the average break-even occupancy rate had fallen to 55 percent, down from 65 percent in 1990. Hotels are now practicing **yield management** (see appendix to this chapter) and charging ever higher prices in high demand markets but also, once again, drastically discounting in weak markets and weak periods. In the United States, ADRs shot up 12.7 percent in 1996–1997, but occupancy started to decline with 140,000 new rooms coming on line in 1998 and over another 100,000 in early 1999 and 2000. Regardless, hotels raised rack rates 5.3 percent in 1998. Essentially, with the use of yield management, most upscale hotels' pricing strategy is "charge **whatever the market will bear.**"[3]

In the mid- to upscale hotel industry, at least, pricing practice remains largely intuitive. Even yield management technology indicates only when to raise and lower rates, not by how much. In the restaurant industry prices remain largely cost-based. This, among other things, has caused numerous failures and takeovers in both industries. We provide this brief history because we think it is possible that history will repeat itself once again with current pricing practices.

Management guru Peter Drucker makes the point in his first three of five "deadly business sins":

The past few years have seen the downfall of one once-dominant business after another. . . .But in every case the main cause has been at least one of the five deadly business sins—avoidable mistakes that will harm the mightiest business.

- The first and easily the most common sin is *the worship of high profit margins and of "premium pricing."*
- Closely related to this first sin is the second one: *mispricing a new product by charging "what the market will bear."*
- The third deadly sin is **cost-driven pricing.** The only thing that works is **price-driven costing.** [Cost-driven pricers argue] "We have to recover our costs and make a profit."

This is true but irrelevant: Customers do not see it as their job to ensure manufacturers a profit. The only sound way to price is to start out with what the market is willing to pay—and thus, it must be assumed, what the competition will charge—and designing to that price specification.[4]

The hotel industry emulates Drucker's three points. Many companies automatically raise rack rates quarterly or semiannually regardless of occupancy ratios or business trends. In the wake of this practice, what follows is a multiple discount process that is, at best, unsophisticated, naive, confusing to the customer, and, in the final analysis, self-defeating. and has forced many hotels into failure. In the late 1990s, the industry has come full circle once again, especially in the upscale market. Travelers know how to bargain and cheerfully pitch brand loyalty out the window if the property down the street is offering a better deal. Table 14-1 provides two reports on how this is done.

The overpriced end of the hotel industry literally forced the growth of the middle-tier properties and spawned the growth of the budget and all-suite chains. As a result of this, only the budget hotels were showing any signs of growth during the early 1990s and many luxury hotels were hemorrhaging money until the late 1990s. Budget hotels offered what many travelers were looking for—clean rooms, convenient locations, and an alternative to high prices. Unfortunately for them, budget

T A B L E   14-1
Obtaining the Best Room Rates

Room Rates from Three Sources[5]

A *Smart Money* magazine reporter reports on obtaining room rates at five different major hotels for a particular weekend using three methods at four different times of day. This is what he got at one of the hotels (the others were similar):

Morning		Lunchtime		Late Afternoon		Night		
Direct	*800 #*	*Direct*	*800 #*	*Direct*	*800 #*	*Direct*	*800 #*	*On-Line*
$239	$495	$450	$450	$290	$250	$239	$239	$285

These are his conclusions:

> The truth is there is no system. Making hotel reservations is every bit as reliable as room service: You never know what you're getting. Whether calling directly, using national toll-free numbers or taking advantage of the Web, you need a little luck and a lot of persistence to get the best deal.

- Never make a room reservation at noon when rates are the highest.
- The 800 number is rarely the best rate. Call the hotel to compare.
- Corporate rates are not necessarily cheaper.
- Though the Web may be the future, it certainly isn't the present. Don't waste your time.
- No matter what you start with, always ask for something cheaper.

Negotiating for the Best Rate[6]

A *Fortune* magazine reporter details his experience on the phone with a luxury class hotel:

> The 800 number reservations agent in Atlanta listens as I tell her my plans to spend a romantic Friday night with my wife. Promptly she suggests a so-called Club room at $385. I politely object. Apparently well trained for such moments, she adds that the price includes hors d'oeuvres, a light lunch and continental breakfast. At night there are cordials and desserts. A special concierge will be at my command as well as an open bar. It sounds alluring, but "I want a deal possibly even more than I want the amenities."
>
> Angling for sympathy and concerned that I not appear cheap, I explain that I can do without the temptations. Scarcely missing a beat, she offers the Deluxe room for only $335. The price includes only the continental breakfast as an extra. I explain a Scottish ancestry. For $285, she says she has another room but it might be facing an adjacent building. "Don't you have any corporate rates?" I inquire. As a matter of fact, they do. In that case, the Club room will cost $275 and the Deluxe, just $245. I've been told, I whisper, that certain corporations get better rates than others. "You mean our volume rates," she says. The Club rate now falls to $235 and the Deluxe rate to $185.
>
> Next, I call the hotel directly and get in-house reservations. No "free grub" offered this time. But the Club room is just $300, the Deluxe room $250, and the "limited view" room only $225. I declare my corporate affiliation. The price drops to $195. I push for a further out. "There's nothing that's going to be lower," she says stiffly.
>
> I try another luxury hotel. Here the 800 number gets the best deal—a Deluxe for $248 versus $340 at the hotel; a Classic room $218 versus $250. I wait and call that night and get the front desk manager. He finds two hitherto unknown classes—a Traditional room at $245 and a Standard room at $205.
>
> Conclusions: Bargain hunting is more art than science. And more like roulette than either. If all this seems chaotic, well, it is. But "amid the madness lies opportunity." But there's a lesson. "Avoid midnight raids on the minibar. A $12 cognac and cashews at $18 a jar can blow the best-earned savings."

hotels overbuilt in the late 1990s and are considered the most vulnerable segment when a downturn in the economy occurs. Budget customers will be able to "trade up" to full service hotels at similar rates during lean economic times. With the average room rate in five-star hotels in New York City exceeding $600, this pricing is a reflection of supply and demand rather than value. When times are bad, upscale hotels seek to eliminate costs, guessing at what the customers "wouldn't miss," in order to compensate for its heavy discounting from high rack rates that are largely unattainable.

THE BASIS OF PRICING

The marketing discipline grew out of the economic discipline. The basic theory of economics, simplistically stated, is that the economy responds to the consumer. The basic theory of marketing is that the consumer calls the shots. When it comes to setting prices, these basic theories need to be remembered. Prices need to be established with the long-term customer, not the short-term margin, in mind.

The case on which we will follow up is well stated by Elliot Ross of the well-known consulting firm, McKinsey & Co.:

> [I]mproving pricing performance without the risk of damaging market repercussions [rests on understanding how the industry's pricing works and how customers perceive prices, based on] information about market and customer characteristics, competitor capabilities and actions, and internal capabilities and costs. . . . Proactive pricers . . . time price changes to the anticipated reactions of customers and competitors rather than to . . . their own analysis of costs.[7]

James Abbey continues the point: Pricing decisions should be based on solid "market research and thorough understanding of the economics of price changes," rather than "intuitive judgments of what the market will bear."[8]

There are five major categories to be considered in developing pricing strategies: pricing objectives, cost-based pricing, competitive pricing, market demand pricing, and customer pricing. We discuss each in turn, but do not go into depth on those areas that are traditional financial concerns, mainly because this chapter is not on pricing per se, but on the role of pricing in marketing. Financial concerns receive heavy treatment in economics and traditional marketing texts.

Our light treatment is not intended to indicate that financial concerns are insignificant. To the contrary, they are critical. We maintain, however, that the role of pricing must be, first and foremost, consumer-based. Cost and profit considerations follow under the heading of "Can we afford to do it?" as has been indicated earlier. Recall from Chapter 1 that profit should be the test of the validity of management decisions, not the cause or rationale for them.

PRICING OBJECTIVES

Objectives are what we want to accomplish. Without them it is hard to determine where we are going or how we are going to get there. Pricing objectives fall into three major categories: financial, volume, and customer objectives.

Financial Objectives

Financial objectives are probably the most dominant, widespread, and enduring pricing objectives in the hospitality industry. Although absolutely essential to success, or even survival, the heavy emphasis on financial objectives tends to overwhelm all other considerations. In some cases this can actually lead to failure; in others, even in successful firms, it can lead to the inability to maximize potential.

Financial objectives take different forms, all interrelated. Profit is the one that usually comes to mind first. We call this **pricing for profit maxi-**

mization, whether the emphasis is on gross profit or net profit. The first problem with the heavy emphasis on profit in pricing is that it tends to ignore many other considerations—in particular, the customer. The second and related problem is that a built-in profit determination may be hard to achieve in the hospitality industry.

In other industries, the relationship among cost, price, and profit is more direct and obvious. In the hospitality industry it is indirect and vague. Product makers can calculate very closely their **variable, indirect,** and **fixed costs.** From that basis they can add on a profit margin per unit. If they are good forecasters they will do well because the products they don't sell today they will sell tomorrow, even if they have to discount them and reduce their profit margin.

In hotels and restaurants, the room or the seat not occupied tonight cannot be sold tomorrow, even at a discount.* Yet a large part of the fixed and **semivariable cost** of selling that room or seat exists, regardless. Even with these problems, there are tools for calculating desired profit margins, which go beyond the scope of this section.

Instead, we are more concerned with the setting of prices based on the thesis that the higher the price, the greater the profit. That thesis will hold true if the price has no effect on patronage. For example, airline terminal bars and lounges are notorious for overpricing and operating with a cost of sales under 15 percent. It is doubtful that this practice has much effect on volume given the nature of the captive market. In most other instances, however, this will not hold true.

High prices alone will reduce volume in most cases. Thus after setting high rack rates, hotels discount to get back the volume at a lower price. From a marketing point of view, something else occurs in the process—the hotel loses customers who are turned off by the high prices, don't know how to negotiate a discount (e.g., as in Table 14-1), or simply don't like being gouged. Even in times of high demand, prices that are too high force many travelers to seek alternatives. Communication technologies, for example, web sites, which are bloated with hotel discounts, are making this even more possible. Customers who opt for these alternatives not only don't come, or don't come back, but they also tell many others. It is because of this common practice of overpricing by upscale hotels that we say that they have spawned the growth of the middle- and lower-tier properties. Essentially, pricing for profit maximization by maximizing prices ignores marketing forces, as Drucker points out above.

Other financial objectives in pricing are **target return on investment** (ROI), **stabilization of prices** and profit margins, and **cash flow pricing** (which seeks to maximize short-run sales to generate cash). All of these objectives have their place in pricing and, in fact, are necessary. Problems arise when one of them becomes the sole pricing objective.

Volume Objectives

Volume objectives are a second set of pricing objectives and take a number of forms. These objectives are particularly prevalent in the hotel industry because it is such a highly **volume-sensitive** business—that is, fixed costs are high but variable costs per room can run as low as 15 percent to 25 percent of departmental income. Once fixed costs have been surpassed, a small gain in volume supports a large increase in profit, as with the airlines as well. In the restaurant business, a **price-sensitive** business (i.e., a small increase in price supports a large increase in profit), variable costs can run as high as 35 percent to 55 percent of sales. Both industries, of course, seek volume (with some noted exceptions, such as where high prices are designed to promote exclusivity). Lower variable costs, how-

---

*This is, as previously noted, referred to as the perishability of services. To counteract this, prices are set accordingly. This practice, unfortunately, ignores the seldom mentioned and also previously noted ease of renewability of these services—the unique ability to sell the same product over and over. To do so means, among other things, setting the price correctly the first time.

ever, provide hotels with the ability to discount deeper to promote volume. Hotel restaurants also are in the unique position of "paying no rent," by contrast with their freestanding competitors.*

One major and commonly used measure of volume is market share, which we have discussed in Chapter 6. Alternatively, this objective may simply be stated as the desired sales growth rate. As a reminder, market share is the percentage of units sold (e.g., occupancy) or dollar volume share of the total business that an individual business is able to obtain within a competitive group. Market share has been shown in other industries to be a leading indicator of profit. It also measures how well one is doing vis-à-vis the competition and also how well in terms of one's own fair share.

To increase market share, a property has to offer something better than the competition. This can be a better product, better service, better location, or better perceived value. One can also be "better" by lowering prices. This may or may not be self-defeating. For a restaurant, a quickly calculated break-even analysis can indicate at which point increased volume will overcome the revenue lost due to lower prices. For a hotel, it is more likely that competition will follow suit and market share will soon return to where it was before. It is probably foolish in most cases in the hospitality industry to lower prices for the sole purpose of increasing market share except, perhaps, in cases of fast-food operators.

Another volume objective is to build business by increasing the customer base. With this strategy,

prices are usually lowered, either temporarily or in special promotions, to attract more customers with the hope that they will become permanent customers. This also can backfire, as it usually does with restaurants that run "twofer" promotions (two meals for the price of one). The reason it backfires is that many consumers who take advantage of the promotion will never return to the property when they have to pay the regular price.

There can be much merit, however, to using price to build the customer base when doing so will build customer loyalty, especially during normally slow periods. For hotels, more customers in the rooms can also mean more customers in the food and beverage outlets.

Another objective is to increase occupancy or seat turnover. This is really no different than talking about increasing sales by lowering the price. Higher occupancy or seat turnover helps to cover relatively fixed labor costs and overhead. Again, for hotels it can mean more customers in the food and beverage outlets. Hotel management personnel are often judged on their occupancy ratios and are often rewarded accordingly, so there is high incentive to price with the objective of increasing occupancy. More frequently today, however, hotel managers are awarded on their REVPAR, which helps to stop them from lowering rates just for the purpose of increasing occupancy.[†]

A final volume objective is the contribution to fixed costs that is made by any incremental business, called a **contribution margin.** If the variable cost of a meal is $3 and the meal is sold for $4, then $1 is available as a contribution toward fixed costs. This is better than zero if the meal is normally sold for $8 but can't be sold. The high fixed costs and

---

*This creates an interesting paradox in many hotels that is counterproductive. The following scenario is common: a sales manager books a large group at a favorable (to the hotel) room rate. To do so, she had to heavily discount the meals. The food and beverage manager and the chef scream—the prices will ruin their food cost percentage—oblivious to the overall profit to be gained from the booking. In most cases, these F&B managers' bonuses are tied into producing a satisfactory food cost. This type of reward compensation forces managers to choose between customers and their own pockets. Some hotels counter this by assigning a portion of room revenues to F&B revenues.

[†]This is changing. Sheraton Hotels, for example, was long noted for its "bottom-line mentality" in awarding bonuses. To change this, bonuses as high as 40 percent of salary for general managers were awarded on four criteria—employee service index (ESI), customer service index (CSI), gross operating profit (GOP), and revenue per available room (REVPAR). Sheraton found that ESI can account for 50 percent of the variance in CSI, which can account for 50 percent of the variance in REVPAR.

volume sensitivity of hotels make this objective even more viable and is the reason for contracting with low rated airline crews or other low rated business in off-peak hours.

This observation is even more apt when one considers the disadvantage that hotel restaurants face when contrasted with their freestanding competitors. The disadvantage is that higher fixed costs are incurred because outlets must be kept open for guest convenience. Local restaurants can close one or two days a week and on holidays; hotels do not always have the same option. Thus it behooves hotel outlets to price for greater volume, although few do. Some hotels must also offer room service in spite of its unprofitability for many.

Volume and profit objectives in pricing often go hand in hand, but this is not always the case. Volume objectives tend to be more oriented to the long term and, when done wisely, to building the customer base.

Customer Objectives

The term *customer objectives* as used here means influence of the customer in a favorable way. This is truly the marketing objective of pricing. There are many ways that pricing can be used to do this simply because it is the most visible part of the presentation mix. We suggest a number of those ways.

One customer objective is to instill confidence in the customer by **price stability.** As we have previously pointed out, this is not common in the hotel industry, other than in some budget properties such as Microtel, Red Roof, and Econo Lodge, and some middle-tier properties such as Courtyard and Hampton Inns. These brands have developed loyal customer bases for this and other reasons. The hotel industry, although it practices it only minimally at upscale levels, is aware of the need for some price stability. Hotel companies have negotiated rates with corporations that remain constant for some period of time. The rates are usually based on the guarantee of a certain number of room nights during the same period.

This allows corporations to better budget their travel expenses when they are confident of a stable price.

Another customer objective is "**inducement to try.**" Restaurant twofers are designed for this purpose, as are other special promotions. Restaurants run **loss leaders** (items on which they take a loss or lower margin with the hope of making up the profit on other items) just as retail stores do. Individual and new menu items may also be priced lower for this purpose. Some weekend and off-peak packages at hotels are another example of an inducement to try. "Opening specials" or **price penetration,** capturing as much of the market as possible, as soon as possble, represent a specific case of inducement to try pricing. Hotels used to open at the highest price they thought the market would bear and avoided initial discounting on the assumption that natural demand would fill the new rooms. Figure 14-2 is an example of inducement-to-try pricing to obtain more customers.

In most marketplaces, where there is greater supply, new demand is not created simply because a new hotel is opened.* The meetings or business traveler market already exists in another hotel, or the traveler stays someplace else because of the tight market. For example, many who would prefer to stay in New York City, where they do business, stay in New Jersey instead. Opening pricing is extremely important; the idea is to get existing customers in competitors' hotels to try the new product, not to scare them away.

Two hotels in New York City opened with the exact opposite introductory pricing strategies and ended up in the same position four years later. The St. Regis and Four Seasons hotels both opened (the St. Regis after a massive renovation) in the New York marketplace at a time when demand for

---

*There seems to be some noted exceptions such as Orlando, Las Vegas, and Hong Kong. Although new hotel building in such areas has sometimes gotten ahead of demand, the additional capacity has helped to increase demand. This is especially true for large convention business. It should be noted, however, that these three locations may have some of the greatest **demand generators** in the world.

F I G U R E   1 4 - 2   Inducement-to-try pricing. Courtesy of Yesawich, Pepperdine & Brown.

guestrooms was soft. The St. Regis priced itself at the top of the market and declared they would rather run empty rooms than discount. In fact, they ran many vacant rooms until the economy picked up in the mid-1990s. Four Seasons opened their hotel with introductory rates of $179, astounding for a five-star hotel of that caliber. By the end of 1998 both hotels were flirting with a $600 average daily rate.

The objective at the St. Regis, rather than inducement to try, is another customer objective called **enhancing the image,** sometimes called **prestige pricing.** The attempt is to make the property appear so special, new, and different that it is worth the higher price. Unless that is really the case, the net result is often lost customers in the long run.

The practice of initial high pricing is also called **price skimming.** The term derives from the notion of skimming the cream off the top, before the competition comes in and forces prices down. Price skimming is sometimes profitable when a company introduces a new product into the market. Price skimming is a popular pricing strategy for computers. The model that came out last year at $4000 can now be had for $1999. For hotels and restaurants, it usually creates the negative, and often lasting, image of being overpriced, and is usually to be avoided. Instead, as with the Four Seasons above, they use price penetration.

"Enhancing the image" is better used when the product is truly unique and special. Four Seasons and Ritz-Carlton are hotel chains that follow this practice to maintain their image of high quality although, as we showed, discounts are often available. Upscale hotels in places like Paris, however, prefer empty rooms to discounting. Some very special restaurants also successfully price high for the same reason, under the philosophy that "If you have to ask the price you shouldn't be here"–also very true in Paris. These are excellent examples of tangibilizing the product through pricing, but there are very few of these opportunities in the marketplace. When these practices are based on ego rather than reality, they are self-defeating.

Another consumer objective in pricing is to **desensitize** the consumer to the price. This is also called **price bundling.** Outstanding examples of this practice are Club Med and the all-inclusive resorts of Jamaica. Club Med started the trend with its "one price covers all" policy, sometimes even including airfare. Alcoholic drinks and incidentals are extra, however, but you "pay" for them with colored beads that you buy (they go on your bill) at the front desk and wear as a necklace. You are desensitized until you check out, but it works.

The all-inclusives have no extra charges; everything is "free" after you have paid one price (substantial) per week. An example of attempts to desensitize in restaurants is the use of fixed price menus with one inclusive price, common in France as ***menu degustation*** or ***prix fixe,*** and other parts of Europe.

A good **price/value** relationship is another customer pricing objective that is a policy for many hospitality companies (see Figure 14-1). This is another form of image enhancement, since the market is generally conceded to be very price/value

sensitive, except for the high expense account customer. Fast-food restaurants in the middle to lower price ranges use this technique all the time in their advertising, as shown in Figure 14-3.

Two other customer objectives are worth mentioning. One is to use pricing to **differentiate** the product, usually with higher prices. If the product appears essentially the same, then price can be used

F I G U R E   1 4 - 3   KFC in India uses fast-food advertising to show price/value relationship.

as a consumer perception mechanism to differentiate one product from another: The 12-ounce prime New York sirloin for $24.95 certainly must be better than the same item for $19.95 somewhere else. Alternatively, Red Lobster frequently uses promotions such as 30 shrimp for under $10 ($9.99 to be exact). Another objective in the same vein is to introduce or promote added services and/or physical facilities. Concierge floors in hotels are priced in this manner, as are flambéed desserts prepared at tableside in restaurants. While it is sometimes difficult to justify the price differences for these services in the formal product, other core elements such as "prestige" may justify the cost to the buyer.

COST-BASED PRICING

Cost-based pricing comes in a number of versions in the hospitality industry. Most popular among these are **cost plus pricing, cost percentage** or **markup pricing, break-even pricing, contribution margin pricing,** and **$1 per thousand pricing.** We cover each of these briefly.

Cost Plus Pricing. This method involves establishing the total cost of a product, including a share of the overhead, plus a predetermined profit margin. Its common use in pricing food and beverages is to relate the profit margin to the selling price. Thus if desired profit is 20 percent of selling price, an item that costs $4, plus $2 labor and $2 overhead, would be priced at $10. This results in $2 of profit for that item. Each product or product line is allocated an appropriate share of every type of expense as well as its own variable cost. The intent is that every product should be profit-generating.

This method ignores the notion that total income is a combined effort in which some products will not generate as much profit as others but will contribute to the whole. It is also subject to misallocation of costs such as depreciation, maintenance, and so on. Cost plus pricing does not allow

for flexibility in pricing decisions, nor does it take into consideration consumers' perceptions of a product's value. It is totally cost-oriented and ignores demand. Attempts to apply different gross margin percentages to different menu items to account for different labor costs have done little to overcome the deficiencies of this method.

Cost Percentage or Markup Pricing. This method is heavily favored by the restaurant industry. It features either a dollar markup on the variable ingredient cost of the item, or a percentage markup based on the desired ingredient cost percentage, or a combination of both. A bottle of wine that costs $10 might be subject to a $5 markup, making the selling price $15. The markup percentage would give a 66.6% cost percent to selling price ratio. If, on the other hand, a 50 percent wine cost was desired, the bottle would be marked up by $10 to make the selling price $20. A common combination of both would be to mark the wine up 100 percent plus $2, making the selling price $22. Room service liquor follows a similar, if somewhat illogical, pricing strategy. The fifth of Johnny Walker scotch that costs $20 across the street in a liquor store is offered through room service at $100 to protect the 20 percent target beverage cost of the hotel.

The foodservice industry appears to be enamored by this method of pricing. Food cost and liquor cost percentages become the standard by which results are measured. The major fallacies of this method are: (1) it is totally cost-oriented; (2) it ignores consumer perceptions of value, particularly in times of widely fluctuating costs; and (3) it tends to price high-cost items up to a level that customers are unwilling to pay.

Break-Even Pricing. Break-even pricing is used to determine at what sales volume and price a product will break even, where costs are equal to sales. It distinguishes between fixed costs and **variable costs.** The break-even point is graphically plotted for several prices using the same fixed and variable costs. By plotting the revenue generated at various prices, a comprehensive picture of profit can be created if the demand is known at various levels. Break-even points can be calculated by dividing fixed costs by selling price minus variable cost to determine how many units need to be sold to break even.

Figure 14-4*a* to 14-4*c* demonstrate the process. Figure 14-4*a* shows a hypothetical break-even analysis for price-sensitive restaurants. In this case fixed costs are relatively low and unit variable costs are relatively high. Because of these factors, sales quickly pass the fixed cost line but the profit margin remains relatively narrow regardless of the quantity sold. This leaves relatively little room for discounting for purposes of increasing volume. Figure 14-4*b* shows the break-even point for several different prices. If demand at a certain price is equal to or greater than the break-even point, then that price would be profitable.

Figure 14-4*c* demonstrates a break-even analysis for volume sensitive hotels. The fixed cost line in this case is higher, and it takes longer for the sales line to pass it. Once past it, the profit margin widens quickly as variable costs remain a relatively small percentage of unit sales. There is more room for discounting to increase volume once the fixed and variable cost lines have been passed by the sales line.

Break-even analysis is a fairly efficient method of determining profit margins at various price levels if—and this is a big if—sales volume can be accurately predicted at the different price levels. To predict this volume knowledge of consumer perception and demand is still needed.

Contribution Margin Pricing.

We have discussed this previously as a volume objective, and it is depicted in Figure 14-4*d*. By contrast with Figure 14-4*a* and 14-4*b*, the variable cost line is interjected into the plot at the same place as the sales line, starting at the zero intersection. This demonstrates the concept of "contribution," showing that if the product sells at a higher price than its variable cost, then it makes a contribution to fixed cost even when sales are not high enough to produce a profit.

The technique is very useful for hotels in soft periods of demand. Room prices can be discounted substantially, if that is what it takes to have them occupied. Even though no profit results, a portion of the fixed cost that would occur if the room was not occupied would be covered. The success of this technique must be assessed by examining the total revenues from rooms sold. After all, selling more rooms at discounted prices may have the same effect as selling fewer rooms at higher prices.

Contribution margin pricing is also another version of markup pricing that can be used beneficially in pricing food and beverages to overcome the problem of over high prices on high cost items. For example, a bottle of wine that cost $50 could be priced with a contribution margin of $25 for a selling price of $75. Wine cost percentage would then be 67 percent, a very high and forbidding percentage by industry standards. However, the contribution margin would be higher than on two $10 bottles sold at $20 each with a 50 percent wine cost. There is a saying that goes "you bank dollars, not percentages."

$1 per Thousand Pricing.

This is a unique method for establishing the selling price of hotel rooms. Although it should serve strictly as a rule of thumb, it is still a widely used measure in the hotel industry. The rule is that the average room rate in a hotel should be $1.00 per every $1000 of construction cost per room. Thus if a hotel cost $80,000 per room to construct and furnish, the average selling price of the rooms should be $80.00.

This rule of thumb is somewhat archaic in today's world and totally ignores consumer perception and demand. It should be used more as a starting point than anything else. After the hotel is built, the rates are adjusted according to other factors.

COMPETITIVE PRICING

One of the most direct methods of determining price is to base it on what competitors charge,

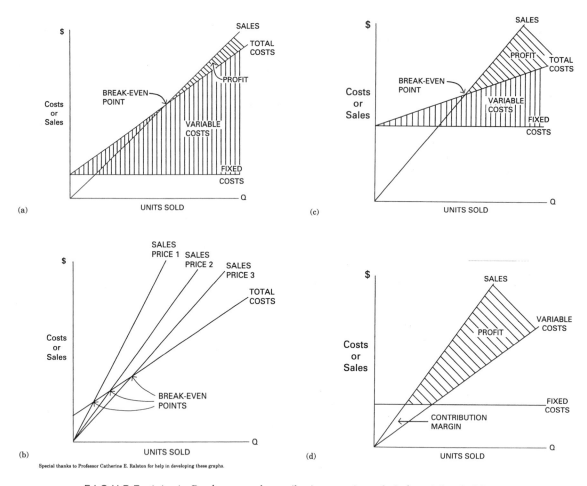

FIGURE 14-4   Break-even and contribution margin analysis for pricing decisions.

Special thanks to Professor Catherine E. Ralston for help in developing these graphs.

sometimes called the **going rate.** One has little choice but to stay in line with other properties offering *the same product in the same product class.* Without valued differentiation, it is difficult to get higher prices, and lower prices will probably be met by competitors. Competitors' prices are readily available, at least the stated prices, making it easy to use them as a benchmark. For example, the New Orleans Hilton, because of its size and location next to the convention center, is the **price leader** among convention hotels in New Orleans. All other convention hotels are priced below the Hilton to remain competitive.

Competitive pricing is viable as long as there is

no consumer perception of significant differences among the entities, as long as one's cost structure allows pricing at that level, and assuming competitors' prices are set correctly to begin with. This means that the market must be willing and able to buy at that level or, better, it means determining what the customer thinks is a fair value for the price.

For example, a new upscale hotel may price its rooms competitively with existing upscale hotels. That seems to work fine as long as the demand exists. If, however, present upscale hotels are running at low occupancy and the market has largely traded down, this may be sheer folly. It might be advantageous to position by pricing somewhere in between the middle tier and the other top tier properties, with the advantage of a better product than one and a lower price than the other. If existing upscale hotels react by meeting this lower rate, the consequences will be the same. A positive effect, however, might be that at least the upscale properties as a group would take business back from the lower tier.

The other side of competitive pricing is that the *augmented* product is rarely ever the same, even in the same product class. This will make little difference—*unless* the customer perceives it to be so. One way to create that perception is with pricing as a tangible aspect of the presentation mix. When one prices above the direct competition, a statement is made that a better product is being offered. The reverse is true if one prices below. In the final analysis this is only a starting point; the market will make the final decision. Thus it is inherently foolish to attempt to bait the customer with pricing if the product is not there to support it.

A good example is a hotel in New York City that was running an average room rate of $159.00. New ownership and management took over and decided to go upscale after slightly refurbishing the hotel. Rack rates of $219 and $259 were posted. The market quickly perceived that the refurbishing was inadequate to justify this kind of price increase and occupancy dropped. Not until rack rates were dropped to $179 did the hotel regain its market share. The same situation can also work in reverse: The same company opened a refurbished smaller hotel in a different location, and priced rooms at $179. The market saw an incredible value as comparable hotels in the area were already at $219. Rates were successfully increased to $239. These two situations in the same company are examples of ignoring the market when setting prices, an all too common mistake in the hotel industry.

In restaurants there is far more variation in the product relative to the same product class. Atmospherics are probably more important along with the menu items, the chef's preparation, the quality of food and drinks, and other variables. Nevertheless, the need to maintain a strong pricing relationship with competitors is important. Restaurants have more opportunity to differentiate their product and should price accordingly, provided the market perceives that differentiation and is willing and able to pay for it.

Both restaurants and hotels will sometimes use penetration prices initially to create awareness and trial, steal customers, and build volume. Once the business is established, it is normal for prices to be increased. Sometimes this works, and sometimes it backfires and business is lost, at which point it is far more difficult to lower prices and recapture the business. The image of being overpriced or having poor price/value is an enduring one with the consumer.

In setting prices, the marketer must always make conscious predictions about competitive reactions. Will they meet the prices? What will be the effect if they do/don't? Peoples Express Airlines has become a classic textbook case. By drastically reducing airfares, Peoples captured enormous market share until the bigger carriers met them at the same price levels with a superior product. This eventually led to the demise of Peoples. On the other hand, Southwest Airlines has remained one of the most profitable carriers with low costs and low prices that the large carriers have been largely unable to combat. It has done this by carefully focusing on the markets and segments it serves, which Peoples did not.

The decision of whether to meet, ignore, or undercut a competitor's price moves is a situation specific one. We can only caution here that the marketer should conduct a thorough analysis of the complete situation—the product, the market, and the competition—before establishing prices or reacting to the prices of others. This is not a time for seat-of-the-pants judgments. In fact, Table 14-2 provides a good list of competitive information needed in developing a pricing strategy.

MARKET DEMAND PRICING

The term *market demand* covers a broad range of factors to be considered in any pricing decision.

TABLE 14-2
Competitive Information for Pricing Strategies[9]

1. Published competitive price lists and advertising
2. Competitive reaction to price moves in the past
3. Timing of competitors' price changes and initiating factors
4. Information on competitors' special campaigns
5. Competitive product line comparison
6. Assumptions about competitors' pricing/marketing objectives
7. Competitors' reported financial performance
8. Estimates of competitors' costs—fixed and variable
9. Expected price retaliation
10. Analysis of competitors' capacity to retaliate
11. Financial viability of engaging in a price war
12. Overall competitive aggressiveness

The appropriate term for the consideration of all these factors is **demand analysis.** Demand analysis should be a major portion of any feasibility study because it is the most critical element in establishing a market. Demand analysis means more than determining if demand for a product exists; it means, instead, asking whether there is a market sufficient in size that is willing and able to buy this product at what price. This is also the foundation of yield management, which we discuss in an appendix to this chapter.

Sufficient demand means that there is a large enough market that wants the product. Let's simplify the problem and say the product is a Rolls-Royce automobile. Able to buy means those who actually have the means to buy it. For a Rolls-Royce the market is now considerably smaller. Willing to buy means those who are also willing to buy it at that price. Now we have a very small market.

With this information (and much else, of course) the makers of the Rolls Royce can make a pricing decision. The target market is very small so large quantities will not be sold, eliminating economies of scale. To make a reasonable profit or return on investment, the car will have to be priced considerably higher than its variable cost. Will the target market pay this inflated price? The willingness and ability exist. In fact, for this market, another 10, 20, or 30 thousand dollars is not going to make much difference. The car can thus be priced at the appropriate level.

The same process applies to steak dinners, lobsters, flambéed desserts, vacations, hotel rooms, suites, or any other product that is put out to market. If there is not sufficient market willing and able to buy, the product is doomed to failure. It doesn't matter what the costs are, how much advertising you do, what the guarantee is, or anything else. The critical question is simply: "What is the market acceptance level of price?"

The answer is not the simplest to find. Many don't find it until after the product has been marketed, for better or worse, but a careful analysis of the market beforehand can make life a great deal easier when the pricing decision is being made. The example was given above of a hotel in New York that tried, and failed, to price above the market. This is the same hotel described in the discussion on atmospherics in Chapter 13 as having made the same mistake in putting in a French bistro restaurant. In these cases the market was relatively easy to identify, but management chose to ignore it and go with its own whim.

There is another concept of demand analysis that is called **demand or price elasticity.** The concept is covered fully in economics texts so it will not be discussed in detail here.* Generally speaking, high elasticity means that the higher the price, the lower the demand, and vice versa. In the case of the Rolls Royce, we could say that within the target market, the product is inelastic—a few more thousand dollars is not going to affect demand. We cannot ignore the elasticity concept and we cannot ig-

---

*The simplest and most common equation for elasticity is percent change in price divided by percent change in quantity sold equals degree of elasticity, that is, the proportionate change in demand relative to the change in price represents the degree of elasticity. If lowering or raising price has little effect on demand, demand is considered inelastic, and vice versa.

nore that this concept must be applied to the appropriate target market. This is especially true in the cases of hotels and restaurants where there are numerous alternatives. Alternative options increase the elasticity of the product. This is exactly why hotel rooms are subject to major discounting in order to obtain sufficient business.

The situation is further convoluted by what people say and what they do. In a study conducted on hotel attributes as perceived by hotel guests in six major hotels in an eastern city, 19 percent of business travelers and 31 percent of pleasure travelers at one hotel (small, upscale) indicated that price was a determinant factor in choosing a hotel. At another hotel (large, convention type), 51 percent of business travelers and 72 percent of pleasure travelers said that price was a determinant factor. Yet, and this is an important yet, only 1 percent of all travelers at the first hotel and only 9 percent of those at the second hotel said that price/value was the reason they chose that specific hotel.[10] The reason for this kind of price discrepancy is the price/value bundle, which we discuss in a moment.

There are a number of other points in regard to market demand that affect pricing that we do not discuss in detail, but list in Table 14-3. This list is not all inclusive but only suggests elements of the identified and appropriate target markets that must be considered.

CUSTOMER PRICING

Here, again, we refer to the target market. Because we have discussed the customer in some detail already, we do not reiterate all the elements that need to be considered in pricing the product. The reader knows by now that in using any marketing tool, such as pricing, the customer is the first consideration.

Price/Value

In establishing prices there are some elements that are particularly pertinent in regard to the customer. The first of these is the perceived **price/value** relationship, as it is commonly called. Given that the customer is willing and able to buy, this is the first price consideration in a purchase decision. It may not be articulated in exactly those words, but whatever words and by whatever criteria, it is this element that will establish the correct pricing levels.

T A B L E 14-3
Demand Pricing Considerations

Usage: How is the product used? Business purposes, pleasure, or personal? What are the users' lifestyles? Do they use it because it is convenient or do they make a special effort to come here? Do they buy on price? Do they shop for the best price? Is it the main usage in this area or an alternative? Do they use it regularly or just for special occasions? Do they use the whole product or just part of it? Do they use it seasonally, cyclically, at certain times, on certain days, during certain periods? Are there different target market differences? How many are on expense accounts? Use credit cards? Come through agents who receive commissions?

Alternatives: What are the competitive options? Upscale, downscale? Other locations? What are nonprice alternatives such as staying with friends, or staying home?

Demand Generators: Where are they? How much do they generate? At what level?

Demand Satisfaction: Is there unfulfilled demand or is the market saturated? What is the market acceptance level? Is the quality level satisfied? What is the generic demand as opposed to the brand demand? Are the available product/service mixes appropriate? How many customers are in the market? Is the number increasing, decreasing? Do demand differentials reflect differential costs?

Economic Conditions: Good? Bad? Inflationary? Is promotional and discount pricing in vogue? Will we have to compete?

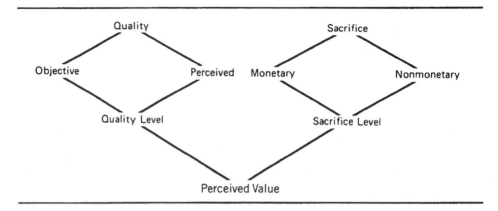

FIGURE 14-5 The relationship among quality, sacrifice, and value.

There are many criteria to serve the customer in the price/value appraisal. Each customer will have different tastes and preferences. Each customer will make different trade-offs such as location for price, prestige for price, service for price, quality for price, and so forth. All will evaluate in terms of the quality of the entire experience (i.e., the augmented product), but each will evaluate the price/value bundle by different criteria.

The hospitality industry places special emphasis on the price/value relationship. It is not at all uncommon for an executive or a manager to state, "We give price/value," or "Our distinction is the price/value we give," when asked to identify the facility's marketing strength. Often, however, the concept of price/value is in the mind of management or in the product quality level rather than in the mind of the consumer.

Price/value is a complex consumer construct that needs to be better understood, because it includes three other constructs. First is quality, which may be objective or perceived quality. Second is sacrifice, which includes both monetary and nonmonetary sacrifice. Third is perceived value—the perceived relationship between quality and sacrifice. It is the final perceived value on which decisions are made to buy McDonald's or Lutèce, Ritz-Carlton or Comfort Inn. These relationships are shown in Figure 14-5, where perceived value is the

end result of the combination of quality versus sacrifice, as was shown in Chapter 1.

In practice, quality is most often operationally or physically defined by management, and is objective in nature, giving rise to such statements as "Our service is the best," or "Our atrium lobby is the highest in the world." Quality as perceived by the consumer, on the other hand, is more likely to be the result of customer experiences, especially in the case of hospitality services. The objective quality of the atrium lobby may be negated by the perceived quality if the consumer is disturbed by noise resounding across the atrium. A rude desk clerk or waiter, to give another example, can instantaneously change a "fair" objective price to an "unfair" perceived price.

Sacrifice is both monetary, where money is paid, and nonmonetary, as with inconvenience, time, and experience. Thus the meal or room, and their respective objective qualities, may justify the monetary price. The perceived quality, on the other hand—such as an experience with a rude employee, a noisy atrium, a long wait for the elevator, the raucous music in the lounge, or the menu with print too small to read—may well not justify either the monetary (price) or the nonmonetary (experience) sacrifice. If management can truthfully say, "Our unique difference is greater *perceived* value" (at any price), then and only then has the ultimate objective been reached.

There is much talk in the hospitality industry about quality, as we have discussed. Too often, however, quality is not measured by guest perception. Only by using guest perception as the standard—and matching objective quality to perceived quality—can management establish the right price that results in the right so-called price/value relationship. This in turn will lead to information on how to add value, in a true sense, that increases the price/value relationship and/or truly justifies the raising of prices. This leads us to a concept called **value pricing** or **price sensitivity measurement.**

Value pricing in food service had its inception, nationally and scientifically, at Taco Bell in 1988. It is based on research originally conducted by Dutch economist Peter H. Van Westendorp. It was further developed as Price Sensitivity Measurement (PSM) by Kenneth Travers and others,[11] but had been largely ignored in the hospitality industry until Taco Bell picked up on it. The process, explained briefly in Table 14-4, puts a price value on a product as determined by the perception of the target market which, in the final analysis, is the only way to set prices.

Through value pricing, Taco Bell learned to bundle its products, for example adding sour cream, including a soft drink, and so on, in a way and at a price where the consumer perceived "value." For the fast-food industry giants, value pricing and bundling have reduced the former standard practices of discounts, coupons, direct mail as key weapons in the fast-food wars.

Expectation Pricing

As we know from Chapter 1, consumers purchase problem solutions based on expectations. Let's turn that around and say that consumers also have in mind a price they expect to pay for a given solution. This is called their **reference price.** Reactions to prices will vary around this reference or **expected price,** based on some kind of prior experience or knowledge. This is an important concept with which to deal.

We know from the research on customer satisfaction that satisfaction occurs when the actual experience is equal to or greater than that which is expected. Thus, contrarily, consumers would be also satisfied when the price paid is the same or less than that which he or she expected to pay for what was received. The old adage, "You get what you pay for," has been proven incorrect too many times but, nevertheless, still forms a basis for consumer expectations. Satisfaction occurs when the customer feels he got what he paid for.

As explained in Table 14-4, research has also shown that consumers, in some arbitrary fashion, establish an upper price level at which they deem the product to be too expensive, and a lower price level below which the quality of the product would be suspect. This is based on expectations. In between is the "indifference" price, the price perceived as normal for that product in a given market, given one's expectations. There are certain hotels and restaurants at which we would expect to pay different prices. When we are "surprised" by an unexpected price, we may tend to become somewhat irate. Thus it is the responsibility of the price-setter not to surprise the customer, such as by charging $100 for a night at a Comfort Inn.

Expectations should be built into the pricing decision. Research can determine what the market thinks the product should cost. This can be especially useful in the pricing of services where a cost basis is lacking for developing an expectation. Findings may indicate that the service can be priced higher; contrarily, a lower than expected price may offer competitive advantage. Knowledge of price expectation can help avoid both overpricing and underpricing, such that the quality is suspect, or that the product is positioned as "cheap" and retains that position later when the price has been increased, thus later appearing overpriced.

Psychological Pricing

Prices cause psychological reactions on the part of consumers just as atmospherics do. As noted, high prices may imply quality and low prices may imply inferiority. This is especially true for services, be-

TABLE 14-4
PSM—Price Sensitivity Measurement[12]

PSM is based on psychological and sociological principles and aims to examine price perception by determining levels of customer resistance as they relate to quality perceptions and the market range of acceptable prices for a specific product or service. For each specific product or service four questions are asked. The first two questions determine the Indifference Point (IDP, Graph I). This is the price at which an equal number of respondents feel the product or service is cheap, as feel it is expensive.

1. At what price on the scale do you consider the product or service to be cheap?

2. At what price on the scale do you consider the product or service to be expensive?

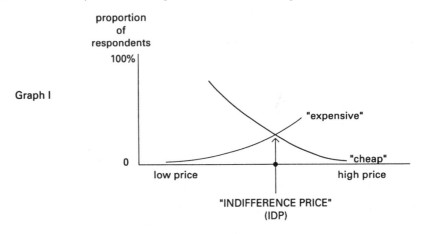

The second two questions determine the Optimum Pricing Point (OPP, Graph II). This is the price at which consumer resistance to purchase is at its lowest, that is, an equal number feel the product or service is too cheap as feel it is too expensive.

1. At what price on the scale do you consider the product or service to be too expensive, so expensive that you would not consider buying it?

2. At what price on the scale do you consider the product or service too cheap, so cheap that you would question the quality?

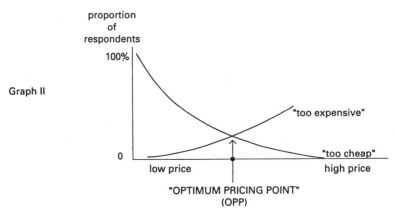

(continued)

TABLE 14-4   *(Continued)*

When the four cumulative distributions are combined it can be determined if there is "stress" in price consciousness (Graph III). The closer the OPP is to the IDP, the less price conscious are the respondents. As the gap widens, the greater is the number of consumers who feel the "normal" price is too high, that is, they are more sensitive to price.

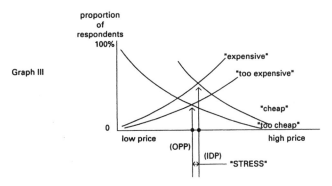

The final manipulation gives the Range of Acceptable Prices (RAP, Graph IV). The "too cheap" and "too expensive" curves are graphed with the *reversed* cumulative distributions of the "cheap" and "expensive," which are then labeled "not cheap" and "not expensive." The intersection of these two curves is the Point of Marginal Cheapness (PMC). This is the point where the number of respondents who feel the product or service is too cheap is equal to the number of respondents who feel it is not cheap.

The intersection of the "not expensive" and "too expensive" curves is the point of marginal expensiveness (PME). This is the point where the number of respondents who feel the product or service is too expensive is equal to the number of respondents who feel it is not expensive.

The Range of Acceptable Price (RAP) has the PMC as its lower price limit and the PME as its upper price limit. It would be unwise to price outside this range unless there is real change in the perceived value or positioning of the product or service. Thus, for example, Taco Bell found that it could move price up (i.e., create great price value) by adding sour cream to tacos and changing the perceived value.

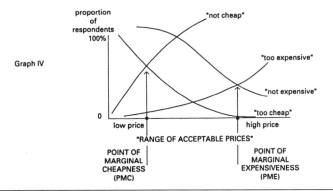

cause of their intangibility. Thus higher priced services may sell better whereas lower priced services may sell poorly, contrary to the standard economic model. Psychological reactions, however, do not necessarily correspond to reality and it is not unusual for consumers to feel that they have made a mistake.

This is also true in the hospitality industry because of the "visibility" factor. Being "seen" at an upscale restaurant or hotel is very important to some customers. For example, a businessman might buy inexpensive furniture for his apartment and drink ordinary wine at home. This same businessman, trying to make an impression on peers and customers, will rave about the antique furniture in the lounge and the expensive wine ordered with dinner—in other words, he wants to be seen with the product that offers the highest affordable visibility factor.

Buyers and nonbuyers of products also have different perceptions of price. This contrast can be demonstrated best with the case of upscale restaurants. Many such restaurants are perceived by those who have never been to be far more expensive than is actually the case. Commander's Palace, one of New Orleans' finest restaurants, used large advertisements in the local paper detailing their attractively priced lunch specials to counteract this. In pricing it is important to understand the price perceptions of nonusers as well as of the users.

Another psychological pricing technique is called **price-lining.** This technique clumps prices together so that a perception of substantially increased quality is created. For example, a wine list might have a group of wines in the $8 to $10 range and have the next grouping in the $14 to $16 range. The perception is a definitive increase in quality, which may or may not be the case.

Still another version of psychological pricing is called **odd numbered pricing.** This is a familiar tactic to all of us. Items sell at $6.99 rather than $7.00 to create the perception of a lower price. Sometimes this is carried to extremes, such as a computer that sells for $6999.99 or a car advertised at $22,999. This tactic is often used in menu and hotel room pricing.

All these differences in consumers' perception might seem to make pricing an impossible task. Perhaps that is why so often hotels and restaurants tend to ignore the customer and price according to other factors! Consumer-based pricing is not impossible, however. Target marketing allows us to select relatively homogeneous markets for whom the product and the price are designed.

The marketer should also be aware, very aware, as to how the customer uses price to differentiate competing products and services. This is a key to positioning with price. Value perception is always relative to the competition, whether the value perceived is real or imagined. It is the marketer's job to understand this process.

As an example of what we have just said, consider the case of a major hotel chain that conducted price research in one of its major market areas. Table 14-5 shows some of the findings and conclusions of the research.

Veblen Effects

There is a contrary phenomenon to almost everything we have said so far in this chapter. A century ago, Thorstein Veblen's *The Theory of the Leisure Class* coined the term "conspicuous consumption" to describe the human tendency to use purchasing as a way of raising social status (sometimes called **Veblen effects.**) John Kenneth Galbraith's *The Affluent Society,* in the 1950s, argued that the modern corporation *creates* consumer desires with advertising and needless brand proliferation. In 1998, Juliet Shor continued the theme with her book, *The Overspent American.*

For these authors, the result is a materialistic race no one can win, in contrast to most economists who view growth in consumer spending as a sign of rising living standards. Viewing consumption as status seeking has considerable implications. Luxury items like furs, jewelry, designer clothes, or a Mercedes may be purchased more to impress others than for any other reason. If this is the case, then there may be potential advantages to maintaining high hotel rates and restaurant prices.

T A B L E   14-5
Research Results on Pricing Effect in a Market

The research revealed a steady loss of regular-rated room nights and revenue—that is, there was enough increase in discounted transient room nights to make published rack rates virtually meaningless. Moreover, many of these rooms were being sold at rates below the corporate rate. This trend had led to declining average rates overall, with almost half the room nights being sold at deep discounts. Although published and corporate rates had been increased dramatically, discount rates had remained flat.

In regard to customers, this research also had some interesting findings. For one, the pricing strategy was building loyalty and repeat business with the "wrong" target markets. Customers were found to have a high degree of rate awareness that influenced their value perception and intention to return; corporate- and regular-rate customers felt the hotels were overpriced. The indifference price was found to be as much as $25 lower than the regular or corporate rates being charged. For discount customers, however, it was slightly higher than what they were paying. In addition, corporate- and regular-rate customers gave the hotels lower value ratings, and the higher the rate they paid the less likely they were to return. Market share of high-rated customers was being lost to competitors. Furthermore, reservation incentive systems designed to obtain higher rates from customers were, in fact, damaging long-term profitability by alienating customers. One important conclusion of the findings was that by reducing high rates and raising discount rates, the customer mix could be changed so as to produce increased profits in the long run.

Flying the Concorde to Paris, staying at the Ritz, and dining at Taillevent may satisfy many needs, but most likely "conspicuous consumption" is one of them. To lower prices at these and similar places would, in effect, be counterproductive.

On the other hand, what looks conspicuous to one person may just be good value to another. Other than individual hotels and restaurants, and there are some like the above in virtually every major city or capital in the world, does this also apply to hotel chains (there are no restaurant chains of this ilk that we know of, but certainly many individual restaurants) like Four Seasons, Ritz-Carlton, Mandarin Oriental, Peninsula, and others? In other words there may, in some instances, be a case for high prices that can be made that subliminally bypasses the price/value relationship.

Value-Added Services

Value-added services are those that are added to the basic product/service that the customer buys, to enhance the perception of value. These are worth evaluating because in some cases they may not add true value; they may simply increase the cost base, or may eventually be passed on, in the form of higher prices, to a customer who doesn't really want them or perceive a higher value.

Developing a product/service for customers' specific needs, that is, augmenting the standard product, is a part of relationship marketing. Business services in a guest room, for which an additional charge is sometimes made, and **turndown service** at no charge, are perfect examples. Many hotels, however, instead of tailoring added services to individual needs, sometimes provide customers with more services than they want or need at prices that don't reflect the value or their cost. Unfortunately, management sometimes does not even know which services customers with similar needs really want, which should be offered as part of the standard product, or which should be offered as value options for which some consumers would willingly pay extra. Furthermore, because of the intangibility of many services, management often doesn't know the cost of providing them, and, no matter how homogeneous a target market, one size does not fit all.

Because hotel managements rely almost solely on measures of customer satisfaction, they are often misled. Customers are always happy to get something for nothing and they express satisfaction of the overall offering. The property, however, has to absorb the costs, of which they may be unaware, that may or may not have created real value in the first place.

The solution to all this is called **flexible service offerings**—particular services valued by individual customers. A hotel should first "inventory" these services, what is being provided to whom and on what basis. They should then apply **activity-based costing** on a segment-by-segment or a customer-by-customer basis. These acts apply especially to group bookings, where services are often added just to get the booking. The same thing should be done for any new services that are being considered.[13]

Customers then need to be asked the value of the service to them. This leads to **activity-based pricing.** The following options are now available: (1) do not offer the service, (2) give the service away at no additional charge, (3) raise the price equal to the cost of providing the service, (4) raise the price less than the cost of providing it, and (5) raise the price slightly higher to camouflage a price increase on the standard product.

This approach allows hotels to fit the service to customer needs, as well as notify customers that they do not have to pay for something they don't want. Some hotels today have turndown service on request only—but only after realizing how much it was costing them and how many customers didn't want it. Instead, the hotel industry argues over the merits of value-added services versus discounting. Different views are apparent and often based on guesswork. Some of these are reported in Table 14-6. Although these statements were made in

---

TABLE 14-6
Views of Discounting Versus Value-Added Services[14]

Thomas Lattin, hotel accounting consultant for Coopers & Lybrand in Houston, opposed discounting. "A guestroom should not be worth less on weekends than it is on weekdays" (an opinion that goes totally against common wisdom and reality because it ignores the two different markets).

Frank Camacho, vice president–marketing, North America and research director, Sheraton Hotels, also opposed discounting but added, "The direction is now going toward 'value-engineering'—that is, offering very selective added benefits," such as coffeemakers in guest rooms. Camacho recommended "price sensing" to segments such as "senior couples, people on vacation alone, individual business travelers and others."

Robert Dirks, vice president–marketing, Hilton Hotels, "value-marketing is the way to go."

Barry Parrish, vice president–marketing, Howard Johnson believes in "action incentives" such as their Business Traveler Club, which offers discount coupons with retailers, room upgrades, vacation and airline discounts.

Jeff Angus, vice president–sales, Red Lion Hotels, "discounting, not value-added marketing, is a more effective way to boost business. Customers want to know what their bill will be in the morning. They are not as concerned with what they received during their stay."

Mark van Hartesvelt, senior vice president–marketing, Guest Quarters, "People are still into price." Guest Quarters found that a promotion that added breakfast and a Polaroid camera at a $15.00 premium did not work well.

Geof Rochester, vice president–marketing, Radisson Hotels, says to use both but under different circumstances: discount to bring in new customers and use the value-added approach to upsell a room to loyal customers.

Bob Gilbert, vice president–marketing, Richfield Hotel Management, recommends "packaging, in which value-added services are offered to business travelers who are willing to pay a premium."

William Watson, senior vice president–marketing, Best Western, Discounting works best and makes the most sense at the luxury end, while value-added promotions are best at middle range or lower properties."

Raymond Lewis, Jr., executive vice president–marketing, Holiday Inn Worldwide, "You need to provide the right price for the right customer at the right time. Discounting and value-added approaches can both be useful, but you don't want to give the value-added benefit to the price oriented person."

1993, you can expect to read similar ones in the not-so-distant future.

The Other Side. Having said all that, the other side of the coin is hotels that charge exorbitantly for services that are needed and expected. According to Smith Travel Research, a lodging research firm, in 1998 "extras" have increased 20 percent and now account for one-third of the typical hotel bill including food and drinks, and U.S. hotels are taking in an extra $5 billion a year on them. Here's a news item that explains this.

Hit by lower occupancies, hotels are taking a "nickel and dime approach for add-on fees to a whole new level." They're increasing fees or adding new charges for everything from the mini-bar to the telephone. "Certainly these areas generate quite a bit of business," says Dieter Huckestein, president of hotel operations for Hilton Hotel Corp., "but we don't want to get to the point where we're charging for your pillow and soap." Some hotels, though, are getting pretty close. "It's like they're picking your pocket and you know it's happening," says one customer.[15]

These increased charges are hitting everything in the auxiliary category including telephone, minibar, laundry, dry cleaning, room service, parking, and added-to-your-bill tipping. More than a few customers are becoming quite irate and choosing to go elsewhere. Hotels, on the other hand, claim they are just covering costs. If so, they need to do a little PR to let the customers know it, rather than giving them a big surprise at check-out time.

INTERNATIONAL PRICING

Pricing is an even more complex variable of the marketing mix in the international marketplace. There are two main reasons for this beyond the usual complexities of pricing. First, the monetary exchange rates fluctuate on a daily basis. These rates fluctuate radically during either national or international economic cycles, and affect every international visitor as well as local guests. Second, pricing tactics by locally owned competitors can send rate structures into a tailspin.

The president of one international hotel company with worldwide properties once said to one of the authors, "We're not in the hotel business; we're in the monetary exchange business." While this statement was not to be taken literally, it demonstrates the concerns of a company operating internationally. Probably one of the greatest problems in this segment is pricing both for the native of a host country and for the international traveler, each of whom may have totally different perspectives of the price/value relationship.

Various different practices also occur in various different countries. French hotels, for example, quote "straight" rates; in other words, for the ordinary traveler the rack rate (or rate posted with the government by law) is usually the rate you pay.* Thus the bargaining process we recited earlier in the chapter rarely occurs in France, regardless of occupancy. At least you know what you are going to pay without all the hassle. Thus France, or any other country, may become either a bargain or costly, depending on the exchange rate between that country and the one you are coming from at the time that you travel.

Traveling with exchange rates in mind is tricky business. Consider the following scenario: Once, an American could book a room in an American

---

*This is also true in much of Europe. Many European countries also use an official or unofficial rating system based on the "number of stars system." There is minimum overlap in the rates between hotels with different star ratings. The ratings also indicate the physical facilities available. Thus customers know pretty well what the property offers, and at what rate range, when they choose a one-, two-, three-, four-, or five-star hotel, rankings which have different meanings than in the United States. Examples in Paris of a five-star hotel are the Ritz; four-star, Le Meridien; three-star, Novotel; and two-star, Ibis (all U.S. ratings). One-star properties are close to hostels. There are efforts, however, to adopt a uniform rating system, such as that used to rate hotels by the official Hotel guide used by travel agents, and by the World Tourism Organization. Just about all hotels and restaurants in much of Europe add a 10 to 15 percent service charge for each and every service purchase.

company-operated hotel in Acapulco through an American travel agency for $120 per night, or could go to Mexico, exchange dollars for pesos, go to the hotel, and obtain the same room for $60. What may seem frustrating, or even devious to the American consumer, is a major headache for the operator who is trying to make a profit while serving markets with totally different monetary values.

The same scenario is repeated worldwide, one way or another, in various international markets. It is no wonder that the tourist is bewildered, but it is no less wonder that the hotel company has a difficult problem on its hands. Now consider the same scenario when the market mix of the hotel is from many different countries, each with its own rate of exchange against the currency of the host country. The rate of exchange is also affected by the prevailing inflation rate in that country.

Second, pricing tactics by locally owned competitors in developing countries can send rate structures into a tailspin. Consider the pricing tactics of "unscrupulous" competitors. These owners are primarily profit-driven, not to mention high-rate-oriented. When business is good, everyone gets top price. When business is bad, many local owners operating in their own countries, as well as some foreign chains, will do anything to get business—which here means to cut room rates. With "deep pockets" for survival, these hotels discount to a level at which their international counterparts, who need to show a profit, cannot compete.

Pricing a hotel room in the international market can be extremely risky, yet this is a marketing tool that cannot be ignored. Heavy discounting when there simply isn't enough demand for the supply ends up being self-defeating for all. As an alternative destination for pleasure travel, for example, Singapore competes with Hong Kong. If the currency exchange rate in one of these countries is unfavorable, the international pleasure traveler may decide to go to the other instead. Thus foreign country destination hotels compete on currency exchange rates over which they have no control. Table 14-7 describes the situation just discussed when it happened in Switzerland.

In the food and beverage areas a somewhat dif-

TABLE 14-7
The Effects of Currency Exchange in Switzerland[16]

The strong franc has hammered many Swiss industries but nowhere is the impact more apparent than in the tourism sector that makes up 6 percent of Swiss GDP and provides one in 11 Swiss jobs. With the franc up 12 percent on the dollar, 4.3 percent against the mark, and 40 percent against the lira, Americans, Germans, and Italians, among others, are avoiding Switzerland. Hotel nights were down 7 percent from a year ago, including slumps of 31 percent in Italians, 20 percent in Britons, and 9 percent in Americans. Total room nights this year are expected to be down by nearly 5 million to 7 million.

Many resorts are diversifying to lure year-around visitors and lessen their dependence on the ski season. Hotels which usually offered rooms on a take-it-or-leave-it basis are now far more flexible. Many have either lowered prices or began offering package deals with restaurants or ski resorts. A study conducted by the Swiss national Tourist Office showed that a 1 percent rise in the franc's value—against, for example, the lira, pound, or peseta—results in a 1.5 percent decline in overnight stays from those countries. Even the Swiss, who generally are half of all hotel stays in the country, are heading elsewhere. Look for them in the Western Hemisphere instead, "flexing their francs."

Business travel has also been affected. More businessmen come to Zurich just for the day in order to cut their costs. Downtown business is off substantially while travelers stay at the airport to avoid the 47 franc taxi ride downtown.

The Davos tourism chief says the strong franc is forcing the tourist industry to "change its whole attitude" and face up to other woes that it usually "sweeps under the rug." Rather than cut prices, however, some hotels are offering free nights for so many nights stayed. "The Italians are the best customers. They buy high-class items. But they can get them for 30 percent to 40 percent less in Italy."

T A B L E   14-8
Source of Hotel Revenues in Different Countries[17]

	Sources of Revenues (Ratio to total sales)			
Country	Rooms	Food	Beverage	Other
United States	66.8%	19.6%	5.9%	7.7%
France	63.5	22.1	8.0	6.4
Germany	53.8	26.9	13.0	6.3
United Kingdom	47.9	31.7	13.5	6.9
Mexico	55.8	22.6	11.2	10.4
Australia	55.4	24.5	12.3	7.8
Hong Kong	48.6	29.7	7.7	14.0

ferent situation exists. In much of Europe and in parts of Asia, "eating out" approximates a national pastime (at least for the middle and upper classes), far more so than in North America. This causes high demand and the prices reflect it. Even so-called moderate restaurants can be quite expensive, and some of the better ones are simply exorbitant. The natives seem to accept it, but for international travelers it can come as quite a shock. Add to this an unfavorable currency exchange rate and the shock becomes even greater. Where hotel dining is more customary, the percentage sources of revenues can change quite drastically, as shown in Table 14-8. We don't have exact figures from Japan but we know that in upscale hotels the rooms percentage is even lower than Hong Kong's.

THE LAST WORD ON PRICING

We close this chapter with some final conclusions. First, Table 14-9 provides some guidelines from a customer pricing perspective on information that should be obtained for developing pricing strategies. Second, Table 14-10 summarizes the pitfalls of pricing that have been found to occur most frequently. Because pricing is the most flexible part of

the presentation mix so, too, does it require constant evaluation. Those who evaluate their pricing should check their pricing strategies against this list. Finally, we provide some final comments on some hotel pricing practices.

Hotel Pricing

In an appendix to this chapter we discuss yield management, a current practice in the hotel indus-

T A B L E   14-9
Information Needed for Pricing Strategies

1. The customer's value analysis of the product/service
2. The price level of acceptance in each major market
3. The price the market expects and the differences in different markets
4. The product's position on the life cycle curve
5. Seasonal and cyclical characteristics of the industry
6. Economic conditions now and in the foreseeable future
7. Customer relationships
8. Channel cost to figure in calculations and the markup at each level
9. Advertising and promotion requirements and costs
10. The product differentiation that is needed

TABLE 14-10
Common Mistakes in Pricing

1. Prices are too cost oriented. They are increased to cover increased costs and don't allow for demand intensity and customer psychology.
2. Price policies are not adapted to changing market conditions. Once established they become "cast in cement."
3. Prices are set independent of the product mix rather than as an element of positioning strategy. Integration of all elements of the marketing mix is essential.
4. Prices ignore the customer psychology of experience, perception of value, and the total product. These are the true elements of price perception that will influence the choice process.
5. Prices are a decision of management, rather than marketing.

In the final analysis, the best price is the one that makes the best overall contribution.

try, especially in U.S. chains, in pricing its rooms. While this practice—attempting to maximize revenue on each room sold at each point in time—may be efficient in price setting, it has also added to the confusion to the customer when seeking hotel room prices.

The confusion started in the 1980s with rack rates that eventually became virtually meaningless except to a few poor souls who didn't know how to get a better rate. (This was essentially the case in the United States but has now spread, to a lesser extent, overseas.) Today, in the upper end of the market in the large chains, there may be at least eight rates for any given room at any given point in time. These are the rack rate, the 800 number rate, the web rate (either/or the hotel's site or sites like those of Best Fares and multiple discount brokers—see Figure 14-6 for an example), the call-the-hotel rate (which could be as many as ten different prices), the membership rate, the corporate rate, the travel agent rate, and the rate you negotiate at the front desk, sometimes called the "walk rate" (the final rate to keep you from walking away when there's an empty room available).

Similar accommodations can vary as much as $100 a night and few guests pay the same price for the same types of rooms.[18] Which rate you get, as we illustrated in Table 14-1, may depend on how good you are at ferreting out the lowest rate—something many hotels won't tell you without a great deal of effort even when they spend a great deal of money advertising it. Unlike the airlines, which have the same practices but quote only one rate at a time, the hotel industry has yet to get its act (or its computers) together.

The retail industry went through the same cycle. "List price" no longer has any meaning—it's the discount price and/or the sale price (sometimes called the street price) but again, like the airlines, it's the same price. Some large retailers, such as Sears, Wal-Mart, and K-Mart, have gone to what they call "everyday low pricing," with some success, to try to counter the consumer learned experience of "wait for the sale price." The hotel industry needs to do something similar as there is virtually no price stability at upscale and some midscale properties. (Interestingly, while a restaurant may have "specials" certain days of the week, one does not go in, or call, to negotiate a price.)

First, "fair" prices need to be set based on value pricing as discussed earlier in this chapter. These may change seasonally or under certain conditions, but need to be consistent regardless of who is quoting the price. (Wyndham Hotels may be a leader in this, as shown in Figure 3-4.) Second, these prices should not be discounted (or raised) other than for specific reasons (such as seasonal, weekends, large groups) as cruise lines do, and at those times they should also be consistent. A possible exception to this might be "last minute" rates, but these should be known and available to all. Finally, the value must be in the price; that is, not

For a great hotel at a great price

Atlanta	Outstanding Value and Selection	Fast, Efficient, Convenient Service	A Great Information Resource
Boston	Quikbook travelers enjoy a wide choice of moderate, superior and deluxe hotels in seven major cities. We've negotiated room rates that are up to 60% off the regular rates. These reduced rates are exclusively for Quikbook customers. And, unlike some discount hotel reservation services, Quikbook has no membership fees or service charges. You simply guarantee your reservation with a credit card and pay the hotel directly when you check out.	Quikbook has developed a state-of-the-art reservations system using the latest in communications technology. You can call one of our agents during business hours. Evenings and weekends, you can get information through our Fax-on-Demand service. Or, launch into cyberspace and visit our website where you'll find lots of terrific information on Quikbook cities and hotels. Booking is easy through our 800 number, via fax or email.	Since 1988, we've been providing thousands of satisfied Quikbook customers with great hotels at great prices. Check out the enclosed city planning guides which contain useful information about Quikbook cities and the hotels available. But remember, we update our hotel values continually so, when you call, ask a Quikbook agent for the latest information and the hottest deals.

Chicago

Los Angeles

New York City

San Francisco

Washington, D.C.

FIGURE 14-6 Quikbook is one of numerous hotel discount brokers.

in a lot of unnecessary amenities and services that the target market doesn't want and for which it isn't happy to pay.

SUMMARY

Pricing is a complex marketing tool but it is, first and foremost, a marketing tool. Thus by definition, pricing should be customer based and customer driven first. Pricing is also a tangible aspect of the product/service offered. As such, it can be utilized to change and manipulate customer perception. The effective marketer must understand this process.

The next step in establishing prices is to identify the target market objectives in terms of financial objectives, volume objectives, and customer objectives. The marketing mix strategy should be based on these objectives and the customers' needs and wants. Cost and competitive pressures establish constraints but cost-oriented methods of pricing such as cost plus, cost percentage, break-even, and contribution margin pricing ignore the need for price-driven costing. Prices must also take into account overall market demand for the industry's products and services.

Finally, it is the customers themselves who should determine the appropriate pricing strategy and actual setting of the pricing schedule. Marketers must understand customers' expectations and how they perceive the price/value relationship.

KEY WORDS AND CONCEPTS

Activity-Based Costing: Determining the cost of providing a value-added service.

Activity-Based Pricing: Pricing or nonpricing of providing a value-added service.

Break-Even Pricing: Pricing above the point at which costs are equal to revenue.

Cash Flow Pricing: Maximizing sales at a low price to generate cash.

Contribution Margin: The contribution that price makes to fixed costs, over and above variable costs.

Cost-Driven Pricing (also Cost-Based Pricing): Pricing based on the costs involved, rather than on the market.

Cost Percentage Pricing: Calculating a price based on a cost percentage.

Cost Plus Pricing: Pricing based on cost plus a profit margin.

Demand Analysis: Measuring the market to calculate existing or future potential demand.

Demand Elasticity: See Price Elasticity.

Demand Generators: Sources of demand, for example, businesses, office buildings, highways, events, gaming, amusement parks, and so on.

Desensitize Pricing: Bundling products and services at one price so the buyer is not sensitive to the price of any one portion of the bundle.

Differentiation Pricing: Pricing used properly to differentiate your offering, in consumers' perceptions, from the competition's.

Enhancing the Image: High pricing to create an upscale image.

Expectation Pricing: Attempting to match the price expectations that consumers have in mind when buying a product.

Fixed Costs: Costs that don't change regardless of sales, for example, insurance and real estate taxes.

Flexible Service Offerings: Value-added services offered only to customers who value them.

Going Rate: The generally accepted rate that competitors charge.

Indirect Costs: Costs that are part of selling the product but not in the product itself, for example, advertising.

Inducement to Try Pricing: Special prices intended to get people in the door.

Loss Leaders: Low priced items to attract customers who hopefully will buy other higher priced items.

Markup Pricing: Marking up the prices over the cost or adding a price based on some rule of thumb.

Menu Degustation: Literally, a "tasting" menu, offering small servings of many different things at one price.

Odd Numbered Pricing: Prices such as 99 cents in the last digits, rather than being rounded up to the next whole number, to give a lower cost perception.

One Dollar per Thousand Pricing: An archaic concept that ADR should be $1.00 for every $1000 of construction cost.

Prestige Pricing: See Enhancing the Image

Price Bundling: Packaging items together at one price to avoid sensitivity to the cost of individual items.

Price-Driven Costing: The price is based on the market after which the product is developed at the appropriate cost.

Price Elasticity: A measure of demand based on price movement.

Price Leader: The dominant player in the marketplace, the one who establishes price barriers that others have to follow.

Price Lining: A psychological technique that clumps prices together to affect perception.

Price Penetration: Pricing low to penetrate the market and capture as much business as possible as quickly as possible.

Price Sensitive: (business) A business with high variable costs where an increase in price is the primary way to increase profits on the same volume (consumer).

Price Skimming: Charging high prices to skim off the top of the market before having to lower prices.

Price Stability: Instilling customer confidence by keeping prices stable.

Price/Value Pricing: Creating an appropriate balance between price and perceived value.

Pricing for Profit Maximization: When the basis of the pricing mix is how much profit can be made.

***Prix Fixe* Menu:** A full menu from start to finish at one fixed price.

Product Driven Pricing: The product drives the price because that is all the customer will pay for it.

Psychological Pricing: Pricing that takes into consideration what may be in the customer's mind or how they react.

Reference Price: An expected price based on a prior experience or knowledge.

Semivariable Costs: Costs that are somewhat fixed regardless of sales units, but can be varied in some circumstances, for example, servers and staff payroll.

Stabilization Pricing: A company keeps the price of a product stable at one level where it has a known profit margin.

Target Return on Investment (ROI): The return expected in profit from the cost of the investment.

Turndown Service: The practice of some upscale hotels of, nightly, turning down the bed, checking the towels, emptying wastebaskets, and so on.

Twofers: Two meals for the price of one.

Value-Added Services: Services added to the standard product, sometimes charged for, sometimes not, to increase the perceived value.

Value Pricing: Pricing based on consumer sensitivity of the price/value relationship in a product.

Variable Costs: Costs that vary directly with each unit sold, for example, food cost.

Veblen Effects: The theory of conspicuous consumption, that people buy expensive things to raise their social status.

Volume Sensitive: A business with high fixed costs but low variable costs so that larger volume creates a larger profit percentage, for example, hotels, airlines.

Whatever the Market Will Bear: Charging the price that people will pay because they have little other choice.

Yield Management: Sometimes called revenue management, the practice of pricing according to demand cycle patterns, for example, hourly, daily, weekly, monthly.

DISCUSSION QUESTIONS

1. What pricing lessons can the hospitality industry learn from the boom times of the early 1980s, the tough times of the early 1990s, followed by the boom times of the mid to late 1990s?

2. Discuss the three types of pricing objectives (financial, volume, and customer), how they are different, and how they overlap.

3. Why is using only cost percentage pricing methods not recommended as a marketing-driven option, especially in the hospitality industry?

4. Discuss why it is possible for the hotel industry to have room rates that can change on a daily basis. How would you deal with a guest who complains about her room rate because she has found that her friend is paying $20 less per night for the same type of room?

5. Is the maintenance of a stable price a viable objective? Why?

6. Discuss your personal pricing elasticity in terms of restaurants, that is, at what point in the price/value mode will you trade down?

7. Discuss how psychological pricing can make a product seem to have a higher price/value relationship.

8. Choose two common mistakes in pricing and apply them to a real-life hospitality establishment.

GROUP PROJECTS

1. Obtain a copy of *The Wall Street Journal* or other major newspaper and locate the foreign exchange rates. Calculate the impact on different markets traveling to different countries, based on the currency of your own country (e.g., what does it cost an Italian to go to France, Thailand, or Japan, and stay in the same price hotel in U.S. dollars?).

2. Define a certain type of room for a certain date in a certain hotel(s). Using at least the eight means mentioned in the chapter, plus bargaining, see how many different rates you can get.

3. Interview the managers of two or three hotels or restaurants. Determine how that property establishes various prices at various times., e.g., rooms, food, wine, liquor, and other services. Written or orally, evaluate these practices in the context of this chapter.

REFERENCES

1. Martin L. Bell, *Marketing: Concepts and Strategy.* Boston: Houghton Mifflin, 1971, p. 857.

2. Subhash C. Jain, *Marketing Planning & Strategy,* 5th ed. Cincinnati: South-Western College Publishing, 1997, p. 400.

3. Statistics in this paragraph are from Bjorn Hanson, hospitality expert, of Coopers & Lybrand and taken from Kathleen Morris, "Lodging Prognosis 1998," *Business Week,* January 12, 1998, p. 121.

4. Peter F. Drucker, "The Five Deadly Business Sins," *The Wall Street Journal,* October 12, 1993, p. A20.

5. Abstracted from Eric R. Tinson, "Rooms with a Price," *Smart Money,* February 1998, pp. 91–92.

6. Paraphrased from Richard S. Teitelbaum, "Sleep Like a Prince, Pay Like a Pauper," *Fortune,* February 19, 1996, pp. 114–115.

7. Elliot B. Ross, "Making Money with Proactive Pricing," *Harvard Business Review,* November–December 1984, pp. 145–155. Copyright 1984 by the President and Fellows of Harvard College, all rights reserved.

8. James Abbey, "Is Discounting the Answer to Declining Occupancies?" *International Journal of Hospitality Management,* Vol. 2, No. 2, 1983, pp. 77–82.

9. Jain, *op. cit.,* p. 397.

10. Robert C. Lewis, "The Basis of Hotel Selection," *Cornell Hotel and Restaurant Administration Quarterly,* May 1984, pp. 54–69.

11. Kenneth Travers, *PSM: A New Technique for Determining Consumer Sensitivity to Pricing.* Los Angeles: Plog Research, no date.

12. Robert C. Lewis and Stowe Shoemaker, "Price Sensitivity Measurement: A Tool for the Hospitality Industry," *Cornell Hotel and Restaurant Administration Quarterly,* Vol. 38, No. 2, 1997, pp. 44–54. The research in this article measured PSM with association meeting planners.

13. Some of the thoughts in this section are adapted from James C. Anderson and James A. Narus, "Capturing the Value of Supplementary Services," *Harvard Business Review,* January–February 1995, pp. 75–83.

14. Excerpted from Laura Koss, "The Great Marketing Debate: Discounting vs. Value-Added Services," *Hotel & Motel Management,* November 1, 1993, pp. 57–59.

15. Thomas Goetz, "Hotel Amenities: They'll Cost You," *The Wall Street Journal,* October 9, 1998, p. W6.

16. Excerpted from Charles Goldsmith, "Strong Swiss Franc Puts Tourism Industry on a Slippery Slope," *The European Wall Street Journal,* September 22–23, 1995, pp. 1, 5.

17. *Hotels,* June 1993, p. 52

18. Chris Scribner, "Competitive Hotel Market Gives Travelers Room to Negotiate," Knight-Ridder/Tribune Business News Web site, September 6, 1998.

Fourteen Appendix

YIELD MANAGEMENT

In 1988 some players in the hotel industry introduced a pricing concept called yield management, now often called revenue management. This concept was copied from the airlines, which, it is claimed, change rates as many as 80,000 times in a single day through central computer reservation systems.

Under yield management, sometimes called revenue management, systems, discount prices are opened and closed based on fluctuating demand and advance bookings. Like airline passengers, hotel customers under this system pay different prices for the same room depending on when and how their reservation is made. Through the sophistication of computer technology, different prices are set depending on demand, day by day or hour by hour. The basic concept is to make reservations available to various market segments based on the value of each segment.

For example, when demand is soft, discounts requiring advance bookings remain available or are reopened for sale shortly before the dates that are not fully booked. When demand builds, the discount rates are removed so that customers then booking will pay higher rates. In other words, all levels of pricing are controlled by opening and closing them almost at will, with any variation in demand. It is said that the competitive advantages of yield management are enormous:

> Yield management can dramatically increase revenues; maximize profits; greatly improve the effectiveness of market segmentation; open new market segments; strengthen product portfolio strategy; instantly improve cash flow; spread demand throughout seasons and times of day; and allow management to price according to market segment demand.[1]

Yield management in hotels has not quite lived up to all those rosy predictions, although some companies claim increased revenues of 5 to 10 percent after instituting it. All sizable hotel chains, and even some individual properties, now have yield management systems in some form or other (property management systems (PMS) to computer reservation systems (CRS)). The practice in the hotel industry, however, has been far different from that with the airlines. In this appendix we briefly discuss the practices and some of the reasons for differences. In one form or another, yield management is here to stay and it is well to be aware of its nuances.

What Yield Management Is

Yield management is a systematic approach to matching demand for services with an appropriate supply, to maximize revenues. Before yield management this was largely limited to balancing group with individual demand, based on complementary booking times. Today, through computer technology, the attempt is to juggle all bookings and rate quotations so that on any given night the maximum revenue potential is realized.

Yield management plans the ideal business mix for each day of the upcoming year and prices the rooms accordingly. It then adjusts the mix and prices on an ongoing basis as reservations do or do not develop. Table 14.A-1 shows the buildup of sold inventory for a 300 room hotel.

In the model shown in the table, a booking pace is built, day by day, for May 1, 2000. This hotel has forecast a 75 percent occupancy on this day one year in advance. The yield management system will monitor the pace for each day and price accordingly. If bookings on April 1, 2000 are at 200 rooms and the forecast was for 170 rooms, the pace is

TABLE 14.A-1
Yield Management Business Mix

Day	Rooms Booked		
	Transient	*Group*	*Total*
May 1, 2000	5	0	5
November 1, 2000	10	15	25
March 1, 2001	25	75	100
April 1, 2001	50	100	150
April 29, 2001	75	95	170
April 30, 2001	155	90	245
May 1, 2001 (Forecast)	135	90	225

stronger than anticipated and prices would be increased. Similarly, if the bookings for that same day were at 150, pricing would become more flexible and would be lowered in some instances.

There are several factors that make the use of yield management suitable to the hotel industry. First, a hotel room is a perishable product, so it is sometimes better to sell it at a lower price than not to sell it at all, because of low marginal production costs and high marginal capacity costs (i.e., contribution margin pricing). Second, capacity is fixed and cannot increase to meet more demand. Third, hotel demand is widely fluctuating and uncertain, depending on the days of the week and seasons of the year. Fourth, different market segments have different lead times for purchase. A convention group might reserve hotel rooms three years in advance, a pleasure traveler two months, and a businessman a week ahead. Fifth, hotels have great flexibility in varying their prices at any given time.

These factors are very similar to the airline industry and represent the requisite conditions for a successful yield management program. Although an operational tool, yield management requires hotels to be market-oriented. Knowledge of market segments, their buying behavior, and the prices they are willing to pay is essential for maximum success.

Why Hotels Are Different

Only certain aspects, however, of the airline-based yield management techniques can be used in hotels, because there are serious differences. The premise of airline yield management is that each seat has a certain level of demand. Obviously, when demand is high, the price for the seat should be also, and vice versa. While this may seem to be an ideal scenario for hotel pricing, other factors intervene.

A hotel room is very different from an airline seat. The configuration of a hotel room inventory could have twenty different categories of rooms, for example, some rooms that face the water, some near the elevator, others on high floors, some facing the parking lot, as well as different types of beds. The differentiation in available rooms within a hotel can thus be immense. On the other hand, an airplane has only economy, business, or first class—even window, middle, or aisle seats are priced the same, and you don't necessarily get what you want. Hotel customers aren't as amenable.

There is a wide range of service choices among hotels at the same destination. Ritz-Carlton is right down the street from Days Inn. Each offers very different levels of service. Consumers say something about the image they want to convey by their choice of venue as well as about the price they are willing and able to pay where on Continental, American, at least the seating experience is similar. Airlines, overall, have yet to differentiate themselves in any outstanding way. Passengers choose airlines for where they are going when they want to go (other than some diversion due to frequent flyer mile rewards). In contrast with impersonal airline seats, a hotel room is a personal experience. As well, hotel guest nights are often multiple. They may span both low yield and high yield nights, rather than one flight. Thus a high yield rate one night may be a low yield one the next.

Hotel guests have choices. If they don't like the rate at one hotel, they can usually easily switch to another. Airlines, however, can match a competitor's rates instantly. Airline choices are very limited and often non-existent at the same place and time. Hotels have many competitors; airlines have few.

Yield Management Practices

Hotels may charge rack rates, which they rarely get at other times, during busy time periods. The customer has little choice, and while the yield could be very high for a particular period, the long-term impact can be disastrous. After paying $275 for a room that is normally $150, the customer may not return again, until perhaps during the summer, when the hotel offers the same room for $100. With airlines, there is little choice. Hotels practicing yield management, like the airlines, also reopen lower rates as the reservation date comes closer

with rooms remaining unfilled (which is most of the time). Thus the room buyer can often call the day before, or even at the front desk at check-in, and get a lower rate than quoted a month earlier. For these reasons, yield management in hotels is a far more sensitive practice than with airlines.

The essential rules of this process for hotels have been said by W. Lieberman to be as follows:

- Set the most effective pricing structure.
- Limit the number of reservations accepted for any given night or room type, based on profit potential.
- Negotiate volume discounts with groups.
- Match market segments with room type and price needs.
- Enable reservations agents to be effective sales agents rather than merely order takers.[2]

To those rules we have added:

- Provide reasons for discounting, such as advance purchase time, payment in advance, nonrefundability, length of stay, and so on, for a variety of market segments. Marriott has done this deliberately to put the trade-off decision in the hands of the customer (Figure 14.A-1). In industry jargon this is called "fences." Many hotel chains use a push strategy through travel agents to fill last minute empty rooms.
- Be consistent across CRS, property reservationists, travel agents, and other intermediaries so that quoted rates are the same. This, as we have seen, has not been done to this date.

Some booking systems have incorporated a set of rules called inventory "nesting." Nesting assures that high value rates are never closed for sale when lower value rates are available. In other words, any rooms allocated to discounts can also be sold at higher prices; if you know how to bargain, you win; if you don't, you get stuck. In another technique called "continuous nesting," instead of allocating a certain number of rooms to each rate program, a minimum rate for acceptance is

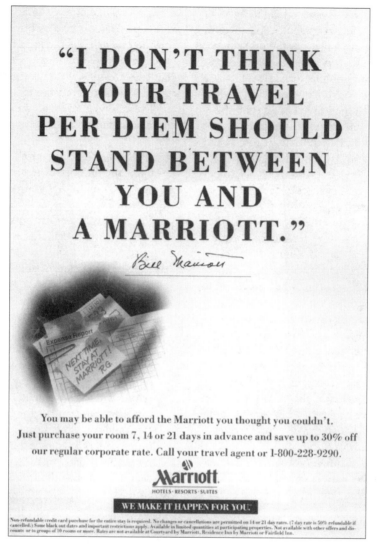

FIGURE 14. A-1 Marriott advertises discounting for advance purchase and payment—no changes, no cancellations, no refunds (in the fine print).

established. Each reservation request is compared to the minimum rate, called the "hurdle" rate. Any request below the hurdle rate is rejected. A hurdle rate is set for each future date by room category. In continuous nesting, the total price for a multiday stay is compared to the sum of the hurdle rates across those days. If the total price does not exceed the sum of the hurdle rates, it is rejected. For example, if the hurdle rate is $100, $200, $150 for Tuesday, Wednesday, Thursday, respectively, someone wanting all three nights would have to pay $450 or $150 per night. All this leads to a variety of acceptances/rejections of room requests by various segments, the length of stay, and the rates they are willing to pay, but is useful in accepting/rejecting a discounted group booking.

While the practice of yield management has its applications for the hotel industry, the authors feel strongly that a marketing approach needs to be employed in conjunction with yield management. The operations approach to yield management is to offer the same room at different rates to the customer depending on what the market will bear, similar to the airlines. For all of the reasons a hotel stay is different from an airline flight, so too should be hotel marketers' approach to yield management.

The yield management system of a hotel should be set up to offer different categories of rooms for different prices. A hotel has an opportunity to create many different types of guest rooms, some more desirable than others. An effective hotel yield management system will open and close categories of rooms, giving the customer greater value for higher pricing. Customers understand when the standard rooms for $99 are all sold out, and the club level for $125 is now available. An operations mentality would offer the standard room for both $99 and $125, depending on demand for the day. A marketer would sell all of the standard rooms for $99 and create value for customers with $125 club rooms in high demand times.

This is a simple example. Just imagine the complexity of systems that keep track of every future date, numerous rate categories, continuous changes in the environment, various sources of reservations, and different market segments. The large number of variables required to forecast demand accurately make it essential that a sophisticated software system be used. (Figure 14.A-2 shows one of many suppliers.) Hoteliers, however, should remember that final decisions should be made by marketers and not by a computer.

Benefits of Yield Management

We have only touched on the rudiments, which are sufficient for an introduction to the process. Now we look at the benefits.

Yield. Yield is the ratio between actual and potential room revenue. Actual revenue is that received from room sales. Potential revenue is what a hotel would have received if their rooms were sold at full price or rack rates. Keep in mind, of course, that for this to be realistic, the full price rates must be realistic. Rack rates that are rarely achieved have little meaning for true yield ratios. Also realize that, unlike the example in Table 14.A-1, a hotel will have any number of different rates, including suite rates. All these must be calculated to determine a true yield ratio. Table 14.A-1 also ignores incremental revenue of food and beverages which, unlike the airlines, cannot be ignored. Yield takes into account both occupancy and room rates and can be illustrated by the example in Table 14.A-2.

As the table shows, a hotel can reach the same, better, or poorer yield through different combinations of average rates and occupancy. Effective yield management requires hotels to have access to many kinds of information, but the most basic element is demand forecasting. Hotels must be able to forecast the demand for each rooms category from each of its market segments, for any date in the future (the near future, at least). Thus customer purchase behavior must be well understood—especially the lead time for purchase and price elasticity.

For example, business travelers as a group are willing to pay more for lodging, and their bookings are usually made in the days immediately preceding their trip. On the other hand, tourists will make reservations well in advance of their trip and will expect lower rates. The yield management system should be able to estimate the number of rooms that will be demanded by each segment for any given day. It is then up to hotel management to set prices accordingly.

Yield management, if used effectively, allows a hotel to manage its limited inventory better in order to maximize revenues. Short-term gains, however, must not substitute for long-term profits. Loyal and repeat customers will not appreciate the lack of room availability or special rates to which they are accustomed. They are likely to be more interested in price stability, so it may be a mistake not to honor a long-term customer's request for their usual rate. Hotel employees who are affected by yield management systems, especially in reservations, sales, and front office departments must be involved in the process so that they understand

FIGURE 14. A-2 TIMS Corp. is a supplier of yield management software.

that outside the promoted objectives of yield management, that is, to maximize revenues, it is still critically important to keep loyal customers.

The Customer

The customer's reaction to yield management practices in hospitality is a quite complex one and not fully known by scientific research at the time of this writing. It is, however, one that needs to be thoroughly examined. Combined with the pricing practices of the hotel industry that we have discussed in this chapter, it is for certain that the customer is confused and frustrated by the dickering process and never really knowing if, "I got the best deal." As one news item reported, "For travelers in search of bar-

T A B L E   1 4 . A - 2
Calculating Yield

Hotel A has 500 rooms and an average rack rate of $180.00. On August 1st it had an occupancy of 70 percent, or 350 rooms sold, at an average rate of $140.00. (REVPAR figures are shown only as a point of comparison.)

Yield = *Revenue Realized divided by Revenue Potential*

Revenue Realized = $140 × 350 rooms sold = $49,000   REVPAR = $98.00

Revenue Potential = $180 × 500 = $90,000   Yield = $49,000 divided by $90,000 = 54.4%

The same yield, or a higher yield, can be realized if Hotel A sold fewer rooms at a higher rate or more rooms at a lower rate:

Average Rate	*Rooms Sold*	*Revenue Realized*	*Yield*	*REVPAR*
$160.00	306	$48,960	54.4%	$98
$120.00	408	$48,960	54.4%	$98
$170.00	300	$51,000	56.7%	$102
$130.00	400	$52,000	57.8%	$104

gains, the recession of the nineties is hotel heaven. Getting a great deal, however, takes bargaining."[3]

The restaurant industry does not yet practice "yield management," with possibly the exception of "early bird" dinners. Maybe it should. Many restaurants are booked to capacity on Saturday nights with empty tables abounding on Monday nights. Why not raise prices on Saturdays, or give discounts on Mondays? How would the customer react? We don't know the answer to that one but it seems only fair that if hotels can do it, so too can restaurants. Perhaps it would help spread out the business.

The ultimate question, of course, lies in the perception of the customer and it might be sheer folly to attempt such a course of action without first learning what the customer's reaction might be. One might surmise that, if the customer was asked, the response would be negative. The issue, we suspect, is embedded in what is perceived as "fair." This is the same issue that the hotel industry is already grappling with but, perhaps in too many cases, is ignoring from the customer's perspective.[4]

Side Effects. As this process has driven management to get the highest yield, it has also put more burden on the customer. For example, if the customer passes the hurdle rate for a three-day stay and then wants to check out a day early, the new practice by some properties is to fine him $50 or more. On the other side, at least one person booking a small group found that she had to pay $2700 to buy a fourth night that she didn't want. Some companies have ended their relationship with hotels because of their tight cancellation or early departure levies. Other companies have started to negotiate these factors before signing contracts. At least one hotel in the United States made the equivalent of 10 percent in room revenue just from cancellation fees, no-show charges, and early departure fees.

Guests at many hotels can now expect to sign a form agreeing to pay an early departure fee if they leave early. These fees were started by Hyatt in 1995 and, as you can imagine, are despised by business travelers, who often have changes in plans. Even, however, as hotels collect more money for rooms that might go unused, they are still over booking travelers and making some "walk." Not happy campers, these folks![5]

All in all, many are raising ethical issues about

all these hotel practices, including yield management, while apparently largely accepting it from the airlines.

Does Yield Management Really Work?

Yield Management System Measurement

When a hotel with an installed yield management system experiences in its first year a healthy growth in revenues from bookings, compared to the previous year when it did not use a system, who or what should get credit for the improved revenue performance? An argument can be made that the system really delivered benefits. However, the Sales & Marketing Department can claim that the new advertising campaigns and direct mail brought in greater volume. The Guest Services Department may claim that higher guest satisfaction ratings generated considerable repeat business. The hotel's management team may point to the fact that the property was operating in a much improved local economic environment.

Considering all of these factors—and the activities enacted to affect revenue performance—one could even ask whether or not the yield management system is actually delivering benefits. Consequently, measuring the impact of the yield management system is essential to correctly attribute what revenue increases are a result of the system or are a result of other factors. Successful measurement can only occur when the hotel measures its performance working with the yield management system, and compares it to the revenue performance it would have received without the system, everything else being equal. Let's take a look at five of the more well known measurement approaches.

1. Historical Revenues Trends Analysis

The hotelier plots daily revenues from the past several years and searches for any type of trends. The patterns are used as a basis for making future projections. By comparing the future projections with any deviation from the projections, the amount of deviation, in theory, may be tied to the system.

This approach, however, fails to account for the impact of new events that happened after the system was installed—new marketing campaigns or the introduction of a web site, for example—which were not done in the past. It still makes it impossible to see what revenue change is due to the system or to other factors.

2. "After the Fact" Review

A process is used to estimate what the unconstrained demand would have been or may have been. The process considers demand "on the books" and, after there is no more hotel capacity, it attempts to figure the amount of demand turned down. The hotelier then speculates, with the best business mix after the fact, how much revenue the property would have generated.

That amount is compared to the actual amount of revenues. This difference or "gap" offers a possible measure for improvement. The "gap" before is weighed against the "gap" after the system installation. The difference perhaps illustrates the system's impact. Simply, this approach only teaches the hotelier how to be wiser after the event, instead of making the best decisions for future booking opportunities. This approach cannot separate what the system is doing and what is being affected by changing market conditions and other factors.

3. Comparison of Hotels Within a Competitive Set

Revenues from a period after system installation are compared to a similar period prior to installation. To consider the effect of extraneous factors on revenues, the comparison is tracked against any demand fluctuations from a similar hotel (without the yield management system) in the same competitive set, with nearly the same demographics. The failing is that it is impossible to imagine two hotels that would experience identical effects from the extraneous factors, and it is highly unlikely they would share the same pricing strategies directed or the same marketing mixes.

4. Computer Simulation in Controlled Environments

To isolate the changes in market conditions and the business environment, system measurement was attempted in a controlled environment, using computer simulation. A yield management practice with basic demand data is deployed. First, booking decisions from the yield management practice are based on simulated human decisions, which result in bookings accepted and not accepted. Next, the booking decisions are based on yield management system decisions. Again, bookings are accepted and not accepted. Accepted bookings from both decision scenarios translate into revenue, and the compared revenues between the two illustrate how the yield management practice may deliver results.

Computer simulation cannot understand truly how the humans would have acted. Even if the measurement shows benefits in a controlled environment, how can the hotelier be assured that there will be benefits in the "real" world? It is impossible to predict in a controlled setting how the users would interact with the system.

5. True Scientific Measurement

If demand does increase due to marketing programs or an improvement in economy after the yield system installation, occupancy will increase, and there will be more sold-out nights. But what if there is no increase in demand compared to last year, while an effective yield management practice is put into place? As a result of the yield management system, it is anticipated that there will be a reduction in the number of turn downs multi-night stays. And the proper overbooking of rooms leads to a decrease in the amount of empty rooms on sold-out nights.

Thus, occupancy will increase through the better yield practice. The scientific measurement approach is the tool with which it can be precisely determined whether the occupancy increased because of the yield management practice or due to marketing programs or improved economic conditions. It begins by identifying periods where the system does not restrict the hotel or resort in accepting bookings. This starts the process by which a look at what is occurring in the marketplace and in the local economy is gained.

Only scientific measurement isolates the impact of the marketing programs and economic factors from the impact of the yield management solution. It shows what room revenue increases can be attributed to the yield management solution.

REFERENCES

1. James C. Makens, "Yield Management: A Major Pricing Breakthrough," *Piedmont Airlines* (in-flight magazine), April 1988, p. 32.

2. W. Lieberman, "Debunking the Myths of Yield Management," *Cornell Hotel and Restaurant Administration Quarterly,* February 1993, pp. 34–41.

3. Andrew Allentuck, "Dickering Can Save You Dollars," *The Toronto Globe and Mail,* February 23, 1998, page D5.

4. See, for example, Sheryl E. Kimes, "Perceived Fairness of Yield Management," *Cornell Hotel & Restaurant Administration Quarterly,* February 1994, pp. 22–29.

5. Parts of this section are abstracted from Danielle Reed, "Hotels Penalize Late Arrivals, Early Departures," *The Wall Street Journal,* August 18, 1998, pp. B1–B2.

C H A P T E R

Fifteen

◆

THE COMMUNICATIONS MIX: FOUNDATIONS AND ADVERTISING

―――――――― *Overview* ――――――――

This chapter starts with a repeat of the definition of the communications mix and the purposes it serves. A brief scenario demonstrates all the elements of the mix.

COMMUNICATIONS STRATEGY Certain strategies should guide the communications effort. These are based on objectives and influenced by the stage of the consumer's knowledge and the type of influence that should be used.

RESEARCH FOR THE COMMUNICATIONS MIX Proper research can save a great deal of wasted money by identifying the needs and objectives of the communications mix, as well as the success rate of any campaign.

PUSH/PULL STRATEGIES These strategies deal with "pushing" the product down through the distribution channels, or pulling it up through them.

WORD OF MOUTH The most powerful form of communications in the hospitality industry, and it's free, but it's also uncontrollable.

DATABASE MARKETING Also called direct mail or direct marketing, database marketing enables a company to target and profile its customers and more directly aim the communications effort. It is also a tool for obtaining new customers.

BUDGETING THE COMMUNICATIONS MIX This is a complex exercise with complex variables. There is no one accepted method. Each individual property has its own budget plus, if it is part of a chain, those imposed by corporate or the franchisor.

ADVERTISING Advertising is paid mass communication, which often has an unknown effectiveness. Nevertheless, it is important to understand its role and what it should accomplish. To do this one needs to subscribe to certain "rules." Advertising needs to be evaluated both before and after the fact. Collateral falls into the same domain.

INTERNATIONAL ADVERTISING   Given the obvious cultural differences, global communications faces the dilemma of standardizing to save money or adapting to different cultural scenarios. Both methods are used in the hospitality industry and both have their risks.

◆

The communications mix is what we have come to know as traditional marketing. Again, it is useful to repeat the definition given in Chapters 4 and 12:

> All communications between the firm and the target market that increase the tangibility of the product/service mix, that establish or monitor consumer expectations, or that persuade customers to purchase.

Some elements of this definition need further explanation. Note the phrase "between the firm and the target market": This tells us that communications are a two-way street. It is not simply what the firm does to communicate, but it is also the feedback from the target market that tells the firm how well it is communicating and how well it is providing the services promised. This, of course, is part of relationship marketing.

Second, the definition says that communications "increase the tangibility of the product/service mix." As we have seen, the presentation mix does the same thing. The difference is that the presentation mix did this with tangible physical evidence of the product. Communications do it with words and pictures, not facets of the product itself.

Third, communications "establish or monitor consumer expectations." Not only do communications create expectations, but they also provide warning when expectations change or are not being met.

Finally, marketing communications "persuade customers to purchase"—we hope. Although interim communications, particularly in advertising and public relations, may have other specific purposes, such as to create awareness, enhance a corporate image, and so on, the ultimate goal of all marketing communications is to induce purchase.

THE COMMUNICATIONS MIX

The communications mix contains five elements: advertising, sales promotion, merchandising, public relations and publicity, and personal selling. We discuss each of these in turn. First, in Table 15-1 we relate an example to demonstrate the elements of the mix.

This story dramatizes the kinds of problems that arise in marketing communication. The Johnsons felt frustrated because they were not satisfied with the restaurant. They wished they had complained to the management. In that wish, they were typical of consumers who feel reluctant and frustrated in not communicating their true feelings to business organizations.

The restaurant owners also felt frustrated. Apparently people were not returning to the restaurant and there had to be some reason why. On the other hand, the owners knew their food was superior and their atmospherics were unique. They wished that they had spent more time talking to their customers to see what they liked and disliked about the restaurant. In that wish, they were typical of business owners who feel they could do a better job of communicating with their customers but who don't know how.

The example illustrates a lack of effective marketing communication. The restaurant has frustrated its customers by not being responsive to

---

TABLE 15-1
Communications Mix in Practice

Jim and Paula Johnson saw a news item in the paper that a new restaurant was going to be created in a long-abandoned, historic, old stone mill down by the river. "It's about time," they thought, "that this town had a new restaurant. This one sounds intriguing. Any restaurant in an old stone mill has to be an exciting concept and it would have to have good food."

Jim and Paula forgot about the restaurant, except when someone mentioned it during a bridge game or in casual conversation, until about six months later. Then they saw a half-page ad in the newspaper. The ad announced the grand opening of the Old Stone Mill restaurant on the next Friday night, featuring fine cuisine and excellent service. There was an enticing picture of the old stone mill by the river. They couldn't go Friday, but immediately made reservations for the next night, Saturday, when the grand opening special drink prices and hors d'oeuvres would still be featured.

On Saturday night they drove with some friends to the restaurant. They had difficulty finding it because the roads down by the river were confusing and not clearly marked. They finally found the restaurant but couldn't find any nearby parking spaces. It was a clear night with almost a full moon, however, and they found the walk to the restaurant invigorating. They looked forward to a great meal and a great experience. When Jim and Paula got to the restaurant they found a long line waiting to get in. Because they had reservations, they passed by the line and went into the cocktail lounge. They had come early to take advantage of the special offer. They found the lounge packed, with no seating space available. The special hors d'oeuvres had all been devoured. They tried to find someone to take their drink order, to no avail, so they went looking for the hostess. They were 30 minutes early for their reservation, but the hostess told them there would be a two hour wait for their table. "What the heck," they said, "it's always this way on Saturday night anywhere," and decided to wait. They were seated an hour and 45 minutes later.

They waited a long time for a waiter. The waiter suggested a menu item that he said was a special and a unique creation of the restaurant owners. Jim and Paula both decided to order it. They then waited a similar length of time until they were served. The waiter explained that the special dish required extra care and time to prepare. On the table, however, was a table tent featuring a carafe of house wine and some shrimp canapes at a special price. They ordered this to have while waiting for their dinner and it came quickly. By the time the meal came, they were filled up on the canapes, salad, bread, and cheese, and were not very hungry. The meal was delicious but they had lost their appetites. They wanted to have another wine with dinner, but were never brought a wine list so didn't order it. Later, when they learned of the wine prices, they were just as happy that they hadn't. They didn't complain but, as they left, vowed never to go there again and to tell their friends what kind of experience they had had.

A month later, the ad rep from the local paper visited the same restaurant to solicit some advertising. The owners were glad to see him because they were having real problems. The restaurant had opened to rave reviews, although one restaurant critic mentioned the slow and inefficient service. At first, it was so busy that they couldn't keep up. Lately, however, business had dropped off dramatically. There had been very few complaints; in fact, almost everyone praised the food, the decor, and the concept. The owners figured that what they needed now was a good advertising campaign.

---

their needs. Customers complain to each other by word of mouth, but don't communicate their feelings to the restaurant management. Both parties would like to have a favorable relationship with the other but don't know how to go about it. What the restaurant needs now is a communications strategy. The anecdote demonstrates all the elements of the communications mix: publicity, advertising, promotion, personal selling, and merchandising, as well as word of mouth. By the time we get through Chapter 17, we will have seen how all these elements apply in this anecdote, and how the restaurant owners should develop a communications campaign. This chapter starts the process.

COMMUNICATIONS STRATEGY

Communications strategies are concerned with the planning, implementing, and control of persuasive communication with customers. Strategies are the plan and tactics are the action, as discussed in Chapter 4. This is an important distinction because it is very easy, in implementing marketing communications, to get bogged down in the tactics. When this happens, communication tactics are often not consistent with strategic objectives.

For example, in personal selling we might call on a client hoping to convince him to book his next group meeting at our hotel. Knowing when his next meeting will be held, we might try to persuade him to book that period. That's a tactic. But he has already reserved at another hotel for that meeting. The result is no sale, and we will have to go through the same process for his subsequent meeting.

Instead, we might use strategic persuasion. Our strategic objective is to persuade the client that our hotel, of all hotels, can best serve his meeting needs and solve his meeting problems. We don't mention dates, we don't "sell" our product; we address his needs. Instead of a "no sale," we receive this response: "I've already booked our next meeting, but I'll get in touch with you for the one after that." If our persuasion has been successful, he will.

In advertising, the same concept applies. The first step of a communications strategy is to decide what our objectives are and what we hope to accomplish. These are broad objectives that will serve as an umbrella for all communications efforts; that is, they will permeate the advertising, selling, promotion, merchandising, and public relations. Some, or all, of these elements may also have subobjectives but they will all be subsumed under the main objectives. Similarly, we may have more than one objective at a time. In any case, we want the objectives to be congruent and not in conflict with each other.

There are many possible main objectives. Here, we list just a few: to create an image, to position (both objectively and subjectively), to provide benefits, to offer solutions to problems, to create awareness, to create belief, to stir emotions, to change attitudes, to create expectation, and to move to action. These are all strategic objectives

TABLE 15-2
The Six Stages of a Communications Strategy

Stage	Possible Strategic Element	
1. Whom to say it to	The target market(s)—Those who either use our product or whom we want to persuade to use it	
2. Why to say it	Prior users: Persuade to use more often Offer new benefits Offer specials at slow periods Show improvements Develop relationships Recapture, reposition Adopt as first choice	Non-users: Create awareness Get interested, get attention Make part of **evoked** set Position Arouse desire Provide more information to evaluate, explain features Persuade to use
3. What to say	Awareness, to desire, to buy Awareness, interest, evaluation, trial Logos, pathos, ethos Cognitive, affective, conative	
4. How to say it	Humor, sex, cost/value, bargain, **slice of life**, lifestyle, mood, atmospherics, testimonial, service, quality, action, etc.	
5. How often to say it	Depends a lot on budget, reach, effectiveness	
6. Where to say it	Selecting the media or personal selling that would most likely reach the target market, most effectively and efficiently	

and it is one or more of those objectives that guide the communications process.

The communication process has six broad stages, which are shown in Table 15-2. The first of these stages is "whom to say it to." This stage sets the guidelines in terms of featured attributes, positioning, benefits offered, promises made, and so forth. Consider the ads for two different hotels (Figures 15-1, 15-2), and two different restaurants (Figures 15-3, 15-4) for the purpose of relating the communications process to an actual strategy. Each ad has a different strategic objective.

Whom to Say It to

The first stage is to define the target market. The appropriate research should be done and the needs and wants of the target market clearly identified. The target markets for both Figures 15-1 and 15-2 are golfers, but that's simplistic. Are the target markets the same in needs and wants? Not really. The Grand Cypress Resort's target is the serious, die-hard golfer who probably has a low handicap, plays very serious golf, probably plays 36 holes a day, spends his evenings talking about each hole and how he played it, and wants to improve his game even more. This golfer is probably male. If he brings his wife, the ads tell us nothing about what she would do, unless she also has a low handicap.*

The La Costa golfer, on the other hand, may or may not also be a serious player, but probably plays only 18 holes a day at a resort, possibly with his wife. He may also play tennis with her. But the night is hers—fine dining, entertainment, and dancing are in order.

The target markets for both Figures 15-3 and 15-4 are diners who like good food, but what a differ-

ence! The Pier House diner likes fresh seafood but, more than that, casual uninhibited dining. These diners may be couples or may be friends of the same sex, wear their shorts and sneakers to dinner, drink beer, and eat with their fingers. But, not at the Prince of Wales (Figure 15-4). Here users are definitely couples who dress for dinner, like really fine food and service, drink wine, and want romance and peace and quiet.

Why to Say It

This is where the marketing strategy comes in. At this stage we are concerned with what effect we expect the communication to have, that is, what we want to accomplish. Some of these purposes are shown in Table 15-2.

The strategy for Grand Cypress (Figure 15-1) is to position it as a quiet, sophisticated alternative to other destination resorts in Orlando and to tell the target market, "We take golf seriously here." (Of all the golf resorts you could choose from, why come here?) The ads are probably aimed at nonusers (users will already know this), so the ads need to create awareness, get attention, capture interest, arouse desire, and position. This market will travel some distance for "perfect" golf.

The strategy for La Costa (Figure 15-2) is to position it as a unique resort with an array of facilities and recreational amenities. This market may be users as well as nonusers. For users it says, "Remember the great time you had? Come on back for more." For nonusers, the ad not only needs to create awareness and get attention, it also aims at the emotions—relax, have fun, live it up. This market may be more local (southwest United States) and takes short break vacations.

In Figure 15-3, the strategy is to position the Pier House as an uninhibited, great time, fun restaurant. Here's the place to relax and "live it up." If you've been here before, come back. If you haven't, "You don't know what you're missing."

In Figure 15-4, the strategy is to reposition The Prince of Wales as a preeminent restaurant. For users, "everything's new," including the total dining experience with a new ocean view. "Come back and

---

*For non-golfers, here are some explanations. A round of golf is 18 holes, two rounds is 36. One round can take three to four hours to play. Par for a course, that is how many strokes it should take a golfer to play 18 holes, is usually 72. Golfers who normally take more strokes than that are given handicaps, or extra strokes, so they can compete evenly with better players. Low-handicap golfers take the game very seriously and "replay" almost every hole after the game, usually with alcoholic beverages.

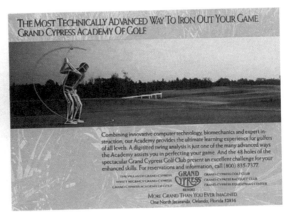

FIGURE 15-1 Grand Cypress Resort's ads illustrate the communications process—appealing to the serious golfer. Courtesy of Yesawich, Pepperdine & Brown, Orlando.

try us now; you'll be amazed." For nonusers, this ad gets attention and creates awareness. It makes the restaurant part of the evoked set the next time they want that perfect, romantic occasion.

What to Say

This stage evolves from stage 2. It deals with the method chosen to achieve the strategic objective. It is based on knowing some things about the target market. It deals with four models of communications strategy. The first two are similar and deal with consumer stages and the second two with the communications effort.

Model A. One thing we need to know about the target market is what "stage" it is in. There are essentially six steps that people move up through to get to actual purchase of a product, plus the actual purchase and repurchase. The steps are not equal: Some may be climbed quite rapidly, or even simultaneously, but when there is more psychological and/or economic commitment involved in the purchase (high involvement), it will take consumers longer to climb the steps, and each step will be more important. The steps the consumer progresses through describe the consumer's state of mind; they are as follows.

1. Has complete unawareness of the existence of the product or service
2. Has mere awareness of the existence
3. Knows what the product has to offer
4. Has favorable attitudes toward the product
5. Has preference for the product over other possibilities
6. Has a desire to buy and is convinced that it would be a wise decision
7. Actually purchases the product
8. Has purchased the product before

Various stages of this model apply to Figures 15-1 to 15-4.

Model B. This leads us to the "adoption process model." This model of consumer behavior contends that adoption, or purchase of a product, is a process. The process starts with awareness, because obviously consumers cannot buy something if they are not aware of it. Awareness can develop simply from walking down a street and seeing a restaurant entrance. It can also develop from see-

FIGURE 15 - 2   La Costa's ad also illustrates the communications process—appealing to golfers with other interests. Courtesy of Yesawich, Pepperdine & Brown, Orlando.

FIGURE 15-3   Pier House's version of the communications process is designed for diners looking for a casual good time. Courtesy of Yesawich, Pepperdine & Brown, Orlando.

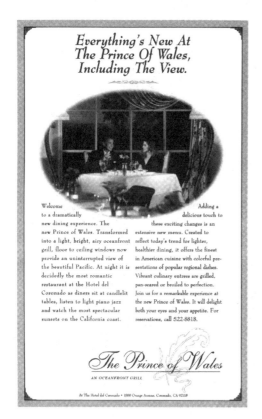

FIGURE 15-4   The Prince of Wales' ad is aimed at users looking for a more elegant dining experience. Courtesy of Yesawich, Pepperdine & Brown, Orlando.

ing a billboard on the highway and, of course, from word of mouth. Apart from word of mouth, awareness in the hospitality industry is usually created by advertising and public relations.

Once the consumer is aware, the next step in the process is "interest." If consumers are interested they seek further information and details about the product, such as the quality, the cost, how to buy it, and so forth. This information may, and often does, come via advertising. In many hospitality cases, however, it may come through the consumer's own initiative—that is, consumers will pay to use the telephone or mail to obtain more information on their own. Personal selling also play an important part in providing information when marketing to groups and meeting planners.

The third step of the model is "evaluation." At this stage consumers ask themselves a number of questions: "Does this product fulfill my needs? Does this solve my problems? Does it do it better than someone else's product? Is it worth the risk?" Advertising, personal selling, and public relations can play important roles at this stage. If the evaluation is favorable the consumer moves on to the next step, trial.

Trial of the hospitality product usually means the same as purchase; there is really no other way to try it. The promotion and merchandising parts of the communications mix are often used to induce trial, beyond that induced by the other mix elements.

If the trial is favorable, the consumers "adopt." They become repeat customers and tell others, thus becoming sources of awareness, information, and evaluation for others who are at various stages of the process. Marketers can influence adoption through performance and relationship marketing, which is why the quality of those two factors is so critical to successful marketing.

Marketers should know what stage of the adoption model their target market is at. This knowledge will strongly influence the communications strategy and objectives that should be based on the two "influence" models. Various steps of this model also apply to Figure 15-1 to 15-4.

Model C. There are three basic rules of persuasion, and they were laid down by Aristotle centuries ago:

- **Logos:** Logic and reasoning (e.g., "where your meetings run like clockwork"). These are rational appeals. (Figures 15-1, 15-4)
- **Pathos:** Emotions (e.g., "where a waterfall cascades down through the lobby"). These are emotional, mood appeals. (Figures 15-2, 15-3, 15-4)
- **Ethos:** Source credibility (e.g., "respected restaurant critic gives it four stars"). These are belief appeals, evidence. (Figures 15-1, 15-4)

For the marketer, these rules represent commonsense treatment in communicating with the target market. Logos, pathos, and ethos are a refinement in stage three of communications strategy, that is, what is the most effective means of persuasion for the target market?

Model D. We next use the stages of the consumer's mind to judge the effect we want the communications to have, and the strategy to obtain that effect. These stages are shown in Table 15-3.

Using these models we can evaluate the four ads as to what it is they are trying to say. The Grand Cypress ad uses logos (logic) and ethos (source credibility—Jack Nicklaus, a famous golfer and course designer). For nonusers it attends to the cognitive and affective stages at either the unawareness or mere awareness level and seeks to move the target to the third (knows what it offers) and fourth (favorable attitude) levels at the interest or evaluation stage. La Costa's ad is based more on pathos. It attends to the affective stage to develop favorable attitudes toward the product and, finally the evaluation and trial stages.

The Pier House ad is clearly aimed at the pathos level. It attends to the affective stage to develop preference for the product over other possibilities and, finally, the trial stage. The Prince of Wales ad deals more with ethos in the conative stage. It aims at creating a desire to buy and the trial stage.

How to Say It

Once the first three stages of communications strategy have been taken care of, the creative juices

TABLE 15-3
Consumer Stages and Their Impact on Communications Strategy

Consumer Stage	Effect Stage	Strategy
Cognitive: The stage of thoughts/beliefs	Create awareness, beliefs, interest, differentiate	Provide information, get attention, inform, remind
Affective: The stage of emotions	Change attitudes and feelings, get involved, evaluate	Position, create benefits and image, stir emotions, arouse
Conative: The stage of motivation and intention	Stimulate and direct desires, adopt	Move to action, reinforce expectation, persuade (see Figure 15-5)

1-800-456-8888

Mirage

Everything you've heard is true.

FIGURE 15-5 Mirage' ad is aimed at the conative stage, propelling action.

at the Prince of Wales it is mood, quality, romance,
atmospherics.

Compare these ads to the consumer trade-off
model in Chapter 1: How do the ads fit this model?
What expectations do they create, what problems do
they solve, what is the price/value relationship and
the risk? Also, consider all four ads in terms of the
definition of the aims of the communications mix:

- Establish communications between the firm
  and the target market.
- Increase the tangibility of the product/service
  mix.
- Establish or monitor consumer expectations.
- Persuade consumers to purchase.

These are the things to be accomplished.
Consider the ads also in terms of selective perception, selective attention, selective comprehension,
selective acceptance, and selective retention, which
we discussed in Chapter 8; and in terms of salience,
determinance, and importance, discussed in
Chapter 11.

How Often to Say It

The next stage is both a consumer-driven and a
budget-driven one. Repetition has been shown to
help selective retention. It has also been shown to
increase "wear-out," that is, the tendency of the
consumer to ignore it after having seen or hearing
it so often. Therefore, this stage requires careful
consideration of when to say it (e.g., television
times, newspaper placement, in-flight magazines),
as well as how often, which will always have a budget limitation.

Where to Say It

Where, as used here, applies to the various components of the communications mix. The examples
used above were advertisements, but only for ease
of illustration. If we use advertising then we must
select the appropriate medium, electronic or print.
Electronic media include television, radio, and

of everyone involved start flowing in the direction
of the advertising copy, the appeals to the customer, the execution stage. Of the many, many options the search is for the one that will work best;
the one that most precisely accomplishes the objectives consistent with the identified target market. Some of the appeal options are humor, fun,
sex, cronyism, price/value, slice of life, lifestyle,
self-improvement, mood, testimonial, and quality.

The creative strategy for Grand Cypress is to
emphasize the product's unique design, physical
ambience, and high quality as well the self-
improvement from the golf academy, and Jack
Niklaus. For La Costa it is mood, lifestyle, experience, activity, "enchantment," special effects,
image, "incredible." The creative strategy at Pier
House is to "conch out," relax, enjoy (lifestyle). And

now the growing home computer on-line services. Print media include newspapers, magazines, billboards, and direct mail. Demographics, geographics, psychographics, annual incomes, and a multitude of other determining factors are reviewed before selection of where to say it occurs.

We might also, of course, use personal selling, promotion, and/or public relations (who goes there?). For Grand Cypress, golf magazines are an obvious medium; perhaps also direct mail to people on a golf association list. For La Costa, consumer and golf magazines would be appropriate, as well as San Diego (30 minutes away) and Los Angeles (90 minutes away) newspapers. For Pier House, local Florida Keys publications would catch the attention of both natives and visitors. Perhaps local radio. The Prince of Wales would also use the local newspaper in San Diego (minutes away) and possibly direct mail.

RESEARCH FOR THE COMMUNICATIONS MIX

If we have to know the target market in order to develop the optimal communications mix and strategy, it follows that the best results will be obtained through research. In the long run, good research will save communications dollars.

We recognize that many properties, particularly individually owned restaurants, will not have such involved communications mixes as those described here. Even these properties, however, will most likely engage in merchandising, sales promotion, and some advertising, if not personal selling; and good public relations can be used by any business. Research is done both internally and externally. The following guidelines apply to even the smallest business, if in somewhat modified form. There are five major questions to be answered.

Where Are We Now?

In other words, how are we perceived? Examples might be "expensive," "luxurious," "good service,"

"good food," "full facilities," "atmospheric," "cheap," "unfriendly," "rundown," "old and tired," or any number of other things. Here are other questions to be asked:

> How do we compare with the competition?
> What do their customers think of us?
> Are they aware of what we have to offer?
> Have they tried us? If not, why not? If so, do they return? Why? Why not? What are their attitudes and feelings?

In short, the research question at this stage is, "How are we seen now?" Management may believe that it has the finest food in town, but if the market doesn't believe this, it really doesn't matter whether it does or not. It is hard to go anywhere if you don't know from where you are starting.

Why Are We There?

This research step calls for an evaluation of the product and previous communications efforts. To embellish on the example above, suppose analysis shows that our food is really not that good. If the objective is to be perceived as having the finest food in town, the product will have to be altered and a new communications effort initiated. If, in fact, we do have the finest food in town, then the communications objective will be to change perceptions. Besides product evaluation, here are other aspects to be researched:

> Are prices perceived as too high?
> What is the real quality level of our service?
> Is the competition doing the same thing, only better?
> Are our attributes and benefits what we think they are?
> Do we really solve consumers' problems? The right ones?
> What puts us in this position?
> What are our strengths and weaknesses?
> What are the users' dissatisfactions?
> What is the profile of users?

What is the usage pattern of users?

Have we communicated what we want to communicate?

The research question at this stage is "How is our product used?" If where we are now is not where we want to be, then we have to find out how we got there. Even if it is where we want to be, we still need to know how we got there. There is nothing like knowing what you are doing right and why.

Where Could We Be?

If where we are now is not where we want to be, then where could we realistically be? Let's say we are not perceived as having the best food in town, but that is where we would like to be: Is that realistic? Do we have the right staff in the kitchen? Can we afford to buy the finest ingredients without raising prices? Would we have to raise prices to achieve the "finest food" objective? Is there a market for it?

That's the product point of view. Perhaps we do have the finest food in town, just what we want to be, but the market doesn't see it that way. Then we would have to ask whether it is realistic to believe that we can change perceptions that, in this case, would be vis-à-vis the competition. Here are some other issues in this stage:

What market position could we achieve?

Are there new buyers and users out there?

Can we increase awareness?

Can we change beliefs or create new ones?

Can we increase benefits and solve other problems?

Do we have the right target markets? Are there others?

Can we create new target markets?

Can we steal from the competition?

The major research question at this stage is "What unmet needs, wants, and problems are there that we have the capability of fulfilling?" The answers to these questions will establish our communication objectives.

How Can We Get There?

Now comes the creative thinking. When this is based on good, solid research, it comes easier and is more likely to work. The first and most obvious question is "What do we have to change?" This could be any part of the product/service mix, or of the presentation mix that is tangibilizing the product/service to the marketplace. Thus we might have to change the product, the service, the price, the atmospherics, the facilities, the employees, or, if we can, the location. We might also have to change the distribution network, or the target markets.

Once we have the product right, and not until then, we can commence with what we have to change, via the communications mix. The Howard Johnson's case described earlier gives an example of trying to persuade with communications before the product is corrected. Howard Johnson's ad campaign, "If it's not your mother, it must be Howard Johnson's," stretched consumer credibility to a limit that very few restaurants could hope to achieve, and which Howard Johnson's never did. Such actions are often fatal; the customer doesn't like to be fooled twice.

Are We Getting There?

This is probably the most neglected stage of communications research. It really means starting over again at the beginning, except that now the field is narrower because we know what we are looking for. This is research to measure results. It asks, "What have we, or haven't we, changed?"

If the objective was to be perceived as having the best food in town, are we now so perceived? The campaign may have brought people, which can be temporary and misleading, but what we want to know is whether we have changed perception, which will have a long-lasting effect.

Some years after the Howard Johnson's campaign above, after Marriott had bought Howard Johnson's and resold the lodging properties to Prime Motor Inns (which went into bankruptcy and sold them to Hospitality Franchise Systems), another communications campaign took place.

This story is told in Table 15-4 to illustrate all of the above points.

PUSH/PULL STRATEGIES

There is one more important element in developing the communications mix. This is especially true in an industry that deals so heavily with other customer providers, or intermediaries, such as travel agents, tour operators, and external reservation systems. We have mentioned these before.

Using a **push strategy** means "pushing" the communications mix down through the distribution channels. For example, a hotel company calls on travel agents, advertises in travel agent publications, provides travel agent bonuses, and so forth. This is intended to get their cooperation in sending customers.

Using a **pull strategy** means going directly to the market who will then go through the distribution channels to book their reservations with an idea in mind of what they want. Ads that say, "call your travel agent" are using this method; that is the company is "pulling" the customer up through the distribution channel. Both methods are common in the hospitality industry and often used simultaneously. The communication question is, "Who are you targeting?" the customer or the intermediary. This will guide the communications message.

WORD-OF-MOUTH COMMUNICATION

The most powerful form of communications, especially in the hospitality industry, is word of mouth. This is particularly true of many individual restaurants and small exclusive hotels that do not formally use any portion of the communications mix.

Elements of the communications mix can, of course, influence word-of-mouth behavior. We may see an ad, read or hear publicity, or talk to a salesperson, and from any one of those experiences develop a perception and expectation. We may then communicate that perception to someone else via word of mouth even though we really have no actual experiences with the product. In this sense, the communications mix affects word of mouth and, indirectly, may persuade someone to purchase or not to purchase.

By and large, however, word-of-mouth behavior originates in actual experience or the word of mouth of others who have had an actual experience. Thus we control behavior more by what we do (relationship marketing) than by what we say. Word of mouth is familiar to all and needs no further discussion here. A strong foundation for good word-of-mouth communication, however, is built by fulfilling the needs and expectations of our customers. When this is not done, an important factor in recapturing a reputation is the way customer requests and complaints are handled, as we discussed in Chapter 3.

DATABASE MARKETING

Database marketing, also called direct mail or direct marketing, is a subset of the communications mix. It's most important usage is the business of managing relevant data on customers to identify them for the purpose of developing a longstanding relationship of repeat business; to send desired messages at the right time, in the right form, to the right people; and to develop the right product that satisfies their needs and wants. Essentially, databases are decision-support systems.

The information in the systems includes internal data on customers and purchased data (list sources) on customers and prospects. The information can be used to generate mailing lists and prospect lists for salespeople and to identify market segments. A direct communications channel with customers and prospects is provided through a computerized customer database. Database marketing augments

TABLE 15-4
The Howard Johnson's Repositioning Ad Campaign

Where are we now? Prime Motor Inns conducted research to answer this question. According to the trade press, Prime's research determined that the negative image accorded Howard Johnson was due solely to the restaurant division; the lodging division was perceived as having a positive image.

We are not familiar with the actual research, but let's consider what it *should* have done. First, go back to the six stages of the consumer described earlier. Awareness was not a problem; just about everyone knew Howard Johnson. Step three is knowing what the product has to offer. Howard Johnson's early motel units were notorious for thin walls, noise, poor maintenance, dark hallways, depressing lobbies, and other negative factors. This generates a research question: Did the consumer now know that at least some of the properties did not fit this image?

Step four is favorable attitude toward the product. If the answer to step three, knowing what the product has to offer, was no, then the answer here is no. If the answer to step three was yes, then the question is, "Do some units with positive conditions create a favorable attitude toward the entire product line?" If the answer was no, then the first step of the campaign should be to create a favorable attitude—after the problems were corrected, of course.

This would mean repositioning. Recall from Chapter 11 that repositioning can mean removing negative images while creating positive ones. One way to help do this would have been to change the name and paint Howard Johnson's famous orange roofs another color, after the negative factors had been corrected, of course.

Prime's research answer, as we have indicated, was "yes"—some units with positive conditions created a favorable attitude toward all units. Prime therefore retained the name and the orange roofs. Frankly, we doubt the validity and reliability of this finding. We think that Prime had some doubts about it too because, as we will soon see, they went to great effort to change the image.

From this point, the research would address the issues in steps five to seven—that is, how do we actually create preference, the desire to buy, and the actual purchase? If Prime had believed what they said they believed, this is where they would have commenced the communications campaign, in stage three, the conative stage, of the model in Table 15-3. Instead, they commenced it in the affective stage.

Why are we there? Howard Johnson had a long history that provided many answers to this question. Even given a positive answer to "Where are we now?" fresh research would have proven very enlightening. If the positive answer was, in fact, incorrect, this would have come out at this step and signalled a change in direction. If it was, in fact, correct, Howard Johnson could have learned at this step why it was correct. This would form the basis of the new communications campaign.

Where could we be? The answers to this question for this example deal largely with positioning. What position could Howard Johnson fill? Did it have to change beliefs to do that? Did it have the right target markets, and so forth? This stage of research is designed to bring realism to the campaign, as opposed to wishful thinking.

How can we get there? This is the ultimate question, the answer to which will drive the communications campaign. For Howard Johnson, in our opinion, it meant a total repositioning aided by a name change. In Prime's opinion, apparently, it also meant repositioning, but with the same name and without any real effort to destroy any previous negative image. Their new ad campaign said, Believe us when we tell you that "We're turning Howard Johnson upside down," with these words literally upside down at the top of the ad. The first paragraph of copy said,

> Your eyes aren't playing tricks on you. We're making so many exciting changes at Howard Johnson, people in the travel industry are starting to say we're turning the place around (or upside down depending on how you look at things).

The last paragraph said,

> Your eyes aren't fooling you, Howard Johnson is turning upside down. And we're so excited by the changes, we're doing flip flops ourselves.

(continued)

T A B L E   1 5 - 4 *(Continued)*

The ad was signed by the CEO. The ad was aimed at corporate travel planners who were, and remained, reluctant to book their clients at a Howard Johnson.

Here's what a Howard Johnson spokesman said about the estimated five million dollar advertising campaign:

Howard Johnson wants to inform the public that the company has changed dramatically . . . to position itself solely as a lodging chain. "What we're saying is, `Hey, folks, we've got a really good product here and don't be discouraged by what we were in the past. Now we're strictly in the hotel business. If you try us, chances are you're going to like us and want to come back.' . . .[W]e wanted a campaign that would cut through all the clutter out there. We wanted our customers to know that something is changing at Howard Johnson."

The new ad campaign is based on research that indicated . . . "A lot of the negative image of Howard Johnson is related to the restaurants."[1]

Note: Among other things, Howard Johnson failed in its communications strategy. Today, it has gained in stature. Under new ownership (Cendant, Inc.), it has divested many of its inferior properties, has built or converted a number of new ones, and has expanded internationally where it does not have to fight a previous image. The roofs, however, are still mostly orange and much of the negative image lingers on in the United States, by those who still remember, and franchise ads still talk about "turning around."

more traditional communications vehicles such as advertising and personal selling.

Database marketing works well with certain market segments of the hospitality industry. Restaurant customers respond well to database marketing, as do weekend package customers for hotels. Individuals tend to respond to database marketing better than organizational customers. There appears to be a correlation between the size of the purchase and the response to database marketing. Dinner for two, which may cost $100, brings a better response from database marketing than it would from a group, which may spend $100,000 in a hotel.

Database information enables companies to target individuals or small microsegments of people. This is very useful for sales and sales management support and for direct marketing programs. Database marketing has three main benefits. It provides a strategic advantage through the more effective use of marketing information internally; it improves the use of customer and market information; and it forms a basis for developing long-term customer relationships, especially with those who account for a large portion of a firm's business.

One form of database marketing is telemarketing, using the telephone to reach customers or prospective customers. This, however, has its limits. In some industries its usage is so frequent that it becomes annoying and counterproductive with many people who are called at home. On business-to-business calls, however, it is more appropriate for setting up sales calls based on information that has been gathered. In this way, databases complement advertising and personal selling. From either of those sources information may be obtained to set up the database, which is then used for further contact.

Proprietary marketing databases are those developed by an individual company for its own use. They provide a competitive advantage in enabling a company to focus on a particular market segment. Examples in the hotel industry are guest history information and frequent guest programs. Preferred room type, pillows, amenities, and other services enable a hotel to be ready to satisfy a customer upon arrival and without hassle. This is a powerful force in relationship marketing. Some systems, such as Ritz-Carlton's, enable any Ritz-Carlton in the world to tap into these preferences after a customer has stayed at any other Ritz-Carlton at another location. Direct mail contact is also facilitated when an event is planned that coincides with certain guests' particular interests. The same is true for restaurants although databases have not yet seen widespread use in these operations.

Customized marketing databases are used to profile prospective customers. Data obtained from outside sources is customized to fit the property's customer profile. Customer information is obtained before the customer is actually contacted so that product information can be customized in advance. Also, contacts can be made with potential customers who have similar profiles to present customers, thus being those who have a greater probability of becoming future customers. Known media use, for example, enables a company to better target its markets through the proper advertising channels. In fact, several customized versions of a promotion or advertisement can be specifically designed for particular market segments.

Database Marketing Components

Database marketing has four fundamental components—strategy, data, information, and knowledge.

Strategy begins with the objectives of the marketing program. Who are the target customers, where do they live, what do they buy, where else do they go, and so on. Once the strategy is conceived and integrated with the other marketing vehicles, such as advertising and public relations, the data is assembled.

Data starts with the actual names, addresses, telephone numbers, dates of departures, preferences, purchase habits, credit card usage, and so on. The initial database should contain data on past customers. New customer prospects, obtained from list sources, can then be added.

The *information* portion of database marketing is the analysis of the data. Demographics and psychographics of customers need to be analyzed. Other factors, such as why they use a particular hotel or restaurant can be added.

The *knowledge* stage of a database program includes segmentation, clustering, and modeling. Segmentation, as discussed in Chapter 10, includes gathering like customers together. For example, a

hotel might have a list of customers who buy weekend packages segmented under a "leisure" code. A restaurant might have a list of customers who attend Sunday Brunch. These segments are then clustered. For example, the leisure traveler may also be a brunch goer at the same property. Or, the leisure customer might come to New York City on weekends in April and live in Northern New Jersey, another cluster.

Once customers are clustered, the search for new lists (and potentially new customers) begins by modeling. The assumption is that if nonusers have similar clusters as current customers, this list source will have a higher yield than a list that has an unknown similarity to current customers.

Using the Database

Database marketing should first be employed to "talk to" past customers. Many property management systems(PMS) in hotels have extensive data on customers that have used the hotel in the past and are familiar with the property. The first step in a database marketing campaign is to assemble the list of past customers. This list may come from the PMS, registration cards, old invoices, credit card companies, or business cards.

The list of past customers is then put on some type of computer program. Simple lists can be assembled on traditional software such as WordPerfect or Lotus. More complex lists need to be built on database programs such as Paradox. Once the list of past customers is organized, certain fields are established to allow the organization to segment the customers. A field is an indication on the database that one characteristic is different from another. Fields can be established for location, date of check out, market segment, amount spent per visit, and so on.

For example, in a hotel there is a major difference between corporate and leisure customers. To make the example simple, a hotel determines that most customers checking out Monday through Friday are corporate, and customers checking out Saturday and Sunday are leisure. These are two different types of customers with two different sets of needs. Fields are set up within the database to allow the marketer to choose corporate and leisure customers to contact.

The hotel then decides to "talk to" both its corporate and leisure customers. Two different **collateral** pieces are developed, one aimed at the corporate customer, the other at the leisure customer. The advertising agency creates two mailers designed to thank the past customers for their business and encourage future usage. For the corporate customer, a newsletter is created to inform them about the different programs within the hotel. The leisure customer is mailed a promotion encouraging return during certain slow weekends.

Once the collateral is developed, the piece is "dropped," or mailed to the customers. To track the database marketing effort, a "trigger" or response mechanism is placed in the collateral to measure success. A trigger might be a special telephone number for the promotion or a certificate to be redeemed in the restaurant. Advertising campaigns work similarly. Database marketing is unique in its ability to be tracked and documented.

Current thinking on database marketing positions it closer to advertising in terms of **tracking.** Advertising can be image oriented, to communicate a positioning statement to a customer, or retail oriented, offering specific prices to be tracked for productivity. Contrarily, database marketing in the past has been tracking driven, needing 2 to 5 percent returns to be considered successful. Database marketing now has an image component like advertising that remains untrackable. For example, many restaurants and hotels routinely send customers newsletters on upcoming programs. These newsletters are untrackable in terms or covers or room nights but nonetheless keep the hospitality entity in touch with its customers.

Once a facility covers its past customers, new customers can be obtained through database marketing. New customers can be found by profiling past customers. The theory behind profiling is that similar customers buy similar facilities. By analyzing the fields of the past customers, a very good pic-

ture of new customers begins to emerge. Past customer fields can yield age, location, income, type of car driven, purchase habits, media usage, local business contacts, number of visits to restaurants in a month, and so on. Given this information, the savvy database marketer seeks lists of similar customers. Table 15-5 provides two examples of using databases for marketing purposes. Table 15-6 summarizes different ways to use a marketing database.

BUDGETING THE COMMUNICATIONS MIX

The amount that a company or an individual property may spend on its total communications effort is not easy to determine. There are no unvarying standards as to how much should be spent in a given product/market situation. This is because the situation is compounded by a complex set of circumstances that are never constant within or among properties or companies. Our concern here will be with individual properties, not entire firms like McDonald's and Burger King, which spend huge amounts and utilize televison, or Marriott and Hilton, which utilize the national print media.

What does the budget consist of? We discussed this briefly in Chapter 7 so this discussion is just an extension of that. Let's start with some common practices. Restaurants do not have marketing departments. If they are individually owned they may or may not have advertising costs. If they do, the amount spent on them is most likely based on "gut feel." How good is business, how well are they known, and how far is their reach? Chances are, those who advertise will spend 2 to 3 percent of sales. In a city where advertising costs are higher, they may spend more. If they are part of a chain or a franchisee, restaurants will pay up to 4 percent of revenue to the parent company that does national or regional advertising for all units in the chain. Any local advertising that they may do on their own comes under the 2 to 3 percent category.

TABLE 15-5
Two Examples of Using a Marketing Database

A hotel in Stamford, CT, built a database of existing customers and sent collateral to encourage repeat usage. The marketing team then wanted to find new customers through database marketing. By profiling its past customers, a picture of likely new customers emerged. The past customer for the leisure segment was a married couple earning a $75,000 household income, 49 years of age with two cars, stayed one night, ate breakfast and dinner in the hotel, and lived within 45 miles of the hotel. The hotel conducted several focus groups of past customers to determine the psychographic reasons for the weekend package purchase. In brief, the customers were looking for a quick getaway for a night.

Armed with this information, the hotel marketing team began to research list sources for similar customers. Lists were purchased that matched the current customer base. A new collateral piece was developed, aimed more at the potential customer and encouraging trial of the hotel, rather than repurchase. The trigger was a coupon for an upgrade to better accommodations upon check-in. This feature allowed the management of the hotel to measure response. The database marketing was successful and was continued as an integral portion of the communications mix.

Many times marketing partners share databases for mutual marketing needs. A hotel in Atlanta approached an area attraction to do some combined marketing. The attraction was busy on weekends, when the hotel was slow. Conversely, the hotel was busy in the middle of the week, the attraction's slowest time period. The two organizations shared customer lists and both received additional business by database marketing to each other's customers. There is no doubt that good database marketing will provide a strong competitive edge in the future.

In the hotel industry similar rules apply, only now reservation costs are added to the equation. A franchised Days Inn will also have no marketing department, may do zero local advertising, but will pay the franchisor a set fee per room, or a percentage of revenue for both advertising and the reservation system. These amounts are contractually negotiated; for example, some recent figures are shown in Table 15-7. These figures are these properties' marketing cost. Again, any local advertising they do will be similar to that of independent restaurants. Also, if they have meeting space they may have salespeople who also come under the marketing costs total.

Major hotels have marketing departments, so this is the more complex case. We'll deal with common practice, which of course will vary among properties. A major hotel will usually base its marketing budget on forecasted sales. This includes the salaries of the marketing and sales staff, fees paid to the parent company (if there is one) for national or regional advertising and for the reservation system. These fees may be percentage based or rooms based or, in the case of advertising, total revenue based. The hotel will also pay to the parent company a fee for any frequent traveler program. (These are usually forecast as a separate item out-side the marketing budget.) Any local advertising is on their own.

What does all this amount to? A good rule of thumb is 5 to 6 percent of forecasted sales for the total marketing budget, which includes all these elements. (For international percentages, please see Chapter 7.) Brand name hotels tend toward the 5 percent figure because of the economies of scale with a large channel of distribution. Independent hotels and resorts tend toward the 6 percent level.

How the money is divided is another issue. Other than contractual fees which are fixed, a property has considerable latitude as whether to spend on advertising, promotions, collateral, research, and so on, and the sales force. A hotel with a large proportion of meetings business will have a larger and stronger sales staff. The director of marketing will negotiate with management as to the department's budget and how and where it will be spent, one choice clearly affecting the other. On a 5 percent budget, a usual split would be,

2 percent salaries and benefits
1.5 percent advertising
1 percent travel/entertainment
0.5 percent collateral/miscellaneous

T A B L E   1 5 - 6
Different Ways to Utilize a Marketing Database

1. Identify best customers (recency, frequency, monetary value).
   - Save money by communicating with best customers.
   - Create customer loyalty by acknowledging the relationship.
   - Identify more potential new customers.
2. Develop new customers.
   - Identify the characteristics of best customers and then purchase lists of similar customers. Overlay information from other sources.
3. Deliver a message consistent with product usage.
   - Segment targeted communications based on customers' purchases, new or infrequent, moderate, or heavy usage.
4. Reinforce customer purchase decisions.
   - Say "thank you" and reassure customers about their experience.
5. **Cross-sell** and **complementary-sell** products.
   - Match product and customer profiles to sell other products that match their lifestyle, for example, a Marriott resort to a business traveler. Find additional needs for services that can be developed.
6. Improve delivery of sales promotions.
   - Target mailings much more effectively.
7. Increase the effectiveness of distribution channels.
   - Deal directly with the customer whatever channel they come through.

Although it is generally accepted that the effects of advertising, other forms of promotion, sales calls, and so on may last over a long period, there is no certainty about the duration of the benefits. The cumulative effect depends on the loyalty of customers, frequency of purchase, and competitive efforts, each of which may be influenced by a different set of variables. Further, promotions may induce competitors to react but it is hard to tell just what that reaction will be until it happens. When it does, the strength of the response may mean additional expenditures to meet it. Hotels also cut rates to compete, or in a down market, but unlike some other industries these are not included in the marketing budget.

There are other methods, or rules of thumb, for determining marketing budgets. More common in hospitality would be budgets based on historical figures, and even budgets arrived at by educated guess. Another method is the one of "How much can we afford?" which seems cautious but is actually a risky approach. Then there is the return on investment approach, which compares the expected return with the desired return, and treats the expenditure as an investment to be recouped over the years. Some promotional costs, of course, produce immediate results. In both cases, however, it may be very difficult to determine the outcome. Then, there is the competitive approach which, essentially, means knowing or seeing what the competition does and reacting to it.

In practice, it is not easy to pinpoint the separate roles of advertising, sales departments, and sales promotions because these three methods almost always overlap each other. A further complexity occurs when an opportunity that hasn't been accounted for in the budget, arises suddenly, such as a group suddenly deciding to come to the city and seeking competitive bids, which can lead to expensive promises and to great sales efforts on the other side of the country. In the final analysis, a hotel may arbitrarily set a figure such as 5 percent of sales as a benchmark, develop the marketing

Franchise Marketing and Reservations Fees[2]

HOTEL & MOTEL MANAGEMENT'S 1998 FRANCHISING

Brand	Parent Company	Segment	Marketing fee	Reservations fee
AmericInn International	AmericInn International	Upscale, limited-service	2%	$0.25 per minute for 800#
Ashbury Suites & Inns	Lodging Hospitality Systems	Upper, Mid Market	2%	Per delivered reservation.
Baymont Inns	Marcus Corp.	Economy	2%	1%
Best Western*	Best Western International	Midmarket	$25,550	$13,140
Budget Host Inns*	Budget Host International	Economy	Included	$39 per unit
Candlewood Suites	Candlewood Hotel Co.	Extended-stay, midprice	None	None
Clarion Hotels, Suites &Resorts	Choice Hotels International	Upscale	1% GRR	1.25% GRR
Club Hotels by Doubletree	Promus Hotel Corp.	Midscale	N/A	N/A
Comfort Inns & Comfort Suites	Choice Hotels International	Limited-service	2.1% GRR	1.75% GRR
Country Hearth Inns	Buckhead America Corp.	Upper economy	1.5%	1% + $1/net reservation
Country Inns & Suites by Carlson	Carlson Companies	Mid tier	2% first year	$5.50/net reservation
Courtyard by Marriott	Marriott International	Upper mid-scale	2% GRR	1.25%
Crowne Plaza Hotels & Resorts	Bass PLC	Upscale	2%	1%
Days Inn of America	Cendant Corp.	Upper economy	Included	2.3%
Downtowner Inns	Hospitality International, Inc.	Mid-scale	1%	$3 per delivered reservation
Econo Lodge	Choice Hotels International	Economy	3.5% GRR	Combined with marketing fee
Embassy Suites	Promus Hotel Corp.	Upscale, all suite	3.5% GRR%	Combined with marketing fee
Fairfield Inn by Marriott	Marriott International	Economy	2.5% GRR	1.5% GRR + $2.95 per res.
Four Points Hotels	Starwood Hotels & Resorts	Full-service	1%	N/A
GuestHouse	Guest House Inns, Hotels & Suites	Upper economy, midmarket	$1.25/room per day	N/A
Hampton Inn	Promus Hotel Corp.	Mid-scale, limited-service	4% GRR	Combined with marketing fee
Hampton Inn & Suites	Promus Hotel Corp.	Upper mid-scale	4% GRR	Combined with marketing fee
Hawthorn Suites	US Franchise Systems	Upper extended stay	2.5%	Included
Hilton Garden Inns	Hilton Hotels Corp.	Midprice	1%	1.7%
Hilton Suites	Hilton Hotels Corp.	All-suite, upscale	1%	1.7%
Hilton Hotels	Hilton Hotels Corp.	Full-service, upscale	1%	1.7%
Holiday Inn	Holiday Hospitality	Full-service	1.5%	1%
Holiday Inn Express	Holiday Hospitality	Limited-service	2%	1%
Homewood Suites	Promus Hotel Corp.	Extended-stay	4%	Combined with marketing fees
Howard Johnson International	Cendant Corp.	Midmarket	2%	2.5%
ITT Sheraton Hotels & Resorts	Starwood Hotels & Resorts	Upscale	1%	N/A
Key West Inns	Key West Inns	Upper economy	1%	1% + $1 per delivered room
Knights Inn	Cendant Corp.	Budget	3%	Combined with marketing fees
MainStay Suites	Choice Hotels International	Midmarket, extended-stay	2.5% monthly GRR	Combined with marketing fee
Master Hosts Inns & Resorts	Hospitality International	Midmarket	1%	$3 per room
Microtel Inns &Suites	US Franchise Systems	Budget	2%	Included
Motel 6 L.P.	Accor Group	Budget	3%	N/A
Marriott Hotels, Resorts &Suites	Marriott International	Full service	1% GRR	Includes fixed &variable fees
Omni Hotels	Omni Hotels	Upscale, full-service	3.5%	Included
Park Inn International	Park Plaza International	Economy	1%	1.5%
Park Plaza International	Park Plaza International	Upscale	1%	1.5%
Platinum Suites	Platinum	Limited-service	1%	1%
Passport Inn	Hospitality International	Budget	1%	$3 per delivered room
Quality Inns, Hotels & Suites	Choice Hotels International	Midmarket	2.1% GRR	1.75% GRR
Radisson Hotels Worldwide	Carslon Companies	Upscale	3.5% GRR	$11 per delivered room
Ramada Franchise Systems	Cendant Corp.	Mid- to upper-midmarket	4.5%	Combined with marketing fees
Red Carpet Inn	Hospitality International	Midmarket	1%	$3 per delivered room
Red Roof Inns	Red Roof Inns	Economy	2.5%	2%
Renaissance Hotels &Resorts	Marriott International	Full service, upscale	1.5% GRR	$3.25 fixed per room
Residence Inn by Marriott	Marriott International	Upper mid-scale	2.5% GRR	N/A
Rodeway Inn	Choice Hotels International	Budget	1.25% GRR	1.25% GRR
Scottish Inns	Hospitality International	Economy	1%	$3 per delivered room
Sheraton Hotels	Starwood Hotels &Resorts	Upscale, full-service	1%	N/A
Signature Inns	Signature Inns	Midprice	3.5%	Combined with marketing
Sleep Inn	Choice Hotels International	Limited-service	2.1% GRR	1.75% GRR
Staybridge Suites by Holiday Inn	Holiday Hospitality	Extended-stay	Included	Included
Suburban Lodge	Suburban Lodges of America	Economy, extended-stay	N/A	N/A
Sundowner Inns	Hospitality International	Economy	1%	$3 per delivered room
Super 8 Motels	Cendant Corp.	Economy	Included	Included
TownePlace Suites	Marriott International	Moderate, extended-stay	1.5% GRR	1% GRR + $2.50 per res.
Travelodge	Cendant Corp.	Midmarket	4%	Combined with marketing fees
Villager Inn & Lodges	Cendant Corp.	Economy, extended-stay	1%	1%
Wingate Inns	Cendant Corp.	Upper midmarket	4%	Included

* Membership company

Key: N/A=Either not applicable or not available at discretion of franchisor,
GRR=Gross room revenue

plan, and then adjust up or down as need be. New openings, special events, and special situations will affect the final budget.

ADVERTISING

Advertising is mass communication that is paid for. It is the most visible element of the communications mix. It has the broadest potential reach of all the components of the communications mix—that is, it can reach the largest mass of people. It can also be the most expensive component. The question is: How effective is it? That is a question that researchers, especially those connected with advertising agencies, have been trying to answer for years. It is an especially pertinent question in the hospitality industry, where word of mouth is such a potent force.

We include in advertising all those things that are part of the public media, such as newspaper and magazine ads; television and radio commercials; websites; billboards; airplane streamers; train, bus, and taxi cards; and so forth, as long as those are paid for by a specific sponsor. We also include collateral, such as hotel brochures, flyers, and pamphlets, and direct mail (not derived from databases), which are not exactly public media but fit into the same genre.

The Roles of Advertising

Advertising, of course, performs the same general role of all communications as a whole: it informs, creates awareness, attempts to persuade, and reinforces buying behavior of present customers. It also can play a major role in positioning, as we have shown. Advertising is subject to the same guidelines that we discussed in the first part of this chapter; the major difference is that it is paid mass communication.

For the hospitality industry, the most important objective function of advertising may be to create and maintain awareness of the company or the property, or some particular component of either such as a new addition or a new service. The most important subjective function is to position the property or the company, as we showed in Figures 15-1 to 15-4.

Advertising also informs, although much hospitality print advertising is not very informative because its constant sameness often fails to differentiate one property from another in the same product class (Figure 15-6). An ad like this does nothing to address the stages we discussed earlier (cognitive, affective, conative), is not persuasive (logos, ethos, pathos), and only, very minimally, addresses the state of complete awareness. It is unlikely that this restaurant will become a part of anyone's **evoked set** as a result of this ad. In short,

CAFFE DE VINCI

"The Italian Art of Pasta"
from homemade lasagna to crabmeat ravioli.

- Private room available for parties
- Full Bar
- Valet Parking
- Outdoor Dining
- Elegant casual atmosphere in a romantic setting

Lunch Monday–Friday
11:30 a.m.–2:30 p.m.
Dinner Nightly
5:30–11:00 p.m.
1009 Kane Concourse
Bay Harbor Islands
(305) 861-8166

FIGURE 15-6 Cafe da Vinci, Bay Harbor Islands, Florida, ran this ad that fails to inform or differentiate.

it is probably money wasted. Much of restaurant (especially fast-food) and hotel chain advertising is done to reinforce behavior and expectation. Companies like Marriott, Westin, Hilton, Holiday, Hyatt, and so on, do chain advertising as a constant reminder to their customers (called **maintenance advertising**) and, of course, to create awareness for potential new customers who may switch.

What Advertising Should Accomplish

Major advertising campaigns in the hospitality industry are conducted only by very large companies with large resources. In the restaurant industry, we are all familiar with the television commercials that emanate from McDonald's (one of the largest advertisers in the country), Burger King, and other fast-food chains.

On the other end of the continuum are the individual restaurants or motor inns that do almost no advertising. In between these two extremes lies a vast group of hospitality operators who do limited advertising on very limited budgets. For these operators, the "more bang for the buck" principle is especially appropriate: Advertising dollars have to be carefully allocated to where they will do the most good. Figure 15-7 is an example of this.

To do the most good, the ideal hospitality advertisement will accomplish five things:

1. It will tangibilize the service element so the reader can mentally grasp what is offered.
2. It will promise a benefit that can be delivered and/or provide solutions to problems.
3. It will differentiate the property from that of the competition.
4. It will have positive effects on employees who must execute the promises.
5 It will capitalize on word of mouth.

We can demonstrate these accomplishments by referring to the Marriott ad in Figure 15-8. Marriott is a national advertiser, but the same principles apply even if you are only advertising in your local newspaper.

FIGURE 15-7 Ebb Tide's ad shows an example of carefully directed advertising by a one-unit restaurant.

The Marriott ad promises a benefit and a solution to one of the most common concerns of hotel meeting planners, getting help when they need it. It differentiates from the competition by immediate identification of the people who can help, something few hotels do. The ad also says that Marriott will keep that promise because there's CEO Bill Marriott himself putting his name on the line. The ad also tangibilizes the service with the red coat. The reader has no trouble conceptually grasping what the benefit will be. The ad has a positive effect on employees because it makes a commitment from the president of the company that he is prepared to back up what he says, thus creating an inspirational effect.

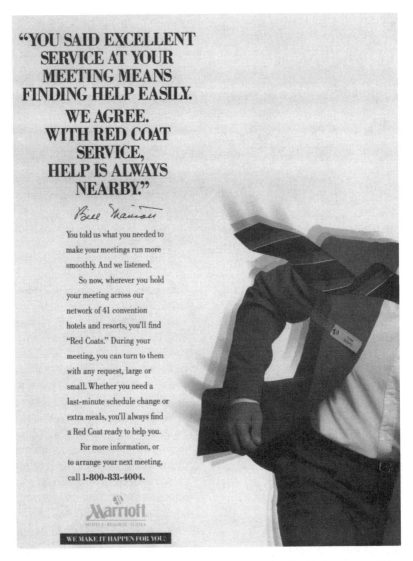

FIGURE 15-8 Marriott's ad demonstrates the five major accomplishments of good hospitality advertising.

Finally, the Marriott ad capitalizes on word of mouth. Even though a reader may not yet have experienced the service, he or she can talk about it. Of course, this word of mouth will be even more positive once the actual experience has occurred.

Note that the Marriott ad is also informative and creates awareness (of a new service). It reinforces the Marriott image for present customers ("See, we're always doing something to make your meeting with us better"), without coming right out and saying it. Many ads strain so hard at doing this that they lose credibility. The ad positions Marriott as service-oriented, as always trying to do something more for its customers. It shows that management cares; Bill Marriott cares about the details of your meeting. Finally, the ad is persuasive. It addresses an issue of frequent concern and says, "We've taken care of that particular problem for you."

It is seldom easy to get all these elements into one advertisement; usually we have to settle for less. Even then, however, one should strive to differentiate with something other than the grandiose claims that characterize some hotel and restaurant ads. Unless there is something truly unique about the property, that kind of ad doesn't fill the requirements given above, and can have negative impact.

Another hotel ad scene shows a couple in a room, usually with the woman sitting on the bed and the man standing in a sliding doorway, or they may be in a swimming pool or on a golf course or in a lobby. While the room, the pool, and the golf course are all part of the product, they do not differentiate from other hotels in the same product class. They don't position the property, they promise no special benefit or problem solution, they don't tangibilize the service, they don't provide reinforcement, they don't have positive effects on employees, they don't generate positive word-of-mouth, they are not very informative, and they hardly persuade the consumer to choose this hotel.

So much for graphics—how about copy? The same rules apply. Ads that simply list the physical facilities of the property (e.g., number of rooms, pools, restaurants, bars, and so on) also do not fulfill the criteria we have given. True, it may sometimes be necessary to provide this information, depending on the target market. Perhaps it does need to be included, but this does not exempt the remaining copy from saying something different.

The Use of Advertising Today

Advertising is traditional marketing. It is so traditional in the hospitality industry that it sometimes lacks creativity, as we have shown. If you cannot make an impact upon the market with advertising, other than to create awareness and provide information as shown in a number of ads throughout this text, it might be better to save your dollars and put them to better use (for instance, in the product or in lower prices, which will generate positive word of mouth, a far more powerful force than most advertising). This is not to say that ad agencies are not creative. It is just that they don't always stick to the basics we have discussed. Note the creative ad in Figure 15-9 that does follow the rules and is quite effective.

The consumer today is constantly bombarded with advertising messages from all directions. The human mind is not capable of paying attention to all these messages. Instead, the mind will selectively perceive, attend to, comprehend, accept, and retain that to which it is most responsive. What the mind is most responsive to are those things we have outlined.

Hospitality properties and services are very similar in the same product class; some would say that they have reached commodity status. The competition is selling the same thing, unique niches are harder and harder to find, services are easy to copy, and aggressive competitors are using innovative positioning strategies. These things mean that it is difficult to gain advertising advantage. In many cases, it may be too expensive to achieve effective awareness and persuasion levels by this means.

All this shows that advertising must be approached with extreme care. Successful advertising is not just copy and graphics, not even just clever copy and graphics, but it derives from a well-planned strategy. Yet there is a strong tendency to look just at the copy and ignore the strategy. Many copy decisions in all industries, in fact, are based on what someone likes rather than how it affects the customer. It is no wonder they say that only half of advertising is effective but no one knows which half!

Evaluating Advertising

Advertising effectiveness is measured in several different ways:

1. A tracking measure is inserted into the ad, such as special 800 toll free numbers, or "Ask for Mary to get the special deal."

FIGURE 15-9 Creative advertising that is effective. Courtesy of Yesawich, Pepperdine & Brown, Orlando.

T A B L E   15-8
Evaluating Advertising by Cost per Thousand

Publication	Circulation	Size of Ad	Cost	Price per Thousand
Conde Nast Traveler	785,262	Full page, color	$38,220	$20.02
Travel and Leisure	1,008,844	Full page, color	$47,583	$21.20
Architectural Digest	815,282	Full page, color	$46,288	$17.61
Departures	362,878	Full page, color	$30,238	$12.00
Town & Country	440,464	Full page, color	$21,000	$20.97
Gourmet Magazine	880,661	Full page, color	$35,393	$24.88

2. Image advertising can be measured by total room nights by destination. For example, room nights from London on a yearly basis may be 1000 before advertising and 1500 afterward. If $50,000 was spent in the London marketplace on advertising, and 500 room nights at $150 were generated for revenue of $75,000, the advertising would be considered marginally successful, given the 30 percent variable cost of the rooms sold.

3. Advertising can be measured by cost per thousand as shown in Table 15-8. In this case, assuming that the customer base is similar, *Departures* and *Architectural Digest* appear to be the best value for advertising, with *Travel and Leisure* and *Gourmet Magazine* being the most expensive "buy."

With more sophisticated computers in hotels and restaurants, the effect an advertising campaign has on business levels can be tracked. After all of the above described phases of the advertising process are employed, the ultimate question is: Did it work?

First, an estimate needs to be made of the cost of the program including all of the components. Ad design, creative work, copy, production, and other costs are combined under the term, "ad preparation." These are added to the media and

agency costs and the total costs are compared to expected results. Table 15-9 shows a calculation for weekend package advertising for a 400-room hotel.

In order to evaluate the potential return on investment for advertising a weekend package for this hotel, the total communications expense is calculated. Step one combines all of the ad preparation with the actual media and agency expense.

Step two determines the net room rate generated by the sale of each weekend package room. Although the price is $100 per room, there is the cost to service the room, pay the travel agent, run the air conditioning, and so on. For this example, a typical cost of 30 percent of the sale price of the room was established.

The final step matches the advertising cost with the results expected. In this case, the hotel has to generate an additional 12 rooms sold per weekend night in order to return the investment. Each additional room sold generates an incremental gross margin of $70 for the property. In this case, the hotel decided that there was a good chance that 12 more rooms per weekend night could be sold. With this type of tracking in place, both the advertising agency and the hotel management have clear expectations of the campaign and the net result after it's over.

Look at a similar model for the hotel's restaurant. Sunday brunch covers have been declining for

TABLE 15-9
Expectations of an Ad Campaign for
Weekend Packages

Step	Figures
Step One	
Ad preparation	$ 2,000
Media placement	15,000
Total communications expense	$17,000
Step Two	
Weekend package room rate ×	$ 100
Departmental profit	70%
Net room rate	$ 70
Step Three	
Total communications expense /	$17,000
Net room rate	$ 70
Room nights needed /	243
10-week media placement	10
Room nights needed per weekend /	24
Two nights per weekend (Fri/Sat)	2
Additional room night sales per weekend night to return advertising investment	12

TABLE 15-10
Expectations of an Ad Campaign for
Sunday Brunch

Step	Figures
Step One	
Ad preparation	$ 2,000
Media placement	15,000
Total communications expense	$17,000
Step Two	
Sunday brunch price ×	$ 20
Departmental profit	15%
Gross margin per cover	$ 3
Step Three	
Total communications expense /	$17,000
Gross margin per cover	$ 3
Covers needed /	5,666
10-weeks media placement	10
Covers needed per Sunday brunch	567

some time. The advertising agency designs a similar campaign to advertise the Sunday brunch. Table 15-10 shows the results of the potential return on investment.

In this case, the hotel wisely declined. The restaurant had only 200 seats, and the return on the advertising investment could never be recovered.

There is no guaranteed way to measure advertising results. This method, however, reduces the risk of spending money unwisely.

Collateral

The same rules discussed above also apply to brochures, direct mail, and other forms of advertising called collateral in the industry. We do not reiterate them here. We add, however, a commentary. Much hotel print advertising has progressed considerably in the past few years beyond the stereotyped ads we have described. Hotel collateral, on the other hand, has progressed only in rare instances and consists of essentially contrived, unreasonable depictions, and standardized copy, both dull and boring. We guess that if you changed the name, address, and picture of the hotel, in at least 75 percent of all hotel brochures you couldn't tell one hotel from another.

Because collateral is a common form of advertising for hotels, we recommend you evaluate the brochure pages shown in Figure 15-10. Do the rules apply? Can we call the first set of pictures **slice of life** depictions?

For authentic American food — made great again every day, we proudly present MAX'S CAFE ● Food ● Spirits ● etc.... The atmosphere is casual, the service anything but. Open daily for breakfast, lunch, and dinner or for light hors d'oeuvres and your favorite cocktails. A special room service menu is also served daily.

FIGURE 15-10 Brochure panels from different hotels—compare the French and the American versions.

FIGURE 15-10 *continued*

INTERNATIONAL ADVERTISING

Communications in the international arena is clearly affected by cultural differences. Coordination of communications efforts with other elements of the marketing mix in foreign markets is more difficult. The quality and the availability of the means and the media vary from country to country and affect the usefulness and success of various techniques.

Global advertising (i.e., advertising using similar copy in different countries) is practiced by many international hotel companies and often fails to dif-

ferentiate. The Holiday Inn at Brussels Airport, for example, prints its collateral in five languages but has about the same copy as a Holiday Inn in Dallas (Figure 15-11). The target market, actually, is the same, assuming no cultural differences. On the other hand, there is nothing wrong with a common theme. Le Meridien carried out its artist Ken Maryanski's caricature theme worldwide, thus immediately identifying its properties (Figure 15-12).

Cultural barriers, however, make implementing

Les chambres offrent une vue panoramique sur la Méditerranée. Chacune possède une décoration et un aménagement personnalisés où raffinement et confort restent les maîtres mots.

The rooms have a panoramic view on the Mediterranean sea. Refinement and comfort are the key words to describe the rooms. Each one of them is personalised and elegantly decorated.

Le Château dispose de trois autres restaurants, "Le Grill du Château" pour des grillades, "Le Café du Jardin" restaurant en plein air et "A votreze chez Justin" pour une cuisine provençale et italienne.

The three other restaurants of the Château are "Le Grill du Château" for grilled dishes, "Le Café du Jardin" an open air restaurant and "A votreze chez Justin" for provencal and italian "cuisine".

FIGURE 15-10 *continued*

FIGURE 15-10 *continued*

a global campaign problematic. In a survey of 100 American advertisers, these barriers were defined as follows:

> Nineteen percent said their biggest mistake abroad was failure to allow for cultural differences.
> Seventy-nine percent develop distinctly differ-ent media plans in each country to reflect cul-tural and linguistic differences.
> Fifty-seven percent redesign the product or the packaging for each individual overseas market.
> Forty percent believe that universal advertising rises above cultural differences only on rare occasions.

FIGURE 15-11 Holiday Inn/Brussels uses standard copy globally.

FIGURE 15-12 Le Meridien used a constant theme internationally.

FIGURE 15-12 *continued*

Because of this, and because of the need to communicate with numerous and dissimilar markets, there tends to be more emphasis on personal selling at the unit level, and less selling at the national level. There is also a greater use of representative firms and consortia than in the United States.

With some classic exceptions, most international hotel properties are relatively new and modern, offer the same basic services, and make the same claims and promises in the same product class. It is truly difficult, as it is in the United States, to differentiate one from the other in advertising copy. Thus many companies, like airlines, stress the destination and put the emphasis on the brand name. The strategy in these cases is largely one of awareness and reminder.

There are some differences. These are not the newer Hyatts, Hiltons, or Sheratons, but the older hotels that have charm, warmth, or historic atmosphere (e.g., Figure 15-13). These attributes are rarely

At Le Meridien Phuket
there's sometimes nothing to do.

There's no hurry, no rush. When you're ready for a little gentle scuba diving, or sailing, or fishing, everything's there.

Until then, just lie by the huge free-form pool and soak up the sun. Sip a long cool drink on your private balcony overlooking the Andaman Sea. Or take an evening stroll to be lulled by the sound of waves on sand.

When you're ready for dinner, the exotic delights of fresh-caught seafood await you. Or Thai specialities with real local flavour. Or finest continental cuisine.

Later you'll be free to attend one of our celebrated theme night celebrations. An added dimension that's earnt Le Meridien Phuket a reputation for inventive incentives.

And more ways to do nothing than anywhere in Asia.

For information and reservations call Chris Reynolds on **312 222 9200**.

Le
MERIDIEN
PHUKET
THAILAND

PREDICTABLY WONDERFUL. WONDERFULLY UNPREDICTABLE.

As befits a storybook island, we've created a storybook resort. Nestled in a private cove, with lush gardens, bright architecture, 4 restaurants and a full menu of sports. It's a place where the senses can be soothed—or delightfully stirred. For reservations and information, call 800-543-4300 or your travel agent.

Le MERIDIEN
L'Habitation Le Domaine
SAINT MARTIN

Over 50 hotels and resorts worldwide. In North America: Boston, Chicago, Montreal, Nassau-Bahamas, New Orleans, New York, Newport Beach, San Diego, St. Martin, Vancouver

FIGURE 15-12 *continued*

The Obvious Choice

For more than 230 years Hotel d'Angleterre has remained the number one hotel in Copenhagen.

It's majestic presence in the centre of Copenhagen's King's Square makes the Hotel d'Angleterre simply the best address in Copenhagen.

130 comfortable and elegant rooms and suites

are all equipped with cable-TV, radio, mini-bar, bathrobes and hairdryers.

La Brasserie, Copenhagen's answer to Cafe de la Paix.

Le Restaurant offers an unforgettable evening with unique French food and superb service.

Banquet and Conference facilities for up to 600 people.

FIGURE 15-13 This D'Angleterre ad sells traditional classic hospitality.

if ever captured in modern hostelries or in their ads. In some cases, however, these attributes may be used to advantage in advertising. In some instances attempts are made to mix the new with the old.

The decision of whether to standardize advertising worldwide or to adapt it to each country and/or each market is a difficult one. The very diversity of the countries and the markets calls on the one hand for diversity in advertising; on the other hand, total diversity would be prohibitively expensive and thus calls for standardization. Nevertheless, each hotel has its own specific collateral and does its own advertising to specific markets. In these cases, every attempt at differentiation should be made. In all cases, advertising by whatever medium should be consistent with the corporate image, should position the establishment in its desired marketplace, and should be a cost-effective method for communicating with the market.

In the final analysis, wherever you advertise, there are certain steps to creating successful advertising. In Table 15-11 are the steps delineated by the president of one of the largest hospitality advertising firms.

SUMMARY

In this chapter we have discussed the foundations of the communications mix and two of its major components, advertising and database marketing. The foundations apply to all aspects of communications and successful implementation depends critically on knowing the target market and conducting the appropriate marketing research.

In small firms, all the parts of the communications mix will often fall within the domain of one person, or one department, thus easing their coordination. In larger firms, there may be both an advertising and public relations firm on retainer, with only personal selling handled mostly in-house. In these cases, a special effort is needed to be certain that all the elements of the communications mix

---

T A B L E   15-11
Steps to Creating Successful Advertising[3]

STEP 1: Set an objective for your advertising.

What do you want your advertising to accomplish? This logical and rather obvious consideration is often not clearly determined at the onset by many advertisers. As a result, they may not design their advertising message or select their media to best achieve these results

- Are you trying to educate prospects about a new product or service?
- Are you trying to win new clients from the competition?
- Are you looking for phone/coupon responses?
- Are you looking for qualified leads?
- Are you trying to build awareness?
- Are you using your advertising to keep your name in front of the public?

Be careful not to fall in the trap of trying to do all or most of these things in one effort. For advertising to be successful it must have a clear and simple objective. If you try to communicate too much, you may end up communicating nothing.

STEP 2: Position your product properly.

What identity or "position" do you want to give your product in the marketplace? You do this by analyzing conditions in the marketplace. Which products are succeeding and which are not? Analyze your competition as well. What consumer demands are they satisfying, which are they not? Lastly, analyze the attributes of your own product or service. What can it offer that consumers want and no one else is currently offering? It is imperative to delineate the "point(s) of difference" for your product.

   What you are striving for is a unique position or identity in the marketplace—one that you can hold secure for a long time to come.

STEP 3: Define your audience carefully.

It is important to determine which segments of the market you can serve best, from a demographic, geographic, and psychographic standpoint. It is also important to determine the geographic sources of your business and who makes the "buy" decision. It is also important to search out "untapped" segments of the market, segments of the population to which no one is currently catering. Remember, this is the age of special interest groups and micro marketing. Seek them out in your advertising message and your selection of media. Avoid being "all things to all people."

STEP 4: Make each ad reinforce your "brand image."

Once you have properly positioned your product and defined the audience you wish to reach, you can now assign your product a personality or "brand image." In advertising this can be carried out by the use of a consistent layout format, typeface, and/or logo and "tag line" (i.e., "Always Coca-Cola.")

   Too often individual ads are created as mutually exclusive elements; ads which preceded them had no common thread to bond them together. A good test for this is to examine all the ads that have been developed for your product(s) over the past year. Do they look as if they might come from one company or six?

   To get the most mileage from your advertising, don't let each ad stand by itself. Make each ad build upon and reinforce the ad it follows, all centering around the "brand image" you have decided for your product.

STEP 5: Make your ad headline and visual compelling.

The main function of your ad headline (and visual, if you have one) is to grab the audience's attention. If it fails to do this, your ad may not have a second chance. Research on readership of consumer print ads indicates that on the average you have about four seconds to accomplish this. Therefore, you should think of the headline and visual in your ad as a

(continued)

T A B L E   15-11   *(Continued)*

billboard on a busy highway with a disinterested audience speeding by at 55 mph. In order to slow down and stop that traffic, your headline must offer a compelling message—one which offers news or a benefit to your audience. Put the message in terms of the audience's needs, not your own. Your visual merely reinforces that message and the body copy elaborates on it. Above all, in your efforts to be compelling, let good taste be your guide. Remember, your brand image is at stake.

STEP 6: Let your prospect's attention focus on your product; not on the message.

How often have you come away from an ad or commercial remembering everything but the product? Don't be too gimmicky in your advertising. Let its creativity guide the prospects toward your product; not distract from it. If your product has clear and simple benefits to your prospects, don't disguise them with creative techniques; make them obvious in your advertising. Remember, successful advertising is good communication. You want your advertising message to telegraph the benefit of your product and achieve the "4Cs"—be compelling, clear, concise, credible and consistent. The underlying essence of any good communication should always constitute getting attention, developing interest and desire, and ultimately motivate action.

STEP 7: Continuously measure your standing in the marketplace.

Does your product perception match that of your consumers? Is your advertising moving the needle in the direction that you want it to go? Is the advertising achieving its intended purpose? These are all measurements which should be taken whether it be through market research, focus groups, sales comparisons, etc.

are synchronized. In either case, the mix should emanate from the marketing need of the firm and be consistent with its overall marketing strategy.

Word-of-mouth communications are a potent force in the hospitality industry and recommendations from persons who have experienced a service play an important role in the customer choice process. Complaints and praise are ways that customers choose to communicate. These can be more effective than any advertising, as well as destructive.

Database marketing allows for "mass customization" of the communications effort. It provides a knowledgeable and responsive marketing system that helps to personalize the customer relationship and focus marketing efforts, to allow target marketing to achieve its ultimate goal of addressing customers' needs, wants, and problems.

It should be clear that good advertising is not simple to orchestrate. While it is easy to employ advertising techniques, it is not so easy to do so successfully. The common theme in the development of advertising is that it's success depends upon the needs of the customer. Advertising should have

clear goals and should be developed after asking the right research questions.

This chapter offers a foundation and a methodology for successful execution of advertising. The most common reason for failure in delivering these subsets of the communications mix is lack of research and planning. With a strong planning process in place and a good research evaluation mechanism, both revenues and customer satisfaction can be maximized. In the next chapter, we continue with the communications mix and four of its other elements, sales promotions, merchandising, public relations and publicity. The last element of the communications mix is personal selling, and we devote all of Chapter 17 to it because of the predominance of its use in the hospitality industry.

KEY WORDS AND CONCEPTS

Affective Stage: The buyer stage of emotions and feelings toward the product.

Cognitive Stage: The buyer stage of beliefs about a product.

Collateral: Promotional material such as brochures, flyers, directions, and so on, used for customer information and to create interest.

Complementary-Sell: To develop or sell a product that is complementary to the main product but not normally part of it.

Conative Stage: The buyer stage of intention or readiness to buy.

Cross-Sell: To sell another product similar to what the customer has already purchased.

Customized Database: A database developed from outside information and customized to fit a company's prospective customer profile.

Ethos: Using credibility to persuade.

Evoked Set: The group of products that immediately come to mind when a person is considering a purchase.

Logos: Using logic and reasoning to persuade.

Maintenance Advertising: Advertising to keep the name in front of the market for quick recognition and as part of the evoked set.

Pathos: Using emotions to persuade.

Proprietary Database: A database developed by an individual company for its own use.

Pull Strategy: To "pull" the customer up through the distribution channel to the product.

Push Strategy: To "push" the product down through the distribution channel to the customer.

Slice of Life: Depiction of people using the product in a normal lifestyle setting.

Tracking: Keeping track of advertising effectiveness by response or other cues.

DISCUSSION QUESTIONS

1. Discuss word-of-mouth communications and how they are affected by the communications mix. Give specific examples. How does this affect the need, or lack of a need, to advertise?

2. Spot the five elements of the communications mix in the anecdote given in the beginning of the chapter. How could the restaurant have communicated better? How could the couple? Is the answer to the restaurant's problem now to advertise? Discuss.

3. Evaluate the ads in the chapter other than Figure 15-1 to 15.4. Discuss the strategy and tactics of these ads and how they are/are not implemented.

4. Select a local restaurant and ask the five major questions that must be answered by market research to develop the communications mix.

5. Why is it so critical to understand the target market before developing the communications mix? Discuss this in detail, with specific examples.

6. Consider a special case of database marketing from your own experience. What information would you want in the database?

7. Pick out some ads from a recent newspaper or magazine. Which are effective? Which are not? Explain.

8. Videotape a hospitality company commercial. Bring it to class and analyze it.

GROUP PROJECTS

1. Consider a local hotel or restaurant and put together an advertising campaign that follows the guidelines laid out throughout this chapter. Be prepared to present this to the class.

2. Conduct a research project for a local establishment that follows the first four guidelines in the chapter under Research for the Communications Mix.

REFERENCES

1. Steven J. Stark, "HoJo 'Dusts Off' Its Image with a $5M Ad Campaign," *Business Travel News,* June 9, 1986, pp. 1, 50.

2. *Hotel & Motel Management,* Franchising Supplement, May 18, 1998, pp. 32–33.

3. Courtesy of Peter Warren, CHME, President, Warren/Kremer/CMP Advertising/Inc.

Sixteen

THE COMMUNICATIONS MIX: SALES PROMOTIONS, MERCHANDISING, PUBLIC RELATIONS, AND PUBLICITY

Overview

This chapter continues with the communications mix.

PRINCIPLES AND PRACTICES OF SALES PROMOTIONS Sales promotions, by definition, are short term. Usually they are in the form of price discounts but may also be in the bundling of products or, common today, frequent traveler points. Basic frequent traveler programs are no longer, in themselves, considered promotions, but we outline them here in a table for those unfamiliar with them; we also show how they can be promotions with added bonuses. For promotions, marketing needs are established just as in any other part the

marketing plan. Promotions are just one way to consider how to fulfill these needs.

GUIDELINES FOR SALES PROMOTIONS Too many sales promotions fail because they do not follow some basic rules. These rules should be considered for every promotion. Sales promotions center on creation of demand. Creativity is called for to differentiate the promotion. Successful sales promotions fulfill certain criteria.

PRINCIPLES AND PRACTICES OF MERCHANDISING Merchandising is designed to stimulate purchase behavior of the customers who are on-premise. Again, the opportunities are endless and the planning and execution need to meet certain criteria. Besides stimulating sales, merchandising also has a long-term goal of increasing customer satisfaction.

PUBLIC RELATIONS (PR) AND PUBLICITY

These unique vehicles of information represent free use of the media. An organization, however, may pay a public relations person or firm to gener-

ate favorable PR. Because of this, PR should always be favorable. Publicity, on the other hand, is news that is generated by events and thus may be favorable or negative. Either one can have more effect than paid advertising because the population generally finds "free" news to be more credible. Thus PR needs to be planned carefully and negative publicity handled very gently.

•◆•

This chapter discusses three more elements of the communications mix: **sales promotions, merchandising,** and **public relations and publicity.** While reading this chapter, the reader should keep in mind the definition and discussion of the communications mix umbrella from the beginning of Chapter 15, as well as that relating to communications strategy and research.

PRINCIPLES AND PRACTICES OF SALES PROMOTION

Sales promotions are marketing communications that serve specifically as incentives to stimulate sales on a short-term basis. Sales promotions can also be effectively used to stimulate trial purchases. In hospitality, they are frequently used to bring in business during off-periods. In most of these cases, the lure is price discounts or the bundling of a product at one price that gives the same perception. In the last few years, we have seen a new lure in hospitality that has increased and is still increasing rapidly in use. This is frequent travel bonuses, often tied in with another company that wants to promote its business such as airlines, car rentals, credit cards, and telephone companies. These promotions are becoming one huge part of the hotel industry's marketing budget at the corporate level, but the costs are then charged back to the individual properties.

When McDonald's offers reduced prices on current fads such as "Teenie Beanie Babies" with a pur-

chase of a Happy Meal, that's a sales promotion. When Palm Springs hotels offer 50 percent off during the summer months, that's a sales promotion. When restaurants offer discount coupons and twofers, that's a sales promotion. When a hotel offers extra bonus points, that's a promotion. One of the most common forms of promotion in the tourism and hotel industries is packaging—a bundling of any combination of travel, rooms, meals, sightseeing, and so forth in one all-inclusive price. These kinds of packages are directed at specific market segments and were discussed in Chapter 8.

Sales promotion involves the development of creative ideas aimed at producing business, or creating a customer, in support of the total marketing effort. Sales promotions must be in tune with overall objectives and must complement other elements of both the communications mix and the marketing mix. Sales promotions, by definition, while they should provide customer satisfaction, are not likely to build long-term customer loyalty in themselves. Obviously, there is nothing wrong with them if they do; it is just that they rarely work that way.

Consider, for example, that Sears department stores have a warehouse sale on appliances—returned merchandise, slightly damaged goods, and so on—a true promotion. You go buy a refrigerator for half price but you do not feel compelled (loyal) to go to Sears to buy a microwave oven at the regular price. The same thing is true of a special weekend rate at a hotel at one-half the regular rate except for one major difference. If you had a great experience you might choose to go to that hotel again at the regular rate. At Sears, the experience really doesn't matter.

Sears also guarantees that you can return any merchandise for any reason, no questions asked. Sears customers pay for that privilege, although the cost is hidden in the purchase price. It is not, however, a promotion; it is a policy designed to build customer loyalty, and it does.

Now suppose that Sears has a permanent warehouse sale "promotion" on all merchandise. All other things being equal, you go to Sears. Now Walmart, K-Mart, and 15 other large chains do likewise. Where is your "loyalty" now?

Although sales promotions are short-term oriented they may succeed in the long term, that is, they may develop repeat business. Long-term promotions, however, rarely succeed in the long term. The reason for this is because long-term promotions become part of the product—that is, they are no longer promotions as originally intended. They become, instead, something you are forced to give customers, or something that customers come to expect, and something that customers must pay for whether or not they want it.

This is what happened with frequent traveler programs—they became part of the product. So now they have reverted back to short-term promotions in the form of bonus points during certain short term periods. Of course, almost as soon as one promotion ends another one is started so they almost come to have the same effect. The result is greater and greater bonus points, as shown in Figure 16-1. Although not truly promotions anymore, ongoing frequent traveler programs are a marketing tool that we can't ignore. As some readers, especially international ones, may not be as familiar with these programs, we lay them out in Table 16-1.

SALES PROMOTIONS AND MARKETING NEEDS

Sales promotions are designed to fulfill a marketing need. It follows, then, that the first thing to be done is to define that need.

FIGURE 16-1 Hyatt's ad demonstrates how bonus point promotions get larger and larger.

There are any number of needs for promotions. To create new business, to create awareness, and to create trial purchase are common ones. Some others are to increase demand in slow periods, to take business from the competition, or to meet the competition in its own promotional efforts. Whatever the reason, there is one major warning with regard to promotions: they should be tied to something positive such as a new or better facility, a new product, or a special time or offering. Further, it is often too easy to jump to offering a promotion when there may be better ways to fill the need.

Promotions tied to negative features—for instance, lack of business when it is expected to be good—tend to backfire. An example of this is restaurant twofers (two menu items for the price of

T A B L E   16-1
Frequent Traveler Programs

Almost all major hotel affiliations offer frequent traveler programs of some kind, at least in North America, but they are catching on elsewhere as well (Figure 16-2). Most of these are tie-in promotions that offer benefits both inside and outside the hotels, such as free room stays, upgrades, car rentals, and airline mileage, the latter becoming increasingly more popular (Figure 16-3). The car rental companies and the airlines reciprocate. Other plans give selections from a full gift catalog as well (Figure 16-4). Most plans award "points" to obtain these "rewards." Some, such as Marriott, offer mileage or room points. The choice is the traveler's. Others, like Hilton, offer both room and airline points.

Points are usually based on dollars spent, sometimes just on rooms, and sometimes also on food and beverages, which helps keep guests in the hotel. Frequent traveler programs have also added promotions within the augmented product. "Bonus points" for certain hotels (such as in Figure 16-1) or time periods promote awareness, trial, or increased usage within the framework of the normal frequent traveler programs. These latter are true short-term promotions that fill short-term needs for individual properties.

Other benefits of these programs, or what are sometimes called corporate rate programs, are more simply termed "privileges" and include guaranteed and preferred rates, guaranteed rooms, speedy check-out, express check-in, free room upgrades, complimentary cocktails and newspapers, free stay for spouse in room, and other amenities. These privileges are more in the context of benefit marketing and do not come under the category of true promotions. They are part of the augmented product for members and most are at little or no additional cost to the hotel. The purpose of both programs is to cultivate the loyal customer, the one who will return to the same property or chain no matter what some competitor offers.

Although the airlines' plans have been touted by the airlines as great successes, it is difficult to know whether that is really the case. Pan American World Airways, now in a reincarnation after bankruptcy, reported losing $45 to $50 million after some colossal blunders when its plan was first inaugurated. The business press regularly reports that most carriers lose as many fliers to rivals' programs as they attract to their own. Research shows that anywhere from 8 to 12 percent of the passengers on any given flight are flying free on frequent flyer miles. Many of these would otherwise be paying passengers, and there are billions of accumulated free miles yet unused, many of which will never be used. Contrarily, Southwest Airlines does not have a frequent flyer program of this type. Instead it offers low fares, a customer-driven culture, and immediate flyer benefits.

For the airlines, and in some hotel situations, free flights/rooms are an opportunity cost. Tony Carpenter, then vice president–operations for Hilton International's U.S. brand, Vista Hotels, reported, "The great unknown factors are how much of the business would you have gotten anyway? And how much loyalty is generated?"[1]—two questions that still have unknown answers. In other situations, such as merchandise and airline mileage awards, hotels have greatly added to their cost basis. In the same article, Mark Lomano, then director of leisure-time industry research for Laventhol and Horwath, stated: "Once you start giving something to a hotel guest, it's very difficult to take it away," that is, it has become part of the product offering. Additionally, it costs major hotel companies hundreds of millions of dollars a year just to manage their programs. There are other drawbacks for hotels.

Hotel Drawbacks

In the first place, hotel guests have many more options than airline flyers. This means that they can belong to everyone's program and still stay where they want depending on where they are at any given time. They can switch back and forth so that everyone wins and everyone loses and the net gain or loss remains the same. Furthermore, the hotel guest is far more fickle than the air traveler and is known to choose hotels by individual property rather than by chain. This, of course, is what the programs are designed to overcome, but they don't help much when the benefits are similar everywhere. We have shown in previous chapters that depending on the survey, hotel guests who put value on these programs in choosing a hotel, range from 2 to 40 percent with most surveys showing about 10 percent. (The latest survey, summer 1998, shows that 8 percent actually choose a hotel for this reason.[2])

The second reason is that staying in one hotel or another is very different from flying one airline or another. The elements of product and service vary far more in hotels than they do in airplanes, not to mention the duration of stay. The frequent hotel customer is far more prone to choose a hotel because it fills specific needs, than in choosing an airline where schedule is the main determining factor.

(continued)

TABLE 16-1 *(Continued)*

This is not to say that frequent travelers don't stay at hotels to accumulate points. Many do. They get free prizes, take free flights, and have free vacations. The question is what are the hotels getting back at a very high cost? One Marriott hotel that we know of averages 8 to 10 percentage points of its occupancy as free guests with Marriott points.

As a group, the hotel industry is giving away something to get the customer it already has, or should have, while trading customers with other frequent guest programs, winning some and losing some, and spending millions of dollars to do it. At the same time it punishes nonfrequent travel members (at least 75 plus percent of the market) by making them pay the bill. Keep in mind, as well, that hotels pay airlines millions of dollars to acquire these points.

With a growing realization that frequent traveler programs may be actually costing more than the benefits obtained from them, many airlines and hotels have scaled back their programs and also made them more restrictive. The most popular ways to do this are: (1) keep raising the number of point required for rewards, (2) set blackout dates when the points can't be used, and (3) allocate only a certain number of seats or rooms, depending on forecasts, for point redemption "freebies," thus not diverting a paying customer. In a volume sensitive business these practices decrease the loss exposure. Note: In 1999, Starwood Hotels found that the biggest gripe on awards was the blackout periods. Their new program eliminated these completely.

FIGURE 16-2 Concorde is a European example of frequent traveler programs.

FIGURE 16-3 Radisson SAS offers frequent flyer points on 23 airlines. (As of November 1999, Marriott offers points on 40 airlines.)

FIGURE 16-4 Holiday Inn's point rewards for frequent travelers.

one). Twofers are designed to generate business by bringing in new customers. In the best situations they succeed in doing this, but the customers they bring in may not be from the designated target market and few of them may ever return.

Although there may be a temporary increase in business, it is obtained at a cost: If food cost percentage is 35 percent, it is now 70 percent. At the same time, regular customers who would normally pay the full price are also dining at half-price. The net gain is minimal, if not negative. This does not mean that twofers cannot be useful for other purposes, such as creating awareness or trial purchase. Usually they will work best at low-priced, family or fast-food restaurants, rarely at upscale restaurants. As Tom Feltenstein states:

The trick is to discount in such a way that you do not sabotage the integrity of your menu. Disguise the lure so that it's perceived as something other than an attempt to discount mainline items.

. . . In the consumer's mind, there is always a correlation between product and price. . . . But over time, discounting is bound to raise questions in the consumer's mind about the integrity of your pricing structure. . . . If you must discount . . . [and] there are times when discounting is a sound promotional technique—then put together a separate package to your regular offering, that will engender no recognizable negative effect on your customer's perception of the value and price of your menu.

. . . [O]nce you get the customer in the store, remember it is going to take more than a cents-off coupon to bring him or her back.[3]

Guidelines for Sales Promotions

There are some general guidelines for promotions that should apply to most cases. The first of these is to define the real purpose of the promotion. That seems obvious enough, but often this guideline is violated. The result is that, after the fact, it is found that even the successful promotion did not meet its objectives.

Be Single-Minded

It is well to keep the purpose **single-minded** and not try to accomplish too many things at one time. Is the purpose to create new business, awareness, or trial; to increase demand in a slow period; to take business away from the competition; to meet the competition; or to sell specialties? Trying to do more than one or two of these things tends to diffuse the promotion, confuse the market, and accomplish none of them. Figures 16-5 is an example of single-mindedness, whereas Figure 16-6 shows a proprty promoting "everything under the sun."

Define the Target Market

Is it first-time users, heavy users, nonusers? What benefits does it seek? What are the demographic and psychographic characteristics? The promotion must specifically focus on the needs of the target market.

What Specifically Do You Want to Promote?

This is not necessarily the tangible item that you may be promoting. For example, you may want to promote a new decor or atmosphere in the lounge, but the promoted tangible item could be a special drink. A hotel might want to promote its rooms on

FIGURE 16-5 The Breakers runs a single-minded promotion to capitalize on a centennial anniversary. Courtesy of Yesawich, Pepperdine & Brown, Orlando.

weekends; the tangible promotional feature could be free breakfast in bed with champagne.

What Is the Best Way to Promote It?

It is not just necessary to give something away or charge a lower price. You may even want to promote higher quality at a higher price. You could offer an additional service, a package price, a future incentive, or something new, like the example shown in Figure 16-7. Before you give something away, or charge less, think carefully about what you will get in return.

Make Sure You Can Fulfill the Demand

This is a critical point. Many customers are alienated and lost forever—the exact opposite intention of the promotional objective—by failure to deliver on the promotion. If you are promoting lobster

FIGURE 16-6 This ad promotes everything but the kitchen sink.

dinner specials, don't run out of lobsters even at the risk of having to let some spoil. If you're offering weekend packages, provide the rooms even if you have to upgrade. The worst thing that can happen is that you'll have a happier customer. At a minimum, do as the retail stores do and provide rainchecks, where customers can use the promotion at a later date; then, when customers collect on them, give something better, just to compensate for the inconvenience. Too many promotions end up losing customers rather than winning them, because management forgets why it is having the promotion in the first place.

Make Sure Reality Meets Expectations

Do this for the same reasons as those just mentioned. Grand-opening promotions for an enterprise that isn't "ready" loses customers instead of winning them. (Recall the restaurant example in Chapter 15.) Don't embellish on what you have to offer; stick to the facts. If you don't have it, don't say it. Also, don't be "picky" on other items. Some managements try to make up for what they are losing on the promotion in other ways, only to create an upset customer.

Communicate Your Promotion and All Related Aspects to the Market

Some promotional literature or ads are so confusing, bury all the conditions of the promotion in the illegible fine print at the bottom of an ad, and/or presume so much knowledge on the customer's part that the customer ignores the ad or gets irritated. Specify clearly all pertinent information such as price, quality, procedure, place, dates, time, and any other necessary detail. When customers

F I G U R E   1 6 - 7   Mövenpick of Toronto runs a promotion for something new with no price reduction.

ask for "it," give it to them; don't play games and say, "There are no more of those left." If you're promoting "children free in the same room," don't hassle with the customer as to whether the child is under 16 or not, or charge $15.00 for a cot—both are no-win situations.

Communicate It to Your Employees

This is critical. Promotions break down too often over failure to do this. Management runs an ad in the local paper about a forthcoming promotion and simply assumes that the employees who have to implement it will know exactly what it's all about and how to handle it. A restaurant we know once ran a promotion of free movie tickets with certain special dinners. None of the waiters or waitresses knew anything about it. When diners asked for their tickets, management was "out of town." The result was a disaster. Front-desk clerks at hotels have the same problem with weekend specials, not to mention reservationists at 800 numbers, who often don't know what it is they are supposed to be promoting.

Finally, Measure the Results

Do this not just in terms of bodies or of dollars. Did the promotion meet its objectives? What were the benefits, gains, losses? Will it work again? If it didn't work, why didn't it? Will there be a lasting effect, or was it a one-shot deal? Some of the best promotion results are nothing more than good will, which will pay off in the future.

Sales promotions can be communicated via advertising, direct mail, tent cards, publicity, personal selling, telemarketing, and various other means. Promotions can be persuasive marketing tools when used wisely and appropriately.

DEVELOPING SALES PROMOTIONS

The use of sales promotions in the hospitality industry centers on creation of demand. A promo-

tion is the development and execution of an event outside the normal day-to-day business.

The goal of a sales promotion is twofold: to increase the satisfaction of the guest while increasing revenues for the hospitality establishment. If the guest is extremely satisfied with a promotion but the costs are so high that money is lost, then the promotion is unsuccessful. Contrarily, if the hotel or restaurant makes a great deal of money but the customers feel slighted, then the promotion is equally unsuccessful.

Normally, there are two types of sales promotions, those centered around established events and those created entirely on their own. A promotion created around an established event might be a Mother's Day brunch, a Bastille Day food offering, a hotel package for Valentine's Day, Christmas shopping, or Easter (Figure 16-8). In these cases hospitality establishments have an opportunity to create excitement for customers, and to build their volumes. Participation can vary from flying in a French chef to cook for Bastille Day to placing a corned beef sandwich on the menu for St. Patrick's Day.

The second type of sales promotion—that created independent of an established event—is more difficult to develop and execute. A good example comes from the Hilton Hotel in New Orleans, told in Table 16-2.

There are many, many variations of promotions. In fact, the number is limited only by the imagination. Table 16-3 describes different promotions reported in the industry press.

Designing the Successful Sales Promotion

What, then, are the steps that need to be taken to ensure a successful promotion?

Identify the Gap. One purpose of a sales promotion from the management perspective is to increase revenues. It makes sense to plan promotions when the facility is not at capacity; the idea is to create new demand. Many promotion are designed

FIGURE 16-8 Le Château Montebello's special Easter promotion.

to build revenues during slack times or sell products that are traditionally in low demand.

The New York Palace completed an extensive renovation in 1997, and repositioned itself at the top of the New York City luxury market. Specifically, the Towers section of the hotel competed head on with the established St. Regis and Four Seasons hotels.

While the physical product was five-star, the customers' perception of the hotel remained confused. Customer research indicated that the St. Regis and Four Seasons were well liked by travelers and changing their behavior would prove difficult. The problem was that the competition was doing a good job and there were no real reasons for their customers to look elsewhere.

Palace management was convinced, however, that once customers tried the Towers they would return. Getting trial usage became the marketing problem to be solved. A sales promotion was created to give the customer a reason to try the Towers. The promotion offered a round trip airline ticket to anywhere in the continental United States on Delta Airlines to anyone staying in the Towers for one night. The tickets were purchased through a special program offered by Delta for $249. Rates in the Towers began at $525 and, with an average stay of two nights, each booking paid for the sales promotion. Future stays created incremental revenue and guest loyalty.

Design the Promotion. There are two areas to address when designing the promotion, that of the customer and that of time. Normally, the customer should be considered before putting any type of promotion together. However, management might design a promotion because of excess inventory. Perhaps some wine was bought in too large a quantity. A wine promotion is created, regardless of the needs of a customer, but the promotion itself is designed to satisfy needs.

The promotion must be consistent with the po-

TABLE 16-2
A Successful Promotion Producing Lasting Results

The New Orleans Hilton, a large convention hotel, was experiencing flat sales of better quality wines sold by the bottle. A newly hired food and beverage manager, with a good knowledge of wines, decided to try selling the better wines by the glass, instead of by the bottle. After all, most of the hotel's guests were conventioneers, and not likely to purchase an expensive bottle of wine. Wines by the glass were offered in one of the restaurants as a test promotion. Within a month the better quality wines were outselling the cheaper house wines by four to one. Customers were looking for better wines but did not want to purchase the whole bottle.

The sales promotion was then instituted in all the food and beverage outlets. The first step was to train all food and beverage servers about the wine and the promotion. Other hotel employees were also informed and recruited into the promotion in novel ways. Bellpersons were given business cards that they could give to guests for a free glass of wine. Housekeepers also put these cards in guest rooms during turndown service and front-desk employees were given wine labels to show to interested guests. In the restaurants, wine displays and table tents were set up in addition to a menu flap that was devoted to wines by the glass.

The hotel was provided all promotional materials by either the winery or the local wholesaler, who also gave a quantity discount for the purchase of the wine. This sales promotion was a resounding success and, in this case, both the customers and the hotel were beneficiaries of an excellent promotion. The hotel was able to build on this promotion to develop a regular feature of better wines by the glass.

---

sitioning of the restaurant or hotel. A disco promotion at the Ritz is not in keeping with the positioning of the hotel. Similarly, a caviar promotion at a family restaurant is equally inappropriate.

The second important aspect in the design of the promotion is the timing and planning. For example, we have seen a restaurant manager decide, the week before Thanksgiving, that a turkey promotion was needed to get business. Last-minute flyers were produced, an advertisement was hurried to the newspaper, and a menu was created. Servers were warned as they came to work that day, and the entire promotion was executed in an unprofessional manner, an obviously failed promotion.

The proper delivery of a promotion includes the integration of a variety of items in the communications mix. Advertising, merchandising, and public relations all need time to be coordinated. Those promotions that do not have the proper timing and planning are usually a failure.

Throughout the design of the promotion, a clear and concise message must be put forth to the customer. While this may not be as necessary for

promotions centered around established events, promotions that are attempting to present a novel concept have to be clear. A St. Patrick's Day promotion can be easily understood by most customers because the event carries with it a certain level of expectation, but a novel promotion may have to be explained to customers and also to all employees.

Analyze the Competition. Competition should be analyzed before a sales promotion is developed. If all of the restaurants in town are offering a turkey dinner for Thanksgiving, what will make this promotion different? A close watch on competitive activity can give the promotion designer a head start on potential problems.

Allocate the Resources. No sales promotion will be successful if customers are unaware of the activity. A major reason for the failure of a promotion is underestimating the resources needed to bring in customers. Just putting the corned beef sandwich on the blackboard of the restaurant will

TABLE 16-3
Some Uncommon Promotional Ideas

Chocolate and Ice Cream Lovers Weekend: The 525 room Hyatt Regency in Tampa, Florida, has an annual ice cream and chocolate lovers Hyattfest for three days, which sells over 250 room nights.

Free Harbor Cruise: The Tidewater Motor Lodge in West Yarmouth, Massachusetts, builds slow Sunday night business with free Hyannis Harbor Cruise tickets. Ads appear in the Boston Globe, which is presented to get the tickets. Twenty plus additional guests per week take advantage of the offer.

Cooking Classes: The 1020-room Acapulco, Mexico, Princess offers cooking class packages to a limited number of 20 guests during low summer season. It has been so successful that there is a waiting list of those who want to book each year. The hotel has also reaped free publicity—articles on the classes have appeared in 75 newspapers and magazines.

Local Radio Broadcasts from the Hotel: Two shows emanating from Atlanta, Georgia's 521-room Waverly Hotel, Big Band Friday Night and a disc jockey session from the lobby during Sunday brunch, brought 40 percent of the hotel's business from local people. Weekend occupancy gained 20 percent since the radio shows began. The promotion also helps local residents remember the hotel for weddings, parties, and gala receptions.

Come Have an Earthquake: Guests at the 80-room Atami Seaside Resort on Japan's Izu Peninsula get to come back at a discount if an earthquake hits during their stay. The return visit is even free of charge if the quake is big enough. Izu happens to be among the world's most seismically active regions. In one week, more than 6000 quakes occurred in the area. Most were nearly undetectable but four ranked 4 on the Japanese scale of 7, rattling dishes and chandeliers. Inquiries from guests dropped off after a particularly bad April. Now guests rattled by an intensity-4 quake get a 50 percent discount and two free meals on their next stay. An intensity-5 or higher quake gives one night completely free. Reservations are now holding up and in the first year only 25 discounts were given.

McDonald's Global Promotion: In 1998, McDonald's kicked off its first global children's meal promotion, tying it to the Disney movie "Mulan." In 110 countries, children received one of eight toys free with the purchase of a Happy Meal. Future promotions are planned with Disney movie tie-ins.

not be enough exposure to have a successful St. Patrick's Day promotion.

All parts of the communications mix should be evaluated for their ability to bring customers to a promotion. Public relations, advertising, and even direct sales can be used to get the message to potential participants. Direct mail can be a cost-effective way to deliver the promotion. In hotels, traditional merchandising methods such as table tents, signage in the elevators, and employee buttons can carry the theme of the promotion.

Establish Goals. How should success be judged? If a sales promotion is to satisfy both the customer and management, how many extra rooms, or covers, or cases of wine can reasonably be expected to be sold? Goals should be set in advance for

evaluating the promotion at the conclusion of the event. Goals need to be realistic, and a measurement form should exist before the promotion takes place.

Understand the Break-Even Point. It is imperative to understand the economic consequences of the sales promotion before its execution. In following the steps outlined above, there may be too many resources allocated to the promotion to ever make meeting the goals financially feasible.

A restaurant promotion might use a $500 advertisement in the local paper to reach the maximum number of potential customers. If the promotion was slated for a Thursday evening in a restaurant that normally sells 75 covers, a realistic goal for a successful promotion might well be 125 customers on the night of the event. However, if the average check for the event is planned at $15, with a gross profit margin of $4.50, the additional profit would be $225, obtained at a cost of $500.

Break-even analysis should be conducted early in the sales promotional planning. We saw one supposedly great promotion developed by a hotel team that at its most successful point—and success was widely anticipated—would have lost $100,000. The greatest "success" of this promotion, had it been carried out, would have been its failure. Both

overallocation and underallocation of resources must be carefully analyzed in relation to the success of the promotion.

Pricing is an important factor in sales promotions and not just because of profits. Is the promotion so expensive to the customer that there will be little demand for the product, or is it so inexpensive that the market will be apprehensive of the quality? Sometimes simplicity may be the way to go (Figure 16-9).

FIGURE 16-9   Red Roof offers a simple, easy, and measurable promotion.

Execute the Sales Promotion. This stage of the promotion is as important as all the others. Execution includes delivery of the product to the customer in the framework of the created expectation. Promotion delivery is more critical than normal delivery because the customer is excited and anticipatory. The promotion has created a demand. Demand has created a special reason to use the product, and customer expectations are unusually high.

Proper execution includes employee participation. The entire staff needs to understand the promotion and its specific involvement. When a bartender shows up for work in the middle of an Oktoberfest without knowing the service steps involved, trouble can be anticipated. Employee involvement, perhaps even in the design stages of the promotion, will increase the chances for optimal delivery of the correct product.

Execution also means maintaining the proper inventory of goods to be sold. If the restaurant runs out of bratwurst during the Oktoberfest and has to substitute hamburgers, the customers' expectations will not be met. Part of the planning process of the promotion is the development of goals. Purchasing should be based on the attainment of these goals, at minimum. It is more desirable to have some waste than to not fulfill expectations.

Evaluate. All sales promotions should have an evaluation mechanism installed. Were the goals met? Were resources optimally allocated?

While these questions are certainly relevant and necessary, they constitute only half the equation designated for success. The second half consists of the following questions: Were the customers satisfied? Were there any unusual complaints? Do comments reflect any information that might be useful for future promotions? All of these questions should be addressed in the evaluation process to allow a total assessment of the event.

When all feedback has been analyzed, the next stage is formulating the next promotion. Perhaps this particular promotion can be held monthly, or yearly. What other promotions can be developed to fill in gap periods or to sell slower-moving products? The process of promotional development begins all over again.

PRINCIPLES AND PRACTICES OF MERCHANDISING

Merchandising is primarily in-house marketing designed to stimulate purchase behavior through means other than personal selling or purchase of time or space in media. In a sense, merchandising is marketing to the captive customer once the customer comes into the hotel or restaurant to purchase a room or a meal. Many customers will buy nothing other than the basic product. The goal of merchandising is to provide opportunities for customers to purchase related or auxiliary products and services.

The goal of merchandising, however, should not be just to stimulate sales; it also has a more long-term goal of increasing customer satisfaction. When the pastry cart is wheeled to the restaurant table at the end of the meal, the goal is to have customers order pastry and increase the check average. It is also to have customers feel even more satisfied because they have finished their meal in a very pleasing manner. If hotel guests order room service, they add to their overall bill. Also, we hope, their stay has been made just a little bit better and we have a few more satisfied customers.

Like everything else, we approach merchandising from a marketing perspective—fulfilling customers' needs and wants and solving their problems. If we are able to do this, the higher check averages and the larger bills will follow. If, instead, we put all the emphasis on the increased revenue we are likely to fall into the same old trap of forgetting about the customer.

The Basic Rules of Merchandising

The opportunities for merchandising in a hotel or restaurant are almost endless and, like sales promotions, are limited only by the imagination. There are a few rules that affect all merchandising which, again, are not unlike those for sales promotions.

Purpose. All merchandising should have a purpose. The commonly expressed purpose—"to increase sales"—is true, but not sufficient. Instead, let's say that the overall purpose is to increase customer satisfaction. Of course, we could also say the purpose is to fulfill needs and wants and solve problems. Much of merchandising does that, but in this case we go a little bit beyond the basic marketing concept.

Sometimes just knowing that something is available, and can be had if wanted, will establish the need or want and/or increase satisfaction even when that thing is not consciously needed or wanted. A good example is the year-round swimming pool in an urban hotel. Proportionally, very few guests use these pools, but research has shown that they like the idea that the pools are there to use if they wish. A positive, however, is turned into a negative when the pool is not open at reasonable times that people want to use it, as sometimes is the case, usually for operational convenience.

The same sense of availability may be true of pastry carts in restaurants for all those people "on a diet." It is human nature to want to feel that we can have something if we want it; merchandising creates that feeling and increases satisfaction.

The other reason we go beyond the basic marketing concept is that merchandising is much involved in the creation of wants. Marketing does not do a great deal to create basic needs, but it can create wants. Restaurant diners might feel a need for chocolate after dinner (might even want it, in fact), but repress that need because it's "fattening." Along comes the pastry cart with all those chocolate goodies; now, they really want it! The same is true of after-dinner drinks and flambéed desserts. Restaurants have tremendous merchandising opportunities. The most powerful one, sometimes neglected, is the menu itself, which can range from the mundane and blasé to exciting and provocative.

By the same token, hotel guests do need to eat; merchandising can make them want to eat in one of the hotel's restaurants. Cards are put up in the elevators, signs in the lobby, and information on the desk in the room. Today, in many hotels, guests also see and hear about the in-house restaurants on the television in their room. In many European hotels, merchandising is practiced upon check-in when the desk clerk asks if the guests would like a dinner reservation made for them.

All merchandising ploys need to have their purpose understood. One purpose, as we mentioned, is to create the feeling, "If you want it, we have it." Another might be to create excitement, as with an exotic drink, a flambéed dessert, or a "spinning salad bowl," which, corny as it was, made Don Roth's Blackhawk Restaurant in Chicago famous. Another purpose might be entertainment, such as that provided by in-room movies, or even sensuality, as provided by the late-evening adult movies. Other possible purposes are convenience (room service), relaxation (aperitifs), contentment (after-dinner cognac), or information (in-room directories).

A merchandising technique used by Marriott in some of its hotels, which can also be used in restaurants, occurs when you are first seated at your dining room table. A waiter or waitress immediately approaches with a basket of house wines, offered by the glass. The customer has immediate service, and a need identified by the customer has been served. Even if there is a delay in ordering the meal, instant satisfaction has been created. Some hotels also use the same approach at breakfast: You are immediately greeted by a server with a pot of coffee in one hand and a pitcher of fresh orange juice in the other.

Compatibility and Consistency. Merchandising efforts should be compatible and consistent with the rest of the marketing effort in terms of quality, style, tone, class, and price. They should reinforce the basic product/service mix, since these efforts themselves are part of the augmented product. Hotels that have an eye on the growing family vacation travel market should consider opening a child care center where parents can leave their children with trained, licensed professional staff. Holiday Inn's Sunspree Resorts offer 24-hour child care service. However, this market and this service may not be compatible in a hotel with a strong transient business traveler base.

Practicality. The rule here is if you can't do it right, don't do it. Failure to follow this rule results in lost customers, not satisfied ones. The child care center is an example where serious problems can result if the service is not offered in a professional way.

Visibility. Let the customer know about it and how to get it. Elevator cards merchandising restaurants often fail to say where the restaurants are or what hours they are open. In today's modern hotels, where restaurants might be anywhere, it can literally be a mind-boggling experience to find one.

Management seems to assume that everyone else knows what it knows about the hotel's layout. In-room directories sometimes are so confusing that the guest either turns to the telephone or gives up. We have even seen directories with full pages on the swimming pool and health club facilities but no indication of how to get there or what to wear on your way. Many people don't use pools simply because they are too embarrassed to go there in a bathing suit and don't want to change in dressing rooms. The Royal Garden Hotel in Trondheim, Norway solved this customer problem by identifying a "swimming pool/health club" elevator specifically for that purpose.

On the other hand, visibility doesn't mean total clutter. Some restaurant tables, or hotel desk tops, have so many table tents, flyers, and brochures on them that there isn't room for anything else and it is too confusing to find what you want. Some people just swoop them off so they can put down their own things.

Simplicity. Make it easy to understand and easy to obtain. Make it clear how much it will cost, how long it will take, when it is available, or any other information that will make it unnecessary for the customer to have to make additional inquiry. Customers tend to just give up when they have to go through too much effort to purchase a service. Something as simple as placing a red heart

next to "heart-healthy" menu items can provide quick information to health conscious customers and increase sales of those items.

Knowledgeable Employees. Make sure everyone knows about it, what it is, how it works, how you get it, what you do with it, and so forth. The key to the success of the any in-house promotion is the knowledgeable employees who publicize it to the customers.

Merchandising is just one more marketing tool for creating and keeping customers. It is also a communications tool because it says to the customer, "Here is what else we can do for you." Wisely used, merchandising is a powerful tool; it should be a revenue-producer and, more important, a customer-satisfier. Too often, it becomes a "customer-annoyer."

Examples of Good Merchandising

Examples of good merchandising techniques abound. One case in point are the business centers within some hotels. These business centers offer a variety of secretarial support services such as typing and dictation, together with copying, fax machines, and computer terminals. Business centers are usually located somewhat off the lobby, with a separate room in which to work. These services cost money for the guests and hotels can make a profit on them. More importantly, they fill a need of the traveling businessperson and create a better guest experience (but not when they grossly overcharge for faxes!).

Another example of good merchandising in a business-related restaurant is the offering of a "45-minute guaranteed lunch" to cater to the limited time of working people. While no additional charge is made for this service, the restaurant has differentiated itself from its competitors by satisfying a need through merchandising.

The emergence of pizza on finer hotels' room service menus is a merchandising opportunity that fills a need of many customers. Many people do not want a full, heavy meal in their room. Some just want to watch television and have something "fun," as if they were at home. The pizza (merchandised often with beer) fills the need of the customer while putting money into the hotels' cash registers (Figure 16-10).

This type of merchandising can only increase revenues. Rarely would you find a customer ordering a lower-priced pizza instead of a steak. Price does not become the deciding factor; instead, the product becomes the reason for the purchase. Those customers who really wanted pizza in the first place might have called for a delivery from

FIGURE 16-10 Flamingo Hilton Hotel in-room merchandising.

outside or gone out of the hotel; either way, the money would have been spent outside the hotel or not at all. More important, once again, you have satisfied a customer by fulfilling a need.

The inclusion of "minibars" in guest rooms both is satisfying to customers and increases hotel profits. Minibars are self-contained units that have beer, wine, mixed drinks, and soft drinks together with snacks for the guest to eat. An inventory is taken of the unit's contents before the guest checks in, and all items consumed are posted to the bill. The probability is low that a guest would call room service for one beer. With a minibar in the room, customers can lean over while watching television or reading, and open a beer at their convenience. Minibars are now featuring many nonfood items such as playing cards and disposable cameras. Again, however, improper merchandising can lose customers. Too many minibar contents are over-priced and customers are not particularly pleased when they have to pay the high prices. Instead, many buy outside and use the minibar as a refrigerator. This is an opportunity lost.*

Merchandising is marketing to the "captured" customer. Unless your hotel or restaurant is alone on a desert island, don't translate capture into captivity. Even on a desert island, you may never see that customer again. Instead, translate capture into opportunity: "Here's an opportunity to make the customer even more satisfied."

PUBLIC RELATIONS AND PUBLICITY

Public relations and publicity are grouped together because of their commonality, which is the "free"

use of the media. For either one, instead of buying space in a newspaper or time on a radio station, the organization obtains it *gratis*, provided the media think the organization is newsworthy or of interest. In that sense, the organization does not control the placement of the information.

Every organization exists in a community, large or small, national, international, or local, which has a direct or indirect influence on its success. It wants to have a positive image in the community and to be seen as a contributor to the overall well-being of society. Effective public relations is the management tool to present the product/service to the media and the community in the best light.

Although publicity can derive from public relations, the difference is that publicity constitutes only the information the media freely and without influence choose to use. Thus publicity may be positive or negative. Public relations, on the other hand, are attempts to control publicity, and to "plant" information in the press or to create a favorable image for reasons other than its formal product. In politics this is called "**spin control**," a phrase we have heard a lot during the Clinton administration.

Public relations, as well as publicity, also occurs through word of mouth. While much of this may be started by the media, other aspects may be spontaneous. For example, a restaurant makes a special effort to employ disabled people. This fact may never strike the media, but the word gets around and the restaurant is looked at as a "do-gooder." This reflects positively on other aspects of the restaurant.

To the listening public, public relations and publicity may be the most believable forms of the communications mix. A salesperson pitching a product, or a slick advertising campaign, may be subject to skepticism from consumers. When an independent source, such as a newspaper, writes about the product in an unbiased setting, credence is lent to the message unmatched by any other media format. A potential customer for a restaurant is more likely to try the veal specialty recommended by a restaurant reviewer than to try the same dish touted by a full-page ad proclaiming its excellence. A negative review can also totally counteract a full page ad.

---

*We have asked some managements why they charge so much for items in the minibar. The answer is unanimous—too many customers abuse the system, raising the costs. For example, they will take out a bottle of beer, drink it, fill it with water, put the cap back on, and return it to the minibar. Some of the newer versions of minibars at least partially prevent this. However, we have not seen the prices going down in these situations.

Public Relations (PR)

Public relations is the planned management of the media's and the community's perception. Although the press certainly cannot be told what to publish, a public relations effort can steer the story toward the best features of the product and away from negative images. Public relations efforts are designed to create stories that capture writers' attention with the hope that the writers will, in turn, communicate "the good news" to the desired readers, or target market. Figure 16-11 is an example of a **PR news release.**

We can demonstrate these points with some examples. After a major hurricane hit south Florida, hotel marketers were put to the test. The Doubletree Hotel reopened 11 days after the hurricane and publicized its decision to set aside 10 percent of its available rooms as complimentary lodging for families who had lost their homes. The hotel Mayfair House created positive press by housing 300 displaced tourists for free immediately after the disaster. After the Mississippi River flooded Des Moines, Iowa, most hotels lost their water supply. The Holiday Inn in West Des Moines still had water and made arrangements for guests from other hotels to take showers there.

Another example is that of McDonald's, a company widely acclaimed for its public relations efforts. For McDonald's, public relations is a major part of the marketing strategy. Ronald McDonald houses for families of ill children at nearby hospitals are nationally famous. When disaster strikes anywhere near a McDonald's some of the first people on the scene are McDonald's employees with coffee and hamburgers for the unfortunate, and for workers on the scene. When a man went berserk a few years ago in a McDonald's in California and shot and killed customers, McDonald's immediately closed the store and provided financial aid to the victims' families. When the company wanted to reopen the store a few months later, the townspeople strongly opposed it. McDonald's quickly complied by closing the store permanently. McDonald's, in essence, "created" these stories and gained a great deal of positive publicity from its public relations efforts.

In such cases and more often in less serious situations, public relations is used to formulate an image in the consumer's mind of what the company or product represents. Public relations engendered publicity enabled McDonald's to capitalize on a possibly negative image. Having Ronald McDonald homes has nothing to do with the production of hamburgers. The story is "created": the company cares for children (and perhaps, one thinks subliminally, has the same care while preparing the food?). McDonald's is a "good guy" in a bad situation.

Doing Public Relations

Public relations is not there just to deal with negative happenings or simply to create positive happenings. Instead, public relations is an ongoing task and an important part of marketing planning. In this capacity, public relations plays the following roles, as summed up by R. Haywood:

> [I]mproving awareness, projecting credibility, combating competition, evaluating new markets, creating direct sales leads, reinforcing the effectiveness of sales promotion and advertising, motivating the sales force, introducing new products, building brand loyalty, dealing with consumer issues and in many other ways.[4]

Public relations also creates images for the local, public, and financial communities as well as for the firm's employees. It creates favorable attitudes toward a firm, its products, and its efforts.

Public relations creates preopening publicity for hotels and restaurants through news releases that the media will carry. The result is that the press attends a grand opening, or "ribbon-cutting." The new business invites dignitaries who make news and in whom the press and the public are interested. On an ongoing basis, PR keeps the press, and hence the public, informed as to what is happening at the property or with the firm. Preopening public relations is extremely important in getting a hotel or a restaurant off to a good start. At this point we are not only marketing an intangible product but also

LAUNCH PRESS RELEASE

<u>The Leading Hotels Of The World Launches</u>
<u>Brand Extension To Focus Exclusively On</u>
<u>Small Boutique Hotels Worldwide</u>

The Small Leading Hotels of the World marks company's foray into boutique luxury segment

NEW YORK, September 29---The Leading Hotels of the World, literally an icon of five-star luxury since its founding over 70 years ago, has entered the luxury boutique hotel market segment with the launch of The Small Leading Hotels of the World.

The Small Leading Hotels of the World will consist of luxury hotels with 100 or fewer guestrooms, each distinguished by customized, personalized services and innovative or classical design. They will be located worldwide.

As a brand extension, each member hotel must operate at the same standards of excellence for which all Leading Hotels are renowned. Rigorous inspection and membership standards set by Leading, coupled with each hotel's keen attention to service and amenities for discriminating guests, will be hallmarks of this new group.

Extensive market research conducted by The Leading Hotels marketing group indicates that the upscale traveler seeks customized, personalized hotel experiences, especially for leisure travel. The brand extension responds directly to these customer driven demands.

"Experience is the status symbol of the Millennium. And this brand extension personifies the definitive 5-star source for the upscale traveler seeking the ultimate in intimate, stylish accommodations," said Small Leading Hotels' Managing Director Marshall Calder.

The hotels, which currently range from the modern and crisply elegant One Aldwich in London to the classic Lancaster in Paris, the famed resort Cap Juluca in Anguilla and the exotic Datai in Malaysia, are rich in distinction and personalized service.

Small Leading Hotels will be located in the world's major cities---from Paris to New York— and chic resort destinations throughout the world.

Information about the individual Small Leading Hotels can be found in the Millennium edition of The Leading Hotels of the World Directory, to be published in December 1999.

The Small Leading Hotels of the World will begin taking reservations for its member hotels effective November 1. For information: 1-800-223-6800 or www.lhw.com or a travel professional.

FIGURE 16-11 Example of a PR release.

one that does not yet exist. Several marketing objectives must be met during this time, including creating name recognition, establishing an image, building excitement, and cementing positive ties to the local community. Preopening public relations must begin at least a year in advance and gather momentum as opening day approaches. Table 16-4 shows a sample timetable for preopening public relations.

Large companies or properties usually have their own public relations firms, which are hired on monthly retainers to maintain favorable publicity for the organization. Even these large companies, however, as well as smaller ones that cannot afford PR agencies, as they are called, must practice public relations in-house on an ongoing basis. Doing this involves employee relations. It also involves relationships with taxi drivers and local police, attitude toward the press, competitive relationships, members of the distribution channels (such as airlines, travel agencies, tour operators), purveyors (who can be excellent carriers of good tidings), shareholders, bankers, and all manner of other publics with which the firm interacts.

Hotel and restaurant managers should belong to the local Rotary, Chamber of Commerce, community task forces, and other groups. One could almost say that everything management does has some aspect of public relations in it. Even the employees of the firm may be excellent public relations elements; in fact, for some firms they may be the most important of all. What your employees say about you and the way you operate reflects heavily on the image that will be created in the public's mind. Public relations serves well in times of need as a defensive weapon; more importantly, it is a continuous and ongoing offensive weapon.

Planning Public Relations

The same rules apply in planning public relations efforts that govern the rest of the communications mix. These include purpose, target market (in this case it may not be the customer at all, but might be the financial community, the industry, employees, intermediaries), setting of tactics, integration with the product service and the firm's overall marketing efforts.

Purpose. The purpose of a specific public relations effort must be established before any further planning occurs. The purpose must be definitive and quantifiable. For example, a restaurant might be under a new management that has to overcome a perception in the marketplace of slow service. In this case, it is unlikely that an advertising campaign would really convince anyone that the service was better. Improving the customers' perception of the restaurant's service would be the purpose of the public relations campaign. The quantifiable measurement, as in advertising, would be the increased number of covers. The subjective measurement would be the change in perception of the service.

A hotel might have a perception in the marketplace of being too expensive for the local customers, and might thus be unused by them. The purpose of the public relations effort would be to dispel the perception by improving the price/value relationship image for the local marketplace. The success of this program can be measured by increased usage of guest rooms by local customers, or in increased restaurant or lounge business outside of usual occupancy trends.

In both these situations, market research should be used to correctly evaluate customer perception, both before and after. Only then can the public relations effort be correctly focused.

Target Markets. When planning public relations, one must consider the benefit to the customer in the target market. Choosing a target market for a public relations effort is as important as choosing the correct market for any marketing effort. You must ask, "How will the target market be influenced to perceive the product?" This involves not only short-term benefits, but long-term ones as well, because hotels and restaurants are a major part of the community in which they exist. They are the most public of all commercial enterprises, so much so that they often become "public places" where people meet. It is these same people, as well,

---

TABLE 16-4

Sample Timetable for Preopening Public Relations for a Hotel

This schedule begins six months before the hotel opening, at which time the announcement of construction plans and the groundbreaking ceremony will have been completed.

150–180 days before opening

1. Hold meeting to define objectives and to coordinate public relations effort with advertising; establish timetable in accordance with scheduled completion date.
2. Prepare media kit.
3. Order photographs and renderings.
4. Begin preparation of mailings and develop media lists.
5. Contact all prospective beneficiaries of opening events.
6. Reserve dates for press conferences at off-site facilities.

120–150 days before opening

1. Send announcement with photograph or rendering to all media.
2. Send first progress bulletin to agents and media (as well as corporate clients, if desired).
3. Begin production of permanent brochure.
4. Make final plans for opening events, including commitment to beneficiaries.

90–120 days before opening

1. Launch publicity campaign to national media.
2. Send mailings to media.
3. Send second progress bulletin.
4. Arrange exclusive trade interviews and features in conjunction with ongoing trade campaign.
5. Begin trade announcement.

60–90 days before opening

1. Launch campaign to local media and other media with a short lead time; emphasize hotel's contribution to the community, announcement of donations and beneficiaries, etc.
2. Send third and final progress bulletin with finished brochure.
3. Commence "behind-the-scenes" public tours.
4. Hold "hard-hat" luncheons for travel writers.
5. Set up model units for tours.

30–60 days before opening

1. Send preopening newsletter (to be continued on a quarterly basis).
2. Hold soft opening and ribbon-cutting ceremony.
3. Hold press opening.
4. Establish final plans for opening gala.

The month of opening

1. Begin broadside mailing to agents.
2. Hold opening festivities.
3. Conduct orientation press trips.

who answer such questions from out-of-towners as "Where should I stay" or "Where's a good place to eat?" Public relations will influence local responses even when the people themselves have never stayed or eaten at the property. Public relations creates an image in the mind of the consumer and reinforces that image in many ways.

Choosing Targeted Media.

Along with identifying a target audience comes the task of reaching these customers. While geographic location of the customers needs to be understood, the correct media to reach that geographic area must be analyzed as well. While a computer trade journal may appear to be a good place to advertise for a corporate meeting, this may not be where a potential vacationer would be reading an article on the benefits of staying in a hotel.

While "selling stories" may sound unusual, good public relations experts will have a network of editors to whom they can do just that by calling upon them personally. This relationship with decision-makers of a media channel can be critical to breaking a story. For this reason, public relations is becoming more of a science, and less of a "hit or miss" type communication effort.

The public relations expert will push a story much as a salesperson sells a product. Calls are made to the editors, they are wined and dined, and thank-you notes and flowers are sent in appreciation of the placement of the story or press release. A press release is a document giving the salient points of a story in a generic industry-wide format. A press release usually contains the contact name of the public relations professional who wrote the story, background information on the facility, and the body copy of the story. It is then "pitched" or "sold" to the media.

Personal contacts are what differentiate a good public relations firm from a poor one. Anyone can write stories and send them to papers and broadcast media, but only a true professional has the contacts to follow up until the article is printed.

Positioning.

A cohesive message must be developed before a public relations campaign is launched. Ideally, the public relations message will integrate with the other forms of the communications mix. If the advertising message is telling customers that service is the main advantage of the product, the public relations stories should also center on that theme. If food quality is the spearhead of the marketing effort, stories on the chefs and their background will augment this effort.

The positioning must also be kept within the framework of the purpose of the public relations effort. If a public relations effort is undertaken to change the customer's perception of slow service, then the positioning should also follow this generic format. It is very easy to get distracted during a public relations campaign and begin many activities unrelated to the purpose or positioning of the product. Positioning is where the "spin" is put on the story.

Developing Tactics

Before the public relations subset is employed, it is important to begin to develop stories on the product itself. The following subject titles represent good starting points in a public relations campaign.

Personnel.

Numerous stories can be submitted based upon the employees who work every day in a hotel or restaurant. The Clarion Hotel in New Orleans received much media attention when an off-duty bellman chased and apprehended the attacker of a foreign tourist who had ventured into an unsafe area of the city.

For restaurants, a background on the chef can provide an interesting story. If the chef has won any awards or trained outside of the country, the local media are often willing to convey the story to their readers.

Customers.

Sometimes customers become a story in themselves. A honeymoon couple from 30 years back checking into the same room can generate empathetic interest. A customer who eats regularly in a restaurant conveys an image of consistency that might cause readers to try the product.

When celebrities or politicians dine in a restaurant or stay in a hotel, the public has a natural curiosity.

Positioning becomes an important element in using customers as a lead story for a hotel or restaurant. Be sure, however, that the customer being featured is the right representative for the desired target market. Publicizing that the latest-rage rock band is staying at the Pierre Hotel in New York could drive away customers who were seeking to have a quiet and inconspicuous stay in Manhattan.

History. A story line developed about the building, neighborhood, or owner's or manager's background can also provide a format of interest to the public. The Vista Hotel in New York City created a "Heritage and History" package that combined visits to the many ethnic neighborhoods of Lower Manhattan, where the hotel is located, with trips to the Statue of Liberty and Ellis Island (the historic immigration gateway) just across the bay.

Measuring Success. As with all communications vehicles, measuring success is important in public relations, but here success is particularly difficult to track. Without special 800 numbers for advertisements, or redemption of coupons of direct mail pieces, public relations has been elusive in its traceability.

A methodology for measuring PR success has been developed based on the premise that "paid" advertising equivalents can be quantified. Put simply, for each column inch of editorial or "unpaid" storyline, the equivalent advertising rate is matched to determine the value of the public relations effort. Table 16-5 shows how a promotion for a prominent New York City hotel tracked this in terms of advertising equivalents.

Guidelines

Additional guidelines for public relations have been suggested by Joe Adams, president of the Adams Group Inc., a national public relations firm.[5]

- PR is not free. This is the most common mistake hotels make. If you don't budget, don't expect results.

T A B L E   16-5
Measuring Public Relations Success

Date	Publication	Circulation	Column Inches	Cost per Column Inch	Advertising Equivalency
2/01/98	Avenue Magazine	80,000	11	$399	$4,389
2/01/98	Cornell Quarterly	6,000	4	$45	$180
2/01/98	Gourmet Magazine	880,774	124	$1104	$136,896
2/15/98	Lodging Magazine	46,000	1	$169	$169
3/01/98	Travel America	416,776	8	$370	$2,960
3/25/98	Barron's	300,000	1	$311	$311
Total		1,729,550			$144,905

The PR release ran in the last quarter of 1997. Many of the prestigious magazines have "closing dates" 90 days prior to publication. A tracking service provided clippings of the publications mentioned above. The column inches were determined by the actual copy and the cost per column inch was determined by each publication's rate card. In this case, the promotion yielded $144,905 of "unpaid" media coverage, or a little over eight cents per person reached.

- Use top PR talent. PR titles are often bestowed on people who have no training or experience in public relations. You can usually buy the services of a good PR firm for what it costs to hire one experienced individual.
- Have a written plan. If you can write it down, you can make it happen.
- PR people must understand your marketing plan. You can't expect results unless you let them in on your plans and objectives. Make sure they understand that PR is a marketing tool.
- Demand regular reports on PR results. A consistent, ongoing PR program should provide consistent, ongoing results.
- If it doesn't sell it's not creative. It takes innovative ideas to get deserved PR coverage.
- Remember: Great public relations depends upon creative management.

Table 16-6 shows an expert's suggested steps for creating a successful PR campaign.

Publicity

When "natural" stories like those above have been fully developed, other methods need to be employed to keep the press interested in the restaurant or hotel. Publicity now needs to be "created" so that editors will continue to have something to write about.

The creation of events is not as simple as it may sound. The purpose of the event needs to be established together with a target medium, and an evaluation of the event needs to follow. Publicity, in this sense, is like promotions, except that publicity is aimed specifically at the media to generate public relations. Promotions can be held without publicity; publicity helps with promotions.

Publicity differs from promotions in the preparation for the event. Targeted audiences (readers) are researched, and the appropriate editors and radio or TV station managers are invited. Again, the personal relationship developed by the public relations expert is critical for successful attendance by the right people.

The event must be organized so that everything goes perfectly. If a promotion is not executed well, the hotel or restaurant is at risk for all of the patrons exposed to the event, plus any other potential customers who hear of it by word of mouth. While this might be catastrophic, it is nothing compared to the potential lost business that one editor could produce by writing in a newspaper with a circulation of 100,000 readers.

At the event, press releases with background information are made available to the press. A prepared press release will answer questions such as the number of seats available in the restaurant, the name of the manager, and so on. The public relations professional will "work the event" by attending and "pitching" the points personally to the attendees. The end of the actual promotion signals the beginning of the placement work for the public relations effort. Thank-you notes and flowers are sent to remind the attendees of the importance of the event. Follow-up calls are made to cajole the writers to place the story in the best light, and to the editors for the actual placement. Having a story placed in a newspaper or on radio/television is not the only measure of success. The physical placement of the story is as important as getting the story into the media.

After all of this work is finished, the last stage of the public relations/publicity effort is the evaluation. Have more customers been generated? Was perception in the marketplace altered to the satisfaction of the management team? The evaluation process is as important as any other phase of the effort. Restaurant covers and rooms sold can be tracked at the property, but changes in customer perception are more difficult to measure.

Handling negative publicity is an art unto itself. Table 16-7 abstracts from an article on a franchisee's and franchiser's cooperation.

T A B L E 16-6
Steps to Creating a Successful Public Relations Campaign[6]

STEP 1: Define what your goal is and whether public relations is the best vehicle to accomplish that goal.

Often sales and marketing people think they need to "do PR" without any clear-cut goal of what public relations can and should be doing for them. At the outset, it is imperative to sit down with the entire team—sales, marketing, operations, and management,—and decide what is missing from the sales and marketing process and what key element can fill that void. What is perhaps most important to remember is that public relations is not a "quick fix" and if you are looking to sell weekend packages for the next two weekends, your goals would be better met by placing advertisements.

Are you opening a new theme park? Want to promote a long-term weekend rate? Or do you simply need to create greater awareness for your product or service? All of these are very viable reasons to implement a public relations campaign.

STEP 2: Take an honest and realistic assessment of the marketplace and your product/company's position in it.

What is the atmosphere in the marketplace where you want to do business? Moreover, what is your product/company's position in it—realistically? Do you have a poor or less than positive image that you want to overcome—or do you have absolutely no image at all that you need to correct? You must create a baseline perception measurement and then determine where you need to go from there.

STEP 3: Formulate your product/company's message.

Before you go out to the media, you need to formulate your product/company's message and decide upon the "key communications points." These are the benefits or points of interest about your product which you want to communicate and which should be reflected in every aspect of your public relations campaign—they also should be integrated into all other corporate communications, marketing, and sales vehicles.

STEP 4: Identify your target audience and the media vehicles which will best help you reach that audience.

Who is the audience that you want to impress—whether it be to promote a great new weekend rate or inform them of a new theme park that is about to open? And what are the best vehicles to reach this audience? If you have only a short lead time between when you are getting the message out and when you need your audience to react, then your media vehicles are more limited—to electronic and some forms of print (e.g., daily newspapers) rather than monthly magazines which work on a longer lead time. Also familiarize yourself with the media that you are targeting to be sure they routinely cover the type of story you are pitching. There is nothing that irks editors more than someone pitching a story to them which has absolutely no relevance to their readership.

STEP 5: Decide how to most effectively deliver that message.

Public relations encompasses a host of strategies which are much too lengthy to detail here. You may choose to create awareness by calling an editor and pitching a story idea about your company over the phone; engaging in a promotion (e.g., giving away a trip to your destination in return for direct exposure among your target audience, having a celebrity at a ribbon-cutting ceremony to re-open a hotel; sending out a news release to your target media; hosting a press conference; inviting journalists to take a complimentary cruise so that they can experience your product first-hand, etc.) Whatever avenue you choose, once again decide what your ultimate goal is (e.g., a story in XYZ Magazine because that publication is read by clients who purchase my product). While it may sound great to get a double-page spread in a bridal magazine by hosting the magazine's editor for a weekend, if your goal is to promote your new corporate rate program, you are getting off track.

(continued)

T A B L E   16-6   (Continued)

A couple of key tips:

- Familiarize yourself with the media outlets you are targeting.
- Make sure what you are pitching to them is "news" and not "fluff."
- Identify a national or regional trend and then tie your company's product or service to that trend.
- Create your own news (e.g., take a survey among your guests/clients and release those results).
- Promote a key executive in the company as an "expert" in the field and try to get him routinely quoted in stories on topics which fit with the company. This lends credibility to the company.

STEP 6: Measure your results.

Many people say that public relations is an "intangible" marketing tool with results that are very difficult to measure and this is true if you are looking to create a particular image or awareness of your product or service rather than a specific call to action. However, if, for example, your budget affords you the opportunity to conduct ongoing market research, then you can test the overall perception of the product or service prior to the campaign's implementation, and then along the way. More common methods are via press clippings and total reader impressions. If you properly defined your target audience and target media vehicles at the outset, and your clippings reflect those targets, then you should be well on your way to implementing a successful public relations campaign—and realizing your goals.

STEP 7: Maintain consistency.

Sometimes executives think PR is something which can be turned on and off at will like a faucet. They think that if they need greater awareness next month they can turn on the PR machine again and then turn it off the month after. That is the biggest mistake one can make. The essence of public relations is in slowly building up an image and a reputation for a product or service and maintaining that perception in the marketplace. Remember, consumers are very wary and they have very short attention spans. You are probably not going to convince them of something overnight and you certainly won't remain top-of-mind for very long after you turn off your PR machine.

SUMMARY

This chapter offers a foundation and a methodology for successful execution of sales promotions, merchandising, and public relations programs. The most common reason for failure in delivering these subsets of the communications mix is lack of planning. Sales promotions usually have short-term objectives. They must be conducted for a specific target market and both employees and customers must be aware of the product/service being promoted. Different products have to be promoted in different ways but, eventually, results must be measured. Merchandising is primarily in-house marketing and the planning process includes assessing the needs of the customer and then providing the product to the customer in a cost-effective manner. With a strong planning process in place, and a good evaluation mechanism, both revenues and customer satisfaction can be maximized.

The public relations effort of a hospitality entity is a very effective element of the communications mix. It may be the most effective element in that it is the most believable for the consumer. A potential customer is more likely to be convinced by reading or hearing a third party's praise for a product than by an advertising campaign.

The public relations campaign should be focused and quantifiable within targeted positioning and purpose objectives. Publicity remains a subset of the public relations umbrella, to be utilized after all "natural" stories have been highlighted by press coverage. Negative publicity requires special han-

T A B L E   16-7
Handling Negative Publicity[7]

A hotel is damaged in a hurricane. A freak accident takes place at a property and someone is killed. A domestic dispute turns violent in a hotel guestroom. General managers must contend with handling the press following these types of incidents. If the property involved is franchised, then this poses a question for the franchiser, who must walk a fine line even though the hotel is privately owned and managed.

The franchiser has limited rights in telling the property's management how to handle the press. On the other hand, a national brand name is on the hotel and the brand identity must be protected. Sometimes a local tragedy can become a national press story, which could leave the public with the wrong image of an entire chain.

Franchisers' PR executives mostly say that while they have crisis management programs, they mostly take their cues from the general managers themselves. Other general managers feel more comfortable in having a franchise corporate office issue statements. Most often the two work together to disseminate information to local and national media.

How should franchise companies best handle media questions regarding events that take place at individual properties? "There needs to be an open dialogue with the press, so that no one thinks a property is trying to hide something," says Scott Brush, an independent consultant. Regardless, the public will look to the brand to make a corporate statement.

A case in point. An 18 year old woman was killed in a freak accident at a Ramada Inn. The woman, who was wet from a downpour, was electrocuted as she slid her card-key into the metal door of her room. The hotel's GM and Ramada's PR manager both released immediate statements saying the case was under investigation and no new information could be provided at the time. Later, negative publicity came from preliminary findings that showed some failure in the guestroom's air conditioning or its supply cord causing the unusually high voltage that triggered the electrocution. Ramada's parent company had no formal crisis management program but consults with the GM and issues statements as needed. It only gets involved as much as the franchisee wants it to. In this case that wasn't enough to stop the adverse publicity.

Radisson has crisis plans in place for each hotel and, in such situations, maintains a channel of communication with the press. If a reporter wants to make a national story out of something, there is no way to stop him. But you can't run away from the issue and say "no comment" says Radisson. Often, Radisson will set up a spokesperson at the property. However, Radisson believes that a hotel should establish its own relationship with the media. Very often, when an accident occurs, the hotel is just as much a victim as the actual victim. Radisson tries to keep a local story from becoming a national story. But if it does, corporate gets very involved and stands side by side with the franchisee to protect the brand and the investment.

Choice Hotels International has a 24 hour crisis hotline for its franchisees. Choice's corporate PR office will also write statements for a property and guide a GM on how to answer press questions. Hilton and Sheraton follow a very similar practice. Corporate can be contacted 24 hours a day through hot lines or beepers.

dling. In the next chapter we continue with the last element of the communications mix, personal selling. We devote an entire chapter to that subject because of the predominance of its use in the hospitality industry.

KEY WORDS AND CONCEPTS

Merchandising: The promoting of additional items for purchase by the customer who is already purchasing something from us.

PR News Release: Favorable news item that is released to the media in hopes that it will be articulated.

Publicity: News that is told by the media, or word of mouth, as a result of some event or happening. It may be positive or negative.

Public Relations: Favorable information that is spread by the media and is often "planted."

Sales Promotions: Special promotions of a short-term nature to sell a product by offering special benefits such as special prices or features.

Single-Minded Promotion: A promotion that has a single focus that can be easily understood by the public.

Spin Control: "Control" or converting negative publicity to a less negative or positive form by those affected.

not done by others. Define the service. Then develop a promotion and merchandising campaign for it internally, and a PR program for it externally.

2. Do the same as #1 for a local restaurant menu item.

DISCUSSION QUESTIONS

1. Develop a hypothetical promotion to sell more California wine in a restaurant using all of the steps outlined for a successful sales promotion.
2. Discuss the basic rules of merchandising using a real-life example.
3. Develop an example of good merchandising for a hotel or restaurant using at least two of the other communications mixes.
4. What are the components of a good public relations plan? Discuss how you might apply them to a local restaurant.
5. Discuss the similarities and differences between sales promotions and merchandising.
6. Contrast public relations and publicity and discuss the implications of each.
7. A major role of public relations may be to deal with unexpected crises that result in bad publicity. Discuss how hospitality organizations can create positive public relations when faced with disasters such as accidental death or serious injury caused by a drunken customer.
8. Develop a preopening public relations plan for a restaurant using Table 16-4 as a guide.

GROUP PROJECTS

1. Suppose you have developed a totally new service for a hotel that you believe is unique and

REFERENCES

1. Reported in David Martindale, "Hotels and Frequent Flyers: The Changing Relationship," *Frequent Flyer*, August 1986, pp. 67–68.
2. A benchmarking survey jointly sponsored by KPMG Peat Marwick, American Hotel and Motel Association (AHMA), and its subsidiary, the Educational Institute (EI). The survey targeted full service hotel companies throughout the United States. Although 67 percent of these hotel respondents thought that frequent traveler programs are effective or highly effective, they reported that their overall contribution to occupied rooms was only 8 percent. Of course, if each hotel averages eight percent of stays due to frequent traveler programs, they are only trading customers and maintaining the status quo. Reported by Kapila K. Arnand, Partner, KPMG, *The Real Estate Report*, 1998.
3. Tom Feltenstein, "How to Discount Your Product Without Sabotaging Your Image," *Nation's Restaurant News*, November 9, 1987, p. F20.
4. R. Haywood, *All About PR*, London: McGraw-Hill, 1984. Quoted in Francis A. Buttle, *Hotel and Food Service Marketing*. London: Holt, Rinehart and Winston, 1986, p. 400.
5. Joe Adams, "Good P.R. Plan Can Be Potent Marketing Tool for Hotels," *Hotel & Motel Management*, June 8, 1987, p. 60.
6. Courtesy of Jane Coloccia, CHME, President, JC Communications, LLC.
7. Abstracted from Laura Koss-Feder, "Crisis Brings Media Scrutiny," *Hotel & Motel Management*, August 14, 1995, pp. 5, 8, 16.

Seventeen

◆

THE COMMUNICATIONS MIX: PERSONAL SELLING

Overview

Personal selling is the only part of the communications mix that involves direct interaction between the seller and the buyer. It is especially suitable when both the product and the buyer's needs are complex. In hospitality it is used primarily by large hotels and chains that deal with meeting planners and corporate accounts.

EMPHASIS ON PERSONAL SELLING Personal selling involves face-to-face contact where the salesperson has high control of the situation with the customer and can get immediate feedback in the negotiation process. The salesperson can then tailor the product to meet customers' needs and solve their problems.

THE SALES PROCESS Starting from scratch the sales process has a definite sequence. *Prospecting* is finding qualified customers. *Qualifying* a prospect

means making sure they are willing and able to buy. The *sales approach* is tailored to the customer by learning what the customer's real problems are. This often requires a lot of *probing. Benefits and features* are presented after learning the customer's problems. Being able to deal with customers' attitudes is a skillful process. The salesperson has to learn to overcome skepticism, indifference, and objections. *Closing the sale* means getting or asking for a commitment. Once the sale is closed, regular *follow-up* is important and, at the time of the event, all *promises made must be kept*.

SALES MANAGEMENT Effective management of a sales force requires setting some parameters and goals. An account management system is used to handle customer accounts, and the sales equation to establish goals for salespeople. The sales action plan is established for reaching the goals.

ORGANIZATION OF THE SALES TEAM   The size of the sales force is based on the number of sales calls planned and the different product lines. Both "inside" and "outside" salespeople are used. Contrarily, more hotels are practicing product line management where a salesperson sells all products to a few large customers such as IBM. All of this means having the right salespeople on the job,

people who have the right ethical standards and motivation.

SALES AND OPERATIONS   These separate but complementary tasks sometimes have conflicts. Internal relationship marketing is important to avoid and resolve them.

●◆●

Personal selling is the direct interaction between a seller and a prospective buyer for the purpose of making a sale. Personal selling may be one of the more challenging aspects of the communications mix. While public relations communicates through stories and the media, advertising communicates through copy and artwork, and merchandising communicates through in-house promotions, the salesperson communicates through direct oral presentation to the customer.

Obviously, every employee should be a salesperson for the organization. In this chapter, however, we discuss selling from the perspective of hospitality organizations that specifically designate people to carry out the direct sales function.

Organized personal selling is not universally used in the hospitality industry. Rarely will you meet a salesperson from the local Pizza Hut, McDonald's, or even Motel 6. On the other hand, full service hotels and restaurants with extensive catering facilities employ salespeople as an essential part of their communications mix.

EMPHASIS ON PERSONAL SELLING

Whether or not personal selling is used by an organization depends on several factors, including the complexity of the products and services offered, the quantities in which they are purchased, and the price that is paid. In the fast-food or budget hotel

case, the products and services are relatively simple: the customer knows what they are; they are usually purchased by individuals or small groups in relatively small quantities; and the price is low. For the buyer it is a low risk, low involvement purchase. Hiring a salesperson would not be cost effective or even productive. The interaction between the buyer and seller is easy and straightforward.

Contrast this to the 1,600-room Hilton in New Orleans. One salesperson may book a group of 500 rooms for three nights at $150 per room night. This is $225,000 worth of room night business alone, negotiated between the salesperson and a meeting planner. In addition, there are food and beverage functions, hospitality suites, general session and breakout rooms, representing possibly another $100,000, and dozens of other details to be worked out. The same is true of a resort such as The Broadmoor in Colorado Springs. These are high risk purchases with high involvement on the part of the buyer who wants every detail to go perfectly. The products and services are complex and need much explanation, negotiation, and confirmation before a contract is signed. A good salesperson will decrease the risk factor by offering assurance and providing examples.

Besides sales managers at the unit level, chains like Marriott, Hyatt, and Hilton employ national and international sales managers to represent the entire chain to accounts that have ongoing needs for many hotels in many locations. Personal selling has been found to be most appropriate when:

- The *product* requires that the customer receive assistance, perhaps personal demonstration and trial, and the purchase decision requires a major commitment on the buyer's part.
- The final *price* is negotiated, not fixed, and the final price and quantity purchased allow an adequate margin to support selling expenses.
- *Distribution channels* are short and direct and channel members require training and assistance.
- *Advertising* media are not effective in reaching and luring the intended markets and the information sought by potential customers cannot be provided thoroughly through advertising.
- The *market* sees personal selling as an essential part of the product.

In each of the above categories, the application to the hospitality product and organizational markets lend themselves to the personal selling portion of the communications mix. Buying the *product* requires a major commitment on the purchaser's part. Even a small meeting in a suburban hotel of only 30 people for 3 days can easily exceed a $10,000 expenditure. Assistance is necessary in application, that is, understanding customers' goals and helping them achieve them. Personal demonstration and trial are common such as site inspections, trial stays, and booking a small meeting before a large one. *Pricing* for meetings, group bookings, and corporate accounts is normally negotiated. *Distribution channels* are short and direct and intermediaries require training and assistance. *Advertising* is inadequate and too expensive to reach and fulfill the needs of the buyer, and explain the benefits. Finally, the *marketplace* sees the salesperson as an integral part of the product. As hotels in the same product class have become, essentially, a basic commodity, it is through salespeople who develop relationships that a competitive edge can be gained.

All the rules of the communications mix apply to sales. However, there are differences between the characteristics of personal selling and the other components of the communications mix, as seen in Table 17-1.

There are several advantages to using personal selling. These include:

1. Selling is really about solving a customers' problem. Customer problems become needs.
2. Personal selling can be used to tangibilize and describe products and services in greater detail.
3. The sales pitch can be tailored to customers' needs. Solutions to customer's specific problems can be offered.
4. Prospective buyers can be identified and qualified before directing personal selling so that communications mix dollars may be more effectively spent.
5. Personal selling can reduce risk and is more effective in getting customers to close the deal and sign the contract.
6. Personal selling is the only part of the communications mix that permits direct feedback from the customer.
7. Personal selling provides an excellent opportunity for relationship marketing.

THE SALES PROCESS

There are several steps in the personal sales process. These include prospecting, qualifying prospects, the sales approach, handling objections, closing of the sale, and follow-up. The sales process also has two other very important aspects that must be kept in mind during the sales interaction—how to sell the product given unique client needs, and what to sell. The successful sales team knows not only how to sell, but what to sell most efficiently.

Prospecting

Prospecting is the term used for finding new customers. The goal of prospecting is to convert unqualified names of customers into sales leads. Sales leads turn into making sales calls, in person or by phone, on qualified customers who are not cur-

TABLE 17-1
Characteristics of the Communications Mix[1]

Communications Mode	Personal Selling: Direct & Face-to-face	Advertising: Indirect and Nonpersonal	Publicity: Usually Indirect and Nonpersonal	Sales Promotion: Usually Indirect and Nonpersonal
Communicator's control over the situation	High	Low	Moderate to low	Moderate to low
Amount of feedback	Much	Little	Little	Little to moderate
Speed of feedback	Immediate	Delayed	Delayed	Varies
Message flow	Two-way	One-way	One-way	Mostly one-way
Control over message content	Yes	Yes	No	Yes
Sponsor identified	Yes	Yes	No	Yes
Speed in reaching large audiences	Slow	Fast	Usually fast	Fast
Message flexibility	Tailored to prospect	Uniform and unvaried	No direct control over message	Uniform and varied

rently using the product. Prospecting is more difficult than calling on existing customers because new customers don't really know the product, although they may certainly have some perception of it. New customers need to be convinced that the product they are currently using does not satisfy their needs as well as your product would. One axiom goes like this:

> If you want to sell your product to our company, be sure your product is accompanied by a plan that will so help our business that we will be more anxious to buy than you are to sell.

It is highly unlikely that a meeting planner will "create" a meeting just because of your facility. The meeting either will already exist, having occurred before at a competitor's hotel or in another area, or will have been partially developed and waiting to be placed in a property. In direct sales, the most common way to get new customers is to take them away from competitors. Prospecting has evolved over the past decade as the real challenge for selling in a competitive marketplace.

"**Cold calling**" (calling on a prospect without notice) used to be the main method to drum up new business. One technique was for a sales team to "**blitz**" an area or office building by making calls, unannounced, on companies within the building. This method is still in place in some organizations, but is not generally recommended. Few like to have a salesperson walk in "cold," and ask to speak to the person that books meetings or banquets. Many salespeople do not like cold calling either, or the risk of rejection that comes with it. On the other hand, some individual salespeople use cold calling, not necessarily "blitz," to successfully set up appointments and obtain pertinent information.[2]

More sophisticated methods of generating leads, or prospects, have emerged. Many sales directors are recognizing the cost of sales calls, and realizing that sending salespeople out on calls without appointments is an expensive way to do business. Depending on the experience of the salesperson, the location, the account, and other variables, a sales call can cost $50 to $500 or more, after salary, benefits, office space, secretarial sup-

GUEST QUARTERS
SUITE HOTELS

M E M O R A N D U M

► To: Audrey A. Mintz

► From: Jack P. Ferguson

► Date: November 9

► Re: Guest Quarters Suite Hotel/Atlanta Perimeter

Audrey:

As we reviewed this morning, the top priority in the NSO Telemarketing Department this week is to qualify the 588 accounts in the FIDELIO system that indicate travel into the Atlanta market. The created questionnaire for this project should accomplish what we want to uncover for the property from the standpoint of:

TRANSIENT, GROUP, EXTENDED STAY, SOCIAL, INCENTIVE/GIFT CERTIFICATE and what **TRAVEL AGENCY** they utilize in their Atlanta area hotel needs.

Audrey, the notes on the PROFILE need to be neat and clear as these will be used by our sales team for the Concentrated Sales Effort the week of December 14-18.

Additionally, use the updated FACT SHEET about the Hotel to verbally walk the customer through the facilities.

JFP/sd
Attachments: ATLANTA PROFILE/ATLANTA FACT SHEET

ATLANTA

F I G U R E   1 7 - 1   Guest Quarters sets up a qualification program.

port, collateral, and travel are factored in as part of the cost of doing business. At even $50 per call, the salesperson becomes an expensive resource, not to be used without a well-devised plan. Direct mail and telemarketing (which also may be called cold calling), or sometimes a combination of both, are used effectively to set up sales calls in advance, and make for concentrated sales efforts with advance notice. Once a face-to-face rapport is established, salespeople often use the telephone as much as possible because of the time and cost for many face-to-face calls.

Qualifying Prospects

In this step, the salesperson determines if prospects are qualified to make the purchase—can they afford it, do they have business in this destination, do they have the authority to make the decision, and just how serious are they? **Qualifying** is done during prospecting, telemarketing, or as a follow-up to direct mail or advertising responses. The qualifying process turns hundreds of names into a few sales leads.

Direct mail responses can also be effective in

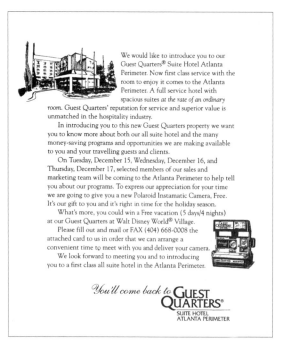

We would like to introduce you to our Guest Quarters® Suite Hotel Atlanta Perimeter. Now first class service with the room to enjoy it comes to the Atlanta Perimeter. A full service hotel with spacious suites *at the rate of an ordinary room.* Guest Quarters' reputation for service and superior value is unmatched in the hospitality industry.

In introducing you to this new Guest Quarters property we want you to know more about both our all suite hotel and the many money-saving programs and opportunities we are making available to you and your travelling guests and clients.

On Tuesday, December 15, Wednesday, December 16, and Thursday, December 17, selected members of our sales and marketing team will be coming to the Atlanta Perimeter to help tell you about our programs. To express our appreciation for your time we are going to give you a new Polaroid Instamatic Camera, Free. It's our gift to you and it's right in time for the holiday season.

What's more, you could win a Free vacation (5 days/4 nights) at our Guest Quarters at Walt Disney World® Village.

Please fill out and mail or FAX (404) 668-0008 the attached card to us in order that we can arrange a convenient time to meet with you and deliver your camera.

We look forward to meeting you and to introducing you to a first class all suite hotel in the Atlanta Perimeter.

You'll come back to **GUEST QUARTERS®**
SUITE HOTEL
ATLANTA PERIMETER

FIGURE 17-2   Guest Quarters uses direct mail to set up sales calls.

qualifying prospects because only those who are genuinely interested in the service will bother to respond to the solicitation. A mailing list is purchased, a mailing piece is developed and mailed with a response card and, often, some kind of incentive. For example, a facility may want to increase its share of a certain market, such as medical meetings. Certain parameters that fit the property, such as size of meeting and geographic preference, are established. A creative direct mail piece is created to generate a response for more information. A sales manager or telemarketer would then follow up the lead, to determine the customer's needs. Figures 17-1 and 17-2 illustrate the first stages of qualifying for a new suite hotel.

Telemarketing is another, more direct method, to generate and qualify leads. This time the prospect is phoned. The telemarketer may just find out if there is a need for the facility and then turn the lead over to the sales manager for professional follow up. Many travel managers are besieged by

sales managers and telemarketers on a daily basis, however, and keep their voice mail on to screen the unwanted invasion of calls. Yet, on the other hand, sales mangers play an important part in fulfilling a travel manager's responsibilities as frequent contact keeps them apprised of the best "deals" with the best product.

Advertising to meeting planners is a common practice for large hotels, resorts, and hotel chains to get them to make the first approach. Media presumably read by these people, such as *Successful Meetings, Meetings and Conventions,* and *Corporate Meetings and Incentives,* as well as national newspapers are used. Such ads may provide special incentives or direct solicitations to the meeting planner (Figure 17-3). Responses are followed up with more information, for example, sending brochures, meeting room specifications, facilities, and so on. (See Figure 9-9 for an example of these details.) Some properties even send out videos to provide more graphic and direct presentations (Figure 17-4). Eventually, a personal sales call, or at least a telephone call, will be in order. It can take many prospects to get a few customers, as shown in Figure 17-5.

The Sales Approach

The sales approach, or communicating personally with customers, is not an easy skill to master. In past years, when the demand for guestrooms was greater than the supply, the selling process was simple—order taking. A salesperson would simply answer the phone or call back customers who had telephoned earlier, and take their orders. The sales process is now very different. In most markets supply exceeds demand and the telephones no longer ring by themselves. A good sales process is what makes the telephones ring.

There is a right way to sell and a wrong way to sell, yet it is still a very personal skill. Many salespeople in the hospitality industry think they are selling by knocking on office doors without appointments (cold calling) and leaving behind a brochure. Today, good salespeople get "inside the

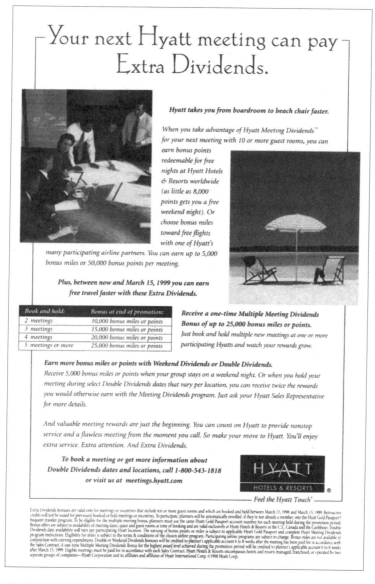

FIGURE 17-3 Hyatt uses a special incentive for meeting planners.

buyer's head." The sales process has evolved to where good salespeople are good problem solvers.

Theodore Levitt has chronicled this progression. In past practice, and perhaps still too often today, the seller tried to unload onto a buyer what the seller decided to offer. "This was the basis for the notion that a salesperson needs charisma, because it was charisma that made the sale rather than the product selling itself." Over time, selling progressed to where the seller "penetrates the buyer's domain to learn about his needs, desires, fears, and the like, and then designs and supplies

Watch Guest Quarters raise it to an art.

It's sad, really, that doing the same thing over and over again doesn't often produce excellence, but merely predictability.

You might arrange your meeting through a big convention hotel, and settle for their routine best. Or, you can insist on something special, like Guest Quarters®.

At Guest Quarters Suite Hotels, we pride ourselves in hosting only smaller business meetings. And we treat each one like it was the most important event we've ever held. Because we believe that every occasion, and every client that we serve, is one of a kind.

Every Guest Quarters Suite Hotel has conference rooms to handle your small meeting. Plus Executive Suites for more private conferences. Our meeting coordinators will help plan everything, from flowers and special menus to all the necessary audio-visual equipment. Whatever the size, our meeting and catering services will please the most sophisticated tastes. Your guests stay in spacious suites, with all the amenities you expect in a first-class hotel. Plus business services like photocopying, fax machines, couriers, overnight shipping and typing. We also offer rentals of personal computers, VCRs and cellular telephones. All to help increase your, and your guests, productivity.

Small meetings. Short notice.

We even offer a "Meetings-In-A-Minute" program, specifically designed to expedite meeting arrangements for groups of fewer than fifty guests on short notice (from one to thirty days). We understand your need for the very best—brief notice or not, and our "Meetings-In-A-Minute" manager can provide excellent suggestions, and helpful tips, while confirming arrangements with just one phone call. We've even designed a "Meetings-In-A-Minute" checklist for you.

Call For Our Free Videotape.

Watch us raise meetings to an art on our video, "Small Business Meetings The Guest Quarters Way." We think it conveys what makes us, and our guests, special. Call today toll-free, or contact me personally, to order your free copy. And watch us make your next small business meeting perfect the first time.

GUEST QUARTERS®
SUITE HOTELS

FIGURE 17-4 An example of a videotape for graphic presentation.

the product in all its forms. Instead of trying to get the buyer to want what the seller has, the seller tries to have what the buyer will want. The 'product' is no longer merely an item but a whole bundle of value satisfactions." The progression process is from need to benefit to feature for the buyer.[3]

Today, once prospected, successful selling is more about long-term relationships between sellers and qualified buyers. It is not just that once you get a customer you want to keep him. It is more a matter of what the buyer wants. He wants a seller who will keep in contact and deliver the promises made to him. Thus there comes to be an interdependence between the seller and the buyer.

It is this lesson that was learned by Ritz-Carlton Hotel Company when it hired a research firm to study its relationships with meeting planners. The research showed that where Ritz-Carlton was falling down was after the sale and before the event, a period of sometimes a year or more. Buyers felt, "Now, that they've got my business they don't care about me," when there was no contact from the hotel until just before the event. Buyers wanted an ongoing relationship during the interim that told them their business was appreciated.

Similarly, some companies, such as Marriott and Hyatt, have a specific account managers who work only a few major accounts such as IBM and Hewlett Packard. These people "live" with these companies so as to get inside their culture and fully understand their needs when planning a meeting or event. This a good example of relationship selling.

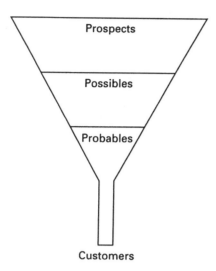

Prospects

Possibles

Probables

Customers

FIGURE 17-5 Many prospects but few customers.

What to Sell

The art of selling begins, like all marketing, by understanding the needs of the customers. This is critical for a successful sale. Once again, the idea is to solve a customers problems. First, one must determine what they are. Sometimes this calls for an interpretation. For example, a customer might say, "I need a good hotel close to the airport for my meeting," that is, one of the customer's problems is convenience. The salesperson's property might not be near the airport and the sale might be lost. Possibly, however, the sale might be saved by offering pickup and transportation—overcoming the distance by offering the convenience. In any event, the salesperson must determine the real problem in order to address it.

Sometimes a customer will express an opportunity, not a need. The salesperson has to understand the subtle difference. While a need is a customer want or desire that can be satisfied by the hospitality entity, an opportunity is a statement of a problem, without the expressed desire to solve the problem. Let's look at the difference:

"I need a hotel with a location near the airport" (need).

"The hotel we use now is too far from the airport" (opportunity).

In the first statement the problem is explicit. The first statement expresses the desire to solve the problem. The second sentence is an opportunity that calls for further interpretation. Suppose the salesperson responds by telling the customer how close their hotel is to the airport. The customer then might reply:

"That's nice, but it doesn't matter. My boss lives on the other side of town and doesn't want to travel all the way to the airport. I personally think the hotel we use now is out of the way, but what can you do?"

What the salesperson interpreted as an opportunity was actually not a conscious need. By addressing a perceived opportunity with a benefit not important to the customer, the salesperson lost the customer's interest. The location of the hotel was a problem for the meeting planner, but not one that he had a desire to solve. It is not uncommon for a salesperson to sell to an opportunity, rather than to a real need, and it is important to know the difference.

Probing

How do you insure that you are not selling just to an opportunity? By asking the right questions of the customer. Asking the customer questions is defined as **probing.**

Probing comes in two forms, **open probes** and **closed probes.** Open probes encourage the customer to speak freely, to elaborate on his or her problems. Closed probes limit the customer response to a yes or no answer, or a limited range provided by the salesperson. Examples of open probes might be:

"Tell me about what is important to you when you select a restaurant."
"What is the nature of your conference?"

In both cases, the customer is encouraged to discuss his or her feelings freely (hopefully revealing some needs). The other probe is called a closed probe, which may sound something like this:

"Is location important to you?"
"Do you prefer chain or independently run restaurants?"

The customer can answer yes or no to the first question, and has a limited option for the second question.

Let's go back to differentiating between needs and opportunities. In order to confirm that an opportunity is a need, use of a closed probe is appropriate. Let's review the selling example already presented.

Salesperson: "Tell me a little bit about your meetings" (open probe).
Customer: "Oh, we have had many lately, but the hotel we use now is too far from the airport" (opportunity)
Salesperson: "Is an airport location important to you in choosing a hotel?" (closed probe).
Customer: "Not really, my boss lives on the other side of town and doesn't want to change now."

The salesperson has avoided talking about something the customer did not need. The salesperson would then open probe further, until a customer need or a new opportunity was identified. In some cases, however, the salesperson might address the objective by further probes (why the boss won't change) and suggest a probable solution, before going on to new opportunities.

Once the need has surfaced, the salesperson has to support the need. Supporting is done in two stages, by acknowledging the need, and then introducing the appropriate benefits and features to the customer. Acknowledging the need tells the customer that the salesperson is someone who understands the problem to be solved, someone who

then introduces the solution (benefit and feature). An acknowledging statement by the salesperson may be:

"I understand your concern for a large ballroom; rear screen projection can take up quite a bit of room."

Benefits and Features

Once the needs of the customer have been established through a series of probes, the customer is introduced to the product benefits and **features.** A feature is a tangible or intangible subset of the product the customer will buy. It is a characteristic of the service being offered. It is also important to recognize those features that differentiate the product from the rest of the competition. These distinctive features should be especially emphasized if they are important to the customer.

The most important thing to remember is that customers do not buy features; they buy benefits. A benefit is the value of the feature to the customer and should be mentioned first to get attention. Unless the benefit is clearly explained, the customer may not understand why the feature is important. A feature might be a ballroom with high ceilings; the benefit to the customer might be that he or she can produce a high tech show because the room's high ceilings can accommodate complicated audiovisual requirements. A feature might be a good location; the benefit to the customer may be that the attendees of the meeting do not have far to drive from the office.

To sell the potential customer on buying the product, the good salesperson will attempt to match the benefits and features to the customer's objectives and needs. Features that may not provide any benefit to the customer should be excluded from the presentation. A primary mistake made in direct sales is to misunderstand the needs of the customer, while simultaneously presenting features and benefits of the product that are unimportant.

One of the authors was training a salesperson

on the selling process, and encountered the following scenario:

Salesperson: "Tell me what is important to you when you choose a hotel for your meetings" (open probe).

Customer: "I want a hotel that can handle a large check-out all at once. The last hotel we went to took $1\frac{1}{2}$ hours for our guests to pay their bills!" (need).

Salesperson: "Was the problem the billing or the time to get (closed probe) through the line?"

Customer: "The time to get through the line."

Salesperson: "I can see why it is important for the group to check out effortlessly. At our hotel, we have video check-out to make leaving the hotel easier."

In this case, the salesperson was doing fine (satisfying the needs of the customer), until she introduced a feature (video check-out), without clearly articulating how the benefit worked. The customer thought that the hotel had a video camera in the lobby to record check-outs. The customer was perplexed as to how this would ease the check-out process. The correct presentation would have been:

Salesperson: "I can see why it is important for the group to check out effortlessly. At our hotel, there is no waiting in line at all (benefit). Attendees can call up their bill on their in room television, and check out right there! (advantage). We have video check-out to make leaving the hotel easier" (feature).

Once the feature was translated into the value for the customer, the customer accepted the benefit.

Like this example, it is sometimes necessary to translate the features of the facility into the benefits because, while the customer may have some idea of the feature being sold, they may be skeptical, have a misunderstanding, or have the wrong impression from previous experience. For example, a health club may not seem to be in need of translation into benefits but there is a big difference in the quality of health clubs in hotels. One of the authors stayed one night in a hotel with a "health club" in a converted guestroom that smelled bad and that sported one 15 year old weight machine and a broken stationery bicycle. The following evening, at a different hotel, the health club had 5000 sq. ft. of space with spas, jaccuzis, state of the art training equipment, personal instructors, and so on. If a health club is relevant to the customer, then the benefits should be explained.

The same holds true for other generic hotel features. A concierge in a Le Meridien Hotel may be sophisticated, multilingual, and resourceful. A concierge in a Ramada Inn may be the manager's secretary. Both are marketed as concierge services, but the benefits to customers are very different. Convention services in one hotel may be a staff of ten, in another the bellman may also set the room. Translating what the features do for the customer is important in the sales process once you have determined what is important to the customer. Figure 17-6 shows a sample benefits/features form to be used in the selling process.

Once the need has surfaced, and been supported, other needs are sought to which the salesperson can respond, by further probing. When it seems that you have uncovered all the needs, and responded to them, it may be time to close the sale.

Customer Attitudes

The salesperson can have an easy customer, like the scenarios outlined earlier in this chapter or, more likely, difficult customers. Recognizing customer attitudes is important for the successful selling effort.

The most common attitudes encountered on a sales call are skepticism or misunderstanding, indifference, and objection. **Skepticism** is when a customer doubts the benefit introduced to satisfy the need. A customer may say "I do not think that

Objective-Benefit-Feature (OBF) Chart

Market Segment: _____

Customer Industry/Organization: _____

Customer Title/Job Function: _____

General Customer Needs (by Priority):

1. _____   4. _____

2. _____   5. _____

3. _____   6. _____

Customer Objectives	Benefits	Features

FIGURE 17-6   A sample benefit/features form for selling.

your food is as good as you say it is." The salesperson would overcome skepticism or misunderstanding in a customer by introducing a "proof source." A **proof source** is a vehicle that proves to the customer that the benefit introduced is as presented by the salesperson. A testimonial letter from another satisfied customer may be the proof needed to convince the skeptical customer that the food is actually as good as the salesperson says it is. A restaurant review from a local food critic may also be a good proof source. An independent source, in writing, may be all that is needed to convince the skeptical customer. A misunderstanding is something that needs to be clarified.

A more difficult customer attitude is **indifference.** When a customer is satisfied with another facility, or has internal options, the customer is considered indifferent. The customer may say "I am already using the banquet facilities at the Fontainbleau Hotel" (i.e., "Why should I change?"). This customer is indifferent and not open to considering alternatives. The salesperson must provide this customer with a reason to consider options. The other type of indifference is internal options. Internal options can be meetings rooms at the office; therefore, the customer would see no need to have meetings at a hotel. In this case, the benefits of not having distractions during a meeting might be emphasized. By meeting off-site, attendees stay focused because they are not in close proximity to their offices.

The solution for handling an indifferent customer is to probe for unrealized needs. These unrealized needs are often the weakness of the competitor. Let's stay with the Fontainbleau example. The well prepared salesperson would know the weakness of the competition, in this case the small size of the parking facility. The salesperson knows that there are never enough parking spaces at this hotel, and would probe to determine if there was a need to satisfy this problem.

The sales conversation might go like this (but probably not this easily!):

Customer: "I appreciate you coming by to see me, but I do not see the reason for the call. I am using the Fontainbleau for my banquets, and I am satisfied at this time" (expressing indifference).

Salesperson: "I see. Do you mind if I ask you some questions anyway?"

Customer: "Go ahead"

Salesperson: "I know that you hold some very large functions. Is it important for you to have enough parking for all of your

quests?" (closed probe for unrealized needs).

Customer: "As a matter of fact, it is. At the last meeting the speaker was late to the podium because she couldn't find a place to park" (expressing an opportunity).

Salesperson: "Then having enough parking for your guests is critical for a successful banquet?" (closed probe to determine need).

Customer: "Certainly."

The salesperson has now uncovered a need and addressed the need by supporting it.

It is easy for salespeople to place a competitor in a bad light. This practice is not recommended, and many customers are turned off by this selling strategy. In the above sales conversation, the professional salesperson referred vaguely to a problem that he knew was a disadvantage of the Fountainbleu, but never directly mentioned the hotel.

The final customer attitude is one of **objection.** Objection occurs when there is a real problem with your product offering that cannot be changed. If the customer wants a hotel near the airport, and yours is not, then you have an objection. If the customer wants a restaurant with a private dining area for a group, and yours does not have one, then you have an objection. Or, the objection that cannot be changed may be on the customer's side. For example, corporate mandates and prescribed hotel lists may dictate that travelers will not be reimbursed if they use your hotel.

Objections are very hard to overcome. It is important to view objections as positive customer feedback rather than as personal reverses during the sales process. Anticipating specific objections is the best way to prepare for them. The strategy for solving the objection is to present benefits already accepted that outweigh the objection presented, or to verify why the objection is important and figure out an alternative. Although the customer many want an airport location, the fact that your hotel is newly renovated, has a better pool, and more flexible meeting space may outweigh the location objection; as might the fact that it is nearer the office and most attendees are driving.

A restaurant customer desiring a private room for entertaining may be presented with more parking facilities, better food, and billing privileges. After all, customers make trade-offs between the different attributes of a product or service to choose the one that offers the best bundle of benefits. After reviewing the entire buy decision, the restaurant customer may be convinced to choose the restaurant without the private dining room. The focus, once again, should be on the objective and needs of the customer. You either overcome the objection by providing a solution acceptable to the customer or agreeing that it cannot be overcome and, therefore, hoping that the pros of using your facility will outweigh the cons.

Closing

The close, or signed contract, should come naturally without having to ask for it. If you've done a good job selling, and if you've handled all objections, solved all the problems, the client may tell you he is ready to sign. Asking for a close prematurely puts too much pressure on the buyer and may lose the sale. **Closing** a sales call entails asking the customer for a commitment. Hence, a sales call close might be getting to meet the decision maker's boss on the next visit, having the customer visit the hotel, or making a presentation to the board that will make the decision.

The ultimate closing is when the salesperson "asks for the business." (This entire process, of course, does not necessarily all take place in one meeting.) At this point, the salesperson summarizes all of the benefits accepted by the customer, and then asks for customer's commitment.

It should be apparent that the sales approach is a difficult one at best. With many new facilities in each market, the selling process is more competitive than ever. The salesperson that has the correct selling skills, and uses them on the sales call will close on a larger portion of business.

Follow-Up

Follow-up means regularly contacting the customer until the event takes place. At that time, one of the most common complaints of meeting planners in the hospitality industry is that the person who made the sale is not around when the services are actually being performed. A convention or meeting may be booked in a hotel 2 to 10 years in advance of its taking place. The promises made by someone who may no longer be at the property, or who may be out trying to sell to another account, still should be kept when the event takes place. Too often, operations says, belatedly, "We can't do that." Also, human error in incorrectly tracing a file can cause untold havoc. To create good word-of-mouth communications and to get customers to come back, follow-up is extremely important. Often, it is the convention services manager who does this (Figure 17-7). Working closely with this person may be as important to the salesperson as working with the customer.

Thus the role of the professional salesperson is evolving. The "order taker" of the mid-1990s became the "order getter" in the late 1990s. Today, successful salespeople will have to be relationship managers. This is especially important in service businesses where trust, credibility, and confidence that promises will be kept, form an essential part of the relationship between the buyer and the sales representative. Of course, the working relationship of the salesperson with operations is also critical, as noted above. Customers sometimes ask the impossible. Sometimes the impossible can be done with the right knowledge and working relationship.

SALES MANAGEMENT

The management of an effective sales force means integrating a variety of skills. Proper account management, organization of the sales team, development of personnel, and motivation of the workforce all combine to make a sales team efficient. The skills necessary to manage the selling process are

FIGURE 17-7 At the Westin/Singapore, the internal service manager "completes the sale" on-premises.

very different than the skills needed to sell. The best salesperson in an organization may be promoted to sales director and fail. The gap between good selling skills and good management skills is a wide one.

Account Management

The management of customers is called **account management.** The method of managing the sales process is called the **account management system.** The account management system balances the resources of the sales team with the profile of the customer base. The account management system allows the sales team to manage its customer accounts like a portfolio of stocks, spending time on the customers that will produce the most business, while balancing many smaller accounts in case one large account is lost.

The foundation of the account management system is the **sales equation:**

Past Customers + New Customers = Goals

Past customers (or repeat guests) provide some of the business, and new customers provide the rest. If the products and services delivered are what the customer expects, new customers will become past customers, making everyone's job easier. First, past customers need to be analyzed and prioritized in terms of the business they provide. An example of this prioritization process is offered below:

Category	Potential Rooms Usage per Account
A	500 +
B	100 to 499
C	less than 100

The past customer base is then placed into each category and each customer account should be called according to its potential business. Customers who provide the most business are called on more than customers who provide less business. The account management system makes sure, however, that the smaller potential customers do get called on a regular basis. Calculations are then made as to the total number of calls that the sales team needs to make to their past customers. These steps are indicated below.

Category	Number of Customer Accounts	Number of Calls per Year	Total Calls per Year
A	150	12	1800
B	300	6	1800
C	500	2	1000
Total	950		4600

This calculation shows that there needs to be 4600 sales calls per year to properly cover the past customer base. Next, the call schedule is calculated, including new customers:

Position	Average Number of Calls/Week	Annualized
Director of Sales	20	960
Sales Manager #1	40	1920
Sales Manager #2	40	1920
Sales Manager #3	40	1920
Total		6720

With the past customers prioritized, and the resources allocated, the sales equation is again utilized to determine if the sales department has the proper perspective on their past and new customers.

Past Customers	+	New Customers	=	Goals
4600	+	2,120	=	6720
68.5%		31.5%		100%

The goals are derived from the resources available. Past customers are calculated from the account management system. New customers, or the prospecting effort, are calculated by subtracting the past customers from the goals. If the goals are less than or equal to the past customers, then new customers (prospecting) are being neglected.

For a mature property, one that has been in the marketplace for at least three years within the same product class and positioning, the above is the ideal model for the allocation of resources. The sales team should focus about 70 percent of its time on past customers, and the remaining 30 percent should be dedicated to finding new customers. In new hotels, restaurants, and catering facilities, the sales equation may be the reverse; with a small customer base the need for prospecting is intensified. Also, in some organizations, an account manager helps to maintain accounts so that the salesperson can be out creating new ones. The sales equation can be used to focus a sales team on its priorities.

The next step of the account management system is to assign revenue potential to each of the accounts. The following example continues the hotel scenario, with the understanding that room nights could easy translate to restaurant covers, airline seats, or other hospitality sales units. Room night revenue potential for each account is determined so the sales team can begin to develop the appropriate action steps needed to fill the gaps in revenues:

Category	Number of Accounts	Room Nights
A	150	75,000
B	300	90,000
C	500	30,000
Total	950	195,000

From this calculation, the Director of Sales can determine that if all of the past customers on the account management system are called regularly, the hotel can potentially book 195,000 rooms from past customers. In most cases the goal, or budget, is higher than that. Let's look again at the sales equation in terms of room nights:

Past Customers	+	New Customers	=	Goals
195,000	+	15,000	=	210,000

Now the selling task is clearer. Set the parameters and call goals, make sales calls on all of the past customers, and the hotel should sell 195,000 rooms. The goal, however, is 210,000 rooms. Therefore the sales team has to prospect, or find, 15,000 new room nights.

Lowest Common Denominator (LCD). Selling 210,000 rooms in one year may seem like an awesome task and, without making the task smaller, it is. So. the next step of the account management system is the breaking down of large tasks into smaller ones, or the **lowest common denominator** (LCD). The following example illustrates how LCD works:

210,000 rooms sold	195,000 past customers
15,000 new rooms	2 night stay
7,500 new customers	50 rooms per year/avg account
150 new accounts	48 weeks per year
3 new accounts per week	3 sales managers
1 new account per week opened per sales manager (LCD)	

The sales team can "go out and sell" 210,000 rooms for the year. Without applying LCD to the problem, the results are usually unfocused. The sales team becomes very busy trying to sell 210,000 rooms, but many times not productively. However, the sales team, after working through the LCD system, can define its strategy—manage the account management system and open one new account per sales manager per week.

Sales Action Plan

The marketing plan is the overall vision for the upcoming year. It encompasses all of the marketing activities, including advertising, public relations, direct mail, and other communication vehicles. The **sales action plan** narrows the broader vision of the marketing plan, and assigns detailed tasks to the sales managers. The sales action plan allows the sales team to take the marketing plan and step it down to the execution phase of the process. It enables the sales team to execute the portion of the marketing plan for which they are responsible. A typical sales action plan is shown in Table 17-2.

The sales action plan follows all of the phases of the account management system—calling on past customers and new customers. Goals are established through LCD for bookings and new accounts. The salesperson can clearly see what needs to be done on a monthly, weekly, and daily basis.

The sales action plan is formatted to accommodate 12 weeks of work. Each quarter, a new sales action plan is written to reflect the next 12-week period's work. This planning process allows the sales team to be flexible, and to change activities to reflect market conditions. The umbrella marketing plan is written to give the direction and overall focus for the sales team. Within the next 12 months, many assumptions made during the formation of the marketing plan may change. The quarterly sales action plan allows the team to adjust its course quickly.

The quarterly plan may also be broken down further into a weekly plan. Figure 17-8 shows a sample format by the week, by the day, and the weekly productivity.

T A B L E   17-2
A Sales Action Plan

Name: Mary Jones   Quarter: 3rd

Sales Equation/Sales Calls

Past Customers	+	Prospecting	=	Goals
100	+	60	=	160/Month
25	+	15	=	40/Week
5	+	3	=	8/Day

Booking Goals

480/Month	120/Week	30/Day

New Accounts Opened

20/Month	5/Week	1/Day

Prospecting Resources

Meeting planner directories, convention and visitors bureau leads, referrals from current customers, newspaper leads, and so on.

Action Plan By Week

Week 1   Sales calls to Hartford _____

Week 2   Make appts for trade show _____

Week 3   Attend trade show _____

Week 4   Develop direct mail for groups _____

Week 5   Sales calls to Boston _____

Week 6   Send direct mail to planners _____

Week 7   Local sales calls _____

Week 8   Local sales calls _____

Week 9   Follow up leads from direct mail _____

Week 10   Follow up leads from direct mail _____

Week 11   Follow up leads from direct mail _____

Week 12   Develop next quarter sales action plan _____

SALES TEAM ACTIVITY REPORT

Name _____   Week Ending _____

SALES ACTIVITY AND RESULTS

ACTION STEPS	DAY	MONDAY	TUES.	WED.	THUR.	FRIDAY	TOTALS	
	DATE						WEEK	MTD
PERSONAL SALES CALLS	OBJECTIVE							
	RESULT							
TELEPHONE SALES CALLS	OBJECTIVE							
	RESULT							
NEW ACCOUNT DEVELOPMENT	OBJECTIVE							
	RESULT							
INTER HOTEL REFERRALS	OBJECTIVE							
	RESULT							
WHOLESALE/VOLUME ACCOUNTS SIGNED	OBJECTIVE							
	RESULT							
SALES CONTACT TOTALS	OBJECTIVES							
	RESULTS							

SEE BACK PAGE FOR PRODUCTIVITY QUOTAS AND RESULTS

KEY ACCOUNT ACTIVITY AND RESULTS

ORGANIZATION	OBJECTIVE	RESULT	ACTION STEP

F I G U R E   1 7 - 8   A sales action plan format.

WEEKLY PLAN

PRIORITIES FOR THIS WEEK:	RESULTS
1.	
2.	
3.	
4.	
5.	

DAY: **DATE:**

	SCHEDULED ACTIVITY	OBJECTIVE	RESULTS	ACTION STEP
8 AM				
9 AM				
10 AM				
11 AM				
12 NOON				
1 PM				
2 PM				
3 PM				
4 PM				
5 PM				
EXPENSES:				

DAY: **DATE:**

	SCHEDULED ACTIVITY	OBJECTIVE	RESULTS	ACTION STEP
8 AM				
9 AM				
10 AM				
11 AM				
12 NOON				
1 PM				
2 PM				
3 PM				
4 PM				
5 PM				
EXPENSES:				

DAY: **DATE:**

	SCHEDULED ACTIVITY	OBJECTIVE	RESULTS	ACTION STEP
8 AM				
9 AM				
10 AM				
11 AM				
12 NOON				
1 PM				
2 PM				
3 PM				
4 PM				
5 PM				
EXPENSES:				

F I G U R E   1 7 - 8   *(Continued)*

WEEKLY PRODUCTIVITY REPORT

Name _____ Week Ending _____

DEFINITE BOOKINGS

ORGANIZATION	NEW	EXISTING	DATES	RATES	COVERS/ SUITE NIGHTS	CATERING / SUITE REVENUE

CANCELLED DEFINITES

TENTATIVE BOOKINGS

ORGANIZATION	NEW	EXISTING	DATES	RATES	COVERS/ SUITE NIGHTS	CATERING / SUITE REVENUE

CANCELLED TENTATIVES

PRODUCTIVITY SUMMARY

DEFINITES		COVERS/ SUITE NIGHTS	AVERAGE RATE	CATERING/ SUITE REVENUE	CATERING/ SUITE REV. QUOTA	**TENTATIVES**		COVERS/ SUITE NIGHTS	AVERAGE RATE	CATERING/ SUITE REVENUE	CATERING/ SUITE REV. QUOTA
	WEEKLY TOTALS						WEEKLY TOTALS				
	MONTHLY TOTALS						MONTHLY TOTALS				
	QUOTAS						QUOTAS				

F I G U R E   1 7 - 8   (Continued)

ORGANIZATION OF THE SALES TEAM

The size of the sales force is determined by the number of sales calls that should be made on a yearly basis. Staffing the sales office should result from a mathematical calculation of sales calls needed to satisfy current customers and those needed to find a reasonable amount of new customers. This is different from the practice in which a salesperson is added only when sales are down, and is eliminated when sales are up. In those situations, resources may be overallocated or underallocated. On a mathematical basis, a salesperson will usually handle between 250 and 350 accounts a year, depending on the market mix of the property.

Once staffing guidelines are established, salespeople are usually organized by geographic territory, market (e.g., business, leisure) event type (e.g., weddings), national accounts (e.g., IBM), and/or product line. For example, in terms of potential customers for a hotel, the city of Cleveland can be divided in half. In order to keep the sales process orderly, one sales representative may be assigned to the east side while another is assigned to the west side.

Product lines are assigned by the type of service within the hotel that the salesperson represents. There are three types of product offerings sold through direct sales: group, transient, and catering. The group product line is for customers who purchase a number of rooms at the same time. The group salesperson may or may not sell the function space simultaneously. A bus tour would be considered a group but would have no need for function space. A corporation might have the same number of guestroom requirements as the bus tour but have extensive meeting space needs. Depending on the size of the hotel, there may be more than one group salesperson; for example, there may be a need for a separate convention salesperson if this is a major market for the hotel.

Transient salespeople sell to customers who have a need to book guest rooms on an individual basis. Corporate sales managers call on corporate travel planners. The catering salesperson normally handles meetings and social events like weddings that don't require a large number of sleeping rooms. This person sells the ballroom space for functions with food and beverage, if possible.

Different organizations, of course, have different organizational structures and duty assignments. One company may have its outside sales force out of the office and cold calling four days a week, with one day in the office writing call reports. Sales leads get passed to inside salespeople who close sales and maintain accounts. Another company may have sales managers who spend half their time inside and half outside. Leads are generated, pursued, and finalized. An inside support person, an account manager, is available inside to maintain accounts. Other companies may have variations of these approaches.

It takes a very disciplined effort to keep an effective sales organization on a focused track. The director of sales needs to cue salespeople as to when business is most needed. For example, weddings may book a ballroom a year in advance. Large groups, such as an Elks Club convention, may also want the ballroom for the same weekend, but also will reserve a large portion of sleeping rooms. If a wedding with a few overnight rooms was already booked for the ballroom, the Elks Club business might be lost. Conversely, if the wedding was turned away and the Elks Club did not choose the hotel, the ballroom might be empty on that date. Such decisions are made on a daily basis.

Product Line Management

Most hotel sales offices are structured to sell the three distinct products that we have discussed. These are transient programs for the individual traveler, such as Marriott's Honored Guest Awards, the group product that offers the customer the opportunity to purchase both sleeping rooms and function facilities for a meeting; and the catering product for the customer who needs function or meeting space without guest rooms (the term for this last type of business is **freestanding**).

Many customer accounts have a need for more than one product, and in some cases a need for all three. For example, a planner at IBM might have occasion to need transient guestrooms, group space, and freestanding function space in the same hotel. Many present methods, however, divide the sales effort and provide for three different salespeople to represent the three products in the same hotel.

Most other industries do not operate in this manner. For instance, you can buy an entire range of automobiles or insurance coverage from the same person. Why, then, does the hotel industry make the same IBM customer talk to three different representatives to buy very similar products in the same location? The customer experience of trying to purchase various hotel products from the same hotel can easily mean negotiating with six to seven salespeople in one year.

The **product line management** approach to sales, in which one sales representative services all three products for the same customer (sometimes called **one-stop shopping**), is a method to gain competitive edge over sales offices organized in the traditional format. Figure 17-9, in fact, shows how Marriott has developed one-stop shopping for IBM. A variation of this is "**meetings express**" sales positions. This "**book 'em and cook 'em**" approach to selling is gradually becoming more commonplace. Specifically, for smaller meetings, the meetings express person sends the contract, blocks the rooms and function space, selects the menu, handles the rooming list, and sends the thank you after the meeting occurs.

Either of the above methods means that customers who have a need for more than one hotel product are handled by the same salesperson in order to offer continuity to the customer during the sales process. Those customers who have only a need for one product (e.g., a wedding) should be handled in the regular manner, in a wedding case by the catering salesperson. The difficulty with the product line approach, and one which has slowed its acceptance, is that each salesperson must be familiar with all the hotel's products and how to sell them.

Development of Personnel

The development of personnel is critical to the success of a sales organization. If the wrong people are hired, businesss will be lost. If good salespeople leave to go to a competitor for better opportunities, which frequently happens, there is additional opportunity to lose business. If a position remains open for any length of time, necessary sales calls to existing and new customers will not be made. Companies need to be conscious of this problem and address the reasons for it. Through better selection and training Ritz-Carlton reduced its sales force turnover from 40 percent to 10 percent, once they had identified the problem that salespeople well trained by other hotel chains did not necessarily fit into the Ritz-Carlton mode.

Other reasons for high turnover include the "move up and out" philosophy. Promotions often involve relocation. If a salesperson is unwilling to relocate, the only other way to further a career is to move to another hotel. Also, salespeople are highly visible, not only to their clients but also in networking functions. This high exposure provides increased opportunities for other positions.

Development of an effective sales staff begins with recruitment. There should be an ongoing effort to locate and know the best salespeople in the marketplace. While new talent can be solicited at the college graduate level, there is still a void at the experienced salesperson level. Organizations such as Hotel Sales and Marketing Association International (HSMAI) are good forums for getting to know the better salespeople in an area.

Training is critical to the development of salespeople. Although there are many existing sales training programs, the challenge is to use them. At least one month of training is necessary for new salespeople to minimally learn the product and understand the needs of customers. Even seasoned salespeople need to be constantly trained through role-playing and sales meetings, to keep their skills sharp. Training also indicates the level of commitment that the company has toward the individual development of a salesperson's career. Figure 17-10

Just One Number Plans Your Next Meeting

FIGURE 17-9 Marriott developed one-stop shopping for IBM.

shows a simplified diagram of a salesperson's relationship qualities.

Ethics

All salespeople should also develop a code of ethics, both personally and through the company. There will be situations when ethical dilemmas will be encountered and salespersons should have certain guiding principles to allow them to conduct their business with honesty and integrity. Several of these issues are shown in Table 17-3.

Another perspective on ethics is provided by Thomas McCarthy, a 45-year hotel marketer who now provides hotel sales seminars. McCarthy asked a group of hotel sales and marketing people if they thought the following situations were ethical.

1. You offer one company, which has an average of ten reservations a month, a $100 rate. The company accepts. On the same day you offer another company the same rate for the same number of reservations. The prospect says it's too high, so you offer a $90 rate.
2. A hotel has a weekend policy that if walk-ins ask for the weekend rate they get it for $69; if they don't ask they are charged $85.
3. A report indicates that an association has signed a contract with another hotel for next year's meeting. Your boss tells you to call the association and offer 50 percent off the other hotel's rate if it will break the contract and come to your hotel.

Results: 1. 37 percent said the action was unethical; 2. 60 percent said the practice was unethical; and, 3. 67 percent said the request was unethical. All three practices are common. McCarthy offers the following two questions to answer when quoting rates:

1. If the public knew about this policy what would be the reaction? If the reaction would be negative, there's something wrong with the policy.
2. If someone asked why one customer got a lower

INTERPERSONAL RELATIONSHIP QUALITY

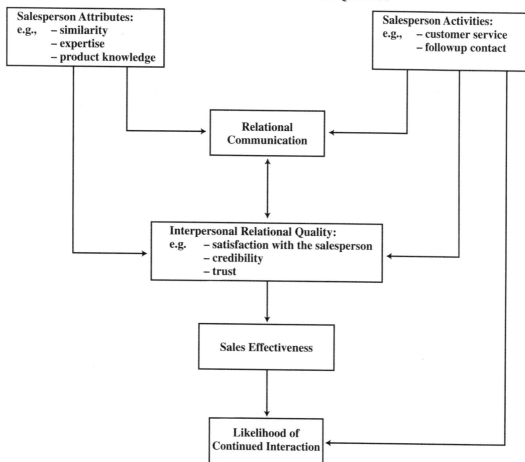

FIGURE 17-10 Diagram of a salesperson's relationship qualities.

rate, could it be explained in a way that a logical person would accept and understand? If not, the practice is probably unethical.[5]

Apply these two questions to the three scenarios above and see what you think.

Motivation

Salespeople need to be consistently motivated to be effective. While this may be true of all job categories, it is especially true of salespeople, who represent the product on a daily basis.

Unlike their counterparts in the operations aspect of the hotel business, salespeople are usually paid salary plus commission or performance bonus. Normally, the operations people are paid a bonus based on the financial progress of the property and, one hopes, customer feedback. Salespeople are paid on their productivity, based upon quotas. Quotas are developed based upon the territory, the market, and the product sold. This quota is normally derived from the budget that the hotel has set for the sales team that year. Once quotas are established, the salespeople are paid for achievement over and above

T A B L E   17-3
Ethical Issues in Personal Selling[4]

The Salesperson's Company
Misrepresentation of call reports.
Misrepresentation of expense accounts.
Use of company assets for personal benefit.
Conflict-of-interest situations.
Disclosure of proprietary company information.
Disparagement of the company.

The Salesperson's Customers and Prospects
Misrepresentation of yourself.
Misrepresentation of your company.
Misrepresentation of your products or services.
Use of high-pressure selling tactics.
Inappropriate gift-giving.
Disclosure of proprietary customer information.

The Salesperson's Competitors
Disparagement of a competitor's company.
Disparagement of a competitor's product or service.
Disparagement of a competitor's sales representative.

the quota. Some incentives are paid monthly, and others quarterly or yearly. It is likely that the more immediate the gratification, the more motivated the salesperson will be.

Productivity, of course, is not the easiest thing to measure because it is not simply a matter of room nights sold and/or revenue gained. To put this in perspective, Table 17-4 cites from an article by Eric Orkin, consultant to the hotel industry in yield management.

Orkin's point is that, "If you use averages to measure performance, people will make decisions to improve the averages whether or not the numbers are good for the hotel. . . . The value of a room night is a reflection of the probability that it can be sold and the rate it can command." If salespeople are motivated by goals, then those goals must be measured by other measures than averages.

Other forms of motivation, such as incentive trips and merchandise, are becoming part of the motivational toolbox of sales organizations. These are also based upon quotas, and may be used when

there is a short-term sales gap that needs to be filled. For an example of a short motivation tool, see Figure 17-11.

SALES AND OPERATIONS

"Sales sells and operations provides" is an expression that describes what is often seen as the relationship between sales and operations. As previously mentioned, that relationship is a critical one and needs further explanation here, because a conflict between sales and operations can be incredibly damaging to a hotel's relationship marketing effort. In fact, this situation represents a real need for internal relationship marketing, discussed in Chapter 3.

Knowledge of the product and of the capabilities of the organization is essential to successful selling. Constant and continuous communications between sales and operations are imperative to effective marketing for a hospitality organization. If what the salesperson sells cannot be delivered, the hotel will in most cases eventually lose the customer (and the salesperson!). It is natural for a salesperson to want to make promises in order to make the sale.

Salespeople have two difficulties in this regard which they need to overcome. One is perception. Operations people see salespeople largely when they are in-house entertaining clients (e.g., having lunch, giving tours) and see their job as a "cushy" one. The second one is that salespeople have no direct authority over operations people, yet they need to make certain that their promises are executed properly. This can cause friction in the lines of authority needed to get the job done and keep promises to customers.

A thorough knowledge of the product and the capabilities of the organization will go a long way toward keeping these promises from creating unreasonable expectations for the customer. If the salesperson is not sure that the hotel can deliver,

T A B L E   17-4
Using Averages to Measure Sales Performance[6]

"In the hotel industry, we use averages to understand how we are doing and to help make decisions. But the premise is unsound: there is no average room night." Consider the following one month's sales chart.

Sales Manager	Room Nights Sold	Average Rate	Total Revenue
Alan	600	$100	$60,000
Barry	583	$103	$60,000
Cathy	700	$ 85.71	$60,000
Debra	680	$ 99	$67,320

Who did the best job? Debra is the revenue leader with a good ADR. Barry has the highest ADR but the lowest room night volume. Alan is in the middle. Cathy has the highest room night volume but may be "giving away" the rooms.

Now consider the following expanded sales chart.

Sales Manager	High-Demand Days Roomnights	ADR	Medium-Demand Days Roomnights	ADR	Low-Demand Days Roomnights	ADR
Alan			600	$100		
Barry	583	$103				
Cathy	250	$103	250	$ 97	200	$50
Debra	680	$ 99				

The picture of efficiency and productivity now changes. Debra is selling high-demand room nights at discount. Barry may be missing opportunities on off-peak days. Alan is okay. Cathy is the star. She is selling low-demand, as well as high-demand days; her ADR is justified because many of her room nights would otherwise have remained unfilled.

then he or she should confirm with operations before making the promise. This not only provides a confirmation, it also gets operations into the act so that there is more likelihood that someone will follow through. The services manager position in large hotels helps avoid these problems. This person works closely with the salesperson and also personally attends to the function when it takes place.

If both parties are truly tuned in to solving the customer's problems, and each party fully understands the problems of the other, satisfactory resolution is almost always possible. This is both internal and relationship marketing practiced at their best. It is the marketing and management leadership of the property or the company that sets the tone and that should make sure that it happens. The salesperson must go back to dissatisfied customers and ask for their business once more.

SUMMARY

The sales process is becoming more complex in the competitive marketplaces of today. The selling process is not unlike the marketing process; understanding the needs of the customer is the primary focus of the sales organization. Understanding the needs of the customers is the foundation of selling. The selling process involves the skilled use of probing, supporting, and closing to manage the sale. Different customer attitudes are encountered on each sales call, they are skepticism, indifference, and objection. All three are handled with professional selling skills.

Having the ability to sell is only half of the selling process. Planning the sales function is also important. Tools such as an account management system, LCD, and a sales action plan all assist the sales manager to

```
$$$$$$$$$$$$$$$$$$$$$$$$$$$$$$$$$$$$$$$$$$$$$$$$$$$$$$$$$$$$$$$$$$$$$$

   HOW TO MAKE MORE MONEY AND SCORE BIG BROWNIE POINTS
   WITH THE D.O.S.


   1ST WAY!  For every actual group roomnight in February booked after
   1/11/99, you will receive $2.00

                   Minimum rate  Monday-Thursday  $79
                   Minimum rate  Friday-Sunday  $69

        Example: Computerland Group 10 roomnights for 3 nights at
        a rate of $89 = $60 for Sales Manager


   2ND WAY!  Whoever exceeds 300 actual group room nights in the month
   of February will receive $100 BONUS on top of the "1st Way" promotion!

   Cathy/Tracy:  If you exceed the budgeted      Club goal of 300
   roomnights in February, you will both receive $100

   Get on your mark, set . . . Book 'em DANNO!!!!!

   (* Please note the rate restriction of $99 over Super Show)

           Amy will be accepting bribes for any inquiry calls!
       Simply put your name and offer in a sealed envelope and return ASAP.


$$$$$$$$$$$$$$$$$$$$$$$$$$$$$$$$$$$$$$$$$$$$$$$$$$$$$$$$$$$$$$$$$$$$$$
```

FIGURE 17-11 An internal memo to motivate a sales force.

focus on what is important. Maintaining a balance of resources to call on past and new customers is critical to the success of the entire organization.

Finding new customers has become a difficult task, each hospitality entity is vying for a smaller base of customers to fill expanding numbers of hotel rooms and meeting space. New methods to find customers, through direct mail and telemarketing, have replaced "cold calling" as methodologies for generating leads.

A sales organization needs to have a clear definition of the markets that it wants to attract, and a recognition that it needs to penetrate competitors' business in order to increase its own. Additionally, the organization has to be knowledgeable and consistent about its goals through the sales organization, and be prepared to sell the customer with appropriate features and benefits. The sales office that organizes the sales team carefully and develops and motivates its people effectively will be the most productive. As the marketplace absorbs more new hotels and demand remains stagnant, the competitive fight for the same business will intensify. Those who establish a strong plan based on the components discussed in this chapter will have the competitive edge necessary to win fair market share.[7]

KEY WORDS AND CONCEPTS

Account Management: Management of customers' accounts.

Account Management System: Management of the sales process.

Blitz: Blitz implies multiple calls more or less at random. The preferred term today is "concentrated sales effort."

Book 'em and Cook 'em: Industry jargon for handling the entire process for small groups.

Closed Probe: Probing with specific questions for specific answers.

Closing: Closing the sales effort by asking for a commitment.

Cold Calling: Calling on a prospective customer without advance notice.

Features: Aspects of a facility that may or may not be important to the potential customer.

Freestanding: Business that uses meeting or dining space, but no bedrooms.

Indifference: When a prospect is happy with current usage and doesn't really care what benefits and features a property has.

Lowest Common Denominator (LCD): The breakdown of new room nights, needed to achieve goals, so that each sales manager has a smaller specific goal to achieve.

Meetings Express: A salesperson who handles all details of small groups.

Objection: A product failing that cannot be changed.

One-stop Shopping: See Product Line Management.

Open Probe: Probing with general questions that allows the person to elaborate problems.

Probing: Asking the prospective customer questions to find out what their real problems and needs are.

Product Line Management: One salesperson sells all products to large user customers.

Proof Source: A credible source used to overcome a prospect's skepticism.

Prospecting: Finding qualified customers who are likely to buy the product.

Qualifying: Making sure a prospect is able and willing to buy.

Sales Action Plan: A plan for the forthcoming quarter for reaching goals.

Sales Equation: Past customers plus new customers equal a sales goal.

Skepticism: When a prospect doubts a sales claim.

DISCUSSION QUESTIONS

1. Describe the correct selling scenario for a customer who responds to your questions like this: "I am currently using a facility with which I am very satisfied."
2. Develop three proof sources for a banquet facility.
3. For an account management system, create a call schedule and a sales equation given the following information:

Account Base:	Category	Number of Files
	A	100
	B	250
	C	300

Positions: Director of Sales, Sales Manager #1

4. Break down the above task to its lowest common denominator.
5. Compose a benefits and features chart for a hotel and discuss how you would use it to address a specific target market.
6. Discuss the needs and difficulties in organizing a sales force by territory and by product line.
7. Define the difference between an opportunity and a need, then give an example of each.

GROUP PROJECTS

1. Assume you are the sales team for the the hotel in question 5. Select three competitive hotels and assess their weaknesses. Prepare four weaknesses per competitor, to be used to overcome the customer attitude of indifference.
2. Make a list of five open questions and five closed questions to ask a potential customer to uncover his or her needs. In class, with a separate group, set up a role-playing scenario where you ask the questions and respond to the answers.

REFERENCES

1. Carl McDaniel, Jr. and William R. Darden, *Marketing.* Newton, MA: Allyn & Bacon, 1987, p. 526. Used with permission.
2. For a positive view on cold calling and how to do it successfully, see Jeffrey H. Gitomer, *The Sales Bible.* New York: William Morrow, 1994, pp. 94–108. Gitomer's recommended opening line is, "Can you help me?"
3. Theodore Levitt, "Relationship Management," in Theodore Levitt, *The Marketing Imagination.* New York: The Free Press, 1986, pp. 111–126.
4. John I. Coppett and William A. Staples, *Professional Selling: A Relationship Management Process.* Cincinnati: South-Western Publishing Co., 1990, p. 365.
5. Thomas T. McCarthy, "Fair Rates Improve Profits and Image," *Hotel & Resort Industry,* January 1994, pp. 12–13.
6. Eric Orkin, "Breaking the Law of Averages," *Lodging Hospitality,* February 1994, pp. 24–25.
7. The nature of this book limits our discussion on personal selling. For further, more complete information, an excellent source is Margaret Shaw and Susan V. Morris, *Hospitality Sales and Marketing.* New York: Wiley, 2000.

C H A P T E R

Eighteen

❖

HOSPITALITY
DISTRIBUTION SYSTEMS

─── *Overview* ───

Distribution systems are conduits for getting the product to the customer or the customer to the product. They have become an increasingly critical marketing tool for the industry, albeit they come in a number of different forms. This chapter is essentially in two parts.

After a brief discussion on how distribution systems work, Part A is about getting the product to the customer through geographic distribution. Part B reverses the order and brings the customer to the product through various distribution channels.

❖

The distribution mix is all channels available between the firm and the target market that increase the probability of getting the customer to the product.

Distribution systems are a set of different organizations, independent or not, involved in the process of making a product or service available for use or consumption. Companies that produce either goods or services need assistance in distributing their products to the end user, the consumer.

Goods-producing firms such as Procter and Gamble, Ford Motor Company, and Coca-Cola must somehow arrange to distribute their product—that is, get it to where the consumer can buy it. In the same sense, but in reverse, hospitality companies like Sheraton, McDonald's, and American Airlines need distribution systems through which their customers can find their products and services in order to buy them.

There is a growing need in the hospitality industry to utilize distribution systems as never before, to make it easier for the customer to find the product. When the demand for hotel rooms and restaurants exceeded the supply, customers managed to find their way to the product offered. This is not the case today, with the proliferation of new hospitality products all vying for the same customer.

HOW DISTRIBUTION SYSTEMS WORK

In a usual manufactured goods situation, the producer of the goods uses a wholesaler or a broker to assist in the distribution of the product, or ships directly to the retailer. A wholesaler is a business unit that buys, or takes on consignment, merchandise from the producer and sells it to the retailer. A broker serves a similar function but may or may not actually acquire the merchandise. The retailer, defined as whoever actually sells the product to the end user, is the point of sale where the consumer can purchase the product. Wholesaler, broker, and retailer are all part of the distribution system.

Companies have found it necessary to utilize these separate distribution systems not only because of the prohibitive costs of developing their own, but also because distributors, particularly the retailer, can get closer to the customer. Ford Motor Company, for example, distributes through its retailers, the local car dealerships, which sell Ford cars to the public. To purchase the real estate, construct the facilities, staff the organizations, and market the cars would be a tremendous burden on Ford's resources.

Procter & Gamble, on the other hand, works through brokers and wholesalers to get its product to the retailers, of which there are tens of thousands, worldwide. Coca-Cola distributes through franchisees who buy syrup in bulk, make and bottle the final product, and deliver it to innumerable retailers. Variations of such distribution systems are endless.

Some systems are **vertically integrated,** partially or fully. In these cases, the supplier of the raw goods and/or the retailers are owned by the manufacturer. An example would be Tandy Corporation, which owns the retailer Radio Shack, and distributes to the stores, the only stores that sell its product. Thus this company is partially integrated, downstream. In hospitality, a unique example would be Nouvelles Frontières (NF) of France. This is a fully vertically integrated company, upstream and downstream, although it does use some resources of others. Figure 18-1 shows how this works. NF owns its own travel agencies, or franchises them, which sell only NF tours and packages, which are sold by no other agency. This is called downstream or forward integration. NF operates its own airplanes (but also uses common carriers); NF owns a number of hotels (but also uses others). This is called upstream or backward integration.

Generic marketing texts call this a vertical marketing system (VMS), the model of which is based on manufactured goods. In this usage, a VMS is any unified combination of suppliers, producers, wholesalers, or retailers. A *corporate* VMS is one like Nouvelles Frontières where one company owns all parts of the system. An *administered* VMS is where one of the members dominates the system by virtue of its power in the chain. A *contractual* VMS is one controlled by contract such as franchising. All three are actually vertical distribution systems (VDS); regardless, these designations really do not fit the service sector. In service industries, like hospitality, the producer and the retailer are one and the same, based on the simultaneous production and consumption concept. Production takes place at the end of the chain, at the outlet, on-site. Thus we don't use the term VMS and we don't consider a franchise to be part of a vertically integrated system. Instead it is both producer and retailer to which the distribution system delivers the customers, which may also be a retailer such as a

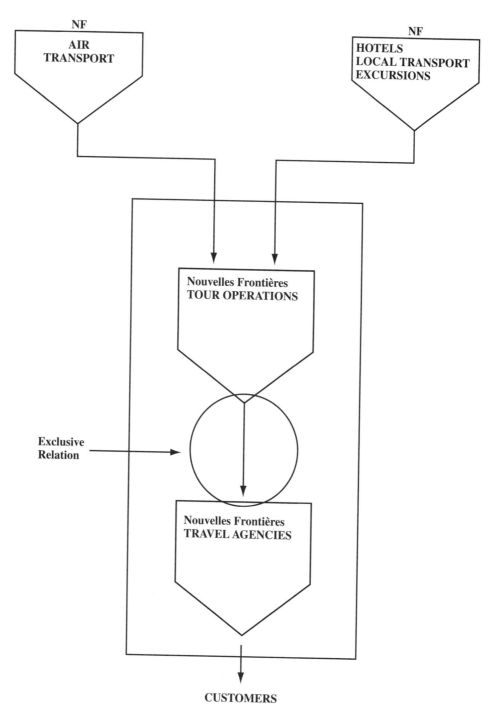

FIGURE 18-1 A fully vertically integrated system.

travel agent. Nevertheless, even then, the hospitality product still has yet to be produced.

In a typical conventional distribution system, the retailer carries many brands, including those of competing companies. Control of the channel lies in the strength of the product being sold. If an item is in very high demand, the producer of this product may be able to set the terms of the system and may manipulate the retailer into carrying and merchandising other and weaker products as well. When the product is weak, the retailers will dictate the terms of the system to reach the consumer.

The same principles apply to the hospitality industry, except that the producer of the product is also the retailer. Thus if the product is strong, the retailer (the property) has control over the wholesaler, for example, a tour operator. If the product is weak, the wholesaler assumes the control. An example in the first case is the Four Seasons Hotel in Nevis in the Caribbean—a very strong product that sets the terms. In the second case, the overbuilt Algarve coast in Portugal is virtually at the mercy of British tour operators, who set the terms. This principle is important in channel management, as we see shortly.

Distribution systems in hospitality have changed dramatically in the past few years, and will continue to change with better technology and the way companies do business as well. Cendant Corporation, a conglomerate, is a good example of the significant change. In the past, owners of lodging properties (the retailers) might approach Howard Johnson or Ramada (the wholesalers) for a franchise affiliation. They now approach Cendant, the wholesaler, which owns the rights to both of these brand names, as well as some others.

In the mid-1970s Howard Johnson's owned, managed, and franchised hundreds of lodging properties and restaurants throughout the United States. The corporate office, located in a suburb of Boston, hosted hundreds of staff to manage the process. Fast forward to the late 1990s. Howard Johnson has increased its hotels, sold off its restaurants, and expanded globally. Howard Johnson no longer owns or manages properties; it just sells franchises and reservations services. The corporate office today has fewer than 15 executives to manage the process and Cendant, as the wholesaler, has the power to dictate the terms.

Although the principles are the same, the distribution system for the hospitality industry differs significantly from those used for manufactured goods, as we have shown above. For one reason, the hospitality product is normally not "moved" to the consumer like a bottle of soda or a tube of toothpaste. For another, the producer (the hotel or restaurant) is also the retailer. Finally, because of the unusually high perishability of the hospitality product, many traditional channels simply would not work. In distribution systems of the hospitality industry, a separate wholesaler or retailer, such as a travel agent, rarely takes physical possession of the product to be marketed and delivered to the end consumer at a later date. (They may, however, take nominal possession, such as a wholesaler who purchases a block of rooms or airline seats to be packaged and sold to the ultimate consumer at a markup.) In hospitality, the manufacturer is not only the retailer, but manufactures and sells the product (delivers the service) simultaneously. The problem, then, is not how to distribute the product to the retailer, but how to get the customer to the retail outlet, that is, make it convenient. Thus arises the need for different kinds of distribution systems to broaden the base of customers and sell the product more efficiently. We separate these distribution systems into two broad categories: Geographic Distribution and Channels of Distribution.

PART A

•◆•

HOSPITALITY GEOGRAPHIC DISTRIBUTION

Overview

Geographic distribution involves owning, managing, franchising, and strategic alliances in key locations where the market is or the market comes. The point is to be in the right locations whether that is a city, a country, a resort area, or a "fast-food row."

OWNING AND/OR MANAGING   These two practices offer the best control over product quality. The two together, however, are becoming obsolete. Today most hotel companies that use geographic distribution are primarily in the business of managing properties owned by others.

FRANCHISING   Franchising allows companies to grow far more rapidly and provides the fran-

chisee considerable support as well as instant brand identity.

STRATEGIC ALLIANCES   These arrangements are also becoming more popular. These are mutually beneficial alliances formed for fast growth, or to fill gaps, and to provide geographic distribution and economies of scope without the capital outlays and without losing control.

RESTAURANT DISTRIBUTION   Besides all the other methods, better dining restaurants are now distributing through delivery systems to homes and hotels.

•◆•

Although there are thousands of hotels and foodservice outlets all over the world carrying many familiar brand names, most of these are not owned by the companies whose names they bear. The industry is really three different businesses: one is development, building, and ownership; next is management; the other is franchising. Some companies do all three. As well, they may be a franchisor (they sell the use of their name), a franchisee (they buy the use of another's name), or both. This disbursement is not so true, however, for restaurant companies. In those cases, growth is largely by franchising. There may be one outlet in a small town and a number of outlets in a major city. Figure 18-2 illustrates some of the complexity with hotels, which we discuss below.

One of many hotel examples is the Embassy Suites in Palm Beach, Florida. This hotel was built by a developer from the midwest, is managed by Servico Management of Florida, which also owns and operates other hotels under different franchise names (Figure 18-3), and carries the Embassy Suites name as well as others, as a franchise affiliation. Servico, however, does not franchise its own name. Servico tried, unsuccessfully, to create its own four-star brand, Royce Hotels, in the late 1980s and early 1990s, but never got the critical mass of hotels needed to stand alone as a brand name.

Major hotel companies such as Hilton, Sheraton, and Marriott are primarily hotel managers who operate hotels for owners who could

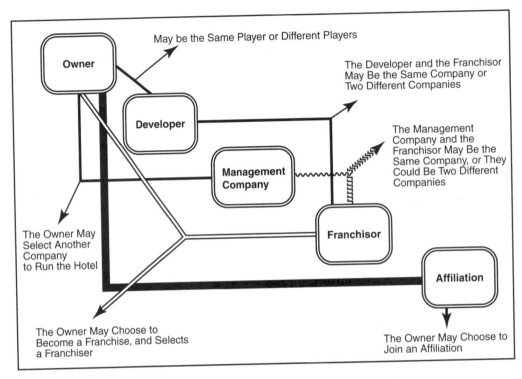

FIGURE 18-2   The players in hotel development.[1]

themselves be an individual, a partnership, a trust, a bank or even an insurance company, or some combination of these. The hotel companies also franchise their names to others. In 1993, in fact, Marriott Corporation divided into two companies: Marriott International, Inc. manages hotels and resorts and franchises its name to those owned by others; Host Marriott is a real estate investment trust (REIT) company that gets favorable tax treatment because it is a REIT, and buys and owns properties, sometimes managed by Marriott International but also by Hyatt, Delta, Four Seasons, and others.

From a chain operator's point of view, it is critical to the successful distribution of a brand name to be in the right geographical areas, as well as specific desirable locations for a specific hotel or restaurant. These are often defined as primary, secondary, and tertiary markets. There are 15 so-called primary cities in the United States, including Boston, New York, Los Angeles, and Chicago. Secondary markets include Hartford, Connecticut; Salt Lake City, Utah; Portland, Oregon; and San Antonio, Texas. Finally, there are tertiary markets such as Des Moines, Iowa; Lexington, Kentucky; and Boise, Idaho. The ranking depends on the size of the market and its buying power. There are also, of course, many smaller or even isolated market areas.

The same is true internationally. Primary international locations are Paris, Frankfurt, London, Tokyo, and Singapore. Secondary ones are Brussels, Amsterdam, Lisbon, Madrid, and Kyoto. In the tertiary category are Cologne, Marseilles, Athens, Stockholm, and Dusseldorf.

Resort locations likewise abound, from the Rocky Mountains to Florida to Honolulu to Bali, to the Cote d'Azur in France, Phuket in Thailand, the Costa del Sol in Spain, and the Fiji Islands. Having a property in Buenos Aires or Mexico City

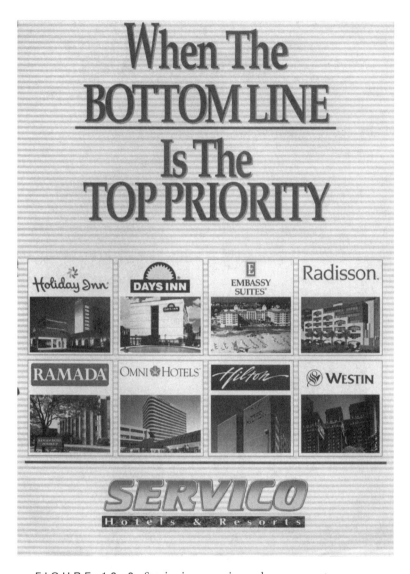

FIGURE 18-3 Servico in an owning and management company.

may be as important to a hotel company as it is for a fast-food chain to have a position on the New Jersey Turnpike, with one big difference—a hotel in Paris may send a customer to a sister hotel in Fiji, whereas there is no similar referral network among sister restaurants.

Upscale hotel chains usually strive to be in the primary markets first, and then move into the other markets. Middle-tier, economy-tier, and restaurant chains may do it the other way around. Certainly McDonald's is in about every level of market conceivable. Pizza Hut is not far behind. The point, of course, is to distribute the product to the right markets—first, by being there and second, by being able to capture the same customer in another place. In order to increase the number of customers in the distribution system, it is necessary to offer the product in a variety of market-

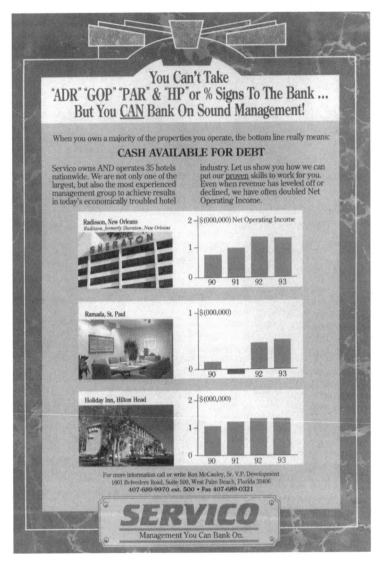

FIGURE 18-3 *(Continued)*

places where the customer either is or goes. Having a presence in the correct marketplace is critical to the success of a distribution channel.

A case in point is the Marriott Marquis Hotel in New York City, which opened in the mid 1980s, a rather late and expensive entry into the New York market. Marriott wanted to capture large conven-tions from the existing network of Hilton and Sheraton hotels. Major convention planners could buy the Hilton or Sheraton product in New York City, Chicago, and Las Vegas, among others. The Marriott product had a market presence in the cor-porate business segment but the hotels were not large enough in size and meeting space to attract the really major conventions and associations. The Marriott Marquis in Atlanta was the first step into this distribution system, but no major player in the convention circuit can maximize its customer base without a hotel in New York City. Thus the individual profit and loss statement of the New York City hotel was not as critical (although it turned out to be quite profitable) as was that hotel's overall contribution to the Marriott convention network nationwide.

More recently, budget and middle-tier chains are behaving likewise—Days Inn is in India, among other places, Best Western is worldwide, Microtel is in South America and Canada, and Howard Johnson is in Israel, Jordan, Egypt, Turkey, Cyprus, and Greece under a franchise agreement, all adding to the distribution system of these chains. Other country companies, such as Accor of France, are also in all parts of the world.

Hospitality companies may use all the methods mentioned above to distribute their products and services geographically—owning (wholly or partially), managing (through management contracts), franchising, and entering into strategic alliances. Although the numbers change almost weekly, Hilton Hotels, approximately, wholly owns about 13 hotels, partially owns 15 hotels, manages another 30 hotels, franchises over 250 hotels, including their mid-level brand Hilton Garden Inns, and has a strategic alliance with Hilton International of the UK (a totally separate company). In addition, hotels use the distribution channels of others, which is discussed in Part B of this chapter.

In any case, the major issues of distribution are (1) where to be so the customer can reach you, and (2) how to get the customer to you. Every hospitality company that wants to expand its product offerings geographically must eventually decide either (1) to make slower progress by owning (at least partially) and managing each unit, (2) to manage without owning, (3) to franchise its name to be managed by others, or (4) to form strategic alliances.

OWNING AND/OR MANAGING

Owning and managing provides the brand name with the best integrity from a product delivery point of view. If a company both owns and manages a facility, the product has a better chance of being consistently maintained and presented to customers in the network. Expansion, however, comes harder when a firm owns and manages all its facilities. The need for capital increases the financial drain and risk, and the opportunities for expansion may overtake the need to own and deliver the product. From a distribution standpoint, the need to expand the name brand identity usually outstrips the financial resources of the company.

Managing is next best to owning and managing for maintaining the quality standards of the product name in the channel of distribution. In many cases, companies manage for a fee while the physical property is owned by others. The fee, however, is not always the sole objective of the managing company. As discussed above, being in the right places in the distribution channel can be equally or more important. For example, Westin or Inter-Continental Hotels' presence in Singapore, at the time their new hotels were built, would probably have been sheer folly from an ownership perspective. Four Seasons manages a hotel in New York City that cost about $1 million a room to build (later sold at less than half the cost) but holds no equity in the property, which meets its standards but which it never could have afforded to build. Many hotel companies today, like Four Seasons and Marriott, are primarily management companies and have virtually gotten out of the ownership costs and risks. This is quite different than only ten years ago.

Another risk, however, emerges when the owning party does not maintain the property at the level desired by the managing company. For example, there may be a Hilton Hotel in a tertiary marketplace. A group of local investors may have provided the money to build the facility; Hilton manages the operation. As the marketplace becomes overbuilt and the tax incentives dry up, cash flow stagnates or dwindles. As the product becomes older in its life cycle, refurbishment becomes necessary to keep it competitive. The original investors can no longer depend on the asset itself to be self-supporting. Even if the hotel is covering its mortgage payments, it is unlikely that additional money has been set aside from operating funds for necessary refurbishment after the normal five- or six-year life cycle.

Hilton would now have to make a decision. Although its name is on the facility, and Hilton customers are becoming less satisfied with the product, the owners may be unable or unwilling to fund the necessary renovation. If the hotel is important enough to the Hilton distribution system, Hilton may choose to provide the funds itself, and wait until the supply/demand imbalance corrects itself and the hotel again becomes profitable. Hilton's other option is to withdraw from the contract and forfeit this marketplace in its distribution system and the related fees generated from the hotel. Four Seasons Hotels, as one example, has financed refurbishments of hotels it manages but doesn't own, choosing not to manage a deteriorated property that carries its name.

Management companies are also changed by owners in a process called **reflagging,** as discussed in Chapter 11. For example, CP Hotels held the management contract for L'Hotel in Toronto but failed to meet earnings projections called for in the contract. The owners went to court and threw out CP. Commonwealth Hospitality was brought in as the new management company with a Crowne Plaza franchise. Also in Toronto, when the Sutton Place Hotel managed by Kempinski went into receivership the lenders brought in Le Meridien as the management company. In Atlanta, a Westin was reflagged as a Marriott after the lender foreclosed. In Paris, a privately owned independent, George V, was reflagged as a Marriott, then a Sheraton, in order to get worldwide brand identity. Some 1500, on average, reflaggings occur every year in the United States.

Finally, to cover all the bases, there are management companies like Servico, mentioned earlier, which operate nothing but management franchises, that is, the Servico name does not appear in the hotel name. Unlike, for example, Marriott, which we could say is in the hotel business (i.e., it wishes to perpetuate its name as a brand or chain and manages hotels owned by others but with its name), companies like Servico are strictly in the hotel management business. Their name doesn't appear on the hotel and they may or may not own either the hotel or the franchise. If not, the owner buys the franchise and hires the management company to manage it. Interstate Hotels Corporation of Pittsburgh is the largest franchise manager of Marriott hotels, as well as franchising and managing a number of other brands.

FRANCHISING

Franchising is a commonly used method for a hospitality entity to increase its distribution network, both to create more revenue and to obtain the geographic presence discussed above. Franchising is also a common method of distribution for non-hospitality companies from Avis Rent-a-Car, Midas Mufflers, and H&R Block tax services to 7-11 convenience stores. Coca-Cola and Pepsi Cola franchise by allowing bottling plants to utilize their mixtures and then distribute their product. This method of distribution has been in common usage since what was called the franchise boom of the 1960s.

Franchising is the usage of a company name by someone else for the purpose of selling that product or service. Briefly, a company creates a product or service. It then offers other companies or persons the opportunity to use the name to market the offering in a variety of geographic areas. The amount of control a franchisor (the parent company) has over the franchisee (the company that buys the name to distribute the product or service) varies as widely as the franchising options available.

The contract between the franchisee and franchisor outlines the terms of the relationship. Items such as marketing support, revenues to the franchisor (usually determined as a percentage of sales—the norm is 4 to 5 percent plus marketing and reservations fees), and duration of the agreement are covered. **Territorial rights** are also negotiated at the same time. A franchisee might obtain rights to a two-mile zone, five-state area, or an entire country, in which no other franchisee of the same product or service can operate. For example, separate franchisees in India have acquired exclusive rights to the Days Inn, Choice International, and Sheraton names in that country.

A leader in franchising for hotels is Bass Hotels and Resorts with its Holiday Inn, Crowne Plaza, Holiday Inn Express, Holiday Select, Holiday Hotels & Suite, Garden Court, and SunSpree Resort (and now Inter-Continental hotels, but not yet franchised) brands. With over 1900 branded properties worldwide, about 95 percent are franchised. Cendant Corporation, however, is the world's largest hotel franchisor with six brand names on properties, none of which it owns. A newer but fast growing franchisor is U.S. Franchise Systems, headed by the inimitable Michael Leven, with three brands (Figure 18-4).

In the fast-food segment of the hospitality industry, the world leader is McDonald's. Other familiar names proliferate. These companies and many others recognize that their ability to distribute their products' name and identity throughout the world is limited by the amount of capital available. Methodically, they have offered their name and their service to potential franchisees. Not only fast-food restaurants go this route; in 1998 T.G.I. Friday's operated more than 470 units in 45 countries, mostly franchised, with an expansion goal of 40 to 50 percent a year.

Major companies need to expose their products to more customers, in effect creating brand-loyal consumers who will buy their product wherever it is available. The rationale is that the more places the customer can buy the product, the more often that customer will become a new customer of the same product in another marketplace. This distribution of the brand name by franchising has become integral in the growth of many major restaurant and hotel chains.

In the United States, over 75 percent (and counting) of all hotels are branded, most by franchising. In Canada, however, only about 20 percent of hotels with 20 or more rooms are branded, but over 50 percent of guest rooms are. Percentages are even lower in other countries, such as in Europe, but this is changing rapidly for all but the very small or very dated properties. The properties with more rooms to fill feel more need for brand identity.

From a distribution standpoint there are two main advantages to being a franchisee. First, it automatically positions the hotel or restaurant in the marketplace where customers already have an image—for instance, McDonald's or a Days Inn. Without a known name, customers have a more difficult time determining the position and eventual product delivery of the facility. Thus branding carries with it a certain amount of risk reduction for the buyer. We noted in Chapter 11 how many hotels are outsourcing their F&B outlets to brand names.

Second, for a lodging property, franchising often provides an immediate reservations network. Primarily for this reason, but also for drive-by recognition, independent properties are becoming unique in roadside and commercial markets in North America. Some claim that, with globalization, the lone hotel not connected to an international system will be lost among the flags. We discussed the details of branding more thoroughly in Chapter 11.

Franchise Support

Traditionally, the franchisor provides the following services with its name affiliation. Additionally, Table 18-1 shows some advantages and disadvantages for both parties.

Technical Knowledge. Each franchise operator does not have to reinvent the wheel. Although there are differences in each local marketplace, many of the

Procreation at its finest: USFS.

Everywhere you look, USFS is reproducing rabbitly. Microtel is the fastest growing all-new construction chain in the budget segment. Extended stay travelers are finding Hawthorn properties in towns and cities from coast to coast. And now, Best Inns & Suites is proudly joining our family of diverse brands. And, as good as things are going, it's just the beginning. To find out how you can join in our remarkable growth, call us at (404) 321-4045.

The Rabbitly Expanding Brands of USFS

©1998 USFS

FIGURE 18-4   Microtel, "rabbitly" growing franchise company.

TABLE 18-1
Advantages and Disadvantages of Franchising[2]

Franchisee Advantages: First consider the advantages that you, as the owner of a hotel and franchisee, would enjoy. These advantages speak to the benefits you would receive by being part of a larger organization, such as brand name recognition, purchasing economies, technical assistance, quality control, reduced financial risk, and a central reservations system.

1. The franchisee enjoys the benefit of an established product or service having consumer acceptance and is therefore free of worries about traditional startup costs, such as developing a market presence. In the case of such companies as Sheraton Hotels, Hilton Hotels, and Holiday Inns, franchisors spend a sizable portion of their advertising budget on national campaigns to keep the public aware of their hotel and restaurant services—for which the franchisee is customarily charged an advertising fee based on the gross revenues of a franchised unit. The brand name recognition, or the fact that customers have heard of the chain and have an image associated with it in mind, of the chain is a key advantage to the franchisee. Moreover, a franchisee saves all the time, effort, and expense that building a reputation would cost, if he were an individual entrepreneur—thus enabling his franchise unit to maintain its competitive edge.

2. A second advantage to the franchisee is the availability of managerial and technical assistance provided by the franchisor. Depending on the policy of a specific franchisor, the range of assistance available may, or may not, include managerial training, site selection, layout and design, furniture, fixtures and equipment purchasing, inventory control, and promotional plans for the grand opening.

3. Another advantage to the franchisee involves franchisor oversight of quality control standards. This is important not only to assure a consistent customer image but also to maintain employee pride in the workplace.

4. In many instances, franchisees benefit financially from the franchisor's advice and guidance on how much inventory to carry, thus avoiding waste and spoilage of perishables, and unprofitable storage of low demand items. Franchisees also benefit from purchasing economies, as the chain as a whole can negotiate better rates for things like soap and towels, as well as credit card fees and phone charges.

5. The carefully designed procedures of a franchised system minimize the financial risks for the franchisee and therefore tend to increase—but not to guarantee—the likelihood of generous franchise earnings.

6. Finally, substantial business is often referred to individual hotels via a central reservations system and chain directories, the cost of which is shared by all units in the chain. This makes the marketing dollars of individual units go much further.

Franchisee Disadvantages: Next, consider the disadvantages that you as the owner or franchisee would face. You would give up the advantage as well as being constrained by the rules of the franchise organization.

1. Failure of the franchisee to read carefully the fine print in the franchise agreement, or failure to secure legal advice before signing such an agreement, may cause a prospective franchisee to succumb to false or misleading sales practices of franchise promoters. Like any other contract, the franchise contract spells out in detail precisely what the franchisor will provide. Consulting with an attorney who understands the practical as well as the legal implications of a franchising agreement will enable a prospective franchisee to focus on those factors most likely to make his or her franchising relationship a successful one.

2. Since franchisors typically realize substantial revenues from franchise fees as well as continuing royalties from franchisees, it may come as a shock to prospective franchisees that the financial obligation up front, when the franchise agreement is signed, can be steep. The ongoing fees also cut into the profit one could make as an independent property.

3. Franchisees may be required to provide certain amenities and facilities such as swimming pools and/or 24-hour front desk service, in order to be part of the chain. These and other service costs to be borne by a franchisee may turn out to be higher than expected, and thus severely diminish the franchisee's expectations of a satisfactory return on the investment.

(continued)

T A B L E 18-1   *(Continued)*

---

4. Territorial rights of the franchisor may overlap those of a franchisee, and thus limit the revenue that the franchisee might otherwise expect to realize. For example, many of the larger hotel chains, early on, granted franchises that prohibited the franchisor from making any other franchise agreements within a specified geographical area. This was designed to protect a franchisee from having the franchisor grant another franchisee the right to operate another unit in the immediate neighborhood (e.g., two Sheratons on the same street). In recent years, however, segmentation of hotel markets has resulted in creation of different hotel brands with separate corporate identities. When such new brands have granted franchises, they have often disregarded the territorial restrictions agreed to by the parent company and its franchisees. Thus, such original franchisees are hurt by competition from another franchisee, in essence from the same company, being permitted to locate within territory originally designated exclusively for the parent company franchisee. For example, say you were granted a Holiday Inn franchise from Holiday Inn several years ago, and were given the exclusive rights to the city of Denver. Suppose, subsequently, Holiday Inn launched two brands, Holiday Inn Suites and Holiday Inn Select. It may be that the rights to those franchises are given to someone else, potentially hurting your sales.

5. With respect to a franchisee's desire to transfer to terminate the franchise, such occasions are generally covered by the language of the agreement. An uncooperative franchisor, however, may withhold approval of such a transaction if, for any reason, the franchisor believes the franchisee to have violated any provision of the franchise agreement.

Franchisor Advantages: Next consider the advantages of franchising from the point of view of the franchisor. Franchising is the ticket to growth for a franchise organization, and its members have a vested ownership interest.

1. Franchisors regard business expansion through a franchising network as the most attractive means of achieving rapid growth without the necessity of having to inject large sums of their own money or of incurring substantial debt through borrowing from banks or insurance companies. Thus, the franchisee's investment in a particular franchise enables the franchisor to share the heavy burden of a rapidly growing hotel or restaurant empire, while at the same time allowing the franchisor valuable time for evaluating market opportunities in a wide variety of competitive environments.

2. Moreover, some franchisors suspect that a manager may be less enthusiastic about the operation of a company owned unit than is the franchisee-manager who is usually a resident of the local community. The personal investment of the franchisee-manager motivates him to work hard pursuit of financial success. Franchising creates motivated owner/managers.

Franchisor Disadvantages: Finally, consider the disadvantages of franchising as seen by the franchisor. Multiple owners can mean lack of consistency and control, and finding qualified franchisees can be difficult.

1. The idea of using the franchisee's money to keep a franchisor's business expansion plan afloat is not without its drawbacks. In the first place, overseeing a quickly expanding chain of hotel franchisees is always a formidable challenge. If less desirable franchisees are allowed to enter the system, it reflects badly on the whole organization.

2. In addition, there can be no guarantee that a franchisee will not discover, sooner or later, that he/she would be able to do just as well—if not better—by operating the business without the franchisor. After the franchise agreement expires, the franshisee may not renew.

3. Furthermore, though the supply of prospective franchisee applicants may appear to be inexhaustible, some franchisors report a dearth of applicants whose experience, financial backing, and motivational drive are sufficiently persuasive to warrant taking a chance on their ability to become successful franchise operators.

---

components of a business are generic. The franchisor provides the procedures for the business.

Managerial Techniques. In some cases, the franchisee lacks management skills. Although procedures may need to be adapted to the local situation, they need not be developed from scratch each time a franchise is sold. Training and procedure manuals are made available by the franchisor. Some franchisors provide full mandatory training programs for their operators. An example of this is McDonald's Hamburger University.

Marketing Support. Clearly the phrase "the sum of the parts is greater than the whole" can be applied here. Franchisees pay a percentage of revenues toward the franchisor's marketing efforts. Each franchisee may market his or her product locally, but being part of a larger organization enables penetration into many cost-prohibitive geographic areas. Local marketing may or may not have to follow guidelines to provide continuity with the rest of the product lines.

Financial Support. Connection with a successful franchisor is sometimes the key to obtaining financing for a business. Lending institutions are more willing to lend money to a project with national affiliation than one of a local entity. The ability of a local operator to obtain business from outside marketplaces is greatly enhanced by a national or regional affiliation. In some cases, such as Microtel, the franchisor sets up a sizable fund from which a new franchisee can borrow to get started.

Safeguards. This broad-based category is a catchall for the support services offered by the franchisor to the franchisee. It includes such things as legal matters, safety regulations, and insurance issues.

Auditing. Most franchises have specific guidelines for operation of their businesses. Some are more stringent than others. The level of service needed to maintain a Days Inn franchise is different from that of a Crowne Plaza or a Sheraton franchise. Normally, there is a systematic evaluation of the franchise to ensure that the customer is receiving the appropriate product and service.

Reservation System. For hotels, a most important reason for franchising is the reservations network. Being a member of a nationwide chain can make the difference between a 50 percent occupancy and a 70 percent occupancy. The franchise affiliation automatically positions a hotel in the local marketplace. Simultaneously, it exposes the hotel to brand-loyal customers.

Traditionally, a toll-free number is provided for the benefit of the customer. This is a great advantage for other intermediaries such as travel agents, as well as the individual customer. Radisson was the first hotel company to offer international numbers, globally toll-free. International lines are staffed 24 hours a day by reservation agents fluent in major languages. Callers in each country dial a local number that is answered by highly trained sales representatives who speak the national language of the caller (see Figure 18-5).

Franchise Practices

Other marketing support from a franchise relationship may include a national sales force that sells the product name to large consumer markets. These salespeople provide coverage in marketplaces where it would not be cost-effective for the local property to enter. The purpose is to sell all of the hotels in the chain to customers who have a need for more than one location.

For example, the accounting firm of KPMG Peat Marwick may need to have training meetings in Dallas, Tulsa, and Jacksonville. Because Peat Marwick is based in New York City, it is more cost-effective to have a member of a hotel chain's national sales organization call on this customer, representing all three locations (which may be managed by three different hotel companies under the same franchise umbrella), than it is for the individual hotels to send their own sales representatives. In many instances, the customers also prefer to deal with one sales representative rather than having to listen to three different sales pitches.

Franchising companies are recognizing the need to provide greater services to their franchisees. As the competition increases for expansion, it is critical to maintain the expansion of the number of franchises. To do this, additional services such as special toll-free numbers for travel agents, one-stop shopping for group bookings, and

Toll-free reservations in the Middle East through AT&T

Depending on where you are calling from, dial one of the access codes
listed below and you will be connected directly to the AT&T system.

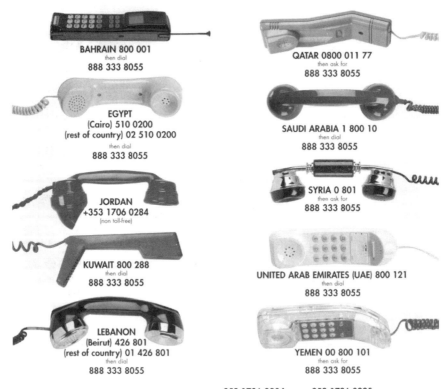

BAHRAIN 800 001
then dial
888 333 8055

QATAR 0800 011 77
then ask for
888 333 8055

EGYPT
(Cairo) 510 0200
(rest of country) 02 510 0200
then dial
888 333 8055

SAUDI ARABIA 1 800 10
then dial
888 333 8055

JORDAN
+353 1706 0284
(non toll-free)

SYRIA 0 801
then ask for
888 333 8055

KUWAIT 800 288
then dial
888 333 8055

UNITED ARAB EMIRATES (UAE) 800 121
then dial
888 333 8055

LEBANON
(Beirut) 426 801
(rest of country) 01 426 801
then dial
888 333 8055

YEMEN 00 800 101
then ask for
888 333 8055

You can also contact Dublin direct (non toll-free) on Tel: **+353 1706 0284** or Fax: **+353 1706 0225**

Radisson ////SAS
H O T E L S   W O R L D W I D E
http://www.radisson.com

Radisson operates over 350 hotels worldwide. Among these you can find 74 Radisson SAS hotels in: **SCANDINAVIA** Aarhus • Copenhagen (4) • Odense • Bergen (2) • Bodø • Kristiansand
Oslo (3) • Stavanger (3) • Tromsø • Trondheim • Göteborg • Helsingborg • Luleå • Malmö • Östersund • Stockholm (6) • Västerås. **EUROPE** Salzburg (2) • Vienna • Brussels • Helsinki • Nice
Paris • Berlin • Dresden • Düsseldorf • Erfurt • Hamburg • Lübeck • Merseburg • Neubrandenburg • Rostock • Wiesbaden • Budapest • Bergamo • Brescia • Lake Garda • Lodi • Milan (2) • Riga
Malta • Amsterdam • Szczecin • Lisbon • Sochi • London · Radisson SAS (1) & Radisson Edwardian (10) • Scotland. **MIDDLE EAST** Kuwait City • Abu Dhabi • Dubai. **ASIA** Beijing • Shanghai

F I G U R E   1 8 - 5   RadissonSAS lets customers or travel agents call toll-free in many languages.

centralized commission disbursement for travel agents, all attempt to differentiate the franchise in the eyes of customers and investors.

Franchising also provides immediate positioning for a restaurant. Pricing, quality of food and

beverage, and general ambience are all preconceived by the sign outside the establishment. Restaurant franchises are usually regulated by the franchisor more than their lodging counterparts. Variation in quality of product in fast-food stores such as McDonald's or Dunkin' Donuts are few. There are, however, a myriad of product and service experiences for travelers at Choice International or Sheraton franchises. Of course, the fast-food operations have managed to successfully create a uniform level of service through simplification and technology, while hotels still must provide a higher level of service through human interaction.

Most customers cannot differentiate between the corporate-owned and managed hotel or restaurant, and that of a franchise. A sales representative of a franchisee in the east is somewhat at the mercy of another franchisee and different management company in the midwest or Europe. Often, sales representatives meet resistance because of problems encountered by customers using the franchise in a different location and managed by a different company.

Hospitality companies have different philosophies of franchising. Marriott, for example, franchises a relatively small amount of full-service hotels for a company its size, but widely franchises its Courtyard and Fairfield Inn products. Contrarily, Holiday Inn has franchised over 95 percent of its product line at all levels. There are also some companies, such as Four Seasons, Fairmont, Mandarin Oriental, Oberoi of India, and Shangri La of Hong Kong, that do not franchise at all. The philosophy of these companies is that the level of service they are attempting to deliver can be maintained only by direct control.

The examples we have given are intended to be illustrative only of the complexity of the owning, managing, and franchising "maze." The "reflagging" phenomenon (i.e., brand switching) that is occurring makes what is true today, false tomorrow (Figure 18-6).

The Signs, They Are A-changing

Since May, new corporate flags wave over these and other hotels as owners and operators re-align their brand affiliations.

Old Brand/New Brand	City	Rooms
Bucksburn Moat House/ Holiday Inn Crowne Plaza	Aberdeen, Scotland	93
Bristol Moat House/Holiday Inn Crowne Plaza	Bristol, England	132
Caversham Hotel Reading/ Holiday Inn	Reading, England	112
Stouffer Riverview Plaza/ Adam's Mark	Mobile, Alabama	375
Econo Lodge/Holiday Inn Express	Greensboro, North Carolina	140
Carambola Beach Resort Rockresort (shuttered)/Radisson	St. Croix, US Virgin Islands	157
Clarion Inn/Sheraton Inn	Napa, California	191
Boston Vista Waltham/Westin	Waltham, Massachusetts	347
Newark Airport Vista/Hilton	Newark, New Jersey	375
Metrodome Hilton/Sheraton	Minneapolis, Minnesota	269
Lake Arrowhead Hilton/ Independent	Lake Arrowhead, California	261
Marriott/Hilton	Gaithersburg, Maryland	301
Renaissance/Hilton	East Brunswick, New Jersey	405
Exel Inn/Comfort Inn	Dallas/Fort Worth Airport	152
Ramada Inn/Courtyard by Marriott	Austin, Texas	98
Holiday Inn Crowne Plaza/ Ramada Plaza	Stamford, Connecticut	377

Source: Company reports, compiled by HOTELS.

FIGURE 18-6 Changing flags—a continuous process.

cially in Chapters 4 and 7, where hotel companies form alliances with telephone, credit card, or other companies that complement each other and have mutually beneficial objectives. They are not, however, in the same business.

Strategic alliances between companies that *are* in the same business, lodging and food service, are becoming increasingly popular. Again, this is a way to gain greater distribution but still maintain independence plus avoid some of the liabilities. An excellent case in point is that of SAS Hotels and Radisson, told in Table 18-2.

Strategic Alliances

There is one more form of what we are calling geographic distribution channels that is different from the others. Typically, these are called strategic alliances. We have mentioned these before, espe-

T A B L E   18-2
A Powerful Strategic Alliance

SAS International Hotels (SIH), a division of the Scandinavian Airline System (SAS), started in 1960 with its first hotel in Copenhagen, SAS's most important gateway city. During the next 28 years SIH owned or leased and operated 21 more hotels in Scandinavia as well as one each in Kuwait, Vienna, and Hamburg. In order to expedite its growth process, in 1989 SIH invested US$500 million for a 40 percent equity position in Inter-Continental Hotels (ICH), then owned by a Japanese company. ICH had more than 40,000 hotel rooms in more than 80 cities worldwide. The advantage to SIH was a worldwide reservation and distribution system in most of SAS' important destinations. The intent was eventual merger.

Unfortunately, because of the Gulf War and a general downturn in the international economy, SIH was forced to absorb 40 percent of ICH's losses and taxes plus pay high interest on its borrowings. In addition, management cultures and approaches proved to be incompatible. In 1992 SIH divested its equity position in ICH, taking a huge write down on its balance sheet, and was facing bankruptcy.

SAS planned a merger with Swissair so SIH entered into a marketing alliance with Swissotels, a subsidiary of Swissair. Swissotels, however, lacked the critical mass that SIH needed to grow internationally. Meanwhile, Radisson Hotels of Minneapolis was trying to penetrate the European market and had a marketing alliance with Movenpick Hotels of Switzerland, also lacking a critical mass. In 1994, SIH and Radisson broke off their separate agreements and formed a strategic alliance called RadissonSAS.

SIH obtained all rights to the name and development of RadissonSAS hotels in Europe, the Middle East, and North Africa. Neither company invested in the other. Radisson got immediate properties, brand identity, and distribution in SIH territory. SIH got immediate brand identity, a global reservation system, and distribution in the western hemisphere. The two companies shared many other **economies of scope.** This is a real strategic alliance that mutually benefits both parties and SIH, now RadissonSAS, now has over 100 hotels in 27 countries plus worldwide distribution.

It is interesting that these two companies have continued this pattern. For example, RadissonSAS has formed strategic alliances with hotel companies in Israel and Italy. Radisson, on the other hand, formed a strategic alliance with Four Seasons Hotels. Four Seasons bit off more than it could chew when it bought the luxury Far East chain, Regent Hotels. Radisson wanted quick growth in that area, as in Europe, and now has all the rights to develop the Regent brand.

In another version, Choice Hotels International, essentially a franchisor, entered into a strategic alliance in 1998 with Flag International, Australia's largest lodging chain, now called Flag Choice Hotels Ltd. Thus Choice gets distribution through 481 Flag properties across Australia, New Zealand, Fiji, and Papua New Guinea. Flag gets master franchise rights and a worldwide reservation and directory distribution system. Marriott has a marketing alliance with New Otani of Japan, giving both companies distribution in each other's territory.

Alliances among airlines are well known. The so-called Star alliance includes United, Air Canada, Thai, Lufthansa, and SAS. The Oneworld alliance includes British Airways, American Airlines, Quantas, Cathay Pacific, and Canadian Airlines. Although these airlines compete with each other on some routes, each sells the others' products, and **code sharing** allows them to book each other's routes, share frequent travel points, and offer "seamless" travel worldwide. Another well-known strategic alliance is that between Coca-Cola and Disney, whereby Disney sells Coke and Coke uses Disney characters in its merchandising. Strategic alliances are increasingly popular as companies seek faster growth, geographical distribution, and economies of scope.

Restaurant Distribution

Other than all the geographic distribution systems we have discussed, restaurants have one other that hotels can't duplicate. Unique in hospitality, they may send the product to the customer. Although there have long been lots of take-home food products and home delivery of pizza, the latest pattern includes hotel delivery. Pizza Hut, Domino's, and the like contract with hotels to deliver pizzas much as they do to homes. More than that, we now have better restaurants doing the same thing through an outside distribution system. Takeout Taxi is one company that delivers meals on behalf of about 750 restaurants, or about 12 in each of the 66 markets it serves in the United States. These restaurants range from local rib joints to big chains like Chi Chi's and TGI Fridays. Takeout Taxi calls itself a marketing company that delivers. It has developed a database of more than 200,000 restaurant customers and uses it to develop highly targeted promotional programs for the restaurants.

Lettuce Entertain You of Chicago (see Figure 10-3), which owns about 30 restaurants, uses a firm called Room Service Deliveries to deliver meals to hotel rooms. Many hotels in city areas, primarily those that do not have a restaurant of their own, have a selection flyer in every room listing 5 to 15 different restaurants and their menus that can be called to order delivery. This service is especially popular in all-suite hotels because the food can be refrigerated and/or reheated. Figure 18-7 shows probably the widest restaurant distribution anywhere.

FIGURE 18-7 K-Pauls worldwide restaurant distribution.

PART B

•◆•

CHANNELS OF DISTRIBUTION

Overview

These are the channels that bring the customer to the product, either directly or as an intermediary. They are outside or external to the hotels and restaurants they use. All these channels overlap and the industry is not absolutely uniform in its use of nomenclature. This can become quite confusing, but we have done our best to sort it out. The channels in this section include consortia, affiliations, reservation companies, representation companies, incentive houses, travel agents, tour operators and wholesalers, discount brokers, and global distribution systems.

STRATEGIES FOR DISTRIBUTION CHANNELS Getting maximum use out of distribution channels means utilizing various tools such as push/pull strategies, promotional tie-ins, and selecting the right channels. A few companies are vertically integrated for this reason.

INTERNATIONAL MARKETS Some distribution channels are more widely used in Europe and Asia than in North America. This is especially true of wholesaler channels.

CHANNEL MANAGEMENT Channels cannot simply be established and left alone. They have to be managed to maximize their use. They also have to be evaluated on a regular basis, channel members have to be motivated, and new members recruited.

•◆•

Channels of distribution include consortia, affiliations, reservations companies, representation companies, incentive houses, travel agents, tour operators and wholesalers, discount brokers, and **global distribution systems** (GDS). These terms represent different distribution systems that can, at the same time, be both quite different and quite similar. Furthermore, the lines between them are not always clear. In general, we can say that none of the companies in these categories own, manage, or franchise, although there are exceptions to that as well. Also, some companies that own, manage, and/or franchise affiliate with other companies that do likewise. The main point to be made, however, is that these channels, unlike those discussed in the first part of this chapter, do not take the product to the customer but, instead, bring the customer to the product.

Perhaps, if we could generalize, we could say that these companies represent distribution channels that are external to companies that are in the hotel operations business. The one major exception to that would be hotel companies' own reservation systems, which are their own distribution channels and well-known, so we don't discuss them here. These other channels are, however, additional marketing tools and very important ones in the distribution process, especially internationally. A given hotel or hotel chain may be involved with all of them. We discuss each one separately, recognizing that there is some overlap among them.

CONSORTIA

A **consortium** of hotels is a loosely knit group of independently owned and managed properties with different names, a joint marketing distribution purpose, and a common consortium designation. Some, however, may belong to chains. The hotel name is primary. Examples of consortia include Leading Hotels of the World and Preferred Hotels & Resorts Worldwide, each of which represents a number of very upscale hotels, Logis de France, which represents almost 5000 family-run hotels of varying sizes in the one- and two-star categories in France, and Inter Europe Hotels which represents three and four-star hotels in eight European countries. What ties these properties together is a joint marketing effort aimed at similar target markets at different times and places. What also ties them together, and differentiates them from strictly reservations networks, is that there is also some measure of control placed upon the membership.

The purpose of the consortium is to open a channel of distribution by maximizing combined marketing resources while retaining individual and independent management and products. Preferred Hotels, headquartered in Chicago, Illinois, is a marketing consortium of over 100 hotels in North America, Europe, the Middle East, and Asia. Preferred has a global reservations network and provides its members with a variety of marketing programs and services. The advantage to the property represented is its ability to retain independent ownership and, therefore, individuality while obtaining worldwide representation in a product class. Customers, in turn, realize that they are not buying a standardized product line. Preferred Hotels maintains very high standards within its membership grouping, and the traveler need not be wary of the potential experience. Hotels are evaluated by an independent third party and must have an 80 percent score to pass (Figure 18-8). Preferred consortium members benefit not only from referrals, but also from advertising, public re-

lations, sales, and direct marketing programs, a reduced credit card fee from American Express, toll-free reservation numbers worldwide, and inclusion in airlines' global distribution systems (GDS) used by travel agents. Similarly, New York based Leading Hotels of the World (LHW) includes over 300 very upscale hotel members, 14 with helipads. Both Preferred and LHW have offices around the world and a waiting list of hotels wanting to join. Some hotels belong to both consortia.

Consortia are more common in Europe than in the United States. As one example, there was Inter Nor Hotels in Norway, since bought by Choice and converted to a corporation, which operated somewhat differently than Preferred. Each Inter Nor hotel was independently owned and managed. It is doubtful, however, that many people knew this. The collateral of each hotel carried the names of the others. Most promotions took place in all hotels simultaneously. Reservations were easily made from one to the other. Each hotel was labeled an Inter Nor hotel as if it were, in fact, a member of a unified chain. There was a "corporate" office in Oslo, which suggested and administered marketing programs for the "chain," evaluated the performance of each unit, arranged seminars to improve marketing and management, and, in general, acted in many ways like the corporate office of a hotel chain.

This type of consortium does not end there; it hooks up with other consortia in strategic alliances, both to provide interchange reservations systems and to broaden the entire network. Inter Nor, for example, hooked up with Danway hotels in Denmark, Arctia Hotels in Finland, Icelandic Hotels in Iceland, and Sara Hotels in Sweden, each of which was also a consortium. These arrangements provided a distribution network of over 100 hotels that not only reserved with each other but also combined on promotions.

Relais & Chateaux is a Paris-based consortium with over 400 elegant, independently owned hotel members, and Relais Gourmands restaurants in 40 countries, including the United States. Its collateral, published in several different languages, describes the consortium as follows:

"WHEN A HOTEL DOESN'T MEASURE UP, INSTEAD OF FIRING THE MANAGER, WE FIRE THE HOTEL."

We admit it's not standard operating procedure at the major hotel chains.

But then Preferred Hotels® and Resorts Worldwide is not a hotel chain.

We're an association of independent hotels.

It's our job to set and maintain the highest possible standards for a group of the finest hotels and resorts around the world. We're very strict when it comes to

our standards. And very unforgiving with member hotels and resorts that don't adhere to them.

Admittedly, this is not an attractive concept to the great majority of hotels.

In fact, it's enough to keep all but the very best from applying. Which perhaps explains why, in a world of more than 300,000 hotels and resorts, at present only 105 are Preferred. They represent the very finest accommodations available anywhere at any price.

Interestingly, they are not necessarily the most expensive hotels in their market.

Ask your travel agent if there's a Preferred hotel where you plan to visit.

Or if you would like a directory listing our 105 current members, please call us at 1-800-447-5773.

PREFERRED
HOTELS® & RESORTS
WORLDWIDE

FIGURE 18-8   Preferred Hotels and Resorts maintains rigorous standards.

. . .[O]ur objectives and procedures do not correspond to a fashion (fashion becomes outdated) but to a need—your's—we have no desire to change except for the better. . . . The Relais & Chateaux do not form a chain, but a product. . . .our clients are not interested in a chain. They look for a product with clearly defined differences, even if the presentation differs from one place to another. . .

In another case, Golden Tulip, a subsidiary of KLM Airlines, owns and manages its own hotels and has a consortium division of other hotels in 48 countries. One problem with consortia, because the only direct control is the right of membership, can be the disparity among properties, both physically and in the way they are managed. Although properties are carefully screened for membership and there is really no desire for look-alikes, problems may still arise. Upscale consortia like Prefered and LHW have very strict controls, but there are many middle or downscale consortia that do not.

These differences among properties are not, of course, unique. Many chains also have them, as we have pointed out. The franchise systems of Hilton and Sheraton are full of them, as are Holiday, Ramada, Wyndham, and many others. This is also true of Ponderosa, Bennigan's, and Friendly's restaurants.

The problem that arises, in any case, is the one of customer expectations and perceptions. While the consortium network is a powerful one in the distribution system, it is also one that must be treated with great care. A chain can blame only itself if one of its units breaks down; most consortia, on the other hand, outside of flagrant protocol violation, must suffer its "wayward children." Such sufferance can be difficult. Conversely, the consortium distribution system represents the maintenance of individuality in a world of chain "sameness," with the advantage of chain marketing clout.

AFFILIATIONS

Many people consider Best Western a hotel chain or a franchise sytem. In fact, this worldwide group is an **affiliation** and membership organization of almost 4000 individually owned properties in 76 countries, under a common umbrella (Figure 18-9). The hotel name is secondary. The variety of product offered to the customer is significant. The overall theme of the affiliation is the price-value relationship of the hotels. Best Western, in any marketplace, will tend, but not always, to offer a clean room for the lowest price. The Best Western affiliation is a very successful channel of distribution. The strong sense of value in all marketplaces keeps customers coming back. Best Western, the largest such organization in the world under a common name, constantly seeks to add new members worldwide. It does not hesitate, however, to drop members who fail to live up to established guidelines. Best Western also painstakingly tries to differentiate itself from traditional franchised hotel chains.

Some hotel companies affiliate with other hotel companies for joint marketing and distribution endeavors, like the Inter Nor example given above. These affiliations have included joint sales and advertising efforts as well as marketing and reservations connections. Consortia and affiliations are similar in organizational structure. The major difference is that in affiliations all properties carry the same names.

RESERVATIONS COMPANIES

Reservations companies are companies that offer member hotels a reservations service in all key areas of the world. These companies usually print an annual directory listing all member hotels and, in some cases, provide marketing support services. Primarily, the company will spend a lot of effort and funds on promoting their company name and image to encourage travel agents and hotels to use their central reservations offices.

There is much overlap among consortia, affiliations, and reservations systems. Unlike consortia, however, there are essentially no entry requirements for reservations companies other than, perhaps, that the properties be within a certain product class range. A charge is assessed by the reservations company for each reservation made. Further, there is no significant central control that polices the properties.

The largest and most comprehensive reservation service has been that of Utell International (Figure 18-10). Now a division of REZsolutions, Inc. after a merger, the company is now, in some ways, also a representation company as it has a sales staff. REZsolutions has a central reservations system, 56 worldwide sales and reservations offices in 38 countries, and connections to 500,000 travel agent/reservations terminals as well as all of the world's major distribution systems. REZsolutions connects 7800 hotels in 180 countries, covering everything from tourist class to deluxe and from small independents to international chains. Members pay, for each reservation, a fee to the air-

FIGURE 18-9   Best Western advertises for affiliations.

line reservation system (e.g., Sabre), REZsolutions, and the travel agent that makes the reservation, as well as a monthly fee to REZsolutions.

REZsolutions is the leading provider to the hospitality industry, worldwide, of technology based systems, distribution networks, private label services, and international marketing programs. It accepts international currency deposits and pays travel agencies in their own currencies. Its "labeling service" for other systems, such as Golden Tulip, means that when you call Golden Tulip what you really get is a REZsolutions agent. Over 95 percent of REZsolutions' business is travel agent based. Its vision is to become the only comprehensive "one-stop shop" for the industry.

Figure 18-11 illustrates a reservations system for small inns that are independent and not branded. These kinds of distribution channels are becoming essential for just about every kind of lodging property in today's global world.

FIGURE 18-10 Utell offers a "visual imagery" reservations sytem.

FIGURE 18-11   InnLink, a small inns reservations company.

Consortia and affiliations also have central reservations networks and some share a reservations system such as Golden Tulip with REZsolution. A hotel is assessed a charge by the reservations system for each reservation made. Many hotel chains, of course, operate their own reservations systems as well. Among the largest and most successful are Holiday's Holidex and the sys-tems of Sheraton's Reservatron, Hilton's Hiltron, Marriott's Marsha, Hyatt's Hyatt Spirit, and Radisson's Pierre. For the small chain or independent hotel, however, or for the company that wants to attract an international market from countries where it does not have properties or a reservation system, it is usually more cost-effective to hook up with a reservations/representation company, or use it to supplement its own system. An example, a region specific reservation company, is shown in Figure 18-12.

REPRESENTATION COMPANIES

A **representation (rep) company** is a channel of distribution that, figuratively speaking, brings a hotel to a marketplace. These companies market a hotel to a customer base for a fee and are hired to act as sales organizations for independent properties that don't have sales or reservations networks of their own. Major chains may also use rep firms to enhance their regional sales efforts. Rep firms have their own sales forces and represent a number of hotels through regional offices in different geographical areas.

Representation companies go much further than reservations companies in promoting their member hotels. Apart from the worldwide reservations network and link to all global distribution systems, they will, for instance, have a sales force actively selling their member hotels; they will print an annual directory featuring all hotels with detailed information on their services and facilities, and print other marketing collateral such as special programs, newsletters, and flyers. They will also undertake aggressive public relations and advertising campaigns on behalf of their member hotels.

Once a representative firm has been engaged, it uses all of the normal communications mix, such as personal selling, direct mail, advertising, sales promotion, and public relations, to get customers to buy certain hotels. Sales calls are the most utilized form of the communications mix, followed by direct mail. David Green and Associates of New York is an example of a representation company that has been in the business for a long time. Newer, more segmented, representation firms, such as Associated Luxury Hotels, have begun to carve niches in the representation marketplace.

Supranational, a European-based firm, is another example. Supranational's purpose is to unify the reservations network without sacrificing the identity of the individual property or chain. It is a very active sales and marketing company. Supranational represents entire hotel companies, as well as a number of independent properties around the world, which are rigorously selected. In total Supranational represents over 700 hotels in over 300 destinations in 44 countries and has 23 reservations offices, worldwide. Thistle Hotels in the United Kingdom, Delta Hotels in Canada, and Omni Hotels in the United States are members of this system. The selling point for customers, usually travel agents, is that by calling the reservations office of the local hotel company of any of the member chains, they can book reservations directly anywhere in the world in any of the member chains' properties. A customer in England can call the Thistle Hotels reservations office in London and make a reservation at the Omni Berkshire Place in New York City. Additionally, Supranational has an active sales force in all key markets and each member hotel group is responsible for selling and marketing Supranational hotels in their local market, that is, each member of the system attempts to market its counterparts, in hopes that the counterparts are doing the same for them. A 4 percent commission on revenue is paid to the partner when this occurs. Supranational is a nonprofit organization operated by hoteliers for hoteliers.

Supranational also publishes a wide range of marketing programs including directories with international hotel classifications, newsletters, city savers, spotlight flyers, guaranted U.S. dollar programs, and incentive programs. Its global distribution system, called SUPROS, is considered to be among the most cost-effective and advanced in the industry. It links into all the major airlines' systems. All told, it has direct links to 240,000 travel agents.

A good rep firm also offers other services such as meeting planners, to consumers, as well as prescreening hotels to be sure they will meet the consumers' needs, checking for space availability, negotiating the most attractive rates, and providing other information about hotels.

One easy phone call reaches 250 hotels in Spain

And, everything else the country has to offer. Marketing Ahead is the specialist of quality tourism to Spain. And we make it so easy for you...just one phone call. From 3 star to 5 star, we represent and can put you in touch with more than 250 hotels in Spain. The right hotels for your clients, whether it be weekend or long-term, luxury or budget travel. Call us, we'll tailor the perfect travel package for your clients' needs.

Some of the hotels we represent:

PARADORES OF SPAIN - (Representation In the Northeast, Mid West and West Coast of the United States)
SEVILLA - Hotel Inglaterra, Hotel Palacio Casa de Carmona
GRANADA - Hotel Alhambra Palace, Hotel La Bobadilla
BARCELONA - Derby Hotels, Hotel Colon, Hotel Condes de Barcelona
MADRID - Hotel Arosa, Hotel Suecia, Hotel Carlos V
IBIZA - Hotel La Hacienda
AVILA - Hotel Palacio Valderrabanos
SAN SEBASTIAN - Hotel Londres e Inglaterra
GALICIA - Gran Hotel La Toja

marketing ahead

Specializing in Quality Tourism to Spain

800-223-1356

433 fifth Avenue • new york, ny 10016 • (212) 686-9213 • (212) 686-0271 FAX

FIGURE 18-12 Marketing Ahead, a region specific reservations company.

Representation firms either operate on a retainer basis or are paid a fee when the group checks out of the hotel. Once a hotel has retained the service of the representative firm, the firm prints a brochure on the facility and markets it in clusters with other hotels in its network. Sales representatives of these companies operate in much the same way as a hotel's sales department. They maintain a client base and files, and make sales calls to convince customers to use a facility in their portfolio rather than an alternative. Having a franchise does not preclude the use of representative firms. Some operators like the opportunity to have as many people selling their hotels as possible.

A representation firm can be more cost-effective for a hotel company than establishing individual sales office in **feeder cities.** A feeder city represents a geographic area from which business is derived, but where a company may or may not have a property of its own. For example, Chicago is a major feeder city for New York City, as are Los Angeles, Paris, and London.

If Chicago was a major feeder city for a hotel in Phoenix, it might not be cost-effective for the Phoenix hotel to have a sales representative make frequent sales trips. Also, setting up a regional office to call on customers can be very expensive. Instead, a representative firm is retained in the feeder city and makes local calls, as the most cost-effective method to build the channel of distribution.

On the surface, representation firms, which are usually located in major metropolitan centers, usually offer a lucrative support system to the marketing distribution effort. Sometimes, however, there are disputes as to where the booking originated. For example, a hotel might have an IBM account in its file system when the representative firm uncovers a piece of business from the same company but from a different contact. The question arises as to whether the firm should be paid for the booking. Details like this need to be worked out before the representation agreement is consummated. If handled properly, this channel of distribution can be an effective addition to distribution efforts.

INCENTIVE HOUSES

Incentive houses are an another example of a strong channel of distribution. These are companies that specialize in handling strictly incentive reward travel. As discussed in Chapter 9, many organizations and firms have incentive contests to reward top-performing employees, salespeople, dealers, or retailers. Travel rewards are a popular form of incentive.

Major corporations often have their own in-house travel departments or individuals to handle incentive arrangements. Many companies have used travel agents. More and more, however, both large and small companies are relying on incentive houses to organize their trips. Carlson Marketing Group is one of the leading incentive travel providers with offices in 30 major cities in the U.S. and in 20 countries worldwide. Maritz travel, based in the midwest United States, is also an established incentive house.

The reason for this specialization is that incentive travel is a special case. For companies that use this kind of reward frequently, there is a constant need for destinations that are new, different, and exciting—in other words, that offer a real incentive. Second, there is a real need for the trip to be letter-perfect. Keeping up with all this, on a worldwide basis, is expensive and time-consuming.

Incentive houses, because of their collective accounts, can parcel out the costs of their expertise. Almost always, someone will have visited and thoroughly inspected the destination, the hotels, the restaurants, and the ground services before putting together the incentive package. The incentive house then "sells" the package to the company and helps the company to "sell" it to those who will seek the reward.

For upscale hotels, particularly in resort areas or foreign destinations, it can be a real boost to the distribution channel to be on the incentive houses' lists. In these cases, a property (and incentive planners deal with individual properties as opposed to chains to be certain of the product) does not simply buy an incentive house's services. In effect, it earns them by doing things right. By contrast with consortia, reservations networks, rep firms, and travel agents, the incentive house's service is paid for by the customer, not the hotel.

In these situations, each channel member is integrally dependent on the others for performance. The incentive house has the corporate customer base. If customers are dissatisfied with the trip, they may choose another incentive house for the next program. Each channel member has to make sure that everything goes as promised. For example, if the ground transportation is an hour late in picking up a group at the airport, the entire trip can be spoiled. Future business may be lost not only to another incentive house, but to another destination.

TRAVEL AGENTS

A travel agent is an **intermediary** in a channel of distribution who makes reservations for a variety of hospitality needs. The travel agent is compensated in the form of a commission, usually based upon the rate of the service purchased. As a rule of thumb in most cases, a 10 percent commission is paid to travel agents who book cruises and hotel rooms, while airlines and rental car firms pay a lesser rate. Travel agencies also form consortia, using the strength of many individual agencies to combine marketing and negotiating clout as a channel member. Table 18-3 shows the status of travel agents at the time of writing.

The travel agent is more of a full-service channel, whereby the hotel booking may be incidental to the airline and ground transportation arranged. Because of this, travel agencies are actively soliciting corporate meeting accounts, especially when they have previously handled a company's individual business travel. By promising more clout in negotiating rates, agencies' role in meeting planning is bound to increase.

The Travel Agent Role

The travel agent is faced with a blizzard of changing conditions in the marketplace. Airlines, collectively, are reported to change fares as many as 80,000 times a day. To recommend a hotel, the agent needs knowledge of location, rates, amenities, dining, entertainment, parking, ground transportation, recreation facilities, and more. The technology of the industry is changing at a furious pace in an attempt to keep up with all this information.

Agencies that were on manual systems only a short time ago now have sophisticated database equipment to manage their bookings, almost 100 percent in the United States but maybe two-thirds

---

T A B L E   1 8 - 3
Travel Agency Statistics[3]

There are over 3300 travel agency locations in the United States and 5000 in Canada doing over $112 billion in sales. The vast majority are single-location offices accounting for two-thirds of airline travel business. The mega agencies, like American Express, account for 25 percent. About 10 percent of bookings are for U.S. hotels, which means travel agents account for an annual $11 billion in hotel sales. They also book 50 to 80 percent of resort occupancies, 85 to 90 percent of international hotel sales, and nearly 100 percent of cruises.

The European and Middle East agency market has over 54,000 agency locations, producing $137 billion in sales and $11 billion in hotel buisness travel bookings. Five countries account for 80 percent of these agencies: the UK, Germany, France, Italy, and Spain. Mega agencies dominate. The Asia/Pacific market consists of over 19,000 agency locations, doing $52 billion in sales. Four central markets—Japan, Hong Kong, Australia, and Korea—account for 80 percent of all travel activity. The Japanese market is dominated by mega agencies. Four account for over half of the business. Japan Travel Bureau competes with American Express for the title of the world's largest travel agency.

that in Europe and Asia. Other automated systems are largely reservation terminals provided by the airlines (e.g., Apollo by United Airlines and Sabre by American Airlines), creating a direct link between travel agents and the airlines controlling this distribution channel. Figure 18-13 is a sample directory page from the Sabre system. Like the hotel systems, these have been called Central Reservations Systems (CRS) but are now being called Global Distribution Systems (GDS). Table 18-4 shows what travel agents would get on their GDS screens for a hotel.

Rates change at a rate unparalleled in the his-tory of travel. The proliferation of hotels offering thousands of packages, incentives, and varying rate structures to varying people at varying times make booking a difficult task at best.

The rental car industry has followed suit with the airlines and hotels, offering special promotions and incentives every day. Many of these promotions have conditions attached to them, such as booking an airline seat 30 days in advance with cancellation penalty clauses. Add to all this the overlapping frequent traveler awards (and the traveler's perplexity among taking airline, hotel, or car rental points), and you have a very complex prob-

FIGURE 18-13   Page from a Sabre system directory.

T A B L E   18-4
GDS Hotel Information on Computer Monitor

HOD19789

PW19789 ROGER SMITH
         LEXINGTON AVE
         NEW YORK NY 10017
         FONE 212-755-1400
         FAX 212-319-9130

AIRPORT - LGA 501
CURRENCY - USD/2

HOD*/*R   TO DISPLAY RATE GRID ONLY
HOD*/-R   TO DISPLAY HOTEL INFORMATION W/O RATE GRID

RAC A1D   A2T   B1D   B2T   C1D   C2T
RAC AJS   AS1   AS2

EXTRAS/OPTS - RA 20.00 RC 20.00 CR   .00   EX 20.00
               FAM-Y MEAL-Y TAX-20

LOCATION - NEW YORK NY
         MIDTOWN MANHATTAN ON EASTSIDE
         NEAR UNITED NATIONS, ROCKEFELLER CENTER, FIFTH
         AVENUE, THEATERS, GRAND-CENTRAL STATION.

COMMUNICATIONS-
         TELEX   NOT AVAIL FAX   212-319 9130 OR 212 758 4061

TRANSPORTATION-
         TAXI LIMOUSINE
         PRIVATE AIRPORT TRANSFER RATES ARE AS FOLLOWS -
         HOTEL TO LAGUARDIA USD 30.00. ONE WAY
         HOTEL TO KENNEDY USD 45.00 ONE WAY
         HOTEL TO NEWARK USD 55.00 ONE WAY
         ALL RATES QUOTED ARE SUBJECT TO CHANGE
         FOR ARRIVALS ONLY PLEASE ADD USD 5.00 SUPPLEMENT.
         PLEASE REQUEST IN SI-FIELD WITH COMPLETE FLIGHT DETAILS.

POLICY-
         CHECK-IN 2 PM / CHECK-OUT 1 PM.
         MAXIMUM 4 PERSONS PER ROOM.
         CHILDREN UNDER 16 YRS FREE IN ROOM WITH PARENTS.
         CONTINENTAL BREAKFAST INCLUDED IN RATE.
         10% COMMISSION PAID WITHIN 48 HRS OF GUEST DEPARTURE.
         TAXES ARE NOT INCLUDED IN RATE.

DEPOSIT/GUARANTEE-
         AX-CB-DC-MC-VS-DS CREDIT CARD GUARANTEE
         ACCEPTABLE WITH VALID EXPIRATION DATE AND
         CARDHOLDER NAME.

CANCELLATION/REVISION-
         MUST CANCEL OR REVISE BEFORE 4PM ON DAY OF ARRIVAL
         TO AVOID PENALTY.

CORPORATE RATE-
         SELL FROM AVAILABILITY AND INCLUDE GUESTS COMPANY
         NAME AND CITY IN SI-FIELD.

(continued)

FACILITIES-

-136 OVERSIZE ROOMS INCLUDING 26 SUITES. ALL ROOMS HAVE REFRIGERATORS AND COFFEE MAKERS / -SUITES ALL FEATURE KITCHENETTES.

-VIP FLOOR 9TH FEATURES MARBLE BATHROOMS WITH JACUZZI, HEATED TOWEL RACKS, BATHROBES.

-PERMANENT AND ROTATING ART EXHIBITS BY MAJOR AND UP AND COMING CONTEMPORARY ARTISTS.

-ROOFTOP TERRACE AND PENTHOUSE SUITE AVAILABLE FOR PRIVATE FUNCTIONS.

-NEARBY EXCELSIOR HEALTH CLUB AVAILABLE TO ADULT GUESTS FEATURES LAP POOL, AEROBIC MACHINES/CLASSES, WEIGHT EQUIPMENT, SUNDECK, COMPLIMENTARY BREAKFAST FROM 7AM TO 11AM.

-LILYS RESTAURANT AND BAR-WHIMSICAL, SURPRISING, ELEGANT, WAP-V. FLAMBOYANT, ENERGETIC, PLAYFUL-SERVES NEW AMERICAN ART CUISINE IN A CASUAL SETTING FROM 6AM TO 10PM.

SERVICES-

-COMPLIMENTARY CONTINENTAL BREAKFAST BUFFET INCLUDED IN RATE.

-24 HOUR ROOM SERVICE.

-ART EXHIBITIONS IN PUBLIC SPACE.

-WEEKDAY NEW YORK TIMES.

-PHOTOCOPY/SECRETARIAL SERVICE.

-EXERCISE AT NEARBY EXCELSIOR CLUB.

-CABLE TV WITH FREE.HBO/VIDEO RENTALS.

-WEEKEND PASSES TO MUSEUM OF MODERN ART OR GUGGENHEIM.

-FAMILY PLAN INCLUDES GIFTS FOR CHILDREN

-VALET PARKING.

-BABYSITTING.

-OVERNIGHT LAUNDRY SERVICE.

ATTRACTIONS-

ST. PATRICKS CATHEDRAL	4 BLOCKS
UNITED NATIONS	4 BLOCKS
CHRYSLER BUILDING	3 BLOCKS
MUSEUM OF MODERN ART	8 BLOCKS
THEATER DISTRICT/TIMES SQUARE	5 BLOCKS
JACOB JAVITS CONVENTION CENTER	1 MILE
MADISON AVE. SHOPPING	2 BLOCKS
GRAND CENTRAL TERMINAL	3 BLOCKS
CENTRAL PARK	15 BLOCKS
GUGGENHEIM MUSEUM	2.5 MILES

INDEXES-

	C	11W	0	LGA
	C	0	0	NYC
	C	17NW	0	JFK
	S	18NE	0	EWR
NY	C	ON	0	CENTRAL PARK
NY	C	OW	0	ST PATRICKS CATHEDRAL
NY	C	OE	0	UNITED NATIONS
NY	C	OS	0	CHRYSLER BUILDING
NY	C	OW	0	MUSEUM OF MODERN ART
NY	C	2N	0	GUGGENHEIM MUSEUM
NY	C	OSW	0	TIMES SQUARE
NY	C	OS	0	GRAND CENTRAL STATION

lem for the ordinary traveler. A good travel agent tries to ease this burden and may well earn the commission on this basis alone.

For some time, travel agents were considered necessary evils by both the airline and hotel industries. Managers felt that commissions were being paid for bookings that would have been received regardless. Supply-and-demand changes in the industry have brought a new significance to the role of this intermediary.

Working with Travel Agents

The travel agent needs clear, concise information on the product, and cooperation with the delivery of the product. The hotel company that can provide the least complicated products to the travel agent, and deliver them to the customer, will likely get the most bookings. The more agents have to decipher very difficult booking procedures, the less likely they are to recommend the facility in the future.

All rates and information furnished to travel agencies on a property need to be as current as possible. Travel agencies have their own customer bases, and will be blamed by their customers for poor service at a facility that they recommended. As one example, the fact that lengthy renovations are planned should be communicated to the travel agents before they hear it from their customers. The short-term loss of revenue from the agents' not booking the facility during the renovation period will appear small when compared with the possible customer dissatisfaction and loss of future bookings.

Cooperation with the agent consists also of paying commissions on a timely basis. The agency has performed the desired service of bringing the product through the channel of distribution. For that service, it needs to be paid. Because many agencies are small, cash flow is very important to their survival. A company or hotel can very quickly get the reputation of being slow or of not paying on commissions. Agencies will go out of their way to avoid recommending the property if they are not receiving their commissions. Contrarily, agents are quick to recommend those who pay commissions promptly.

Further, cooperation with travel agents includes upgrading their important clients at no extra charge, offering complimentary stays to allow them to experience the product firsthand, doing special promotions to gain their loyalty, and, in general, working with them in every way possible. To fail to do this is to bite the hand that feeds you. Hospitality companies today often market directly to the travel agent (Figure 18-14).

A familiarization trip (commonly referred to as **fam trips**) is a popular method used to expose the hotel product to intermediaries in the channel of distribution. A fam trip is just that; the hotel has a group of travel agents visit the facility to familiarize them with the features and benefits. Word-of-mouth advertising is the most believable form of communication. If travel agents are impressed with a facility during a fam trip, they will convey their enthusiasm to customers, and bookings will increase.

Travel agents are also reached through other distribution channels. Advertising in travel agent publications (e.g., *Travel Weekly*) is one such channel, but not necessarily a good one. Travel agents don't have time to read these carefully. Direct mail is another channel that suffers from the information overload syndrome. The best channels, without a doubt, make information readily available to travel agents when they need it. Computer technology is doing this for most. For others, there are worldwide publications such as *Hotel & Travel Index* and *Official Hotel Guide,* now available on CD-ROM, which list, in summary fashion, basic details about hotels—but only the computer or a phone call can provide up-to-the-minute rates.

Travel agents are as important worldwide as they are in the United States. In major destination areas such as Singapore, Hong Kong, and Manila, many agents operate as "inbound" agents—that is, they deal primarily with people coming into the country as opposed to those going out. This means setting up ground arrangements, hotel bookings, local tours, and so forth.

FIGURE 18-14 Westin markets directly to the travel agent.

In North America, travel agencies tend to be larger in size. This is because size is needed to handle the large accounts and negotiate the best arrangements, a necessary ability for being the agent of choice. Further, by banding together in consortia, groups of agencies have been able to bargain collectively with travel suppliers to gain access to preferred rates or other customer benefits. These are subsequently used as enticements to lure and retain business clientele, who could not obtain the same benefits on their own. Through the control of information, agents exert great influence in all segments of the travel market. Allied Percival International (API) is an example of a consortium of upscale travel agencies. API negotiates airline, hotel, and car rental rates on the basis of its combined travel expenditures among all of its participating members. Each member retains their autonomy while benefitting from volume negotiated rates.

Although nearly all U.S. travel agencies possess automated ticketing systems, they process only a small part of their room reservations via those systems. However, this percentage is increasing as the speed of a transaction becomes increasingly critical to an agency's profitability. Figure 18-15 is an ad offering a CRS systems access code, while Figure 18-16 offers hotel reservations through several global distribution system codes.

In fact, travel agents do not so much sell airline seats, hotel rooms, or rental cars as they sell time. A 10 percent commission on a $100 room is $10. A travel agent can access this hotel room through a GDS in three to seven seconds. If that same travel agent had to look up the property in a directory, dial the 800 number, get put on hold, speak to an agent, and then confirm the booking, they would make the same $10 for 10 minutes worth of work. In today's highly competitive environment, agencies that take 10 minutes for a $10 commission will not be in business very long.

FIGURE 18-15 Thistle, a hotel chain providing CRS access to agents.

FIGURE 18-16 Hotel reservations through several GDS codes.

The Travel Agency Future

Ironically, the technology that allows agencies to have access to an increasing volume of information is the same technology that threatens their existence. Once the technology is refined for easy adaptability on personal computers, the channel of distribution will become increasingly direct to the consumer. The new information highways being developed today may eliminate portions of the travel agents' business. No major hotel or chain can afford to ignore this channel and, in fact, in the United States a majority now have Web sites with direct booking ability.

Faxes are becoming a booking method of the past. The Internet has made great strides in the booking process. The lower rated brands, such as Days Inn, are being booked more often than Ritz-Carlton, but the progress is significant. There are companies on the Internet where a customer can set his or her own price for an airline seat, car rental, or hotel room. This company will offer the price to their travel partners, and confirm the booking. Personal computer-based reservation systems such as MailLink, PC Link, and Eaasy Sabre are catching on with business travelers, who like the security of making their own reservations and don't want to spend a lot of time on the telephone.

There are already over three million subscribers to Eaasy Sabre, the PC-based reservation service of AMR Corp., the parent company of American Airlines. Eaasy Sabre is accessed through public data networks such as CompuServe, Prodigy, and America OnLine and gives access to most of the information available to travel agents using the industrial strength Sabre computerized reservation system. Using Eaasy Sabre provides the added convenience of having tickets sent to you through a travel agent, delivered by overnight courier, or available to be picked up at the airport.

MailLink is an electronic mail-based version of TravelFax. PC Link is for stand-alone PC users. Both provide artificial intelligence software that takes a role in finding suitable travel arrangements. This software actually scans the schedules for the user and proposes several choices that fit his or her parameters. These systems are designed to complement the services of a travel agent when using normal type bookings. The future, however, may tell a different story.

Another phenomenon that is occurring in the travel agent world is the "super" travel agent. Take American Express. Through acquisitions, it has become the world's largest travel agency with nearly twice the volume of its nearest competitor. American Express also operates as a full-service tour operator. American Express corporate charge cards generate reams of travel data on everything from a corporate client's favorite carrier to its most frequented destination. This information is used when American Express bids for the company's travel account. Clients benefit from the company's massive purchasing power and its technological sophistication.

Finally, there are more and more Internet companies like bestfares.com and quikbook.com where one can find all kinds of discounts that threaten travel agencies, as well as websites for many hospitality firms. Table 18-5 shows just a few. Personally, however, at least at this time, we have found it far easier, faster, and no more expensive to stick with a good travel agent. We cover today's fast moving technology more thoroughly in Appendix B.

TOUR OPERATORS AND WHOLESALERS

Tour operators differ from their counterparts in channel management options in that they take nominal possession, or secure an allotment, of the hotel inventory to sell it to the public. Tour operators may also take nominal possession of the food and beverage product, by making reservations in a number of outlets at anticipated tour destination points. They may also arrange for ground transportation, side trips, historical site visits, and so on. There are two types of tour operators—wholesalers or tour brokers, and **"ad hoc"** or **series** tour operators. Generally, they all work through travel agent retailers. The word "tour" should not be construed as necessarily meaning groups. These channels book as many, or more, individuals and couples.

The wholesaler or broker blocks space and then uses various combinations of the communications and distribution mixes to market the facilities to individual and group consumers. Brochures featuring a tour, or multiple tours, and all related accommodations are printed and distributed to travel agents or mailed to existing and potential customers, usually on request. The consumer picks up a brochure at a travel agency (an example is shown in Figure 18-17), or responds to an ad.

Advertising in the print media is also a common practice to attract tour customers. Consider, for example, the Liberty Travel ad in Figure 18-18. The

T A B L E   18-5
Websites for a Selected List of Hospitality Organizations (all preceded by www.)

Barbados	barbados.org
British Virgin Islands	bviwelcome.com
Canada Tourism	canadatourism.com
Cayman Islands	caymanislands.ky
Cruising Agency	cruising.org
Cruise World	cruiseworld.com
Four Seasons	fourseasons.com
Greenbrier Hotel	greenbrier.com
Hawaiian Airlines	hawaiianair.com
Hilton Hotels	hilton.com
Jamaica	jamaicatravel.com
Leading Hotels of the World	lhw.com
Mandarin Oriental Hotels	mandarinoriental.com
Marriott Hotels	marriott.com
Mauna Lani Bay Hotel	maunalani.com
Mirage Resorts	mirageresorts.com
Nikko Hotels	nikkohotels.com
Perillo Tours	perillotours.com
Quantas Airline	quantas.com
Renaissance Hotels	renaissancehotels.com
Ritz-Carlton Hotels	ritzcarlton.com
Shangri-La Hotels	Shangri-La.com
Singapore Airlines	singaporeair.com/americas
Waldorf Towers	waldorf-towers.com
Westin Hotels & Resorts	westin.com

part shown is less than half of a full page ad that Liberty Travel runs weekly on the back page of the Sunday New York Times Travel Section with various destinations and promotions. The small box for Hyatt hotels in the Caribbean is paid for by Hyatt. The rest of the page is paid for by American Airlines, other advertised destinations, and Liberty Travel. Hyatt spends about 2 percent of its wholesaler revenue in the Caribbean on this type of advertising. This wholesale market is 30 percent of total rooms and 40 percent of FIT business for Hyatt in this destination. This activity, for Hyatt, does not really fall into the realm of advertising as discussed in Chapter 15. Nothing is stated but the name, location, and price. The activity flows through the distribution

FIGURE 18-17   Aristos, a tour operator and wholesaler cooperative effort.

channels of the wholesaler, in this case GoGo Tours, and the retailer, in this case, Liberty Travel.

GoGo Tours does millions of dollars of business in the Caribbean, as well as elsewhere. It takes an allotment of rooms from Hyatt, for example, at 20 percent off Hyatt's gross rate, in different rate categories, with cutoff time periods to sell them. Other wholesalers work on a "sell and report" basis, that is, they report sales only after they are made, free of a cutoff time. The hotel advises sellout periods. GoGo's inventory appears in the computers of 170 Liberty Travel agencies. GoGo also sells rooms for American Express under its private label. The rooms are sold by travel agents at their regular rates, as if they called the hotel directly. Hyatt, of course, has paid GoGo a commission. GoGo pays a commission to the travel agent. Hyatt pays for the ad and has its own reservations system that books the rooms. Of course, other Hyatt advertising or experience complements this channel.

The wholesaler market includes people using a variety of transportation options. The wholesaler negotiates with the airlines, cruise lines, railroads, hotels, car rentals, and bus companies to develop travel options to be resold as a total package.

Groups come from every realm of the spectrum, from a high school hockey team to an upscale corporate trip to the Super Bowl, to individual travelers. Wholesalers negotiate the best possible deals from the suppliers and then sell at a price to include their profit margins. Figure 18-19 shows a hotel advertising directly to tour operators.

International wholesalers exist both domestically and abroad. Domestic wholesalers under the umbrella of, for instance, "Visit USA" are called inbound operators; they handle tours and groups organized overseas, and manage their customers' travel needs while in the United States. Their outbound counterparts handle the reverse travel internationally. This is true of all countries serving international markets.

Ad hoc groups are organizations that are already formed and want to book a tour to a previously visited or new destination. An example of an ad hoc group would include a Lions Club tour to the Ozarks in Arkansas, or an archaeology club trip to Mexico. The tour operator again takes possession of the inventory of hotel rooms and restaurant seats, but the risk is much lower because a solid booking is in place. A series group, on the

FIGURE 18-18　Liberty Travel advertises the wholesaler and retailer business.

other hand, might be a solicited group of couples or retirees that want to tour the French vineyards.

The tour operator needs the full cooperation of channel members to be successful. Ad hoc groups are the least complicated to administer. The wholesale tours, on the other hand, are very risky; some hotels and restaurants have strict cancellation guidelines and, if the tour doesn't sell, the wholesaler can end up holding a large perishable inventory.

Good channel management can work two ways. If a wholesale tour broker is attempting to coordinate a tour series to a destination, the hotels and restaurants should remain flexible to help in the development of the distribution network. The fall foliage season in New England may not be the time to help a channel member create a new series, since demand for the hotel product at that time exceeds the supply of hotel rooms. If the wholesaler is attempting to bring in business in a less busy time, such as spring, every attempt should be made to

encourage the effort. Short-term decisions regarding cancellation clauses could prejudice an active channel member in the future.

The other side of the coin is that, in times when business is slow, the tour operator will wield clout to obtain the lowest possible rates. In heavy destination areas such as the Algarve coast in Portugal, where extensive overbuilding has occurred, British tour operators have bargained for tens of thousands of room nights to bring room rates down to ridiculously low levels.

INTERNET CHANNELS

The Internet is the latest technological distribution channel advance in direct booking with hotel companies. We discuss this further in Appendix B on technology.

ORLANDO

THE REAL MAGIC IS SELECTING A HOTEL LIKE THIS AT A REASONABLE RATE

You Deliver The Guests, We'll Deliver As Promised

Next time you're booking a Central Florida tour, don't leave anything to chance. Book a **Sure Tour** at the Clarion Plaza Hotel. We'll provide confirmation in one working day, *guaranteed* group room rates, group pre-registration and pre-key, complimentary room and meals for tour escort and driver, and much more! Located in the middle of the attraction action, this exceptional vacation destination features: • Complete guest services • Location 1 mile from Sea World, 10 minutes from Walt Disney World® Resort, 5 minutes from Universal Studios • 5 restaurants & lounges • 24-hour deli • Nightclub with live entertainment • Large, tropical heated pool • Game Room • Ample parking for buses • And much more!

Contact our sales office at 1-800-366-9700

Clarion Plaza Hotel
Orlando

9700 International Dr., Orlando, FL 32819-8114 • (407) 352-9700 • FAX (407) 351-9111

FIGURE 18-19 Clarion Hotel advertises to tour operators.

STRATEGIES FOR DISTRIBUTION CHANNELS

There are two major strategies for increasing usage of the product in a distribution channel. These are the "push" strategy and the "pull" strategy, which we have previously discussed in Chapter 15. To refresh your memory, in the pull strategy, inducements are offered to make the consumer want to "pull" the product down the channel or, conversely, the company pulls the customer up through the channel. Examples of pull strategies in the hospitality industry are the frequent traveler programs. With these promotions, the customer presumably has an increased desire for the product and seeks the appropriate distribution channel.

The push strategy acts in the opposite way, by giving the incentive to the channel member (e.g., the travel agent) to sell the product to the consumer. An example of a push strategy would be to offer a 20 percent commission on all bookings made during a low-demand time period. At twice the normal commission, the travel agent has a reason to push the product over another that may be offering a lower commission. Certain incentives, such as free rooms, free airfare to destinations, and in some instances cash bonuses, have come into use. As competition for channel members' business becomes more intense, we expect the incentives of the push strategy to increase proportionately.

Promotional Tie-Ins

This category of strategies is the catchall for the burgeoning attempts of the industry to expand its market base through intermediaries. Under this umbrella lies the couponing utilized by restaurants and hotels alike. The numerous dining clubs sprouting up throughout the country present a good example of the promotional tie-in channel of distribution. In this method, a number of restaurants participate in a dining club, whereby the intermediary organization prints, markets, and distributes the coupons representing everything from a free dessert to a two-for-one dinner offering. Hotel companies have been represented by various coupon organizations, primarily selling a 50 percent discount off rack or corporate rate to their members, often but not necessarily on weekends and during slow periods. With today's rampant discounting, this, like some car rental discounts, is often not a good deal. One can often negotiate for less, but the coupon buyer customer usually doesn't know this.

Another area of tie-ins for hotels are the airlines. A majority of airline customers eventually become hotel customers. Hotels work with the airline to arrange specific marketing packages to mutual destinations. Now, the channel of distribution grows longer. After the hotel enters an agreement for distribution with an airline, a second channel member, the travel agent, or tour operator, moves in. Each intermediary, while offering new customers, takes a commission.

Hotel and rental car companies are by necessity integrating with the airline reservations systems. By combining technology, these channel members present a unique opportunity to the customers (in this case, travel agents) to take advantage of "one-stop shopping." Through direct access to global distributions systems, agents can make the flight arrangements, get a rental car, and book a sleeping room without ever using the telephone, as we have shown.

None of this channel participation is without cost. Without constant supervision and evaluation, channels of distribution can sometimes become cost-prohibitive. For example, "super-saver" room rates could indeed bring in less than the cost of the channel of distribution. At $49, the commissions paid to the airline network, the travel agent, the contribution to the advertising, the contribution to the frequent traveler plan, and the franchise fee could bring the net revenue to below the cost of providing the service!

Selecting the Channel of Distribution

Selection of the distribution channels is important. The length of the channel needs to be analyzed. In no uncertain terms, shorter is better; the longer the channel of distribution, the more potential problems arise for the management of that channel.

By short or long we refer to the number of intermediaries in the channel. Each intermediary has to make a profit and each one involves some measure of coordination. Therefore, the fewer middlemen involved, the more profit and the less chance for errors. At some point there may seem to be a need to add on channels. If the new intermediary can be reasonably expected to bring in more customers at a profit for the originator, the channel should probably be expanded. If the channel member cannot deliver the needed number of customers and the profit, the decision should be negative.

Vertical Integration

When a company becomes its own supplier of products, it becomes vertically integrated, as in the Nouvelles Frontières example given earlier. This type of distribution needs a large amount of capital to be successful, and this strategy should be considered only if the potential for success is somewhat assured. Another good example in the hospitality industry is Carlson Companies, Inc., shown in Figure 18-20.

Carlson consists of four groups: Carlson Wagonlit Travel, an international network of travel agencies and tour operators; Carlson Marketing, a promotional and incentive group; Carlson Hospitality,

which includes hotels and restaurants and the Radisson Diamond cruise ships; and Carlson Leisure, offering various travel services. Both the Carlson Travel Group and the Marketing Group feed reservations to the hotels and the cruise ships. All customers of the Carlson Travel Network are encouraged to stay in Radisson Hotels in all of the relevant destinations. If a customer has a firm preference for an alternative hotel, however, the travel agency will certainly book that reservation. All this gives Carlson tremendous clout in the travel industry. In a vertically integrated channel of distribution such as this, the company becomes its own source of business.

INTERNATIONAL MARKETS

By and large, certain distribution channels are more heavily relied upon by international hotel companies in foreign lands than in their own home country. Markets are drawn from many geographical areas with many cultural differences as well as different needs and wants. Reaching these markets fully and efficiently by advertising and/or direct selling is cost-prohibitive.

CARLSON HOSPITALITY WORLDWIDE	CARLSON WAGONLIT TRAVEL	CARLSON MARKETING GROUP	CARLSON LEISURE GROUP
Hotels	Carlson Wagonlit Corporate Card	Performance Improvement	Carlson Wagonlit Travel Associates, Inc.
Regent International Hotels	ActOne™ Travel & Expense Management System	Loyalty Marketing	A.T. Mays (U.K.)
Radisson Hotels Worldwide	Carlson Wagonlit Travel Business Advisory Services	Event & Sports Marketing	Carlson Travel Academies
Country Inns & Suites By Carlson		Direct Marketing	Neiman Marcus Travel Services
Restaurants			Carlson Leisure Group U.K.
T.G.I. Fridays			Carlson Vacations
Front Row Sports Grill			Samsonite Travel Expo
Italianni's			Carlson Destination Marketing Services
Friday's American Bar			
Cruise Operations			
Radisson Seven Seas Cruises			
Carlson Hospitality Worldwide	Carlson Wagonlit	Carlson Marketing Group	Carlson Leisure Group

FIGURE 18-20 Carlson is a vertically integrated company.

Hotel companies need someone in local markets who knows the market, knows its needs and wants, knows how to reach it, knows how to communicate with it, and knows how to sell it. Not all countries enjoy full toll-free telephone dialing; thus many companies in other countries depend more on consortia, referral agencies, travel agencies, wholesalers, and brokers for business. As one example, Sol Melia Hotels in Spain relies on wholesalers for 95 percent of their room sales in their resort properties. Most hotels on the Algarve coastline in Portugal, or the beach resort areas in Turkey, do likewise.

Consider southeast Asia: Huge numbers of tourists come to this part of the world as part of tours or on individual travel packages from Europe, North America, Australia, and Japan. Consider Europe, where the largest outside markets are North America and Japan. Consider South America, which draws its bulk business from North America and Europe.

While wholesale distribution channels are essential to international markets, they also cause problems. First of all, channel operators want bargain rates for their clients and often have the clout to get them, as we discussed at the beginning of the chapter. Second, they want commissions. Third, they often make promises that are difficult for properties to fulfill and for which the hotels will subsequently be blamed. Fourth, they can be manipulative. For example, some wholesalers will boycott a hotel if that hotel does business with another wholesaler. When the wholesaler cannot deliver all the business that the hotel needs, the hotel is in a difficult position.

Nevertheless, heavy use of distribution channels is necessary and a fact of life in international markets. Channel members are brought to the destination to see it and be sold on it. These are expenses that have to be absorbed. Even when channel members come on their pleasure trips, large discounts are granted as a matter of routine.

Along with this trend, aiding and abetting it, is vast improvement in the distribution system in Asia. Nineteen thousand travel agency outlets across the Asia/Pacific control upward of $52 billion in sales each year and the number is increasing. Except in Japan, the market is largely controlled by small to mid-sized independents. Most are single location offices, especially in Hong Kong and the Philippines. Although most of Asian agencies use CRS systems, only a pittance of hotel reservations are made that way. Most are still made by telephone or fax directly with local reservations offices or hotels.

International franchising is also used by multinational companies to increase their distribution network. McDonald's, Burger King, Dairy Queen, and Denny's all have international franchisees. Although these franchisees essentially maintain the product line of the franchisor, they may make local adaptations. For example, Denny's serves ginger pork and curried rice in Japan; McDonald's serves wine in France, mutton burgers in India, and beetroot in Austria (and actually sells the catsup for its hamburgers); and Dairy Queen offers a type of bread called roti, and a fried vegetable and meat dish in the Middle East. Many hotel companies manage, franchise, and form strategic alliances internationally, as well, as we discussed earlier.

CHANNEL MANAGEMENT

Good channel management stems from the formulation of a good working relationship among channels from the start. All agreements pertaining to the workings of the channel should be in writing and should be updated as conditions periodically change. There is rarely an all-win situation. If a channel member is not deriving some reasonable value from the network, that member will not participate actively, and distribution will eventually become more difficult and more costly.

For example, a hotel could develop a good working relationship with a representative firm for marketing of the property. The representative firm then markets the hotel through sales calls, brochures, direct mail, and so on. A booking results, and a commission becomes due. If the hotel begins to dispute the validity of the origination of the bookings, or delays the payment, the relationship within the channel of distribution becomes ineffective. The representative firm will not be anxious to market the facility in the future, and will spend its time selling more cooperative hotels. This becomes a no-win situation. The hotel is dissatisfied with the productivity of the channel member, and the representative firm will move on to more lucrative endeavors.

Each channel member seeks to create customers for a profit, but without some give-and-take on a regular basis by all channel members the system becomes tedious and disruptive. The hospitality firms that have carefully selected their partners and are managing them well will be consistently increasing their customer base while others are looking for new channel members.

Evaluation of the Channel

This step is critical for the continued success of any program. If a hospitality entity is unable to tell how many bookings a representative firm produced, or how many coupons were turned in from the dining guide, then intelligent channel management is impossible. Often, channel members can report the statistics. If unit management is unable at least to spot check these numbers, the channel member will be in control when it comes time to negotiate the next agreement.

For example, the hotel that engages in a channel agreement with an airline sets an objective. The objective needs to be set in a quantitative format, to be used in the evaluation process. The success of the channel of distribution might be defined as raising the productivity of the airline reservation service from 100 rooms per month to 120 per month.

It is also beneficial to understand the break-even point of the channel. In the above example, it might take an additional ten rooms per month to cover the additional commissions and some combined advertising costs. After a predetermined amount of time, the channel is evaluated. If it is producing less than 110 rooms per month, careful

consideration might be given to either increasing the marketing support for the program or dropping the channel member completely.

Evaluation is more than just a tally of dinner covers or room nights. A channel may be driving the volume, but if the customer is unhappy, the effort is not only shortsighted but dangerous.

A dining guide can market a two-for-one dinner promotion in a number of different ways. If customers expect two lobsters for the price of one when making reservations, and find out the promotion applies only to chicken, they will be sincerely disappointed. If hotel guests were expecting deluxe accommodations, and agreement with the channel member was to offer a run-of-the-house rooms, the guests who get the inferior rooms will not be happy with their purchase. They may not be unhappy enough to complain but, still worse, they may be unhappy enough not to come back.

The marketing-driven company with good channel management skills will ensure their customer satisfaction throughout the process. If a channel member is producing customers that are consistently unhappy, it would be better never to have used that distribution method in the first place.

During channel management, two ongoing factors are needed to ensure continued success. These are motivation and recruitment. For motivation, it must be recognized that most channel members are carrying many similar products into the marketplace. Travel agents have a variety of hotels and airfares from which to choose. The representative firms have several hotels in their portfolio that match the needs of their customers. The number of promotional tie-ins available to both the consumers and the channel members are mind-boggling. Franchising options for the developers and independent managers are plentiful.

Motivation

Some type of motivation must be continuously offered by the channel leader in order to promote continued success. Unless the product offered is so desirable that there are several channel members bidding on the rights to carry it, motivational techniques are necessary.

The push strategies mentioned earlier are the primary source of motivational support for channel members. Incentive trips for outstanding travel agents or the best franchisee in the system will go a long way toward smoothing operating channels of distribution. Many companies in the consumer goods and industrial products industries have full-time staff members who do nothing but organize and implement channel incentives in order to keep members interested in their products.

Incentives need not be in the form of travel. Consumer goods such as appliances and televisions can make the bonus system easier to attain, and provide short-term gratification for participants. The drawback of the magnificent incentive trip to Europe may be that it takes a year to win, and only a very few employees will ever have a chance to collect the prize.

Although the motivational options available are almost unlimited, an area that also needs attention is that of top management. All of the sales representatives can win trips and toasters, but the president of the company is often ignored. Travel agency owners do not need toasters and trips; what they need is the personal attention that allows their views to surface to someone important. An invitation to dinner by a senior executive of the hospitality company may buy more loyalty than 1000 toasters. Too often, in the rush to motivate a channel member, the owner of the business is left out of the process.

Recruitment

The second ongoing task for the channel manager is to recruit potential new channel members. If this task is not organized and planned, the channel is in perpetual danger. Unfortunately, the danger is subtle because a company may not realize that it is exposed until a member drops out. For example, a travel agency may be one of your best producers in the Florida market. It sends an unusually high number of guests to your hotel because it has done a good job marketing your facility, and has built up a good clientele.

One day the travel agent calls and says it is dropping your facility in favor of your competition down the street. Immediately the reservations slip and business starts falling. This scenario is very realistic for a number of managers. First, the competitor had a good recruitment program in place and replaced its channel member with yours, thereby improving its distribution network overnight. Second, without having had a good recruitment program of its own, your hotel now has to begin the process of finding a strong replacement channel member. As you are now in dire need, the negotiations will swing in favor of the potential new channel member.

There will always be times that a channel member leaves and/or needs to be replaced. This is part of doing business. However, a good channel manager will have alternatives ready and prescreened according to the criteria mentioned earlier in the chapter.

Recruitment is also necessary to provide alternatives to channel members who are not performing satisfactorily. It is far easier to deal with an unsatisfactory situation once you have other options than to have to recruit channel members when at a disadvantage.

Summary

Distribution systems are methods of marketing a hospitality entity that are gaining greater acceptance in an increasingly competitive environment. In a business where the product is perishable and where production and consumption are simultaneous, we need to find many ways to allow customers to easily purchase our products and services.

Geographic distribution strategies such as management contracts, franchising, and strategic alliances allow a firm to enter markets without incurring large capital investment and financial risk. However, firms can lose operational control by lending their names to franchisees all over the world. Regardless, geographical distribution means being in the right places.

Consortia, affiliations, reservations networks, and representation firms bring the customer to the product, especially in faraway places. Incentive houses, travel agents, and tour operators are intermediaries who distribute hospitality services to customers and also bring them to the product.

The backbone of any channel of distribution is channel management. Any marketing-driven organization will take the time to evaluate its current distribution system and organize a cohesive plan for improvement. A competent channel manager should then be assigned to monitor and consistently reevaluate the network to obtain the maximum benefits to the company. This channel manager may take the form of the Director of Sales, the General Manager, or the Resident Manager at the unit level of the hotel. The corporate marketing office should assume responsibility for the chain-wide agreements. Finally, the satisfaction of the consumer is the true test of a channel's success. Without this, none of the steps outlined above are productive or needed.

For hotels, at least, channel management is a far more productive and critical part of the marketing mix today than advertising.

KEY WORDS AND CONCEPTS

Ad hoc Groups: Organizations already formed that book tours.

Affiliation: A group of hotels that carry the same common name, not necessarily in the same product class, or that affiliate with another group, also with a same common name.

Code Sharing: An airline term where different airlines in an alliance can access each other's flight schedules to plan seamless trips for passengers.

Consortium: A group of individual properties with different names that carry a common designation that groups them into the same product class.

Economies of Scope: These occur when two or more business units share resources such as distribution systems, especially reservations, and advertising.

Fam Trip: A familiarization trip for travel agents at low or no cost to introduce them to products.

Feeder City/Country: A geographic location that regularly feeds customers into another city or cities, country or countries.

Global Distribution System (GDS): A computerized reservations system that includes airline, hotels, ground services, and so on, most often used by travel agents.

Intermediaries: Go-betweens that bring the customer and the property together, for example, travel agents, tour operators.

Reflagging: A colloquial industry term for changing management or franchise names.

Representation (Rep) Companies: These companies have sales offices and market to represent different properties under different names.

Reservations Company: Members carry their own names, or chain names, but use a common reservation system, as well as their own.

Series Groups: Various people brought together to form a travel group.

Territorial Rights: The area in a franchise agreement in which the franchisee has the exclusive right to operate properties.

Vertical Integration: When a company makes and sells its own products, it is called backwards or upstream vertical integration. When it controls the use of the product, it is called forward or downstream vertical integration. When it does both, it is called fully vertically integrated.

DISCUSSION QUESTIONS

1. Discuss the advantages and disadvantages of franchising as a method of increasing the channels of distribution.

2. Discuss the similarities and dissimilarities

among consortia, affiliations, reservations networks, and representation firms.

3. Why are channels of distribution inherently different for the hospitality industry than for goods industries?

4. Describe the difference between a push and a pull strategy. When might it be best to use one instead of the other?

5. What are the most important criteria for choosing a channel member and why? Discuss the ramifications.

6. Describe ways and means of motivating channel members and their significance.

7. Why do some hotel companies franchise aggressively, while others not at all?

8. Research the internet websites of five hotel companies. Compare the information provided in terms of effectiveness as a distribution channel.

9. Research the internet websites of an airline, car rental company, and hotel company. Which site makes it easiest to make a reservation, and why?

GROUP PROJECTS

1. Assume your group has a small chain, but growing, of 15 upscale 300-room hotels in 3 countries. Through the Web and internet, compare reservations systems and their cost and effectiveness and determine which system or systems you would use.

2. As hotels have their systems as discussed in this chapter, develop a distribution channel or channels for a restaurant chain with 300 units across the country. Does it make sense?

REFERENCES

1. Harold E. Lane and Denise Dupré, *Hospitality World.* New York: Van Nostrand Reinhold, 1997, p. 350.

2. Ibid. pp. 367–369.

3. Taken from various industry sources, 1999.

MARKETING INTELLIGENCE AND RESEARCH

Overview

This appendix details some marketing intelligence needs of the industry to lay the basis for data collection and research purpose. The greater portion deals with research problems and the research process. By no means is this appendix exhaustive of the topic. Rather it serves more as an introduction to it, or as a refresher. The full treatment can be found in numerous marketing research textbooks.

INFORMATION ACQUISITION This section briefly discusses sources of both external and internal information and information needs.

DESIGNING THE MARKET INTELLIGENCE SYSTEM Setting up a marketing information system is discussed and a model presented showing sources, output, and use.

MARKETING RESEARCH Conducting such research is a way to discover consumers real needs, wants, problems, and demands.

FORMAL MARKETING RESEARCH This section explains the scientific method as well as the different forms of research investigation, including qualitative and quantitative and broad types of data.

THE RESEARCH DESIGN This controls the research process. This section lists some desired objectives and research areas to use to reach them, both critical in setting up the research design.

THE RESEARCH PROCESS This section provides a model and discussion of the entire research process from deciding on the purpose to analyzing the findings.

RESEARCH FINDINGS Questions of validity and reliability must be answered to valuate the research.

USEFUL RESEARCH Some ideas of appropriate usages in hospitality.

Good intelligence is the basis of good marketing decisions. This is not to say that some smart decisions have not been made on intuition alone, but for every one that has, there have probably been a few hundred others that have failed. The world is changing fast and so is the consumer, who has many more choices. This means that marketers also have many more choices. Choices mean decisions, and making more decisions means acquiring more information, even if only to verify intuitive thought. The quality of the decision depends on the quality of the information and how it is used. All the information in the world will not lead to the right decision if it is not properly interpreted and used.

Marketing intelligence flows from many different directions. The trick is to get it routed in the right direction and in a form that is accurate and most useful. At the same time there is the problem of information overload—that is, being bombarded with so much information that it is difficult to sort out what is relevant and what is not. In this appendix, we discuss information sources, as well as their relevance to marketing decisions.

As with many other subject areas in this text, marketing intelligence is not restricted to one chapter. In fact, much of the discussion throughout the text has been about the use of information that is needed to make marketing decisions or to handle marketing problems. One of the best sources of marketing intelligence comes from the customer. That area was covered in Chapter 3 as an important area of relationship marketing. Environmental scanning, discussed in Chapter 5, is another area where intelligence is critical to marketing decisions. Chapter 6 dealt with the use of intelligence for competitive analysis. Chapter 15 discussed research for the communications mix. Chapter 18 pointed out the importance of intelligence received through distribution channels. Both strategic planning and developing the marketing plan, discussed in Chapters 5 and 7, also are framed in the context of intelligence sources.

In this appendix we deal more specifically with intelligence needs and how to meet them.

Essentially, we break down the sources of marketing intelligence into three major areas: the external environment, the internal environment, and formal marketing research.

INFORMATION ACQUISITION

External Information

External information flows through distribution channels, competitors, suppliers, and various local, state, and national agencies and associations, as well as the marketplace. Acquiring some of this is simply statistical data gathering; some goes under the name of research. The question is what data is relevant. There is often a mass of external and **secondary data,** that is, data collected for some other purpose, available.

Distribution channels that can provide information include travel agencies, reservation systems, credit card systems, tour brokers, wholesalers, and so forth. Competitors themselves are a source of information. Besides the sharing of occupancy figures, some hoteliers read others' **reader boards,** call for room rates and/or reservations, and even go so far as to book rooms. Some hotels have their sales reps spend nights each year in competitive hotels and rate the hotels on different attributes relative to their own hotel. These analyses are used to determine the price/value relationship for each competitor, and thus to develop pricing and positioning strategies.

Both hotels and restaurants employ **mystery shoppers.** Restaurateurs eat in each other's restaurants and make comparisons. Suppliers are a great source of information, especially in the restaurant business where they have firsthand information on just how well various restaurant operations are doing. Customers can also reveal a great deal of information about the competition to which they go. Finally, there are government agencies and hotel and restaurant associations. Municipal, state, and federal governments and/or tourist boards all collect readily available information including lists of airport arrivals, out-of-state visitors, countries or states of origin, purpose of travel, length of stay, or whatever.

In the United States, Smith Travel Research is just one hotel research firm that gathers data from hotels all over the country, as we showed in Chapter 6. CREST (Consumer Reports in Eating Share Trends) of Chicago collects data and tracking reports on restaurant chains and different styles of restaurants from fast-food to gourmet. Anderson Consulting, KPMG Peat Marwick, PricewaterhouseCooper, Pannell Kerr Forster, and numerous other consulting/accounting firms, as well as financial analysts, collect data, do research, venture opinions, and publish annual reports drawn from trends and financial data of their clients. Some of this information, in a limited fashion, is available on the Internet. More detailed and complete information is stored in databases, called data warehousing, and is available to subscribers for a fee.

Much of this information is broad-based and may or may not be specifically useful other than for spotting trends and making comparisons. The same is true of the data available from private firms that do research for open publication. But the information is readily available (www.hotel-online.com on the Web gives daily updates on reports from many of these organizations) and can be helpful in keeping industry people informed of what is going on. In foodservice, the National Restaurant Association (NRA) in the United States (www.restaurant.org) provides considerable and current information.

Internal Information

The hospitality industry as a whole has access to more information about its customers than perhaps any other industry in the world. Thus it is somewhat surprising how little is known about those customers. Of course, there is the standard information that most operators gather: occupancy, average room rate, average check, frequently ordered items, and so forth, but the opportunity to know

more about the customer is too often left unseized. This is particularly true considering the huge databases acquired by some companies through their frequent guest programs. These databases, probably the most commendable part of frequent guest programs, are still widely underutilized.

Internal information is obtained by hotels from their guests by placing **comment cards** in rooms or, as also used by restaurants, on restaurant tables or at the cash register (Figure A-1). These cards have their best use in spotting operational breakdowns and complaint trends. Due to the fact that in many hotels, returned comment cards come from less than 1 percent of the occupied rooms, their use for drawing clear conclusions is quite problematic. Due to this self-selected nature of the respondents, guest responses cannot be used as representative, reliable, or valid evaluations against which service standards can be established.

Hotel executives should also know about customer satisfaction, guest history, repeat business, likes and dislikes, idiosyncracies, willingness to return, and many other things about customers. Restaurateurs should know about what items will sell, what their repeat customer ratio is, or why people don't order dessert, preferred seating and, again, many other things. It is clear that information systems in these areas are lacking in many operations. Some hotel companies, like Marriott and Sheraton, do follow up on their guests with a randomly selected sample by mailing surveys to their homes or businesses shortly after their stay, but these are the exceptions, not the rule, and much good information that could be obtained is not. Others collect information sporadically. This is changing, however, as more and more hotel companies use outside research firms to collect customer data. Says Mark Albion, marketing professor at Harvard Business School:

> Mass marketing is no longer the most effective or cost-efficient way to sell. Most companies have to aim their products at more discrete segments of the population. To do that right, you can't know too much about the customer.[1]

1. OVERALL, How would you rate your stay with us?
   Excellent　Good　Fair　Poor　☐ ☐ ☐ ☐

2. What was the primary purpose of your visit?
   Business ☐　　Meeting/Convention ☐
   Banqueting ☐　　Pleasure ☐

3. Was your reservation in order on check in?
   Yes ☐　　No ☐

4. How would you rate the following?
   Excellent　Good　Fair　Poor
   Check in speed/efficiency ☐ ☐ ☐ ☐
   Luggage Porter assistance to/from room ☐ ☐ ☐ ☐
   Cleanliness of room on first entering ☐ ☐ ☐ ☐
   Check out speed/efficiency ☐ ☐ ☐ ☐

5. How would you rate the following in terms of their friendly and efficient service?
   Excellent　Good　Fair　Poor
   Reservation Staff ☐ ☐ ☐ ☐
   Reception Staff ☐ ☐ ☐ ☐
   Concierge Staff ☐ ☐ ☐ ☐
   Luggage Porters ☐ ☐ ☐ ☐
   Housekeeping ☐ ☐ ☐ ☐
   Telephone Operator ☐ ☐ ☐ ☐
   Valet ☐ ☐ ☐ ☐
   Health Club Consultants ☐ ☐ ☐ ☐
   Maintenance Staff ☐ ☐ ☐ ☐

   OVERALL SERVICE
   Please tell us about any staff member who was especially helpful so that we may tell them of your appreciation.
   _____
   _____
   _____
   Additional Comments: _____
   _____

HOUSEKEEPING

6. Was your room kept neat and tidy during your stay?
   Yes ☐　　No ☐

7. Was your bed turned down and your room refreshed each evening to your satisfaction?
   Yes ☐　　No ☐
   Additional Comments: _____

8. ROOM SERVICE
   Breakfast ☐　Lunch ☐　Dinner ☐　Supper ☐
   Excellent　Good　Fair　Poor
   Timeliness of Delivery ☐ ☐ ☐ ☐
   Courtesy/efficiency of Waiter ☐ ☐ ☐ ☐
   Quality of Food and Beverage ☐ ☐ ☐ ☐
   Value for Money ☐ ☐ ☐ ☐

RESTAURANTS AND LOUNGES:

9. Please rate the Restaurants and Lounge that you visited
   Restaurant No. 1 _____
   Breakfast ☐　Lunch ☐　Dinner ☐
   Excellent　Good　Fair　Poor
   Service ☐ ☐ ☐ ☐
   Food Quality ☐ ☐ ☐ ☐
   Menu Variety ☐ ☐ ☐ ☐
   Value for Money ☐ ☐ ☐ ☐

   Restaurant No. 2 _____
   Breakfast ☐　Lunch ☐　Dinner ☐
   Excellent　Good　Fair　Poor
   Service ☐ ☐ ☐ ☐
   Food Quality ☐ ☐ ☐ ☐
   Menu Variety ☐ ☐ ☐ ☐
   Value for Money ☐ ☐ ☐ ☐
   Comments: _____

HEALTH CLUB

10. Did you use the Health Club facilities during your stay?
    Yes ☐　　No ☐

11. To what degree did the Health Club live up to your expectations?
    Excellent　Good　Fair　Poor　☐ ☐ ☐ ☐
    Comments: _____
    _____

BANQUETS/MEETINGS:

12. Did you attend a banquet or meeting during your stay?
    Yes ☐　　No ☐
    If yes, which one? _____
    Breakfast ☐　Lunch ☐　Dinner ☐　Meeting only ☐

13. 　　　　　　　　　　　Excellent　Good　Fair　Poor
    Quality of Food and Beverage ☐ ☐ ☐ ☐
    Efficiency of Service ☐ ☐ ☐ ☐
    Friendliness of Waiting Staff ☐ ☐ ☐ ☐

    GENERAL COMMENTS _____
    _____
    _____
    _____

14. Have you stayed with us before?
    Yes ☐　　No ☐

15. Based on your experience, would you return to us on future visits to London?
    Yes ☐　　No ☐
    Please print or attach Business Card.
    Name: Mr Mrs Ms _____
    Address: _____
    _____
    _____
    Company: _____
    Phone: (Home) _____
    (Office) _____
    Room Number: _____ Dates of stay: _____

FIGURE A-1 A guest comment card.

Yet, consider this:

No one knows you better than Mom. But does she know how many undershorts you own? Jockey International does.

Or the number of ice cubes you put in a glass? Coca-Cola does. Or how about which you eat first, the broken pretzels in a pack or the whole ones? Try asking Frito-Lay.[2]

Neal Geller of Cornell Hotel School conducted research on hotel managers' information needs. He found they had many that were not being fulfilled, and concluded:

The guest is *in* the hotel [restaurant]. He or she made a reservation (or walked in), registered, pro-

vided credit evidence, is beginning to accrue charges, and will eventually settle the bill and check out. The idea is to use all these processes to obtain the marketing data needed, and to do so in a way that creates the smallest amount of inconvenience to the guest. The high technology of today provides the mechanical tools necessary to do the job. It is simply a matter of forethought, redesign, and reeducation for the employees.[3]

DESIGNING THE MARKETING INFORMATION SYSTEM

The first steps in developing a marketing information system are to define the goals and critical success factors of the particular organization, and to identify the information needed to make the decisions to reach those goals. This provides a vehicle whereby management is forced to think about and isolate those areas most critical to it. Identification of critical areas will enable the further identification of the information needed to measure the progress in those areas, and the need to establish a system to provide the information. A good information system should encompass the following:

- The information provided should satisfy users' needs.
- The information must be accurate and objective.
- The information must be summarized to be relevant and to be reduced in volume. One way to do this is to report variance from forecast or exception from expectation, rather than a massive set of all-inclusive data.
- The information must flow quickly and smoothly within the organization and be routed only to those to whom it is pertinent.
- The system must be flexible and capable of being changed as critical factors change.

A seven-step program for accomplishing this is as follows:

1. Establish a project team and steering committee. In a small organization this could be one person.
2. Document business plans and goals.
3. Define the critical success factors of the business.
4. Analyze the information that will be necessary to bring about and to measure the critical success factors.
5. Define the system necessary to provide those information needs.
6. Install the system to be efficient and effective.
7. Monitor the system and its fulfillment and performance, and update as needs require.

A schematic drawing of a marketing information system for hospitality companies is shown in Figure A-2. One part of that system is the formal research. We move on to discuss that area in greater detail because it is the stage of creating information, rather than collecting information, that has been the focus of this appendix thus far.

MARKETING RESEARCH

Marketing research of the consumer is closely aligned with consumer needs, wants, problems, and demands—existing, latent, and incipient. The trick here is to find out the problems and demands customers have when using or wanting to use the product. What do they do when they arrive, walk in or check in, and go to their room or table? What do they do the rest of their stay? These are just a very few of the questions to be answered. To determine incipient demand you cannot always ask customers what their problems are, because they don't always know. Management has a theory about what is important to the customer, but rarely is that theory grounded in scientific research, like the coffee break example we gave in Chapter 1.

You can see that in a situation like that, if we asked the customers what problems they had, they would probably reply "None, everything is just fine." That is because the problems are probably in an initial stage, just beginning to exist. Problems like this are difficult to articulate, so management concludes it is doing the best job possible; because it has satisfied customers, it fails to see the opportunities.

As an example of typical, unscientific research, assume management decided to survey what was important in a coffee break, again. They would make up a list of items and ask respondents to indicate the importance of each one in a coffee break. One of the items would be "quality of coffee," which 98 percent would check as very important. Voila! The most important thing in a coffee break is the quality of the coffee. Management buys the best coffee—situation taken care of, opportunity lost; that is, the research has failed to uncover the real problem.

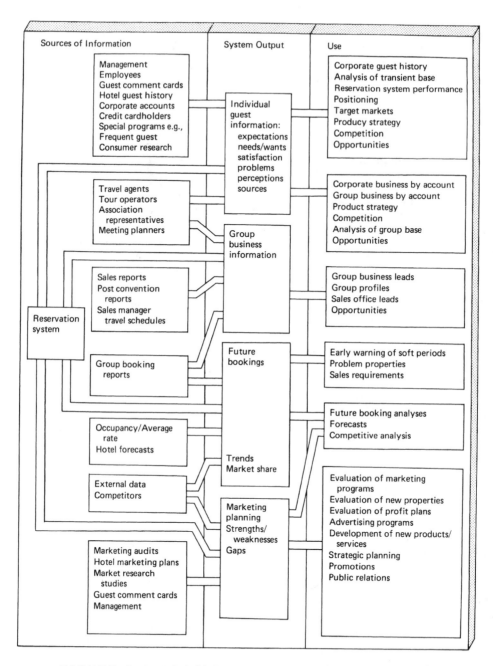

FIGURE A-2 A desirable hospitality management information system.[4]

Research is used to study how people use the product. What do they do, where do they go, how do they do it? It is also used to determine why (for what factors) a customer would/would not return. With this kind of information we can look for opportunities to make it all happen more easily and with less trouble.

FORMAL MARKETING RESEARCH

Formal marketing research, or **scientific research**— and we use the word "formal" to distinguish it from the haphazard collection of data such as that provided by comment cards—is the objective and empirical collection of information about consumers. In this same sense, it means **primary data** as opposed to **secondary data.** Secondary data, however, may be very useful to our purpose. For example, the U.S. Travel Data Center and Tourism Canada gather information on national and state/provincial travel trends. This is information is not specific enough for a firm's customer needs but is useful for environmental scanning. Primary data, on the other hand, are data collected for a specific purpose and constitutes what is called formal, or scientific, marketing research.

Data are not necessarily information. This point is important because research is only as good as its interpretation. There is another important point about business research: Its purpose is to provide information to make decisions; if it doesn't serve that purpose it is a waste of both time and money. An example is given in Table A-1. As competition becomes more intense and creating and retaining a customer becomes ever more difficult, it becomes more and more necessary to know and understand that customer prior to making decisions.

The Gallup examples introduce a very important research element called **intervening variables.** Literally, these are variables that "intervene." In the Gallup eating out case all the "ifs" we introduced, such as who we were with, intervene in our response. If intervening variables are not controlled

for, then the research findings are apt to be worthless, as were Gallup's. Failure to control these is a major failing in much research.

There is another problem with so-called averages in research. In fact, they can be dangerous to interpret unless they come from homogeneous groups or market segments. One way to remember this is to keep in mind the following: Four women are seated at a table. One is pregnant. On average, therefore, each woman is 25 percent pregnant. Basing serious business decisions on averages of heterogenous samples is not recommended.

Proprietary Research

Proprietary research is research conducted for a particular organization for the particular use of that organization as opposed to a general use. It may be conducted by the organization itself or by an outside supplier, a firm commissioned to do the actual data collection, and possibly analysis, for another firm. In the hospitality industry, very few companies conduct their own research. Marriott, Holiday Inn, and others once had research departments and attempted to do this, but now contract with outside suppliers to do it.

Regardless of who does it, the research requirements are the same. Absolute rigor and control are necessary for the findings to have validity and reliability. There are two broad categories of research—qualitative and quantitative. Both have their place; the important thing is to know what that place is.

Qualitative Research

Qualitative research is concerned with obtaining information on consumer attitudes and behavior on a subjective basis. It is largely exploratory in nature and the findings cannot be **generalized** to a larger population. Its purpose is usually to learn more about a subject, to understand how consumers use a product, to test a new product concept, or to provide information for developing further quantitative research.

TABLE A-1
Some Misleading Research Findings

A Gallup study queried a very important subject for hoteliers, whether people prefer to eat in the hotel restaurant rather than going someplace else. Unfortunately, the reported results were meaningless. Gallup's question, posed to a nationally representative sample of adults, asked, "When I stay at a hotel or motel, I usually prefer to eat in the hotel restaurant rather than going someplace else. Would you say the statement is very true, somewhat true, somewhat untrue, or very untrue of your opinion?"

Our own answer (the authors) might be as follows, depending on the hotel or motel, its location, and the reputation and prices of its dining room: for breakfast, very true; for luncheon, very untrue; for dinner, somewhat untrue—all depending, of course, on why we are there, whom we are with, what we are doing, and so forth. How do you interpret our answer? Gallup just lumped everything together, apparently on the assumption that the meal period, time, context, company, and numerous other variables have no bearing on the response. Thus, as we have stated, the findings are meaningless.

Here's another Gallup one: "I expect a hotel or motel to provide me with complimentary toiletries such as shampoo. Would you say the statement is very true, somewhat true, somewhat untrue, or very untrue of your opinion?" We leave this one up to the reader to interpret.

The most common form of qualitative research is the **focus group**. A focus group is six to ten people "typical" (obtained by screening in their selection) of the type of people expected to use the product. These people are brought together in a room where a skilled moderator leads the discussion.

As illustration, suppose a restaurateur was considering a radically new menu. He has a mock-up of the menu made but before he goes ahead with the change he wants to see how his customers might react. He invites eight of his customers on each of four different days of the week to have a free dinner if they will agree to participate in a two-hour focus group. He hires a skilled moderator (he would not do this himself because of his lack of skill and potential bias) who leads the group in discussion. The moderator not only asks questions but also attempts to build a rapport with the group and spends a lot of time "probing." The relationship between the moderator and the group is important because a reluctant group will not provide thorough information.

It is not uncommon to audio- and/or videotape focus groups. Thus more complete analysis is possible after the session is over. Also, while the session is being conducted, the restaurateur and some of his staff may sit behind a one-way mirror and observe the proceedings, watching for special nuances and signs that the moderator might miss.

The other most common form of qualitative research is the personal interview. This constitutes a structured or unstructured exchange in which the interviewer probes for specific comments and reactions. There are a number of pragmatic reasons for using qualitative research, which are shown in Table A-2.

The major problem with qualitative research is that you cannot generalize from it. The best you can say is that this is what "these people" say. It does, however, help in "getting inside the consumer's mind." It helps to define problems, and it forms the basis for quantitative research to follow. Sometimes we think we understand the problem but we really don't; we are unable to put ourselves into the consumer's perspective.

Other times we simply don't know just what the problem is. Comment cards may be positive, customer comments are good, and everything looks rosy, except business is declining. Through qualitative probing it may be possible to uncover some problems that, otherwise, would never reveal themselves.

TABLE A-2
Pragmatic Reasons for Using
Qualitative Research

- It can be executed quickly in a short period of time.
- It is relatively economical.
- The environment can be tightly controlled.
- It permits direct contact with consumers.
- It permits greater depth by probing for responses.
- It permits customers to "open up."
- It develops new creative ideas.
- It establishes consumer vocabulary.
- It uncovers basic consumer needs and attitudes.
- It establishes new product concepts.
- It interprets previously obtained quantitative data

Quantitative Research

Quantitative research deals with numbers. It measures, quantitatively, what people say, think, perceive, feel, and do. Descriptive quantitative research is the kind with which we are most familiar. It tells us how many, how often, and what percentage, such as how old people are, their sex, their income, their education, or whether they like or dislike something. It then tells us frequency and percentages, for example, there are 362 females in the sample (48 percent), they ate in a restaurant 2.3 times last week, and 36 percent of them have at least a college education.

Descriptive data tells us who and what but it doesn't tell us why. It might tell us how many persons in each age bracket ate out, how many times and the relative percentages. From this information we could also determine, statistically, if any differences in eating out patterns by age category were likely to have occurred by chance. But it wouldn't tell us how these factors interact, that is, does the age of an individual predict how many times that person will eat in a restaurant in a given week? As an example, the descriptive data obtained from a comment card like the one in Figure A-1 might tell us that an individual thought the food

and service were fine but not if that was a reason they chose the property.

Descriptive research tells us one or more things at a time, but it does not tell us if there is an implied **causal relationship** between them. Descriptive data doesn't identify the real reasons consumers behave as they do and make the decisions they make. The frequency of consumers renaming an attribute, for example location, does not necessarily indicate its relative determinance in the choice process.

Allowing **multiple responses** on limited choice questions introduces a bias problem that is particularly common in both public and proprietary descriptive research, and sometimes destroys the value of the findings. When the question choices are also biased, it can be seen why some people say, "You can prove anything you want with research."

Inferential quantitative research is a horse of a different color. It allows us to infer to a larger **population** based on the findings from a **probability sample,** a sample where each person in the population being studied (e.g., business travelers) has an equal chance of being selected. As it is rarely feasible to survey everyone in whom we might be interested (called a population), we have to select only a few people from the larger group (called a sample). With inferential statistics, it is possible to draw conclusions about the population on the basis of the sample data.

At the same time, inferential methods enhance the **multivariate analysis** of interaction effects, which requires probability sampling as an underlying assumption. An example would be the measuring various effects in studying why members of a particular market segment might choose a particular restaurant. A sample from the segment could be surveyed and asked to rate the importance in their decision of food quality, service, ambience, location, and price. In multivariate analysis, each of these attributes would interact with the others. The analysis would then reveal "weights," that is, the respective weights of each attribute in choosing the restaurant. This would reveal both the relative relationship of the various attributes as well as the predictive capability of each in choosing the restaurant.

With the findings from the above, assuming we had surveyed a representative sample of all people who choose that restaurant, we could infer to all those people (the population) as to why they make that choice. This would tell us what is important in influencing people to choose the restaurant or, perhaps, why they would not choose it. Thus inferential data is far more powerful and useful than descriptive data. It is also more complex, takes more skill to obtain, requires the use of a computer, and is more expensive both in collection and analysis. Today's software, however, makes the data analysis relatively easy; the potential misinterpretation is the difficult and risky part.

THE RESEARCH DESIGN

For some, research is a scary word. It conjures up visions of spending lots of money, of academic eggheads, and of undecipherable reports. Although all this may occur in some situations, they are hardly typical, nor need they be. More important, marketing research is really the only way to get to know your market. As creating and retaining a customer becomes ever more difficult, it becomes more and more necessary to do research to know and understand the customer. Marketing research is necessary, among other things, to accomplish the following:

Lessen uncertainty
Replace intuition with facts
Stay current with the market
Determine needs and wants
Locate segments and target markets
Plan strategies and tactics
Act in advance for the future
Make business decisions

Some off the areas of marketing research that need to be pursued to accomplish the above are:

Customer perception
Customer awareness
Need for new products and services
Price sensitivity
Communication strategies—image, media, targets, frequency, content, appeals
Product strategies—service, quality, price, needs and wants, renovations, amenities
Market segments—demographics, psychographics, users, benefits, volume, motivations
Consumers—opinions, beliefs, attitudes, intentions, behavior
Demand analysis
Competitors' strengths and weaknesses

This list could easily be continued at some length but that is not necessary here; you will find many additions to it in other chapters. The important point, however, is not the list but the identification of why you are doing the research. It is the answer to that question that leads to good research design.

Developing the **research design** may be the most important part of all research. This is because perfectly executed and analyzed research is virtually worthless if it is not based on the appropriate design. The design is what guides the research from beginning to end. Whether you are conducting research, commissioning it, or reading it, you should understand the requirements of the research design. For that reason we go through it step by step. The first four steps are the most critical ones for building the research foundation. They include specifying the research purpose, defining the research problem, establishing the research objectives, and determining what we expect to find out. The research process is shown in Figure A-3.

THE RESEARCH PROCESS

The Research Purpose

Research design begins with establishing the purpose of the research, which derives from the man-

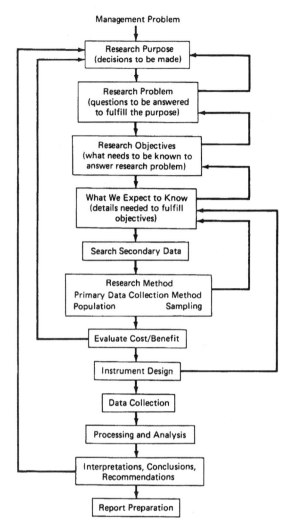

F I G U R E   A - 3   A flow chart of the research process.

do with the findings—that is, what kinds of business decisions you plan to make after you have the results. You might decide to develop an advertising campaign, change your menu, refurbish your decor, run a special promotion, challenge your competition, or any number of other things. Simply knowing that you had new competition, which you probably knew anyway, would not help much in making these decisions. Knowing your purpose will lead to obtaining the information you need to fulfill that purpose. The purpose of the research establishes the parameters of everything that follows in the research design. The first of these is the research problem.

The Research Problem

The research problem means exactly that: the research problem. It doesn't mean the management problem; the existence of the management problem explains why you are doing the research in the first place. The research problem is how to provide the information that addresses the management problem.

We can utilize the same example as before—business is declining. That is the management problem. The research problem is to answer the question "What is causing business to decline?" or, as in the example above, "Why are our customers going to the competition?" The answer to this question will tell us what to do to stop it from declining—that is, how to fulfill the research purpose. These first two steps are so important in designing research that we elaborate further.

Suppose we had said that the purpose of the research was to find out why business is declining and that the problem was to find out why it was declining. We discover that the answer is that our customers are going to competitors so we have the answer to the problem and we have satisfied the purpose. Instead, let us say that the research purpose is to develop a marketing strategy to stop the decline in business. That leads us directly to the problem: What needs to be done to stop the decline in business?

agement problem. For example, you might say the purpose of a research study is to find out why business is declining, which is actually the management problem. You might learn that it is declining because three new competitors have come to town and your former customers are going to them. That would be interesting but it wouldn't tell you what to do about it. What you want to know is how to stop business from declining.

The purpose of research is what you intend to

We now know that learning that our customers are going to new competition is not enough. We need to know why they are going there, or perhaps, why they are not coming here anymore—that is, we need to know what has to be done to stop this desertion. This, in turn, guides the rest of the research design. In fact, it is often useful to state the research problem even more specifically in the form of a question: What needs to be done to stop the decline in business?

Research Objectives

These are the specific objectives—what we want to find out. To follow from the research problem ("What needs to be done to stop the decline in business?"), it is obvious that the sample that we survey is not going to provide the answer directly. We need to infer that from the information we collect. The research objectives, then, might be to find out what people do and why; for instance:

> What are present eating-out habits?
> What are perceptions of our restaurant?
> What do customers look for in a restaurant?
> What would they like to see in a restaurant?

The objectives are to obtain the information we need to address the problem. From the objectives flow the answers to the question "What do we expect to know after the research is completed?

What We Expect to Know

What we expect to know is all the pieces of information that are necessary to fulfill the objectives, for instance:

> Where do they go now?
> How often do they go there?
> Why do they go there?
> How much do they spend there?
> What do they order there?
> Why do they dine out at all?
> What do they think of us?

> What do they seek that they can't find?
> What would persuade them to go to a different restaurant?

It should be clear now that if we simply deal with the issue of why business is declining, we might not come up with answers that would be very useful in changing the pattern. That is why the above four steps are so critical to good research, and why each one must flow from the previous ones. What each step does, in turn, is simply to narrow the boundaries of the research so that it focuses directly on what is needed to make management decisions. This process continues. The first four parameters will establish who the population is, the sample that is needed, the questions that need to be asked, and whether the research should be qualitative, descriptive, inferential, or some combination of these.

Research Method

The remainder of the research design is called the research method. This includes establishing the population, the sample, the sample size, the method of data collection, the questions asked, and the type of analysis that will be applied.

Population. The population is all those people in whom we are interested. This might mean all present customers, all potential customers, or both. It might mean all people who eat at restaurants in this area, or all those who come from another area. It might be all businesspeople, or leisure travelers, or those who eat beef, or those who don't. It might be all those who use a certain restaurant category (fast-food), or a certain restaurant brand (McDonald's).

In the broadest sense, the population is all those people who might spend money to buy our product. The important criterion is that the population be as homogeneous as possible—that is, that its members have similar characteristics along the dimensions we wish to measure. Consider the following example.

The operator of a restaurant wishes to determine the opinions of a particular group of people concerning her restaurant operation. The populations involved could be classified in the following ways:

All people who eat out

People who like to dine out in the type of restaurant operated by this restaurateur

People who have an opportunity to dine at this type of restaurant

People who know about this particular restaurant, and:

- Have never dined there
- Have dined there in the past but do not dine there now
- Dine there now on an irregular basis
- Dine there now on a regular basis

Sample. The **sample** is derived from the population. Because we can't survey everyone, we will have to survey only a few. From these few we hope to learn the characteristics of the many. Selection of the appropriate sample and sample size is beyond the scope of this book. There are prescribed methods for doing this that may be found in any research text. Our main concern here will be with the type of sample.

A **probability sample** is one in which every member of the population has an equal chance of being selected. This means that the sample is collected randomly without any bias as to who is selected. A simple method of randomly selecting a sample group of 50 might be to put all the names in the population in a bowl, reach in, and pick out the 50 names one at a time.

Statistically, it can be shown that a random sample will closely approximate the true characteristics of a population. This is why we can infer from a sample. It can also be shown that we can say, with a certain degree of confidence, that what we have learned could not have occurred by chance, given a certain error tolerance. It is only with probability samples that one can legitimately use inferential analysis.

A **nonprobability sample** obviously means just the opposite—that is, everyone in the population does not have an equal chance of being selected. This may be called a **convenience sample,** in which people are selected simply because they are convenient. We might choose to sample the first 50 people who check out of the hotel one morning. This does not allow us to generalize our findings to anyone else who stays at the hotel. People who check out later, or on another day, might have very different characteristics from these first 50.

Another kind of nonprobability sample is called a **judgmental** sample. In this case, it might be decided that some specified variation is needed, such as a mixture of sexes, age groups, travel purpose, and method of arrival at a hotel. We might choose the first ten of each category who check out. Judgmental samples are often used for focus group selection because focus groups are usually specifically selected to represent certain characteristics. In the cases, subjects are first screened to be certain that they meet certain criteria such as demographics or usage. For example, in the example given above, if we wanted to ask people which hotel had the most comfortable beds in the world (it's been done!), we would first screen them to be certain that they had slept in all the hotel beds in the world.

A **quota** sample is similar. It specifies a certain quota of people or kinds of people. A common method of creating judgmental or quota samples is what is called a mall-intercept. This means, essentially, that we go to a shopping mall and intercept people. If they will respond (many won't), we screen them, by asking, for example, "Do you eat dinner in a restaurant two or more times a week?" If the answer is no, we move on; if it is yes, we proceed with further questions.

Of course, all so-called mall-intercepts don't take place in malls; they may take place in airline terminals, restaurant entryways, or hotel lobbies.

Another type of nonprobability sample is composed of the people who fill out guest comment cards in hotel rooms. This is a biased **default sample.** Although you could argue that everyone who stays in a hotel has the same opportunity to fill out the comment card, this does not constitute a probability sample because the researcher has no means of controlling the probability. The results in a default selection. The bias comes from the fact that the sample would represent only those people who are prone to fill out comment cards. These people may differ drastically from people who never fill out comment cards.

Instrument Design and Data Collection. The data collection design comes next. However, data collection was clearly in mind when the sample was selected because the two are closely interrelated and must be coordinated.

Some written preparation, called the **instrument,** is required before the data is actually collected. For example, a questionnaire has to be prepared if the data is collected by telephone, personal interview, or mail. A mailed questionnaire will require more care in its preparation in terms of format, design, appearance, and other factors that will both induce respondents to complete it and make it easier for them to do so. It is also important that the data collected be easy to tabulate or feed into the computer for analysis. For this reason, there is also a trade-off decision between **closed-ended** and **open-ended** questions.

If focus groups are to be used, a moderator's guide is prepared, first to screen the potential participants to be certain that they fit the criteria established. If we wanted to ask questions about eating out, for example, we would screen to be certain that participants were people who did eat out. The main use of the moderator's guide is during the group process. Although focus groups are generally unstructured, guidelines are used to keep the conversation on course and be certain that the appropriate and important items are discussed.

In other forms of qualitative research such as personal interviewing, the interviewer will also use a guide for the same reasons. Additionally, it may be desirable to ask specific questions and write down specific responses for later analysis.

Questionnaire design is not as simple a task as it may sometimes seem. Questions must be clear and unambiguous. Each question should, as nearly as possible, have the same meaning for all respondents. This means that if an abstract term such as "quality" is used, the word quality should be defined so that everyone interprets it in the same way.

The subject of questionnaire or instrument design is covered in research textbooks and is not, therefore, discussed here. We only caution of the hazards involved, because if you are not measuring what you think you are measuring, you will obtain invalid data and findings. For this reason, too, it is always necessary to pretest the questionnaire. This means trying it out on people who will not be included in the sample in order to get feedback on the wording, the time it takes, the clarity, the understanding of terms, possible omissions, and other factors that might confuse respondents or invalidate the findings.

The decision as to whether to use personal interviews, mail, telephone, or other data collection methods (such as comment cards or individual intercepts) is an important one in the research design. Each one has its trade-offs in terms of time and money. While the budget is always a limiting factor, the most important criterion is whether the method is the one that will provide the most reliable data for the problem at hand. There is no one answer to this because each case is individual and must be weighed on its own merits.

Analysis and Interpretation. The data obtained must, of course, be processed, analyzed, and interpreted very carefully. The method of analysis will have been decided beforehand, including whether it will be done by hand or by computer. Also, the analytical techniques to be used should be predetermined, since these will affect the way questions are asked, the type of response solicited, and how they are measured. Data analysis is also beyond the scope of this book; again, we refer readers to any good marketing research text. Table A-3 includes a minicase and a very brief research design to illustrate the research design points that have just been covered.

TABLE A-3
Minicase Illustrating the Research Design Process

TACO GOURMET

A successful restaurateur decided to start a Mexican fast-food chain offering "gourmet" tacos and other Mexican foods, to cash in on the latest fast-food trend but at a higher level of quality. His pilot effort was called Taco Gourmet. The food quality was superior because he used only the best ingredients. He priced his items about 30 percent higher than the competition for the same items.

Business was excellent the first month, then starting falling off. After three months it was only half of what it had been the first month. The owner noticed that few of his customers were repeaters. He inquired among his friends to see if they had heard complaints. The only complaint that seemed to appear was about the prices. The owner decided to conduct some formal research. After analyzing the situation he asked a consultant to develop a research design. The following is what the consultant came up with:

Purpose of the Research: To determine product and pricing strategies.

Research Problem: What is the market looking for in a Mexican fast-food restaurant?

Objectives:
- To determine quality perceptions of Mexican fast-food.
- To determine the price/value relationships of Mexican fast-food.
- To determine market demand for Mexican fast-food at different price/quality levels.

What We Expect to Find Out:
- Do people know and appreciate the difference between quality and ordinary Mexican fast-food?
- If yes, what is the difference based on?
- How much are they willing to pay?
- How frequently do they eat it?
- Where do they go now? How often? How much do they spend?
- What is the present awareness and trial of Taco Gourmet?
- What is the present perception of Taco Gourmet?
- How much more, if anything, will people pay for "different" Mexican fast-food?

Population: All people over the age of 16 within a five-mile radius who eat Mexican fast-food at least once a month.

Sample: Assuming 50 percent of the population appreciate the difference in quality, with a 5 percent margin of error and a desired confidence level of 95 percent, a sample of 384 is required.[a] With an expected response rate of 25 percent, a probability sample of 1600 names will be drawn from street listings.

Data Collection: Four focus groups divided by sex and age will be convened. Data collected from these groups will be used to develop a written questionnaire to be mailed to the sample.

Data Analysis: Frequency statistics will be derived and data will be crosstabulated by demographics. Regression analysis will be used to predict intention to purchase Mexican fast-food at various price/quality levels.

---

[a] The computation of sample size is done here using the proportional method, which is described in research texts.

RESEARCH FINDINGS

The research design, the sampling, the data collection, and the data analysis must be all rigorously controlled when doing research. Each step is critically important, none more or less so than the others. Two supreme tests are applied to research findings: reliability and validity. Because these tests are so critical we discuss them briefly.

Reliability

Reliability in research means that the findings can be projected to a larger population if it is one of the intents of the research to do so. It means that if we took a similar sample from a similar population we would get similar results. It means that if we asked the same questions in a different way that we would get similar results. Even if reliable, the findings may or may not be valid.

Validity

Findings must be reliable if they are to be valid. **Validity** means that the data must support the conclusions. The conclusions must be valid in that they are based on whether the research actually measured what it is presumed to have measured. Anyone who wants to use research for decision-making purposes should always verify its validity first. Lack of validity is the most common cause of faulty research. Some of the critical forms of validity are as follows:

Face Validity: Is the instrument (questionnaire) measuring everything it is supposed to measure? Is the sample representative of the behavior or trait being measured?

Construct Validity: Is the construct being measured the one we think we are measuring? For instance, if we want to find out why people use a restaurant and they tell us that the most important factor is the quality of food, are they really telling us that this is the reason they choose a given restaurant?

Internal Validity: Are the findings free from bias? Are they true or are they an artifact of the research design—for instance, are there intervening, interactive, additive, or spurious effects that affect the responses and are extraneous to the causal relationship? An example of this is, if 100 people are asked their opinions of a hotel and 50 have been there and 50 have not, then having been to the hotel is an intervening variable—that is, it *intervenes* in their opinion. Such variables must be controlled. In this case, we would control by asking if they had or had not been there. We could then compare the responses from each group to see if they differed.

Common faults of research projects, more or less in the frequency of their occurrence and importance, are listed below.

1. Lack of construct validity
2. Failure to control for intervening variables
3. Unwarranted conceptual leaps, unsupported conclusions, and presumptive judgment
4. Failure to apply tests of statistical significance
5. Errors in sample selection
6. Failure to identify the issues, problem, or purpose of the research
7. Failure to capture the richness of the data (whether because of poor research instruments or poor statistical analysis)
8. Failure to define or limit variables
9. Poor writing
10. Failure to notice spurious relationships[6]

USEFUL RESEARCH

Despite its importance, marketing research will never make up for for bad management, a bad product, poor service, or a product that has no market. Assuming none of these conditions exist, marketing research is appropriate when you don't know, for certain, items like those in Table A-4.

Marketing research forms the basis for decisions, but it does not make them for you. It should

TABLE A-4
Appropriate Hospitality Uses of Research

- Why people choose your property
- Why people choose another property
- Who your real competition is
- How many of your customers come back
- How many don't
- How people "use" your property
- What trade-offs your customers make in choosing
- How to gauge acceptance of a new concept
- Price sensitivity and how much to discount to gain competitive advantage
- Whether your product and pricing strategy is in tune with your market
- Who your target market is
- If your thinking is the same as your customers'
- What are the persuasive appeals for each market and each type of customer
- Whether you are keeping up with changes in your customers' needs and wants
- Whether your customers are truly satisfied
- Whether you are keeping customers with complaint handling or losing them
- Whom your advertising is reaching and affecting—if anybody
- How your advertising is positioning your property in the market's perception
- If you are ahead of market trends or running to catch up
- Many, many other things about your market

be designed to provide specific information to answer the questions to which an operator needs answers. This is not a simple matter. Too much research is conducted without full understanding of what management hopes to learn. On the other hand, too much research is conducted to confirm decisions already made or to feed an ego. When the decision fails the research is blamed.

The results of valid research should be accepted and used, even if they refute existing beliefs. Too much research ends up buried in a file drawer because it did not agree with someone's prior assumptions. Regardless of what management believes, it is customers' perceptions that count.

SUMMARY

It is difficult to overemphasize the importance of

marketing information systems in the hospitality industry today. Whether it is environmental scanning, internal data, competitive analysis, or consumer perception and behavior, the time has come when management can barely survive by intuitive decisions only. Management at every level of a hospitality organization needs information not only to manage effectively but also to act in advance for the future. Management must fully understand what its needs are and develop the systems to fulfill them.

On the other hand, the problem may be one of having too much information. Computer technology and information services provide an abundance of information too unwieldy for ready digestion. The additional problem, then, is one of selection. Effective marketing information systems will come only after defined and selective informational needs are established.

Marketing research is an area of the marketing information system now coming into its own in hospitality. In an industry that is physically closer to its customer than most, the hospitality industry is one that doesn't know enough about its customer. The result has been the loss of customers and the winning of customers by default, or the "trading" of customers. For the firm that wants to keep customers, it is simply going to have to know that customer better. In an industry where brand loyalty is fleeting, switching costs are low, and every product unit has a personal relationship with the individual who purchases it, the value of research should be readily apparent.

KEY WORDS AND CONCEPTS

Causal Relationship: Implies a cause and effect, that one thing leads to another.

Close-Ended Questions: The subject is given limited and specific possible responses, for example, yes or no.

Comment Cards: Cards left in a room or on a table for customers to indicate their satisfaction with various services.

Construct Validity: Whether we are measuring what we think we are measuring.

Convenience Sample: A sample chosen because it is convenient.

Default Sample: A sample without restrictions obtained by default, for example, those who happen to be there or those who choose to participate.

Descriptive Data: Describes people and things (like age, gender, how often) but doesn't show a statistical relationship among data.

Face Validity: Whether we are measuring the right things and the right sample.

Focus Group: A small group of representative people brought together for the purpose of gaining general information and opinions.

Generalize: To generalize to a population is to apply the findings of a sample to the entire population from which the sample is drawn.

Inferential Research: Allows the research to infer findings to a larger population.

Instrument: The questionnaire or question guide used to collect the data.

Internal Validity: Whether the findings are free from bias.

Intervening Variables: Variables that affect a sample's responses that are not part of what the research is trying to learn.

Judgmental Sample: A sample based on judgments of who would be appropriate.

Multiple Responses: When respondents are allowed to give more than one answer to a question, for example, "why do you go to this hotel" with a number of possible reasons that can be marked.

Multivariate Analysis: Using multiple variables in conjunction with each other for determining interactive effects.

Mystery Shoppers: Incognito shoppers who shop for the purpose of collecting information.

Nonprobability Sample: A convenience sample where all members of the population do not have an equal chance of being chosen.

Open-Ended Questions: When respondents are not controlled in any way as to how they respond, that is, they are not given choices.

Population: In research terms, a population is a group of people who will be sampled and researched to measure the patterns of all.

Primary Data: Data collected for a specific purpose.

Probability Sample: A sample where each person in the population has an equal chance of being selected.

Proprietary Research: Research done for one particular firm, as opposed to public research.

Qualitative Research: Research that gets people's subjective opinions but does not show any statistically valid causal relationships.

Quantitative Research: Research that deals with numbers and statistical analysis.

Quota Sample: A sample based on quotas of different categories, for example, male/female.

Reader Boards: "Boards" in hotels that indicate what events are occurring in the hotel that day and what organizations are meeting there.

Reliability: In research this means that the findings would be similar if taken from another similar population, or if repeated.

Research Design: The design that guides the research from beginning to end.

Sample: The portion of the population used to actually conduct the research.

Scientific Research: Research that follows scientific protocol.

Secondary Data: Data collected by others, often but not necessarily public, that can be used as a starting point for information.

Validity: The validity of results makes them usable for sound decisions.

DISCUSSION QUESTIONS

1. Why are management information systems and marketing research more important today than they were 15 to 20 years ago?

2. How is the hospitality industry unique in its ability to gather internal information. Give some examples of how this can be done. Make a list of things you would want to know about your customers if you managed a hotel or restaurant. Discuss how this information would help you make management decisions.

3. Describe how inferential quantitative research is different from descriptive research.

4. Describe the difference between a probability and a nonprobability sample. Be prepared to discuss when you would use each and why.

5. Discuss the different versions of validity, and reliability.

6. For the Gallup survey question cited in the text on whether people expect shampoo in their rooms, discuss what is wrong with the question and how it should be reworded.

GROUP PROJECTS

1. Your group, as a manager of a hotel, have run a special promotion for six weeks. It was an unqualified success. You wonder why and decide to commission some research to find out. Define the research purpose, the research problem, the objectives, what you would expect to know when done, the population, the sample, data collection, and analysis (in general terms).

2. Go to the library and find some published research in a hospitality journal, one example for each of the group, and analyze it in terms of the discussion in this chapter, especially for the research process, the validity, and the reliability.

3. You find that returning customers are becoming fewer and fewer. When you talk to some of them they tell you that everything is fine, yet they don't return. Design the research to uncover the problem.

REFERENCES

1. "Wizards of Marketing," *Newsweek*, July 22, 1985, p. 42.

2. John Koten, "You Aren't Paranoid If You Feel Someone Eyes You Constantly," *The Wall Street Journal*, March 29, 1985, pp. 1, 22.

3. A. Neal Geller, *Executive Information Needs in Hotel Companies*, Peat, Marwick, Mitchell & Co., 1984, p. 7.

4. Adapted from A. Neal Geller, *ibid.*, p. 53. Used by permission.

5. Robert C. Lewis and Abraham Pizam, "Designing Research for Publication," *Cornell Hotel & Restaurant Administration Quarterly*, August 1986, p. 57.

TECHNOLOGICAL ADVANCES
AND FUTURES

Overview

The contributions of technology to marketing in the hospitality industry can not be understated. Just 20 short years ago, one of the authors began his career behind the front desk of a hotel as a management trainee. A room rack, representing each individual room, was stacked in front of the clerks. Each room was "reserved" by placing a colored ducat into a slot. Names for the telephone rack were recorded from the handwritten folios at check in. The night audit was performed from a glorified cash register, the infamous NCR 2000.

The first edition of this book, only 10 years ago, was written on a Compaq "portable" computer that weighed 28 lbs., had no hard drive (all programs were on 5 1/2 inch disks) and a small green five inch screen. Disks of each chapter were sent by Federal Express between the authors, including across the Atlantic Ocean.

Fast-forward to the 1990s, where property management systems handle all of the manual functions of the front desk. Remote check-in is possi-

ble. Sales and catering have technology interfaced with the PMS (property management system), to book live space even by remote while on outside sales calls. Toll-free 800 numbers to hotel reservations offices are being replaced by "call centers" of reservationists. Guestrooms are electronically temperature controlled, key systems by and large are electronic as well. The Internet has become a strong channel of distribution for reservations and information on hotels and restaurants. Consumers can book hotel rooms directly from their wireless Palm Pilots. This edition of this book was written with high speed laptops and chapters transmitted by modem over the Internet.

This appendix is an introductory, by no means exhaustive, review of technology as it relates to hospitality marketing. We realize that some of the technology we describe may well be obsolete, or certainly more sophisticated, by the time you read this book. We want to overcome that problem by describing the benefits of technology as it enhances the experience for the customer. Customers' perception of good service just 10 years ago included bathroom amenities, turndown service, and the size of the mint on the pillow. Service for today and beyond has been defined in terms of ease of doing business. Technology is an integral part of the hospitality experience, as it makes doing business away from the office easier.

This appendix will cover external technology such as global distribution systems (GDS), the Internet, Central Reservations Services (CRS), internal technology including property management systems (PMS), point of sales systems (POS), sales and catering technology, and in-room technology. After that, we will discuss some current applications and some future advances.

External Technology

Global Distribution Systems

Global distribution systems (GDS) are the overall technology platforms that are based in airline reservations systems that reside on many travel agents' desks. Major airlines created their own reservations systems; for example, SABRE was built by American Airlines, System One by Continental Airlines, Apollo by United Airlines, and DATAS II by Delta Airlines. The airlines soon realized that these reservations systems had excess capacity and began using it to distribute complementary travel products such as hotel rooms. Car rental companies soon followed hotels onto the systems, thus providing one-stop-shopping on the GDS for access by travel agents. Initially, the hotel application was cumbersome. Airlines have fewer options from which the customer can choose. A seat is first class or coach, aisle or window. Guestrooms, on the other hand, have a variety of configurations — single, double, queen, king, park view, high floor, and so forth, with many variations in price because of yield management systems. Unfortunately the airline systems databases were not able to cope with the number of permutations required in selling hotel rooms. Instead, they displayed a subset of the room product available, which lead travel agents to mistrust their computerized systems when dealing with hotels. Often the travel agent would get better prices and availability

by telephoning the hotel directly. As a result, the percentage of hotel rooms booked over the GDS has never reached similar proportions to that of airline seats. The GDS companies have subsequently taken steps to address this problem by broadening both the scope and range of products that their systems can distribute.

Windows-based versions of the GDS became available in mid-1999. New versions of the airlines' software have made the booking process easier for the travel agent. Travel agents work for a commission, usually ten percent of the value of the hotel room stay. A two night booking for $200 per night yields the agent $40 in commission. The GDS provides instant booking and can take less than one minute to complete. The alternative is for the agent to place a telephone call, be put on hold, talk to the reservation sales agent, and await the confirmation number to get the transaction completed. This process can take up to five minutes. The commission remains at $40 for one minute of work or five minutes of work. Many travel agencies are forcing GDS use to increase efficiency.

As mentioned earlier, GDS information can be different than that offered at the hotel. Better availability and better rates can still sometimes be found at the hotel level. Special requests, such as suites, early arrivals, and flowers delivered to the room upon arrival are still not managed well in the electronic booking mechanism of the GDS. Thus, many travel agents still place telephone calls for their VIP customers.

At its inception, the GDS represented a closed, dedicated connection of terminals in travel agencies displaying information about airlines, hotels, car rentals, cruises, and other travel products. Now the GDS has been reduced to only one component of a much larger ecosystem of networked travel information. The GDS now offers a multidimensional flow of information and transactions.[1]

Consolidation of the GDS industry soon followed the trend in hotel companies. The original GDS companies have merged and joined forces to create fewer but stronger distribution systems. The major service providers of the GDS are Amadeus, SABRE, Galileo, and Worldspan. These providers represent 80 percent of the market with smaller providers such as Infini, Axess, Gemini, and Abacus filling in the remaining 20 percent.[2] Two companies provide the facilities to interface the GDS with hotel reservations systems. These Ultraswitches are named WizCom and THISCo. The Ultraswitch makes all of the GDSs talk the same language to the individual hotel chains software. For example, Hilton has to be able to communicate rate and availability changes simultaneously to Amadeus, SABRE, Galileo, Gemini, Worldspan, Infini, Axess and Abacus. The Ultraswitch provides this service to the hotels and GDSs.

The GDS has provided another medium for hospitality marketers to get their message out to the travel community. Special advertising vehicles are available on the GDS for hotels to market special promotions. Headlines are offered in each system, which require a travel agent to read and acknowledge the message before "signing-on." New technology is now emerging to make these sign-on messages available simultaneously with the hotel's web-site. This multipurpose application will shift the GDS to a Global Distribution Network (GDN).

The Internet

The Internet is quickly becoming a major channel of distribution for the hospitality industry. In 1998

there were an estimated 100 milli worldwide with up to 20 million c time. Almost two million web sites tence. Hospitality companies are rep creases of 200 to 400 percent in usage year.... .... will soon produce the highest online revenues of any industry type, including personal computer hardware, groceries, flowers, books, software tickets, music and clothing. Pegasus Systems claimed in 1999 that 44,000 people per day accessed the web site TravelWeb (www.travelweb.com), which contains links to over 50 hotel chains, such as Hyatt and Best Western, and books every type of hospitality business.

Travelocity (www.travelocity.com) is another alternative. Through its web site one can book hotels (35,000), bed and breakfasts (20,000), flights, cars, and cruises. Both Travelocity and TravelWeb are considered "booking engines" for the Internet. Independent hotel web sites can "link" to a booking engine, thereby giving their customers instant access to inventory and confirmation numbers. These booking engines are linked directly with the GDS. Still another alternative (www.hotelreservation.com) is a listing of independent, non–chain affiliated, hotels. A novel approach to marketing travel on the Internet comes from www.priceline.com. On this web site the customer sets the price they are willing to pay for an airline seat or a hotel room, and the computer checks all availability, worldwide, in an attempt to match the needs of the customer with willing providers.

The American Hotel and Motel Association estimates hotel bookings on the Internet by individuals were over $360 million in 1998 and will grow to $2.9 billion in 2002.[3] As of this writing, the primary use for the customer is gathering information. Making reservations on the Internet is still a cumbersome process and many customers are reluctant to give their credit card numbers to guarantee guestrooms for fear of misuse. The trend for booking on the Internet, however, is compelling for hotels to cultivate, primarily because of cost. The use of third party organizations that provide the link to the global distribution systems can cost from 5 to 15 percent of the booking. These costs are significant and drop dramatically by providing direct access to the hotel inventory over the Internet. Many travel agencies view the Internet as a threat to their business. As customers are becoming increasingly sophisticated in their use of the Internet, the need for the travel agent may be reduced in the future. In essence, every traveler with a personal computer and modem has access to booking rooms electronically. This position was formerly held exclusively by the travel agencies and their GDS access. As a sign of the growing trend for consumers to book directly on the Internet, some airlines are offering additional frequent flyer miles for these transactions. Clearly, the cost of the frequent flyer miles, if redeemed, is significantly less than the commission due the travel agent on the airline seat sold.

Starwood Hotels and Resorts has taken a unique approach to the travel agency community concerning Internet bookings. Starwood's web page offers the consumer the opportunity to reward the travel agent without involving them with the bookings. According to Doug McKenzie, Starwood's vice president-luxury brand management, the end user has a choice to select their travel agency from an extensive list on Starwood's web site. A commission is sent to the agency as a result of the Internet booking.

Marriott has again taken a leadership role in marketing on the Internet. According to Mike Pusateri, Marriott's Vice President for Interactive Sales and Marketing, their strategy on the Internet is to convert information seekers into reservations bookers. Marriott's Web Site received 11,000 hits per day and averaged $1.5 million in sales monthly in 1998.

A successful web site will not only provide information on the hospitality entity, but will also be linked to similar web pages. A consumer searching the net tends to look at category types in the intended destination, such as luxury hotels, to fulfill their lodging needs. Consumers of luxury lodging are unlikely to "surf" the web page of Days Inn. Leading Hotels of the World has a web page linking and describing all 300 plus hotels in its consor-

tium (Figure B-1). Smart marketers would have their individual hotel, for example the Hotel Bel-Air in Los Angeles, linked to this web page. While Leading Hotels provides some information on the Hotel Bel-Air, more curious consumers should be able to electronically connect to the Hotel Bel-Air's web site for further information.

Two common problems with web site marketing management are current information and fulfillment. Laws governing the information provided on the Internet are still in their infancy stages. Many web sites carrying information on various properties are created and forgotten, many containing outdated material. The marketing management of the hospitality web site needs to constantly search for materials provided under its name through others' links, and request/provide updated information to the web site owner.

Once a web site is active, it begins to receive "hits" and "looks" from consumers on the World Wide Web. "Hits" to a website are different than "looks" at a website. A hit will bring the viewer to the home page of a website. Subsequent looks will give the viewer more information. In general, the hotel marketer is looking to create a booking or give essential information in no more than three clicks of the mouse; the initial hit and two looks are all that most viewers are willing to give to a site. Many contacts with the web site are just that, a quick hit and on to the next subject. Many website requests require response to e-mail for information, fulfillment of brochures, etc. Hospitality marketing organizations are now reorganizing to provide the resources to fulfill this new source of customer inquiry. A hotel company web site is shown in Figure B-2.

Central Reservations Systems

The central reservations system (CRS) function, which allows booking from an 800 number, is integrated with both the GDS and PMS. The CRS was created so that individual hotel chains could provide consolidated access to their worldwide inventory by toll-free telephone calls. A well-managed

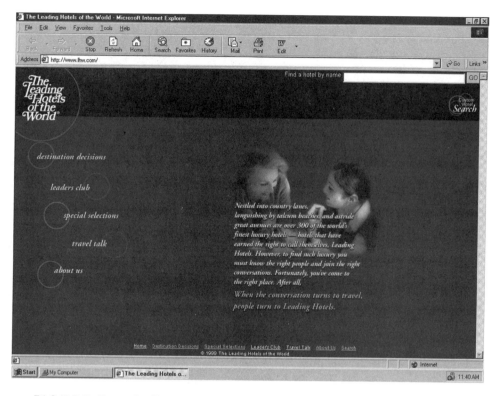

FIGURE B-1 Leading Hotels of the World: A hotel consortium's home page web site

CRS will offer the customer the same availability and rates that are available on both the GDS and at the hotel. Ideally, the local hotel will be electronically compatible with the CRS to ensure similar information is available to the customer. Unfortunately, even at the time of this writing, many hotels communicate manually with the CRS, resulting in incorrect information, availability, rates, and slow response time.

All major hotel chains, worldwide, now communicate from their call centers (CRS) and GDS directly to the individual hotels. Other consortia brands such as Leading Hotels of the World and Preferred Hotels and Resorts are quickly developing this technology for their customers.

As with other technology applications, the CRS functionality is being consolidated and outsourced to reduce cost. The voice reservations of

Leading Hotels are now being handled by REZsolutions. Although the call is answered "Leading Hotels of the World" a REZsolutions employee is indeed handling the call. This is called "private label" service. Many hotel chains are reviewing the cost to maintain their own CRS and outsourcing of this function has become an alternative that is both cost effective and maintains service levels.

The seamless connectivity of the CRS system is a future benefit to the customer, in this case the travel manager or travel agency. Using the airlines' systems, such as Worldspan, a travel agent can view a hotel's inventory directly. Seamless connectivity allows two way inventory management; the travel agent sees the same inventory that the reservations manager on property sees in the PMS. Room categories are booked based upon availability and rates

FIGURE B-2   Radisson: A hotel company's home page web site.

are shown for each category. Travel managers and agents are able to provide the most accurate information to their travelers with seamless connectivity. While all major hotels do not yet offer seamless connectivity, most are moving in that direction. Most hotels chains are now offering "single image inventory," whereby the inventory is held at the CRS level, but a different availability of inventory is maintained at the property level.

Internal Technology

Property Management Systems

Property management systems (PMS) cover the primary technology at a hotel. A hotel's PMS can be as simple as a check-in/check-out terminal or as complex as a system that ties in all revenue areas and produces instant reports on all of these areas, an integrated PMS. The PMS has traditionally been located in a mini-main frame computer somewhere on property. New technology is now allowing the PMS to run on networks of personal computers. All facets of the check-in/check out process are computerized. Room types are "blocked" electronically by rate or guest preference.

Many management companies and franchisers are struggling with different hotel brands that use many different PMSs. As these different PMSs don't "talk" to each other, the result is maybe unusable data, and savvy marketers are working to integrate all common brands within one PMS. Both Cendant, the master franchisor for well known brands such as Howard Johnson, Ramada, Super 8,

Travelodge, Knights Inn; and Choice Hotels International, which franchises brands such as Comfort Inn, Quality Inn, Clarion, and Econolodge, have recognized the need for consolidating their PMSs to provide standardized marketing data. As each franchise may be independently owned and managed, compliance is difficult in a worldwide program. Cendant has invested $ 75 million in a product named "Project Power-Up" to consolidate the marketing data from each property. The result will be assurances that all revenues are reported to the master franchiser, operational data is standardized, a single-image inventory system is available for the travel agent to view, the ability is provided to offer property to property reservations, and accessibility to central databases is available for marketing to new customers. Choice Hotels International is doing the same with its Enterprise Hospitality Solutions product. An industry group called Hospitality Industry Technology Integration Standards is attempting to create acceptable standards for all PMSs, no matter what company develops them.

The marketing advantages of the PMS technology from a customer perspective is guest history. Guest history allows the PMS to keep track of customers' needs. Most PMSs build guest history files in the computer based on previous stays. Some of the more sophisticated customer oriented companies, such as Ritz-Carlton, manage an international database of guest history, whereby a customer leaving a hotel in Florida can expect the same amenities upon arrival that night in Chicago.

Customer preferences such as foam pillows, king bed, The Wall Street Journal upon arrival, or park view rooms are recorded by reservations and the front office. When the guest re-books, these preferences appear on the file and are delivered upon arrival. Many travel departments of corporations or travel agencies obtain customer profiles from their travelers, and then forward them to the hotels, airlines, and rental car companies as a means of giving more personal service. A properly executed guest history program enhances the cus-

tomer experience and retains customers. Many five star hotels have a full time employee dedicated to guest history. Most hotels, however, utilize very little of the capacity of the guest history function of their PMS. Also, in many hotels, old data and inconsistent management of the data are two common problems in the administration of guest history programs. Figure B-3 illustrates some other PMS uses with software provided by CLS.

Future applications of guest history will include not only room preference but will be enhanced by information about menu selections, gift shop purchases, movie rentals, and ancillary purchases within the hotel during a guest's stay. New technology and falling hardware costs have now provided improved storage capabilities, allowing "full folio" archiving of records for future analysis.

Point of Sale Systems

Point of sale systems (POS) are the food and beverage arms of the PMS. Often, separate software will be 'interfaced' with the central PMS to manage the food and beverage function. POS systems now allow a waiter to order from a terminal in the restaurant directly into the kitchen. Valuable information such as menu preferences, average waiting time per entree, and availability of certain entrees, all providing better service to customers, are obtainable from the POS system. For hotel restaurants, all transactions for cash, house accounts, credit cards, and room service are all channeled into the PMS, instantly available to the guest for balance inquiry. POSs are now being integrated with PMS companies, for example by the Micros-Fidelio partnership. Micros was a leader in POS, while Fidelio specialized in both PMS and sales and catering software.

POS systems are slowly becoming part of some restaurateurs' marketing strategies. Frequent dining programs can be managed with POS. Customer preferences can be stored in a similar fashion to guest history in the PMS. Diners can be greeted by name, seated at their favorite table, and

FIGURE B-3 PMS uses with CLS company software.

offered the menu, for example, "sans boeuf" (without beef), with the new software available on POS.[4]

Sales and Catering

Another component of the PMS is the sales and catering software. Software providers such as Delphi or Fidelio have created systems to manage the selling process of both rooms and catering space for the hotel. Each customer is assigned a file with a profile of the needs of the customer and the volume of anticipated business. The call reports, or records of sales conversations, are managed through a word processing function and attached to the file. When a customer requests space, the software looks into the inventory of the hotel and shows how many guestrooms are available and at what rate. The function rooms, previously managed in a diary by manual entry, are electronically displayed for the salespeople. If the business is confirmed, space is blocked, and a contract generated within seconds. Modems and fax machines allow contracts to be transmitted immediately to the customer. Portable computers can be used similarly to book business from a trade show or a remote office.

Customers benefit from this technology by getting quicker answers to their inquiries. The pace of business today is accelerating, and meeting planners need immediate answers. Sales and catering technology allows a salesperson to book a meeting and get a contract on a planner's desk in less than 15 minutes. Many hotel companies share these sales contacts among other hotels in their organization. Customers again benefit from this technology by having better-informed salespeople calling on them for business in other locations. Figure B-4 shows the Delphi sales and catering software system network. It is not that long since all these things were done manually, if at all.

Note in Figure B-4 the ability to bring up competitors' profiles. This enables the marketing department to look at competitors' strengths and weaknesses as well as tracking lost business to competitors. This helps to identify patterns that may develop over time such as one competitor, in particular, that appears to attract a certain type of account.

According to Delphi, their revenue management system, ". . . enables a property to analyze a piece of business from many different angles to assure you are getting the best possible rate based on time of year, amount of business already booked, number in party, and type of function. It also empowers you with the tools you need to document that profitability to management."[5]

In-Room Technology

As discussed earlier, hotel guests are looking to have better business functionality in their guestrooms. In-room technology has contributed to the marketing of hotel rooms with these services. Many times e-mails need to be answered, letters have to be printed, faxes need to be sent, etc. Technology services for guests have evolved rapidly over the past few years. Business centers performed many of the above-described services as they began to appear in hotels during the early 1990s. These business centers offered desktop computers for use by guests, together with printers and fax machines. Hotels are now offering in room business services, such as two-line telephones to accommodate modems and calls to and from the room. In-room faxes are quite common in business hotels; many also serve as printers for personal computers. Voice mail has replaced traditional message delivery systems in hotels. In-room safes with electronic locks now offer an electric plug inside the safe, to allow the re-charging of laptop computers while maintaining security. The customer now has the ability to plug in their computer, check their office e-mail, print a document, and receive a fax while ordering room service! In short, the technology has moved from the office, to the lobby, to the guestroom of the hotel over a short period of time. The Ritz-Carlton chain does all this one better—it has a "technology butler" on hand for anyone confused by all the "gizmos and gadgets" in their room. Likewise, Inter-Continental Hotels have employees

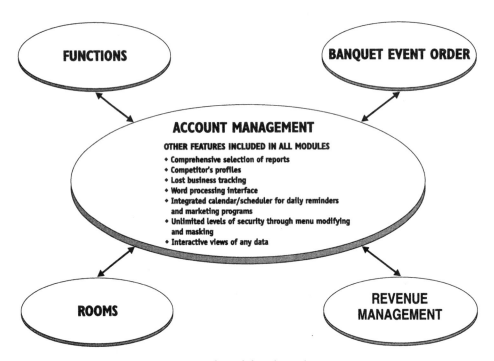

FIGURE B-4 The Delphi Sales and Catering System.

designated as CyberAssist Coordinators in each of its 138 hotels world-wide.

Electronic controls for lighting, do not disturb signs, and room temperature now maybe condensed into a small box at bedside, allowing the customer to manage the environment without leaving the bed. Even movie watching has evolved dramatically over the years. From movies on television, to VCRs in the room, to Spectravision movies offered at designated times, to On-Command Movies offered at a time that is convenient to the guest, the methodology of movie viewing in rooms has changed significantly. Marriott has even named their technologically advanced rooms "Rooms That Work."

Also on television, at many hotels guests can readily access interactive guest information systems. Players such as InfoTravel, City Key, Lodgenet Entertainment, CNN Text, WebTV Networks, and others offer various in-room guest services. Some offer information on local dining,

shopping, attractions, sports, recreation, and entertainment. Others provide categories such as places to eat, things to see and do, services, and getting around. CNN Text is essentially a newspaper that can be read on the television. It is widely used in Europe where teletext television sets are the standard. English is the primary language but headlines and news summaries can be accessed in the European language of selected major national newspapers. Where available, guests can also access the Internet through their in-room television sets.

Some technology has not been well accepted by the customer. Video checkout was touted by experts as the answer to long lines at checkout. Customers are able to review their bill on the television in their room, and pick up a copy at the front desk upon departure. Usage at large hotels, where checkout lines are a major annoyance, remains below 10 percent. Other forms of technology have not worked. The technology for video conferencing was available in the early 1980s.

Many industry leaders feared a significant negative impact on their business. The idea for video teleconferencing was that the chairman of a company headquartered in Chicago could deliver his annual state-of-the-company speech from his office to many different sites throughout the world. Hoteliers were concerned that the annual meeting in Chicago that bought 500 rooms in the city would dissipate as attendees stayed in their offices for the meeting. This, of course, never happened. The need for personal contact in a business setting has not been replaced by technology.

Expensive CD-ROMs were developed by hotels in the mid-1990s to allow customers to view the hotel in a more dynamic setting than a brochure. Most sit unused on the shelves of the travel agencies, who are too busy to look at them. The Internet has replaced the CD technology, now everything an agent needs to know is easier to obtain on the "net."

Some Other Technology Uses

There are many various applications of all this technology, of course, so here we mention just some of the most recent advances. Although these applications include both external and internal technology advances, these examples show the general trend toward using the advancing technology in different ways.

Microtel

US Franchise Systems' Microtel Inn and Suites, a fast-growing budget chain with over 500 newly built or being developed properties in just two years, in 1998, and aiming for 1000 by the year 2000, was one of the first hotel chains to use the Internet as its network for global distribution. Its cutting-edge central reservation system (CRS) called FIRST (Fast Internet Reservation System Technology), an extension of its original reserva-

tion system, also makes it the first budget chain to offer full Internet booking capabilities down to last-room availability for both guests and travel agents.

Microtel's web site (microtelinn.com) makes it incredibly easy to book a reservation. Besides offering instant confirmation (many hotel systems do not do this, in fact with some you may have to wait two days) it provides information on locations and services including maps and directions, nearby restaurants, entertainment, and meeting facilities. Data on rates and availability come directly from the FIRST reservation system so one is always guaranteed up-to-the-minute information. In addition, on-line users can, at this time,

- Respond with direct feedback to the customer service department through e-mail,
- Request a Microtel directory,
- Get the latest news on the company and its stock, and
- Respond to a special survey for those with disabilities to provide the chain new insight into understanding handicapped travelers' needs.

Forthcoming are e-mail newsletters to customers and brochures that can be downloaded.

REZsolutions*

The world's largest reservations firm provides "Electronic Showround," an Internet product that displays 360-degree views of properties (www.hotelbook.com). REZsolutions, which we mentioned in Chapter 18, in fact, offers a very complete technology platform covering most of the areas we have discussed as illustrated in Figure B-5.

---

*As this book goes to press, it has been announced that Pegasus Systems, Inc. has agreed to acquire REZsolutions, Inc.

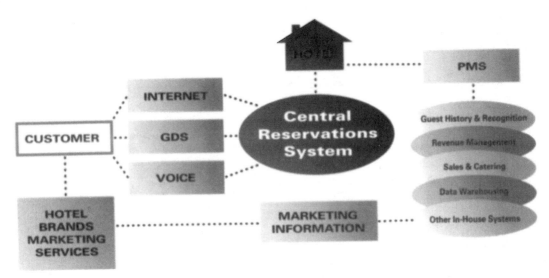

The data generated by our IT systems can be channeled back into planning and development, thus optimizing business from the worldwide market through REZsolutions' extensive worldwide network and marketing solutions.

FIGURE B-5   REZsolutions offers a complete information technology platform as shown.

Restaurant Choices

The Great Canadian Restaurant Survey (www.restaurant.ca) and the A La Carte Guide to North America (www.westweb.com/alacarte) are two examples of restaurant directories. In the first case, the viewer first selects a city—Toronto, Montreal, Vancouver, or Quebec City. The next screen provides choices—specific areas within the city, type of cuisine preferred, price range, special features desired, and consumer ratings from responses to the Survey. The next screen lists the restaurants that meet the criteria. The A La Carte guide listing includes over 300,000 restaurants categorized by city, state, or province, and cuisine. It is basically a yellow pages on the net.

Mi Amore Pizza & Pasta, Lompoc, California, maintains a marketing database that tracks customers and their purchases. If regulars haven't been there in 60 days, the PC based system sends out a postcard to lure them back with a discount. New menu items are suggested to customers based on their profile. Each year the database prints out a list of best customers for personally signed Christmas cards. The delivery database has more than 10,000 customers in it and growing (in a town of 11,000). Employees simply enter a phone number into the cash register and the computer automatically builds a database. The restaurant's goal is to build an individual relationship with each customer. Sales are increasing 20 to 30 percent a year.

Hotel Practices

A recent survey of hotel companies with full service properties throughout the United States found that heavy usage of technology was still no match for traditional methods of booking rooms. Some findings are reported in Table B-1. We include

TABLE B-1
Hospitality Benchmarking Survey[6]

Usage:

• Use airline GDS systems	86%
• Use on-site yield management system	72%
• Use centralized yield management system	60%
• Have chain web site	67%
• Have hotel specific web site	38%
• Use guest comment cards	97%
• Amount returned	3.8%
• *Hire outside firm to do satisfaction studies	84%
• *Request guests to complete satisfaction survey on check-out	67%
• Do not survey past repeat guests who do not come back (*We also doubt the other 37%.)	63%
• *Management acknowledges in-house repeat guests	87%
• *Recognition of repeat guests through guest history tracking	86%
• Have frequent stay program	82%
• *Automatic free upgrades for repeat guests	79%

Channels as a contribution to occupancy:

• On-premises sales department	25%
• On-premises reservations office	21%
• Central hotel chain 800 number	15%
• Travel agents, companies	12%
• Global distribution systems	10%
• Guest frequent stay programs	8%
• Local convention and visitors bureau	4%
• Hotel company national sales force	4%
• Walk-ins	1%
Total	100%

some nontech findings as well to show some potentials for technology use. (Authors' Note: Those with an asterisk we frankly find very suspect, based on our own experience and that of many frequent travelers we have talked to. Of course, because of the research design, the percentages may be accurate in terms of "doing it." What they don't tell us is how frequently they are done.)

The Future

Many technological advances are now in existence but sparsely used. We expect to see much greater use of these capabilities in the future. [7]

- Data warehousing—a database that consolidates information from multiple disparate systems into a universally accessible and usable format for a defined user group
- Sophisticated digital images, video, and sound
- Electronic brochures with three-dimensional pictures of property and facilities
- Customer surveys with Internet response for data to build customer loyalty through incentivized on-line questionnaires to create customer profiles and discover attitudes
- Gathering competitive intelligence
- Virtual reality hotel tours
- Contact of inactive customers
- Hotel company updates on new products, services, offers and benefits, and customer reaction to them
- Cross-selling of other products and services and brand extensions
- Members only offerings to loyal customer base
- Direct feedback after a stay—comments, complaints, suggestions
- Public relations releases
- Value-added services
- Internal marketing for employees, including mission statement

While some of these functions are being attempted by many hospitality companies, most are analyzing these and many other options as they move their companies ahead with available technology. Frankly, technology is moving so fast who knows what will come next? But the positive side, we are certain, will deal with building loyal relationships.

References

1. Jay A. Castleberry, Christian Hempell and Gretchen Kaufman, "The Battle for Electronic Shelf Space on the Global Distribution Network," in Arthur Andersen, *Ideas and Trends*, August 5, 1998.

2. Robert M. Coyne and John D. Burns, "Global Connectivity," Hotel and Motel Management, April 22, 1996, p. 28.

3. John Cahill, "Internet," Lodging, June 1998, p. 75.

4. Mark Hamilton, "Restaurant Frequency & Loyalty Systems Come of Age," The Hotel and Restaurant Technology Update, Summer 1998, p. 20.

5. Delphi Sales Brochure, Newmarket Software Systems, Inc., Portsmouth, New Hampshire.

6. Hospitality Benchmarking Survey, jointly sponsored by KPMG Peat Marwick, American Hotel & Motel Association, and the Educational Institute. Reported in KPMG, *The Real Estate Report*, Summer 1998.

7. Some of these ideas are taken from research conducted by David C. Gilbert, Jan A. Powell-Perry and S. Widijoso, all of the School of Management Studies for the Service Sector, University of Surrey, Surrey, England and reported in a research paper, "A Study of the Hotel Industry's Application of the Internet as a Relationship Marketing Tool," July 1998.

Cases In Hospitality

USING THE CASE METHOD

•◆•

The primary reason for using case studies in business courses is their verisimilitude, or their approximation of reality. Although cases will not give us all the information we would like to have, or possibly all that we could have in the real world, where we still never have all that we would like to have, they come as close as possible to that situation in an academic setting. Similarly, as in the real world, we have in cases more information than we need, or at least more than is relevant to the present situation. We must then separate the wheat from the chaff, the relevant from the irrelevant. We must define the problem(s); understand its causes, symptoms, ramifications, consequences, and repercussions; organize the facts; analyze and synthesize them; formulate possible solutions; evaluate them; verify them; and choose and defend a particular solution or application.

Thus what the case process really does is to bring theory, concepts, and facts into a stage of application and implementation. You may, for example, understand perfectly well the concepts in this book of marketing planning, environmental impacts, competitive advantage, relationship marketing, consumer behaviors, segmentation, positioning, and the hospitality mix, but these will mean a lot more to you when you have to actually apply them. In the case method of learning, you get a chance to do this. A case study chronicles the events that managers had to deal with and charts the manager's response or the manager's dilemma. Each case is different because each organization and each situation is different, but you will learn to appreciate and analyze the problems faced by many different hospitality companies and to understand how managers tried to deal with them.

There are two things that are inherent in using cases in education. One is that you have to *think!* By that is meant that doing case studies is not an exercise in memorization. As in the real world, there is no place to look up answers and there is no one right answer. Instead, you have to *read between the lines,* assimilate and synthesize various pieces of information, apply concepts and theories, and project all this into a realistic situation. This takes a lot of *thinking!*

And it takes *time!* You cannot read a case a few hours before class and expect to offer good analysis and solutions. Top executives cannot do it so why think that you can? Although good intuition is a great skill if you have it, it still has to be based on thorough analysis and synthesis of concepts applied to facts.

The second inherent factor in using case studies in the classroom is *interaction.* While much can be learned from the information that is in a case, and much can be learned from the cognitive process of analyzing the case, the ultimate test will come in being able to *articulate* and *explicate* this process. You may be the genius who has the secret to eternal life but if you cannot (1) articulate it, and (2) persuade someone to use it, then it will amount to naught. You may be asked to do this in writing, and you may be asked to do it orally. Regardless, being able to articulate is an important part of the case method learning process.

The other part of interaction, which many of us too often forget, is called *listening.* Sometimes we want to show how smart we are (or get points) by espousing our views without listening to those of others. Interaction is a two-way process. Listen and reply to others rather than ignore their points of view in favor of your own. Ask questions of them and of the instructor. It was Voltaire who said, "Judge a man not by his answers, but by his questions." Good executives listen and ask questions before making important decisions.

THE LEARNING CURVE

By the time you have reached this course, it is likely you will have gone through various stages of learning. You will have learned to memorize "buzz words," definitions, and key facts, and you will have learned to regurgitate this *knowledge* on multiple choice and true and false exams. Chances are you have also learned to *apply* this knowledge in written papers/exams to show that you *comprehend* it. In some cases you may even have been asked to *analyze* it. If you have had case studies in other courses, you may have been given a list of three to five case issues to address.

Some or all of this may also apply in the courses that use this book. With cases, however, it is time to go to a higher level of learning. As cases are used in courses because of the verisimilitude to actual situations, then arriving at solutions for those cases should also approximate the verisimilitude of decision making. Once you're in the "real" world of employment, you may not, at least immediately, be the executive who makes final decisions. In fact, you may be one to six levels down but, nevertheless, you may be asked to provide a recommendation.

However a real life case comes to you, at the top or the bottom, it will not come with a few neat questions that you only have to answer or with the information all neatly sorted out. Instead, you will have to decide what is irrelevant, what the real issues are, what the critical facts are, how they fit in this company, what the alternatives are, and what the recommended course of action should be. You may even have to consider who will implement this decision and how it will be done, as many decisions involve change that affects many people, and the

best decision will fail if it is not properly implemented. And you might have to present this to your boss on one or two pages, or in a ten-minute presentation, then defend it.

All this means going to a higher level of learning. Bosses do not have time to read through, or listen to, a barrage of garbage, especially if it is irrelevant or if they already know it. Instead, they want you to *synthesize* and *evaluate* your analysis, and be prepared to support it, so they can make a decision. The case studies in this book are intended to help you learn these skills.

Although the cases in this book are far more complex, let's start by considering a simple decision. Or is it so simple? The fast-food store across the street from yours has come out with a "Double whammy, slam banger, triple treat" hamburger at $2.29 that is stealing your market. But your specialty is chicken. What should you do?

Consider just a few of the issues that might be involved in this decision: Mission—what business are you in?—short-term tactics versus long-term strategy, ethics, other competitors, bargaining power of buyers and suppliers, efficiency, quality, innovation, customer responsiveness, barriers to imitation, sustainable competitive advantage, cost leadership, differentiation or focus strategy, resources, capabilities, employees, diversification, cultures, organizational conflict, implementation, and control.

After you've *analyzed* all these factors, and more, based on *application* of your *knowledge* and *comprehension*, piece by piece, you need to boil it all down and bring it back together. This is called *synthesis*. After synthesis, you *evaluate*. That is, you make value judgments. Will it work? What is the upside? What is the downside? What if it doesn't work?

Synthesis

This stage of learning, new for many, requires a little additional explanation because it is not an easy task.

In analysis we learn to break a problem down into its many parts such as the marketing, the financial, the organizational, and the environmental components. Many students, and managers, are good at this, but what they often do not do is put the pieces back together again. Too often the ability to analyze is valued over the ability to synthesize. In other words you have to boil it all down, concisely and succinctly, in a relatively few words that can be easily understood and evaluated. Mastering this ability will stand you in good stead in this class and throughout your entire career. Many companies, in fact, tells us that this is one of the most important capabilities they are looking for in managers.

ANALYZING CASES

There are a number of ways suggested for analyzing cases. Which way is best depends a great deal on the type of case, the information in the case, what kind of decisions and/or applications are to be made, and finally, what works best for you. One thing, however, is fairly unanimously agreed upon: Read the case through first without taking notes, marking the case, or in any way trying to break it down. The idea, first, is to get the total picture.

The second time through, mark the case or make notes on what is pertinent and relevant. Depending on the case, you will need to define the problem(s), gather the facts, analyze the information, do a SWOT analysis (an analysis of Strengths, Weaknesses, Opportunities, and Threats, which is covered in Chapter 4 and which your instructor will explain more thoroughly), define alternatives, synthesize, arrive at solutions, and evaluate them. These steps are fairly standard for handling any problem-oriented case. Some cases in this book may be used more as discussion cases. In these cases, arriving at a solution is not as critical; in fact, the case may lack enough information to do that, and part of your job may be to determine what information is needed and how to go about getting it, and what went wrong and why.

Case Analysis Process

The following is a checklist model that breaks down the parts, one by one, to get at the real issues and to see where they lead. You will find this method very useful in dissecting the cases. The checklist asks the questions to which you will need answers, either now or later.

1. Why is there a problem?

   The answer to this should be factual and measurable. This is usually what management sees as its problem, for example, occupancy is down, covers are off, we are losing market share, there is a chance to grow, we want to make an investment, the environment is changing, there is new competition, quality is down, and so on. Note an important distinction: This is *why*, not *what*. The answer to this question—and this is important—is not the solution to the problem. It is simply why the problem exists, and you need to identify that first in order to guide your direction in looking for a solution.

2. What is(are) the critical question(s)? What is the root problem?

   At this stage you need to find the question that will lead to the answer after having done the analysis. To make this clear, we will work backwards in a simple example. Suppose the "why there is a problem" above is, "We've been open six months and are only doing forty covers a night." The root problem, jumping to a hypothetical solution, turns out to be that the market doesn't know we exist; that is, there is a lack of awareness. The critical question we would have asked is "Why aren't more people coming here?" Root problems address causes, not symptoms or solutions.

   Notice that this question could have had many answers: The product is poor; it is perceived as overpriced; word of mouth is negative; we haven't targeted the right market; we're trying to do something we don't have the capabilities for doing; we lack distinctive competence; the positioning is wrong; the competition is undercutting us; and so forth. First, as you see, we have to ask the *right* question. Then we proceed with,

3. What are the critical factors? What has to be changed?

Now we are into gathering the facts, and sorting the wheat from the chaff. Here we have to analyze the data. (Don't skip over those exhibits! They may contain important information!) We are really just gathering information at this stage, but we want it to be the right information, which is why we define the critical question first. Once we have done this, but before we analyze it, we need to ask another question.

4. Are there any conditions for the solution?

This is important because is helps to keep us from going astray. For example, in a case with a deteriorating hotel property, students will often define the solution as "renovate." If renovation means $50 million, however, and the owner is not able or willing to spend it, then that "solution" is not much help. Conditions may be values or beliefs. Sometimes these may be overcome, sometimes not. It is important to know what they are. The best solution is useless if it can't be implemented.

5. Situation analysis.

This is where we look at all the elements of the system and analyze each part for strengths, weaknesses, opportunities, and threats (SWOT analysis). Strengths and weaknesses are internal to the company and need to be carefully explored. For example, a weakness might be a location that we can't change, or a product design that we can change. Some weaknesses we have to live with and plan our strategy accordingly. Others we try to turn into strengths. Even a so-called poor location can sometimes be turned into a strength.

Opportunities and threats are external to the company, which sometimes has little, if any, control over them. We want to exploit opportunities and, again, try to turn threats into opportunities. For example, a down economy is a threat but there may be specific market groups that can be taken away from lower rated competitors at a competitive price to ride out the storm.

If information is not available, you may have to infer it from the best information you have and decide if it is worth going after additional information.

When you have addressed these issues, and many more, and decided which ones are critical factors in the case, you should then look at them more closely. What you have done is determined the "facts," or at least the facts as they can best be determined. This is from information in the case, or information you have inferred from the case. As far as you know, it is the best information you have.

Now you need to ask: What assumptions can I make from this information? What further questions do I need to ask? What is missing? Is it worth the time and effort to get it? Is research needed? When you have answered these questions, and done the additional work called for, you can then say, "Okay, what tentative conclusions can I draw from this?" For example, you might have made the assumption that there is a one-time opportunity in the marketplace. Your conclusion, then, would be that you need to analyze this opportunity.

From the situation analysis, you should be able to identify not only problems and causes, but also the opportunities and what it takes, and what it precludes, to take advantage of those opportunities or to ward off threats.

Now, and only now, if this is a solution-oriented assignment, should you start thinking about alternatives. If you think about them earlier, you are likely to bias your analysis. For example, a case might say that the company wants to integrate upstream. You start thinking that a solution is the right acquisition. As you proceed through the analysis you look for information to support that alternative, which may not be the right one at all.

The only difference when cases are used as discussion cases is that the solution may be somewhat elusive for lack of information. Your situation analysis, however, does not change. You are more likely looking for what could have been done differently or how what was done worked or didn't work.

FINALLY

After you have done all this work, you need to put it all in perspective. Whether you have been told to turn in the work or not, *organize it!* For many students, this may be the most important thing you will learn in a case course. Frankly, if you cannot organize your thoughts in a way that others can follow, explicate them succinctly, and articulate them clearly, you will not go far in business, no matter how smart you are, or what your GPA is.

Check your work against your original questions. Why is there a problem? Does your solution address it? Did you answer the critical question(s)? If not, you may have the wrong answer—or the wrong question. Did you satisfy the conditions for solution? What are the risks? Are the resources available? What are the advantages and disadvantages—no solution is ever perfect or without some problem. This, of course, is synthesis. You are putting the big pieces back together to make a cogent and succinct argument. Now evaluate it. What will happen if you do? What will happen if you don't? Who is going to implement it?

If you can answer these questions, you should be ready to go into the classroom, or put down on paper or, in the real world, present to your superiors, a cogent, clear, concise, succinct argument for your position—and hold your own against anyone. Holding your own does not mean refusing to listen to other viewpoints, failing to consider new information or a new way of looking at the information, or not accepting an alternative that may be better than yours. This is all part of the process. Even the President's cabinet disagrees, yet decisions have to be made.

What holding your own means is, do not be shy; speak up; do not be afraid to argue and defend your position; and do not be afraid to compromise and accept someone else's position. Thinking clearly, using and analyzing the best information available, synthesizing and evaluating it, explicating, and articulating are what the real world is all about. What better place is there to learn it than here?

C A S E

One

◆

THE AIRLINE MARKET*

"I will give you my position in about a week," said Jean Valjean,

General Manager of the Le Centre Hotel, and he put down the phone and looked at the letter before him. The letter was from SKS Airlines requesting a one-year contract for 40 rooms each night at $72.00 per night. The problem facing Jean was a simple one: Does he take SKS and fill the 40 rooms for 365 days at $72.00 or does he refuse the business so that he can sell the rooms some nights for up to the full rack rate of $185.00? Last year the hotel had 95 percent occupancy or above for 135 nights; overall occupancy was 68 percent with an ADR of $108.00, but on near or sell-out nights the hotel could usually get rack rate on incremental room sales. This year was expected to be about the same.

---

*This case was originally prepared by Professor W. M. Braithwaite, University of Guelph, Guelph, Ontario. It has been revised and disguised for use here. All figures in are C$. For conversion purposes, one C$ equals about U.S. $0.70.

BACKGROUND OF THE HOTEL

Le Centre Hotel was located in the downtown area of a Canadian city in Quebec. It was viewed as a four-star corporate/convention hotel. It had 800 rooms including the Towers—a prestigious five-story hotel within a hotel. The Towers had its own check-in facilities, lounge, and special amenities, and contained 140 rooms including 16 suites. The balance of the hotel offered a choice of king, queen, and double beds with an additional 24 suites and 6 rooms especially equipped for the handicapped.

The hotel operated three restaurants. Le Mistral on the 37th floor offered gourmet French cuisine and an exceptional wine list. It had a seating capacity of 84. Le Shoppe on the third floor was open for breakfast, lunch, and dinner and had a seating capacity of 260. L'Expresso, an European style "express" restaurant on the promenade level, was for people in a hurry. It had a seating capacity of 60. In addition to the restaurants the hotel had five lounges. Other features of the hotel included a five story glassed-in atrium, glass enclosed year-round pool and health club with gymnasium, sauna, whirlpool and massage. The hotel had a multilingual staff.

COMPETITION

For airline crews, all hotels in the area were Le Centre's competitors because airlines historically chose hotels based on price and location, as long as they met a minimum level of comfort and services. SKS, however, preferred four-star hotels near shopping and entertainment facilities. This made competitive about ten properties located in the downtown area, so the decision would be made based on price and service. Jean was well aware that a number of competitors had expressed interest in the SKS business. He was also aware that if he took the contract and satisfied the SKS crew that he would have more negotiating power when the contract came up for renewal next year when the room rate could be increased. In the hotel business, it was always easier to renew existing room contracts than to solicit new ones.

THE PROPOSAL

Le Centre's target market included all forms of corporate groups, professional associations, and conventions. The SKS proposal appeared to be a good opportunity for Le Centre because it guaranteed 40 rooms per night (two overseas flights a day)for the entire year plus potential clients from their flights. The contract, if accepted, would require the hotel to have clean rooms immediately upon check-in, and to control the crews' wake-up calls. These services were standard tasks for Le Centre. However, because of the late departure of aircraft toward Europe, check-out time for SKS would be between 4:00 and 6:00 P.M. while the inbound crews would be arriving sometime between 9:00 and 10:00 P.M.

the same night. This meant the hotel had to have extra maids on duty to have these rooms ready within two to four hours. In addition, when flight schedules were changed, this meant changes in wake-up calls. This extra service posed a problem during the summer months when the hotel was full of regular guests and the staff was reluctant to provide extra service to the crews at the expense of the other guests who were paying the full rack rate.

Experience with other airlines had shown that airline crews spend less money in the hotel than other guests during their stay, an average of about $15.00 each on food only. This was because their usual stay was only one night. If they had leisure time, such as if they were grounded for additional days, they preferred to explore the city; hence, food and beverage purchases were largely made outside the hotel.

SALES AND COST DATA

Jean knew he would have to work fast on this proposal. He called in his assistant, Colette Chabot, and asked her to collect all the data required to estimate the comparative revenue and costs that would be involved to make a decision whether to accept the SKS offer.

Colette began with an analysis of room statistics for the previous year. These showed that, if the proposal had been in place, the number of regular guest rooms that would have been lost was equivalent to 105 nights sold out and 30 nights at an average of 97 percent occupancy. Analysis of the food and beverage statistics, not including banquets, for the previous year showed food revenue of $33.00 per occupied room and average beverage revenue of $22.50. The hotel's standard cost percentages were 36 percent for food and 32 percent for beverages.

In analyzing the probable effect on operating costs, Colette found that, on about 150 nights the SKS contract would require the equivalent of one additional front desk clerk for eight hours at an average hourly rate of $12.20. Fringe benefits were calculated at 35 percent of all payroll costs. In addition to this cost, Colette estimated the following variable costs per occupied room:

Housekeeping: One half hour per room at $10.60 per hour for the evening shift (part-time maids were available at this rate)
Laundry and Linen: $1.25 per occupied room
Utilities: $1.50 per occupied room
Amenities: $2.50 per occupied room.

Colette turned this information over to Jean for final analysis and a decision. As Jean sat in his office contemplating this information, he was reminded of a discussion at a recent meeting of general managers of all Le Centre hotels when they were told that one of the company's objectives for the coming fiscal year was a 12 percent return on investment. He was also very aware of the serious cash flow problem facing his hotel at that time. For the last fiscal year cash flow was negative by more than $2 million. With a $50 million long-term mortgage at floating rate interest and $4.2 million in annual municipal taxes to pay, the SKS business promised a steady and certain cash flow every week.

Two

ANDIAMO'S RESTAURANT*

I don't believe in advertising," John Quinn, co-owner of Andiamo's, stated. "You need lots of money to advertise and it's better to promote things in-house. Andiamo's has done the same amount of business since we stopped advertising. If I had the money to spend again, I would build a banquet room to increase our capacity to do business."

Andiamo's was a small, moderately priced restaurant featuring northern Italian cuisine. It was located on a side street in the college town of Ithaca, New York. The decor was "simple, high tech, and NY chic."

Andiamo's had two storefronts: one featured a deli decor where passersby could observe fresh pasta being made, the other exposed the restaurant. As guests entered Andiamo's they passed the deli counter that displayed the artfully arranged antipasto ingredients and desserts. There was also a show kitchen that was separated from the dining room by a long white counter. A striped awning and white tile floor provided the visual division be-

tween the two areas. All final preparation of the food was done in the "show kitchen" to allow the customers to see for themselves "just how fresh the food is." The dining room was off to the left and down two steps. A very simple white decor gave the feeling of a modern, elegant restaurant.

BACKGROUND

Peter Schore, the other co-owner, held a bachelor's and a master of science degree in hotel and restaurant management. Prior to opening Andiamo's, he had been a food and beverage manager of a major, international hotel chain and had been a teacher at a culinary school. Schore wanted to fulfill his dream of opening a restaurant. He purchased an inn outside Ithaca, NY, where people would "take a Sunday drive to go and eat."

Schore wanted to start another more commercial venture in a city or large, suburban area. After vacationing in Italy for three months, he decided to open a restaurant featuring northern Italian cuisine. Schore chose Ithaca for three reasons: he

*Helaine Rockett researched and contributed to this case. Names and location have been disguised.

resided there, he liked the town, and he wanted the restaurant to be a neighborhood place for fine food at moderate prices. After weeks of searching, Schore discovered a location that was exactly what he wanted. He was most surprised when informed that a Mr. Quinn had recently approached the owner to discuss a similar proposition.

John Quinn had owned and operated a successful soup and salad style restaurant in Ithaca for the past seven years. He recognized that the latest trend in gourmet pasta restaurants was uniformly popular elsewhere in the country and believed that an ethnic restaurant of that type would also prosper in the Ithaca area.

Schore and Quinn agreed to join forces and combine their talents to develop Andiamo's. Since both of the principal partners recognized that a co-manager setup could be potentially problematic, they agreed to the following division of responsibilities:

1. Quinn would be in charge of all recordkeeping, advertising/promotion, cost control, and maintenance, as well as the general supervision of the front of the house.
2. Schore would manage the back of the house to include food purchasing, storage, preparation, and presentation.
3. Each of the comanagers would function as manager 50 percent of the time (20 to 30 hours a week).

GETTING OPEN

Andiamo's was started with a budget of $87,000. The white china was secondhand, the furniture was purchased at auction, and most of the equipment was also used merchandise. Plumbing, electrical, and equipment hookup problems increased expenses to $148,000.

Quinn and Schore recognized that different meal periods would attract different customers, so they attempted to target their advertising to capture the appropriate markets. A brainstorming session produced the following consensus:

Meal Period	Target Market
Lunch	Intown and regional businesses
Dinner	Remote areas
Afternoon snack	Students, shoppers, locals
Brunch	Remote areas
Late night snack	Students, locals
Take out	Locals

Type of Media

13 local newspapers within a 30-mile radius

1 free valley newspaper

New York Times

New York Magazine

Local radio station

In October, Andiamo's literally "just opened the doors." Two weeks prior to the opening, Quinn and Schore had placed advertisements in three surrounding newspapers with an ad simply stating "Andiamo's." One week before the opening the ad was amended to read "Andiamo's—Fine Italian Cuisine."

Arrangements had been made to host a press party and a grand opening party for Ithaca's Chamber of Commerce members, but the "endless hours" involved in opening the restaurant, as well as a cash shortage, necessitated that plans for these events be scrapped. The co-owners did visit the admissions offices of the surrounding colleges, the local conference center, and all of Ithaca's downtown merchants to familiarize them with Andiamo's and to invite them for a complimentary cocktail.

Andiamo's served much the same menu for lunch and dinner, although the luncheon portions were smaller and the prices lower. Besides the appetizer and full dinner menu, there was also a separate pasta menu. Both beer and wine, but not liquor, were available, with a rather extensive Italian wine list with selections ranging from $14.00 to $39.00 per bottle, plus a $9.50 house wine.

ANDIAMO'S CONCEPT

Andiamo's was conceived as an establishment that served only "the freshest possible food made from scratch." It was intended to be a moderately priced restaurant in a neighborhood setting. The owners insisted they were "not interested in making a fast buck or a tremendous return;" they just wanted "to do reasonably well."

Operations

A year later, in October, Mark Jaslow became the manager of Andiamo's. He had been employed as a cook in New York City for the past six years and was just finishing his hotel and restaurant management degree at Cornell University. Mark had originally been hired as the cashier/assistant manager seven weeks before. Upon his promotion, the co-owners retired from active management and assumed their new roles as "directors of investment and operations," and also as restaurant consultants.

Mark described the business level in the previous spring and summer as "booming." From November on, however, business began to decline. In an effort to improve the bottom line, manpower hours, laundry expenses, and advertising dollars were either decreased or, in the latter case, eliminated entirely. Lunch was eventually discontinued in December when advertisements for luncheon specials failed to significantly impact business. The owners decided that the amount of overhead simply exceeded the amount of sales revenue.

Jaslow staffed two to three wait persons and no busperson on weekdays, and four wait persons and one busperson on weekends. Andiamo's also employed a full-time chef and sous-chef, and a part-time pasta maker and baker. All employees had been employed at Andiamo's's for over one year and all were very efficient, according to Jaslow.

Andiamo's could accommodate 76 patrons at the 22 tables in the restaurant. Jaslow stated that in a good week the average turnover rate was below once on Sundays and week nights, two times on Fridays, and three times on Saturdays. The average check for dinner was $22.00 per person and about 20 percent of the total was beer or wine.

According to Jaslow, close to 90 percent of the guests were repeat customers, and 10 percent had been recommended by friends. The clientele was described as mostly upper middle class couples in the $30,000–$50,000 income bracket from the surrounding cities within half an hour of Ithaca. Based on the menu, clientele, and atmosphere, Mark classified the restaurant as "gourmet."

In its first full year of operation, the restaurant averaged $11,500 per week in sales volume, with $7000 coming in on the weekend nights. Food, beverage and advertising costs are shown on the abbreviated income statement (Exhibit 2-1).

EXHIBIT 2-1
Abbreviated Income Statement

Sales			
Food			
Served	473,143		
Take-out	15,479		
Food sales	488,622		
Wine and beer	120,292		
Total Sales	608,914		
Cost of Sales			
Food	135,511		
Wine and beer	49,440		
Total Cost of Sales	184,951		
Advertising	13,921		
Promotion	2,928		
	16,849		
Other Costs			
Total other operating costs		354,945	
Total Costs		556,745	
Profit Before Occupation Cost			52,169
Occupation Costs			58,965
Profit (Loss) Before Depreciation			(6,796)

Marketing

When asked his views on the marketing/advertising scenario, Quinn stated, "I feel our market is within a half hour drive of Ithaca. Because of easy accessibility to Route I80, we see Andiamo's as capturing the transient vacationer who might be enroute to ski, camp, or fish. People from the city heading to the country want to stop in a somewhat cosmopolitan, interesting town."

The major problem, according to Schore, was how to divert those travelers from the superhighway and into Ithaca. "We could never afford to construct a billboard on Route I80, so I decided to attend a Chamber of Commerce meeting to determine how Ithaca is promoting itself." At the meeting, Schore discussed his concerns with the members, and was instrumental in the creation of the Ithaca Publicity Committee.

This committee drafted a marketing proposal and designed a brochure to distribute to ski areas, campgrounds, tourist agencies, and other tourist spots. The committee members visited local merchants and sold $200 advertising blocks to finance the brochure. In return, the merchants were promised valuable exposure. Exhibit 2-2 shows the framework of the marketing plan.

Competition

There were 45 restaurants in Ithaca ranging from McDonald's to gourmet operations. Schore believed that the direct competition for Andiamo's were those that were medium priced and had a

---

EXHIBIT 2-2
Chamber of Commerce Marketing Plan

Campaign Objectives

To attract more people downtown for shopping, dining, and entertainment:
By projecting "Main Street Ithaca" as a vibrant business community with traditional and contemporary elements that blend to give "Main Street Ithaca" broad appeal.

Target Markets

- Area residents
- Residents of major highway communities
- Colonial America buffs: Shaker Community, Historical New York
- Business conference and workshop attendees: hotels and motels conference centers, convention bureaus, major corporations, and university centers
- Academic travelers: prospective students and parents, visiting parents, academic conferences, and returning alumni
- Cultural event attendees: theater at colleges and university, chamber concerts, regional theater, orchestras, and so on.
- Summer camp: staff and visiting parents
- Antiques buyers and collectors
- Skiing area patrons
- Craftspeople and buyers
- Country inn devotees

Promotional Campaign

Develop Identity: Through consistently used logo—"Main Street Ithaca"

(continued)

E X H I B I T 2-2 *(Continued)*

Press Releases: Widely distributed to announce "Main Street Ithaca" Campaign and enumerate reasons to visit Ithaca

Brochure/Business Directory: Distributed within two-hour driving radius to:
- Other Chambers of Commerce
- Tourist booths
- College visitors and conferences
- Hotels and motels
- Cultural events
- Summer camps
- Recreational areas
- Historical areas

The Directory would also be mailed to:
- Ad respondents
- Area resident mailing list
- College mailings
- Special interest lists

Advertising Campaign: Promoting "Main Street Ithaca" with brochure request element
- Local Media—Large ads with elements of directory alternated with smaller institutional identification ads.
- New York, New England, and Northeast periodicals and newspapers and other media in two-hour driving distance. Also special interest periodicals, general tourism guides, and periodicals.

Preliminary Budget

Brochure development, production, and mailing: Ad layouts	$11,000
Local and regional media advertising	14,000
National travel and special interest publications	15,500
Approximate first-year budget:	40,000

Underwriting the Campaign

Mix of:

1. *Directory Listing:* Consisting of Businesses on Main Street (Market to State Streets) and on Side Streets (one block north and south of Main)

   Category
   Name   Address   Phone Number
                One line description
                100 participants @ $250   ($5.00 a week)

2. *Corporate and Institutional Sponsors*
   Listing under Sponsors
   $300 Minimum No Maximum
   Open to all businesses first year under sponsorship of Downtown Business Association.

somewhat unique atmosphere. He identified seven restaurants in the area as competition:

Type of Menu	Atmosphere	Price
1. Vegetarian	Cafe	Low
2. Cheese raclette	Traditional	Medium
3. American-mixed	Inn	Medium-high
4. American-mixed	Traditional	Medium
5. Chinese	Oriental	Medium-high
6. Seafood	Traditional	Medium
7. Vegetarian	Traditional	Low-medium

Mark identified as competition three different restaurants that were within the Ithaca town lines:

Type of Menu	Atmosphere	Price
1. French	Traditional	High
2. Italian	Ethnic	Medium
3. American	Cafe	Medium-high

Advertising

Advertising continued through most of the first year until all ads were eventually canceled in November. Seventy-five percent of the ads simply stated "Andiamo's" and included a description of its food with the address and hours of operation. The remaining 25 percent of the ads were more informative, with specific details about the food and often a unique gimmick to attract customers to the establishment. One example was a coupon ad that ran in the valley's free newspaper with a circulation of 29,000. Only ten coupons were redeemed.

An informal, unscientific study of 25 residents within a ten-mile radius of Ithaca conducted in February of the second year revealed that none of the respondents recognized the name "Andiamo's," nor did they know what it was or where it was located.

HEDONISM II*

Gary Williams, general manager of Hedonism II, enjoyed the sunset from the deck of the resort's Rick's Cafe as he thought about yesterday's board meeting. The discussion at the meeting had centered around expanding the resort's rooms and adding a swimming pool for nudists. Gary's concern was what this would do to their position in the marketplace and their perceived image. He had been noting for some time how Club Med was changing its image from a place for "swinging singles" to one for families. Hedonism II had been patterned after Club Med. "Was it now time," Gary wondered, "to follow a different path? What would this do to our market? What would it do if we don't and follow Club Med instead?"

Hedonism II was situated on 22 acres of landscaped gardens at the northern end of the Seven Mile Beach in Negril, a resort community on the western tip, famous for its sunsets, of Jamaica in the Caribbean Sea. By law, there were no buildings taller than palm trees in Negril. The resort had 280 rooms located in a multitude of two-story buildings. It had just about every known Caribbean resort amenity with the exceptions of golf and cruises.

Hedonism II was one of the SuperClubs. SuperClubs was a marketing organization that promoted five resorts in Jamaica and one in St. Lucia. It operated a network of sales representatives and ran advertising campaigns across North America to market the resorts. It was innovative in the sense that each property was marketed to a separate target market: Couples Jamaica and Couples St. Lucia attracted couples seeking romance; Jamaica Jamaica targeted couples, singles, and families (with children over 16); Boscobel Beach drew families of all ages; Grand Lido was aimed at the sybaritic market; and Hedonism II targeted fun-loving couples and singles. Only Couples St. Lucia and Boscobel Beach did not offer a nude beach or nude sunbathing.

THE HEDONISM II PACKAGE

Originally, the Hedonism II package was an all-inclusive holiday that included everything except drinks. Similar to Club Med, guests purchased

*Kate Taylor and Judy Atkin contributed to this case.

plastic sharks' teeth, which were strung around the neck, to buy drinks. This idea, however, had recently been dropped in favor of a total all-inclusive package at this and other SuperClubs.

Hedonism II attracted over 45 percent repeat guests. To encourage this, many "perks" were offered. For example, there were weekly repeat guest cocktail parties, yearly reunions, and 3 free nights for all guests who have paid for 14 or more nights in the previous year. Some guests had been known to stay there as many as ten times a year. This strong and loyal customer base was continually acknowledged.

THE MARKETING PLANS

The original marketing strategy developed by Hedonism II was to position against Club Med, a well-established, worldwide, and original all-inclusive resort concept started in 1950. Today, there were more than 100 Club Meds in over 30 countries but none in Jamaica. This was only because Club Med rotated its staff every six months and Jamaican law required hiring a certain number of Jamaicans. Club Med staff came from all over the world and were unable to obtain Jamaican work permits.

Generally, although their resorts vary, Club Med targeted office workers, executives, and professional people. In the 1980s, some Club Meds gained a reputation as a wild, sex-oriented vacation. In the late 1990s a new attitude was developing in North America about the negative aspects of promiscuity. Club Med rethought its positioning and started to focus more on sports and family vacations in order to evolve in response to changing times and needs.

Club Med was a formidable competitor and had locations on other Caribbean islands, locations that drew 80 percent of their market from the United States and Canada. Hedonism II's first strategy was to "piggyback" Club Med. Brochures identified it as an alternative to Club Med. A later marketing strategy called for a breakaway from Club Med. Hedonism II marketed on the intangibles of the resort by using pictures and language that stressed the hedonistic approach. Another change was to adver-tise the clothes-optional aspect of the resort. Brochures indicated that there was a nude beach, and there was quite a bit of nudity in the photographs.

Marketing was positioned against Club Med but without mentioning it in the advertising or brochures. Emphasis was still on the intangibles, such as shown in Exhibit 3-1. Billboards, newspapers, and magazine ads featured a half torso with sharks' teeth strung around the neck, as shown in Exhibit 3-2. This was designed to create curiosity and encourage people to contact their travel agents for information. Currently, there was less of a focus on nudity and more focus on sports, but the clothes-optional aspects were still identified.

The original target market for Hedonism II was singles between the ages of 20 and 40, affluent and adventurous, fun loving and casual. Presently it was couples and singles between 25 and 45 with the same characteristics and who wanted excitement, relaxation, and a full array of activities. The actual breakdown was as follows: 65 percent singles, 35 percent couples, 60 percent males, 40 percent females, average age—summer 28, winter 39.

OCCUPANCY

Throughout the 1980s Hedonism II ran year-round occupancies in the 80 to 86 percent range. In the 1990s, after Club Med changed its target market strategy, occupancies began falling into the mid to low 70s. Occupancy ran highest from January to May and slumped lowest during the hurricane season from September into December, but rarely fell below 50 percent. Management and the Board of Directors became concerned about the overall decline.

FUTURE PLANS

Hedonism II, like Club Med, had kept in touch with its customers' changing needs and wants. In response to these it was planning a full service restau-

On Pleasure:

The dictionary will tell you that Hedonism is the seeking of pleasure as a way of life. Not a bad definition, but not very imaginative. And we wish the word "pleasure" was a verb rather than a noun.

We believe that pleasure—the feeling of pleasure—is the most normal and natural of all states and that it is a great deal more natural than its opposite alternative!

We believe, too, that pleasure comes in many forms and that it is most gratifying when it involves all your parts—mind, body, spirit, soul.

It is holistic, not secular.

This is what sets Hedonism II apart from any other Caribbean experience and why we don't consider ourselves as an hotel. We don't look like one. We don't act like one.

Hedonism II is a tropical village by the sea where adults share the pleasures of mind, body, spirit, soul.

There are no children. No formality. No need for money of any kind. And it is the freedom from money, beads, signing chits, etc., that forms an important element of the Hedonism II experience: it breaks down the barriers that usually exist between the guest and the traditional hotel.

Freedom from any concern for money also liberates your mind; it frees your spirit and does wonders for your soul! You simply enjoy <u>everything</u> we have to offer without a second thought. And the absence of commerce allows natural friendships to develop freely between guest and guest and guest and staff.

Hedonism II is <u>the</u> place to meet kindred people who <u>expect</u> life to be enjoyable. Because there is no formality the sharing of the experience occurs naturally as it is happening. People who come together as couples rekindle their relationship and mingle easily with singles. And with singles many a lasting romance has found its beginnings here.

Hedonism II can engage you in enough activity to keep you on the go all day and most of the night. In this respect we follow the dictum of Oscar Wilde that "Nothing succeeds like excess." But we also believe you should be able to take it all in at your own pace. It's your holiday, not ours, and we never forget it.

Please consider this to be your passport to the best holiday of your life. Above all, enjoy, enjoy.

EXHIBIT 3-1 Hedonism II Stresses the Intangible in Words.

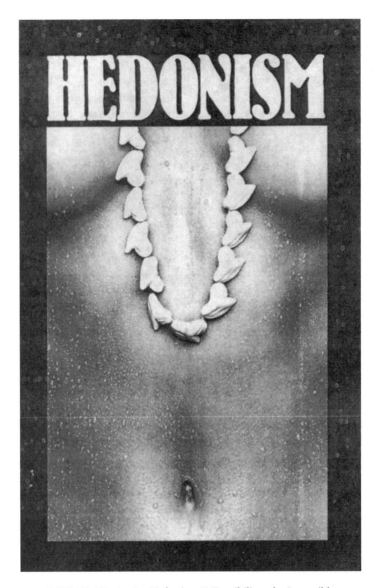

EXHIBIT 3-2   Hedonism II Tangibilizes the Intangible.

rant for those who desired a sit-down meal; presently, there was only a buffet. Sales managers in the United States and Canada were continually creating new travel incentives for customers and travel operators such as Canadian dollars at par with the U.S. dollar, and all-inclusive airfare similar to Club Med packages. The resort also planned 70 more rooms on the "nude side" of the hotel plus a nude swimming pool. With the high prices of all-inclusive holidays, and more and more of them coming on the market, Hedonism II was constantly trying to add extras that would maintain and enhance the value perception. A long-term plan was to copy the hedonism concept on another Caribbean island.

Gary Williams wondered what all this meant in terms of the future.

CASE

Four

LE CIRQUE 2000 RESTAURANT

The New York Palace Hotel, located at 50th Street and Madison Avenue in New York City, had been acquired from Helmsley Hotels by the royal family of Brunei. An extensive renovation was in the planning stages. Food and beverage offerings were determined to be a critical component in the repositioning of the hotel.

Under prior management, the early luster of the Helmsley Palace had waned. The city's first five-star hotel when it opened in 1980, the hotel set a new standard for luxury hospitality service. When the royal family bought it, however, the Palace had not been renovated since opening and was in dire need of refurbishment. Its business had gone down-market in the early 1990s, with a customer base that included airline crews, FIT rates of $99, and numerous bus tours.

Despite a decline in the hotel's room product and the quality of its market mix, the food and beverage facilities remained impressive. Three outlets were located in the historic Villard Houses, a part of the hotel that had been constructed in 1882. The Gold Room served high tea, the Trianon Room was very French and served a full French à la carte service, and the Hunt Bar offered a traditional, wood paneled New York City ambience. The lobby bar, Harry's, was a local favorite. Despite a reasonable volume of business, the food and beverage department was losing in excess of $4.5 million per year. In the mid-1990s, the management of the hotel was given complete license from the royal family to make a decision on the food and beverage offerings after a complete hotel renovation. The center of focus was the Trianon Room.

COMPETITIVE ANALYSIS

There were two primary upscale hotel restaurant competitors in the city. These were Lespinasse at the St. Regis and Les Célébrités at the Essex House, each a few blocks away. Nearby freestanding restaurant competitors, all upscale, included the following:

Restaurant Name	Style	Location
Gloucester House	Nouvelle Seafood	50th street, next door
Giambelli	Italian	50th street, close by

Restaurant Name	Style	Location
Cinquanta	Nouvelle French	50th street, close by
Dolce	Continental	49th Street, one block away
Sushisay	Japanese	51st Street, next door
Tse Yang	Chinese	51st Street, next door
La Grenouille	French	52nd Street, two blocks

Within a five-block walking distance there were an additional 76 restaurants from which hotel guests could select. Many of the competitive offerings were world-class level, giving The New York Palace customer numerous choices close to the hotel. The Trianon at the Palace was not really any longer a direct competitor with any of these restaurants, given the hotel's existing, down-market customer base. In fact, the average checks of the other restaurants in many cases exceeded the nightly room rate at the Palace.

STRATEGY

The Palace management considered that any cuisine imaginable should be considered for future postrenovation of the Trianon Room and the hotel. Numerous meetings were held at the Palace to decide what the concept for the postrenovation New York Palace food and beverage should be. Initially, discussions led toward hiring the top chef available in the world, fitting out the most expensive kitchen in North America, and positioning the restaurant head to head against Lespinasse and Les Célébrités. All indications, however, were that those restaurants, while famous and serving excellent food, lost money as freestanding entities.

The objective of The New York Palace management was to provide a world-class dining experience for its customers, while maintaining the financial integrity of the operation for the ownership. Discussions eventually turned toward leasing the space to a well-known restaurateur.

While several operators were being reviewed, an unique situation was unfolding at the famous Le Cirque restaurant.

Le Cirque

The restaurant, Le Cirque, owned by Sirio Maccioni, was located at the Mayfair Baglioni Hotel at 65th Street and Park Avenue. Like the Helmsley Palace, the Mayfair was in need of renovation to retain its positioning in the New York marketplace. The ownership then decided to change the complexion of the building, from a hotel to condominiums.

Sirio Maccioni was contemplating a change in his business as well. Having been named "The Best Restaurant in North America" by *Conde Naste Traveler* in 1995, Le Cirque had reached a milestone after 22 years of operation. Sirio had noticed that his current customer base was aging with his restaurant. The atmosphere of a classic French restaurant, complemented by a circus motif, was getting old. The millennium was just around the corner, and Sirio felt a new look was necessary to reposition his restaurant for the future.

A courtship between Maccioni and The New York Palace management began and lasted almost a full year, before the two parties came to an agreement. The 65th Street Le Cirque location closed three months later, and work began on the new location at the Palace. A world-famous restaurant designer, Adam Tihany, was commissioned to design the new restaurant, now to be called Le Cirque 2000.

Sirio's vision for his new restaurant was a 100 percent change from both the old design and menu. While retaining just a few signature items on the menu, such as the Dover sole and crème brûlée, most of the menu, service, and atmosphere were marked for change. After employing the well-known Cambodian-born and French-trained chef Sotta Khunn, and world-famous pastry chef Jacques Torres, the restaurant was poised to leap into the millennium with new vision and talent. The strategy was also to completely change the complexion of the Le Cirque customer from the staid, matronly Park Avenue gentry to the new, energetic, younger customers of midtown Manhattan.

PUBLIC RELATIONS CHALLENGE

A "World Tour" of the new concept was designed for the summer before the restaurant opened. The purpose of the tour was twofold: to introduce the idea of a new Le Cirque to the public and to gauge the media interest in the upcoming transformation. Dinners were hosted in Munich, Berlin, London, Paris, and Montecatini Terme, Italy (Sirio's hometown) to introduce the new concept. The media attention was incredible. Every major publication in each city covered the event. CNN television followed the World Tour and reported on its progress.

Most hospitality-related public relations efforts are aimed at gaining publicity by creating events for the media to write about. Le Cirque had a unique opposite problem: there was too much publicity surrounding the upcoming opening. The Le Cirque 2000 story had been building momentum since the closing of the 65th Street location. The press was clamoring to get the inside scoop on the new restaurant. The trial balloon of the World Tour aroused media overload on the story. Management of both The New York Palace and Le

Cirque hoped to maintain both short- and long-term relationships with all the media. A negative story in any one of the major publications could be disastrous.

The dilemma facing both the management of The New York Palace and Le Cirque 2000 was to keep all of the press involved and happy with stories to be written about the opening. The problem was that each publication, including *The New York Times, Crains New York Business, The New Yorker, New York Magazine, Conde Nast Traveler, Gourmet,* and *Travel and Leisure,* wanted an exclusive story on the restaurant. Management feared that if they gave an exclusive story and information access to only one publication, remaining publications could be offended and possibly write unfavorable stories about the new restaurant. With such a dynamic change in concept, everything was on the line for Le Cirque. Both the Palace and Le Cirque would face serious challenges if the restaurant did not initially do well in the press. The scenario was likened to the opening night of a Broadway play; bad reviews can kill even the best show. The New York Palace and Le Cirque were in what appeared to be a no-win situation.

Management of both The Palace and Le Cirque wondered how to resolve this unique dilemma in public relations. In essence, they wondered if there might be a way to spread out the publicity opportunities among all the press and keep everybody happy.

THE HÔTEL PALACE*

Danilo Moriconi swivelled his desk chair and stretched his clasped fingers into the morning sunlight streaming through the lace curtains of his office window. His knuckles cracked one after the other. He had just read the managing director's response to a critical letter to the editor in the largest regional newspaper, *Die Tagesblick,* and was feeling quietly self-satisfied. Although the original complaint letter had been something of a public relations disaster for the Hôtel Palace, he was content with the hotel's official response, which had upheld both the hotel's integrity and his own, and with the overall outcome of recent events. Surely God was smiling on the Hôtel Palace again and, despite the current economic climate, Moriconi felt sure that a new era was dawning for the venerable hotel and for his career. The next 75 years—or at least the next few years—would certainly witness the return of the Palace to its former glory, and Moriconi felt that the hotel was finally back on track again.

THE PALACE AT SEVENTY-FIVE

The Hôtel Palace had just celebrated its seventy-fifth anniversary under the economic cloud of a major recessionary period. As part of its celebration, it offered a special promotional rate of Swiss Francs (ChF) 75.00† per person inclusive of breakfast and dinner in the hotel's renowned dining room to anyone celebrating his or her seventy-fifth birthday during the same year, an unprecedented special offer in an establishment unaccustomed to discounting. The "Merci" package was advertised as a gesture of gratitude to local people who had supported the hotel through its many years.

Although the hotel was internationally famous—a member of Leading Hotels of the World—and a recognized institution within Switzerland, its market base of wealthy foreign aristocrats had deteriorated to a point where it achieved less than 40 percent annual occupancy of

---

*This case was written by Jeffrey B. Catrett, Professeur Hôtelier, Ecole Hôtelière de Laussane, Switzerland. Names have been disguised.

†For conversion purposes use one ChF equals C$1.00, FF 4.15, DM 1.25, Dfl 1.4, UK .42, U.S. $0.68

its 160 rooms. Its once numerous permanent residents, who maintained apartments at the hotel for seasonal occupancy, had dwindled to a handful of octogenarians. Younger affluent travelers had developed interests in adventure and experience tourism not readily available in the well-established city/resort region surrounding the hotel, and the remaining regular visitors to the region preferred to invest in condominiums or real estate. Few transient guests were willing to pay the hotel's rack rates, which started at ChF 350.00 (app. U.S. $238.00) per room.

The hotel's physical plant had deteriorated to an appallingly low level as a result of the property's poor financial showing (the hotel lost several million francs annually) and the owners' resulting unwillingness to reinvest in furniture, fixtures, and equipment. In fact, the Palace almost certainly would have declared bankruptcy and closed were it not supported by a prestigious international sporting association whose patronage of banqueting facilities and restaurants kept the hotel looking at least somewhat successful. The owners therefore continued to operate the hotel as a trophy property in the hope that new management might be able to reposition the hotel in line with modern tastes and needs.

THE MANAGEMENT TEAM

The Palace had been operated for the last five years as part of a smaller "collection" of hotels owned by Swissair, the prestigious national air carrier, composed of several disparate international properties ranging from newish four-star airport hotels to five-star palaces. Ownership had recently insisted upon replacement of the hotel's general manager, who had operated the hotel for the chain unsuccessfully since the management contract had been signed five years earlier. During the last year, the hotel management team, headed by a new managing director, Jakob Aebersold (who had been released by a famous palace hotel in St. Moritz,) had hired Karin van den Welden, a sales account executive with two years experience at Nestlé. The Palace was just beginning to experiment with promotions and discounting, a move strongly resisted by Moriconi and other Palace veterans.

The hotel's staff was oddly divided between associates who had been with the hotel for several decades—the concierges, porters, and waiters—and hotel school trainees. The management team was composed of Aebersold, the managing director; Moriconi, the assistant director; and François du Champs, the vice director, who also served as food and beverage director; along with a director of rooms division, a director of human resources, and a financial comptroller who coordinated accounting operations with an outside accounting firm. The director of human resources, Heidi Lutz, who had come over with Aebersold from the St. Moritz property, doubled as his personal assistant and public relations manager. A handful of assistant managers were engaged in actual supervision of employees. Aebersold had been in his position for approximately one year and was under pressure to increase the hotel's profitability. He was given to fits of extreme temper and was often seen literally jumping up and down with his fists clenched shouting at associates and other managers. This behavior was often exhibited in the hotel lobby and restaurants as well as in private and departmental offices.

Aerbersold was secretly resented by both Moriconi and du Champs, both of whom had been with the hotel for many years and who had been passed over for promotion. Moriconi had emigrated to the country 20 years earlier as a young apprentice and believed that his émigré status was the reason for his failure to be promoted. In the early years, he had been awed by the spectre of the Swiss hotelery. But as time went by and he watched his beautiful hotel progressively disintegrate, his southern temperament had boiled at the agonizingly slow pace of events in Switzerland. Although the company had invested in so-called "Management of Change Seminars," the only changes Moriconi perceived were short-term, quick-fix schemes to increase revenue, which ruined the hotel's image, taking it further and further away from the vaunted position of its heyday years. Moriconi believed that a grand hotel was an institution that must remain aloof from the swirling tides of economic and demographic trends if it were to maintain its integral character. The company, he believed, had increasingly sold the hotel out to a class of clientele that could not appreciate its essential finesse and charm and that would only be dissatisfied with the expensiveness of the offer, without consideration for the renovation work needed to maintain the product.

With respect to his own career, Moriconi had grown wary of the antiforeigner sentiment and local hotel chauvinism prevalent in the region. He had painstakingly established close connections to important people within the international sporting association, however, and his tenure was in little jeopardy. Du Champs was considered by many, including himself, to be the token Swiss French on the management committee. In a company headquartered in Zurich, he felt he had little chance to gain a general manager's position. He accepted his fate with a kind of permanent sulk and was rarely seen around the hotel.

A FORAY INTO MARKETING

Miss van den Welden had enlisted the support of the chain's corporate Marketing Department, dominated by former marketers of Swissair, in providing an internal relationship marketing and upselling instruction course to associates. The program was administered on a compulsory basis to all line-level staff both in the Rooms area and in the hotel's outlets, and was also attended by line-level associates and assistant managers. Attendees were not paid for the time they invested in the course, which was given in the hotel ballroom. Tipped associates were told that the course would increase their gratuities, and nontipped associates were assured that the course would serve as an important credit on their résumé. The course was introduced by Miss van den Welden but was led by airline sales staff and stressed both

the importance of building relationships with potential return guests and of upselling hotel products and services. At the conclusion of the course, each staff associate and assistant manager was tested on the material, and each earned a nationally recognized certificate. The course was completed just two weeks before the beginning of the seventy-fifth anniversary celebrations.

THE UNFOLDING GALA

When the first big night arrived—a Saturday night during a normally busy period in the early fall—invited local dignitaries and socialites as well as representatives of the international sports association were ushered into the hotel's many banquet rooms for specially prepared dinners and speeches. The press was in attendance, and the event was covered extensively in regional papers and magazines, including *Die Tagesblick*. Additional banquet staff had been enlisted from local hotel schools to aid in the preparation and service.

The hotel's restaurant, La Rotonde (16 Gault Millau points out of a possible 20*), was reserved mainly for persons who had been attracted by the "Merci" package offer. La Rotonde's long-time maître d'hôtel and president of the national maître d' Association, Antoine Rey, had recently stormed out of the restaurant as a result of a personality clash and power struggle with Aebersold, vowing to take away La Rotonde's return guest base and ruin its reputation in the local community. Older waiters resented the loss of the Maître d' whom they believed had been largely responsible for maintaining the reputation of the restaurant and ensuring their substantial incomes (13.04 percent of revenue plus considerable incidental tipping.) Some younger waiters were relieved at the removal of this traditional autrocratic manager,

---

*Gault Millau is a famed and prestigious restaurant rating company based in Paris. Very few restaurants are rated 16 or above.

however, and welcomed the arrival of a young Austrian, Hans-Rudolph Scheer, a hotel school graduate who had been hired to fill the position.

THE FAVRE INCIDENT

Mr. and Mrs. Marcel Favre arrived for dinner in the restaurant on the first night of the seventy-fifth anniversary celebration dressed in their finest attire—expensive if somewhat poorly tailored clothing—and proudly presented their coupon for the menu being offered as part of their "Merci" package. (The coupon was valid for the fixed menu, which included coffee but no beverages.) Mr. Favre had celebrated his seventy-fifth birthday during March of the same year and was looking forward to his first Hôtel Palace experience. After many years of farming, he had sold his land for a handsome profit and was enjoying his retirement with his wife of over 50 years. They were graciously received by Scheer, who escorted them to a table in a station manned by one of the hotel's most experienced waiters, Antonin Propescu.

The Favres took note of the fancy menu cards with the history of the establishment, the Gault Millau rating, and the prices printed exclusively on the gentleman's card. Mr. Favre ordered the prix fixe menu for himself and his wife and selected a bottle of lower-priced local wine when the waiter presented the wine card—a wine he recognized, which was widely available in local supermarkets. During the course of the meal, the Favres remarked that Propescu seemed somewhat cool and distant, but decided that this apparent hauteur was probably considered appropriate in such a distinguished restaurant. Propescu made several attempts to offer another bottle of wine, but the Favres remained with their initial selection throughout the dinner. All-in-all, the experience was somewhat formal for their taste, but they savored the luxurious surroundings and were impressed with the excellent food quality.

At the conclusion of the dinner, Mr. Favre asked Propescu's advice in selecting "something special" as an after-dinner drink for the couple to toast the occasion. He told Propescu, with a wink, that the Favres had been accustomed to their own home-made eau de vie, but wanted something "a little better" for this important occasion. Propescu did not present the card, but indicated with a flourish that he had "just the thing for a special evening," mentioning the name of a French vintage unfamiliar to the Favres. He returned with two glasses and a delicious dessert wine, which the couple enjoyed immensely. At the conclusion of the meal, Propescu indicated deferentially that he would place the beverages on the couple's hotel bill. Although the evening had been somewhat stiff, and the Favres had felt somewhat out-of-place, they retired for the night satisfied with their one and only Hôtel Palace experience.

At check-out the following morning, they were told that the hotel's computer was not functioning properly. The Reception trainee politely requested an imprint of Mr. Favre's credit card and said that a copy of the bill would be sent to them in the mail within a few days.

Two weeks later, Mr. Favre received the bill as well as a major shock. The dessert wine—a Château d'Yquem—had been charged to the bill at ChF 200.00 per glass. The "special after-dinner drinks" had cost almost three times as much as the rest of the experience combined. Mr. Favre duly called the hotel to complain.

SERVICE RECOVERY?

Mr. Favre's first complaint was answered by an Asian reception trainee who asked him in awkward French if they had, in fact, consumed the drinks. When he replied that they had, the trainee responded by saying that there was nothing she could do—the credit card had already been charged, and it was the hotel's policy only to alert the accounting firm if disputes were made as to the validity of charges. Mr. Favre placed a second and angrier call to the hotel and asked to speak to someone responsible for the restaurant. After some time, his call was transferred to a Banquet Maître d', the only person of responsibility from the Food and Beverage Department on duty during the afternoon. Against a din of background noise, the Banquet Maître d' explained that he was supervising a function at the moment and that Mr. Favre would have to call the Maître d' for La Rotonde in a few days, after the check and bill could be secured from the accounting firm. He promised to have Scheer look into the matter. Mr. Favre then called the hotel a third time and demanded to speak to the managing director. He was told, after several minutes on hold, that Mr. Aebersold was not available, but that the assistant director, Mr. Moriconi, would return his call within the hour.

Moriconi called back 45 minutes later after investigating the incident, announced himself, and listened respectfully to Mr. Favre's complaint. Mr. Favre argued that he had not been advised of the charge for the Château d'Yquem at the time of the service and would never have selected such an expensive option if he had been aware of its price. He suggested that he would be willing to pay a reduced amount for the drinks, but that he felt he should not and could not pay the full price for something he had not directly ordered. While relating his frustrations, Mr. Favre became increasingly abrasive, using rough language in an incredulous tone of voice. He finished by relating his fury at having been mishandled by the reception trainee and the Banquet Maître d' and having to wait beside his telephone for a management response.

After letting Mr. Favre speak his mind, Moriconi responded in a tone of cool, controlled authority. The Hôtel Palace, he explained, was well-known throughout the community as a hotel with certain standards and, of course, certain prices—a hotel for connoisseurs. The special "Merci" package had been arranged to allow members of the local community to share in a special moment in the hotel's history. Moriconi defended the actions of the waiter Propescu by pointing out to Mr. Favre that he had asked specifically for "something special" as an after-dinner drink in an environment where "something special" certainly meant "something expensive." Propescu had mentioned the name of the wine and would assume normally that Mr. Favre's

failure to ask for the wine card or the price meant that he knew the wine and its reputation for quality and expense. Moriconi suggested that it would have been inelegant and patronizing for the waiter to discuss prices openly and inappropriate and equally patronizing to offer a low-priced substitute when "something special" was requested.

Favre responded somewhat sheepishly that he had not wanted to appear ignorant when Propescu mentioned the vintage. Moriconi proceeded by agreeing with Mr. Favre's assessment of the hotel's awkwardness in responding to his calls but pointed out that the Palace was a large establishment with a complex internal hierarchy and a variety of levels of experience. Nevertheless, he assured Mr. Favre that the hotel would take steps to remedy its clumsiness in reacting to customer concerns. In the end, however, Moriconi summarily rejected Mr. Favre's offer to pay a discounted price for the Château d'Yquem, pointing out that the wine had been consumed and that the hotel had incurred the associated costs. Mr. Favre reacted angrily saying that he would refuse to pay and threatening that repercussions would follow. Moriconi calmly replied that the Palace would not be threatened, and the charge would remain on the card.

THE FALLOUT

The next day, an inflammatory letter to the editor composed by Mr. Favre was published in *Die Tagesblick*. In it, he described in detail his own personal background, the events as they unfolded, and his impressions of the insensitive response given by Palace management. After several days of contemplation and consultation with his PR assistant, Aebersold responded with a letter that expressed the hotel's regret that Mr. Favre had been upset by the matter but also expressed anger that the incident had been reported in a one-sided and disproportionate manner. Aebersold affirmed the hotel's right and responsibility to maintain its position as an upholder of taste and standards within the community, noting that high prices were necessary to keep the hotel open, providing the services expected by that community. La Rotonde, the letter asserted, was clearly a gourmet restaurant, and Mr. Favre, it concluded, had been treated with the same discretion and in the same manner as would any guest in La Rotonde regardless of social station.

CONCLUSION—
A SMALL VICTORY

The fog, traditional for this time of year, had thickened around Moriconi's office, and the sun had been reduced to a small distant bright spot in the heavens. Moriconi swiveled around toward the jumble of reports he would need to consider for the week's upcoming meetings and absently stroked the leg of his fine Italian Renaissance writing table. The room had grown darker, but his spirits had not dimmed. Although he had had to put up with a few of Aebersold's trademark fits, it had been worth it. It was a small but important victory for an old hotelier, and he had learned to relish these small victories and bide his time. For the first time in many weeks, he found himself actually looking forward to the endless round of meetings. Though it would be subtle and slow, change—at least the kind of change Moriconi yearned for—was definitely in the air.

Six

RAISE THE NUMBERS!*

The Plaza Royal Hotel was built in 1929. The hotel had been successful as a top of the line property and over the years had developed a loyal clientele. In recent years, however, major competition had entered the market and was seriously threatening the hotel's market share. These new properties include those operated by Hilton International, Sheraton, and Four Seasons, among others. In the face of this competition, management recognized that the property had deteriorated and was in need of major refurbishing if it was going to maintain its market status.

The company commenced a three-year, $100 million renovation program that would completely refurbish all 1200 rooms as well as the lobby, food and beverage outlets, meeting rooms, and back of the house service areas. Rather than take the risk of losing customers to competitors, who might not return when the renovations were completed, it was decided to remain open and keep in operation any rooms or portions of the hotel that did not have to be shut down for construction.

By next year, 600 rooms would have been renovated but not without considerable difficulty. Customers were often forced to step over piles of lumber, around construction equipment, and through mazes of boxes, to get to their rooms. This had caused a considerable amount of dissatisfaction and numerous customer complaints. In fact, it was known that a number of regular customers had decided to go elsewhere, at least for the duration of the renovation period. Many, however, said they would return when it was finished.

At the same time, the economy had taken a downturn. Hotel occupancies, citywide, had dropped. This caused even more intense competition among hotels for the existing business. With another one to two years to go with its renovation program, Plaza Royal management was struggling to maintain its forecasts. Of particular concern was the corporate market, and the sales staff was working hard to maintain the hotel's share of this segment.

Corporate group room nights were estimated to finish the year with 33,500. Corporate transient room nights would be about 90,000. Because of the renovation program and resultant periodic loss of meeting space, the next year forecast for corporate

---

*Vicki Tindle contributed the information for this case. Names have been disguised.

group room nights was lowered to 30,000. The corporate transient forecast was raised to 95,000 to compensate for this loss.

The sales department wasn't too sure just how it was going to meet these projections. The projected corporate transient rate was to remain at $128 per night. This compared to a $122 rate at the Sheraton, and a $164 rate at the Four Seasons. Hilton's corporate transient rate ranged from $118 to $138, and it had vowed to keep these rates throughout the next year, in view of the economy. These three hotels were perceived as the major competition for the corporate market in the city.

The Plaza Royal sales staff had little difficulty competing with its $128 rate for the newly renovated rooms. In fact, the refurbishing was so successful that it felt it could probably obtain even higher rates for those rooms. However, there would be only 600 of them to sell for much of next year and they couldn't always guarantee them. Further, even though the rooms were very satisfying, customers still had the problem of ongoing construction in public areas and hallways, along with the attendant dust, confusion, and noise.

For some customers, the quality rooms at $128 were worth the trade-off of the renovation confusion. For others, they were not. Worse, however, was the situation when a customer was placed in an unrenovated room and still had to endure the renovation mess. These customers were becoming increasingly difficult to keep.

In November the sales staff scheduled an all day meeting to plan its strategy for the next year; namely, how to maintain even 30,000 corporate group nights and how to increase corporate transient nights by 5000. Also on the agenda was a longer term consideration: How to keep and/or get back the customers being lost because of the renovations, after the renovations were completed.

The Director of Sales began the meeting by reading a memo she had just received from the corporate office. They weren't very pleased, she read, about the forecast projecting a loss in corporate group nights, or the increase in corporate transient nights of only 5000. However, they were somewhat persuaded that perhaps these figures were realistic in view of the renovations going on. To make up for the loss of revenue, however, they wanted the corporate transient rate for next year to be set at $142 per night.

Seven

•❖•

RAISE THE GOAL!

John Brady returned to his office to figure out what to do next. As sales manager of a large resort in Florida, he was responsible for the group market. Up to now, he thought he was doing well, making calls on his customers and booking business.

At a sales meeting prior to his return to the office, the director of sales had increased John's goals. Apparently, the corporate office of the hotel company was displeased with his results and had held a meeting with the director of sales. Now it was John's problem.

John's first thought was to look at his account management system. It looked like this for the current year:

Category	Number of Accounts	Room Nights	Average Rate
A	75	12,000	
B	75	5,000	
C	200	10,000	
Total	350	27,000	$ 90.74

John's previous goal for a year had been 25,000 room nights, which he had been achieving on a consistent basis. Now, his goal has been raised to 30,000 room nights, at a $100 average rate. He cal-culated what he had to do for the upcoming year, with his Sales Equation:

Room Nights

Past customers	+	New customers	=	Goals
27,000	+	3,000	=	30,000

Clearly, John needed to find more rooms for the upcoming year. Of his 350 accounts, the breakdown by subsegment is described below:

Group Files

Segment	Number of Files	Average Rate	Number of Rooms	Booking Lead Time
Corporate	150	$120	10,000	3 months
Tours	150	$ 70	15,000	6 months
Associations	50	$100	2,000	1 year
Total	350	$ 90.74	27,000	

John was constrained by time and felt he could only call on 350 accounts a year. Any more, and his prospecting time would be reduced to nothing. John had to get back to his director of sales within a week to let him know what he was going to do about increasing his quotas for the upcoming year.

CASE

Eight

THE RIVERSIDE RESTAURANT*

It had been a cold and blustery day and the weatherman was forecasting a blizzard. Reservation cancellations had begun flooding in to the Riverside Restaurant by late afternoon, and by 7:00 o'clock it was obvious that the evening's business would be negligible.

Manager Joseph Cantone took advantage of this rare opportunity to leave the floor and retire to his office. He began reviewing financial records and was pleased to see that the Riverside had continued to increase its sales volume in each of the past three years. On a less encouraging note, he realized that the restaurant had not produced the substantial profits necessary to achieve its financial objectives.

BACKGROUND

The Riverside Restaurant was located in North Caldwell, Idaho, approximately 20 yards off the heavily trafficked Route 44. Caldwell had once been a familiar way station for east-west travelers on the Old Oregon Trail as early as the mid-eighteenth century. It was approximately 15 miles from Boise, Idaho, the state capital, and just off I84 that crossed the state. The transportation access to Caldwell was excellent and was probably the area's greatest asset for retaining present industry and attracting new businesses.

The town's approximately 25,000 citizens had increased by about 12 percent in the last five years, growing at a rate one and one half times that of the state. Statisticians predicted that the population would jump by another 11.5 percent over the next four years. The events of recent years had tended to decentralize the community and progressively change its character from a self-sufficient manufacturing town to a bedroom community.

The Riverside Restaurant had been solely owned by Orly Cantone. Cantone started his restaurant career as a busboy at the competing Lafayette House and was eventually promoted to head waiter. He decided to create a roadside restaurant that specializing in prime rib. The Riverside was known for its superior prime rib to the present day. Orly also had owned the Riverside Pub in South Caldwell. His sons, Joseph and Robert, purchased the two restau-

*Names and location have been disguised

rants from him when he retired. Currently, Joseph managed the Riverside Restaurant, while Robert managed the Riverside Pub.

Word-of-mouth advertising had always been responsible for the growth of the Riverside. Orly Cantone had never advertised the restaurant or promoted his specials in any way, and Joseph felt the same way. "When people walk into our restaurant," he said, "we try to take care of them. Customers do not want their guests to be dissatisfied. Food has to be good. Service has to be polite. At lunch time, it has to be fast. We do our best to provide a relaxed and comfortable dining experience with quality food and genial service while providing an acceptable price/value relationship. People who have dined with us have had a favorable experience and tell their friends and relatives. It's as simple as that."

THE RESTAURANT TODAY

The Riverside Restaurant was a stately, old mansion that had been the showplace of North Caldwell in the mid-1800s. It was a three-story, white Victorian structure with four dining areas and a cocktail lounge. The main dining room, called the Lounge, was decorated in a pink and maroon motif and seated 70 people. It was adjacent to the cocktail lounge, which seated 30 and was for cocktails only, except when customer requests or dining room overflow necessitated serving dinner in this room.

The nonsmoking dining room, also decorated in pink and maroon, had a capacity of 40 and was located next to the stairway leading to the second floor. This area was separated from the other dining rooms and hallways and was most popular. The River Room was a 125-seat function room located behind the nonsmoking area and was used for à la carte service on Saturdays and holidays only. The room was done in blue and gold and was an ideal spot for rehearsal parties and wedding receptions. Finally, there was the 15-seat private dining room, which was located on the second floor. It was increasingly popular with business groups, particularly in the spring.

The Riverside had existed for almost 40 years and had witnessed the rise and fall of many area restaurants. Five years ago, there were at least a dozen pizza parlors in North Caldwell, each of which had a long waiting line. Now only a handful remained. There were also many Chinese restaurants in the area, but most also eventually failed.

The Riverside menu featured prime rib, steak, and various seafood items. Dinner prices ranged from $12.50 to $18.95 and included a selection of relishes, crackers, and homemade cheese as well as a house salad. The best-selling entrée had long been the prime rib, which was available for as little as $17.95 with beverage and dessert. Upon request, the house policy was to offer an additional serving of prime rib, but few customers requested seconds since the entrée portion was generous.

The restaurant's luncheon menu was in the $8 to $12 range and offered smaller portions of some of the dinner items as well as soups, sandwiches, and salads. A banquet menu was available for parties of 25 or more.

Joseph Cantone was hesitant to embrace "trendy" cuisines, since he feared that they would lead to his restaurant's downfall. Although he had agreed to revise the Riverside menu a few years ago in response to the strong demand for seafood, beef remained a popular selection. Nonetheless, seafood soon overtook beef as the top seller.

The Riverside tried to position itself as a moderately priced meat and potatoes restaurant that did not attempt "gourmet" preparations. Joseph remarked, "I don't want to be perceived as an elegant restaurant which only the well-to-do can afford. I also have no intention of expanding to a chain operation, which would require more managerial and financial capabilities than we currently have. I want to improve what we are doing. Wouldn't it be great to see the whole restaurant reserved by 12:00 on Saturday?"

CUSTOMERS

According to Joseph Cantone, the Riverside attempted to appeal to everyone. "When you do that," he said, "what you have is wholesome food which is served nicely at a reasonable price." For some reason, however, the restaurant was not popular among residents of North Caldwell. Cantone suggested that perhaps they were afraid to try the restaurant because of its "ritzy-looking" building.

Demographically, the Riverside customers were predominantly male, with over 75 percent of all female diners accompanied by a male companion. More than half were in the 40 to 60-year-old age bracket. One-third of all sales volume was generated by corporate bookings. Cantone cultivated this patronage with membership in various social and civic organizations. Credit card sales represented 60 percent of total sales.

At lunch time, approximately 80 percent of the clientele were businesspeople, whereas that percentage dropped to 20 percent at dinner. For the most part, dinner regulars were residents of the surrounding communities who had patronized the Riverside for many years. These guests were set in their ways, and the waitresses frequently complained about their demanding natures.

FINANCIAL PERFORMANCE

The restaurant's peak periods were predictable, with Tuesdays and Wednesdays generally proving to be the slowest nights. The restaurant served an average of 150 to 250 covers on Sundays through Thursdays, 450 on Fridays, and approximately 600 on Saturdays.

Joseph Cantone considered his product to be underpriced relative to the market. He chose not to raise his prices since he felt they should reflect the financial attitude of what he considered to be an economically depressed community. Joseph alluded to his current situation with the following comment. "Our dollar volume has increased every quarter for the last three years. However, the increase in volume did not keep pace with the inflationary trend. Additionally, we did not achieve the desired return on gross sales."

MANAGEMENT

When he first purchased the restaurant from his father, Joseph immersed himself in the minute details of operating the establishment and interacted personally with everyone from the dishwashers to the vendors. Recently however, he had begun to delegate more of the operational details to his unofficial assistant manager, Veronica Terinese. Veronica was a veteran waitress who had gradually taken over the hiring and scheduling of the wait staff. She began at the Riverside ten years ago and had become a go-between for Joseph and the service personnel. She kept track of the daily performance of the restaurant by recording the number of covers and the average checks on her personal computer. She also compiled sales abstracts for use in future menu planning.

A strong emphasis was placed on quality control of service. Joseph established the service standards, monitored their execution, and actively solicited feedback from his customers. He also held frequent staff meetings to discuss service related problems. Veronica Terinese was proud of the Riverside staff. "You just have to make sure you don't lose any of your good people," she said. Many of the waitresses had been at the Riverside for 10 to 15 years, although an increasing percentage of the staff were college students and young mothers.

The Riverside had no sales or marketing staff per se, since Joseph did not feel that employing a salesperson would prove cost-effective. As a result, a considerable part of the sales effort was made by Joseph himself.

"Our base is too limited to support a major marketing program," he said. "In order to attract the Boise market, we would have to go out and hire professionals who are knowledgeable of that specific market. Our business simply does not warrant that type of activity." On a local level, Joseph acknowledged that it would be relatively inexpensive to advertise in the area media. However, he contended that it might change the restaurant's image.

COMPETITION

Joseph Cantone considered everyone in food service from a McDonald's to a Chinese restaurant to be his competitor. However, he was not concerned about those who offered two-for-one specials as a means of attracting new business. "They will steal your customers for a while," he said, "but they are not building loyalty. The customers will return when the special ends."

Of the 22 restaurants in North Caldwell and the several others within 10 to 20 miles, only a few could be identified as direct competitors. There was no other restaurant in North Caldwell that was comparable in level of service and atmosphere, although a similar new establishment was slated for construction across the street within the next year. The primary competitors were identified as the Riverside Pub, the Lafayette House, and Benjamin's.

The Riverside Pub: The Riverside Pub was a sister restaurant to the Riverside and was located five miles away in South Caldwell. When it was opened in 1979, the establishment attracted many of the Riverside customers, since the Pub was closer to Boise and was therefore more convenient for many. Except for minor variations in decor, the two facilities were extremely similar. Menu, prices, and level of service were virtually identical. The customer base of the Pub was primarily businessmen, with some local residents and college students as well.

The Lafayette House: The Lafayette House first opened in 1784 when it was a popular tavern on the Old Oregon Trail. It was located in North Caldwell, five miles north of the Riverside, on Route 44 and was easily accessible from all directions. The facility had six dining rooms and a cocktail lounge. The Lafayette House attracted businesspeople and locals on the strength of its word-of-mouth advertising. The atmosphere was somewhat rustic and the establishment was known for its excellent facilities for small or large banquets accommodating a maximum of 200 people. Entrée prices ranged from $16.00 for shrimp scampi to $20.50 for filet mignon, with prime rib prominently featured at $18.50. Like at the Riverside, entrées included fresh relishes, tossed salad, and assorted rolls.

Benjamin's: Benjamin's was 12 miles from the Riverside. Since the restaurant opened in 1978 the seating capacity had been increased to 650 people. Presently, there were three dining areas, a lounge, and a ballroom that accommodated 250 guests. After dinner, many of the guests enjoyed dancing in the Library Lounge, which featured live entertainment five nights a week. The best-selling entrée at Benjamin's was the Prime Rib at $18.95. Other items included poultry, seafood, and beef with filet mignon at $20.95 as the most expensive. Side dishes were offered à la carte with prices for salads or vegetables ranging from $2.25 to $4.50. The major markets for Benjamin's were the businesspeople and the special occasion diner. The establishment's reputation had been built on its ability to provide either intimate dining for families and friends or a large scale business function. There were many repeat customers, who had generally become acquainted with Benjamin's through word of mouth, although some were first attracted by infrequent newspaper ads.

CONCLUSION

Despite the fact that sales volume had increased over each of the last three years, Joseph Cantone was not altogether satisfied. His restaurant had not kept pace with inflation and his real profit was declining. Cantone wondered if this was the case with his primary competitors and pondered this dilemma as the snow outside continued to fall.

Nine

◆•◆

THE SUPERIOR INN AND CONFERENCE CENTER*

It was a beautiful morning in February when Susan Newton replaced Howard Creel and assumed the position of director of marketing of the Superior Inn and Conference Center in Omaha, Nebraska. Howard had already reviewed the competitive situation with Susan and presented her with a marketing plan that covered the rest of the year. Although he sincerely wished her the best of luck, Howard was anxious to return home and await his movers. True to character, Susan wanted to talk.

The Superior Inn was a 30-year old property that had averaged a 64 percent occupancy the year before at a $79.66 average rate in a highly competitive market. This level of business represented an actual market share of 9.8 percent, which fell far short of the property's fair market share of 14.29 percent. The question foremost in Susan's mind was this: "What would it take to improve the over-

all occupancy picture to at least the point where the hotel received its fair market share of the potential business?"

THE CITY OF OMAHA

Omaha, Nebraska, was a fast-growing metropolis located at the crossroads of the nation. It was considered to be the agricultural capital of the world as well as its largest livestock market and meat-packing center. Omaha was one of the nation's largest producers of quick frozen foods and was notable as a transportation, communication, and insurance center. The city was presently in the midst of a diversification and expansion program with the goal of lessening its dependence on agriculture.

Omaha was readily accessible by all means of transportation. It was situated at the intersection of Interstate 80, which ran across the United States from the east coast to the west, and Interstate 29,

---

*Bharath M. Josiam contributed to this case. Names and places have been disguised.

which ran north-south. Several major airlines operated a total of more than 100 daily flights in and out of Omaha, and Eppley Field was about 12 miles from the downtown area. Eight railroads made Omaha the fourth largest railroad center in the country.

HISTORY

The Superior Inn and Conference Center was built in 1970 by the Kraus Corporation. Initially, the Hotel Kraus was the showplace of the area. Unfortunately, however, the cumulative effect of successive owners and franchisers eventually took its toll on the hotel. A series of investors proceeded to bleed the property, rather than reinvest in capital improvements. As a result, the Superior Inn became sorely in need of extensive renovation.

In 1988, the Innstar Corporation purchased the facility and began a physical overhaul. Innstar decided that the existing franchise had a poor image that was not unlike that of a truck stop. A Superior Inn franchise agreement was signed. In 1998 Ozark Innkeepers assumed ownership of the hotel.

It was hoped that the combination of the Superior Inn franchise and the change in ownership would be a real shot in the arm for the hotel's momentum. Ozark Innkeepers spent $1 million renovating 100 of the 185 guestrooms, the lobby, and some of the meeting space, but there was a great deal more to be done. It was disheartening, moreover, that the expected surge of business due to the renovation had failed to materialize. Nonetheless, Susan Newton was enthusiastic about the impact the renovation would have on her clients.

THE SUPERIOR INN AND CONFERENCE CENTER

The Superior Inn and Conference Center was a U-shaped, low-rise building with 185 sleeping rooms. The 100 rooms in the "Executive Wing" had been completely renovated. The hotel was located in the southeast section of town and was easily accessible from either Interstate 80 or US Highway 275. The hotel did not provide limousine service to the airport, which was about 12 miles away.

There was a private courtyard adjoining a spacious and canopied patio between the two wings of the building. Features included an olympic-sized heated outdoor pool, patio bar, and barbeque pit. The landscaping and groundswork had been partially redone in recent months and quotations were being received on the remainder of the project. This area was conveniently located to the lower lobby, the ballroom, and the lounge, and was extremely popular from May through October for parties and receptions.

The main lobby was large and had been renovated within the last year. It lent itself well to convention groups for either mass registration or just plain congregating. The lower lobby was connected to the main lobby and also served as a registration area. In addition, the lower level could also be utilized for either coffee breaks or as a display area.

Guestrooms ranged in price from $91 to $104 single, and from $98 to $112 double, depending on bedding. Suites were available for either $145 or $195 per night. Each room or suite included a Touch-Tone telephone as well as cable TV hookup, complete with remote control. The hotel did not offer room service.

MEETINGS AND BANQUETS

Meeting facilities at the Superior Inn were well conceived with a good balance of various sized rooms and one of the largest ballrooms in the area. The Omaha Ballroom seated 650 guests for a banquet and could accommodate a maximum of 900 people theater-style, although its room dividers were not soundproof. There were a total of 13 rooms in all, and most were in urgent need of renovation. A charge was assessed for room rental if no meal was served at the function.

Meeting room equipment was generally dated and in need of replacement. The approximately

500 chairs and 30 banquet tables were in particularly bad condition, and the audiovisual equipment was not remotely state-of-the-art.

Banquets at the hotel were noted for their good food and service. However, the lack of proper equipment created problems when it necessitated the "borrowing" of crockery and cutlery from the restaurant when Banquets was busy. Meetings and banquets accounted for about 20 percent of total revenue.

EFFIE'S

The restaurant at the Superior Inn was named in remembrance of its first manager, Effie Hathaway. Effie's had a maximum capacity of 75 and was comfortably decorated with overstuffed chairs and well-cushioned banquettes along the walls. However, the room had not been physically improved in many years and the wear and tear was pronounced. Effie's was located in between the lounge and the kitchen.

The menu consisted of basic American fare with an emphasis on the agricultural products native to the region. Beef was well-represented along with a wide variety of vegetables, but fish and seafood items were noticeably scarce. Management generally attempted to offer a middle-of-the-road selection since Effie's was the hotel's only restaurant.

The market for the restaurant varied significantly by meal period. Breakfast business originated almost entirely in-house, and only 5 percent of breakfast customers were not registered at the Inn. Lunchtime business was about a 50–50 mix, and dinner patrons were 70 percent guests of the hotel. Effie's represented about 18 percent of total revenue.

HARRY'S

The lounge at the Superior Inn was warm and friendly with a forest green and pale yellow decor accented by polished brass. Unfortunately, Harry's had not aged well and was seriously in need of major renovation. At present, the lounge seated 58 people and was open from the hours of 11:00 A.M. to 1:00 A.M., seven days a week.

There was a small alcove off the lounge that was regularly used as a serving station. A cook was scheduled to man this area during each weekday lunch period, handcarving the meats for overstuffed delicatessan sandwiches. The alcove was also staffed during cocktail hour when complimentary hors d'oeuvres were available.

Harry's boasted live entertainment on weekend nights when a three-piece band played Top 40 hits. There was a 8 × 8 foot dance floor in the center of the room, which was generally quite crowded.

Approximately 30 percent of the lounge's clientele was drawn from the local market, with the remaining 70 percent originating in-house. Business was particularly strong when conventioners arranged to congregate in the lounge. Harry's sales accounted for about 10 percent of total revenue.

THE MISSION STATEMENT

Howard Creel had prepared the hotel's new Mission Statement as follows:

We are a highly successful, full service conference center providing the finest service, highest quality of food, and the cleanest, most comfortable rooms in all of Omaha. Because of our excellent reputation, location, and value, we cater not only to a strong association/convention market but to the corporate and transient market as well.

In order to remain successful and to maintain our strong positive image, we must continue to provide the finest food, beverage, and entertainment in the area at the best value. We must continue ongoing renovations and keep abreast of the changing marketplace. We must be trendsetters and not trendfollowers, and must strive to keep our employees motivated and well-trained. A good attitude is the answer.

If we are able to achieve all of this and continue our strong public relations efforts, we will reach new markets and will in turn increase revenues in all areas of the hotel.

MARKET SEGMENTS

Susan Newton disagreed with Howard Creel, who felt that the Superior Inn could not afford to pick and choose its guests, particularly in response to the highly competitive environment. Creel had attempted to increase sales by targeting virtually all segments, but Newton felt that the property should create a niche for itself rather than attempting "to be all things to all people," as she put it. The rooms revenue and occupancy by segment is shown in Exhibit 9-1.

Susan was particularly interested in the corporate market, which currently represented only 16.4 percent of total rooms revenue. Creel's one solitary assistant had been assigned to this segment for the past two months and had spent a great deal of time making initial contacts with potential corporate clients. A special rate was offered to those area businesses that produced more than 50 room nights per month, and the secretaries who reserved the room nights were invited to a private party. Susan also wondered about the Superior reservations system, which generated about 8 percent of total rooms occupancy.

Susan Newton felt that the hotel was well positioned in the association market where most of the groups were voluntary organizations on limited budgets. Howard Creel had focused on this segment personally and counted many associations as regular, repeat guests of the hotel. The good reputation of the Food and Beverage department was an added plus in appealing to this segment.

The Superior Inn periodically received inquiries in regard to bus tours and their room requirements. Susan Newton was not interested in pursuing this market, since it conflicted with the many associations that also required weekend rooms. Exhibit 9-2 illustrates day of week average occupancies, which were fairly consistent throughout the year.

Finally, there was the transient market, which accounted for 42.8 percent of revenue. Newton was dissatisfied with the current system for identifying the subsegments of this market and was committed to instituting a better tracking system in the future. For the meantime, however, defining the unique characteristics of this market would continue to be a highly subjective proposition.

ADVERTISING

All advertising for the Superior Inn–Omaha was handled by the General Manager himself. At the moment, advertising was restricted to spots on the local radio stations and a few print ads in the local and area newspapers. Almost all of these ads featured the lounge and/or the restaurant.

EXHIBIT 9-1
Revenue and Occupancy Percentages

Segment	Revenue (%)	Occupancy (%)
Transient	42.8	37.6
Social	1.8	1.5
Tour	3.4	4.6
Association	34.1	41.2
Corporate	16.4	12.3
Military/ Government	1.5	2.8

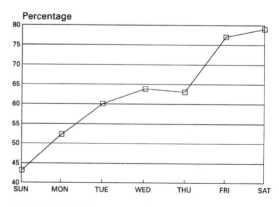

EXHIBIT 9-2 Day of Week Occupancies.

The Superior Inn headquarters handled the advertising intended to build and promote the "Superior Inn image" on the national level. These advertisements appeared in major newspapers and periodicals and on national television.

COMPETITION

As evidenced by its occupancy and average room rate (Exhibit 9-3), the Superior Inn was challenged by competitors on all fronts. Newton considered the competition to be both the full service establishments such as the downtown Marriott and the Ramada right across the road, and the no-frills properties like the Suisse Chalet. Exhibit 9-4 provides pertinent information about competitive properties in the same approximate price range.

Newton was firmly of the opinion that the only way the property could hold its own in the face of such intense competition was to offer good food, prompt and courteous services, and clean and well-maintained rooms at a reasonable price. She was optimistic about the future, since the renovations were progressing at a good pace.

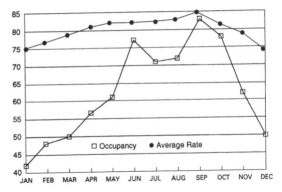

EXHIBIT 9-3 Average Occupancies and Room Rates.

CONCLUSION

Whereas Susan Newton was trained in marketing, Howard Creel was an old school salesman who believed that you can sell anything if you are aggressive enough. Newton recognized that a hard sell was not the answer and believed a policy of segmentation and diffentiation was desirable.

The question to Newton was this: how to develop a marketing plan in order to increase market share by smoothing the peaks and valleys of the hotel's recent performance. With this in mind, Susan Newton sat back to plot her strategy.

EXHIBIT 9-4
Competitive Property Comparison

Hotel	Single Rack Rate	Rooms	Outlets[a]	Banquets[b]	Location	Other
Superior	$91–$104	185	1R, 1L	13 rooms, 900	Off highway	No limo
Suisse Chalet	$69–$78	86	1R, 1L	5 rooms, 1000	Off highway	Billboards
Ramada	$92–$108	120	1R, 1L	4 rooms, 200	Off highway	Billboards
Sheraton	$110–$135	263	1R, 2L	15 rooms, 900	Rte. 29	Limo
Hilton	$102–$115	178	2R, 1L	7 rooms, 450	Airport	Undercuts
Holiday	$93–$106	168	2R, 1L	8 rooms, 700	Highway	Renovated
Best Western	$92–$106	181	1R	17 rooms, 375	Highway	Limo
Howard Johnson's	$95–$108	114	1R, 1L	3 rooms, 100	Highway	No limo

[a]Number of restaurants and lounges.

[b]Number of banquet rooms, maximum capacity theater-style.

Ten

◆

SOJOURN IN JAMAICA*

It was a balmy evening in March when the Air Jamaica 727 touched down at the Montego Bay airport in Jamaica. As Mr. and Mrs. Saltzer stepped off the flight they marveled at the 75 degree weather, the short sleeve shirts everyone was wearing, and the bright moon in the sky. They had boarded the plane at John F. Kennedy Airport in New York where the temperature was 10 degrees above zero, the ground was covered with snow, and the wind was howling. They were happy to leave all this behind and planned to totally forget it for the next two weeks as they enjoyed a sojourn in Jamaica.

It was a short taxi ride to the Elegant Hotel just outside of Montego Bay. They had chosen the hotel from an ad in a popular magazine which read, "Where Adults Go When They Run Away from Home. If you're looking for Jamaica's most spectacular vacation setting, no other place comes close." They were soon there, checked in and unpacked. Having had dinner on the plane, they went downstairs to explore the hotel, after which they stopped for a drink at the circular bar off the lobby.

"Wow," they thought, "this is going to be neat. We really made the right decision." They then retired to bed so as to get an early start in the morning.

THE NEXT MORNING

The Saltzers were up bright and early and looked out over the grounds from the balcony of their room before going downstairs for breakfast. The hotel was shaped like a U facing the ocean and from their room in the center they had a broad view of the ocean with extensions of the U projecting out on either side of them. Immediately below them, the Saltzers could see a large inviting pool with a pool bar with the bar stools in the water. To their right of the pool was a large dining area with about 30 round tables with umbrellas, about 10 of which were occupied. In this section, and closer to the hotel, was an extensive breakfast buffet setup. Further out, beyond this area and the pool, was a beach house where sports facilities were offered, and beyond this the sandy beach with sailfish, other boats, and water sports equipment.

*Names have been disguised.

The Saltzers headed for the outside dining area as soon as they got downstairs. Although they only wanted juice and coffee and not the buffet, (they were on European plan), they wanted to sit out in the sun, watch the ocean, and forget the New York weather. The maître d' quickly seated them as far out toward the ocean as possible. He then suggested that they partake of the buffet at their leisure. "We only want juice and coffee," they responded. "Oh," he said, "in that case you can't sit here." "What do you mean we can't sit here?" said Mrs. Saltzer. "This is only for people having the buffet," replied the maître d'. "Then where can we sit?" said Mr. Saltzer. "You have to go inside to the coffee shop," was the reply.

Reluctantly, the Saltzers got up and went inside to the coffee shop. They found a booth on the outside of the room by a window. There was no sun shining on them but they could peer out and see the ocean in the distance. "Oh, well," they said, "we'll be out there soon enough." A waitress came and handed them two menus. "Just orange juice and coffee," they said. "Oh," she replied, "if you just want orange juice and coffee you can't sit here."

"Why not?" they said. "This room is only for people ordering from the menu," was the reply. "Then where can we sit?" "You can sit in the other room at the counter."

The Saltzers went into the other room. There was no sun, no ocean, no windows, and no view. "How do we know we're not still in New York?" they said. They decided to skip breakfast and head for the waterfront.

At lunchtime, the Saltzers ran into the same problem. There again was a buffet outdoors which 30 or 40 people were partaking of, and they were told they had to go into the bar restaurant if they didn't want the buffet. They found this restaurant to be empty except for one other couple. They sat down and waited about 20 minutes for the waitress. When she came they ordered two club sandwiches. These came about 45 minutes later; the delay almost caused them to miss their planned trip into the interior of Jamaica on a train where they visited the Appleton rum distillery.

THAT EVENING

The train was not air-conditioned, and although the Saltzers enjoyed the trip, they returned to the hotel at 5:00 P.M. very hot and perspiring from the 90 degree weather. They went straight to their room, put on their bathing suits and headed for the pool. On one side of the pool was the pool bar, on the other side were lounge chairs. The Saltzers put their robes, towels, reading materials, and so on on two lounge chairs and jumped into the pool. After swimming for a few minutes, they swam up to the pool bar and sat on two of the stools which were otherwise empty. They ordered two of the hotel's signature rum drinks.

"Sorry, the bar is closed," said the bartender, pointing to a sign above the back bar which stated that the bar closed at 6:00 P.M. "But it's only 5:35," they protested, pointing to the clock above the back bar. "I know, but it takes us time to check out and close up." "Come on," they pleaded, "we just got here. Give us a break." "Well, okay, let me see your chits." "What chits?" "The small cardboard piece you got when you checked in that show that you are a registered guest and can charge to your room." Oh, yeah," they said. "they're in our room. We didn't think of them. Besides, if we had them in our bathing suits they'd be soaking wet by now." "Well, I have to have your chits," said the bartender. "Do you think we just parachuted into the pool?" said Mrs. Saltzer.

The bartender finally agreed to call the front desk and verify that the Saltzers were guests of the hotel. After he did this he served them their drinks and proceeded to close up the bar. At about 6:00 the Saltzers, still hot, went back into the pool. At the end of the pool was a very large sign which someone else in the pool called to their attention. The sign read, "Pool closes at 6:00." "That's ridiculous," thought Mr. Saltzer as he kept on swimming, "no one closes a pool at 6:00 in Jamaica when the temperature is 90 degrees, especially at an expensive resort like this."

At about 6:05 a man, obviously a hotel employee, walked along the end of the pool where Mr. Saltzer was swimming and where the sign was and, catching Mr. Saltzer's attention, said to him, "Do you see that sign?" "No, I can't read," said Mr. Saltzer. The man went away. About 10 minutes later he returned carrying two large buckets in each hand. He dumped them into the pool about five feet from Mr. Saltzer, who realized that the pool was being chlorinated. He got out quickly.

The Saltzers had dinner in the hotel dining room that night. They weren't sure if it was a good dinner or not. By this time they were so upset that they just picked at their food. After a brief discussion they decided to check out the next morning although they didn't know where they would go.

The next morning they packed their bags and carried them downstairs to the lobby where they found about 40 people waiting in line to check out.

There was one desk clerk behind the desk handling these checkouts. Also behind the desk, however, were three other employees engaged in conversation but not helping with the checkouts.

After about an hour the Saltzers reached the head of the line. "Why are you checking out today when your reservation is for two weeks?" asked the desk clerk. "This place stinks," said Mr. Saltzer. "Gee, that's what a lot of people are saying," said the desk clerk, "Why do *you* say that?" "Just give us our bill," said Mr. Saltzer.

As the Saltzers rode in the taxi toward Ocho Rios, about 50 miles down the northern coast line, looking for a place to finish their vacation, the Saltzers discussed the comments they had heard from others while standing in line to check out. "I guess we were lucky," they said, "even if it did cost us $500 for two nights."

C A S E

Eleven

◆◆◆

BUTLER'S HIDEAWAY*

Jonathan Butler sipped his Piña Colada on the sundeck of his terrace overlooking the Caribbean sunset and felt very pleased with his decision to create Butler's. Butler's Hideaway had opened five years before with a mission to offer the most discriminating of guests a vacation hideaway. Located on the island of Grand Cayman in the British West Indies, which is well known for its beautiful seven-mile beach, magnificent waters, peace and quiet, political stability and strong economy, Butler's had been a smashing success.

Grand Cayman Island was only a 75 minute flight from Miami International Airport. This was one of the important strengths highlighted by the feasibility study conducted by Pannell Kerr Forster before the investment was made. Mr. Butler, an investor not a hotelier, felt that the product Butler's was offering was working very well.

An award-winning architect had been selected to design Butler's to complement the colors and rhythm of the tropics with a distinctly opulent and luxurious flavor. Butler's overlooked a magnificent seven-mile beach. The Great House included 20 rooms and 20 suites. Also in the Great House was a Cartier boutique, a Carita beauty salon, and a sun and sundries store. A beautiful lounge had a waterfall that cascaded down to a freshwater pool, bar, and casual restaurant called Pimms, which served breakfast and lunch. The fine dining room was fronted by famous chef Roger Vergé and offered both lunch and dinner.

There were also 20 villas in the complex, some with one bedroom and a few with two bedrooms. Each included a private pool exquisitely designed to meander through the villa's own dining terrace. A fully equipped kitchen was concealed with a service entrance in order that room service might be of the highest standard and served with discretion. Butler's had become known as one of the great hideaways for the elite.

The finest of personalized service was offered at Butler's; all guests had a personal concierge who coupled as their driver. A water sports center chartered luxury motor yachts for those wishing to visit neighboring islands or seek well-known snorkeling or diving spots.

---

*Sheena Smyth contributed to this case. Some names and places have been disguised.

CURRENT STATUS

Butler's had just had its best year. Its average annual occupancy was 74 percent and its average daily rate was $450 European Plan, $340 in the Great House and $850 in the villas. Although the past two years had been tough years due to international turmoil and weak economies, Mr. Butler felt they were right back on track as he looked at the customer profile. Butler's clientele was the rich and famous. It included celebrities, CEOs, private bankers, high level executives, dignitaries, and entrepreneurs. Thirty percent came through Leading Hotels of the World, 15 percent through travel agents, 20 percent through selected American and European wholesalers, while 10 percent were corporate bookings, and 25 percent were direct. Sixty-five percent came from the United States, 20 percent from Europe, and the rest from around the world. The average length of stay was 6.5 days, 5 days for Americans and 8 days for Europeans.

Repeat business had grown to 34 percent. Butler's prided itself on remembering all the whims and fancies of each guest staying with them. This demanding clientele seemed to be very happy with the facilities of the hotel and the services provided.

Serious competition in the region included Cap Juluca on Anguilla, La Samanna on St. Martin, and Manapany on St. Barthelemy. None of these were large resorts and there seemed to be plenty of business for all.

Advertising for Butler's was handled by Yesawich, Pepperdine & Brown, one of the leading agencies in the hotel industry. Mr. Butler was very happy with their services, which included differentiated advertising, press kits and press trips, media blitzes, news releases, and special event promotions. He felt that their efforts were timely, cohesive, and targeted.

The General Manager of Butler's, Kathryn, had been there since it opened. Mr. Butler was very pleased with her performance. It was not easy in Grand Cayman to find the staff profile needed to accommodate these clients. She always planned ahead and had a great sense of her customers' wants and needs, likes and dislikes.

Training was high on the list of priorities. Total Quality Management had been implemented two years before and was now working very well. Most of the staff had been handpicked by Kathryn. As labor costs were extremely high in Cayman, the quality of service generally found was, to say the least, "challenging." Kathryn always seemed on top of things, however. The restaurants were profitable and had a good following from lawyers, bankers and other professionals living locally on the island.

FUTURE PLANS

Mr. Butler was considering opening a second Butler's and was conducting research on another Caribbean island. He was, however, somewhat alarmed by some of the information being sent to him. A Pannell Kerr Forster study stated, "The status element has diminished; it is now being replaced by personal pleasure. Trading up is out!"

Peter Yesawich, president of Yesawich, Pepperdine & Brown, had recently written, "The images of luxury, opulence and indulgence do not play with the image of today. The consumer mindset of the '90s is extremely conservative."

Mr. Butler was quite disturbed by these consumer trends. He was not going to make a decision unless it was founded in fact and decided to research further. He called some of his advisors and was told, "Focus on the genuine, real, authentic; there seems to be an aversion to glitz."

Mr. Butler did not feel comfortable asking Kathryn to conduct focus groups with the delicate level of his clientele but he knew she was always sensitive to their needs and wants. He asked himself if he was thinking from the customer's perspective.

Mr. Butler did not want to signal anxiety to his partners or customers, but further research informed him that the concept of luxury as a motivator no longer worked. Indeed, in the Yesawich, Pepperdine & Brown and Yankelovich Partners Leisure Travel Monitor, an annual research survey, he found some disturbing trends in American society.

Activity	1995	Present[a]
Shopping in prestige stores	24%	15%
Wearing designer clothing	26%	14%
Driving expensive cars	39%	29%
Staying at luxury hotels	29%	15%

[a]Margin of error +/− 3%.

All indicators on Grand Cayman, however, looked positive. His colleagues on the board of the hotel association were very happy with the current situation and future forecasts for business. Mr. Butler felt that he had carved out a niche in the market that would be hard to lose providing all services were in place and the product was desired. On the other hand, as Americans brought him 65 percent of his business, how could he afford to ignore the market mood in the States and not to look at these trends?

"Are we at the top of the life cycle?" he thought. "Do we need to reposition? Can we risk it to stay as we are? Can we risk it to change? What should he do about his second project that he had in mind?" "No one pays rack any more," he repeated to himself. "The crisis is moving from west to east." He looked around his fine dining restaurant and decided to discuss his concerns with Kathryn.

Twelve

•◆•

THE GLORIOUS HOTEL*

The 100 million dollar plus, 650-room Glorious Hotel, originally budgeted at $80 million, was under construction in Chicago, Illinois, when management decided to plan marketing strategy a year in advance of opening with a two-day session led by a hotel strategic marketing consultant. Plans for the session were scrapped, however, when management decided that (1) the consultant's fee of $3000 a day was too high, and (2) management already pretty well knew what its strategy would be.

The Glorious Hotel in Chicago was, after all, joining a prestigious line of luxury hotels bearing the Glorious name in San Francisco; San Jose, California; New York City; Dallas; and New Orleans. Like those hotels it would be a member of the prestigious reservations network, Leading Hotels of the World. All of these hotels were considered luxury properties with some holding the AAA 5-Diamond Award and some the Mobilguide 4 Star Award. The Chicago property, like the others, which ranged from 550 to 750 rooms, would also have strong meeting and convention facilities.

In fact, Glorious corporate considered itself to be a premier operator of large luxury hotels. Richard Smith, chairman and chief executive officer of the Glorious Hotel Management Company, responded to an interview as follows:

Q: How do you accomplish a high level of personal service in hotels large enough to host major conventions? Doesn't "large hotel" conflict with "personal service?"

Smith: Not when you put yourself in your guests' shoes. Our hotels are designed to attract people of quality. Therefore you put into effect the services you believe persons of quality want.

Q: Do customers understand what they're getting when they stay at "luxury" properties?

Smith: This is very confusing. The only thing luxury about a new hotel may be that it's new. This doesn't make a luxury hotel. It takes a lot of years, a lot of experience.

Q: Is the size of your hotels in this age of

*Names have been disguised.

Smith: By being a large hotel most people don't think it's possible to give personalized service to guests. I disagree. It's no harder to keep 500 rooms clean than 100.

Q: How can you deliver personalized service to individual travelers and cater to groups at the same time?

Smith: To us, every guest coming into the hotel is recognized as an individual traveler. We don't look at anyone as being a member of a convention. They're all individual people who want luxury service.

Q: How involved do you get in the fine details of running Glorious Hotels?

Smith: I get right into what tablecloths are put in a restaurant, the china, the stemware. I read all the menus before they're put in a room. I go through every detail, but everybody's ideas are listened to.

Q: How do you keep yourself from becoming insular in your hotel business?

Smith: I don't think any ideas are new, just repeats from years ago. All you do is take other people's ideas, convert them to match your own ideas and philosophies, and try to accomplish the same thing.

THE GLORIOUS EXPERIENCE

An attendee at a convention held at The Glorious in Chicago stayed at the hotel over a year after it opened and related the following experience.

I checked into the hotel at around 10:00 P.M. From the doorman on through the desk clerk and the bellman, the personnel were very efficient and friendly. Riding up in the elevator, I asked the bellman where I could still get something to eat. His answer was the Primavera restaurant. Suggesting that I didn't want a full dinner but more of a snack, he said I should go to the Primavera lounge where "trendy" and "boutique" properties a detriment to selling? that would be available until 11:00 P.M. I set my bag in my room and headed straight for the lounge.

The Primavera lounge was separated from the restaurant by a 15-foot corridor. Coming from the elevator or escalator from the lobby floor, one came first to the bar. One could go around the outside of the bar to reach the restaurant, or could go through the bar, out the other end, across the 15-foot corridor, and into the restaurant (Exhibit 12-1). I went straight into the lounge, which had about 125 seats plus some dozen bar stools.

I had hardly entered the lounge when I was jarred by walking in front of a large screen television on which the Denver Broncos were engaging the Buffalo Bills in the weekly fall Monday night football event. I noticed two people sitting at the bar and a couple in the far, far corner at a table. The bar and lounge area were otherwise empty, and none of the four were watching the football game. This surprised me as I had already ascertained that the hotel was full.

There were a waitress and bartender on duty. I stood for awhile until they finished a conversation and the waitress came over and asked if she could be of help. I understand, I shouted over the football game, that I can get a snack here. She reached to a table, picked up a menu and handed it to me, and said, "Sit anywhere," and returned to the bar. I sat at a table behind a large pillar so as to block out the television screen, but not the noise. After about ten minutes the waitress came to my table to take an order.

"The menu says wine by the glass," I said, "What wine is it?" "I'll find out," was the reply. She returned in about five minutes. The wine was a cheap Italian at $8.00 a four ounce glass. I ordered it along with some shrimp and pasta. She left and I looked around. There were bowls of peanuts on some of the tables so I got up and retrieved one from another table. Unfortunately, they were too soggy for my taste. The waitress came back with the wine. "Do many people come in to watch the football game?" I asked. "Do you mean employees or guests?" she responded. "Are you ever busy here," I asked. "Well, yeah, sometimes," she said.

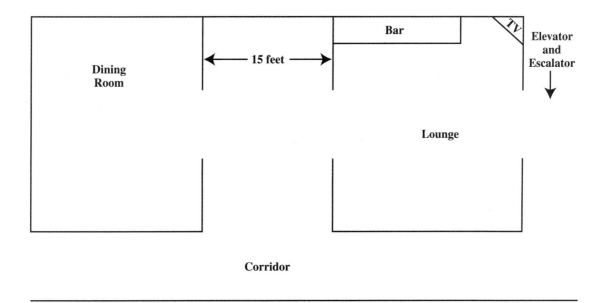

E X H I B I T 1 2 - 1 Layout of the Restaurant/ Lounge Area.

While I enjoyed my supper I saw about 20 people walk into the lounge and look around. Two stayed, one of whom watched the football game. I learned what she meant by employees later. Four or five at a time would come in and watch the game for about five minutes and leave. When I asked the waitress about this she explained that there was an employee pool on the game.

I returned to my room and made a number of observations. The bedside light and radio were on. What a nice touch, I thought. The clock radio later went off by itself. The bed, of course, was turned down. This was no small feat as the covering quilt was a heavy and expensive one that had been placed in one of the two very plush and comfortable chairs by the desk/side table. There were four pillows on the queen bed and they seemed to be of very high quality, as well. On the night stand next to the bed was a chocolate basket—yes, a basket made out of chocolate—which contained six very rich and expensive, albeit delicious, chocolates. I estimated this to have a cost of at least five dollars. There was also a card from the General Manager welcoming me.

The room itself had an excellent layout unlike any I had seen. The room itself was quite large—I estimated over 400 square feet—in the shape of a parallelogram, with a large desk, two very comfortable chairs, a long dresser, and separate well-built television table. It was all of high quality and in very good taste. There was a full vanity section, followed by a bathtub and basin section, then by a large walk-in shower, and finally by a toilet section. Each section could be shut off from the others. There was an automatic light in the closet and, bless it, removable hangers! I couldn't have been more delighted and wasn't surprised when I read on the back of the door that the room rate was $280 single, $340 double, even though I was only paying the convention rate of $135.

In fact, the room was loaded with additional amenities. There was a tiny TV over the wash basins; unfortunately, I was never able to get clear reception on it. There was no pay TV, all was included but no special movies were offered. There were two gorgeous terry cloth robes in the closet. The room had a phone by the bed plus a "state-of-the-art" one on the desk that looked like you could conference call Congress on it. Being unsophisticated about these things I didn't try; the only problem I had was when trying to give the hotel's number to my daughter who lived in Chicago, it was nowhere to be found.

There was a stand-up electric shoe polisher plus an offer of a free shoeshine if you hung your shoes on the door knob between 11:00 and 6:00. I tried it and it worked! There were three large pink bars of soap, one each in the basin, tub, and shower, a "French Mill" soap, "Glorious" shampoo, hair conditioner, and body lotion, a shower cap, a sewing kit, and a notice of the number to call if you wanted anything more. I didn't use this as I took most of these amenities home in my suitcase. The large bars of soap, although hardly used, were replaced daily. The only minor annoyance was that, in the large walk-in shower, surprisingly, there was no place to put the soap other than on the floor.

At 8:30 the next morning, after being surprisingly awakened by the clock radio alarm at 6:00 A.M., I went to the Primavera restaurant for breakfast. This time I walked around the lounge, which was immediately adjacent, dark and empty, to the restaurant. There were about 15 people waiting in line, mostly singles, but a very jovial maître d' who kept asking things like how many in your party, are you having a nice stay, sorry for the delay, have a nice day, to those departing, and similar friendly expressions. The reservation phone rang frequently. The maitre d' was quick to answer it with, "Thank you for calling Primavera. This is Daryl Patten. How may I help you?"

After about 20 minutes I was seated at a table for four complete with table linen, silver, service plate, and crystal. After about seven minutes a waiter came and removed the other three place settings. Five minutes later he came back for my order—orange juice and coffee.

The conference was a great success and the luncheons that went with it were excellent, although perhaps a tad more than I normally eat in the middle of the day. The only minor annoyance was that in the middle of each eight round was a beautiful and expensive flower arrangement, for example, birds of paradise. These made it impossible to talk, eye-to-eye, with people across from you at the table.

Oh, yes, there was one other thing. The second night I decided to work in my room and order room service. I couldn't quite understand why a bottle of Smirnoff was $64.00 and a grilled steak was $26.00, so I ordered a Becks and sent out for a pizza.

All in all, the Glorious is a great hotel for $135. It was interesting to read in a trade publication, after I returned home, that the Glorious was barely doing 50 percent overall occupancy, in a city running almost 70 percent overall, and might have to be "repositioned as second-tier luxury" property. In the same article the GM of the Glorious was quoted, "Tiers are establishing themselves. Only some hotels will get top rates. It will depend on name recognition and the strength of their marketing programs." To boost occupancy levels, the article stated, many high-end hotels in Chicago were charging "rates significantly lower than what is needed to pay their debts" with a "backing off from published rates . . . and heavy discounting off rack rates on commercial group business." One industry spokesman was quoted in the article as saying, "It is difficult if not impossible for large luxury hotels to deliver the personal services that guests who pay $200 or more for a room expect."

EMPIRE SZECHUAN RESTAURANT*

"How was your dinner here?"

"Very good, it was excellent."

"Thank you very much for coming."

After saying "Good night" to a customer, Charlie Gao, manager of the Empire Szechuan Chinese restaurant, stepped out from behind the counter and looked through the dining room window. The street was busy, cars were passing back and forth. This had been a busy day for most people, but not for his restaurant. Seat turnover tonight was one and a half, not even up to two. It had been three or four when the restaurant first opened.

Charlie recalled that the first month's business was so busy that queues lined up along the counter waiting to get seats. Gradually, sales volume had slipped at both lunch and dinner. Only six months later, business was so disappointing that shares in the restaurant had been sold three times over. "Something must be wrong," he thought, but

whenever he asked for feedback from customers, he always received compliments.

HISTORY

Charlie Gao was the manager as well as the principal owner of the Empire Szechuan restaurant, holding 40 percent of the stock. Other minor partners were in New York City. Working in the restaurant industry for ten years, Charlie had obtained substantial cooking and waiting experience as well as some management knowledge. He had been a manager in several Chinese restaurants including Jade Beach, a Chinese restaurant in a casino in Atlantic City, and Szechuan Empire on Broadway at 97th Street in New York City. After he had accumulated enough money, he decided to fulfill his fantasy of opening a restaurant of his own. He found some partners among his career friends.

Eventually, Charlie got his opportunity in

---

*Jane Lin contributed to this case.

Amherst, Massachusetts, a town of 20,000 permanent residents known for its high involvement in education. With five colleges in the Amherst area (Smith, Mount Holyoke, Amherst, Hampshire Colleges, and the University of Massachusetts), the additional population was largely made up of students, particularly during fall and spring semesters. The Empire Szechuan opened in the heart of Amherst featuring Hunan/Szechuan regional style cooking.

Charlie's research revealed that the average income in this area was quite high. He also learned that there were four other Chinese restaurants in downtown Amherst. Chinese restaurants also existed in Hadley, which was five miles away, and in Northampton, which was nine miles away. He considered that only Panda East in Amherst would be his immediate, main competitor. From observing Panda East's operation, Charlie was quite encouraged.

People in the area seemed to love Chinese food. He was surprised to learn that Amherst Chinese Food, a family owned, family operated restaurant, whose owner had never received proper training in the restaurant business and who knew little about restaurant operations, had been successful in this little town for 15 years. The future really looked promising!

With his ten years experience, his advantages in location, plus the acquisition of a chef who used to work at Panda East, Charlie firmly believed that his "empire" would conquer this town easily. As Panda East had been very successful, Charlie designed his menu after the menu of Panda East.

The restaurant was small, but comfortable. It had one dining room with a seating capacity of 70. There were eight booths lining the walls. In the center were some square tables seating four or two. Both walls were decorated with glass, which made the restaurant look more spacious.

COMPETITION

Panda East: In downtown Northampton a Chinese restaurant named Panda Garden had been operating successfully for a number of years. It featured four main regional styles of Chinese cuisine: Hunan/Szechuan, Beijing (Mandarin), Shanghai, and Cantonese. Many customers from the Amherst area had asked the manager to open another Panda restaurant in downtown Amherst. He opened Panda East in 1996 with two spacious dining rooms seating 130 people. Successful, as it had been in Northampton, the restaurant drew much of the local Chinese food business to its premise.

Amherst Chinese Food: Located on Main Street, not far away from Empire Szechuan, was Amherst Chinese Food. After getting his Doctor's degree in Plant Science at the University of Massachusetts, Mr. Chang, the owner, opened the restaurant in 1990 with the idea of making enough money to buy a farm. His mission statement was clear: "To offer healthy, fresh, Chinese food to the community." He further stated, "We welcome everyone here to be comfortable whether in jeans or tuxedo." His farm supplied all the vegetables needed, and local people perceived this restaurant as one which served healthy (no MSG), fresh family-style food. The seating capacity was 130. This restaurant enjoyed a substantial repeat business, and its sales volume had increased despite the opening of Panda East and Empire Szechuan.

Hunan Garden: Hunan Garden was located on Route 9, about a mile east of Amherst. As its name indicated, it served mainly Hunan/Szechuan style food. This restaurant had been acquired by the Ngs family in 1995 and had been quite successful until the arrival of Panda East and Empire Szechuan. Due to this stiff competition, it was promoted heavily among college students, who had been chosen as its target market. It ran frequent student specials, issued coupons, and served a buffet at a tempting price of $7.25 from Monday through Thursday.

Kim Toy Chinese Foods: This was the oldest Chinese restaurant in the area and had opened in 1976. It was owned and run by an elderly couple. The restaurant had only 20 seats and opened only from 4:00 P.M. to 8:30 P.M. As there was not much business, the owners handled cooking, serving, and washing dishes themselves and employed no other staff.

OTHER PROBLEMS

Business for Empire Szechuan had never stablized, but only went down shortly after opening. One disadvantage was that the restaurant did not have a liquor license. Charlie believed that if he got this license, business would increase greatly but licenses were scarce and you had to "know someone." Customers could, however, buy beverages at a package store around the corner and bring them in to drink at no additional charge. Another disadvantage was the size and layout of the restaurant. This discouraged parties of more than 6 people.

Most guests who came and tried the new restaurant did not return. Except for the above two disadvantages, Charlie Gao had no further explanations for his declining business. In fact, he believed that the food prepared in his restaurant was finer than that served in Panda East. One example of this was Ginger Chicken from the old menu of Empire Szechuan in New York. According to the standard recipe, the main ingredient for this dish, chicken, should be slices from the breast, and Empire Szechuan prepared this dish accordingly. At Panda East they used ordinary chicken slices.

Charlie admitted that his portions were not as large as those served at Panda East, although the price range was the same. In Charlie Gao's view, if customers sought real fine Chinese cuisine, they would not care about this little difference.

REPOSITIONING

Charlie Gao decided that he would not be successful just by copying what Panda East was doing. He decided to reposition his product.

First, he redesigned the menu. He decided to bring what had been successful in New York City, Empire Szechuan style, to this little town. On his new menu, he especially stated: Empire Szechuan, New York Style. To differentiate from the other Chinese restaurants, Charlie designed a Special Diet Menu that included no salt, sugar, cornstarch, or MSG.

Charlie also tried to improve the product from the service aspect. He had all experienced waiters, asked for feedback from customers, and embellished his product. Beside serving tea and ice water, as most Chinese restaurants did and as most customers expected, Charlie also offered crispy noodles while customers were waiting for their order. As a lunch special, beside serving free rice and free soup, as Panda East and other Chinese restaurants did, Empire Szechuan attached two free eggrolls to the lunch package and kept the price the same. To attract even more business, Charlie also planned to convert the basement into a banquet room. Empire Szechuan also had seasonal specials and chef's specials that were not on the regular menu.

The recovery was slow in coming. Overhead exceeded revenue. At this point, beside the lack of a liquor license and the restaurant not being large enough, Charlie concluded that another reason for his slipping business was that it was very hard to change customers' habits. He believed that once one went to a place to dine, they would stick to it unless they were not satisfied.

ADVERTISING AND PROMOTION

Prior to opening, and at the beginning of its operation, Charlie set a promotion budget of $4000 a month and promoted heavily in the *Daily Hampshire Gazette, Amherst Bulletin, The Collegian,* and other local newspapers, trying to create awareness. After two months, the budget was cut to $2000 per month, and then to $700 per month. Currently, after only a half a year of operation, Charlie hardly did any promotion except for delivering menus to some supermarkets. He considered that awareness had been created.

CONCLUSION

How, Charlie thought, was he going to rejuvenate the business? How could he boost the volume again? What was the best strategy for this restaurant, which had only been open for six months, to adopt?

Charlie Gao stepped out of the door. It was a bit chilly. It was spring now. Summer was coming. When summer came, this town, with its population largely made up of students, would be empty and quiet. If he did not do something soon, he could foresee that his business would go nowhere but down and down, worse, and worse. . . .

C A S E

Fourteen

◆◆◆

THE CUSTOMER'S COMPLAINT*

123 Main Street
Boston, Massachusetts
Gail and Harvey Pearson
The Retreat House on Foliage Pond
Vacationland, New Hampshire

Dear Mr. and Mrs. Pearson:

This is the first time that I have ever written a letter like this, but my wife and I are so upset by the treatment afforded by your staff that we felt compelled to let you know what happened to us. We had dinner reservations at the Retreat House for a party of four under my wife's name, Dr. Elaine Loflin, for Saturday evening, October 11. We were hosting my wife's brother and his wife, visiting from Atlanta, Georgia.

We were seated at 7:00 P.M. in the dining room to the left of the front desk. There were at least four empty tables in the room when we were seated. We

were immediately given menus, a wine list, ice water, dinner rolls, and butter. Then we sat for 15 minutes until the cocktail waitress asked us for our drink orders. My sister-in-law said, after being asked what she would like, "I'll have a vodka martini straight-up with an olive." The cocktail waitress responded immediately, "I'm not a stenographer." My sister-in-law repeated her drink order.

Soon after, our waiter arrived, informing us of the specials of the evening. I don't remember his name, but he had dark hair, wore glasses, was a little stocky, and had his sleeves rolled up. He returned about ten minutes later, our drinks still not having arrived. We had not decided upon our entrées, but requested appetizers, upon which he informed us that we could not order appetizers without ordering our entrées at the same time. We decided not to order appetizers.

Our drinks arrived and the waiter returned. We ordered our entrées at 7:30. When the waiter asked my wife for her order, he addressed her as "young lady." When he served her the meal, he called her "dear."

At ten minutes of eight we requested that our salads be brought to us as soon as possible. I then

*"Talkback Answering the Customer's Complaint: A Case Study," *Cornell Hotel and Restaurant Administration Quarterly.* Copyright © Cornell University. Used by permission. All rights reserved. The names of the people and the restaurant have been disguised.

asked the waiter's assistant to bring us more rolls (each of us had been served one when we were seated). Her response was, "Who wants a roll?", upon which, caught off guard, we went around the table saying yes or no so she would know exactly how many "extra" rolls to bring to our table.

Our salads were served at five minutes of eight. At 25 minutes past the hour we requested our entrées. They were served at 8:30, one and one-half hours after we were seated in a restaurant that was one-third empty. Let me also add that we had to make constant requests for water refills, butter replacement, and the like.

In fairness to the chef, the food was excellent and, as you already realize, the atmosphere delightful. Despite this, the dinner was a disaster. We were extremely upset and very insulted by the experi-

ence. Your staff is not well trained. They were overtly rude, and displayed little etiquette or social grace. This was compounded by the atmosphere you are trying to present and the prices you charge in the dining room.

Perhaps we should have made our feelings known at the time, but our foremost desire was to leave as soon as possible. We had been looking forward to dining at the Retreat House for quite some time as part of our vacation weekend in New Hampshire. We will be hard-pressed to return to your establishment. Please be sure to know that we will share our experience at the Retreat House with our family, friends, and business associates.

Sincerely,
Dr. William E. Loflin

LE CHATEAU FRONTENAC*

Le Chateau Frontenac Hotel in Quebec City, Quebec, Canada was a classic "grande dame" hotel. Built in 1893 it had always epitomized elegance, architectural beauty, and the grandeur of what a hotel could be before modern construction overtook the industry. Simply standing in the lobby with its high atrium and regal tapestries, one could feel the charm of another era.

The main competition for Le Chateau Frontenac were the more modern, more convention type hotels of Loew's Concorde (450 rooms), Hilton International (540 rooms), Radisson (375 rooms), and Holiday Inn (300 rooms). All of these had been built in the last 15 years and none had the charm of the Frontenac, but they did have more efficient facilities and physical plants. While they all targeted the business traveler, summer tourists, and group business, as did the Frontenac, they did not attract the "traditionalist" traveler, who was drawn to the Frontenac.

Le Chateau Frontenac had undergone numerous refurbishings in its lifetime and was due for another. A decision was made, at the same time, to add 66 more rooms to the existing 544. The refurbishing and addition were done over a six year period at a cost of $50 million† with the new rooms replicas of the old ones. Le Chateau Frontenac now stood in its finest glory with a sizable debt, 610 rooms, and a need to fill them.

HOTEL DEMAND

Hotel demand in Quebec City was largely tourists and tours from May through October, as this was the most classic French city in North America, steeped in history and tradition, as was Le Chateau Frontenac. There was much to see for culture buffs, great antique stores, and outstanding restaurants. Convention season was September and October with the rest of the year mostly business travel. Le Chateau Frontenac had 80 to 95 percent occupancy during the tourist and convention seasons at $195 ADR, and 50 to 55 percent the remainder of the year at $155 ADR.

---

*Alex Kassatly, Executive Assistant Manager at Le Chateau Frontenac at the time of this incident, contributed to this case.

†For conversion purposes one C$ equals about U.S. $0.70.

With 66 more rooms now, management wondered how to increase revenue to pay their cost. November to April had little hope as the market was quite static at that time. May through August the hotel took only upscale tour groups at an average rate of $175 to $215. Now, anxious to fill its extra rooms during high season, management contacted a group of tour operators.

These contacts revealed that the hotel could capture additional tour groups and easily fill the hotel in high season if it offered a $149 rate for about 100 days. This meant about 75 rooms sold per day for about 100 days that would otherwise likely remain empty. Management called an executive staff meeting to discuss the wisdom of this decision.

Sixteen

◆

THE MARKETING OF "LITTLE ENGLAND"*

Earlyn Shuffler, President of the Barbados Tourism Authority (BTA), reviewed his speech for the last time. He still had a few minutes before the start of the annual BTA board meeting, at which he was presenting a review of activities for the past year and recommendations for the future. On his way to the board room, he reflected on the events of the previous year.

Last September, the appointment of a new three-member BTA executive committee, with Allan Batson retaining the chairmanship, signaled the end of a long-standing controversy surrounding the government's management of the island's tourism industry, which had seen various structures and numerous directors coming and going. The "executive," as the new committee was com-

monly called, consisted of Earlyn Shuffler, President; Thomas Hill, Vice President Sales and Marketing; and Errol Griffith, Vice President Finance and Corporate Affairs. All of these individuals had extensive experience in their respective fields and were well equipped to face the daunting task that lay ahead. This newly appointed team, soon nicknamed the "Dream Team" by the media, were viewed as saviors of the flagging tourism industry, with the ability to recapture lost ground, increase visitor arrivals and spending, and develop an effective marketing plan for the island.

CARIBBEAN TOURISM

The entire Caribbean region (see map at back of book), including some not truly Caribbean islands such as the Bahamas and Bermuda, received over 14,000,000 stay-over visitors in the previous year. Of these, approximately 60 percent originated from the

*This case was written by Lisa M. Jebodhsingh under the supervision of Dr. Margaret Shaw, School of Hotel & Food Administration, University of Guelph, Guelph, Ontario. © Lisa M. Jebodhsingh and Margaret Shaw. Used by permission. All rights reserved.

United States, 18 percent from Europe, 6 percent from Canada, and 16 percent from other markets. There were over 165,000 hotel rooms in the region and tourism receipts were almost U.S.$12 billion.

Each island of the Caribbean conducted its own marketing campaign, and each was responsible for attracting visitors to their shores. Continued efforts by the Caribbean Tourism Organization, the Caribbean Hotel Association, and a number of private sector entities, however, resulted in a number of the islands collaborating on a joint marketing campaign. The outcome of this effort was the Caribbean Vacation Planner, a full color book that contained basic tourist information about 34 islands in the region and aided travelers in planning their Caribbean vacation. This was the only instance of cooperation and collaboration in Caribbean tourism marketing.

BARBADOS

Barbados, affectionately known to visitors and locals alike as "Little England," was the most easterly of the islands of the Caribbean, 166 square miles in size, with a population of slightly more than 254,000. Barbados gained its independence from Britain in 1966, and was considered to be one of the best governed and most politically stable islands in the region. The island earned its nickname due to its resemblance in parts to the English countryside, and the adoption of certain characteristically English traditions, for example, afternoon high tea.

Barbados is bordered by the Caribbean Sea on its west coast and the Atlantic Ocean on its east coast. The relative calm of the Caribbean Sea made the west coast of the island ideal for swimming, sailing, and snorkeling, while the turbulence of the Atlantic Ocean transformed the east coast to a haven for surfers. A wealth of attractions was offered to visitors to the island, ranging from tours of old plantation houses to a day at the races, from a wander through the coolness of underground sea caves to a canter through the countryside, from a day of frolic cruising on the popular pirate ships to an elegant dinner at one of the many top restau-

rants. The more adventurous visitors tried parasailing or deep sea fishing, while others preferred to relax on one of the many beaches.

In the past Barbados had been viewed as an elite destination, catering to the upper income end of the tourism market. According to Allan Batson, Chairman of the BTA, however:

> Barbados has rededicated itself to providing a well-rounded product, from economy hotels and villa accommodations, to world-class luxury resorts, offering value at all three price ranges—budget, mid-range, and luxury. We now target travellers in each of these three categories with offerings to appeal to their individual sense of value and style.

In recent years, tourism had become the mainstay of the economy, replacing sugar as the largest foreign exchange earner, and was the second largest employer. The island had close to 6000 hotel rooms, including apartment hotels. The winter tourist season ran from mid-December to mid-April, and the summer season from mid-April to mid-December. Traditionally, the winter season was the peak season for arrivals, with visitors from North America and Europe flocking to the island to escape the chill of winter. In recent years, however, peak arrivals had been experienced in the months of July and August during the annual "Crop Over Festival." This month-long festival had gained international recognition and signified the end of the harvesting of the sugar crop, hence the name "Crop Over." It culminated in a day of costumed revelry, food, and entertainment enjoyed by visitors and locals.

In the year just passed, Barbados received a total of almost 927,000 visitors and tourist expenditure was estimated at U.S.$679,500,000, making a net contribution to the island's gross domestic product of about U.S.$233 million. Of the total number of visitors, approximately 442,000 were stay-over visitors, an increase of 3.9 percent over the previous year. These visitors spent at least 24 hours on the island, and between 30 and 40 percent of them had visited Barbados at least once before. Stay-over visitor arrivals for January to May, and July, were lower than the corresponding months the year before. In June, and August to December, however, monthly stay-over arrivals consistently exceeded the previous year. The percentage by month of total stay-over visitors is shown below.

Europe had provided the largest number of stay-over visitors to the island, contributing 44.3 percent of the total, a 2.9 percent increase over the previous year. The United States contributed 25.3 percent of the total stay-over visitors, an increase of 2.7 percent over the previous year. Arrivals from other areas, their percent of total, and percent of increase over the previous year, are shown in Exhibit 16-1.

American Airlines and British West Indian Airways (BWIA) were the two main carriers providing airlift from the United States; there were no charter services from that country. Flights arrived daily from New York, Miami, and San Juan. Air Canada, Canadian Airlines, and charter airlines Air Transat, Royal Airlines, and Canada 3000 provided scheduled and charter service from Canada. British Airways was the major carrier from the United Kingdom, along with numerous charter airlines providing air access from the UK and other European countries.

Cruise passengers on land trips accounted for about 485,000 of the total visitors, a 5.5 percent increase. These visitors spend less than 24 hours on the island and spent approximately U.S.$45 million of the total visitor expenditure. It was estimated that stay-over visitors spent approximately U.S.$1435 each during their visit, while cruise passengers spent on average U.S.$93 each while on the island.

COMPETITION AND ACCOMMODATIONS

In a macro sense, all warm weather destinations, especially islands similar to the Caribbean Islands

E X H I B I T   16-1
Past Year Stay-Over Visitors to Barbados

Area	Stay-Over Visitors	Percent of Total	Percent Increase
United Kingdom	126,621	28.6%	2.6%
Other Europe	69,232	15.7	4.4
Canada	53,373	12.1	2.1
United States	111,983	25.3	2.7
Other	80,898	18.3	9.4
Total	442,107	100	3.9

(for example, Hawaii, Tahiti, Fiji) were competition for the Caribbean and Barbados. In a micro sense, however, given the present markets and their distance, the scope of competition could be narrowed considerably even within the Caribbean region. Bermuda, for example, was north enough that the winter was its off-season. Other islands in the region had different attractions and characteristics. The Bahamas, Puerto Rico, Aruba, and Curacao had large chain hotels and offered gaming as a major incentive. Cuba, Haiti, Dominican Republic, Puerto Rico, Trinidad, and Jamaica were all quite different in character and ethnicity. Thus the prime competition for the same markets could be narrowed down to some of the Lesser Antilles and the Windward Islands. Exhibit 16-2 shows the approximate number of hotel rooms in each of these destinations and the approximate visitor expenditure for the most recent year.

THE BARBADOS TOURISM AUTHORITY (BTA)

The BTA was a statutory agency of the Barbados Ministry of Tourism. It was funded by an annual subvention from the central government, most recently of U.S.$15 million, of which approximately 70

Jan.	Feb.	Mar.	Apr.	May	June	July	Aug.	Sept.	Oct.	Nov.	Dec.	Total
8.1	8.3	8.9	8.6	7.0	6.8	10.0	9.2	6.9	7.6	8.5	10.1	100%

EXHIBIT 16-2
Hotel Rooms and Visitor Expenditures
of Major Competition

Islands	Hotel Rooms	U.S.$ Expenditures (Millions)	Expenditures Per Available Room
Anguilla	978	58	59,304
Antigua/Barbuda	3317	448	135,061
Barbados	5685[a]	680	119,613
British Virgin Islands	1224	214	174,837
Dominica	757	35	46,235
Grenada	1428	67	46,919
Guadeloupe	7798	443	56,809
Martinique	7220	431	56,695
Montserrat	710	21	29,577
St.Kitts/Nevis	1593	87	54,614
St. Lucia	2954	255	86,324
Sint Maarten/St. Martin	3710	464	125,068
St.Vincent/Grenadines	1215	57	46,913
U.S.Virgin Islands	5461	1045	191,357

[a]Luxury 24.8 percent, A Class 5.4 percent, B Class 3.4 percent, Guest Houses 1.5 percent, Apartment hotels 64.9 percent.

percent was dedicated to marketing costs and the remaining 30 percent to administrative costs. Total actual expenditures were about $U.S.17 million. The authority also managed overseas offices in the United States, Canada, United Kingdom, and Germany. A global advertising agency was contracted by the BTA to create and execute its advertising campaigns, and a global public relations firm was contracted to support these advertising campaigns.

The primary role of the BTA was the marketing of Barbados' tourism product. The official role, as dictated by the government and the Barbados Ministry of Tourism, consisted of the following:

• To promote, assist, and facilitate the development of tourism in Barbados.
• To design and encourage marketing strategies for the effective promotion of the tourism industry in Barbados.

• To seek to enhance the provision of adequate and suitable air and sea passenger transport services to and from Barbados.

In partial fulfillment of these duties, the BTA also engaged in sports promotion, hotel and restaurant registration, licensing and classification, public relations and public awareness programs, media relations, press releases, crime/damage control, international media tours, facilitation of tourism partners, travel agent familiarization visits, and cooperation with private sector partners. An annual marketing plan was also prepared by the BTA as part of its annual report, which outlined the strategies and projections to maintain Barbados as a desirable tourist destination. With the appointment of the new executive, this marketing plan became confidential, and was no longer made available to the public.

In recent years, Barbados' position in the marketplace had deteriorated, as reflected by stagnation in the level of stay-over visitor arrivals. Reasons cited for this included the strength of the Barbadian dollar (BDS$2 = U.S.$1); the inability to compete on cost with other warm weather destinations, for example, Mexico and Cuba; mild winters in North America; well-publicized instances of crimes against visitors; and hurricane devastation that reduced visitor arrivals throughout the region. These difficulties, however, were also faced by other Caribbean destinations that experienced surges in arrivals substantially greater than those in Barbados.

There was an apparent lack of recognition of the island in the marketplace due to a recent history of lackluster marketing. This lack included travel agents and tour operators in the island's main markets. The controversy that surrounded the BTA from its inception resulted in a perceived absence of leadership in the Barbados tourism industry. Efforts at promoting the island and attracting visitors were hindered by this perception and, consequently, there was a general lack of confidence in the island by the recipients of these efforts. In addition, marketing efforts were not limited to the BTA, the official marketing body of the Barbados tourism product. There were also instances of advertising and promotion by other stakeholders in the industry, for example, the Barbados Hotel and Tourism Association, St. James Beach Resorts, and the Elegant Resorts of Barbados. These also served to undermine the authority of the BTA. According to the Minister of Tourism, Billie Miller:

An analysis of the past performance of the management of Barbados' [tourism]...abroad reveals there has been wastage, ineffective use, duplication of effort, limited sharing of information, and a lack of complementarity.

Earlyn Shuffler, president of the BTA, saw his role as a facilitator for the industry:

I am to provide leadership by example; to build a strong management team and be the primary facilitator in bringing all sectors of tourism together to make Barbados the preferred warm weather destination in the Caribbean.

Prior to the appointment of the new executive there were a number of government-backed marketing strategies already in place for the island (Exhibit 16-3). In order to achieve some of their goals, the new executive of the BTA developed a number of additional strategies. Their main obstacle, however, was the lack of current, comprehensive market information. Thomas Hill, vice-president sales and marketing of the BTA, believed:

The product is here, it has always been here, it is an excellent product and improves as time goes on. But what we have to determine now is how do we take that to the rest of the world and convince them that this is the place to visit?

As part of the new strategies, the BTA launched a U.S.$2.3 million advertising campaign in the United States in an attempt to recapture some of their lost market share. The campaign focused on

EXHIBIT 16-3
Marketing Strategies in Place Before the Hiring of the New BTA Executive

United States
- A super value package
- Barbados Welcomes VISA in collaboration with VISA International—VISA cardholders received promotional material with their monthly statements
- Increased advertising and public relations
- Educational tours to the island of 800 travel agents by this year end
- Strategic alliances with British West Indies Airways (BWIA) and American Airlines

United Kingdom
- Promotional tour to the United Kingdom in November
- Participation at World Travel Market in November
- Road shows with Kuoni and British Airways

Other Europe
- Educational tours in Barbados for travel agents
- Participation in Travel Trade Workshop, Switzerland
- Participation in Carib 2000, and all Caribbean travel fair in Paris
- Radio advertising in Germany
- Spot advertising in media

Canada
- Promotional tour to Montreal, Toronto, Calgary, Edmonton, Vancouver
- Sponsorship agreement with Hamilton Tiger Cats football team
- Negotiating with the Toronto Raptors basketball team to use Barbados as their official destination
- Program with Regent Holidays (tour operator) to bring visitors from Vancouver, Quebec, and Toronto

the theme "Imagine yourself in Barbados" and depicted scenes of visitors enjoying themselves in Barbados. The BTA also branched into new markets, and sought entry into the South American market through linkages with Brazil. This venture failed to reach its full potential with the loss of airlift between Brazil and Barbados. British West Indian Airways (BWIA), the airline that provided transportation from Brazil to Barbados, canceled this route shortly after its introduction due to lack of profitability for the airline and underusage of the route.

"Barbados is concerned about market share." said Jean Holder, secretary-general of the Caribbean Tourism Organization. "During the past decade there has been a significant loss of market share [from] important markets [for Barbados]." Barbados was a traditional warm weather destination, offering doses of "sun, sea, and sand." In an attempt to diversify and recapture some of its lost market share, a number of product offerings were expanded with the intention of capturing specific niches, which are shown in Exhibit 16-4. With these products, the island was able to offer a wide range of activities throughout the year, shown in Exhibit 16-5, catering to a variety of tastes.

"Was this enough? Do we really have a strategy to move the island forward?" wondered Mr. Shuffler. Reports so far for the year indicated an increase in arrivals to the island. "Was this due to the efforts of the BTA?" He wondered what decision the board would reach after he presented his report. "Whom should we target, and what should we offer? Can we really support so many different products? What should the plan of action be for the future?"

EXHIBIT 16-4
Specific Niche Markets Targeted

Niche Market	Activities
Sports	Cricket, field hockey, horse racing, wind surfing, golf, yachting, soccer, body surfing, bridge, chess, surfing, running, cycling, and swimming were available.
Culture	Offerings included Paint it Jazz Festival (past performers included Roberta Flack), Holetown Festival, Holders Opera Season (past performers included Luciano Pavarotti), Oistins Fish Festival, De Malibu Congaline Carnival, Gospelfest, Crop Over Festival.
Weddings/Honeymoons	In the UK, Barbados was voted top wedding destination. There were no residency requirements and couples could be married on the day of their arrival on the island.
Heritage	Old slave huts, plantation houses, churches, and sugar mills formed part of heritage tours.
Diving	Natural reefs and sunken wrecks provided underwater attractions.
Filmmaking	A Film Credential Industry brochure was being compiled for use as a marketing tool. This followed the filming of several episodes of "The Bold and the Beautiful" in 1995, and the U.S.$1.1 million Malibu Coconut Rum ad that was filmed on location on the island.
Ecotourism	Harrison's Cave, Turner Hall Woods, and Welchman Hall Gully were touted as part of the eco-product

E X H I B I T   16-5
Monthly Activity Schedule

January	Wind Surfing World Championships
	Paint It Jazz (jazz festival)
	Mount Gay International Regatta
	  (sailing)
	Barbados National Trust
	  (heritage tours, January–April)
		July	Carnival/Crop Over (Carnival,
			  July–August) Caribbean Storytelling
			  Festival

February	Flower Show Holetown Festival (cultural festival)	August	International Schools Netball Festival Banks International Hockey Festival Tulip Rally (international car rally)

March	Cockspur Gold Cup Race
	  (horse racing)
		October	Sir Garfield Sobers Seniors
			  Cricket Festival

April	Holders Opera Season
	  (opera and Shakespeare season)
	Oistins Fish Festival (cultural festival)
	Caribbean Atlantic Cricket Cup
			Sun, Sea, Slam International
			  Bridge Festival
			International Triathlon
			Pro Am Cricket Festival

May	Gospelfest (international Gospel week
	  of activities-
		November	Sprite Caribbean Surfing
			  Championships

June	Aqua Splash (aquatic-based
	  competition and show)
	Shell June Rally (international car rally)
		December	Run Barbados Road Series
			United Barbados Open Golf
			  Tournament
			Red Stripe Series Regional Cricket

C A S E

Seventeen

◆

THE REGAL HOTEL*

Diane Frank was recently appointed Director of Sales at the Regal Hotel. Her General Manager, Jim Jeffreys, had been at the hotel a little over a year. Jim and Diane were having an informal discussion late Monday afternoon:

Jim: Well, Diane, you've been here just over a month now, how do you feel about your new position as Director of Sales?

Diane: Jim, I'm excited about the job, its responsibilities, and the challenge we have ahead of us to turn around our occupancy and profit figures.

Jim: So am I, and we certainly have our work laid out for us. As you're aware, next year's Marketing Plan is due at the home office by the end of the month. I know you've done some preliminary work on it, and it's time to pull it together. Could you have it ready for me by the end of next week? I'd like to go over it with you and have a final copy by the third week in November.

Diane: I don't see any problem with that deadline, Jim. I have my staff working on the rough drafts for their respective markets now. I've also had the opportunity to review recent occupancy levels, average rates, the competition, etc., and feel good about developing a sound marketing strategy for next year.

Jim: Good. You know what direction I think we should take, yet I'd like your independent input as much as possible. Oftentimes, new blood and fresh eyes can better see target areas we might have overlooked. Is John (Executive Assistant–Rooms) being helpful with the transient figures and any input you might need?

Diane: Yes, he is. All the staff is being very cooperative and giving me the support I was hoping for.

Jim: Great. Let me know if you run into any problems or need any help. Our

*This case was contributed by Margaret Shaw, Ph.D., University of Guelph, Ontario, Canada. All names and figures have been disguised. All rights reserved.

Marketing Plan is critical to the overall success of the hotel.

THE PRODUCT

The Regal Hotel was a 500-room first-class property in the capital city of a midwestern state. It was managed by the Royal Hotel Corporation, a national hotel management company. The two principal owners of the hotel were a national insurance company and a large real estate development firm. The Royal was one of six hotels the Royal Hotel Corporation had opened in major secondary cities across the United States in the past three years. Located in the heart of the downtown business district and state capital buildings, it was built as part of a major new complex that included the hotel, an office building, and 29 retail shops, predominately clothing stores. The office space housed 20 firms employing approximately 250 persons.

The hotel had 18 function rooms ranging in size from 500 to 7100 square feet, accommodating up to 1000 persons in one room for a general session theater-style meeting. The Presidential and Governor's Suites were plushly appointed, board of director styled rooms, located on the third floor of the hotel. The Regal did not have the physical capability to hold major exhibitions and trade shows. However, it was conveniently located across the street from the State Capital Convention Center, which had 30 meeting rooms and 140,000 square feet of unobstructed exhibit space. Overall, the physical condition of the hotel was excellent.

The Regal had several food and beverage operations. Jackson's, located on the second lobby level, served breakfast, lunch, and dinner seven days a week, and offered a wide range of moderately priced entrée choices. Lunch, cocktails, and dinner were also served every day in the hotel's rooftop lounge, the Crow's Nest. King Arthur's restaurant offered round the world gourmet dining, and included an extensive wine cellar. A complete room service menu was available from 6:30 A.M. to 11:30 P.M. daily. The average food checks for Jackson's, the Crow's Nest and King Arthur's were $9.00, $20.00, and $32.00, respectively. A new "Light Lunch" restaurant was to open soon on the third floor lobby level. It was hoped this would generate traffic for the retail shops as well as capture the existing noontime shoppers with the appeal of a quick and easy light lunch.

CAPITAL CITY

This midwestern capital city had a metropolitan population of 600,000 people. The local business community included major headquarters for approximately 200 corporations, regional and local offices for an additional 250 corporations, 50 national insurance companies, and a large number of national fraternal organizations. Many of these firms were located on the perimeter of the city as well as in downtown locations. Situated just north of the city was the main campus for State University with an enrollment of 22,000 students.

Like many cities in the United States, Capital City was in the process of a major revitalization program. There was an active and cooperative spirit in the community for the redevelopment of the downtown area. One of the major coordinating bodies was the Commission for Metropolitan Development, a not-for-profit organization promoting the revitalization and use of the downtown core. General planning and generation of funds for this extensive program was masterminded by the Commission, and was supported by other agencies and organizations.

City projects completed in the past five years included the Convention Center Complex, major new office buildings, improved transportation systems, a sports arena for major sporting events (with a seating capacity of 15,000), and an international marketplace (similar to the Quincy Market of Boston); all located in the center of the city.

Projects under construction included a major addition to the Convention Center, a track and field/velodrome sports complex adjacent to the University, the resurrection of the train station area, and the preservation of a historic theater. The development of a multimillion dollar 250-acre urban park just west of the city was in its final planning stages.

The convention center expansion would be a dome-shaped building with a seating capacity of 60,000 with the potential to host major sporting events including basketball, hockey, and major league football. This expansion would also provide an additional 150,000 square feet of exhibit space and 19 additional meeting rooms. The project was scheduled to be completed in two years.

A major new 600- to 800-room convention hotel was expected to break ground within the next 18 months. The building site was two blocks from the Regal. The hotel was being developed by a regional development firm. Several national hotel chains had bid for the management contract of the hotel, and an announcement was expected by the end of the year.

Convention delegates to the city had more than doubled in the last four years from 200,000 to 500,000 delegates. Over 3,000,000 visitors traveled to Capital annually. The city had identified national association business and amateur athletic sporting events as their principal target markets. The Convention and Visitors' Bureau was the major solicitor for the citywide events. In support of their active marketing program, the Bureau's budget had increased from $300,000 to $1,200,000 in the past three years.

The Regal management worked closely with the community in support of the redevelopment program. The General Manager, Director of Sales, and Director of Public Relations were involved daily with various local committee meetings, hosting leading contributors, and generating enthusiasm among the hotel employees. They were well aware that the growth and vitality of the city would lead to the growth and success of the Regal Hotel.

Jim Jeffreys had been appointed General Manager of the Regal Hotel a year earlier. He was the third general manager for this property, and had a strong hotel sales and marketing background. Jim had held several positions as sales manager and director of sales for the Royal Hotel Corporation. This was his first assignment as General Manager. Jim felt strongly about total dollar contribution and net profit as a basis for judging the success of the hotel.

Diane Frank was the Director of Sales. She had initial sales training with a competitor of the Royal Hotels. Eighteen months ago she had been appointed Director of Sales of an east coast Royal Hotel property and promoted to her present position in mid-September. A graduate of the School of Hotel Administration at Cornell University, Diane had gained an excellent reputation for her marketing skills and salesmanship abilities.

SALES AND MARKETING

The Regal Hotel catered to both the convention and transient markets. The principal convention markets were national, regional, and state associations, and corporate accounts. Their transient business was drawn primarily from recommendations of the local business community.

Sales

The primary function of the sales department at the Regal was to book convention business. They also targeted transient accounts (i.e., high volume corporate accounts). Larger groups at the Regal tended to be the association accounts (200 to 450 persons). Convention planning for this market was usually 18 to 24 months in advance. The small- and medium-sized groups (association, corporate, tour and travel) were more likely to plan 3 to 15 months in advance, and ranged in size from 15 to 250 persons. Group booking activity at the Regal had con-

EXHIBIT 17-1
Regal Hotel Business Mix

Market Segment	Past Year		First Ten Months Current Year	
	Room Nights	Percentage	Room Nights	Percentage
National associations	20,670	19.3	17,820	20.6
Regional associations	8,150	7.6	8,605	10.0
State association	19,210	17.9	16,185	18.7
Corporate	10,900	10.2	14,270	16.5
Tour and travel	2,050	1.9	5,350	6.2
Government	1,012	0.9	690	0.8
FIT	45,246	42.2	23,402	27.1
Totals	107,238	100	86,322	100

Note: Association, Corporate, and Tour and Travel reflect group business; Government and FIT reflect transient business.

centrated on the association market. The business mix for the past year and the forecast for the current year are shown in Exhibit 17-1.

There were four salespersons on the sales staff at the Regal. Each sales person was assigned a specific market segment (see Exhibit 17-2), and was responsible for drafting the section of the marketing plan pertaining to his or her respective market. Quarterly updates on progress to date and possible revised action plans were submitted to the Director of Sales (i.e., changes in planned sales trips, results of a sales blitz, unexpected changes in market conditions).

Public Relations, Advertising, Special Promotions

In addition to personal selling, other areas of marketing activity at the Regal Hotel included public relations, advertising, and special promotions. The primary responsibility of the Public Relations department at the Regal was to handle all media relations, plan and coordinate special events, and work closely with the sales department on special promotions directed to specific target markets.

Highlights included summer concerts in the lobby, monthly artist programs, and the arrangement of special luncheons for local business leaders with the Chef. The "Chef's Table," as it had come to be known, was one of the more successful PR activities to contribute to the hotel's occupancy. A direct relationship could be seen between the corporate executives having attended a luncheon and the resulting increase in business from their respective firms.

The advertising schedule for next year had been finalized. This schedule was primarily a balance between local media selections and chain allocations. Local media emphasis had been placed on King Arthur's Restaurant and corporate transient room business.

Promotional activities included direct mail solicitation to special market segments (i.e., state and regional associations), weekend package promotions to the local community, and exhibitions at major convention trade shows such as the Meeting Professionals International and American Society of Association Executives for group business promotion.

A summary of the marketing budgets for the past two years, along with next year's projections,

EXHIBIT 17-2
Current Salesperson Assignments

Salesperson	Assigned Market Segment	Allocation of Time	
		Selling	*Administration*
Director of sales	National associations (east coast)	40	60
Sales manager # 1	National associations (Chicago), state associations (state capital)	80	20
Sales manager # 2	State associations (other midwestern states), regional associations	85	15
Sales manager # 3	National and regional corporations	85	15
Sales manager # 4	Local corporations (group and transient), tour and travel	85	15

are shown in Exhibit 17-3. A plan to increase the sales staff by one member is reflected in part in the next year's payroll increase.

Market Surveys

Two market surveys had just been completed to help determine the geographic market source of the Regal Hotel's business—the American Express Lodging Market Analysis and a Geographic Market Survey from internal sources of the Royal Hotel Corporation.

The American Express survey indicated that the three most important feeder cities for the Regal were Chicago, New York City, and Capital City, comprising over 40 percent of the guest profile.

(The sample population included American Express users only.) This survey also revealed below average use of the Regal from several major secondary cities in the midwest including Cleveland, Cincinnati, and Detroit. Excerpts from the internal geographic survey also suggested that Chicago, New York City, and Capital City were the principal geographic markets for rooms business at the Regal.

OCCUPANCY STATISTICS

The Regal Hotel had experienced fluctuating occupancy rates for the past three years. Exhibit 17-4 shows the total room night occupancy, occupancy

EXHIBIT 17-3
Summary of Marketing Budgets

Expenditure	Previous Year	Current Year	Next Year
Payroll	$ 314,000	$ 330,000	$ 400,000
Advertising	299,000	305,400	320,000
Promotions	2,400	4,800	19,000
Public relations	2,200	10,000	12,000
Other	220,000	138,000	164,000
Chain allocation	230,000	260,000	287,000
Total	1,067,600	1,048,200	1,202,000

EXHIBIT 17-4
Roomnights, Occupancy Percentage, Average Daily Rate—Summary Statistics

		Jan.	Feb.	Mar.	Apr.	May	Jun.	Jul.	Aug.	Sept.	Oct.	Nov.	Dec.
Year 1	RN	6602	7640	9987	11110	11875	9541	6417	7604	9233	10702	9365	6310
	% Occ.	42.6	54.6	64.4	74.1	76.6	63.6	41.4	49.1	61.6	69.0	62.4	40.7
	ADR	$79.80	$72.66	$71.84	$75.04	$ 85.20	$ 76.20	$ 71.74	$73.48	$82.04	$ 82.24	$83.90	$86.02
Year 2	RN	5795	7125	10862	8769	10700	10969	7444	10121	9472	11710	7992	6279
	% Occ.	37.4	50.9	70.1	58.5	69.0	73.1	48.0	65.3	63.1	75.6	53.3	40.5
	ADR	$85.76	$89.48	$90.74	$88.20	$99.94	$83.20	$85.94	$88.48	$92.60	$ 90.72	$94.36	$91.48
Current Year	RN	7004	6454	9192	9590	9690	7628	5872	8813	9962	12117	—	—
	% Occ.	45.2	46.1	59.3	63.9	62.5	50.9	37.9	56.8	66.4	78.2	—	—
	ADR	$92.76	$99.30	$101.82	$97.26	$111.72	$106.54	$103.20	$99.56	$104.68	$106.96	—	—

Year	Occupied Rooms	Occupancy Percentage	Average Rate
Year 1	106,404	58.30%	$ 77.92
Year 2	107,238	58.70%	$ 90.26
Current Year	86,322*	56.80%*	$102.28*

(* First 10 Months Only, i.e., Year-to-Date)

percentages, and the overall average rates since the hotel's first full year of operations. The current variable cost per room was roughly $24.00. Exhibit 17-5 shows group and transient occupancy figures and their respective average rates for the past and current years.

COMPETITION AND PRICING

Four first-class hotels, including the Regal, had entered the market in Capital City in the past five years. As noted earlier, a new 600- to 800-room convention hotel would be built soon in close proximity to the convention center. The city had also attracted several low budget motor inns in the recent past, particularly in the suburban areas. Six hotels, including the Regal, were considered first-class properties in metropolitan Capital City—three downtown and three suburban.

The Regal considered itself to have two principal downtown competitors: the Capital Holiday and the Adams Hotel. Both were managed by national hotel management firms. The 450-room Capital Holiday was located in the heart of the

E X H I B I T   17-5

Group and Transient Room Night Occupancy and Average Daily Rate—Summary Statistics

		Last Year		Current Year	
		Transient	*Group*	*Transient*	*Group*
January	Occupancy	3790	2005	3804	3200
	Average Rate	$ 92.40	$73.20	$101.80	$ 82.40
February	Occupancy	4230	2895	4032	2422
	Average Rate	$ 96.04	$79.90	$104.40	$ 90.80
March	Occupancy	4890	5972	4490	4702
	Average Rate	$106.54	$77.80	$113.90	$ 90.30
April	Occupancy	3972	4797	4215	5375
	Average Rate	$ 93.20	$84.40	$106.30	$ 90.20
May	Occupancy	3140	7560	4420	5270
	Average Rate	$115.66	$93.40	$113.80	$110.00
June	Occupancy	3497	7472	3520	4108
	Average Rate	$ 95.62	$77.40	$111.60	$102.20
July	Occupancy	3501	3943	3322	2550
	Average Rate	$ 94.44	$78.40	$115.20	$ 87.60
August	Occupancy	3971	6150	4270	4543
	Average Rate	$ 95.40	$84.02	$109.00	$ 90.70
September	Occupancy	3647	5825	3641	6321
	Average Rate	$ 96.54	$90.14	$112.44	$100.20
October	Occupancy	4018	7692	3990	8127
	Average Rate	$ 93.76	$89.12	$114.36	$103.34
November	Occupancy	4390	3602	—	—
	Average Rate	$ 96.04	$92.30	—	—
December	Occupancy	3257	3022	—	—
	Average Rate	$ 98.04	$84.40	—	—

downtown business district. The Holiday's function facilities were similar to the Regal's and up to 1000 persons could be accommodated theater-style in its main ballroom. Though routine maintenance and periodic renovations had been carried out at the Holiday, the Regal was considered to have a superior product with respect to both its physical attributes and quality of service. The Capital Holiday catered to state, regional, and national associations, group and transient corporate business, transient government business, and tourist groups. There was apparently no particular market segment that dominated their business mix. Nor were there any major promotional or public relations activities in the local community.

The Adams Hotel originally opened with 250 guestrooms. Because of its success, an additional 200 guestrooms had recently been added. The hotel had excellent function space, including modern audiovisual equipment permanently installed in many of its meeting rooms. The hotel had superb parlor suite accommodations for small business meetings. The Adams Hotel advertised and promoted heavily to the corporate market for both group and transient business in the downtown area. Other targeted markets included state, regional, and national associations, and educational business from the nearby State University. The Adams Hotel was considered the Regal's major competitor.

The recent published rates for these three properties are shown in Exhibit 17-6. The estimated current averate rate for each was as follows:

Regal Hotel	$102.00
Holiday Hotel	$84.00
Adams Hotel	$92.00

Though it was difficult to determine group and transient average rates for the competitors, it was reasonable to assume that special transient promotion rates and group convention rates were considerably lower than the Regal's. The Regal had recently lost several convention bids because of rate quotations ranging $10.00 to $15.00 higher than their competitors.

EXHIBIT 17-6
Published Rates for Downtown First-Class Hotels in Capital City

Hotel			*Published Rate*		
			Current Year		
Regal Hotel	Single	$100.00	$116.00	$128.00	$146.00
	Double	$124.00	$140.00	$152.00	$170.00
Holiday Hotel	Single	$100.00	$104.00	$108.00	
	Double	$120.00	$124.00	$128.00	
Adams Hotel	Single	$100.00			
	Double	$120.00			
			Last Year		
Regal Hotel	Single	$ 84.00	$ 96.00	$110.00	
	Double	$108.00	$120.00	$134.00	
Holiday Hotel	Single	$ 70.00	$ 84.00		
	Double	$ 90.00	$104.00		
Adams Hotel	Single	$ 72.00	$ 80.00	$ 90.00	
	Double	$ 90.00	$100.00	$110.00	

SUMMARY

The Regal Hotel was a first-class property considered by many to be the finest and most expensive in the area. However, occupancy and profit figures for the hotel were still fairly low. Jim and Diane were under pressure to plan and implement a successful marketing strategy to increase the profit of the hotel. Diane called a meeting for 4:00 P.M. Wednesday to meet with the sales staff. She suggested they not make plans for dinner; it would be a long meeting. Sandwiches would be brought in. The meeting was held in the Governor's suite and began as follows:

Diane: Ladies and gentlemen, we have a problem. I have reviewed your drafts, and they are not acceptable.

Dave: You asked us to write up our marketing plans, and that's what we did.

Diane: I asked you to prepare a marketing strategy and outline your action plans, not simply "write." From what you gave me, I see little difference between this year's plan and last year's. If we are intending to implement the same strategy, there would be no point in just rewriting it.

Joane: What's wrong with last year's plan?

Diane: That's exactly why I called this meeting, Joanne. For the next several hours, as a group, we are going to review our current situation at the hotel, examine our current markets, look hard at our competition, explore new market possibilities, and so forth. Then, we will determine what we should be doing, not necessarily where we are at the present time. Shall we begin?

CASE

Eighteen

◆◆◆

A WORLD SERIES OF YIELD MANAGEMENT*

You are the front office manager of a 500-room commercial hotel in an urban location. Your property caters mostly to traveling business people during the week and to families and tourists on the weekend. The hotel has three food and beverage outlets on site, including a coffee shop for fast-service breakfast and lunch, an informal dining room serving Italian cuisine, and a very popular sports bar. The sports bar and restaurant has a large screen TV and frequently hosts sports celebrities as guests. The room seats 200 people and is decorated with signed posters, photos, and sports gear. The menu includes an assortment of finger foods, hot and cold sandwiches, and a variety of alcoholic and nonalcoholic beverages.

The hotel is a franchise of a well-known hotel chain and is managed by a management company. Most of the ownership of the hotel is held by institutional investors, including a large insurance company. The property is 10 years old and has had an excellent financial track record.

The fall season is particularly strong for this hotel, as it services many business meetings and transient business guests during the week. Weekends have lower occupancies and lower average rates than do Monday through Thursday, but business is still solid. It is now part way through September and the fall season has promised to be stronger than any of the previous five years, albeit at lower rates. A summary of occupancy and average rate for the month of October for the last five years is as follows:

	Past Year	Prior Year	Prior Year	Prior Year	Prior Year
Occupancy	85%	86%	83%	74%	77%
Average Rate	$130	$125	$125	$110	$120

As the front office manager, you are now reviewing the projected occupancy for October of the current year. You are faced with an unusual dilemma; you must decide which guests to accommodate. The city's major league baseball team very

*This case was written by Denise Dupré and is used by permission of John Wiley & Sons.

possibly may be a contender in the World Series, but the actual contenders may not be known for sure until the Tuesday before the Series begins. If it is a contender, games 1 and 2 will be played at home on Saturday, October 18, and Sunday, October 19. If needed (the first team to win four games wins the series), games 6 and 7 will be also be played at home on Saturday and Sunday, October 25 and 26. (October 20 through 24 are travel and away games.) The hotel rooms in the city will most certainly sell out on those dates at top rates. As of September 15, for these days, 400 of the hotel's 500 rooms in your hotel have already been sold at an average rate of $125 for the weekdays (Mon–Thu) and 300 have been sold for the weekend days (Fri–Sun) at an average rate of $90.

The sales and marketing department has requested a block of 100 rooms to accommodate a very loyal business group from the night of Sunday, October 19 through the night of Saturday, October 25, a seven-night stay. This group would expect to pay their corporate rate of $100 per room. Four evening banquets, other meals, beverages, and various meeting rooms will be needed during the course of their stay. The group would like to book immediately.

Reviewing historical booking patterns, you note that the hotel would typically sell an average of 80 rooms to transient guests on Monday, October 20, through Thursday, October 23, and 120 rooms on Saturday and Sunday, October 18 and 19, and on Friday, Saturday, and Sunday, October 24, 25, and 26. These transient guest typically book rooms three to seven days in advance for weekdays and two to three days in advance for weekends. The average rate for these sales would be expected to be $110 on weekdays and $80 on weekends.

If the World Series games are, in fact, played in the city, you would easily expect to be able to charge the full rack rate of $160 on all remaining rooms; however, you would not anticipate those bookings to be made until the last minute. As you review the roster of guests already booked in that October period, you note a large concentration are from one city—the fans of the likely opponents in the World Series. If the home team is not a finalist, or if the series is over in four games, you anticipate a large number of cancellations. The hotel has a 24-hour cancellation policy. If the other team is not a finalist, the rooms will be replaced by fans of the team that is the finalist.

Nineteen

HOLIDAY INN ENTERS SALZBURG*

Walter Foeger looked at the stack of information before him. His new Holiday Inn, now under renovation, would open in about a year in Salzburg, Austria. The questions of who the market would be and how to position the hotel were at the top of his mind. He had to make decisions soon, before the renovation went much further.

Walter had negotiated an "open" management contract with Holiday Inn management, a subsidiary of Bass Hotels and Resorts, based in Atlanta, Georgia, USA. "Open" meant that he had the option to position mid-market as a Holiday Inn, or up-market as a Crowne Plaza. He was fully aware that Bass preferred a Crowne Plaza, the upscale hotel in its product line, other than Inter-Continental. But Walter had no illusions. He had observed the positioning problems of some of the other Crowne Plazas in Europe, such as the one in Amsterdam, and wasn't sure that an upscale position was the right one for the Holiday Inn in Salzburg. He was investing a lot of

his resources in his first hotel and wanted to be sure of its success.

As a Crowne Plaza, which tries to be a five-star property in Europe although a three- to four-star in the United States, the hotel, Walter knew, would have to be a better product with more amenities. Walter was willing to commit the resources to do this if the market called for it, but that wasn't his greatest worry. As a man who had made his money in importing and exporting, he was well aware of the need to reach the right market segments and to position to offer the best value in the product class.

Walter had calculated that renovating as a basic Holiday Inn would cost him about ATS 1,200,000 per room, while a Crowne Plaza would cost him about ATS 1,600,000 per room, in order to compete in the upscale market.*

The size of the hotel was already established and configured for 199 rooms including seven suites.

---

*Karsten Rosel, former Manager, International Sales, Holiday Inns Europe, Wiesbaden, Germany, contributed to this case. Some facts have been altered to facilitate the use of the case.

*For conversion purposes, ATS 100 (Austrian schillings) equaled approximately U.S.$8.80, DM 14.2, and GBP 5. For ease in using the case, other figures are given in U.S. dollars converted at U.S.$0.088 = ATS 1 or, conversely, ATS 11.36 = U.S.$1.

What was still in doubt were the choice of room furbishings and the quality and type of public space, food and beverage outlets, meeting rooms, recreation facilities, and other services. The difference in construction cost of $7 million meant to Walter a higher average ADR of at least $35.00.[†] "Can I do this in this market?" he wondered as he pondered the information that had been collected for him.

LOCATION

Salzburg, Austria, is located in the heart of Europe, no more than a two-hour flight from the furthest major European city, London (Exhibit 19-1). It was in the middle of Austria, capital of the Salzburg province, and had a population of about 135,000.

[†]Walter used the old rule of thumb of $1.00 per $1000 construction cost.

Salzburg was an interesting area for tourism because of its historical and cultural significance. The city also contained 12 conference or exhibition centers. Approximately 30 fairs occurred in the city each year, but only four really affected the hotel business. Salzburg also had a very heavy motor coach traffic, but very few stopped overnight. There was an excellent variety of tourist packages and a large choice of cultural highlights, such as all-day excursions in "Salzburger Land" and Mozart events.

The Salzburg economy was generally strong, with unemployment less than 3 percent. Approximately 120 companies in Salzburg had annual gross revenues of over $100 million.

The soon-to-be Holiday Inn's location in the city center opposite the Congresshall and the Mirabellgarden was considered to be a unique selling point. It was one kilometer from the train station and seven kilometers from the airport. The downtown area was in easy walking distance. The property had originally been the long-standing 208-room Hotel Pitter, a well known three- to

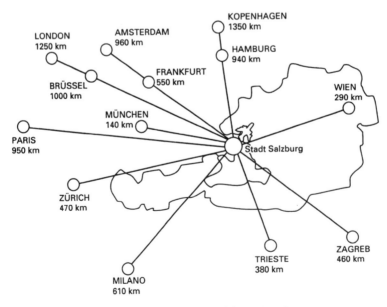

EXHIBIT 19-1 Salzburg, Austria

four-star hotel that had fallen on hard times. Walter had maintained the existing frame of the building but had gutted the interior for renovation.

THE HOTEL

The preliminary plans for the renovated and refurbished five-story hotel showed the following configurations.

Rooms: Seven suites; 36 standard double/double; 7 executive standard; 61 queen; 8 executive queen; 5 king; 15 executive king; 58 single; 2 wheelchair accessible.

Outlets: Two restaurants, one 2400 square feet, the second 900 square feet. These would be served by one kitchen. There would also be a cocktail bar and a lobby bar.

Recreation: Indoor swimming pool, sauna, steam bath, solarium.

Meeting Facilities: Four conference rooms; one boardroom; one ballroom. Capacities from 10 to 300. All on same floor and adjacent.

Parking: Ample parking was available outside.

Walter still had time, but not much, to change these configurations.

THE MARKET

The Salzburg market was essentially divided into low, medium, and high seasons. January, February, October, and November were low season, when city occupancy usually ran 20 to 30 percent. Medium season was March to June, September, and the first half of December, when occupancy ran about 50 percent. High season was July, August, and the last half of December, when there were numerous festivals, Christmas, and strong tourism. The city ran at close to 100 percent occupancy during high season and hotels typically did one-third of their annual occupancy at that time.

Overall, about 20 percent of the market was transient corporate, 15 percent groups and congress, the balance being tourism. The top four feeder markets were the USA, Germany, Italy, and Great Britain followed by France, Spain, Switzerland, and Japan. Eighty percent of these markets were tourism. A feeder market for commercial business was also Vienna.

Fifteen companies in Salzburg had subsidiaries or mother companies in other countries and were considered major potential commercial accounts:

Aqua Engineering	Porsche GmbH
BMW Austria	Puma GmbH
Brenntag Austria	Raab Karcher
Conoco Austria	Schosswender Werke
Ford Motor Company	Teekanne GmbH
Melitta GmbH	Wacker Chemie
Mercedes Benz GmbH	Wrigley Austria GmbH
Mannesmann Demag	

COMPETITION

Walter's staff had completed a competitive analysis. Ten hotels were found to be in the 5-star category and 22 in 4-star. Many were quite small, locally owned, and had limited facilities. Although all these were in some way competitive, for reasons of location, condition, size, facilities, reputation, and international affiliation, Walter's group decided that the Holiday Inn's positioning should be weighed against only eight. Brief descriptions of these eight are given in Exhibit 19-2. All eight hotels offered room service and had CRS (computer reservation systems). More details appear in Exhibit 19-3 on the five hotels presently operating that were considered, in the final analysis, to be the main competitors.

Walter analyzed these figures one more time before he called in his executive team to make a final decision.

5-Star

Sheraton Hotel: One hundred sixty-five rooms; 8 years old; rack rate $135–$445.

Advantages	*Disadvantages*
• Next to Congresshall (city center)	• No swimming pool or leisure facilities
• Has established position in market	
• Well-known cuisine	
• Aggressive sales force	
• International reservation system	
• Listed in company directories of Hoechst, Siemens, BASF	

Radisson Hotel: Sixty-two rooms; opening in six months; rack rate $167–$600.

Advantages	*Disadvantages*
• Magnificently restored houses	• No pool or leisure area
• Very luxurious	• No parking
• Old Town district	• Limited banquet capacity
• International reservation system	

Osterreichischer Hof: One hundred twenty rooms; first opened in 1866; rack rate $141–$431.

Advantages	*Disadvantages*
• Downtown location	• No pool or leisure facilities
• Very traditional hotel	• No parking space
• Loyal clientele for many years	• No sales force
• Major renovation two years ago	
• Belongs to famous Hotel Sacher in Vienna	

Goldener Hirsch: Seventy rooms; converted baroque; rack rate $229–$572.

Advantages	*Disadvantages*
• Baroque center of city	• No parking
• Ciga hotel chain	• Limited meeting facilities
• Leading Hotels of the World	• No pool or leisure facilities
• Famous bar for celebrities	
• Gault et Millau award restaurant	
• Furnished with authentic folk art masterpieces	

(continued)

EXHIBIT 19-2 *(Continued)*

4.5-Star

Penta Hotel: Two hundred fifty-seven rooms; one year old; rack rate $141–$343.

Advantages	Disadvantages
• Spacious banquet capacity	• Bad location, out of city center
• 550 parking places	• No cosy atmosphere
• Local sales force	• Price dumping advocate
• Pool, gym, sauna	

Best Western Kaserhof: 65 beds; converted manor house; rack rate $116–$310.

Advantages	Disadvantages
• Lovely garden	• Limited conference space
• Three restaurants	• City outskirts

4-Star

Novotel: One hundred forty rooms; four years old; rack rate $110–$189.

Advantages	Disadvantages
• Good parking space	• Weak product quality
• Local sales force	• No pool or leisure facilities
• City location	
• Works closely with local companies	

Dorint Hotel: One hundred forty rooms; four years old; rack rate $97–$185.

Advantages	Disadvantages
• Sauna, gymnasium	• No swimming pool

EXHIBIT 19-3
Final Competitive Analysis in Salzburg

	Sheraton	Oster. Hof	Penta	Novotel	Dorint
Rooms	165	120	257	140	140
Building	modern	traditional	modern	modern	modern
Renovations	ongoing	2 years ago	new	none	none
Parking	indoor	none	indoor	in & outdoor	outdoor
Hotel Staff	157	220	230	60	75
Sales Staff	5	0	4	1	1
Reservations Staff	1.5	2	3	1	1
Rooms Quality (1–10)	8	7	5.5	4	4.5
Rooms					
doubles	144	65	247	137	120
singles	—	45	—	3	—
Suites	21	10	10	—	20
Restaurants	2	5	2	1	1
appearances (1–10)	1. 8	6–8	1. 7	4	4.5
	2. 6		2. 5		
capacity	1. 100	80–150	1. 140	80	120
	2. 40		2. 85		
cuisine	1. traditional	1. traditional	1. continental	standard	standard
	2. bistro	5. rathskeller	2. coffee shop		
Bars	1	2	1	1	0
appearance (1–10)	8	8	6	4	—
capacity	50	80	100	25	—
Banquet Rooms	4	6	15	3	3
appearance (1–10)	7	6	5	3	3
maximum capacity	150	300	1000	260	140
NEXT YEAR'S RACK RATES (off-season rates discount at least 50%)					
single $	158–282	172–268	191–268	110–136	97–150
double $	205–335	229–308	229–308	136–189	132–185
max. comm'l. discount	50%	20%	60%	30%	30%
group rate $	137 pp	negotiable	negotiable	55 pp	63 pp
suite $	400–700	352–660	negotiable	—	160–238
Forecasted Year Occ. %	65	65	45	70	60
Forecasted Adr ($)	169	184	157	145	138
Estimated Mix %					
individual	40	55	25	45	60
business	35	25	20	25	20
group	15	10	35	15	10
congress	10	10	20	15	10

CASE

Twenty

$\bullet\text{\Large\textbf{◆}}\bullet$

THE UPPER CRUST RESTAURANT*

Rick Maple, the general manager of the Howard Johnson Newton Hotel, sat at his desk and breathed a deep sigh of frustration. He had just received the month end figures for the hotel's main food and beverage outlet, the Upper Crust Restaurant, for April. Sales for the month were about $81,000. This figure was substantially less than the $110,000 that had been budgeted. Figures for previous months showed similar discrepancies.

Madison Simpson, the restaurant manager, walked into Mr. Maple's office and acknowledged the disappointment showing on Rick's face. "We have to do something," Mr. Maple said to Madison. "The restaurant is simply not generating enough volume." Both Maple and Simpson had earned B.S. degrees in hotel and restaurant administration. They now knew they faced a major challenge, using what they had learned in an attempt to generate higher volume for the Upper Crust Restaurant.

HISTORY AND BACKGROUND

The Upper Crust was an upscale restaurant specializing in seafood and New England style cuisine.

The name was used for the signature restaurants in the Sheraton Tara hotel chain. There were Upper Crust Restaurants located in eight Sheraton Tara hotels in Braintree, Danvers, Framingham, Springfield, and Newton, Massachusetts; Nashua, New Hampshire; Portland, Maine; and Parsippany, New Jersey.

Tara Hotels was the largest franchisee of the Sheraton Corporation in the New England area. The hotels were owned and operated by The Flatley Company, based in Braintree, Massachusetts. They were positioned in the marketplace as upscale properties, catering to higher rated groups and corporate travelers. The physical hotel product was above that of normal Sheraton standards.

The Howard Johnson Newton was a 261-room property located literally above the Massachusetts Turnpike in Newton, Massachusetts, six miles west of Boston, but carefully sealed away from the noise, traffic, and congestion of the turnpike. The turnpike was the main interstate highway into Boston from suburban areas and western Massachusetts. The hotel was formerly managed by Dunfey Hotels under the same Howard Johnson franchise. Although the property was now owned by Flatley, it still carried the Howard Johnson sign on its exterior, as well as the Tara sign, and would continue to do so for two more years because of the franchise

*Eric Jhanji and Felix Moy researched and contributed to this case.

agreement. Until the Howard Johnson sign was removed from the exterior of the property, the hotel would continue to cater to lower rated market segments such as mid-range commercial travelers, airline crews, and sports teams, who were attracted to the Howard Johnson name by its low prices.

After purchasing the property, The Flatley Company began to renovate the interior of the hotel in order to bring it up to Tara standards. The front desk area, the lobby, 50 percent of the rooms, and the Upper Crust Restaurant had been renovated.

At the time of the purchase, the main food and beverage outlet in the hotel was known as Oscar's, the third name the restaurant had in the past five years. Prior to Oscar's, it had been a Red Coach Grille, which had been a subsidiary product line of Howard Johnson. Oscar's was an independently owned, mid-scale restaurant. Flatley eventually purchased Oscar's and ran the restaurant as such for a year. The concept was then terminated and the restaurant was closed for renovation. It reopened six months later as the Upper Crust. The decision had been made by The Flatley Company to renovate and open the Upper Crust despite the fact that the hotel had not yet become a Tara. When the lobby and the front desk area were being renovated, management believed that it was in the best interest of the property to renovate the restaurant at the same time, prior to the forthcoming name change of the hotel.

PROBLEMS FACED BY MANAGEMENT

From a marketing perspective, management faced the following problems with the Upper Crust:

1. The Upper Crust was an upscale restaurant situated in a property that catered to low rated group segments, and would continue to do so for another two years.
2. How would upper middle class customers from the Newton area communities be attracted to an upscale restaurant located in a hotel still perceived to be a Howard Johnson?
3. How would lower rated hotel guests be attracted to an upscale hotel restaurant?
4. Attached to the north end of the property, and accessible through the lobby of the hotel, was an independently owned "pub-like" restaurant known as Appleby's. This restaurant specialized in light, lower-priced foods such as hamburgers, chicken wings, and sandwiches. Appleby's operated under a ten-year contract with the owner of the entire Gateway Plaza property, which included the hotel. Its business boomed because it attracted the in-house lower rated market segments that were staying in the hotel.
5. Financial data indicated that business of the Upper Crust Restaurant was not meeting The Flatley Company's expectations.

THE RESTAURANT

The guiding principle of the Upper Crust was stated on the cover of the lunch and dinner menus:

Once upon a time the custom of the land was for kings and nobles to entertain frequently at court. Guests from far and near were invited and the gaming and feasting lasted for a week. Huge banquets were held and every night the great halls of the castles rang with the sounds of celebration.

The feasting boards were set up in the shape of a "T" with the king and his ranking nobles occupying the head table. And, when the occasion called for a very special feast, the cooks were commanded to prepare giant meat pies, concocted from choice mutton, pork or beef. These giant pies were carried steaming from the galley directly to the king. He and his royal followers were served the choicest parts of the meat pie . . . the upper crust. And so it came about that those who receive special treatment are called the Upper Crust. We chose it as the name of our restaurant because we believe that our patrons are something special and deserve royal treatment.

A newly renovated restaurant with luxurious surroundings and a warm and inviting atmosphere, the Upper Crust was divided into three main sections: the Lounge, the Tapas, and the main dining room.

The Lounge: In the lounge area there was a large sit-down bar, as well as a big screen TV, which regularly displayed major sporting events. Light snack foods, as well as pizza, were available. A monthly calendar of events for the lounge was displayed at the bar, as well as in the lobby of the hotel. Some of these events included BBQ Nite, Deli Nite, the Mexican Fiesta, and the Oriental Express.

Tapas: The Tapas section was a Spanish concept. This section could be seen at the end of the main aisle upon walking into the restaurant. It contained a long, L-shaped counter with eight seats, and was very attractively decorated. In Spain, the Tapas is known as "A traditional Spanish appetizer that originated when city and town people congregated together for conversation and good times." Spanish style appetizers were available in this section.

Main Dining Room: The main dining room consisted of 145 seats. It was elegantly designed. The coverings of the banquette seats were very attractive, and the carpeting and drapes were plush. In one corner of the dining room there was a grand piano for live entertainment during dinner hours. In another corner there was a harp, which was played during the Sunday Brunch. In addition, a small private dining room, which could accommodate up to 14 people, was situated at the back of the main dining room. This was ideal for small meetings and private dinners.

The Upper Crust had a total of sixty employees including an executive chef, two sous-chefs, and five line cooks. Newly hired employees were required to study staff and service manuals, which were prepared by the restaurant manager. In addition, they were required to pass a written exam and familiarize themselves with all aspects of the operation. The restaurant had recently experienced problems relating to a high rate of employee turnover. This was due to the low volume of business, as well as to the numerous employment opportunities available in the surrounding areas.

MENU DESCRIPTION

Breakfast at the Upper Crust was a traditional, American-style offering. Prices ranged from $8.95 for a continental breakfast to $10.75 for bagels and lox. In addition, an à la carte selection was available.

Lunch at the Upper Crust offered a diverse array of tempting foods. In addition to New England style appetizers, soups, salads, burgers, and sandwiches, a wide variety of entrées were available. Some of these included Chicken Citrone ($11.25), Seafood Frittata ($10.95), and Stir Fry Chicken ($10.95). A special lunch treat was the Carvery Buffet, which included a variety of several meats, salads, seafood dishes, and fruits for $12.95.

Dinner at the Upper Crust included an excellent selection of entrées, as well as an appealing variety of appetizers, soups, and salads. Appetizers included Veal Ravioli ($7.50), Escargot Tara ($9.95), and Oysters Bienville ($9.95). Soups included Clam Chowder ($3.50), Seafood Gumbo ($3.95), and Onion Soup ($4.50). Entrées ranged in price from $16.95 for Chicken Zinfandel to $21.95 for Grilled Tournedos Aux Fine Herb. Some popular favorites were Boston Scrod ($14.95), Veal Pommeroy ($17.75), and Fillet of Salmon ($19.95).

The Upper Crust was open seven days a week for breakfast, lunch, and dinner. The lounge was open nightly until 1 A.M.

MARKETING—CURRENT STRATEGIES AND TACTICS

Madison Simpson identified his main markets by meal period as follows:

Breakfast: Predominantly an in-house market with very few people from outside the hotel.

Lunch: Much of the lunch business came from local companies in the Newton area. Individuals, as well as small groups of businesspeople formed a large portion of this market. In addition the retired, elderly community in the Newton area also was considered a part of the lunch market.

Dinner: Much of the dinner business stemmed from the surrounding communities including, especially, Newton. This clientele was generally upper middle class in terms of socioeconomic status. They ate out quite often and were quite fussy and demanding in terms of their expectations.

The in-house business generated by the Upper Crust was quite small. Management felt that this was because it was an upscale restaurant located in a hotel that still attracted lower rated market segments. Madison anticipated a 25 percent increase in the restaurant's volume once the hotel officially became a Tara. This assumption was based on the fact that the property would then be catering to higher rated market segments who would frequent the Upper Crust more often, thus increasing the in-house business.

In the meantime, however, Madison emphasized that much of the marketing being utilized revolved around creating awareness of the restaurant for the outside area communities outside Newton. In order to achieve this, various marketing and promotional tactics had been employed.

COMPETITION

Management felt that The Upper Crust competed against other foodservice operations in the Newton area, as well as in the nearby suburbs of Boston. It did not compete against restaurants located within the city of Boston where there was a large choice from which to choose.

The assumption could be made that any operation that sold food, beverage, and/or liquor in the Newton area was a competitor. Management, however, perceived three hotel restaurants as their primary competition. These restaurants were located in the Sheraton Needham, the Marriott Newton, and Embassy Suites in Cambridge, four, two and six miles away, respectively. The Upper Crust, however, was very reasonably priced compared to these competitors.

ADVERTISING

Various advertisements had been run in local area newspapers such as *The Newton Graphic, The Wellesley Townsman,* and *The Needham Times.* A general advertisement introduced the restaurant to the community and also provided some descriptive information on the cuisine. This ad was run quite frequently. Another frequently run advertisement was one that offered a $10 discount off a second entrée when a first was purchased at full price.

During the summer, a grand opening party had been held in the restaurant. Prominent politicians, area business leaders, and media people had been invited. The purpose of this event had been to gain exposure for the restaurant in the Newton area.

Another promotional tactic utilized was the Sunset Dinner. This was a complete dinner including soup, salad, entrée, beverage, and dessert for a price of $10.95, $12.95, or $14.95. These dinners were served from 5 P.M. to 6.30 P.M., Sunday through Thursday. This was a form of discounting designed to attract guests from the outside. The emphasis was on price/value.

A separate telephone line, independent of the hotel, was established for the restaurant in order to separate its identity from Howard Johnson's. When customers called to inquire about the restaurant, they were told that it was located in the Howard

Johnson hotel, which would soon become a Tara hotel.

A large sign was placed above the Massachusetts turnpike, as a way to capture the attention of commuters. The high volume of traffic made this an appealing tactic.

Special promotions were run throughout the year as part of a company-wide Upper Crust promotion for all eight restaurants of the same name in different Flatley Hotels. For example, a "Seafood Festival" was run in February, when seafood dishes such as Gulf Shrimp, Red Drumfish, and Stone Crab Claws were offered.

CONCLUSION

Mr. Maple and Mr. Simpson both understood that it was largely their responsibility to attract more customers from the outside community to the Upper Crust. Although they knew that business would improve once the hotel become a Tara, this alone was not enough. "In order to generate the kind of volume desired by the corporate office, we must think of new ways to attract people from the area communities," said Mr. Simpson.

Twenty-One

•◆•

THE MOORING RESTAURANT*

The Mooring Restaurant was located in the Mystic Hilton Hotel in the southeastern shore town of Stonington, Connecticut. It was approximately 130 miles from New York City and 90 miles from Boston. This prime location made it easily accessible by boat, Amtrak, by car off Interstate 95, and by plane via the Groton–New London Airport. The hotel used its location as a convenience aspect in marketing the hotel to many business clients and families, as shown in Exhibit 21-1.

The Town of Stonington was a small, seaside lower middle class town of 17,000 inhabitants with an average yearly per capita income of $18,536 and an average age of 40. Its seaport charm and history, along with that of its somewhat larger sister city of Mystic, attracted many tourists during the summer season, when the population tripled. These tourists came to visit the famous Mystic Seaport, Olde Mistick Village, and Mystic Marinelife Aquarium, located across from the Hilton. Also located in and around the Mystic area were a number of large companies such as Dow Chemical, Pfizer, and General Dynamics.

---

*Kevin Durfee and Melissa Pappas contributed to this case.

THE MYSTIC HILTON

The Mystic Hilton was a relatively new franchise property of Hilton Hotels. It was operated under management contract by the Fisher Hotel Group, which also operated the deluxe Bostonian Hotel, located in the Faneuil Hall marketplace in Boston. Frank Fisher's overall mission for his hotels was to operate "small urban luxury hotels, such as the Bostonian."

The Mystic Hilton was the only major hotel in the area, with 184 rooms and a year-round occupancy of 76 percent. Occupancy was greatly higher in the summer tourist season and much lower in the winter season. Winter weekends were close to full occupancy, however, as the hotel aggressively promoted winter weekend getaways. In addition, the hotel hosted many business clients and conventions which made up approximately 40 percent of hotel revenues. The average age of the hotel guests was between 30 and 50 years.

Every hotel, motel, bed and breakfast, and lodging place in the area offering a place to sleep was competition. In a micro sense, however, the Old

EXHIBIT 21-1   Location of Mystic Hilton Inn

Mystic Motor Lodge and a Comfort Inn were the only product class competitors for the Hilton.

Frank Fisher did not believe in having any small, coffee shop style restaurants in his hotels. He believed that a hotel restaurant must draw people in from the outside and that it must be an integral part of the overall package to help market the hotel. Fisher hotel restaurants must be high quality, service conscious, fine dining establishments. Fisher Group was experienced in running these types of hotel restaurants and had been very successful with their 4-star Seasons Restaurant in the Bostonian Hotel.

THE MOORING RESTAURANT

The Mooring was one of two restaurants located in the Mystic Hilton. It was easily accessible through the hotel lobby entrance but there was no separate entrance to the restaurant from the outside. The only physical evidence of the restaurant on the outside of the hotel was the Mooring logo on the Hilton sign at the beginning of the driveway entrance. The other outlet in the hotel was the Soundings Lounge, which offered a limited menu consisting of mostly appetizers and sandwiches.

The Mooring was initially modeled after the inside of a ship. It sported wood floors and tables and an overall nautical appearance. This design, however, created a dark noisy atmosphere that was not conducive to the luxury restaurant that Frank Fisher had imagined, so it was remodeled. The physical plant and atmospherics of The Mooring were exemplified in a brightly lighted room with large windows overlooking a small courtyard plaza. Linen tablecloths, fine china and silver, a wine table display, carpeted floor, soft background music, and comfortable upholstered chairs made up The Mooring's atmosphere to appeal to a more discriminating diner. Through the use of atmospherics, the Fisher Group created an environment that they hoped would affect the buyer and increase the purchase probability.

The restaurant seated approximately 108 people and served three full-service meals a day. Lunch and dinner menus varied in respect to both entrees and price. The average lunch item was $9.00, while the average cost of a dinner entrée was $22.00. Through the use of price the restaurant positioned in the upscale market, differentiated itself from the competition, and created a perception of its product.

The restaurant served 120 to 150 covers per day, midweek, almost on a year round basis: 20 to 30 breakfasts, 60 to 70 lunches, and 40 to 50 dinners. On weekends it served about 40 breakfasts, 40 lunches, and 120 dinners.

Management marketed the restaurant to a variety of segments. The primary market for lunch was business clientele, attracted by the guaranteed 30-

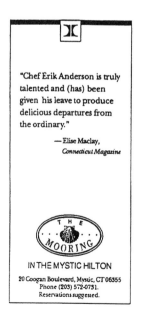

"Chef Erik Anderson is truly talented and (has) been given his leave to produce delicious departures from the ordinary."

— Elise Maclay,
Connecticut Magazine

IN THE MYSTIC HILTON

20 Coogan Boulevard, Mystic, CT 06355
Phone (203) 572-0731.
Reservations suggested.

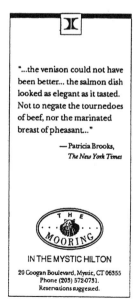

"...the venison could not have been better... the salmon dish looked as elegant as it tasted. Not to negate the tournedoes of beef, nor the marinated breast of pheasant..."

— Patricia Brooks,
The New York Times

IN THE MYSTIC HILTON

20 Coogan Boulevard, Mystic, CT 06355
Phone (203) 572-0731.
Reservations suggested.

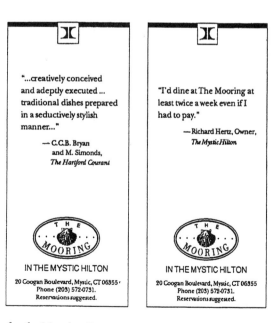

"...creatively conceived and adeptly executed ... traditional dishes prepared in a seductively stylish manner..."

— C.C.B. Bryan
and M. Simonds,
The Hartford Courant

IN THE MYSTIC HILTON

20 Coogan Boulevard, Mystic, CT 06355
Phone (203) 572-0731.
Reservations suggested.

"I'd dine at The Mooring at least twice a week even if I had to pay."

— Richard Hertz, Owner,
The Mystic Hilton

IN THE MYSTIC HILTON

20 Coogan Boulevard, Mystic, CT 06355
Phone (203) 572-0731.
Reservations suggested.

EXHIBIT 21-2 Accolades for the Mooring Restaurant

minute Express Lunch consisting of soup and sandwich. The dinner crowd was a varied mix with no specific market segments. The restaurant did not attract many families. The front desk often suggested to price-sensitive families staying in the hotel that they eat at the more moderately priced Skipper Jack's nearby.

The Mooring was a very good restaurant, in keeping with Frank Fisher's desires. The restaurant had received many very favorable reviews from local newspaper and magazine critics regarding the food preparation and service. These accolades were displayed prominently in various locations throughout the hotel, including several at the restaurant entrance and the front desk area. Exhibit 21-2 shows samples.

The restaurant also did a fair amount of advertising. This was done locally from May to August, plus special holiday promotions, as well as in Connecticut, Rhode Island and New England monthly magazines, and in newspapers in the nearby cities of Hartford, New London, and Providence.

Frank Fisher wanted to use The Mooring restaurant as a prime marketing tool for the hotel. The restaurant, however, was not attracting much business, despite its excellent reputation, and was losing money.

C A S E

Twenty-Two

◆

HOTEL PLAZA PRINCESS*

John Phillips, general manager of the Toronto Hotel Plaza Princess, wondered how he could increase occupancy and raise prices to their original level. The hotel had opened with a single corporate rate of $245 but only a 22 percent occupancy during the first four months. Occupancy increased to 55 percent when the rate was dropped to $208 after the first summer.

BACKGROUND

The Plaza Princess Hotel (PPH) was owned and operated by the parent company of the same name. It claimed to be the world's leading deluxe hotel chain. PPH contended that 85 percent of its customers were business travelers, 40 percent of all guests at a specific hotel were repeat visitors to that

hotel, and it was the first choice of frequent international business travelers, according to an in-flight survey.

The chain had over 100 properties located in 48 countries around the world. Over the past 50 years, the company had achieved a reputation for personalized service, luxury product, and geographic scope, making it a recognized name among international business and leisure travelers. PPH had a strong foreign presence but its image in the North American market was considerably weaker.

The Toronto property was built for about $60 million and was fully owned by PPH. It was one of Toronto's premier boutique hotels and was located in the upscale downtown area of the city also known for expensive restaurants and boutique shops. There were 213 guestrooms, including 12 suites, plus 7 meeting rooms, a business center, a fitness center, an indoor rooftop lap pool, and a sundeck. There was also an upscale lounge and dining room. Guest services included laundry, valet and shoe shine service, 24-hour pressing, twice daily maid service and turndown, 24-hour room service, concierge, guest relations service, and valet parking.

---

*David Blake and Paul Kuno contributed to this case. All rates are given in Canadian dollars. For conversion purposes one C$ = U.S.$0.70. Names have been disguised.

COMPETITION

The Plaza Princess Hotel had five competitors in the same product class. All were in the same approximate area except for the King Edward, which was farther downtown. A comparison of these properties for the past year on price, number of rooms, average occupancy rate, and market share is shown in Exhibit 22-1. Mr. Phillips, however, felt that not all of these properties were competing for the same customer.

Mr. Phillips felt that the main competitive advantage for the PPH was its facilities. The hotel was less than a year old and had a very high quality product with exclusive guest services. Mr. Phillips asked his marketing director, John Visconti, to rank the competition based on the condition of the facility and the guest services offered for the corporate market. His report follows:

The Four Seasons has the same guest services and competes for the same business market segment. It is a luxurious facility with an image of the best upscale hotel chain in North America. The Toronto property has a refurbished lobby and front desk but the rooms are beginning to look tired and run down. (Mr. Visconti rated it as an eight out of ten.)

The King Edward and Sutton Place have refurbished facilities but each lacks essential customer services for the corporate transient segment. (He rated Sutton Place a six but downgraded King Edward to a five because of its location.)

The Park Plaza has two towers. One has been recently refurbished but the other is very run down. It also lacks essential guest services. (It was rated a four.) The Renaissance is being refurbished and promises an upgraded facility next year. However, it also lacks essential guest services.(It was also rated a four.)

The PPH has superior facilities with a lavish marble entryway, mahogany paneling, and rooms that cater specifically to the business traveler with oversized desks, and a separate shower and bathtub in each bathroom. Extensive guest services also ranks the PPH higher than the competitive properties, except the Four Seasons, which has the same services. PPH rates a nine out of ten.

Mr. Visconti felt that the area drew four major market segments. They were the tourist/entertainment, corporate transient, government, and upscale conference segments. Major attractions for the tourist/entertainment segment were generally farther downtown, except for the very upscale boutiques that attracted buyers. The PPH area was home to many of the large businesses in the downtown area and attracted the corporate transient

EXHIBIT 22-1
Competitive Analysis

Hotel	Rooms	Occupancy(%)	Corporate Rate($)	FMS(%)a	AMS(%)b
Plaza Princess	213	55	208	12.4	11.2
Four Seasons	382	87	275	22.3	31.8
King Edward	318	75	215	18.6	22.8
Sutton Place	280	65	198	16.4	17.4
Park Plaza	264	45	176	15.4	11.4
Renaissance	256	22	170	14.9	5.5c
Totals	1713	61		100.0	100.0

a FMS (fair market share) is the number of rooms of each hotel divided by the total number of rooms in all hotels.
b AMS (actual market share) is the number of rooms occupied of each hotel divided by the total number of rooms occupied.
c The Renaissance periodically closed rooms for refurbishing during the year.

market. Government was a large segment because of Queens Park, just south, which was home of the provincial government. The upscale conference market was attracted to the area because of its quality and upscale hotels.

PPH targeted the corporate transient and corporate group markets specifically. The Four Seasons, King Edward, and Sutton Place were hotels that were competing for these same segments. The Park Plaza and the Renaissance, because of their lower prices, were getting a majority of the government segment. The tourist/entertainment market, because of its diversity, was spread among all downtown hotels.

Mr. Phillips wondered how to position the PPH for the future. If they stayed at their present price level, other hotels might steal their present customers. If he raised prices to attract the upscale business market, he was afraid that occupancy would again drop as it had before.

CASE

Twenty-Three

•◆•

THE MT. HIEI HOTEL*

The Mt. Hiei Hotel was about 20 minutes drive, at an uncrowded hour, east of Kyoto, Japan, adjacent to a national park and an important shrine. Lake Biwa, Japan's largest lake, was off to the east. The southern exposure rooms had usable balconies from which one could view Kyoto in one direction and Lake Biwa in the other. The northern exposure rooms on the front of the hotel were more modest and faced the park and shrine in the near distance. The hotel was surrounded by tended lawns and gardens but not the ornamental shrubbery that was so popular in Japan.

The hotel was built in 1959 as an upscale resort for wealthy Japanese families. The surrounding area of Kyoto, Kobe, and Osaka was well-known for many years as a wealthy market. Some smaller cities were likened to Beverly Hills, California for per capita income. The hotel had 74 rooms, 69 in the traditional Japanese style. The rooms were quite large, especially considering the time of con-struction and the customary Japanese hotel room size.

When the hotel opened, the rich-poor dichotomy in Japan was greater than in the 1990s. The initial room rate, double occupancy, was equal to about US$335 per person, in the early 1990s, prohibitive to most then and now. Occupancy, however, although it varied by season, was about 80 percent. Customers were mainly Japanese families who stayed more than just a few days, especially in the summer when they enjoyed the escape from the oppressive hot and sultry lower elevations.

General Manager of the hotel was Mr. Kusano who began his career at Mt. Hiei as a pageboy. According to him, "The rich and influential guests came in the early 1960s. They were elegant people who met with each other, chatted, and walked about in a relaxed environment, enjoying just being there. The hotel was a wonderful vacation haven, especially since there were currency restrictions for Japanese traveling abroad. Now that I am General Manager, I'd like to bring back the wealthy and elegant clients of those early days. I want to relive that grandeur at first hand—as the GM."

*We gratefully acknowledge the contribution of this case by Professor William Kaven, School of Hotel Administration, Cornell University.

MT. HIEI HOTEL TODAY

Changes in Japanese disposable personal income had brought changes in Japanese tastes and spending. Lake Biwa and its major city, Otsu (700,000 population), had high-rise hotels, marinas, amusement parks, and excursion boats not unlike Mississippi River paddle wheelers. Many new resorts were being built around Japan and over 11,000,000 Japanese traveled abroad annually.

Present occupancy at Mt. Hiei was about 42 percent with July and August over 88 percent. Summer business was mainly families with an average age for adults of over 40 years. The average stay was one night.

The rest of the year the customer mix at Mt. Hiei was about 60 percent individual travelers. The other 40 percent was composed of incentive groups, corporate training groups, and junior high school student groups on escorted trips to see Kyoto's historical sights.

The average rate for individual travelers was about US$135 per night, per couple. Eighty percent were from the surrounding area and the rest were from the Tokyo area. The group travelers provided an average rate of US$70.00 per person, three to a room, with breakfast and dinner included. The meal segment of the price was valued at US$12.00 for breakfast and US$36.00 for dinner. This left US$22 per person for the room.

Incentive group customers, being rewarded by their employer, usually stayed two nights. Corporate training meetings and conferences, held by firms such as Matsushita, could last as long as 10 to 15 nights. The high school students usually came in April and stayed two nights. This was an annual Kyoto phenomenon when motor coaches brought thousands of exemplary, polite, uniformed students from all over Japan for a two-day whirlwind tour of palaces, shrines, temples, and gardens. This annual deluge caused a competitive pricing frenzy among Kyoto area hotels and ryokans (traditional Japanese inns or small hotels whose floors are covered with tatami).

The food and beverage department played a strong role at Mt. Hiei, as was common in most Japanese hotels. This resulted from the Japanese custom of entertainment away from home, and the importance that the Japanese placed on eating and drinking with families, friends, and colleagues. At Mt. Hiei food and beverages accounted for 60 percent of revenue, rooms accounted for 25 percent, and other services for 15 percent.

In addition to the main dining room, grill room, and bar in the hotel, there were two additional special facilities. The first was a large, covered and glassed-in barbecue area adjacent to the hotel and usable year around. The local definition of barbecue was for each customer to grill his or her own steak over charcoal braziers installed in the middle of round tables which seated about eight people, while chatting and drinking at the same time. The barbecue area was used by groups on outings or business meetings as well as by in-house guests.

The second facility was a detached building, the Eizankaku Japanese Inn. The Inn contained a few Japanese-style rooms that could serve as private dining rooms or sleeping rooms, but the building was used mainly for Japanese banquets. The building was small but the atmosphere was inviting for the Japanese traditional style of entertainment. The customers were usually male and from organizations, clubs, or firms on a special outing. Most were transported to and from the hotel on a chartered bus. They first enjoyed a hot public bath, then dressed in cotton kimonos provided by the hotel and sat around having a good time chatting, drinking, singing, eating, and relaxing. The sameness of the attire and the convivial atmosphere served to eliminate rank and rancor; old wounds were often erased. Such outings were common in Japanese organizations.

PLANS TO IMPROVE THE OPERATION

The hotel's owner was determined to improve profitability. The physical plant was upgraded at substantial cost by renovating the lobby and reception area, adding new rugs and wall hangings. Guest rooms were refurbished and refurnished but hallways and stairways were not included in the renovation. Upon completion, a six-person promotion department set out to increase guest traffic and make the hotel profitable.

The promotion effort was short-lived and unsuccessful, so a different direction was pursued. Payroll costs and expenses were reduced. Contracts were let to outside suppliers for all possible labor functions of the hotel, including food and beverage operations, housekeeping, and maintenance.

The leasing of the food and beverage operation presented several problems. The hotel was in a sparsely populated area that did not allow for possible outside customers other than the booked banquets. Also, qualified employees were very scarce in the area. This made it difficult to use part-time staff. Further, public transporation up Mt. Hiei was infrequent and costly for the few hours of work that part-time employees might get. Finally, and most important, was the status of the head chef, whose entire career had been tied to Mt. Hiei Hotel. He was an influential top executive with an excellent reputation whose replacement was not feasible even under the best of circumstances.

When profit did not return after renovation, promotion, and cost-cutting, a contract was let for the selling function to an outside professional sales organization. This organization was active in con-

tacting group buyers and produced an increase in the numbers of guests such as the junior high schoolers, incentive groups, and training meetings, but all at low rates. This further decreased the average room rate.

Mr. Kusano was deeply concerned about the hotel and its decline in customers, revenue, and profit. He very much wanted the hotel to be popular, full, and profitable. He felt the hotel was efficiently run; it only needed the customers to make it profitable. Mr. Kusano yearned for the return of the elegant clientele and the wonderful feeling of customers enjoying their stay with him as general manager.

"I think that the hotel may need some added attractions to bring back those elegant customers," said Mr. Kusano. "But the owner is not interested in adding anything to the hotel as it is losing money anyway. The pity is people have changed; they don't know how to be real guests in a fine hotel. I see people now coming into this hotel in their designer label clothes and carrying plastic sacks. They sit down on our chairs, open their sacks and bring out Bento* and eat it right here. There is nothing I can say as I am not here to teach them manners."

---

*Bento are small Japanese wooden box lunches consisting generally of rice with pickled vegetables and fish or meat.

C A S E

Twenty-Four

•◆•

LITTLE THINGS MEAN A LOT

"Eureka!" cried Jim Jackson to his wife Joan. "We won a free weekend from the drawing at that party we went to last week! A weekend at the Meadow Lodge Resort with deluxe accommodations in a Signature Service room. We also get a free Sunday brunch. All we have to do is call the concierge. Let's go next week; I need a break."

The Meadow Lodge Resort was not far from where Jim and Joan Jackson lived. Next to it was a a modern athletic center with, among other things, four tennis courts. Tennis was the Jacksons' favorite sport. The resort also featured indoor and outdoor swimming pools and other health center amenities. The Jacksons had often talked about going there for a weekend just to get away from the "rat race."

FRIDAY NIGHT

The Jacksons arrived at Meadow Lodge about 5:00 P.M. on a Friday afternoon in early June. They planned to play some tennis, do a little swimming, take a whirlpool and sauna, drink wine at the out-side pool patio cafe, catch up on some reading, watch a recent movie and, in general, just relax. They arrived in their room full of anticipation.

"Oh, oh," said Jim, as they entered the room. "There's only one comfortable chair in the room for reading." He called housekeeping and another one was delivered promptly. There was still, however, only one reading lamp for the one chair. He tried to position the deck lamp for the other chair but it didn't provide enough light. Also, there wasn't any table for either chair on which to put a drink or a coffee cup. "So much for reading," he said, as he positioned the desk chair so at least one of them had a "table."

The Jacksons proceeded to unpack and put their clothes in the two dresser drawers. It wasn't that easy as the drawers had no runners and kept going askew and falling out. "I wonder where they got this furniture," said Joan. Jim picked up the TV program to see if he could catch the French Open tennis tournament. "This program starts tomorrow," he said. "They've already replaced this week's." He called housekeeping again. The same program was delivered. "I think I know where there's this week's," said the houseman, who quickly went and got one. "Let's play tennis," said Jim. After tennis, they decided to have a drink on the outdoor pool patio, but found it closed.

When they returned to their room the phone rang. It was a friend of the Jacksons who lived nearby. They had agreed to meet him for a drink at 8:00. "Meet you in the piano lounge," said Jim. "The room directory says it's open until 10:00; it should be nice and quiet." They went downstairs, met their friend, and went into the piano lounge, which was part of the lobby but sectioned off with comfortable chairs and couches. There was no one else there. As they sat down the piano player said, "The bartender just went home. If you go in the bar and ask, they'll bring you a drink."

The three got up and went in the bar. "We can't stay here," said Jim. There was a TV blaring some nonsense in one corner and a large TV screen doing the same in the center, although there was only one couple in the room, and they weren't watching it. They tried to find a corner to get away from the TV but there was no escaping. They asked the bartender to serve them in the piano lounge. He said he couldn't do that but offered to give them drinks to take out themselves. Jim signed the check and as they walked out they picked up some munchies on a table by the bar. "Do you want that charged to your room?" said the bartender. "We thought they were free snacks," they said. "That's okay," said the bartender, "Go ahead and take them and I won't charge you." They went back to the lounge to have their drinks and enjoy the music but the piano player left at 9:00, about the time they got there.

At 9:45 the Jacksons' friend left and they headed for the casual restaurant, which closed at 10:00. The hostess greeted them with, "We close in 15 minutes." "Does that mean you'll throw us out at 10:00?" Joan asked. "No, but we close in 15 minutes," was the response as she led them to a table, repeating the admonishment one more time. There was only a party of two in the restaurant that looked like it could seat 150. The hostess seated them in a dark corner close by the kitchen entrance. "Do you have another table?" they asked,

and were led to a table near the door. They ordered a light meal quickly and finished promptly.

The Jacksons went back to their room and turned on a pay movie. It was too fuzzy to watch so they turned it off and went to sleep. The next morning the desk clerk removed the charge from their bill and told them if it happened again to call maintenance.

SATURDAY

The Jacksons got up at 7:00 A.M. and made some coffee in the in-room coffeemaker. They found orange juice and cream in the minibar but it was so warm they were hesitant to use it. "Let's go for a swim," said Joan. "Check first to see if it's open," said Jim. Joan looked in the room directory and saw that the pool opened at 7:00. "But it's closed from 8:30 to 9:00," she said. "What's the point in going, it's already after 8:00. I wonder why they would do that with all these people in the hotel on weekend packages?" They decided to spend the day driving around the countryside instead.

Back in their room, the Jacksons had a glass of wine and tried to decide where to go for dinner. Not wanting to get back in the car and drive again, they decided to go back to the same restaurant. This time they went earlier, about 8:00. There was a party of six and a deuce in the dining room. They were seated in the same dark corner next to the six and they once again asked to move. They were moved again near the door and right in front of where the buffet was being set up for Sunday brunch. "What's the use?" they said. The hostess, a different one, overheard them and came back to ask if they would like to move. "Yes," they said. "We'd like to sit near a window." The hostess went and talked to the waitress who, shortly after, came to take their order. "The hostess said we could move." "Well," was the reply, "she talked to me but I'm the only one on tonight and that section is closed." The pained expression on the Jacksons' faces must have moved her as she finally said,

"Well, all right," and took them to a window table. She wasn't too pleasant, however, the rest of the meal. The Jacksons finished dinner and went to their room where they finally found a movie to watch that was clear.

SUNDAY

Sunday, the Jacksons slept late. They packed their bags before going downstairs to have their free Sunday brunch in the same dining room where they had been twice for dinner. This time there were about 20 people in the room. They were led to the same dark corner table. As they muttered, the waitress overheard them. "Would you like to move?" she asked. "We'd really like to sit by the window on such a beautiful day," they replied. "Fine," she said, "but I'll have to set up the table because that section is closed." "Never mind," replied the Jacksons, "we'll stay here." The brunch was delightful.

After brunch, the Jacksons checked out. "Well, that's the last time for that place," said Jim as they pulled out of the driveway, "even if it was free." "Not really," said Joan, as she looked at the bill. "We spent over $200. Besides, it wasn't so bad. It's a nice hotel and the people were certainly nice and responsive when you asked." "I know," said Jim, "but it's the little things that make the difference."

C A S E

Twenty-Five

⬩◆⬩

LE MARQUIS DE NAPOLEON*

The Napoleon Hotel was a deluxe four-diamond (AAA rating) hotel located in the heart of downtown Philadelphia, owned and operated by a French hotel chain. It was within short walking distance of the financial district, the government center, the main business district, Liberty Market, and cultural and historical landmarks. It was also attached to Napoleon Place, a 175-store shopping mall that included boutique as well as major department stores, and a food court with 25 counter-style service restaurants.

The hotel had a distinct European atmosphere. It contained 500 rooms constructed around four atria with about 130 guest rooms in each atrium. All rooms were furnished in a combination of antiques and classic European designed furniture. Room service was available around the clock and evening turndown service with a French chocolate was standard in all rooms. The hotel had a large indoor swimming pool with a sun terrace and a fully equipped health and fitness club. There were also

16 function rooms plus a grand ballroom seating 600. The hotel had averaged 65 percent occupancy the previous year with an ADR of $198.

The Napoleon Hotel had two restaurants and one bar. The Lobby Bar was a large lounge/bar located right off the hotel lobby. It was very open, comfortable, and inviting. Entertainment was provided. Cafe Rouge was an informal dining room/coffee shop that specialized in French Bistro cuisine and American food. It had a light, casual, relaxed atmosphere and was open from 7:00 A.M. through 11:00 P.M. It was especially popular among hotel guests at breakfast. At lunch and dinner guests came from both inside and outside the hotel.

LE MARQUIS

Restaurant Le Marquis de Napoleon was the hotel's flagship award-winning restaurant. The food was French nouvelle cuisine. A sample menu is shown in Exhibit 25-1. Other details are given below:

- Winner of Mobil four-star award
- 17 Gault Millau Toques

---

*Emily Hartman researched and contributed to this case. Names and places have been disguised.

Les Hors d'Oeuvre

Rouleau de Printemps de Thon aux Pousses de Soja Marinées, Wasabi Vinaigrette 9.00
Raw Tuna in a "Brick", Marinated Bean Sprouts, Wasabi Vinaigrette

Salade de Crevettes et Topinanbour à l'Huile de Curry et Graines de Vanille 13.50
Louisiana Shrimp on Jerusalem Artichoke Salad and Curry Oil

Ravioli de Confit de Canard, Salade d'Epinards Nouveaux au Foie Gras, Vinaigrette au Jus de Viande 16.00
Confit of Duck in a Crisp Potato Slice, Spinach and Foie Gras Salad, Meat Juice Vinaigrette

Salade Fantaisie aux Asperges 9.50
Seasonal Salad with Fresh Asparagus, Enoki Mushrooms and Truffle Dressing

Chaussons de Sarasin aux Crabes, Huile de Crustacés 11.00
Buckwheat Pancakes with Crabs and Shellfish Oil

Les Potages

Soupe de Moirilles Fraîches aux Herbes de Printemps 7.50
Morel Soup flavored with Fresh Herbs and Asparagus

Bouillon de Galanga et Shiitake, Quenelles de Crevettes 8.50
Galanga and Shiitake Broth with Shrimp Dumpling

Les Mets de la Mer

Dos de Sandre Poché au Jus de Celeri en Branche 26.50
Yellow Pike Poached in Celery Juice

Saumon en Coque de Shiitake, Jus au Champignons 29.00
Salmon in Shiitake Caps with a Light Mushroom Juice

Homard du Maine à la Polenta Liquide, Vinaigrette au Miel et Romarin 34.50
Maine Lobster with a Liquid Polenta, Honey and Rosemary Vinaigrette

Flétan Poêlé au Hachis de Fèves, Artichaut et Olives Noires à l'Huile de Corriandre 28.00
Halibut topped with Fava Beans, Artichokes and Black Olives

Les Entrées

Côtelettes d'Agneau dans une Pomme en Robe, Vinaigrette au Basilic 32.50
Lamb Stuffed Potatoes, Goat Sour Cream, Basil Vinaigrette

Lapereau Mitonné au Jus d'Oignons Nouveaux, Pâtes Croustillantes 28.00
Young Rabbit with Fried Pasta and Onion Juice

Noisettes de Veau aux Huiles de Poivrons Rôtis 33.00
Veal Saddle with Roasted Pepper Oil

Terrine de Boeuf et Pommes de Terre, Bouillon de Légumes au Paprika 29.50
Beef and Potato Terrine, Vegetable and Paprika Broth

Crotin Chavignol Gratiné et sa Salade d'Endive 8.00
Glazed Crotin Chavignol with Endive Salad

EXHIBIT 25-1   Sample Menu of Le Marquis de Napoleon

- Best of city award four straight years
- Philadelphia Magazine Hall of Fame restaurant
- American Express/Travel Holiday Award
- Esquire Magazine's 100 best new restaurants award
- Philadelphia Eagle four-star award
- Open every night except Sunday, 6:00–11:00 P.M.
- Seats up to 90 people
- Private dining room seats up to 14 people

The Le Marquis menu was created by a world-renowned French chef and was changed on a quarterly basis. Press releases were sent to local newspapers announcing the changes; any other advertising was by word of mouth. No promotion was done in-house for the restaurant except for a small ad on the back of the room service menu in each room, plus placards in the hotel elevators. The restaurant served dinner only.

Le Marquis employed a full staff of seven chefs, seven waiters, five buspersons and a manager. All were nonunion employees and were skilled professionals in their fields. All were on duty every night, although some would be sent home on slow nights.

The average customer at Le Marquis was over age 30, was not a hotel guest, and was dining there for a special occasion, business or pleasure, but usually to celebrate an event.

The main competition for Le Marquis came from restaurants located in other Philadelphia hotels, all of which were relatively nearby. This was because there was a dearth of first-class freestanding restaurants in the downtown city area. Le Marquis management felt that it was distanced from the competition because of its physical facilities, both the restaurant and the hotel, the quality of its food, and its excellent reputation. Exhibit 25-2 shows comparative figures among these restaurants.

On average, Le Marquis did about 45 covers a night with an average food and beverage check of $71.69. Top management, however, was not at all happy with the current situation, which last year showed a loss of $204,000. Jean Claude, the food and beverage manager, had his job on the line and was searching for solutions, including opening for breakfast and lunch. He acknowledged that the restaurant had some weaknesses, namely location (the hotel was two blocks from the city's "war zone"—an unattractive run-down area of strip shows, cabarets, etc.), high prices, high employee turnover, and a general unawareness among potential customers. He examined last year's financial statement for further clues (Exhibit 25-3), keeping in mind that management was adamant about positioning the restaurant as "the finest dining room in the city of Philadelphia."

E X H I B I T   25-2
Comparison with Competition's Signature Restaurants

Hotel	Daily Average Covers		Average Food Check($)		Average Time Spent (minutes)		Dinner Choice %	
	Lunch	Dinner	Lunch	Dinner	Lunch	Dinner	à la carte	Menu
Meridien	40	60	26.00	47.00	90	120	70	30
Ritz-Carlton	40	60	24.00	45.00	90	160	100	0
Adam's Mark	40	55	20.00	42.00	60	120	70	30
Marriott	79	80	11.32	30.29	50	90	50	50
Philadelphian	55	75	14.00	40.00	60	120	100	0
Liberty House	35	50	20.00	35.00	60	120	40	60
Napoleon	NA	45	NA	50.04	NA	150	60	40

EXHIBIT 25-3
Financial Figures for Le Marquis

	Jan.	Feb.	Mar.	Apr.	May	June	July	Aug.	Sept.	Oct.	Nov.	Dec.	Total
Food ($)	61,160	61,829	67,313	68,623	64,749	61,025	48,472	42,433	57,246	66,523	56,684	67,365	723,422
Beverage ($)	19,856	24,814	27,760	29,274	30,662	27,885	22,020	21,242	26,416	31,080	24,437	27,488	312,934
Total Revenue ($)	81,016	86,643	95,073	97,897	95,411	88,910	70,492	63,675	83,662	97,603	81,121	94,853	1,036,356
Food Cost ($)	23,614	23,619	25,646	26,557	33,151	28,743	22,249	18,017	22,555	26,674	24,771	27,499	304,095
Beverage Cost ($)	6,715	7,866	9,105	9,631	9,808	9,035	7,002	6,925	8,506	9,915	7,991	9,263	101,762
Total Cost of Sales ($)	30,329	31,485	34,751	36,188	42,959	37,778	29,251	24,942	31,061	37,589	32,762	36,762	405,857
Gross Profit ($)	50,687	55,158	60,322	61,709	52,452	51,132	41,241	38,733	52,601	60,014	48,359	58,091	630,499
Total Payroll and Benefits ($)	59,299	61,214	57,815	61,052	57,301	51,694	48,725	54,255	47,404	55,270	55,185	65,544	673,758
Total Other Expense ($)	14,231	14,976	10,593	13,922	12,688	13,410	15,434	11,412	15,702	12,707	11,152	14,606	160,833
Departmental Profit ($)	(22,843)	(21,032)	(8,086)	(13,265)	(17,537)	(13,972)	(22,918)	(26,934)	(10,505)	(7,963)	(17,978)	(21,059)	(20,4092)

Dinner Covers	1141	1185	1381	1340	1312	1231	949	862	1139	1338	1167	1412	14,457
Average Daily Dinner Covers	47	49	57	55	54	51	39	36	47	56	48	45	46
Average Food Revenue per Cover ($)	53.60	52.18	48.74	51.21	49.35	49.57	51.08	49.23	50.26	49.72	48.57	47.71	50.04
Average Beverage Revenue per Cover ($)	17.40	20.94	20.10	21.85	23.37	22.65	23.20	24.64	23.19	23.23	20.94	19.47	21.65
Average Total Revenue per Cover ($)	71.00	73.12	68.84	73.06	72.72	72.23	74.28	73.87	73.45	72.95	69.51	67.18	71.69
Average Cost of Sales per Cover ($)	26.58	26.57	25.16	27.01	32.74	30.69	30.82	28.94	27.27	28.09	28.07	26.04	28.07
Average Payroll per Cover ($)	51.97	51.66	41.86	45.56	43.67	41.99	51.34	62.94	41.62	41.31	47.29	45.71	46.60
Average Other Expenses per Cover ($)	12.47	12.64	7.67	10.39	9.67	10.89	16.26	13.24	13.79	9.50	9.56	10.34	11.12
Average Total Cost per Cover ($)	91.02	90.86	74.70	82.96	86.09	83.58	98.43	105.11	82.68	78.90	84.92	82.09	85.80
Net Revenue per Cover ($)	(20.02)	(17.75)	(5.86)	(9.90)	(13.37)	(11.35)	(24.15)	(31.25)	(9.22)	(5.95)	(15.41)	(14.91)	(14.12)
Room Occupancy (%)	40.1	39.1	67.0	67.4	68.6	77.4	71.2	80.4	78.8	87.2	61.7	39.0	65.0

C A S E

Twenty-Six

HOLIDAY INN CHATTANOOGA*

Graham MacLeod, General Manager of the Holiday Inn Chattanooga was staring out of his tenth floor, makeshift office overlooking the city when the telephone rang. He listened as his secretary responded to the call: "Good morning, Holiday Inn Chattanooga. . . . No, this isn't the Skyline Inn. . . . No, we haven't been reinstated by Holiday Inn, we're owned by a different company now. . . . I know this used to be a Holiday Inn before it was Skyline, but Pavilion Hotels purchased the property over six months ago. . . ."

For the past three months, MacLeod had become increasingly aware of the uphill battle he faced to overcome the negative image inherited from the Skyline Inn. He was fully confident, however, that his brand-new renovated and refurbished hotel would prove successful since it would be the only true businessperson's hotel in Chattanooga. The only question that remained in MacLeod's mind was how long it would take to bury the Skyline connection.

*William Romeo researched and with Nancy Charves contributed to this case. Names and location have been disguised.

BACKGROUND

In 1978, the hotel was built by the Holiday Inn Corporation, which owned the property until it was sold in 1988. Holiday Inn had begun striving to upgrade its image as well as increase its profitability. The run-down Chattanooga property did not fit the corporation's plans. The decision was made to sell the hotel rather than refurbish it.

The hotel was purchased by Dr. Robert Chung, who created the Skyline Inn. Dr. Chung was a multimillionaire computer engineer turned hotelier. Chung was a brilliant man, but his talents were not well-suited to a service industry. During his stint as owner, he was known for his unwillingness to finance renovations. As a result, the hotel's reputation suffered. The perception of the Skyline Inn grew progressively worse and occupancy levels fell to 40 to 45 percent. Robert Chung finally sold the hotel in 1998 when he acknowledged the deteriorating reputation of the property.

Pavilion Hotels was chosen as the management company for the property under the franchise, once again, of Holiday Inn. The new owners planned to invest $10.5 million in improvements to the property. The intended result would be a first-class, quality facility.

Chattanooga was a city of about 200,000 in the southeastern part of Tennessee. It was well-situated near the intersection of Interstate 75 and Route 24, and Chattanooga Airport was only ten miles to the south. Downtown Chattanooga had been revitalized significantly over the past several years and was clearly on the upswing. It boasted numerous newly constructed office towers and rehabilitated buildings. There were over 500 specialty shops located within a 30-mile radius of Chattanooga and the Mid-America Mall, the largest shopping mall in Tennessee, was just five miles from downtown. Chattanooga's urban facelift was further assisted by increasing industrial growth. Six new major industrial sites would eventually accommodate the area's strong demand for commercial expansion. These sites ranged from one-half mile to eight miles from the hotel.

The most significant current development was the $150 million Monarch Place, which would include a 26-story office tower and a 12-story atrium lobby Sheraton Hotel. This building included 350,000 square feet of office space in addition to the 300-room first-class hotel that Sheraton would operate there. The property would have convention facilities for 1500 people as well as an executive boardroom, four hospitality suites, a complete health club, and a full-scale business center.

Consultant Christopher Griffin summarized the city's potential by stating, "Chattanooga has the potential to someday be the mecca of Tennessee—if we cultivate it and not get greedy and choke. There is enough for everybody, and we have so much going for us. Chattanooga will have the brightest red carpets you have ever seen. Believe me, Memphis will know that Chattanooga is here."

PAVILION HOTELS

Pavilion Hotels was an individually owned company that had expanded from one original hotel to the present ten properties. Pavilion operated properties that extended from Little Rock, Arkansas to Raleigh, North Carolina under a variety of franchises. Within the next two years, Pavilion planned to add ten more hotels to its portfolio for a total of 20.

The company had recruited many top leaders in the hospitality field, all of whom were young but experienced, and the group had developed a reputation as an up-and-coming company. Pavilion Hotels was a people-oriented organization, which recognized that the attitude of its employees was the key. Its philosophy was to listen to employees of the hotel because they were its representatives. One Pavilion executive summed up their philosophy by stating, "Theorywise, people are inherently good by nature, and with a little pat on the back, they will perform to the best of their ability."

HOLIDAY INN—CHATTANOOGA

The Holiday Inn Chattanooga was located in the north end of the city at the intersection of Interstate 75 and Route 24. Although the facility was still in the midst of major renovations, Director of Sales Ray Flynn was optimistic. He believed that the completed project would produce an upscale, corporate transient facility that would have no equivalent in the area. "We're brand new," he said. "Everything's been redone. By June 1st, no other hotel will be able to say that. When business people arrive, they will know that there's new plumbing, wiring, lighting fixtures—everything from stem to stern. They won't have to worry about a thing."

Once completed, the 12-story hotel would consist of 250 first-class rooms. Each would contain such amenities as a state-of-the art telephone system, a computer connection modem, a fax machine, and a VCR video component. The rooms were all to be furnished with nongeneric walnut furnishings and a large, well-lit workstation. Two hundred rooms would have a king-sized bed. All were to be decorated in good taste with only top quality furnishings.

The eleventh floor of the hotel would offer three executive suites and two executive boardrooms. The Presidential Suite, which overlooked the entire city of Chattanooga, was the largest on the floor and consisted of three full-sized rooms as well as a kitchenette. The remaining two suites were the Governor's Quarters and each consisted of two rooms. All of the property's suites were positioned on a corner of the building in order to provide maximum visibility.

The Holiday Inn Chattanooga would also provide guests with an Olympic-sized indoor swimming pool and a full facility health club. The club would feature a jacuzzi, sauna, and Nautilus system.

Business Facilities

Management considered that the hotel's business center would be one of its major differentiating points. The Holiday Inn Business Center was to be truly "an environment designed for results." As the customer entered the hotel, the business center would be immediately visible through the smoked glass doors. This effect was intentional, since it emphasized the commitment of the hotel to the business customer.

The Center would contain three high-performance state-of-the art PCs attached to top quality printers and high speed modems. There would also be a facsimile machine, and dictaphone. Complete secretarial services and a Federal Express office would be available, along with three private consultation rooms. Holiday Inn had fully committed to the Business Center in the hope of wooing the business traveler, particularly the one who appreciated the attention to detail.

Function space at the Holiday Inn would be less extensive than that of competitive hotels. The largest room would accommodate a maximum of 100 people. In addition there were seven small conference rooms, which would hold up to 20 people each. The hotel's marketing plan anticipated that most function business would originate locally. It was planned that room rentals would require a sleeping room commitment, except during the off-season periods. Weekend banquet business was expected to consist of weddings, reunions, and association business.

Other Facilities

The rooftop restaurant, which once rotated atop the hotel, had received a facelift along with the rest of the hotel. The dining room no longer revolved and the entire top of the hotel was currently in the process of being squared off. "The Squared Circle" had been selected as a name in remembrance of the past.

The restaurant, which seated 112 guests, offered a casual and relaxed atmosphere. It was a multi-purpose facility, which would serve breakfast, lunch, and dinner, with an emphasis on traditional Southern cooking. Graham MacLeod did not anticipate that the restaurant would see much activity on the weekends, but he was philosophical. "What The Squared Circle does on the weekends is a bonus," he said. "Our main concern is to take care of the individual corporate traveler."

Adjacent to the restaurant was the Squared Circle Lounge. The 104-seat lounge was planned to feature live entertainment each evening with various local pianists at the baby grand. The decor focused on brass and mirrors which encouraged eye contact, and there was an abundance of stand-up space. Management described the lounge as "fun, yuppie, and conducive to meetings."

The Corporate Travelers Club constituted another extra to be provided by the hotel. This amenity was especially geared toward the individual corporate traveler and included the following:

- *The Manager's Table:* For purposes of camaraderie, guests would receive an invitation to dine at the Manager's Table with other club members.
- *Pre-Ordered Breakfast:* Club members would be offered the option of utilizing doorknob menus to request breakfast for the next morning.
- *Complimentary Newspapers:* These were to be delivered each morning.
- *Turndown Service:* Beds would receive turndown service every night.

- *Other Perks:* Use of the health club was to be complimentary, as was each eleventh night as a guest of the hotel.

The Pricing Policy

The establishment of rates at the Holiday Inn was in direct relation to the occupancy of the hotel. When demand was high and there was a major attraction in the city, only the rack rate would be available. At other times, when the city was quiet and occupancy was low, a potential guest could negotiate with the front office manager in order to obtain a bargain rate.

Management recognized that a hotel room was a perishable commodity, and every effort would be made to prevent a potential customer from bypassing the Holiday Inn and patronizing the competition. Forecasted average rates were as follows:

Corporate	$112.50
Rack	$145.00
Group	$100.00
Suites	$195.00

Occupancy percentages were predicted to be 56, 62, and 73 percent, respectively for each of the first three years. The hotel's private consultant was not concerned about occupancy during the slow periods. "There's an old saying," he said. " 'Let's schedule it for January or February because it's quiet.' Well we've changed our tune. If it's quiet, let's not meddle with it. Bring them in here when it's busy. Bring them in when the hotel is full. Because when you're doing that, you are telling people that you care enough about them to pay for rooms at another hotel when we are booked. Why bring them in when the place is a morgue?"

COMPETITION

According to the General Manager, the Holiday Inn Chattanooga currently had only two direct competitors: the Marriott and the Hilton West. The marketing plan, however, included the Holiday Inn Chickamauga, the Quality Inn Lookout Mountain, and the Ramada Inn South on the list of competitors.

The Marriott was located in the heart of downtown Chattanooga and catered to both the corporate traveler and the convention market. The Hilton West was situated off Interstate 75, five miles north of the downtown section. This hotel catered to essentially the same two markets as the Marriott. MacLeod acknowledged that the proposed Sheraton convention hotel would become the third major competitor upon completion. Exhibit 26-1 gives details on the competition. Presently, the fair market share of the Holiday Inn Chattanooga was 20 percent in relation to its five competitors. Once the new Sheraton opened, the percentage would drop to 16 percent.

MANAGEMENT PHILOSOPHY

Graham MacLeod and other members of the management team planned to operate the hotel with an exciting, aggressive, and innovative style. They believed that their positive energy and enthusiasm would rub off on the entire staff, thus distinguishing the Holiday Inn Chattanooga from the competition.

The management team also attempted to instill a caring attitude in the employees. Each felt that it was imperative to constantly remind the guest that he or she was welcome, and planned to instruct their staffs to follow through with this approach from the second the guest set foot on the property until the moment of departure.

Mr. MacLeod stated that the Holiday Inn aspired toward two primary objectives. First, to achieve an occupancy of 70 to 75 percent and, second, to be perceived as a quality yet reasonable businessperson's hotel.

The Marketing Plan defined the Mission Statement as follows:

E X H I B I T   26-1
Holiday Inn Chattanooga Competition

Hotel	Rooms/Suites	Rates	Meeting Space[a]	Location	Amenities
Holiday Inn Chattanooga	250/3	$100–145	100	Downtown	Full business center, indoor pool, health club
Marriott	265/9	120–155	1000	Downtown	Indoor pool, health club, concierge floor
Sheraton West	268/5	115–150	900	5 miles north	Indoor pool, VIP floor
Quality Inn	185/0	85–110	600	6 miles east	Outdoor pool
Holiday Inn Chickamauga	154/2	105–125	350	9 miles north	Indoor/outdoor pool and health club
Ramada Inn	124/1	100–125	200	5 miles east	Outdoor pool
Sheraton	308/8	150–175	1500	Downtown	Indoor pool, full health club, racquet ball courts, concierge floor, business center

[a]People that can be accommodated

Our product is unique to the Chattanooga area and we have arrived at the ideal time in terms of demand. The location is superb and we must now begin to concentrate on guaranteed satisfaction of service. Both the professionalism of the staff and the consistency of the service will be critical if the previously held opinions of the facility are to be erased.

A copy of the Mission Statement was also distributed to all employees so that they would be repeatedly reminded why the hotel was in business. A burgundy card with decorative gold lettering was inscribed with the following:

"Our Mission is:
• To be metropolitan Chattanooga's *BEST* at providing FIRST CLASS GUEST SERVICE and price/value satisfaction to the traveling executive.
• To become known as an organization whose managers direct the staff with dignity and respect.

Our Staff is:
• Dedicated to the individual guest's comfort level.
• Committed to impeccable excellence in product quality

MARKETING

Because of the limited meeting/function space, management recognized the need to target different markets than either the Marriott or the Hilton West. Holiday Inn's management identified the individual business traveler market as the prime niche for the hotel They also agreed that it would not be a group-oriented property. Thus the hotel's target market was defined to include corporate transients, airline crews, and the weekend traveler, although convention overflow business would certainly be welcomed.

Since Chattanooga was not considered to be a weekend destination, minimal interest was anticipated from the leisure traveler. This particular segment generally visited the city because of specific Civic Center activities, and MacLeod was optimistic that some of this business would come his way due to his past support of the Civic Center. Four weekend packages had been developed to lure whatever weekend business existed, with special focus on lovers, singles, shoppers, and country western enthusiasts.

Within the next month, the Holiday Inn would begin negotiations with various airlines. It was hoped that this would lead to several contracts that would produce 8 to 10 percent of the hotel's customer base. According to MacLeod, airline revenue was a highly desirable means of increasing guaranteed cash flow during the uncertainty of the first year.

The Holiday Inn Chattanooga positioned itself as a mid-priced, upper-middle market property. In order to ensure that the customers' perceptions outweighed their expectations, the hotel was priced just below the Marriott while offering a higher quality property.

The focus of the hotel's advertising would be to reach the corporate travel market. Therefore, it would be concentrated in the larger air carrier magazines and with popular car rental agencies. Piedmont and Delta airlines, Budget and Hertz car rental were to receive the bulk of the advertising dollars. MacLeod was investigating the possibility of installing a direct telephone line from the airport to the hotel.

Three weeks prior to the reopening, the Chattanooga Holiday Inn had done very little advertising. The only significant piece was small and appeared in the Travel section of the major Tennessee newspapers. However, advertising was expected to increase once the hotel opened. Additional efforts to reach the corporate traveler would be via newspapers, billboards, and trade and business journals. The sales staff had already initiated frequent direct mailings.

It was estimated that the Holiday Inn Reservation System, Holidex, would account for 20 percent of all reservations. The Holiday Inn Chickamauga was expected to lose 8 to10 percent of its market base to the refurbished hotel.

CONCLUSION

Graham MacLeod realized that he had a lot to do in the weeks before the Holiday Inn Chattanooga opened its doors. Most importantly, it was essential that he develop a reasonable plan of attack to overcome the hotel's image problem. He sat back in his chair and sighed, "I only wish that we had never become a Holiday Inn franchise; then things would be much easier."

Twenty-Seven

PROMOTING SUNDAY BRUNCH

John Elder, Director of Sales for the Hilton Inn in Pittsfield, Massachusetts, a city and environs of about 60,000, looked over his brunch cover statistics with dismay. Total Sunday brunch covers at the 175-room hotel had steadily declined over the past two years from 5012 to 4574 to 3935, a 21.5 percent decline. Something, he thought, needs to be done.

A number of new restaurants had recently opened in Pittsfield and had begun to penetrate the lucrative brunch market. Tom Harding, food and beverage director of the hotel, felt that this competition was the major cause of the decline. The Hilton Inn had often served 150 for Sunday Brunch in the past. These figures were now reached only on special occasions such as Mother's Day. Tom felt that there was potential to do 250 covers, which was about the room's capacity for brunch.

Sunday Brunch was served in the Emerald Room, located on the top fourteenth floor of the Hilton Inn. The view from any seat in the restaurant was spectacular, offering views of the Berkshire Mountains from all four sides. The food presentation was traditional, a full all-you-can-eat buffet with salads, breakfast items, a carving station, and well arranged with ice carvings and other attractive presentations.

The profit margin on Sunday Brunch was slim and was presently about 10 percent of the $16.95 selling price, based on current sales. Alcoholic beverage sales, however, raised the average check to $19.50 and the contribution margin on beverages was 65 percent. Tom figured he could double the present number of covers with the same labor force and fixed costs and make a margin on the additional covers of 50 percent, plus the beverage margin. He also figured that above that number, to maximum capacity of 250, the profit margin would be about 40 percent after adding additional labor, plus the beverage margin.

The target market for Sunday Brunch was both in-house guests and local customers. Research disclosed that the local customers lived within a ten mile radius, had household incomes of $40,000 plus, and were an average age of 45. Many younger couples were frequent brunch goers as well. Middle-age customers with small children at home were not targeted.

The executive committee of the hotel decided they should reintroduce Sunday brunch to the local community. It believed that many of the customers who had been to the brunch were merely trying other restaurants. It was decided that a promotion, lasting six months, was needed to induce new trial or repurchase by former customers.

After some brainstorming, "The Get Rich Quick Brunch at the Emerald Room of the Hilton Inn" was developed. The idea was that each customer would have an opportunity to win a lottery. A lottery ticket would be given to each customer and there would be a weekly minimum payout. Legal ramifications of the promotion were researched and found acceptable.

John Elder and Tom Harding felt comfortable that the promotion would work. After convincing the executive committee of this they were assigned to work out the details.

John and Tom had decided that lottery tickets, given to each brunch customer, would be valued at $2.00. Should, they wondered, this be included in the current brunch price, charged for as an extra, or should the brunch price raised $2.00 to cover it? How much should the weekly payout be? How would they promote the lottery and how much would that promotion cost? What were the merchandising opportunities? Could they get some local PR and publicity? Tom brought the Lotus program up on his computer screen as John started working out the communications details.

Twenty-Eight

THE PLAZA HOTEL IN BUENOS AIRES*

Alex Fiz, assistant operations manager of the Plaza Hotel, looked at the memo before him that he had just received from the hotel's general manager. It was brief and to the point: "What's happening? We are losing market share and there are two more competitors coming next year. How are we going to position ourselves in this environment?"

BACKGROUND

The Plaza Hotel was an independent hotel located in the heart of the city of Buenos Aires, close to the business district, shops, restaurants, and theaters. The Plaza was an historical grand hotel with superb service and attention to details (Exhibit 28-1). Built in 1910, the hotel was a classical building that had been maintained in first-class condition. It offered a very traditional, luxurious, old-fashioned image compared to the luxurious modern style offered by its competition. It was the only member of Leading Hotels of the World in Argentina.

Buenos Aires, sometimes called "the Paris of South America," was a city of 13 million inhabitants and the capital city of Argentina. It was famous for its night life and cosmopolitan atmosphere. However, the city had only a small tourism market with an unusually short stay average. Most tourists stopped there only on their way to other tourist destinations. From a corporate point of view, it was an "interesting" city but, being "far away from everything," made it difficult for the city to attract businesses. Market demand was not growing nearly as fast as the hotel supply.

From its opening until 1988, the Plaza did not have direct competition. Between 1988 and 1995, however, three new hotels of international chains entered the market—Sheraton, Kempinski, and the Alvear Palace, a Summit International Hotel. In

*We are grateful to Alex Fiz for information used in developing this case. Some facts have been disguised.

IN BUENOS AIRES
WHY THE PLAZA?

- Because it is the symbol of hotel excellence with over 80 years of prestige, catering to the most discriminating guests including royalty and outstanding world personalities.
- Because it is ideally located for business and pleasure.
- Because it offers 300 totally refurbished rooms and suites, 11 conference rooms, 4 restaurants, including the "Plaza Grill", the oldest in town, the famous Plaza Bar, The Health Club and a beautiful brand new Pool.
- Because its service is second to none.
- Because it is the only member of "The Leading Hotels of the World" in Argentina.

10% Commission. We honour immediately.

One of
The Leading Hotels of the World

Florida 1005 - Buenos Aires - 1005 - Argentina
Tel.: 312-6001/09 · Cables "PLAZOTEL"
Télex: 22488 PLAZA AR · Telefax: (54-1) 313-2912

Reservations
The Leading Hotels of the World: (800) 223-1230
Utell International: (800) 44-UTELL
Loews Representation International: (800) 223-6800

EXHIBIT 28-1   The Plaza Hotel in Buenos Aires

spite of this, the Plaza was able to maintain its position and occupancy at the top of the market. Then, in 1998, a luxury Park Hyatt opened in a renovated turn-of-the-century mansion. This was shortly followed by a luxurious, modern Caesar Park with atrium lobby, operated by Westin, in the same area.

All six of these hotels were located close to each other in the center of the city, although some had specific location advantages that attracted certain markets. The Plaza was seriously threatened by the two newest hotels. It began losing customers to both of them, as well as to the Sheraton. A number of top suite customers defected to the Hyatt, while the Caesar Park was cutting rates to create awareness. All these hotels competed head-on for the same corporate clientele.

Next year, an Inter-Continental and a Crowne Plaza were due to open, adding more supply in the already highly competitive market. Inter-Continental pricing was expected to be very aggressive and include "price-dumping" to create awareness.

THE PLAZA HOTEL

The Plaza Hotel had 300 rooms, including 30 suites, 215 deluxe, and 55 standard. The suites were priced at $500 but usually sold at the corporate rate of $185.* The hotel's approximate occupancies, with the desired rate for each segment, were as follows.

Rack rate (deluxe)	10%	$240
Corporate	35%	$185
Agencies	10%	$160
Groups	30%	$150
Honeymoon	4%	$225
Local market	6%	$100
Complimentary	5%	

*All prices in the case are given in U.S. dollars.

Eighty percent of the Plaza's business was repeat. This had been a very loyal clientele but it was beginning to diminish. Thirty percent of business was from the United States, 40 percent from Europe, 15 percent from South America, and 15 percent from the Far East and other. The local market was very difficult to attract because it could not afford the prices.

Leading Hotels of the World delivered 35 percent of the Plaza's business and 10 percent came from the Utell International network. The rest of the business was direct. The biggest customer was Coca-Cola, three blocks away, which booked 2000 room nights a year.

Alex looked at the other information he had collected to show the last three months' figures,

which were typical of the market situation (Exhibit 28-2). He noted that the high level customers were going to the Hyatt and Caesar Park and that Sheraton's high occupancy and low ADR were greatly affected by its 240 crew rooms at $62.00 a night. He also noted that the other locally owned and operated hotel, Alvear Palace, had a very large portion of the government market, which paid full rates.

Alex knew that the Plaza had to maintain a 60 percent occupancy at an ADR of $130 just to break even. That point was perilously close and he realized that some new strategies were needed, especially with Inter-Continental and Crowne Plaza opening next year.

E X H I B I T   2 8 - 2
Buenos Aires Market Information

Hotel	Rooms	Rack Rate ($)		April		May		June		June REVPARS
		Single	Double	OCC (%)	ADR($)	OCC (%)	ADR($)	OCC (%)	ADR($)	
Plaza	300	240	240	63.9	142	52.2	143	54.6	142	77.53
Kempinski	203	180	215	48.7	110	41.1	126	34.7	116	40.25
Sheraton	757	205	225	84.5	107	84	112	85.1	105	89.36
Caesar Park	170	295	295	51.1	223	34.8	225	46.2	198	91.48
Hyatt	163	295	295	68	227	63.1	225	65.4	229	149.77
Alvear Palace	248	220	50	64.5	182	55	186	67	175	117.25

Twenty-Nine

HILTON INTERNATIONAL / TORONTO*

"The average room rate is $10 to $12 lower than last year. We really have to drop our rates to maintain occupancy and we haven't even been able to do that."

Philip Stratton, Front Office Manager at the Hilton International/Toronto, reflected on the state of city's hotel market. The predicted slump in the economy had arrived and the Hilton was facing the consequences. Its room rates had been the lowest in the city among comparable first-class hotels, yet occupancy was down from last year. Philip hoped that the existing price war would not intensify in the coming spring season.

THE HILTON INTERNATIONAL

The 600-room Hilton was located in the heart of the city's entertainment and business area. It pro-

vided direct access to major business towers through a three-and-a-half mile underground shopping mall walkway. Facilities included a heated indoor/outdoor swimming pool with sauna, a health club, 24-hour room service, covered underground parking, and convention and meeting facilities for groups up to 1100. Standard amenities included color cable TV, AM/FM radios, first run movies, minibars, alarm clocks, oversized beds, and individual climate controlled rooms. The hotel also operated three restaurants and two lounges.

THE ENVIRONMENT

Citywide occupancies had suffered a plunge from 78 to 66 percent in the past year, although average room rates in the product class continued to rise, going from $118.75 to $135 in the same period of time. The hotel industry was not optimistic that the mar-

---

*Helen D'Olveira contributed to this case. Some names and figures have been disguised. All dollar amounts are in U.S. dollars.

ket would rebound in the near future. Additionally, 750 more rooms were soon to be added to the city's 16,000 room supply including a new 450-room Marriott two blocks north of the Hilton.

Philip did not expect the Marriott to compete directly for the same markets as the Hilton. The Hilton was better located to the financial district for most business travelers. The Marriott, attached to a major shopping complex, would be more likely to appeal to tourists and out-of-towners than business travelers. Regardless, Marriott was known for grabbing market share and Philip was concerned with what its tactics would be. Rather than guess, he believed that all he could do was wait until it opened. More serious, at the moment, was what the Sheraton right around the corner was doing.

The Hilton's main city center competitors had already cut their rack rates by as much as 50 percent. Exhibit 29-1 shows these competitors and the winter specials each was promoting.

PRICING STRATEGY AT THE HILTON

The previous fall, with both winter and more recession materializing, Hilton management felt that its conservative clientele (40 percent group, 30 percent tourists, 30 percent individual business travelers) would not relish paying room rates much over $125. It decided to lower rates much below rack before the competition did it first. Rack rates ranged

from $149 to $279 single and $179 to $299 double, depending on the type of accommodations.

Input was obtained from the International Sales Office and all members of the executive committee. It was agreed that the winter special would be $109.00 per room, single or double occupancy. A variety of promotional packages were also designed (Exhibit 29-2). Since only about 1 percent of all daily occupied rooms ever sold at rack rate, this tactic was not seen by management as being a particularly radical move.

NOW WHAT?

In February, the Toronto Hilton had the highest occupancy rate among its major competitors (Exhibit 29-3), although its occupancy was five percentage points below the previous year. In late March, the Royal Plaza cut its rates to $99.00 per room, single or double. In response, Hilton management decided to forego a planned spring increase to $125.00 and decided to maintain the $109.00 rate until at least the end of June.

In an attempt to combat the low rate, Philip developed a reservation call strategy for direct calls (about 30 percent of calls came through the international Hilton 800 number) and trained all the Hilton reservationist accordingly. Reservationists receiving a call first asked a number of questions to help identify tastes, and hence room rates that the caller might find acceptable, such as:

EXHIBIT 29-1
Hilton's Main Competitors' Winter Specials

Hotel	Room Rate (S/O)	Inclusive	Daily Parking Rate
Hilton	$109	Continental breakfast	$10
Sheraton	$129	Full breakfast	$18
Westin	$99	Room only	$16
Royal Plaza	$99	Coffee/newspaper	$17
Crowne Plaza	$109	Room only	$16

EXHIBIT 29-2
Promotional Packages at the Toronto Hilton

Package Name	Dates	Available	Rate	Amenities	Comments
Warm Winter	1/7–4/15	Mon–Sun	S$109 D$129	Hot chocolate	500 mugs to first 500 at this rate
Interline Staff (airline employee)	2/5–5/31	Mon–Sun	S$75 D$95	None	Subject to availability
Bounce Back & Romance Break	2/5–4/31	Mon–Sun	S/D$109	None	Based on availability
Enroute Hotel Clearing Center	3/8–6/1	Mon–Sun	$5 off minimum day rate	None	Calls must come through hotel hotline
Doubleheader Baseball Package	4/13–9/28	Fri only	S$169 D$189	2 field-level tickets	Subject to availability, $35 deposit
American Express Dinner for 2	2/4–7/31	Fri –Sun	$109	Continental breakfast and dinner	Must be requested
Bounce Back	10/1–4/30	Fri–Sun	S$109 D$129	Continental breakfast	Arrivals on Friday only
Bounce Back	Same	Thur–Sun	Same	Same	Arrivals Thursday, must stay through Saturday
Bounce Back (junior suite)	Same	Same	S$199 D$219	Continental breakfast	Guaranteed junior suite
Bounce Back (executive floor)	Same	Thur–Sun	S$189 D$209	Same	Thursday arrival, must stay into weekend
Double Your Adventure	11/15–3/31	Mon–Sun	S$109 D$129	None	"Passport" at Check-in[a]
Romance Break (regular room)	10/1–4/30	Same	$265 including tax and gratuities	Wine, gift, full breakfasts	Guaranteed kingsize bed, $209 for extra night
Romance Break (junior suite)	Same	Same	$299 including tax and gratuities	Same	Guaranteed junior suite, $265 for extra night
Romance Break (executive floor)	Same	Same	$329	Same	Guaranteed executive floor, $289 for extra night
Hilton Gold Card Members (weekdays)	Same	Sun–Thurs	S$145 D$169	F&B discounts	Can book up to 10 rooms
Hilton Gold Card Members (weekends)	Same	Fri–Sun	S$99 D$119	F&B discounts	Only Fri–Sat
Senior Hilton Honors Club	10/1–12/31	Mon–Sun	S$109 D$129	None	

[a]"Passport" refers to a special coupon booklet containing discounts valid for a variety of stores and restaurants in the city

EXHIBIT 29-3
February Occupancy Rates for Hilton and
Main Competitors

Hotel	Number of Rooms	Occupancy (%)
Hilton	601	67
Crowne Plaza	587	42
Royal Plaza	1438	48
Sheraton	1398	59
Westin	964	57

Are you a corporate client?
Will you be attending a convention while in town?
Will you be arriving on a weekday?
How many nights would you like to stay?
How many people will be staying in the room?
Would you like to reserve for any other times or
   at another Hilton?

Each day Philip set a minimum daily rate, based on anticipated occupancy, that was conveyed to all reservationists. Reservationists were encouraged to quote the rack rate, but were allowed to quote a lower rate down to the minimum daily rate. Management approval was required to go lower than the minimum. If management was not available, however, reservationists were entrusted to use their discretion in quoting lower rates acceptable to the caller. Philip believed this flexibility contributed greatly to the relatively high occupancies that Hilton enjoyed in the city. He found no indication that the flexibilty was abused. In fact, reservationists seemed to like the responsibility.

As spring approached, Philip was not sure what price reaction to expect from his competitors. He concerned himself with maintaining the relatively high occupancy rate he had successfully established in the winter season. Finally, there was still the nagging thought of the Marriott opening in the fall with its special opening prices. Philip decided to call a strategy meeting to formulate some plans to deal with these issues.

Thirty

MERCHANDISING POWER BREAKFASTS

Le Meridien Hotel in Boston, Massachusetts, sat on the edge of the financial district of the city. Its Cafe Fleuri served "power breakfasts," a term given to breakfast meetings of businesspeople who got together to negotiate "deals." Power breakfasts had come to replace the three-martini lunch as the social/business setting where the power brokers "wheel and deal." Wheeling and dealing was the name of the game in the financial districts of cities like Boston and New York because these were where most of the big deals were made. Of course, for every big deal there were a hundred little ones that also got negotiated. For this purpose, Le Meridien was ideally located, and Cafe Fleuri was the ideal spot to be.

In fact, for Hugues Jaquier, General Manager of Le Meridien, the success of breakfast in Cafe Fleuri had become a problem. Cafe Fleuri seated 180. Each morning, from Monday to Friday, it served 250 to 300 covers with an average check of $14.50. (The breakfast menu is shown in Exhibit 30-1.) This was no small feat as power breakfast eaters were not prone to quick turnover. In fact, 90 percent of these breakfasts were "locals" from the surrounding business community who had "staked out" their own tables so that even Le Meridien hotel guests had a hard time getting into the restaurant.

Many hotel guests, however, were accommodated with a buffet breakfast that was served in a Le Meridien ballroom. This arrangement handled 100 to 400 breakfasts each morning from Monday through Friday. Power breakfast people, however, didn't want buffet. They wanted to be waited on as they whispered and negotiated and grabbed at every rhetorical opportunity. The buffet breakfast concept, moreover, also was not popular with some hotel guests, who preferred a quick juice and coffee breakfast and thus had to wait to get into Cafe Fleuri.

There was another problem. The entrance to Cafe Fleuri was a small waiting space that accommodated only about 15 or 20 at a time, standing room only. This small space made it difficult for people waiting for a table. From this space one could look down over a railing upon the escalator by which people got to Cafe Fleuri. At the bottom

FRESH FRUITS, JUICES, AND CEREALS

Papaya or mango juice $3.15
Freshly squeeze orange or grapefruit juice $3.25
Apple, grape, tomato or prune juice $2.95
Half grapefruit $3.50
Seasonal melon $4.00
Yogurt with fresh fruit $5.50
Fruit salad or fresh berries $5.25
Cold cereal, oatmeal, porridge, or granola $3.00
Cereal with fresh fruit $5.00
Muesli cereal $3.75

*OUR
CREATIVE SPECIALTIES*

Smoked salmon plate with
condiments and toast
$13.25

Scrambled eggs with tomato
and basil
$8.25

Blueberry or strawberry crêpes
$7.50

Omelette of smoked salmon
$9.25

Omelette of onions, peppers,
tomato, and prosciutto
$8.50

Toasted bagel with cream cheese
$3.50

*With smoked salmon $9.50

LE PARISIEN

Juice of your choice
Breakfast pastries
Coffee, decaffeinated coffee, tea,
hot chocolate, milk or skim-milk
$8.25

LE JAPONAIS

Misochiru soup
Yaki Nori (seaweed)
Japanese pickles
Broiled salmon with vegetables
Steamed rice
Green tea
Please allow 30 min. for preparation
$17.00

Croissants or muffins $3.75
Danish $3.25
White or whole wheat toast $2.25
Six grain toast $2.50

Additional charge
The 5% State Tax will be added to your bill. Gratuity not included.
Please refrain from cigar and pipe smoking.

*JACQUES MANIÈRE
LOW CALORIE BREAKFAST*

Plain yogurt with
fresh fruits
Omelette with steamed
turkey breast and mushrooms
Plain toast
1/2-oz. of butter
295 calories
$12.50

*OMELETTES, EGGS
AND GRIDDLE*

Two eggs, any style $5.00
With ham, bacon or sausage $7.50
Mushroom omelette $7.25
Eggs benedict $8.50
Ham and cheese omelette $7.50
Banana or blueberry
pancakes $8.50
Pancakes, French toast
or waffles with maple syrup $6.25
*With strawberries and whipped
cream $2.15
*With ham, bacon or sausage $3.75

BEVERAGES

Coffee, decaffeinated coffee,
tea, hot chocolate,
milk or skim-milk $1.95

Le
MERIDIEN
BOSTON

250 Franklin Street, Boston, MA 02110 617 451-1900

EXHIBIT 30-1   Cafe Fleuri Breakfast Menu

of the escalator was a fairly large space that was a combination entryway coming from the hotel lobby in one direction, and from the street side entrance of the hotel in the other direction. As many came into this area from both directions, they were uncertain of whether to proceed up the escalator to wait for Cafe Fleuri seating, or to go elsewhere.

THE PROPOSED SOLUTION

Le Meridien also had a famous French dinner restaurant called Julien, arguably the best French restaurant in Boston. It was on the same level as Cafe Fleuri but separated from it by a short walk-

Julien Breakfast
$15.00

Freshly squeezed orange or grapefruit juice
The Julien Baker's Basket with assorted
jellies and preserves

Your choice of one of the following:

• • • •

*Brittany-style crêpes with sauteed apples
and strawberries
*Daily low calorie specialty inspired by
Chef Jacques Maniere
*Julien French toast
*Scrambled egg with Vermont ham and fresh herbs
or with bacon and sausage
*Shirred eggs with asparagus tips and
Nova Scotia grave lax
*Soft boiled eggs with toasted French bread
*Three egg omelette with onions, peppers and mushrooms
*Half melon in season
*Fresh fruit compote puree, salad of fresh fruits
or seasonal berries
*Yoplait yogurt or Petits Suisses with fresh fruits
*Hot Red River cereal, nutril grain, granola, Swiss muesli

• • • •

European blend coffee, selection of loose teas,
Swiss hot chocolate,
milk, skim millk, half and half, decaffeinated coffee,
espresso, decaffeinated espresso, cappuccino

• • • •

Parisien Breakfast
$9.50

Freshly squeezed orange or grapefruit juice
The Julien Baker's Basket with assorted jellies
and preserves
European blend coffee, selection of loose teas,
Swiss hot chocolate,
milk, skim milk, half and half, decaffeinated coffee,
espresso, decaffeinated espresso, cappuccino

Le
MERIDIEN
BOSTON

MAKE IT YOUR BUSINESS
TO BREAKFAST.
AT JULIEN.

Served Monday through Friday
from 7:00 — 10:00 AM
Parisien Breakfast $9.50
Julien Breakfast $15.00

PUT THE NEW JULIEN BREAKFAST
ON YOUR AGENDA.

For More Information:
Please call (617) 451-1900

EXHIBIT 30-2 Promotional Flyer for Breakfast at Julien

way. Julien seated 90 but was far more distinguished in its decor than Cafe Fleuri. Tables were further apart and chairs were high back, offering far more privacy. The room was warmly decorated with wood, a thicker carpet, more discreet lighting, and, "All in all," thought Hugues Jaquier, "it lends itself far better to power breakfasts; especially as it now sits idle during that time. If this room could be used for breakfast," thought Hugues, "it wouldn't solve my coffee and juice customer problem but it would certainly take some pressure off Cafe Fleuri, and my customers would love it!"

From June through August the concept of a Julien breakfast was developed and preparation

Dear Guest,

As you may already know, the Julien Restaurant is one of the most
renowned dining rooms in all of Boston.

Which is why it gives me great pleasure to let you know that we have
recently introduced the Julien breakfast. Available weekday mornings,
the Julien breakfast is designed for professionals who appreciate not
only a healthy start, but a quite and civilized one as well -- with
freshly-squeezed juice, daily newspapers, wireless telephone, and
whatever else you need to get your day off to a productive beginning.

If you would like to sample Boston's newest business breakfast
firsthand, our captain will be more than happy to reserve a table for
you. Simply call the Julien (extension 7120) or our Concierge
(extension 3) for reservations.

In the meantime, I thank you for your patronage and wish you a most
pleasant stay in the Boston area.

Sincerely,

Francois Chockaert
Food & Beverage Director

250 FRANKLIN STREET
BOSTON, MASSACHUSETTS 02110
TEL. (617) 451-1900 · TELEX: 940 194
TELECOPY: (617) 423-2844
────────────────────────
TRAVEL COMPANION
OF AIR FRANCE

EXHIBIT 30-3 Letter Left on Pillows at Turndown Service.

Hugues Jaquier
Managing Director
Directeur Général

[date]

Dear [gender] [last]:

Once more, I am delighted to welcome you back to Boston and, of course, to the Meridien.

In case you weren't aware of it, I also wanted to take this opportunity to let you know that we are now serving breakfast in our Julien restaurant. Available weekday mornings, from 7 am until 10 am, the Julien breakfast is geared for professionals like yourself who appreciate not only a healthy start, but a quiet and civilized one as well - with freshly-squeezed juice, daily newspapers, wireless phones and whatever else you need to begin your day.

If you would like to sample what I'm sure will become Boston's most popular business breakfast, our captain will be more than happy to reserve a table for you. Simply call the Julien (extension 7120) or our Concierge (extension 3) for reservations.

In the meantime, I thank you for your continued patronage and, as always, I hope that you will contact me personally if there is any way in which I may be of assistance to you.

Most sincerely,

Hugues Jaquier

HJ:eml

250 FRANKLIN STREET
BOSTON, MASSACHUSETTS 02110
TEL. (617) 451-1900 - TELEX: 940 194
TELECOPY: (617) 423-2844

TRAVEL COMPANION
OF AIR FRANCE

EXHIBIT 30-4 Welcome Back Letter for Regular Guests.

HOTEL MERIDIEN

ANNOUNCING A BREAKFAST THAT'S GOOD FOR BUSINESS.

The new Julien breakfast
offers healthy cuisine that's
good for your body and an
atmosphere that's good
for your business.
Put a Julien breakfast on
tomorrow's agenda.

7:00–10:00 AM
Monday through Friday
Continental Breakfast $9.50
Full Breakfast $15.00

Information: (617) 451-1900

Le
MERIDIEN
BOSTON
Julien Restaurant in the Hotel Meridien. 250 Franklin St., Boston.

E X H I B I T   3 0 - 5   Newspaper Ad Promoting the
Julien Breakfast.

was made for a September 15 opening. The idea
was to have a health-oriented breakfast for well-to-
do business people. It was to be good value at a low
price with 100 percent fresh product, low calories,
and top quality service. Latest editions of the world
financial press would be available for perusal.

First, the menu was developed and intentionally
priced to be no higher than that in Cafe Fleuri. It was
put on the back of a flyer, which was to be used in-
house and in mailings (Exhibit 30-2). Also for in-

house, posters were made for the lobby and elevators,
with the same Ken Maryani drawn caricatures used in
all Le Meridien advertising. In addition, breakfast at
Julien was to be featured on the in-house TV channel,
and a letter was to be left on pillows after turndown
service (Exhibit 30-3). A similar letter was prepared as
a "welcome back" for regular guests (Exhibit 30-4).

Externally, commercials were prepared for radio
stations WEEI and WRKO. Print ads were prepared
for the *Boston Business Journal,* the *Boston Business Magazine,* and the *Boston Globe* newspaper
(Exhibit 30-5). A letter was also sent to major corporate offices (Exhibit 30-6), and a letter mailed to
chief executives of financial companies with a personal invitation from Hugues Jaquier. Finally, press
invitations were sent out.

The planning was perfect and the execution
flawless. "We've got a sure hit," said Hugues as he
stood at the entrance to Julien on opening morning, September 15. "All I've got to do now is figure
out what to do with my juice and coffee customer."

Four months later, in January, Hugues had figured out what to do with the juice and coffee customers and, if nothing else, had accommodated
some of his hotel guests who wanted to get out and
away. This did not, however, relieve much of the
pressure on Cafe Fleuri and the covers in Julien
were averaging only 15 to 20 each morning.

Hugues Jaquier
Managing Director
Directeur Général

Ms. Canice H. McGarry
Organization Development
Massachusetts Housing Finance Agency
50 Milk Street
Boston MA 02109

Dear Ms. McGarry,

I am pleased to announce that, beginning on Monday,
September 18, we will introduce breakfast service
in the Julien Restaurant.

Designed to meet the demands of our business
clientele, the Julien breakfast - served from 7:00
am until 10:00 am, Monday through Friday - will
provide a quiet, private setting and a prix fixe
menu including such specialties as Brittany-style
crepes with fresh fruit; Julien French toast; a
wide selection of egg dishes; and lighter fare
including yogurts, cereals and daily low-calorie
dishes inspired by Jacques Maniere.

I would like to invite you and a friend to be my
guests for a complimentary breakfast in the Julien
on whatever weekday morning is most convenient for
you between September 18 and 29. Please make your
reservation at least 24 hours in advance, by
calling the Julien Restaurant, and present this
letter upon your arrival.

In the meantime, thank you for your continued
interest in our hotel and I look forward to seeing
you very soon.

                    Sincerely,

                    Hugues Jaquier

HJ:eml

250 FRANKLIN STREET
BOSTON, MASSACHUSETTS 02110
TEL. (617) 451-1900 · TELEX: 940 194
TELECOPY: (617) 423-2844

TRAVEL COMPANION
OF AIR FRANCE

EXHIBIT 30-6 Letter Sent to Corporate Offices.

Thirty-One

❖

L'AMITIE RESTAURANT*

"Something is wrong, Jim," said Bruce Johnson, the manager of L'Amitie Restaurant. "It just doesn't make sense. Our customers tell us they love us. In fact, we hear nothing but compliments. Read the comments in the guest book that people sign on the way out; they indicate nothing but praise. Newspaper reviews have also been excellent. One writer in Baltimore has stated that we are one of the best restaurants in the state. Yet business is going nowhere but down. Slowly, to be sure, but surely. Customer counts are down. And worse, we're losing from $20,000 to $25,000 a month."

"Okay, Bruce," replied Jim McLean, the backer and principal owner of L'Amitie, "I'm well aware of the figures and it's my pocket the money is coming out of. We've gone over the costs item by item and they're certainly not out of line compared to national operating figures. Our food cost stays constant around 31 percent and our beverage cost at 19 percent. What's killing us of course is our labor cost at 35 percent. But we can't cut labor unless we reduce the service level we're trying to provide. And

that would defeat our whole purpose of being here. Clearly we have to find a way to do more volume."

"Well, we've certainly advertised enough," replied Bruce. "Just look at the figures of what we've spent. I'm beginning to think there just aren't enough people in this meat and potatoes town who appreciate good food. Maybe we'll have to change our concept. But how do we know? And how do we know what to change it to? And how do we know if it will work? Do we really know why people come or don't come here? If they don't come here, where do they go? After all, there's only one other French restaurant in the area that competes with us and they can't all go there. Maybe we're just not meeting the demands of the market. I think we had better learn something about the market before we go off half-cocked again. I suggest we do a market research study. What do you think?"

HISTORY OF L'AMITIE

L'Amitie Restaurant had been open just two years. It had been well planned and well executed and al-

*Names and locations have been disguised.

most no expense had been spared. Almost everyone would agree that it was an elegant restaurant. The owners were especially proud of the elegant bathrooms with their gold fixtures.

Jim McLean was the principal owner of L'Amitie. Bruce Johnson and his wife were minor partners and managers of the restaurant. Jim McLean was in his sixties and essentially retired from business. He had accumulated a small fortune as one of the original McDonald's franchisees. After he sold his franchise back to McDonald's, he decided he would like to own a truly different type of restaurant for more upscale tastes, but he did not want to be involved in active management. His search for an active and managing partner eventually led him to Bruce Johnson and his wife. Bruce Johnson was 36 years old. He was the graduate of a four-year university hotel program. After college, Bruce had worked for awhile for Radisson hotels in food and beverage. He subsequently went to work for T.G.I. Friday's restaurants and opened three of their new units. Along the way he had obtained substantial cooking experience as well as management knowhow. At the age of 27 he decided he wanted to operate his own restaurant.

The Johnson's first attempt at their own operation was a restaurant on the Maryland coast that they leased on a year-to-year basis. The realistic operating season, however, was only four months. They ended the first season $50,000 in debt. Two years later they had paid off the debt and were making a profit. Three years later the Johnsons felt they had outgrown the location. They were looking for an expansion location in Baltimore when they heard of Jim McLean's search for a partner. The partners shared a common dream—to establish a top class French restaurant.

Jim McLean had lived in this same Newport, Delaware community all his life and had many friends there. When he decided to open an upscale restaurant he conducted his own survey among his friends. This told him that what people in the area wanted was a French restaurant. Money was no obstacle and Jim was willing to spend what it took. On the other hand, he was not inclined to build an ego monument either. A man of humble origin, he had never had a financial failure, and he was determined that his new restaurant would also be profitable.

THE RESTAURANT

Under construction, the new restaurant grew from an original 2500 square feet to about 7000 square feet with two dining rooms that seated a total of 135 people. There was also a sizable kitchen, office and storage space, and room in the basement for later conversion to small banquet rooms. A nationally known food and wine consultant was retained at a sizable fee to advise on the name, the menu, the layout, the style, the decor, and the promotion of the restaurant. A continental chef with an excellent reputation was hired. The introduction to the menu was carefull worded as follows.

Our Philosophy
We pride ourselves on being a restaurant dedicated to quality. Certainly, by today's standards, any experienced traveler knows our offerings are more than affordable. L'Amitie is for those who appreciate the finer things in life. It is a restaurant built upon attention to detail. With rare exceptions, we make everything on premises. Many of our items are now available for you to take home. Our palmier cookies have been served at a wide variety of functions, from recitals in Baltimore to a meeting with the Governor at the State House. The legend of our rolls has been covered numerous times by the Baltimore papers. Our pride continues. . . . Our fresh herbs are cultivated in our own greenhouse.

Christine's soups are now available by the quart, and we now do regular off-premises catering.

For those of you who are looking for that "special" place for your next private party, consider L'Amitie. We do have certain size restrictions. However, our specialities include executive and business breakfasts, cocktail receptions, luncheons, and small dinner parties.

Thank you for welcoming us into this community. We are proud to be here.

Your Hosts

Active Members of: National Restaurant Association
Chaine de Rotisseurs
Les Amis d' Escoffier
Maryland Restaurant Association
Greater Baltimore Chamber of Commerce
American Culinary Federation, Inc.

As one entered L'Amitie, one first passed through a massive double door under an eye-catching kiosk roof. The only external identification of the restaurant was a highly polished brass plate with the name L'Amitie on it. Immediately inside was a wide entrance hall with a maître d's desk at the end. In back of this desk were floor-to-ceiling wine racks. To the right was a room seating 40. This room had banquettes along the front of the building. Behind the banquettes and in the center of the wall, there was a small cut-glass window to the outside. Across the room was an elegant polished rosewood bar with eight stools.

On the other side of the entrance way was a dining room seating 95 persons on two levels. The front of the room was again banquettes, but there was no window to the outside. Both rooms were furnished with French provincial tables, chairs, and other decor. Bruce Johnson was quoted in an interview as saying, "We designed the restaurant to be like a French chateau, with one dining room for casual meals and another room for formal dining." The formal room to the left had linen table cloths; the informal room had no cloths or placemats. Both rooms had fine crystal, silver and china, and fresh flowers on every table.

The restaurant property itself was part of a small strip shopping center in the wealthiest suburb of Wilmington, Delaware built and owned by Mr. McLean. On one end of the strip and next to L'Amitie was a bank. On the other end was an inexpensive but quality family restaurant, and a branch of an upscale area department store. In-between were small exclusive shops. L'Amitie was indistinguishable from its neighbors in this strip except for the front brick facade in place of windows, the kiosk, and the brass name plate. It was not readily recognizable as a restaurant. In fact, some had said that it looked more like a funeral parlor.

THE AREA

The suburb of Newport in which L'Amitie was located had one of the highest per capita incomes in the state. It was about five miles from the center of Wilmington and was a bedroom community for a blend of corporate executives and small business owners.

The lifestyle, however, was very conservative. The remainder of the greater Wilmington area (population about 150,000) was a changing scene but one that clung to tradition. Almost on the Maryland state line, 8 miles to the southwest, was the well-to-do community of Newark, many residents of which commuted to Baltimore, 50 miles away, as well as to Wilmington. Other areas of Wilmington were more middle class and some were strictly working class. Across the Delaware River, about six miles from Newport, were a number of other communities in Salem County, NJ. Many of the residents of this area worked in the Wilmington area. Exhibit 31-1 shows a map of the area.

According to *Restaurant Business' Restaurant Growth Index* (RGI), eating and drinking sales in the Wilmington area were $249 million, but the population was somewhat less likely to eat out than the national average. The RGI index of 106, where 100 means that supply exactly equals demand, indicated that the market growth potential was slightly higher than the average American city.

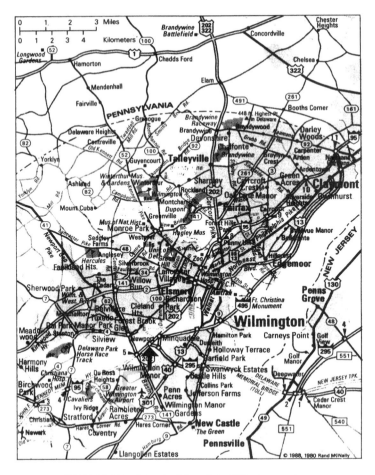

EXHIBIT 31-1   Map of the Wilmington Area.

THE DEVELOPMENT

When L'Amitie first opened, they did no advertising. This was because the consultant had said that her name was so famous that people would come from the publicity alone. When very few came in the first two months, the partners decided that they had better do something. According to Bruce Johnson, a rumor started soon after opening that L'Amitie was so elegant, dinner cost $100 per person. Actually, meals with beverage averaged just under $45 per person at dinner.

Creative advertising was commenced with a decidedly French flavor. For example, when a brunch was introduced on Sunday it was advertised as Le Bon Brunch. Buffets were called Le Bon Buffet. The restaurant was described as "Bon Elegant" versus "Bon Stuffy" to dispel the $100 check rumor. Area newspapers were the primary media used. Brunch checks came to average $18.00 a person.

Business at L'Amitie picked up after advertising was commenced. Average dinner covers reached 60 per night, partly due to an average of 125 on Saturdays. L'Amitie opened for luncheon with menu items priced from $8.95 to $12.95, and business was excellent almost from the start. Check averages at luncheon eventually grew to $18.00 per person.

Other changes took place as time progressed. Management discovered that the local definition of French food was Caesar salad, quiche, crepes, and so forth—not nouvelle or classical cuisine. Adaptations were made without sacrificing the integrity of the food. A prime rib buffet was introduced on Sundays. An eight item early bird dinner menu for those who arrived before 6:30 P.M., with all entrées priced at $14.95, was added to meet the demands of customers who wanted lower priced meals. Originally it was planned to serve this menu in the casual (bar) dining room, but it was found that status conscious customers didn't want to sit in the "discount" room. Early-bird check averages were at first around $15.00 per person; business was brisk and early birds eventually became 60 percent of the total dinner covers during the week, with a $22.50 check average.

The menu was accompanied by an excellent wine list starting at $24.50 per bottle for Muscadet, Alsace riesling, Entre-deux-Mers, Rosé d'Anjou, white Zinfandel, and a Côtes du Ventoux from the Rhone valley. For around $30.00, one could obtain Vouvray, Macon, California Chenin Blanc, Sauvignon Blanc, Fumé Blanc, Gewurtztraminer, Tavel rosé, or a red Graves, Medoc, or Beaujolais Villages. Other listings ranged from California Chardonnay, Pouilly-Fuissé, Grand Cru Chablis, Santenay, and Chateau Talbot for $35 to $45.00 to Chateau Latour 1982 at $225.00. No half bottles were offered.

As business developed at L'Amitie, a number of customers became regulars. Others never returned or did so only on special occasions. Business stabilized for a short period at about $105,000 per month. About 10 percent of this was from off-premise catering, 11 percent was liquor sales, and 13 percent was wine sales. The casual or bar dining room was seldom used, for meals or for drinking.

After 12 months business began to slip. Some tie-in direct mail coupon campaigns were initiated with little effect. Two-for-one dinners were very popular for a six week period with those who "seemed to come out of the woods" but did not fit L'Amitie's clientele image. Business resumed its slide when they were discontinued. Customer comments continued to be good but customer counts fell at both lunch and dinner. Management tried various new approaches but none seemed to have any more than initial impact, if that. Revenue dropped to an average of $90,000 a month, including 10 percent from outside catering, with about two-thirds of this at dinner and one-third at lunch and Sunday brunch.

CONCLUSION

"Well Bruce," said Jim in response to the question about doing a research study, "we are a one-of-a-kind restaurant in this area, that is for sure. All of our competition is lower priced, less formal, and more casual, and none of them have food or service that reaches our level. This certainly defines for us a unique niche in the market place. We have made some accommodations to the meat and potato crowd by taking the tuxedos off our waiters and by introducing buffets, brunch, early-bird specials, and so forth. We have a loyal clientele; we just don't have enough of it. Comments on our food and service continue to be excellent. Yet, obviously, business is slipping and we are losing money, so we must be doing something wrong. I'm not opposed to change and I'm not opposed to a research study. But I am opposed to throwing good money after bad. What is this study going to tell us? What do we expect to learn? The table top study conducted by our advertising agency a few weeks ago told us that we're doing everything right and nothing about what we should change (Exhibit 31-2). As a result, the agency thinks we have to put even more emphasis in our advertising on the quality of our food and our French ambience. We've thought this all along. How is this study going to be any different?"

"Because," Bruce said, "this time we'll do it scientifically. We can't afford to sit here and do nothing, that's for sure. Let's at least get a proposal."

EXHIBIT 31-2
Table Top Questionnaire and Findings

We'd like to make L'Amitie even better for you and your guests. If you'd be good enough to answer the questions below, we'd appreciate it very much. It's totally confidential of course.

About L'Amitie

Did you consider your meal _____ excellent _____ good _____ fair _____ poor?

Do you find the service _____ excellent _____ good _____ fair _____ poor?

Do you dine here _____ once a week _____ once a month _____ less frequent _____ first time?

Compared to other fine restaurants, do you think our prices are _____ too high _____ just right _____ lower than most?

Your favorite entrée at L'Amitie is: _____

About You

Where you reside(town,zip) _____

Occupation _____

Approximate household income _____ less than $25,000 _____ $25,000–$50,000 _____ over $50,000

Favorite type of restaurant _____ French _____ American _____ Italian _____ Mexican _____ Other

Dine out _____ times per week

Business meals per week _____

Are they primarily _____ lunch _____ dinner?

Merci!

You can drop this card in the convenient box near the door or mail it to us.

TABLE TOP QUESTIONNAIRE FINDINGS

Survey conducted 11/23 to 12/31; 836 covers, 292 returned.

Considered Meal: Excellent 176, good 97, fair 17, poor 2.

Considered Service: Excellent 235, good 55, fair 3, poor 0.

Dine Here: Once a week 15, once a month 53, less frequently 111, first time 106.

Think Prices Are: Too high 61, just right 195, lower than most 20.

Household Income: <$25,000 9, $25,000–$50,000 69, >$50,000 138.

Favorite Type of Restaurant: French 168, American 42, Italian 57, Mexican 10, Chinese 13, German 1.

Number of Times Dine Out per Week: 456, business 390, lunch 211, dinner 119

Favorite Entrée at L'Amitie: Veal 29, lamb 28, duck 15, fish 13, seafood 9, chicken 8, veal and lobster 7, steak 7, sole 6, scrod 4.

Occupation: Businessperson 32, doctor 17, executive 14, teacher or self-employed 12, vice-president or retired 7, administrator, attorney, accountant, or consultant 5, psychologist, sales rep, insurance, advertising, or waiter 4, secretary, district manager, professor, investor, marketing, or real estate 3, engineer, psychotherapist, homemaker, entrepreneur, nurse, stockbroker, artist, public relations, salesman, contractor, designer, florist, or restaurant manager 2, retail manager, lawn service, manufacturer, union rep, computer analyst, economist, barber, tennis pro, fashion designer, dentist, machine operator, book dealer, or auto dealer 1

Specific Comments:

Excellent service—will definitely return.

First time ever I didn't get change from gift certificate. Will use credit for my last time at L'Amitie. Pure parsimoniousness.

Waitress very nice. Too much hovering and speediness by waiters.

For every entrée in a French restaurant there should be an intermezzo course and place plates used.

Heat your coffee (2), warm your bread.

L'Escargot's prices are lower.

Only wrinkled tablecloths were less than excellent.

Portions too small (4).

Suggest less chocolate on dessert menu.

Veal Oscar not up to expectation, chocolate mousse too small.

Keep early bird special!

Mousse in the cake not good, all else superb.

Carla great waitress (3).

Quality was superb (5)!

Yellow pages advertising deceiving as far as attire and atmosphere.

Have dined here many times and always found excellent but disappointed in early bird special.

Prices too high for liquor (2).

An elegant restaurant must offer the courtesy to take guests' coats and bring them upon leaving.

Needs fresh flowers. Too noisy.

Enjoyed the evening, will return.

Miss the country room menu.

People should be well-dressed in main dining room.

Enjoyed our first experience, look forward to returning.

Choice of menu is excellent.

Enjoy early diners' specials.

Charles is the greatest (3)!

Reinstate Caesar salad and croissants at lunch.

More veal dishes for dinner.

Croissants disappointing, cold and overdone.

Roast of lamb should be carved at table.

TABLE TOP QUESTIONNAIRE SUMMARY BY ADVERTISING AGENCY

The purpose of this questionnaire was to ascertain certain demographic and lifestyle characteristics of L'Amitie's customer base, as well as to develop a benchmark for customer satisfaction, dining habits, and so on.

Customer satisfaction levels at L'Amitie are very high in terms of food, service, and price. It appears that no substantive changes are indicated. The high "just right" answer to the pricing question, however, deserves some notice in that customers ordinarily feel that most restaurant prices are too high. Combined with the high household income scores, L'Amitie should not be reluctant to inch its prices higher. People tend to equate quality with price—prices that are too low (or even "just right") may be perceived as indicating a lower quality.

In analyzing the residence information provided by respondents, it is readily apparent that the bulk of L'Amitie's business comes from the Wilmington area. However, given that L'Amitie has been in this market for two years, and has been a fairly steady advertiser, it must be assumed that awareness is as high as can be expected in the Wilmington market, based on dollar expenditures to date. In other words, L'Amitie's message has reached nearly as many people as affordable within budgetary constraints.

The resultant traffic levels are the product of this awareness level. Therefore, raising the traffic level will require raising the awareness level within the Wilmington market. This will, in part, be accomplished via word of mouth. However, it can be assumed that lower advertising levels will result in lower traffic levels and conversely. Only by experimenting with increased ad levels will it be known whether there is a wider market in Wilmington.

It is possible that increased ad levels may not draw the increase in traffic necessary to offset the additional expenditure. In other words, it is possible that L'Amitie has already drawn as much as it will from Wilmington.

This assumption is somewhat supported by the high percentage of out-of-state customers. According to the figures, there were 46 percent as many out-of-staters as there were Wilmington residents, 41 percent as many as there were Wilmington area residents. L'Amitie, in other words, has a strong pulling power from the demographically and psychographically different markets of nearby Maryland and New Jersey. This may indicate a strength that L'Amitie has not tapped; a potential reservoir of business that is more accustomed to and receptive to the L'Amitie dining experience.

The occupational information offers some support to this hypothesis. From the figures derived in the study, occupations were categorized into three major groupings: businesspeople (129), professionals (53), and others (19).

The business/professional marketplace, while widely varied and diverse, represents a major strength to L'Amitie. This data strongly suggests that future marketing plans be aimed at maximizing L'Amitie's impact upon this market. Interestingly, the northern Maryland region represents a strong bastion of business/professional people, certainly much stronger than does the Wilmington market.

In general, these people tend to be more mobile, more adventuresome, and more discriminating in their choices of food, eating, and entertainment.

With its strong out-of-town pulling power and an apparent softness in its "hometown" markets, it may behoove L'Amitie to consider making a strong push for attracting this more affluent and receptive out-of-town customer. Considering the truly unique nature of the establishment, this suggests that L'Amitie make a conscious decision to become a "regional" restaurant rather than a local one. It must be understood, however, that such a decision would require a substantial advertising and public relations effort at first.

C A S E
Thirty-Two

THE MERRY WEEKEND*

Anthony Bronson, vice president of marketing for the Tara Hotel chain, had given careful thought to the proposed agenda for the upcoming general managers' meeting to discuss weekend packages at "nontraditional properties." The meeting had been planned following corporate research that revealed pertinent facts regarding the weekend customer. Bronson saw a need to develop a more appropriate and competitive weekend package plan other than the one presently offered at Tara's more "traditional" properties.

Since the purchase of some Dunfey owned and franchised hotels, the need had grown for a more cohesive and uniform image for these properties that would better represent the Tara Hotel Company. Tara Hotels was the largest franchisee of the Sheraton Corporation in the New England area. They were positioned in the market place as upscale properties, catering to higher rated groups and corporate travelers. The physical hotel product was above that of normal Sheraton standards.

Most of the former Dunfey properties were Sheraton franchise hotels, as were the original Tara hotels, but they had had no capital improvements for the past three years. It was planned to renovate and upgrade each facility to make it consistent with the present image of the original Tara properties. In the meanwhile, these hotels were more "inn-like" than "hotel-like" and presented some serious marketing problems.

One particular problem of the new acquisitions was the sale of Merry Weekend packages throughout the company. These packages had been developed for the traditional Tara properties and had proven to be very successful. They sold for $79.00 to $89.00 for two, per night, depending on the property, and are described in Exhibit 32-1.

It was suspected that loss of established Merry Weekend customers was beginning to take place within the company due to dissatisfaction with the product offering of the nontraditional properties. Merry Weekend customers were known to be loyal customers who went from property to property to enjoy their Merry Weekends. When they went to the new properties expecting the same facilities, they found that the same product wasn't there. In fact,

*John Wolper of Mercyhurst College researched and contributed to this case. Some names have been disguised.

The Tara Merry Weekend

What royal memories are made of.

Your everyday routine is demanding. It's important to take a little time to get away.

Relax. We have the solution. A Tara Merry Weekend. It's a great way to get away and live like royalty for 3 days and 2 nights at one of 12 exciting locations.

Choose a castle, country or resort setting. From the romantic, rocky coast of Maine or the idyllic countryside of New Hampshire to the white-duned beaches on Cape Cod, or cosmopolitan ambience of Boston and beyond.

Your Tara Merry Weekend for two includes a sumptuous Saturday breakfast, complimentary fresh fruit basket, use of pool and health club facilities,* and a lavish Sunday brunch.

Join us for a Tara Merry Weekend and be treated like royalty. For reservations call the Tara Hotel of your choice.

*Additional charge for golf, tennis and racquetball. No indoor pool at Lexington.

A thoughtful treat for your favorite couple.

Tara Merry Weekend gift certificates are also available. Simply call the Tara Hotel of your choice for complete information.

EXHIBIT 32-1 Brochure Description of the Merry Weekend Package.

Tara reservationists were reporting irate phone calls after customers had been to the new properties.

This problem had occurred before when the Danvers property was purchased from Radisson Hotels. At that time, three Tara hotels had the castle motif and there was a known 20,000 Merry Weekend customers. Advertisements and direct mail were aimed at these customers to lure them to the Danvers property before it was renovated. Many tried the property, taking business away from the other Taras. This also resulted in considerable dissatisfaction. Tara customers now had seven traditional Tara properties from which to choose, in addition to the five nontraditional properties, but the known Merry Weekend customer base had increased only to 23,000. Thus the increase in hotels had not brought a proportionate increase in Merry Weekend customers.

BACKGROUND

Tara Hotel Company was owned by The Flatley Hotel Company of Braintree, Massachusetts, a di-versified construction company with diversified real estate holdings. After constructing four traditional Tara hotels, built with an Irish castle motif, The Flatley Company purchased six other properties from Dunfey Hotels, the one from Radisson Hotels in Danvers, and constructed one contemporary atrium lobby hotel.

Since opening the first Sheraton Tara, the Tara Hotel division had developed a reputation for excellent physical products. The Sheraton Tara group of hotels offered its guests the finest in comfort with first-class guestrooms, restaurants and coffee shops, ballrooms, meeting rooms, recreational facilities, indoor and outdoor swimming pools, saunas, steam baths, exercise rooms, and a PGA golf course, but not all facilities were available at all properties, as shown in Exhibit 32-2. Each hotel was designed with the business traveler in mind. In addition to the appropriate facilities, the nationwide Sheraton reservation line provided a strong system for confirming rooms to travelers outside New England.

CUSTOMER RESEARCH

Tony Warhola, director of market research for the Tara hotel group, had conducted a customer survey to learn the likes and dislikes of some of the Merry Weekend customers. The study was designed to determine customer satisfaction of Merry Weekend packages, to identify the most appealing promotional benefits, to assess competitors' package usage, and to develop a Merry Weekend customer profile. The study was conducted at the Nashua and Framingham properties. The survey questions, responses, and a summary of the findings can be found in an appendix to the case.

After completion of the survey, Bronson gathered data for the past four months and for the same months of the previous year, just prior to the general managers' meeting, in an attempt to draw some conclusions from company sales information on the Merry Weekend packages. A comparison of the sales in the six traditional Tara hotels, plus Hyannis, which was a semiresort with Tara stan-

EXHIBIT 32-2
Tara Hotels Inventory

Location	Rooms	Dining and Entertainment	Swimming Pool		Racquet-ball	Tennis	Golf	Sauna	Health Center
			Indoor	Outdoor					
Nashua, NH	350	Restaurant, Pub and lounge	Y	Y	Y	Y		Y	Y
Braintree, MA	400	Two restaurants, pub and lounge	Y	Y	Y			Y	Y
Framingham, MA	375	Two restaurants, pub and lounge	Y	Y	Y			Y	Y
Danvers, MA	367	Two restaurants and lounge	Y	Y	Y	Y	Y	Y	Y
Springfield, MA	300	Two restaurants and lounge	Y		Y			Y	Y
Parsippany, NJ	400	Two restaurants pub and lounge	Y	Y	Y			Y	Y
Hyannis, MA	224	Restaurant and lounge	Y	Y		Y	Y	Y	Y
Bedford, NH	200	Restaurant and lounge	Y	Y					
Lexington, MA	115	Restaurant, pub and lounge		Y					
Portland, ME	220	Restaurant and lounge	Y					Y	
Newton, MA	261	Restaurant and lounge	Y					Y	
Warwick, RI	125	Restaurant and lounge	Y					Y	

dards, versus the other five purchased properties, was revealed in this analysis (Exhibit 32-3).

Bronson distinguished between "Tara" and "non-Tara" hotels based on the current facilities offered at each property. The key difference between the two hotel groups was the offering of full or limited service. Merry Weekend customers didn't care whether the hotel looked like a castle; they wanted the health club, Upper Crust, and Jester's Court restaurants, and other full service amenities of the traditional Taras. Typical outlets at these hotels are described in Exhibit 32-4.

Bronson also evaluated the strengths and weak-nesses of the chain. Among the strengths he found were:

- The excellent location of all properties
- The excellent services offered
- The extensive marketing research being conducted
- The competitive prices in the traditional Tara hotels
- The positive image of the Tara properties
- The good facilities provided in Tara properties
- The repeat customers, especially those with established brand loyalty to Tara hotels.

E X H I B I T 32-3
Summary Results of Merry Weekend Packages

Tara Hotels Merry Weekend Analysis (Number of Rooms)[a]

Hotel	Nov. LP	Nov. PY	Dec. LP	Dec. PY	Jan. LP	Jan. PY	Feb. LP	Feb. PY	Totals LP	Totals PY
Taras										
Nashua	984	850	316	300	1,067	1,008	934	1,629	3,301	3,787
Braintree	708	410	280	260	395	576	881	1,065	2,264	2,311
Framingham	991	850	314	289	817	911	1,087	1,092	3,209	3,142
Danvers	198	150	73	70	228	200	405	350	904	770
Springfield	24	0	13	0	42	0	156	0	235	0
Parsippany	175	0	76	0	189	0	399	0	839	0
Hyannis	230	36	86	92	414	427	438	503	1,168	1,058
Total	3,310	2,296	1,158	1,011	3,152	3,122	4,300	4,639	11,920	11,068
Non-Taras										
Bedford	146	34	45	42	84	137	98	273	373	486
Lexington	37	44	32	329	16	16	38	57	123	446
S. Portland	359	250	103	67	154	11	327	333	943	661
Newton	21	26	3	3	15	10	24	39	63	78
Warwick	0	0	0	0	0	0	0	0	0	0
Total	563	354	183	441	269	174	487	702	1,502	1,671
Grand Total									13,422	12,739
% Tara									88.8	86.9
% Non-Tara									11.2	13.1
Inventory										
% Tara	72.3	[2,416 Rooms]								
% Non-Tara	27.7	[921 Rooms]								
Total	3,337 Rooms									

[a]LP: latest period. PY: previous year.

Among the weaknesses Bronson found were:

- The prices of the non-Taras being perhaps too high in respect to the facilities they offered
- The poor facilities and small room sizes of the non-Taras
- The confused image of the non-Taras because they were recently purchased from Dunfey
- Lack of customer awareness of ownership of non-Tara properties
- The transition period while non-Taras upgraded to Tara levels with inconvenience and disservice to guests
- Losing customers of the Tara hotels after they had patronized the non-Tara hotels
- Offering Merry Weekenders seven traditional Taras instead of four.

Bronson saw the opportunities for the Tara Hotel Company to be:

Because everything is here.

The Upper Crust
Restaurant

Our Haute Cuisine makes every dinner a festive event! Specialties include prime ribs, steaks and ocean-fresh lobster as well as veal, lamb, poultry and seafood dishes. Cheeses, relishes and hearth breads are included with your repast, and a dessert cart brings a selection of sweets to your table. Dinner served daily from 5 P.M. to 10:30 P.M., and reservations are available Sunday through Thursday. Also, a bountiful brunch is served each Sunday from 9:30 A.M. to 2 P.M.

Knaughty Knight Club

Knightly Entertainment in a romantic setting of candlelight and arched ceilings. Complimentary hot hors d'oeuvres, cheese and fruit served Monday through Friday from 5 P.M. till 7 P.M. when the dancing begins. Popular cabaret groups (a new one every two weeks) provide live entertainment Monday through Saturday nights.

Jesters Court
Cafe

Regal Repasts cheerily served amid informal surroundings. Satisfying even the heartiest of appetites throughout the day, Monday through Saturday. Intriguing entrees such as Sole Oscar, Wiener Schnitzel and London Broil top the varied luncheon menu, served 11:30 AM - 5 PM. Dinner from 5 PM - 11:30 PM features international favorites, including veal marsala and scallopini, tournedos aux champignons, shrimp Mario. And exquisite desserts cap the evening.

Z.J.'s Pub
and Game Room

The Game's The Thing in a casual environment where you'll joust and jest amid dramatic archways and spectacular murals. Imbibe refreshment while you impress the joyous throng with your skills at backgammon and cribbage, checkers and chess. Open daily from 11 A.M. to 1 A.M., with complimentary hors d'oeuvres, cheese and fruit tray served Monday to Friday from 4 P.M. to 7 P.M.

Sheraton Tara Hotels
The Flatley Company
BRAINTREE • FRAMINGHAM • NASHUA, N.H.

E X H I B I T 3 2 - 4 Descriptions of Tara Outlets.

- Building on the existing reputation of the Tara image
- Maintaining existing repeat customers
- Identifying new markets through research
- Capturing markets through price value in the non-Taras

Bronson also saw threats in other hotels offering very competitive value packages, and the loss of Merry Weekend package customers within the Tara system because of disappointment at non-Taras and confusion from offering existing customers different products from which to choose.

The company used its current base of names and addresses from the traditional Tara properties to help promote the Merry Weekend packages at the new traditional Taras and at the non-Tara ho-

tels. Some of these customers, after buying the package at a non-Tara, never came back to either a non-Tara or a Tara.

Without a distinction of services and facilities, Merry Weekend promotions continued to market the packages to known past customers. Little research, or even thought, had been given to the promotion of these packages and their consequences at the newly added properties.

THE GENERAL MANAGERS' MEETING

The meeting began promptly at 1:30 P.M. and was conducted by Bronson. Key corporate staff and general managers from the traditional and non-Tara properties were in attendance. The agenda read as follows:

1. Overview of the situation
2. Identification of problem
3. Analysis of competitive offerings
4. Product development
5. Marketing of product—advertising and direct mail

Each general manager and his director of sales spent 30 minutes discussing their situation. They identified the loss of their customers to new traditional Tara properties as well as the customer dissatisfaction with the non-traditional Tara product. Two additional hours were spent analyzing competitive offerings, discussing the product, the customers, and prices.

In addition to the survey results reported and discussed at the meeting, the round-table discussion about the customers who came to non-Tara properties indicated that a majority of these weekend guests loved to receive free in-room gifts, enjoyed shopping but liked to stay in the hotel for other activities (in fact, would sit in the lobby for hours feeling that the more time they spent in the hotel the more they received their money's worth), liked coupons for discounts in the restaurants and lounges, liked to have their picture taken with the Beefeater doorman (Exhibit 32-5), and arrived by automobile. Most non-Tara managers suspected that most of their weekend customers belonged in the blue collar category.

A basic problem discussed was that the Merry Weekend package was not working well at non-Taras because they had fewer facilities to offer the customers. Competition was also a major topic of discussion, centering around key competitors, especially the large chain-affiliated hotels. These hotels recognized the contribution to revenues of weekend packages in their overall sales strategy. Like the Sheraton Tara properties, they were highly dependent on business travelers and occupancies plunged on weekends. They courted the markets aggressively through advertising and very attractive prices.

Bronson wanted to have a new package ready for sale throughout the Tara system by May 30 to insure customer awareness and support any opportunity for a strong presale market for the upcoming summer season. Those at the meeting recognized that the company had to respond quickly and effectively if it was going to meet the competitive challenge. Management recognized the difficulties of competing in each hotel's respective market because of the varied degrees and methods of competition. If the non-Tara hotels were to remain competitive, they would have to compensate somehow for their physical failings.

The meeting came to a close with optimistic enthusiasm regarding the new strategies that were to be put in place.

Now You Can Enjoy Your Tara Merry Weekend at Even More Castles.

Tara Hotels is pleased to announce the addition of seven new properties. In Newton, Lexington and Hyannis, MA; Warwick, RI; Bedford, NH; South Portland, ME; and Parsippany, NJ. And coming soon to Springfield, MA.

Sheraton Tara Hotel
  Braintree, MA 617-848-0600
Sheraton Tara Hotel
  Danvers, MA 617-777-2500
Sheraton Tara Hotel
  Framingham, MA 617-879-7200
Sheraton Tara Hotel
  Lexington, MA 617-862-8700
Sheraton Tara Hotel
  Springfield, MA 413-781-1010
Sheraton Tara Hotel
  South Portland, ME 207-775-6161
Sheraton Tara Wayfarer Hotel
  Bedford, NH 603-622-3766
Sheraton Tara Hotel
  Nashua, NH 603-888-9970
Sheraton Tara Airport Hotel
  Warwick, RI 401-738-4000
Tara Newton—A Howard Johnson's Hotel
  Newton, MA 1-800-654-2000 or 617-969-3010
Tara Dunfey Hyannis Hotel
  Hyannis, MA 1-800-THE TARA or 617-775-7775
Tara Hotel
  Parsippany, NJ 201-515-2000

For Sheraton reservations: 1-800-325-3535

Treat yourself to a Tara Merry Weekend

E X H I B I T   3 2 - 5   Merry Weekend Brochure Cover.

APPENDIX 32A: MERRY WEEKENDER CUSTOMER SURVEY RESULTS

Purpose of Research

- Determine customer satisfaction with weekend package.
- Identify most appealing benefits of weekend packages.
- Assess competitor package usage.
- Develop Merry Weekend customer profile.

Methodology

Surveys distributed to all Merry Weekend customers on two weekends at the following properties:

- Nashua only on November 13–15
- Nashua and Framingham on November 20–22

In total, 129 surveys were completed of the 273 distributed for a respectable response of 47 percent.

Two properties with the most Merry Weekend business were selected. In April, a mail survey will be conducted with all Merry Weekend customers from January of last year through March of this year. This later study will be representative of all Merry Weekend customers for all properties.

The present study developed from discussion concerning the January promotion to all Merry Weekend customers; specifically, we wanted to know if a third night free with a Merry Weekend package was an appealing benefit. This opportunity to survey customers allowed the capturing of additional information for directional purposes and also is the foundation for the mail survey to be conducted in April.

Therefore, since this study does not represent all Merry Weekend customers, the results are directional only and should not be generalized to all Merry Weekend customers. However, the results that follow are very useful and give us a good idea and direction to follow.

Survey Questions and Results

1. How often have you used this Merry Weekend Package in the last TWO years (including this weekend)?

First time today	52%
Two	9
Three	23
Four	7
Five	5
Six	1
Seven to nine	3
	100% (base = 129)

2. In the last two years, how often have you extended your Merry Weekend stay from 2 nights (Friday and Saturday) to 3 nights (Friday, Saturday, and Sunday?)

Never	73%
Once	10
Twice	10
Three times	7
	100% (base = 60)

3. During your Merry Weekend stays, how often do you eat dinner in the hotel's restaurant?

Friday night only	25%
Saturday night only	52
Both Friday and Saturday	23
	100% (base = 60)

4. Please rate the following characteristics of the Merry Weekend packages with 5 being excellent and 1 being poor.

	%Very Good or Excellent	Average Rating
Cocktail Party	76%	4.1
Fruit Basket	68	4.0
Saturday Breakfast	81	4.1
Sunday Brunch	100	4.4
Value Overall	79	4.1
(base = 60)		

5. Which one factor was most important to you when selecting this Merry Weekend Package?

Location	41%
Price	23
Repeating	10
Friends	6
Other	9
Restaurant	4
Pool	4
Spa	3
	100% (base = 129)

6. How did you become aware of Merry Weekend Packages?

Repeat Customer	29%
Referral	26
Newspaper Ads	13
Gift Certificate	12
Called Hotel Directly	12
Friends	4
Other	4
	100% (base = 129)

7. Have you purchased any other weekend packages offered by a hotel other than Tara Hotels?

Yes	32%
No	68
	100% (base = 127)

8. Who were these packages offered by?

Marriott	37%
Sheraton	17
Hilton	17
Holiday Inn	12
Hyatt	10
Westin	5
Omni	2
Other	4 (base = 41)

9. Below is a list of benefits hotels have used in weekend packages. On a scale of 1 to 5, with 5 being very appealing, how appealing are these benefits to you?

	Percent appealing or very appealing		
	First Time MW Customers	Repeating MW Customers	All
Free dinner for two in hotel's restaurant	96%	89%	93%
Free tickets to local theater, museum	38	33	34
Free third night MW stay	42	59	50
Free use of pool and health spa	67	64	65
Free in-room movies	73	68	71
Free brunch	96	94	95

	Average Rating		
	First Time MW Customers	Repeating MW Customers	All MW Customers
Free dinner for two in hotel's restaurant	4.7	4.7	4.7
Free tickets to local theatre, museum	3.1	2.8	3.0
Free third night MW stay	3.3	3.6	3.4

| | Average Rating | | |
	First Time MW Customers	Repeating MW Customers	All MW Customers
Free use of pool and health spa	4.0	4.0	4.0
Free in-room movies	4.1	3.9	4.0
Free brunch	4.8	4.8	4.8

10. What one addition would you like to see to the Merry Weekend Package?

Addition		Willing to Pay (% yes)
Dinner for two	43%	68%
Free third night	6	83
Lounge entertainment	5	100
Later check-out	4	25
Free HBO	4	0
Theater tickets	4	75
Better service	2	100
Golf	2	100
Champagne on arrival	2	50
AM coffee in lobby	2	50

Single Mentions: Coed Steam Room, more activities, whirlpool for two, children's play area, all night room service, refrigerator in room, free massage (base = 95)

Customer Profile

11. In the last year, how often did your work require you to travel which included overnight stays in hotels?

Number of Overnights	Customers
None	57%
One	6
Two	12
Three	4

Number of Overnights	Customers
Four	2
Five–nine	11
Ten +	8

100% (base = 115)
Average = 2.4 nights

12. Age

Under 30	16%
30 to 39	26
40 to 49	41
50 to 59	12
60 to 69	4

100% (base = 127)
Average age = 41

13. Income

Under $35,000	17%
$35,000 to $49,999	41
$50,000 to $69,999	27
$70,000 or more	15

100% (base = 123)
(Median income $47,682)

Conclusions

The customer profile of the MW customer is not surprising as this was very close to our educated guess. The percentage of first time (52%) MW customers strongly suggests that there is new business to be captured. Additionally, the 32% of the customers who have used competitor's weekend packages suggests that "brand loyalty" can be established either by adding amenities to the package or by simply reminding the customer of our package through direct mail or other forms of advertising.

"Third Night Free" is an appealing benefit as one of every two customers indicated this benefit to be appealing or very appealing, although this benefit did not appear as appealing as other benefits. One problem with assessing the appeal of this benefit is the actual description of a third night free without biasing the question for a positive response (for example, assigning a dollar value for the free night.) Also, one other problem is that benefits rated were already being offered, while a third night free is a new idea for a package.

With 77 percent of the customers already having one dinner meal in the hotel, the suggestion of having dinner for two included in the package (even with a higher MW price per day) would "cut into" the food and beverage revenue. Since only 23 percent have both dinner meals at the hotel, our objective should be to increase this percentage.

CASE

Thirty-Three

❖

CAFE DI CARLO*

"Call it being in the wrong place at the wrong time. The building was being offered to me and I didn't know what to do with the space. So I decided to put up some sort of dining establishment, just for the fun of it."

Bonni Di Carlo was the sole proprietor of the Cafe DiCarlo restaurant, located in the center of Amherst, Massachusetts, a town of 20,000 permanent residents and 30,000 college students. Bonni began her career in the foodservice business by developing a "pizza joint." With the University of Massachusetts (UMASS) and Amherst College close by, the restaurant was an immediate success with students as the major market. After almost seven years of catering to a "loud and obnoxious group," Bonni felt that she needed a change. This was when the concept of Cafe DiCarlo was born, an upscale Italian restaurant.

This change involved not only a makeover in menu but also in facility, design, staffing, management philosophy, and market positioning. The lay-

out and design of Cafe DiCarlo was conducive to a warm and intimate fine dining experience. Entering the low-level restaurant, one immediately took comfort in the warm wooden floors, tables and seats, the brick columns, and the wide array of artwork displayed. All the artwork was provided by local artists who exhibited their work for six weeks at a time in hopes of selling it. In the background a wide range of music, jazz to opera to new age, could be heard. On the whole, Cafe DiCarlo could be described as a creative, artsy interior design catering to the intimate dining experience. The dining area consisted of 13 tables of varying sizes, seating a total of 40.

Cafe DiCarlo was designed so as to promote privacy and a sense of being one-on-one. "I want the customer to feel as if he or she is walking into their friend's dining room...they should feel relaxed and enjoy the fine dining atmosphere and experience," said Bonni.

Bonni had the intention of continuing to cater to the UMASS and Amherst College market. The only difference, however, was that she did not want to attract the "pizza and beer" crowd. Instead, she hoped to attract students who preferred to dine in

---

*Nicole Panlilio, Alice Tse, Shari Alone, and John Griffin contributed to this case.

783

a classier place, where they could take their parents, and generally have a pleasant and quiet evening out—a place where they could relax, dine unhurriedly, and enjoy good food, good wine, and efficient service. Bonni believed that students would be eager to come to a "more casually elegant restaurant such as this one."

THE REALIZATION

Bonni closed the pizza operation right after she bought the building. Four months later, Cafe DiCarlo—Fine Italian Dining, opened its doors in the same space. To Bonni's surprise and disappointment, the students were neither anxious nor excited about the new restaurant. In fact, Cafe DiCarlo's actual patrons were mostly professors, graduate students, foreign students (mostly European) and a few local, elderly couples, most of whom came for dinner.

To counter this, Bonni initiated a promotional "Pasta Night" on Wednesday evenings when students could "choose from a variety of additions" to create their own pasta dinners, starting at $4.95. She ran an ad in the local, daily student newspaper for one month (Exhibit 33-1).

The purpose of the promotion, Bonni said, was "not to make money but to let the restaurant be known." The promotion, however, was quite unsuccessful. Bonni decided to scrap the idea and be happy with her present patrons and regulars who frequented the establishment. About 70 percent were repeat customers.

Competition was not a major concern for Bonni. She viewed a nearby so-called gourmet continental restaurant with a comparable atmosphere that also focused on the noncollege market as her major competitor, along with two other nearby Italian restaurants that had more traditional family-oriented concepts and drew from all segments of the local market. In Northampton, eight miles away, there was one Italian restaurant somewhat similar to Cafe DiCarlo, as well as a

EXHIBIT 33-1 Cafe DiCarlo ad to attract students

more sophisticated 40,000 population. Bonni had not tried to reach this market, so didn't consider this restaurant as competitive.

MARKETING EFFORTS

Bonni embarked on another promotion. This time it was geared toward the senior citizen market. Bonni wanted to increase the poor luncheon and afternoon sales by offering senior citizens a daily special of two entrée choices (pasta), with freshly baked bread, a house salad, and a beverage included. These were served for only $5.95 and only between the hours of 11:00 A.M. and 4:00 P.M. The promotion was quite successful in that it somewhat boosted luncheon and afternoon turnover. It also made more people aware of the restaurant.

Other efforts at increasing market awareness were ads that were run in various publications at the beginning of each semester for about two weeks to a month (Exhibit 33-2). Other ads ran during the semester to attract theater goers (Exhibit 33-3). Both these ads introduced a somewhat lighter fare at lunch. The restaurant also served as an art gallery. All works of art displayed on the walls were for sale. Walk-throughs and browsing were encouraged in the afternoon.

When asked whether or not her target market had changed, Bonni Di Carlo replied, "No. We still want and are attempting to attract the UMASS and Amherst College students. We believe that placing ads in the college newspapers is sufficient enough to accomplish this." Bonni really did not put much

EXHIBIT 33-2 Cafe DiCarlo awareness ad

EXHIBIT 33-3 Cafe DiCarlo theater-goer ad

effort and thought into marketing aside from these ads. In fact, she had a very small budget for it—about $500 a month. Most ads were "fun" ads for special promotions, changes in menu, and holiday specials. The ads focused on food rather than the creative concept and the dining experience.

THE FUTURE

Eighteen months later, the Cafe was still an unknown commodity to the general public. Cafe DiCarlo offered a new seasonal menu. A new chef who, for the past ten years, had lived in Italy and worked in a family-style restaurant in Tuscany, was hired. This, Bonni hoped, would help to project a family-style image for the restaurant. While most Italian restaurants seemed to bow to customer demand, Cafe DiCarlo was dedicated to educating the customer. The menu was not Italian American but actual dishes as they were prepared in homes in Italy. Price-wise, the menu was far-ranging (Exhibit 33-4).

The next summer Bonni expanded the operation to include a 50-seat outdoor area at the back of the restaurant. A slightly different menu was offered outside. Bonni also planned to expand into the second level of the building. She was a little hesitant because of the possibility of losing the privacy and personable atmosphere that Cafe DiCarlo possessed. Further, she wasn't sure just who her market would be, especially when she wasn't yet able to fill the first floor.

Bonni Di Carlo wanted to classify her restaurant as a fine dining establishment. On the other hand, she also wanted to attract the college students, as

---

ENTREES

all entrees are served with vegetables or roasted potatoes

GAMBERI alla DIAVOLA
shrimp in a peppery tomato sauce with cherry tomatoes
and sauteed fresh spinach
16.95

CAPE SANTE con VERDURE alla GRIGLIA
scallops with braised greens in a sherry cream sauce with fresh herbs
15.75

PESCE del GIORNO
Fish of the Day
Priced Accordingly

GALLETO al FORNO
Rock Cornish Game Hen
roasted with olive oil, fresh rosemary
and white wine, served with potatoes
12.25

PETTO di POLLO con CARCIOFI e FUNGHI
Breast of Chicken
sauteed with mushrooms and artichoke hearts
in a tangy vermouth and butter sauce
12.95

CASSOULET TOSCANA
Tuscan Stew
a rich stew made of fresh vegetables, kidney beans
and plum tomatoes with sweet Italian sausages
10.95

SCALLOPINE di VITELLO con SPEZZIE
Veal Scallopine
in a rich white wine and butter sauce with minced fresh herbs
16.75

COSTOLETTE d'ABBACCHIO DORATO
Prime Lamb Chops
marinated in fresh herbs with lemon - breaded - then baked
16.95

BISTECCA AL PEPE
sirloin steak with cracked black pepper in a
rich red wine mustard glaze
18.95

SCALLOPINE di VITELLO con SPEZZIE
Veal Scallopine
in a rich white wine and butter sauce with minced fresh herbs
16.75

COSTOLETTE d'ABBACCHIO DORATO
Prime Lamb Chops
marinated in fresh herbs with lemon - breaded - then baked
16.95

BISTECCA AL PEPE
sirloin steak with cracked black pepper in a
rich red wine mustard glaze
18.95

E X H I B I T   3 3 - 4   Cafe DiCarlo dinner menu

---

long as they are not "rowdy and obnoxious." Essentially, they are the largest group of people in Amherst for nine months of the year. As things are, Bonni is barely breaking even and needs to increase her market share or attract new markets.

Thirty-Four

HILTON INTERNATIONAL: BRANDED SERVICE CULTURES*

For many years, Hilton International hotels were largely dependent on Americans traveling abroad. More recently, however, Hilton International's goal has been to develop a core consistency of domestic guests in each of its markets, attracting a steady stream of international business travelers by responding to individual customers' personal and cultural needs. Hotel firms have traditionally considered themselves to be good at meeting the expressed direct wishes of their guests. The 1990s, however, have brought increased attention to indirectly expressed needs as a new fruitful source of competitive advantage of service branding initiatives based on cultural and national characteristics.

Geoffrey Breeze, vice president for corporate marketing, glanced at his watch. He realized that it was already 9:00 A.M., time for the corporate meeting to start. He and Andrew Bould, se-

nior vice president of sales and marketing, were to submit their report to Mr. David Jardis, the CEO of Hilton International, dealing with their view on the possible evolution of the Japanese *Wa No Kutsurogi* program, and its potential adaptation to other cultures. They knew that Mr. Jardis would base his decision on their analysis, and that they could greatly influence the entire international strategy of the chain.

BACKGROUND

Hilton International (HI) was formed in 1949 as a separate subsidiary of the United States' Hilton Hotel Corporation with the opening of the Caribe Hilton International in Puerto Rico. In 1964, with 24 overseas hotels, HI was spun off as an independent publicly owned company with its shares traded on the New York Stock Exchange. The agreement covering the spin-off gave the U.S.

---

*Cecille Gouailhardou, Olivier Passieux, Eric Roca, and Jean-Denis Vaultier researched and contributed to this case.

Hilton Hotel Corporation (commonly called *Hilton Domestic*) the exclusive right to use the name Hilton in the United States, and Hilton International the exclusive right to use the Hilton name throughout the rest of the world. The only connection between the two companies that remained was the jointly owned Hilton worldwide reservations system, which handled 5 million reservations annually.

In 1967, HI was acquired by Trans World Airlines and became part of the Transworld Holding Company. In 1987, HI was acquired by the American Allegis Corporation (formerly and subsequently United Air Lines), but within a matter of months Allegis divested it. HI was then last acquired in 1987 by the British Ladbroke Group, one of the United Kingdom's largest companies. HI benefitted from Ladbroke Group management style, financial backing, and sales and marketing techniques. In the mid-nineties, HI was operating over 160 hotels in almost 50 countries. Independent research purported that HI had the most powerful hotel brand name in the world and was the first choice for business travelers abroad.

Ladbroke, at that time, planned an aggressive growth strategy for HI, with the opening of about 40 more hotels in at least seven new countries by the year 2000. This strategy was based on management contracts, joint ventures, or partnerships with regional or national hotel developers. Focusing on a broader international market, this expansion represented significant marketing challenge for the company.

NEW CUSTOMER RESPONSIVENESS

Competition among hotels in the international arena became stronger and more vigorous in the 1980s and 1990s as new types of customers with many different lifestyles flooded the market place. To determine the optimal service for the future, HI commissioned customer and employee surveys to identify market needs and expectations. One part of this was the views of employees on job related issues and, more importantly, on what services they believed their customers wanted them to provide. This research was instrumental in shaping a program designed to create a more contemporary service-led organization.

As a result, HI attempted to communicate a change of culture to consumers and staff by launching a global advertising campaign entitled, "Take Me to the Hilton." This program led to the "Hilton Promise" that every HI employee would give superior and distinctive service, service that guests would remember and for which they would return. The main emphasis of the promise was that the service provided would be worldwide. One of the different service clusters initiated was that addressed to Japanese customers.

HI's promise aimed to achieve the company's new objectives by, (1) developing unique branded offerings that capitalize on the new service culture, by developing products that respond to individual customers' needs, and (2) creating a service-driven culture globally.

SERVICE BRANDING

The first step in recognizing the needs of customers was illustrated by the "Hilton Club" concept. Hilton Club was designed to meet the needs and requirements of frequent international users with the following benefits:

- A guaranteed room on bookings made 24 hours prior to arrival.
- Priority bookings through special Hilton Club telephone lines.
- Upgrade to superior room, on availability.
- Flexible arrival and departure times.
- Complimentary spouse accommodation.
- Fast check-in/check-out procedures.
- A Hilton Club Manager to ensure personalized service.

- Coordinated garment pressing and shoeshine on weekdays.
- Complimentary newspapers and magazines in the member's own language.
- Complimentary hot or cold beverage every day.
- A 20 percent discount on business support services provided by the hotel.
- Preferential fee for members' partners.

Utilizing HI's confidential global database and computerized reservation system, Club members' preferences (e.g., favorite beverage, guest room category and location, reading materials, and special dietary requirements) were instantly communicated to a hotel's Hilton Club staff prior to arrival. Membership in the Hilton Club guaranteed that special comfort, as well as tangible benefits, were consistently delivered on a global basis. At the same time the "Meeting 2000" concept was introduced at all HI hotels (Exhibit 34-1). Similar concepts have emerged in international chains such as Forte's *Venue Guarantee* and Marriott's *No Risk Meeting*.

THE JAPANESE MARKET

HI was the only foreign company with a worldwide representation to operate hotels in four major cities in Japan (Tokyo, Osaka, Tokyo Bay, Nagoya), with a total 2530-room capacity. This presence in the Asian market increased the Japanese clientele in HI hotels all over the world. The Japanese segment represented 21 percent of the global clientele of the company, the same as American guests. Moreover, independent research showed that Hilton was the

* A dedicated meeting Service Manager, available throughout the day to provide organizers with reliable support and help.

* A business and Meeting Service Center, located close to the main function area, providing full communications services : typing, fax, photocopying, translation and courier services. Specialist services, such as graphic design and photographic processing, are made available as required.

* Boardrooms furnished to the highest standards with a wooden boardroom table and special Hilton 8 Hours Chairs, designed to ensure maximum comfort;

* Technically trained staff to deal with any equipment problems on the spot.

* A wide range of all-purpose meeting rooms, all equipped with hard top tables, comfortable chairs and individual wardrobes.

* A selection of Break Out Rooms for small working groups.

* Express check-in for residential delegates at the Business and Meeting Service Center.

* Flexibility to eat and take breaks at any time of the day and to choose from a selection of menus ranging from a highspeed meal, to a working lunch served in the meeting room, to a Hilton Healthy Choice, an option that guarantees not to slow customers down.

* In-room telephones with a direct line to the Business & Meeting Services Center as well as outside direct dialing.

* Flexible pricing with costs carefully budgeted.

* A Hilton Working Wall Room, available in most hotels, with an integrated audio visual system including TV, video, 35 mm slide projector and computer capability (all controlled by one simple remote panel).

EXHIBIT 34-1 Hilton Meeting 2000 Features

clear first choice for Japanese business travelers worldwide. For its outstanding performance in the Japanese market, both domestically and internationally, Hilton was presented with the "Service Industry Success Award" by the "Opportunity Japan" campaign, an initiative sponsored by the Japanese Department of Trade and Industry and the British Overseas Trade Board. At this point, HI launched the world's first service brand for the Japanese traveler, called *Wa No Kutsurogi*.

Japanese Cultural Trends

The Japanese public, long famous for its homogeneity, was moving toward a more heterogeneous society. According to a survey by the Japanese prime minister's office, the number of Japanese who think of themselves as "average," or representative of the masses, was in decline. This trend toward a more diverse society had several effects. In terms of consumption, it appeared as individualism and a strong desire for differentiation. This supposed a greater degree of freedom and creation of one's own sense of values, by choosing one's own way of life. This was directly opposed to traditional Japanese conformity.

WA NO KUTSUROGI SERVICE

Since Japanese guests made up one of the largest segments of HI's total guest profile, an extensive consumer research program was conducted in Japan. The goal was to find out what Japanese customers who traveled internationally wanted HI hotels to provide. The culmination of this research was the devlopment of a Japanese service brand, *Wa No Kutsurogi*, meaning "comfort and service the Japanese way." This program allowed HI to reinforce Hilton market leadership on a global basis, as Japan represented one of the most exciting travel opportunities of the decade. The *Wa No Kutsurogi* service was initially implemented in 43 HI hotels around the world.

The research indicated that the key requirements of Japanese guests were to feel secure, to feel at home, to make the most of their limited time overseas (no time wastage), and to maintain high standards of cleanliness and efficiency. The *Wa No Kutsurogi* program included services "to combine the specific elements of the Japanese service culture with Hilton's renowned style of hospitality," and to apply a "home away from home" Hilton concept to the Japanese market.

Each Hilton hotel operating the *Wa No Kutsurogi* was inspected by local Japanese companies, in order to endorse the hotel's ability to deliver Japanese service. The inspection was done with a checklist given to the Japanese inspector by HI (Exhibit 34-2) and was to be repeated annually with approval shown by a "Certificate of Recognition."

In France, for example, the *Wa No Kutsurogi* service was implemented in the Hilton Paris Suffern, a ten-minute walk from the Japanese owned Nikko Hotel, which was known for its attractiveness to Japanese clientele and which had a full Japanese restaurant. Japanese clientele represented 3 percent of the Hilton's total customer base and was essentially composed of business travelers and groups. The *Wa No Kutsurogi* service was systematically provided to Japanese, but only to those paying full rate. It included the service of Japanese tea in the room, the availability of a *yukata* (a lightweight gown) and Japanese slippers, a receptionist speaking fluent Japanese, and the offering of Japanese meals on the room service menu.

The Hilton Paris Suffern was annually inspected by international Japanese representatives living in Paris, to check the conformity of the program. Fifteen successful inspections were required for the hotel to be part of the program, which guaranteed the maintenance of a network of excellence.

IMPLICATIONS FOR FURTHER PRODUCT INNOVATION

Research conducted specifically to test the reactions of other nationalities to the features of the

HILTON

和のくつろぎ
S E R V I C E

Thank you for taking part in our hotel's site Inspection

Hilton 'Wa No Kutsurogi' Service is a very special programme, and only those hotels which are endorsed by our customers are entitled to participate.

Please tour the hotel to check the availability of the following services and facilities. Simply tick the boxes provided.

If the hotel fulfils these standards, we would be honoured if you would sign the Certificate of Recognition.

Front Desk Services

☐ **Japanese Speaking Staff**
  - *On hand Front of House at peak times*
  - *Available via pager (including 24 hour emergency cover)*
  - *Liaise with local organisations and agencies*

☐ **Safety Deposit Boxes**
  - *Good security*
  - *Easily accessible*
  - *Sufficient quantity*

☐ **JCB Cards welcomed**

Guest Rooms

☐ **Information in Japanese**
  - *Folder with information in Japanese, including hotel directory, room service menu, telephone guide, laundry list and questionnaire*

☐ **Safety Instructions in Japanese**
  - *Fire/evacuation instructions in Japanese on display*

☐ **Telephone Assistance**
  - *Hotel switchboard directs appropriate calls to Japanese speaking staff*
  - *Switchboard has 24 hour rota for all call forwarding*
  - *Japanese speaking staff are equipped with pagers*

☐ **Bottled Still Mineral Water**
  - *Bottled still mineral water available in room*

☐ **Hairdryer**
  - *In the room*

☐ **Handshower**
  - *Facility available (or installation plans underway)*

☐ **Alarm Clock**
  - *In the room or received at check in*

☐ **Newspaper Delivery**
  - *Japanese or English language newspaper available for early morning delivery at specified time*

☐ **Green Tea Service**
  - *Available on request and advertised*

☐ **2 Hour Pressing**
  - *Advertised*

☐ **Twin bedded rooms**
  - *Available*

Food & Beverage

☐ **Oriental Food Selection**
  - *Available at main restaurant*
  - *Available on room service menu*

☐ **Menus in Japanese**
  - *Bilingual menu on request in main restaurant*

☐ **Japanese Drinks**
  - *Available (Includes premium beers)*

Available for Corporate Rate Guests

☐ **Slippers**
  - *Disposable or reusable*

☐ **Bathrobe**
  - *Provided in the room*

☐ **Yukata**
  - *Provided in the room or on request*

E X H I B I T 3 4 - 2   Hilton's *Wa No Kutsurogi* Inspection List

Japanese service brand revealed that Hilton guests generally expect to find a more cosmopolitan mix of people staying in a Hilton than in other international hotels. The degree of acceptance among Hilton guests for subtle forms of customization, based on cultural and/or national characteristics, suggested that there were numerous possibilities for extending, refining, and formulating further service brand variations.

Evidence suggested that economic trading partnerships were growing larger and stronger, and that it would be important to monitor closely the dynamics of changes affecting the international hotel business. The impetus for change, HI felt, would come from the European and Pacific Rim countries, and from the large underdeveloped areas of the world like Latin America and Africa where, in some places, newly liberated economies and people would make a difference in global developments. In this context, HI concentrated on the origin of the guest in order to develop services that meet culturally different needs.

Hilton International caters to customers with more and more different national origins. According to management, the number of guests that cross at least one country border to stay in a Hilton will increase from 51 percent to 75 percent by the year 2000. The implication of this would be that HI would need to continually extend and refine its service branding approach in order to respond to the inevitable cultural transfer that would gather pace in the years ahead.

Before entering the meeting room, Mr. Jardis talked to Geoffrey Breeze about an article he had just read in a global marketing journal. Theodore Levitt, marketing guru at Harvard Business School, stated that:

> Many of today's differences among nations, as to products and their features, actually reflect the respective accommodation of multinational corporations to what they believe are fixed local preferences. They believe preferences are fixed, not because they are, but because of rigid habits of thinking about what actually is. Most executives in multinational corporations are thoughtlessly accommodating. They falsely presume that marketing means giving the customer what he says he wants, rather than trying to understand exactly what he'd like. So they persist with high cost, customized multinational products and practices, instead of pressing hard and pressing properly for global standardization.*

As the meeting was about to start, Geoffrey Breeze thought about this and the importance of his presentation. He knew that it would have a crucial impact on the way Hilton International would market its product toward international customers in the years ahead.

---

*Theodore A. Levitt, "The Globalization of Markets," Harvard Business Review, May/June 1983, pp. 92–102.

C A S E

Thirty-Five

CENTER PARCS FRANCE*

Sitting in an airplane, Mr. Harry Loeffen, the Dutch president of Center Parcs France, was gazing out of the small window at the waters of the channel separating England and France. Mr. Loeffen was on his way back from London, where he had attended the board meeting of Center Parcs International. During the meeting, each country's president was given Center Parcs' objective in regard to profitability and future growth in their country. Mr. Loeffen was given the objective of opening three more Center Parcs in France in order to increase the total number of French parcs to five by the year 2005. Also burning in his mind, was the discussion about whether to take the Center Parcs concept to North America. He hadn't even thought of that one before.

Mr. Loeffen had proudly presented to the board the high performance records of the existing two properties in France, which had been operating at more than 90 percent occupancy. Now his mind was occupied with the challenge before him—to success-

fully expand Center Parcs France. He also recalled the conversation he had had with the president of Center Parcs Germany, his counterpart in that country. Mr. Hormann had mentioned how difficult it was to open Center Parcs in Germany due to stringent government regulations, even though Germans love nature-oriented activities. Mr. Loeffen had never talked to Mr. Hormann before. He honestly didn't know what went on in the German division. Come to think of it, the French division didn't even promote the German Center Parcs.

BACKGROUND

The Center Parcs concept was developed in 1968 by a Dutchman, Mr. Piet Derksen, the founder of a concern called "Sporthuis Centrum." The first village built with the Center Parcs concept, however, didn't open until 1980 in The Netherlands. It was a tropical paradise called "De Eemhof." The village served as the original of which 13 carbon copies had been made in the years that followed. European expansion of the concept began in 1981,

---

*Eizo Morita, Joern Uwe Sroka, Margreet Yntema, and Claire Zwinglestein researched and contributed to this case.

when Center Parcs opened its first village outside The Netherlands, in Belgium.

In 1989, the British brewery company, Scottish & Newcastle, acquired Sporthuis Centrum, including its Center Parcs concept. At that time there were 13 Center Parcs holiday villages. Today, there were still only 14 villages: 6 in The Netherlands, 2 in Belgium, 3 in Great Britain, 1 in Germany, and 2 in France, as shown in Exhibit 35-1. The total number of bungalows, as they were called, was about 9000 units, accommodating over 40,000 guests. All the Center Parcs villages were identical; thus there was no localization of the product.

The opening of the French market in 1988, with a village in Normandy, had not been easy. It had taken the company two years to reach its commercial and financial goals. Mr. Loeffen believed this was partly due to the fact that the market was not ready for such a concept, as the French are "rather conservative and reluctant to try new concepts." The village in Normandy (Les Bois-Francs, 13), however, did become a success, and in 1993 Center Parcs opened a second village in Sologne, France (Les Hauts de Bruyere, 14). Business was so good that the property in Sologne was expanded from 3200 beds to 3700 beds by 1997.

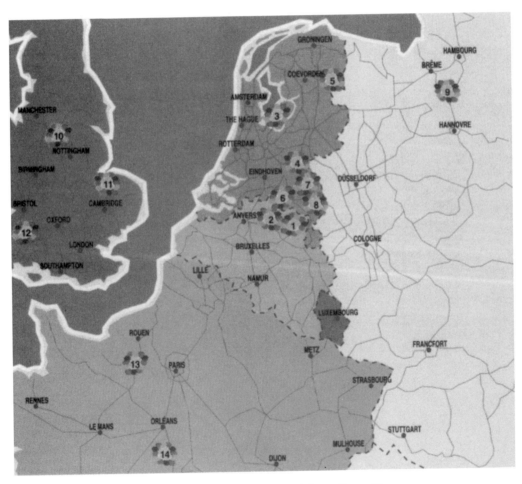

E X H I B I T   3 5 - 1   Locations of Center Parcs villages

THE CENTER PARCS PRODUCT

The Center Parcs concept was unique in Europe. Every village was built on a parcel of between 100 to 300 hectares of woodland and water, not far from a major demand generating area. The land surrounding the buildings had a natural beauty and, should a property not be optimal in its natural resources, Center Parcs planted extra shrubs, trees, and other foliage. Each village consisted of approximately 600 self-contained bungalows of from one to five bedrooms, located within the parc in such a way that no bungalow overlooked another. The most prominent feature of a Center Parcs was a huge glass dome. Inside this dome, Center Parcs built a "tropical paradise" with various water-based activities (artificial wave pool, water slides, etc.), and with an environment consisting of many real tropical plants. The temperature inside the dome was kept at 22 degrees C; the temperature of the water was kept at 29 degrees C. Apart from the water-based activities, Center Parcs also offered a variety of active recreational facilities such as tennis and squash courts and bicycles for rent. In fact, all automobile parking was on the periphery of the site, and bicycles and walking were the only means for getting around inside the village.

Shops and restaurants surrounded the artificial environment of the recreational complexes, with small supermarkets, boutiques, banks, and a range of dining facilities, which varied from fast-food to gourmet. All this together provided a year-round pleasant atmosphere in the foul weather of northern Europe. A list of facilities and activities is shown in Exhibit 35-2, and Exhibit 35-3 shows typical Center Parcs layouts.

CENTER PARCS COST AND PERFORMANCE

The acquisition of Sporthuis Centrum, and thus Center Parcs, by Scottish & Newcastle brought strong financial backing with it. All new Center Parcs were to be built with the equity of Scottish &

Newcastle. With an 85 percent average occupancy rate, a typical Center Parcs village took three years to break even, including preopening costs. A typical village, with all the facilities and infrastructure mentioned and a minimum of 600 bungalows, should take 20 years to amortize the FF 800 million investment.* On average, each Center Parcs had an occupancy of 90 percent after the first few months. The previous year, the two French sites had had an average occupancy of only 87 percent, but next year's forecast was for 90 percent again.

The previous year, the average revenue generated by the two French villages was FF 600 million and the gross operating profit was FF 300 million per site. Of this amount, 54 percent came from the rental fees of the bungalows, and 46 percent from visitors' personal spending for bicycle rentals, food, and so forth.

Center Parcs International intended to expand its operations in Europe by adding one village a year, and was considering expanding outside of Europe. Three new sites were to open in France by 2005. The company's plans were based on certain assumptions, as follows. Today's guest seeks:

- A certain "affective cocooning" (being with family or friends) and convivial service (everything organized, with numerous activities to please the entire party)
- Activities to flee loneliness and to improve self-fulfillment
- A green environment of natural beauty and quiet where he/she can behave like Robinson Crusoe.

The company assumed further that new companies wanting to invest in big resorts will have high capital needs for construction and operation. The break-even point was a critical issue so the property had to be perfectly adapted to market demand. To amortize these investments, high economies of scale needed to be achieved with high volume of sales. Thus, the future resort had to be multiprod-

---

*For conversion purposes use one US\$ = FF 6, one C\$ = FF 4.

The Choice Is Yours...

Each of the following can be found at Longleat, Elveden and Sherwood:

SUBTROPICAL SWIMMING PARADISE INCLUDING:
- FLUMES
- SOLARIUM
- VIEWING AREA
- WAVE MACHINE
- WILD WATER RAPIDS

SANCTUARY IN THE SPA
- FINNISH SAUNA
- PRIVATE POOL
- SAUNA
- TURKISH BATH

HEAD TO TOE HEALTH & BEAUTY AT AQUA SANA INCLUDING:
- AROMATHERAPY MASSAGE
- EYEBROW/EYELASH TINTING
- FACIALS
- FIGURE TREATMENTS
- HAIRDRESSING
- QUICK TAN SUNBEDS
- REFLEXOLOGY
- WAXING

INDOOR SPORTS AND LEISURE FACILITIES
- AEROBICS AND STEP AEROBICS
- BADMINTON
- CHILDREN'S PLAY AREA
- FENCING*
- FITNESS STUDIO
- RACKET BALL
- ROLLERSKATING
- SHORT TENNIS
- SNOOKER
- SQUASH
- TABLE TENNIS
- TENNIS
- TEN PIN BOWLING

OUTDOOR SPORTS AND LEISURE FACILITIES
- BOWLS (SEASONAL)
- CHILDREN'S PLAY AREA
- CLAY PIGEON SHOOTING*#
- CROQUET (SEASONAL)
- CYCLING
- FIELD ARCHERY*#
- FISHING
- FIVE-A-SIDE FOOTBALL

- HORSE RIDING LESSONS*#
- JUNIOR SPORTS HOUR
- NATURE WALK
- PETANQUE/JEU DE BOULES
- PONY TREKKING*#
- PUTTING GREEN (SEASONAL)
- SOCCER COACHING*
- TARGET ARCHERY (SEASONAL)*
- TENNIS
- TOURNAMENTS AND TEAM GAMES
- VOLLEYBALL (SEASONAL)

WATERSPORTS
- CANOEING
- FISHING
- JUNIOR SURF, SAIL AND SKIM
- PEDALOS
- SAILING
- WINDSURFING

RESTAURANTS & BARS INCLUDING:
- CHEZ PIERRE
- COUNTRY CLUB
- COUNTRY PANCAKES
- CRISPINS
- FAMILY RESTAURANT
- LAGOON BAR AND SNACKS
- LE CAPRICE
- LEISURE BOWL
- PIZZERIA/TRATTORIA
- SPORTS BAR

SHOPS
- CHILDSPLAY (CHILDREN'S SHOP)
- PARCMARKET
- SPORTIQUE (SPORTS BOUTIQUE)
- TREATS (SWEET SHOP)
- WINKEL VAN SINKEL (GIFT SHOP)

SERVICES
- BABYSITTING
- BANKING FACILITIES
- KINDERGARTEN (3 - 12 YEAR OLDS)
- LAUNDERETTE
- MEDICAL CENTRE
- 24 HOUR RECEPTION SERVICES

And of course over 400 acres of delightful woodland and meandering waterways.

When you register at Reception you will receive a comprehensive guide called "Making The Most Of Your Stay", giving you full details of the facilities available at your chosen Village, with opening times and prices. There is also an information service available on your television giving you the most up to date information on Village activities.

Please note that all facilities are subject to availability. Please see paragraph 19 on page 42. *These activities may be booked at Leisure Booking Points and are supplied by subcontractors to Center Parcs. # These activities take place outside the Village.

EXHIBIT 35-2   Facilities and activities of a typical Center Parcs Village

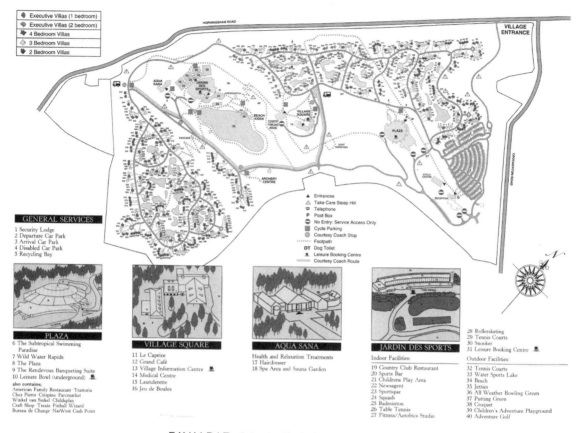

GENERAL SERVICES

1 Security Lodge
2 Departure Car Park
3 Arrival Car Park
4 Disabled Car Park
5 Recycling Bay

PLAZA

6 The Subtropical Swimming Paradise
7 Wild Water Rapids
8 The Plaza
9 The Rendevous Banqueting Suite
10 Leisure Bowl (underground)

also contains:
American Family Restaurant ·Trattoria
Chez Pierre ·Crispins ·Parcmarket
Winkel van Sinkel ·Childsplay
Craft Shop Treats ·Pinball Wizard
Bureau de Change ·NatWest Cash Point

VILLAGE SQUARE

11 Le Caprice
12 Grand Café
13 Village Information Centre
14 Medical Centre
15 Launderette
16 Jeu de Boules

AQUA SANA

Health and Relaxation Treatments
17 Hairdresser
18 Spa Area and Sauna Garden

JARDIN DES SPORTS

Indoor Facilities:
19 Country Club Restaurant
20 Sports Bar
21 Childrens Play Area
22 Newsagent
23 Sportique
24 Squash
25 Badminton
26 Table Tennis
27 Fitness/Aerobics Studio
28 Rollerskating
29 Tennis Courts
30 Snooker
31 Leisure Booking Centre

Outdoor Facilities:
32 Tennis Courts
33 Water Sports Lake
34 Beach
35 Jetties
36 All Weather Bowling Green
37 Putting Green
38 Croquet
39 Children's Adventure Playground
40 Adventure Golf

EXHIBIT 35-3 Typical Center Parcs layout

uct, geared to multimarkets, that is, a diversified product with many activities, indoor and outdoor, with a wide range of prices. To be successful, three markets would have to be targeted: the proximity market including short breaks, the long-stay holiday market, and the residential market.

THE EUROPEAN SHORT BREAK MARKET

The traditional definition of a short break was a trip of one to three nights duration. *The European Travel Monitor,* the only existing pan-Europe survey of western Europe travel trends, showed a 5 percent increase over a five-year period in the volume of trips of one to three nights. Using a wider definition of

short breaks, trips of up to seven nights, the volume of trips had increased by 25 percent over a five-year period. (Exhibit 35-4 shows details by country.) Research showed a trend toward longer short breaks while, at the same time, long holidays were getting shorter. With major travel markets such as France, Germany, and the UK following the short break trend, the total short break market in Europe accounted for some 26 million trips a year, or 17.5 percent of the total holiday market in Europe.*

The German tourism market, with a 600,000 existing client base, accounted for around one-third of the total West Europe tourism volume; thus it generated three and a half times more trips

---

*Reservations at Center Parcs were taken for only one of three time periods: 3 days (Thur–Sun), 4 days (Sun–Thurs), 7 days (Thur–Thur or Sun–Sun).

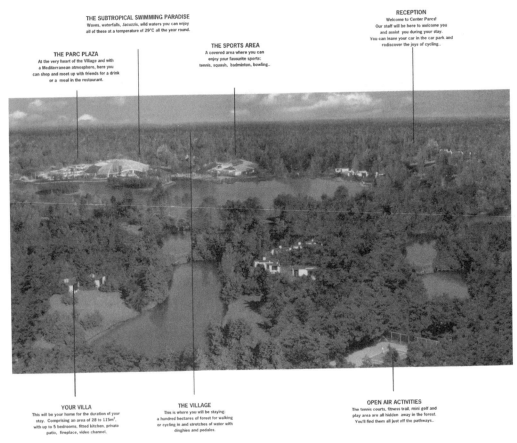

THE SUBTROPICAL SWIMMING PARADISE
Waves, waterfalls, Jacuzzis, wild waters you can enjoy
all of these at a temperature of 29°C all the year round.

RECEPTION
Welcome to Center Parcs!
Our staff will be here to welcome you
and assist you during your stay.
You can leave your car in the car park and
rediscover the joys of cycling..

THE PARC PLAZA
At the very heart of the Village and with
a Mediterranean atmosphere, here you
can shop and meet up with friends for a drink
or a meal in the restaurant.

THE SPORTS AREA
A covered area where you can
enjoy your favourite sports:
tennis, squash, badminton, bowling..

YOUR VILLA
This will be your home for the duration of your
stay. Comprising an area of 28 to 115m²,
with up to 5 bedrooms, fitted kitchen, private
patio, fireplace, video channel.

THE VILLAGE
This is where you will be staying:
a hundred hectares of forest for walking
or cycling in and stretches of water with
dinghies and pedalos.

OPEN AIR ACTIVITIES
The tennis courts, fitness trail, mini golf and
play area are all hidden away in the forest.
You'll find them all just off the pathways..

EXHIBIT 35-3 *(Continued)*

outside the country than the UK, its closest follower. The top countries in volume besides Germany were the UK and Sweden, followed by Belgium, France, and Italy. The major advantage of attracting the short break market was the easing of existing seasonal peaks. Short breaks were mostly taken over the weekends in periods outside school holidays, thus allowing travelers to take advantage of discounted air and rail travel prices.

Destinations

The majority of short breaks were to neighboring countries with adjoining borders. Fifty percent of all trips were taken with private cars, followed by bus and plane. Due to their central location within Europe, and partly due to Germany's high short break volume, France and Austria were Europe's major destinations. The French market was one of the few in Europe that had realized a constant growth in the past five years. Together, all West Europe destinations accounted for 89 percent of the total European short break market. Major destinations for West Europe short breaks (one to three nights) were as follows:

Destination	Percent of Market
France	18
Austria	11
Germany	8
Netherlands	7

**% change in total volume of holidays according to
length of trip in nights**

	1 - 3	4 - 7	Total
Austria	2	42	7
Belgium	-33	18	-11
Denmark	0	22	3
Finland	52	-19	5
France	20	38	6
Germany	16	23	5
Greece	-56	-11	-20
Iceland	-17	4	-30
Ireland	38	-20	-19
Italy	-14	58	42
Netherlands	-44	10	3
Norway	35	37	45
Portugal	-2	26	7
Spain	-21	-12	7
Sweden	-2	-10	-11
Switzerland	66	44	28
UK	16	29	30
Overall	**5**	**25**	**10**

E X H I B I T   3 5 - 4   Five year trends in length of West Europe holiday trips

Destination	Percent of Market
Italy	7
Sweden	6
Denmark	6
Belgium/Luxembourg	5
Switzerland	5
Spain	4
UK	4
Total West Europe	89
Other Mediterranean	2
Eastern Europe	8
Long haul	2
Total	100

Future Trends

The general trend in the West European short break market was toward shorter and smaller packaged tour programs that were booked shortly before the trip, or not pre-booked at all. Mainly in countries such as Germany, UK, Switzerland, and The Netherlands, tailor-made holiday programs and "mix-and-match" programs had gained in popularity. These à la carte programs usually included a choice of the individuals' preferred transport mode. They also had the advantage of catering to individual tastes while usually still being cheaper and easier to purchase than trips that needed to be individually put together. These products could be booked at the last minute, without lengthy preparations, allowing travelers to choose arrival dates and length of stay.

Programs and products of tour operators also had come to include, in addition to city breaks, "Go-As-You-Please" type programs including different types of hotel accommodation and leisure parks, as well as weekends centered around golf and other sporting activities. Some 25 percent of Episodes' (a French short break tour operator) packaged programs for theme park weekends in

France were sold to people living outside of France. Since most new short break products were offered by big tour suppliers, rather than by the independent travel trade and destinations, the connection to well-organized travel agents and reservation systems was becoming more important. According to the travel trade, 50 percent of all short break trips were booked through the travel trade, up from only 25 percent ten years previously, and this percentage was likely to increase further, given the growth in pan-European competition.

Another identified trend was the fact that, although spending of younger people on short breaks had decreased, elderly people had been increasing their spending on short breaks. The building of the channel tunnel between the UK and France further appeared to increase the volume of the short break market, as the UK short break demand for destinations in France had long been an established feature of the UK tour operating scene. The UK region of Dover and the French region of Nord Pas de Calais, which were connected by the tunnel, had agreed upon a mutual plan for regional development, including tourism.

CENTER PARCS IN FRANCE

Young families constituted the core of Center Parcs' clientele. These families were in higher income brackets of the market. The parents were generally aged between 25 and 50 years. Center Parcs also attracted business tourists by hosting seminars and conferences with their meeting facilities. Of the French village visitors, 93 percent were of French origin and, of these, 54 percent were drawn largely from Paris and its surrounding regions. Over 2 million bed nights were spent in Center Parcs France in the previous year. Center Parcs' total number of individual guests in all parcs reached over 3 million, with geographical distribution as follows: 1,100,000 Dutch, 728,000 British, 600,000 German, 472,000 French, 275,000 Belgian, and another 5500 from other countries.

Marketing and Distribution

As there existed no product that was similar to the Center Parcs concept, Center Parcs did not have direct competition. According to Mr. Loeffen, however, all French theme parks, as well as any short break destinations, were indirect competitors.

Each Center Parcs village had an annual communications budget of FF 43 million, which was spent on communicating to their target markets through, primarily, television and radio commercials. These ads provided the customer with a phone number for obtaining a brochure with more detailed information. From the brochure, the prospective French village guest could make a reservation through the central reservations office located in Paris. The total number of brochures printed annually was about one and a half million, resulting in a total of over one half million calls. Twenty-five percent of all calls received in the Paris reservation center resulted in direct reservations.

Although the Paris reservation center could take reservations for Center Parcs villages outside of France, this was not actively promoted by Center Parcs France. Fifty percent of guests came to Center Parcs through their marketing campaigns; the other half came through recommendations of family or friends. This approach permitted Center Parcs to avoid paying commissions to travel agents, who produced only 3 percent of the reservations.

Recent advertising campaigns conducted by Center Parcs France showed that awareness of the Center Parcs concept still needed to be increased. This became apparent when Center Parcs tried a more emotional television theme, which failed due to insufficient product knowledge.

In the past, Center Parcs had counted largely on the quality of its product to retain customers. Since one of the company's goals, however, was to fill up the remaining 10 percent occupancy available, Mr. Loeffen wanted to increase the repeat customer base through guest service improvements. Center Parcs was assessing a change in the check-in procedure that gave repeat guests the key to their cottage right at the entrance of the village thus avoiding a trip to the reception area. Gifts such as pralines and bottles of champagne were also being offered to repeat guests.

STRATEGY AND FUTURE DEVELOPMENT

Center Parcs management was assessing four potential sites for the development of future villages in France. These sites were located in the Bourgogne (near Dijon), the Lorraine (near Strasbourg), the Nord Pas de Calais (near Lille), and the Rhone Alps

area (near Grenoble). For the Rhone Alps area, an adaptation of product to weather conditions was under consideration. Exhibit 35-5 provides demographic details for the different sites, and Exhibit 35-6 shows their locations.

After his arrival back in Paris, Mr. Loeffen decided to organize a meeting with his management team to discuss the issues raised during the London board meeting. Knowing that each Center Parcs investment would cost FF 800 million, he and his executive staff would have to evaluate potential expansion sites with much urgency and come up with a comprehensive plan.

Demographic Data on Selected Regions

Regions	Bougogne	Lorraine	Nord Pas de Calais	Rhone Alpes	France
Habitants	1,613,000	2,305,726	3,965,058	5,350,701	56,555,700
GDP per capita(FF)	121,000	102,228	97,638	N/A	121,988
Industrial Sector as % of GDP					
Industry	25%	28%	27%	N/A	24%
Agriculture	10%	2%	2%	N/A	3%
Services	60%	64%	66%	N/A	68%
Public Works	5%	6%	5%	N/A	5%

Breakdown of Population by Age Group

Age Group	Bougogne	Lorraine	Nord Pas de Calais	Rhone Alpes
0-14	19%	17%	21%	20%
15 -24	16%	17%	23%	15%
25 - 34	16%	18%	14%	15%
35 - 44	15%	12%	14%	15%
45 - 54	10%	7%	8%	11%
55 - 59	5%	4%	5%	5%
60 - 69	10%	15%	8%	10%
70 and +	9%	10%	7%	9%

E X H I B I T   3 5 - 5   Demographic data on selected regions

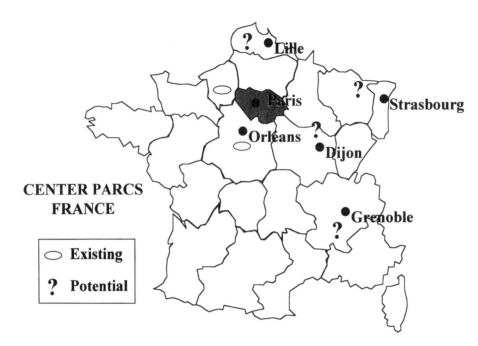

CENTER PARCS FRANCE

⬭ **Existing**

? **Potential**

EXHIBIT 35-6   Location of selected regions

While Mr. Loeffen was walking around the offices, one of his executive staff told him the story of a resort complex located in Kyushu in southern Japan, called Seagaia. This resort not only had pools under a dome, but the dome could be opened and closed. Mr. Loeffen thought that such a concept was amazing and became even more aware of how the resort business was changing.

Perhaps, Mr. Leffen thought, the Center Parcs management in other countries or at headquarters was going through the same thought process and could provide some insight. All issues under consideration in France were applicable to other Center Parcs. If so, he thought, should we work together? We have always operated independently of each other so far. And then there was this North American thing that kept coming to mind, although it was really none of his business.

C A S E

Thirty-Six

❖

TO BE OR NOT TO BE*

Hans Turkel looked out the big picture window of his office on the top floor of the Pigeon Bay Inn, observing the pleasure boats leisurely cruising around Lake Erie. "That's where I should be," he thought, "instead of sitting here trying to figure out which way to go." In fact, his half-million dollar "yacht," moored in the bay, had been there throughout most of the summer, as he wrestled with the decision of how and by whom, this hotel should be managed. Windsor Management, which was bidding for the contract, wanted a decision soon. And Hans wanted to get out of the day-to-day operation of the hotel. Yet, somehow, he couldn't seem to come to a decision.

Pigeon Bay Inn was built in 1989 in Kingsville, Ontario, a small town on Lake Erie. It was the only American Automobile Association four-diamond rated hotel on the Windsor peninsula in southwest Ontario, Canada. This peninsula, except for a nar-

row waterway, bordered the state of Michigan and the city of Detroit, which was directly across the waterway from the city of Windsor.

The hotel had been described as "an elegant car needing a tune-up." When the original owners ran into financial difficulties during construction of the hotel, it had been finished without attention to detail. The hallways, for instance, were poorly lighted, and the hallway ceilings resembled office ceilings. The rooms, on the other hand, had been elegantly finished. Each room had its own character. The bedrooms were furnished with antiques and many had fireplaces, canopy beds, and whirlpool bathtubs. Pigeon Bay boasted an exercise room, sauna, indoor swimming pool, swimex pool (a pool in which guests could swim against a current), whirlpool, and gift shop. It had 137 guestrooms, a restaurant, a lounge, 16 hour a day room service, and 19 function rooms seating 8 to 250 persons. The fine dining room had the capacity to seat about 75 people.

A little over three years ago, Hans Turkel, a private investor who had become wealthy though various real estate deals, along with several "silent" investors, had purchased the hotel when the original owner ran into more financial difficulty. Hans was not a ho-

*Susan E. Menzies researched and contributed to this case. All names and locations have been disguised. All dollar amounts are in Canadian dollars. For conversion purposes use one C$ = U.S.$0.70.

telier, but he assumed the management of the hotel from day one. The many attractions and uniqueness of Kingsville enabled Pigeon Bay to maintain occupancies and rates much higher than the somewhat remote area might indicate. Although he believed the hotel had potential, Hans Turkel thought that the Pigeon Bay projected a sterile atmosphere. He wanted the hotel to establish a distinct personality by embracing the history and ambience of the area. He also believed that the hotel needed to improve guest service and put more emphasis on the service delivery. Most of all, however, Hans Turkel wondered about who should manage the hotel.

THE SITUATION

As of May 1, beginning of the fiscal year, the new owners of Pigeon Bay had contracted Windsor Management Services (WMS) for a limited period to review and run operations. Windsor Management Services was a management company subsidiary of Windsor Hotels and Resorts. It managed hotels both on a temporary basis and long-term basis, with and without the Windsor name. Time constraints and the need for professional management led the investors to hire WMS as an interim manager for the hotel. Now, WMS was urging Hans Turkel to give them a long-term contract or to flag Pigeon Bay as a Windsor hotel, but Hans had his reservations about both ideas.

Pigeon Bay Inn was close to the center of downtown Kingsville, a town of approximately 8000 year-round residents. It overlooked Pigeon Bay and a marina. Situated on Lake Erie, Kingsville was surrounded by the grape-growing and wine-producing region of southwest Ontario. It was about 45 minutes from Windsor, Ontario, 60 minutes from Detroit, and offered convenient summer ferry service to Sandusky, Ohio.

Kingsville was a historic town, the first capital of the Windsor peninsula, and the site of a historic fort and one time battle scenes. Admiral Perry had sailed the waters and anchored in Pigeon Bay. Efforts to preserve the historic beauty of the town were evident in the picturesque old buildings, tree-lined streets, and open park commons. The town bustled with tourists in the summer. Much of the activity centered around one of North America's most famous theater events, the Noel Coward Festival. The Festival was a 30-year tradition in Kingsville. It ran from mid-April to mid-November and brought people from a 300-mile radius.

Although there were various winter activities at the hotels and in the Windsor region during the winter, these activities did not typically attract winter vacationers. Occupancy levels varied by season at Pigeon Bay. June through October was high season; April, May, and November were shoulder seasons; and December through March was low season. The main source of business in the low and shoulder seasons was conferences and groups, which peaked from September through November and, to a lesser extent, between January and May. Although the largest sources of customers were Windsor and Detroit and the rest of the peninsula region, Hans Turkel felt that more of the nearby state of Michigan had the potential for increased business.

MARKETING PIGEON BAY INN

Marketing efforts in the past had focused predominantly on personal selling augmented with print advertising, direct mail, and telephone follow-up. Marketing approaches tended to concentrate on corporate accounts. Most marketing efforts, however, were ad hoc with little strategic thrust. In Hans Turkel's words, "We're order takers." A special events calendar with a critical path, along with various media buys and associated deadlines, was planned on a bimonthly basis. Media selection was typically based on historical knowledge of corporate market buyers (e.g., meeting planners), using media that had worked in the past. A breakdown of market and geographic sources was as follows:

Market Source	Percentage
Corporate/Group Tour	71.5
Referral	8.7
Friend	5.7
Repeat	4.1
Walk-ins	3.0
Other	7.0
Total	100%

Geographic Source	Percentage
Detroit	33.1
Windsor and Southwestern Ontario	27.3
Southern Ontario	10.9
Other Canada	7.5
U.S. nearby states	15.4
Other international	5.8
Total	100%

The corporate market consisted of professional conferences and meetings. Marketing promotion efforts directed at this market included personal sales, advertisements in trade and business publications and directories, familiarization tours, direct marketing efforts, limited trade show activity, offering of corporate rates, and other related activities.

There was little systematic development of this market and its extent and size was unknown. This made it difficult to determine the Inn's market share of conferences and meetings. The extent to which this market used various media sources for choosing a hotel was also unknown. Further, group tours, a separate and distinguishable market, was lumped in with the conference and meeting occupancy figures. This made it difficult to delineate these markets.

Independent travelers or transients made up the balance of the customers. Marketing efforts directed at this target market included brochures, advertisements (primarily in Detroit and Windsor media), and direct mailings of promotional materials. These guests were believed to be upscale, although their demographics had not been established. Customer information collected consisted

of name, address, and telephone number. The extent of repeat business was also unclear and was not recorded in the hotel's database.

Pigeon Bay sold nearly all of its rooms on a package basis to both groups and individual guests. There were some 25 packages. These were also modified by number of guests and room type, creating a total in excess of 400 different packages. This created confusion in the marketplace as well as with reservations and, eventually, check-in.

COMPETITION

Pigeon Bay was the most modern and largest of only four full service hotels in the Kingsville area and had somewhat of a monopoly in the local market. Building site restrictions in Kingsville posed a major barrier to market entry of potential competitors. The hotel's main competition, however, was considered to be those hotels within a two- to three-hour driving distance of Detroit and Windsor that served the small (fewer than 250 people) upscale conference market. Other than hotels in the immediate area, no other specific competitors were identified. Quality comparison of Pigeon Bay, according to its management, with its local competitors is shown in Exhibit 36-1.

WINDSOR HOTELS AND RESORTS

Windsor Hotels and Resorts was a Canadian company that owned and/or managed 23 hotels throughout the country, including one in Windsor, under the Windsor flag. It had also expanded internationally to places like the Caribbean, the Far East, and Orlando, Florida, and had ambitious plans to expand further. Windsor was also a member of Supranational, a representative company with a reservation system for almost 600 hotels in 50 countries with 23 worldwide reservations centers. Windsor's sales network included the largest group

E X H I B I T   36-1
Comparative Ratings of Pigeon Bay Inn and its Local Competitors[a]

	Pigeon Bay Inn	*Old Village Inn*	*King's Ransom Inn*	*Vineyard Inn*
Location	2	3	1	4
Meeting facilities	1	3	4	2
Guestroom product	1	4	2	3
Overall ambience/experience	2	3	1	4
Value	1	3	2	4
Service	1	2	3	4
Total score	8	18	13	21

[a]A ranking of 1 indicates the most favorable; 4 indicates the least favorable.

sales force in metropolitan Detroit, and salespeople in Toronto, Ottawa, Montreal, and Vancouver. As a Windsor flag hotel, Pigeon Bay Inn would be represented at trade shows by Windsor Hotels.

Using the Windsor name would be one means of differentiating Pigeon Bay from its competitors. Windsor was a brand name that many people recognized. Windsor Management Services felt that the Windsor name would be a positive addition to Pigeon Bay's already established reputation. WMS suggested that the hotel could maintain its identity by using the Windsor name as a tag line rather than a prefix, "Pigeon Bay Inn, a Windsor Hotel."

Although there were benefits, there was a price for the services Windsor offered if the hotel was branded as a Windsor. Fees would include a charge of $9.25 for each room booked through the central reservations network. WMS assumed that Windsor would account for 90 percent of transient reservations and that the average length of stay would be 1.5 nights. There would be a once a month charge of $220 for access to Windsor's chain-wide guest history database. The cost charged for Windsor's national sales force would be $420 per room per year, or $4795 per month. Additionally, the Windsor regional, or local, marketing team efforts would incur a charge of $2000 per month. WMS felt that with both the Windsor regional and national sales forces, Pigeon Bay could operate without an outside salesperson and therefore save

$2500 per month. Management fees included a base fee of $7500 per month plus 30 percent of net operating profit remaining after deducting base net profit and base fees, up to 3 percent of gross revenue. Base net profit was set at $1,050,000 the first year (seven months), $2,100,000 the second year, and $2,300,000 each year thereafter. As an independent hotel managed by WMS, but not branded as a Windsor, or using other Windsor services, management fees would be a flat $9000 a month.

WMS proposed that, under Windsor management or a Windsor flag, strategy would be to simplify the package offerings for individuals so that both guests and hotel staff could understand them. They would be reduced to four categories: High Demand, Regular Demand, Low Demand, and Asked For. The first three would vary only on the room rate and could be turned on/off depending on season, day of the week, and demand. The fourth category would include all advertised or published packages which would have a special offering and availability, as well as a room-only offering. Other "added-value" packages would be offered throughout the year.

Another key strategy would be to try to maximize group rooms and group rates during certain periods, but reduce group bookings and go after higher rate transient use in certain other time periods in order to maximize revenue. This, WMS felt, would have the effect of changing the next ten months' (April 30 was the end of the fiscal year) sales mix to that shown in Exhibit 36-2, under WMS management, or to that in Exhibit 36-3, if operated as a Windsor Hotel with a Windsor flag.

If Pigeon Bay were to be a Windsor flagged hotel, WMS felt more substantial change would occur in two key areas that would benefit the hotel and substantially increase revenues and profitability. These two areas were:

Windsor's Reservations Network: The hotel would gain immediate listing in all major airlines reservations systems (currently not accessed), the reservations system of Supranational, as well as access to Windsor's other hotels and their guest referrals. Through the Windsor CRS, guests calling for a reservation would have guaranteed access 24 hours a day, 365 days a year, linked directly to the hotel to ensure sale up to the last room at rates specified by the hotel.

Windsor's Sales Network: Windsor had the largest group sales force in Detroit in addition to its cross-Canada network. These offices were supplemented by sales and marketing specialists in Windsor hotels who maintained contact with all of the major meeting planners and corporate travel managers.

WMS felt that the association with Windsor would increase transient business through the reservations and hotel network, and group business through the sales network, especially in the shoulder and off seasons. Exhibit 36-4 shows the hotel's results from the takeover to the present date. Exhibit 36-5 shows WMS's projections if managed by WMS, and Exhibit 36-6 shows projections if flagged and operated as a Windsor.

A MAJOR DECISION

Privately, Hans Turkel was concerned that Windsor was not suited to managing higher-end hotels like the Pigeon Bay, especially in guest service delivery, as all their hotels were primarily marketed to group tours and the meetings market at low rates.

TOTAL	# SOLD	RATE	REVENUE	PERCENT
HIGH PACKAGE	1,523	155.02	236,099	5.2%
REGULAR PACKAGE	409	120.00	49,080	1.4%
LOW PACKAGE	378	98.28	37,150	1.3%
ASK FOR PACKAGE	1,685	114.38	192,724	5.7%
HIGH RATE	774	155.00	119,970	2.6%
REGULAR RATE	295	130.00	38,350	1.0%
LOW RATE	286	112.71	32,235	1.0%
ASK FOR RATE	870	109.33	95,117	3.0%
GROUP INCENTIVE	295	110.40	32,568	1.0%
GROUP CORP.	12,812	110.35	1,413,846	43.6%
GROUP GOVT.	1,148	93.48	107,319	3.9%
GROUP TOUR	610	116.46	71,041	2.1%
GROUP ASSOC.	3,342	96.25	321,653	11.4%
GROUP OTHER	4,947	106.42	526,450	16.8%
TOTAL	29,374	111.45	3,273,601	100.0%
OCCUPANCY %		67.6%		
PACKAGE	3,995	128.92	515,053	13.6%
RATE	2,225	128.39	285,672	7.6%
GROUP	23,154	106.80	2,472,876	78.8%

EXHIBIT 36-2 Forecasted sales mix with WMS management (June 18–April 30)

TOTAL	# SOLD	RATE	REVENUE	PERCENT
HIGH PACKAGE	1,573	154.70	243,349	5.1%
REGULAR PACKAGE	459	120.00	55,080	1.5%
LOW PACKAGE	378	98.28	37,150	1.2%
ASK FOR PACKAGE	1,935	113.32	219,274	6.3%
HIGH RATE	774	155.00	119,970	2.5%
REGULAR RATE	295	130.00	38,350	1.0%
LOW RATE	286	112.71	32,235	0.9%
ASK FOR RATE	920	108.82	100,117	3.0%
GROUP INCENTIVE	295	110.40	32,568	1.0%
GROUP CORP.	13,312	109.89	1,462,896	43.4%
GROUP GOVT.	1,148	93.48	107,319	3.7%
GROUP TOUR	610	116.46	71,041	2.0%
GROUP ASSOC.	3,342	96.25	321,653	10.9%
GROUP OTHER	5,347	104.75	560,100	17.4%
TOTAL	30,674	110.88	3,401,101	100.0%
OCCUPANCY %		70.6%		
PACKAGE	4,345	127.70	554,853	14.2%
RATE	2,275	127.77	290,672	7.4%
GROUP	24,054	106.24	2,555,576	78.4%

EXHIBIT 36-3 Forecasted sales mix as a Windsor hotel (June 18–April 30)

	FIRST 8 MONTHS		SECOND YEAR		THIRD YEAR		FOURTH (PAST) YEAR	
ROOMS AVAILABLE		32,120		50005		50142		50005
TOTAL OCCUPIED ROOMS		23,126		35004		33564		31360
% TOTAL OCCUPANCY		72.0%		70.0%		66.9%		62.7%
AVERAGE PAID RATE		$122.31		$113.97		$114.41		$110.00
REVENUE:								
ROOMS	2,826	47.73%	3,989	48.82%	3,840	47.62%	3,450	46.98%
FOOD & BEVERAGE	2,552	43.10%	3,521	43.09%	3,570	44.28%	3,246	44.20%
TELEPHONE	74	1.25%	114	1.40%	122	1.51%	118	1.61%
OTHER	469	7.92%	547	6.69%	531	6.59%	530	7.22%
TOTAL REVENUES	5,921	100.00%	8,171	100.00%	8,063	100.00%	7,344	100.00%
OPERATING INCOME:								
ROOMS	2,000	70.77%	3,046	76.36%	3,032	78.96%	2,621	75.96%
FOOD & BEVERAGE	160	6.27%	564	16.02%	924	25.88%	739	22.76%
TELEPHONE	(44)	−59.46%	(11)	−9.65%	9	7.38%	7	5.79%
OTHER	376	80.17%	356	65.08%	299	56.31%	316	59.62%
GROSS OPERATING INCOME	2,492	42.09%	3,955	48.40%	4,264	52.88%	3,682	50.14%
OVERHEAD EXPENSES								
GENERAL & ADMIN.								
ADVERT. & PROMOTION	543	9.17%	722	8.84%	692	8.58%	643	8.76%
REPAIRS & MAINTENANCE	225	3.80%	210	2.57%	538	6.67%	612	8.33%
UTILITIES	200	3.38%	206	2.52%	235	2.91%	288	3.92%
TOTAL OVERHEAD EXPENSES	147	2.48%	246	3.01%	262	3.25%	289	3.94%
GROSS OPERATING PROFIT	1,115	18.83%	1,384	16.94%	1,727	21.42%	1,832	24.95%
TAXES & INSURANCE	1,377	23.26%	2,571	31.46%	2,537	31.46%	1,850	25.19%
HOTEL INCOME (LOSS)	489	8.26%	363	4.44%	401	4.97%	441	6.00%
	888	15.00%	2,208	27.02%	2,136	26.49%	1,409	19.19%

EXHIBIT 36-4 Pigeon Bay Inn as an independent since takeover: historical results (000's)

Regardless, he faced an important decision. He knew it was necessary to assess the pros and cons of (1) hiring Windsor Management Services to run the hotel, (2) continue operating the hotel as an independent, or (3) becoming a Windsor affiliated hotel.

It was hard to determine in which direction to proceed, but Hans Turkel knew he should look to the future. He wanted to do what was necessary to maintain the hotel's currently favorable situation. Either a WMS management contract or a Windsor flag would solve a lot of problems. On the other hand, he liked the idea of being a full independent and he didn't like paying management fees. And then there was that boat out there! Hans had to make a decision soon among the three alternatives as Windsor management had requested an early decision.

	FACTOR	JUNE	JULY	AUG	SEPT	OCT	NOV	DEC	JAN	FEB	MAR	APR	TOTAL	%
TOTAL PAID OCCUPIED		1453	3724	3783	3998	3608	2843	1232	1848	1975	2150	2760	29374	
WAGES AND BENEFITS														
WAGES	13.50%	2664	7305	10184	10184	10184	10184	10184	10184	10184	10184	10184	101625	23.04%
BENEFITS		440	1033	1375	1375	1375	1375	1375	1375	1375	1375	1375	13847	3.14%
TOTAL WAGES AND BENEFITS		3104	8338	11559	11559	11559	11559	11559	11559	11559	11559	11559	115472	26.18%
OPERATING EXPENSES														
ADVERTISING		14395	21084	9360	9360	9360	9360	9360	9360	9360	9360	9360	119716	27.14%
ASSOCIATION DUES		0	295	397	397	397	397	397	397	397	397	397	3868	0.88%
BROCHURES		0	1718	2222	2222	2222	2222	2222	2222	2222	2222	2222	21716	4.92%
COLLATERAL		0	0	5889	5889	5889	5889	5889	5889	5889	5889	5889	53001	12.02%
CONTRACT LABOUR		93	0	167	167	167	167	167	167	167	167	167	1596	0.36%
DONATIONS		0	0	200	200	200	200	200	200	200	200	200	1800	0.41%
ENTERTAINMENT		0	0	600	600	600	600	600	600	600	600	600	5400	1.22%
ENTERTAINMENT MGMNT		0	0	600	600	600	600	600	600	600	600	600	5400	1.22%
DIRECT MAIL		0	0	2056	2056	2056	2056	2056	2056	2056	2056	2056	18504	4.20%
F & B MARKETING		193	500	1497	1497	1497	1497	1497	1497	1497	1497	1497	14166	3.21%
DRY CLEANING		0	0	250	250	250	250	250	250	250	250	250	2250	0.51%
LOCAL ADVERTISING		1692	4684	0	0	0	0	0	0	0	0	0	6376	1.45%
PRINTING & STATIONARY		0	0	350	350	350	350	350	350	350	350	350	3150	0.71%
PROMOTION MANAGEMENT		3323	5802	3695	3695	3695	3695	3695	3695	3695	3695	3695	42380	9.61%
SIGNS ON PREMISES		0	13	100	100	100	100	100	100	100	100	100	913	0.21%
SIGNS OFF PREMISES		0	0	200	200	200	200	200	200	200	200	200	1800	0.41%
TELEPHONE		0	338	400	400	400	400	400	400	400	400	400	3938	0.89%
TRADE SHOWS		0	0	772	772	772	772	772	772	772	772	772	6948	1.58%
TRAVEL & AUTO		0	0	1411	1411	1411	1411	1411	1411	1411	1411	1411	12699	2.88%
TOTAL OPERATING EXPENSES		19696	34434	30166	30166	30166	30166	30166	30166	30166	30166	30166	325621	73.82%
TOTAL ADVERTISING & PROMO		22800	42772	41725	41725	41725	41725	41725	41725	41725	41725	41725	441093	100.00%

EXHIBIT 36-5   Pigeon Bay Inn projections if managed by WMS (a) June 18–April 30 monthly advertising and promotion budget

	JUNE 18 TO APRIL 30 1st Year (317 Days)		MAY TO APRIL Year 2		MAY TO APRIL Year 3		MAY TO APRIL Year 4		MAY TO APRIL Year 5	
ROOMS AVAILABLE	43429		50005		50142		50005		50005	
PAID ROOMS OCCUPIED	29374		35004		36102		36004		36004	
% PAID OCCUPANCY	67.6%		70.0%		72.0%		72.0%		72.0%	
AVERAGE PAID RATE	$111.45		$114.96		$118.41		$121.96		$125.62	
REVENUE:										
ROOMS	3,276,002	47.68%	4,024,002	47.70%	4,274,823	47.70%	4,391,037	47.70%	4,522,768	47.70%
FOOD AND BEVERAGE	3,337,304	48.57%	4,096,202	48.56%	4,351,523	48.56%	4,469,823	48.56%	4,603,918	48.56%
TELEPHONE	72,490	1.06%	88,974	1.05%	94,520	1.05%	97,089	1.05%	100,002	1.05%
GIFT SHOP	119,267	1.74%	146,388	1.74%	155,512	1.74%	159,740	1.74%	164,532	1.74%
OTHER	65,374	0.95%	80,241	0.95%	85,242	0.95%	87,559	0.95%	90,186	0.95%
TOTAL REVENUES	6,870,437	100.00%	8,435,807	100.00%	8,961,620	100.00%	9,205,249	100.00%	9,481,406	100.00%
OPERATING INCOME:										
ROOMS	2,495,824	76.19%	3,098,482	77.00%	3,312,988	77.50%	3,403,054	77.50%	3,505,146	77.50%
FOOD AND BEVERAGE	814,221	24.40%	1,024,051	25.00%	1,109,638	25.50%	1,139,805	25.50%	1,173,999	25.50%
TELEPHONE	(3,712)	-5.12%	4,449	5.00%	4,726	5.00%	4,854	5.00%	5,000	5.00%
GIFT SHOP	32,623	27.35%	39,525	27.00%	41,988	27.00%	43,130	27.00%	44,424	27.00%
OTHER	52,335	80.05%	64,192	80.00%	68,194	80.00%	70,048	80.00%	72,149	80.00%
GROSS OPERATING INCOME	3,391,291	49.36%	4,230,698	50.15%	4,537,534	50.63%	4,660,891	50.63%	4,800,717	50.63%
OVERHEAD EXPENSES										
GENERAL & ADMIN.	429,071	6.25%	505,753	6.00%	520,925	5.81%	536,553	5.83%	552,650	5.83%
MANAGEMENT FEE (a)	124,789	1.82%	108,000	1.28%	108,000	1.21%	108,000	1.17%	108,000	1.14%
ADVERT. & PROMOTION	441,093	6.42%	522,256	6.19%	537,924	6.00%	554,061	6.02%	570,683	6.02%
REPAIRS & MAINTENANCE	214,727	3.13%	255,358	3.03%	263,019	2.93%	270,909	2.94%	279,037	2.94%
UTILITIES	247,039	3.60%	293,524	3.48%	302,330	3.37%	311,400	3.38%	320,742	3.38%
TOTAL OVERHEAD EXPENSES	1,456,718	21.20%	1,684,891	19.97%	1,732,198	19.33%	1,780,924	19.35%	1,831,111	19.31%
GROSS OPERATING PROFIT	1,934,573	28.16%	2,545,807	30.18%	2,805,337	31.30%	2,879,967	31.29%	2,969,606	31.32%
OTHER EXPENSES										
TAXES	362,204	5.27%	416,278	4.93%	428,766	4.78%	441,629	4.80%	454,878	4.80%
INSURANCE	19,750	0.29%	22,378	0.27%	23,049	0.26%	23,741	0.26%	24,453	0.26%
TOTAL OTHER EXPENSES	381,954	5.56%	438,655	5.20%	451,815	5.04%	465,369	5.06%	479,331	5.06%
OPERATING PROFIT	1,552,619	22.60%	2,107,152	24.98%	2,353,521	26.26%	2,414,598	26.23%	2,490,275	26.26%
NON-OPERATING EXPENSES	240	0.00%	0	0.00%	0	0.00%	0	0.00%	0	0.00%
HOTEL INCOME (LOSS)	1,552,379	22.60%	2,107,152	24.98%	2,353,521	26.26%	2,414,598	26.23%	2,490,275	26.26%

(a) WMS management fee of $9000 per month
Note: Three percent inflation rate assumed

EXHIBIT 36-5   Pigeon Bay Inn projections if managed by WMS (b) Five year projections if managed by WMS

	FACTOR	JUNE	JULY	AUG	SEPT	OCT	NOV	DEC	JAN	FEB	MAR	APR	TOTAL	%
TOTAL PAID OCCUPIED		1453	3724	3783	3998	3608	2993	1382	2098	2125	2450	3060	30674	
WAGES AND BENEFITS														
WAGES	13.50%	2664	7305	10184	10184	7684	7684	7684	7684	7684	7684	7684	84125	18.17%
BENEFITS		440	1033	1375	1375	1037	1037	1037	1037	1037	1037	1037	11484	2.48%
TOTAL WAGES AND BENEFITS		3104	8338	11559	11559	8721	8721	8721	8721	8721	8721	8721	95609	20.65%
OPERATING EXPENSES														
ADVERTISING		14395	21084	9360	9360	9360	9360	9360	9360	9360	9360	9360	119716	25.85%
ASSOCIATION DUES		0	295	397	397	397	397	397	397	397	397	397	3868	0.84%
NATIONAL SALES & MRKTG (a)		0	0	0	0	4680	4680	4680	4795	4795	4795	4795	33220	7.17%
DATA BASE MARKETING (b)		0	0	0	0	220	220	220	220	220	220	220	1540	0.33%
REGIONAL OFFICE (c)		0	0	0	0	2000	2000	2000	2000	2000	2000	2000	14000	3.02%
BROCHURES		0	1718	2222	2222	2222	2222	2222	2222	2222	2222	2222	21716	4.69%
COLLATERAL		0	0	5889	5889	5889	5889	5889	5889	5889	5889	5889	53001	11.45%
CONTRACT LABOUR		93	0	167	167	167	167	167	167	167	167	167	1596	0.34%
DONATIONS		0	0	200	200	200	200	200	200	200	200	200	1800	0.39%
ENTERTAINMENT		0	0	600	600	600	600	600	600	600	600	600	5400	1.17%
ENTERTAINMENT MGMNT		0	0	600	600	600	600	600	600	600	600	600	5400	1.17%
DIRECT MAIL		0	0	2056	2056	2056	2056	2056	2056	2056	2056	2056	18504	4.00%
F & B MARKETING		193	500	1497	1497	1497	1497	1497	1497	1497	1497	1497	14166	3.06%
DRY CLEANING		0	0	250	250	250	250	250	250	250	250	250	2250	0.49%
LOCAL ADVERTISING		1692	4684	0	0	0	0	0	0	0	0	0	6376	1.38%
PRINTING & STATIONARY		0	0	350	350	350	350	350	350	350	350	350	3150	0.68%
PROMOTION MANAGEMENT		3323	5802	3695	3695	3695	3695	3695	3695	3695	3695	3695	42380	9.15%
SIGNS ON PREMISES		0	13	100	100	100	100	100	100	100	100	100	913	0.20%
SIGNS OFF PREMISES		0	0	200	200	200	200	200	200	200	200	200	1800	0.39%
TELEPHONE		0	338	400	400	400	400	400	400	400	400	400	3938	0.85%
TRADE SHOWS		0	0	0	0	0	0	0	0	0	0	0	0	0.00%
TRAVEL & AUTO		0	0	1411	1411	1411	1411	1411	1411	1411	1411	1411	12699	2.74%
TOTAL OPERATING EXPENSES		19696	34434	29394	29394	36294	36294	36294	36409	36409	36409	36409	367433	79.35%
TOTAL ADVERTISING & PROMO		22800	42772	40953	40953	45015	45015	45015	45130	45130	45130	45130	463042	100.00%

(a) Includes $4,795 per month for national sales force, starting in January
(b) Includes $ 220 per month for access to guest history database
(c) Includes $2,000 per month for regional sales force

E X H I B I T   3 6 - 6   Pigeon Bay Inn as a Windsor hotel brand (a) June 18–April 30 monthly advertising and promotion budget

	JUNE 18 TO APRIL 30 1st Year (317 Days)		MAY TO APRIL Year 2		MAY TO APRIL Year 3		MAY TO APRIL Year 4		MAY TO APRIL Year 5	
ROOMS AVAILABLE	43429		50005		50142		50005		50005	
PAID ROOMS OCCUPIED	30674		36254		37105		37504		37504	
% PAID OCCUPANCY	70.6%		72.5%		74.0%		75.0%		75.0%	
AVERAGE PAID RATE	$110.88		$118.00		$121.54		$125.19		$128.94	
REVENUE:										
ROOMS	3,403,502	47.60%	4,277,928	48.40%	4,509,751	48.40%	4,694,952	48.40%	4,835,801	48.40%
FOOD AND BEVERAGE	3,480,756	48.68%	4,237,326	47.94%	4,466,950	47.94%	4,650,392	47.94%	4,789,904	47.94%
TELEPHONE	75,675	1.06%	92,123	1.04%	97,115	1.04%	101,104	1.04%	104,137	1.04%
GIFT SHOP	124,532	1.74%	151,600	1.72%	159,815	1.72%	166,378	1.72%	171,370	1.72%
OTHER	65,694	0.92%	79,973	0.90%	84,307	0.90%	87,769	0.90%	90,402	0.90%
TOTAL REVENUES	7,150,159	100.00%	8,838,950	100.00%	9,317,938	100.00%	9,700,595	100.00%	9,991,613	100.00%
OPERATING INCOME:										
ROOMS (a)	2,619,751	76.97%	3,315,394	77.50%	3,495,057	77.50%	3,638,588	77.50%	3,747,745	77.50%
FOOD AND BEVERAGE	885,047	25.43%	1,084,755	25.60%	1,143,539	25.60%	1,190,500	25.60%	1,226,215	25.60%
TELEPHONE	(2,362)	-3.12%	4,606	5.00%	4,856	5.00%	5,055	5.00%	5,207	5.00%
GIFT SHOP	35,083	28.17%	40,629	26.80%	42,830	26.80%	44,589	26.80%	45,927	26.80%
OTHER	52,323	79.65%	63,818	79.80%	67,277	79.80%	70,039	79.80%	72,141	79.80%
GROSS OPERATING INCOME	3,589,842	50.21%	4,509,203	51.02%	4,753,559	51.02%	4,948,772	51.02%	5,097,235	51.02%
OVERHEAD EXPENSES										
GENERAL & ADMIN.	432,574	6.05%	509,362	5.76%	524,643	5.63%	540,382	5.57%	556,593	5.57%
MANAGEMENT FEE (b)	92,289	1.29%	166,693	1.89%	161,279	1.73%	200,082	2.06%	215,698	2.16%
ADVERT. & PROMOTION	463,042	6.48%	552,000	6.25%	568,560	6.10%	585,617	6.04%	603,185	6.04%
REPAIRS & MAINTENANCE	214,812	3.00%	255,446	2.89%	263,110	2.82%	271,003	2.79%	279,133	2.79%
UTILITIES	261,187	3.65%	308,096	3.49%	317,339	3.41%	326,859	3.37%	336,664	3.37%
TOTAL OVERHEAD EXPENSES	1,463,904	20.47%	1,791,597	20.27%	1,834,930	19.69%	1,923,942	19.83%	1,991,274	19.93%
GROSS OPERATING PROFIT	2,125,939	29.73%	2,717,606	30.75%	2,918,630	31.32%	3,024,830	31.18%	3,105,961	31.09%
OTHER EXPENSES										
TAXES	362,204	5.07%	416,278	4.71%	428,766	4.60%	441,629	4.55%	454,878	4.55%
INSURANCE	19,750	0.28%	22,378	0.25%	23,049	0.25%	23,741	0.24%	24,453	0.24%
TOTAL OTHER EXPENSES	381,954	5.34%	438,655	4.96%	451,815	4.85%	465,369	4.80%	479,331	4.80%
OPERATING PROFIT	1,743,985	24.39%	2,278,951	25.78%	2,466,814	26.47%	2,559,460	26.38%	2,626,631	26.29%
NON-OPERATING EXPENSES	240	0.00%	0	0.00%	0	0.00%	0	0.00%	0	0.00%
HOTEL INCOME (LOSS)	1,743,745	24.39%	2,278,951	25.78%	2,466,814	26.47%	2,559,460	26.38%	2,626,631	26.29%

(a) includes central reservation fee of $9.25 per room booked (estimated)
(b) includes base fee of $7500 per month plus 30% of net profit (estimated)
Note: Three percent inflation rate assumed

EXHIBIT 36 - 6   Pigeon Bay Inn as a Windsor hotel brand (b) Five year projections if flagged as a Windsor

Thirty-Seven

$\bullet \blacklozenge \bullet$

LETTER TO THE EXECUTIVE VICE PRESIDENT

Mr. John Sharpe,
Executive Vice President, Operations
Four Seasons Hotels Limited,
Toronto, Ontario M5S 9Z9

Dear Mr. Sharpe:

I was pleased to stay at the Four Seasons in downtown Toronto the night of March 3. As I would have expected, treatment was beyond reproach and the entire staff was not only friendly and helpful, but totally efficient. After all, this is the Four Seasons reputation.

As the hotel industry, however, continues to put more and more emphasis on service, service, service, I sometimes find that little nuances that don't show up on guest comment cards, or are not significant enough to "complain" about, make a considerable difference in a guest stay. (I still call them service albeit without personal contact.) In fact, in this case, had I been staying longer I would have picked up the telephone and, I'm sure, all would have been rapidly corrected. As you well know,

most guests don't complain; they simply don't come back. Of course, much of this comes from the high expectations that one has when staying at a Four Seasons. So, I thought I would pass on to you how Four Seasons failed to meet my expectations on a one night stay.

The room, 2707, was large, delightful, understated and in excellent taste, on a corner with two large windows. In front of one window, a perfect place for reading, was a coffee table and *one* comfortable chair. There was plenty of room for a second chair but one of us had to use the not-so-comfortable desk chair to sit there, much to our surprise. The overhead light had a lightbulb missing, and the total wattage made reading somewhat difficult. The desk light had two 60 watt bulbs, better than too many hotel rooms that have only one, but two 75s or 100s would have been far preferable for someone doing close work, or with 60 year old eyes.

I have read somewhere that Four Seasons was the first to introduce shampoo to bathroom amenity packages. My own research has shown me that people, especially women, are very reluctant to put a shampoo in their hair when they don't know what it is. Generic shampoos are out, brand names are in, and a no-name is a surprise at any first-class hotel.

I am a regular sauna user and can easily stay 20 minutes or better in a sauna at usual temperatures of 160–200 degrees Farenheit. But 230 degrees drove me out in five minutes and there was no control to change it. I have only seen a sauna that hot once before, and that was in Bangkok where the sauna was also empty in spite of the large contingent of Japanese using the health club.

Yours truly,

Phyllis Spooner

Thirty-Eight

❖

THE HOLIDAY INN COMMENT CARD

Your hotel is somewhat run-down, to say the least. It is tired and tawdry. You should really do something about it as I, for one, will not return. Especially bad are those old bedspreads, which are straight out of the '60s, not to mention being torn and soiled. Also, your coffee is horrible! This has nothing to do with the '60s because there is certainly better coffee on the market today. I would expect better from a Holiday Inn.

Dorothy Rupert
222 Main Street
Fargo, North Dakota

CASE
Thirty-Nine
◆•◆

WINNING BACK THE CUSTOMER*

For four years, the 438-room Somerset Hotel hosted the training meetings of ABC Pharmaceutical Company. These meetings were held throughout the calendar year for periods of one to three weeks, as ABC trained its salespeople, and had some very specific requirements, as shown in Exhibit 39-1. For the Somerset this business represented some 4000 room nights a year plus ancillary business that came from other divisions of ABC. Thus, the Somerset sales department was shocked to learn that ABC was going to take its next year's business to the Hilton Hotel nearby.

Mike Fornolo, director of sales, immediately tried to establish the reason for this defection. Although the reason was never made totally clear, Mike learned that there had been some billing mistakes, that ABC had found it a hassle to get them corrected, and that some of them had continued to occur. ABC also seemed to feel that, given the volume of business, Somerset's rates were too high.

Finally, ABC seemed to have the impression that Somerset management and staff had come to take the business of ABC for granted after the first two years. ABC felt their trainees were treated like second-class citizens, and that there was poor response to problems.

After a year at the Hilton, ABC took its business to the nearby Holiday Inn, indicating there must have been some dissatisfaction at the Hilton. Mike Fornolo decided to make another try for the business and visited the ABC sales training director, Mr. Smith, to determine his needs. In September Mike made a proposal to ABC, as shown in Exhibit 39-2. After delivering the proposal, Mike called Mr. Smith three times, but no calls were returned. On the fourth call he spoke to Mr. Smith, who denied receiving the messages that Mike had called. He told Mike that ABC was returning to the Hilton, that he did not feel that the Somerset was truly interested in the business, and that the rate was unrealistic based on the volume of business.

In March of the following year, Audrey Haywood became a sales manager at the Somerset and took over the ABC account. At that time Audrey called ABC to introduce herself, told them

*The details of this case were contributed by Susan Morris when she was Director of Marketing at the Somerset Hotel. Names have been disguised.

EXHIBIT 39-1
Corporate Training School Characteristics

- Dates are committed and rates negotiated in the fall for the following year.
- Number of trainees each session ranges from 8 to 20 individuals.
- Guestrooms are often double occupancy and need to be clustered together near a study/hospitality room.
- Trainees tend to be young, single, aggressive, athletic, mix of male and female.
- Proximity of the hotel to the company's training facility, where the training is actually conducted, and means of transportation to the facility are very important.
- Expenses are paid for by the company, which tends to be very price sensitive.
- There are minimal catering requirements.

that ABC had been the Somerset's first major client and would never be taken for granted. Until August, Audrey had various contacts with Mr. Smith at other meetings at the Somerset that he attended.

In August, Audrey received a message to call ABC regarding bidding for the next year's business. Her account activity log for the rest of the year read as follows.

August 6	Left message to call me back.
August 9	Set up appointment with Jones, #2 person. Told me they were taking bids from Somerset, Hilton, Holiday Inn, and Ramada.
August 10	Met with Jones. Reviewed needs of ABC. Discussed benefits of Somerset. Had "good vibes."
August 12	Delivered proposal for Jones (Exhibit 39-3). Neither Smith nor Jones available to see me.

EXHIBIT 39-2
New proposal for ABC Business by Mike Fornolo

Dear Mr. Smith:

Thank you for your time at your office the other day. I appreciate your filling me in on ABC Company's training needs for next year. We at the Somerset are very excited about the possibility of hosting your next year's sales training program. At this time I can offer you the following:

Sleeping Rooms: $99.00 per room per night (single or double) for your sales training program.
For your relocating managers: $90.00 per room, per night, based on a minimum stay of 14 consecutive nights.
Study center/work room: $95.00 per day

As I mentioned at your office, we would be able to offer your in-house trainees a discount in our restaurant, but we can discuss that further at a later date.

Mr. Smith, this is purely a "nuts and bolts" proposal that I do not feel fully describes how much the Somerset and I want to be your host next year. I can personally commit to you that my hotel will do the best job for you, for your people, and for your company. I would like to have ABC Company training business come back. Hopefully, you will give us a chance.

If you have any further questions or concerns, please do not hesitate to call. I look forward to speaking with you again.

Yours truly,
Somerset Hotel
Michael Fornolo, Director of Sales

EXHIBIT 39-3
New Proposal for ABC Business by Audrey Haywood

Dear Mr. Jones:

It was a pleasure to meet with you recently regarding the possibility of the Somerset Hotel hosting the ABC Company sales training schools next year. Thank you very much for inviting us to bid for your training program. In reponse to your requests, there are several objectives that I would like to address:

Objective 1: To provide an environment conducive to the training schools while keeping the costs reasonable.

Somerset Hotels are well-renowned for their excellence, both in terms of the quality of our facilities and the level of service we provide. This Somerset Hotel is no exception. To assist you in maintaining the budget designated for the training schools, we are pleased to extend the following rates:

Single/double occupancy: $95.00 (regularly $127/$142)
Resource room: $95.00 (regularly $129)
As you can see, we are offering ABC a very significant discount.

I understand that, upon occasion, there are ABC Company managers who are relocating to this area. We are glad to extend a $95.00 rate to these individuals (minimum stay: 30 days).

Objective 2: A hassle-free training school that flows smoothly.

It is our ambition to look after all the logistics of the training schools so that you may focus on the purpose of the training. We will assure that the following details are looked after.

1. Welcome letters explaining the services and facilities available to attendees are presented on check-in (sample enclosed).
2. Wake-up calls are timely.
3. Messages and mail are received promptly.
4. Attendees' rooms are located in the vicinity of the resource room.
5. Bills are presented in a comprehensive format and on a timely basis.

Recognizing that this is a problem that you have encountered in the past, I have enclosed a sample Master Bill. Please note that we provide a one page summary of the room, tax, and incidentals incurred by each attendee.

Objective 3: Treat the attendees like VIPs.

Your attendees will feel very well accommodated in our guestrooms. The rooms have two double beds as well as radios, alarm clocks, HBO, in-room movies, climate control, and spacious washrooms.

Attendees may have breakfast in our bright and cheery King's Wharf Restaurant or enjoy a light, continental breakfast in our lounge. Both breakfast and dinner menus are enclosed so that you may see the variety and the low prices that are offered.

Recognizing that there will be opportunity for those attending the training schools to relax, we offer several alternatives. At the end of the day, attendees may soothe their weary muscles or do a full work-out in our Health Club complete with exercise rooms, hydrotherapy pool, and saunas. We also have an indoor/outdoor pool, shuffle board, and two tennis courts that are lit at night. For those looking for a different kind of relaxation, there is nightly entertainment in our Main Brace lounge.

Bob, we hope that this letter has given you an indication of how we at the Somerset Hotel can help you make next year's training schools the most successful yet. We trust that we will receive your utmost consideration and look forward to a favorable reply. If everything meets with your approval, please sign and return the enclosed copy of the proposal to my attention no later than August 31.

We are hopeful of establishing a long-term relationship between the Somerset and ABC Company. I hope to meet with you to further discuss our proposal. In the meantime, if you have any questions or concerns, please give me a call.

Best regards,
Somerset Hotel

Audrey Haywood, Sales Manager
cc: A. Smith, Director of Sales Training

August 13	Telephoned to see if proposal received and if any questions/concerns. Neither one available.
August 14	Dropped off Somerset signature chocolates, postcard, and notes. Neither one available.
August 17	Left message to call back.
August 19	Left message to call back.
August 28	Found out from Jones that business was going to Hilton. Basically, they felt that all was going well there, so why change?
September 4	Sent follow-up letter to Jones and received note from Smith (Exhibit 39-4). Thoughts: ABC unwilling to take risk? What incentive or motivation can we offer? Do they have trust in Audrey Haywood? Do they have trust in Somerset?
December 18	Sent Christmas card to Smith.

The next year, Audrey Haywood, now director of sales for the Somerset, renewed her efforts. Her account activity log reported the following.

August 18	Met with Smith re the next year's bid for business. When I mentioned our rate quotes for the two previous years, he was surprised and actually checked his files. He had the impression they were higher. He stated that his goal for trainees was to ensure they would be able to rest, enjoy, and have a hassle-free stay.
August 25	Delivered proposal. Same as previous year except raised rate $1.00. Competition has changed with the introduction of Embassy Suites to the scene.
September 6	Called to find out decision.
September 12	Left message.
September 16	Smith called to say that they had chosen Embassy, liked size of the rooms. (Note: Embassy rooms have a bedroom and sitting room so that two people sharing have some privacy. Price is the same as standard hotel room. Amenities include two televisions, VCR, refrigerator, sink, and microwave. Room rate includes breakfast and evening cocktail reception but Smith says not interested in these. Drawbacks are one restaurant, one lounge with no entertainment or dancing. Room service hours restricted. Health club facilities and hours very limited. All bills are generated in Atlanta so local hotel cannot respond to problems efficiently. No washers or dryers for guest use, no bell staff, no telephone operators, no concierge.)
November 18	Sent Thanksgiving card.
December 16	Sent Christmas card.

The following year, Audrey Haywood's account activity log recorded the following.

March 7	Called Smith and he actually answered his telephone! Strange

---

E X H I B I T   3 9 - 4
Handwritten Note Received from Mr. Smith

Audrey—Thank you very much for the Somerset Chocolates! A beautiful touch. I'm sure that by now you're aware we will not be using your facilities next year for our schools but appreciate all your efforts and attention to detail in this regard. Thanks again—Andrew Smith

---

conversation. Said he didn't understand why I bothered calling him; it was obvious we did not need his business; our quotes were totally out of line (I repeated quotes of $95 and $96 and asked if that was out of line); accused me of trying to find out what he was paying at Embassy; was surprised by our rates, thought they were higher; thought all of ABC's business (we host other meetings) should be pulled out of Somerset.

March 8   Sent Smith letter of response (Exhibit 39-5)

April 11   Smith's secretary booked a meeting at Somerset for June because, she said, we have hosted similar meetings, successfully, for sister companies of ABC. Smith not involved in planning this.

June 13   Meeting went well. Spoke to Smith 2–3 times. At one point he said, "You really want my business, don't you?" After the meeting, called and sent him a letter requesting feedback. Silence.

July 15   Sister company to ABC, whose business we did host, informed me that parent company was pressuring them to use Hyatt, which was owned by parent company. Double the commute time from their facilities, didn't want to go there. I offered price incentive to stay at Somerset, offered to provide even lower rate if both companies came to Somerset. This put a different slant on bidding process and the competition.

October 17   Going to Hyatt next year.

EXHIBIT 39-5
Follow-Up Letter to Phone Call

Dear Mr. Smith:

Just a note to say thanks for the time you extended me on the telephone recently as we discussed the ABC Company sales schools. I am pleased that the Embassy Suites is working out well for you. They really do have a great product, especially the oversized rooms, which provide trainees with a little more breathing space. Maybe we need to start knocking down walls at the Somerset!

I was disappointed to hear that you have the impression that the Somerset does not want your business. It is difficult not to take your comments personally, as I feel that I have worked very hard for the last two years to get to know the needs of the sales schools and to put together proposals that respond to those needs. You mentioned that our pricing has not been in the same ballpark as other hotels. I have enclosed copies of our bids for the last two years. . . . I did not realize that our quotes of $99.00 and $95.00 were out of line.

Mr. Smith, I would like to apologize if you found my efforts to be overzealous, or if I have in any way led you to think that the Somerset does not want your business. Quite to the contrary, I have tried to show our enthusiasm by keeping in touch with you, putting together competitive proposals, and demonstrating our service by assuring that the ABC Company management meetings go off without a hitch.

I would like to request that you keep us on your list of hotels to be considered for next year's sales training schools. I have not given up hope that one of these years, you and I will sign a contract together.

In the meantime, if I can be of assistance, I am at your service.

Best regards,

Somerset Hotel
Audrey Haywood, Director of Sales

C A S E

Forty

◆

WAS IT WORTH IT?*

The Grand Canyon Hotel in Palm Springs, California suffered, as did all Palm Springs hotels, during the summer off-season. To a lesser degree, occupancy was also low during the shoulder seasons of spring and fall. Unlike some Palm Springs hotels, the Grand Canyon stayed open during these periods and did the best it could with the market it could draw. Management, however, felt that the hotel had more to offer if it could find the market to which to offer it, and could offer it a very affordable price during this time of year.

The marketing department was assigned the task of developing a package that would draw a new market during, to start, the spring shoulder season. The hotel had the usual amenities of Palm Springs resorts including a golf course and multiple tennis courts. It also had an unproportionately high number of suites. The marketing department felt that these were the facilities to feature, but it needed something extra. The extra turned out to be a Lincoln Town car for customers who were flying in to the Los Angeles airport and would have to make the commute to

Palm Springs, over 100 miles away. This was also made available, however, at the Palm Springs and Ontario, California airports. A package was developed that featured a suite, Lincoln Town car with unlimited mileage for the entire stay, unlimited golf and tennis, and breakfast daily for $129 per person, per day, double occupancy, any length stay. An additional attraction for the Canadian market was Canadian dollars at par with U.S. dollars if the package was prepaid, a savings of about 25 cents on the dollar. Ten percent commission was promised to travel agencies.

Ads were primarily aimed at travel agents. They ran for four weeks in all major travel agent publications. Additionally, they ran in Sunday travel sections of Chicago and Vancouver, British Columbia, newspapers. Faxes were also sent to travel agencies, primarily in the Midwest and the East Coast. The response was excellent. Spring weeks quickly filled up, increasing the normal 30 to 40 percent occupancy to over 70 percent.

Management and the marketing department were pleased with the results. In fact, 800 couples took advantage of the promotion over an eight week period with an average stay of 2.5 nights at U.S. $245 a night (after factoring in the effect of the

*Names disguised.

Canadian dollar discount). Management felt, however, that further evaluation was needed. The promotion had not been inexpensive. First, there was the advertising expense; on top of this was the travel agents' commission on an already low rate. A further additional cost was the Lincoln Town cars. Management's first question was: Was all this worth it, or could we have done as well with nor-

mal off-season discount rates and without the extra expenses?

The second question was: What made the promotion a success? Was it the total package, or individual parts of it? If the latter, which parts? Management didn't have the answers to these questions and decided that the only way to get them was to commission some research.

Forty-One

❖

BRIDGEPORT INN AND CONFERENCE CENTER*

According to John Phillips, CEO and president of Bridgeport Conference Services, the typical meeting planner devotes only 20 percent of his time to planning meetings. In most cases, the individual responsible for the organization of the meeting is also a participant who finds it difficult to both host the event and make a suitable contribution. "He's not a 'pro'," explains Phillips, "so we try to take the worry away from him to let him concentrate on the business at hand. Our aim is to make him look like a hero."

A consulting firm profiled the conference center segment of the hospitality industry, based on a small sampling of executive conference centers, as shown in Exhibit 41-1.

BRIDGEPORT CONFERENCE SERVICES

A large and highly developed marketer of meetings at conference centers was Bridgeport Conference

Services, Inc., operating nine properties around the country. The emphasis at Bridgeport Conference Centers was on self-contained meeting packages with exceptional services to enhance the productivity of meetings. As opposed to a hotel in a major metropolitan area complete with all the distractions, Bridgeport Conference Centers were located in natural settings away from the hustle and bustle of the city.

The centers offered extensive recreational activities, which invigorated the body as well as the mind. The advantage of the self-contained facility was that meeting participants tended to discuss related business matters while enjoying the leisure activities, thus increasing the overall productivity of the meeting. Bridgeport Conference Services catered to Fortune 500 companies, which normally demanded first-class dining, accommodations, and amenities and looked toward executive conference centers to improve the productivity of their meetings.

Bridgeport Conference Services performed most external marketing functions at the regional and national level, rather than at each of the individual properties. Bridgeport Conference Services

---

*Scott Flagel and Karl Grover contributed to this case. Names have been disguised.

EXHIBIT 41-1
Profile of Executive Conference Centers

Meeting Types: Executive conference centers were most often used for training sessions (44 percent of all meetings, with a mean group size of 28), management planning (27 percent of meetings with a mean of 23), and sales meetings (16 percent of meetings with a mean of 44.)

Sources of Business: Most conference center meetings were sponsored by business organizations (82 percent), although trade and professional associations accounted for 9 percent of the business at participating centers, and academic institutions and government bodies occasionally met at the centers.

Occupancy: Although some conference centers did play host to transient traffic in order to boost business during slow periods, average annual occupancy among the centers was still low at 59 percent. December and January were the slowest months; March and October the busiest.

Traffic Patterns: Conference centers reported that meeting participants most often arrived on Sunday or Wednesday and stayed through Friday. An earlier trend toward weekend meetings appeared to be reversing, except in resort areas where a Friday arrival was common. Conference centers handled an average of 5 to 12 meetings each week.

Recreational Facilities: Most executive conference centers offered tennis, swimming, golf, an exercise room, and a game room; some also boasted facilities for bowling and horseback riding. (Although most centers allowed meeting participants unlimited access to these facilities, some derived additional revenue from recreation.)

Operating Statistics: Revenues and operating expenses of executive conference centers compared with those of convention hotels found most operating ratios to be similar. At 8.5 percent of sales however, marketing costs at executive conference centers were almost twice those of convention hotels (4.9 percent)—presumably reflecting the need to communicate both the existence of a new facility and a fairly new concept to prospective clients.

---

believed this was beneficial for the company because interested parties could contact one central office to obtain information on any or all of the properties.

All of the centers operated by Bridgeport Conference Services were closed to transient guests, with the exception of the Bridgeport Inn at Bridgeport Village. This facility was open 365 days a year to the general public whenever rooms were available and not used by conferences.

THE BRIDGEPORT INN

The Bridgeport Inn at Bridgeport Village was conveniently located close to the major metropolitan areas of the Northeast United States, yet completely removed from the noise and distractions of city life. The Inn itself was located in Bridgeport Village, a self-contained community that also boasted a 3000-unit condominium complex, a shopping bazaar, a professional building, and a bank. The physical structure of the Inn reinforced the natural atmosphere.

The meeting rooms of the Inn, and the very heart of its business, were fixed in size, not having the retractable walls that allow for greater flexibility. The missing thin, retractable walls, trademarks of many downtown convention hotels, were replaced with soundproof walls that did not allow the outside world to enter. The meeting rooms were equipped with comfortable chairs, table space, screens, and state-of-the-art audiovideo equipment that, along with coffee breaks, were included in the price of the room.

The 121 guestrooms were also fitted in the rustic mold, with a camp-like firmness to the beds and custom furnishings in the bright and airy rooms. Most of the rooms had two twin beds, although more and more were being converted, in response to customer requests, to include queen-sized beds and private sitting areas. Deluxe facilities at the Inn included a golf course, outdoor swimming pool, tennis courts, health club with saunas, billiard room with connecting pub, and a beautiful restaurant and lounge called Woody's.

The Bridgeport Inn was owned by the Bridgeport Village Developers and operated by Bridgeport Conference Services, Inc. Joseph Biden, the general manager of the property, believed that there were problems inherent in this type of arrangement. For example, plans for an expansion of 80 rooms and an indoor fitness facility consisting of a swimming pool, racquetball courts, and an improved health club had been discussed again and again with no definite decision being made. Biden felt that the expansion would not only be beneficial in the long run, but actually essential if they intended to maintain their competitive position in years to come.

The pricing strategy of the hotel was to offer an all-inclusive price that included a room, three meals a day, coffee breaks, meeting facilities, and use of all recreational facilities with the exception of golf, where there was a minimal greens fee. The conference rack rate was $225 per person double occupancy and $285 single occupancy, which was comparable to city hotels offering the same services.

The hotel split its markets into two categories: conferences, which had a 50 percent repeat factor, and transient social customers, who returned 60 percent of the time. The conference markets comprised almost three-fourths of all business and were very diverse demographically. The conference market also generated the greatest percentage of the Inn's revenue.

ORGANIZATION

The Conference Manager of the Inn served as the liaison between the regional sales office and the property's clients. There was no sales department for conferences on the premises. When arranging with a future meeting planner, the conference rep-resentatives acted as consultants to the company planner. This was beneficial to the client because the representatives were very experienced in meeting particular meeting requests.

The Operations Manager had created strategies to encourage better utilization of the food and beverage outlets, such as promoting sports-oriented theme nights in the lounge to the mostly male guests. Woody's restaurant catered to the local market and also those social guests not on a meal plan, in addition to the American Plan conference guests. Business was brisk on the weekend nights, and Sunday brunch was also popular with the locals.

The general manager, Mr. Biden, was the final member of the executive staff. He was pleased with the performance of the hotel, but would have liked to add an on-site sales position to the budget. All executive committee members agreed that a salesperson who was based at the Inn would be better equipped to make a sale than one who was geographically distant.

THE COMPETITION

Because of the success of hotel concepts similar to the Bridgeport Conference Centers, there had been an increase in competition from two separate sectors. The first form of competition was from hotels that had shifted their marketing efforts toward executive conferences when they recognized the potential for revenue.

The second form of competition was from companies invading the niche that Bridgeport had carved out. An example of this was the Arrowwood facility, which was located not far away in Rye, New York. Arrowwood was built at an average room cost of $250,000 and boasted the latest in audiovisual equipment and indoor recreational facilities, although at a higher price than Bridgeport. More competition like this was expected as more and more companies attempted to jump on the executive conference bandwagon.

DEMAND

The occupancy rate for the Bridgeport Inn at Bridgeport Village had hit a peak two years before at 69 percent. Mr. Biden believed that the occupancy rate was still well above the industry average, but was nonetheless concerned with the negative trend in occupancy.

He was convinced that decisions by the developers had triggered this downward spiral, stating that "not adequately renovating the existing facility and not proceeding with the expansion/addition has contributed to the occupancy problem. The addition of 80 rooms would help meet the demand of weekday requests for conferences and the indoor facility would attract more winter guests."

For the conference market, January and February had the lowest weekday occupancy, but the remaining months were consistently higher. Weekend occupancies, however, fluctuated drastically, due to special packages and other incentive plans. The impressive weekend occupancy rates for January and April were a little misleading because room rates were discounted considerably in those months.

For the social market, the biggest demand fluctuations occurred between summer and winter months, and between weekdays and weekends. The hotel had much more to offer the social guest in the summer. Although overall weekend occupancy had improved over the last five years, it still ran a poor second to weekday occupancies. Occupancy information for the previous year is shown in Exhibit 41-2.

THE MARKETING FUNCTION

Mr. Biden was concerned about the negative trend. He had done what he felt was necessary at the local level, but any long-range actions were subject to approval of both Bridgeport Village and Bridgeport Conference Services.

E X H I B I T 41-2
Occupancy Information

Social Market			
Month	Weekday	Weekend	Total
January	8.0	23.5	12.8
February	9.9	27.3	16.1
March	9.8	37.7	17.9
April	13.3	26.9	18.3
May	17.7	49.7	28.0
June	7.3	56.8	20.5
July	17.3	59.6	33.6
August	13.8	44.7	21.8
September	15.7	53.1	30.4
October	9.8	50.4	25.5
November	8.9	47.4	19.0
December	5.1	22.4	18.6
Average	11.4	41.6	21.9

Conference Market			
Month	Weekday	Weekend	Total
January	57.0	33.3	49.4
February	49.6	6.6	34.2
March	61.5	8.2	46.0
April	61.2	19.5	45.9
May	61.9	5.1	43.6
June	71.8	13.8	56.4
July	65.1	5.6	42.1
August	59.8	3.1	45.2
September	74.0	5.0	54.6
October	83.4	10.0	59.8
November	68.5	9.5	46.2
December	72.0	2.2	37.6
Average	65.5	10.2	46.8

Note: Weekday occupancy is Sunday night through Thursday night and weekend occupancy is Friday and Saturday night.

A problem, however, existed among Bridgeport Village Developers, Bridgeport Conference Services, and the management of Bridgeport Inn in terms of short-range versus long-range objectives. Management had felt constraints in having to set objectives that adhered to short-term goals while also keeping long-range objectives in mind.

The marketing function of Bridgeport Inn was somewhat diversified. First, there was the corporate marketing department that handled all but local group sales, advertising and corporate strategy. In fact, 88 percent of conference bookings went through the main sales office at corporate, which handled all but on-the-spot arrangements. This was designated corporate procedure even to the point that if the Inn received inquiries, it was required to refer them to the corporate office.

Then there was the network of interaction between the corporate marketing department and the Inn's catering and conference sales force, which at times could become somewhat tense. Finally, operations management had the responsibility of marketing the restaurant and lounge both internally to in-house guests and conferees, and externally to the local community. The overall marketing function was covered by all three of these divisions, but there was no one person involved and responsible for the mass marketing activities of the Inn.

Mr. Biden noted that, in spite of the decline, the customer repeat rate was over 50 percent of the total business. He wondered if this was good or bad; was the Inn losing customers, potential customers, was the overall market declining, or a combination of all three? He summed up the situation by saying, "Our bottom line is fantastic in terms of profit, but we have to correct the problems at hand. Only then will we be able to make meeting planners look like heroes."

Forty-Two

◆•◆

NOW YOU WANT ME!*

John Sessions and his family drove up in front of the well-known Super Resort Hotel for a much looked-forward-to two week stay, but a puzzling series of events curtailed it. Their car was parked by resort personnel which, they later learned, meant a 15- to 25-minute wait each time they wanted to pick up the car. This became a daily ordeal despite repeated pleas that somehow the service be speeded up.

John and his wife, two sons, 13 and 14, their daughter, 19, a girlfriend, 20, and John's mother and sister had reserved four concierge floor rooms. Although the reservations had been made months in advance, and repeatedly confirmed by the hotel for four concierge-level rooms, with an inside door connecting two of these rooms and two double beds in three of them, they were forced to accept no connecting rooms, two rooms with king beds, and one boy had to sleep on a rollaway cot.

USING THE RESORT'S FACILITIES

On the first day, the daughter and her friend went to the highly touted health club to see the exercise

facilities, but were told they would have to pay $25 each just to look—even though their group was paying well over $1000 a day for their rooms. They did not pay and thus did not see the facilities.

On the second day, the family needed some laundry done. It was left outside the door, early, for guaranteed pickup, as requested. Returning after breakfast, they found the laundry still there. A phone call to housekeeping brought an apology, an immediate pickup, and an emergency delivery to an outside laundry service. John's confidence in the hotel's reliability suffered another dip.

On day three the family decided to eat lunch at one of the resort's nicer restaurants. They were told, "Sorry, we're closed for the week. Please go to another restaurant." They did go to another restaurant where they could sit outside on a warm, sunny day. "Sorry," they were told, "outside seating is only available in the summer." They went inside where they were seated in the back, facing the wall, rather than in the empty front area with its beautiful water view.

The two boys became ill. The hotel called a doctor, who charged $150 each to examine them, would give no prescription, and told them to come to his office in two days—for another $50 each.

*Names have been disguised.

Thanks, but no thanks, they said and recovered on their own.

On the fourth day one of the boys walked into the concierge lounge for a soda and was told he was not allowed in without a parent. John then accompanied his son to the lounge for a soda.

On the sixth morning John walked into the concierge lounge for breakfast with his two sons. "Sorry," he was told, "rules and regulations. Nobody under 18 allowed to eat here," although they had been eating there for almost a week. "You should rethink your policy," suggested John to the attendant. She assured him that "Your children have been perfectly behaved and are no problem, but we must enforce the policy." The following day, that attendant's superior encountered John, severely upbraided him, and said the policy would be enforced under all conditions with no exceptions.

NOW YOU WANT ME!

Not too surprisingly, John called a nearby competing resort, obtained guarantees that he would encounter no such problems there, and checked his family out of the first resort. As they left, the hotel's general manager pleaded with them to stay, apologized profusely, and admitted that everything they had suffered had been due to the hotel's negligence. He also offered to waive the lounge policy for children under 18. John thanked him, drove two miles to the other hotel, and enjoyed a great week's vacation at a far lower price.

A busy and harried staff? Hardly. The hotel was at 30 percent occupancy when all this occurred.

On returning home, John's wife wrote to the general manager of the hotel, related the incidents and asked how they could call themselves a hotel geared for family-type holidays. The general manager replied immediately.

> Please accept our apologies for not properly communicating our concierge lounge policy and for the subsequent frustration and embarrassment experienced by your family. As an expression of our good faith, and in the hope that you will one day return to our hotel, we are enclosing a $1814.40 check. . . . We also invite you to enjoy a complimentary brunch for six people. . . . We want you to be assured that your experience was a gross exception to the norm. Your letter has been shared with the appropriate personnel and corrective action has been taken.

CASE

Forty-Three

•─•─•

PLANET HOLLYWOOD MOSCOW*

Berlin, March 6th: Almost fighting to escape the Berlin crowd, Arnold Schwarzenegger climbed into the limousine. He sat close to Robert Earl and said, "Wow, what a warm welcome. I knew that Sly and I were famous in the eastern countries, but this is definitely crazy!" Robert Earl nodded, but he already had in mind the next opening—Moscow.

Robert Earl watched his two partners enjoy a sip of Napa champagne while he thought of all the way Planet Hollywood had come in such a short time, and how Keith Barish and himself had convinced the cream of the Hollywood movie industry to join them in this crazy adventure that had led them to open their thirtieth restaurant in Berlin, formerly in East Germany. As the businessman he was, Earl's thoughts went back to the worries caused by the opening to come—Moscow.

Indeed, launching Planet Hollywood, a truly American concept, in a country that had been an enemy during the Cold War would not be the easiest thing in the world. Earl wondered how he

would deal with the local Mafia and racketeers, and how production standards could be ensured with yet unreliable suppliers and unskilled or unmotivated staff. Could Moscow inhabitants afford a single hamburger at Planet Hollywood? Then he remembered, "McDonald's did it; why not me?" But that was without the current considerations. "What if the Communist party comes back into control?" Trying to share his partners' enthusiasm, he sipped at his champagne and promised himself to talk about this with Keith Barish as soon as he set foot on American soil.

THE PLANET HOLLYWOOD CONCEPT

Planet Hollywood was the result of the ideas of Keith Barish (producer of several hit films such as *The Fugitive, Sophie's Choice,* and *9½ Weeks*), and the catering expertise of Robert Earl, founder of the successful Hard Rock Cafe concept. Planet Hollywood was the only chain dining experience inspired by the world of films and television. It

---

*Sandra Tardio, Charles Petit, and Anshu Agrawal researched and contributed to this case.

was a trendy idea that provided, at a reasonable price, food, drink, and a unique Hollywood ambience.

Planet Hollywood restaurants were decorated with some of the world's most valuable movie and television memorabilia such as Stallone's flying Lamborghini from *Judge Dredd,* the bus from the movie *Speed,* and the swords Richard Gere and Sean Connery had used in *Lancelot.* Many artifacts owed their origin to four of the shareholders: Arnold Schwarzenegger, Sylvester Stallone, Bruce Willis, and Demi Moore, as well as other movie industry players.

The restaurants also featured a diorama dedicated to films and television. Also to be seen were walls with hand prints of the likes of Paul Newman, Clint Eastwood, Tom Arnold, and others. To add to the ambience, there were trailers of coming attractions shown on the state-of-the-art audiovisual systems. These were complemented by custom design videos with music from movie sound tracks. All units included a merchandise store that sold a range of apparel such as hats, T-shirts, shorts, vests, denim and leather jackets, all adorned with the company's logo. These stores typically produced 40 percent of a unit's revenue.

The menu featured California's "new classic cuisine" such as pasta, salads, burgers, pizza, smoked and grilled meats, and fish. Cocktails were all named after famous movies. The restaurants also had special table d'hôte menus for gathering and banquet functions.

Staff and Training

Training of personnel was very important to the company, since it saw as one of its competitive advantages the warm welcome, personalized and fast service that guests receive. These were basic to the success of the concept. Thus, all personnel were intensively trained by the American Planet Hollywood staff, who followed each step of the waitstaff while they were serving customers. This process was a nine-day training period followed by an exam. Managers went through a month and a half training period in the United States. An international staff was emphasized in each location, with 50 percent being local and 50 percent being foreigners whenever possible.

Company Structure

Keith Barish, chairman, and Robert Earl, president, were the major shareholders of the company. The American headquarters in Orlando, Florida exercised strict control over all operations. Every decision made by a manager abroad had to be confirmed by an American counterpart. Data concerning sales and personnel were sent to the United States daily; weekly and monthly reports were also transmitted. The European headquarters was in London; this imposed a certain intricacy in the financial systems as European properties had to comply with local rules, as well as the British and American ones.

Marketing

Heavy emphasis was placed on the marketing and communications strategy. The company identified three different target markets: individuals, companies and groups, and the tourism professionals who organized them. Public relations campaigns were based on spontaneous visits of the stars to the different chain units. Costs of these visits were drawn from the PR budget, generated huge publicity, and resulted in a direct increase in patronage on the following day. In general, communications was based on specific occasions and events taking place.

Tourism professionals were targeted with the objective of increasing group business. Planet Hollywood hoped to put its restaurants on their agendas, hoping that they would become repeat customers. Some incentives offered were gift certificates, no waiting, and transportation to and from airports. Companies were targeted through personal contacts with the aim of attracting meetings, product launches, and so forth.

HISTORY

The first Planet Hollywood opened in New York City in 1991 in a nineteenth century building on West 57th Street, one block from Carnegie Hall. In less than three years the idea had grown from one location to more than a dozen, and soon came to include Chicago, Washington, DC, Phoenix, Aspen, San Francisco, Atlanta, Orlando, Reno, Miami, Lake Tahoe, New Orleans, Beverly Hills, San Diego, Atlantic City, Dallas, and the Mall of America in Bloomington, Minnesota, among others, in the United States; soon added were Paris, Hong Kong, Barcelona, Prague, Amsterdam, Vienna, Rome, Sydney, Australia, Tokyo, and Berlin, among others. Moscow was next on the list. The goal by the turn of the century was 50 units worldwide.

The company not only brought in movie stars as shareholders (they were paid in stock), but paraded out plenty of stars for each of its grand openings, which sometimes attracted star-gazing crowds as large as 35,000. Actors, sports figures, and other celebrities were brought into Planet Hollywoods for signings, special charity events, anniversary celebrations, and other promotions. In fact, stated Keith Barish, "If you happen to be in New York you might see one of these celebrities seated next to you. A lot of things can go wrong when you make a movie. They don't all turn out like *The Fugitive*. But with Planet Hollywood, every time we open one it's a success. You know in advance that you are going to have a hit."

THE RISKS IN MOSCOW

Things had changed in the relationship between the United States and Russia, but the anticipated boost in the Russian economy had not occurred. Shops were still often empty or filled with things that people either didn't need or couldn't afford. Customers still queued for vital ingredients such as

flour, bread, and milk. The average Russian income of 500,000 rubles, about $U.S.100, represented little buying power. Thus, the affordability of a meal at Planet Hollywood by even the mid to upper social class was questionable.

Robert Earl knew all this as well as the risks of rackets from the Mafia and other local gangs. In fact, one report had it that in one year 634 local Mafia gangs asked for 10 to 50 percent of the revenues of their "protected partners." None of this would facilitate the work of the local general manager, probably an expatriate or a Russian with an American education.

For customers, Earl expected an unusual clientele mix made up of local Mafia representatives and racketeers, local politicians and important government employees, foreign and local businessmen and, of course, foreign tourists.

In regard to operations, there were also a number of key issues. First of all, how and where would they find suitable personnel? The populace that would produce job applicants was well known for its lack of skills, motivation, and absenteeism. Certainly, this would affect the high quality standards of production and service. Longer than usual training programs would be needed for reasons of both work qualifications and language. Further, it was typical in the country to work only six hours of a supposedly eight-hour day. Language problems could also be a barrier for high spending tourists and foreign businessmen. Then, there was the question of theft by employees to feed their own families or sell in the black market.

Another worry was that of the reliability of local suppliers. Were they capable of regularly providing sufficient volume of quality ingredients? Or, Earl thought, should he get involved in the production process as did McDonald's? There was also, perhaps, the necessity to import some ingredients. Other issues were concerns of hygiene standards and power failures.

Finally, there was the question of security. The local manager would have to cope with local gangs trying to reap some of the benefits of the operation. Otherwise it would not be unlike the Mafia to come in and trash the entire place, or scare customers. Russian crime was notorious for its frequency and very little was to be expected from the local police, since bribery was a common practice. Walking in the streets after 10:00 P.M. was quite risky. Then, finally, there was the local black market that would counterfeit logoed Planet Hollywood items.

Financially speaking, there were plenty of additional concerns. One was whether the government would allow repatriation of profits the restaurant would realize. Another was negotiations with suppliers in a country with an inflation rate that could be as high as 2000 percent a year. This would also affect the payment of local wages.

There were also the customers' eating habits. Food had become a major obsession in Russia, where 80 percent of a typical Russian's monthly income would go toward food purchases. Regardless, they had somewhat different eating habits. For example, meat and other animal products such as butter were consumed less as price liberalization had led to considerable price increases for these rare products. Consumption of potatoes and sugar, on the other hand, had increased tremendously. The typical daily food consumption of the average Russian included cabbage, potato, eggs, sausage, and beet root. Food had also become a means to demonstrate one's social scale.

THE DECISION

With all these problems facing him, Earl wondered if he had gone mad. And he still saw his biggest problem as that of the government and the possible return of the Communists to power. This time his decision was not as easy as the past ones. The country itself was not the most welcoming. On the other hand, it had an amazing market potential that cried out to be satisfied. For all these reasons, and at least a U.S.$15 million investment just to start, was it worth all the risks? Trade-offs would have to be made, but where and how?

C A S E

Forty-Four

◆◆◆

A HASSLE-FREE HOTEL
IN BERMUDA*

Margaret Manley and Laura Ferncroft, two widowed sisters in their 60s, decided to have a last "fling" in Bermuda, where Laura had previously lived for 20 years with her late husband. They chose the upscale Hamilton Princess Hotel on the waterfront in the capital city of Hamilton. This was February, off-season in Bermuda, commonly called "Rendezvous Season" by the Bermuda Tourist Board in its advertising, so they knew it wouldn't be too busy. The Princess Hotel had been there for decades and was considered a "classic."

Laura arranged the trip with her travel agent and obtained a one week package rate that included breakfast and a superior bedroom. Arriving at the hotel they found the central hotel doors blocked by ladders and the doorman busy chatting to the workmen. Their taxi driver took them through the automatic lefthand door. Registration, even with no one ahead of them, took a good 20

minutes, as the clerk left the desk twice for lengthy periods, with no explanation. A welcoming attitude was definitely not in evidence. "Well, we're off to a good start," said Margaret, sarcastically, as they headed for their room.

It was an attractively decorated room in the older part of the hotel, and looked out on a spacious lawn and garden area. On the right one had a view across the harbor to the north shore of Warwick parish. After unpacking, Margaret, an inveterate reader, sat down with a book she had started on the plane. Unfortunately, she couldn't see the print in the evening dusk. After checking all the light bulbs in the room, she found none greater than 60 watts. Housekeeping was contacted for some 100 watt bulbs which took an hour to arrive.

Before dinner, Laura decided she would enjoy a relaxing hot bath, but when she went to push the lever for the drain stopper, it wouldn't budge. After some substantial effort, she called and carefully explained the problem to Housekeeping, who said Maintenance would be contacted. Forty minutes

---

*This case was contributed by Barbara Brooks.

later, the maintenance man arrived, and Laura noted he carried no tools. After fiddling around the tub for a few minutes, he decide to get his tool kit—another 15 minute delay. About 20 minutes after restarting work, he announced, "All set now." Laura, ever cautious, said, "Let me try it." She did and was still unable to move the lever. It turned out the maintenance man had worked on clearing the drain and not on the lever at all. Laura had taken it for granted that, since he had asked no questions, he had been told what the problem was. "Oops," he said, "I'll have to replace that fixture," and left again. In about 15 minutes he was back and 30 minutes later the lever was fixed. Of course there was no time for the pre-dinner bath.

Dinner Time

Margaret and Laura then went downstairs for dinner. There were three choices listed in the room directory—a quite pricy fine dining room, a theme bar and grill, and a bright casual dining room with a reasonable menu, high ceilings, and windows that looked out on the harbor. Not caring for the first two, they chose the latter but when they arrived at the door it was locked and the room was dark. Looking around in amazement, they finally noticed a small sign on the door, "Closed for Renovations." They decided to go out for dinner.

The last straw for that evening was Laura's discovery, when attempting to take a pre-bed bath, that there was no hot water! "Oh, just run the bath for 15 minutes and it will get hot," they were informed. The cause was cited as a computer breakdown. After 20 minutes of wasted water, the temperature hadn't changed from barely lukewarm, so Laura gave up and endured a tepid bath. In the midst of it the bathroom fluorescent light fixture

started to flicker badly, one tube conking out completely, resulting in a half lighted bathroom. "What a marvelous way to end one's first day in this supposedly classy hotel," she cracked to her sister.

BREAKFAST

The next morning, Margaret and Laura had breakfast in the dining room. When a check was given them after finishing, Laura explained to the waiter that breakfast was included in their package. "I don't know about that," he said. "I'll have to check it out." They waited about 10 minutes until he returned and told them they were listed as on the European Plan. "This is too much," said Laura, "particularly since our plan is prepaid." Margaret and Laura went to the front desk where it took about 20 minutes for a rather indifferent clerk, then the front office manager, then an assistant manager, to check the situation. This consisted of all three staring at a computer screen, indifferent to the guests who, by that time, were sorely in need of some friendly reassurance while waiting. It was finally discovered that the Air Canada package did indeed include breakfast. Nonetheless, at the end of the week, when Margaret and Laura were checking out, they found seven breakfasts on their bill. They repeated the previous process until the clerk agreed to remove the charges. It took Laura only a couple of minutes to figure out the amount on a piece of paper, but it took the clerk a good five minutes to make the adjustments on the computer. "So much for that rendezvous," they said to each other as they took a cab to the airport. "At least we'll be able to 'dine out'* on this for ages."

---

*An English expression for a good story to tell at dinner with others.

Forty-Five

◆◆◆

THE RIDEAU GOLF AND COUNTRY CLUB*

"What happened to the good old days? There are kids running around all over the club and slowing down play, they're loud and. . ."

"These women! Get them off the course, they're slow! It took me over four and a half hours to play a round.—it's absolutely ridiculous! Not only do we have to put up with them on the course, but now they're in our lounge, too!"

"How am I supposed to eat my dinner, when the dining room was closed again for yet another wedding. I pay good money to be a member of this club, and when I want to use the facilities, I want them to be available. I don't want non-members taking up my space. What was the priority in this place? Members or money?"

"My son, Alfred, really enjoys the junior clinics, and now we play golf as a family on the weekends. We think it was a great place for him to spend time in the summers, and we love the family. . ."

Brian Murray sipped his morning coffee on the patio of the golf lounge as he sifted through these and other similar customer letters in preparation for the quarterly Board of Directors meeting. It had been three years since he had become General Manager of the Kingston Rideau Golf and Country Club. In those three years, Brian had worked hard to fight dropping membership by implementing new programs and changing certain operations. Much of his work had yielded increases in membership in certain demographic categories, but not without severe resistance from the long-time members who continued to foster a long-standing, traditional Old Boys' Club culture. Judging from the reaction of the members through these and other similar letters, he wondered which direction the meeting, and his club in general, would take.

*This case was contributed by Andrea DeVito, Krista Leesment, and Brenda York, and developed under the supervision of Margaret Shaw, Ph.D., University of Guelph, Ontario, Canada. All rights reserved. All dollar amounts are in Canadian dollars. For conversion purposes, one Cdn$= .70 US$. Names have been disguised.

PROFILE OF KINGSTON

Kingston had a population of 136,415 and was located in Eastern Ontario just south of six-lane cross-country Highway 401, approximately half way between Toronto and Montreal. The city had a very high number of tourists during the summer who were drawn to Kingston by its many museums and historical sites. Kingston was also a world-class sailing destination, and hosted many sailing regattas on Lake Ontario, on which it was situated. Kingston was home to approximately 25,000 students who attended either Queen's University, Royal Military College, or St. Lawrence College. Kingston was also one of Canada's ten top retirement destinations. It was a prime location for retirees due to its low cost of living and its proximity to many of Ontario's major centers and "cottage country" (Rideau Canal, Thousand Islands).

Exhibits 45-1 and 45-2 show that Kingston's highest population distribution was in the 30–44 years of age category and that the average individual income was $24,747. Average household income was $47,101, as shown in Exhibit 45-3.

CURRENT TRENDS IN THE GOLFING INDUSTRY

Canada's golf industry had experienced rapid growth in the past ten years. According to the Royal Canadian Golf Association, the number of golfers in Canada had increased from 3.8 million in 1990 to 5.2 million in 1998. Canada had the highest golf participation rate per capita in the world, with a national average participation rate of 19.4 percent. A huge influx of new Canadian golfers had a major impact on the industry. Some of the most obvious trends were: an increase in both female and junior golfers, an increase in the demand for more public golf courses, and a shift toward market diversification by private courses.

Golf was still predominantly a male pastime in Canada. Men accounted for 73% of total golfers; however, this number had been dropping steadily as women became increasingly more interested in the sport. In 1990 only 18% of Canadian golfers were women, this number had grown to 27% in 1998.

The average age of Canadian golfers was 39, a result of an increasing number of junior players taking up the sport accompanied by a relatively stagnant senior participation. In 1990, there were 325,000 junior golfers aged 12 to 17 and 331,000 senior golfers aged 65 and older. In 1998, there were 359,000 junior golfers and 329,000 senior golfers. Research showed that average rounds played increased dramatically with age. Although the number of junior golfers had increased, the number of rounds they played per year was significantly less than the senior and intermediate age category golfers. Male juniors played on average 11.2 rounds of golf per year and seniors played ap-

E X H I B I T   45-1
Population Distribution by Sex and Age in Kingston

Age (years)	Males	% of Total	Females	% of Total	Males and Females	% of Total
Under 14	13,380	9.81%	12,950	9.49%	26,330	19.30%
15–29	17,045	12.49%	16,110	11.81%	33,155	24.30%
30–44	16,615	12.18%	16,950	12.43%	33,565	24.61%
45–59	10,385	7.61%	10,350	7.59%	20,735	15.20%
60–74	7,330	5.37%	8,685	6.37%	16,015	11.74%
75+	2,340	1.72%	4,275	3.13%	6,615	4.85%
Total	67,095	49.18%	69,320	50.82%	136,415	100%

EXHIBIT 45-2
Population Distribution by Income in Kingston

Income Range	Males	% of Total	Females	% of Total	Total	% of Total
Under $9,999	8,885	8.99%	16,280	16.74%	25,165	25.45%
$10,000–$19,999	8,960	9.06%	14,915	15.08%	23,875	24.15%
$20,000–$29,999	8,585	8.68%	9,525	9.63%	18,110	18.32%
$30,000–$39,999	8,785	8.88%	5,320	5.38%	14,105	14.27%
$40,000–$49,000	5,860	5.93%	2,250	2.28%	8,110	8.20%
$50,000 and over	7,505	7.59%	1,995	2.02%	9,500	9.61%
Total Pop. >15 years	48,590	49.14%	50,285	50.86%	98,875	100%
Average Income ($)	$31,165		$18,545		$24,747	

proximately 37.3 rounds. Exhibit 45-4 depicts demographic profiles of Canadian golfers in more detail.

In many areas of the country, there had been an insufficient supply of public courses. As a result, more and more public courses were being constructed. Semi-private courses had become very popular, accounting for 50% of all rounds played in 1998. This was followed by public courses with 31% of play, and private courses with 19% of play.

Changing demographics had forced many private courses to rethink their position in the market. There was a greater demand for private courses that catered to families, juniors and women. Many private clubs were opening their doors to occasional public golfers. For example, at St. George's, a private golf course in Toronto, management had chosen to make their course available to non-members on Sunday afternoons and evenings when member demand was low. More and more private courses were making changes that would allow them to capitalize on emerging industry trends. Brian MacDonald, director of membership development for the Royal Canadian Golf Association, had said that, "without programs to introduce and keep people in the game, the industry will have trouble maintaining or increasing what it has right now."

EXHIBIT 45-3
Population Distribution by Household Income in Kingston

Household Income Range	# of Households	% of Total Households
Under $10,000	3,330	7.07%
$10,000–$19,999	7,600	16.14%
$20,000–$29,999	6,860	14.56%
$30,000–$39,999	7,060	14.99%
$40,000–$49,999	6,650	14.12%
$50,000–$59,999	5,825	12.37%
$60,000–$69,999	4,375	9.29%
$70,000 and over	9,590	20.36%
TOTAL	51,290	100%
Average Income ($)	$47,101	

HISTORY OF THE RIDEAU GOLF AND COUNTRY CLUB

Rideau Golf and Country club was first established in 1917 as a golf course with only 6 holes. In 1929, Stanley Thompson, a reputable golf course architect, who had designed world class courses such as those at Jasper Park Lodge and Banff Springs Hotel, expanded Rideau into an 18-hole golf course.

In order to generate year-round income, in 1961 Rideau added curling rinks to the club. The curling

EXHIBIT 45-4
Selected Demographic Profiles of Canadian Golfers

Age Range (Years)	%	Age Range (Years)	%	Household Income	%	Golfers who are Members at Private Clubs	%
Male 12–17	8%	Female 12–17	3%	<$30,000	17%	Yes	13%
Male 18–34	25%	Female 18–34	11%	$30,000–$49,999	25%	No	87%
Male 35–49	23%	Female 35–49	8%	$50,000–$74,999	25%	**TOTAL**	100%
Male 50–64	12%	Female 50–64	4%	>$75,000	33%		
Male >65	5%	Female >65	1%	**TOTAL**	100%		
TOTAL	73%	TOTAL	27%				

club was considered the secondary product at Rideau.

The club had traditionally catered mainly to males; this had discouraged female membership. This dated focus had contributed to the existent Old Boys' Club culture that was now evident at Rideau. The golf lounge was originally open only to men, but in 1986 the lounge opened its doors to women. Still, men typically kept to one side of the lounge and women to the other. Although there were no formal rules for this division of sexes, there was a planter that informally acted as a divider in the room. On occasions, when the planter had been removed, members had said that they were uncomfortable because it seems that the women might be "taking over" the lounge.

In 1995, as a result of a battle fought and won by Rideau member Dr. Brenda Billings, female membership fees were raised so that they were equivalent to men's fees. The women, then, were granted the right to tee off during any of the club's operating hours, rather than restricting them to off-peak hours, as had previously been the case. In an attempt to attract more members, Rideau's management had also recently implemented a junior program for golfers under 18 years of age. This program consisted of sponsoring junior clinics for members as well as for juniors from the Kingston area. As a result, junior membership had more than doubled in a 10 year period.

Rideau's management team was trying to in-crease the number of out of house functions, such as weddings, Christmas parties and business meetings. These non-member functions had become an important source of revenue for the golf course. The dining room was closed to membership in order to accommodate many of these functions. Some members had expressed dissatisfaction because they felt that their membership fees were substantial enough that they should not have to be inconvenienced by non-members. Brian Murray was having difficulty balancing the needs of members, and the lucrative revenue generated by the non-member functions. He was hesitant to turn non-member functions away, because revenue from internal membership use of the dining room was on the decline.

Culture of the Club

Rideau Golf and Country Club was perceived in the community as an exclusive, private club that attracted, and catered to, many of Kingston's elite. The course itself had a strong reputation in golfing society. In 1996, Rideau Golf and Country Club had been ranked as one of the top fifty golf courses in Canada, and one of Canada's top five most underrated courses by Score Magazine.

The President and Board of Directors were members of the club. They were nominated, and subsequently voted in, by Rideau's shareholders each year. The Board of Directors was comprised of ten male members and two female members. The average age was 57, with only two just under 50. In 1950, 100 shares of stock were issued to each member. Since then, the number of shares had been split several times in an attempt to diversify power. When shares were split, existing shareholders were given purchase priority. The majority of original shareholders opted to capitalize on this opportunity. As a result, for numerous years the same 100 people had maintained voting control over the Board of Directors and, consequently, the golf course in general.

The predominant internal culture at Rideau could best be described as an Old Boys' Club atmosphere. Traditions and values that were established in 1917, when the club first opened, continued to exist. Many of the current members had been at the club for numerous years and, in many cases, their parents and grandparents were members during the early years of the club. A strong, personal commitment to the club had developed among such members. They felt at home, and enjoyed the numerous annual tournaments, ceremonies, and social events that were mainstays at Rideau. These traditions were also very attractive to new members who were seeking an excellent, challenging course combined with business and social opportunities.

On the flip side, with such a strong "old school culture" there existed a sense of conservatism and resistance to change. This stubborn attitude was probably a reflection of members' ages and their self-perceived status in society. Often new, innovative-thinking management found this culture intimidating since the members felt, due to their long-standing history at the club, that they knew better than the management what would and would not work. As a result, Rideau's management had felt a great deal of resistance from the members toward any attempted or actual changes the club had made to adjust to modern times. For example, the Board of Directors and members debated for a full year over whether or not to install

an elevator at the club (they finally did install it). Another time, management faced intense heat from members when they announced that member fees would increase by $2 per month in order to plant more flowerbeds at the clubhouse. There were many members that still believed that the golf lounge should had remained a men's only lounge and that women's tee off times should still come second to men's tee off times. These same members had also been known to complain if young, attractive women were not hired to serve in the golf lounge for the summer. The Board of Directors was unwilling to consider the addition of a swimming pool, health club, or tennis courts. Such changes would be similar to those of other private clubs that were attempting to attract a younger membership by catering to families.

Membership at Rideau was on the decline. This could have been due to the predominant old age of the members, but was also due to the club's inability to accept change, which was inevitably driving away many of its potential new members. It was important to note that the culture issues evident at Rideau were predominant in the golf membership; almost no culture problems existed within Rideau's curling population.

CLUB LAYOUT AND DESIGN

Rideau accommodated both golf and curling memberships and, as such, was open year-round. There were several eating and drinking facilities at Rideau that were open to members only. These included the Dining Room: dinner only, formal atmosphere and fine dining, overlooking Lake Ontario; Club Cafe: casual restaurant for lunch and dinner; Golf Lounge: overlooks the 18th hole, open during the golf season, lounge food like sandwiches, burgers, and beer; Curling Lounge: similar to golf lounge, open in the winter, often used for receptions and special events year-round; 10th tee: snack shop booth located at the 10th hole; Other Amenities: driving range, practice putting and chipping green, men's and women's locker rooms, co-ed sauna, and boardroom.

Rideau had a par of 70 and was 6,982 yards long with 18 holes. The course was considered to be one of the best in eastern Ontario. Rideau's tight fairways and small greens made it an extremely challenging course. There was an abundance of water and mature tree growth, making the course aesthetically pleasing. The course was extremely well manicured; much of this could be attributed to the computerized underground watering system. Rideau's speed of play was relatively slow, due to its aging membership.

Rideau owned a significant amount of undeveloped land. They had recently received a bid from the city to purchase the land for $800,000. The land was large enough to accommodate another 18-hole course. The city would have liked to use the land as a public park. Rideau currently did not have enough money to develop a second course, but decided to hold onto the land for future expansion.

MEMBERSHIP

There had been a decline in both golf and curling memberships since 1987. The number of golfers had decreased from 881 in 1987 to 825 in 1998, and the number of curlers had decreased from 424 in 1987 to 370 in 1998. However, substantial increases were evident in both the female and junior categories. The number of female members was 244 in 1987, and was projected to be 375 by the end of 1998. The number of junior members would be 120 by the end of 1998, up from 49 in 1987. The membership data are listed in Exhibit 45-5.

Membership Profile

Exhibit 45-6 summarizes the golf membership distribution at Rideau. Upon examination of this exhibit, it is evident that the majority of Rideau golfers were seniors (384). There has also been notable declines in the number of intermediate golfers (168 in 1987 to 103 in 1998). This decline was attributed to the shift of these golfers from the intermediate age category to the senior age category. There has also been a significant increase in junior golf memberships. In 1998, Rideau had 100 junior golfers compared to 41 in 1987. A large number of the members were retirees who had migrated from Toronto or other places outside Kingston. The remaining senior golfers were comprised of independent businesspeople and people affiliated with the universities and the hospital.

EXHIBIT 45-5
Membership Figures at Rideau Golf and Country Club

		1987 Total	%	1990 Total	%	1993 Total	%	1996 Total	%	Projected 1998 Total	%
GOLFERS	Male	678	50.04%	649	48.40%	502	39.31%	466	36.78%	450	36.14%
	Female	162	11.96%	178	13.27%	247	19.34%	262	20.68%	275	22.09%
	Junior	41	3.03%	52	3.88%	73	5.72%	92	7.26%	100	8.03%
	Total	881	65.02%	879	65.55%	822	64.37%	820	64.72%	825	66.27%
CURLERS	Male	334	24.65%	312	23.27%	297	23.26%	281	22.81%	250	20.08%
	Female	82	6.05%	88	6.56%	93	7.28%	98	7.73%	100	8.03%
	Junior	8	0.59%	12	0.89%	15	1.17%	18	1.42%	20	1.61%
	Total	424	31.29%	412	30.72%	405	31.71%	397	31.33%	370	29.72%
SOCIAL MEMBERS		50	3.69%	50	3.73%	50	3.92%	50	3.95%	50	4.02%
TOTAL		1355	100%	1341	100%	1277	100%	1267	100%	1245	100%

EXHIBIT 45-6
Golf Membership Distribution at Rideau Golf and Country Club

	1987		1990		1993		1996		Projected 1998	
	Total	*%*	*Total*	*%*	*Total*	*%*	*Total*	*%*	*Total*	*%*
Senior Golfers (>46 years)	383	*43.47%*	374	*42.55%*	361	*43.92%*	378	*46.10%*	384	*46.55%*
Husband/Wife Golfers (>46 years)	102	*11.58%*	92	*10.47%*	96	*11.68%*	102	*12.44%*	106	*12.85%*
Husband/Wife Golfers (19–45 years)	78	*8.85%*	74	*8.42%*	76	*9.25%*	54	*6.59%*	48	*5.82%*
Intermediate Golfers (19–45 years)	168	*19.07%*	182	*20.71%*	128	*15.57%*	109	*13.29%*	103	*12.48%*
Junior Golfers (<18 years)	41	*4.65%*	52	*5.92%*	73	*8.88%*	92	*11.22%*	100	*12.12%*
Non-Resident Member	26	*2.95%*	24	*2.73%*	12	*1.46%*	17	*2.07%*	15	*1.82%*
Corporate Social	50	*5.68%*	50	*5.69%*	50	*6.08%*	50	*6.10%*	50	*6.06%*
Clubhouse	33	*3.75%*	31	*3.53%*	26	*3.16%*	18	*2.20%*	19	*2.30%*
TOTAL	881	*100%*	879	*100%*	822	*100%*	820	*100%*	825	*100%*

REVENUE

Membership revenue was comprised of approximately 80% annual fees and 20% entrance fees. Total revenue, and golfing and curling revenues, had declined in the last few years. For example, curling revenue went from $83,991 in 1987 to $76,000 in 1998. In 1993, golfing revenue was $1,008,928, dropping to $985,000 in 1998. Overall revenue declined to $1,398,000 in 1998 from $1,417,764 in 1996.

Internal food and beverage revenue was generated via sales to members at the golf course. On the other hand, external food and beverage revenue originated from non-member functions, such as wedding receptions, Christmas parties, and business meetings. Internal food and beverage revenue, although higher than external food and beverage, had decreased from $216,400 in 1993 to $202,200 in 1998. However, external food and beverage revenue had steadily increased from $72,600 in 1987 to $134,800 in 1998. Revenue figures for Rideau are listed in Exhibit 45-7.

As a private golf club, Rideau had two sets of fees. The first set was the entrance fee. It was a one-time payment that a customer paid upon becoming a member. In certain instances, Rideau allowed members to pay the entrance fee in installments over a five-year period, but, in doing so, these members paid a higher total price. Junior members (18 years of age and under) were exempt from paying an entrance fee. However, as a golfer grew older, he or she was subject to the entrance fee of the membership category that corresponded to his or her age.

The second fee was the annual fee. Paying this fee allowed members unlimited golf, full clubhouse privileges, and coverage of the members' required fees in the Ontario Golf Association and Canadian Golf Association. Exhibit 45-8 is a list of the two sets of fees charged to each member according to age range.

Rideau Golf and Country Club was a seasonal business. The curling season began in September and ended in April. The golf season usually ran from late April to late October; however, on occasion members might still be golfing in December.

EXHIBIT 45-7
Revenue Figures for Rideau Golf and Country Club

| | 1987 | | 1990 | | 1993 | | 1996 | | Projected 1998 | |
	Total	%	Total	%	Total	%	Total	%	Total	%
Curling	$83.991	7.17%	$79,662	6.41%	$79,433	5.68%	$78,834	5.56%	$76,000	5.44%
Golfing	$826,218	70.52%	$884,948	71.20%	$1,008,928	72.15%	$1,006,750	71.01%	$985,000	70.46%
F & B - Internal	$188,760	16.11%	$192,580	15.50%	$216,400	15.47%	$210,680	14.86%	$202,200	14.46%
F & B - External	$72,600	6.20%	$85,660	6.89%	$93,670	6.70%	$121,500	8.57%	$134,800	9.64%
TOTAL	$1,171,569	100%	$1,242,850	100%	$1,398.431	100%	$1,417,764	100%	$1,398,000	100%

EXHIBIT 45-8
Fees for Members at Rideau Golf and Country Club

Entrance Fees		Annual Fees	
Senior Golfers (>46)	$7,000	Senior Golfers (>46)	$1,787
Husband/Wife Golfers (>46)	$12,000	Husband/Wife Golfers (any)	$3,301
Husband/Wife Golfers (19–45)—one-time	$5,100	Intermediate Golfers (19–45)	$1,228
Husband/Wife Golfers (19–45)—5-year	$5,590	Junior Golfers (>18)	
Intermediate Golfers (19–45)—one-time	$3,000	-Parents are members	$371
Intermediate Golfers (19–45)—5-year	$3,500	-Parents are not members	$530
Social	$500	Social	$380
Clubhouse	$100		

Exhibit 45-9 shows a time line for the golfing and curling seasons. In the fall, overlap occurred between golf and curling. During this time there were some staffing issues and decisions to make regarding hours of operation. Management had solved this problem by closing the golf lounge during the slow weekday periods and serving both curlers and golfers from the curling lounge bar. Although, this might not have been the ideal situation, it did minimize labor and operation costs.

COMPETITION

There were no other private golf courses in the Kingston area, with the exception of Crestwood, a 3,124-yard, 9-hole course with a par of 36. This private course catered mainly to the military personnel in the Kingston area by offering members who were in the military significant membership fee dis-counts. However, the development of a private golf course was being considered for a senior residential area in Bath, Ontario (15 minutes from Kingston).

There were three semi-private golf clubs located in Kingston's vicinity. (Note: semi-private golf clubs combine private memberships with public golfing privileges, but the members had first priority and special advantages at these clubs.) Foxland was a semi-private 18-hole course, 5,020 yards long and the par was 70. It was considered a relatively simple course with a fair level of maintenance and offered limited amenities and member services. Membership fees were $500 a year, and public one time green fees were $18.

River Ridge had 18 holes and par was 71, the course was 6,293 yards long. The membership fees were close to $750 per year and one-time, public green fees were $20. The level of course maintenance was good, and difficulty of the course was medium. Additional amenities included a public lounge, public restaurant, and pro shop.

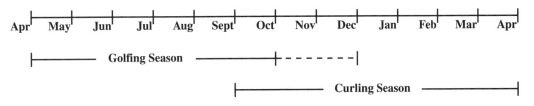

EXHIBIT 45-9 Timeline for golf and curling

Canton Meadows had a 6,044-yard course with an 18-hole par of 72. Membership fees were $850 per year and one-time public green fees were $20. The course was rated fairly difficult and was maintained very well. There were two restaurant/lounges at the club. One was open only to members and the other was open to the public. Both the members and the public were welcome to book the banquet room for special social functions, but member functions took priority.

Fishcreek Golf Course was the only public municipal run course in Kingston. The 5,200-yard course was poorly maintained and offered no other amenities other than a pro shop. It was rated an easy 18-hole course, with a par of 70. One time, public user green fees were $12.

Rideau had higher junior and female membership than ever before, but why were its revenues decreasing? Why was there such backlash from some members over the new direction that the club was trying to take? Brian wanted to please his existing clientele, but he was sure that opening the doors to an increasing number of women and junior members would ensure growth for the club. Hopefully, the meeting would shed some light on the issues that Rideau was facing. Maybe it was just a matter of time before the club's new direction translated into success at Rideau. Maybe some drastic changes were in store. Brian knew that, in a few hours, his vision for the future of Golf and Country Club would become clear and hoped that this vision would be successful.

CURRENT SITUATION

As Brian Murray entered the boardroom, he mulled over the customer letters in his mind.

C A S E

Forty-Six

Yogen Früz®*

It was early evening in the fall of 1998. The busy summer season had come to an end and Chris Desjardins was reviewing the advertising campaign used that summer. He had sent out surveys to evaluate the effectiveness of the campaign to the more than 80 franchised outlets across Canada. Slowly the completed surveys were being filled out and returned to him at the Yogen Früz head office in Markham, Ontario. As advertising and marketing director of Yogen Früz Canada Inc., Chris was concerned about the effectiveness of his most recent advertising campaign and had already started thinking about how he would proceed with advertising for 1999.

Chris had been part of the Yogen Früz team for several years. As a young company, Yogen Früz was an exciting, dynamic and fast-paced place to work. The company was still headed by its original founders, Michael and Aaron Serruya. It all started in August 1986, when the two brothers, only 21 and 20 years old, opened up a frozen yogurt concession in the newly built Promenade Mall in their home town of Thornhill, Ontario, north of Toronto.

By 1998, Yogen Früz stock had been traded on the Toronto stock exchange for four years and operations had expanded to 88 countries worldwide. In 12 years, a single concession stand in a mall had grown into a multimillion dollar company. Furthermore, Yogen Früz had taken the lead as the world's largest frozen yogurt chain and one of the fastest growing foodservice franchises in the world. The revenues of Yogen Früz Worldwide from 1995 to 1997 are shown in Exhibit 46-1.

THE COMPANY

The idea to open the concession had come from Aaron Serruya when he was co-owner/operator of Sharon's Bagels in Miami Beach. Aaron watched as two frozen yogurt stores, The Country's Best Yogurt (TCBY) and I Can't Believe It's Yogurt (ICBIY), opened up on either side of his store. He

EXHIBIT 46-1
Yogen Früz Revenue Stream

Source	Revenue per Year					
	1995		1996		1997	
	U.S.$	%	U.S.$	%	U.S.$	%
Canada	$4,641,880	51	$4,525,301	15	$5,745,450	12.5
United States	$2,134,361	23	$18,522,781	62	$26,088,917	57
International	$2,409,494	26	$6,990,541	23	$14,057,378	30.5
Total revenues	$9,185,735	100	$30,038,623	100	$45,891,745	100

and his brother Michael approached TCBY and attempted to purchase the Canadian franchise rights. The chain responded that they were busy expanding in the United States and had no plans to move into Canada for another year or two. The brothers decided to tackle the Canadian market themselves, before the American competition moved in. Aaron sold his shop in Florida and the brothers received a $90,000 loan from their father to finance the business. The first concession in Thornhill opened up only nine months later. It was given the European sounding name Yogen Früz. Although literally it has no meaning, the name was thought to complement the premium product as it represented yogurt and fresh fruit.

The Product

After extensive research the Serruyas concluded that the most cost-effective method of dispensing frozen yogurt was to use a machine that would allow portion-controlled frozen yogurt to be individually mixed with fresh fruit on demand. The mix-on-demand method minimized waste and made the product more visually appealing. The unique, low-fat product they developed had a richer, more robust flavor than the soft-serve products sold by competitors in the United States, and a more premium image. Frozen yogurt was perceived as a frozen dessert for health and calorie conscious people.

Target Markets

The brothers determined that their key target market would be middle income women aged 18 to 48, including mothers with kids. The secondary target market was teens. It was felt that women would be more receptive to frozen yogurt than men because of the greater concern among women about controlling calorie and fat intake. Consumer education about the product was a challenge from the onset as many people were unfamiliar with frozen yogurt. Yogen Früz combated this with in-store sampling and couponing. "When we first opened in Calgary," said Aaron Serruya, "we couldn't give the stuff away. People wouldn't even take free samples. They were all saying, 'Oh no, I don't like yogurt.'" Today, Alberta is Yogen Früz's number two Canadian market.

Locations

Initially the company determined that shopping malls were the best venue for the Yogen Früz concept. With long, harsh winters in Canada, climate controlled malls ensured demand all year long. In fact, December, with the influx of Christmas shoppers in the malls, proved to be the busiest time of the year. Furthermore, the simple method of preparation of the product meant Yogen Früz concessions could be opened in only 250 square feet of retail space.

Franchising

The first franchised store opened in London, Ontario, in 1987, almost a year after the Promenade Mall unit. Soon after other franchise offers came pouring in. Master franchise territories were developed in the various provinces for immediate rapid expansion. Once the company became more established, all of the master franchises were bought back so that all of the franchises throughout the country were under direct control of the head office.

Franchisees were required to have $100,000 and to operate the franchise themselves. To keep control of the franchise network, all advertising, site location, lease negotiation, and sourcing of supplies and equipment was conducted through the head office. By 1998, there were over 80 full Yogen Früz stores in malls across Canada.

Growth Strategies

By the early 1990s, the Serruyas realized they were quickly running out of shopping malls in Canada within which to expand. At that point they started to consider other distribution channels in which to market their product. One strategy was to sell franchises internationally. It was determined that growth in Canada would come from co-branding with other foodservice outlets and introducing frozen yogurt outlets to nontraditional locations.

The management of Yogen Früz had begun to realize that frozen yogurt was a product that attracted impulse sales. Consumers did not necessarily seek out the product, but rather they purchased it because it was available. It was determined that the more places the product was available, the more potential there was to sell it. Nontraditional growth or joint venturing with other fast-food companies became one of the strongest areas of expansion for Yogen Früz.

Co-branding was first developed with the donut industry. It was discovered that frozen yogurt and donuts complemented each other well. Donut stores did 60 to 70 percent of their business between 7 A.M. and 11 A.M. when Yogen Früz did al-

most none. In the afternoon and dinnertime, when sales for yogurt pick up, sales for donuts slow down.

In 1992, Yogen Früz entered a piggyback agreement with Country Style Donuts, a division of Maple Leaf Foods Franchise Operations. In addition to introducing the Yogen Früz concept to a whole new market, the deal allowed the chain to sell a limited line of Country Style Donuts and coffee in specific franchises. By 1998, Yogen Früz had over 300 licensed locations in foodservice outlets in Canada including Country Style Donuts, Pizza Hut, Mr. Sub, Blimpie, and independents.

Several prominent nontraditional locations were established in an attempt to place the Yogen Früz brand in high-traffic locations, where a preexisting facility created a low cost of entry. Yogen Früz was established in high profile locations such as Toronto's Skydome, the African Lion Safari in Cambridge, the Toronto Airport, and Ottawa's Corel Centre, as well as in two hospitals.

THE COMPETITION

In 1987, when Yogen Früz started franchising its operations, the U.S. chains Zack's and TCBY were attempting to establish a foothold in the Canadian market. Baskin-Robbins had already launched its own successful soft-serve frozen yogurt chain, Yogurty's Yogurt Discovery. As the first entrant into the Canadian market, Yogen Früz was able to maintain its leadership position.

In 1991 Yogen Früz bought out Yogurty's and most stores in Canada were converted to the Yogen Früz brand. In 1996 Yogen Früz acquired the ICBIY franchise in the United States, before it had a chance to expand to Canada

When Yogen Früz opened shop in 1987, TCBY was the largest franchiser of frozen yogurt in the United States. When TCBY came to Canada, the retail format used was to open stand-alone street-level outlets in major cities, as they had done in the United States. This strategy failed to account for potential low winter demand in Canada due to the cold weather. Thus TCBY only established a very minor presence in Canada and was never a serious competitor to Yogen Früz.

In 1998, Yogen Früz had no direct competitors in the frozen yogurt segment in Canada. The closest competitor, also in malls, was Baskin Robbins with approximately 200 franchises. While Baskin Robbins' primary product was ice cream, it also served one yogurt-based product. Laura Secord and Dairy Queen were also considered competitors although they only served ice cream.

PRODUCT MATURITY

By the mid-1990s, the Yogen Früz product was widely available in Canada. However, sales in frozen yogurt were declining. According to *The Centre for Advertising Services,* U.S.* per capita consumption of the "other frozen dessert category," which included frozen yogurt (desserts other than ice cream), jumped four pounds between 1985 and 1993. Consumption hit a record high in 1993 as frozen yogurt peaked in popularity. Since 1993, however, consumption had been on the decline. This slump was attributed in part to the rising popularity of low-fat and nonfat ice cream. Analysts predicted that frozen yogurt was passé.

In order to counteract declining sales in the frozen yogurt segment, Yogen Früz decided to diversify the product portfolio of the franchises to attract more customers, including men. Nonfat yogurt was introduced in 1993, ice cream was introduced in 1994, and Fruitty Ice was launched in 1995. Yogen Früz then started opening larger "superstores" that offered ice cream and coffee in addition to frozen yogurt. This diversification lead to a 20 to 70 percent increase in sales, according to Aaron Serruya.

In 1997 a new yogurt-based product was introduced at the franchise level—the Smoothy Früz®.

Smoothies were identified as the fastest growing area of the frozen dessert business. Smoothies were made in dairy and nondairy versions, with non-fat Yogen Früz, Tropicana juices, and Snapple. The customer also had a choice of four healthy additions, including ginseng root powder, vitamin and protein powders, wheat germ, and wheat grass juice supplement, to augment the nutritional value. Smoothies were intended as a snack or, because of their nutritious ingredients, as a meal replacement. In fact, because they were a nutritional breakfast alternative, many mall-based operators added sales early in the day, thus lengthening the typical sales day.

In the 1998 season, Yogen Früz' closest competitor, Baskin Robbins, also introduced a line of smoothies. The Baskin Robbins' smoothie was also made from yogurt and fresh fruit and cost $3.18. Baskin Robbins' smoothies came in four flavours including Berries Gone Banana, Just Peachy, Very Strawberry, and Aloha Berry Banana. See Exhibit 46-2 for a complete list of Yogen Früz yogurt products available.

COMMUNICATIONS MIX

In 12 short years, Yogen Früz had achieved tremendous success, both in Canada and internationally. As director of marketing and advertising, Chris Desjardins played an important role in ensuring the continuing success and longevity of the Yogen Früz brand. His task at hand, however, was to determine how best to communicate the values of the Yogen Früz brand to existing consumers, potential consumers, and potential franchisees in Canada.

Advertising

Up until the 1997 summer season, Yogen Früz had primarily relied on word of mouth and in-store point of purchase advertising to promote its product. The rationale was that the purchase of frozen yogurt in a mall was usually an impulse decision. Point of purchase advertisements were necessary to

---

*The Canadian frozen dessert market generally follows trends in the United States.

EXHIBIT 46-2
Yogen Früz Product Line

Yogen Früz			Früzer Shakes	
Size	*Price of Cup*	*Price of Waffle Cone*	*Size*	*Price*
Small	$2.10		Regular	$2.49
Medium	2.65	3.18	Large	2.99
Large	3.15	3.69		
Extra Fruit	.50			

Flavors

Strawberry/Raspberry/Blueberry/Blackberry/Cherry/Cranberry/Kiwi/
Peach/Pineapple/Banana/Honeydew/Cantaloupe/Mango/Papaya/
Chocolate/Cheesecake/Orange
Available in Non-Fat and Low-Fat

Toppings		*Take Home*	
Toppings, fruit	.50	Small family pack	4.99
Toppings, candy	.50	Large family pack	7.99
Hot fudge	.60		
		500 ml pre-pack— Chocolate Chocolate, Cookies n Cream, Strawberry Sundae	3.99

Smoothy Früz		*Fruity Ice*	
Flavor	*Price*	*Size*	*Price*
Strawberry Sensation	3.49	Small	.99
Mighty Berry	3.49	Medium	1.49
Strawberry Peach Passion	3.49	Large	1.69
Raspberry Rush	3.49		
Strawberry Banana Classic	3.49		
Pineapple Orange Sunset	3.49		
Extra natures additions— ginseng root powder, protein powder, wheat germ, wheat grass, lecithin	.50		

Flavors

Lemon Lime/Grape/
Strawberry Kiwi/
Cherry/Orange/
Pineapple/Blue Raspberry

(continued)

EXHIBIT 46-2 *(Continued)*

Drinks and Novelties	Price	Freshly Squeezed Juices	Price
Juice	1.10	Small	1.60
Water	1.10	Medium	2.15
Pop	1.10	Large	2.55
		Jumbo	3.35
Strawberry Sorbet	1.25	**Varieties**	
Lemon Sorbet	1.25	Orange Juice/Carrot Juice	
Blast Bars	1.75	Pink Grapefruit Juice/	
Tropicana Bars	1.89	Cherry/Orange/	
		Carrot and Assorted Vegetable Juices	

communicate the product benefits when the consumer was deciding whether or not to make the purchase. One series of ads stated, simply, "Sorry. We don't have any (fat). We apologize for the inconvenience." The effectiveness of point of purchase ads was measured by increase of sales in the particular product category. For example, after the no-fat campaign was launched, sales of non-fat products rose 400 percent. The only other form of advertisement that had been used was billboards on public transportation. Yogen Früz budgeted $250,000 in 1997 for their total communication budget in Canada.

Television

In April 1997, Chris and the Yogen Früz team decided for the first time to use broadcast media to promote the brand and develop brand awareness within Canada. Walsh and Associates Agency was hired to produce a television commercial for the price of $80,000. The money for the commercial did not come from the communication budget for that year since the commercial was to be used in markets outside of Canada as well. The commercial was entirely visual, with a music-video feel, so that it could be easily used in foreign markets. The commercial stressed lifestyle and brand awareness and the slogan "One World One Taste" was developed for the commercial. In Canada, the Yogen Früz commercial

was launched coast-to-coast on some of the country's most popular television stations during the peak season from May to August. The commercial schedule and cost breakdown for British Columbia are shown in Exhibits 46-3 and 46-4.

The goal of the television commercial was primarily to target an audience of women 18 to 49. It was aimed secondarily at teens and students. The commercials aired on YTV and Much Music nationally, and in spot markets on CityTV, The New VR, CFTO, ONTV, CFMT in Toronto, as well as CICT in Calgary, WBS in Edmonton, and BCTV and CHER in Victoria. It was expected that commercials would reach more than 7 million Canadian homes. The money used to air the commercial came from the communications budget. The total cost to air the commercial across the country was $227,908.93. The Yogen Früz commercial was supported by numerous on-air promotional giveaways, product samples, and gift packs.

At the end of the 1997 summer season, Chris was unsure about the success of the television commercial. He was not sure if the high cost of producing the ad, and airing it during times of high viewership made this type of advertising worthwhile. No type of follow-up research was conducted after the launch of the commercial as it was deemed unnecessary, and none of the marketing budget had been allocated to research. Thus

EXHIBIT 46-3
Television Schedule (British Columbia May 8–Sept 1)

British Columbia

	Week Beginning Monday	May				June					July				August					Total
		05	12	19	26	02	09	16	23	30	07	14	21	28	04	11	18	25	01	
YTV (National)																				
Flipper	Sun, 1–2 pm	2	2	2	2	2	2	2	2	2	2	2	2	2						26
Goosebumps	Thurs, 8–8:30 pm	1	1	1	1	1	1	1	1	1	1	1	1	1						13
Sunday Late Movie	Sun, 12–2:30 am	2	2	2	2	2	2	2	2	2	2	2	2	2						26
Prime Rotation	Mon–Sun. 6:30–11:30pm	4	4	4	4	4	4	4	4	4	4	4	4	4						52
Late Night Rotation	Mon–Sun. 11:30–2:30am	3	3	3	3	3	3	3	3	3	3	3	3	3						39
Night Owl Rotation	Mon–Sun. 2:00–6:00 am	6	6	6	6	6	6	6	6	6	6	6	6	6						78
MUCH Music (National)																				
MUCH Megahits II	Sat., 11:00–11:59 am	1	1	1	1	1	1	1	1	1	1	1	1	1						13
MUCH Megahits II	Sat. 5:00–6:00 pm	1	1	1	1	1	1	1	1	1	1	1	1	1						13
MUCH Megahits II	Sun. 5:00–6:00 pm	1	1	1	1	1	1	1	1	1	1	1	1	1						13
Electric Circus	Fri. 1:30–3:00 am	1	1	1	1	1	1	1	1	1	1	1	1	1						13
Electric Circus	Fri. 10:00–11:30 am	1	1	1	1	1	1	1	1	1	1	1	1	1						13
Electric Circus	Fri. 9:30–11:00 pm	1	1	1	1	1	1	1	1	1	1	1	1	1						13
Full Rotation	Mon–Sun, 12:00 am–12:00 pm	18	18	18	18	18	18	18	18	18	18	18	18	18						234
BC TV 8																				
Oprah Winfrey	Mon.–Fri. 3:57–5:00 pm						1	1	1	1	1	1	1	1	1	1	1	1	1	13
CTV Afternoon Rotation	Mon.–Fri, 1:00–3:00 pm					3	3	3	3	3	3	3	3	3	3	3	3	3		39
CHEK (Victoria)																				
Jenny Jones	Mon.–Fri. 11:00 am–4:30 pm	5	5	5	5	5	5	5	5	5	5	5	5	5						65
		47	47	47	47	50	51	51	51	51	51	51	51	51	4	4	4	4	1	663

E X H I B I T 46-4
Television Times and Cost (British Columbia)

YTV-BC		MUCH MUSIC-BC	
DEMO	W18+	DEMO	A18-34
LENGTH	30 Seconds	LENGTH	30 Seconds
WKLY. OCC	18	WKLY. OCC	24
WKLY. AUD	88,900	WKLY. AUD	48,900
WKLY. Kelowna/Kamloops Rtgs	5	WKLY. Kelowna/Kamloops Rtgs	5.9
WKLY. Prince George Rtgs	17	WKLY. Prince George Rtgs	4.2
WKLY. Vancouver Rtgs	7	WKLY. Vancouver Rtgs	7.4
WKLY. Total Rtgs	29	WKLY. Total Rtgs	17.5
CPM	$9.21	CPM	$12.51
WKLY. COST	$820.00	WKLY. COST	$612.00
TOTAL WEEKS	13	TOTAL WEEKS	13
FLIGHT DATES	05/May/97 × 13 Wks	FLIGHT DATES	05/May/97 × 13 Wks
TOTAL SPOTS	234	TOTAL SPOTS	312
TOTAL AUD	1,155,700	TOTAL AUD	635,700
CAMPAIGN COST	$10,660.00	CAMPAIGN COST	$8,606.00

Kelowna/Kamloops, Prince George, Vancouver

WBS-BCTV		WBS-CHEK VICTORIA	
DEMO	W18-49	DEMO	W18-49
LENGTH	30 Seconds	LENGTH	30 Seconds
WKLY. OCC	4	WKLY. OCC	5
WKLY. AUD	77,000	WKLY. AUD	15,000
CPM	$9.74	CPM	$14.61
WKLY. COST	$750.00	WKLY. COST	$219.23
TOTAL WEEKS	13	TOTAL WEEKS	13
FLIGHT DATES	09/Jun/97 × 13 Wks	FLIGHT DATES	05/May/97 × 13 Wks
TOTAL SPOTS	312	TOTAL SPOTS	65
TOTAL AUD	1,001,000	TOTAL AUD	195,000
CAMPAIGN COST	$9,750.00	CAMPAIGN COST	$2,850.00

Kelowna/Kamloops, Prince George, Vancouver

Chris was not even sure if the commercial had resulted in increased awareness for the brand.

Radio

Before the 1998 summer season, Chris was approached by Garfield Ogilvie of the Radio Marketing Bureau, Inc. Garfield gave Chris a presentation on the effectiveness of radio advertising. The Radio Marketing Bureau claimed that almost 80 percent of Canadian adults listen to radio every weekday. Radio therefore delivers high, affordable frequency or repetition, which helps build brand awareness. As radio stations target niche markets, advertisers can target the particular niche to which their product is most appealing. Unlike television, radio offers year-round coverage with no summertime decline.

Chris was impressed with the presentation and materials presented by the Radio Marketing Bureau and opted to produce the following radio commercial for the 1998 summer season:

Yogen Früz
Hey—have you heard the news? It's the summer of the Smoothy Früz.
The coolest cool, the smoothest smooth,
Refresherate yourself with a Smoothy Früz.
Now you can take a tasty break any time of day,
Non-fat, real fruit—made the Yogen Früz way
The coolest cool, the smoothest smooth,
Refresherate yourself with a Smoothy Früz.
From Yogen Früz.

The cost of airing a television ad was more expensive than the previous year. Thus radio was a cost saving alternative. The radio commercial cost $4000 to produce and a total cost of $129,334 to air across the country. The commercial was entirely musical and stressed not only the Yogen Früz brand name, but also promoted awareness of the Yogen Früz Smoothy Früz, considered to be a product with high sales potential. The radio commercial was aired on second- and third-rated stations, in terms of audience, across the country. The type of music played by the selected stations was primarily easy rock and mix. The detailed schedule and cost of airing the commercials is shown in Exhibit 46-5.

Evaluation of Campaign

It was the end of the 1998 summer season and once again Chris was unsure how to evaluate the success of the latest advertising campaign. He had sent out surveys to the franchises across the country requesting the opinions of the franchisees on the success of the recent advertising campaign. The results of the surveys already returned to him were mixed. There was no clear consensus amongst the franchisees on which choice of media was most effective—television or radio. If anything, the franchisees felt that point of purchase advertisements were the most effective, since frozen yogurt is an impulse purchase. An example of the survey completed by franchisees is found in Exhibit 46-6.

Chris noted that when Baskin Robbins launched their smoothy at the beginning of the 1998 summer season, it was accompanied by a media campaign via television advertising as well as flyers and promotional offers. Baskin Robbins developed in-store advertising as well, which depicted pictures of the four varieties of smoothies with the slogan, "Real Fruit, BR Smoothy—Smart Treat."

WHAT REALLY WORKS?

Each year, Chris set his communications budget at 4.4 percent of the previous year's revenues. But which form of media provides best dollar for dollar value, wondered Chris? Which type of advertising reaches our target market most effectively? What type of advertising is most suited to a product in the product life cycle stage in which Yogen Früz found itself? Chris considered TV more youth oriented and very expensive. Radio allowed him to reach a very specific target market and, while still expensive, was a cheaper alternative to television. Point of purchase ads had always been considered effective, but were they enough? Was it possible to extend the product life cycle of Yogen Früz through advertising? Chris mulled over these issues as he left the office after another long day, and promised himself to do a detailed pros and cons analysis of each form of media.

EXHIBIT 46-5
Coolest Cool Smoothy Früz® Radio Schedule

Area	Start Date	Station	Promotion	Spots Per Week	Number of Weeks	Cost Per Week	Total Cost
Toronto	22 June	Hits 103.5	Yes	37	4	$2,160.00	$8,640.00
Toronto	22 June	530 AM	Yes	12	4		$6,500.00
Toronto	22 June	Hits 103.5	Hit Summer Rush	200 + 100 530 AM			
Toronto	22 June	EZ Rock 97.3	5000 coupons, 3 Prizes	35 (5 nights)	4	$2,512.50	$10,050.00
Toronto	22 June	CISS FM 92.5	20M Coupons, 20 Smoothy Packs	30 (10 nights)	4	$2,700.00	$10,800.00
Toronto	29 June–13 July	MIX 99.9	Yes	17	2	$3,060.00	$6,120.00
London	29 June	EZ Rock Q 97.5	Yes	18	3	$2,164.00	$6,492.00
Owen Sound	29 June	CKNX 101.7	20 Packs	17	4	$765.00	$3,060.00
Calgary	29 June	KISS 96.9	Yes	30	4	$1,530.00	$6,120.00
Calgary	29 June	CKRY 105.1	Yes	18	3	$1,980.00	$5,940.00
Edmonton	29 June	CFMG 105 EZ Rock	Yes	23	3	$1,020.00	$3,060.00
Edmonton	29 June	CKNG 92.5	Yes	21	3	$1,974.00	$5,922.00
Ottawa	22 June	KOOL CKKL 93.9	20 Packs	18	4	$1,476.00	$5,904.00
Ottawa	22 June	Majic CJMJ 100.3	20 Packs	15	4	$1,700.00	$6,804.00
Ottawa	22 June	The Buzz 1200AM	Yes	15	4		
Kitchener	22 June	CHYM 96.7	Yes	16	3	$1,664.00	$4,992.00
Thunder Bay	22 June	CJSD 94.3	Yes	15	4	$735.00	$2,940.00
Kingston	22 June	The Boroler 102.7	Promotions Only				
Vancouver	22 June	CKZZ FM 95.3					
Total							$129,334

EXHIBIT 46-6
Promotion Evaluation of Smoothy Früz®

Please fill out this evaluation form and mail or fax it back to the Y.F. Marketing Department by the end of September. This will help us to evaluate the promotion and help us make decisions regarding future marketing programs.

Address: 8300 Woodbine Ave. 5th floor, Markham, Ontario, Canada L3R 9Y7 Our fax number: (905) 479-5235

1. Do you feel customers are more aware of Smoothies this year?
2. If yes why are they more aware of Smoothies?
3. Do your customers order by the name "Smoothy" or Smoothy Früz®?
4. Did the new counter top menu help in marketing your Smoothies?
5. Did you use the new Duratran for your menuboard? _____ If no, Why?
6. How many Smoothies do you sell per week? _____
   What increase in numbers have you had this summer%? _____
   Smoothies are what % of your weekly sales? _____
7. What is the break down of Dairy Smoothies over Non-Dairy Smoothies? Dairy Smoothies _____ %
   Non-Dairy Smoothies _____ %
8. What is your most popular flavour? _____ Your least popular flavour? _____
9. Has the introduction of Smoothies by your competition affected your sales?
10. Are the customers aware that Yogen Früz® offers the biggest variety of Smoothies and dairy or non-dairy Smoothies?
11. Did any of your customers mention that they have heard our radio commercial?
12. Do you feel that Radio is a better way to reach your customers in the summer than T.V.?
13. What is your overall opinion on the Radio advertisements and promotions?
14. Did you try to promote Smoothies in the morning?
15. Did you do anything special in your store to help promote Smoothies?

    Store location: _____

    Franchisee: _____

C A S E

Forty-Seven

◆●◆

HEROES TAP AND GRILL*

Mike Monroe was troubled and angry as he locked the doors of Heroes Tap and Grill for what he feared could be the last and final time. Heroes would not be open for 30 days due to the recent charges of serving alcohol to minors and exceeding maximum capacity. "It figures this would happen at the worst time imaginable," he thought to himself. Over the past year and a half business had been declining steadily, and they were struggling to break even. Mike wasn't sure the restaurant would be able to survive 30 days of no business activity whatsoever. As he picked up his coat and left to go home, Mike thought back to when Heroes had first opened five and a half years earlier. Then, the house had always been full. People used to line up and wait for an hour to get a table. He had worked so hard to please people, and felt he had something for everyone at his establishment. What could have

gone wrong? Why was patronage so low? What could he do to save his restaurant? Even more important, could his restaurant be saved at all?

THE RESTAURANT

Heroes Tap and Grill was owned by Mike Monroe, and his wife Barbara Brooks, in the college town of Prince George, British Columbia. Mike was a graduate of the College of New Caledonia's Hotel and Food Administration Program. In addition, Mike and Barb each had many years of experience within the restaurant industry, both as minimum wage employees in the front and back of the house, and as managers. However, Heroes was the first restaurant the two had owned and operated.

The city of Prince George was located in central British Columbia, Canada, and had a population of about 70,000. The College of New Caledonia had an enrollment of 10,000 plus students in the fall and winter semesters, and 4000 during the summer.

There were only two malls within the city of Prince George, Westwood Mall and Chesire Road

---

*This case was contributed by Erin O'Brien and developed under the supervision of Margaret Shaw, Ph.D., University of Guelph, Ontario, Canada. All rights reserved. Names and places have been disguised. All amounts are in Canadian dollars. For conversion use one C$ = U.S.$0.70.

Mall. Heroes was located in Chesire Road Mall, the largest of the two by far. People would travel from all areas of Prince George not only to shop at this location, but also to attend the Cineplex Odeon movie theater located on the second floor of the mall (one of the two movie theaters in Prince George).

The mall was situated in close proximity to the College. It was only about a 20 minute walk to the mall from campus, and it was also easily accessible by bus. Buses left from both the college center and from the central downtown square.

The mall had operating hours of: Monday–Saturday, 9:00 A.M.–9:30 P.M., and Sunday 12:00–5:00 P.M. Heroes was not required to adhere to the same operating hours. It was open for business Monday–Saturday 11:00–1:00 A.M., and Sunday 11:00 A.M.–8:00 P.M.

Heroes was located on the second floor of the mall, situated directly across from Cineplex Odeon The restaurant had a chalkboard at the entrance on which they would display a list of the movies currently playing in the theater, and their start times.

Mike wanted the restaurant to have a very relaxed atmosphere. The interior was woodsy with wine-colored covering on the seats, brass railings, and a large number of booths. Pictures of popular "Heroes," such as Marilyn Monroe, Clint Eastwood, and Elvis, covered the walls of the restaurant.

There was a seating capacity of 200 people, which included a "boardroom" facility. The boardroom was separated from the restaurant by beautiful glass doors and could be rented out for parties, meetings, and occasion dinners. When this room was not rented out it was used as part of the restaurant during regular business hours. Potential existed to expand the capacity of the restaurant during the summer months by means of a patio. However, it was, at the time, in need of much work, and the owners felt it would be best to put off the improvement/use of the patio until a later date.

There was a large upraised rectangular bar situated at the rear of the restaurant. Televisions were placed in the four corners around the bar so they could be viewed from any angle. The sports channel was shown on the televisions at all times, but the sound was kept off unless there was a big game or match. Lively upbeat music played throughout the restaurant, but customers could also choose a selection of music from the jukebox found directly across from the bar.

There was also a pool table, dart board, shuffle board, dance floor, and DJ booth all located in the rear of the restaurant near the bar.

The Clientele

Within just a few months of opening, the restaurant was experiencing great success, at both the lunch and dinner hour, without any advertising. Mike and Barb found that their clientele appeared to be primarily families shopping within the mall, as well as a large number of movie goers, stopping in either before or after the show. They didn't have as many students frequent the restaurant as they had expected, but they were quite pleased with their success and felt it best to focus on the customers they had.

They had also managed to obtain a regular bar crowd. This consisted of men who would often gather in the evenings/afternoons to watch sports, or to take advantage of the happy hour, as well as mall staff who would often come up to Heroes after work for dinner and/or drinks.

The Menu

The Heroes menu was printed on a brown paper bag. There was a wide selection of items offered. These ranged from inexpensive appetizers and sandwiches to full entrée dinners offering a choice of soup or salad, and starch (rice, baked potato, house pasta, or fries). Some of the most popular menu features were: All you could eat soup and salad priced at $5.99, Make your own pasta, and Make your own pizza.

A kid's menu was also available for families with children ten years of age or younger. This menu was printed on a separate page, which was covered with cartoon characters for the kids to color (crayons were supplied to each child with a menu). When items were ordered from this menu, the child would receive a free beverage, free ice cream for desert, and a free balloon on exit.

A variety of specials were offered on a regular basis. Each day there was a pizza of the day, soup of the day, appetizer of the day, pasta of the day, a lunch special, and a nightly special. On Friday and Saturday evenings two nightly specials were available. There were also daily specials available from Monday to Thursday and following are some examples;

Monday: Two for one 16 oz. T-bone steaks (full entrée) for $19.99.
Tuesday: All you can eat pasta for $8.99–had to be the pasta of the day.
Wednesday: All you can eat chicken wings for $8.99.
Thursday: Brontosorous ribs (full entrée) for $16.99.

The Bar

A happy hour was available at the bar daily from 3:30 until 5:00 P.M., when customers were given a free four-slice pizza, with any three toppings, for every pitcher of draft beer purchased. There were also bar snacks, and two for one appetizers (available from 9:00 to 11:00 P.M.), offered at the bar but not available on the restaurant menu.

COMPETITION

Competition was not a major concern of Mike's when Heroes Tap and Grill was first opened. There were no other restaurants within the mall, only the fast-food outlets found in the mall's center. In addition there were very few restaurants in the area surrounding Cheshire Road Mall, only an East Side Mario's and a Pizza Hut, which were located in two separate strip malls across the street. Mike had considered one potential threat, the Potted Pigeon. While it was not located directly near Heroes, it was a similar restaurant in its relaxed style, and in the types of food it served. It was situated closer to the college and was also the only restaurant to accept the College's meal card. However, seeing as the majority of their customers were not students, at the moment anyway, it was not a major issue. Besides, Mike thought having some competition is healthy. "It keeps you on your toes," he said.

THE FIRST TWO YEARS

While business remained steady throughout the first couple of years, Mike noticed some bothersome trends that were occurring in his business. The most disturbing of these was the incredible slow period from January to April. While this was common for most restaurants, due to the tightening of purse strings following the Christmas season, Mike felt that his situation was even more severe because of his location in the mall. The number of customers in the mall (Mike's main client base) was very low, as were the number of people going to see movies. Mall customers dropped by 40 percent and, at times, as much as 50 percent below the norm for September to January.

To counteract this trend Mike decided to implement a number of changes. First, he allowed the two for one appetizer special, previously only offered to the bar patrons, to be available to all customers of Heroes (between 6 and 9 P.M.). He also introduced a two-for-one dessert special, by which any customer who produced a movie stub (for that night) could receive two desserts for the price of one with the purchase of any beverage. Mike already had a number of regulars who came into Heroes to watch sports or play pool, so he felt there was opportunity to expand on his bar business. To do so he invested in a large screen TV on which to show hockey, football, and other sports games.

Mike also observed over these two years that more and more students were coming into the restaurant. He recognized that it was primarily to take advantage of the all you can eat specials: the soup and salad deal, the all you can eat pasta (Tuesday nights), and the all you can eat wings (Wednesday nights). While the majority of customers still came from the mall crowd, Mike wondered if the students couldn't be the solution to his problem from January to April. He began to advertise Heroes in the two student newspapers, *The Crest* and *The Caledonian*. Mike then applied to obtain a meal card contract with the College's Express Centre, and was granted a three-year contract to begin the first of the school year.

The Express Card

At the College of New Caledonia, students living in any of the on-campus residences were required to purchase a meal plan. Off-campus students were not required to purchase the plan but were given the opportunity to do so. Students chose from meal plan options ranging from a light meal plan ($500) to a full meal plan ($1100), per semester. When the card was used to purchase food, it was swiped at the cash register and a number of points were deducted, like a debit card. This meal card was accepted in all of the campus cafeterias and until this time had been accepted in only one restaurant off campus, The Potted Pigeon. The meal card could not be used to purchase any alcoholic beverages.

For restaurants interested, the meal card contract was obtainable (by application) from the Express Centre, a department of the Hospitality Services at the College. When reviewing the potential clients, the Express Centre evaluated a number of factors including,

1. The "fit" of the restaurant in terms of suiting and meeting students needs.
2. The feasibility—does the restaurant attain enough of its business from students to warrant the use of meal cards?
3. Will the restaurant be able to make money for the Centre?

If the above factors were met, the restaurant in question would then offer a bid (a percentage of sales they were willing to pay back to the Centre). Heroes was found to fit the requirements, and was granted a three-year contract, agreeing to pay the Centre nine percent of Express card sales each year.

A further benefit of having the meal card was the free advertising done by the Express Centre for those restaurants accepting the meal card in their establishment. For example, table cards promoting Heroes Tap and Grill were displayed on the tables in all cafeterias. Restaurants accepting the meal card were also listed in brochures that were mailed out to students both on and off campus, and in the packages for new incoming students. In addition, for a minimal monthly fee, advertisements for the restaurant would also be run in a monthly publication released by the College's Hospitality Services department.

THE NEXT YEAR

Mike had been unprepared for the impact the meal card would have on his business. He had expected patronage by students to increase, of course, but he did not realize by how much. The first September with the card was the busiest month Heroes had yet seen. Not only was the mall busy with "back to school" shoppers, but the college students were pouring in. Having five or six nightly reservations for groups of 40–50 students was not uncommon. Unfortunately, not all ran smoothly. There were numerous complaints of slow service, long waits for food, and food coming at inconsistent times. The restaurant was often understaffed, and the majority of the kitchen help were young, inexperienced teenagers. This led to frequent mix-ups in the kitchen and the inability of waitstaff to offer excellent service.

Business toned down to a more manageable level in October, but Mike was excited by the success, and felt he had found his new market. There were, however, a few things that concerned Mike.

The first was the fact that students could not purchase alcohol on their cards. He had noticed that, for the most part, the students coming in were not spending their money at the bar, but more often they took advantage of the "unlimited refills" offered on the soft drinks.

Another major concern was the staff. Mike's customers had always commented on the pleasantness and promptness of his staff, and he believed this was what brought many of his return customers back. The majority of servers had worked at Heroes since it opened and had come to know the regulars very well. It was not uncommon for the wait and bar staff to greet customers by name, but now servers often grumbled about having to serve the large groups of students. The most common complaint was the lack of tipping by the students. Tipping on the meal card was not permitted and often students would come in with no cash as all they needed to pay for their meal was their card. Mike feared the staff did not give the students the same level of service they did to other customers, and also wondered what impact the situation would have on their morale. He had noticed staff booking off Tuesdays and Wednesdays, the two nights most frequented by students, saying they were not available to work those evenings.

Another issue of concern arose when the next summer turned out to be much slower than the summers of the three previous years. Mike attributed the lag to the students going home for the summer months, and decided it would be beneficial to focus on reaching more of the mall/family crowd during these months. A number of things were done in an effort to do just that.

First, Mike introduced a new summer menu, which offered various items that were not available at other times of the year, such as a fresh fruit plate, strawberry spinach salad, and a mango and kiwi chicken dish. In addition, he began once more to focus on increasing bar business. He began implementing promotions within the mall in hopes of getting in a drinking crowd during the summer months, consisting of both mall staff as well as mall patrons. He developed a plan to host theme night "parties" at Heroes throughout the summer. One example was a Hawaiian luau night. On these nights the restaurant would be decorated accordingly, drink and food specials would be offered, and a DJ would be brought in. To promote the night, stores in the mall were asked to display posters. These posters would also be displayed within the restaurant about a week in advance of the "big night." In addition, two staff would walk throughout the mall for about an hour every day, about a week in advance, handing out free Hawaiian leis, and informing people of what the "party" was about, and the type of drink and food specials that would be available. The nights were somewhat successful, attracting mainly mall employees, and Heroes staff who were off and would bring in their friends.

THE FOURTH AND FIFTH YEARS

The next two years proved to be a tough period for Heroes. Competition increased dramatically. Three new restaurants and a new coffee pub went up in the immediate area: Up the Creek, The Red Rooster, Swiss Chalet, and Walter's Coffee Pub, not a full service restaurant but one that served light food dishes as well as a variety of specialty deserts. More detailed descriptions are given in Exhibit 47-1.

Other problems were also arising. Staff turnover was incredibly high, with 50 percent of Mike's former staff leaving to work at the Red Rooster restaurant. Mike was faced not only with the problem of finding new staff, but also the time and money to train them.

Customers, and subsequently sales, began to decline dramatically. Students were now the main clientele, about 75 percent, but their numbers were decreasing. Mike knew he would lose even more of this business in the future as East Side Mario's and Up the Creek were expected to have meal card contracts by September. Few families frequented the establishment. Those that did come were mainly seen only at peak shopping periods (i.e., September and

EXHIBIT 47-1
The Competition

Restaurant	Type	Segment	Independent or Chain	Meal Card?	Other Amenities	Price Range
Potted Pigeon	American food	Casual theme, popular with students and a younger crowd	independent	yes	Yes—two pool tables	$6.99–$13.99
Pizza Hut	Pizza joint	Young families, price conscious, casual theme	chain	no	No	$4.99–$12.99
East Side Mario's	Italian/American	Family restaurant, midscale, fun/boisterous atmosphere	chain	Yes—next Sept	No	$8.99–$18.99
Swiss Chalet	Primarily spit roasted chicken	Family restaurant, casual theme, as the name suggests—like a Swiss Chalet	chain	no	No	$5.99–$10.99
The Red Rooster	BBQ food, ribs, chicken, beef	Midscale, open concept kitchen, caters to mid 20s to late 30s age group	chain	no	No	$8.99 $18.99
Walters Coffee Pub	Coffee, light lunch, deserts	Quick—service, casual theme, varied clientele from late teens to seniors	chain	no	No	$1.99–$7.99
Up the Creek	American food	Casual theme, fireplace, camping atmosphere, early 20s to middle age.	chain	Yes—next Sept	No	$6.99–$16.99

November/December). Mike was at a loss. He wasn't sure how he could or should compete with this new competition.

Mike knew he needed an edge. His first decision was to introduce a delivery service to students living in residence (so they could still use their meal card) as none of the other establishments offered this service. The delivery service was a success, and very well liked by the students; however, it was not making the money Mike needed to turn things around.

The second decision was to introduce Wacky Wednesdays, a new concept in an attempt to bring in the students, not to eat, but to get them spending their money at the bar. Mike felt Wednesday was appropriate as students were still coming in for the "all you could eat" wings. The new Wacky Wednesday special was a 32 ounce draft beer for the price of a 16 ounce one, or a double bar shot for the price of one, starting at 9:00 P.M. It took some time for the idea to catch on. At first it attracted mainly mall employees and staff. Then Mike brought in a DJ on Wednesday nights and began promoting the special in the student newspapers. Eventually, more and more students began pouring in; some nights there would be lineups at 9:00 waiting to get in. The dance floor in the restaurant was packed, and it was not uncommon to meet the maximum legal capacity of the restau-rant. Mike raised the price of the drinks to $4.25 for either a 32 ounce or double shot, and the students kept coming.

Staff had commented to Mike a number of times concerning the regulars feeling alienated by this new atmosphere. More than one server had heard the line, "It's just not like it used to be." Not only regulars complained, but other customers did as well. On more than one occasion, a table seated at 8:30 on a Wednesday night would become frustrated and annoyed at 9:00 when the DJ came on and dance music began to blare. Yet, as the night became more and more popular, Mike decided to take advantage of this and, in the summer, invested in improving the old patio attached to the restaurant. He put in a separate bar outside so that more customers could be fit into the restaurant on Wednesday nights.

Unfortunately, Wednesday evenings were now the only nights when the restaurant was busy. The rest of the week the restaurant was practically empty. Mike couldn't figure it out. Nothing had really changed at Heroes except for the implementation of Wacky Wednesday. Yet, not only were the families and mall patrons not coming in, the students were no longer coming in to eat either. Even the before and after movie business had dwindled. Something needed to be done and soon, but what? Mike had 30 days to figure it out.

C A S E

Forty-Eight

◆

FAST EDDIE'S*

"What do I think my biggest challenge is?" Mike Gorski sat on the other side of the table in the donut store across the street from his Elgin Street, Cambridge, burger operation. He pondered for a moment, then replied, "Probably people. Managing people. Whether it's construction people, employees, franchisees—having the right people at the right time. If I had consistently better people this company would run better. I could open and run stores more easily. . . ." Mike's voice trailed off as his mind moved on to the next subject he wished to discuss.

In the 11 years since its inception, the *fast eddie's* burger operation had grown from its one store operation in Brantford, Ontario, to seven stores located in the Ontario communities of London, Cambridge, Simcoe, and Brantford, with another slated to open soon in Waterloo. *fast eddie's* began

as, and continued to be, a Canadian, family-owned and operated chain, a fact the company proudly promoted.

Even before the inception of *fast eddie's,* the Gorski family had a history of fast-food store ownership. Mike's father, Ted, had owned several McDonald's franchises north of Toronto and had employed his children in the stores from an early age. The franchises were sold in 1979. Son Mike and daughter Jania went on to obtain business degrees from McMaster University in Hamilton.

While in Texas in the mid 1980s, Mike Gorski became aware of a drive-through burger operation named Short Stop. He became intrigued with the concept of a rapid, pared down burger store, and returned home to discuss the family's possible return to the fast-food business.

Mike and other members of the Gorski family refined and later launched the *fast eddie's* concept. The idea was simple—the service of a fairly basic menu of burgers, fries, and drinks in a drive-through setting. The most immediate and unique elements of the concept were that there was no interior service offered (not even an indoor service counter for walk-up orders) and two drive-

*This case was contributed by Elizabeth Duncan, Caroline Langelier, and Geoffrey Smith and developed under the supervision of Margaret Shaw, Ph.D., University of Guelph, Ontario, Canada. All rights reserved. All dollar amounts are in Canadian dollars. For conversion purposes, C$1 = U.S.$0.70.

through windows (one on each side of the building). "Two windows, no waiting." The company dedicated itself to selling a faster and better quality product at a substantially lower price than its competition.

Mike Gorski was *fast eddie's* and *fast eddie's* was Mike Gorski. To say that he was involved with the company was an understatement. His passion neared religious zeal and was both infectious and intimidating. He and his sister Jania (president and vice president operations, respectively) maintained a close, hands-on focus on the chain and were constantly in the stores "flipping burgers" with the rest of their "restaurant family." One of the criteria for selecting a new restaurant location was proximity to the head office in Brantford, enabling the Gorskis to travel daily to most or all of the stores. The personal involvement in the chain also went to the heart of the product.

THE PRODUCT

One of the cornerstones of the company was the production and service of a product superior to that of the burger competitors—the national burger chains. In pursuit of this goal, Mike had been deeply involved with his various suppliers in the development of the burger patties, buns, and fixings. Historically, Mike had allied himself with local suppliers for community reasons, but also to permit him regular personal contact with the suppliers themselves. During the 11 years of operation, a number of changes had been made, all directed toward product improvement.

Each of the elements of the various burgers was regularly and rigidly reviewed for quality. This process had resulted in, among other things, the substitution of full leaf lettuce for the original shredded and bagged iceberg that was more commonly used in the fast food industry. The personal input into product development extended to the buns, ketchup, sauces, cheese, and meat. Mike wanted his customers to "open up the bag and smell the quality." He wanted his customers to immediately make the value connection between his product's quality, his low "shock pricing," and the speed of service.

This passion for excellence had resulted in the changing of meat suppliers, from a southwestern Ontario firm to Cardinal Meats of Mississauga. Subsequent to observing deterioration in the quality of the patties being supplied by the original meat packer, Mike confronted the company about his concerns. Their silence spoke volumes. After laboratory testing confirmed Mike's suspicion that there was a problem, the contract was voided and the successful relationship with Cardinal was initiated. Once again, Mike personally worked with Cardinal in the development of the specifications for the new patties. The contract with Cardinal called for random, independent testing of the product, to be initiated by *fast eddie's* and paid for by Cardinal. Mike featured Cardinal on the poster ads for burgers located outside his restaurants.

Beyond the food product, *fast eddie's* was unique among its fast-food competitors in other ways. Like many others, such as McDonalds, *fast eddie's* had drive-through windows, but unlike the others, there was no inside accessibility for customers.

Each *fast eddie's* outlet was built in a long, narrow configuration totaling 800 to 900 square feet, and was equipped with two drive-through windows to permit faster processing of customers. The menu was posted prominently on the center rear of the building, with ordering pillars located on both the left and right sides of the structure. After ordering, the motorist proceeded forward and along either of the two sides of the building to receive service at the drive-through window. Money and food were handled at the same window, unlike some national fast-food burger chains where they were handled separately. Although there were two essentially identical drive-through options, approximately 80 percent of the automobiles used the "right hand side" window, 20 percent used the "left hand side" window. This 80/20 split of traffic flow somewhat defeated the purpose of the building design. In addition to the two drive-through windows, each store was equipped with two front windows to accommodate walk-up business. The pedestrian customer was offered no protection from the elements while ordering or waiting for the food. There were service targets for this aspect of the operation, but there were no sensors in place to specifically monitor performance in this area.

OPERATIONS

fast eddie's competed well with its burger competitors and generally beat its "sandwich" competitors in terms of speed. For example, over one heavy service period, 12:00 to 2:00 P.M., times were as follows,

Store	Average Service Time
fast eddie's	44 seconds
Burger King	38 seconds
Tim Horton's	150 seconds

The corporate goal was to complete service to the customer within 40 seconds of arrival at the drive-through window (as measured by sensing devices in the concrete pad beneath the window). The hourly/daily, and weekly results were posted in the individual restaurants as well as being forwarded to the head office. The service time targets figured prominently in the performance measurement of the stores.

The *fast eddie's* concept called for a specific exterior configuration consisting of the building itself, three traffic lanes, and some customer parking space to permit the on-site consumption of the food (Exhibit 48-1). The store still under development in Waterloo diverged from this concept and, worthy of note, it was the first store to be opened in an already existing building. This location, built into a renovated service station, would have only one drive-through window, and its dimensions would be quite different from the standard store.

Each store operated with an average of four to six employees per shift, but most commonly with five employees plus a manager during peak times. Two employees took/served orders and operated

---

EXHIBIT 48-1
Layout of *fast eddie's*

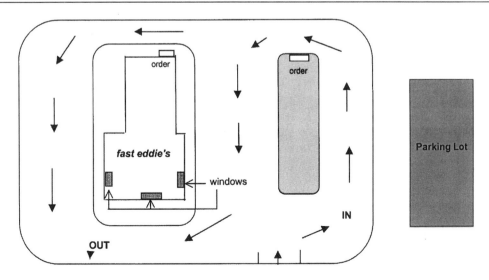

cash; the remainder prepared the food. There was a shift manager and/or store manager in the unit at all times. It was common for a supervisor (a corporate employee) or a Gorski family member to be present and working in a store during many of the hours of operation.

Hours of operation for the stores were from 10:30 A.M. through 11:30 P.M., seven days a week. Most sales took place during typical lunch and dinner periods as well as Thursday and Friday evenings, and Saturdays. The stores usually operated with full staff during these periods, operating with as few as three employees during the least busy periods. Two of the stores were located within a block of large secondary schools, which increased demand at the walk-up windows. This important customer base was highly sensitive to weather, academic commitments, and holidays. The drive-through burger business itself was cyclical; there was a 40 percent drop in sales for the ten-week period in January through March of each year.

Marketing

It was Mike Gorski's position that the startlingly low prices, "shock pricing" as he put it, would drive an initial purchase at the store and the superior quality would bring the customer back. It was for this reason that he was so focused on quality.

Mike also felt that location was critical, and he easily and passionately launched into descriptions of how and why he had chosen sites for the existing stores. Each *fast eddie's* was within eyesight of at least one (and often more than one) nationally known fast-food store—McDonald's, Burger King, Wendy's, Tim Horton's, and others. Again, the Waterloo store was somewhat different. It was located beside a Swiss Chalet store and across the street from a small independent burger store, with the "burger nationals" being further down the street. Each of the stores, without exception, was located on a high-traffic street in a retail commercial area.

fast eddie's relied heavily on word of mouth to sell itself. The company spent an average of 2 percent of revenue on promotion, with very little being spent in traditional advertising venues such as radio and print media. Over the years, a number of articles had appeared in local area newspapers about the chain (featuring Mike in particular) but the company did not generally advertise in this medium. Instead, the chain primarily promoted itself through cents-off or bonus offer coupons distributed to target households through the Penny Saver direct mail coupon package. The process was repeated three or four times per year and was targeted to bring in customers in the four to six week period following distribution, during the slower sales periods for the company. In order to validate the coupon, the customer had to write a comment about *fast eddie's* service on the reverse side. In addition, the chain offered a "happy hour" weekly—hamburgers were offered at 39 cents from 4:00 P.M. to 7:00 P.M. on Thursday nights. Corporate business cards had printed coupons for free "Crazy Frys" and burgers on their reverse sides.

The chain regularly featured a discount on one of the higher value burgers. Each restaurant used the adjustable portion of its menu sign to advertise its participation in a particular burger promotion. The burger promotion campaign offered another example of Mike's commitment to quality. Management determined whether a particular store could accommodate the anticipated influx of additional customers as a result of the promotion without compromising service standards. In one case, the older of the two stores in Cambridge had a significant proportion of new employees, and it was felt that the store could not meet corporate standards if traffic was increased. Mike decided to exclude this store from sandwich promotions for a period of four weeks, allowing for additional training and the ability to meet service time standards. A similar decision was made to exclude a new Cambridge store from participation for its first three months of operation, while managers and staff gained experience.

fast eddie's emphasized its small chain, Canadian image. The "dot" on the "i" in the name was a maple leaf. The chain promoted its willingness to participate in community fund-raising activities using a notice on the drink and French fry cups. A company representative attended community events/parades and handed out promotional gifts and materials.

HUMAN RESOURCES

fast eddie's head office management team consisted of seven people: the President (Mike Gorski), the Vice President Operations (Jania), the Vice President Finance (Monika), two supervisors of operations (Matt and Steve), the office manager Stacey, and one administrative support person (Jennifer). There was a restaurant manager at each of the seven restaurants plus a total of 40 to 45 full- and part-time employees at the store level operation.

Mike involved himself in all aspects of the operation, but his primary responsibilities lay in marketing, managing suppliers, locating potential new store sites, talking to possible franchisees, and motivating his managers to perform. Monika, as Vice President Finance, dealt with the financial management of the business and Jania, like Mike, was deeply involved in the daily operation of the chain in her capacity as Vice President Operations. Both Jania and Mike visited most of the stores on a daily basis. Their presence was constant and the attention was personal. Not surprisingly, the mention of formal or even informal succession planning generated a distant stare from Mike, and an admission that no ready answer to the problem came to mind. *fast eddie's* was driven by Mike, his attention to detail, and his daily presence in the *fast eddie's* outlets, and to a lesser extent by Jania Gorski.

The two supervisors of operations, Matt and Steve, each had considerable experience in the retail and restaurant fields and had been with *fast eddie's* for five and eight years, respectively. Together they were responsible for the supervision of all locations, including inspection, report preparation, and replacing store managers as required.

The store managers were responsible for the day-to-day, minute-to-minute operation of their respective sites. The job required at least 60 hours per week and encompassed the management of staff, hiring, on-the-job training of employees, and ordering of supplies. All seven managers had previous restaurant experience prior to joining *fast eddie's* and were paid a salary of $32,000 plus performance bonus. All but the most recently hired manager had been with *fast eddie's* for at least five years, and all raved about the company.

Mike launched easily and passionately into the topic of management training. He felt it was critical to his operation. There was ongoing training available on a biweekly basis in the form of video and lecture, with hard copy take-aways for each manager's store manual. According to Mike, it was his management program, called "PROACTIVES" (People, Results, Operations, Appearance, Communication, Training, Inspire/Value, Emotion, Systems)that was at the heart of his success, and his store managers carried the program with them in the form of laminated cards.

The PROACTIVES system put specific targets for service, food handling, and personnel issues directly in the hands of the supervisors, and portions of the PROACTIVES program were posted in various areas in the store for all employees to see. The management process was constantly being reviewed and refined by Mike, and his conversation was peppered with academic references from the human resources and management fields.

More recently, Mike had focused his energy on the training of line employees, after he noticed the relatively long time it took to bring a new hire up to full operating capacity. This issue was critical, as the PROACTIVES program called for a hard line on quality issues and contributed to an already high turnover rate typical in fast-food frontline employees. Apart from the obvious desirability of a new hire coming up to speed rapidly, Mike felt that this was also critical in his quality drive, as it would give his managers a degree of comfort in releasing an unsatisfactory employee if s/he knew that a new hire could be integrated rapidly.

After study, Mike concluded that the company

training efforts had been too broad in focus. Rather than using classroom techniques to teach employees about the company and its policies and expectations, he created an on-the-job skill based training program. The new focus dropped the training time from days to one to two hours. The company "education" program continued after the initial skill training, but a new hire could be "up and running" almost immediately.

All line employees were paid minimum wage on an hourly basis, but were also eligible to participate in a modified profit-sharing plan. This program was based on store performance. Managers were provided with weekly store data (sales, time scores, etc.) as well as monthly corporate figures. All employees were entitled to access this information but, according to Mike, few bothered to do so. Some data (time targets/performance, etc.) was posted prominently within the restaurants. Credits within the program were cashable upon exit from the company but did not constitute company shares, per se.

COMPETITIVE ENVIRONMENT

fast eddie's was the only drive-through restaurant in Ontario with a two-window configuration. However, each store was strategically located within a "fast-food alley" and, as such, was engaged in a fiercely competitive environment. *fast eddie's* sought to differentiate itself through unique physical structure, shock pricing, speed of service, and quality of product. See Exhibit 48-2 for a comparison of pricing among a number of burger stores.

FUTURE GROWTH

The start-up funds for *fast eddie's* came from the Gorski family. Mike contributed $87,000 of his own money. Retained earnings of over $1.5 million were used to finance additional stores. The consol-

EXHIBIT 48-2
Competitive Pricing of Fast Food Restaurants

	fast eddie's	*McDonald's*	*Burger King*
Hamburgers			
Basic	$0.69	$0.99	$0.99
Cheeseburger	$0.79	$1.19	$1.14
Double cheeseburger	$1.97	n/a	$2.69
Double Burger Works	$1.97	$2.99	$2.39
Chicken Works	$1.97	$2.99	$2.99
Monster	$2.97	$2.99	$3.79
Fries			
Medium	$0.89	$1.15	$1.45
Large	$1.29	$1.99	$1.85
Crazy Fry	$1.69	n/a	n/a
Soft Drinks			
Small	$0.79	$1.29	$1.29
Medium	$0.89	$1.59	$1.49
Milkshakes			
Small	$1.29	$1.79	$1.59
Large	$1.49	$2.19	$1.99

idated income statement for the firm is shown in Exhibit 48-3. The total revenue from operations for the next year was projected to be $6.8 million. This compared to $5.9 million for the current year.

Average sales per restaurant in the April to December period were $2580 per day, compared to $1554 per day in the slower winter months. On average 3000 to 3500 cars per week passed through each location with the average sale being $5.56. Continued growth was a corporate goal and the

EXHIBIT 48-3

	1997	1998	1999 (estimate)
New Outlets Opened	1	1	1
Total Outlets	6	7	8
Sales	5,130	5,895	6,795
Food cost			
Food	1,910	2,211	2,541
Paper	233	267	308
Total	2,143	2,478	2,849
Gross Profit	2,987	3,417	3,946
Labor			
Line Staff	1,023	1,191	1,364
Management	192	224	256
Head Office	190	190	190
Total	1,405	1,605	1,810
Operating Expenses			
Advertising	110	126	145
Utilities	106	123	141
Uniforms	14	16	18
Training	25	25	25
Auto	9	11	12
Business Taxes	74	85	98
Garbage Removal	32	37	42
Equipment Maintenance	285	333	380
Cleaning Supplies	69	81	92
Administrative Expense	32	37	42
Depreciation	284	333	380
Total	1,040	1,207	1,375
Operating Profit	542	605	761
Interest on long Term Debt	0	0	0
Income Before Taxes	542	606	760
Income Taxes	156	175	236
Net Income	386	431	524

question under discussion was whether to continue to finance future expansion or whether to expand through franchising the concept.

To this end, and in response to inquiries from interested members of the public, a franchise package was developed. Mike's figures estimated a start-up cost for a new restaurant of between $575,000 and $825,000, depending on the cost of site preparation (Exhibit 48-4). The *fast eddie's* concept had historically called for a newly constructed, free-standing structure with a specific traffic lane configuration. Success with the new Waterloo store might alter the corporate position; however, this remained to be seen.

fast eddie's expected that a new store would operate at a loss in the first year of operation. This was not atypical in any business. Mike's initial prediction that it would take approximately three years for a unit to perform at its peak had turned out to be accurate.

The company received 15 to 20 inquiries about franchising each month, most likely originating from the solicitation on the *fast eddie's* paper bag. Each prospective franchisee was given a short preliminary interview by telephone and was sent a franchise package. Less than two per month were returned and Mike stated that, in his opinion, only one application to date had been worthy of significant follow-up on his part.

"They're babies. They have no business sense." Mike pulled some completed applications from his briefcase. The poorly completed papers reflected an equally poor understanding of the time and financial commitment required to operate any business, let alone a fast-food restaurant. Mike was concerned that permitting inexperienced, would-be entrepreneurs to take on this type of operation was to doom them and the chain to mediocrity or failure. He spoke with derision of the rapid (and seemingly uncontrolled) expansion by other retail food operations and was clearly not interested in traveling that route.

Mike wanted to maintain close control over the quality of his product and service and was concerned that the prospective franchisees that had come forward to date were unwilling to make the personal commitment to the business he required of them. He openly stated that those who have applied to date were not generally of the "quality" of operator he would be willing to trust with his "baby."

Mike was aware that should he choose to proceed with franchising, he would have to go out and actively seek appropriate franchisees rather than wait for them to appear at his doorstep. For the moment he seemed unwilling to go this route and appeared content to permit "the mountain to come to Mohammed." At the same time, Mike was unhappy with the results his "wait and see" strategy had achieved. Thus he asked himself.

Should he continue to expand *fast eddie's*? If so, should he continue to expand through retained earnings or through franchising? Should he relinquish any measure of control to the franchisees?

EXHIBIT 48-4
Start up Costs of a *fast eddie's* Restaurant

	Low	Medium	High
Land	$200,000	$250,000	$300,000
Building	$200,000	$250,000	$300,000
Equipment cost	$150,000	$175,000	$200,000
Training/Inventory/Etc.	$ 25,000	$ 25,000	$ 25,000
Total	$575,000	$700,000	$825,000

Forty-Nine

•❖•

DELPHI OR FIDELIO?*

Joseph Bennett, President of Reddington Hotels, sat back in his chair during a recent Marketing Information System (MIS) meeting at his company. Reddington Hotels needed to standardize its software systems in order to capture customer profiles. Customer profiles would be input into the various hotels' computer systems, reveal who the decision-makers were, the volume of bookings, history of the accounts, and so forth. By standardizing and sharing information, Reddington would then have a unique customer base. Instead of customers "belonging" to the company's various franchises, the customers' data would be able to be shared among all Reddington Hotels. The accounts for Reddington Hotels would all be available for all the salespeople. With a standard system in place, information sharing on customers would become a reality. Salespeople being transferred between Reddington Hotels would be familiar with the system and always able to access the data.

Reddington Hotels was formed during the early 1990s as an owner/management company and had 140 hotels throughout the United States. The portfolio was built from displaced real estate that had been owned by insurance companies, banks, and pension funds. The mix of hotels fell into the following segments: 23 full service, 72 limited service, and 45 budget.

The franchise affiliations varied with the hotels. Reddington managed Sheraton, Radisson, Howard Johnson, and independent hotels. Mr. Bennett had called the meeting with his senior sales, marketing, and MIS executives to discuss the possibility of a single software computer system for the entire company. Some hotels had simple computerized systems and others were operating property management systems (PMS) in their properties under various names.

While there were significant advantages in having the same technology platform in all hotels, there were significant issues that needed to be resolved before going forward. The first was a choice of systems. There were two primary systems available to Reddington Hotels—Delphi and Fidelio. The Delphi sales system was created by an individual in New Hampshire during the 1980s and had grown exponentially during the years. Fidelio was created

*Names have been disguised.

by Inter-Continental Hotels during the same time period and was later spun off as a separate company.

A benefit grid showing where each system was stronger was created to guide the executives in their decision-making process:

Benefit	Delphi	Fidelio
1. U.S. Distribution	X	
2. International Distribution		X
3. Sales Systems	X	X
4. Support Systems	X	X
5. Property Management System		X
6. Interface	X	X

Reddington had determined that the six benefits were all important but had yet to determine which were more important. Delphi had an advantage with stronger domestic distribution where all of the current Reddington Hotels were located. Fidelio had better distribution internationally. The sales systems, which include customer profiles, traces, function book, and yield management were judged to be equal. The support systems including training and software upgrades were also deemed to be similar.

Fidelio offered a complete technology package, meaning the sales computer system linked into a front office PMS to show current rooms inventory. Fidelio offered both the sales system and the PMS although they could be purchased separately. Delphi could interface with Fidelio's PMS as well as others. Delphi did not offer a PMS component of the technology platform. Fidelio could interface with non-Fidelio PMS.

Mr. Bennett steered the meeting to begin to determine the weighted benefit of each element to the organization. From a scale of 1 to 10 with 1 being least important to 10 being most important, he asked his executives to rate each benefit individually. The sum total of the weighted benefits would then assist his team in choosing a sales computer system.

Fifty

MARKETPLACE TO GO*

In 1980, John Delano opened the first Farmers' Restaurant in Dallas, Texas. Offering full-service casual and fine dining with an emphasis on fresh farm product and seafood, the restaurant became a quick success. The 1980s saw the addition of more than 20 additional Farmers' Restaurants in Dallas, Fort Worth, Austin, Houston, and other major cities in the southwest United States. In 1991, the success of these restaurants led to the development of a new concept called Farmers' Market Restaurants. The first was opened in Dallas. This new European market-style restaurant was a variation of the already successful Farmers' concept.

The Farmers' Market concept was unique. The restaurants were set up to look and act just like a European market where, for example, bakers made bread from scratch, and cooks prepared an omelet as directed by customers. All food was prepared on location and there was no traditional "back of the house" kitchen. Raw materials, such as 50-pound bags of potatoes, were worked into the display. There were no waiters; when customers arrived at a Farmers' Market they were

shown to a table and then were given the freedom to wander among the various food stations, choosing their own food and bringing the meal back to the table. The use of these food stations gave the restaurant a greater flexibility to adapt to local tastes and trends that other restaurants did not have. Guests were given a card that was stamped at the various food stations and used as a guest check when they paid on the way out of the restaurant. The concept was immediately successful and quickly expanded into other cities where Farmers' Restaurants already existed.

John Delano soon realized that about 30 percent of Farmers' Market business was take-out, and he recognized another potential concept in the "home meal replacement" (HMR) market. In 1998 four prototype "Marketplace to Go" outlets were introduced in Dallas in a joint effort with Dixie, a large supermarket chain in the southwest. The Marketplace to Go outlets were located at the entrance of each Dixie store and occupied approximately 1500 square feet. They were set up to look exactly like a traditional Marketplace restaurant with the only difference being a limited seating area that could accommodate ten to fifteen patrons, who might wish to stop for a coffee or light lunch while shopping. Dixie customers first had to pass through the Marketplace to Go outlet in order to reach the aisles of the supermarket. The Marketplace to Go outlets mainly served take-out food, in a retail environment, that was ready to eat or prepackaged with an emphasis on its quality and freshness. The Marketplace to Go operations competed with other take-out restaurants in the HMR market by supplying entire dinners for customers on their way home from the supermarket. Mr. Delano had high hopes for the Marketplace to Go concept. The four original outlets were operated at a slight loss but, according to Mr. Delano, they would begin to turn a profit in another year as high overhead costs were spread out over more outlets.

Mr. Delano had announced his intention to grow rapidly over the next two to three years. The company anticipated opening four to five new flagship Marketplace to Go outlets in key North American cities. Boston, Chicago, St. Louis, San Francisco, and Atlanta were some of the cities being considered. Lease negotiations for several high-profile supermarket locations were underway. The company also intended to vigorously pursue further Marketplace to Go outlets on a stand-alone basis. The key to this expansion outside of Dallas was the acceptance of the Marketplace to Go concept in Dallas. There were only a few market-style rivals in North America, including Eatzi's in Dallas, and Harry's Home Market in Atlanta, Georgia.

THE HMR CONCEPT

Mr. Delano met with his Marketing Director, Chris Murphy, a recent graduate from the hospitality graduate program at the University of Houston. Chris had worked for Mr. Delano for a number of years, first as a busboy, then as a waiter and, after completing his master's studies, assumed the role of Marketing Director of Delano, Inc. The purpose of the meeting was to discuss the future plans of the Marketplace to Go concept.

"Chris, I know we have a good thing going with this Marketplace to Go concept, but I need some

hard facts to convince the shareholders at next month's meeting," remarked Mr. Delano. "I agree that this concept will work," replied Chris, "but the first thing we have to do is agree on a definition of HMR." Chris explained,

> The way I see it Mr. Delano, the way consumers are buying food products from supermarkets is changing. There is more of an inclination to buy ready-to-eat products that require little or no preparation. That is what HMR is all about. But, more specifically, HMR products must have several core values: they are home-style comfort foods, primarily for home consumption; they are easy and convenient to obtain and consume; they are quick service, complete meals and meal components, preparation-free, high quality, cost effective, and appropriate for family sharing. It is the kind of food consumers would cook for themselves at home, if they had the time, skill, or motivation.

"I see you're putting your masters degree to good work Chris, and I agree with your definition of HMR. But I still need some hard facts to convince the shareholders that this is a good idea," said Mr. Delano. "No problem," replied Chris, "there are a number of things that would suggest this is a great idea to pursue." Chris explained further:

> A slew of recent statistics confirms that the HMR trend is not a fad. The North American lifestyle is changing. There is an increase in the number of dual income families which, in turn, is leaving families with less time to cook for themselves. These are the catalysts pushing the HMR trend. A recent study from the National Restaurant Association shows that 57 percent of take-out restaurant meals are purchased because consumers say they don't have time to eat in a restaurant anymore. Additionally, consumers said they are either too pressed for time or too fatigued at the end of the day to cook. It would also be wise to inform the shareholders of the changing demographic profile of North America. Baby Boomers comprise 38 percent of the North America population. This particular segment is characterized by its willingness to pay for quality and the lack of spare time. Also, it is a fact that today more women

are entering the workforce and the size of families in North America is shrinking. What this amounts to is two-income households with few children and very little free time. All of this points to the tremendous opportunity for HMR to catch on in North America. In fact, it is predicted that, by the year 2005, more than 50 percent of the average consumer's food spending will be on prepared meals purchased outside the home, and taken back home for consumption.

"That confirms what I've thought all along. It looks like its clear sailing from here on in," said Mr. Delano. "Now that we know there is a market for HMR, we should be able to duplicate our success in Dallas in other major cities across North America." Chris thought briefly about Mr. Delano's comments and said: "With all due respect Mr. Delano, there definitely is a market for HMR, but knowing that does not guarantee our success in other cities." "Of course it doesn't," said Mr. Delano, "but all we have to do is choose the prime locations. In fact, lease negotiations are already under way in New York City."

"What does he mean by prime location?" Chris thought to himself. He decided he should speak up now, before it was too late. "But Mr. Delano, we have four very different locations in the city of Dallas alone. How do we know the locations we are negotiating for are the prime locations?" Mr. Delano replied, "You're right Chris. I guess what we need to know is how our four locations measure up in terms of revenue performance, and then we will know which of our locations are best." Chris then said, "Not only that, but we need to know who we are serving at each location, and what we are doing right, and what needs improvement. Then we will be able to make a better decision on where we should locate the new outlets."

Mr. Delano was impressed and said, "Chris, I don't know what I'd do without you. I'm putting you in charge of conducting a market study of the four original locations. Remember Chris, the shareholder's meeting is only in one month, and I'm looking for some good information". For a brief moment, Chris regretted making his previous comments. He knew he had a lot of work ahead of him but said, "Splendid idea, Mr. Delano. I'll report back to you in three weeks time." "Good job, Chris, that's why I pay you the big bucks," said Mr. Delano.

THE MARKET STUDY

Chris used two main sources of information for his market study. The first was an in-person consumer survey that was administered to Dixie's customers at each of the four Dallas locations. From the consumer survey, as well as discussions with Dixie managers, it was determined that the majority of Marketplace to Go customers originated within two miles of the supermarket. From this, it was decided that the distance of 0–2 miles would be used as the trading area of each location. Chris decided to contract the services of Home Research, a social market research company in Dallas, to gain further insight into each of the trading areas. He used the information gathered by Home Research as his second main source of information. Exhibit 50-1 shows the Home Research results for each of the four locations in Dallas. Each location was about five miles from any other.

Chris also wanted to get a sense of the business-residential mix of each of the primary trading areas. The Home Research finding for this are shown in Exhibit 50-2.

Given the Home Research data, Chris now turned to the other main source of information, his own consumer survey. A total of 440 personal interview questionnaires were conducted as shown in Exhibit 50-3. The survey was constructed and pretested before any data was collected. The interviews took place within the Dixie stores, but not within the Marketplace to Go outlets themselves. This was done to gain insight into why some Dixie customers chose not to shop at the Marketplace to Go outlets.

Exhibit 50-4 presents the relevant demographic information of Dixie's customers who said they had previously purchased from the Marketplace to Go outlet.

EXHIBIT   50-1

Home Research Findings of Population within 0–2 Miles Each Location

Location	A Location	B Location	C Location	D Location
Population:				
Males	30,421	39,664	63,606	20,932
Females	24,889	58,466	91,534	17,829
Total	55,310	98,130	155,140	38,761
Female age percent				
20–29	21	25	22	18
30–49	39	65	67	34
50 +	40	10	11	48
Household Structure:				
1 person	5065	8120	23,815	3390
2 person	7745	8545	19,890	4985
3 person	4510	3765	10,635	2600
4–5 person	5930	5570	13,540	3865
6+ persons	1180	765	3310	420
Households Income:	55,825	88,426	54,148	77,084

Chris designed the survey to determine very specific information. For example, he wanted to know the household composition of current Marketplace to Go customers.

Exhibits 50-5 and 50-6 summarize the household composition in each of the four locations.

Another key piece of information Chris wanted to know was where the customers were coming from just prior to arriving at the supermarket. Interestingly, over 75 percent of customers at the B and C locations said they were at work prior to the

supermarket, whereas the majority of the customers at the A and D locations came from home.

The consumer survey also indicated that all four Dixie locations were rated by customers to be very good to excellent in terms of food quality, product selection, and customer service. However, customers at all locations were less satisfied with the value received from the Marketplace to Go products. Furthermore, price was cited as the main reason for not purchasing from the Marketplace to Go outlets. Similarly, price was cited as the aspect they

EXHIBIT   50-2

Findings of Business-Residential Mix

Location	A	B	C	D
Households	34,260	38,160	100,140	10,640
Businesses	1142	2671	8345	2660

EXHIBIT 50-3
Survey Collection Distribution

Location	Weekday AM	Weekday PM	Saturday all day	TOTALS
A Area Customers	32	40	39	111
B Area Customers	40	32	35	107
C Area Customers	34	35	41	110
D Area Customers	40	37	35	112

liked least about the Marketplace to Go outlets followed by congestion at the entrance of the outlets.

Chris was curious as to whether customers were purchasing more, less, or the same amount of HMR products than they did three years ago. It was found that HMR products appeared to be gaining in popularity among those surveyed at all locations, with just over 50 percent of customers saying they were buying more HMR products, and only a small percentage saying they were buying fewer HMR products.

Chris needed one more piece of information to complete his market study. He needed to know how well each of the locations had perform since it's opening. To obtain this information, Chris spoke with the unit managers at each of the four

EXHIBIT 50-4
Demographic Results from Consumer Survey

Location:	A f	A %	B f	B %	C f	C %	D f	D %	Totals f	Totals %
Gender:										
Males	15	28%	22	36%	27	42%	12	15%	76	29%
Females	39	72%	38	64%	37	58%	70	85%	184	71%
Age:										
20–29	5	9%	7	11%	10	16%	9	11%	31	12%
30–39	21	39%	23	38%	29	45%	17	21%	90	34%
40–49	20	37%	18	30%	15	23%	33	40%	86	33%
50 and over	8	15%	13	21%	10	16%	23	28%	54	
Mother Tongue:										
English	37	67%	48	79%	51	80%	80	95%	216	82%
Other	18	33%	13	21%	13	20%	4	5%	48	18%
Residence:										
Owned	42	76%	48	80%	35	56%	65	80%	190	73%
Rented	13	24%	12	20%	28	44%	16	20%	69	27%

f = the frequency of response

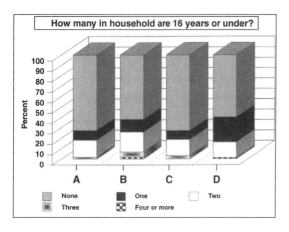

EXHIBIT 50-5 Age Demographics.

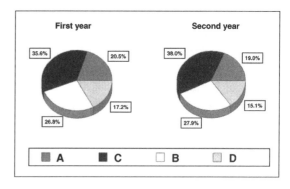

EXHIBIT 50-7 Relative Revenue Contribution of Each Location for Two Years Since Opening.

locations. Exhibit 50-7 shows the percentage revenue contribution of each Marketplace to Go outlet.

The Meeting with Mr. Delano

As promised, Chris met with Mr. Delano three weeks after their initial meeting and presented him with the market study. "Good to see you Chris. Let's see how valuable that master's degree really is," said Mr. Delano. Chris handed him the market study and sat patiently as Mr. Delano leafed slowly through the pages.

"Chris, it looks like you've done some hard work here. My only problem is that I'm still not sure in what kind of communities we should be locating the new Marketplace to Go outlets. Who exactly is our target market, and what we are doing well to serve them?" asked Mr. Delano. "I think what we need is a little more analysis here. Why don't you take a couple of days and try to come up with some common performance factors for our most successful locations. That should give us a better idea of who we are serving and where we should be located."

"I'll get right on that Mr. Delano. I'll see you in a couple of days," replied Chris.

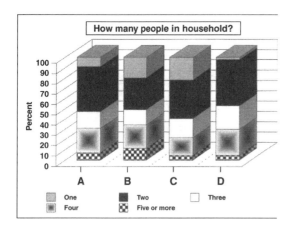

EXHIBIT 50-6 Family Size Demographics.

Fifty-One

ELECTRONIC DISTRIBUTION AT GROUP ACCOR*

Jean Blanc had recently taken over as Vice President for Electronic Distribution at the hotel division of Group Accor. His newly created post was a reflection of the importance that the company was placing on this area. Already, Jean-Marc Espalioux, Accor's CEO, had made technology his top priority. He had allocated a 500 million franc budget over three years to an investment program with the aim of improving service and efficiency by upgrading and refining the Group's management and reservation tools. His enthusiasm was echoed throughout the group. For example, Philipe Brizon, Chairman of Novotel, had been quoted as saying that, "The hospitality industry was experiencing a real revolution in terms of channels of distribution, and strategically it was about time for us to get equipped."

*This case was contributed by Peter O'Connor, Assistant Professor, Hospitality Information Technology, Institut de Management Hotelier International, Groupe ESSEC, Cergy Pontoise, France

To date, however, Accor as a whole had failed to take advantage of these opportunities. Despite an elaborate infrastructure, only three percent of overall booking volumes originated through electronic routes, with a further two percent being processed by the telesales centers. Furthermore, processing these bookings was seen as troublesome by the individual properties, both in terms of the effort required in managing the process and the costs involved.

ACCOR HOTELS

Beginning in 1967 with just a single hotel in northern France, Group Accor had grown to become one of the largest lodging, restaurant and travel companies in the world. Accor operated over 2600 hotels with over 290,000 rooms. Accor employed over 120,000 people in 126 counties around the globe, and was also involved in restaurants, contract catering and, through partnerships, in car rental agencies and travel agencies. The Group's total sales volume in 1995 was over 40,000 million francs (or over US$ 6 billion), yielding an EBIT (Earnings before Interest and Tax) of over 3.5 million francs. Approximately two thirds of this profit was generated by the Group's hotel activities.

Like many hotel companies, Accor did not concentrate on a single market segment. It operated across the entire spectrum of the industry from upscale, luxury hotels down to budget operations. Its Sofitel brand services the more upmarket customer, Novotel, Mercure and Ibis brands were aimed at the mid-price market, while Etap, Formule1 and Motel 6 (in the United States) target the economy customer. The characteristics of each of Accor's major brands are shown in Exhibit 51-1. Also in the United States, in mid-1999 Accor purchased the budget Red Roof chain.

ELECTRONIC DISTRIBUTION OF ACCOR HOTELS

Given its importance as one of the world's largest hotel companies, Accor had a comprehensive central reservations department, encompassing both a worldwide network of telesales centers (with offices in Amsterdam, Evry, France, Frankfurt, London, Madrid, Milan, New York, and Perth) and a computerized reservation system known as "ResInter" which is illustrated in Exhibit 51-2.

As can be seen in Exhibit 51-2, Accor was connected to all of the major GDS via the WizCom switch, serviced the information and booking requirements of the telesales centers, and was accessible directly to the public over both the Minitel Videotext system (a French telephone service) and the Internet. In the latter case, however, no rates

---

E X H I B I T   51-1
Brand Characteristics of Group Accor Hotels

Sofitel is Group Accor's upscale product, with 113 hotels (4 star, ARR 1600 FF) in prime locations in leading business and leisure destinations in over 40 countries. It targets an international business and leisure clientele that are looking for a pleasant environment, high quality facilities, and personalized service.

Novotel encompasses 317 properties (3 star, ARR 900 FF) in 50 countries and is positioned at the upper end of the mid-priced category, and targets business clients during the week and the leisure market during weekends and holidays.

Mercure again focuses on the mid-price traveler in both the business and leisure markets, but offers a more limited service than its Novotel cousin. The brand has 387 hotels (2,3,4 star, ARR 600 FF) in 30 countries, but is mainly focused in and around Europe, and encompasses three different categories—Grand Hotel Mercure, Hotel Mercure and Relais Mercure—depending on comfort level, price, and location.

Ibis is the largest European hotel chain, with 452 properties (2 star, ARR 430 FF) including 293 in France, 46 in Germany, 10 in Portugal, 8 in the UK and a growing presence in the rest of the world. Usually located in city centers, along major roads and near airports, the brand is focused on the mid-priced market, offering travelers quality service at attractive prices.

Etap is positioned at the top of the economy sector (179 properties, 1 star, ARR 300 FF) with basic, functional and clean lodgings at very low prices. Each room has an en-suite shower and toilet, can sleep up to three people, and has a television. No restaurant facilities are provided, and units are usually located on major roads or at major intersections.

Formule1's concept (312 properties, 1 star, ARR 250 FF) is practically identical to that of Etap (basic accommodation at very low prices). However rooms do not have en-suite facilities, and only have one bathroom for every four rooms. Again there are no restaurant facilities, and properties are located along major roads.

Motel 6 (782 properties, U.S. 2 star, ARR 350 FF)is once again a budget concept, offering cheap, no-frills accommodation with full bath, along major roads in the US market. Red Roof was purchased with the intent to integrate its 322 properties into Motel 6.

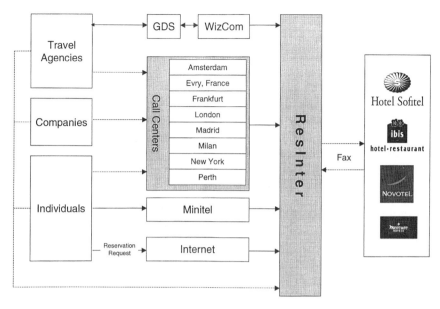

E X H I B I T   5 1 - 2   ResInter—Accor's Central Reservation System.

were displayed on the system and the customer could only make a "reservation request," which then had to be processed manually at the central reservations office, and a response sent by email. ResInter could process reservations for up to 405 days in advance, and handled 19 different room types and 62 different pricing levels for the 1235 hotels available on the system. It processed bookings for over 2.5 million room nights, of which 1.3 million originated over the GDS and the remainder through its other channels. Sources of reservations for ResInter were 71 percent travel agents, eight percent tour operators, nine percent companies, and 12 percent individuals.

CHALLENGES FOR RESINTER

Accor had traditionally had a philosophy of decentralisation. In the view of the founders, the role of top management was to liberate their employees so that they could do their jobs, rather than constrain them with tight management control. Such an ap-

proach was in contrast to the emphasis on centralization and reliance on hierarchy that typified the United States hotel industry. Nowhere was this more noticeable than in the operation of their reservation system.

ResInter sold its hotels based on the "allocation" method. Hotels informed their nearest central sales office of the number of rooms that they had available for sale by ResInter on each date in the future, along with the rate at which they were to be sold. These rooms were effectively regarded as sold at the individual property level, although they could be taken back and the date "closed out" nearer to their consumption date. Problems arose because availability, rates, and reservations were being managed at two separate, remote locations. With an effective communications system, these two inventories could be kept in synch. With the ResInter system, however, all communication between the central system and the individual properties (and vice versa) was done using fax. Hotels had to fax the sales office to modify allocations or rates, and reservations were also sent to the properties over fax. As a result, there was much duplication of effort, particularly in manually updating the computer systems at either end, and errors often occured, resulting in the systems becoming out of synch.

A more appropriate solution would have been to have an interface between ResInter and the Property Management System at each property. In Accor's case, however, creating such a link would be difficult because of the diversity within the chain both in terms of hardware and the PMS systems being used. A wide variety of different hardware platforms, operating systems, and PMSs were being used through out the group, depending on the size of the property, its brand, its location, and even on the preference of the general manager. In addition, many of the smaller properties were not automated at all and thus still needed the fax based system.

Another key issue was how to distribute the budget brands. Despite their relatively basic image, the budget sector was especially important for Accor, contributing nearly two-thirds of EBIT. However, the three budget brands—Etap Hotel, Formule1, and Motel 6—were not distributed electronically (apart from over a dedicated system on the Minitel in France). Given the growing competition in this sector, however, and the importance of the budget market for the profitability of the group as a whole, there was a desire to make these properties as accessible to the marketplace as possible.

Given each of these challenges, Jean was faced with a dilemma. He must quickly redevelop the electronic distribution strategy of the group to reflect both the desired new emphasis of the CEO and new developments in technology. Where should his priorities lie?

C A S E

Fifty-Two

GUEST HISTORY AT RITZ-CARLTON*

Ritz-Carlton is acknowledged as one of the leading hotel companies in the world in terms of customer service. It has won countless awards, including being chosen by Global Finance readers in 1997 as the best hotel chain in North America. The strategy that lies behind this success is simply to offer the best customer service possible by anticipating guest's needs. This is reflected in the company's mission: "to provide the finest personal service" and "fulfil even the unexpressed wishes and needs of its guests." Ritz-Carlton's outstanding level of customer service is achieved by having a common set of goals and procedures throughout the world, known as the Gold Standards, in which all members of staff are trained and followed passionately. In fact, staff are the key to Ritz-Carlton's success. Each member is carefully selected and matched to

their particular position, and then extensively trained both in the technical components of their position and also in the company's customer service philosophy. Each is empowered "to move heaven and earth" to insure that the customer is satisfied and that any complaints are quickly and efficiently resolved.

Technology is used extensively to support the efforts of employees. Using a computerized system known as CLASS (Customer Loyalty Anticipation and Satisfaction System), Ritz-Carlton is able to turn guest preference data into actionable information, which employees can subsequently use to provide a more personalized level of service. The goals of the system are lofty—to give 100 percent reliability and consistency in recognizing repeat guests, fulfil guest preferences and anticipate their needs, and to help personalize each guest experience.

Each employee carries a guest preference pad, on which they can write guest preferences. These are consolidated and entered into CLASS on a daily basis, and consequently available to employees at

*This case was contributed by Peter O'Connor, Assistant Professor, Hospitality Information Technology, Institut de Management Hotelier International, Groupe ESSEC, Cergy Pontoise, France.

any of the 33 Ritz-Carltons immediately. "The idea is that if a guest wants the Pittsburgh Press in his room where ever he goes, or wants rocks in his pillow the next time he stays with us, he won't have to express that desire," says Bruce Speckhals, Vice President of Information Systems. CLASS is integrated with MARSHA, the Marriott Central Reservation System on which the Ritz-Carlton properties are now distributed, and bookings are linked to guest profiles during the reservation process. At each property, the guest recognition manager prints a guest recognition report on a daily basis and circulates it to each department. Thus, arriving guests are immediately recognized as repeat customers, their needs anticipated, and selective elements of their stay customized in line with their preferences in order to provide more personalized service.

The system also helps Ritz-Carlton to create loyalty programs that recognize the value of repeat guests. Returning customers are classified into one of three groups. Repeat customers have less than twelve stays within a year, key repeat customers have more than twelve stays in one or two properties within a year, and loyal customers have more than twelve stays in at least three properties within

a year. CLASS allows the company to determine the travel patterns and revenue contributions of each guest, and make projections as to their lifetime value. Thus one of the keys to the success of the overall system is linking the reservation to the guest profile, a process that is managed by the guest recognition manager at each property. Despite the wealth of data available for direct marketing purposes, however, Ritz-Carlton has only comparatively recently begun to exploit this opportunity. Moreover, as the trust and confidence of its customers are so important, guest data is never sold or passed on to outside companies. Direct marketing is coordinated on a global scale to record who has received what and when, and to insure that the amount of mail that an individual receives is carefully managed.

Is the system successful? According to independent research, over 90 percent of Ritz-Carlton customers say that they would come back. The question now for Ritz-Carlton is how to maintain this competitive advantage. With the continuing reduction in the costs of technological based systems, an opportunity exists for its competitors to use similar systems and similar levels of recognition for their customers.

GLOSSARY

•◆•

Ad hoc group A tour group of customers, headed for a specific destination, that stays enroute at a hotel overnight. The enroute stay is a stopover and not part of the reason for the tour.

Account Management System Methodology for managing customer accounts in a sales office.

Airline market Housing of airline employees and crew members by a hotel on a contractual basis, normally over a period of at least one year. Also known as "base business."

Area of Dominant Influence (ADI) Specific geographic population bases determined by television audience but also used by newspaper and magazine media for distribution coverage.

Atmospherics In a positive sense, the conscious designing of a concept to create certain effects in buyers; the effort to design buying environments to produce specific emotional effects in the buyer that will enhance purchase probability. May also be negative.

Attitudes Affective component of the belief-attitude-behavior triad; emotional responses toward beliefs.

Augmented product The totality of all benefits received or experienced by the customer when purchasing the product.

Average check The method of tracking the spending habits of food customers, derived by dividing the total money collected within a meal period by the number of customers served. Some establishments include liquor purchased in the calculation.

Average Room Rate (ARR) The method to track the spending habits of rooms customers, derived by dividing the total money collected for room rent on a given day by the number of rooms sold; also called Average Daily Rate (ADR). Establishments may or may not include complementary rooms, out-of-order rooms, and day-use rooms in the calculation.

Behavioral differences The ways in which one segment (customer) behaves differently from another. Can lead to conflict among segments.

Belief Something we think is fact (something we believe) about an object, for whatever reason or derivation. A belief is cognitive.

Benefits Serve the needs and wants of the consumer; what a feature can do for the customer; the reason that a customer needs or uses the feature or product.

Bimodal or strongly-skewed life cycle Two possible configurations of the product life cycle when it does not always follow a bell-shaped curve.

Break-even pricing Pricing to cover at least fixed costs beyond variable cost per unit.

Bus tour Travelers arriving at a hospitality establishment by motorcoach, as part of a total tour package.

Business purpose To create and keep a customer.

Business traveler Customer who utilizes a hospitality product because of a need to conduct business in the particular destination. This person usually travels alone or with a limited number of individuals.

Business Center A service offered by the hotel that includes some of the following: fax, secretarial services, copiers, conference rooms, computers, shipping, etc.

Cannibalized market An offering by the same company of a similar product to the same customer in the same market; giving the consumer an alternative to the existing hotel or restaurant, under the same ownership, when a customer gained is also a customer lost.

Cash flow pricing A strategy to maximize short-run revenues to generate cash.

Catering salesperson Handles meetings, banquets, and social events (such as weddings) that require few sleeping rooms.

Channels of distribution The means used to get the product to the customer; in hospitality it often means creating awareness and availability in order to get the customer to the product, often through other entities.

Chapter 11 bankruptcy The court protection of an existing business entity from its creditors. When a business is no longer viable and/or solvent, the courts will assist in the reorganization and/or the orderly distribution of assets to creditors. Chapter 11 is voluntary on the part of the organization to gain protection before it is forced into involuntary bankruptcy, usually so it can continue to operate. United States only.

Close Gaining a verbal or written commitment from the customer.

Closed probe A communications method used during a sales call to direct customers who may not be aware of their needs or cannot express those needs well.

Closing The customer makes a commitment to buy.

Cognitive dissonance A theory that recognizes a customer's potential uncertainty after the purchase decision has been made. A customer may believe that his or her choice of product was wrong, incorrect, or a mistake.

Collateral A term used in advertising to include brochures, fliers, cocktail napkins, matchbooks, and other promotional materials.

Communications mix The variety of methods used to tell the consumer about a product, including advertising, merchandising, promotions, public relations, and direct selling.

Communication strategy The purpose, or desired effect, of the communication to the marketplace before it has been decided how to say it.

Comparative group A target market that a customer may try to emulate. For example, teenagers may consider a rock band as a comparative group and make their product choices accordingly.

Compensatory models The purchase decision model that assumes the willingness to trade one feature for another in order to make the buy decision.

Competitive intelligence Includes information-gathering beyond industry statistics and trade gossip and involves close observation of competitors to learn what they do and why they do it.

Competitive strategy The firm chooses its competition and when and where it will compete. The firm then targets all its marketing forces towards the identified competitor(s).

Conceptitis A word we have coined to describe those people who are afflicted with total immersion in design concepts with little regard for how the customer will use the product.

Conference Center hotel A hotel that specializes in the meetings market.

Conjunctive model Consumers might establish a minimum acceptable level for each important product attribute and make a choice only if each attribute equals or exceeds the minimum level.

Consortium A loosely knit group of independently owned and managed hotels (or other companies such as travel agencies) with a joint marketing distribution process.

Construct validity Measuring what you think you are measuring; for example, ensuring the behavior pattern being measured is actually significant to the customer's buy decision.

Consumer demand Consists of the existing, latent, and incipient demand of consumers having a need for a specific product.

Contribution margin pricing A version of markup pricing that can be used to price a product. A margin is assigned to an offering above the variable cost to establish the price. The contribution is to fixed cost after the variable cost has been covered, even when there is no absolute profit.

Control The feedback loop of the marketing system, which includes research and marketing intelligence that tells if the system is working right.

Convention or conference services manager Hotel personnel assigned to handle conventions and conferences and their needs while at the hotel.

Core product What the customer is really buying, often abstract and intangible attributes.

Cost percentage or markup pricing Favored by the restaurant industry, this method features either a dollar markup on the variable ingredient-cost of the item, a percentage markup based on the desired ingredient cost percentage, or a combination of both.

Cost-plus pricing Establishing the total cost of a product, including overhead, plus a predetermined gross profit margin.

Cottage industries Small companies and businesses supply a major product offering and/or sell directly to the consumer.

Cover Generic term applied to a meal served; for instance, 20 customers in a restaurant are 20 covers.

Customized product The design of a product to fit the specific needs of a particular target market.

Data collection, external The assembling of information from environmental sources—such as currency rates, international terrorism, population growth, demographics, and so on—that may indicate trends that affect the purchase decisions of customers.

Data collection, internal The assembling of information within the context of the hospitality establishment—such as average room rate, menu preferences, and so on—that may indicate trends that affect the purchase decisions of customers.

Data collection, primary The assembling of information directly from the consumer, as in consumer research.

Data collection, secondary The assembling of information from other sources that have collected it for another purpose.

Demand analysis An analysis of a market to determine whether it is ready, willing, and able to buy a specific product.

Demographic segmentation Customer definition based on geographic location, income, race, age, nationality, and so on.

Descriptive data Information that tells us who and what, but not why.

Descriptive quantitative research Research that tells us how many, how often, and what percentage, such as how old people are, their sex, or their income; provides means, standard deviations, and other statistics.

Designated Market Area (DMA) Developed by the A.C. Nielsen, a research company, these are geographic areas serviced by television stations. Data include demographic characteristics that can be used for reaching specific audiences; also used generically as a target market area.

Determinant attributes Attributes that determine choice.

DEWKS Acronym for couples of dual employment, with kids; about 50 percent of U.S. married couples.

Differentiation The ability to convey to a customer a tangible or intangible advantage of one product over a competitive one.

DINKS Acronym for couples with a double income, no kids; about 18 percent of U.S. married couples.

Director of Marketing (as commonly applied) Within the hierarchy of a hospitality entity's organizational chart, the department head responsible for producing revenues, usually through the utilization of the communications mix. This position is normally found in larger hotels and restaurant chains. The Director of Marketing reports to the General Manager and oversees the position of Director of Sales, if applicable.

Director of Sales In smaller hospitality entities, the same job description as Director of Marketing applies. In larger organizations, this position reports to the Director of Marketing and heads the direct sales effort.

Disjunctive model The consumer establishes a minimum level of expectation based on only one or a few attributes.

Distribution strategy The process by which a hotel determines its options for channels of distribution.

Edifice/Oedipus complex An emphasis on the edifice or building as the primary selling point in the product and/or communications mix. When used pejoratively, the hotel structure fails to differentiate itself from other hotels in both a physical and positioning sense, thus losing any possible differentiation in the customer's mind. In Greek mythology, Oedipus was banished from the kingdom as a child; as an adult he returned and, ignorant of his heritage, murdered his father and wed his mother. In psychology, the term *Oedipus complex* is used to define a male who has a fixation for his mother. In the sense described above, the term "edifice complex" is used colloquially as a play on words to mean *not* recognizing the real reason people buy hotel rooms because of a fixation on the physical property.

Elasticity The economic model that establishes the relationship between pricing of a product and demand for the product.

Environmental scanning The analysis of trends that may affect both the production and the purchase of a product by the customer.

Expatriate Person who lives and works in a country not of his or her own origin or nationality.

Expectancy-value model Assumes that people have a measurement of belief about the existence of an attribute and that each attribute has an importance weight relative to the other attributes.

Expectation pricing Pricing according to what it is believed people expect to pay, regardless of intrinsic value.

External information Data gathered from distribution members such as suppliers, vendors, and local, state, and national agencies and associations.

Facilitating goods Tangible goods that accompany an intangible product or service to facilitate its purchase; for instance, airport limo service or an 800 reservation phone number.

Family life cycle Spans the basic stages of life (e.g., single, married, married with children, married with grown children, widowed), and how these stages affect the purchasing decision.

Feasibility study The thorough evaluation and determination of a business venture and its ability to perform in a marketplace. Market feasibility indicates market demand; financial feasibility indicates financial performance.

Feature A tangible or intangible component of a product that is offered to solve the customer's problem.

Fern bars A trendy concept of the 1970s that features an atmosphere filled with plants, brass, and glass.

Focus group An assemblage of typical customers used to discuss and critique products (typically determined by the use of screening techniques). A moderator normally leads the discussion of five to ten people.

Food and Beverage (F&B) The term applied to the department within a hotel that manages the food and beverage products.

Foreign or Free Independent Traveler (FIT) A visitor from another country, or simply any individual without a preset itinerary such as a package or tour; variously used in the industry.

Formal product The basic product customers think they are buying, such as a hotel room or a meal, as opposed to the core product.

Franchisee An organization or person that purchases a brand name to distribute the product or service.

Franchising A method for a hospitality entity to

increase its distribution network, both to create more revenue and to obtain increased geographic presence. Management of the hospitality entity that is franchised is not retained by the parent company.

Franchisor   The parent company of a franchising distribution network.

Freestanding   A slang term for a customer who needs function or meeting space without accompanying guestrooms. This term can also be applied to food and beverage outlets not associated, or positioned not to be associated, with a host hotel.

Frequent-flyer programs   Programs that reward the airline passenger for repeated patronage with free mileage credit toward future flights and other awards such as rental cars and hotel rooms.

Frequent traveler   By industry definition, a traveler who spends at least ten nights per year in a hotel room for any number of reasons; also called frequent guest.

Frequent-traveler programs   Emulation of frequent-flyer programs that offer free hotel rooms, upgrades, and other benefits and prizes for repeat patronage.

Functional strategies   The "what" of the strategic system; that is, "what" we are going to do specifically within the marketing mix to reach the customer.

General Manager (GM)   This position is normally the head of the individual hospitality entity, such as a restaurant or hotel.

Global Distribution Systems (GDS)   These are the electronic booking processes by which hotel, car, and airline reservations services are made worldwide.

Goods   Tangible, physical factors over which management has direct control; or, in other industries, manufactured goods.

Grazing restaurants   A concept of restaurants where the customers are offered a variety of foods throughout the day and night; the customer is allowed to walk up to many food sta-

tions in the restaurant, sampling more than just one entree—hence the term *grazing*. Also used as a customer behavior where the customer may "nibble" at any time rather than at set meal periods.

Ground services   Ancillary services such as transportation, tours, sight-seeing, etc., at a destination for arriving travelers.

Group product line   For customers who purchase a number of rooms, catering, and related services

Group market segment   Five or more single attendees at a meeting whose purpose is business and/or pleasure, usually within the facilities of the hotel.

Group salesperson   The member of the hotel sales force who handles the needs of customers booking ten or more hotel rooms at a time, and generally accompanying meeting space.

Hassle-free   A common industry term that describes a customer's experience as being without any problems or hang-ups.

Heterogeneity   Variation and lack of uniformity in a service being performed; also, variation of consumers in the marketplace.

Hospitality marketing mix   Contains four major submixes: product/service mix, presentation mix, communications mix, and distribution mix.

Hospitality product   The goods and services offered by the hospitality entity. The goods and services include guestrooms, food, beverages, health clubs, pools, and so on, and all services, whether included in the price or priced separately.

Importance attributes   Items that are important to the consumer in making a choice of product, or in consuming the product, but are not necessarily determinant.

Inbound operator   A channel of distribution that handles international travel to the host country from all locations outside the country; also handles ground services when the traveler arrives.

Incentive houses Companies that specialize in handling the needs of organizations that reward their employees with travel.

Incipient demand Demand for which even the customer does not yet recognize there is a need (i.e., the demand is in its embryonic stage).

Incongruities Discrepancies between what is and what ought to be.

Inferential quantitative research This method allows the extrapolation of findings from a survey sample to a larger population base; for this sample, each person in the population being studied must have an equal chance of being selected in the sample.

Innovators A consumer term identifying those who are the first to try a new product.

In-plants Travel agencies that are located on the premises of a customer.

Intangible Unable to be perceived by the sense of touch; used in marketing as unable to be perceived by the five senses or easily grasped conceptually.

Intention The conative stage of the buying process—what people intend to do.

Internal Information Data collected from sources within the organization, such as occupancy, average room rate, average check, number of covers, frequently-ordered menu items, and so on.

Internal marketing Applying the philosophies and practices of marketing to people who serve the external customers so that (1) the best possible people can be employed and retained, and (2) they will do the best job of serving the customer. Management emphasis is equally on the employee, the customer, and the job as it is on the product.

Internal marketing concept Organization's internal market of employees can be influenced effectively and motivated to customer-consciousness, market orientation, and sales-mindedness by a marketing-like internal approach and by using marketing-like activities internally.

Internal Rate of Return (IRR) The method of determining the percentage of profit needed for projects funded with existing cash.

Internal validity Reported research findings that are free from bias and are valid in their conclusions.

Judgmental sample A nonprobability sample using a specified variation. Subjects are "screened" to ensure they meet criteria specified.

Latent demand A consumer need for which no suitable product is available to satisfy the need (e.g., fast-food before McDonald's).

Leader Someone who has followers.

Lowest Common Denominator (LCD) The sales process by which large tasks are broken down into the smallest (most manageable) pieces of work to be completed by a salesperson.

Loss leaders Items that are offered to customers at low (loss) prices to create traffic, and the potential purchase of a more desirably priced item; for example, a soup special may be priced at 50 cents in the hope that the customer will also order a sandwich.

Macro competition Anything that is competing for the same consumer's dollar that you are, regardless of the product similarity; for instance, a new car might compete with an extended vacation.

Market demand The measurement of the amount of demand in the marketplace. See *Demand analysis.*

Market positioning Creating an image of a product in the marketplace in the consumer's mind.

Market segmentation Assumes a heterogeneity in the marketplace and a divergent demand. Segmentation divides the market into various segments, with homogeneity along one or more common dimensions.

Market share The determination of a hospitality entity's actual success rate in attracting customers. Once a determination of total supply for the product is made, each competing business has a "fair" market share; that is, its proportion of the total supply. Its proportion of actual sales is its "actual" market share. The market share establishes who has sold more or less than their fair share of the available supply.

Marketing Communicating to and giving the target market what they want, when they want it, where they want it, and at a price they are willing to pay.

Marketing concept The theory that the customer has a choice and does not have to buy a product, or your product—hence the need to market or attract the customer to the product.

Marketing mix Traditionally, the "Four Ps"—product, price, place, and promotion; in hospitality the product/service, presentation, communication, and distribution that directly affects the consumer.

Marketing opportunity Exists when the needs (problems) of the customer are not being satisfied, or could be enhanced.

Marketing orientation The philosophy, foundations and practices of marketing as evidenced in the philosophy of the firm.

Marketing-oriented management The philosophy that customer needs are primary to all processes; for example, when designing a product before the sale, when delivering a product after the sale, and while the customer consumes the product.

Marketing plan Working document that the hospitality enterprise develops for action during the forthcoming year. A situation analysis and all phases of the communications mix should be addressed as needed.

Marketing system Makes marketing orientation and marketing concept work. Comprises leadership, opportunity, planning, and control.

Maslow's hierarchy Higher-level needs do not become primary until lower-level needs have been fulfilled.

Master strategy Shapes objectives after developing and weighing alternatives; specifies where the firm is going and is the framework of the marketing effort. Normally a long-term planning process.

Micro competition Any business that is competing for the same customers in the same product class; that is, is a direct competitor with a similar product in a similar context.

Mission statement The statement that delineates the total perspectives or purpose of a business. It states why the business exists, the competitors, the marketplace, and how the business serves its constituents.

Multiple brand strategy The strategy of a firm that crosses over a variety of levels of consumer needs for the same product; for example, Marriott Hotels offers five brands of hotels, from deluxe J.W. Marriotts for the non-price-sensitive guest to the Fairfield concept for the price-sensitive budget traveler.

New markets The attempt to increase the customer base of a business by developing new markets through the solicitation of current nonusers, or fulfilling unfulfilled, latent, or incipient demand.

Non-contact employees Those employees who have little or no direct contact with the customers; dishwashers and laundry workers are two examples of non-contact employees.

No-equity deals The management of a hospitality entity without significant capital investment on the part of the managing company.

Noncompensatory models When the customer perceives no trade-off of attributes (e.g., conjunctive or disjunctive models); for example, some customers would not accept a double-bed guestroom in lieu of a promised king-bed guestroom even if the price were much lower.

Nonprobability sample Everyone in the population does not have an equal chance of being selected: includes judgmental, quota, or convenience samples.

Nontargeted prospecting Using list of potential clients to make "cold" calls (i.e., calls with no advance contact).

Normative beliefs The thought process that certain individuals or groups should conform to a particular behavior.

Objective positioning The process of creating an image about a product that reflects its physical characteristics and functional features.

Odd-numbered pricing A pricing methodology employed to create a perception of a lower price by charging, for example, $6.99 rather than $7.00.

Open probe A question phrased by a salesperson to encourage a customer to speak freely.

Opening specials A pricing methodology used as inducement to try the product in the initial phases of the product life cycle; also called introductory pricing.

Operations orientation A work ethic within a hospitality entity that focuses on the internal mechanism of the organization rather than the customer. Sometimes, similarly, called the F&B mentality because of that department's historical emphasis on controlling cost and running a smooth operation before consideration of customers' needs or wants.

Opportunity analysis Matching product strengths to opportunity while avoiding threats caused by product weaknesses.

Organizational customer A customer who buys the hospitality product for groups of secondary customers with a common purpose.

Outbound operator A channel of distribution that handles international travel from the host country to all points of destination outside the country.

Package market Offering to consumers a combination of room and amenities for an inclusive price.

Penetration pricing A company drastically reduces prices to initially create awareness and trial of product, eventually stealing customers and building volume.

Perception What is real to the consumer; that is, what the consumer perceives or believes.

Perceptual mapping Process that helps to determine the positioning strategy relative to the competiton by "mapping" competitive positions or product attributes.

Perishability A characteristic of a product that indicates the length of time available for sale to a customer, after which it perishes. An automobile may have a perishability of a year before a new model is introduced—even then it can be sold at a reduced price; a hotel room-night has one day, after which it can't even be given away.

Perpetuability A word we have coined to describe the characteristic and ability to perpetuate repeated sales of the same product, e.g., a hotel room or an airline seat. Although the room-night has perished, the same product can be sold the following day.

Personal constructs Devices that individuals use to interpret or make sense out of what they confront. Personal constructs are on a bipolar continuum; for instance, good–bad.

Physical plant The term for the actual building and its components that house the hospitality entity.

Physical supports Materials necessary for the production of a service (e.g., a reservations system). From this support, both the contact personnel and the customer will draw services.

Planning Defining what has to be done and allocating the resources to do it.

Porte cochere A covered carriage entrance at the front of a building.

Positioning The consumer's mental perception of a product, which may or may not differ from the actual physical characteristics of a product or brand.

Positioning strategy The planning by the hospitality entity to maintain, enhance, or change the consumer's mental perception of the product.

Presentation mix All elements used by the firm to increase the perception of the product/service mix in the mind of the consumer.

Presentation strategy The idea that the presentation mix must be consistent with the product/service and the overall master strategy.

Press release A document prepared for the press

providing the salient points of a story that the hospitality entity would like published.

Price A statement of value, usually in monetary terms, that can be used to express the cost of a good or service.

Price lining This technique clumps prices together so that a perception of substantially increased quality is created (e.g., $79, $99, and $119 rooms).

Pricing skimming The pricing of a product at the high end of the scale to create a perceived value, skim off the top of the market, and then eventually reducing the price to include a larger number of potential consumers.

Pricing objective The desired results of a pricing strategy, which should be consistent with the hospitality entity's other marketing objectives.

Primary reference groups Small, usually intimate groups whose behavior patterns may directly influence individuals within the group.

Proact Opposed to react; act before the event rather than afterward (commonly used in strategy vernacular).

Probing Method to determine the needs of the customer through a series of inquiries.

Product An offering of a business entity as it is perceived by both present and potential customers; a bundle of benefits designed to satisfy the needs and wants, and solve the problems of specified target markets. A product is composed of both tangible and intangible elements; it may be as concrete as a chair or a dinner plate, or as abstract as a feeling. The utility of a product derives from what it does for the customer.

Product awareness Whether consumers are familiar with a product or even know it exists.

Product differentiation Perceived difference in a product when compared with others.

Product life cycle The description of the various stages that a product experiences during its tenure in the market; these phases include an introduction or embryonic stage, growth stage, mature stage, and stage of decline.

Product orientation An organizational approach to marketing that focuses on the product itself and assumes that the product will sell itself; for instance, emphasis on atrium lobbies or swimming pools as the product the customer is buying (related to *Edifice complex*).

Product parity The competition is selling the same thing, or the consumer perceives no difference between offerings.

Product strategy Deals with the benefits the product provides, the problems it solves, and how it differentiates from the competition.

Production line orientation An organizational approach based on how fast, how many, and how cheaply to produce a product to get it to the market in bulk at the lowest possible price.

Product/service The totality of what hospitality companies offer their customers, including goods, services, and environment.

Product/service mix Combination of products and services, whether free or for sale, aimed at satisfying the needs of the target market.

Profit center concept The idea of breaking a larger organization into smaller, more manageable pieces by assigning profit contribution goals to individual departments.

Profit Impact of Marketing Strategy (PIMS) Program that is a computerized cross-sectional study based on about 200 pieces of data supplied by more than 450 companies in more than 3,000 businesses. This program has shown that the profitability of a business is affected by 37 basic factors that explain more than 80 percent of the profitability variation among the businesses.

Proprietary research When research is conducted for a particular organization for the specific use of that organization as opposed to general use.

Prospecting The methodology used in finding new customers; an example would be making sales calls on customers who are not currently using the product.

Psychographers People who correlate factors into relatively homogeneous categories using classification terms for consumers' lifestyles, such as homebodies, traditionalists, swingers, and so on.

Psychographic segmentation Lifestyle patterns combine the virtues of demographics with the way people live, think, and behave in their everyday lives to divide them into market segments, i.e., by their attitudes, interests, and opinions (AIO).

Psychological pricing Pricing strategy utilized to elicit consumer reactions such as perceived quality or value.

Public relations The organized attempt by a business to get favorable stories concerning their product or services carried by the media.

Publicity The format used in public relations to "create" a story. Stories are created through organized promotions.

Pull strategy Inducements are offered to make the consumer want to purchase a product or "pull" the product down the channel of distribution.

Push strategy Inducements are offered to the channel member to sell or "push" the product down the channel of distribution.

Probability sample One in which every member of the population has an equal chance of being selected.

Qualitative research The process of obtaining information on consumer attitudes and behavior on a subjective basis. This research is largely exploratory in nature and the findings cannot be generalized to a larger population. An example is the use of focus groups.

Quantitative research The process of obtaining information on consumer attitudes and behavior on an objective basis. This research is factual in nature and the findings sometimes can be generalized to a larger population.

Rack rates Regular published rates for hotel rooms, almost always discounted except in periods of very high demand.

Reference groups/Referents Groups that form small pockets of influence that affect consumers.

Relationship marketing The emphasis on retaining existing customers through building good relationships.

Reliability In research, findings can be projected to a larger population if it is the intent of the researcher to do so; also, if the study is repeated, similar findings will emerge.

Repositioning Changing the position or image of a product to consumers in the marketplace.

Representative firm Channel of distribution that brings a hotel to a marketplace, they market a hotel to a customer base for a fee.

Research design The process of establishing the total objectives and method of research to be conducted.

Research problem The designation of the problem of the research; that is, stating what the research is going to answer (not necessarily the same as the management problem).

Research purpose What you intend to do with the findings; what kind of business decisions you plan to make after you have the results.

Reservation networks Central reservations systems that serve multiple companies or properties.

Retail market Middlemen such as travel agents who sell directly to the consumer; a member of the distribution mix.

Return on Assets (ROA) The ratio of profits to assets that is generated by a business.

Return on Investment (ROI) The ratio of profits to investment that is generated by a business.

Revenue management See *Yield management.*

Run-of-the-house room The generic term for the random assignment of guestrooms to customers. Customers are not promised a certain type of room before their arrival at the hotel.

Sales equation The mathematical process by which the past customers, new customers, and budget expectations are calculated.

Sales action plan Format to organize and manage a sales department to create and maximize dales.

Salient attributes Those attributes that readily

come to mind when you think of a product or product class.

Sample   A group derived from the population at large; from it we hope to learn the characteristics of many based on a few.

Segmentation   The dividing of a large customer base into smaller homogeneous categories, based on a variety of applicable factors.

Selective acceptance   The theory that customers accept only information that they choose to accept, that they select from a variety of information only what is applicable.

Selective attention   The theory that customers attend to only what is of particular interest to them.

Selective comprehension   The theory that customers will try to comprehend, digest, and evaluate something only if they are still interested in it after attending to and accepting it.

Selective retention   The theory that customers retain in memory for future reference only what suits their particular interest after attention, acceptance, and comprehension.

Selling orientation   To practice "hard sell" techniques; the emphasis is on selling what you have to offer and persuading the customer to buy, rather than on the needs of the customer.

Service   Nonphysical, intangible attributes that management controls (or should), including friendliness, efficiency, attitude, professionalism, responsiveness, and so on.

Service augmentation   The marketing strategy to add to a generic product by enhancing services; for instance, the perception of a hotel room may be enhanced by the availability of a shoe-shine service.

Share of mind   Marketing jargon associated with positioning; it means that the positioning has been established in the consumer's mind.

Simultaneous production and consumption   Unique service characteristic whereby consumption depends on participation of the seller and the seller requires the participation of the buyer.

SMERF   A market segment that covers the social, military, ethnic, religious and fraternal customer base.

Soft opening   Product introduction begins a few days to a few weeks before the official opening.

Standard Metropolitan Statistical Area (SMSA)   Area that the government defines as a large economic area in terms of supposed economic boundaries. Government produces data on these areas such as population, ethnic mix, income, and so on.

Standard product   The attempt to provide a similar experience to the customer despite different locations or managers; for example, McDonald's offers a standard hamburger throughout the United States.

Strategic Business Unit (SBU)   Units of a business that have a common market base. Each SBU serves a clearly defined product-market base with its own strategy.

Strategic marketing   Long-term view of the market and the business to be in; marketing management stresses running that business and seeks to optimize objectives within the constraints established by the strategy.

Strategic planning   Developing a plan for how to get from here (situation analysis) to there (objectives). It is concerned with setting business objectives, the match between products and markets, the choices of competition, the allocation of resources, and planning ahead to reach the objectives.

Strategic thinking   Synthesis as opposed to analysis in strategic planning.

Subjective norm   People's perception of the social pressures put on them to perform or not perform in a particular way.

Subjective positioning   The perceived image that does not necessarily belong to the product or brand, but is the property of the consumer's mental perceptions.

Suitcase party   Customers come to a hotel with their suitcases packed, and during the evening, an exotic weekend away is awarded randomly, and the couple is whisked away to their destination.

Tactics   The step-by-step procedure of executing the details of a strategic plan.

Target marketing   The marketing strategy to aim a product or service at one portion of a specific market segment.

Target markets   Homogeneous markets that allow for more detailed analysis and evaluation of potential customers of a segment.

Technology orientation   Belief that success in the marketplace is a result of the finest technological development. This thought process is similar to the business philosophy exemplified by Polaroid for many years. Also akin to atrium lobbies with lakes and waterfalls.

Tour series   Prearranged link of stopovers for customers traveling by bus, usually carrying a theme.

Transient salespeople   The salesperson who is designated to sell to organizations that have a need to book guestrooms on an individual basis.

Trial   This stage of product introduction attempts to get the consumer to try a product.

Two-fer   Restaurant promotion that offers two meals or drinks for the price of one.

Vertical integration   Company becomes its own supplier of products (for instance, Holiday Inns had a subsidiary that sold hotel furnishings) or its own distributor (for instance, Radisson Hotels and Carlson Travel Agency belong to the same company).

Walked customers   Resulting from overbooking hotel rooms, customers' reservations are not honored and they are sent to a different hotel.

Wholesale tour operator   Middlemen who create hospitality packages, such as group tours, and sell to the customer through retail agents. A member of the distribution mix.

Word-of-mouth advertising   The marketing strategy that satisfied customers are the best form of communication. Satisfied customers will tell potential customers of their experience, thus increasing the customer base.

Yield management   The concept of maximizing the revenue yield by raising or lowering prices depending upon the demand. Often called *revenue management.*

NAME INDEX

•◆•

A. C. Nielsen Research, 298
Abacus, 609, 610
Abbey, James, 406, 432
Absolut vodka, 292
Acapulco Princess, 491
Accor. *See* Groupe Accor
Accor Lake Manyana Hotel, 316
Adams, Joe, 503, 508
Adams Group Inc., 503
Agrawal, Anshu, 833
Air Canada, 556, 689
Air France, 99
Air Transat, 689
Ala Moana Hotel, 259
Albion, Mark, 589
Albrecht, Karl, 17
Alice Fazooli's, 32
Allied Percival International (API), 573
Allie's Restaurants, 95, 106
All Nippon Airways (ANA), 310
Alone, Shari, 783
Alvear Palace Hotel, 749, 751
Amadeus, 609, 610
Americana Dutch Hotel, 117
American Airlines, 277, 539, 556, 575, 576, 608, 689
American Allegis Corporation, 788
American Automobile Association (AAA), 288
American Express, 201, 202, 260, 261, 306, 333, 568, 575
American Hotel & Motel Association, 130, 274, 610
American Hotels, 35
AMR Corporation, 575
Anderson Consulting, 589
Angus, Jeff, 424
Anthony's Pier 4 Restaurant, 385
Apollo Reservations System, 569, 608
Apple Computer, 88
Araskog, Rand, 16, 17, 18
Arctia Hotels, 559
Aristos Tours, 577
Arrowwood Conference Center, 27, 29, 265
Arthur Andersen Worldwide, 171
Asia Hotel, 117
Asian Airlines, 131

Associated Luxury Hotels, 565
Atami Seaside Resort, 493
Atkin, Judy, 639
Aurora Restaurant, 372
Avis Rent-a-Car, 333, 548
Axess, 609, 610

Bahama Breeze Restaurants, 179, 344, 370
Bally Casinos, 17
Banff Springs Hotel, 384–385, 386
Barbados Hotel and Tourism Association, 691
Barbados Tourism Authority, 687
Barbizon Hotel, 334
Barish, Keith, 833, 834, 835
Baskin Robbins, 851, 852, 859, 856
Bass Breweries, 95, 99
Bass Hotels & Resorts, 95, 141, 344, 549, 707
Bass PLC, 13, 141
Baton Rouge Convention and Visitors Bureau, 276
Batson, Allan, 687, 688
Bay Street Restaurants, 332
Bell, Martin L., 402, 432
Benchmark Hospitality, Inc., 270
Benjamin Hotel, 334
Bennigan's Restaurants, 332, 561
Berkshire Hilton Inn, 345
Best Fares, 428
Best Inns, 35, 95
Best Western Hotels, 242, 349, 424, 547, 561, 562, 610
Beverly Hills Hotel, 366
Beverly Hotel, 334
Beverly Wilshire Hotel, 333
Binkley, Christina, 18
Blackhawk Restaurant, 496
Blake, David, 723
Blanc, Jean, 885
Bloch, Robert, 344
Blue Elephant Restaurant, 343
Boca Raton Hotel and Club, 140
Boccaccio Restaurant, 291
Boeing Aircraft, 132
Bollenbach, Steve, 17, 18
Borden, Neil, 358, 379

Boston Market, 147, 159, 368
Bowen, T., 56, 59-60, 66, 70, 72, 78, 82, 82
Braithwaite, W. M., 629
Brasserie, 292
Breakers Hotel, 189, 485
Bridgeport Conference Services, Inc., 825-829
Bridgeport Inn and Conference Center, 825-829
Brinker International, 344
Bristol Hotel, 99, 367
British Airways, 99, 556, 689
British Ladbroke Group, 788
British West Indian Airways (BWIA), 689, 692
Brizon, Philipe, 885
Broadmoor Resort, 510
Brooks, Barbara, 837
Brush, Scott, 506
Burger King, 89, 97, 126, 134, 159, 244, 292, 298, 302, 331, 333, 364, 374, 582
Business Development Research Consultants, 349

Cabañas, Burt, 270
Caesar Park Hotel, 750
Cafe da Vinci, 463
Cafe Di Carlo, 783-786
Cafe Fleuri, 757-758
Camacho, Frank, 17, 424
Cambridge Suites, 403
Canada 3000 Airlines, 689
Canadian Airlines, 556, 689
Canadian Pacific Hotels, 68, 114, 128, 129, 146
Caneel Bay Resort, 58, 383
Capriccio Restaurant, 291
Caribe Hilton International Hotel, 787
Carlson Companies, Inc., 581
Carlson Group Marketing, 63, 132
Carlson Hospitality, 95, 581
Carlson Leisure, 581
Carlson Marketing Group, 567, 581
Carlson Wagonlit Travel, 581
Carlyle Hotel, 238
Carlzon, Jan, 19, 32, 48

SUBJECT INDEX

•◆•

WORLD MAPS

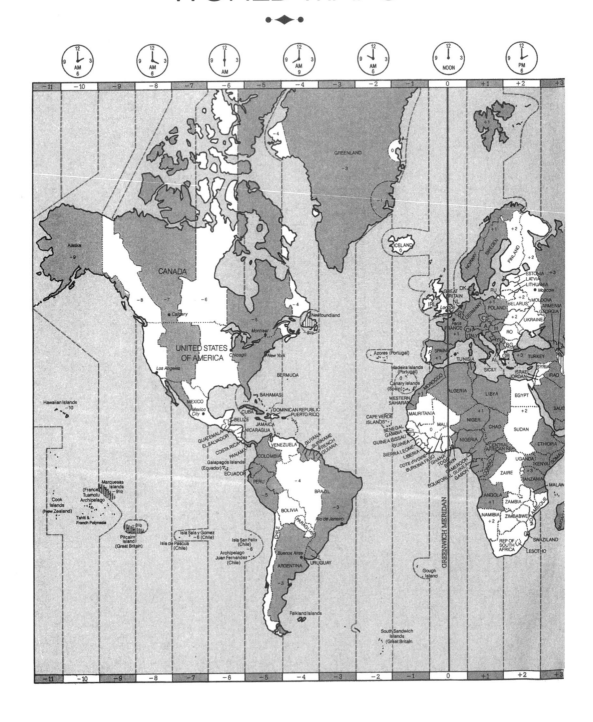

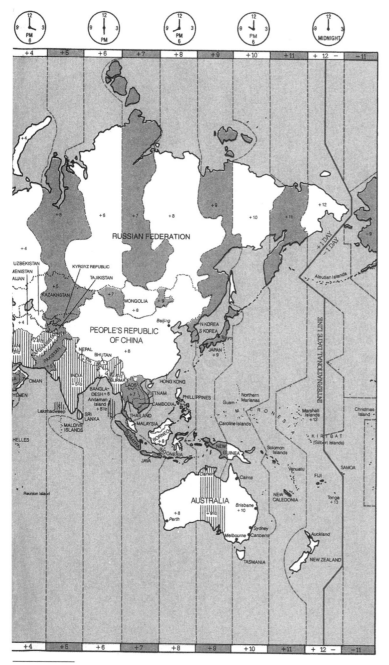

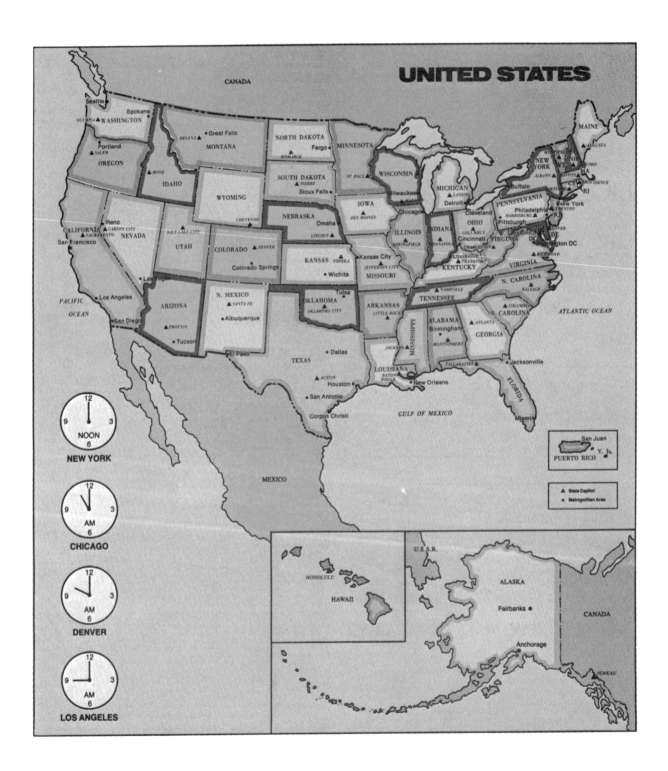

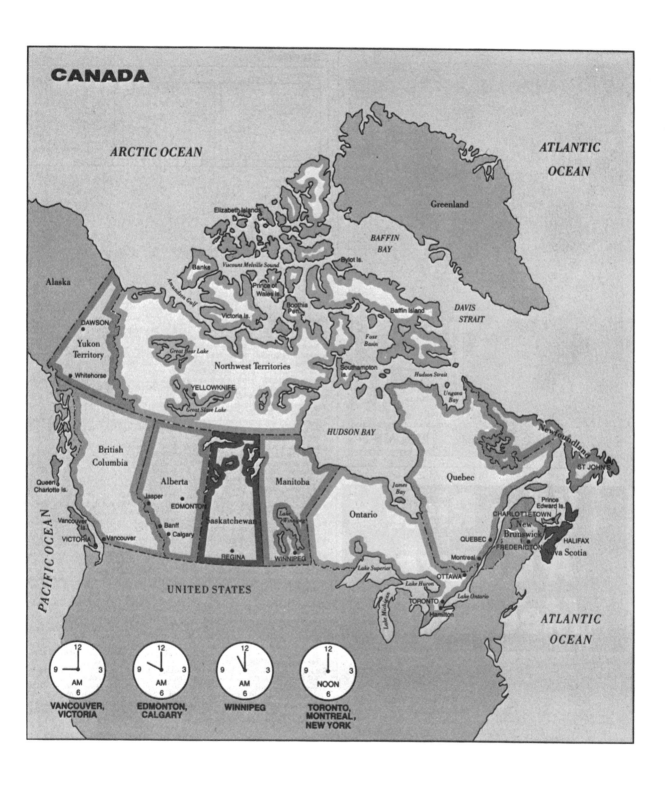

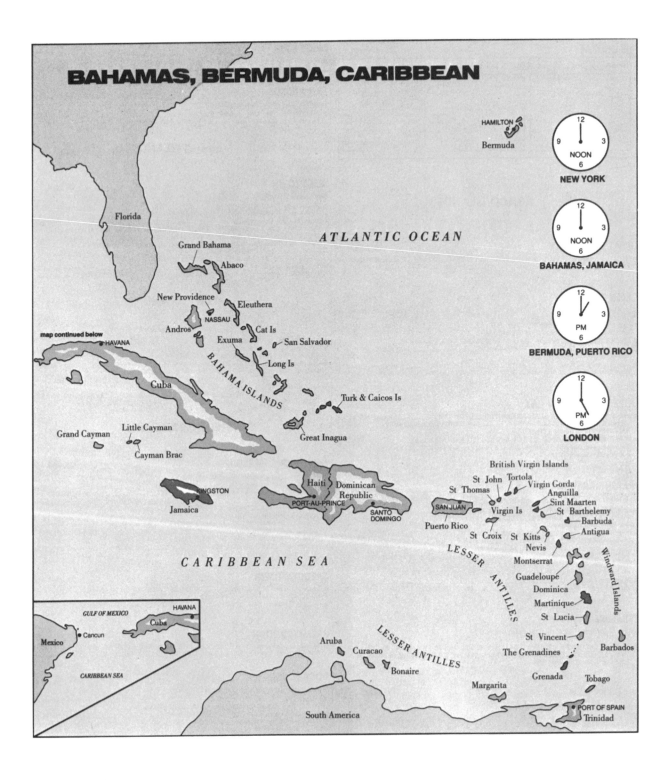

BAHAMAS, BERMUDA, CARIBBEAN

HAMILTON
Bermuda

NEW YORK
NOON

BAHAMAS, JAMAICA
NOON

BERMUDA, PUERTO RICO
PM

LONDON
PM

Florida

ATLANTIC OCEAN

Grand Bahama
Abaco

New Providence
Eleuthera
NASSAU
Andros
Cat Is
Exuma
San Salvador
Long Is

map continued below
HAVANA

Cuba

BAHAMA ISLANDS

Turk & Caicos Is

Grand Cayman
Little Cayman
Cayman Brac

Great Inagua

British Virgin Islands
St John
Tortola
Virgin Gorda
St Thomas
Anguilla
Sint Maarten
SAN JUAN
Virgin Is
St Barthelemy
Puerto Rico
Barbuda
St Croix
St Kitts
Antigua
Nevis
Montserrat

KINGSTON
Jamaica

Haiti
Dominican
Republic
PORT-AU-PRINCE
SANTO
DOMINGO

Guadeloupe
Dominica
Martinique
St Lucia

Windward Islands

CARIBBEAN SEA

LESSER
ANTILLES

St Vincent
The Grenadines
Barbados

GULF OF MEXICO
HAVANA

Mexico
Cancun
Cuba

Aruba
Curacao
Bonaire

LESSER ANTILLES

Grenada
Tobago

CARIBBEAN SEA

Margarita

PORT OF SPAIN
Trinidad

South America

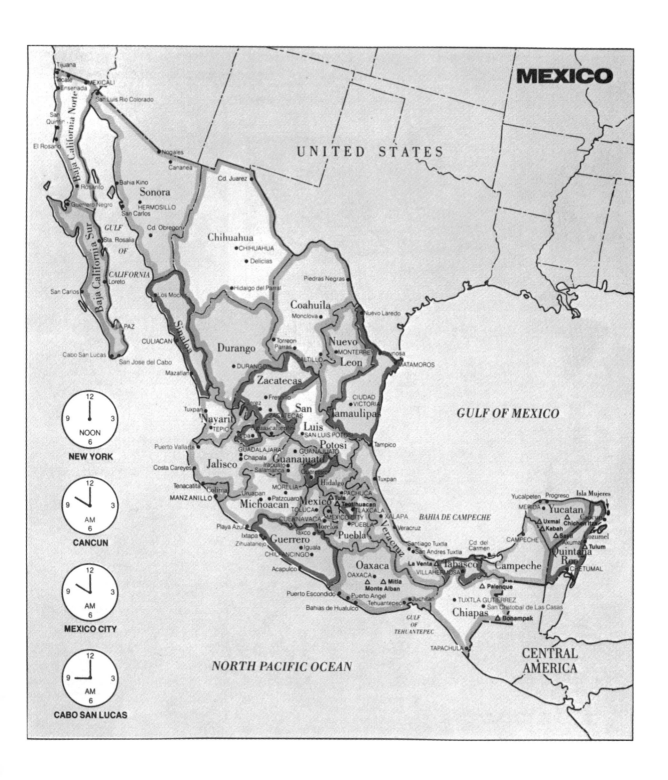

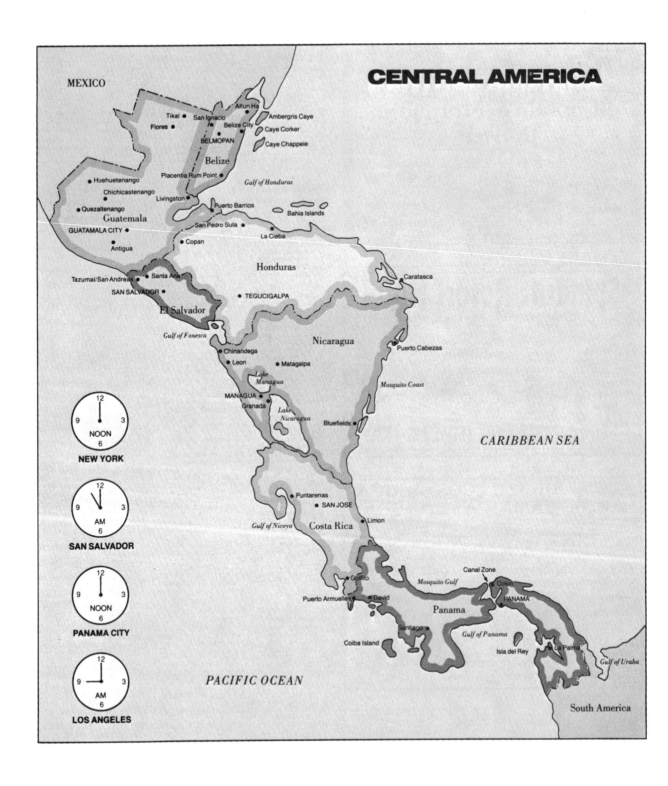

CENTRAL AMERICA

MEXICO

Tikal •   Altun Ha
San Ignacio •
Flores •   Belize City •
  BELMOPAN
  Belize

Ambergris Caye
Caye Corker
Caye Chappele

Huehuetenango •
Chichicastenango •
  Placentia Rum Point •
Quezaltenango •
  Guatemala
GUATAMALA CITY •
Antigua •
• Copan

Livingston •
  Puerto Barrios •
San Pedro Sula •
La Cieba •

Gulf of Honduras

Bahia Islands

Honduras

• Caratasca

Tazumal/San Andreas •
SAN SALVADOR •
  • Santa Ana
  El Salvador

• TEGUCIGALPA

Gulf of Fonesca

Nicaragua

• Puerto Cabezas

Chinandega •
Leon •
  • Matagalpa

Lake Managua

MANAGUA •
Granada •
  Lake Nicaragua

Bluefields •

Mosquito Coast

CARIBBEAN SEA

Puntarenas •
• SAN JOSE
• Limon

Gulf of Nicoya   Costa Rica

Golfito •
Puerto Armuelles •   • David

Mosquito Gulf

Canal Zone
  • Colon
  PANAMA •

Panama

Santiago •

Coiba Island

Gulf of Panama

Isla del Rey

• La Palma

Gulf of Uraba

PACIFIC OCEAN

South America

NOON
NEW YORK

AM
SAN SALVADOR

NOON
PANAMA CITY

AM
LOS ANGELES

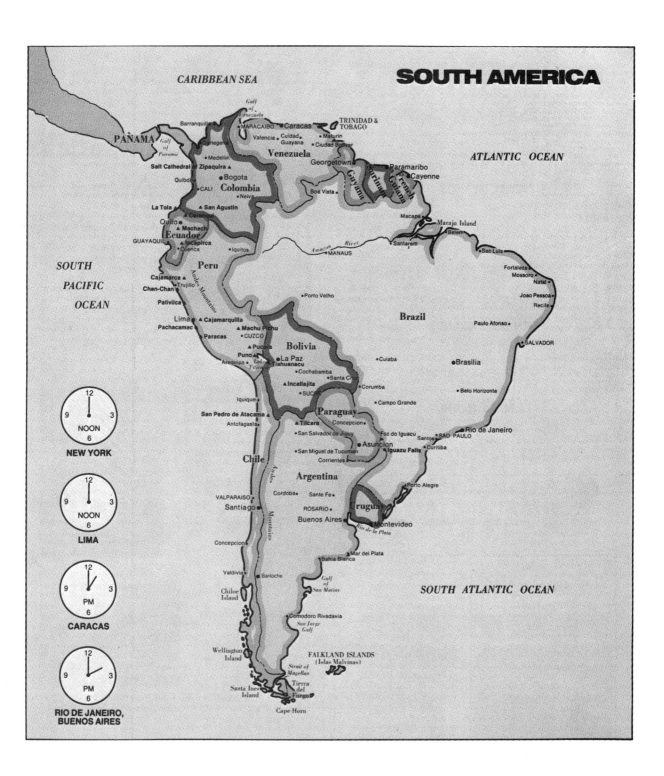

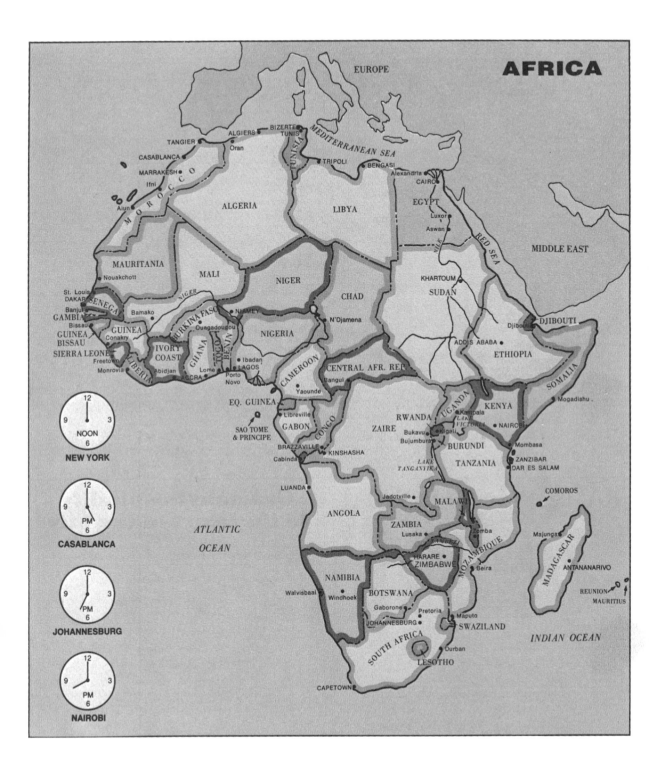

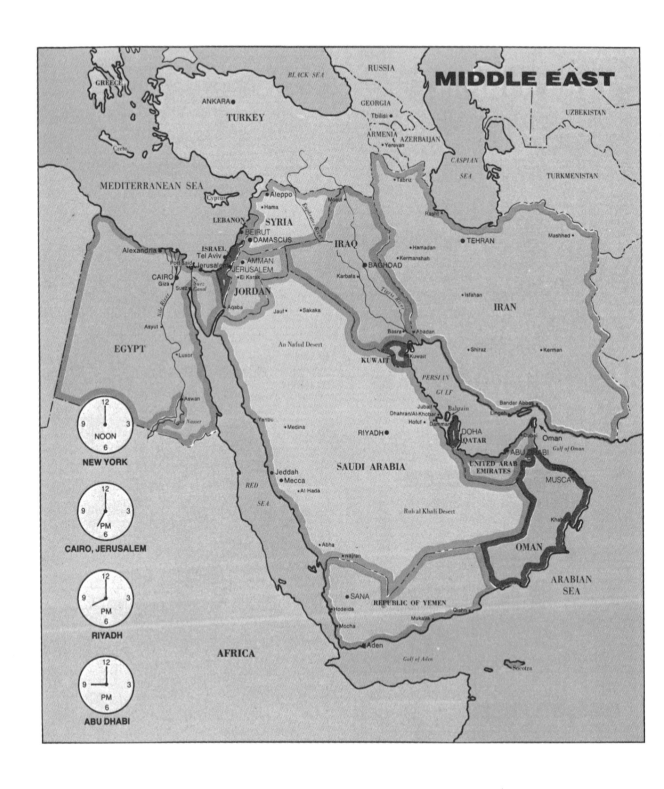

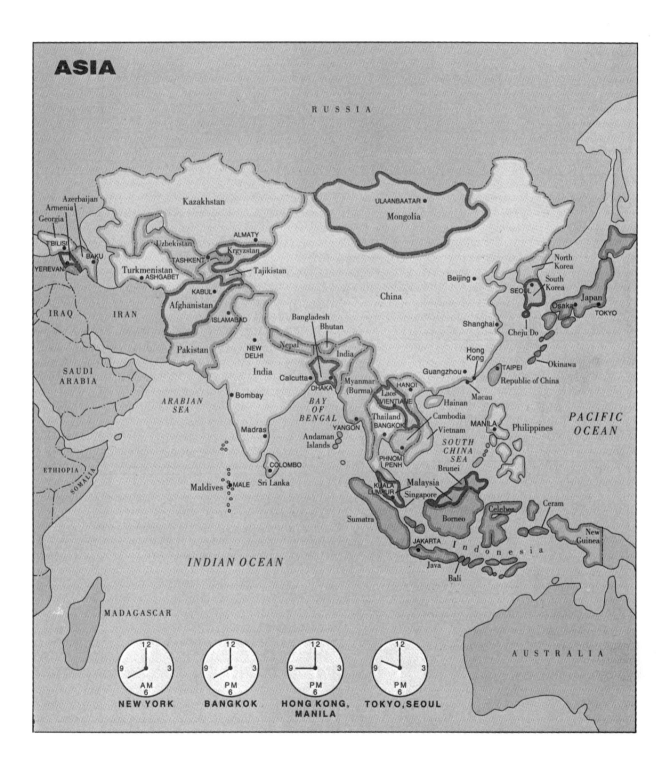

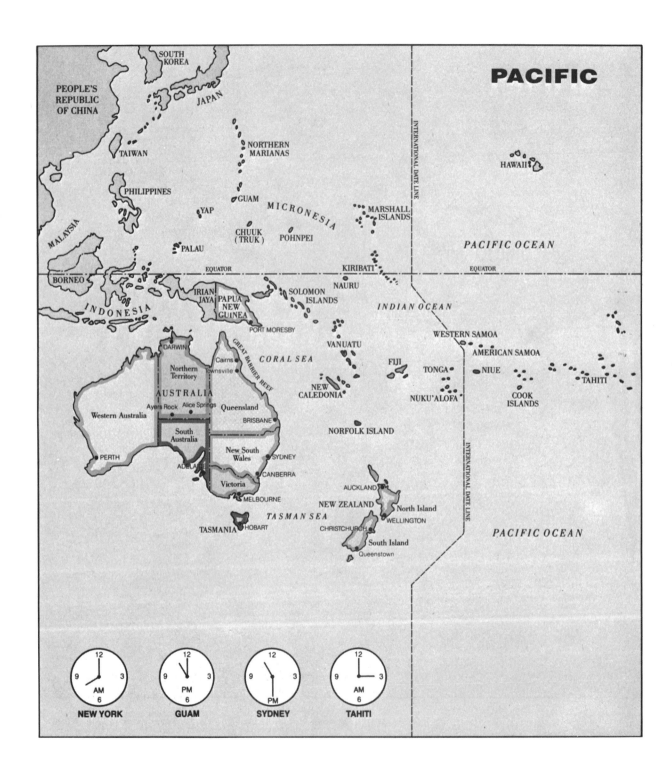